# Hitler, the War, and the Pope

**Revised and Expanded**

## Other Books by Ronald J. Rychlak

*Environmental Law* (with David Case) (Oceana's Legal Almanac Series: *Law for the Layperson*), Oxford University Press, 2010.

*Righteous Gentiles: How Pius XII and the Catholic Church Saved Half a Million Jews from the Nazis*, Spence Publishing, 2005.

*Trial by Fury: Restoring the Common Good in Tort Litigation*, monograph 8 in the Christian Social Thought Series, The Acton Institute, 2005.

*Mississippi Criminal Trial Practice* (with Marc Harrold), Thompson/West, 2004.

*Real and Demonstrative Evidence: Applications and Theory*, Lexis Publishing Company, 1995; second edition, 2003.

*Gaming Law: Cases and Materials* (with Robert M. Jarvis et al.), Matthew Bender & Co., 2003.

# Hitler, the War, and the Pope

**Revised and Expanded**

**Ronald J. Rychlak**

Our Sunday Visitor Publishing Division
Our Sunday Visitor, Inc.
Huntington, Indiana 46750

The Scripture citations used in this work are taken from the *Second Catholic Edition of the Revised Standard Version of the Bible* (RSV), copyright © 1965, 1966, and 2006 by the Division of Christian Education of the National Council of the Churches of Christ in the United States of America. Used by permission. All rights reserved.

English translation of the *Catechism of the Catholic Church* for the United States of America copyright © 1994, United States Catholic Conference, Inc. — Libreria Editrice Vaticana. English translation of the *Catechism of the Catholic Church: Modifications from the Editio Typica* copyright © 1997, United States Catholic Conference, Inc. — Libreria Editrice Vaticana.

Quotations from the *Positio* and *Actes et Documents du Saint Siège relatifs à la seconde guerre mondiale* are used with permission, copyright © 2010 Libreria Editrice Vaticana. Unless noted differently, other quotations from papal and additional Vatican documents copyright © 2010 Libreria Editrice Vaticana.

Every reasonable effort has been made to determine copyright holders of excerpted materials and to secure permissions as needed. If any copyrighted materials have been inadvertently used in this work without proper credit being given in one form or another, please notify Our Sunday Visitor in writing so that future printings of this work may be corrected accordingly.

ISBN: 978-1-59276-565-2 (Inventory No. T847)
LCCN: 2010921978

**Cover design:** Amanda Falk
**Cover art:** Shutterstock
**Interior design:** Sherri L. Hoffman
**Interior images:** Document images in the Appendix courtesy of the author. He would like to thank Bill Doino, the Congregation for the Causes of Saints, and Pave the Way Foundation for their assistance.

PRINTED IN THE UNITED STATES OF AMERICA

To Claire:
*"Practically perfect in every way"*

*"To this day, Auschwitz does not cease to admonish, reminding us that* anti-Semitism is a great sin against humanity, *that all racial hatred inevitably leads to the trampling of human dignity."*

POPE JOHN PAUL II

(*CROSSING THE THRESHOLD OF HOPE*, P. 97; EMPHASIS IN ORIGINAL)

# Table of Contents

# Foreword

*By Renato Cardinal Martino*

In September 2009, the human family somberly marked the seventieth anniversary of the start of World War II, underlining the need to remember the bloodiest conflict in the twentieth century so as not to repeat it. The following pages are an appropriate extension of this remembrance. In his new edition of *Hitler, the War, and the Pope*, Professor Ronald Rychlak once again offers a synthetic historical account of the inner dynamics of World War II, and the singular role played by the Catholic Church, and specifically by Pope Pius XII, in rescuing untold numbers of Jewish men, women, and children from the terror of Hitler's Nazi regime.

The detail and depth in which Rychlak exposes the historic realities of Hitler's rise to power and the Third Reich's ensuing program of dehumanizing destruction and extermination are supported by intensive research and accurate historical evidence. As one can glean from this insightful and rich account, there was no "safe haven" for any person who did not fit Hitler's insane image of the "perfect man." Christians and Jews alike were his targets for obliteration. Indeed, one of his primary objectives was to bring down the Church itself:

> I promise you that, if I wished to, I could destroy the Church in a few years; it is hollow and rotten and false through and through. One push and the whole structure would collapse.... I shall give them a few years reprieve. Why should we quarrel? They will swallow anything in order to keep their material advantages... we need only show them once or twice who is the master. Then they will know which way the wind blows. They are no fools. The Church was something really big. Now we are its heirs. We, too, are the Church. Its day has gone. (Chapter Five: Hitler's Rise to Power and the Concordat, p. 67)

Hitler, like other figures before him throughout the course of history who attempted to stamp out Christianity (Roman emperors, dictators, totalitarian regimes, and other notorious political ideologues), was ultimately proven to be unsuccessful in his campaign. The famous words of Tertullian once again ring true: "The blood of the martyrs is the seed of Christianity" (*Apologeticus,* 50).

Rychlak unveils the truth about the Nazi's deceptive agenda for change following the Weimar years of German defeat, national humiliation, political violence, and severe economic and social dislocation, and how Hitler's false promises of hope and renewal were, in fact, death-dealing plans for a diabolism the likes of which no one could have imagined. It would not be long, however, before the Third Reich's true colors began to be seen, and many German citizens, religious leaders, and members of Hitler's own party began to express their disillusionment and discontent with all that was unfolding before their eyes. Severe punishment, including deportation to concentration and death camps, awaited these dissenters. Among them were Catholic and Protestant clergy who, among others, suffered greatly at the hands of the Nazis.

The Holy See, through its network of diplomatic relations, became quickly engaged in the attempt to halt the budding international crisis called Nazism and Hitler's reign of terror. Recognizing that the Jewish people were among Hitler's most vulnerable victims, the Roman Pontiff, Pius XII, himself an experienced Vatican diplomat, spared no effort, diplomatic and otherwise, to save countless Jewish people who were in harm's way. The evidence is clear: Pope Pius XII employed every available means at his disposal to protect and rescue those at risk during the Nazi regime. Professor Rychlak's research offers fresh insights into the debate on *Hitler, the War, and the Pope*, and I am grateful to him for presenting this expanded edition of his important work.

*Renato Cardinal Martino is president emeritus of both the Pontifical Council of Justice and Peace and the Pontifical Council for the Pastoral Care of Migrants and Itinerant People. He served sixteen years as the Holy See's permanent observer to the United Nations.*

# Foreword

*By Rabbi Eric A. Silver*

In a meadow outside Runnymede, England, there is a memorial erected by the American Bar Association commemorating the signing of Magna Carta on that spot in the year 1215, when the English barons compelled King John to sign a document granting certain rights to his subjects. Over the years, most of the clauses have been revoked or superseded by newer and better laws, but four still remain in effect. It is the fourth of these that will concern us here: "We will not deny or defer to any man justice or right." For all the negative press received by lawyers in recent years, even the most cursory inquiry will reveal that the overwhelming majority of those in the profession are guided by, and hold in highest regard this, the twenty-ninth clause of Magna Carta.

Enter Ronald Rychlak, lawyer, professor of law, devout Catholic, and a man committed to ensuring that justice and right are granted to a man whose death occurred over half a century ago, a man for whom he seeks justice, for he is guided by the words of English jurist William Gladstone: "Justice delayed is justice denied." But one can go further back in history, for the quote is also found in the Mishnah, compiled some sixteen centuries before Gladstone. One may therefore view the impulse toward ensuring that justice not be delayed as a Jewish imperative, in addition to a civil one. To be sure, a sense of urgency about justice must inform legal thinking in any society seeking to be regarded as just and fair, and the Mishnah simply presages what has come to be taken for granted in any well-ordered system of jurisprudence.

This is the second time that I have been asked to write a foreword to a book about the role of Pope Pius XII during the period of the Holocaust. It might seem strange indeed that a rabbi would be engaged in such a task, inasmuch as matters such as canonization are internal matters decided upon by the appropriate arms of the Roman Catholic Church, and rabbis are seldom, if ever, consulted in these matters. So, one might well ask, what is a rabbi doing here at all?

The answer is to be found in the Book of Deuteronomy, chapter 16, verse 20, where we read: *Justice, justice shall you pursue.* In the original Hebrew, the idea is expressed in but three words: *tzedek tzedek tirdof,* and the rabbinic literature spends considerable time analyzing them.

To begin, it is held that the Torah speaks with an economy of words, and when a repetition or a redundancy occurs, it is regarded as being only superficial, so that closer examination reveals it to be not a repetition or a redundancy at all. In this case, we might simply find the words: *tzedek tirdof* — pursue justice.

Better yet, we could follow the accepted Hebrew word order, putting the verb at the beginning of the sentence, so that it would read: *tirdof tzedek* — pursue justice. This is how the Bible would ordinarily express the concept, and it would seem to make the point clearly enough. But the reversal of normal Hebrew word order, as well as the repetition of the word "justice," convey a meaning transcending the simple text. Justice is something that must not merely be accepted, and simply to seek after justice would be equally inadequate. In order for it to be justice, real justice, it must be pursued — a fierce and relentless pursuit is indeed the only thing that will ensure due process, else we have only partial justice, and partial justice is false justice. The rabbis ask rhetorically: "Why is the word *justice* written twice? To show that justice must be pursued, whether it is for you or against you, whether it is in behalf of the Jew or the Gentile." More importantly, the pursuit of justice must be carried out *with* justice. In Hebrew, the repetition makes it an absolute. It *must* be absolute. It must be done in the proper fashion, and above all, it must not compromise.

Further, it is these two works, the Torah and the Mishnah, the Written and the Oral Teaching, that comprise the corpus of divine revelation within Judaism. Everything else is commentary. Justice must be pursued, and justice may neither be delayed nor denied.

It is altogether fitting, therefore, that the latest submission for the quest into the truth of the role of Pius XII during the time of the Holocaust be the result of the efforts of a professor of law, a man whose professional efforts are directed toward teaching others how to engage in the practice of law, how to ensure justice for their clients and for society as a whole. I do not overstate the case when I say that the very safety and stability of our society depend on what men and women like Professor Rychlak are doing, for in a society of laws, we depend upon good and wise people to procure justice for us.

It is, after all, why I am writing these words. As a rabbi, and as a Jew, the matter of canonization of saints does not affect me. As a believer, I have profound respect for the faith of others, but that is as far as it goes. As a Jew, however, my passion for the pursuit of justice demands that I speak out when I see it violated. My regard for the Catholic faith and my respect for my Catholic friends would not direct me to be silent in the face of injustice, and my love for my own Jewish faith demands that I speak out equally strongly when an injustice is perpetrated against a truly righteous man — a saint, if you will — for the same Torah that insists that I pursue justice also demands that I not stand idly by.

I know Ronald Rychlak, and I know him to be a man of uncompromising integrity, a lawyer, a man who sees events through the eyes of a legal scholar, and a man who asks questions that will lead him and others to the truth. A witness in a trial is sworn to tell the truth, the whole truth, and nothing but the truth. Conjecture, hearsay, partial truths, and outright lying are equally out of place. The reasoning here is fairly simple: if we are content with anything less than the full truth, then justice has not been served. As a lawyer, he asks the questions that others might not, because he views the situation as he might a courtroom drama, where the quest for truth and justice take on special meaning.

Rychlak has accomplished what no one else has attempted: he has sought to go beyond rhetoric and opinion, these existing in abundance, and has sought to treat the issues as if they were being presented in a courtroom. I think that is the problem we are faced with today: an overabundance of rhetoric and opinion, and not very much justice. By pushing firmly for fact over opinion, Rychlak serves the cause of justice admirably. What can we know? What can be established as factual evidence? What would a judge and jury accept?

Once this is done, then the rhetoric and opinion are seen in their proper perspective, having their origin in a Communist plot to discredit the man who viewed the Soviet system as the embodiment of evil. They could not attack him in his lifetime, for their arguments would have been easy to refute. Indeed, during the lifetime of Pius XII, accolade after accolade was heaped upon this Righteous Gentile who had risked so much to rescue Jews in their hour of peril. It was only after God brought Pacelli home that the attacks began, and the attacks are seen under Rychlak's relentless inquiry to consist of lies, slander, malice, a desire to thwart justice. These lies have served to raise doubts in the minds of good and honest people who, thinking that if there is smoke, there must be fire, call for delays in a process that should have proceeded to its well-deserved conclusion years ago. Rychlak has set out to clear away the fog and obfuscation surrounding the record of the wartime Pope.

Let those who doubt but read Rychlak, follow his exquisitely organized courtroom-like arguments. What Professor Rychlak brings to the forum are facts, not rhetoric; dates, not conjecture; evidence, not slander. When the facts are considered — *the facts* and not the rhetoric, *the facts* and not the hearsay, *the facts* and not the slander — the sum of the matter will be seen to reflect the energies of a man who did everything humanly possible to thwart the Nazi plan for the extermination of the Jews, and then some.

This rabbi hopes and prays that the cause for the canonization of Pope Pius XII will proceed with all due speed. Catholics deserve that, and Jews deserve as well to know the great good that this man performed during his papacy. The world owes Ronald Rychlak a debt for bringing the truth to light.

*Eric A. Silver is a retired naval officer and rabbi residing in Cheshire, Connecticut. He is active on the North American Board of Rabbis and has served on the National Rabbinic Cabinet of the United Jewish Communities. He is passionate about building bridges of understanding among people of different faiths.*

# Foreword to the First Edition

*By John Cardinal O'Connor*

None of us can look back upon the last century without a sense of remorse. The phenomenon of "man's inhumanity to man" in the twentieth century is unparalleled and unpardonable. Indeed, it was the century in which Adolf Hitler and his minions seduced a nation, brought about a devastating world war, and inflicted that horror, the Holocaust. Millions upon millions perished and the words of the Lord God spoken so long ago in the Book of Genesis echo in our ears: "Your brother's blood cries out to me" (see Gen 4:10). I lived through most of that century. I lived through the Second World War. I lived through the Holocaust. And I, like so many others who have crossed the threshold of the twenty-first century and the third millennium, ask myself, "How could this darkness have enveloped us?" I believe that I shall never know the answer this side of heaven. However, I take tremendous consolation in the fact that there were virtuous men and women who were as lights in that darkness, men and women who did all within their power to fight evil and to protect the innocent. In particular, I am consoled by the heroic virtue of Pope Pius XII, upon whom was placed the cross of shepherding the Church in those most difficult of days.

I am indebted to Professor Ronald J. Rychlak for this book, *Hitler, the War, and the Pope*. In his well-crafted pages, he tells us the story of Eugenio Pacelli, a saintly priest, a skilled diplomat, and a consummate churchman, who was elected pope only months before Hitler's invasion of Poland. The darkness was settling upon Europe, even as the papal tiara was placed upon his head. As the war began and escalated, and as Hitler's atrocities against the Jewish people began to be known, Pope Pius XII did all within his power to negotiate peace and to save as many Jewish people as he could. As the war ended, the voices of a free world, from the United States to Europe to Israel, sang the praises of Pope Pius XII.

Yet, a half-century later, Hitler haunts us still. His so-called Final Solution and his ghastly brutality still pique our consciences. Recently, a plethora of books and articles have been published in an effort to cast light on the darkness that was Hitlerism. It comes as no surprise, then, that one whose stature loomed as large as that of Pope Pius XII should come under close scrutiny. Therefore, Professor Rychlak's book comes at a most opportune time.

I am reminded of the words of Thomas Jefferson in his *Notes on Virginia*: "A patient pursuit of facts, and a cautious combination and comparison of them, is the drudgery to which man is subjected by his maker, if he wished to attain sure knowledge." Professor Rychlak has subjected himself to this drudgery of detail by patiently pursing the facts. With due caution, he has combined and compared them for us so that we might attain knowledge of the part played by Pope Pius XII when darkness fell all around him. The portrait that emerges is one of an extraordinary pastor facing extremely vexing circumstances, of a holy man vying against an evil man, of a human being trying to save the lives of other human beings, of a light shining in the darkness.

JOHN CARDINAL O'CONNOR
Archbishop of New York
February 28, 2000

*Author's note: Shortly after these words were written, Cardinal O'Connor died on May 3, 2000.*

# Preface

The decade that has passed since publication of the first edition of *Hitler, the War, and the Pope* has been exciting from a personal perspective and rewarding from a professional perspective. Certainly, the controversy over the wartime leadership of Pope Pius XII has been much "hotter" than it was in the previous ten years. Moreover, due to the first edition, I found myself in the midst of much of the controversy.

I wrote the first edition to solve my personal curiosity that had been piqued by a colleague, George Cochran, who had said that Pius XII was a Nazi. Anytime over the past ten years when I got dejected because some false allegation was taking all of my time and leading people to a false conclusion, my wife would console me by reminding me that I had accomplished my original goal of figuring out what happened, and that I had persuaded George of the Pope's innocence of the charge.

When the page proofs of the first edition were released, George gave a copy to a priest/law professor with whom he taught summer school at Fordham. When I visited New York in September 2000, that priest, Father Robert Araujo, invited me to lunch with Archbishop (now Cardinal) Renato Martino, who was at that time the Holy See's permanent observer to the United Nations. My great friend and colleague John Czarnetzky joined me at the lunch. As soon as we were done eating, Archbishop Martino asked John and me to work with the Holy See Mission to the United Nations. That invitation resulted in an incredibly rewarding professional experience that has continued under the Holy See's new permanent observer, Archbishop Celestino Migliore. It also opened up an incredibly rich area of legal research, and John and I are eternally grateful to Cardinal Martino, Archbishop Migliore, and Father Araujo.

This book has led to several new friendships. Bill Doino and Dimitri Cavalli, who helped me research the first edition, are great friends and excellent Pius XII scholars in their own right. Ion Mihai Pacepa, the highest-ranking intelligence official ever to have defected from the former Eastern Bloc, has also become a great resource and a good friend. Father John Jay Hughes and Father Vincent Lapomarda, S.J., provided many important insights. Gary Krupp of Pave the Way Foundation has also become a close friend and a significant contributor to the Pius XII debate. I'd like to thank him and his wife, Meredith, for many things, including introducing me to His Holiness Pope Benedict XVI.

Father Peter Gumpel and Father Paul Molinari, recently retired from the Congregation for the Causes of Saints, are wonderful men, great friends, and invaluable resources. In addition to the people already mentioned, Monsignors James Reinhart and Anthony Frontiero from Cardinal Martino's staff became good friends, as did Michael Novak, Jody Bottum, and Rabbi David Dalin. I got to meet Sargent Shriver when Wil Colon (owner of Genesis Press) and I flew to Washington to meet him. Shriver bought about three hundred copies of the first edition to provide to the American bishops. The book also brought me closer to my former and current pastors, Father Kevin Slattery and Father Joe Tonos, who are wonderful men and good friends.

Unfortunately, I've lost some friends whom I met through the Pius XII debate. Scott Robey, my former teacher and coach, was motivated by the first edition to write a motion picture script. We renewed old acquaintances shortly before he passed away. Avery Cardinal Dulles corresponded with me for several years, and we shared a few wonderful meals together before he died. Several of my favorite memories over the past decade relate to dinner, conversation, and cigars shared with the late Father Richard John Neuhaus at his Manhattan home.

I would like to thank several others who helped this project come to fruition. The University of Mississippi School of Law has always been supportive of my work. Robert Khayat, Sam Davis, and my colleagues at the law school are all due a significant degree of thanks. Bob Lockwood found the Genesis Press edition of the book and convinced Greg Erlandson of Our Sunday Visitor to bring out a paperback edition. That was very important in terms of getting the book widely distributed. Paul Gallo of SuperTalk Mississippi radio network has also been a great promoter of the book.

Many readers corresponded with me after the first edition came out. Sometimes it was a brief note; other times it was a detailed exchange. Some comments encouraged me and made me realize the importance of getting the truth of this matter known. Others forced me to engage in deeper research that paid dividends in this edition. In all cases, I ended up thankful for what I learned.

The most important people in the process, of course, are in my family. Unfortunately, since the last edition we lost my wife's father, Paul. On the other hand, the birth of my youngest daughter, Olivia, also took place in these last ten years. She, Joseph, Lindsey, Susanna, Mary Helen, and Sally are lights in my life. My children are my motivation, and my wife is my inspiration. I have been blessed.

# ONE

# The Papacy and the World

The heart of the Catholic Church is at the Vatican, the smallest sovereign state in the world. Vatican City is on the west bank of the Tiber River, lying within the Italian capital city of Rome, and almost completely surrounded by walls that were built in the sixteenth century. The city covers about 108 acres, but most of the outdoor sights can be seen in a comfortable hour-long walk. The Vatican also has extraterritorial jurisdiction over Castel Gandolfo, the papal summer residence near Rome, and thirteen churches and other buildings in Rome.

The Vatican's population consists primarily of employees of the Holy See, the central government of the Catholic Church.[1] The Vatican flies its own flag, mints its own coins (Euros and associated denominations), maintains a police force, a court system, two jails, a fire department, and provides postal services. The Vatican also has its own newspaper, railway station, telephone system, five radio stations, and a bank with financial resources in Italy and abroad.[2] At one time, the Vatican had its own army, but Pope Paul VI disbanded the Noble Guard and the Palatine Guard in 1970. True military might had disappeared long before that. Today, about one hundred members of the Swiss Guard are a largely ceremonial remnant of earlier military prowess.

The leader of the Catholic Church is the Pope, the Bishop of Rome. The Catholic Church teaches that Jesus Christ conferred the position of primacy in the Church upon the apostle Peter and on him alone. In defining this doctrine, the First Vatican Council cited three New Testament passages, called the "Petrine" texts:

> **Matthew 16:18-19:** "And I tell you, you are Peter, and on this rock I will build my Church, and the gates of Hades shall not prevail against it. I will give you the keys of the kingdom of heaven, and whatever you bind on earth shall be bound in heaven, and whatever you loose on earth shall be loosed in heaven."
>
> **Luke 22:32:** "But I have prayed for you [Peter] that your faith may not fail; and when you have turned again, strengthen your brethren."
>
> **John 21:17:** He said to him the third time, "Simon, son of John, do you love me?" Peter was grieved because he said to him the third time, "Do you love me?" And he said to him, "Lord, you know everything; you know that I love you." Jesus said to him, "Feed my sheep."

According to Catholic teaching, these texts signify that Christ himself named Peter as head of the Church, with the authority to pronounce infallibly on matters of faith and morals. The Pope is the successor of Peter, and the powers that were conferred on Peter pass down in perpetuity to his papal successors. The Pope is aided by the cardinals and a bureaucracy known as the Roman Curia. When the cardinals are called together to deal with questions of major importance, they are referred to as the College of Cardinals. Upon the death of the Pope, the cardinals who are under eighty years of age elect his successor.

When elected, each new Pope inherits his many official titles: Bishop of Rome, Vicar of Jesus Christ, Holy Father, Successor of St. Peter, Prince of the Apostles, Supreme Pontiff of the Universal Church, Primate of Italy, Archbishop and Metropolitan of the Roman Province, Sovereign of the State of Vatican City, and Servant of the Servants of God. His ministry is to serve, and his role of authority is to teach and govern in the name of Christ.

In addition to being the head of the Church, the Pope is also a head of state. The Holy See signs treaties and makes international agreements with other countries. Papal nuncios (ambassadors) are sent to most countries, and elsewhere apostolic delegates (who do not have formal diplomatic functions) watch over and inform the Pope of the state of the Church in their assigned regions. The Vatican has its own secretary of state, maintains a mission (embassy) and has a permanent observer to the United Nations, and regularly participates in international conferences and agreements.[3]

In terms of international relations, most popes have had similar goals. Preservation of peace, care for the impoverished, and religious freedom are usually among the more important objectives. Perhaps the most controversial popes of the twentieth century — at least in terms of world politics — were the Nazi-era popes, Pius XI and Pius XII. Because of the official neutrality of the Vatican during the war and concern on the part of the Holy See about the spread of Communism across Europe, some historians have argued that Pope Pius XII, in particular, failed to provide the moral guidance that was needed at this time of great crisis. Others have even suggested that he wanted the Germans to win.

Several questions must be addressed in order to evaluate Pius XII's role in World War II. They include: Was he anti-Semitic? Was he blinded by a hatred of Communism? Did he come under the influence of Adolf Hitler? Would more aggressive use of the bully pulpit have diminished Jewish suffering? These are complicated questions that demand careful answers.

The best way to analyze the wartime performance of Pius XII is by viewing the world from the perspective of the Vatican during that era. In particular, one must evaluate the situation in Europe during the 1920s and 1930s; the personal history of the key figures involved; international developments throughout World War II; and the perception of those closest to the situation, especially the Jewish victims of the Nazis. It is also worth considering the genesis of criticisms that were not voiced until decades after the war. Once these factors have been studied, the picture of the Vatican and its wartime leader becomes much clearer, and the difficult questions concerning the role played by the Pope in World War II can be answered with a fair degree of certainty.

Pope Pius XII, the Church's 260th Pope, was born in Rome on March 2, 1876, as Eugenio Maria Giuseppe Giovanni Pacelli. Two days after his birth, he was baptized into the Catholic faith by his grand-uncle, Monsignor Giuseppe Pacelli. According to one report, another priest, family friend Monsignor Iacobacci, held the baby in his arms and said: "Sixty-three years from today the people in St. Peter's and all Rome will loudly praise this *bambino*."[4] (Pacelli was elected pope on his sixty-third birthday.)

The Pacelli family had been supplying the Holy See with lawyers since the early years of the nineteenth century. Eugenio's grandfather, Marcantonio Pacelli, moved to Rome in 1819 to enter the service of the Holy See. He was promoted by Pius IX to undersecretary of the interior in the Papal States, and he held that post until 1870. While at the Vatican, Marcantonio helped to establish the Vatican's newspaper, *L'Osservatore Romano*.

Eugenio's father, Filippo Pacelli, was a distinguished Vatican lawyer.[5] He served as a counselor to the Holy See, particularly in financial matters when he headed the Bank of Rome. He was made dean of the Consistorial College, which was composed of twelve lawyers who contributed outstanding service to the Church. He also belonged to the so-called Black Nobility. Members of this group stood by the Church and defended the rights and honor of the Pope during the time of the "Roman Question," when the Vatican was in conflict with Italy (1870-1929).[6] Eugenio's brother, Francesco Pacelli, also a lawyer, was right-hand man to the Vatican secretary of state, Cardinal Pietro Gasparri, during the negotiations with Benito Mussolini that led to the historic Lateran Treaty and the end of the Roman Question.[7]

Eugenio's mother, Virginia Pacelli, was a very religious woman who taught her son the importance of prayer as soon as he could talk. He became a devout child, but not without the typical interests of all children. He learned to play the violin and continued to love music throughout his life. He also enjoyed having stories told to him. Many of the stories, of course, were religiously oriented. One day, his uncle told him the story of a missionary priest who was persecuted and ultimately crucified by his tormentors. Eugenio told his uncle that he, too, would like to be a martyr, "but without the nails."[8]

The Congregation for the Causes of Saints has an essay that Eugenio probably wrote when he was thirteen or fourteen years old. In it, he comments on his body, his moral character, and his attitude toward life:

> I am of normal height, my body thin, my face somewhat pale, my hair dark brown and soft, my eyes very dark, my nose aquiline. There's not much to be said about my chest, which, in all frankness, is not broad and powerful. Lastly, as for my legs they are long and thin; my feet cannot be called small.

He sums up: "Physically, I am pretty much an average boy." The teenaged Pacelli goes on to note that he is sometimes overly excitable, but he is working on controlling that. He adds that he does not like to be corrected, but that he quickly forgives those who offend him, because he is striving to attain more fully a spirit of generosity.

A former classmate once described the young Eugenio as follows: "You would not call him a genius, but rather a consistent worker.... He was a lovable and courageous boy."[9] When he was in the seminary, Eugenio "found time for the lighter moments of student life," including a starring role in the play seminarians put on during carnival time.[10]

His relatives thought that Eugenio might follow family tradition and become a lawyer, but his religious influence was stronger. At the age of eighteen, he attended a four-day Church retreat. When he came home, his mind was made up. He would be a priest.

Eugenio was accepted into a prestigious seminary in Rome, the *Capranica*. Within a very short time, he distinguished himself as one of the best students in his class.[11] He particularly excelled in languages, eventually becoming fluent in Latin, Greek, English, French, German, Spanish, Portuguese, Hebrew, and Aramaic. Eugenio took additional courses at another great institution, the *Gregoriana*, or Gregorian University. This intense program of studies, the dankness of the old buildings, his meager diet, and the demanding schedule caused Eugenio's health to suffer seriously. He developed a hacking cough, and the family doctor warned that he was on the brink of tuberculosis.

These health problems nearly ended Eugenio's study and his religious career, but he had been noticed by Pope Leo XIII, who permitted young Pacelli to live at home while completing his courses. This was a rare, if not unprecedented, dispensation.[12] Frail health, however, still plagued Eugenio and prevented his participation in the school's graduation ceremony. Instead, he was ordained on Easter Sunday, April 2, 1899, by Francesco Paola Cassetta, auxiliary bishop of Rome, in the bishop's private chapel. The new, twenty-three-year-old priest celebrated his first Mass the next day in the Basilica of St. Mary Major, the largest Marian church in Rome. Father Pacelli was then assigned to the parish of the Chiesa Nuova, where he had previously served as an altar boy. He did not, however, abandon his studies; he followed family tradition and studied law. He already possessed a doctorate in theology, and in 1902 he would be awarded a doctorate in canon and civil law.[13]

Pope Leo XIII had a program for training exceptional young clerics to serve in the Vatican diplomatic service, and two years after Pacelli was ordained, Cardinal Gasparri, secretary of the Congregation of Extraordinary Ecclesiastical Affairs (and future Vatican secretary of state), invited Pacelli into this program. Leo died in 1903, but the next year, the new Pope Pius X named Pacelli a monsignor and assigned him to a team that was charged with codifying the laws of the Church.[14]

For the next decade and a half, Monsignor Pacelli worked with the Congregation of Extraordinary Ecclesiastical Affairs on the codification project.

In 1904, he was named house-prelate of the congregation. In 1911, he became undersecretary of state. He also served as the Pope's *Minutante*, editing and correcting the Pope's speeches and minutes, and as the Holy Father's personal envoy to the Austro-Hungarian emperor. At the same time, he continued to say Mass, hear confessions, and instruct underprivileged children in religious matters.[15]

In 1914, Pope Pius X named Cardinal Gasparri the new Vatican secretary of state, and Pacelli was promoted to the post Gasparri vacated, secretary of the Congregation of Extraordinary Ecclesiastical Affairs. Pope Pius X died later this same year and was replaced by Pope Benedict XV. When the First World War broke out, the Vatican became a relief station for suffering victims of war. Pacelli and Gasparri were charged with maintaining liaison with the hierarchies on both sides of the conflict, answering appeals for aid from all over Europe, and organizing a war relief program. Together, they helped thirty thousand French and German prisoners return to their homes.[16]

In the summer of 1917, the papal nuncio to Bavaria, Archbishop Giuseppe Aversa, passed away. With Germany at the center of a war that affected most of Europe, this post was too important to leave vacant for long. The Pope needed to send a replacement immediately. Pacelli was already well known to both the secretary of state and the Pope, so he became Benedict's choice to represent the Holy See in Munich.[17]

Before undertaking his new position, Pacelli was consecrated as bishop by Pope Benedict in a special ceremony in the Sistine Chapel.[18] He was at the same time elevated to the rank of archbishop. He was then sent off to Munich and into a very difficult situation. The British envoy to the Holy See, Sir Henry Howard, wrote in his diary that this move "will be a dreadful loss for our British mission to the Vatican for he is the *one man* who can be trusted implicitly; however, it is also consoling that there should be such an honest man at Munich at present."[19]

As nuncio to Bavaria, Pacelli's job was to try to ease the suffering, stop the fighting, work on a new concordat (treaty or agreement) with the German state of Bavaria, and establish diplomatic relations with the rest of Germany. To these ends, in June 1917, Pacelli went to Berlin to introduce himself to Reich Chancellor Theobald von Bethmann-Hollweg. While in Germany, Pacelli visited many other German officials, including Kaiser Wilhelm II.

Earlier popes had acted as arbiters in wars, and Benedict XV wanted to do so now. Without taking sides, he put out an appeal to the governments to end the "useless slaughter."[20] He laid out a plan to be presented to German leaders by Pacelli (who had helped draft the plan), but the new nuncio's efforts did not bring an end to the fighting. Kaiser Wilhelm II spent most of the meeting lecturing Pacelli on how the Vatican should deploy its soldiers in the event of an attack.[21] All that Pacelli could accomplish was to convince the kaiser to end the practice of bringing Belgians to Germany as semi-slave laborers.[22] Pope Benedict's proposal did, however, prepare the way for Woodrow Wilson's settlement plan a year later.[23]

For the remainder of the war, Pacelli concentrated on carrying out Benedict's humanitarian efforts. (He has been credited with helping sixty-five thousand prisoners of war return home.)[24] Pacelli soon became a common sight in the streets of Munich, handing out food to those who were impoverished. Benedict emptied the Vatican treasury, as he carried out his efforts to alleviate suffering. He spent so much of the Church's funds that at the time of his death in 1922, there was not even enough money to cover the expenses related to his funeral and the ensuing conclave.

War ended only when it became obvious that Germany would have to seek a treaty, and the German people demanded that Kaiser Wilhelm II do so. Inspired by the Communists in Russia, revolutionaries staged uprisings throughout Germany in November 1918. In Pacelli's region of Bavaria, a short-lived Soviet Socialist Republic was proclaimed.[25] Wilhelm II abdicated and fled to the Netherlands that same month. Germany seemed to be on the verge of a Communist takeover, but the Social Democrats and other more moderate parties were able to establish a parliamentary republic, which negotiated an armistice. The terms specified that the German army would immediately evacuate all occupied territory; surrender great quantities of war material, including all submarines; and intern all other surface warships as directed by the Allies.

---

A few weeks before he was sent to Munich, while Pacelli was still serving as undersecretary of state of the Holy See, Nahum Sokolow — author, journalist, and board member of the Zionist World Congress — came to Rome to inquire about the Holy See's position on the establishment of a Jewish homeland in Palestine. Pacelli warmly received Sokolow and expressed openness toward his cause.[26] To Sokolow's surprise, Pacelli then asked Sokolow whether he wanted to meet the Pope. Pacelli arranged for a forty-five minute private audience with Benedict XV. The Pope said the Zionist initiative was "providential" and "in accordance with God's will." He released Sokolow with the words: "I am sure we will be good neighbors."[27]

One week later, in the Sistine Chapel, Pope Benedict XV ordained Pacelli as an archbishop. The following week, Pacelli was on a train to Munich where he would be the Pope's sole representative to Germany. He soon had to deal with a very difficult situation.

Zionist settlers in Palestine were in danger. The Turks suspected the Jews of collaboration with the British, who had supported an Arab revolt and engaged in warfare with the Ottoman Empire. Cemal Pasha, the commander-in-chief and governor of Syria, had overseen the Ottoman Empire's deliberate and systematic destruction of its Armenian population, resulting in the deaths of about 1.5 million Armenians during 1915 to 1917. In 1917, Pasha turned brutally against the Jewish-Zionist settlements in Palestine. He threatened widespread massacre. More than eight thousand Jews were forced to leave their homes. Assaults and murders were becoming common. Reuters news agency reported a "massive expulsion of Jews who could face a similar fate as the Armenians."[28] The Zionist office in Copenhagen expressed concern that the Jews of Palestine would face the same fate as the Armenians: extermination by hunger, thirst, and disease.

On November 15, 1917, Cardinal Secretary of State Gasparri sent a message to Pacelli. It stated: "The Israelite Community of Switzerland asked the Holy Father to commit himself to the protection of the sites and the Jewish population of Jerusalem. He asks Your Excellency[,] through us, to influence the German government accordingly in the name of the Holy Father. Card. Gasparri."[29] The following day, Pacelli wrote to the Bavarian Secretary of State:

> The undersigned Apostolic Nuncio has the honor to inform Your Excellency that the Israelite Congregations of Switzerland asked the Holy Father to appeal for the protection of the sites and the Jewish population of Jerusalem. His Eminence, the Cardinal Secretary of State had ordered the undersigned to act accordingly and with all care and to draw this subject to the attention of the Imperial Government. The Undersigned requests from Your Excellency to enforce the realization of this purpose with everything in your capacity. In advance gratefully, signing with the assurance of my highest appreciation, Eugenio Pacelli, Archbishop of Sardes, and Apostolic Nuncio."[30]

The German leadership complied with the requests and sent a démarche to the Ottoman government.[31]

The importance of the German démarche, which was urged by Pacelli and the Vatican leadership, cannot be overstated. Turkish troops in Palestine were at this time under the command of a *German* general, Erich von Falkenhayn. As his biographer explained: "An inhuman excess against the Jews in Palestine was only prevented through Falkenhayn's conduct, which has a special significance in respect to the German history of the 20th century."[32] Dr. Jacob Thon, head of the Zionist office in Jerusalem, wrote in December 1917:

> It was a special stroke of good fortune that in the last critical days General von Falkenhayn had the command. Cemal Pasha in this case — as he announced often enough — would have expelled the whole population and turned the country into ruins. We and the whole population, Christians as well as Muslims, must remember P. [Pacelli] with deep gratitude, since he saved the civil population from doom when he prevented the planned evacuation of this area.[33]

As others have concluded, Pacelli "had every moral right to feel that he had been instrumental in safeguarding both Jerusalem Jewry and the holy sites from almost certain destruction."[34]

Nuncio Pacelli met with Sokolow again, when the Zionist leader visited Berlin in 1925. After that meeting, Pacelli sent a letter (dated February 15, 1925) to Cardinal Secretary of State Gasparri in which he reported:

Mr. Nahum Sokolow, President of the Executive Committee of the Zionist organization, when he was travelling through Berlin a few days ago, insisted to see me. During the brief conversation, which I felt was completely constructive and in full agreement, he, being a Jew, expressed his feelings of veneration and respect for the Catholic Church, and I remembered that in the beginning of 1917, when he visited Rome, he was received repeatedly by Your Eminence and had the honor to be received in a private audience by His Holiness. Therefore I recommend that when he returns in the current year he would be particularly pleased if he could be sympathetically received by Your Eminence and possibly receive your assurance of your attention and care. Although I know that the intention of this gentleman, although it is interesting, does not fall into the responsibility of this Nunciature, I feel it was my duty to recommend the above mentioned to the good will of Your Eminence.[35]

The following year, Sokolow returned to Berlin, and he wanted to see Pacelli. Although Pacelli was severely ill and at the hospital at that time, his physicians agreed to let Sokolow visit Pacelli's bedside for five minutes. Pacelli, however, did not let Sokolow leave for nearly ninety minutes. "It was obvious how interesting and uplifting the conversation with the Nuncio was, a discussion of historical questions, Jewish as well as Catholic," wrote German Zionist Kurt Blumenfeld, who waited for Sokolow in the hospital library.[36]

---

The Paris Peace Conference was organized by the victors at the end of the First World War. In attendance were seventy delegates, representing twenty-seven victorious Allied powers. Despite his humanitarian efforts, Pope Benedict was excluded from the postwar peace conference due to the Vatican's official neutrality.[37] Neither Germany nor any other defeated power was permitted to attend. Because the victorious nations often had conflicting proposals, the sessions were tumultuous and the final proposals were controversial. The four major powers — Britain, France, Italy, and the United States — dominated the proceedings.

American President Woodrow Wilson proposed a conciliatory settlement based on fourteen points, many of which had been in Pope Benedict's plan a year earlier. Wilson warned of the consequences of imposing harsh terms on the losing side:

> Victory would mean peace forced upon the loser, a victor's terms imposed upon the vanquished. It would be accepted in humiliation, under duress, at an intolerable sacrifice, and would leave a sting, a resentment, a bitter memory, upon which terms of peace would not rest, not permanently, but only as upon quicksand.[38]

He continued: "Only a peace between equals can last; only a peace the very principle of which is equality and a common participation in a common benefit."[39]

Most of the nations at the conference, however, were unwilling to permit survival of a strong Germany.

After three and a half months of argument, the Allied leaders finally reached agreement. The Versailles proposal called for Germany to admit guilt, give up territory, and disarm its military.[40] Germany's Saar and Rhineland districts were to be placed under Allied occupation for fifteen years, and they were to remain perpetually demilitarized, as was a belt of territory thirty miles deep along the Rhine. All of Germany's overseas possessions were to be occupied by the Allies and organized as "mandates," under the supervision and control of a newly formed League of Nations. The former emperor and other German war leaders were also to be tried as war criminals (this provision was never enforced).

A number of other provisions were designed to insure the rest of the world against possible future German aggression. The new League of Nations was organized to make the peace secure, administer former colonies of the defeated powers, and foster general disarmament. The German army was limited to one hundred thousand men and was not to possess any heavy artillery; the general staff was abolished, and the navy was to be reduced. The new Austrian republic was reduced to its essential Germanic core, leaving it only one-quarter of its former size. Germany was prohibited from uniting with Austria, even by means of a customs union. No German air force would be permitted, and the production of military planes was forbidden.

The Germans would also have to pay for the damages caused by the war. In fact, the Allies demanded reparations in excess of what Germany could realistically pay. In addition to providing compensation for all civilian damages caused during the war, Germans had to pay reparations of great quantities of industrial goods, merchant shipping, and raw materials. This burden, it was thought, would prevent Germany from being able to finance any major military buildup. What it actually accomplished was to provide Adolf Hitler with an issue that would unify his supporters throughout the next two decades.[41]

The German delegation denounced the plan, claiming it was in violation of the armistice negotiations and that the economic provisions would be impossible to fulfill. They argued that the Allies had proposed one set of terms to end the fighting, but now a completely different set of demands was being made. Nevertheless, they were over a barrel. The German army was unable to regroup. (Despite Hitler's later claims to the contrary, the German army did not want to continue fighting at this time.) The German delegation took the proposal back to Berlin, where it was also denounced by Chancellor Philipp Scheidemann.

The Allies maintained a naval blockade of Germany, and it soon became obvious that Germany would have to sign the treaty. The Socialist Republican leaders resigned rather than sign the treaty. (They also had problems at home and had been forced to use the military to maintain order and suppress revolts.) Shortly thereafter, a freely elected constituent assembly met in Weimar to write a constitution that would give governing power to the German Reichstag.[42] On

July 31, 1919, the Weimar Republic was established, and Germany was organized into a federal republic consisting of seventeen separate states.

The new German Chancellor, Gustav Bauer, sent another delegation to Versailles. After informing the Allies that Germany was accepting the treaty only because of the need to alleviate the hardships on its people caused by the "inhuman" blockade, the Germans signed the proposal. Hitler would later argue that this capitulation to foreign demands invalidated the Weimar Republic's claim to represent Germany. When National Socialism swept across Germany, Weimar's leaders (particularly the Social Democrats) came to be called the "November Criminals."[43]

# TWO

# Hitler and the Postwar World

Adolf Hitler was born the day before Easter, April 20, 1889, in the small Austrian village of Braunau am Inn. He was the fourth child of a marriage between Klara Pölzl and Alois Hitler (his third marriage).[1] Klara was an affectionate mother, and she nursed sickly Adolf until he was almost five years old.[2] Alois, on the other hand, a retired customs officer, drank heavily and was a strict disciplinarian who regularly beat his sons. Adolf's older brother ran away from home at the age of fourteen, leaving Adolf as the primary target of his father's temper.

Young Adolf was a choir boy who liked to read western novels and play "Cowboys and Indians." He was at the top of his class as a young boy, but he changed as he got older. He became moody and broke off with most of his friends. He studied yoga, hypnotism, astrology, and various other forms of Eastern occultism.[3] His teachers reported that he was lazy and undisciplined. He spent much of his time alone, reading or drawing. Art provided an outlet from the real world.

When Hitler was thirteen years old, his father died. Five years later, his mother died. This was a devastating loss. For the rest of his life, he would keep his mother's picture with him. Even as a grown man, he kept her picture next to his bed.

At the age of eighteen, Adolf received an allowance from his parents' pension and set off to Austria's largest city, Vienna, to become an artist. Vienna was one of the brightest and most cosmopolitan cities in Europe, but it was not an easy place for an outsider.[4] Adolf sought admission to the Imperial Art Academy, but his application was denied twice. Letters he wrote during this time indicate that he was lonely, ill, and in need of money. When times were particularly rough, he spent nights in the park or slept in doorways. At other times, he lived in a boarding house and managed to scrape out a living by selling small watercolors and drawings. (Perhaps more important to his standard of living was a loan or gift of money that he received from his aunt, Johanna Pölzl.) He was described as slight in build, poorly nourished, with hollow cheeks and shabby clothes.[5] He seems to not have had any romantic interest in a city full of romance. In fact, at least one friend considered him an outright misogynist.[6]

Hitler studied and illustrated Austrian architecture, especially the palaces and monuments that had been designed and built in tribute to the thousand-year Reich of the Holy Roman Empire. He also enjoyed going to Vienna's opera house, which featured music that paid tribute to Germany's noble past. Richard Wagner's operas, in particular, were noted for their portrayals of heroism, despair, hope, treachery, tragedy, and fate.[7] Listening to *Der Ring des Nibelungen* or *Parsifal,* and at the same time studying monuments to Austria's former glory,

Hitler came to believe that Aryans were a superior race of people.[8] He envisioned Germany once again becoming a true empire.

Although Vienna had some serious problems with anti-Semitism,[9] Hitler's anger at this time was not directed toward Jewish people. Rather, "two subjects above all aroused his aggression": Communists and the Jesuits.[10] His anger toward the Jesuits is thought to have developed through the influence of Georg Ritter von Schönerer, a vehemently anti-Catholic politician who lived in Vienna.[11]

Schönerer founded a movement that was known by its slogan: "Away-from-Rome."[12] As it grew in popularity, many Catholic followers converted to Protestantism. Simultaneously, a new faith called *Theosophy* spread across Europe. This was a mixture of various Gnostic, Egyptian, and Hindu beliefs combined with the myth of Aryan superiority.[13] Followers recognized one another by an ancient Eastern symbol of good luck and fertility, the swastika.[14] Schönerer's nationalistic faith combined with Theosophy, and the result was an apocalyptic vision promising a new world subject to German domination — an empire inhabited by noblemen and cleansed of all Judeo-Christian influence.[15]

Hitler may have been shaped by the politics in Austria, but he had no intention of serving in the Austrian military, which, he complained, was composed of Czechs, Slovaks, and Croats. He moved to Munich to avoid the draft, but the authorities caught up with him. On January 19, 1914, the day before he was supposed to appear at the Austrian military barracks at Linz, Hitler was served a summons by the Munich police and escorted to the Austrian consulate. If convicted of draft evasion, he could receive a fine, one year of prison, and he would still have to perform his military service. With the help of a lawyer and a self-serving letter of explanation, however, Hitler avoided punishment and was found physically unfit for duty. By 1921, he would rewrite this episode of his life, saying only, "on August 5, 1914, my request to the King having been granted, I reported to the 1st Bavarian Infantry Regiment in order to join the German Army."[16]

For all of his resistance to joining the Austrian army, at the outbreak of war Hitler enlisted in the German army and thrived as a soldier. He was a company runner in the Bavarian infantry, fighting in France and Flanders throughout World War I. He took messages back and forth to headquarters and was often at the front lines. This was a dangerous assignment, typically given to intelligent, brave, and physically fit young soldiers. Hitler was wounded in 1916 and gassed in 1918. It was during the war, he later claimed, that Providence first came to his aid when a voice told him to evacuate a trench just before an explosion killed everyone who remained in it.

In 1914, Hitler was awarded the Iron Cross, Second Class. Toward the end of the war, when he was a corporal (his highest rank),[17] he was awarded the high honor of the Iron Cross, First Class, for volunteering and successfully completing what had appeared to be a suicide mission. As the war closed, Hitler was receiving treatment for temporary blindness caused by a British gas attack.

After the war, Hitler returned from a military hospital to Munich, where he underwent an army-sponsored course of political education for soldiers who were returning home. The program featured Pan-German nationalism, strong anti-Semitism, and a good deal of anti-socialism. Hitler had been shocked by his country's defeat. He was now convinced that Germany had been betrayed by the Jews and Marxists. His feeling grew into an obsession. Eventually, he would combine these fanatic beliefs with his oratorical skills and nearly achieve world domination.

————

Pacelli remained in Munich following the war, with the added responsibility of representing the Vatican not only to Bavaria, but also to the Weimar Republic, which was centered in Berlin. He put together a largely German staff, selected a German nun for his housekeeper (Sister Pascalina Lehnert, who would remain in his service until his death), a German priest as his top aide, and another for his confessor.[18] He also developed a close circle of German clerical advisers, mainly Jesuit priests. Eventually, he was able to preach and lecture in German.

Germany's new, democratic government faced serious trouble from the beginning. With six major political parties, and several minor ones, it was hard to form effective coalitions. The German people felt that democracy had been imposed upon them, and the new government's task of paying war reparations to the Allies was highly unpopular. All of this contributed to German resentment, and Hitler was not the only would-be dictator to try to take advantage of the situation. Communists, monarchists, and nationalists each occasionally resorted to violence in their efforts to overthrow the republic.

The Vatican was concerned about the political struggle that was taking place in Germany. The Church had long opposed Communism, and the possibility of a Communist Germany was a significant concern for the Holy See. Pacelli mounted the pulpit of the Munich cathedral to speak out in strong language against the postwar menace of Bolshevism.[19] Because of this, he was threatened with physical violence several times. This risk became extraordinarily serious in April 1919, when Communists took over the Bavarian government and declared it a separate Communist state.

With the Communist takeover, almost all diplomats in Munich packed their bags and fled to Berlin. "Only Nuncio Pacelli announced that he was staying at his post."[20] He soon became a target of Communist hostility. He regularly called in protests, pointing out that as a representative of a foreign nation, his possessions were inviolable under international law.[21] Finally, the rogue leadership decided to assassinate the problematic Catholic leader.[22] One time a car, in true gangster fashion, sped past his house, spraying it with machine-gun fire, but Pacelli was not home.[23] Then, as reported by Bishop (later Archbishop) Fulton Sheen:

On April 29 at 3 P.M., Commander Seiler of the Red Army of the South and his aide-de-camp Brongratz ... appeared at the door of the archbishop's house in company with a group of Red sailors. The thugs, gaining entrance to the house by threatening the servant with hand grenades, made their way to the library and awaited the appearance of their prey. Seiler took up his appearance closest to the door with a pistol drawn; the gunmen stood around him in a semicircle, some with drawn guns, some with hand grenades. Suddenly the wanted man appeared.

With a blasphemy, Seiler threw out his pistol hand; it hit the pectoral cross on the man's breast. This tall, lean figure, grasping the pectoral cross and facing the raised guns, said in soft, low tones, "I am not afraid; I am in God's hands. But you gain nothing! I am interested only in saving my people."

Under the gaze of those spiritual eyes, no one dared pull a trigger. Neither Seiler nor Brongratz nor the others knew why they did not shoot; when they got back to headquarters, they were unable to explain ... why they did not kill that man. They were never able to explain why a pair of eyes, a lean figure holding a cross, and a soft voice should be more powerful than their guns and their grenades. There was only one thing that was certain. From that day on, that man would be afraid of absolutely nothing in the world.[24]

A few days later, many of the intruders returned, unarmed, to apologize, ask forgiveness, and return a stolen automobile.

Another attack came when Pacelli was riding home in his car after a meeting with the archbishop of Munich. An angry mob descended on the car, yelling and threatening to turn the car over. Pacelli ordered the driver to open the roof. After initial reluctance, the driver agreed. Pacelli then stood on the back seat to address the astonished crowd. "My mission is peace," he said. "The only weapon I carry is this Holy Cross. I do no harm to you, but only good things. Why should you harm me?" He then raised his hand and blessed the crowed. When he sat back down, the mob moved out of the way and let the car pass.[25]

When word of Pacelli's bravery spread throughout Munich, he was held in even greater awe than before. It was said of him that "he fears absolutely nothing and no one."[26] When the Communists were ousted from power in May 1919, police began rounding them up. Knowing of the several incidents in which he had been involved, the police asked Pacelli to help identify suspects, but he had no desire for revenge. He always managed to be unavailable when asked to help identify those who had sought to harm him.[27]

On January 22, 1922, Pope Benedict XV succumbed to influenza. At the ensuing conclave, one of Pacelli's close friends from his days in Rome, Cardinal Ambrogio Damiano Achille Ratti, was elected pope. He chose the name Pius XI. Cardinal Gasparri, who had brought Pacelli into the Vatican's diplomatic service, was retained as secretary of state. Two of Pacelli's closest friends were now in the top two offices of the Church.

The Catholic Church was strong in Germany, but it had splintered in the mid-1800s. Whereas countries such as Poland (90 percent), Italy (95 percent), Hungary (67 percent), Luxembourg (94 percent), Austria (85 percent), Belgium (75 percent), and France (93 percent) were largely Catholic, Germany was predominantly Protestant (about 65 percent). The Protestant Reformation, which began under the leadership of Martin Luther, was centered in Germany. When the Catholic Church excommunicated Luther, German noblemen welcomed him. Luther is well known for having translated the Bible into German, and his influence in Germany probably exceeded his influence in any other country.[28] As such, in the pre-war years, Protestants outnumbered Catholics by about a 2-to-1 ratio. Regardless of the denomination, however, the influence of churches in Germany was waning as secular philosophies grew in popularity.[29]

The majority of Christians in Germany considered themselves patriotic, and they would fight for what they saw as their nation's interest. This nationalism caused some religious people to welcome the rise of Nazism. Anti-Semitism was also quite prevalent and would certainly have had an important influence on many people. Hitler knew this, and he considered anti-Semitism "a useful revolutionary expedient."[30] Most Germans rejected the extreme forms of hatred found in Hitler's later actions and statements,[31] but one account of the attitude of a typical German family is as follows:

> Just as the average Protestant was middle class and "national," he was also anti-Semitic. Today you can hardly speak of "harmless" anti-Semitism, but at that time we saw the antipathy toward the Jews as harmless. All of us.... I was raised to believe that, until the Jews rejected Jesus, they were a loyal people, a wonderful people. They were farmers and shepherds. Then God rejected them, and since that time they have been merchants, good for nothing, and they infiltrate everything, everywhere they go. And against that you had to defend yourself. In the Nazi Party program it said that Jews should not be permitted to be citizens. Most Germans held that to be a matter worth consideration.[32]

For those Christians who sympathized with the Nazis, anti-Semitism and nationalism merged to form an Aryan version of Christianity, which Hitler would later exploit to its full advantage.

Germany in the 1920s was ripe for a man with the dynamic oratory skills that Hitler possessed. Geographically, the nation was split, with the Polish Corridor separating East Prussia from the rest of Germany. Financially, it had not only to rebuild its own economy and industry, but also pay reparations to other nations. In the past, Germany had been able to obtain raw materials from its colonies. These colonies now, however, were supplying France and Britain, while Germany was paying money to those same nations. Berlin was filled with beggars. (Pacelli said that the sight of starving, homeless children in the streets of Germany sent an actual, physical pain through his heart.)[33] Disgruntled Germans were ready to listen to anyone who offered solutions, and Hitler did just that.

Today, many people wonder how a short, dark-haired man could have impressed so many people with the concept of the ideal blond, blue-eyed Aryan. (Indeed, none of the top Nazi officials looked like this ideal.) Although it does not appear so in black-and-white photographs, Hitler's hair was brown, not black, and his eyes were blue.[34] While the Soviet autopsy of his charred remains showed him to have been 5 feet 5 inches tall, his followers set forth the claim that he was 5 feet 9 inches. Moreover, when filmed, he was always made to appear taller than he really was.

Hitler's publicity machine made him seem bigger than life. He was the first German politician to fly from one place to another so that he could appear in several towns in one day. His slogan was "The *Führer* over Germany." He did not drink or smoke; he avoided caffeine; he was a vegetarian, and he ate moderately — though he had an affinity for pastries and cream puffs. He also wrote several plays and the libretto for an opera. In order to maintain the tremendous following he had among German women, his love interests, including Eva Braun, were hidden from the public, and it was suggested that he was celibate.[35] A true politician, Hitler would kiss babies and show friendship to small children. He was an animal-lover who opposed hunting, animal experimentation, and vivisection. (A 1934 post-card showed him feeding two small deer.)[36] Those who knew him personally also reported that he was a good-natured host who enjoyed entertaining people in his country home.[37] It was said that he had a good sense of humor and that he laughed a lot. He also played the piano and had a serious interest in art and classical music.

Hitler's introduction to National Socialism came on September 12, 1919, when he joined the German Workers' Party in Munich. At first, he was a civilian informer for the army, which was very interested in this group. The small party was, like many others in postwar Germany, comprised primarily of unhappy, alienated war veterans who blamed Germany's misfortunes on foreign interests and Jews. The party was particularly attractive to marginalized people, shop-keepers and artisans caught between big labor and big business, small farmers losing out to larger enterprises and middlemen, former university students who blamed the "system" for their unemployment, and the numerous former soldiers who were having a hard time adjusting to civilian life.

By February 24, 1920, Hitler was acting as the party's propaganda chief. On the first of April that year, the German Workers' Party changed its name to the National Socialist German Workers' Party (*Nationalsozialistische Deutsche Arbeiterpartei*), and this title was abbreviated to the word Nazi. On July 29, 1921, Hitler was named its president. The army then began to supply him with money and members.

The National Socialists had several beliefs and aims. First and foremost was a belief in Aryan German race superiority and a violent hatred of Jews. The

Nazis also believed in an extreme nationalism that called for the unification of all German-speaking peoples. (Later, this would lead to the occupation of Austria and Czechoslovakia.) They also believed in a form of corporative state socialism and the glorification of strength and discipline. It was similar to Fascism, which had preceded it in Italy.

---

From the beginning, the Catholic Church had a rocky relationship with the National Socialists. In 1920, Clemens August Graf von Galen (the future bishop of Münster) declared that Nazism contained ideas "which no Catholic could accept without denying his faith upon cardinal points of belief."[38] On October 1, 1921, the *Bayerischer Kurier* quoted Nuncio Pacelli as saying: "The Bavarian people are peace-loving. But, just as they were seduced during the revolution by alien elements — above all, Russians — into the extremes of Bolshevism, so now other non-Bavarian elements of entirely opposite persuasion have likewise thought to make Bavaria their base of operation." This was Pacelli's first published warning to people about Nazism, but it was not his last. In May 1924, he wrote that Nazism is perhaps the most dangerous heresy of our time. In fact, of the forty-four public speeches that Nuncio Pacelli made on German soil between 1917 and 1929, at least forty contained attacks on National Socialism or Hitler's doctrines.[39] Other Catholic leaders joined with him. German bishops warned against Nazism on five occasions between 1920 and 1927,[40] arguing that National Socialism was totalitarian, racist, pagan, and anti-Christian. Even Pope Pius XI, in 1925, warned not only against Communism, but against "every political conception which makes society or the State an end in itself, from which naturally, fatally indeed, it finishes in absorbing or destroying private rights."[41]

Father Rupert Mayer was a highly decorated Catholic military chaplain during the First World War. He later became interested in the Nazi Party, and he even addressed some crowds along with Hitler. As he came to know the party, however, he had a dramatic change of heart. In 1923, he spoke on the theme "Can a Catholic be a National Socialist?" He proceeded to tell a greatly disillusioned audience that the answer was no. He was howled down and not allowed to speak further. When the party suffered a major defeat shortly thereafter, Father Mayer was given much of the blame.[42]

Although there was general unrest and concern over the National Socialist movement throughout the nation, Germany gave Pope Pius XI little cause for alarm in the early years of his pontificate. Pacelli reported back to Rome that Hitler was unlikely to achieve any real power. The Nazis were not yet strong enough to be a serious threat, and the Church's interests were safeguarded by a strong Catholic Center Party in the Reichstag and throughout the nation.[43] There was, however, a desire to improve diplomatic relations with the German capital city of Berlin.

Despite years of diplomatic overtures, no nunciature (embassy) had been established in Berlin, primarily because of Protestant opposition and fear of offending Bavaria, which had (and wanted to keep) the Munich nunciature. By 1920, however, things had changed. It was to the advantage of both sides to negotiate a new agreement. In August 1920, Pacelli met with German President Ebert in Munich. This was the beginning of relations between the Vatican and the government of the Weimar Republic. Within a month, the Weimar government announced its intention to establish a German embassy at the Vatican. Shortly thereafter, Pacelli traveled to Berlin to meet other German officials. The Germans named an ambassador to the Papal Court, and the Holy See named Pacelli as nuncio to the Weimar Republic (in addition to his duties as nuncio to Bavaria.)

Although the Weimar Republic was represented in Rome, so was Bavaria. Thus, there arose a question as to where the papal nunciature should be maintained. The Bavarians were anxious to keep Pacelli in Munich. They knew that the Vatican wanted to conclude a concordat with the republic (though this was almost impossible due to the semi-autonomous nature of German states in matters such as this), and they did not wish to see their individual agreement with the Vatican disappear into a treaty dealing with Germany as a whole. The Bavarians argued that Pacelli should remain and first complete the concordat with Bavaria, which, they said, could serve as a model for a later agreement between Berlin and Rome.

Vatican Secretary of State Gasparri announced that Pacelli would remain in Munich for the time being. This pleased Pacelli, who preferred to keep his permanent residence in Munich in order to see the Bavarian concordat through to completion. He also resisted the move (and would continue to do so until 1925), at least in part, because Munich was a Catholic city, whereas Berlin was more Protestant, anti-clerical, and the Socialist parties were very strong. Many Protestants, liberals, and Socialists already suspected the Holy See of unfriendliness to Germany and the republic's secular principles. There was also the possibility of an increase in anti-Vatican sentiment if the nuncio's presence in Berlin became too visible. Pacelli therefore retained both posts and regarded the "short distance" between Berlin and Munich as only a minor inconvenience.

---

Like National Socialism in Germany, the Fascism that took hold in Italy grew from hostility toward that nation's experience in World War I. Following the war, there was disunity throughout Italy. Italy had gained little for its efforts on the victorious side. Internal disorder, labor unrest, and diplomatic frustration created a volatile situation. Had Mussolini (a former Socialist) not captured the imagination of the young war veterans, it is quite possible that a Bolshevik revolution would have taken place in Italy as it had in Russia. In fact, many of Mussolini's followers were former Communists.

On March 23, 1919, Mussolini formed the *Fascio di Combattimento* (Fascist) Party in Milan. The name was taken from the ancient Roman symbol of power, *fasces* — a bundle of rods bound together with a protruding blade. (An example can be seen on the back of an American Winged Liberty (Mercury) head dime, last minted in 1945.) The symbolism is that there is strength in unity. Strict law and order, as well as glorification of the state, were bedrock principals of the Fascist Party. A number of ex-servicemen joined the party because of its strong nationalistic stance. Some industrialists and landowners also supported the Fascist Party because it stood in opposition to the Communist Party, which had picked up a significant following.

In 1921, just days after Germany unconditionally accepted Allied demands for reparations, Mussolini and thirty-four other Fascists were elected to the Italian Parliament. Later that year, Mussolini renamed the Fascist Party as the National Fascist Party and declared himself its leader, or *Il Duce*. For the rest of that year and much of the next, Fascists clashed with various groups, especially Communists and Socialists.

In October 1922, Mussolini rounded up about four thousand of his followers and led a march on Rome. Mussolini's Fascists wore black shirts and carried bayonets. When they reached Rome, the Blackshirts waited for an order to attack, but it never came. Though he would later claim to have seized power with his might, for the most part Mussolini's men were cheered by the crowds, and King Victor Emmanuel III agreed to Mussolini's demands before the men ever reached Rome. (Mussolini himself traveled to Rome on a train.)

Pius XI had been pope for less than nine months when Mussolini was named prime minister in 1922. Mussolini immediately began directing violence against many institutions, including the Catholic Church. Nevertheless, he was not yet all-powerful. He suppressed the Communists, but the Socialist and Catholic Popular parties together still outnumbered the Fascists in parliament, and their combined strength would have been capable of thwarting Mussolini's plans. Such an alliance, however, was not to be.[44]

Pius XI thought that the Church's cause would be better served by a nonpolitical Catholic body with influence in all branches of the national life. Hence, he fostered and expanded Catholic Action, a movement designed to associate the laity more closely with papal aims. Catholic Action soon acquired a very large membership, especially in the professions and the universities. It also ran its own charitable and youth organizations. Catholic Action came to embrace all forms of activity — social, pastoral, and educational. It was not designed to be political, but Pius XI felt that it could accomplish more important social reforms than a political party could.

Not all of Mussolini's political opponents went away overnight, but without an alliance with other parties, Christian political power nearly vanished. Individual parties were unable to counter the growing Fascist movement, especially in light of the violent tactics that Mussolini used against them. In fairly short time, serious opposition withered away, and Mussolini was free to impose his dictatorship.

Like Adolf Hitler, Mussolini was acutely aware of the impact of religion on politics. He was an avowed atheist, and early in his political life he expressed extreme contempt for Christianity. In 1908, he described priests as "black microbes who are as fatal to mankind as tuberculosis germs." In 1919, he wrote: "Detesting as we do all forms of Christianity... we feel an immense sympathy with the modern revival of the pagan worship of strength and courage."[45] At one point, the Church banned Mussolini's newspaper, and at another time Pope Benedict XV protested against Mussolini's "terrible blasphemies."[46]

By the early 1920s, Mussolini's view of the Church had changed, likely out of political opportunism. Italy was overwhelmingly Catholic, and he did not want to create a conflict with such a large constituency — or with the Vatican, which (despite the lack of diplomatic relations) was a powerful influence within Italy. In 1923, Mussolini married his common-law wife. He also increased the amount that the government paid to the clergy. Over the next two decades, he would constantly struggle with the Vatican as he acted on his territorial ambitions, but he no longer openly condemned the Church.

————————

About the same time that future Axis nations Germany and Italy were experiencing so much social upheaval, a future Allied nation, the Soviet Union, was having similar problems that would shape world history for decades to come. Moreover, of particular interest to the Vatican, in the Soviet Union religious people in general — and Catholics more often than not — were the subject of state-sponsored persecution. As Eugenio Pacelli got more involved in Vatican affairs of state, he came to know of the atrocities that were unknown in the West until decades later.

While Hitler was still a remote threat, Catholics in the Soviet Union were being systematically murdered by the Communists. It is true that the Soviet mass murders were different from the Nazi ones. There was no plan to kill off an entire group of people, but there was an all-out effort to destroy religion.

A Soviet citizen could be religious only if his faith did not hinder him from being, above all, a Soviet patriot. That, as it turned out, was impossible. On January 13, 1918, a decree on the separation of church and state deprived all churches of their land and legal rights, in effect outlawing them. Religious marriage was abolished. The family was declared obsolete. Over the next five years, thousands of Ukrainian priests, monks, nuns, and lay Catholics were sent to prison or to Siberia. Many of these prisoners were shot, and others were allowed to die of starvation, cold, and disease in what the Soviet authorities called "corrective labor camps."[47] Sometimes they were tortured before they died.

Having already confiscated church buildings and land, in February 1922 the government issued a decree that all church valuables, including sacred objects, would be confiscated. Clergy and faithful laypersons fought against this confiscation. In the three months that followed, 1,414 bloody clashes between church people and government troops were recorded. During 1922 alone, a total of 8,100 priests, monks, and nuns were executed.[48]

Needless to say, the Soviet persecution did not go unnoticed in the Vatican; yet the Church had no desire to lose its contacts with Russia. In fact, the Church sought to improve lines of communication. The Pope asked Pacelli to begin preliminary discussions in Berlin with the Russian ambassador about the possibility of sending an apostolic delegate to Moscow and working toward a concordat between the two nations.[49] Lengthy talks were held throughout the fall of 1924, but nothing came of the initiative.[50]

A renewed persecution of Catholics in the Soviet Union led to another unsuccessful attempt to reach an agreement. The Soviets eventually informed Pacelli that Moscow was not interested in a concordat or any form of bilateral agreement. Pius XI came to believe that with Stalin in power there could be no diplomatic relationship between Moscow and the Vatican.[51] Their relationship was to be one of bitter hostility. Moreover, this hostility was not tied to a particular nation; rather, the basic ideology of Communism was incompatible with Catholicism, if not with organized religion itself.

In 1930, Pius XI personally and openly protested against the anti-religious excesses of the Communist regimes. He also ordered a Mass in St. Peter's for all of those who had been killed in the Soviet Union. In 1937, he issued a strong condemnation of Communism in his encyclical *Divini Redemptoris* (of the Divine Redeemer, commonly called "On Atheistic Communism"). "Communism is intrinsically wrong," proclaimed the papal document, "and no one who would save Christian civilization may collaborate with it in any field whatsoever."[52] This would create some difficult questions for the next pope, when the Soviet Union joined the Allies in their war against Hitler's National Socialism.

# THREE

# The Spread of Nationalism

In October 1922, the same month that Mussolini's Blackshirts marched on Rome, Germany faced a financial crisis. On the twenty-third, German Chancellor Joseph Wirth proposed to his cabinet that Germany declare bankruptcy. The mark had been falling so dramatically that prices had risen 100 percent in the previous month. Public baths in Berlin were closed to save coal. Germans were openly expressing their reluctance to pay war reparations. The government's ability to lead was called into question.

The payment of reparations placed an enormous strain on a country already exhausted by more than four years of war. In early 1923, Germany fell behind in deliveries of coal and timber, prompting French and Belgian forces to move in and occupy the industrial Ruhr province. Germany immediately condemned the occupation as a violation of international law and stopped all reparation payments to those two nations.

Chancellor Wilhelm Cuno urged a program of passive resistance to the occupation. Workers in Ruhr mines and factories went on strike, but this led to greater instability. In addition, industrial output plummeted, which brought on economic collapse. French and Belgian forces then occupied industrial installations, requisitioned coal, took over the transportation system, confiscated salaries, and did away with the private ownership of some businesses. The resistance continued, however, and in retaliation French forces cut off shipments of coal to other areas of Germany, putting even more pressure on an already distressed economy. More than one hundred fifty thousand Germans were displaced from the occupied area, primarily due to suspicion of sabotaging the national rail system. This resulted in what was essentially an undeclared state of war between France and the Rhineland.

Pacelli negotiated with the German leaders in Berlin.[1] They had been unwilling to condemn sabotage, even when it resulted in violence. Pacelli argued that condemnation was necessary in order to favorably dispose other nations toward Germany and to help with later reparation negotiations. He explained that the Vatican had often come to the aid of the Weimar Republic when it sought support in international matters, but that the German leaders now had to condemn the violence if they expected the Vatican to do anything further on Germany's behalf. The Berlin leadership ultimately condemned the violence, but the protests continued.

By June 1923, the German economy was at the breaking point. In just three weeks, the German stock market lost about half of its value and inflation reached its peak.[2] Prior to the First World War, a German mark was worth about 25 cents. In October 1922, when Germany was already considering bankruptcy, a U.S. dollar bought 4,000 marks. By June 1, 1923, that same dollar could buy 74,500 marks. Two weeks later it would buy 136,000 marks. Many Germans blamed the crisis on reparations and the occupation of the Ruhr. Protesting German workers slowed production to such a level that coal, traditionally a major export, had to be imported. Additionally, displaced workers from the Ruhr placed even more strain on the economy. By late June, reserves held by the central bank were depleted.

The financial distress took its toll on the political scene. On October 3, 1923, the Berlin cabinet resigned, and Chancellor Stresemann was appointed as the first constitutional dictator of the Weimar Republic (a precedent that would later help Hitler seize total control of the nation). The economy, however, did not improve. The exchange rate hit 12 billion, then (overnight) 40 billion marks to the dollar. By the beginning of November, one loaf of bread cost 140 billion marks. By mid-November, a single dollar could buy 4 trillion marks. Germany was reduced to a nation of scavengers.

The German government tried to counter the problem by issuing a new mark, worth a trillion of the old ones. Unfortunately, this tended to add to the confusion, because there were then three official currencies in circulation: the new one, the old one, and an even older one. To help take care of this problem, the German government instituted even more governmental regulations. Germans were prohibited from buying foreign currency; foreign traders had to accept "blocked marks," which could be spent in Germany only, at a discounted rate; and travelers were searched for currency violations at the national border.

Ultimately, currency control would turn Germany into a sort of police state almost a decade before Hitler became dictator. Letters were opened, accounts were reviewed, and a siege, wartime economy took over even though Germany was at peace.[3] On November 23, 1923, following a "no confidence" vote in the Reichstag, the Stresemann government resigned. A new government took over power, but it also went through many difficult periods as the German economy continued to stumble.

————

As Pacelli watched the confusion and disorder that was so devastating to the German people, Adolf Hitler made his move. For several years, he had been holding meetings and gathering a following. An early poster advertising one of his rallies read, in part, as follows:

> Fellow Citizens: Come today, Sunday, March 6, 1921, 10 A.M.
> to a GIANT PROTEST DEMONSTRATION at the
> CIRCUS KRONE
> Speaker A. Hitler on:
> "LONDON AND US?"

Protest against the Peace Treaty of Versailles which has been foisted upon us by the single guilty party of the war, namely the Jewish-international stock exchange capital. Protest against the latest Paris dictate, and finally protest against the Reich Government, which once again makes the most colossal promises without consulting the German people.

\* \* \*

Admission 1 Mark. War invalids free. No Jews admitted.[4]

To his followers, Hitler was seen as a bright new leader who could avenge the defeat of 1918 and lead the Germans to a new era of prosperity by leaving the current government behind. "Democracy," said Hitler, "is a rule by crazy brains. The [Weimar] Republic is a monstrosity."[5]

In October 1923, the *Christian Science Monitor* published a front-page exclusive interview with Hitler, referring to him as the "leader of the German Fascist movement."[6] In it, Hitler complained about Germany's surrender of the Ruhr to France, saying that he would have rather seen it turned into a desert. "If I had been at the head of the government, the Ruhr district would have been burned down as Moscow was burned by the Russians. The French would never have found a single bridge or tree there."[7] The interviewer noted that this "Bavarian Mussolini" was "not to be taken lightly." Hitler stared hard into the interviewer's face, made excited gestures, and raised his voice until "he almost shouted." He then gave away his plans for his future role in Germany: "What has been possible in Italy also is possible in Germany, where the German people, given a Mussolini, would fall down on their knees before him and worship him more than Mussolini has ever been worshiped in Italy."[8]

Nuncio Pacelli recognized the threat. In 1923, he wrote to the Holy See to report that a militant group ("followers of Hitler and Ludendorff") were persecuting Catholics and Jews.[9] He referred to this group (not yet known as Nazis) as "right-wing radicals." He also praised the "learned and zealous" Cardinal Archbishop Michael von Faulhaber of Munich, who was attacked because he "had denounced the persecutions against the Jews."[10] The following year, on May 1, in a handwritten draft report to Secretary of State Gasparri, Pacelli wrote: "Nazism is probably the most dangerous heresy of our time."[11] In another handwritten report dated three days later, the future Pope Pius XII wrote: "The heresy of Nazism puts state and race above everything, above true religion, above the truth and above the justice."[12]

---

Bavarian dictator Gustav Ritter von Kahr was scheduled to appear in a giant Munich beer hall along with most of the other Bavarian leaders on November 8, 1923. While von Kahr was speaking, several hundred storm troopers surrounded the hall and Hitler entered. Protected by a machine-gun crew, Hitler climbed on a table and fired a shot into the ceiling. Proclaiming that the "National Revolution" had begun, Hitler forced the Bavarian leaders to join him in a private room. With gun in hand, he urged them to turn the Bavarian dictatorship into a national one, with a march on Berlin, similar to Mussolini's march on Rome.[13] After a coerced agreement, the group broke up. The next day, Pacelli telegraphed to Rome: "Last night Hitler with his armed bands declared that the Bavarian government had fallen.... The belief is, to put it shortly, that order can be restored, but probably not without bloodshed."[14]

Hitler's forces took over the Munich army headquarters, but soon thereafter von Kahr posted signs explaining that this was a result of extortion and moved his headquarters to a new location. The next morning, Hitler led a column of storm troopers to army headquarters, but they walked into a trap. The police blocked them off in a narrow street. Guns were fired, and sixteen of Hitler's men were killed. Many more were wounded. Most of the survivors ran away or were arrested. Hitler was not shot, but his bodyguards threw him to the ground so forcefully that he dislocated a shoulder.

On November 12, Pacelli sent two messages to Rome. The first said: "Situation still critical. The Nationalists rouse the people against the clergy, especially [Cardinal] Faulhaber."[15] Then word came that Hitler had been arrested three days later in a villa forty miles outside of Munich. Pacelli sent a second telegram to Rome: "Hitler imprisoned. Peace seems to be reestablished."[16] Two days later, Pacelli sent a detailed report on the putsch in which he emphasized the fundamentally "anti-Catholic" nature of the nationalist movement.[17]

Adolf Hitler's trial for the failed Beer Hall Putsch began in February and ended on April 1, 1924. He was found guilty of high treason and sentenced to five years in prison. Reporters accurately noted, however, that this was merely a slap on the wrist. He would be eligible for parole in six months. Moreover, at trial Hitler portrayed himself as the spirit of German nationalism and the enemy of Marxism. Newspaper accounts transformed him into a national hero. He vowed not to let prison destroy him. "You may pronounce us guilty a thousand times over," he said, "but the goddess of the eternal court of history will tear to tatters the brief of the state prosecutor and the sentence of this court."[18]

On April 24, Pacelli reported to Rome on a "vulgar and violent campaign" being waged in the press against Catholics and Jews by Hitler's party.[19] He concluded that this movement regarded Catholics and Jews as its worst enemies. In fact, his report to Rome on Ludendorff's trial (March 3, 1924) explained that the defense argued that the Catholic Church and the Pope were Germany's worst enemies.[20]

From this time on, updates on National Socialism were always present in Pacelli's reports to Rome due to the threat that it clearly posed to Christianity and the Catholic Church.[21] He also repeatedly complained that many Catholics were being "cheated and misled" because they did not realize that "nationalism is perhaps the most perilous heresy of our time."[22]

Hitler was very well treated in prison. He had his own room in the fortress at Landsberg, with a magnificent view over the River Lech. He spent much of his time dictating his book *Mein Kampf* ("My Struggle") to his old friend Rudolf Hess, who was also being held for his participation in the failed coup. (Hess later became deputy leader of the Nazi Party and minister without portfolio in Hitler's government, and in 1939 he became the third-ranking Nazi in Germany.) During this time, the German economy continued to struggle, and the National Socialist ideas advanced by Hitler became attractive to more and more Germans.

Hitler was released from prison on Christmas Eve 1924, after only eight months of incarceration. His anti-Semitism was more virulent than ever. The National Socialist Party had been banned after the failed Beer Hall Putsch, but this played right into Hitler's hand by preventing rivals from taking it over. Although he was prohibited from making public speeches, Hitler soon obtained permission from the government to reorganize the party. He renounced the use of force and promised to gain power only through legal means. He did, however, vow to destroy the Weimar Republic with the weapons of democracy.[23] If out-voting the opposition took longer than out-shooting them, at least the result would be guaranteed by the German constitution. Sooner or later, he reasoned, the Nazi Party would gain a majority in the Reichstag, and after that, Germany.

---

For Pacelli, the 1920s brought many international issues affecting both Germany and the Church. The Allies had invaded portions of Germany during the First World War, and some borders were redrawn. Of all the areas in dispute along Germany's eastern borders, the situation in Danzig, Poland, was the most controversial. In order to give Poland access to the sea, the Treaty of Versailles gave the nation a narrow corridor through former German territory to the port city of Danzig (better known today by its Polish name, Gdansk), which was made a free city under the supervision of the League of Nations.

The population of Danzig spoke German and was overwhelmingly Catholic. That became important when the city government requested incorporation into a German Catholic diocese. Rather than incorporate Danzig, however, the Pope (who was accused of being pro-Polish due to his prior service as a nuncio in Poland) named a German-speaking Irish priest, Eduard O'Rourke, as administrator for Danzig. O'Rourke was given the powers of a diocesan bishop. In this way, German interests in Danzig were maintained without all the difficulties that actual incorporation of the free city into a German diocese would have involved.[24]

For several years, Pacelli had been the Holy See's representative to both Bavaria and to the Weimar Republic. He had offices in both Munich and Berlin, but he maintained his official residence in Munich and returned there as often as possible. A concordat with Bavaria was signed in March 1924, and the more important issues were now centered in Berlin. Despite some Protestant resentment at seeing a representative of the Pope in Berlin, the Weimar government made clear that it urgently desired his presence in Berlin on a more full-time basis. Vatican Secretary of State Gasparri agreed, and Pacelli made the move to the German capital on August 18, 1925.[25]

Pacelli had been greatly admired during his more than eight-year stay in Bavaria. There were numerous expressions of sorrow at his departure. In addition to banquets in his honor, newspaper editorials praised his achievements. The official farewell party took place on July 14, 1925. Rarely has any city experienced such an outpouring of respect, admiration, and love for a foreign dignitary as took place in the Bavarian capital for Pacelli.[26]

In moving from Munich to Berlin, Pacelli went from an area loyal to Rome to one that was skeptical of Rome's intentions. He had some reluctance about the move.[27] Nevertheless, the move was necessary so that he could concentrate on the Vatican's long-desired concordat with Germany. Pacelli quickly took an active part in the life of the city and formed acquaintances and friends in all circles. He selected a large home surrounded by park-like grounds so that he could entertain representatives of other nations on a regular basis. Soon, high German officials, politicians, aristocrats, students, and workers were regular visitors to the nunciature.[28] With his well-informed opinions, outgoing personality, social grace, and quick wit, Pacelli was very influential throughout Berlin, even in non-Catholic circles. He had the reputation of being "the best informed diplomat in Germany."[29]

———————

In July 1925, Hitler's *Mein Kampf* was released. It was dedicated to his followers who were killed in the street the day after the Beer Hall Putsch. It became "the oft-cited but seldom read bible of the Nazi movement."[30] In it, Hitler called for a national revival and a battle against Communism and Jews. It was part personal testament, part manual for the National Socialist German Workers' Party, and part demagogic appeal to the German people. Pacelli must have taken special note of Hitler's analysis of religious institutions in general, and the Catholic Church in particular. As explained by one author:

> Though Hitler often invoked God or Providence when he spoke, he was a thoroughly lapsed Catholic. Hitler considered Christianity incompatible with the new National Socialist age — it was "merely whole-hearted Bolshevism, under a tinsel of metaphysics." He deplored the survival of religious observance among German ministers and generals, "little children who have learnt nothing else." He regarded Christianity and communism as two sides of the same coin, sharing in St. Paul a common Jewish ancestor. Hitler took the German nation as his religion.[31]

In *Mein Kampf,* Hitler spent a good deal of time discussing the political use and misuse of religion in times of international conflict. He was unhappy with what

he perceived to be a lack of patriotism on the part of German churches during earlier conflicts, while he claimed that opponents used the churches for anti-German
reasons. He focused primarily on the Pan-German movement, a late-nineteenth-
century call to unify all German-speaking people and separate them from non-
Germans. This "goal had been correct, its will pure," Hitler wrote.[32]

In the nineteenth century, the Pan-Germans fought openly and bitterly
with the Catholic Church, as Bismarck struggled to bring Catholic institutions
under Prussian state control.[33] Hitler believed that direct confrontation with the
Church offended the spiritual nature of the people and caused them to reject the
Pan-Germans. He adopted the Pan-German attitude about the Catholic Church,
but he hid his war against it.[34] When others were too strident in their opposition
to religion, Hitler distanced himself from their positions.[35] In fact, he found ways
to use the Church for his own purposes.

According to Hitler, when others wanted to reshape Austria into a "Slavic
state," they used religious institutions "without the slightest qualms," for that
purpose:[36]

> Czech pastors were appointed to German communities; slowly but surely they
> began to set the interests of the Czech people above the interests of the churches,
> becoming germ-cells of the de-Germanization process. The German clergy did
> practically nothing to counter these methods.... [They were] completely use-
> less for carrying on this struggle in a positive resistance to the attacks of the
> adversary.[37]

Like the Pan-Germans, Hitler was angered that Catholic officials were
unwilling to support German causes over Catholic or universal issues. He argued
that "the Catholic clergy as such was grossly infringing on German rights."[38] He
wrote:

> Thus the Church did not seem to feel with the German people, but to side
> unjustly with the enemy. The root of the whole evil lay... in the fact that the
> directing body of the Catholic Church was not in Germany, and that for this
> very reason alone it was hostile to the interests of our nationality.[39]

Therefore, Hitler concluded that "Protestantism as such is a better defender of
the interests of Germanism."[40] He did, however, note that it would be hard to
persuade Protestants to adopt his anti-Semitic position.[41]

Hitler, who once described Christianity as the worst trick the Jews had
played on humanity, originally proposed a new German religion, based on the
old Germanic gods, to take its place. The existing churches put an end to this
part of his plan, at least for the time being, but relations between Germany and
the Vatican suffered. Hitler proposed to correct his problem with the Catholic
Church's lack of German identity, not by nationalizing the Church, but by culti-
vating the national identity within the Church. He wrote of the "value of large-
scale propaganda."[42] He explained:

Let the German people be raised from childhood up with that exclusive recognition of the rights of their own nationality, and let not the hearts of children be contaminated with the curse of our "objectivity," even in matters regarding the preservation of their own ego. Then in a short time it will be seen that (presupposing, of course, a radically national government) in Germany, as in Ireland, Poland, or France, the Catholic will always be a German.[43]

By carefully crafting a national Catholic Church, Hitler felt that "an astute tactician" would be assured of a strong following.[44]

To do what he proposed, Hitler said it was necessary to understand the current strengths and weaknesses of the existing German churches. His opinion was that German churches were so involved in a Catholic/Protestant dispute that they were blind to the true threat to Germany — the Jews. "[T]he Jew… now again he succeeds in causing the two German denominations to assail one another, while the foundations of both are corroded and undermined by the poison of the international world Jew."[45] Hitler, in fact, argued that Jews deliberately created rifts between the Christian churches in order to take advantage of them. Thus, the "desired goal" of Jews was that "Catholic and Protestants wage a merry war with one another, and the mortal enemy of Aryan humanity and all Christendom laughs up his sleeve."[46] Clearly, it was racial purity, not religion, which was most important to Hitler.

Before Hitler came to power, Jews were integrated into the German culture. Under the Weimar Republic, Jews in Germany were treated better than in most other European nations.[47] They had constitutional protections, and many of them married Gentiles. This particularly concerned Hitler:

This contamination of our blood, blindly ignored by hundreds of thousands of our people, is carried on systematically by the Jew today. Systematically these black parasites of the nation defile our inexperienced young blonde girls and thereby destroy something which can no longer be replaced in this world. Both, yes, both Christian denominations look on indifferently at this desecration and destruction of a noble and unique living creature, given to the world by God's grace.[48]

The origin of Hitler's extreme hatred of Jews will probably always be a matter of speculation, but whatever it was, he used every means at his disposal to annihilate the Jewish race. To do this, he had to attract a strong following. He looked to practices in the Catholic Church, not as a means of currying favor with the Lord, but as a way to capture devoted adherents.

Hitler once explained, "I have always learned a great deal from my opponents." He then went on to identify Marxists, Freemasons, and the Catholic Church as examples of opponents from whom he had obtained "illumination and ideas."[49] "There has been nothing more impressive in the world than the hierarchal organization of the Catholic Church," he said. "I have taken over many elements of it in the organization of my party."[50] The first point that

Hitler claimed to take from the Catholic religion related to celibacy and personal strength. Priests and nuns, of course, take a vow of celibacy. Hitler thought that this made them stronger. The "very significance of celibacy... is not at all recognized by most people. It is cause of the incredibly vigorous strength which resides in this age-old institution."[51] Hitler's propaganda machine went to great lengths to hide his romances from the public (and some who were fairly close to him thought that he was indeed celibate at least until shortly before his death).

A second point that he claimed to take from the Catholic Church related to maintaining faith in a dogma, regardless of whether the evidence points in different directions:

> Here, too, we can learn by the example of the Catholic Church. Though its doctrinal edifice, and in part quite superfluously, comes into collision with exact science and research, it is nonetheless unwilling to sacrifice so much as one little syllable of its dogmas. It has recognized quite correctly that its power of resistance does not lie in its lesser or greater adaptation to the scientific findings of the moment, which in reality are always fluctuating, but rather in rigidly holding to dogmas once established, for it is only such dogmas which lend to the whole body the character of a faith. And so today it stands more firmly.[52]

Hitler, of course, held to his core beliefs (such as extermination of the Jews), even to the point of damaging his war effort.

Finally, Hitler looked to the Catholic Church for guidance on a matter in which he was to become recognized as a true master — the means of persuasion:

> At night, however, [people] succumb more easily to the dominating force of a stronger will.... The same purpose, after all, is served by the artificially made and yet mysterious twilight in Catholic churches, the burning lamps, incense, censers, etc.[53]

Hitler would later perfect the torchlight parades that won him so many followers.[54] Some of these events were so enthralling that anti-Hitler people, even Jews, sometimes found themselves swept up in the emotion of the moment.

This Nazi interest in the Catholic Church as a model for building individual strength continued into the war years. "I have learned above all from the Jesuits," said Hitler.[55] Heinrich Himmler, leader of the German S.S., had several books about the Jesuits and spoke of training his elite Waffen S.S. combat troops along Jesuit lines (without, of course, the Christian influence). He even sent his principal officers to the Wewelsburg Castle in Westphalia for a type of "spiritual exercises," based on the Nordic ideals, the Holy Grail, and the Teutonic Knights of old. He hoped that they would learn the inner subjugation of will and intellect that would make them expert soldiers. Hitler jokingly called Himmler "our very own Ignatius Loyola."[56]

Despite the discussion of religion, *Mein Kampf* was not a holy book;[57] it was a blueprint for future action. After being freed from prison in December 1924,

Hitler spent the rest of the decade trying to implement these ideas and build his power base. He trained with a professional stage magician to learn gestures and body positions that would help him make better presentations. He also worked on rebuilding the Nazi Party. An improving economy stalled his efforts, but fortunately for him (and unfortunately for the rest of the world), on October 29, 1929, the Wall Street stock market crashed, leading the world into the Great Depression. Germany, still dependent on outside loans, saw them all dry up. Unemployment soared, and the economy tumbled. The unrest led to Communist revolts and fighting in the streets. Hitler knew that all of these matters would work in his favor.[58]

# FOUR

# The Lateran Treaty

Mussolini was called "the most blasphemous journalist in Europe,"[1] but he understood the political importance of religion. Not only in gaining power, but also in running the country, support from the Church was crucial in a country as Catholic as Italy. As he would later (December 1934) write in the French newspaper, *Figaro*:

> History of western civilization from the time of the Roman Empire to our days shows that every time the State clashes with religion, it is always the state which ends defeated. The simple, passive resistance of the clergy and the faithful is sufficient to foil the most violent attacks on the part of the State.[2]

Mussolini was determined not to "clash" with the Church. In the mid-1920s, he increased clerical stipends, reintroduced Catholic teaching into schools, and reformed laws relating to charitable institutions.[3] By far, however, the most important development regarding the relations between Italy and the Vatican was the signing of the Lateran Treaty in 1929.

Benedict XV, who reigned from 1914 to 1922, renewed the old practice of making agreements or signing concordats with nations so that the Vatican could safeguard Church interests and better oppose anti-Christian forces. As nuncio, Pacelli had successfully negotiated concordats with three German states, and he laid the groundwork for a fourth with all of Germany.[4] Now, the Holy See needed to strengthen its relations with the Catholic nation of Italy, which surrounded Vatican City on all sides.

The Pope had once been the temporal ruler of the states of the Church, which comprised a considerable portion of central Italy. His last remaining territory was taken away when Italian government troops seized Rome in 1870.[5] The ancient city had been the papal capital; it was now made the capital of the Italian Kingdom.

In order to conciliate the Holy See, in 1871 the Italian government enacted the "Law of Papal Guarantees."[6] Under these provisions, the Pope and his successors were guaranteed possession of St. Peter's, the Vatican and its gardens, the Lateran Palace, and the Villa of Castel Gandolfo. The Pope was also granted sovereign rights within these possessions, including the inviolability of his own person and the authority to receive and send ambassadors. In addition, he was granted free use of the Italian telegraph, railway, and postal systems, and provided with an annual subsidy of approximately $645,000.

The reigning Pope at that time, Pius IX, refused to recognize the Law of Papal Guarantees because it was a legislative act by the Italian government, not a negotiated treaty or concordat. He and his successors declined the annual subsidy, proclaimed themselves "prisoners of an usurping power," and did not leave Vatican City or even show themselves in public.[7] In October 1926, Mussolini had an intermediary express to Pope Pius XI his strong desire to enter into negotiations for the purpose of eliminating the hostility between the Church and the nation of Italy.[8] These negotiations culminated in 1929 with the signing of the Lateran Treaty.

The Lateran Treaty actually consisted of three documents, which Cardinal Pacelli's brother, Francesco, helped negotiate. In the first document, the Holy See recognized the Kingdom of Italy and surrendered territorial claims in exchange for Italy's recognition of a sovereign and independent Vatican City State. A second document provided compensation for Church property that had been seized in 1870. The third document, the true concordat, defined the rights and obligations of both the Church and the state.

Much of the Church's teaching was incorporated into the 1929 concordat, and the Italian government agreed to all of the Church's most important religion-oriented issues: Catholicism was declared the sole and official religion of Italy. All issues involving religion and politics were to be settled according to Church law. Catholic education was made compulsory in all schools, the government recognized Church schools and universities, Church holy days were made state holidays, and the state agreed to pay salaries to priests and bishops. Papal colleges, while not given extraterritorial privileges, were free from taxation and guaranteed against expropriation. Ordained priests, moreover, were exempted from military obligations. Church marriages were given civil effect, and divorce was made subject to the restrictions of canon law.[9] Catholic Action, the Pope's lay organization, was granted freedom for all its activities so long as it conformed to directives from the Holy See. The Church was given autonomous government and legislative power as well as the right to establish its own police force, civil service, postage services, flag, currency, radio station, and a railway station. Papal churches, palaces, and other buildings outside the Vatican were given the territorial immunities normally reserved for foreign embassies. The Pope was granted free communication with his bishops throughout the world, and he was free to appoint Italian bishops, subject only to political objections of the state.[10] Italy also provided money to the Vatican.

When Pope Benedict XV died in 1922, the Vatican had to borrow $100,000 to cover the expenses of his funeral and the conclave to elect his successor. With the Lateran Treaty, the Church received a cash payment of 750 million lire and one billion lire in state securities.[11] This was intended as compensation for the property seized from the Church in 1870. The approximate value of this settlement was $92.1 million, which did not approach the true value of the seized property, but some commentators have suggested that it saved the Vatican from bankruptcy.[12]

In exchange for Italy's agreement to recognize the Vatican as an independent sovereign state and to guarantee its protection, the Vatican essentially agreed to divorce itself from secular politics.[13] This killed any hope of reviving the Catholic Popular Party, which had once posed a threat to Mussolini, but which had disappeared by 1927. Pius XI, however, was never a proponent of Catholic political parties. He preferred to work with concordats and his organization Catholic Action. He was pleased with the Italian concordat as it was written, and his assessment that "we have given back God to Italy and Italy to God" was widely shared.[14]

On February 11, 1929, Vatican Secretary of State Gasparri and Mussolini met at the Lateran Palace and signed the documents. The Vatican thus officially became the smallest sovereign state in the world, with an area of only slightly more than a hundred acres and less than five hundred citizens. After the signing ceremony, the Pope appeared on the balcony and blessed the crowds in St. Peter's Square. The Italian Chamber of Deputies voted that February 11, the date of the signing of the Lateran Treaty, would replace September 20, the anniversary of the taking of Rome in 1870, as a national holiday.[15]

While there was some expression of disappointment with the Church for having reached an agreement with Mussolini, he was not an unpopular world figure. Not only had he "made the trains run on time," but Mussolini had also accomplished many things for the Italian people.[16] By engaging in big deficit spending (though he had come to power promising a balanced budget), Mussolini built 1,700 seaside summer camps for children, provided prenatal clinics for expectant mothers, instituted the eight-hour workday, and provided insurance for the elderly, unemployed, and the disadvantaged.[17] From the Church's perspective, it was also important that he had placed crucifixes in every classroom and provided chaplains to Italian soldiers.

In the late 1920s and early 1930s, many people saw Mussolini as a positive influence on Europe. Among his admirers were Albert Einstein (a Jew who fled Germany to escape racism), Mohandas Gandhi (who called Mussolini "a superman"), George Bernard Shaw (a Socialist), the archbishop of Canterbury (who called Mussolini the "one great figure in Europe"), Winston Churchill (who told Mussolini, "I am sure I would have been with you from the beginning to end," if they had been countrymen), and even Sigmund Freud (a Jew who called Mussolini a "cultural hero").[18] He also attracted the attention of future Fascist leaders, Juan Perón and Adolf Hitler (who adopted the brown shirts for his storm troopers, in imitation of Mussolini's black shirts).[19]

Fascists from around the world tended to view the treaty with the Catholic Church as a betrayal by Mussolini.[20] Perhaps regretting that he had gone so far along the path of conciliation, in the month following its signing Mussolini publicly stated: "Within the State, the Church is not sovereign, nor is it even free... because it is subordinate... to the general law of the State. We have not resurrected the Temporal Power of the Popes, we have buried it."[21] In referring to Christianity, Mussolini said, "This religion was born in Palestine but became Catholic in Rome. If it had stayed in Palestine, it would very likely have remained one of the many sects that flourished in those perfervid surroundings... and would probably have died out leaving no trace."[22] Pius XI used harsh terms to criticize Mussolini's pronouncements and explained that Catholicism was distinct, separate, and in significant ways inconsistent with Fascism.[23]

A decade after the signing of the Lateran Treaty, Pius XII (Pacelli), in *Summi Pontificatus* (On the Unity of Human Society), wrote of its importance:

> We can, in this first Encyclical directed to the whole Christian people scattered over the world, rank among such friendly powers Our dear Italy, fruitful garden of the Faith, which was planted by the Princes of the Apostles. For, as a result of the Lateran Pacts, her representative occupies a place of honor among those officially accredited to the Apostolic See. "The Peace of Christ restored to Italy," like a new dawn of brotherly union in religious and in civil intercourse, had its beginning in these Pacts.[24]

Although the Church forged a working agreement with Mussolini, neither Pacelli nor Pius XI sympathized with Fascism.[25] The Pope was one of the first world leaders to condemn the anti-Christian teachings of Fascism (at a time when other statesmen were still vying for Mussolini's favors). Moreover, as some scholars have concluded, the Church, "by obtaining the freedom of action necessary to exist as a viable spiritual power in Italy, gained more than it lost."[26]

The Lateran Treaty did not cause Pius XI to let up on his criticism of Mussolini or Fascism in general.[27] Moreover, Mussolini did not view the treaty with the Holy See as any sign of mutual respect. Before long, he began asserting the right to place his friends in high positions within the Church, and his men openly attacked the lay organization Catholic Action. Fascists seized the Vatican newspaper, *L'Osservatore Romano*, and suppressed other newspapers.[28] In addition, despite the Lateran Treaty's provision for Catholic religious education in public schools, Mussolini now insisted that public education remain solely the prerogative of the state and that it be kept outside the province of the Holy See. He tried to outlaw all Catholic youth groups, and Italian university professors were forced to swear loyalty to Fascism (only eleven refused).[29] While Mussolini sometimes attended military Masses, he exhibited extreme contempt for the religious services.[30]

By 1931, things had gotten very bad. First, the Fascist newspaper *Lavoro Fascista* ran a series of articles attacking Catholic Action as being anti-Fascist and contrary to Italian laws. Then, in May and June, Fascist-inspired anti-papal demonstrations swept across Italy. Catholic buildings were pillaged, Catholic publications were burned, and protestors in the street chanted, "Down with the traitor Ratti [Pope Pius XI]" and "Kill him!"[31] Mussolini himself repeated his famous slogan, "Everything in the State, nothing apart from the State, nothing against the State," but with a foreign journalist he went further, adding: "The child, as soon as he is old enough to learn, belongs entirely to the State, to it alone."[32] Pius XI was compelled to respond, and he did so with the encyclical *Non Abbiamo Bisogno* (on Catholic Action in Italy).

Unlike most encyclicals, which are written in Latin, *Non Abbiamo Bisogno* was written in Italian, to make it more accessible to the Italian people. The Pope signed it on June 29, 1931, and Monsignor (later Cardinal) Francis J. Spellman of New York smuggled it out of Italy and released it in Paris, rather than the traditional Vatican release. Pius XI feared that Mussolini, who controlled the press, would prevent its distribution if it were released in Italy.[33] In the encyclical, Pius XI did not expressly condemn the Fascist Party or the regime, but he did warn against "pagan worship of the State."[34] He rejected a revolution that "tore young people from the Church and Jesus Christ, and nurtured their young to vigor to hate, to violence and to irreverence." He also disputed Mussolini's charges that groups like Catholic Action were political in nature and that Mussolini's political foes headed the organizations (which would have been a breach of the Lateran Treaty).

Mussolini had no doubt about the Pope's meaning. In retaliation, the Fascists forced fifty thousand Catholics to either resign from Catholic Action or lose their jobs, effectively bringing that organization to an end.[35] Some in the Vatican feared physical reprisals against the Pope or Secretary of State Pacelli, who was said to be the driving force behind the Pope.[36] Mussolini, however, contented himself with periodic petty insults (once threatening to build a giant mosque and import thousands of Muslims to worship in Rome) and continuing persecution of Catholic institutions.[37]

In reaching an accord with Italy, Pius XI was treating Italy the same way he treated other nations. Even if a state might stand to gain more in the short term than the Church, governments do not last, and eventually the Church would be better positioned if it had a relationship with the people. Thus, the Pontiff was confident that the Church would emerge triumphant in the long run if it had an agreement. In fact, despite the horrid treatment of the Church in Communist nations, the Vatican (through Pacelli) tried to obtain a concordat with the Soviet Union in the mid-1920s,[38] and it did conclude one with the predominantly Socialist government of Prussia in 1929.[39]

Although it was a common provision in the concordats that the Vatican signed with other countries, one provision of the Lateran Treaty proved particularly controversial:

> With regard to her sovereignty in the field of international relations, the Holy See declares that she wishes to remain extraneous to all disputes concerning temporal affairs between nations, and to international congresses convened for the purpose of settling such disputes, unless the contending parties call upon her to serve as the mediator of peace. Nevertheless, she reserves the right to exercise her moral and spiritual power in every case. As the result of this declaration, the Vatican State will always be considered neutral and inviolable territory.

Thus, while the Holy See is always officially neutral, it never relinquishes the right to speak on moral truths.

# FIVE

# Hitler's Rise to Power and the Concordat

Hitler was a mystery to most people in Munich. He gave spine-chilling speeches in the beer halls, but his past was unknown. He was not from Munich, though he spoke like he was. It was rumored that he was from Bohemia, that "Hitler" was not his real name, that he was Jewish, and that he was being supported by others in the movement who would one day reveal themselves as the true leaders of National Socialism.[1] This aura of mystery might have contributed to his ascent to power, which came as a surprise to many foreign diplomats.

Though he was not yet recognized as a threat, in the 1920s Hitler built a power base that was poised to take over Germany. To do this, he relied on a select group of men. Perhaps the most important was Joseph Goebbels, his minister of propaganda. Goebbels paved the way for the National Socialists to be accepted as a legitimate political party, and he continued shaping public opinion even after the Nazis took control. He did not simply censor undesirable information or commentary; he exploited the media in a carefully orchestrated campaign to advance Nazi ideals. He produced motion pictures focusing on nature and Darwin's "survival of the fittest" theory. Animals that killed their deformed young were said to be practicing proper race theory. Weak and deformed humans were depicted as a drain on the nation. Jewish people were similarly portrayed. Slowly, Goebbels began to shape national opinion.[2]

Unlike the Communists in Russia who promoted class warfare, Hitler tried to offer something to all Aryan Germans. To the industrialists, he offered protection from nationalization. To the unemployed, he offered massive social programs. To disgruntled war veterans, he offered scapegoats (the Weimar officials who signed the Treaty of Versailles) and promised to restore Germany's might. Hitler offered solutions to all, primarily by blaming the Jews for the nation's troubles. They, he argued, profiteered from the war while others were dying. This fit well with the party line on race theory.

Despite their propaganda efforts, the Nazis never received an absolute majority of votes in any free election during the Weimar Republic. The first Nazi to win public office in Germany was Wilhelm Frick, who became the minister of the interior for Thuringia in January 1930, the month *after* Pacelli left Germany.[3] In September of that year, the sitting German government suffered a major defeat in the legislative elections. Hitler's National Socialists won 107 seats and became the second-most-powerful party in Germany.

Rather than concentrating on complex economic questions, Hitler turned Germany's fiscal woes into an issue of national independence. His oft-repeated theme was: "It is not an economic question which now faces the German people; it is a political question — how shall the nation's determination be recovered?"[4] Hitler proclaimed to cheering audiences that he would scrap the Treaty of Versailles if he came to power.

French troops were still in the Rhineland in early 1930. They were scheduled to stay there until 1935 to assure that Germany would abide by its obligations under the Versailles Treaty and not rearm itself. German Foreign Minister Gustav Stresemann, however, negotiated an early pullout of the French troops in 1930. In exchange, Germany committed not to send any forces to the left bank of the Rhine and to respect a demilitarized zone extending about thirty miles east of the Rhine River. Cardinal Pacelli expressed regret to the French ambassador that France had not more strongly opposed such a violation of international agreements.[5] History may well have been different if the French troops had stayed longer.

————

As Germany was about to fall into Hitler's control, changes were also taking place in the Vatican. Vatican Secretary of State Gasparri had been in charge of the Holy See's international relations for many years, but at age seventy-seven it was time to turn these tasks over to a younger person. This was a very important position. The secretary of state counseled the Pope on both foreign and domestic issues. As such, the position has been likened to a combination of prime minister and foreign secretary.[6] The Pope accepted Gasparri's recommendation and selected the fifty-three-year-old Eugenio Pacelli.[7]

In 1929, Pacelli was informed of the Pontiff's decision to call him home to Rome, elevate him to the cardinalate, and soon thereafter appoint him as Vatican secretary of state. Pacelli was not anxious to leave the country where he had served so long. He was concerned that his work in Germany was not really done. He could see that Hitler and the National Socialists presented a serious threat. His housekeeper, Sister M. Pascalina Lehnert, in her personal memoirs, recorded:

> A distressing thought disturbed the Nuncio on his departure from Germany: The continuing progress of National Socialism. How perceptive he had been already at that time in judging Hitler and how many times he had warned the German people of the tremendous danger that threatened them! They did not wish to believe him. People of every rank and class let him know at the time of his departure what they expected of Hitler: the ascent and greatness of Germany.
>
> On one occasion I asked the Nuncio if he did not think that this man could have some good in him, and that... he [Hitler] could perhaps help the German people. The Nuncio shook his head and said: I would be very, very much mistaken in thinking that all this could end well. This man is completely

obsessed: all that is not of use to him, he destroys; all that he says and writes carries the mark of his egocentricity; this man is capable of trampling on corpses and eliminating all that obstructs him. I cannot understand how many in Germany, even among the best people, do not understand and are not able to draw the lesson from what he writes and says. Who among these has at least read his horrifying book *Mein Kampf*?[8]

Pacelli argued that there were matters dealing with church-state relations that he had not yet resolved, and he asked that the Pontiff put off the appointment. Pius XI, however, was determined that Pacelli return to Rome.

In Berlin, there was a repetition of what had occurred in 1925 when Pacelli left Munich. Testimonial dinners and newspaper editorials expressed sadness in both government circles and among the general public. President Paul von Hindenburg, a Protestant who would play an important role in Hitler's political rise, hosted a farewell luncheon for the departing nuncio. At it, he raised his glass and offered a toast: "I thank you for all you have accomplished during these long years in the cause of peace, inspired as you have been by a high sense of justice and a deep love of humanity; and I can assure you that we shall not forget you and your work here."[9]

Pacelli left Berlin for the last time in December 1929. For his departure, the Weimar government provided him with an open carriage to take him to the train station. Thousands of people lined the road to wish him a fond farewell. They carried candles and called out their best wishes. Pacelli could not hide his emotion. As he gave blessings to the crowd, tears ran down his face.[10]

In Rome, on December 29, 1929, Pacelli received the red hat of the cardinalate. The aging Gasparri then began to teach Pacelli about the office of secretary of state, which he would be called upon to fill the next month. ("The informed gossip was that Pacelli took over the post of Cardinal Secretary of State only unwillingly.")[11] Among the new secretary's first acts was to send a letter back to Germany, to Cardinal Schulte, the archbishop of Cologne. The letter, which was also published in the *Roman Catholic Diocesan Journal*, encouraged the German bishops to fight for religious principles and against the rising star of Hitler.[12]

———

Pacelli was considered "refined, witty, intelligent, and a brilliant conversationalist."[13] He was said to be universally respected, liked by the people, and someone to whom the Italian government would listen. As secretary of state, Pacelli strove to be of one mind with Pope Pius XI. In fact, the Pontiff said: "Cardinal Pacelli speaks with my voice."[14] This unity of purpose would be crucial in the coming years, as conflicts with the Nazis were already beginning to take place.

Germany was about one-third Catholic and two-thirds Protestant. "To its credit, the Catholic church stood against Hitler with a greater solidarity than the Protestants."[15] Up until Hitler seized full control, "any Catholics who joined the

Nazis risked the severe disfavor of the Church."[16] In 1930, Cardinal Adolph Bertram of Breslau expressed his opposition to National Socialism and refused a religious funeral for a well-known party official. In a widely publicized statement, Bertram criticized as a grave error the one-sided glorification of the Nordic race and the contempt for divine revelation which was increasingly taught throughout Germany. He warned against the ambiguity of the concept of "positive Christianity," a highly nationalistic religion that the Nazis were encouraging. Such a religion, he said, "for us Catholics cannot have a satisfactory meaning since everyone interprets it in the way he pleases."[17]

Norms published by the Episcopal Ordinaries of Mainz in September 1930 stated that it was forbidden for all Catholics to join Hitler's party; Nazis were not allowed to take part as a group in funerals or other similar functions; and Catholics who remained in the party were not allowed to receive the sacraments (i.e., they were excommunicated).[18] The following month, L'Osservatore Romano carried an article entitled "The Party of Hitler Stands Condemned by the Ecclesiastical Authorities."[19] Similarly, the bishops of Berlin and Westphalia condemned the Nazis in pastoral letters. In the spring of 1931, the Bavarian bishops also condemned National Socialism and described it as heretical and incompatible with Catholic teaching.[20] Similar statements were made by bishops in Cologne, Paderborn, and the upper Rhine.[21]

Nazi leadership in Germany was upset by the condemnations. In April 1931, Hitler sent Hermann Göring, the top National Socialist in the Reichstag and one of Hitler's three "general secretaries," to Rome as a "political commissioner."[22] Göring had good contacts with Mussolini's government, and Hitler thought that he might also be able to smooth things out with the Vatican. He wrote a letter invoking Hitler's name and asking for an audience with Pacelli, but the Holy See would not accord him such an honor. He was granted an audience with an undersecretary.[23] A report of the meeting shows that the Nazis claimed that they were not opposed to the Catholic Church and that they were upset about things German bishops were saying and doing (like denying Easter Communion to Hitler's followers).[24]

In response to these criticisms, the Nazi press cited some of Pope Leo XIII's pronouncements about the relations of practicing Catholics to political parties, to bolster the argument that Catholics could be National Socialists. Pacelli ordered a lengthy article to be published in the Vatican newspaper, L'Osservatore Romano. The article defended the Catholic Center Party, corrected the Nazi Party's distortions of Leo's pronouncements, and said that a Christian should not belong to any political party that works against Christian ideals.[25]

At the local level, the dispute between the Church and National Socialism got ugly. For instance, one parish priest said of Nazi officials during a Mass one Sunday: "Let those stinking [Nazi] bastards come at me, two thousand of them if you like, and I'll bash in all their skulls so that their brains squirt out. It'll make enough soup for a week."[26] Another priest spoke to school children about the

Nazi Brown Shirts: "The Brown Shirt is supposed to be a shirt of honor, isn't it? Yes, Brown's the word. Like something else that's Brown — and stinks!"[27] When Nazi authorities complained, Secretary of State Pacelli merely confirmed that some priests were making such statements.[28]

---

Despite the tension between the National Socialists and the Catholic Church, Hitler was moving closer to national prominence. The German constitution provided for an elected president who could appoint a chancellor. These were the two most powerful positions in the government. Paul von Hindenburg, a popular war hero, had been president since the mid-1920s, but Germany experienced an almost constant stream of new chancellors in the late 1920s. The six million jobless men in Germany woke up with little to do each morning, except for the daily routine of street fighting. This, in turn, led to political unrest and a continuing series of elections, and by the early 1930s, even Hindenburg's position was insecure.[29]

In March 1932, Hitler forced a runoff with Hindenburg for the German presidency. Fear of the redistribution that might come with a Communist takeover concerned many German industrialists, and Hitler played on these fears to obtain financial support.[30] (Hitler's political opponents even made a short animated film suggesting that he was in the industrialists' pocket.) Hindenburg defeated Hitler, but Hitler drew 37 percent of the vote and called it a victory for National Socialism. The Nazis were clearly a national power. Hitler pledged to cooperate with the government. In return, the government lifted a ban that had been placed on Nazi storm troopers.

In May 1932, Hindenburg withdrew his support from Chancellor Heinrich Brüning and replaced him with a conservative Catholic, Franz von Papen. Papen, however, failed to obtain a popular mandate in two Reichstag elections. Instead, the German political scene became even more difficult as both ends of the spectrum grew in strength and hardened in resolve. Addressing the National Socialist Reichstag members, Hitler said he could no longer tolerate the present government and that a total Nazi victory was just a matter of time.

In June, the German leadership acceded to a long-standing Nazi demand and announced that they would no longer pay war reparations.[31] In July 1932, the Nazis doubled their strength in the German parliament, becoming the biggest party in the Reichstag. With their rise to power, however, came much rioting and fighting between Nazis, Communists, and Socialists. In one seven-week period there were 461 riots in Prussia alone. Eighty-two people were killed and about four hundred were injured.[32]

On August 24, a Nazi newspaper in Berlin was banned for inciting riots, but only six days later Nazi leader Hermann Göring was elected president of the Reichstag (similar to speaker of the house). The next month, Chancellor Papen dissolved the Reichstag after a vote of no confidence.[33]

In November 1932, new elections cost the Nazis thirty-five seats in the Reichstag. Communists picked up most of those seats. The strength in Communist ranks deeply concerned those close to President Hindenburg (in his mid-eighties and considered senile by some).[34] They determined that obtaining Hitler's support might be one way to shore up the crumbling government. Hindenburg offered Hitler a limited chancellorship of Germany, but Hitler refused and Kurt von Schleicher was named chancellor in December. When Schleicher failed to win much support, Hindenburg was forced to return to the one prominent political figure who could unite support behind him.

On January 30, 1933, after a month of secret meetings with Hindenburg and Papen, Hitler was named chancellor of Germany.[35] Hindenburg had been persuaded that he could control Hitler, as the latter had no experience in government and only three National Socialists were members of the new government.[36] This proved to be a serious mistake. With the announcement of Hitler's appointment, Communists rioted, but many more Nazis celebrated. Hitler's storm troopers marched in a torchlight parade. At least a few deaths were reported.

Once in power, Hitler did restore a degree of order to Germany. The street fighting was largely eliminated. Anyone who dared to challenge the government faced immediate imprisonment (or execution) without benefit of trial. It was harsh, but many found the relative peace to be a welcome relief from the constant rioting and fighting between opposing political parties that had scarred the Weimar Republic. Moreover, Hitler benefited from a much improved economy.

Hitler was anxious to promulgate many new laws as quickly as possible. Before he had been in office for seven months, he had already placed 497 new laws and ordinances on the books, "a remarkable feat of enthusiasm and industry."[37] He promised that churches would be free, that he would resist Bolshevism, and that he was committed to peace. The minutes of a Reich cabinet meeting of March 15, 1933, reveal that the new leadership thought that "the question of coordination of political Catholicism into the new State is of special importance."[38] Eight days later, Hitler said: "The government sees in both Christian confessions the factors most important for the maintenance of our Folkdom.... The Government will devote its care to the sincere living together of Church and State."[39] This tricked some people, but not Pope Pius XI or his secretary of state.[40]

The British chargé d'affaires at the Holy See, Ivone Kirkpatrick, in a letter to Sir Robert Vansittart, dated August 19, 1933, explained an encounter he had had with Pacelli at this time:

> Cardinal Pacelli... deplored the action of the German Government at home, their persecution of the Jews, their proceedings against political opponents, the reign of terror to which the whole nation was subjected. I said to His Eminence that I had heard the opinion expressed in Italy and elsewhere that these events (persecution of Jews, etc.) were but manifestations of the revolutionary spirit. With the passage of time and the responsibilities of office, Herr Hitler would

settle down, temper the zeal of his supporters and revert to more normal methods of government. The Cardinal replied with emphasis that he saw no ground for such easy optimism. It seemed to him that there was no indication of any modification in the internal policy of the German government.[41]

At a party in Rome, one of Pacelli's old friends said that it was good that Germany now had a strong leader to deal with the Communists. Pacelli responded: "Don't talk such nonsense. The Nazis are infinitely worse."[42] Just two weeks after his promise of peace, Hitler said: "One is either a German or a Christian. You cannot be both."[43]

Despite these feelings, Hitler wanted to keep organized religion on his side. He spent these early months trying to build a reputation as a legitimate, moderate statesman. Except for the statements in *Mein Kampf* (which were carefully edited in translated editions), he refused to make negative statements publicly about the Christian churches.[44] When Nazis openly criticized religion, they claimed to be attacking "negative Christianity," which was said to be devouring German moral principles. The Nazi alternative, as set forth in their party platform, was "positive Christianity." In 1939, one British author summarized the favored German position:

> The German Christians do not, at least in intention, question or repudiate the Christian faith. They assent to the ancient creeds of the Church and the Confessions of the Reformation, though they regard these in language and substance as having little relevance for the present day. They represent themselves as good Lutherans.[45]

In this way, the Nazis were able to misuse Christianity and defend the supremacy of the German people.[46]

During the spring of 1933, Hitler's representatives met frequently with members of the Church's hierarchy:

> As astute politicians they desired to avoid the direct antagonizing of any large section of the people unnecessarily, and they were doubtless aware that their strength would be enormously increased if they could avail themselves of the potential enthusiasms of religion. Of the antipathy of the Catholic Church as an institution they were already persuaded, but they had good hopes of Protestantism, and they might hope to become strong enough to make the Catholic Church revise its first unfavorable judgment. They declared themselves to be Christian, therefore, but to be neutral as between the various denominations of Christians.[47]

Hitler claimed to support religious schools. Character, he said, could be built only on the basis of religion, and character would be needed in the German men of the future. He also promised to permit the Catholic organizations to continue in operation as long as they promoted Christian ideals. He stressed the great importance he attached to working closely with the Catholic Church. His anti-Bolshevist stance and his promise to make Christianity the basis of German morality, and also to make the family the basic unit for the nation, certainly were pleasing to the Catholic hierarchy.[48]

In the first meeting of the new Reichstag, Hitler expressed the government's commitment to Christian principles and said he looked forward to developing amicable relations with the Holy See. He stressed the fundamental agreement between National Socialism and Christianity. He said he was convinced that without Christianity one could neither run a personal life nor a state, and that Germany in particular needed the kind of religious and moral foundation only Christianity could provide. Things looked so promising that Protestant churches across Germany formally acknowledged their acceptance of Hitler and his regime on March 26.[49] Two days later the German bishops lifted the ban on Catholics joining the Nazi Party (though they expressly noted that they were not withdrawing their condemnations of Nazism, and their statement "was joined with an uncompromising denial of the core of Nazi ideology.")[50] Secretary of State Pacelli, upon reading the episcopal act of submission, expressed his dismay.[51]

Hermann Göring, a German World War I flying hero, was an early follower of Hitler. He was now Prussian minister of the interior, and in that role he made a filmed statement in which he said, "I shall sweep clean and remove from office all those Communists and Catholics who are opposing our national endeavors."[52] Soon thereafter, the National Socialists set out to do just that.

———————

On February 1, 1933, Hitler won a vote to dissolve the Reichstag, with a new election to be held in March. Two weeks later, German Catholic Organizations published an article in a Berlin newspaper entitled "A serious word in serious times." It said: "What happened in our country since last year is a national disaster." The article went on to say it was a sin "to call for hate and revenge and to deny rights to those who are different."[53]

At the end of February, less than a week before new Reich elections were scheduled, the Reichstag building was set on fire and sustained heavy damage. Though there has always been speculation that the Nazis set the fire to frame their political rivals, Hitler blamed the arson on a Communist conspiracy.[54] The following month, a young man named Marinus van der Lubbe, identified as a Communist, was arrested for arson. (He would receive the death sentence in December and be executed a month later.) Regardless of whether the Nazis had anything to do with setting the fire, they certainly took advantage of it.

Hitler induced President Hindenburg to sign a decree "for the protection of the people and the state" that suspended the constitutional guarantees of individual freedom, freedom of the press, private property, and the privacy of mail.[55] Writing in 1939, one author explained that "this decree was nominally directed against the Communists, but it has been constantly employed against the Church."[56] It made it virtually impossible for Church leaders to use the mail or telephone, permitted the homes of pastors and bishops to be raided, led to the sequestration of large sums of money from the Church, and resulted in the suppression of many Catholic periodicals.[57]

Under the new decree, Hitler's storm troopers, the S.A. (*Sturmabteilung*), served as the police force. They could now search homes without a warrant, confiscate property, and outlaw the meetings of groups that might oppose them. They rounded up Communists and anti-Hitler Catholics.[58] Hundreds of people were incarcerated until the investigation (and election) was over. Hermann Göring had all one hundred Communist members of the Reichstag arrested, preventing them from campaigning in the crucial week before the election. Communist newspapers and meeting halls were also shut down, as Berlin took on the appearance of a police state. From this point on, there were no real limits on Hitler's power. Little wonder he said that the burning of the Reichstag was "a gift from the gods."[59]

On March 5, 1933, with many of their opponents in jail or intimidated, the Nazis and their Nationalist allies won a majority in the Reichstag. One week later the flag of the German Republic was lowered, and the empire banner was flown alongside the swastika. This month would see the opening of the first concentration camp at Oranienburg, outside of Berlin.[60] Other camps were preparing to open, including one at an old power factory near Dachau. The camps had become necessary due to all of Hitler's political enemies that were being taken into custody and filling the prisons. Hitler was establishing his Third Reich, which, he said, would follow in the tradition of the Holy Roman Empire and the unified German Empire established by Bismarck and would last for a thousand years. Its establishment was considered a "major defeat for the powers of Jewry, capital, and the Catholic Church."[61]

On March 10, the German Bishops' Conference in Fulda appealed to President Hindenburg, expressing

> our most serious worries which are shared by large circles of the population.... We as Bishops have to ask with tremendous seriousness whether the movement which came to power [the Nazis] will respect the Sanctuary of the Church and the position of the Church in the public life.... The hour has come when we have to appeal to you with the urgent request for your protection of the Church and the ecclesiastical life and action.[62]

Unfortunately, on March 23, the Reichstag adjourned, giving Hitler's cabinet the power to rule by decree.[63] (In 1930, the Reichstag had granted Chancellor Heinrich Brüning's request to govern by means of emergency powers, setting the precedent.) The Enabling Act granted Hitler dictatorial powers for an initial period of six months, though it never ended while he was alive. This act formalized the authority that he had already assumed with the emergency order in February.[64] President Hindenburg technically had the authority to dismiss the chancellor, but this was not a realistic possibility.

Hitler had achieved what none before him had dared to try. He did away with the separate powers of the individual states and brought them all under the central authority of the Reich. For the first time in German history, the federal character of the nation was destroyed and the Reich was truly unified.[65] In his last address to the disbanding Reichstag, Hitler announced that "treason toward the nation and the people shall in the future be stamped out with ruthless barbarity."[66] Soon, no form of dissent would be tolerated.[67]

Pope Pius XI proclaimed 1933 to be a holy year.[68] When he inaugurated it on April 2, he held out hopes of peace and prosperity. Unfortunately, the year was certainly not holy in Germany. On March 28, Hitler banned Jews from businesses, professions, and schools. On April 1, he called for a boycott of Jewish-owned businesses. The National Socialist leadership then proceeded to enact some four hundred anti-Jewish laws.[69] Laws were passed barring "non-Aryans" from the legal profession and parts of the medical professions, establishing a 5 percent quota of Jewish students in public schools, and prohibiting Jews from voting, serving in the government, appearing in motion pictures and plays, or publishing books.

The 1933 boycott attracted worldwide attention. The idea was that "Jewish businesses" would be identified and Aryans would avoid patronizing them. Those who violated the boycott would at least be publicly humiliated. Jewish and non-Jewish people from around the world led a public outcry denouncing this action and threatening to boycott German goods. The Vatican filed a formal protest. The Nazis, of course, used all of this to their benefit.

Billboards went up around the nation with sayings such as "Jews the world over are trying to crush the new Germany."[70] Signs were placed in store windows reading, "Germans defend yourselves against Jewish atrocity propaganda, buy only at German Shops!"[71] Joseph Goebbels, the minister of "Popular Enlightenment and Propaganda," said that the boycott would remain in place as long as Jews around the world were boycotting German goods and accusing Germany of atrocities.[72] The Nazis were so effective in turning the international uproar to their favor that German Cardinal Michael von Faulhaber wrote to American Cardinal George William Mundelein, archbishop of Chicago, urging him to use his influence to stop press reports about German atrocities, lest things be made worse in Germany. Faulhaber also wrote Cardinal Pacelli, telling him that it was impossible to confront the government on the racial issue without persecution of the Jews becoming persecution of the Catholics.[73]

In May, the Nazis broke up all trade unions and began purging the country of non-German books with huge bonfires. German students, from universities that had been regarded as among the finest in the world, gathered to burn books with "un-German" ideas, including those by Sigmund Freud, Albert Einstein, Jack London, and H. G. Wells.[74] Curricula were revised in the German schools to teach "race science" and other theories related to the superiority of the Aryan race.[75] Many university professors were removed from their positions, including writer Thomas Mann, theologian Paul Tillich, and Nobel Prize winners Gustav Hertz and James Franck. Pope Pius XI responded by assigning many Jewish intellectuals to teach in the colleges over which he had control.[76]

————

While Hitler was baptized into the Catholic faith, he was not a Christian. His real faith was National Socialism, and the Nazis viewed Christianity as an outmoded superstition that would eventually wither away. "The religions are all alike," Hitler said within a year of coming to power, "no matter what they call themselves. They have no future. Whether it is the Old Testament or the New, or simply the sayings of Jesus… it's all the same old Jewish swindle." Even the Ten Commandments, he said, "have lost their validity."[77] He spoke of both Protestants and Catholics with contempt, convinced that all Christians would betray their God when they were forced to choose between their nation and their faith.[78]

In 1933-34, Hitler predicted that a "new age of magic interpretation of the world is coming, of interpretation in terms of will and not of intelligence."[79] "Man is becoming God — that is the simple fact. Man is God in the making…. National Socialism… is the will to create mankind anew."[80] He saw his job as helping this evolution take place. To accomplish this, he promised that he would not be prevented "from tearing up Christianity root and branch, and annihilating it in Germany."[81] Of course, as British historian Michael Burleigh has written: "Hitler was a lazy, dilettantish autodidact rather than a systematic thinker, so one should not strain to discover coherence or consistency in his views on religion or much else."[82]

Regarding the Catholic Church in particular, Hitler was confident that he could bring it down:

> I promise you that, if I wished to, I could destroy the Church in a few years; it is hollow and rotten and false through and through. One push and the whole structure would collapse…. I shall give them a few years reprieve. Why should we quarrel? They will swallow anything in order to keep their material advantages… we need only show them once or twice who is the master. Then they will know which way the wind blows. They are no fools. The Church was something really big. Now we are its heirs. We, too, are the Church. Its day has gone.[83]

Hitler knew that there might be resistance among the older Catholics, but he felt that he could accomplish his goals by focusing on youth. "As long as youth follows me, I don't mind if the old people limp to the confessional."[84] He privately disclosed:

> I shall make them appear ridiculous and contemptible. I shall order films to be made about them. We shall show the history of the monks on the cinema. Let the whole mass of nonsense, selfishness, repression and deceit be revealed:

how they drained money out of the country... how they committed incest. We shall make it so thrilling that everyone will want to see it. There will be queues outside the cinemas.[85]

Hitler had no compunction about being duplicitous, because as he saw it, "Conscience is a Jewish invention. It is a blemish like circumcision."[86]

Because the Nazis were not open about their view of religion, many German church officials welcomed the morality of the Third Reich. Hitler, they anticipated, would lead a return to piety, virtue, idealism, discipline, morality, and patriotism. He would put an end to vice and licentiousness, to agnosticism and godlessness. Under a Hitler government, they thought, Germany would experience a true rebirth of spirituality. Weimar had become associated with defeat and national humiliation, political violence, severe economic and social dislocation, and a political leadership with no real executive policy-making capabilities. Many religious people saw Weimar as a non-Christian system devised by criminals. The Nazis promised to rectify all of these problems. They were so persuasive that some religious leaders — even those who would later be deported to concentration camps for their anti-Nazi sermons — did not initially take issue with the Nazi regime.[87]

Bishop Theophil Wurm, the Lutheran state bishop of Württemberg, eventually became an outspoken opponent of National Socialism. At the beginning, however, like many Christian leaders in Germany, he welcomed the establishment of an authoritarian government. Even before the fall of Weimar, he argued that Germany's only choice was a dictatorship by Hitler or a dictatorship by Moscow.[88] A few months into Hitler's chancellorship, Wurm proudly noted that National Socialism was living up to its promises. The new regime deserved praise for crushing "at great sacrifice" the "terror" of the far left and for waging a struggle against "the disruptive influences in our cultural life."[89] In April 1933, he wrote a letter to the Lutheran clergy of Württemberg in which he expressed his sense of profound relief at the rise of Nazism. He said that Germany was like a "beleaguered city" in which, after a "very dangerous period of confusion and division," a "united and purposeful leadership" had emerged as a result of the "cooperation of responsible men."[90]

Over the next several years, Wurm began to find fault with Hitler's government. In 1934, he was twice put under house arrest for his outspokenness. On December 6, 1938, shortly after *Kristallnacht* ("Night of Shattered Glass"), when Nazis went on a violent rampage, Wurm protested in a letter to the minister of justice.[91] In 1940, Wurm repeatedly wrote to government officials urging changes in official policies, especially those concerning genocide.[92] In 1943, he began writing officials to protest "the way in which the struggle against other races and nations is being waged." What the Germans were doing, he said, violated God's commandments and shamed a "cultured people." These actions, he warned, "could bring a terrible retribution against our nation."[93]

Finally, in July 1943, Wurm wrote Hitler, protesting against the "Final Solution" of the "Jewish question." He urged Hitler, "in the name of God and for the sake of the German people," to stop "the persecution and annihilation to which many men and women within the German sphere of authority are being condemned without a judicial verdict." He wrote: "Measures adopted for the extermination of the other non-Aryans are in clearest violation of God's commandment and undermine the foundation of all Western thought and life, namely, the God-given right to human existence and to human dignity in general."[94] The extermination measures, Wurm also argued, disgraced the German name. The *Führer* did not reply.

None of Wurm's protests ever caused the Nazis to change their behavior. In 1944, he was banned from public speaking and from publishing his work. In a private letter, he argued that National Socialism had now become the political embodiment of moral corruption. "A deliverance of the German nation is [impossible], unless its leadership acknowledges its injustice and atones for that injustice."[95] In the meantime, as a man of religion, he could only wait, trust, and pray. Only God could change the system of government established under the Third Reich.

Like the Protestants, many Catholic leaders were not opposed to Hitler when he first came to power. Catholic doctrine seemed incompatible with National Socialism, but Hitler made many promises that sounded good. Just as important, Catholic leaders were well aware that Communists were waging a war of annihilation against Christianity in the Soviet Union. Communists were now trying to spread atheism in Germany. Many Catholics saw Hitler as the best barrier to the spread of Communism. Moreover, Catholic officials had long condemned Weimar's indifference to Christian values; its attempt to restrict the role of religion in national affairs; its advocacy of secularism and materialism; its tolerance of immorality; and its flirtation with radicalism and Bolshevism.[96] These Church leaders truly believed that Weimar had been established by a wrongful rebellion against legitimate authority, that the republic placed the interests of the parties above the welfare of the people, and that it acquiesced in the military weakness and humiliation of Germany. These concerns meant that there was little sympathy for Weimar as it was collapsing.

On the other hand, German Catholics were able to identify with the Jews. Both groups were religious minorities, and they both were charged with insufficient patriotism or even disloyalty to the nation due to their allegiance to religious leaders outside of Germany. This caused Nazi leaders to denounce Jews and Catholics for being "international" or "cosmopolitan" in their allegiance and for serving the interests of alien forces.[97] (The leaders of the Catholic Church also knew that there were several influential groups within the National Socialist party that regarded Catholicism as a sworn enemy.)

This kinship with the Jews, though distant, caused Catholic leaders to be less than enthusiastic about National Socialism.[98] On June 8, 1933, a pastoral letter from all the German prelates said: "[W]e believe that a unity of people can be realized not through the identity of blood but rather through the identity of belief, and that the exclusive emphasis on race and blood with regard to membership in a State leads to injustices which burden the Christian conscience...."[99] Once the Third Reich was well established, however, the German Catholic Church sought to get along with the new order. Hitler's government, for its part, tried to reassure Church leaders by proclaiming support for religious ideals and values.

––––––––

On July 20, 1933, Germany and the Holy See signed a concordat, and the Vatican ratified it on September 10.[100] It has been incorrectly reported that this was "Nazi Germany's first international treaty."[101] In fact, the Four-Powers Pact between Germany, France, Italy, and Great Britain was signed in Rome on June 7.[102] The Soviet Union, on May 5, 1933 (more than two months before the concordat was signed), renewed a trade and friendship agreement with Germany,[103] and on that same day the British Parliament voted to accept an Anglo-German trade agreement.[104] Moreover, Hitler's representatives were fully accredited and recognized by the League of Nations and took part in the disarmament discussions in Geneva, which also came before the signing of the concordat.[105] In other words, Italy, France, the United Kingdom, the Soviet Union, and the whole League of Nations recognized the new German government before the concordat was signed. Moreover, in August 1933, one month before the concordat was ratified, Germany and Palestinian Jews signed the Haavara Agreement relating to the emigration of German Jews to Palestine.[106]

Pius XI believed in establishing diplomatic agreements with many nations. Under his leadership, the Church reached agreement with twenty-one countries, including Czechoslovakia, Austria, Italy, Germany, Poland, Yugoslavia, Latvia, and Lithuania.[107] As nuncio in Germany, Cardinal Pacelli had been largely responsible for negotiating the agreements with Bavaria (1924), Prussia (1929), and Baden (1932). He had also started negotiations with the Weimar Republic for a concordat with the whole of Germany and had attempted to secure an agreement with the Soviet Union.[108] As a lawyer and diplomat, Pacelli agreed with the Pope that this was the best way of preserving the Church's freedom of action.[109]

The Holy See's concordats with individual German states had little meaning now that Hitler had centralized power and control over Germany. The Church had been working toward agreement with Germany long before Hitler rose to power. In fact, Pacelli had worked toward such an agreement ever since he was appointed papal nuncio to Bavaria. Eventually, those efforts came back to haunt him:

> In October 1924, Pacelli again approached the Reich government under Wilhelm Marx and suggested that it should resume the concordat negotiations it had

broken off. By mid-November the new draft was ready, but it was not pursued further. Only nine years later, in the spring of 1933 did Hitler's negotiator, [Former Chancellor] Franz von Papen, take *this precise draft* with him to Rome.[110]

Now the Church found itself in a bind. Hitler, who never intended to keep his promises, wanted to stay on good terms with the Church and was happy to accept all of the Church's long-standing demands.[111] ("I will be one of the few men in history who have deceived the Vatican," he boasted shortly before the concordat was signed.)[112] Moreover, Papen (a Catholic whose primary role in the early years of the Reich was to obtain the support of the Church),[113] made it quite clear that if the Church were to reject the terms it had agreed to nine years earlier, Hitler would simply impose his own rules and blame the Pope for having rejected a very favorable treaty.[114] Papen also noted that the agreement with Germany was similar to agreements the Holy See had signed with other nations.[115]

In a private conversation with Ivone Kirkpatrick, British chargé d'affaires to the Vatican, Pacelli denied that the treaty constituted an approval of Nazism. In fact, he expressed "disgust and abhorrence" of Hitler's reign of terror. Hitler, however, put pressure on the Vatican during negotiations by arresting ninety-two priests, searching sixteen Catholic Youth Clubs, and shutting down nine Catholic publications, all within three weeks.[116] Kirkpatrick reported to the British Foreign Office on August 19, 1933:

> These reflections on the iniquity of Germany led the Cardinal [Pacelli] to explain apologetically how it was that he had signed a Concordat with such people. A pistol, he said, had been pointed at his head and he had no alternative. The German government had offered him concessions, concessions, it must be admitted, wider than any previous German Government would have agreed to, and he had to choose between an agreement on their lines and the virtual elimination of the Catholic Church in the Reich. Not only that, but he was given no more than one week to make up his mind.... If the German Government violated the Concordat — and they were certain to do that — the Vatican would have at least a treaty on which to base a protest.[117]

The French ambassador at the Vatican, François Charles-Roux, believed that neither Pacelli nor the Pope were under any illusions about Hitler's word, but as Pacelli stated to him: "I do not regret our concordat with Germany. If we did not have it, we would not have a foundation on which to base our protests." In any event, as Pacelli joked to a British diplomat, the National Socialists "would probably not violate all of the articles of the concordat at the same time."[118]

Mussolini, who had reached an agreement with the Church four years earlier, supported the treaty because he felt that it would strengthen the German position.[119] He stated that together with the Four-Powers Pact, the concordat made Germany's diplomatic position much stronger. (Hitler also signed a similar agreement with Protestant churches.)[120] Not all Nazis, however, agreed. Joseph

Goebbels, Reinhart Heydrich, and others in the party objected until the end and may even have tried to sabotage the process by creating violent incidents involving the clergy and Catholic organizations.[121]

Some critics have argued that Pacelli, as part of the concordat negotiations, withdrew support from the Catholic Center Party in Germany, transferring power to the Holy See. This action, according to the critics, silenced the one entity that could have stopped the National Socialists from coming to power.[122] The facts do not support this conclusion.

The Center Party did not consist exclusively of Catholics, but it advanced the Church's interests in Germany until Hitler's rise.[123] By early 1933, however, Hitler largely stripped it of power. It could not stand up to Nazi pressure,[124] and it embarrassed the Holy See by supporting the Enabling Act,[125] albeit "with reservations" and "under pressure of necessity and on the understanding that the law was to remain in force for six months only."[126] In fact, some members had considered forming a coalition with the Nazis in 1932, just for survival.[127] It was almost eliminated by the Nazis in March 1933.[128] For the next three months, Nazis brutalized the remaining members of the Center Party as well as other Catholics.

On July 5, 1933, two weeks before the concordat was signed, the party membership decided to dissolve voluntarily in the hope that this would stop the persecution.[129] When Pacelli read about this in a newspaper, he said:

> Too bad that it happened at this moment. Of course the party couldn't have held out much longer. But if it only had put off its dissolution at least until after the conclusion of the concordat, the simple fact of its existence would have still been useful in the negotiations.[130]

He explained in a letter written in mid-July 1933: "Above all it must be remembered that the Centre and the Bavarian Volkspartei have dissolved themselves on the basis of a decision entirely independent of the Holy See."[131] As reflected by this statement, the party was not negotiated away with the concordat.[132] There was, however, a concession regarding political activity.

Pius XI, like all popes since at least Pius X (reigned 1903-1914), agreed with removing clergy from direct political involvement.[133] Pius thought that the Church could be more effectively defended by the terms of the concordat than by parliamentary action.[134] Moreover, the Pope was concerned about the legitimacy of direct political activity by the clergy, and he looked with more favor on the lay organization Catholic Action.[135]

The relevant provision, paragraph 32 of the concordat, said: "[T]he Holy See will prescribe regulations which will prohibit *clergymen and members of religious institutes* from membership in political parties and from working on their behalf" (emphasis added). The supplemental protocol relating to this paragraph said: "The conduct enjoined upon the pastors and members of religious institutes in Germany does not entail any limitation of the prescribed preaching and interpretation of the dogmatic and moral teachings and principles of the Church."

Critics have argued that direct political involvement by Catholic clergy could have held Hitler in check, but that Pacelli, the 1917 Code of Canon Law, and the concordat all served to restrict this possibility in order to centralize the Vatican's authority. This criticism is based upon four assumptions: (1) that Pacelli made the decision, not Pius XI; (2) that the party would have remained viable; (3) that the party would have opposed Hitler; and (4) that the concordat effectively silenced the German bishops. Three of these four assumptions are demonstrably false, and the fourth is far from certain.

As for the assumption that Pacelli was the driving force behind the concordat, the critics credit (or blame) Pacelli for decisions that were far beyond his control. They suggest that Pacelli was the instigator of all the international moves that took place while he was secretary of state. That is not, however, the way that diplomats saw it at the time. Reporting back to London on the prospects of the 1939 papal election, the British minister to the Holy See, Francis D'Arcy Osborne, wrote that "it was always [Pacelli's] task to execute the policy of the late Pope rather than to initiate his own."[136] (Pope Pius XI signed the concordat on September 9, 1933.)[137] In fact, Osborne reported that Pacelli had not garnered the ill will typically found between the secretary of state and other cardinals precisely because he only carried out Pius XI's objectives.[138] Pacelli took pride in executing the will of Pius XI. The Pontiff himself said: "Cardinal Pacelli speaks with my voice."[139] Either young Pacelli dominated the Church's international policies years before he had any true authority (as the critics assert) or he carried out the will of his superiors (as Pope Pius XI and others who actually knew Pacelli reported). All relevant evidence points to the latter scenario.[140]

Regarding the claim that the Catholic Center Party would have remained viable but for the concordat, that too must fail. Hitler's power was sufficiently secure, and his means sufficiently brutal, that by March 1933 no religious institution — in fact, no political party — could stand up to him.[141] The Catholic Center Party was seriously weakened and almost eliminated by the Nazis in March 1933.[142] An editorial written by the editors of the American Catholic magazine *Commonweal* and published on April 5, 1933, reported that

> nothing other than the overthrow of Hitlerism by the German people itself will bring justice to the Jews, and to other oppressed minorities, including the Catholics. The German Catholic bishops have condemned the ultra-nationalism of the Nazi party, and that condemnation still stands, even although the Center party has been forced to vote for its own suppression.[143]

Even if the Catholic Center Party had survived, it is not certain that it would have opposed Hitler.[144] "The party was split and many Roman Catholics were attracted by the early achievements of the Nazis, as were most Germans."[145] The German nuncio reported in March 1933: "It is alas undeniable that the Catholic people with few exceptions have turned to the new regime with enthusiasm and have forgotten the disciplinary standards published by the episcopate...."[146] Today one wonders how this could have been possible. At the time, however, Hitler promised to provide economic prosperity, free Germany from the Treaty of Versailles, end daily street fighting, clean up the vice, and promote social justice.[147] Add to these matters that Hitler's socialistic programs were purportedly designed to help people in need, and he promised to respect the rights of the Church, and it becomes easier to see how some Christian people might have been attracted to his policies.[148]

The assumption that German bishops would have been outspoken against the Nazi regime, but were silenced by the concordat, is wrong. As the Nazis began to put pressure on German Catholics, and Catholic laypersons were subject to arrest and beatings, the German bishops backed off from the earlier sanctions that they had placed on National Socialists.[149] Even before the concordat was completed, the bishops issued episcopal statements supporting the new regime.[150] Eventually, the bishops voted to ask the Vatican to ratify the concordat without delay.[151] Archbishop Gröber of Freiburg came to Rome in order to take part in the concordat negotiations. As Pacelli explained in a letter to his assistant, Monsignor Lorenzo Schioppa, Gröber said the bishops were unanimous in agreeing that the concordat was "the last hope of avoiding a much worse *Kulturkampf* in Germany than the one in Bismarck's time.[152]

The bishops understood that because of the supplemental protocol they would not be silenced by this concordat.[153] The concordat, in fact, did no more than assert traditional Church teaching (predating the 1917 Code of Canon Law and surviving Vatican II) when it limited the participation of clergy in party politics.[154]

Despite the removal of Catholic clergy from direct participation in the political process, they were not restricted from making statements that addressed basic human rights, and many did make such statements about the Nazi government.[155] Moreover, Catholic laypersons were in no way restricted from political activity by the terms of the concordat. The political restrictions, set forth in paragraph 32 of the concordat, applied only to "clergymen and members of conventual orders."

The agreement with Germany was very similar in this respect to the Lateran Treaty signed with Italy in 1929 and to instructions given to the French clergy in the mid-1920s. The Church did not in any way agree to restrictions on its right to involve itself in politics whenever "the fundamental rights of man or the salvation of souls requires it."[156] As such, the Catholic clergy was not silenced.[157] Perhaps most importantly, by the time that the concordat was signed, there was only one party left in Germany — the Nazi Party. Because of the concordat, Catholic clergy had a clear basis to resist when pressured to join the Nazis.[158] Many Protestant ministers, unprotected by such an agreement, were coerced into joining the party.

---

On July 26 and 27, 1933, the Vatican newspaper, *L'Osservatore Romano*, carried a two-part article by Pacelli in which he vehemently denied any assertion that the concordat indicated approval of National Socialism and instead explained that it was intended to protect the Church's interests in Germany.[159] Between April 1,

1933, and June 1936, the Vatican filed more than fifty protests against the Nazis, several of which dealt with maltreatment of the Jews.[160] The first one, dated April 1, 1933, dealt with the anti-Jewish boycott, and the ninth one, filed on September 9, 1933, asked for protection of Jews who had converted to Catholicism.[161] Protests regarding the treatment of Catholic institutions, however, eventually slowed. "[I]n the war years there were no longer the steady protests with regard to the Catholic Schools or associations, for these had virtually ceased to exist."[162] The Nazis never replied, but the Holy See circulated the protests to the bishops in Germany, so that they would know what the Vatican was doing.[163]

Before long, the concordat was being used by the Holy See as a weapon in its battle against the Nazis. As Protestant Reverend Martin Niemöller, who spent seven years in prison for his opposition to Hitler and the Nazis, said:

> In the struggle that has ensued, the Catholic Church, because of its stronger international position, has done heroic work. And by means of the concordat between the Pope and the Hitler government the Catholic Church was put in position to counteract the Nazis' vicious propaganda against Catholic history and Catholic dogma.[164]

German Foreign Minister Joachim von Ribbentrop testified at Nuremberg that he had a "whole deskfull of protests" from Rome.[165] Of course, since the Nazis controlled the press, few of these protests were published within Germany during the Nazi era.[166]

The Vatican issued so many complaints regarding violations of the concordat that by 1937 the Nazis were trying to disavow it.[167] Hitler later promised to "put a swift end" to the concordat.[168] On February 17, 1938, *Das Schwarze Korps*,[169] the official paper of the S.S., contained an article protesting that the concordat presupposed the old Germany resting upon a federation of states, a party system, and a liberal outlook. The argument continued that since this agreement was based largely on the Weimar constitution of 1918, not the Third Reich of Adolf Hitler, a number of clauses were obsolete. As such, the concordat was out of date, and should be abandoned.[170] The article argued that in 1933 Hitler had expected the moral support of the Church in his work of national reconstruction, but he had not received this support. Instead, pastoral letters, sermons, pamphlets, and encyclicals had insulted the government.

In 1937, the storm trooper publication, *Der S.A. Mann*, wrote that the Vatican's purpose in negotiating the concordat was to bring the National Socialist government to its knees: "The Vatican was ill-advised in 1933 to suppose that with a Government that had scarcely begun its work one could settle a Concordat with the idea of using it to make impossible the development and fulfillment of this work."[171] It went on to say that:

> Cardinal Pacelli's idea was to save the Centre Party, not indeed as a party, but as "the sum of the Catholic organizations." In fact, "he wanted to block the

way to any future development of National Socialist cultural politics, and he thought the trick would not be observed in Berlin." Hence right upon right was demanded in the Concordat with a view to an ultimate political domination of the clergy.... The Church made a surprisingly favorable bargain with the new Government — on paper.[172]

*Der S.A. Mann* accused the Church of "open sabotage" that should release the government from its obligations.[173] Later, Hitler promised to end the concordat following the war, saying that "it will give me the greatest personal pleasure to point out to the Church all those occasions on which it has broken the terms of it."[174]

Reporting from Berlin in 1940, William Shirer wrote of the concordat in the past tense and noted that German Foreign Minister Joachim von Ribbentrop went to Rome in March of that year to obtain a new concordat.[175] (He also noted that "Germany didn't observe the last concordat, persecuting the church whenever it pleased.")

The concordat, which may on the surface seem to indicate friendly relations between the Holy See and Nazi Germany, was in fact an indication of precisely the opposite, as the historical record now plainly reveals.[176] It was not a recognition of Hitler's Third Reich. It did not indicate the Holy See's support for Nazism, and in no way did it suggest that Pope Pius XI, Pope Pius XII, or the Holy See supported the German cause in World War II. The *Palestine Post*, the predecessor of today's *Jerusalem Post*, favorably reported: "Jews must be treated with Christian charity, is the injunction which the Vatican has transmitted to Germany in the memorandum accompanying the ratification of the Concordat."[177]

The concordat was Hitler's attempt to take advantage of the Vatican. He accepted long-standing demands, forced the Holy See to agree to them, and then ignored his commitments. Ultimately, however, this proved to be but one more serious miscalculation made by Germany's evil leader. The concordat came back to haunt the Nazis, as Pope Pius and the Catholic Church used it to shield Jewish victims and resist Nazi advances.[178] Within a decade, Hitler would express his intent to terminate the accord.

In addition to a general opposition to racial laws, the Church would not accept that a person who had been duly converted to Catholicism was still a Jew. To the Church, the issue was one of faith, not race. Accordingly, as part of the concordat, German officials agreed to regard baptized Jews as Christians. This would end up being one of the most important agreements between the Vatican and the Third Reich — one that saved the lives of thousands of Jews, officially baptized or not.[179]

---

On July 30, 1933, the first steps were taken to dissolve the Catholic Youth League. This same month the Nazis began serious enforcement of their racial laws. Jewish people were fired from civil service jobs. Within a month, Nazis were arresting large numbers of Jews and political prisoners (primarily Communists and Socialists) and sending them to concentration camps for infractions such as insulting the state, offending storm troopers, or consorting with German girls. Hitler's chief negotiator, Vice Chancellor Franz von Papen, wrote in 1945: "Hitler sabotaged the Concordat."[180]

On August 28, 1933, the German Catholic bishops issued a joint pastoral letter to be read from the pulpits of all Catholic Churches in the nation. Quoting from the Gospel of Matthew, the letter said that: "the messengers of Christianity are to be the 'salt of the earth,' and 'the light of the world,' and 'should let their light shine before the people.' The Church should be as 'a city on the hill,' visible from afar in the life of the people."[181] Hitler responded on September 11 that he was not against Christianity itself, "but we will fight for the sake of keeping our public life free from those priests who have failed their calling and who should have become politicians rather than clergymen."[182] Four days later, proving that words had no effect on the Nazis, they passed the Nuremberg Laws, which defined German citizenship and paved the way for later anti-Semitic laws.[183]

After the war, Fabian von Schlabrendorff, a Protestant member of the German resistance, wrote a memorandum to U.S. General William ("Wild Bill") Donovan, in which Schlabrendorff reported:

> Immediately after Hitler had seized the power, National Socialism showed itself as an ideology plainly opposed to Christianism. Only a minority among the princes of the Catholic Church[,] like for example Bishop Berning from Osnabrück and later Cardinal Innitzer from Vienna[,] tried to show a friendly attitude towards Hitler. The majority of the princes of the Catholic Church left no doubt in their declarations and pastoral letters that there was no bridge between Naziism [sic] and the Catholic Church. As the years went by, the attitude of the Catholic Church became ever clearer. The rejection of Hitler became more and more obvious.[184]

He went on to explain: "Because of the hierarchic organizations of the Church, the denunciation of Hitler was propagated by the majority of Catholic clergy in the land. The result of this was that the enmity towards Hitler was promulgated not only by the high clerics but was also carried to the masses by the low clerics."[185]

Donovan, in his own report for the OSS War Crimes Staff, which was approved by the Nuremberg Prosecution Review Board, examined the relationship between the German Catholic leadership and the Nazis as they came to power:

> During this period the relations between the Nazi Party and the Catholic Church were extremely bitter. . . . On their part, the German bishops, stigmatizing the Nazi movement as anti-Christian, forbade the clergy to participate in any

ceremonies, such as funerals, in which the Nazi Party was officially represented, and refused the sacraments to party officials. In several pastorals, they expressly warned the faithful against the danger created to German Catholicism by the party.[186]

Donovan explained that the bishops' endorsement of the 1933 concordat between the Holy See and Germany did not indicate any sympathy for the Nazis. Rather, they thought that such an agreement might moderate the Nazis, as had happened in Italy following the Lateran Treaty:[187]

> The Church had been making agreements with foreign governments for centuries. It did not view them as endorsements of the existing government. Pope Pius XI explained his thinking in 1937, in his encyclical *Mit brennender Sorge* (*With Burning Anxiety*): When, in 1933, We consented... to open negotiations for a concordat, We were prompted by the desire... to secure for Germany the freedom of the Church's beneficent mission and the salvation of the souls in her care, as well as by the sincere wish to render the German people a service essential for its peaceful development and prosperity. Hence, despite many and grave misgivings, We then decided not to withhold Our consent for We wished to spare the Faithful of Germany... the trials and difficulties they would have had to face... had the negotiations fallen through. It was by acts that We wished to make it plain, that the pacific and maternal hand of the Church would be extended to anyone who did not actually refuse it.[188]

As Pius XI told a meeting of bishops in Rome in May 1933: "If it is a matter of saving a few souls, of averting even graver damage, we have the courage to negotiate even with the devil."[189]

From the perspective of the Vatican, the German concordat was very favorable — one of the best that it had ever signed.[190] The state essentially met all of the demands that the Church had long made of the Weimar Republic, including: independence of Catholic organizations, freedom of the Church, freedom for Catholic schools, free communication with Rome, Church control over religious orders and ecclesiastical property, and religious education in public schools (taught by teachers approved by the bishop).[191] Only minimal restrictions were placed on ecclesiastical appointments (bishops were to be appointed by Rome, subject to political objections by the Reich government; clergy were to be appointed by bishops, the only requirement being that they be German nationals).

A public statement made by Hitler about the rights of the Catholic Church, which was made official policy with the signing of the concordat, was released to the press on July 9, 1933. It read:

> 1. The dissolution of those Catholic organizations which are recognized by the present treaty and which were dissolved without instructions by the government of the Reich is to be rescinded immediately.

2. All coercive measures against priests and other leaders of the Catholic organizations are to be annulled. A repetition of such measures in the future is inadmissible and will be punished in conformity to the existing laws.[192]

The Vatican also received the long-sought right to maintain theological faculties at state institutions and to establish seminaries. In short, with the concordat, "the Catholic religion in Germany was placed on an even footing with the Protestant faith and was guaranteed the same rights and privileges as the latter."[193]

In June 1933, after negotiations for the concordat were well underway, the archbishop of Munich, Cardinal Faulhaber, cautioned that Hitler wanted an agreement with the Vatican for propaganda purposes. He said that Hitler "sees what a halo his government will have in the eyes of the world if the Pope makes a treaty with him." He argued that Catholic people would not understand the Holy See making a treaty with the Third Reich when "a whole row of Catholic officials are sitting in prison or have been illegally ejected."[194] Critics often cite this language. Later, however, Faulhaber learned all of the reasons why the Church had agreed to the concordat. He said: "With the concordat we are hanged, without the concordat we are hanged, drawn and quartered."[195] Faulhaber became an outspoken opponent of Hitler, and support from Pius was one reason for his outspokenness.[196]

The concordat did tend to reassure German Catholics, and the Nazis fully exploited it for propaganda purposes.[197] According to the minutes from a meeting of the Conference of Ministers on July 14, 1933, Hitler saw "three great advantages" to the concordat:

1. That the Vatican had negotiated at all, while they operated, especially in Austria, on the assumption that National Socialism was un-Christian and inimical to the Church;
2. That the Vatican could be persuaded to bring about a good relationship with this purely National German State. He, the Reich Chancellor, would not have considered it possible even a short time ago that the Church would be willing to obligate the bishops to this State. The fact that this had now been done was certainly an unreserved recognition of the present regime;
3. That with the concordat, the Church withdrew from activity in associations and parties, e.g., abandoned the Christian labor unions. This, too, the Reich Chancellor would not have considered possible even a few months ago. Even the dissolution of the Center Party could be termed final only with the conclusion of the concordat now that the Vatican had ordered the permanent exclusion of the priests from party politics.[198]

As such, Hitler was anxious to secure the agreement, and he was willing to do whatever it took to obtain it.

The signing of a concordat is sometimes mistakenly assumed to signify a close relationship between the government and the Holy See. That, however, is not the case. The modern tradition of the Vatican is that if relations, no matter how strained, are maintained, there is a possibility of influencing the government and of protecting Catholic interests. Without some form of relationship, the Holy See cannot effectively protect and minister to its people. As one commentator noted:

> This is the precise opposite of the fact; a country which was on ideally good terms with Rome would not need to have a Concordat at all; and the existence of such a document implies that the two signatory parties are, in a more or less degree, distrustful of each other's intentions. It is an attempt to regularize a difficult situation by tying down either party, on paper, to a minimum of good behavior.... **Nothing could be more absurd than to represent [the Concordat of July 1933] as if it meant that the New Germany and the Vatican were working hand in hand.**[199]

Peter Godman, who reviewed archival documents that concern the relations between the Holy See and Germany from 1923 to 1939 concluded: "The notion that [Pius XI or Pacelli] harbored sympathies for National Socialism, because they continued to negotiate with its leaders, must be rejected."[200]

———

In June 1933, shortly after the Vatican signed the concordat with Germany, another religion attempted to forge a working relationship with the new regime. On the eleventh of that month, the Nazis put into place a law prohibiting the International Bible Students Union and its subsidiaries because of agitation by the Jehovah's Witnesses against the state.[201] In response, on the twenty-fifth, the Jehovah's Witnesses convened a hastily organized convention at the Sporthalle Wilmersdorf in Berlin. Some five thousand delegates attended.

Like Catholics, the Jehovah's Witnesses were internationalists in a religious sense. They were also generally tolerant of other races, regarded secular authority as evil, and were openly anti-militaristic. They expressed the view that: "Being no part of the world, we take no part in the wars of the nations."[202] All of these factors caused the nationalistic, racist, and militaristic Nazis to despise them. Thus, with Hitler's ascent to power, the government unleashed an immediate wave of persecution against the Jehovah's Witnesses. The 1933 Jehovah's Witnesses convention was an attempt to bring an end to this persecution so that the Witnesses could go on doing their work.

The Berlin *Sporthalle* was bedecked with Swastika flags for the convention, and the representatives adopted a "Declaration of Facts" ("*Erklärung*"), which attempted to assure the new government that it would receive full cooperation from the Jehovah's Witnesses. Among the most controversial provisions were the following:

It is falsely charged by our enemies that we have received financial support for our work from the Jews. Nothing is farther from the truth. Up to this hour there has never been the slightest amount of money contributed to our work by Jews. We are faithful followers of Christ Jesus and believe upon Him as the Savior of the world, whereas Jews entirely reject Jesus Christ and emphatically deny that he is the Savior of the world sent of God for man's good. This of itself should be sufficient proof to show that we receive no support from Jews and that therefore the charges against us are maliciously false and could proceed only from Satan, our great enemy. The greatest and most oppressive empire on earth is the Anglo-American empire. By that is meant the British Empire, of which the United States of America forms a part. It has been the commercial Jews of the British-American empire that have built up and carried on Big Business as a means of exploiting and oppressing the peoples of many nations.

\*\*\*

Instead of being against the principles advocated by the government of Germany, we stand squarely for such principles....

\*\*\*

The people of Germany have suffered great misery since 1914 and have been the victims of much injustice practiced upon them by others. The nationalists have declared themselves against all such unrighteousness and announced that "Our relationship to God is high and holy."

\*\*\*

We therefore appeal to the high sense of justice of the government and nation and respectfully ask that the order of prohibition against our work and our literature be set aside, and the opportunity be given us to have a fair hearing before we are judged.

Over two million copies of the declaration were printed, and each delegate was asked to help distribute 250 copies to judges, mayors, and other government officials.

The cover letter mailed to Hitler blamed "clerical, especially Catholic, quarters" for the untrue charges that had been made against the Witnesses, and said that "commercialistic Jews and Catholics" in the United States were "the most eager persecutors of our Society's work."[203] The letter expressly rejected "the slanderous claim that the Bible Students are supported by Jews," and went on to say that the "Bible Students are fighting for the same high, ethical goals and ideals" expressed by the National Government. "Respecting the purely religious and apolitical goals and objectives of the Bible Students, it can be said that these are in compete harmony with the similar goals of the National Government of the German Reich." The letter then delved into politics that might have been attractive to Hitler. It argued that the "Anglo-American World Empire... — especially

England — is to be held responsible for the League of Nations and the unjustified treaties and burdens placed on Germany."[204]

On June 27, 1933, one day after the Witnesses began sending copies of the Declaration of Facts by registered mail to German officials, the Prussian state banned Jehovah's Witnesses, and the police began to carry out widespread raids on their homes and places of business. The next day, the Society's property was seized and occupied. Their printing plant was closed on orders of the government. The Jehovah's Witnesses' property at Magdeburg was confiscated, and the staff of 180 was forced to leave. Hitler declared: "I dissolve the 'Earnest Bible Students' in Germany; their property I dedicate to the people's welfare; I will have all their literature confiscated."[205] Between two million and three million marks' worth of Watch Tower books, booklets, paintings, Bibles, and other material was confiscated and destroyed by the Nazis.[206]

Never again did the Jehovah's Witnesses seek to curry the favor of the National Socialist regime. The Watch Tower Society henceforth opposed Nazi policies, refusing to take up arms and remaining strictly neutral toward the government.[207] For this, the Witnesses were required to wear a marker similar to the Star of David worn by the Jews. Eventually, more than 2,000 Jehovah's Witnesses were sent to concentration camps.[208] A total of 635 died in prison (203 of these were actually executed; the rest died due to the harsh conditions).[209] The 1934 *Jehovah's Witness Yearbook* reported: "The Papal hierarchy is really behind the persecution of God's people in Germany." In reality, however, the Witnesses were imprisoned for two primary reasons: they refused to take up arms, and they had loyalties to another, higher regime.

———————

The Catholic Church did not normally interfere with what it considered to be the internal matters of another sovereign nation. It was, however, fundamentally opposed to racist theories. In 1928, the Vatican issued a statement declaring that the Church "just as it reproves all rancors in conflicts between peoples, to the maximum extent [*quam maxime*] condemns hatred of the people once chosen by God, the hatred that commonly goes by the name of anti-Semitism."[210] On April 4, 1933, the Holy See sent a letter, signed by Secretary of State Pacelli, informing Monsignor Cesare Orsenigo, the nuncio in Germany, that some requests had come to the Pope asking for his "intervention against the danger of anti-Semitic excesses in Germany."[211] The letter continues: "Given that it is part of the traditions of the Holy See to carry out its mission of universal peace and charity toward all men, regardless of the social or religious condition to which they belong, by offering, if necessary, its charitable offices, the Holy Father asks your Excellency to see if and how it is possible to be involved in the desired way."[212] In 1938, Pius XI wrote a letter instructing those in the universities and seminaries to "make use of biology, history, philosophy, apologetics, legal and moral studies as weapons for refuting firmly and completely the... untenable assertions" of race and state put forth by the Nazis.[213] The Pope wanted racial theories to be scientifically refuted so that the clergy would be able to oppose them on rational as well as religious grounds.

German bishops continually complained, either individually or as a collective group, about concordat violations and Nazi policies.[214] Despite assurances to the contrary, Hitler launched a strong campaign to separate churches from schools and youth organizations. He threatened to remove children from parents who refused to follow a Nazi program. "We shall rear them as needful for the Fatherland," he said during one storm trooper review.[215] In 1933, 65 percent of Munich parents sent their children to Catholic schools. By 1937, it was only 3 percent.[216] Hundreds of Catholic schools were converted to secular institutions. Secretary of State Pacelli, in a formal protest, asserted that "a planned attack is in progress against the Catholic schools."[217]

Once organized religion had served its purpose, Hitler wanted to bring it to an end as quietly as possible. In December 1933, he issued an order that all church youth groups be dissolved and that all young people be sent to Nazi Party youth organizations (the Hitler Youth for boys; the League of German Maidens for girls).[218] All other youth organizations were forbidden to take part in organized sports, wear uniforms, or march in formation. This legislation led to some violent clashes between the Catholic Boy Scouts and the Hitler Youth.[219]

Weekly meetings of the Hitler Youth were held on Sunday mornings, which prevented children from going to church services. In those areas where churches were permitted to conduct youth activities, Gestapo regulations were often formulated so that actual compliance was impossible. To receive permission to hold outings, for instance, churches had to submit a list of participants, their dates of birth, whether they belonged to the Hitler Youth, how long the activity would last, where it would take place, and a detailed description of what was planned.[220] This application had to be submitted months in advance of the planned outing, and Hitler Youths were not permitted to attend unless they had written permission from their Hitler Youth leader. Such rules virtually eliminated church-related youth groups. Cardinal Pacelli, speaking to a representative of the Reich government, said: "We are very much afraid that a German religion could arise."[221]

In October 1933, Hitler pulled Germany out of the League of Nations, withdrew from the disarmament conference, and committed himself to rearming Germany. He justified these moves by claiming that Germany had been treated unfairly under international policies. "The men who today lead Germany have nothing in common with the traitors of 1918" who signed the Treaty of Versailles, argued Hitler.[222] The next month, he offered German voters a referendum, but since all other political parties had been outlawed, no opposition appeared on the ballot and the Nazis captured about 93 percent of the vote.

While Pacelli tried to moderate tensions between the Pope and German officials, his private writings and letters from the mid-1930s reveal the contempt he felt toward Nazism. He referred to Nazis as "false prophets with the pride of

Lucifer," and "bearers of a new faith and a new gospel."[223] For a religious man and future Pope, there could not be a more damning charge. For their part, the Nazi press published a drawing showing Cardinal Pacelli embracing an unattractive French Communist Jewish woman. To the Nazis, there were few allegations that could have been more offensive.

Throughout the rest of 1933, the Nazis consolidated their power. In November, they took over the largest press in Germany. In December, the storm troopers became an official arm of the Reich. Four hundred thousand "imperfect" Germans were identified for the sterilization program, which was condemned by Pope Pius XI and the Austrian bishops.[224] Those bishops "denounced National Socialism in set terms" and condemned both the Sterilization Law and the radical anti-Semitism and excessive nationalism of the Nazi movement.[225] The year was such that the Nobel Committee decided not to award a Peace Prize.

# SIX

# Hitler Battles the Churches

In May and June 1934, S.S. chief Heinrich Himmler circulated a fifty-page memorandum on the religious bodies in the Reich. Under the heading "Hostile Clergy," it reported:

> The most dangerous activity of countless Catholic clergy is the way in which they "mope about," spreading despondency. Favorite topics are the "dangers of a new time," "the present emergency," "the gloomy future." Prophecies are made about the speedy downfall of National Socialism or at the very least mention is made of the transience of all political phenomena, compared with the Catholic Church which will outlive them all. National Socialist achievements and successes are passed over in silence.
>
> There is thus a deliberated undermining of the very basis of the National Socialist programme of reconstruction, the people's trust in the leadership of the state.[1]

Before long, Hitler had anti-Nazi Catholic priests imprisoned on immorality charges. Erich Klausener, leader of Catholic Action, was murdered in a June 1934 purge. Hundreds of priests and Catholic officials were arrested or driven into exile, while others were accused of violating currency regulations or morality rules.[2] The campaign was "intended to destroy the loyalty felt by Catholics for their clergy and especially for members of religious orders."[3]

In mid-June 1934, Hitler announced that Germany would not pay its remaining foreign debts. World reaction was restrained, so Hitler was able to help shore up the German economy without creating new international problems. That same month he also acted to secure his political power within Germany.

June 30, 1934, came to be known as the "Night of the Long Knives." In one night, Hitler eliminated his rivals with more than a hundred summary executions.[4] Hitler's storm troopers, the S.A., had been indispensable to Nazi might, but Hitler feared that they had evolved into a personal army for Captain Ernst Roehm, S.A. chief of staff.[5] Roehm was now the greatest threat to Hitler's power. In addition, German military leaders were unwilling to submit to Hitler's rule until he assured them that the army, not the S.A., would be the primary military force in Germany.

Hitler claimed that the storm troopers were poised to stage a revolt and suggested that they might have been working with Russia. (Roehm, according to some accounts, was now demanding a "second revolution" that would make good on Nazi claims to socialistic ideals.)[6] Hitler also circulated the rumor that Roehm was plotting his assassination. In retaliation for these offenses — real or imagined — Hitler had Roehm executed. Although Hitler had previously accepted Roehm's homosexual activity, Nazis now circulated the story that he had been found in a compromising position with another man.[7] Karl Ernst, leader of the Berlin storm troopers, was also murdered. Former Chancellor Kurt von Schleicher and his wife were both killed, supposedly because they resisted arrest. More than a hundred other officials and storm troopers were also slain or committed suicide.[8]

Hitler used this opportunity to rid himself of Catholic opposition leaders. Erich Klausener, president of the Berlin Catholic Action and a known opponent of Nazism, was shot and killed. Dr. Edgar Jung, another leader of Catholic Action, was also killed. Adalbert Probst, president of the Sporting Association of German Catholics, was summoned to Berlin under a pretext. His wife received his ashes in the mail a few days later. Michael Gerlich, editor of one of the most widely read Catholic newspapers in Germany, *Der gerade Weg*, was found dead in prison. The bishops' palaces in Würzburg, Rottenburg, and Mainz were sacked, and shortly thereafter more than five hundred priests and religious were arrested, many of whom died in jail.[9]

Prior to the Night of the Long Knives, three German bishops (Wilhelm Berning, Conrad Gröber, and Nikolaus Bares) met with Hitler to try to establish a better line of communication between the Church and German leadership.[10] On June 29, the bishops and German negotiators completed a draft agreement that — if one were to believe Hitler — appeared to work out many of the disputes that existed over matters such as the proper role for Catholic youth groups and Catholic lay organizations. Following the bloodshed that came with the Nazi rampage, however, Pope Pius XI vetoed any such accord.[11]

While the S.A. was not disbanded following the Night of the Long Knives, it was relieved of most of its powers. Authority had been promised to the military, but Hitler betrayed them and instead gave it to the executive arm of the National Socialists, the black-shirted S.S. (*Schutzstaffel*) headed by Heinrich Himmler.[12] The S.S. was an elite corps of men who were bound together by their racial and elitist self-understanding. Rather than pledging themselves to the Reich, members of the S.S. were devoted exclusively to Hitler. "Every Catholic in Germany was keenly aware that the elite SS would not even admit Catholics — only those who repudiated the Church."[13] These were the men who would later organize the concentration camps and direct the Nazi effort to exterminate the Jews.

Explaining his "blood purge" in a speech shortly thereafter, Hitler said, "Everyone must know for all future time that if he raises his hand to strike the state then certain death is his lot."[14] Any remaining limitation on Hitler's power ended in August with President Hindenburg's death. Hindenburg had held Hitler in check at least twice in the past. Now there truly were no limits. The role of kaiser, president, parliament, and chancellor were all now filled by one man.

With his new powers, Hitler could make war and peace, create and abolish laws, execute suspects, and pardon convicts. He was both legislator and executive, and he would reshape the courts in his image as well.

———

In the Soviet Union, too, political upheaval defined the times. After vanquishing first their Trotskyite rivals and then, by 1929, the Bukharinites, Stalin and his followers were ready to put their plans into full swing. On December 27, 1929, Stalin announced the goal of the liquidation of the *kulaks* (wealthier peasants) as a class. It is estimated that about 13 million people were rounded up and shot or deported. "Deportation" meant that those who were considered "class enemies" were packed into cattle cars and shipped to Russia's Arctic wasteland, where almost certain death awaited them.[15]

In Ukraine, 7 million people were starved to death on the Kremlin's orders. Farmers who took grain or vegetables from their own land were shot. Dead bodies littered the streets of Kharkov, the capital. "It was," eyewitnesses later recalled, "as if the Black Death had passed through."[16] Before he was finished, Stalin would be responsible for 20 million deaths.[17] According to the head of the Russian parliamentary commission on rehabilitation, "from 1929 to 1953... 21.5 million people were repressed. Of these a third were shot, the rest sentenced to imprisonment where many also died."[18]

While the Soviets were eliminating their "undesirables," they were also waging an all-out battle against the source of most peasants' strength: the Church. In 1929, a law was passed that strengthened the state's control over the parishes.[19] Propagation of religion now became a crime against the state.[20] Priests and their families were deprived of civil rights. As "disenfranchised persons," they did not have the right to ration cards, medical aid, or communal apartments. Many prelates were arrested, tortured, and killed.[21] The children of clergy were not allowed to attend schools or higher educational institutions.[22] Thus, they were forced to renounce their parents in order to obtain an education, if not simply to live.

Hundreds of churches of all denominations were destroyed, including many of historical significance. The churches that survived had their bells removed, so that their ringing would not disturb the workers. Very few Catholic churches in Russia at the time of the revolution survived, and those that did were maintained primarily to convince foreign visitors that there was still religious freedom in the Soviet Union.[23]

Although Soviet abuses were not widely known until after the war, those in the Vatican had good information. In 1930, Pope Pius XI published an open letter protesting "the horrible and sacrilegious outrages being perpetrated against the Catholic Church in Russia."[24] He specifically noted the murders of priests, the moral blackmail of workers, and the indoctrination of and moral corruption of children. As Vatican secretary of state, Cardinal Pacelli knew of these Soviet abuses.[25] This knowledge created a problem a few years later when Stalin's Soviet

Union joined the Allies in the war against Hitler's Germany, and Pacelli — as Pope Pius XII — had to make difficult decisions concerning the allegiance of his church.

————

On January 13, 1935, the German inhabitants of the coal-rich Saar, occupied by the French since the end of the First World War, voted on a return to Germany. There had been some doubt about whether an overwhelmingly Catholic region, comprised mainly of miners and industry workers, would choose to return to a Germany run by a dictator who had crushed trade unions, harassed the Church, and destroyed the democratic republic. The inhabitants, however, resented being held captive by occupying forces even more. They voted 477,000 to 48,000 to return.[26] On March 1, France transferred the Saar back to Germany in the hopes of appeasing Hitler.

When German troops marched into the Saar, they were enthusiastically greeted, and the feeling was reciprocated. Hitler proudly welcomed the inhabitants of the Saar back to Germany. In a radio broadcast from Berlin, he promised the world that with the return of the Saar he had no further territorial claims on France.[27] This was important to the French because they thought that it meant he had dropped his claim to Alsace and Lorraine, which had been areas of dispute between the two countries.

Three days after the transfer of the Saar, citing Germany's aggressive behavior and rearmament, Great Britain announced a new intensified defense policy.[28] This, however, did not slow Hitler down. By mid-month, Germany declared that it was reinstating the military draft. This was a clear breach of the Treaty of Versailles, but the German press hailed the move. Mussolini followed with expanded conscription the next week.

The world situation was in such an unstable state that in October 1934, Pius XI dispatched Pacelli to be his legate to the Eucharistic Congress in Buenos Aires.[29] This broke a tradition that had kept the Vatican secretary of state close to home for well over a century, but sending its most-trusted representative signified the Vatican's deep concern about world events. (Pius XI also told others that he was sending Pacelli around the world because he would one day be pope.)[30]

In a letter dated March 12, 1935, to Cardinal Carl Joseph Schulte of Cologne, Pacelli referred to the Nazis as "false prophets with the pride of Lucifer," and "bearers of a new Faith and a new Evangile," who were attempting to create a "mendacious antimony between faithfulness to the Church and to the Fatherland."[31] There are also reports from this time of Pacelli privately referring to the new regime in Germany as "diabolical."[32] As the Nazis became more certain of their political strength, the persecution of the Church and religious people intensified.

By 1935, Church leaders in Germany were regularly subjected to physical violence; hundreds of priests and other Church officials were arrested, driven into exile, accused of immorality, or charged with violating currency regulations.[33] The trials, which ran for years, were designed to destroy the reputations of monks and nuns by showing their "perverted and immoral" lifestyles. Many of the trials were designed and publicized as a propaganda campaign to convince Catholic parents not to send their children to Catholic schools.[34] Propaganda Minister Goebbels even lowered the height of newsstands so that children could see the lurid photographs and anti-Catholic cartoons that accompanied the stories. The *New York Times* reported one incident in May 1936: A priest was summoned to a "sick call" at a hotel room, and when he arrived, photographers were there to film him with a prostitute hired by the Gestapo.[35]

It became serious enough that Pope Pius XI appointed the bishop of Trier, Franz Bornewasser, to conduct an investigation. Bishop Bornewasser found that fewer than one out of five hundred accused priests or religious were actually guilty of the charges.[36] In July 1935, Minister of State Adolf Wagner said: "In the days that lie immediately ahead of us the fight will not be against either Communists or Marxists, but against *Catholicism*. Everyone will find himself faced with the serious question: German or Catholic? This struggle will not be easy."[37] The *New York Times* reported that Christmas 1937 would see "more than a hundred Protestant pastors and several thousand Catholic clergymen in prison." [38]

Catholics were forbidden to hold public meetings, even for purely religious purposes.[39] Convent nuns were declared redundant, and some six hundred teaching nuns were told to seek civilian employment. Church properties were ransacked, Catholic meetings were broken up, and scurrilous stories continued to appear in the Nazi press. Attempts by the Nazis to remove crucifixes from schools in Bavaria led to such an outcry that several local officials rescinded the orders.[40]

The Nazi press was quite outspoken in its opposition to the Catholic Church. *Deutsche Volkskirche*, a Nazi political magazine, reported on a Church conference as a "devilish beginning," to various "treasonable activities" by "these Jewish-Roman Jehovah priests."[41] One passage said: "All accommodation between the Roman Church and National Socialism is impossible; there can only be a struggle for victory or defeat."[42] Another article in *Völkischer Beobachter* reported that the "Catholic Congress" held in Prague on June 30, 1935, was designed to arrange for closer cooperation between Catholicism and Bolshevism.[43] The following day, the same paper reported that the Vatican was negotiating with the Soviet Union for a concordat.[44] Even the magazine of the Hitler Youth tried to smear the Church by claiming it was closely associated with Communism.[45]

———

When Nuncio Pacelli wrote to Rome in 1923 complaining about the Nazi persecution of Catholics, he noted that the attacks "were especially focused" on the "learned and zealous" Cardinal Faulhaber, who "had denounced the persecutions against the Jews."[46] Pacelli and Faulhaber formed a close friendship during those years. Later, when Pacelli was pope, Faulhaber was his most important adviser on German matters.[47]

In 1935, at an open meeting, Nazis called for Faulhaber to be killed.[48] In February 1936, Nazi police confiscated and destroyed one of his sermons. This happened twice again the following year.[49] On October 25, 1936, members of the Hitler Youth hurled insults at him as he was entering his car.[50] In August 1938, the Nazis ransacked his office.[51] In late November 1938, after he had given a speech, a uniformed detachment arrived in front of his residence and threw stones at the windows. They shouted, "Take the traitor to Dachau," and shattered window frames and shutters.[52] In May 1939, demonstrations against Faulhaber took place throughout Bavaria, and posters were hung saying: "Away with Faulhaber, the friend of the Jews and the agent of Moscow."[53] After the war began, Faulhaber relied upon Pius XII's encyclical *Summi Pontificatus* (On the Unity of Human Society)[54] in an address condemning Nazis, resulting in a headline reading "Cardinal Faulhaber Indicts Hitlerism" in the London *Tablet*.[55]

Reverend Martin Niemöller, a noted German Protestant leader who spent seven years in concentration camps for his opposition to Hitler and the Nazis, said that Faulhaber's sermons showed him "to be a great and courageous man."[56] Niemöller went on to say that Faulhaber's "sermons are monuments to the Christian faith, and they will be remembered forever."[57]

In his 1945 memorandum to General Donovan, Fabian von Schlabrendorff praised Faulhaber for openly stating his opposition to the Nazis and influencing other Catholics to do the same. Schlabrendorff reported that "decisive credit" for the Catholic opposition to Nazism "ought to be given to Cardinal von Faulhaber from Munich and whose personal sermons branded Nazism as the enemy of Christendom."[58] After the war, Rabbi Stephen S. Wise, one of the leading American voices for the Jewish cause, called Faulhaber "a true Christian prelate" who "had lifted his fearless voice" in defense of the Jews.[59] In fact, Wise said that Faulhaber had been a much better friend to the Jews of Europe than even the widely heralded Martin Niemöller.[60]

Faulhaber wrote Secretary of State Pacelli, describing the persecution of the Jews as "unjust and painful."[61] He was especially troubled that "also those [Jews] who have been baptized for ten or twenty years and are good Catholics, even those whose parents were already Catholic, are still legally considered to be Jews, and are to lose their positions as physicians or lawyers."[62] Nevertheless, he did not want to engage in direct confrontation with the Nazi authorities. He cautioned Pacelli that for the time being it was impossible to oppose the government on the racial question because of the threat that it would present to his Catholic followers.[63] Such requests for silence, from those Catholic leaders closest to the situation inside Nazi Germany, helped shape Pacelli's thinking on this matter.

———

As world attention was drawn to the events in Germany, the Nazis promised to stop their campaign of hatred against "Jews, Catholics, and reactionaries."[64] Reports out of Germany, however, were not promising, especially for the Jews.

Prior to Hitler's rise to power, Jewish people in Germany were treated as well, if not better, than they were in any other European nation.[65] Things had deteriorated with the early boycott of Jewish businesses and limitations on entry to professions, but the situation was about to get even worse. A series of laws promulgated at the Nazi Party meeting in Nuremberg in September 1935 essentially segregated Jews from the rest of the German people. These "Nuremberg race laws" held that people with one Jewish grandparent were not allowed to call themselves German. Jewish speech, newspapers, and even prayers were censored. Lest the Aryan race be further "defiled," marriage between Jews and other Germans was prohibited. Laws were enacted that prohibited Jews from settling in some German towns. Aryan Germans were forbidden from cooperating with Jewish people, and purchasing goods from a Jewish merchant was considered treason. Needless to say, many Jewish businesses were driven into bankruptcy. Vatican Radio condemned the injustice and inhumanity of these new laws.[66]

Hitler announced that Jews were not entitled to vote or participate in German politics. In addition, Jews were prohibited from employing German women under the age of forty-five, raising the German flag, or dating Aryans (arrests of Aryan girls who mixed with Jewish boys resulted in both being sent to concentration camps for the crime of "race defiling.")[67] Plans were even announced to buy out all Jewish businesses, though it seems unlikely that a true purchase was ever seriously contemplated.

Catholic and Protestant leaders immediately protested these actions. Hitler himself responded. On September 11, 1935, the German leader pronounced that the party had no intention of waging war against Christianity. On the other hand, he cautioned that under no circumstances would the National Socialist state tolerate

> the continuance or fresh beginning of the politicizing of the denominations by roundabout ways. Here let there be no mistake about the determination of the Movement and the State. We have already fought political clericalism once and driven it out of Parliament, and that, too, after a long struggle, in which we had no power of the State behind us, and the other side had all the power. Today it is we who have this power; and we shall never wage the war as a war against Christianity or even against one of the two denominations; but we shall wage it in order to keep our public life free from those priests who have fallen short of their calling, and who think they have to be politicians, not pastors of the flock.[68]

One right still allowed to German Jews was emigration, and 150,000 (30 percent of Germany's Jewish population) did so between January 1933 and November 1938.[69] By 1939, 80 percent of Jewish people under the age of forty had left.[70] (Unfortunately, as it turned out, thousands of German Jews fled to Poland, where a terrible fate awaited them.)[71] In 1936, Vatican Secretary of State Pacelli established an organization to help Jewish refugees as they fled from Nazism.[72]

Within Germany, the Catholic Church took a leading role in opposing the racial laws. On February 9, 1936, Bishop Galen of Münster made a speech at Xanten, which became very well known. In it, he said:

> There are fresh graves in German soil in which are lying the ashes of those whom the Catholic people regard as martyrs for the Faith, since their lives gave witness to their most dutiful and loyal devotion to God and the Fatherland, to the nation and the Church, while the dark secrecy which surrounds their deaths is most carefully preserved.[73]

The Nazis fought back, protesting that while Catholic priests should thank God that the National Socialists had swept away "the Jewish-Bolshevist underworld," they were instead sheltering "the corrupters of our race."[74]

Catholic leaders outside of Germany also condemned the racial laws. Polish Cardinal Augustyn Hlond spoke of "the very many Jews who are believers, honest, just, kind, and philanthropic… who are ethically outstanding, noble and upright." Cardinal Hlond continued: "I am against that moral stance, imported from abroad, that is basically and ruthlessly anti-Jewish." He then spoke of Catholic teaching on anti-Semitism: "It is contrary to Catholic ethics. One may not hate anyone. It is forbidden to assault, beat up, maim, or slander Jews. One should honor Jews as human beings and neighbors…. Beware of those who are inciting anti-Jewish violence. They serve an evil cause."[75]

The protests grew so common that the Nazis accused the Catholic Church of acting on behalf of the Jews.[76] Hermann Göring complained that

> Catholic believers carry away but one impression from attendance at divine services and that is that the Catholic Church rejects the institutions of the Nationalist State. How could it be otherwise when they are continuously engaging in polemics on political questions or events in their sermons… hardly a Sunday passes but that they abuse the so-called religious atmosphere of the divine service in order to read pastoral letters on purely political subjects.[77]

Adolf Wagner, Bavarian minister of the interior, said that "there will be no peace in Germany until all the political priests are driven out and exterminated."[78]

Many still find it hard to understand how Hitler could have convinced an advanced, industrial nation like Germany to follow his outlandish racial theories, but the same month that he imposed these new racial laws (September 1935), he was also able to announce that the number of jobless had fallen from six million to one million.[79] Strict economic controls caused a short-term expansion in the economy, and living standards improved dramatically. Five years earlier there had been daily rioting in the streets, life savings were wiped out overnight by inflation, and no one had a job. Now unemployment was virtually eliminated; industrial production soared; inflation was under control; and the economy, fueled by expenditures for rearmament and public works, flourished.[80] Unencumbered by the obstructions inherent in a democracy, Hitler revived a collapsed economy in five years. He erased the shame of Germany's defeat in World War I by reclaiming the Rhineland and discarding the unfair Treaty of Versailles. He gave millions of Germans attractive vacations through his *Kraft durch Freude* ("strength through joy") program. He established training schools for those who were unskilled and brought the nation to full employment. He brought crime under control. He built freeways and promised the production of a car that ordinary Germans would soon be able to afford.[81]

Germans, in fact, enjoyed the highest standard of living in all of Europe.[82] In 1937, Winston Churchill noted that Hitler's accomplishments were "among the most remarkable in the whole history of the world."[83]

As late as 1951, 42 percent of adult West Germans and 53 percent of those over thirty-five believed that the pre-war years of the Third Reich were the "best" that Germany had experienced in that century.[84] Even in the British Parliament, National Socialism was hailed as Europe's only protection against the spread of Communism.[85] Such things would never begin to justify Hitler's evil actions, but they might help to explain the difficulty Germans had in challenging him. And, of course, those who did challenge him (including many priests and ministers) were immediately arrested and frequently executed.

————

As Hitler shaped German minds to his way of thinking, he imposed his will in many different areas. He made sports compulsory in all schools. Non-belief in Nazism was made grounds for divorce. Two great enemies of Nazism were joined together, as Germans were called upon to resist "Jewish Bolshevization."[86] As countries around the globe pointed fingers at Germany, Hitler condemned the Soviet Union as an instigator of war. He also tightly controlled the media.

Hitler used the most modern medium, radio, to its fullest advantage. Nazi leadership saw this as the most effective way to influence the masses. German radio quickly became the voice of the Nazi Party, as the airwaves were flooded with speeches by or about Hitler and National Socialism. (Jazz music — a free form of expression — was banned.)[87] To ensure wide dissemination of Nazi propaganda, Hitler ordered the production of small, cheap radios. By the end of the decade, 70 percent of German families owned radios, the highest percentage in the world.[88]

In the early 1930s, Hitler's homeland of Austria was experiencing social upheaval on an only slightly smaller scale than Germany had in the preceding years. Hundreds of rioting workers in Vienna were killed when the Austrian army attacked them with machine guns and howitzers.[89] The Socialist mayor of Vienna was placed under arrest, as were many other party leaders. As reports began to circulate that Hitler would annex Austria, leaders in Britain, France, and Italy issued a joint statement calling for Austrian independence.

Austria was ripe for exploitation, and it came first from within. Chancellor Engelbert Dollfuss suspended parliamentary government in March 1933 and put in place a revised constitution largely based on Mussolini's ideas of a corporate state. In April 1934, perhaps inspired by Hitler's actions the year before, Dollfuss seized full dictatorial powers. He had the authority to send anyone suspected of working for an outlawed political party to a concentration camp without a trial.[90] He used spies and informers to keep tabs on the people. The diminutive chancellor at one point even ordered an end to jokes about his size.

On July 25, 1934, less than a month after the Night of the Long Knives (and shortly after the Holy See and Austria had signed a concordat), Austrian Nazis took the government by surprise, murdered Dollfuss, and held the Austrian cabinet hostage.[91] The rebels were soon arrested, however, and the attempted takeover collapsed when Mussolini (a long-time protector of Austria) dispatched troops to the Austrian border. Nevertheless, the Nazis obtained what they sought — increased political power.

In February 1935, Hitler met with Dollfuss' successor, Kurt Schuschnigg, who was bullied into signing a written agreement.[92] A few days later, several Nazis were put in high positions within the Austrian government. Within a week, Hitler demanded self-determination for Germans in Austria and Czechoslovakia. On February 22, the Austrian Nazi Party chief and seventy-two aides were arrested and charged with conspiracy to overthrow the Austrian government. This set the stage for serious conflicts to come a few years down the line.

Hitler's aggression in Austria did not go unnoticed. Secretary of State Pacelli had predicted that Austria would be the Nazis' first victim.[93] Following Dollfuss' assassination, the Vatican newspaper ran a series of page-one articles in which National Socialism was equated with national terrorism and said to have come from a gang and not a party.[94]

———

In February 1936, Hitler presided at the inaugural of the Volkswagen factory at Fallersleben, Saxony.[95] Modeled on Henry Ford's concept of cars for common people, Hitler hoped to emulate Ford's success with this new "people's car." (He had already laid out plans for a nine-hundred-mile-long, nationwide highway system.) In addition to providing employment and a consumer product that was popular with the masses, the automotive industry gave Hitler large factories that could be used to build military vehicles. It was almost impossible to determine whether an automotive plant was tooled to produce engines for Volkswagens or to produce airplane engines. When the order came for these factories to begin building planes, they were already equipped to do so; British factories required much more time for retooling.[96]

In early 1936, Nazi Minister of Propaganda Joseph Goebbels declared: "The German people are a truly poor nation. We have no colonies and no raw materials."[97] He warned that Germany would soon need new territories. In March 1936, one year after Hitler re-established obligatory military service in violation of the Treaty of Versailles, the German army entered the Rhineland. His generals argued that the move would be suicidal, but Hitler disagreed. He claimed that the move was necessary due to the recently completed mutual assistance pact between France and the Soviet Union and similar discussions between France and Great Britain. World leaders condemned the move, but Hitler told adoring crowds that Germany needed only to please God and itself.[98]

In retrospect, this might have been a prime opportunity to stop Hitler's expansionist plans. Pacelli told the French ambassador that France should have opposed this violation of international agreements.[99] France's prime minister and foreign minister both urged the commander of the French army, General Maurice Gamelin, to eject the Germans.[100] Gamelin, however, overestimated German manpower and was unwilling to take on such a force. British Prime Minister Anthony Eden later said that this was the act of appeasement which he most regretted.

———

From the time he wrote *Mein Kampf,* Hitler regarded organized religion as important to his politics. He needed influence in the churches because he thought it impossible to replace churches with party ideology.[101] He did, however, feel that Christian churches could learn to adapt to the political goals of National Socialism. In his March 23, 1933, speech to the Reichstag, Hitler paid tribute to the Christian faiths as "essential elements for safeguarding the soul of the German people," promising to respect the churches' rights, and declaring that his government's "ambition is a peaceful accord between Church and State."[102]

One of Hitler's favorite stories about religion came to him from a delegation of visiting Arabs.[103] They told him that when the Muslims attempted to penetrate beyond France into Central Europe during the eighth century, they were driven back at the Battle of Tours.[104] Had the Arabs won this battle, they said, Germany would be Islamic today. Moreover, much of the world probably would also have been converted, for their religion believed in spreading the faith by the sword and subjugating all nations.[105]

This prospect intrigued Hitler. Such an approach to religion was, he thought, perfectly suited to the Germanic temperament. Hitler felt that the conquering Arabs, because of their racial inferiority, would have been unable to contend with the harsher climate and conditions of Germany. They could not have kept down the more vigorous Aryans, so Islamized Germans would ultimately have led a Muslim German Empire. Hitler concluded his historical speculation by stating:

> You see, it's been our misfortune to have the wrong religion. Why didn't we have the religion of the Japanese, who regard sacrifice for the Fatherland as the highest good? The Muhammadan religion too would have been much more compatible to us than Christianity. Why did it have to be Christianity with its meekness and flabbiness?[106]

Clearly, the theory of the religion did not much matter, only the possibility of exploiting it. If Christianity was not to his liking, he would change it.

Hitler was born to a Catholic family, but since Protestants comprised two-thirds of the citizens of Germany, he had to keep them loyal. In 1934, he told a group of Protestant church leaders that inwardly he felt closest to the Evangelical Church.[107] Despite his professed admiration for all Aryans, Hitler had little respect for the masses. "You can do anything you want to them," he once said about devout Protestants. "They will submit... they are insignificant little people, submissive as dogs, and they sweat with embarrassment when you talk to them."[108] He was also able to tap into certain anti-Semitic teachings of Martin Luther.

Like Hitler, Luther was a ferocious believer in absolute obedience to political authority. (In *Mein Kampf*, Hitler called Luther one of the great heroes of the German people.)[109] Luther wanted to convert Jews to Christianity, but when he failed to accomplish that, he developed strong anti-Semitic feelings. He called the Jews "venomous," "bitter worms," and "disgusting vermin." He wrote a book entitled *On the Jews and Their Lies*, which was a favorite of the Nazis.[110] In it, he expressed his desire to rid Germany of its Jews and to take their wealth. He also had this advice:

> First, to set fire to their synagogues or schools and to bury and cover with dirt whatever will not burn, so that no man will ever again see stone or cinder of them. This is to be done in honor or our Lord and Christendom.... Second, I advise that their houses also be razed and destroyed.... Third, I advise that all their prayer books and Talmudic writings, in which such idolatry, lies, cursing, and blasphemy are taught, be taken from them. Fourth, I advise that their rabbis be forbidden to teach henceforth on pain of loss of life and limb. Fifth, I advise that safe-conduct on the highways be abolished completely for the Jew.... Sixth, I advise that usury be prohibited to them, and that all cash and treasure of silver and gold be taken from them and put aside for safekeeping.[111]

Luther wrote that the Jews have been for fourteen hundred years and still remain "our plague, our pestilence, and our misfortune."[112] The Nazis circulated statements like this, as Italian Fascists cited anti-Semitic statements from the Jesuit periodical *Civiltà Cattolica*,[113] to argue that their political philosophy was not incompatible with Christianity. However, that would not have mattered to Hitler anyway. He once said: "The heaviest blow to humanity was the coming of Christianity. Bolshevism is Christianity's illegitimate child. Both are inventions of the Jews."[114]

The Nazis hoped eventually to replace organized religion with their own brand of "Nazi Christianity."[115] The most extreme version of this was set forth in a 1930 book by Alfred Rosenberg called *The Myth of the Twentieth Century*.[116] The book, published by Hocheneichen-Verlag Press (owned by Hitler),[117] was a cross between the Bible and *Mein Kampf*. It was very anti-Semitic, strongly anti-papal, and anti-Christian in spirit. Rosenberg argued that Germany was surrounded by enemies and had been infiltrated by Jews seeking to destroy the Aryan race and by Christians who were draining Germany's national pride. According to Rosenberg, Germany's honor was constantly at odds with the forces of internationalism, including the Christian churches, especially the Catholic Church, which had been "judaized and asianized."[118] Rosenberg mocked the Pope as "an infallible God; a medicine man; papacy is servitude," and he argued that "the Christian-Jewish plague must perish."[119] As was written in 1939: "Of the *Myth of the Twentieth Century* it is impossible to write with real respect. It is a monument of pseudo-scholarship full of absurdities, misstatements, and bizarre theories."[120]

Even though the Pope put it on the index of prohibited books in February 1934,[121] and the Church published a devastating answer to it in October of that year,[122] *The Myth of the Twentieth Century* sold hundreds of thousands of copies. It was widely regarded as the standard text for party ideology.[123] During the war, Rosenberg drew up a thirty-point program for the National Reich Church. The following selected points were certainly sufficient to put any other churches on notice as to where the Nazis stood:

1. The National Reich Church of Germany categorically claims the exclusive right and the exclusive power to control all churches within the borders of the Reich: it declares these to be national churches of the German Reich.
5. The National Church is determined to exterminate irrevocably... the strange and foreign Christian faiths imported into Germany in the ill-omened year 800.
7. The National Church has no scribes, pastors, chaplains or priests, but National Reich orators are to speak in them.
13. The National Church demands immediate cessation of the publishing and dissemination of the Bible in Germany.
14. The National Church declares that to it, and therefore to the German nation, it has been decided that the Führer's *Mein Kampf* is the greatest of all documents. It not only contains the greatest but it embodies the purest and truest ethics for the present and future life of our nation.
18. The National Church will clear away from its altars all crucifixes, Bibles, and pictures of saints.
19. On the altar there must be nothing but *Mein Kampf* (to the German nation and therefore to God the most sacred book) and to the left of the altar a sword.
30. On the day of its foundation, the Christian Cross must be removed from all churches, cathedrals and chapels... and it must be superseded by the only unconquerable symbol, the swastika.[124]

Hitler, while approving of the impact that *Myth of the Twentieth Century* had, privately called it "stuff nobody can understand."[125]

When Hitler came to power, there were at least twenty-nine major Protestant denominations.[126] Hitler, however, wanted to have one single organization, probably because it would be easier to influence.[127] As such, it was soon decreed that the diverse churches be united into a single "German Evangelical Church."[128] Leaders of this church called for a synthesis of *Volkstum* (German national identity) and Christianity. A constitution for the new church was formally recognized by the Reichstag on July 14, 1933. One of the first issues for the new religion was election of the first "Reich Bishop."

The constitution for the new church provided that it would be led by a Lutheran bishop and that there would be a "spiritual cabinet" made of leaders from other denominations who would advise the bishop.[129] Representatives of the twenty-nine Protestant denominations originally selected Friedrich von Bodelschwingh, a clergyman widely known for his social welfare work. Bodelschwingh had no real political ties, and the Protestant leaders hoped that he would be satisfactory to Hitler. Unfortunately, Ludwig Mueller, an army chaplain and adviser to Hitler, also wanted the post.

Mueller was a member of the German Christians. This "church" had been founded in 1932, with encouragement from the Nazis. (They called themselves the "storm troops of Jesus Christ.")[130] Their first act was to issue a statement of guiding principles mirroring the Nazi position on German nationalism and race. Among the declarations were: "We see in race, folk, and nation orders of existence granted and entrusted to us by God.... Faith in Christ does not destroy one's race but deepens and sanctifies it.... We also demand that the nation be protected against the unfit and inferior." The statement's ninth principle provided:

> As long as the Jews possess the right of citizenship and there is thereby the danger of racial camouflage and bastardization, we repudiate a mission to the Jews in Germany. Holy Scripture is also able to speak about a holy wrath and a refusal of love. In particular, marriage between Germans and Jews is to be forbidden.

Most of the clergy in this new religion appeared in jackboots and Nazi Party brown shirts. In 1933, the "German Christians" could claim three thousand out of a total of seventeen thousand Protestant pastors in Germany, and the percentage of churchgoers was probably even greater.[131] ("Hardly any" Catholic priests, on the other hand, "endeavored to serve Hitler by openly preaching Nazi policies or ideological goals."[132] When, in 1943, a Catholic priest proposed creation of a German Catholicism, he was excommunicated by the Vatican.)[133]

With support from his church, Mueller was able to force a referendum on the new structure of the German Evangelical Church.[134] On the eve of the election of delegates who would ratify the constitution of the new church and select the bishop, Hitler took to the radio to urge the election of German Christians who supported Mueller. It worked; the German Christians ended up dominating the new church, and Mueller was made Reich Bishop.[135]

Hitler spoke approvingly of this "positive Christianity," which would, he said, contribute to the German struggle. He earned some goodwill by reaching out to Christians and appearing to be conciliatory. Church leaders liked his many references to world freedom. As others have concluded, "apparently he hoped that the people would feel good about him in the beginning, even if they didn't feel so good about him later on."[136]

The German Christians staged a massive rally in Berlin. The Berlin district leader of the German Christians proposed the abandonment of the Old Testament, "with its tales of cattle merchants and pimps," and the revision of the New Testament with the teaching of Jesus "corresponding entirely with the demands of National Socialism."[137] Resolutions were drawn up demanding "One People, One Reich, One Faith," requiring all pastors to take an oath of fidelity to Hitler, and insisting that all churches exclude converted Jews.[138]

This dramatic redefinition of Christianity was far too much for many Protestant leaders and led to the formation of the "Pastors' Emergency League." Headed by the Reverend Martin Niemöller, the group was able to limit some of the German Christians' revisions.[139] In particular, the Pastors' Emergency League was able to eliminate the "Aryan Paragraph" (which would have segregated all Christians with any Jewish blood) from the constitution of the new Protestant church. Still, the whole issue of making Hitler's dogma part of the foundation of a religion caused a major division in the German Protestant community.

Niemöller's 1933 autobiography, *From U-Boat to Pulpit*, told the story of how he had gone from U-boat commander in World War I to become a prominent Protestant pastor. Niemöller, like many religious leaders, openly supported the Nazis as they gained power in Germany. He also welcomed Hitler to the chancellorship in 1933. In fact, he sent Hitler a telegram congratulating him on Germany's withdrawal from the League of Nations and thanking him for his "manly act and clear statement in defense of Germany's honor." [140] The telegram ended with an expression of "loyal and prayerful support." At the close of Niemöller's book, he added a note of satisfaction that the Nazi revolution had finally triumphed and that it had brought about the "national revival" for which he had so long fought.[141] The book received high praise in the Nazi press and became a best-seller. Niemöller even took part in Berlin's "Brown Synod" of September 1933. It was called this because of the numerous Protestant pastors and church leaders who took part while in Nazi uniform. In fact, Niemöller took the minutes of the meeting.[142]

Niemöller eventually came to resent what Hitler was doing to Christianity, and he became the leader of the "Confessional Church," which sprang up in opposition to the German Christians. The Confessional (or Confessing) Church opposed the Nazification of the Protestant churches, rejected Nazi racial theories, and denounced the anti-Christian doctrines of the Nazi leaders.[143] In 1934, the Confessional Church declared itself to be the legitimate Protestant church of Germany and set up a provisional church government.[144] Thus, there were then two groups — one associated with Bishop Mueller and the other associated with Niemöller — claiming to constitute the Protestant church in Germany. Shortly after its founding, the Confessional Church included about a third of all Protestant clergymen in Germany. The Nazi government, of course, suppressed the Confessional Church (250 members were arrested following one service),[145] and its numbers dropped dramatically. By the end of 1935, the Gestapo had arrested seven hundred Confessional Church pastors.[146] In 1937, all five members of the Confessional Church's executive committee were arrested. While some members of this church spoke against Hitler, they had no lasting impact.

Confessional Church realists recognized that "any open profession of political opposition to the Nazi state would be imprudent, if not suicidal."[147] Nevertheless, many in the clergy thought that a simple confession of faith, which questioned certain Nazi theories, but did not challenge Nazi authority, might be acceptable. Thus, in April 1934, the Confessional Church clergy issued the "Barmen Confession," which served as a declaration of the basic beliefs of the Confessional Church.[148]

The Barmen Confession did not criticize Nazism as a political movement. Germany had as yet not seen the worst of Hitler, and loyalty to the state was deeply ingrained in the German psyche. "At this point the fervent hope was that both God and Caesar could be served without choosing between one or the other. Eventually that hope was shattered."[149]

Perhaps the most important statement in the Barmen Confession was: "We reject the false doctrine that the state, going beyond its special mandate, should and could become the sole and entire order of human life and thereby also fulfill the vocation of the church."[150] The Barmen Confession also challenged as heretical the suggestion that God is revealed not only in Scripture but also in the German people.

Christians who were sympathetic to the Nazis denounced the Barmen Confession, as in the following German Christian response:

> We as believing Christians thank God our Father that he has given to our people in its time of need the *Führer* as a "pious and faithful sovereign," and that he wants to prepare for us in the National Socialist system of government "good rule," a government with "discipline and honor." Accordingly, we know that we are responsible before God to assist the work of the *Führer* in our calling and in our station in life.[151]

This mixture of religious and political faith in Hitler would secure his power within Germany for many years to come.

Two years after the Barmen Confession, in May 1936, ten prominent members of the Confessional Church, including Niemöller, drafted a letter to Hitler criticizing the deification of the *Führer* and the totalitarian structure of the Nazi state. They directed a "simple question" to the leader of the nation, namely: "whether the attempt to de-Christianize the German people, either with the continuing participation of responsible statesmen or merely with their looking on and doing nothing, is to become the official course of the government."[152]

The letter went on to state: "If blood, race, nationality, and honor received here the dignity of eternal values, then the Protestant Christian is compelled by the First Commandment to reject this valuation.... If, within the framework of the National Socialist view of the world, an anti-Semitism that requires hatred of Jews is forced on a Christian, then the Christian commandment to love one's neighbor opposes that within him."[153] One of the drafters later explained that they thought Hitler simply did not know about the injustices, and that he might put them to an end if he were informed.[154]

A copy of this letter was smuggled to Switzerland, where it was leaked to the press. The Nazis then claimed that those who had composed it were disloyal and unpatriotic, and that they were collaborating with Germany's enemies.[155] Church leaders — even those who had been critical of the Nazis — rushed to dissociate themselves from the letter. "Eventually more than eight hundred pastors were arrested, and at least a few died in concentration camps."[156] The Nazis now had complete administrative control over the Evangelical churches. In the end, the letter had no effect on the Nazis' maltreatment of German Jews.

Like the others, Niemöller was arrested and put on trial for "agitory" speech, slander, and opposition to government laws. To Niemöller is credited the famous verse:

In Germany they came first for the Communists, and I didn't speak up because I wasn't a Communist.

Then they came for the Jews, and I didn't speak up because I wasn't a Jew.

Then they came for the trade unionists, and I didn't speak up because I wasn't a trade unionist.

Then they came for the Catholics, and I didn't speak up because I was a Protestant.

Then they came for me, and by that time there was no one left to speak up.[157]

Although he testified at his trial in February 1938 that he disliked Jews (having preached in 1937 about their "dark and sinister history" and the curse that was upon them for having "brought the Christ of God to the cross"), he was convicted.[158] In September 1939, he wrote to Admiral Raeder from the Sachsenhausen concentration camp asking to be released so that he might return to active duty with the armed forces of the Third Reich. "If there is a war," he later explained, "a German doesn't ask if it just or unjust, but he feels bound to join the ranks."[159]

———

The mid-1930s brought indications of war to come. Italy had unsuccessfully attempted to conquer Ethiopia in 1896. In 1935, Mussolini decided to avenge that defeat. He believed that a victory there would strengthen Italy's position in the Middle East. It would also reveal him as a true military leader.

Ethiopia, also called Abyssinia, lay in Africa adjacent to Italian Somaliland. A dispute arose, perhaps manufactured by Mussolini, regarding the border between these two areas. In October 1935, Mussolini made his move. With mechanized troops facing poorly armed Ethiopians, Mussolini's forces did not take long to finish the job. In spite of appeals for help issued by the Ethiopian emperor, Italian forces captured the capital in May 1936, and Mussolini claimed victory. Over half a million Ethiopians were killed. Mussolini was then able to unite Ethiopia with the Italian colonies of Eritrea and Italian Somaliland into one large colony which he named Italian East Africa.

During the Ethiopian war, Mussolini controlled the press and silenced the opposition. After the war, the reaction of other countries was a clear example of appeasement. Although the League of Nations briefly imposed an embargo against Italy, it was of little consequence. "Italy at last has her Empire," Mussolini announced. "It is a Fascist empire because it bears the indestructible sign of the will and power of Rome."[160] Ethiopia was formally annexed, and King Victor Emmanuel III of Italy assumed the title of emperor. Mussolini announced that Italy was now satisfied and ready for peace.

Some critics have said that Pope Pius XI supported the Italian aggression, suggesting that he favored it because it could expand the Church's influence. Actually, prior to the invasion, he "spoke out strongly on at least three occasions, condemning unprovoked aggression as a crime against the moral law."[161] He called the invasion a "crime so enormous, a manifestation of such folly, that We hold it to be absolutely impossible that nations could again take up arms against each other.... But if anyone should dare to commit this heinous crime, which God forbids, then We could not but turn to Him with bitterness in Our hearts, praying *Scatter the peoples who want war*."[162] He led prayers for peace, with direct reference to the Italian-Ethiopian conflict.[163] In September, when receiving Catholic hospital workers, the Pontiff spoke of his "unutterable grief" at this "war that is simply one of conquest."[164] Additionally, when Mussolini ordered Rome illuminated to celebrate Italian victories, Pius kept Vatican City dark, drawing criticism from the Fascist press.[165]

Writing from Rome in October 1935, *New York Times* reporter Anne O'Hare McCormick took note of Pius XI's efforts against Italy's aggression:

> Three times since the Papal Secretary of State [Pacelli] inaugurated the three-day prayer for peace in the Catholic world at Lourdes last July, the Pope had prayed for peace with direct references to the Italio-Ethiopian conflict. Late in August, while addressing an international congress of nurses, he expounded the doctrine of the church in regard to aggressive war. A month later he denounced the crime of war, particularly war of conquest, to 15,000 war veterans gathered in Rome. The third time, it is learned on good authority, he spoke to Mussolini himself.[166]

In December of that year, McCormick noted that the Pope rejected the Italian justification for the war as being necessary for population expansion and as a defense of the nation's frontier.[167] She explained the Pope's special interest in the Ethiopians:

Add to this the special interest the present Pontiff takes in the Ethiopians. The only college within the confines of Vatican City has been built for students from Ethiopia, forty of whom now study in peace and safety in the heart of enemy country, under the direct protection of the Pope. Pius XI has been on cordial terms with the [emperor of Ethiopia] ever since, as Ras Tafari [Haile Selassie,] the present Emperor of Ethiopia visited the Vatican ten years ago.[168]

Surely, neither Mussolini nor any other reasonably well-informed world leader of that era thought that Pope Pius XI supported Italy's invasion of Ethiopia.

————

Pope Pius XI spent much of the 1930s grooming Secretary of State Pacelli to one day succeed him as Pope. In 1935, Pius XI organized a huge peace pilgrimage to Lourdes, just before the outbreak of the Ethiopian war. On April 28, he had Pacelli address 250,000 pilgrims. The cardinal spoke of the National Socialists and said that they were:

in reality only miserable plagiarists who dress up old errors with new tinsel. It does not make any difference whether they flock to the banners of the social revolution, whether they are guided by a false conception of the world and of life, or whether they are possessed by the superstition of a race and blood cult.[169]

The *New York Times* called the address an "attack on both Hitlerism and communism."[170]

That same year, Pacelli's closest colleague, Undersecretary of State Alfredo Ottaviani, published a textbook on canon law. As others have noted, this book was an indication of how Pacelli thought. In the book, Ottaviani "named and shamed the Fascist and National Socialist theoreticians."[171]

Secretary of State Pacelli also made an unprecedented trip to the United States in 1936, creating quite a sensation. Air transportation was still quite rare, but the future Pope crisscrossed the nation on planes. Pacelli went to the top of the Empire State building, saw the Liberty Bell, drove to Mount Vernon, and met with President Franklin D. Roosevelt. Everywhere Pacelli went, people loved him. A flight attendant called the cardinal "the most considerate passenger I ever had."[172] When airline officials apologized for a late arrival, he said: "No apologies. I caught up on my reading."[173] An account of a reception given in his honor in New York stated: "To all, the Cardinal guest of honor gave his smiling attention, his ready wit, and his serious consideration, and America loved him for it."[174] In her memoirs, Rose Kennedy, mother of John F. Kennedy, wrote about traveling with the cardinal:

He was not a handsome man, yet his eyes shone with such intensity and compassion, in his bearing there was an unearthly sense of important purpose that I truly felt I was in the presence of a mortal who was very close to God. At Hyde Park there were cars waiting to take us the additional few miles to the President's home.... Suddenly, about halfway there, there were hundreds of children — from local and nearby parochial schools — lining the road, all rosy cheeked and excited and waving their little U.S. and papal flags. The cardinal could have waved and smiled and passed by; but instead that humane and godly man stopped our caravan, left his car and — with the red robes of his cardinal-ate moving with the shift of autumn breezes — passed among the children, smiling and patting heads, and with his right hand making the Sign of the Cross or raised in a gesture of benediction. I shall never forget the future Pope Pius XII striding in his robes among those children on a rural roadside near the Hudson River in apple-and-pine tree country in New York State. It was such a happy and spontaneous gesture.[175]

In South Bend, Indiana, students wondered how the prelate would pronounce the name of their institution. He stood on the stage, and "In a decided South Bend accent, all heard him speak the flat English Name, 'Noter Dame!' The students went wild; a new hero had appeared on their horizon, and Cardinal Pacelli was 'all right.' "[176] Pacelli avoided meeting with Roosevelt during his campaign for re-election, but they had lunch together after Roosevelt won. Afterward, Pacelli joked with reporters: "I enjoyed lunching with a typical American family."[177]

The future Pope developed a great fondness for the United States. He liked to reflect on his trip to America. "He spoke of his airplane flight across the great American Continent and of the largeness of the view, the tolerance, the free atmosphere of America. Evidently the freedom struck him most. No other atmosphere, he implied, was so conducive to the free practice and free growth of religion."[178]

At some point after his trip to the United States, Cardinal Pacelli repaid the hospitality of the Americans by hosting visitors from the United States. After an early morning Mass, he invited them to his apartment for breakfast: One later described the event:

But if his breakfast was meager, it was more than compensated for by the sparkling conversation at the table.... It was a merry, witty interlude. Shielded behind heavy glasses, his eyes played such hide and seek that often it was difficult to discover when he was joking, but no humorous slip or opportunity for a jest was allowed to pass without his pouncing on it. The young guest summed it up in these words: "He is the most impressive man I have ever met — intensely spiritual, but his mind is so keen that he misses nothing of all that is going on around him."[179]

Of course, being aware of what was going on meant that he understood the world situation. While he was still in the United States, Pacelli was asked about the situation in Germany. He immediately went from a hearty laugh to a gesture of helplessness, and said, "Everything is lost."[180]

---

In October 1936, Hitler began establishing alliances that would be important in the event of war. He sent military aid to Franco's rebels in Spain, and the

Reich was the first international power to recognize the Italian conquest of Ethiopia. In November, Hungary and Austria both recognized the Italian Empire, and Italy supported Hungary's right to rearm. That same month, Rome and Berlin both recognized the Franco rebel government in Spain, while the United States abandoned its embassy in Madrid. (Pius tried to mediate the situation in Spain, where during the thirty months of war, more than seven thousand priests and religious were slaughtered.)[181] The British government warned Hitler that it would fight to protect Belgium. The most important development of late 1936, however, was the formation of the Axis.

In November 1936, Count Galeazzo Ciano visited Hitler. Ciano was Italy's foreign minister, as well as Mussolini's son-in-law (husband to his daughter, Edda). The visit resulted in the announcement on November 25 that Germany, Italy, and Japan had signed an anti-Communist pact, pledging cooperation in defending against the spread of Communism. It was called the "Axis" because Mussolini said Europe would revolve on the axis of Germany and Italy. Mussolini urged France and Britain to join in with them.[182]

Hitler often said that he regretted having allied with the "so-called yellow race" and was sorry about the loss of life sustained by the white race in East Asia, but he respected Japan's military power.[183] Mussolini, who at first objected to inclusion of Japan, would later explain that agreement with Japan was "in perfect line with the Tripartite Pact. The Japanese are a proud, loyal people which would not remain indifferent in the face of American aggression against the Axis powers."[184] In Japan, Prince Fumimaro Konoye explained: "It is natural that Germany and Italy, who were making a new order in Europe, should make common cause with Japan. The division of the world into several spheres of co-existence and mutual prosperity would benefit all nations."[185]

Reactions to the Italian alliance with Hitler were mixed inside the Vatican. It meant that Mussolini might have more influence with Hitler, causing Germany to moderate some of its positions. Pius XI was hopeful for such a result. In fact, about a week after the pact was concluded, Mussolini sent a memorandum to Hitler urging, among other things, a détente between the Third Reich and the Holy See.[186] Ultimately, however, Hitler had more success swaying Mussolini than the other way around.

———

In March 1937, Pius XI issued three encyclicals concerning international relations. Two of them would prove to be of particular importance. In *Divini Redemptoris* (of the Divine Redeemer, although it is better known as "On Atheistic Communism"), he attacked Communism, which was beginning to spread throughout Europe and other parts of the world. He wrote:

> This Apostolic See, above all, has not refrained from raising its voice, for it knows that its proper and social mission is to defend truth, justice and all those eternal values which Communism ignores or attacks.... With reference

to Communism, Our Venerable Predecessor, Pius IX... as early as 1846 pronounced a solemn condemnation... against "that infamous doctrine of so-called Communism which is absolutely contrary to the natural law itself, and if once adopted would utterly destroy the rights, property and possessions of all men, and even society itself." Later on, another of Our predecessors, the immortal Leo XIII, in his Encyclical *Quod Apostolici Muneris*, defined Communism as "the fatal plague which insinuates itself into the very marrow of human society only to bring about its ruin."[187]

In 1931, Pope Pius XI had written: "No one can be at the same time a sincere Catholic and a true Socialist."[188] With this 1937 encyclical, Pius XI made clear that Communism was even more anti-Christian in its orientation.

The Pope wrote that Communism was historically evil, that Communist governments were out to destroy religion, were godless, were violent, denied the individual and the family, and reigned by terror. He also complained that the world press failed to report Communist atrocities. He concluded that "Communism is intrinsically wrong, and no one who would save Christian civilization may collaborate with it in any undertaking whatsoever."[189]

Pius also issued an encyclical in March 1937 dealing with Hitler's National Socialism. The Vatican under Pope Pius XI had already issued several strong condemnations of anti-Semitism. On March 25, 1928, an official decree of the Holy Office proclaimed:

> Moved by the spirit of charity, the Apostolic See has protected the people [of Israel] against unjust persecutions, and since it condemns all jealousy and strife among peoples, it accordingly condemns with all its might the hatred directed against a people which was chosen by God; that particular hatred, in fact, which today commonly goes by the name anti-Semitism.[190]

In the spring of 1933, as the Nazis were just beginning to exercise their newfound power, Pope Pius XI met with several prominent Jewish leaders. The *Jewish Chronicle of London* — the leading English-language Jewish newspaper in Europe — reported:

> The Pope received in audience a delegation [of Jewish leaders]... and had a long private talk with them about the situation of the Jews in Germany. It is understood that the Pope was extremely concerned about the sufferings imposed on the Jews, and expressed his sympathy with them and his desire to be of help. Rabbi da Fano, who is eighty-six years of age, is a personal friend of the Pope and was his teacher of Hebrew when the Pope was Director of the Catholic Ambrosian Library in Milan.[191]

The Church's opposition to anti-Semitism and racism was well recognized by the Jewish community. In September 1933, the *Jewish Chronicle of London* again reported:

The Pope, having received reports of the persistence of anti-Semitic persecution in Germany, has publicly expressed his disapproval of the movement. He stated that these persecutions are a poor testimony to the civilisation of a great people. He recalled the fact that Jesus Christ, the Madonna, the apostles, the prophets and many saints were all of the Hebrew race, and that the Bible is a Hebrew creation. The Aryan races, he declared, had no claim to superiority over the Semites.[192]

Vatican opposition to anti-Semitism and racism continued to be reflected in directives from the Holy See, speeches by Pius XI and Cardinal Pacelli, and statements on Vatican Radio and in *L'Osservatore Romano*. By 1937, however, it was clear that the long list of informal condemnations of anti-Semitism and Nazism would not suffice.

The German bishops were scheduled to make their regular five-year visit to Rome in 1938. Given the situation, however, they moved the trip up by a year. The bishops reported that the National Socialists were completely ignoring the concordat and persecuting Catholics.[193] "For the Church it is at the moment a matter of life and death; bluntly, they want its annihilation."[194] They did not, however, think that a "counter-offensive" was feasible. "Instead of this, the visitors appealed to the Vatican to intervene energetically in cases where the concordat was breached."[195]

The German bishops asked for a formal document to be published condemning National Socialism. They were, however, unanimous in their opinion that "if a doctrinal statement should be issued it should on no account provoke a repudiation of the concordat by the Nazi State."[196] Since Pacelli was the best-informed Vatican official on German matters, Pius XI asked him to work with Cardinal Faulhaber, archbishop of Munich, in drafting the document.[197] Faulhaber wrote the first draft of the encyclical by hand. He used a pastoral tone based upon the theme of suffering, and he abstained from harsh judgments.[198] Pacelli added sections and edited others, making it more confrontational.[199] Within seven weeks, it was ready for the Pope's signature.

*Mit brennender Sorge* ("With Burning Anxiety") was one of the strongest condemnations of any national regime that the Holy See ever published, and "the harshest statements against Nationalism were Pacelli's."[200] It condemned not only the persecution of the Church in Germany, but also the neo-paganism of Nazi theories. It denounced racism and was directed right at Nazi Germany. The encyclical stated in part that:

Whoever exalts race, or the people, or the State, or a particular form of State, or the depositories of power, or any other fundamental value of the human community however necessary and honorable be their function in worldly things — whoever raises these notions above their standard value and divinizes them to an idolatrous level, distorts and perverts an order of the world planned and created by God; he is far from the true faith in God and from the concept of life which that faith upholds.[201]

The document took a brazen swipe at Hitler and Nazism when it said:

> None but superficial minds could stumble into concepts of a national God, of a national religion; or attempt to lock within the frontiers of a single people, within the narrow limits of a single race, God, the Creator of the universe, King and Legislator of all nations before whose immensity they are "as a drop of a bucket" (Isaiah XL, 15).[202]

The encyclical praised leaders in the Church who stood firm and provided a good example to others. It concluded that "enemies of the Church, who think that their time has come, will see that their joy was premature."[203] When the German Catholic hierarchy later thanked Pope XI for the encyclical, he politely declined, pointing to Pacelli and saying: "Thank him; he has done everything. From now on, he will deal with everything."[204]

Unlike most encyclicals, which are written in Latin, *Mit brennender Sorge* was written in German. It was smuggled out of Italy, copied, distributed (120,000 copies were distributed in the Münster diocese alone),[205] and read from the German pulpits on Palm Sunday, March 12, 1937.[206] No one who heard the pontifical document read in church could have any illusion about the gravity of these statements or the significance of its having been written.[207] The resistance, including Count Claus von Stauffenberg, a Catholic officer who was later executed for his attempt to assassinate Hitler, read the encyclical and was encouraged.[208] A shortened version of this encyclical was translated into English and published under the title "To the German People" in a popular anthology of Catholic literature.[209]

The reading of the encyclical was like a bomb going off in Germany.[210] *Newsweek* magazine reported:

> On Palm Sunday, priests read their 21,000,000 German Catholics a papal encyclical which had been smuggled across the border. It bluntly charged that the Nazis had violated their 1933 Concordat with the Vatican, that civil officials were trying to undermine the Catholic religion; it condemned the ideology of race, blood, and soil as articles of faith.

\* \* \*

> Pius' proclamation echoed the bitterness of four years of Church-State strife. Catholicism, like Protestantism, has paid a high price for its resistance to "coordination." Arrests of 3,500 priests and religious for all the offences in the Nazi lexicon pointed in only one direction: a frantic effort to tear away the clergy's cloak of piety and nobility. More than anything else, the Reich wanted to break the Church's grip on the minds of 2,000,000 German children. Patriotism must replace Catholicism as the religion of the youth; Germany's totalitarian future depended on it.[211]

Naturally, the Nazis did not take the papal rebuke lightly. As *Newsweek* reported, *Mit brennender Sorge* soon led to a "fight to the finish."[212]

The only reason *Mit brennender Sorge* was read to anyone was because the Nazis were caught off guard. By the time Palm Sunday Mass was over, Gestapo guards were at the church doors to confiscate copies.[213] The prosecution report for the postwar Nuremberg trials said that all available copies of *Mit brennender Sorge* were confiscated, twelve printing offices were closed, people convicted of distributing the encyclical were arrested, and the Church-affiliated publications that reprinted the encyclical were banned. Later on, the mere mention of the encyclical was made a crime in Nazi Germany.[214]

The day following the release of the encyclical, the Nazi press struck back. *Völkischer Beobachter* carried a strong counterattack on the "Jew-God and His deputy in Rome."[215] *Das Schwarze Korps* called it "the most incredible of Pius XI's pastoral letters; every sentence in it was an insult to the new Germany."[216] An internal German memorandum dated March 23, 1937, called the encyclical "almost a call to do battle against the Reich government."[217] The German ambassador to the Holy See was instructed not to take part in the solemn Easter ceremonies, and German missions throughout Europe were informed by the Nazi Foreign Office of the "Reich's profound indignation."[218] Nuncio Orsenigo feared that the encyclical would unleash an open period of religious persecution.[219]

Hitler was enraged by the encyclical.[220] He verbally attacked the German bishops at a mass rally in the Berlin *Lustgarten*.[221] He warned that the German state would not tolerate any challenge to its authority. When churches "attempt by any other means —writings, encyclicals, etc. — to assume rights which belong solely to the state, we will push them back into their proper spiritual activity."[222] Hitler also dictated a letter to the Pope, complaining that the Vatican had gone to the people instead of coming to him.[223] Pacelli sharply rebuffed German protests, noting that the German government had not been cooperative in the past when the Vatican complained about various matters.[224] The Nazis threatened to cancel the concordat due to *Mit brennender Sorge*, but they decided not to do so. Instead, they waged a propaganda campaign against the Church and subjected several priests to currency or morality trials. At Koblenz, 170 Franciscans were prosecuted for corrupting the youth by turning their monastery into a "male brothel," and a Hitler Youth film was circulated that supposedly showed priests dancing in a bordello.[225] In April 1937, Berlin Nazis put one thousand monks on trial.[226] In May, Hitler was quoted in a Swiss newspaper as saying that "the Third Reich does not desire a *modus vivendi* with the Catholic Church, but rather its destruction with lies and dishonor, in order to make room for a German Church in which the German race will be glorified."[227]

The month after *Mit brennender Sorge* came out,[228] April 1937, Winston Churchill took note of Germany's increased military might and aggressive tendencies. He told the House of Commons: "We seem to be moving, drifting steadily, against our will, against the will of every race and every people and every class, towards some hideous catastrophe." Many times he warned the pacifist-minded government that Britain was not keeping up with Germany's military preparations.[229]

Critics of Pope Pius XII often suggest that had he only been more outspoken in his condemnations of Nazis and their anti-Semitism, he could have lessened the harshness of (if not prevented) the Holocaust. The lesson from *Mit brennender Sorge*, however, suggests otherwise. Not only did the Nazis retaliate against the Church, the persecution of Jews also got worse after this encyclical was released.

———

This Nazi retaliation for *Mit brennender Sorge* led to a notable statement made by Cardinal Mundelein. In front of five hundred Catholic prelates and priests assembled for the quarterly diocesan conference at Preparatory Seminary on May 18, 1937, Cardinal Mundelin excoriated the Nazi government. He said:

> Perhaps you will ask how it is that a nation of 60,000,000 people, intelligent people, will submit in fear and servitude to an alien, an Austrian paperhanger, and a poor one at that, I am told, and a few associates like Goebbels and Goering, who dictate every move of the people's lives, and who can, in this age of rising prices and necessary high cost of living, say to an entire nation: "Wages cannot be raised." Perhaps because it is a country where every second person is a government spy, where armed forces come and seize private books and papers without court procedures, where the father can no longer discipline his son for fear that the latter will inform on him and land him in prison.[230]

Mundelein also denounced the Third Reich for its ongoing "monk trials," designed to portray Catholic priests and brothers as homosexual pederasts to justify the closing of all Catholic schools and forcing Catholic schoolchildren into "non-confessional" schools. As the press reported at the time, Mundelein's statement "provoked the Hitlerites to fury."[231]

The *New York Times* reported that before a crowd of twenty thousand National Socialists, Joseph Goebbels, the minister of propaganda, responded to Cardinal Mundelein, "in the most scathing public attack on the Christian confessions delivered to date by any member of the government":

> Most of the attack was directed against the Catholic Church.... He trembled with rage as he spoke of reports of religious persecution in Germany appearing in the foreign press, while the crowd drowned his voice in shouts of "Traitors!" ... Goebbels spoke for two hours, ranting that clerical immorality was causing "hair-raising moral chaos" in the country. "And I can declare," he continued, "in the fullest measure to the German people now listening to me that this sex plague must and will be ruthlessly extirpated. And if the Church has proved itself to be too weak for this task, then the state will carry it out!"[232]

The Nazis wanted the Vatican's secretary of state to arrange for an apology from Mundelein, but "Cardinal Pacelli refused to accept the Reich's demand for an apology."[233] The Vatican's reply was that the statement was made on the cardinal's own initiative, but this "does not mean that the Vatican disapproves...

because what the Holy See thinks of the German religious situation has been so clearly expressed [in *Mit brennender Sorge*]."[234] Addressing the German ambassador to the Vatican, Diego von Bergen, Pacelli used some of the insight that he picked up on his visit to the United States in 1936: "We are neither willing, nor are we able to restrict the freedom of speech of an American citizen who wishes to expose the falsities of a foreign government. Freedom of speech is an American birthright."[235] Pacelli's advice to Pius XI was that "the Holy See must not . . . deplore Mundelein's speech. This would be an act to make National Socialism still more arrogant, especially Hitler who thinks in his self-delusion that the entire world should knuckle under to him."[236]

*Newsweek* magazine interpreted the Vatican's response as follows: "Cardinal Mundelein spoke for himself, but his opinion of Nazism is higher than ours."[237] It went on to explain that over the years Pius XI's "disapproval" of the Nazis had grown to "outright enmity."[238] The Germans temporarily broke off normal relations with the Holy See.[239]

On March 3, A. W. Klieforth, the American consul general to Cologne, Germany, reported to Washington on the new Pope's political leanings. Klieforth had met Pacelli two years earlier. He said that the new Pontiff's "views, while they are well known, surprised me by their extremeness."

> [H]e opposed unalterably every compromise with National Socialism. He regarded Hitler not only as an untrustworthy scoundrel but as a fundamentally wicked person. He did not believe that Hitler was capable of moderation, and in spite of appearances would end up in the camp of the left-wing Nazi extremists where he began his career.[240]

Pacelli also supported the German bishops' opposition to National Socialism even at the cost of losing the support of young German Catholics.

———

France's Popular Front government, supported by the Communist Party, extended an invitation to the Pontiff to visit France in 1937. The Pope's health prevented him from making the voyage, so he asked Pacelli to go in his place. Pacelli had already made a strong impression in France during an earlier visit to Lourdes, when he had protested against the "superstitions of race and blood," which underlie Nazi theology.[241] This time, in a speech at Notre Dame Cathedral in Paris, he spoke of "that noble and powerful nation whom bad shepherds would lead astray into an idolatry of race."[242] He struck out against the "iniquitous violence" and the "vile criminal actions" being perpetrated by German leaders, and he denounced the "pagan cult of race."[243] The Nazis knew what he meant. The Reich and Prussian minister for ecclesiastical affairs wrote to the German Foreign Ministry that Pacelli's "unmistakable allusion to Germany . . . was very well understood in the French Popular Front and the anti-German world."[244] Other German leaders also complained about the political nature of

Pacelli's statement.[245] Pacelli's appearance was lauded in the French press, and French leaders sought to normalize relations between the Holy See and the French government.[246] His words, however, did not have any positive impact on world events. In August, the Soviets put thirty churchmen on trial for a Fascist plot, and teachers in Berlin were instructed on the need to teach anti-Semitism. In September 1937, a huge Nazi rally in Nuremberg attracted international attention as Hitler was awarded a prize by the National Socialist Congress for his scientific services to the German people. The event was the largest display of Nazi power in history, with over six hundred thousand soldiers on parade. The clear anti-Semitic message did not stop a large international diplomatic corps from attending, including Mussolini and an American representative.[247]

———

At the Vatican in late 1937, Pacelli took another step toward his destination. At a consistory on December 16, Pius XI elevated five new cardinals. Pacelli was present, and Pius made an oblique reference and gestured toward Pacelli. While it was unclear to most of those at the consistory, he later explained that he knew his time was running short and that it was his desire that Pacelli succeed him.[248]

# SEVEN

# The Violence Spreads

In early 1938, Hitler's armies had not yet crossed a frontier. The Rhineland province had been remilitarized, and the Saar had been reincorporated into Germany (by an overwhelming vote of the residents), but not a single foreign soldier had been injured by these moves. Hitler himself was calling for peace.[1] (Later that year, writer Gertrude Stein promoted Hitler for the Nobel Peace Prize.)[2] About two hundred Jewish people had been murdered by the Nazis, most in the first fourteen months of Hitler's rule.[3] Jews, however, were permitted to leave Germany, and they did so by the tens of thousands. The number of Jews (and others) in concentration camps was decreasing, but things were soon to become dramatically worse.[4]

Mussolini had protected Austria in the past, particularly when Hitler threatened it in 1934. When Hitler again threatened Austria in early 1938, Pius sent the Italian nuncio to ask Mussolini to promise to once again support Austria. Mussolini, however, refused to make any commitments.[5] The Vatican openly scolded Mussolini for this reluctance.[6] Hitler needed no further encouragement.

In March 1938, Hitler moved troops to the Austrian border. Austria was Hitler's native land, and he was quite popular there. Austrian leader Kurt Schuschnigg called for a referendum on the Nazi issue, but that vote never took place (Hitler would win a 99 percent approval in his referendum the next month).[7] On March 12, German troops moved in. On the fourteenth, Hitler returned to Vienna and proclaimed a union (*Anschluss*). Austria, with its population of 7,008,000 was incorporated into Germany, and its name was officially changed to Ostmark. Schuschnigg and his supporters were arrested. On March 26, Hermann Göring warned all Jews to leave Austria. Thirty-four thousand arrests were reported by April 2.

Austria was at this time between 85 and 100 percent Catholic. It had entered into a well-received concordat with the Vatican in 1933, and the Holy See was strongly opposed to its annexation into Germany. At the direction of Secretary of State Pacelli, *L'Osservatore Romano* published a series of front-page articles in defense of Austrian independence.[8] When the *Anschluss* took place, an undersecretary at the Vatican complained to the British minister that it was "a disaster caused by German vainglory, Italian folly, and Anglo-French weakness."[9]

The Germans introduced their anti-religious laws into Austria and did what they could to suppress the churches. For example, in Innsbruck and the villages of North and South Tyrol, from the time that Austria was annexed until April

1940, 5 churches and 24 chapels were closed, 3 priests were sent to concentration camps, 55 were arrested, 48 were forbidden to visit the schools, 100 were refused permission to teach religion to children, and 93 were deprived of their state subsidy. Moreover, 52 Catholic schools were closed, as well as 170 other education institutions of various kinds. Seven convents and other Church properties were seized and adapted to non-Catholic uses, and a large number of Catholic associations were disbanded and their buildings seized by the Gestapo. This was typical of the situation throughout the nation.[10]

Austrian Jews were, of course, subjected to even greater persecution from the Nazis. In the first few days following the *Anschluss*, all Jewish businesses were branded with large red inscriptions that identified them as being owned by Jews. Aryans who were caught patronizing such shops were forced to wear a sign around their necks proclaiming "I, Aryan swine, have bought in a Jewish shop." Jews were deprived of their civil rights, including the right to own property, the right to be employed or to hire others, the right to work in any profession, and the right to enter restaurants, cafés, or public parks.[11] Within a month, more than five hundred Jewish people committed suicide in Austria.

Pius XI was particularly troubled by the annexation of Austria because, with the exception of socialist Vienna, Austria had been on especially good terms with the Church. For many years, the nation's leader was a priest, Monsignor Ignaz Seipel. After Seipel's death, Chancellor Engelbert Dolfuss put in place a new constitution based on Pius XI's 1931 encyclical, *Quadragesimo Anno* (on reconstruction of the social order). He also enshrined the terms of the 1933 concordat into law. After Germany occupied Austria, Hitler refused to respond to Vatican questions concerning the continued validity of the concordat.

In November 1937, shortly after the release of *Mit brennender Sorge*, the Austrian bishops made a public declaration of sympathy for the German cardinals and bishops. They also made it clear that they rejected Nazism.[12] The *Anschluss*, however, changed everything.

Shortly after Austria was annexed, the archbishop of Vienna, Cardinal Theodor Innitzer, met with Hitler, and he made a declaration of loyalty coupled with a request for protection of the Church.[13] The bishops issued a welcoming statement that said: "We acknowledge with joy that the National Socialist movement has done and is doing great things in the area of national and economic construction, and also in social policy for the German Reich and people, and specifically for the poorest strata of the people."[14] These statements were duplicated and widely published.[15] A report on the matter, translated into English, was sent to Ambassador Joseph P. Kennedy, to be forwarded on to the White House. In the report, Cardinal Pacelli strongly disassociated the position of the Austrian bishops from that of the Vatican.[16]

The attitude of the Austrian bishops was in accord with much of the feeling throughout Austria, where the German troops had been greeted as heroes rather than conquerors. Father Falkan, a Catholic parish priest, said, "I must admit that

I was glad to see the Nazis come to power, because at that time I felt that Hitler as a Catholic was a God-fearing individual who could battle communism for the Church."[17]

Catholic leadership in Rome was not deceived. Vatican Radio immediately broadcast a vehement denunciation of the *Anschluss* and the reaction of the Austrian Catholic Church.[18] Pius XI ordered Archbishop Innitzer to report to Rome.[19] (Nazi officials tried hard to keep him in Vienna.)[20] Before meeting with the Pope, Innitzer met with Pacelli, who had been outraged by the Austrian cardinal's words and actions. This has been called one of the "most tempestuous" meetings of Pius XI's pontificate.[21] Pacelli made it clear that Innitzer had to retract his statements.

According to the British minister to the Holy See, Sir D'Arcy Osborne, Innitzer "was severely hauled over the coals by the Vatican" and "told to go back and eat his words."[22] A German official in Rome, who saw Innitzer shortly after his meetings, reported: "I have the impression that the Cardinal, who seemed very exhausted from the conversations in the Vatican, had had a hard struggle there."[23] The same official reported later the same day that the retraction of the earlier statements "was wrested from Cardinal Innitzer with pressure that can only be termed extortion."[24]

Innitzer was made to sign a new statement issued on behalf of all of the Austrian bishops, which provided: "The solemn declaration of the Austrian bishops on 18 March of this year was clearly not intended to be an approval of something that was not and is not compatible with God's law."[25] The Vatican newspaper reported that the bishops' earlier statement had been issued without approval from Rome.[26] Before long, Innitzer was recognized as a true enemy of the Nazis.[27]

On Friday, October 7, 1938, a group of young Nazis pounded on Innitzer's door and shouted that he should be taken to a concentration camp. The police intervened, and the rioters left. The next night, another hostile demonstration began against the archbishop's residence. Soon rocks were thrown, and every window in the building was broken. The police were called, but before they could arrive, the rioters kicked in the heavy door and entered the palace, smashing everything they found. The invaders beat the archbishop's secretary into unconsciousness, entered the chapel, and smashed a statue. They then broke into the cardinal's study, where they forced open his desk and destroyed a crucifix. The cardinal's purple robes, pectoral cross, and ring were removed and used for a bonfire. All the furniture was broken, the paintings were torn down, and art objects were ruined. Vienna's newspapers contained not a word about it.[28]

After receiving word of the attack on Cardinal Innitzer, Pius XI could no longer contain himself. On October 21, in one of his last public appearances, Pius personally attacked Hitler, likening him to Julian the Apostate (Roman Emperor Flavius Claudius Julianus), who attempted to "saddle the Christians with responsibility for the persecution he had unleashed against them."[29]

In April 1938, Cardinal Pacelli gave to Joseph P. Kennedy, then U.S. ambassador to Britain, a report to be forwarded on to President Roosevelt. In it, Pacelli made clear that the Nazi program struck at the "fundamental principle of the freedom of the practice of religion," and he warned about the emergence of a new Nazi *Kulturkampf* against the Catholic Church. He told Kennedy that any political compromise with the Nazi regime was "out of the question."[30]

This same month, Pius XI ordered that in all Catholic universities, the sciences — from biology to philosophy, including the juridical sciences — refute Nazi racist theories. The letter from the Sacred Congregation of Seminaries and Universities (now the Congregation for Catholic Education), whose prefect at the time was the Pope himself, was sent on April 13, 1938, to the rectors and presidents of all Catholic universities worldwide. It was signed by Monsignor Ernesto Ruffini, secretary of the congregation (and a future cardinal). It began by recalling the Pope's address on Christmas Eve 1937, in which he denounced the persecution that the Church was suffering in Germany. It went on to say that "the Holy Father's principal affliction" was that pernicious doctrines were being promoted, falsely called scientific, "for the purpose of perverting spirits and uprooting authentic religion."[31]

In announcing the appointment of several Jewish scholars to positions of importance in the Vatican, Pius XI said: "All human beings are admitted equally, without distinction of race, to participate, to share, to study and to explore truth and science."[32] As a commentator noted, "This was the spirit that guided Pius XI in gathering to the bosom of the Vatican the great Jewish scholars cast out by fascist Italy."[33] That spirit would make itself known to the world several more times before the Pontiff passed away the following year.[34]

In May 1938, Hitler visited Mussolini in Rome and tension between the Vatican and the Nazis reached a new level. Mussolini hoped to ease tensions between Germany and the Holy See (so as to make planning for the visit easier), so he had a report published saying that the Pope would receive Hitler.[35] Secretary of State Pacelli immediately had a denial published in the Vatican newspaper, in which he made clear that the Pope intended nothing of the kind.[36] Pius XI, along with Pacelli, left the city for the Pope's summer home three days before Hitler arrived. This was two months before the Pontiff usually left Rome. ("The air here makes me feel sick," he said to those seeing him off.)[37]

Mussolini ordered Rome to be well decorated for the *Führer's* visit. ("Rome certainly does Brown up well," wrote an American seminarian in Rome.) The Vatican protested against the original plan to decorate the churches.[38] Pius XI ordered that all Vatican museums be closed and that no members of the German delegation be admitted into Vatican City. He also left orders for the clergy not to take part in the many festivities that the Romans had planned to celebrate Hitler's visit.[39] Roman officials unsuccessfully tried to avoid the sparsely populated and dimly illuminated Vatican City on the parade route.[40]

The Vatican's newspaper, *L'Osservatore Romano*, "studiously ignored" Hitler's visit.[41] From his summer retreat, Castel Gandolfo, Pius held a public audience at which he listed among his sorrows that on the feast of the Holy Cross, people in Rome were hosting "the symbol of another cross which is not that of Christ."[42]

May 1938 was also the month that Mosche Waldmann, a delegate from the pre-state Jewish community in Palestine, visited Rome. Waldmann met with Roman Chief Rabbi David Prato, who was on "constant conversational terms" with Pacelli.[43] Prato believed that the "opposition of the Vatican to the neo-paganism of National Socialism [was] fundamental."[44] Waldmann concluded that the Holy See was not yet prepared to endorse the establishment of a Jewish state in Palestine, but he also noted that the Vatican no longer assisted only those Jews who had converted to Catholicism, but also Jews themselves.[45]

On May 21, 1938, Pacelli sent a letter to Cardinal Tisserant, secretary of the Sacred Congregation for the Eastern Church, regarding a contemplated Polish law that would have made Kosher slaughtering illegal. Pacelli explained to Tisserant that he had undertaken steps in opposition to the law because it would "represent for the Jews a true persecution."[46]

A few days later, Pacelli left for Budapest, to speak at the International Eucharistic Congress. While there, in the wake of the *Anschluss*, Pacelli made a moving address in which he explained:

> Face to face with us is drawn up the lugubrious array of the military godless shaking the clenched fist of the Anti-Christ against everything we hold most sacred. Face to face with us spreads the army of those who would like to make all peoples of the earth and every individual human believe that they can find prosperity only by receding from the Gospel of Christ.[47]

The Germans refused to send a delegation to the International Eucharistic Congress when they learned that Pacelli would be there. He had, after all, berated them the year before when he went to France for the Pope. In fact, the Germans permitted no news of the Congress to be transmitted in Germany, even though Pacelli gave one of his two addresses in German (as Pius XI had released his anti-Nazi encyclical, *Mit brennender Sorge*, in German for wider distribution in that nation.)[48] Certainly, had the Nazis been able to link the Pope to their anti-Semitic views, they would not have missed the chance.

---

Italy did not adopt racial laws until July 1938, sixteen years after Fascism came to power. Until then, Italian Jews were as likely to belong to the Fascist Party as were any other Italians.[49]

Mussolini put off the imposition of racial laws for as long as possible, perhaps due to the Lateran Treaty and his desire to maintain good relations with the Vatican. Italian Jews were protected by a constitutional provision that was widely praised as a model of Fascist tolerance and enlightenment.[50] The Union of Jewish Communities even struck a special gold medal and presented it to Mussolini.[51] In fact, the "close bond" between Fascist Italy and Jews influenced most Italian Jews to stay in Italy, rather than emigrate to Israel/Palestine or the United States, as many German and Eastern European Jews did.[52]

Mussolini issued his "Aryan Manifesto" July 14, 1938. This pseudo-scientific document had been commissioned by Mussolini, but it was signed by a group of "racial experts." It announced the discovery of an Italian race and set forth the following racial precepts:

1. Human races exist.
2. There are great and small races.
3. The concept of race is purely biological.
4. The population of modern Italy is of Aryan origin and its civilization is Aryan.
5. It is a myth that other peoples have mingled with the Italian population during the modern era.
6. There now exists an Italian race.
7. The time has come for Italians frankly to proclaim themselves racists.
8. It is necessary to distinguish between European Mediterranean people and Africans and Orientals.
9. Jews do not belong to the Italian race.
10. The European physical and psychological traits of Italians must not be altered in any way.[53]

The day after Mussolini announced the new policy, Pius XI used uncompromising terms of condemnation, calling it "a true form of apostasy. It is no longer merely one or another erroneous idea; it is the entire spirit of the doctrine that is contrary to the Faith of Christ."[54] In addition, the Pope said that "it is forgotten today that mankind is only one large all-inclusive general race."[55] Secretary of State Pacelli met with the Pope and then recorded in a handwritten note his disgust with the racial laws, noting that he was disturbed that the Italian government was importing German anti-Semitism into Italy.[56]

From July 6 to July 15, delegates from thirty-two nations and observers from twenty-four organizations met in Évian-les-Bains, France, to discuss the issue of Jewish refugees. This meeting, known as the Évian Conference, was convened at the initiative of President Roosevelt. At the conference, nations that might have offered to accept more Jews who were then leaving Germany declined to do so. Australia was represented by the minister for trade and customs, T. W. White, who expressed a far-too-common attitude: "It will no doubt be appreciated also that as we have no real racial problem, we are not desirous of importing one by encouraging any scheme of large-scale foreign migration.... I hope that the conference will find a solution of this tragic world problem."[57] After the conference, Chaim Weizmann, who would become the first president of the State of Israel, said: "The world seemed to be divided into two parts — those places where the Jews could not live and those where they could not enter."[58]

On July 21, Pius XI openly declared: "Catholic means universal, not racist, nationalistic, separatist.... The spirit of Faith must fight against the spirit of separatism and exaggerated nationalism, which are detestable, and which, just because they are not Christian, end up by not even being human."[59] Two weeks later, Pius XI made a public speech in which he said: "The entire human race is but a single and universal race of men. There is no room for special races. We may therefore ask ourselves why Italy should have felt a disgraceful need to imitate Germany." This was reprinted in full on the front page of the Vatican newspaper on July 30, under a four-column headline. The sub-headline mentioned both "universal concepts" and the "great human family."[60]

Other articles condemning National Socialism, racism, or anti-Semitism appeared in 1938 issues of *L'Osservatore Romano* on April 2,[61] July 17,[62] July 21,[63] July 23,[64] August 13,[65] August 22-23,[66] October 17-18,[67] October 20,[68] October 23,[69] October 25,[70] October 26,[71] October 27,[72] November 3,[73] November 13,[74] November 14-15,[75] November 16,[76] November 17,[77] November 19,[78] November 20,[79] November 21-22,[80] November 23,[81] November 24,[82] November 26,[83] December 25,[84] and January 19, 1939.[85] As one contemporary commentator explained:

> The Vatican newspaper, *Osservatore Romano*, had been forthright and downright in its denunciation of Hitler for his excesses against the Jews, his sterilization law, his restrictions upon the freedom of speech and assembly and freedom of religious worship. This little newspaper, published within the Vatican state, was one of the few remaining in Europe that dared to criticize Hitler or Mussolini. Even the French press had become respectful toward Hitler, and in Poland, Norway, Sweden, Denmark, the Netherlands, Finland, Hungary, Rumania, Jugoslavia and Czechoslovakia, newspapers were silent on Hitler. His name did not appear in Lithuania. But the Vatican newspaper fulminated and poured its criticism upon his head, even while he was in Italy. The newspaper had been just as persistent in its attacks upon Mussolini.[86]

Secretary of State Pacelli oversaw *L'Osservatore Romano* and Vatican Radio. "Without exaggerating the international impact of these labours, they provide more than enough evidence that the future Pope had no tenderness towards National Socialism."[87] A. C. Jemolo, a noted opponent of Italian Fascism during the war years, wrote:

> It may be recognized without qualification that there was no heretical principle, no proposition against dogma, against orthodox history or against morals which was even tentatively advanced by Fascist men or journals of any authority, which was not immediately refuted by pontifical acts, by very authoritative ecclesiastical reviews or by the *Osservatore Romano*....[88]

As World War II loomed and then broke out (from 1938 to 1940), the United States State Department's political positions were published verbatim in *L'Osservatore Romano*, much to the chagrin of the Italian fascists and Hitler.[89] After the war, Piero Calamandrei, a left-leaning political activist, who was no friend of the Church, stated to the Italian Constituent Assembly that: "At a certain moment, during the years of greatest oppression, we were aware that the sole newspaper in which it was still possible to find some accent of liberty, of our own liberty and of the common liberty of all free men, was the *Osservatore Romano*."[90]

The Nazis certainly understood where the Pope stood. The German paper, *Völkischer Beobachter*, responded to his condemnation of the "Aryan Manifesto" in its August 2, 1938 edition:

> The Vatican has rejected the racial doctrine from the very beginning, partially because it was first proclaimed publicly by German National Socialism and because the latter drew the first practical consequences from this knowledge; for the Vatican adopted a political stance of opposition towards National Socialism. However, the Vatican also had to reject the racial doctrine because it contradicts its dogma of the equality of all men, which is again a consequence of the Catholic claim for universality, which incidentally, it shares with liberals, Jews, and Communists.[91]

Pius sent Mussolini a handwritten letter asking that Jewish Catholics be exempted from the provisions of this new racial law. Thinking that this would "make the law confessional instead of racial," Mussolini left the letter unanswered.[92] (Fascists claimed that the racial question was political, not religious, and therefore was outside the Church's legitimate province.) Pius also wrote King Victor Emmanuel III, arguing that Mussolini was trying to destroy Italy's concordat with the Holy See.[93]

The Pope's speeches thereafter were not reprinted in the Fascist press, which regularly distorted his comments. Mussolini warned Jewish people that more severe measures would be adopted unless "the improvised and unexpected friends who are defending them from so many pulpits" cease their campaign.[94]

Perhaps due to the Vatican's influence, most Italian people refused to cooperate with the anti-Jewish laws. Except for one brief period, Jewish relief organizations operated openly during the racial campaign until the German occupation of Italy in September 1943. In fact, the Jewish rescue organization, the Delegation for Assistance to Jewish Emigrants (DELASEM), made many trips into Italian-occupied areas to bring Jews back into Italy, with the full cooperation of the Italian government.[95]

When Mussolini began enforcing the anti-Semitic legislation, Italian Church authorities instructed Catholics to be charitable to the Jews.[96] Many Jewish people were "converted" with falsified baptismal certificates so that they might be protected under the terms of the Lateran Treaty. The Church often focused on legal arguments concerning marriage regulations and how they constituted a breach of the Lateran Treaty. In a Christmas allocution delivered later that year, Pius XI condemned the "inhuman and therefore anti-Christian" racial laws.[97] The Pope also taunted Mussolini, arguing that he changed his attitude about the Jews largely "in imitation of Germany."[98]

While many Catholics were swayed by anti-Semitic laws, some groups and individuals stood out for their opposition. Members of Catholic Action printed fliers and leaflets in a campaign against Fascism. This so angered the secretary of the Fascist Party that he ordered that the printing presses be broken, leaflets confiscated, and Catholic Action members beaten and expelled from the party (meaning that many would lose their jobs).[99]

---

In an effort to appease its threatening neighbor to the west, the Polish government considered a bill in 1938 that would have prohibited the killing of animals by cutting their jugular vein. This, of course, would have made it virtually impossible to prepare or obtain kosher meat in that nation. In a letter dated April 6, 1938, Cardinal Tisserant suggested to Secretary of State Pacelli that he contact the papal nuncio in Poland, Archbishop Filippo Cortesi, and try to stop this legislation. Pacelli wrote back to Tisserant that "such a law would constitute a true persecution of the Jews."[100] He then contacted Cortesi and instructed him to condemn this act of persecution and anti-Semitism.[101]

Cortesi replied to Pacelli on May 7, saying that he, too, thought the legislation in question was anti-Semitic. Cortesi, however, assured the secretary of state that the bill would not be turned into a law. It had passed only one branch of the parliament, and it never did become law. The nuncio agreed, however, that in this pre-war time period, "as Your Eminence observed, we must condemn every act of persecution and of anti-Semitic violence."[102] Later, when the Nazis threatened the Jews of Rome, Pacelli (Pope Pius XII) protected the Torah and other ritual objects and helped ensure that the Jews could properly slaughter their animals.[103]

---

On November 9-10, 1938 (the fifteenth anniversary of Hitler's 1923 putsch), one of the most violent nights in Berlin's history took place. Storm troopers were set loose on the Jewish population. Young Nazis went on a rampage, killing Jews at random, smashing windows, destroying homes and businesses, and burning synagogues. The riot came to be called *Kristallnacht* ("Night of Shattered Glass") because there were so many broken windows. About six hundred synagogues were burned, more than seven thousand Jewish shops were ransacked, and thirty-five thousand Jews were arrested. More than ninety people, most of them Jewish merchants, were killed in the rioting. Most rioters in Berlin wore civilian clothes but drove Nazi Party cars and wore the boots of party members.[104]

*Kristallnacht* has been identified as the beginning of the true war against the Jews. Soon, Jews in Germany and occupied nations were packed into ghettos, forced to wear the yellow Star of David for identification, and subjected to ever-harsher restrictions and persecution. In the following days, thousands of Jews were sent to concentration camps. This led to a mass exodus, as 150,000 Jews emigrated from Germany between *Kristallnacht* and the beginning of World War II.[105]

The morning after *Kristallnacht*, Catholic priest Bernhard Lichtenberg, provost of St. Hedwig's Cathedral in Berlin, spoke out from the pulpit, closing each of his services with a prayer for the Jews:

> What took place yesterday, we know; what will be tomorrow, we do not know; but what happens today, that we have witnessed; outside, the synagogue is burning, and that, also, is a house of God.... Do not let yourself be led astray by such un-Christian thoughts, but act according to the clear command of Christ: "Thou shalt love thy neighbor as thyself."[106]

Because of his outspokenness, Father Lichtenberg was sentenced to two years in prison. After prison, he was seized by the Gestapo and sent to Dachau. He died on the way there. In 1995, Pope John Paul II beatified him (along with Father Karl Leisner), the first step toward sainthood.[107]

A few days after *Kristallnacht*, a twenty-seven-minute long national radio broadcast in the United States was carried on both CBS and NBC (the only two major broadcast networks at the time). It emanated from the Catholic University of America, in Washington, DC, and featured Father Maurice Sheedy, head of the university's Department of Religious Education; Monsignor Joseph Corrigan, the university's chief executive; and three current or former trustees of the school: Archbishop John Mitty of San Francisco, Bishop Peter Ireton of Richmond, and the former governor of New York, Al Smith.[108] Bishop John Gannon of Erie, Pennsylvania, also spoke. This broadcast called on politicians in Germany to stop persecuting Jews, and it called on Catholics to pray for the stricken Jews. Archbishop Mitty delivered a declaration of solidarity with the Jews. Bishop Gannon said: "[I]n the face of such injustice toward the Jews of Germany, I express my revulsion, disgust and grief." Newspapers the following day had headlines such as: "Prominent Churchmen Denounce Oppression of Jews by Germans," "Catholic Churchmen Join Pleas for Jews," and "Noted Laymen, Clerics Voice Nazi Protest."[109]

The same month that *Kristallnacht* took place in Germany, racial laws in Italy were tightened with passage of the "law for the defense of the Italian race."[110] This law prohibited interracial marriages involving Italian Aryans, and declared that such marriages would not be recognized. Civil recognition of Church marriages had been one of the most important aspects of the Lateran Treaty, and this seemed a clear breach, despite Mussolini's attempts to argue otherwise. Pius XI was the first official to file a protest, which was reported in the Vatican newspaper,[111] but he had no influence with the dictator.[112] His protests, however, may have been part of the reason why Italians were never very willing to enforce racial laws.[113]

Relations between Italy and the Vatican deteriorated significantly after the racial laws were put in place. On January 2, 1939, Mussolini warned the Holy See that he would not tolerate any opposition to his racial policy. Later that same year, Mussolini expressed his displeasure over Pius XI's comments regarding anti-Semitic policies and threatened the security of the Vatican.[114] Police were stationed outside the Vatican City gates, and they reported on all visitors. Lay Vatican employees were recruited to watch the movements of prelates. Mail was opened, and telephone conversations were monitored.

For several days following *Kristallnacht*, *L'Osservatore Romano* ran a series of front-page articles reporting on the atrocities.[115] On November 13, under the headline "*Dopo le manifestazioni antisemite in Germania*" ("After the manifestations of anti-Semitism in Germany"), the Vatican newspaper noted the moral outrage expressed in many countries around the world over the pogrom. It even quoted the critical dispatches of the Jewish-owned Havas News Agency.[116]

Pius also instructed three prominent cardinals — Ildefonso Schuster of Milan, Pierre Verdier of Paris, and Joseph-Ernest Van Roey of Belgium — to publicly condemn Nazi racial theories. "Very close to us, in the name of racial rights, thousands and thousands of people were tracked down like wild beasts, stripped of their possessions... [when all they were doing was] seeking in vain in the heart of civilization for shelter and a piece of bread," said Cardinal Verdier. "There you have the result of the racial theory." *L'Osservatore Romano* published all three statements along with a strong attack on totalitarianism delivered by Michael Cardinal Faulhaber of Munich.[117]

---

On September 6, 1938, in a statement that — though barred from the Fascist press — quickly made its way around the world, Pope Pius XI said:

> Mark well that in the Catholic Mass, Abraham is our Patriarch and forefather. Anti-Semitism is incompatible with the lofty thought which that fact expresses. It is a movement with which we Christians can have nothing to do. No, no, I say to you it is impossible for a Christian to take part in anti-Semitism. It is inadmissible. Through Christ and in Christ we are the spiritual progeny of Abraham. Spiritually, we are all Semites.[118]

The Nazis and Fascists did not permit the Pope's words to be reprinted in nations where they controlled the press, but these words quickly circled the globe.[119]

The *Tablet* of London, the Church's semi-official newspaper to English-speaking nations, ran the remarks on September 24, 1938, under the headline "Italy: The Holy Father on the Jews." Secretary of State Pacelli repeated the statement in a public speech he gave shortly thereafter in Rome;[120] the *New York Times* carried a front-page story on the statement;[121] and Jacques Maritain, perhaps the leading Catholic philosopher of the era, wrote an important and beautiful essay that was translated into English and published in the *Virginia Quarterly Review* by the spring of 1939. He wrote: "Spiritually we are Semites — no stronger word has been uttered by a Christian against anti-Semitism, and this Christian was the successor to the Apostle Peter."[122]

The victims of the Nazis certainly took note of the Pope's commitment. In January 1939, the *National Jewish Monthly* reported that "the only bright spot in Italy has been the Vatican, where fine humanitarian statements by the Pope have been issuing regularly."[123] The February 1939 issue of the *National Monthly*, published by B'nai B'rith, put Pope Pius XI on its cover, along with the headline: "Pope Pius XI attacks Fascism." Inside the journal, on page 207, under the title "Pope Assails Fascism," it stated: "[R]egardless of their personal religious beliefs, men and women everywhere who believe in democracy and the rights of man have hailed the firm and uncompromising stand of Pope Pius XI against Fascist brutality, paganism and racial theories." Even the United States Congress passed a joint resolution acknowledging Pius XI as a symbol for "the re-establishment of the rule of moral law in human society."[124]

The Nazis, on the other hand, were less than happy. In December 1938, the Hamburg magazine *Volk im Werden* published an article which said:

> In the constant battle against the Church of Rome, it is necessary that the National Socialist movement be vigilant, so as to preserve unaltered the inheritance of its ideas.... Our "joy" has nothing in common with the Catholic Christian "blessedness," and our socialism is precisely in direct contrast with Catholic charity. There is no need to emphasize that national unity and solidarity must be constantly reinforced and protected against Catholic universalism.[125]

The article went on to argue that "Rome is continuing its campaign to conquer the German soul" through its social works. "And so we conclude: the social activity of the Church begins with the Jewish-Christian concept of the cursing of work, and presents as its remedy 'supernatural sanctification,' by means of the mystical body of the Church.... [S]ocial Catholicism has thus become a weapon and an instrument of the super-national Church of Rome."[126]

———

As 1938 drew to an end, frantic preparations for war swept across the globe. British leaders drew up a national plan providing instructions for what each person should do in case of war. Germany and France both increased military preparedness. Italy disavowed its 1935 pact with France. In Spain, Franco restored the citizenship of ex-King Alfonso XIII and took final control of the nation. Fascist Baron Hiranuma took over as Japanese prime minister. Germany demanded the return of colonies to Japan and Italy, warning the United States not to interfere. Western diplomats noted that the Holy See was more clearly lining up on the side of the democracies.[127]

# EIGHT

# The Pre-War Pope

In 1938, Pius XI was very ill. He spent six months convalescing at Castel Gandolfo. Cardinal Pacelli repeatedly urged the ailing Pontiff to slow down. Pius indignantly replied, "The world would be far better off with a dead pope than with one who cannot work full time."[1]

Pius XI's final public comments on the world situation focused on Hitler's threatened aggression. Though he was nearing death, he could read the writing on the wall. He warned Italian Catholics not to trust Germany. He met with British Prime Minister Neville Chamberlain and Lord Halifax and told them what he thought of the regimes in Italy and Germany, the duties of the democracies, and the urgent need to help the refugees.[2] He also notified American and Canadian bishops of his displeasure at the reluctance of Catholic universities in their countries to hire more European Jewish scholars and scientists, and he asked them to remedy this situation.[3]

With the tenth anniversary of the signing of the Lateran Treaty at hand, Pius XI summoned the whole Italian episcopate to Rome. He reportedly planned to undertake a major emigration and resettlement project in São Paulo, Brazil, and to make a stinging indictment of Fascism.[4] On January 9, 1939, Secretary of State Pacelli sent out messages to the archbishops of the world, instructing them to petition their governments to open their borders to Jews fleeing persecution in Germany.[5] The following day Pacelli wrote to American cardinals, asking them to assist exiled Jewish professors and scientists.[6] Unfortunately, Pope Pius XI never made his planned speech. At five in the morning on February 10, 1939, one day before he was scheduled to give his address, Pius XI passed away in his sleep.

On February 13, the Alliance Israélite Universelle wrote to Rome: "Never shall we forget the kindness and courage with which the late pope has defended all victims of persecution, irrespective of race and religion, in the name of those eternal principles whose noblest spokesman he has been on earth.... He has truly earned our eternal gratitude and everlasting admiration."[7] Bernard Joseph, on behalf of the Executive of the Jewish Agency (the future Government of Israel) published a piece, saying this about Pius XI:

> In common with the whole of civilized humanity, the Jewish people mourn the loss of one of the greatest exponents of the cause of international peace and goodwill.... More than once did we have occasion to be deeply grateful for the attitude which he took up against the persecution of racial minorities and, in particular, for the deep concern which he expressed for the fate of the persecuted

Jews of Central Europe. His noble efforts on their behalf will ensure for him for all time a warm place in the memories of the Jewish people wherever they live.[8]

The British representative to Rome reported that the fallen Pontiff's courage at the end of his life ensured that he was "one of the outstanding figures of the world."[9]

The reaction in the Axis nations was quite different. On February 16, 1939, just days before he passed away, the official publication of the Nazi S.S. labeled Pius XI as "the sworn enemy of National Socialism."[10] Upon his death, *Das Schwarze Korps* eulogized him as the "Chief Rabbi of the Christian World."[11] According to the *New York Times*, Germany fulfilled "the requirements of diplomatic usage," but it did nothing beyond noting the Pope's passing.[12] Mussolini remarked: "At last that stiff-necked old man is dead."[13]

During the seventeen years of Pius XI's reign, he had tried to protect the spiritual mission of the Church by concluding bilateral concordats with no less than twenty-one countries. However, at the time of his death, the world's stability was in great jeopardy. Aggressive and evil theories were spreading across the globe. The same month that the Pope died, twenty-two thousand Americans attended a pro-Nazi rally in New York City's Madison Square Garden.[14] Pius XI's successor would assume the leadership of the Catholic Church at one of the most difficult periods in history.

---

On a number of occasions, Pius XI indicated that Cardinal Pacelli would make an ideal pope, going so far as to say that if he were sure the conclave would elect Pacelli as his successor, he would retire.[15] This made Pacelli a likely candidate, but his health remained a concern.[16] Moreover, there is an old Vatican saying: He who enters a conclave a pope, will come out of it a cardinal.[17]

There was a tradition of electing Italians, and Pacelli was strongly supported by the so-called democratic group within the Curia.[18] He had a great deal of support due to his experience in dealing with leaders of other nations. He had been a nuncio for thirteen years and secretary of state for almost ten years. He also had been closely involved in the preparation of several encyclicals and had negotiated many concordats, including one with Germany. Pacelli had also been denouncing Nazi breaches of the concordat for several years, and he felt that Nazism posed a threat to Christianity similar to the one posed by Communism. As such, the German government used all possible pressure to bring about the election of a more friendly pope.[19]

On February 16, 1939, the German ambassador to the Holy See, Diego von Bergen, addressed the Sacred College of Cardinals in what was expected to be a customary expression of sympathy over the death of Pius XI. Rather than merely offering condolences, however, the ambassador spoke of an "upbuilding of a new world which struggles to rise on the ruins of the past which in many respects no

THE PRE-WAR POPE | 127

longer has a *raison d'être*."[20] As the *New York Times* reported, it was a clear request for a pope more sympathetic to Hitler's expansionist plans.[21] The British Legation to the Holy See reported back to London that it contained a "blackmailing note" and was "a veiled warning against the election of Cardinal Pacelli."[22]

The Germans viewed Pacelli unfavorably because they feared that he would continue the same policy that he had followed as secretary of state. The French foreign minister expressed his hope that Pacelli would be elected for that very same reason.[23] A private note from the British Legation to the Holy See read, "I should like to back Pacelli if we were in a position to do so, but we are not."[24] The cardinals let everyone know that the choice of a successor to Pius XI rested with God, and not the Rome-Berlin Axis.[25]

On the way into the conclave, Pacelli stumbled and fell to the ground, injuring his arm. He was helped to his feet by Jean Cardinal Verdier of Paris, who joked in Latin: "*Vicarius Christi in terra!*" ("The Vicar of Christ on earth").[26] The pun proved prophetic, as Pacelli was elected pope on the first day of the conclave, March 2, 1939. Although the balloting is officially kept secret, it is now believed that Pacelli was elected on the second ballot with about forty-eight of the sixty-five votes cast being in his favor.[27] He did, however, request the confirmation of a third vote, and he was unanimously elected.[28] (According to an unidentified cardinal who was in the conclave, as the votes were coming in for Pacelli: "I have never seen anyone look so pale and yet continue breathing.")[29]

The cardinals, who in voting are notionally the parish priests of Rome, are electing their bishop. At the time of Pacelli's election, war appeared inevitable. As such, one of the most important considerations was how the new Pope would deal with world unrest. Ultimately, the debate over whether they needed a "spiritual" or a "diplomatic" pope was settled in favor of "the most experienced and brilliant diplomat available."[30]

Of all the diplomats in the cardinalate, Pacelli was certainly the most accomplished. He had been groomed for this office almost from the moment his predecessor was elected. Not long before his death, Pius XI said: "We commend to our brethren of the Sacred College the high esteem and lofty opinion we hold for the ability and high-mindedness of our chief collaborator, thrice worthy as our successor in this Apostolic See."[31] Pacelli was known for "cool and critical" thinking, was considered a "modern man," and was seen as "a veritable prince of diplomats."[32] He had traveled widely throughout the world as Pius XI's secretary of state and had the overwhelming support of the foreign cardinals.

Following the vote, the traditional signal, white smoke, was seen rising above the Vatican and a huge crowd assembled to await the announcement. "*Annuntio vobis gaudium magnum! Habemus Papam!*" ("I announce to you a great joy! We have a Pope!"). The excited crowd raised a long and deafening roar. "The most eminent and reverend Lord Eugenio...." The announcement was drowned out by another explosion from the crowd as the people joyfully finished the name: "Pacelli! Pacelli!"[33]

It was reported at the time that Pius XII was cautious, suave, and tolerant, as opposed to Pius XI who was impulsive, bristling, and authoritarian.[34] Pacelli, it was said, "takes a long time to make a decision of importance. Once it is made, however, one may be sure that it is the result of profound analysis and meditation."[35] Pacelli was "ascetic in his personal habits, omniscient in his intellectual aspirations, endowed with the gift of total recall, unswerving in his devotional activities, affable though reticent, thoughtful of subordinates, and eloquent and impenetrable as a personality."[36] Moreover, Pacelli "looked like a casting director's dream of a pope, lean, remote, scrupulously ascetic in gesture and expression."[37]

The choice of Pacelli was welcomed in every country in Europe and the Western Hemisphere, except Germany.[38] The headline across the top of the *Baltimore Sun* read: "Election of Pacelli Surprise and Disappointment to Followers of Hitler."[39] The headline in the *Dodge City Daily Globe* was "Anti-Nazi Cardinal Elected Pontiff."[40] As reported in the *New York Times*:

> The election of Pius XII... brought nearly general applause around the world. Statesmen and the press, laymen and churchmen, hailed him as a man equipped by experience and wide travels to meet the issues of the day and hour. In Washington and London it was held that the new Pope would encourage all forces seeking to lift the threat of war and totalitarianism. In Paris even Socialists and Communists praised Pope Pius XII as a probable barrier to Fascism. The Fascist nations — Italy and Germany — were divided in their opinion. In the Italian press the selection was praised. But the German press, which had opposed Cardinal Pacelli's election, charging that he favored the Western democracies, was at first silent, but later expressed an attitude of watchful waiting.[41]

The report continued: "Today once more the Catholic church, on the broad issue, stands side by side with the democratic people in defending the integrity of the human spirit and the brotherhood of mankind against the spiritual servitude of the new barbarians."[42] A wartime biography of Pacelli reported on his election that "diplomats in Rome from the great majority of countries (always with the exception of Germany) were delighted with the choice."[43] The Washington correspondent for the *New York Times* noted that "Persons in official and semi-official life generally expressed gratification at the election of Cardinal Pacelli."[44]

The news in Poland was received "with great joy."[45] In England, it was said that "no choice could have been more welcome to this country.... It is regarded as a sign, if not a guarantee, that the Vatican will continue to throw its worldwide influence against totalitarian ideas wherever they exist."[46] From Paris, the *Times* correspondent reported: "The election of... Pacelli as Pope was received in France... with the greatest possible satisfaction. His elevation is regarded as a guarantee that the firm policies of Pius XI both in regards to spiritual matters and political ideologies will be vigorously defended by the Vatican."[47]

Even Communist papers endorsed Pacelli's election. The French Communist paper *L'Humanité* wrote: "It is Pius XII. Will he not along with the name also take up the work of that man whom he served as Secretary of State during the last years? For when it was a question of the nonsense of racial doctrine, Nazi persecution and the attacks of Fascism and freedom of conscience and human dignity, Cardinal Pacelli and the Pope were not to be separated."[48] The *Daily Worker*, the paper of the Communist Party in the United States, praised Pacelli's first statement (a call for peace) and contrasted the Church with Nazi racial policies.[49]

According to the Jewish press: "Pius XII has clearly shown that he intends to carry on the late Pope's work for freedom and peace... we remember that he must have had a large part to play in the recent papal opposition to pernicious race theories and certain aspects of totalitarianism."[50] The *New York Times* quoted the grand master of a Jewish organization, the Independent Order of Abraham, who said after Pacelli was elected pope: "Everybody knows the liberal tendencies of Cardinal Pacelli, and every Jew in this country should honor him, for we all know that the new Pope thinks along the lines of human rights. The Church is to be congratulated in selecting Cardinal Pacelli for its leader."[51]

The lead editorial in the *Canadian Jewish Chronicle* explained that "although the election of two hundred and sixty-one pontiffs has hitherto been a matter of indifference to Jews... the election of the two hundred and sixty-second pope was one which elicited considerable interest."[52] This was so because, regardless of his qualifications,

> [t]he election of Cardinal Pacelli is more than merely a tribute to personal talent. It is the choice of a policy.... The frantic attempt, therefore, which has been made by Nazis and Fascists to influence the election, by speech, suggestion, and counsel, in favor of a cardinal friendlier to Hitler and Mussolini... was ultimately foiled. The clumsy advice which... Germany's Ambassador to the Vatican, recently gave to the College of Cardinals... has already received an answer as unequivocal as the advice was arrogant. The plot to pilfer the Ring of the Fisherman has gone up in white smoke.[53]

In Jerusalem, the *Palestine Post* reported: "The cordial reception accorded the election, particularly in France, England and America — and the lukewarm reception in Germany — are not surprising when we remember the large part he [Pacelli] played in the recent papal opposition to pernicious race theories."[54] The *Jewish Chronicle* (London) reported in its March 10 edition that "among the congratulations received [by the Holy See] are messages from the Anglo-Jewish Community, the Synagogue Council of America, the Canadian Jewish Congress, and the Polish Rabbinical Council."[55] The president of the Rabbinical Council of America heralded the election of Pacelli as "most welcome."[56]

"It seems that the only dissenting voice raised against the choice of Cardinal Pacelli as the new Pope was heard in Germany."[57] Papers sympathetic to the Nazis bitterly complained about the "prejudiced hostility and incurable lack of comprehension" shown by the Holy See on the racial question.[58] *Das Schwarze Korps*, the official publication of the S.S., wrote:

We do not know if Pius XII, though young enough to see the developments in Germany, is intelligent enough to sacrifice many old things of his institution. As nuncio and secretary of state, Eugenio Pacelli had little understanding of us; little hope is placed in him. We do not believe that as Pius XII he will follow a different path.[59]

The morning after Pacelli's election, the Berlin *Morgenpost* reported: "The election of Cardinal Pacelli is not accepted with favor in Germany because he was always opposed to Nazism and practically determined the policies of the Vatican under his predecessor."[60] That same day, the *Frankfurter Allgemeine Zeitung* wrote: "Many of [Pacelli's] speeches have made it clear that he does not fully grasp the political and ideological motives which have begun their victorious march in Germany."[61] *Graz*, an Austrian Nazi paper, said Pacelli was "a servile perpetrator of Pius XI's doomed policy."[62] In an effort to undermine his authority within Germany, the Nazi journal *Das Reich* wrote: "Pius XI was a half-Jew, for his mother was a Dutch Jewess; but Cardinal Pacelli is a full Jew."[63]

According to the March 4, 1939, entry in Joseph Goebbels' diary, Hitler considered abrogating the concordat in light of Pacelli's election as pope.[64] A few weeks later, the German Reich's Chief Security Service issued a secret report which said:

> Pacelli has already made himself prominent by his attacks on National Socialism during his tenure as Cardinal Secretary of State, a fact which earned him the hearty approval of the Democratic States during the papal elections.... President Roosevelt said in his cable of congratulations: "With great joy I learned of your election to the papacy. I recall with pleasure our last conversation during your visit to the U.S.A."[65]

By the following year, there were reports that Hitler wanted to "drive His Holiness out of Italy and then to have his election announced as invalid...."[66] Pacelli's election, however, would not dissuade the Nazis from their desired path.

At the time Pacelli was elected, Germany had already annexed Austria, was within days of seizing control of all of Czechoslovakia, and was threatening Poland. Nevertheless, protocol required the new Pope to send brief, personal messages to all heads of states with whom the Vatican had diplomatic relations, and a note to the man threatening to start a war might provide an opportunity to advance the cause of peace.[67] Between his election and coronation, Pius XII met with the four German cardinals in an attempt to develop a plan to stop the Nazi persecution of the Church in Germany. They all agreed to try a conciliatory approach.[68] There was, however, a limit. The new Pope vowed: "We cannot sacrifice our principles. Once we have tried everything and if they still persist in their desire for war, then We will defend Ourselves. But the world should note that we have done everything to live in peace with Germany."[69] He then sent Hitler a letter which read as follows:

To the illustrious Herr Adolf Hitler, *Führer* and Chancellor of the German Reich! Here at the beginning of Our pontificate We wish to assure you that We remain devoted to the spiritual welfare of the German people entrusted to your leadership. For them We implore God the almighty to grant them that true felicity which springs from religion. We recall with great pleasure the many years We spent in Germany as Apostolic Nuncio, when We did all in Our power to establish harmonious relations between Church and State. Now that the responsibilities of Our pastoral function have increased Our opportunities, how much more ardently do We pray to reach that goal. May the prosperity of the German people and their progress in every domain come, with God's help, to fruition![70]

Although the letter was written in an attempt to reach an understanding with Germany, this language was very common and similar to the language used in letters to other world leaders. "Not a single word could be construed as approbation of what Hitler stood for."[71] It was simply diplomatic protocol coupled with an attempt to end the hostilities. When Pius XII met with the German ambassador, however, it became clear that no accord would be possible. The meeting ended with Pius telling the ambassador that he was aware of Nazi abuses and would not tolerate them.[72] Hitler was apparently the only world leader who did not respond to the new Pope's letter.[73]

Pius then made the first clear move to justify the faith that the Jewish press had placed in him. He appointed Cardinal Luigi Maglione as secretary of state for the Vatican. As the *Zionist Review* (London) reported:

Pope Pius XII has given the Nazis and Fascists another unpleasant surprise. On the eve of his coronation His Holiness announced the appointment of Cardinal Luigi Maglione as Secretary of State for the Vatican. Cardinal Maglione... is known as a staunch Liberal and as a friend of the democratic powers. His appointment confirms the view that the new Pope means to conduct an anti-Nazi and anti-Fascist policy.[74]

Along with Pope Pius XII, Monsignor Domenico Tardini,[75] and Monsignor Giovanni B. Montini,[76] Cardinal Maglione played an important part in Vatican diplomacy and efforts to restore justice to the world until his death in 1944.

The coronation of Pope Pius XII took place on March 12, 1939. Due to the Vatican's dispute with Italy, there had not been a traditional ceremony in over a century. This coronation, however, was one of the most magnificent that Rome had ever seen. It was the first to be broadcast on radio, the first to be filmed in its entirety, and delegations were sent from almost every nation of the world. The American ambassador to England, Joseph P. Kennedy (accompanied by his son John, the future president of the United States), was the first ever official representative of the United States at the coronation of a pope.[77] The patriarch of Constantinople announced that for the first time in history, the Greek Orthodox Church would be represented at the coronation. Germany was the only major power that did not send a representative, though the German ambassador to the Holy See did convey the congratulations of the Reich and its leaders.[78] (A memorandum by an official in the Reich Protocol Department pointed out that following the election of Pope Pius XI, the German leadership sent "most cordial congratulations," but that in light of Pacelli's "well-known attitude" toward Germany, congratulations to the new Pope "are not to be conveyed in a particularly warm manner.")[79]

Addressing the cardinals, Pius XII explained he would devote his papacy to the struggle for peace. The Pope's supreme title, *"Pontifex maximus,"* means "the great builder of bridges." Pacelli had taken the name Pius (in Latin, meaning pious, kindhearted, and gentle; in Hebrew signifying conciliation) in honor of his predecessor, but clearly the outbreak of war was utmost in his mind. Even before the coronation, Pius developed his plan for peace. He selected as his coat-of-arms a dove holding an olive branch in its beak. His device was *"Opus Justitiae Pax"* ("The work of justice is peace"). His first message on Vatican Radio was a pledge to work for unity and a plea for peace throughout the world.[80] Pius XII came to be called the "Herald of Peace," as he regularly prayed in public for matters such as eternal rest for all who died in the war, and comfort for the exiled, refugees, prisoners, the displaced, and all who suffered.[81]

Pius XII subscribed to the same doctrine of impartiality for the Holy See that was exercised by Pope Benedict XV during World War I.[82] Throughout the war, he tried to improve the conditions for prisoners of war, displaced persons, and those in concentration camps, regardless of their nationality. (Government officials in Germany and Russia so resented this activity that they dismissed the Vatican's representatives from occupied territories.) Vatican diplomats distributed medicine, books, rosaries, and other items — including Christmas presents — to prisoners of war in every country. They also spoke with the prisoners, took messages to concerned families, and tried to improve conditions for the interned of all nations. Most of all, Pius consistently struggled to bring peace to a world afflicted by war.

On the day after his coronation, Pius held a series of meetings with U.S. Ambassador Joseph Kennedy. Afterward, Kennedy wrote to his superiors at the Department of State indicating that the new Pope held a "subconscious prejudice that has arisen from his belief that Nazism and Fascism are pro-pagan, and as pro-pagan, they strike at the roots of religion." Pius was greatly disturbed by the "trend of the times." Nevertheless, Kennedy deemed it prudent to keep these opinions private, and he urged the Pope to enter into negotiations with the Reich. The Pope's final remark was: "The Church can only do so much, but what it can do, it will."[83]

Unfortunately, Hitler did not let problems with the Vatican slow down his aggression. On March 15, 1939, just three days after the coronation in Rome, and despite assurances to the world made only months earlier, Hitler invaded interior Czechoslovakia (beyond the area he had won in negotiations) and divided it into two states. This finally caused British Prime Minister Neville Chamberlain to abandon his appeasement stance and offer military alliances to the two countries now threatened by Germany (Poland and Romania) and to Greece, which was threatened by Italy.[84] (It was to honor the pledge to Poland that Britain went to war against Germany later in the year.) Unlike the German Czechs in the annexed Sudetenland, who were seen as Aryans and treated rather well, those who lived in the newly occupied protectorate states of Bohemia and Moravia (including six million Catholics) were treated quite harshly. As always, religious institutions were singled out for persecution.

----

The so-called hidden encyclical of Pius XI is a story told by many papal critics.[85] The typical version is that Pius XI was prepared to make a strong anti-Nazi statement. He commissioned a draft, but he died before releasing it. His successor, Pius XII, decided not to issue it. Critics then argue that had Pius XII not "hidden" this encyclical, much suffering would have been avoided.

The true story of the "hidden encyclical" is that there never was an encyclical or even a draft encyclical. Pope Pius XI asked for a paper from the American Jesuit John LaFarge. The thought was that this might eventually be used as the basis for an encyclical. LaFarge was not an expert theologian or historian, so he sought help from two other priests, Father Gustav Gundlach from Germany and Father Gustave Desbuquois from France.[86] This resulted in three different papers, one written in French, one in English, and one in German.[87]

The source upon which most critics rely, Georges Passelecq and Bernard Suchecky's *The Hidden Encyclical of Pius XI*, deals with the French and the English papers, but not the German one. That book also makes clear that Pius XI was not the author of any of the documents. In fact, as that book further makes clear, there is no evidence that either he or Pius XII even saw these documents. A copy of the German paper was sent to Pius XI, but by that time the Pope was already gravely ill. When it was found after his death, there were no notations suggesting that he ever reviewed it.[88] The book also explains that the paper disappeared immediately after Pius XI's death, and the men who were working on the project believed (indeed were certain) that Pius XII had *not* seen it.[89] He therefore could not have hidden it.

The primary author of the German draft, Professor Gustav Gundlach, S.J., helped Pius XII with his first encyclical, *Summi Pontificatus* (On the Unity of Human Society),[90] which was released on October 20, 1939, just after the outbreak of war. Not surprisingly, *Summi Pontificatus* (which urges solidarity with all who profess a belief in God and — contrary to the claims of some critics — expressly mentions Jews) contains language that is similar to the paper on which Gundlach had worked. In fact, the Vatican correspondent for the *New York Times* later wrote: "Stripped of its religious references, the encyclical was tantamount to a declaration of war on Germany and Russia."[91]

One of the problems that modern critics have had with the traditional story of the hidden encyclical is that the so-called original draft contained some anti-Semitic statements. Critics of Pius XII are sometimes reluctant to attribute such sentiments to Pius XI. Critic John Cornwell resolved this problem in his book *Hitler's Pope* by accusing Pacelli of having written the draft when he was secretary of state, then of having buried it when he became pope. (In fact, Cornwell even suggests that Pacelli suppressed the encyclical while he was still secretary of state, during Pius XI's illness.) Thus, Cornwell criticizes Pius twice — first for writing it, then for suppressing it. It is really too great a stretch of logic to be considered legitimate. There is absolutely no evidence that Pacelli had anything to do with drafting or hiding the hidden encyclical.

# NINE

# 1939 and the Outbreak of War

The lead article in the February 1939 issue of *Reader's Digest* explained the situation in Germany for the Catholic Church on the verge of World War II. Entitled *Nazi Scapegoat Number 2* and written by S. K. Padover, it painted an ugly picture that too many modern commentators have forgotten:

> Nuns in Nazi prisons, priests in concentration camps, Catholic leaders shot, Cardinals' homes wrecked — Americans read such news and, shocked at the barbarism of the Reich, are puzzled besides.... As Hilaire Belloc, the eminent Catholic writer, admitted, the conflict between Catholicism and Nazism is "beyond all reconciliation." One or the other must destroy its opponent. The *Völkischer Beobachter*, principal Nazi party organ, in its Vienna edition of October 15, 1938, says flatly, "We are armed to continue the battle against Catholicism until the point of total annihilation." German Catholics are facing the same fate as the Jews. They are Nazi Scapegoat No. 2.[1]

That same year, supposedly in response to a letter from the parents of a severely handicapped child, Adolf Hitler announced the formation of a special Reich council to deal with "mercy death" for the severely handicapped. In the spring, Nazi officials, doctors, and directors of several established institutions met to consider the creation of euthanasia centers. This was the beginning of the Nazi racial purification program.[2]

A "euthanasia" program had long been part of the Nazi plan.[3] In 1929, at the Nazi convention in Nuremberg, Hitler proposed the annual "removal" of seven hundred thousand to eight hundred thousand of the "weakest" Germans as a means of rapidly improving the overall health and capabilities of the German race.[4] He also wanted to eliminate millions among the "inferior races that breed like vermin."[5] This led to the creation of the "Reich Commission for the Scientific Registration of Hereditary and Constitutional Severe Disorders," and doctors soon began conducting the experiments that would lead to the gas chambers of World War II.[6]

One of the first steps was official recognition of the "right to die," which aroused only minimal opposition.[7] Then, in 1939, doctors began to give "mercy deaths" to the "incurably sick."[8] Carbon-monoxide chambers were built to carry out the euthanasia program. Next came deformed children, who were said to adversely affect the race and not to have very happy lives anyway.[9] At first, these children were identified while still very young (not more than three years old), but the age gradually edged up to seventeen and then to adulthood. Moreover, the standards also changed. Originally, only the severely deformed were included in the program. Eventually, children with misshaped ears, bed wetters, and those who were found difficult to educate were marked for elimination.[10]

Between December 1939 and August 1941, about five thousand children and one hundred thousand adults were killed by lethal injections or in gas chambers that were built to look like shower rooms.[11] The victims were all deemed to have a "life unworthy of living" because they were physically or mentally handicapped, deformed, or otherwise considered "undesirable."[12]

Bishop Clemens August Graf von Galen of Münster (in the Rhineland) took a leading role in opposing Nazi racial laws from the very beginning. On February 9, 1936, he made a public anti-Nazi speech at Xanten Cathedral. In response, the Nazis charged that Galen was trying to shelter "the corrupters of our race."[13] During the war, it was written of him that

> [w]ithout the slightest regard for his personal safety, he has not hesitated to write or telegraph Hitler direct whenever he has violated the Concordat. The Bishop has gone in person to the highest authorities in the land in order to lodge a long series of vigorous protests against the persecution of the Catholic Church, and, risking his very life, he has publicly stigmatized the Gestapo and its chief, Himmler, as murderers and despots.[14]

When word of the euthanasia program first leaked out to the German populace, widespread outrage led by religious leaders spread throughout the country. In August 1941, Galen became the first prominent German clergyman to denounce the program when he mounted the pulpit and asked:

> Do you or I have the right to live only as long as we are productive?... Then someone has only to order a secret decree that the measures tried out on the mentally ill be extended to other "nonproductive" people, that it can be used on those incurably ill with a lung disease, on those weakened by aging, on those disabled at work, on severely wounded soldiers. Then not a one of us is sure anymore of his life.... Woe to humanity, woe to our German people, when the sacred commandment "Thou shalt not kill" is not only violated, but when this violation is tolerated and carried out without punishment![15]

Secretly duplicated, the speech quickly spread across Germany. Galen came to be known as "the Lion of Münster." His reputation for standing against the Nazis became international when news of his bold sermons filtered out to the international press.[16]

When these sermons were brought to the attention of Pope Pius XII, he wrote to Galen that they had brought him "a consolation and a satisfaction which We have not experienced for a long time as We walk down a sorrowful path with the Catholics of Germany."[17] As pope, Pius did not speak as freely as Galen had, but he noted that letters Galen had mailed to the Holy See had laid the groundwork for his 1942 Christmas message.[18] After the war, Pius named Galen a cardinal, both as a tribute to his brave stance against the Nazis and as a sign that Germany "still had a place among the nations of the world."[19]

On December 2, 1940 — well before Galen's famous sermons against euthanasia — Pius XII published an official Vatican statement in the Catholic press that unequivocally condemned the killing of "life unworthy of life."[20] He then wrote to Bishop Konrad von Preysing (who was a personal friend),[21] noting the Vatican statement and explaining that it was at that point up to the German bishops to see what could be done.[22] Preysing saw to it that the decree went into every diocese in Germany, and it was favorably and publicly commented on by the German bishops. On March 9, 1941, in a public sermon, Preysing cited Pius XII, "whom we all know — I should say from personal experience — as a man of global horizons and broadmindedness [who] has reaffirmed the doctrine of the Church, according to which there is no justification and no excuse for the killing of the sick or of the abnormal on any economic or eugenic grounds."[23] Other German bishops followed suit,[24] culminating in Galen's famous sermons of July and August of 1941.

Many commentators argue that Galen's protests were successful in ending the euthanasia program and that the Nazis did not retaliate. In fact, the euthanasia campaign was not ended, but continued under greater secrecy until the end of the war.[25] Moreover, there was retaliation. Galen was from an old and well-established family. His arrest by the Nazis "would be to plunge the whole of that area... into passionate and probably open rebellion."[26] Therefore, the Nazis retaliated against priests who served under Galen. As one of Galen's successors, Reinhard Lettmann, the bishop of Münster, explained: "After having preached these sermons the Bishop was prepared to be arrested by the Gestapo.... The Bishop was deeply dejected when in his place twenty-four secular priests and thirteen members of the regular clergy were deported into concentration camps, of whom ten lost their lives."[27] In 1942, Hitler expressed his plans for Galen:

> I am quite sure that a man like the Bishop von Galen knows full well that after the war I shall extract retribution to the last farthing. And, if he does not succeed in getting himself transferred in the meanwhile to the Collegium Germanicum in Rome, he may rest assured that in the balancing of our accounts, no "T" will remain uncrossed, no "I" undotted.[28]

Hitler vowed that "[t]he Bishop of Munster will one day face a firing squad."[29] The Nuremberg prosecution report shows that Galen was at times forbidden to speak to the public or to give blessings.[30] In fact, as a result of his outspokenness, Galen's diocese suffered a far higher death rate than most others.[31] In fact, during the war, Münster was reduced to ruins, and Galen was left homeless and forced into a temporary shelter, where he was left essentially under house arrest.[32]

Following Galen's protests, the German euthanasia program took on a lower profile,[33] but at the same time, the Nazis began a similar program on a vastly greater scale in Poland.[34] (In fact, according to one account, the euthanasia program only appeared to slow down because the killing resources were redirected to Jewish victims.)[35] Euthanasia continued throughout the war. In the autumn of 1941, the staff at Hadamar, one of the euthanasia centers, celebrated the cremation of its 10,000th corpse with a special ceremony, followed by music, dancing, and drinking.[36]

The execution techniques that were developed in these euthanasia hospitals would soon be adapted for use on those who were deemed racially valueless.[37] The euthanasia doctors would move on to their new patients. The "scientific" techniques they had developed were refined and perfected until, in the gas chambers of Auschwitz, it would be possible for these doctors to eliminate thousands of people in one day.

Hitler was confident enough of his ability to eliminate the Jewish race that on January 30, 1939, in a speech before the Reichstag commemorating the sixth anniversary of his coming to power he announced:

> Today I will once more be a prophet: if the international Jewish financiers in and outside Europe should succeed in plunging the nations once more into a world war, then the result will not be the Bolshevizing of the earth, and thus the victory of Jewry, but the annihilation of the Jewish race in Europe![38]

No one then knew how close he would come to carrying out this threat.

As these pages are being written, the Catholic Church is considering Galen for sainthood. The Church has already recognized his "heroic virtue," and he was beatified by Pope Benedict XVI on October 9, 2005, in St. Peter's Basilica.[39] As such, he is now considered "Blessed." Perhaps the final assessment, however, should be left to the Jewish Anti-Defamation League, the world's leading organization fighting anti-Semitism. The ADF "commended the Vatican for clearing the way for the beatification" of Galen. A press release said:

> "Cardinal von Galen, ignoring great personal risks, refused to remain silent in the face of Nazi atrocities," said Abraham H. Foxman, ADL National Director, and Rabbi Gary Bretton-Granatoor, ADL Director of Interfaith Affairs. "He is credited with stopping advancement of Nazi euthanasia programs and was a passionate advocate speaking out against the persecution of European Jewry."[40]

---

Ahmed Zog was elected president of the Albanian Republic early in 1925. The National Assembly proclaimed him king in 1928. Under his leadership, Albania strengthened its ties with Italy. By the late 1930s, however, the relationship was strained. In early 1939, the two nations were engaged in peace negotiations. King Zog, however, balked at Mussolini's demand that the Italian navy be given permanent access to Albanian harbors and that military garrisons be established along Albania's Greek and Yugoslavian borders. When Mussolini could not win these concessions at the bargaining table, he decided to take them by force.

On Good Friday, April 7, 1939, Italy invaded Albania, citing the need to protect Italians residing there from roving armed bands. The invaders gave no notice and faced almost no resistance. King Zog was driven into exile, and Albania became an Italian protectorate.

On Easter Sunday, Pius XII condemned both the Italian attack on Albania and the German invasion of Czechoslovakia. He blamed the current state of war on those who neglect justice: "How is peace possible in this world, if acknowledgment of just interest as well as unanimous efforts toward social progress are lacking? If solemnly given promises are broken without any hesitation?" He said, "Justice requires that all men acknowledge and defend the sacrosanct rights of human freedom and human dignity, and that the infinite wealth and resources with which God has endowed the whole of the earth, shall be distributed... for the use of all His children."[41] The statement prompted the Anglican bishop of Chichester to publish a letter expressing his "profound gratitude to the Pope" in the *London Times*.[42] The German press, on the other hand, carried not a word about the statement.[43]

Mussolini at first said that Pius could "go ahead and protest, if only to save his own soul...."[44] By July, however, he sent Count Ciano to present an ultimatum to the papal nuncio. In his diary, Ciano recorded: "Either [*L'Osservatore Romano*] will cease its subtle propaganda against the Axis or we shall prohibit its circulation in Italy. It has become the official organ of the anti-Fascists."[45]

Pius, who was deeply concerned about the Hitler-Mussolini pact, wanted desperately to avoid another big war. Thus, he did not negotiate in a public forum. Instead, less than two months after he was elevated, he asked Germany, Italy, France, and Britain to attend peace talks at the Vatican. Rumors soon circulated that Pius wanted Warsaw to soften its stand against German demands on Danzig and the Polish Corridor.[46] The talk became so widespread that Secretary of State Maglione wrote to Lord Halifax of England, assuring that Pius never intended to take "the initiative in proposing to the two governments a concrete solution of the problem," but had merely urged the parties to act calmly and with moderation.[47] Peace talks never took place, however, at least in part because French and Polish leaders were afraid that the only way to attain peace would be to make concessions to Germany.

On May 22, Italy and Germany signed a new ten-year agreement, the "Pact of Steel," which — according to Hitler — created "an invincible block of 300 million people." The agreement bound the two nations economically, politically, and militarily. It also attracted worldwide attention. Britain called an extra session of Parliament to discuss it. The Vatican saw it as a dangerous sign of the forthcoming war. In an address to the cardinals on June 2, 1939, Pius XII said:

> The Church is not dominated by the interests of one party. She will not become embroiled in the dangerous temporal conflicts of the States but, with the anxiety of a mother, she will attempt to secure peace in moments of great danger,

to quiet the frenzied passions of the fighting parties. She will do everything possible in order to stop the war now threatening the world and to forestall its disastrous consequences.[48]

Throughout the war, the Pope would abide by this plan, which he had laid out prior to Germany's invasion of Poland.[49]

———

Despite the limitations imposed by the Versailles Treaty, Hitler spent much more money ($50 billion to $100 billion) on the German military machine in the 1930s than other nations spent on their military.[50] As a dictator, Hitler did not need to gather political support for his programs, and he did not worry about the economic consequences of the huge deficits he ran up. British and French leaders were unable to convince a majority in their respective nations of the need for similar spending.[51] As such, by 1939, Germany was far better prepared for war than were most other nations. Still, the combined strength of England and France might have been able to dissuade Hitler from his ambitious plans, if only they had reached an agreement with the Soviets. The Germans, however, beat them to the punch.

On August 23, 1939, Hitler put together the final piece of his plan for a military invasion of Poland. He had been held in check because he feared that the Soviets, who would not like an aggressive German army right at their border, would strike back if he invaded Poland. He got the assurance he needed by signing a nonaggression pact with Stalin. The pact was supposed to assure peace between the two nations for five years. All it really did was assure Germany's invasion of Poland.

Since one of Hitler's primary goals was the containment of Bolshevism, Stalin might naturally have sided with the Western Allies. They, however, would have demanded that he agree to protect Poland. Not only did Hitler ask less of the Soviets, but he was also willing to give Stalin a prize. After the war, it was disclosed that the nonaggression agreement had a secret additional protocol that assigned to the Soviets a "sphere of influence" that included Finland, Estonia, Latvia, part of Romania, and eastern Poland — despite a nonaggression agreement that the Soviet Union already had with Poland.[52]

Stalin appears to have meant to carry out the agreement with Hitler. Over the course of the next year, the Soviet Union sent many supplies and raw materials to Germany. Hitler, however, never intended to honor his pledge. He later admitted that this was simply a way of stalling for time; he breached the agreement with a massive invasion of the Soviet Union less than two years later.

Recognizing the dangerous world situation, Pius broadcast appeals for peace on Vatican Radio on August 19 and August 24, 1939. Speaking to "you leaders of peoples, politicians, men of arms, writers and broadcasters" he pleaded: "The danger is tremendous, but there is still time. Nothing is lost by peace; all is lost by war." He urged "by the blood of Christ… the strong [to] hear us that they may not become weak through injustice… [and] if they desire that their power may not be a destruction."[53] As he made his appeal, entitled *To Those in Power and Their Peoples*, the new Pope clearly identified the cause of the current state of world affairs. As one correspondent later wrote, Pius "was pointing the finger at Hitler."[54]

On the afternoon of August 31, the Pope sent identical notes to the governments of Germany, Poland, Italy, France, and Great Britain "beseeching, in the name of God, the German and Polish Governments... to avoid any incident."[55] He begged the governments to support his appeal and added: "The Pope is unwilling to abandon hope that pending negotiations may lead to a just pacific solution."[56] Unfortunately, other nations did not see this as a realistic alternative.[57]

A year earlier, Hitler said that he would have no more territorial demands and that he understood Poland's need for a port. Now, however, he railed against the Polish Corridor that separated East Prussia from the rest of Germany (and provided Poland with its only access to the sea). Poland already permitted German trains and cars free transit across the corridor, but that did not satisfy the German dictator. The free city of Danzig, under the protection of the League of Nations, had a large German population. It had been "torn from the Fatherland," Hitler argued. (Privately, he also thought that Poles were an inferior race that needed to be eliminated.) He began a propaganda campaign to convince his nation that the Germans in this area were being mistreated by the Poles.[58]

Previously, Hitler had encountered world leaders who were willing to accommodate him. Chamberlain was only the most visible proponent of appeasement. Now, however, Hitler ran up against people who were determined to make no concessions. Poland had been restored as an independent nation following the First World War. At that moment in time, neither Russia nor Germany were great powers. As those nations grew in power over the next twenty years, Polish leaders became concerned. They now felt that Poland's only chance was to behave defiantly.[59]

In the early morning hours of September 1, 1939, German forces staged an incident along the border of the two nations. Hitler took to the airwaves to denounce the "Polish attack" and to announce the annexation of Danzig to the Reich.[60] At that very time, German planes began a massive bombing assault, as German tanks rumbled across the border.[61] This *blitzkrieg* ("lightning war") attack came with a speed unparalleled in earlier warfare. German mechanized troops smashed through Polish towns and villages, reducing them to rubble as Poles on horseback charged modern tanks.

Luigi Cardinal Maglione, Vatican secretary of state, telephoned the Pontiff to tell him of the invasion. After answering in his customary manner, *"E'qui Pacelli"* ("Pacelli here") and hearing the news, the Pope retreated to his chapel, fell to his knees and poured out his grief in prayer.[62] Working with his chargé d'affaires in Warsaw, Pius helped organize Polish Jews for a passage to Palestine.[63] Over the next few months, Pius XII's apostolic delegate in Istanbul, Angelo Roncalli, prepared thousands of baptismal certificates for arriving Jews in the hope that such papers would permit passage into the country.[64]

The Poles were almost powerless to resist aggression by the world's finest fighting machine. Screaming dive bombers terrorized Polish cities. Much of the Polish air force was destroyed in the first few hours. Long columns of German tanks smashed the Polish cavalry. Hundreds of thousands of Poles were captured, injured, or killed. Though civilians rallied to defend their country, German victory in Poland was assured from the outset as German forces used military bases in Czechoslovakia so that the attack could come from the north and the south. Within weeks, much of Poland was occupied; German victory took only twenty-eight days. At a fairly small cost, Hitler had acquired twenty-one million more subjects and vast agricultural and industrial resources.[65]

The Nazis built almost all of their death camps in Poland. Jews from all over Europe were sent there in cattle cars to be eliminated. About six million Jews died in these camps. Other groups were also marked for extermination, particularly Gypsies and Poles. It is estimated that three million Catholic Poles died in the Nazi concentration camps, and another two million were sent to Germany as slave labor for the Reich.[66]

The campaign against Christian Poles is often overlooked, but Hitler's first prisoners and victims in Poland were thousands of intelligentsia, members of the resistance, and clergy.[67] As Hitler's private secretary, Martin Bormann, explained:

> All Polish intelligentsia must be exterminated. This sounds cruel, but such is the law of life.... [Polish priests] will preach what we want them to preach. If any priest acts differently, we will make short work of him. The task of the priest is to keep the Poles quiet, stupid, and dull-witted.[68]

Thousands of Polish priests were sent to the concentration camps by the Nazis; two-thirds of them — about 2,500 — died there.[69] The primate of Poland, August Cardinal Hlond, fled first to Rome, then to France. When he attempted to go back to his diocese, the German ambassador sent a note to the Vatican saying that Hlond was an enemy of Germany and did not have permission to return.[70] Archbishop Adam Stefan Sapieha soon took on the role of leader of the Polish Church within the occupied nation.[71]

On September 3, 1939, two days after the invasion and in compliance with mutual defense treaties they had signed with Poland, the nations of Great Britain, France, New Zealand, and Australia all declared war on Germany. Within a week, Canada would also declare war, and the United States would declare its neutrality. It was too late for Poland, but the days of appeasement were over. Hitler found himself in a much larger war than he had expected.[72]

---

As German troops continued their advance into Poland from the west, to the surprise of everyone (except Hitler), Soviet troops marched in from the east. There were occasions of confusion, with Poles thinking that perhaps the Soviets were there to support them in the war against Germany, but such was not the case. Seven hundred Soviet soldiers and thousands of Poles were killed in the fighting.[73] The Polish government and high command escaped into exile on September 18, but the fighting continued. Hour after hour, Warsaw radio broadcast the Polish National anthem. Finally, on September 27, it went silent.

Germany and the Soviet Union divided Poland between themselves. The Soviets were ruthless in their occupation of the eastern half of Poland. Anyone who might be able to rally civilians to revolt — including military officers, intellectuals, politicians, and priests — was systematically eliminated. Poland once more disappeared from the map. John F. Kennedy, writing in 1945, expressed his view of Soviet brutality, and perhaps revealed an ignorance of German brutalities, when he wrote: "In many ways, the 'SS' were as bad as the Russians."[74]

The Soviet Union's expansionist plans were not limited to Poland. Pursuant to their secret agreement with Hitler, the Soviets demanded the right to establish naval and military bases in the republics of Estonia, Latvia, and Lithuania.[75] Soviet troops invaded those nations in October.[76] The following year, they were incorporated into the Soviet Union as constituent republics.[77]

Finnish authorities refused to permit Soviet military bases in their nation, so on November 30, without a declaration of war, about one million Soviet troops invaded Finland.[78] The Soviets were particularly brutal toward Finnish civilians. President Roosevelt sharply condemned "this dreadful rape" and referred to Stalin's regime as "a dictatorship as absolute as any other dictatorship in the world."[79] The League of Nations expelled the Soviet Union, making it the only country ever expelled from the League for aggression.[80]

By the following March, the Finns had to accept the Red Army's treaty terms and cede territories in southern and eastern Finland to the Soviet Union. The Finnish president bitterly remarked, as he signed the treaty, "Let the hand wither that is forced to sign such a treaty." A few short months later he suffered a stroke and was paralyzed on his right side.[81]

---

While the prospect of fighting for Hitler was troubling for many Germans, national loyalty was seen as something separate from Nazism. The idea of refusing military service simply did not occur to most people.[82] At the beginning of the war, it seemed possible to be respectable soldiers. A document called the "Ten Commandments of the German Soldier" was printed in the payment books. The commandments included instructions such as a prohibition on plundering and orders that civilians and unarmed prisoners should be treated decently. Later in the war, however, Hitler had that page torn out of the books.[83]

Early in the war, the German bishops issued a pastoral letter calling on Catholic soldiers to do their duty "full of the spirit of self-sacrifice." They also called on "all devout Catholics in civilian life to pray that God's Providence may bring the war to a victorious conclusion, with a peace beneficial for *Volk und*

*Vaterland.*"[84] This was never the Vatican's attitude, and it did not take long for the bishops to change their minds. In 1941, they issued another pastoral letter condemning the continued persecution of the Church in Germany.[85]

After the coronation of Pope Pius XII, at least some Nazi leaders thought that a working agreement with the Church might be possible.[86] With the outbreak of aggression, however, such hope evaporated, and Hitler even briefly recalled his ambassador to the Vatican.[87] Theodor Groppe, a general who was dismissed from the German army because he opposed Nazi propaganda against the Catholic Church, warned Pius that Hitler had vowed: "I will crush Christianity under my heel as I would a toad."[88]

In 1930, the bishops of Berlin and Westphalia condemned the Nazis in pastoral letters.[89] In that same year, the bishop of Mainz affirmed that "every Catholic is forbidden to be a member of the Nazi Party."[90] In the spring of 1931, the Bavarian bishops also condemned National Socialism and described it as heretical and incompatible with Catholic teaching.[91] Similar statements were made by bishops in Cologne, Paderborn, and the upper Rhine.[92] "In 1931, the bishops of Bavaria, the upper Rhine, Köln, and Paderborn all issued statements proclaiming the incompatibility of National Socialism and Catholicism," and by the end of that year "the entire German episcopacy had declared itself against the movement."[93]

The 1932 common pastoral letter contained an "all-inclusive" prohibition on Nazi Party membership.[94] The bishops "emphasized the Nazi threat to religious liberty, and they attacked Nazi racist policy."[95] They also forbade uniformed groups of National Socialists from attending Mass. In 1933, the common pastoral letter attacked the pagan emphasis on blood and race.[96] Hitler responded on September 11 that he was not against Christianity itself, "but we will fight for the sake of keeping our public life free from those priests who have failed their calling and who should have become politicians rather than clergymen."[97] Four days later, proving that words had *no effect* on Hitler, the German government passed the Nuremberg Laws, which defined German citizenship and paved the way for later anti-Semitic laws.

Both the 1934 and 1935 joint episcopal letters reminded Catholics that the Ten Commandments and the moral law bound all races. All people were subject to sin, and the Nordic race was no exception.[98] A number of bishops, including Clemens Count von Galen, stressed the universality of the moral law for all races in their 1934 individual letters. In their 1935 joint memorandum to Hitler, the bishops bluntly accused the government of attempted race breeding.[99]

A fairly constant theme of reports from the nuncio in Berlin (Archbishop Cesare Orsenigo) was concern that this resistance was driving Germans away from the Church.[100] On April 13, 1940, he wrote:

> I consider it my duty to point out that a part of the clergy has adopted an almost openly hostile attitude towards a Germany at war. This attitude of the clergy goes as far as a desire for complete defeat. This attitude of the clergy, which unfortunately remains no secret, arouses not only the displeasure of the gov-

ernment, but gradually also that of the entire people, as the people are almost all of them enthusiastic for their leader; and therefore I fear a painful reaction will follow one day which will isolate the clergy and even the church from the people.[101]

While Nuncio Orsenigo's attitude has been subject to question,[102] "his assessment was certainly closer to the truth than the assumption that Germany's Roman Catholics — about one third of the total population — were like so many divisions that the Pope could throw into battle against Hitler."[103]

A report from the Nuremberg prosecutor's office outlines dozens of cases where Catholic priests were persecuted due to their opposition to the Nazis.[104] It also shows that the Nazis took steps to silence the Church:

> On 28 October 1935 the Propaganda Ministry imposed censorship before publication on all Church periodicals, and on 30 November 1935 this was extended to all writings and picture material multigraphed for distribution. After 1937, the German Catholic bishops gave up all attempts to print their pastorals, and had them merely read from the pulpit.[105]

Of course, sometimes it was impossible even to read statements from the pulpit. The Bavarian bishops' pastoral letter of September 4, 1938, was confiscated and forbidden, as was the pastoral letter of the Bishops' Conference of Fulda, dated August 19, 1938.[106]

Hitler certainly did not see the Catholic clergy in Germany as his allies. In 1941, he complained bitterly about the Catholic clergy turning against the state.[107] He claimed that many priests were leaving the Church (for the state) but added that he would be unable to convert the Pope.[108] In 1942, Hitler said: "The evil that's gnawing our vitals is our priests, of both creeds. . . . It's all written down in my big book. The time will come when I'll settle my accounts with them. . . ."[109] On August 11, 1942, he expressed his frustration:

> I'll make these damned parsons feel the power of the State in a way they never would have dreamed possible! For the moment I am just keeping my eye on them; if I ever have the slightest suspicion that they are getting dangerous, I will shoot the lot of them. This filthy reptile raises its head wherever there is a sign of weakness in the State, and therefore it must be stamped on whenever it does so. We have no sort of use for a fairy story invented by the Jews. . . . The foulest of the carrion are those who come clothed in the cloak of humility, and the foulest of the foul is Count Preysing! What a beast! . . . The uselessness of the parson is nowhere better illustrated than here at the front. Here we have enemies who are dying by the million — and without a single one of these liars. The Catholic Church has but one desire, and that is to see us destroyed.[110]

Hitler also called Christianity one of the two great scourges (along with the pox) in history, and complained bitterly that "the priests continue to incite the faithful against the State."[111]

Hitler verbally attacked the German bishops at a mass rally in the Berlin *Lustgarten*.[112] His attitude toward clergy is reflected in several semi-private statements like this one: "Now, the priests' chief activity consists in undermining National-Socialist policy."[113] In 1934, S.S. chief Heinrich Himmler circulated a fifty-page memorandum complaining about hostile clergy.[114] His plan was to let "each petty little district" have its own pope.[115] One high-ranking Nazi (Reinhard Heydrich) even went so far as to comment, "Here we see what a bitter and irreconcilable enemy we have in the Catholic Church."[116]

One charge often made by modern critics is that the German clergy collaborated with the Nazis by turning over documents that could be used to identify who was or was not Jewish. Actually, much of this information was already available to the Nazis by virtue of the German census. To the extent that information was uniquely in the hands of the clergy, and was demanded by the Nazis (with severe threats), the collaboration of the German Catholic clergy was far from wholesale. In 1946, Monsignor Johann B. Neuhäusler, who himself was imprisoned in Dachau, published a massive series of primary documents demonstrating extensive Church resistance to Nazi anti-Semitism, including refusal to hand over genealogical records.[117]

In order to show collaboration with the Nazis by Catholic clergy, critic Daniel Goldhagen quotes the Nazi Military Bishop Franz-Justus Rarkowski, but he was the exception that proved the rule. As an initial point, Rarkowski was virtually forced upon the Church by the Nazis (under the threat of having no military ordinary or military chaplains). Moreover, the Church banned him from participation in the German episcopacy. When he made a statement favoring the German cause early in the war, Vatican Radio responded:

> The German episcopate has so far avoided taking a position on this war that would transcend their pastoral duty towards the faithful. If the army bishop [Rarkowski] has read or heard what the Head of this Church has repeatedly and unequivocally said about the injustice done to Poland, he must be aware of the discrepancy between his position and that of the Holy See.[118]

Vatican Radio went on to declare that "Hitler's war is not a just war and God's blessing cannot be upon it,"[119] and "It almost looks as if the army bishop sometimes finds it easier to align himself with the Nazis than with his church."[120]

---

In a report dated December 10, 1939, Cardinal Hlond informed Pope Pius that numerous Polish priests had been killed, imprisoned, or deported; Catholic schools, hospitals, and orphanages were closed; priests were compelled to say a prayer for Hitler after Sunday Mass (the only day Mass was permitted); Church money was confiscated; and many churches were closed "under the pretext of being unsafe for use."[121] He concluded by saying: "In a word, the finest Polish dioceses with their seven million Catholics are doomed to be lost to the Faith."

The cardinal's second message to Pius was even clearer as to the intent of the Nazis:

> It goes without saying that the Nazi aim is to de-Christianize as rapidly as possible these countries which are attached to the Catholic faith and the results are as follows: 95 percent of the priests have been imprisoned, expelled, or humiliated before the eyes of the faithful. The Curia no longer exists; the Cathedral has been made into a garage... the bishop's palace into a restaurant; the chapel into a ball-room. Hundreds of churches have been closed. The whole patrimony of the Church has been confiscated, and the most eminent Catholics executed....
>
> Apparently, it has to be admitted, Hitlerism has succeeded in its designs.[122]

Reports also informed the Pontiff about the Nazis' maltreatment of Polish citizens, noting specifically mass executions and the imprisonment of tens of thousands of Poland's civilian leaders, including many Catholic priests.[123]

From the earliest weeks of the war, the Allies (especially the French and Polish governments) asked the Holy See to condemn both Nazi and Soviet aggression in Poland.[124] Many Polish priests, including the primate of Poland, also called for a condemnation of the occupying forces.[125] The first papal response came in a speech presented in French to the Belgian ambassador to the Vatican on September 14, 1939. Pius decried the invasion of Poland as "an immeasurable catastrophe," pleaded for civilian populations, and warned against the use of "poison and asphyxiating gases."[126] On September 26, speaking to a group of German pilgrims, he said: "You have come to Us in a very grave hour. It is so grave, and the future so dark that at present We can see and say only this: the war which has just broken out is, for all peoples who will be drawn into it, a terrible scourge of God.... Pray that God may shorten the misery of war and restore peace."[127] On September 28, Vatican Radio broadcast Cardinal Hlond's plea: "Martyred Poland, you have fallen to violence while you fought for the sacred cause of freedom.... On these radio waves... I cry to you. Poland, you are not beaten."[128]

---

Upon receiving orders from the Vatican, Bishop Fulman of Lublin called together the priests from his and other nearby dioceses. He told them that "the new Jewish reserve the Nazis have set up here in Lublin is a sewer. We are going to assist those people as well as our own, as well as any man, woman or child, no matter of what faith, to escape; and if we lose our lives, we will have achieved something for the Church and for God."[129] Bishop Fulman's activities led to severe retaliation from the governor-general of occupied Poland, Dr. Hans Frank. Bishop Fulman was incarcerated, and he saw many of his priests die in the concentration camp. Following one execution, Frank addressed Fulman:

> "You have been helping the enemies of the Third Reich," Frank snapped. "You advise and guide subversive elements, you comfort the dogs who deserve to die, you help the Jews to escape. We shall exterminate all enemies of the Reich,

including you, Bishop, down to the lowest of your kind. When we have finished with Poland, when we have finished with Europe, not one of you will be left.... Not one. No Pope. No priest. Nothing. *Nichts.*"

"God have mercy on you," Bishop Fulman repeated.

"God better have mercy on *you*," Frank mocked. "You obey the orders of the Vatican, and for that *all* of you will die."[130]

Indeed, many Catholic priests, religious, and laypersons did pay with their lives for following directives from the Pope.[131] In fact, by the end of the war there probably was not a single Polish family that had not "lost someone close at Auschwitz or at another camp."[132]

Early in the war, Archbishop Sapieha (who headed the Catholic Church within Poland during the war) asked the Pope for a forceful statement in support of Poland and against the Nazis.[133] In 1942, Pius had a letter smuggled into Poland, to be read from the pulpits. Pius XII's messenger, Monsignor Quirino Paganuzzi, reported what happened next:

As always, Msgr. Sapieha's welcome was most affectionate.... However, he didn't waste much time in conventionalities. He opened the packets, read them, and commented on them in his pleasant voice. Then he opened the door of the large stove against the wall, started a fire, and threw the papers onto it. All the rest of the material shared the same fate. On seeing my astonished face, he said in explanation: "I'm most grateful to the Holy Father... no one is more grateful than we Poles for the Pope's interest in us... but we have no need of any outward show of the Pope's loving concern for our misfortunes, when it only serves to augment them.... But he doesn't know that if I give publicity to these things, and if they are found in my house, the head of every Pole wouldn't be enough for the reprisals Gauleiter Frank will order."[134]

Sapieha declined to read the letter because he realized that such a statement would have no lasting positive impact and could bring about severe repercussions.

Pius later cited his experience with the message to Sapieha in a letter that he wrote to Bishop Preysing of Berlin:

We leave it to the local bishops to weigh the circumstances in deciding whether or not to exercise restraint, to avoid greater evil [*ad maiora mala vitanda*]. This would be advisable if the danger of retaliatory and coercive measures would be imminent in cases of public statements by the bishop. Here lies one of the reasons We Ourselves restrict Our public statements. The experience We had in 1942 with documents which We released for distribution to the faithful gives justification, as far as We can see, for Our attitude.[135]

Pius did not, however, completely decline to talk about Poland. On June 2, 1943 (the feast day of St. Eugenio), in an address to the cardinals which was broadcast on Vatican Radio and clandestinely distributed in printed form within Poland, the Pope, at the request of Archbishop Sapieha, expressed in new and clear terms his compassion and affection for the Polish people and predicted the rebirth of Poland:.

> No one familiar with the history of Christian Europe can ignore or forget the saints and heroes of Poland... nor how the faithful people of that land have contributed throughout history to the development and conservation of Christian Europe. For this people so harshly tried, and others, who together have been forced to drink the bitter chalice of war today, may a new future dawn worthy of their legitimate aspirations in the depths of their sufferings, in a Europe based anew on Christian foundations.[136]

Archbishop Sapieha wrote from Kraków that "the Polish people will never forget these noble and holy words, which will call forth a new and ever more loyal love for the Holy Father... and at the same time provide a most potent antidote to the poisonous influences of enemy propaganda."[137] He also said that he would try to publicize the speech as much as possible by having copies printed, if the authorities would permit it. After the war, Pius named Sapieha a cardinal.

———

Most of the world learned of Pius XII's feelings toward the Nazis with the release of his first encyclical, *Summi Pontificatus* (On the Unity of Human Society), on October 20, 1939. In it, Pius wrote of "a world in all too dire need of help and guidance... a world which, preoccupied with the worship of the ephemeral, has lost its way and spent its forces in a vain search after earthly ideals."[138] He condemned the "Godless State" and deplored "the forgetfulness of that law of human solidarity and charity which is dictated and imposed by our common origin and by the equality of rational nature in all men, to whatever people they belong."[139] His reference to an "ever-increasing host of Christ's enemies"[140] was a swipe at both Germany and the Soviet Union. He went on to condemn racists, dictators, and treaty violators.[141]

Like most of Pius XII's statements, the words were guarded, but there was no question about the nations he was discussing. Poland was identified by name, and the other nations were easy to identify.[142] In a clear slap at Nazi racial theory, Pius also said that within the Church there was "neither Gentile nor Jew."[143] An October 28, 1939 edition of the *New York Times* reported: "It is Germany that stands condemned above any country or any movement in this encyclical."[144] As Cardinal Hinsley of Great Britain explained in a radio message the following year, "Certainly no Catholic can have the remotest leaning towards the Nazi creed after the Encyclical of Pius XII in which its guile and violence were unmasked."[145]

Nazi authorities in Germany restricted the publication of *Summi Pontificatus*, permitting only heavily edited versions "in which the sense of some of the passages most adaptable to the Nazi arguments about the war was given, coupled with one or two impertinent reprimands to His Holiness for not being more severe with Germany's enemies."[146] As a wartime author explained, "Even diplomatic observers quite used to regarding suppression of detail as a normal thing were surprised at the extent of the official German excisions. The passage about Poland was cut completely. So were the references to the need for respecting international agreements and the right of national independence."[147]

"This Encyclical," wrote Heinrich Mueller, head of the Gestapo, "is directed exclusively against Germany, both in ideology and in regard to the German-Polish dispute; How dangerous it is for our foreign relations as well as our domestic affairs is beyond dispute."[148] Reinhard Heydrich, leader of the S.S. Security Office in Warsaw, wrote: "[T]his declaration of the Pope makes an unequivocal accusation against Germany."[149] Von Bergen, the German ambassador to the Holy See, was told that Pius had ceased being neutral.[150] In occupied Poland, Nazi police destroyed a monument to Pope Pius XI, which had been on the cathedral.[151] Eventually, the Nazi military in Poland reprinted the encyclical, but they changed the wording, substituting "Germany" for "Poland."[152]

The Western powers certainly saw this encyclical as an endorsement. A report from the British Legation to the Holy See noted that *Summi Pontificatus* contained a "frank condemnation of statolatry and its consequences" similar to the condemnation of Nazism that was found in *Mit brennender Sorge*.[153] The minutes of a meeting of the British high command report:

> The Encyclical itself is perhaps, in some ways, the most important document the war has yet produced and the wider its circulation the better from all points of view.
>
> * * *
>
> I am strongly in favor of instructing Mr. Osborne to convey, if possible to the Pope himself, an expression of H.M. Government's appreciation of the sentiments expressed in the Encyclical. To this might be added a personal message from the Secretary of State.[154]

A headline in the London *Daily Telegraph* on October 28 read: "Pope condemns Nazi theory."[155] The *American Israelite* reported on the Pope's "denunciation of Nazism."

The president of France praised the new Pope's encyclical, and Polish Cardinal Hlond wrote to offer his thanks:

> This official and solemn statement, together with the unforgettable paternal allocution of September 30, will be greatly treasured by Poles. It will also be, for the rising generation, a source of the great strength in the Faith and the traditional attachment to the Holy See, especially when it is seen in the light of the many and far-reaching works of relief that Your Holiness has initiated, and conducts with papal generosity on behalf of the Polish people, condemned even in their own country to extermination by misery, hunger and disease.[156]

Later, French planes dropped eighty-eight thousand copies of this encyclical over western Germany in a propaganda battle.[157]

---

Ironically, even *Summi Pontificatus* has become a point of controversy. In June 1938, more than a year before the outbreak of World War II, when Pacelli was still the Vatican secretary of state, Pope Pius XI commissioned an American priest, Father John LaFarge, to draft a paper for an encyclical attacking racism and anti-Semitism. LaFarge worked on his document for several months, as did two other Jesuit priests, German professor Gustav Gundlach and French Father Gustave Desbuquois. Pacelli was elected pope in March 1939, and his first encyclical, *Summi Pontificatus*, was written with the help of Father Gundlach (who drew heavily on his own earlier work).[158]

By the time Pope Pius XII released his encyclical, however, many things had changed. Relations between the Vatican and the Axis powers had deteriorated; racial laws were now being enforced in Italy; all of Czechoslovakia had been occupied; Poland had been invaded; and World War II had broken out. It was, therefore, harder for a neutral nation to be blunt about matters that had taken on an international flavor. If Pius abandoned his neutral position in his first proclamation, it would have ruined any chance he might have had to help the warring nations negotiate a peaceful resolution. Thus, his encyclical was less adamant than the paper prepared for his predecessor, but with good reason.[159] Nevertheless, the differences between Pius XII's encyclical and the paper prepared for Pius XI have added to the controversy surrounding this issue.[160]

---

Pius sought to unite Catholics throughout the world in a crusade of prayer for peace. He also called upon them to provide money, food, and clothing to help the victims of the war. He said that whatever money was given to him would be spent to relieve the poor and needy, and that is what he did. During the war, there was no heat in the papal apartment. Pius felt that since the poor lacked coal, he, too, would make a sacrifice.[161] In a November 1939 radio address, he explained that "when Catholics are not aware of their duty with regard to the non-Catholics throughout the world, this is a defect in their Catholic mentality."[162] That same month he issued an encyclical on the 150th anniversary of the establishment of the hierarchy in the United States, in which he condemned the "modern blind thirst for pleasure."[163]

Yitzhak Isaac Halevy Herzog, chief rabbi in the Holy Land, sought an audience with Pius XII in 1939 on "certain matters of a non-political nature which are of most vital importance to Jewry."[164] The Pope did not meet with Rabbi Herzog, but he did arrange for the rabbi to have an audience with the cardinal secretary of state.[165] The rabbi's concern was forwarded to the Pope, who established committees to help Catholic-Jewish refugees, and he also organized the emigration of some three thousand "non Aryans" to Brazil.[166] After the war, Rabbi Herzog offered his thanks for Pius XII's "life-saving efforts on behalf of Jews during the Nazi occupation."[167]

Shortly after the outbreak of war, Pius XII established the Pontifical Relief Commission, with agencies in Norway, Denmark, France, Belgium, the Netherlands, Greece, and Yugoslavia. An office was also established in Lisbon for the purchase and distribution of supplies from the United States.[168] These agencies worked throughout the war to help alleviate suffering. The Vatican's efforts to provide food and clothing to people in occupied countries was frequently hindered by Allied or Axis efforts to avoid providing any benefit to the enemy.[169] Thus, the Allies refused to lift the blockade against Germany and some German-occupied nations.[170] Similarly, when the Vatican tried to send money and supplies to occupied Poland, the effort was derailed by German authorities. Later, when the Germans agreed to allow the American Commission for Polish Relief to send supplies to Poland, the Vatican was also able to funnel in provisions.

Pius opened the Vatican Information Bureau in September 1939, based on a similar organization formed by Benedict XV during World War I. It started when a Polish family asked the Vatican secretary of state to find family members who had been deported. The volume of requests for information grew as the war spread. The office was originally staffed with only a handful of clerks, but the bureau had to hire many more people to handle the increasing number of petitions. Soon, the office was receiving a thousand letters a day asking for help in locating prisoners and other war victims. Eventually, as many as six hundred people were hired to answer the correspondence. Vatican Radio sent out up to twenty-seven thousand messages a month trying to locate missing persons.[171] After the war, the Vatican offered a similar information service, providing the names and addresses of German prisoners to their families.[172]

———

In late 1939, with Poland fully under control, Hitler turned his attention to the West and began preparing for war. Many in the German populace, however, feared that Hitler would lead Germany to ruin. Some of them began considering ways to thwart him.[173] One of the most serious threats against Hitler came from the German high command, where some officers began plotting to overthrow him and to put a new government in place.[174]

The reaction by other nations to an anti-Hitler coup was a serious concern to these conspirators. If they were to stage a revolt, the British and French might take military advantage of it, occupy Germany, and mete out harsh justice to the German people, even though they had deposed Hitler. It was therefore necessary to reach an understanding with the Allies.

The German resistance was in regular contact with the Vatican.[175] Pius was the only leader of a neutral government who was trusted by the German resistance.[176] Although the leaders of the planned coup — Colonel Hans Oster,

General Ludwig Beck, and Major Hans Dohnanyi — were Protestants, they recruited Dr. Josef Müller, a leading Munich lawyer and a devout Catholic, to travel to the Vatican to ask the Pope to broker a peace agreement between Britain and the anti-Nazi Germans.[177] The conspirators arranged to have Müller inducted into the German Intelligence Service so that he could explain the many trips that he would be making to Rome.[178]

Müller set up a chain of communication (through Pius XII's close adviser Father Robert Leiber)[179] in order to avoid drawing suspicion.[180] Müller asked the Pope to contact the British authorities on behalf of the resistance.[181] Although he was concerned about breaching neutrality, Pius said that "the German opposition must be heard in Britain," and the voice would be his.[182] According to Müller, Pius "told me through Fr. Leiber that not as the Head of the Vatican State, but as a Pope his conscience not only allows but obliged him to offer his life and the Church for peace."[183] Word of this spread quickly among the conspirators, and they used papal cooperation to convince other Germans to join in the conspiracy.[184]

Over the course of several months, the Pope relayed messages between Müller and the British minister to the Holy See, Sir Francis D'Arcy Osborne.[185] On several occasions, Müller also brought messages to Pius from sources inside Germany concerning military plans and movements. Pius forwarded these warnings to the threatened governments.[186] As others have noted, "Never in all history had a pope engaged so delicately in a conspiracy to overthrow a tyrant by force."[187] In his autobiography, Müller wrote that it was obvious "how dearly the Holy Father wished to restore a Germany of law, order and peace, which ceased to be the nightmare of its neighbors — a Germany without Hitler."[188] He also wrote: "The Pope wanted nothing more urgently and dearly than a Germany liberated from Hitler and Nazism. There is no other way to explain his brave support of the German Military Opposition."[189]

The Nazi authority learned of Pius XII's work with the resistance, but only after it was too late for them to do much about it. A declassified Nazi document prepared by S.S. General Ernst Kaltenbrunner, chief of the S.S. Security Service ("*Sicherheitsdienst*," or S.D.), dated November 29, 1944, reflects Pacelli's involvement with Müller and the resistance. It contains information extracted from arrested conspirators about the anti-Hitler opposition. It explains that in the fall of 1939, Müller got in contact with Father Leiber, and from Leiber, Müller "received a lot of information on the position of the Pope and the enemy powers. He discussed possibilities of a peace and learned from Leiber that the condition for a peace agreement would be a change of the regime in Germany."[190] The report also notes that "Müller later came in close personal contact with Pacelli after meeting him several times and also discussing politics with him. Pacelli always treated him with openness and politeness."[191] The report concluded that in carrying out this work with the Pope, Müller was "working for the oppositional group (the German Military Resistance)."

The Pope's involvement in this clandestine work was prompted by his distrust of Nazism and his perception of its bitter attitude toward Christianity. He specifically told the British ambassador that "the German principals are in no way connected with the Nazi Party."[192] On December 4, 1939, the French ambassador to the Holy See was received by Pius XII in a private audience. The ambassador later reported: "The religious situation in Germany preoccupied him more than ever. Anti-Christianity was apparently congenital to Nazism (he said), incorporated in it."[193]

On January 12, 1940, in a private letter to Lord Halifax in London, Osborne wrote that the Pope had been approached by an intermediary who said that a German offensive was planned for February, but that a group of German generals were prepared to overthrow Hitler and reach a peace settlement if they were assured of certain terms.[194] Those terms included "restoration" of Poland and Czechoslovakia, but retention of the *Anschluss* with Austria. Osborne reported that the Pope felt it his duty to pass on this information, but that he was not expressing any personal opinion on the terms of the proposal.[195] He recognized the risk and urged absolute secrecy (even to the point of not informing his own secretary of state). He thought, however, that this was an important matter, and he was willing to do whatever was necessary to bring about peace.[196]

The British were cautious about the message from Germany. (Osborne reported that "the whole thing was hopelessly vague.")[197] They had previously received false messages of this sort, designed by the Nazis to determine whether any Germans were cooperating with the British.[198] Osborne reported back to the Pope that the British wanted more assurances regarding the overthrowing of Hitler. Pius seemed to understand that the British could not take the rather nebulous and uncertain proposals very seriously unless there were more details from inside Germany.[199]

In the first week of February 1940, Pius arranged for a secret meeting with Osborne. He was discreetly led to the Pope's personal apartment dressed in his normal work clothes, not the formal dress that was typical for papal audiences.[200] The Pope reported that he had again been approached by the German intermediary and that the Germans once again proposed overthrowing Hitler. This time, however, there were more details. The proposal was to establish a military dictatorship for a period of time, to be replaced by "a democratic, Conservative and moderate Government," decentralized and federal in nature.[201] The Rhineland and Westphalia would remain united to Prussia; Austria would be within the federation, but Poland and non-German Czechoslovakia would be independent. The Germans wanted to use this plan as the basis for future negotiations.[202]

The British leadership, like the Holy See, was very concerned that a coup might lead to a Communist takeover in Germany.[203] Nevertheless, they replied that if they were certain that the principals behind this offer were capable of carrying out the plan, they would be willing to consider the proposal after consultation with French leaders.[204]

Unfortunately, the conspirators came to fear that Nazi officials had caught wind of their plot, and they were reluctant to reveal their identities to the British officials.[205] Additionally, Hitler's early and impressive military campaigns made it much more difficult to gather support inside of Germany for his overthrow.[206] On March 30, 1940, Pius told Osborne that he had heard no more from the Germans since passing on the last message. The "generals' plot" was not to be.

Pius had certainly done his part in getting the British to agree with the anti-Nazi German conspirators. "All agreed that the British terms were generous to Germany. That the English would have lived up to them had the Nazis regime toppled was guaranteed by the faith and honesty of the Holy Father."[207] As others have observed: "The plot thickened for some five months and ultimately failed only because of a lack of trust between the British and the German plotters, not because of any hesitancy on the part of Pius XII to take part in so dangerous a conspiracy."[208]

Müller also brought the Pope some documentation that Pius would send, not to the British, but to Mussolini. These documents related to S.S. crimes committed against Jews and non-Jews in Poland. Pius showed these documents to the Italian ambassador to the Holy See and asked that Mussolini be told about them. The ambassador warned that Mussolini would resent papal involvement, but Pius said that he would be responsible before mankind if such atrocities were to happen in Italy. He would not be intimidated, even if it meant that he would be sent to a concentration camp.[209]

In the following years, there were several times when the Nazis almost uncovered the Pope's involvement with the resistance, and the Vatican expected that this would happen.[210] In such a case, "the pope certainly would have been a hunted (if not dead) man, and terrible retaliation would likely have been visited on the Vatican and Catholics throughout Europe."[211] In the autumn of 1942, a Munich businessman was arrested for smuggling foreign currency across the border into Switzerland. He told Himmler's men about Müller's trips to the Vatican and the plot to get rid of Hitler (but the whole truth was not known by the Reich leaders until 1944).[212] Certainly this sealed Hitler's view of Pope Pius XII.[213]

In 1939, Pius sent Hitler a letter congratulating him for surviving an attempt on his life.[214] Some commentators have looked to this letter as a sign of pro-Nazi sympathy. Hitler, however, did not see it the same way. "He would much rather have seen the plot succeed," Hitler said.[215] When his aids pointed out that Pius XII had been a friend to Germany when he was nuncio, Hitler responded, "That's possible, but he's no friend of mine."[216]

———

Relations between the Vatican and the United States government, though informal, were very good at the time the war broke out. Pius XII (then Secretary of State Pacelli) met President Roosevelt on his 1936 trip to the United States, and the two men had become friends.[217] Their wartime correspondence reveals a deep and mutual respect. At Christmastime 1939, Roosevelt named Myron C. Taylor as his "personal representative" to Pope XII (not an ambassador to the Vatican).[218] This was a compromise for the formal diplomatic relations that Pius wanted, but which might have been seen in America as giving preference to one religion over another.[219]

Taylor was the former chairman of the board of the United States Steel Corporation, and he was already serving on a presidential commission for the alleviation of the suffering of refugees. He was a personal friend of Roosevelt, and he had entertained Secretary of State Pacelli on his visit to the United States in 1936. He also owned a villa in Florence. Importantly, he was a Protestant. This made it easier for the president to justify sending a representative to the leader of the Catholic Church.[220]

In his letter to the Pope suggesting this arrangement, Roosevelt said that this would help "our parallel endeavors for peace and the alleviation of suffering."[221] In Pius XII's return letter to Roosevelt, he said that the president's pledge to join the Vatican's struggle for peace was "an exemplary act of fraternal and hearty solidarity between the New and the Old World in defiance against the chilling breath of aggressive and deadly godless and antichristian tendencies, that threaten to dry up the fountain head whence civilization has come and drawn its strength."[222] This language, so close to that used in *Summi Pontificatus* to indict the Nazis, must be read in the same light. In fact, the American ambassador to Italy reported back on Christmas Eve that

> The Pope today after referring to a violation of "international and divine laws" told the Sacred College of Cardinals that he was deeply gratified by the appointment of Myron C. Taylor.... The Pope remarked, "This is Christmas news which could not be more welcome since it represents on the part of the eminent head of a great and powerful nation a worthy and promising contribution to our desires to a just and honorable peace and for a more effective work toward alleviating the sufferings of the victims of the war."[223]

Roosevelt and Pius saw some things differently when it came to the best way to bring about ultimate peace, but they always agreed as to the unjust nature of Hitler's aggression.[224]

Throughout the war, Taylor carried written and verbal messages between these two world leaders.[225] (Mussolini, in fact, later came to blame Taylor for a network of military intelligence in which he thought the clergy participated.)[226] Following Roosevelt's death, Truman reappointed Taylor, and he stayed in this position until his resignation on January 18, 1950. Following the war, Pius wrote that the "solution of urgent problems, the interchange of important information, [and] the organization of American relief," would have been "unthinkable and almost impossible" but for this relationship which permitted President Roosevelt and the Pope to coordinate their efforts on so many projects.[227]

The Pope gave the world a five-point peace program in his 1939 Christmas address. Pius called on Catholics the world over, and especially in comparatively comfortable America, to care for and share with the needy and alleviate the suffering of refugees and war victims. He also blamed the hostilities on the way treaties and commitments were violated. He said the "unlawful use of means of destruction, even against non-combatants and fugitives, against old people, women, and children, and the utter contempt for human dignity, liberty, and human life result in deeds which call for the vengeance of God."[228] It made no explicit reference to Germany, but only Germany and Russia were guilty of the atrocities that Pius condemned. Propaganda Minister Joseph Goebbels, in his diary, wrote: "The Pope has made a Christmas speech. Full of bitter, covert attacks against us, against the Reich and National Socialism. All the forces of internationalism are against us. We must break them."[229]

TEN

# 1940 and the Nazis Press On

By January 1940, approximately fifteen thousand civilians had died in Nazi-occupied Poland, though the Germans tried to conceal the real situation. As word of Nazi atrocities began to leak to the outside world, there was much denial and disbelief. The Holy See, however, was well informed. It knew that innocent people were being subjected to severe abuse, though the "Final Solution" had not yet been decided upon.

Vatican Radio was an important source of uncensored information. In 1931, Secretary of State Pacelli hired Guglielmo Marconi, the inventor of wireless broadcasting, to install a 10-kilowatt transmitter on the highest point in Vatican City. It was refurbished and its power greatly enhanced in 1937. It broadcast messages in a variety of languages, including Italian, German, English, French, Spanish, and Latin. During the war, its steel tower became a symbol of hope for freedom and justice.[1] The Nazi authorities monitored it, but it was a capital offense for regular Germans to listen to it.[2]

Vatican Radio was especially effective at rapidly responding to false claims put out by Axis leaders. When Hitler proposed a "new order" with a federation of European states under the control of Germany and Italy, a Vatican Radio broadcast said that "[i]t is a world order which is as dry as the desert, an order which is the same order as the order of the desert. It is being achieved by the exploitation of human life. What these falsehoods call life is no life. It is dissolution — it is death."[3]

On January 19, 1940, Pope Pius told Monsignor Montini, the future Pope Paul VI, that Vatican Radio must broadcast a report on the conditions of the Catholic Church in German-occupied Poland.[4] The first report, broadcast in German, took place on January 21. On January 22, Pope Pius XII himself read a report on Vatican Radio, based on information provided by Cardinal Hlond:

> The new year brings us from Warsaw, Cracow, Poznan, Pomerania, and Silesia an almost daily tale of destruction, destitution, and infamy. The testimony is unimpeachable; eyewitnesses tell of the horror and inexcusable excesses committed upon a helpless and homeless people. A violent assault on justice and decency is going on in that part of Poland which has fallen to Germany, a persecution which is one more contemptuous to the law of nations, one more grievous affront to the moral conscience of mankind.[5]

The next day, in England, the *Manchester Guardian* reported: "Tortured Poland has found a powerful advocate in Rome.... [*Vatican Radio* has warned] all who

158

care for civilization that Europe is in mortal danger." A January 25 headline
in the *New York Times* reported: "VATICAN CONTINUES ATROCITY
CHARGES; Report on Poland Gives Names of Priests Who Have Been Murdered by Nazis."[6] Later, word reached the Vatican that due to this broadcast, the
Nazis "imprisoned, shot, or tortured to death countless Polish clergymen."[7] As
others have explained:

> Some of the most courageous broadcasts aired by Radio Vatican at this time
> were those that unveiled the horrors of the Nazi Holocaust. On January 20,
> 1940, an American Jesuit became the first announcer in world radio to report
> the imprisonment of Jewish and Polish prisoners in "sealed ghettos." From that
> point on, Vatican Radio continued to feature stories on concentration camps
> and other Nazi torture chambers. From 1940 to 1946, Vatican Radio also ran
> an Information Office, transmitting almost 1.25 million shortwave messages
> to locate prisoners of war and other missing persons. Later the radio station
> combined its information services with the International Refugee Organization,
> forming a team Tracing Service to reunite war-torn families and friends.[8]

In March, the *American Israelite* reported that Pius XII was "taking actions that
were obviously a rebuke to Jewish anti-Semitism."[9]

During the war, it was not known how involved the Pope was with Vatican Radio. When Axis leaders complained about broadcasts, Vatican officials
responded that Vatican Radio was run by the Jesuits as an independent concern.[10] Research into the Vatican's wartime records, however, shows that Pius
XII personally authored many of the intensely anti-German statements beamed
around the world. In other cases, directives were found from the Pope regarding
the content of the broadcasts.[11]

The late Father Robert Graham, one of the people assigned to go through
the Vatican's wartime records, described Vatican Radio's role:

> Research into the broadcasts during the crucial period 1940-1941 reveals a mas-
> sive denunciation of persecutions and oppressions in Germany and in the Ger-
> man occupied territories.... Some of the most important of them were due to
> the initiative of Pius XII. A note from Msgr. Montini, substitute in the Secre-
> tariat of State, refers to the start of this campaign. Under a January 19, 1940,
> date he notes a directive from the Pope [on the appalling situation in Poland]:
> "Provide information to Vatican Radio for German broadcast."[12]

As Pius XII knew, these broadcasts had concrete results because they inspired
the resistance to stand in support of the victims, regardless of their nationality or
background. Father Graham said: "I was stupefied at what I was reading. How
could one explain actions so contrary to the principle of neutrality?"[13] (On February 28, 1940, Pius met with the American ambassador to Italy for forty-five
minutes and conveyed military information about the situation as he knew it in
Germany.)[14]

Vatican Radio broadcasts regularly prompted vigorous protests from Mussolini and the Germans.[15] The Nazis called it the "Voice of the Pope," and Propaganda Minister Goebbels vowed to silence it. Even papal critic John Cornwell reported that Vatican Radio "attracted a flow of protests implying that the Holy See was continuously breaking the terms of the Reich Concordat" by its reporting on events in Poland.[16] The Germans ultimately decided that due to the hostile and anti-German attitude of the Vatican's press and radio, Catholic priests and members of religious orders in occupied Poland would be prohibited from leaving that country.[17] Pius sent a message that said: "The Church will go on as before. The Nazi machine is making war on the Church. The Church will fight with its own weapons."[18]

In his memoirs, Harold Tittmann, U.S. representative to the Pope, explained why these broadcasts eventually had to be toned down:

> In October 1939, the Jesuit-operated Vatican Radio started to broadcast first-hand accounts of atrocities perpetrated by the Nazis in Poland.... However, the Polish bishops hastened to notify the Vatican that after each broadcast had come over the air, various local populations suffered "terrible" reprisals. The thought that there were those paying with their lives for the information publicized by the Vatican Radio made the continuation of these broadcasts impossible.[19]

Eventually, the superior general of the Jesuits gave the order to desist: "How I hated to give the order to stop these broadcasts, especially since I am a Pole myself. But what else could I do? They (the Nazis) have the power, and they use it as they please."[20]

It was clear by now that the Church was strongly opposed to Hitler's National Socialism. On January 26, 1940, under the headline "Vatican Radio Denounces Nazi Acts in Poland," an American Jewish newspaper reported: "The Vatican radio this week broadcast an outspoken denunciation of German atrocities in Nazi [occupied] Poland, declaring they affronted the moral conscience of mankind."[21] This same month, the United Jewish Appeal for Refugees and Overseas Needs donated $125,000 to help with the Vatican's efforts on behalf of victims of racial persecution. The *Jewish Ledger* of Hartford, Connecticut, called the donation in support of the papal efforts an "eloquent gesture" that "should prove an important step in the direction of cementing bonds of sympathy and understanding" between Jews and Catholics.[22]

Critic Daniel Goldhagen quoted a Vatican Radio broadcast of January 1940, trying to make the point that the Vatican was concerned only about Polish Catholics and could not spare a good word for Jews. He then asked rhetorically: "Why, as a moral and practical matter, did [Pius XII] speak out publicly on behalf of the suffering of Poles, but not of Jews? No good answer."[23] In doing this, Goldhagen badly misrepresented the truth.

As an initial matter, the radio broadcast quoted by Goldhagen did not limit itself to Christian Poles. It merely refered to "Poles." Writings of that time sometimes distinguished "Poles" and "Jews," using the former designation to refer only to Polish Christians, but this was far from always the case. Moreover, Goldhagen implied that Jews were never mentioned on Vatican Radio. This is simply false.

Goldhagen seems to have taken his Vatican Radio quote from Pierre Blet's *Pius XII and the Second World War*. That book is a quite helpful summary of the *Actes et Documents* collection, but it is a *summary*. Had Goldhagen actually researched the Vatican Radio transcripts from January 1940 (the month upon which he focuses), he would have found that Jews were expressly and clearly identified. A widely-reported-upon broadcast from January 26 stated the following:

> A system of interior deportation and zoning is being organized, in the depth of one of Europe's severest winters, on principles and by methods that can be described only as brutal; and stark hunger stares 70 percent of Poland's population in the face, as its reserves of food-stuffs and tools are shipped to Germany to replenish the granaries of the metropolis. Jews and Poles are being herded into separate "ghettos," hermetically sealed and pitifully inadequate for the economic subsistence of the millions destined to live there.[24]

The report confirmed the worst of the earlier reports of "horror and inexcusable excesses."[25]

Similarly, on July 30, in response to a speech given at the National Socialist Congress at Nuremberg, Vatican Radio instructed listeners to look to the teachings of St. Paul that were repeated by Popes Pius XI and Pius XII in *Mit brennender Sorge* and *Summi Pontificatus*. The doctrine of human equality, said the broadcast, was the very heart of Christian revelation. That destiny was common to all men — Germans, Poles, *Jews*, and Christians alike.[26]

Vatican Radio was able to target its four shortwave bands to areas that were the focus of German propaganda. Thus, when the Germans flooded Spain with the claim that National Socialism was compatible with Christianity, Vatican Radio reduced the number of English broadcasts and increased Spanish broadcasts to tell the Spaniards about the religious conditions in Poland, Austria, and Germany.[27] On October 15, 1940, Vatican Radio denounced "the immoral principles of Nazism,"[28] and it returned to this topic on November 19, when it responded to an editorial in the Madrid newspaper *Alcazar*, which had said that "National Socialism is primarily a religious movement based on Christian principles."[29] The Vatican Radio broadcast reviewed Nazi attacks on Christianity, the Catholic Church, religious leaders, Church doctrine, religious education, and also discussed other matters such as the closing of monasteries in Austria and the confiscation of religious property.[30] Part of the broadcast went as follows:

> With violence and with singular ability this [Nazi] literature has attacked Christianity and the Catholic Church both as a whole and in its personnel and institutions. It has even attacked the most essential dogmas of the Church. This attack has been carried out with the greatest possible efficiency while the Church has

been hindered from the self-defense it should properly have employed. As to the education situation, if National Socialism is a Christian movement as the *Alcazar* alleges, what is the explanation of the fact that, whereas in 1933 almost the entire Catholic Youth was educated in Catholic schools, the whole magnificent school organization is now practically nonexistent?[31]

The broadcast went on to note the closing of monasteries in Austria, the deportation of priests in Poland, and the refusal to recognize the validity of Church wedding services. A *New York Times* headline proclaimed: "Vatican Says Nazism Is Foe of Christianity; Lists Persecutions in Reich to Support Charge; Vatican Sees Nazis as Church's Foes."[32]

On October 25, 1940, in response to German news reports concerning the Church in Poland, Vatican Radio revealed that 115 parishes had been deprived of their clergy, 200 clergy from the Poznan diocese had been placed in concentration camps, the cathedrals of Poznan and Gniezno had been closed, most larger seminaries had been taken over, and the Catholic University of Lublin had been closed (with many members of the theology faculty being suppressed).[33] The broadcast concluded by reporting: "The Catholics of Poland have grave need of the Catholics of the whole world to sustain them in their trial."[34] On November 2, the Nazis filed a protest with the Vatican, complaining that recent transmissions were "against Hitler, against Nazism," and "in contrast with neutrality."[35] Removing any doubt about the validity of those charges, in a March 30, 1941, broadcast, Vatican Radio explicitly condemned "the wickedness of Hitler."[36] The Vatican ordered its Polish priests to "assist all who need help regardless of race or creed."[37]

Most Vatican Radio broadcasts are not easily accessible to researchers. There are, however several ways to learn about these broadcasts. The broadcasts of Pius himself have been published in a twenty-volume set extending over his entire pontificate; many other transcripts (translated from original broadcast transcripts provided by the Jesuits who ran Vatican Radio) were published in the *Tablet of London*; and — of greatest interest — a small, underground newsletter from Vichy France published several transcripts without editorial comment. The Vichy publication was known as *La Voix du Vatican* ("The Voice of the Vatican").[38]

The broadcasts were directed to French listeners, and the "voice" of most of these broadcasts was Father Emmanuel Mistiaen.[39] In addition to reassuring the French that they would eventually emerge from the horror of Nazi occupation, Father Mistiaen continually reminded his listeners that mankind was indivisible and that there were no superior or inferior races. His broadcasts resulted in several protests and threats from the German government (which also regularly jammed the broadcasts).[40]

---

In March 1940, Hitler sent his foreign minister, Joachim von Ribbentrop, to meet with Mussolini. *Il Duce* told Ribbentrop that the Church was not a particularly useful friend and that the Pope was not really dangerous. He went on, however, to explain that he knew from personal experience that the Pope's enmity could be unpleasant.[41] Ribbentrop decided to request an audience with the Pope. The Vatican was not anxious to grant the request, but as Pius explained to the Archbishop of Breslau:

> To avoid the danger of any policy being misunderstood and despite the perplexi-
> ties existing in many respects, We granted a private audience, allowing Our-
> selves to be guided here by the consideration that a personal conversation with
> one of the *Führer's* closest collaborators might offer Us the possibility of estab-
> lishing a useful contact for restoring the best living conditions for the Catholic
> Church in Germany and also for the future of the war and of peace.[42]

A caravan made its way to the Vatican. The German cars were adorned with papal colors and Nazi swastikas. The Vatican, however, downplayed the event. "Few people saw Ribbentrop arrive in Saint Peter's Square."[43]

Ribbentrop, dressed in his Nazi uniform, marched into the Pope's office and gave the Pope a lecture on German might and the folly of the Vatican having sided with the democracies.[44] Pius then pulled out a ledger and — in German — recited a long list of outrageous abuses by the Nazis in Poland, giving the precise date, time, and details of each. The *New York Times* reported that "the Pontiff, in the burning words he spoke to Herr Ribbentrop... came to the defense of the Jews in Germany and Poland."[45] He also said that Vatican Radio broadcasts would continue as long as the Nazi atrocities did.[46] Ribbentrop did not satisfy the Pope's request for assurances of better treatment in the future, but he did promise to take the matter under consideration.[47] Pius then terminated the audience. Rib-bentrop reportedly felt faint as he left.[48] As one report put it, Ribbentrop "took home nothing but 'a delicate snubbing' and a nervous breakdown."[49]

On April 9, 1940, German troops swept across the Danish border. Accord-ing to the Germans, the occupation of Denmark was not a military conquest, but a friendly occupation called *Inschutznahme* ("protection"). According to legend, King Christian X and several religious leaders, including Catholic priests and the bishop, demonstrated solidarity with the Jews by wearing the yellow star in pub-lic.[50] Privately, the Danes hid and eventually smuggled almost the entire Jewish population of eight thousand to safety.[51] Pius XII was noted for his contribution to the effort.[52] "In fact, under Pius XII's pontificate, many Catholic clergymen and nuns took greater risks and suffered far more on behalf of the Jews than did King Christian of Denmark"[53] The week after the invasion, Pius issued his "Call to Prayer for the Restoration of Peace Among Nations," which called on Catho-lics around the world to pray daily for peace in the month of May.[54]

---

Although the anti-Hitler coup that had been planned in late 1939 never came to fruition, some of the conspirators still believed that Nazi aggression had to be stopped. They sent a message to the Vatican concerning the German plans to invade Holland, Luxembourg, and Belgium.[55] When Pius learned of the plan, he agreed to pass the message on to the Allies. He had it sent by coded radio signals to the nuncios in Brussels and The Hague, then it was forwarded to the Allied leaders in London and Paris.[56] On May 3, 1940, Cardinal Maglione sent identical telegrams to the nuncio in Brussels and the internuncio at The Hague warning that an attack was imminent.[57] The following month, the Germans expelled both of these nuncios.[58]

The telegrams from the Holy See read: "From a source that can be considered trustworthy, we have learned that, unless something prevents it or happens in the meantime, an offensive will shortly occur on the western front; it will also affect Holland, Belgium, and perhaps Switzerland."[59] A similar report was verbally given to François Charles-Roux, the French ambassador to the Vatican. On May 6, he telegraphed his government: "Once again the pope and Msgr. Montini informed me and my counselor that, according to information coming to them from a foreign country, the Germans will unleash an offensive to the western front within a very short time (a week)." He added in a letter of the same date that the offensive would be simultaneously launched against France, Belgium, and Holland.[60] The British representative to the Vatican also sent a similar message back to his home office on May 6, though he mentioned that he gave it little credence.

Although the warnings reached the Allies about one week before the Nazi invasions took place, Western forces failed to capitalize on the information. On May 10, 1940, German troops moved into the Low Countries (the Netherlands, Belgium, and Luxembourg). Luxembourg was occupied without any significant resistance. The Dutch mined bridges, blocked roads, and flooded large areas, but it was too little, too late. German tanks moved rapidly, and paratroops landed on the Dutch countryside as infantry troops pushed forward.[61] The Dutch were overwhelmed in five days. Their government fled to England.

The Belgians lasted only two weeks longer than the Dutch. King Leopold III ordered his troops to cease resistance and to lay down their arms in unconditional surrender on May 28, 1940. For this action, he was condemned by French Premier Paul Reynaud (who knew that France was vulnerable to attack through Belgium), but the king had been relying on British support. When the support was not forthcoming, the Belgian king had little choice.

The invasion of these small, neutral nations deeply offended the Pontiff. On the very night of the invasions, he personally drafted three messages that were then sent, via telegrams, to the Queen of Holland, the King of Belgium, and the Grand Duchess of Luxembourg. The messages referred to these nations becoming involved in the war "against their will and against their rights."[62] The telegrams were printed on the front page of *L'Osservatore Romano* on May 12.[63] (All 180,000 copies were either sold or confiscated shortly after they were delivered to the newsstands; news carriers were savagely beaten.)[64] Though these messages were primarily expressions of condolences, there was little doubt about where the

Pope stood. For instance, in the message to King Leapold of Belgium the Pope wrote:

> At a time when the Belgian people, for the second time and contrary to its will and its law, see its territory exposed to the war's cruelties, We, profoundly moved, send to Your Majesty and to your whole beloved country assurances of Our paternal affection; in asking God that this difficult trial come to an end through the reestablishment of Belgium's full liberty and independence. From the bottom of our heart We grant Your Majesty and your people Our apostolic blessing.[65]

Similarly, the telegram to Queen Wilhelmina of Holland asked "the supreme arbiter of the destiny of nations, to hasten with his all-powerful help the reestablishment of liberty and justice."[66] To the Grand Duchess of Luxemburg, Pius wrote that "the people of Luxemburg, despite their love of peace, find themselves in a tempest of war, Our heart is close to them, and We implore from Heaven aid and protection so that they may live in liberty and independence."[67] As French ambassador Charles-Roux later wrote, the messages were "a public affirmation of the guilt and the responsibility of the German government."

Italian code-breakers intercepted and decoded the Pope's messages to the invaded nations even before they were published. Mussolini took them as a serious personal affront.[68] He called the papacy "a disease wasting away the life of Italy" and promised to "rid himself of this turbulent priest."[69] The Fascist newspaper *Regime fascista* declared that Pius XII had incited "the Catholic King of the Belgians to cause the blood of his people to flow, in order to help the Jews, the Freemasons, and the bankers of the City of London."[70] Myron Taylor, Roosevelt's representative to the Pope, wrote to the president that "the Pope is under fire from the political forces in Italy. The *Osservatore Romano* is assailed openly and even the Pope since his three messages... has been openly attacked. It is true that he needs all the support that can be given him...."[71]

Mussolini's ambassador, Dino Alfieri, personally filed an official protest on May 13, charging that Pius had taken sides against Italy's ally, Germany.[72] The Pope responded that his conscience was at ease, saying: "We are not afraid to go to a concentration camp."[73] He added:

> The Italians are certainly well aware of the terrible things taking place in Poland. We might have an obligation to utter fiery words against such things; yet all that is holding Us back from doing so is the knowledge that if We should speak, We would simply worsen the predicament of these unfortunate people.[74]

As he frequently explained to the German bishops, while he was neutral, he was not indifferent to violations of justice.[75] The American Jewish press noted that "Pope Pius XII has been moving cautiously for this is a time of war — when heads of religions and states must act with calm and consideration."[76]

Relations between Italy and the Holy See were now severely strained.[77] A headline in the *New York Times*, dated March 14, 1940, proclaimed: "Pope Is

Emphatic About Just Peace... Jews' Rights Defended." Fascist youths protested his stance.[78] A group even mobbed Pius XII's limousine and shouted "death to the Pope!" as he was traveling to a Roman church for Mass.[79] By the end of May 1940, the French ambassador to Italy reported: "Pius XII did not conceal from me that he had used up all his credit; the Duce refused to listen to him and no longer reads his letters."[80] The Italian minister of foreign affairs, Galeazzo Ciano, wrote in his diary on May 12, 1940:

> The telegrams sent by the Pope to the rulers of the three invaded states have incensed Mussolini, who would like to curb the Vatican, and is inclined to go to extremes. In these last few days he often repeats that the papacy is a cancer which gnaws at our national life, and that he intends, if necessary, to liquidate this problem once and for all. He added: The Pope need not think that he can seek an alliance with the monarch, because I am ready to blow both of them up to the skies at the same time."[81]

The next day's entry in Ciano's diary indicates that Pius XII had been approached by one of Mussolini's representatives, but the Pope refused to cooperate. "[H]e is even ready to be deported to a concentration camp, but will do nothing against his conscience.... He cannot be accused of cowardice or indifference to human suffering."[82]

---

On the day after the Dutch surrendered, the Germans began turning their attention to northern France. Nazi propaganda had been favorably received in France, perhaps because Hitler had only authorized an expurgated French translation of *Mein Kampf.*[83] Robert d'Harcourt was one of the few voices warning the French about the dangers to be found in Hitler's teachings. In the late 1930s, he published several pamphlets explaining Hitler's tactics and his aims. As secretary of state, Pacelli sent him a handwritten note thanking him for taking these actions.[84] In general, however, the French did not know what lay in store.

Marshal Philippe Pétain, a French World War I hero, succeeded Paul Reynaud as prime minister of France on June 16, 1940, two days after the fall of Paris. The Nazis installed a friendly government on July 1, in the town of Vichy in central France. France was thus split into the occupied north and unoccupied Vichy France in the south. The former undersecretary of defense, General Charles de Gaulle, exiled in England, called on his compatriots to resist the Germans.

On October 24, 1940, Marshal Pétain met with Hitler. One week later, he proclaimed: "It is with honor, and in order to maintain French unity... that in the framework of an activity which will create the European new order, I today enter the road of collaboration."[85] Pétain was attracted to the notion of a strong, authoritarian government. He stood for the protection of private property, social harmony, and order. Believing that France had been overwhelmed through "moral decadence," he asked for and received full executive and legislative powers, without restriction. This was at first greeted with widespread support from the public.[86]

Most of the nation's seventy-six bishops embraced Pétain's "National Revolution," which promised a return to the spiritual and moral values espoused by the Church.[87] Alfred Cardinal Baudrillart, the rector of the Catholic Institute in Paris, called Hitler's mission a noble and inspiring one. Religious instruction, outlawed since the separation of church and state in 1905, was revived in public schools. Teachers were instructed to teach morality and spiritual values. Pétain replaced the familiar socialist-sounding device *"Liberté, Fraternité, Egalité"* ("Liberty, Brotherhood, Equality") with the more conservative *"Travail, Famille, Patrie"* ("Work, Family, Homeland"). The Vichy government also provided support for religious education, and crucifixes were hung on public buildings.

Shortly after the Vichy government came into being, Pierre Cardinal Gerlier, archbishop of Lyons, reflected the feeling of many French people when he said that "if [France] had remained victorious, we would possibly have remained the prisoners of our errors. Through being secularized, France was in danger of death."[88] This did not reflect the attitude of the Pope. In July 1940, he addressed a letter to the Church in France in which he expressed "the profound echo raised in Our fatherly heart by the calamity which has plunged France into mourning."[89] He said that he could not "remain apart from your misfortunes while throughout France the tears flow... abundantly."[90] He went on to relate his concern, assure the victims of his prayers, and promise them of better days to come. As others have noted, "From the very first day... the opposition between the orientation of the Vichy government and the thought of Pius XII was evident."[91]

---

In the summer of 1941, foreign Jews were rounded up and deported from Vichy with the full cooperation of Vichy officials.[92] Eventually, some forty thousand citizens were murdered and sixty thousand more were deported to concentration camps for "Gaullism, Marxism, or hostility to the regime." One hundred thousand others were deported on racial grounds.

The highest dignitaries of the Church immediately denounced these deportations and this treatment of Jewish people. Pope Pius XII "spoke with exceptional decisiveness against the over-valuation of blood and race."[93] On August 1, 1941, a Vatican Radio broadcast did the same:

> A great scandal is presently taking place and this scandal is the treatment suffered by the Jews; it is why I desire that a free voice, the voice of a priest, should be raised in protest. In Germany the Jews are killed, brutalized, tortured because they are victims bereft of defense. How can a Christian accept such deeds... these men are the sons of those who 2,000 years ago gave Christianity to the world.[94]

Continuing with this theme the following spring, a broadcast quoted Cardinal Van Roey, the primate of Belgium, condemning Nazi race theory.[95] When the first mass deportations began from the unoccupied zone in the summer of 1942, Archbishop (later Cardinal) Saliège lodged the first public episcopal protest.[96] He also drew up a memorable statement for the priests in his diocese to read from the pulpits and to be broadcast on Vatican Radio:

> Why does the right of asylum no longer exist in our churches? ... In our diocese, horrible scenes are taking place in the camps.... Jews are men. Jews are women. Not everything is permitted against them, against these men, these women, these fathers and mothers of families. They are part of mankind. They are our brothers like so many others. A Christian cannot forget it.[97]

Arthur Cardinal Hinsley of Great Britain took to the airwaves and informed Europe that in Poland alone the Nazis had massacred seven hundred thousand Jews.[98]

As soon as deportations began, Papal Nuncio Valerio Valeri contacted Pétain, head of the Vichy government, demanding that they be put to an end. Pétain said, "I hope that the Pope understands my attitude in these difficult circumstances." The nuncio replied, "It is precisely that which the Pope cannot understand."[99] Vatican Radio condemned "this scandal... the treatment of the Jews."[100]

Vatican Secretary of State Maglione told the French ambassador to the Vatican "that the conduct of the Vichy Government toward Jews and foreign refugees was a gross infraction"of the Vichy government's own principles, and was "irreconcilable with the religious feelings which Marshal Pétain had so often invoked in his speeches."[101] As reported by the *Tablet* (London), on July 10, 1942, Pope Pius XII "spoke with exceptional decisiveness against the over-valuation of blood and race."

Responding to the arrest of thirteen thousand Jewish Parisians in July 1942, the French bishops issued a joint protest:

> The mass arrest of the Jews last week and the ill-treatment to which they were subjected... has deeply shocked us. There were scenes of unspeakable horror when the deported parents were separated from their children. Our Christian conscience cries out in horror. In the name of humanity and Christian principles we demand the inalienable rights of all individuals. From the depths of our hearts we pray Catholics to express their sympathy for the immense injury to so many Jewish mothers.[102]

The text was delivered immediately to Pétain, and each bishop was charged with communicating it to his clergy. The *Jewish Chronicle* reported that "Catholic priests have taken a leading part in hiding hunted Jews, and sheltering the children of those who are under arrest or have been deported to Germany."[103]

Critic Daniel Goldhagen claimed that Pius XII "clearly failed to support" this protest. Actually, at his direction the protests were broadcast and discussed for several days on Vatican Radio.[104] Church teachings on the equality of all and the error of trying to make distinctions between Jews and Gentiles were broadcast into France, in French, on Vatican Radio. Cardinal Gerlier, who publicly condemned Nazi atrocities and the deportation of Jews, explicitly stated that he was obeying Pius XII's instructions to oppose anti-Semitism when he made these statements.[105]

In August 1942, Archbishop Jules Gérard Saliège, from Toulouse, sent a pastoral letter to be read in all churches of his diocese. It said: "There is a Christian morality that confers rights and imposes duties.... The Jews are our brothers. They belong to mankind. No Christian can dare forget that!"[106] At the request of Pius XII, Vatican Radio broadcast Saliège's letter twice and made comments on it for six consecutive days.[107] As the Vatican newspaper put it: "Saliège became a national hero, a symbol of spiritual resistance and courage."[108] (When the war ended, the American Jewish Committee gave him an award for saving so many Jews, and Pope Pius XII named him a cardinal.)[109]

Pius also instructed his nuncio to issue another protest and recommended that religious communities provide refuge to Jewish people.[110] On August 7, 1942, Nuncio Valeri sent a ciphered message to Maglione, reporting: "I have spoken quite frequently to the foreign minister... and with the head of state himself (Pétain) about this very sad problem." This was sent just a day after a *New York Times* headline proclaimed: "Pope Is Said to Plead for Jews Listed for Removal from France."[111] Three weeks later, a headline in the same paper told the sad story: "Vichy Seizes Jews; Pope Pius Ignored."[112]

On September 10, 1942, D'Arcy Osborne, the British minister to the Vatican, cabled Anthony Eden, the British foreign secretary, detailing the Italian Fascist press attacks and threats against the Church, which Osborne wrote were "a reproach for the Vatican's protest against the anti-Jewish policy of the Vichy Government."[113] Two days later, Osborne telegrammed the British Foreign Office: "The Pope today confirmed to me that the Nuncio at Vichy had protested against persecution of Jews in France."[114] In fact, the American press reported that the Pope protested to the Vichy government three times during August 1942.[115] The result of the protests, unfortunately, was that they angered the new Vichy leader Pierre Laval, and he reaffirmed his decision to cooperate in the deportation of all non-French Jews to Germany.

The *Canadian Jewish Chronicle* ran the following headline on September 4, 1942: "Laval Spurns Pope — 25,000 Jews in France Arrested for Deportation."[116] In an editorial dated August 28, 1942, the *California Jewish Voice* called Pius "a spiritual ally" because he "linked his name with the multitude who are horrified by the Axis inhumanity." In a lead editorial, the *London Jewish Chronicle* said that the Vatican was due a "word of sincere and earnest appreciation" from Jews for its "intervention in Berlin and Vichy."[117] The editorial went on to say that the rebuke that Pius received from "Laval and his Nazi master" was "an implied tribute to the moral steadfastness of a great spiritual power, bravely doing its manifest spiritual duty."

According to the *Geneva Tribune* of September 8, 1942, Vichy ordered the French press to ignore Pope Pius XII's protests concerning the deportation of Jews.[118] Despite this order, word spread rapidly due to the courageous attitude of the Catholic clergy. In fact, just weeks later, the *New York Times* reported: "The moral prestige of Marshal Pétain is undermined by the mounting resistance of French Bishops and clergy to Vichy's surrender to German pressure notably expressed in resistance to the deportation of refugee Jews."[119] In early 1943, the bishop of Clermont ordered that a joint letter of the French episcopate defending "the human person," which had been inspired by the deportation of Jews, be read at all Masses.[120]

———

On September 14, 1942, the Vatican Radio theme was "Let us not betray our brothers." There was no doubt about who was to be considered a brother: "Jesus Christ ... first turns his attention to the flock of his own beloved Jewish people, to all those of his race who helped to save the world, among them his mother, his friends, his disciples. He gazed at the Jewish people with an everlasting love...."[121] Similarly, a broadcast from a couple of months earlier asked the anti-Semites:

> Why this vicious campaign, why always lash out against the harmless and not the ferocious? Really did the former do everything? Did he carry the weight of Israel's crimes? Are you sure? Of course not. You know that it isn't. And yet you lie and mislead your fellow man.[122]

When Lord Bishop Bruno de Solages from Montauban spoke up against the deportation of Jews, he made clear that he considered Vatican Radio to be the authentic voice of the Pope. That helps account for all of the rescuers who have cited Vatican Radio as one of their inspirations. Leaders of the French resistance even produced an underground newsletter, *La Voix du Vatican*, which reprinted transcripts from these broadcasts.[123]

French Catholic philosopher Jacques Maritain was in the United States in 1940 when his nation fell to Germany. That fall he wrote the book *France My Country, Through the Disaster* to counter the collaborationist propaganda in Vichy France. The U.S. Army Air Corps airdropped copies into Vichy, and it became the "first breviary of the Resistance."[124] He continued to write and speak against the Nazis and the Holocaust. As he explained in a Vatican Radio broadcast:

> What the world gives us to contemplate in the great racist prosecutions is that Israel is itself engaged on the way of Calvary, because it activates and stimulates earthly history, and because the slave masters do not pardon it for the demands it and its Christ have introduced into the heart of the temporal life of the world, for they will always say No to tyranny and to the triumph of injustice.[125]

Following the war, Maritain moved to Rome, as France's envoy to the Holy See.

As it did in other nations, the Church in France helped produce thousands of false documents that were used to deceive the Germans, and special efforts were made to protect Jewish children. Working with Jewish groups, French Christian organizations saved thousands of Jewish children in France.[126] At one point, a group of Protestant and Catholic social workers broke into a prison in Lyon and "kidnapped" ninety children who were being held with their parents for deportation. The parents were deported the next day. The children were sheltered in religious institutions under the protection of Pierre Cardinal Gerlier with the assistance of Father Pierre Chaillet, a member of the cardinal's staff. When Gerlier refused a Nazi order to surrender the children, Vichy leaders had Chaillet arrested. He served three months in a "mental hospital" before being released.[127]

Despite all of these efforts, critics routinely turn to a document known as the "Bérard Report" in order to paint the Vatican in a bad light. This matter began in August 1941, when Marshal Pétain asked the French ambassador to the Holy See, Léon Bérard, to ascertain the views of the Vatican on the collaborationist Vichy government's anti-Jewish legislation.

Henri Cardinal de Lubac, who lived through the German occupation of France, has two chapters about the Bérard Report in his book, *Christian Resistance to Anti-Semitism: Memories from 1940-1944*. Lubac explains that Pétain was being pressured by the Catholic hierarchy in France to abandon the anti-Semitic laws, and he wanted a statement from the Vatican that he could use to silence French Catholics. Thus, in a letter dated August 7, 1941, he asked for a report on the Holy See's attitude toward the new legislation.

The response came in a long memorandum from Ambassador Bérard. Rather than providing an authoritative source, Bérard cited "someone in authority" and gave a long justification for that position, based on Church history, including the writings of St. Thomas Aquinas. The key phrase is as follows: "As someone in authority said to me at the Vatican, it will start no quarrel with us over the statute for the Jews." Bérard assured Pétain that "the Holy See had no hostile intention." He claimed that the Vatican did not wish to "seek a quarrel."[128]

It is, of course, highly suspect for a diplomatic report to go into historic Church teaching rather than relying on diplomatic sources. Lubac said that "[i]f the ambassador had been able to obtain from any personage at all in Rome a reply that was even slightly clear and favorable, he would not have taken so much trouble to 'bring together the elements of a well-founded and complete report' obviously fabricated by himself or by one of his friends."[129] Moreover, the historic discussion in the memo omitted many more recent authoritative statements against anti-Semitism. Those authoritative statements, of course, would not have served Pétain's purposes.

As others have concluded, Bérard drafted this memorandum to meet Pétain's needs, not to reflect the Church's actual position. Bérard's report was dated September 2, 1941. On September 13, at a reception at the Parc Hotel in Vichy,

Nuncio Valeri criticized the anti-Semitic legislation and said that the Holy See had made clear its opposition to racism. Citing Bérard's report, Pétain suggested that the nuncio might not be in agreement with his superiors.

Valeri immediately wrote the Vatican's secretary of state, Cardinal Maglione, and asked for more information. Then, around September 26, Valeri called upon Pétain and was given a copy of the Bérard Report. In exchange, the nuncio gave Pétain a note concerning the "grave harms that, from a religious perspective, can result from the legislation now in force."

On September 30, Valeri wrote to Maglione, enclosing a copy of the Bérard Report. He explained the conversation at the Parc Hotel as follows: "I reacted quite vigorously. . . . I stated that the Holy See had already expressed itself regarding racism, which is at the bottom of every measure taken against the Jews."

Maglione wrote back to Valeri on October 31, explaining that Bérard had made exaggerations and incorrect deductions about Vatican policy. He fully approved of the note that Valeri had given to Pétain and encouraged Valeri to continue efforts to discourage the rigid application of the anti-Semitic laws. Valeri then drafted a note of protest that he sent to Pétain.[130]

As such, what we know for certain is the following: if Pétain *ever* thought that Bérard's account was legitimate, the Vatican's true position was immediately brought to his attention, before the commencement of mass deportations. As Lubac concludes, "[F]rom the very first day . . . the opposition between the orientation of the Vichy government and the thought of Pius XII was patent."[131]

The archbishop of Lyons, Cardinal Gerlier, who had earlier welcomed the Vichy government, now wrote protests that were read from pulpits throughout his diocese and were broadcast throughout the nation despite Nazi censorship.[132] The cardinal declared that the French state and church were now divided, and he refused to bless those who volunteered to fight for Vichy forces or to say Mass for those who died fighting for that cause.[133]

Rabbi Stephen S. Wise, perhaps the leading Jewish voice in the United States during the war, wrote in 1942:

> It appears to be more than rumor that His Holiness Pope Pius XII urgently appealed through the papal nuncio to the Vichy government to put an end to deportations from France, and the appeal of the Pope is said to have been reinforced by petition and protest from the Cardinal Archbishops of Paris and Lyons. . . . If such papal intervention be factual, then Pius XII follows the high example set by his saintly predecessor, whose word in reprobation of anti-Semitism, "spiritually we are all Semites," will never fade out of the memory of the people which does not forget but forgives.[134]

Late in June 1943, Vatican Radio warned the French people that "he who makes a distinction between Jews and other men is unfaithful to God and is in conflict with God's commands."[135]

A statement by Bishop Pierre Théas of Montauban, read in all the churches of his diocese, was representative of the attitude of the Catholic leadership:

> Hereby I make known to the world the indignant protest of Christian conscience, and I proclaim that all men, whether Aryan or non-Aryan, are brothers because they were created by the same God; and that all men, whatever their race or religion, have a right to respect from individuals as well as from States.[136]

Many Catholic priests sheltered Jews and urged their parishioners to do the same. When the Nazis discovered this, the priests were arrested for their efforts (and typically sent to concentration camps where many died).[137]

The widespread bravery of Catholic priests in their opposition to Nazism was illustrated in a wartime book written by a member of the French underground.[138] Because the book *Paris-Underground* came out in 1943, the author changed the names of the people involved, but she attested that the basic facts were "a matter of record."[139] One of the important characters was a Catholic priest, Father Christian. According to the book, he was very involved in underground work, including passing information to Britain and hiding refugees. At one point, he was found by a German officer in a private home where he had been hiding British soldiers. He invented a cover story, and the Nazi believed it. The officer then offered the priest a ride in his car.

"Thank you, Captain," Father Christian answered, "but I am afraid my parishioners would not understand if they saw me arrive with a German officer. You realize, of course, how they feel."

"Yes, indeed," said Captain Weber stiffly. "They do not yet understand that we have come to save their country from degradation."[140]

Not only did the priest refuse to ride with the Nazi officer, but the officer also understood why the ride was declined: French people knew that the Catholic Church was opposed to what the Nazis were doing.[141]

---

Father Pierre-Marie Benoît of Marseilles, a Capuchin priest, turned his monastery into a veritable rescue factory. Inside, he and his workers printed passports, identification cards, certificates of baptism, and employers' recommendation letters for Jews.[142] Outside, he helped smuggle many Jewish people into Spain and Switzerland. Eventually, he earned the name "Father of the Jews."[143]

In July 1943, Father Benoît was summoned to Rome by the Italian government. He took advantage of the trip to present a plan to Pius XII. After thanking the Holy Father for his work on behalf of French Jews and forwarding "the appreciation they feel toward the Catholic Church for the charity it has shown them," he proposed a plan to offer more help. Benoît wanted the Church to gather information on the whereabouts of Jews deported from France, particularly to Auschwitz; obtain more humane treatment of Jews in French concentration camps; work for the repatriation of Spanish Jews who were residing in

France; and transfer some fifty thousand French Jews to North Africa, where they would be safe. The Pope readily agreed, and helped Benoît obtain pledges of support from Britain, the United States, and Jewish organizations in the Allied nations.

Unfortunately, Benoît's project failed. With the surrender of the Italian forces to the Allies, German troops swept into the Italian zone of France, ruining any chance for cooperation with occupying forces. That was not, however, the end of his efforts. As thousands of Jews fled across the Alps to safer countries, Benoît again approached the Vatican. With its help, he convinced the Spanish government to authorize its consuls in France to issue entry permits to all Jews who could prove Spanish nationality. In case of doubt about nationality, the final decision rested with Benoît.[144]

Later in the war, Benoît (operating under the name of Padre Benedetto) went to the International College of Capuchins in Rome, where he worked with a Jewish rescue organization, the Delegation for Assistance to Jewish Emigrants (DELASEM). Beginning in April 1944, DELASEM operated from its headquarters in Benoît's residence, and he helped that organization keep in touch with the International Red Cross, the Pontifical Relief Commission, the Italian police, and other civil authorities. Benoît and others in Rome helped DELASEM manufacture false documents and establish contact with sympathetic Italian, Swiss, Hungarian, French, and Romanian officials. After the war, he received an award from the Italian Jewish Union for his work in protecting about one thousand Jews in Rome.[145]

---

In 1942, French forces in North Africa disregarded orders from Vichy and sided with Allied forces led by General Dwight D. Eisenhower, thus joining in the struggle against the Axis. This led to the German occupation of the whole of France in November 1942. The Vichy government was forced by the German authorities to move first to eastern France and finally, as virtual captives, into Germany.[146] In the face of the onslaught, the Vichy regime finally disintegrated.[147]

Even before the liberation of Paris in August 1944, Charles de Gaulle was named president of the new provisional government of France (after having served as commander-in-chief of the Free French forces). On May 29, 1944, he sent a handwritten note to Pope Pius XII:

Dear Holy Father:

Placed at the head of the French Republic's provisional government, I am happy to bring Your Holiness assurances of our people's filial respect for and their attachment to the Apostolic See.

The trial endured by France for many years now, the suffering of each of its children, have been lessened by the witness of your fatherly affection. We foresee an end to the conflict.... In accord with what you have taught us, we believe that the most underprivileged deserve our greatest care....We are resolved to save [the French people], and we very much hope to do so while benefiting from the special kindness that Your Holiness indeed wishes to extend to France.

May Your Holiness deign to bless our undertakings as well as the faith of the French people whose witness I place at Your feet.[148]

In June 1944, de Gaulle visited Vatican City for a meeting with the Pope to discuss the future of Europe, France, Germany, and Italy. The Vatican recognized that Vichy would soon disappear, and de Gaulle was treated as the head of the French government (resulting in a protest from the ambassador from Vichy).[149] As de Gaulle later described it:

The Holy Father received me. Under the kindness of the welcome and the simplicity of the moment, I was grasped by how sensible and powerful was his thinking. Pius XII judges everything from a perspective that surpasses human beings, their undertakings and their quarrels.... This is why the Pastor had made the church a domain reserved to himself personally and where he displays the gifts of authority, of influence, of the eloquence given him by God. Pious, compassionate, political — such does this pontiff and sovereign appear to me because of the respect that he inspires in me.[150]

De Gaulle returned to a liberated Paris in late August 1944. As part of the new government's procedures, all diplomats who had represented their countries to the Vichy government, including Vatican nuncio Bishop Valerio Valeri, were expelled.[151] De Gaulle, however, made it clear that he appreciated the nuncio and the Holy See's efforts during the occupation, going so far as to grant Valeri an audience.[152] De Gaulle informed the former nuncio that he was aware of all the good things that he had done for France and that he regretted the nuncio's departure, which was "solely due to events that unfolded during these past years."[153] He awarded Valeri the Grand Cross of the Legion of Honor and had military honors paid to the departing diplomat.[154] Despite sending Valeri home, de Gaulle had no desire to sever relations with the Holy See.[155] Valeri was replaced by Pius XII's personal choice, Archbishop Angelo Roncalli, the future Pope John XXIII.[156]

As war spread throughout Europe, the Pope became especially concerned about protecting his people and his nation — the Church and Vatican City. During the early months of the war, Mussolini remained neutral, but it was clear that he was contemplating Italy's entrance into the war.

On April 19, 1940, Roosevelt's envoy Myron Taylor was sent from his residence in Florence to Vatican City to discuss ways to keep Mussolini out of the war. Taylor asked about a presidential letter to Mussolini and suggested that Pius might also play a role. He gave Maglione two questions and waited in Rome for an answer from the Pope. The following day, Taylor cabled the response back to the United States: Yes, the president should immediately send a message to Mussolini, and yes, the Pope would undertake a parallel endeavor. The Pope, however, noted that his efforts and those of President Roosevelt should remain independent and not appear to be a coordinated action.[157]

On April 24, Pius sent a message to Mussolini urging that Italy be kept out of the war.[158] Unfortunately, the joint efforts of the president and the Pope could not stop expansion of the war.[159] On June 10, 1940, Italy declared war on France and Great Britain and invaded southern France. Speaking of Italy, President Roosevelt said: "The hand that held the dagger, has stuck it into the back of its neighbor."[160] As others have written: "The same dagger pierced the very heart of Pius XII."[161] Citing "the almost incredible events of the past two weeks," President Roosevelt asked Congress for more than a billion dollars in additional defense appropriations. He also called for the annual production of 50,000 warplanes.[162]

Several Italian bishops sided with their nation and rallied around Mussolini, but Vatican Radio came out strongly against the aggression. Axis propaganda, however, made it appear that the Pope supported Italy's aggression. As a Protestant correspondent wrote of this matter during the war:

> The Pope who had strained every nerve to bring peace had become the subject of Axis machination. It was true that the Nazis hated the Pope because of his condemnation of their racial, military and humanitarian policies. He had also condemned them for violating treaties. But in Italy, he had cherished a hope for neutrality for Italy's own sake. The former expressions of regard for the Pope now changed to vicious attacks. The Pontiff was forced to issue a rebuttal.
>
> "An untruthful press," he said, "is no less murderous than armoured cars."[163]

Three days after Italy's entrance into the war, Pius XII issued the encyclical *Saeculo Exeunte Octavo* (on the independence of Portugal). In it, he again emphasized his vision of the Church's role during the war:

> Following in the footsteps of Him who "went about doing good and healing" and obeying the command of Him who said, "heal the sick" and "make disciples of all nations," the missionary not only speaks learnedly and wisely of the Kingdom of God, but also attempts to heal bodies infected with disease and misery.[164]

The provisions of the Lateran Treaty were supposed to assure the freedom and neutrality of the Vatican, but the war would not be kept out of Rome. Pius XII gave up his annual vacations during the war, abandoning his summer home so that he could stay in Vatican City.[165]

When his efforts to keep Italy out of the war failed, Pius next sought assurances from both sides that the Vatican's neutrality would be respected. Since Italy was allied with Germany, one of the Pope's first concerns was securing a promise that Allied forces would not bomb Rome.[166] Because Axis powers stored great quantities of munitions in Rome, it was a likely Allied target. There were also many important military targets on the outskirts of Rome, including three airfields and a munitions plant. As such, the Allies promised to respect the Vatican's neutrality, but did not promise to avoid Rome altogether.[167] Germany was more certain in its pledge to try to avoid damaging Italian cities.[168] Of course, there would have been little reason for Germany to plan an attack on Italy early in the war. (Later, German forces would occupy and ultimately threaten to raze the city.)

During the war, the Vatican provided sanctuary to Jews, German deserters, Poles conscripted by the German army, anti-Fascist Italians, and diplomats from nations at war with Italy. Before Italy's entry into the war, many European Jews fled to that nation. After it got involved in the war and Jews were put at risk, Pope Pius XII sent instructions to St. Raphael Verein, a Catholic organization that had long been active in helping emigrants leave Europe for the New World. He told the organization to give aid to Jewish refugees who had come to Italy from Austria, Poland, Hungary and other nations. Before long St. Raphael Verein had a very efficient program in place. With the German occupation, open operations became impossible. (The last plane carrying Jewish refugees left Rome on September 8, 1943.) St. Raphael Verein then turned to the task of assigning the Jews left behind to hiding places. By 1945, this organization had given assistance to some twenty-five thousand Jews.[169]

All of this resistance work made the Vatican a likely target for the German military. In fact, President Roosevelt wrote Pius and told him that British aircraft and weapons captured by Axis powers were being saved for the purpose of attacking the Vatican while placing the responsibility on the Allies.[170] All Vatican apartments were fitted with heavy curtains for blackouts. The Vatican built several air-raid shelters as well as a steel armored room to protect rare books and manuscripts. Vatican firemen made inspections each night. Air-raid sirens went off several times a day, and the Vatican had many blackouts. These precautions paid off when bombs did fall on the Vatican later in the war.[171] (Pius refused to enter the shelters even during bombings.)

Allied diplomats in Italy, including the ambassadors from France, Great Britain, Poland, and Belgium, all moved into Vatican City after Italy declared war. German intelligence suspected that the Allies used the Vatican as a secure base for espionage. In order to avoid a breach of neutrality, the diplomats were forbidden from having political discussions in public, their mail was read, their phone calls were monitored, they could not receive visitors without permission, and they were not permitted to leave Vatican City. Interestingly, in June 1944, when Italy threw in with the Allies, the German ambassador to Italy moved into the Vatican, as the French, British, Polish, and Belgian representatives returned to their embassies in Rome.[172]

The Vatican was an important vehicle for uncensored information during the war. *L'Osservatore Romano*, the official Vatican newspaper, became the most widely read source of news in Italy. It had a circulation of about 20,000 before the war, but it increased to about 150,000 by 1940, and priests often read it from the pulpit.[173] Fascist persecution of those who purchased it resulted in circulation dropping back down to around 10,000 later in the war.[174] The newspaper was denounced by the Nazis and the Fascists, who charged that it was the "evident mouthpiece of the Jews," that its primary readers were Jews and Masons, and that it, like the Vatican, had "joined the cause of the Allies."[175]

While neither the Vatican newspaper nor the radio broadcasts were completely shut down by the Nazis, L'Osservatore Romano was often confiscated and radio broadcasts were frequently jammed.[176] Both were regularly misquoted. When Vatican Radio engaged in counterpropaganda, the Nazis sometimes made threats against the Vatican. Nonetheless, the Vatican press played a very important role throughout the war.[177]

———

In addition to using Vatican Radio and L'Osservatore Romano to spread the truth about the Nazis, Pope Pius XII played an interesting role in the publication of a book in 1940. As discussed earlier, in late 1939 and early 1940, Dr. Josef Müller carried messages back and forth from anti-Hitler conspirators to the Pope.[178] This included information regarding a proposed coup and German military movements. Pius forwarded this information to the Western governments.[179]

The Nazis, of course, realized the position of the Catholic Church. Gestapo spies observed sermons and reported back to Nazi officials.[180] They suppressed Catholic books for containing pro-Jewish messages.[181] Members of the "German Faith Movement," who had the backing of the Nazi Party, called the Catholic Church satanic, dangerous, and fraudulent.[182] Jesus was dismissed as a "Jewish Reformer," and Hitler was declared to be the one true Lord.[183]

Pius helped smuggle to London several documents that were published in The Persecution of the Catholic Church in the Third Reich. This book is a collection of protests, reports, and accounts that demonstrate the abuse suffered by the Church at the hands of the National Socialists throughout the 1930s. To review these reports is to wonder how German Catholic leaders were able to stand as firmly against the National Socialists as they did. If Pius had any lingering doubts about the relationship between Hitler's followers and the Church in Germany, this information cleared them up.[184] The Pope's efforts to ensure that this information was made known in England, a nation that was actively engaged in war with Germany, is a clear signal of his true sympathies.

———

In September 1940, Hitler traveled to the French town of Hendaye to meet with the Spanish leader General Francisco Franco. Hitler wanted Spain to enter the war, and he offered Franco arms, raw materials, and colonies. Spain, however, had not yet recovered from its civil war; it did not need a new foreign one.

Besides, Franco's revolution had been against Communism. How could he now side with Hitler, who was cooperating with the Soviet Union? Pius also urged his bishops in Spain to use their influence to try to keep Spain out of the war.[185] Hitler did not give up easily, but Franco would not budge. Hitler ended up ranting about Franco and his "Jesuit swine" foreign minister.[186] (Later in the war, Franco opened Spain's border to Jews who were fleeing Nazi persecution. Pope Pius XII was able to help thousands reach safety in Spain.)[187]

In November, Hitler met with Vyacheslav Molotov, the Soviet foreign minister (and nominal premier), in Berlin. This resulted in the Soviets proposing a "border and commercial" accord with the Axis powers, a highly ironic result given that the supposed purpose of the Axis was to stop the spread of Communism. (Mussolini, though Hitler's truest ally, was unable to prevent him from signing the short-lived treaty.)[188] The two nations had already signed a nonaggression pact and divided Poland, and they had signed a series of commercial agreements, so this additional step seemed quite reasonable, even if it was hard to reach the precise language of agreement. Hitler, however, was primarily concerned with securing his eastern front until he was ready to attack. Like many others, the Soviets reached an accord with Hitler only to find that he never intended to carry through with his promises.

In December, *L'Osservatore Romano* published an article in response to a brochure that was then being circulated in Italy. The brochure, entitled *Germans and the Catholic Faith in Poland*, claimed that the German authorities had not interfered with religious activities in Poland, that church buildings remained open, and that the Nazis had even assisted in the building of some new Church buildings.[189] The Vatican newspaper, however, pointed out that at least one bishop had been exiled, numerous clergy had been imprisoned, the religious press (including publishers of prayer books) had been restricted, secondary schools and universities had been shut down, Poles were either prohibited from or limited in the times and places where they could enter churches, and even *German* Catholics in some areas were completely prohibited from taking part in religious services.[190] Clearly, the Vatican was incensed with the treatment of the Church by the Nazis. The cover of *Time* magazine, dated December 23, 1940, said: "Martyr of 1940; In Germany only the cross has not bowed to the swastika."[191]

On Christmas Eve, Pius XII took to the radio to condemn once more the evils in the world. He said:

> We find ourselves faced with actions as irreconcilable with the prescriptions of positive international law as they are with natural law and even with the most elementary sentiments of humanity, actions which show us into what a polluted, chaotic circle the juridical sense, led astray by purely utilitarian considerations, can sink. It is in this category that we place: premeditated aggression against a small, hardworking and peaceful people under the pretext of a nonexistent danger that they neither intended nor were capable of; atrocities...; illegal use

of destructive force even against noncombatants, fugitives, the elderly and children; a contempt for human dignity, freedom and life that gives rise to actions that cry out for vengeance before God; anti-Christian and even atheistic propaganda.... The memory of the short-lived duration of negotiations and agreements in the end paralyzes any effort capable of leading to a peaceful solution.[192]

There is no doubt that these were references to Hitler's aggression.[193] Commenting on the address, an editorial in the *New York Times*, dated December 25, 1940, stated that Pius XII's "moral order" "in a word, is in complete contradiction to Hitler's Order."[194] Hitler, however, prevented this message from reaching people in occupied areas.[195]

In Poland, German troops began herding Warsaw's Jewish population into an area behind an eight-foot wall in the city's ghetto district. Nazis claimed that this would give the Jews a new life and also protect Poles from diseases spread by war. In reality, this was simply preparation for the Final Solution. The priests in all of Warsaw's Catholic churches exhorted their parishioners to bury their prejudice against Jews and to beware of the "Jew-hatred preached by their common enemy."[196]

# ELEVEN

# 1941 and New Enemies

Nazi ideology and German forces were very tough on the Catholic Church. As Pope Pius XII wrote in February 1941, in a letter to the bishop of Limburg (the Netherlands): "The statements about the 'new order' for the Church that have been propagated by a certain party show that it has as its aim the equivalent of a death sentence for the Catholic Church in Germany."[1] In his Easter message of April 13, 1941, broadcast from the Vatican, the Pope again called for peace and just treatment of the people in all of the occupied nations.[2] He began with a profession of his belief in prayer:

> In this tempest of misfortunes and perils, of afflictions and fears, our most powerful and safest haven of trust and peace is found in prayer to God, in whose hands rests not only the destiny of men but also the outcome of their most obdurate dissensions.
>
> * * *
>
> Yes, let us pray for early peace. Let us pray for universal peace; not for peace based upon the oppression and destruction of peoples but peace which, while guaranteeing the honor of all nations, will satisfy their vital needs and insure the legitimate rights of all.[3]

Importantly, he prayed not just for any peace, but "peace that will be just, in accordance with human and Christian norms."[4]

As he did throughout the war, the Pontiff expressed confidence in the ultimate success of prayer. "[U]nder the vigilant providence of God and armed only with prayer, exhortation and consolation, we shall persevere in our battle for peace in behalf of suffering humanity." He asked that "the blessings and comforts of heaven descend on all victims of this war." He then asked the occupying powers to respect the occupied nations:

> With all due esteem we ask the powers which occupy the foreign territories during this war to treat the population in these countries according to the voice of their conscience and their own sense of honor. Be just, humane and cautious. Do not impose on them burdens which you, in similar circumstances, would think unjust. The glory and the pride of prudent commanders is helpful charity; the treatment of the prisoners of war and of the population in the occupied countries is the safest criterion and a most definite characteristic of the height of civilization among persons and peoples. Remember that God may, perhaps,

bless or curse your own motherland according to your behavior toward those who fell the victims of your victory.[5]

Pius concluded by saying that "very dear" to him were all the victims: "children of the Church of Christ, those with faith in the Divine Savior, or at least in Our Father Who is in Heaven." In context, of course, that referred to Catholics, Protestants, and Jews.

Clearly this talk was directed at the Axis powers, particularly Germany.[6] In fact, German and Italian representatives criticized the Pope, the Gestapo confiscated printed copies of the remarks, and Goebbels vowed to silence Vatican Radio,[7] which the Nazis called the "Voice of the Pope."[8] Goebbels is noted to have remarked four days after the message that Vatican Radio, which broadcast the message, was more dangerous than a Communist transmitter and had to be silenced.[9]

British officials acknowledged that "the independent stand taken by the Vatican Radio is of the greatest importance to our propaganda generally and to our appeal to German Catholics in particular."[10] In May, Secretary of State Luigi Maglione revealed that special powers would be given to papal representatives around the world, in case the Pope would "not be able to communicate" with them.[11]

When the Catholic faithful were permitted to hear these broadcasts, they reacted accordingly. French priest-rescuer (and later cardinal) Henri de Lubac paid tribute to the Pope's radio station, describing the profound impact it had upon the French resistance.[12] Similarly, Michel Riquet, S.J., an ex-inmate of Dachau who was recognized for saving Jewish lives, stated: "Pius XII spoke; Pius XII condemned; Pius XII acted.... Throughout those years of horror, when we listened to Radio Vatican and to the Pope's messages, we felt in communion with the Pope in helping persecuted Jews and in fighting against Nazi violence."[13] Riquet repeated these sentiments in 1965, when he led a pilgrimage of French Catholics to Israel.[14]

British propagandists used Pope Pius XII's Easter statements for military purposes.[15] Rather than simply repeating the Vatican broadcast, British authorities "reinforced" and re-transmitted it from London, while giving the impression that it was coming from and on behalf of the Vatican. (More than once during the war, the Vatican had to warn people that statements being attributed to it — from both sides — were not valid.)[16] In addition, British intelligence put out the word that a Christian-oriented radio station that broadcast Allied propaganda into Germany was actually an arm of Vatican Radio.[17] This, of course, had at least the appearance of being a breach of the Vatican's promises and agreements it had made with Italy and Germany. It also put the Vatican in jeopardy without the Pope's consent.

Bishops in Poland reported that these broadcasts were causing the Nazis to increase the persecution of their victims, especially Catholics.[18] As a result, Pius directed that Vatican Radio be perfectly objective (meaning that most broadcasts avoided discussing Germany).[19] The British government, which lost a formidable source of propaganda, issued a protest to the Holy See:

> The sudden silence on a subject of imperative concern to Catholics can only be attributed to successful pressure on the Vatican by German authorities, and his majesty's government cannot but regard the decision of the Vatican to yield to this pressure as highly regrettable and inconsistent with the best interests of the Holy See and the Catholic Church. There can be no doubt that with the United States, the Allied cause will prevail and the Christian ideal triumph over pagan brutality. What then will be the feeling of the Catholics of the world if it may be said of their Church that, after at first standing courageously against Nazis paganism, it subsequently consented, by surrendering silence, the rights and the principles on which it is based and by which it lives?[20]

There were also some complaints filed by priests who had previously broadcast their sermons but were now prohibited from doing so.

The Vatican's response was threefold. First, Pope Pius assured the British minister to the Holy See, Sir D'Arcy Osborne, that there was no agreement between the Vatican and the Germans concerning future broadcasts. The Pope also, however, explained that he could not ignore the persecution of innocent Catholics that these broadcasts always seemed to prompt. Finally, Pius complained about the British use of his proclamations for propaganda purposes, to the detriment of Catholics in Germany.[21]

Despite these answers, there was some concern in the Vatican that the suspension of radio broadcasts might be seen as some sort of alignment with the Nazis. As such, the secretary of state prepared a long memorandum, which was personally reviewed and corrected by Pius XII, for distribution to the Holy See's representatives in France, Switzerland, Spain, Argentina, Brazil, and the United States. It pointed out that in those areas occupied by the Germans, Catholic schools and churches were closed, religious houses were invaded and searched, priests were arrested, bishops were kept away from the people, and religious teaching and worship was impeded in a thousand ways.[22] With this type of treatment being accorded Catholics in Nazi-occupied areas, and with a defiant attitude at the upper echelons of the Holy See, it is not surprising to find that by January, Vatican Radio was again broadcasting anti-Nazi messages.[23]

---

In June 1941, Hitler breached the nonaggression agreement he had signed two years earlier and invaded the Soviet Union to seek *lebensraum* ("living space") for the German people.[24] Hitler believed that Providence intended for Slavs (*Untermenschen*) to be servants of the godlike Aryans. (Medieval Latinists had used the word *sclavus* for both slaves and Slavs.)[25] In order to make conquered areas of Russia "fit" for German settlers, criminally convicted Jews, Poles,

Gypsies, Russians, and Ukrainians were not to receive normal sentences; they were to be executed.[26] Educated Slavs, like the clergy, were a potential threat and had to be eliminated.

Vyacheslav Molotov, the Soviet foreign minister, broadcast an address in which he said, "This war has been forced upon us, not by the German people, not by German workers, peasants and intellectuals, whose sufferings we well understand, but by the clique of bloodthirsty Fascist rulers of Germany who have enslaved Frenchmen, Czechs, Poles, Serbians, Norway, Belgium, Denmark, Holland, Greece and other nations."[27] Of course, none of the Nazis' earlier aggression seemed to matter to the Soviets until their nation was invaded.

Hitler said the attack was necessary to combat the Russian-British threat to Europe and called it the biggest military attack in the history of the world. He wanted the Pope's blessing on the invasion, and some observers expected one.[28] Hitler claimed that it was a "crusade" into the godless Soviet Union.[29] (Monsignor Domenico Tardini, head of the Vatican foreign office and an outspoken opponent of Hitler, replied: "Nazism has conducted a veritable persecution against the church and continues to do so. Consequently the swastika is not the cross of a crusade.")[30]

Volunteer regiments of Frenchmen, Spaniards, Italians, Croatians, Hungarians, and Slovenians signed on to go with the German troops for the invasion. A sizable contingent of priests from the Vatican's Russian seminary in Rome also planned to accompany the German troops, with the hope of opening long-closed churches in the Soviet Union.[31] French Cardinal Baudrillart traveled to Rome to ask a papal blessing for French volunteer soldiers. The cardinal said their task was "to free the Russian people." Pius, however, demanded an immediate withdrawal of the request for a blessing and ordered Cardinal Baudrillart to make no further public statements on the war whatsoever.[32]

Minutes from the British high command, dated September 10, 1941, state: "His Holiness is heart and soul with us in the struggle against Nazism, and his attitude as regards the 'anti-Bolshevist Crusade' leaves nothing to be desired."[33] In an address he gave in late June 1941, Pius denounced the suffering of "old people, women, children, the most innocent, the most peaceful, the most defenseless."[34] He also spoke of religious persecutions "which the very concern for those who suffer does not allow one to reveal in all their painful and moving detail."[35]

Mussolini was furious at the Pope's refusal to support the Axis.[36] In Berlin, a report on intercepted Vatican documents said that "the pro-Polish attitude of the Pope and of his secretary of state are clearly seen — an attitude which has been at least insinuated in his public declarations."[37] An intelligence report on Pius XII's June 21 address stated: "A few days after the outbreak of Germany's struggle against the Bolsheviks, the Pope had not one word to say against them. This fact alone shows clearly that his words in this allocation do not refer to Bolshevism but are directed exclusively against National Socialist Germany."[38] The British representative to the Vatican later sought and obtained permission from Pius to report on the Pope's refusal to support Hitler's "crusade." That the Pope had maintained neutrality even against atheistic Bolshevism, it was thought, "would make an excellent impression in London."[39]

The Nazi leadership continued to feel nothing but hostility toward Christianity and the Catholic Church. In a report written to top Nazi and provincial leaders in June 1941, Martin Bormann wrote:

> The ideas of National Socialism and of Christianity are irreconcilable. The Christian churches are built on the ignorance of their believers.... National Socialism rests on scientific foundations.... That is why the German emperors' struggles against the popes always failed.... Now, for the first time in German history, it is the Führer who holds the spiritual reins firmly in his hands [and] the people must be progressively alienated from the churches and the clergy. The churches must never recover the least influence over the national destiny. Their power must be broken forever.[40]

Hitler was quoted saying: "After the war... every Catholic State will have to elect its own pope, and the Christian-Jewish past is now approaching its end."[41]

In public prayers on August 29, 1941, the anti-Nazi provost of Berlin's cathedral, Bernhard Lichtenberg, offended the Nazis by praying for persecuted Jews, prisoners of war, and all the victims of the war.[42] The nuncio in Germany, Archbishop Cesare Orsenigo stated, in his report dated November 12, 1941, that this led to the priest's arrest.[43] In October, Lichtenberg was assigned for deportation to Dachau, and he died on the way there.[44]

----

With German tanks advancing, Stalin turned to British Prime Minister Winston Churchill for help. In a radio address to his people little more than a week after the German invasion, Stalin praised Churchill and other heroes of the West, without mentioning typical Soviet heroes. He reopened the churches and called up fifteen million men for "The Great Patriotic War." Churchill said that Britain would help the Soviets in any way possible to obliterate the "bloodthirsty guttersnipe." He stated his "one single, irrevocable purpose... to destroy Hitler and every vestige of the Nazi regime."[45] The two nations signed a "Mutual Assistance" agreement on July 12, 1941.

Despite their history of abuse and oppression, the Soviets were invited to sign the Atlantic Charter.[46] That document's first point declared that signatories "seek no aggrandizement, territorial or other." It did not matter that the Soviet Union had already annexed the Baltic states, divided Poland with Hitler, and had been expelled from the League of Nations for its invasion of Finland; the Soviets were to be full-fledged partners with the Western Allies.

Pius XII now found himself in the awkward position of privately siding with atheistic Soviet Russia, overwhelmingly Protestant Britain (with its vast, mainly non-Christian empire), and the predominantly Protestant United States, against

Hitler's largely Catholic "Fortress Europe."[47] Moreover, the Pope's predecessor, Pius XI, had written in *Divini Redemptoris* (of the Divine Redeemer) that no one who wanted to save Christian civilization could collaborate with Communists.[48] Yet, here it was: the Allies had made the Soviet Union a full partner in the war against Hitler's National Socialism.

The Pontiff's preference for the Allies over the Axis is reflected in a top secret message, dated September 17, 1941, to the German Foreign Ministry. In it was a translation of the Italian ambassador to the Holy See's report on a meeting that he had had with the Pope a day earlier. When Ambassador Attolico brought up the subject of the Soviet Union, Pius cut him off:

> But if I should talk of Bolshevism — and I would be fully prepared to do so, continued Pius XII, should I then say nothing about Nazism? The situation in Germany, he told me, has become infinitely worse since the day of his departure from Berlin. Even if the *Führer* has ordered the "suspension" of the persecutions, this does not mean that Christ has been readmitted to the schools from which He was removed... or that the German children will no longer be made to recite that parody of the Our Father in which they thank Hitler for their daily bread.[49]

The secret message went on to quote a serious question that Pope Pius asked of the Italian ambassador:

> I was told long ago that in Germany they already had it in mind to do away with the Vatican, because there was no place for it in the new European order, etc., etc. Now, I am assured that even in his meeting with Mussolini the *Führer* stated that it was necessary to "put an end to" the Vatican. Is that true?[50]

The Italian ambassador issued a firm denial and said that this "seemed to make the Pope feel good and almost relieved, thus showing how much his conviction, I might say almost his nightmarish fear, of new and more ruthless persecutions weighs on his mind...."[51] The ambassador went on to explain that the Pope thought that he might one day "be driven out of Rome. But — mark me — he does not speak it out of fear."[52]

The United States was officially still neutral, but the lend-lease trade law essentially extended credit to Great Britain. American Catholics were very concerned about extending a similar benefit to a Communist nation.[53] President Roosevelt wanted Pope Pius to help change their minds. On September 30, 1941, he wrote to Pius:

> In so far as I am informed, churches in Russia are open. I believe there is a real possibility that Russia may as a result of the present conflict recognize freedom of religion in Russia, although, of course, without recognition of any official intervention on the part of any church in education or political matters within Russia. I feel that if this can be accomplished it will put the possibility of the restoration of real religious liberty in Russia on a much better footing than religious freedom is in Germany today.[54]

The Americans summoned the apostolic delegation in Washington to the White House to offer assurances that the United States was only doing what was necessary to fight the Nazis and was not changing in its fundamental distrust of Communism.[55] Roosevelt's representative to the Pope, Myron Taylor, was sent back to Rome. He pleaded with the Pontiff to clarify (if not change) Catholic teaching regarding the propriety of cooperating with the Soviets, especially as that teaching was reflected in Pius XI's encyclical *Divini Redemptoris*.[56]

Taylor argued that in order to avoid a deep split among Catholics in the United States, the Holy See would have to come out with a statement on *Divini Redemptoris*.[57] Cardinal Maglione answered that "[t]he Holy See has condemned and still condemns Communism. It had never uttered a word, and it cannot do so, against the Russian people. It has also condemned Nazism."[58] Maglione did not think that the Pope needed to further clarify this matter, but he promised to assure the apostolic delegation in Washington that they did not need to worry about supporting Roosevelt in the war against Hitler.[59]

In a letter dated September 20, 1941, the Vatican Secretariat of State explained to the apostolic delegate in Washington, Archbishop Amleto Cicognani, that in *Divini Redemptoris* Pius XI had condemned atheistic Communism, but "not the Russian people to whom, in the same document, he sent expressions of good wishes and compassion."[60] The apostolic delegate was instructed to have one or more respected bishop make the following public statement:

> The attitude of the Holy See with regard to the Communist doctrine is and remains what it always has been. However, the Holy See has nothing whatsoever against the Russian people. It is now the Russian people which has been unjustly attacked and is suffering greatly as a consequence of this unjust war. This being so, Catholics should not have any objections to collaborating with the United States government to help the Russian people by giving the latter such help as they need.[61]

The apostolic delegate appointed the auxiliary bishop of Cleveland, Michael Ready, to head up the campaign to clarify *Divini Redemptoris* in the United States.[62]

This understanding of *Divini Redemptoris* fit well with the American position that Soviet dictator Joseph Stalin was opening the way to religious freedom in Russia and helped dissolve American Catholic opposition to extending the lend-lease program.[63] In fact, during the rest of the war, religious activity in the Soviet Union significantly increased.[64] After the war, in an address to the College of Cardinals and the diplomatic corps, Pius XII said: "We took special care, notwithstanding certain tendentious pressures, not to let fall from our lips or from our pen one single word, one single sign of approval or encouragement of the war against Russia in 1941."[65]

Many prominent Catholic Americans were happy to announce their support of providing aid to Russia (and Soviet propaganda forces were used to amplify their voices). They included: Colonel William J. Donovan, Father John A. Ryan of Catholic University, and Michael Williams, editor of *Commonweal*. Perhaps the most outspoken supporter of this support was Bishop Joseph P. Hurley of St. Augustine, Florida. In a radio address entitled "Papal Pronouncements and American Foreign Policy," Bishop Hurley explained:

> Crusade forsooth! Not God, but the enemy of God, wills it; its standard is not the Cross, but the swastika which a great Pontiff called "this foe of the Cross of Christ"; the rape of Poland is scarcely a recommendation for Christian knights; and the recluse of Berchtesgaden is badly cast for the role of Peter the Hermit.... America's attitude toward this new war should not be swayed by Nazi propaganda; it must be based on purely strategic considerations. The Nazi remains Enemy No. 1 of America and of the world.[66]

Hurley likened President Roosevelt's Catholic critics to little children: "We have suffered long from their tantrums.... Years ago they established the crank school of economics; latterly they have founded the tirade school of journalism; they are now engaged in popularizing the ostrich school of strategy."[67]

The position of most people in the Vatican (which was shared with the future president of the United States, Harry Truman)[68] was summed up by the assistant secretary of state, Monsignor Tardini, who said it was "one devil chasing out the other."[69] Camille M. Cianfarra, a correspondent for the *New York Times*, wrote that "the Vatican was hoping that the German-Soviet War would give the British Empire and the United States time to increase their military preparedness."[70] Winston Churchill might have been thinking of the Church's concerns when he said, "I have only one purpose, the destruction of Hitler.... If Hitler invaded Hell, I would make at least a favorable reference to the Devil in the House of Commons."[71]

Pius was well aware that the Soviet Union was capable of everything Hitler had done to this point, and more. Moreover, the Soviets had been doing these bad things longer and had publicly identified their aim of destroying religion. From 1928 to 1953, a period when Stalin headed the Soviet Union, most historians estimate that he was responsible for twenty million deaths.[72] This includes victims who were shot, who died in the Gulag, and those who died in man-made famines. Stalin was responsible for starving to death at least five million Ukrainian peasants in 1932-1933 (the *Holodomor*, "death by hunger"),[73] the extermination of perhaps six and a half million kulaks (well-off peasants), the execution of one million party members in the Great Terror of 1937-1938, and the massacre of all Trotskyists in the Gulag.[74] In other words, Joseph Stalin killed more, perhaps millions more people, than did Hitler. He also had conducted an all-out effort to rid his country of the Catholic Church. As Richard Overy explained in his book *Why the Allies Won*:

> In his Navy Day Address on 27 October Roosevelt told his audience that he had in his possession a secret document which showed a Nazi plan to "abolish

all existing religions," to supplant the Bible with *Mein Kampf*, and to replace the Cross with a sword and swastika. Roosevelt was also armed with a personal assurance from the new Pope, Pius XII, that the encyclical condemning communism could be bent sufficiently to allow Catholics to support aid for the suffering Russian people. American Christians of all denominations could now rally to the cause with a clear conscience.[75]

Throughout its entire existence, the Soviet Union suppressed religion, primarily in countries that had been largely Catholic. It was the first nation in history to make a "dogma of the non-existence of God."[76] The Holy See warned the British and the Americans that Stalin had not changed his goal of eliminating religion just because the Soviet Union had joined in with the Allies. (Hitler, by contrast, was much more circumspect in his dealings with the Church. His attitude was that Catholicism must be eliminated after the war was won, but he never had an open and announced policy of eliminating religion.)[77] The Allies, of course, did not want the Pope to bring up Stalin's persecution of the Church, and Pius agreed not to, probably because by bringing it up he would have openly appeared to be taking sides.

The Vatican's concern about the Soviets caused some observers to speculate that the Holy See favored Germany over the Soviet Union.[78] Pius was pressured to oppose Marxist expansion. Late in the war, Nuncio Roncalli, the future Pope John XXIII, wrote to express "panic" at the Soviet offensive into the West. In April 1944, the prime minister of Hungary came to Rome with a desperate plea for the Pope to put himself "at the head of a peace initiative capable of halting the Soviet advance that was about to engulf the Christian peoples of Europe." The Pope, however, refused to do anything to support the Axis. He said that Germany had changed and that it was "infinitely worse" than when he had been there as nuncio.[79]

---

On December 2, 1941, a powerful Japanese naval attack force received orders to proceed with their plans. The undetected force arrived off the Hawaiian Islands on the morning of December 7. Sunday was selected because the Japanese leadership expected the Americans to be less prepared on their day of rest and worship.[80] They hit Pearl Harbor in two successive waves of more than 350 Japanese bombers, torpedo planes, and fighters. Altogether, 18 American ships were sunk or disabled. In less than two hours, the Japanese dealt the United States the single most staggering blow in its military history. Fortunately, the American aircraft carriers — Japan's true target — were on missions elsewhere, and the attack failed to destroy any of them. The Japanese lost only 29 planes.

On the day following the attack, President Roosevelt told a joint session of Congress that December 7 was a date "which will live in infamy."[81] He requested a declaration of the existence of a state of war between Japan and the United

States. Congress immediately voted in favor of the declaration. Almost simultaneously, Japanese naval and air forces attacked Wake Island, Guam, British
Malaya, Singapore, the Dutch East Indies, Burma, Thailand, and the Philip-
pines. On December 11, Germany and Italy declared war on the United States.

In his Christmas address, "Christianity and the World Crisis," presented to
the Sacred College of Cardinals on December 24, 1941, Pope Pius XII greatly
expanded on the plan for peace that he had set forth in 1939:

> In a new order founded on moral principles, there can be no place for (1) open or
> subtle oppression of the cultural and language characteristics of national minor-
> ities, (2) contraction of their economic capacities, (3) limitation or abolition of
> their natural fecundity. The more conscientiously the state respects the rights of
> its minorities, the more safely and effectively it can demand from its members
> loyal observance of their civil rights which are equal to those of other citizens.

The Pope argued for respect of the minorities within a state and for respect
of the state by the minorities. Once each side showed such respect, he argued,
peace would naturally follow.

Understood in the context of the time, the Pope was advocating the preservation of four national rights of minorities that were being threatened by National
Socialism: culture, language, economic capacity, and the right to rear children.
He stressed his "solidarity with all the persecuted people of Europe, including
the Jews." In fact, in an allusion to Nazi Germany's violent anti-Semitism, Pius
said: "Within the limits of a new order founded on moral principals, there is no
place for open or occult oppression of the cultural and linguistic characteristics
of national minorities." He ended the address with a reaffirmation that he loved
"with equal affection all peoples, without any exception whatsoever."[82]

As Hitler was announcing his need for more land and raw materials, the
Pope condemned the "narrow, selfish considerations which tend to monopolize
economic wealth and raw materials in general use, to the exclusion of nations
less favored by nature."[83] Property, the Pope argued, is a right *and* a duty. Private
rights had to be limited by the public good, and these same principles must be
applied to international relations. As Hitler longingly eyed resources that might
be captured militarily, the Pope explained that selfish economic policy was at
the heart of the world's current economic problems. Similarly, as Germany was
arming itself for aggressive war, Pius urged disarmament, both physically and
spiritually. He wanted people to forgo not only their weapons, but also their
*wish* for weapons. While Hitler was breaking treaties and violating concordats,
Pius explained that true peace could take place only when international obligations were fully respected (through the establishment of an effective international
organization).[84]

Commenting on this message, the Reich's ambassador noted that it was
directed at both Hitler's Germany and Stalin's Soviet Union.[85] Mussolini was
angered because, as Count Ciano recorded in his diary on Christmas Day 1941,

"he found that out of the five points it contains at least four are directed against the dictatorships."[86] As the *New York Times* editorialized on Christmas Day 1941, the Pope had placed himself squarely against Hitlerism:

> *The voice of Pius XII is a lonely voice in the silence and darkness enveloping Europe this Christmas.* The Pope reiterates what he has said before. In general, he repeats, although with greater definiteness, the five-point plan for peace which he first enunciated in his Christmas message after the war broke out in 1939. *His program agrees in fundamentals with the Roosevelt-Churchill eight-point declaration.* It calls for respect for treaties and the end of the possibility of aggression, equal treatment for minorities, freedom from religious persecution.... The Pontiff emphasized principles of international morality with which most men of good-will agree. He uttered the ideas a spiritual leader would be expected to express in time of war. Yet his words sound strange and bold in the Europe of today, and we comprehend the complete submergence and enslavement of great nations, the very sources of our civilization, as we realize that *he is about the only ruler left on the Continent of Europe who dares to raise his voice at all.* The last tiny islands of neutrality are so hemmed in and overshadowed by war and fear that no one but the Pope is still able to speak aloud in the name of the Prince of Peace....
>
> In calling for a "real new order" based on "liberty, justice and love," to be attained only by a "return to social and international principles capable of creating a barrier against the abuse of liberty and the abuse of power," *the Pope put himself squarely against Hitlerism.* Recognizing that there is no road open to agreement between belligerents whose reciprocal war aims and programs seem to be irreconcilable," *he left no doubt that the Nazi aims are also irreconcilable with his own conception of a Christian peace.* "The new order which must arise out of this war," he asserted, "must be based on principles." And that implies only one end to the war.[87]

Pope Pius XII would say and do even more the following year.

# TWELVE

# 1942 and the Final Solution

At the beginning of 1942, the Vatican faced a demand from the German government that it make no further appointments of bishops, archbishops, or other high administrative dignitaries in Reich-occupied areas without consulting the German government. In response, the Vatican's secretary of state not only itemized a long list of treaty violations by the Germans, he also attacked the Nazi government for acting "contrary not only to existing Concordats and to the principles of international law ratified by the Second Hague conference, but often — and this is much more grave — to the very fundamental principles of divine law, both natural and positive."[1] As such, the Church under Pius XII would not submit to the Nazi demands. Later in the year, Hitler considered recalling his ambassador to the Vatican.[2]

On January 20, 1942, Reinhard Heydrich, second-in-command of the S.S., convened a conference in the Berlin suburb of Wannsee. At the meeting, fifteen top Nazi bureaucrats and members of the S.S. met to decide on the resolution of the "Jewish Question."[3] Persecution was already widespread, but now the "Final Solution" — extermination of all Jews — was made official policy. Poland, the European nation with the greatest Jewish population, was already under Nazi control.[4]

On January 22, 1942, a Vatican Radio broadcast gave a dramatic description of German atrocities in Poland and said that Poland was in a state of terror and barbarism. As reported in the American press two days later: "Vatican City radio station made two broadcasts today, adding many details to the atrocities that supposedly are being committed in German-occupied Poland. It is now clear that the papacy is throwing the whole weight of its publicizing facilities into an exposé of conditions which, yesterday's broadcast said, 'profoundly pained' the Pope."[5]

This broadcast is noteworthy in that the Pope had expressly toned down radio condemnations of the Nazis in Poland following his broadcast on the preceding Easter,[6] but he did not hesitate to tell the world what the Vatican had learned about the Nazis and their maltreatment of Polish victims. The Germans threatened reprisals if broadcasts like this continued.[7]

German-occupied Poland was where 4,600,000 inhabitants, primarily Jews and Catholics, bore the brunt of the Nazi's plans for the future. The Wartheland area (*Warthegau* — derived from the river Warta, which flows through the region) was annexed outright by Germany. In addition to being the first place where Jews would face mass extermination, this was an experimental area for Hitler's plan to eliminate Christianity.[8]

The Nazi plan for Christianity in Wartheland was set forth in a document dated March 14, 1940 (though this document did not come to light until more than a year later).[9] In a thirteen-point plan, the Nazis proposed to reduce all churches to the status of corporations. In other words, religious associations would be permitted, but not churches. Only adults could become members of these associations; there would be no youth groups. Germans and Poles could not meet together, and the Catholics could have no relations with the Holy See. The minimum age for marriage was fixed at twenty-eight for men and twenty-five for women. For Polish workers deported to Germany, marriage was prohibited.[10] Poles in Germany also were prohibited from possessing Catholic prayer books in their native language.[11]

Within Germany, the Nazis had already consolidated most Protestant Churches into a single German church.[12] In 1941, they announced the formation of the "Roman Catholic Church of German Nationality in the Reich District Wartheland." The government would control church finances, the Gestapo would regulate worship times, and the church's role in the region would be radically altered.[13] Of course, the Nazis had to undertake some drastic measures in order to implement such plans.

By early October 1941, more than half of the two thousand pre-war clergy in the Wartheland had been imprisoned, deported, or expelled, and the arrests were continuing.[14] At least seven hundred priests were incarcerated at Dachau, and more than four hundred nuns were interned in a special camp at Bajanowo.[15] The Vatican was prohibited from having a nuncio in Wartheland,[16] but the extent of Nazi abuse is reflected in Charge No. 17 against Governor-General of Poland Hans Frank at the Nuremberg war crimes trials. Submitted by the Polish government, the charge provided in part:

11. The general situation of the clergy in the Archdiocese of Poznan in the beginning of April 1940....

> 5 priests shot,
> 27 priests confined in harsh concentration camps...,
> 190 priests in prison or in [other] concentration camps...,
> 35 priests expelled into the Government General,
> 11 priests seriously ill in consequence of ill-treatment,
> 122 parishes left entirely without priests.

12. In the diocese of Chelmno, where about 650 priests were installed before the war only 3% were allowed to stay, the 97% of them were imprisoned, executed or put in concentration camps.

13. By January 1941 about 7000 priests were killed, 3000 were in prison or concentration camps.[17]

In addition, three Polish bishops died in German concentration camps.[18]

Wartheland was a test case for what the Nazis would do everywhere if they won the war.[19] All Catholic clubs and organizations were dissolved; all cultural, charitable, and social organizations were abolished; there was no longer a Catholic press, not even a single Catholic bookstore.[20] Those who lived under these conditions were only too aware that mere words would have no positive effect on the Nazis. For instance, Bishop Karl Maria Splett of Danzig was entrusted with the interim administration of the Polish Diocese of Kulm.[21] Upon learning of calls for resistance that came from Polish leaders in exile, Splett wrote to Pius:

> At my inquiry the Gestapo told me that Cardinal Hlond had called for resistance among the Polish population over the Vatican radio station, and the Gestapo had to prevent him.... They say that Cardinal Hlond called the Polish people to rally round its priests and teachers. Thereupon, numerous priests and teachers were arrested and executed, or were tortured to death in the most terrible manner, or were even shipped to the far east.[22]

The lesson was that strong words from the pulpit meant only more suffering for those in need of help.[23]

———

Polish Catholic clergy strongly resisted the Nazis, and they suffered greatly for it.[24] In 1940, the Germans decided to put all priests from the concentration camps into one location where they could be tightly controlled. They were kept together in Dachau Barracks 26, 28, and 30 (later they were squeezed into Barracks 26 and 28 which had room and beds for 360, even though there were rarely fewer than 1,500 priests interred there). These barracks were ringed with a barbed-wire fence, which restricted the ability of priests to minister to other prisoners during their few free hours.[25]

These Dachau priests worked in the enormous S.S. industrial complex immediately to the west of the camp, but the Nazis had other uses for them as well. Some were injected with pus so that Nazi doctors could study gangrene; others had their body temperature lowered to study resuscitation of German fliers downed in the North Atlantic; one priest was crowned with barbed wire and a group of Jewish prisoners was forced to spit on him.[26] Father Stanislaus Bednarski, a Pole, was hanged on a cross. In November 1944, three priests were executed "not because they were criminals," as one judge stated, "but because it was their tragedy that they were Catholic priests."[27]

As the tide of the war began to turn, and the Germans needed to get all the labor possible out of the prisoners, the S.S. decided to use these generally well-educated prisoner/priests as secretaries and managers. With priests in the offices where they could manipulate labor schedules, they were able to engage in forms of sabotage. Thus, a planned gas oven at Dachau never became functional due, at least in part, to the efforts of these imprisoned Catholic priests.[28]

Priests at Dachau were not marked for death by being shot or gassed as a group, but over two thousand of them died there from disease, starvation, and general brutality. Early in the war, priests were treated slightly better than other prisoners at Dachau. The Nazis did this in order to create resentment among the prisoners and to keep the priests isolated. Later, as the war went on, only Jews were treated worse than priests in the concentration camps.[29] When Pope Pius XII or the German bishops were critical of Hitler or the Nazis, the treatment got much worse. "That's a fine kettle of fish your Pope got us into," said one Protestant minister following one round of particular brutality. The worst week of treatment followed a Vatican Radio broadcast critical of the Nazi regime.[30]

One year, the Nazis "celebrated" Good Friday by torturing sixty priests. They tied the priests' hands behind their backs, put chains around their wrists, and hoisted them up by the chains. The weight of the priests' bodies twisted and pulled their joints apart. Several of the priests died, and many others were left permanently disabled. The Nazis threatened to repeat the event if their orders were not carried out.[31]

Father Jean Bernard of Luxembourg was one of the rare priests incarcerated at Dachau who survived.[32] (Of the 2,800 Polish priests sent to Dachau, only 816 survived until April 1945.)[33] In his memoirs, Father Bernard reported that there was so little food that he risked the ultimate punishment in order to steal and eat a dandelion from the yard. The prisoners would secretly raid the compost pile, one time relishing discarded bones that had been chewed by the dogs of Nazi officers. Another time, the Nazi guards, knowing what the priests intended, urinated on the pile. For some priests, this was not enough to overcome their hunger.[34]

It was said that sores never healed in Dachau, but despite the unsanitary conditions and brutal treatment, priests were usually better off in the priest block than they were in the infirmary. The infirmary was more of a place to die than to receive proper treatment. When Father Bernard was first admitted to the infirmary, his beds had three bunks. "You have to go up to a top bunk," explained one attendant; "you can still climb pretty well. When you can't manage anymore, you'll get a middle bunk, and then one at the bottom."[35] They received so little food that Father Bernard once ate his bunkmate's ration before reporting that the man had died.[36]

On March 2, 1943, Cardinal Maglione sent a long letter protesting the Nazi persecution of the Catholic Church in Poland to German Foreign Minister Joachim von Ribbentrop. The letter cited atrocity after atrocity. "No less painful was the fate reserved for the regular clergy," the cardinal wrote. "Many religious were shot or otherwise killed; the great majority of the others were imprisoned, deported or expelled."[37] In an allocution to the Sacred College on June 2, 1945, which was also broadcast on Vatican Radio, the Pope noted the death of about two thousand Catholic priests at Dachau.[38]

The Vatican's efforts to win freedom for its bishops and priests imprisoned in Dachau were all frustrated, though no one doubts the Holy See's desire to win their freedom. Pope Pius XII used no different technique in his efforts to help Catholic priests than he did when trying to help Jewish paupers.[39] In each case, his words and actions were calculated so as to achieve the best results for the victims.

---

In January 1942, Japanese officials contacted the Holy See with the intent of establishing diplomatic relations. The Vatican's positive response upset American leaders, who filed a protest.[40] The Vatican secretary of state, Cardinal Maglione, explained that the Asian territories overrun by Japan contained eighteen million Catholic people. As such, the Holy See felt that it needed to have diplomatic relations with the Japanese government. It was simply a reflection of the role of a neutral church in the time of war.[41] (Moreover, the Vatican's presence in Japan eventually proved helpful to the Allies when its contacts were used to provide relief to British civilian internees.)[42] After a meeting with Cardinal Spellman of New York, President Roosevelt agreed that the Holy See really had no alternative in this matter.[43]

In April 1942, American forces in the Pacific suffered a serious defeat at Bataan. The Americans responded with bombing raids over Tokyo and other Japanese cities. Bombing of British cities continued, and Allied forces intensified their air raids over Germany. In May, the first RAF one-thousand-bomber raid was directed against Cologne, destroying much of the city. In the summer, the U.S. Army Air Corps joined in the operations. The German Luftwaffe, which might have provided some defense for the German cities, had decreased in effectiveness since the Battle of Britain.[44]

This expansion of the war into civilian areas particularly concerned the Pope. In his message of May 13, 1942, to the warring nations, Pius condemned cruelty and violence, pleading for the protection of civilian populations. Unfortunately, the warring nations did not listen to the Pope's words. As Pius later mentioned to the British chargé d'affaires, the Nazis suppressed the statement in Germany.[45]

On June 9, 1942, in German-occupied areas of the Soviet Union, the Nazis enacted a new law on "religious tolerance."[46] Despite its name, it was actually a measure designed to regulate religion and restrict churches. Hitler told his inner circle: "The formation of unitary churches for larger parts of the Russian territory is... to be prevented. It can [only be] in our interest if each village has its own sect which develops its own image of God."[47] German authorities not only reviewed sermons for proper subject matter but also censored the texts.[48] All religious organizations were required to register with the German district commissar. The commissar was given the right to remove any priest suspected of political unreliability. Religious organizations had to limit their activities or they could face penalties ranging from fines up to the dissolution of the church community.[49] It was similar to what was happening in Poland, and it reflected Hitler's eventual intent for all areas under his control.

---

Edith Stein was born on Yom Kippur 1891, in the Prussian town of Breslau (now Wroclaw, Poland). Although she was brought up in a Jewish family, she quit practicing her faith by her teenage years and considered herself an atheist.

She attended the University of Breslau, then transferred to the University of Göttingen to continue her studies in philosophy. It was the study of philosophy that brought her to Christianity.

In 1921, at the age of 29, Edith read the autobiography of St. Teresa of Ávila, founder of the Discalced Carmelite Order of Catholic nuns. St. Teresa's grandfather had been a Jewish convert to Catholicism, and Edith felt a kinship. Edith joined the Catholic Church in 1922 and eventually became a leading voice in the Catholic Women's Movement in Germany.

By the early 1930s, Edith was well known in the German academic community. She was a professor at the German Scientific Institute of Pedagogy in Münster. While on a trip during Holy Week 1933, she stopped in Cologne at the Carmelite convent for the Holy Thursday service. It was here that she decided to relinquish her life as an author and lecturer to become a nun in the Carmelite Order. She later wrote:

> I told [the Lord] that I knew it was His cross that was now being placed upon the Jewish people; that most of them did not understand this, but that those who did would have to take it up willingly in the name of all. I would do that. At the end of the service, I was certain that I had been heard. But what this carrying of the cross was to consist in, that I did not yet know.[50]

On October 15, 1934, Edith Stein took the name Teresa Benedicta of the Cross and entered the Carmel of Cologne.[51] When support for Hitler became an important issue, she revealed her Jewish background rather than offer her vote to the National Socialist leader.[52] This act was to cost her life in 1942.

After *Kristallnacht*, when Nazis in Germany terrorized so many Jews, Edith moved to a convent in Holland to spare her sister Carmelites possible trouble over her Jewish origin. (Her biological sister Rosa followed shortly thereafter.) When Holland fell to the Nazis and the deportations started in the Netherlands, converts to Christianity were exempted. Nevertheless, the leaders of the Christian churches in Holland, both Protestant and Catholic, agreed to issue a public protest against the deportation of Jews. The Nazis replied that the holy men should keep quiet or things would get worse.[53]

The Catholic leadership in Holland was not about to be silenced by a threat from the Nazis. Dutch bishops had warned their followers about the dangers of Nazism as early as 1934, and in 1936 they ordered Catholics not to support Fascist organizations or they would risk excommunication. They forbade Catholic policemen from hunting down Jews, even if it meant losing their jobs.[54]

The Catholic archbishop of Utrecht had a letter read in all of the Catholic churches on July 26, 1942, condemning the treatment of the Jews. The letter stated, in part:

> Ours is a time of great tribulations of which two are foremost: the sad destiny of the Jews and the plight of those departed for forced labor.... [A]ll of us must be aware of the terrible sufferings which both of them have to undergo, due to no

guilt of their own.... [W]e have learned with deep pain of the new dispositions which impose upon innocent Jewish men, women and children, the deportation into foreign lands.... [T]he incredible suffering which these measures cause to more than 10,000 people is in absolute opposition to the Divine Precepts of Justice and Charity.... [L]et us pray to God and for the intercession of Mary... that He may lend His Strength to the people of Israel, so sorely tried in anguish and persecution.[55]

Rather than making things better, this statement led to Nazi retaliation.[56]

On July 30, 1942, a memorandum from the general-commissar stated: "If the Catholic clergy can thus ignore negotiations, then we in turn are forced to consider the Catholic full-blooded Jews as our worst opponents and to take measures to ship them off to the East as quickly as possible."[57] Since Protestant leaders had refrained from making statements that outraged the Germans, Jews holding Protestant baptismal certificates were not deported. Jewish converts to Catholicism (including Edith Stein and her sister) and Jews with false Catholic baptismal certificates, however, were deported.[58] On the trip, various eyewitnesses recalled Edith comforting and consoling others. When her sister became disoriented, Edith told her, "Come, Rosa. We go for our people."[59] She was last seen with her sister, both of them praying and smiling. No survivors reported on her final moments. She was put to death at Auschwitz on August 9, 1942, along with her sister and at least six other German nuns.[60] She was canonized as St. Teresa Benedicta of the Cross by Pope John Paul II in 1998 and named as co-patroness of Europe in 1999.

According to sworn eyewitness testimony, Pius XII was considering having *L'Osservatore Romano* publish a protest against Nazism when the events from Holland were reported back to him. There was no nuncio in Holland at the time, since he had been expelled by the Nazis, so Pius learned of these events from newspapers and radio accounts. Aware that a statement from the Holy Father would provoke even greater retaliation than was generated by the statement of national bishops, he picked up pages of writing that he had been working on, walked over the to stove, and burned them.[61]

Of particular importance to the papal critics is another letter written by Stein in 1933. The letter was only recently made public (though it had been known about for some time). It makes the case for a papal statement regarding Nazi persecution of Jews and Catholics; as such it has been used to argue that Stein was angry about the papal approach to the war (the letter was written to Pius XI, though critics also use it against Pius XII).[62] It turns out, however, critics were wrong in thinking that Stein wanted a papal encyclical on the matter. As explained by the Vatican analyst for CNN when the letter was made public in 2003:

> She wrote this letter in April of 1933, complaining about Nazi persecution of the Jews to Pius XI. Now, a lot of people have long believed that in that letter she asked the Pope to write an encyclical letter. That's a major papal document con-

demning the Nazis. And the fact that Pius didn't do it has been used as part of the campaign against him. What we now know, as of yesterday morning, once that letter is on the record, is that she did not make any such request. So at least in that way, it resolves a historical debate in favor of the Vatican's position.[63]

Responding to Stein's letter, Pacelli wrote to her abbot, thanking him for forwarding her message to the Vatican. The secretary of state told the abbot: "I leave it to your discretion to let the sender [Stein] know in a suitable way that her message has been duly put before His Holiness."[64]

It was long known that the Holy See sent Stein a papal blessing. It was not known, however, that the Pope had *already* sent a message to the papal nuncio in Berlin on April 4, 1933, instructing him to intervene with the new government on behalf of the Jews.[65] In other words, Pope Pius XI had anticipated Stein's concern and acted on it before he got her letter. Because it was a delicate diplomatic matter, the reply did not explain all of this to Stein, who was a layperson, not yet a nun, at the time of her letter.[66]

Contrary to what the critics would have their readers believe, Stein was not upset with the Vatican. She did, after all, become a nun after these events. Additionally, later in 1933, she sent a gift to the Holy See — her new two-volume translation of St. Thomas Aquinas' writings. Later, when Pacelli became Pope Pius XII, Stein was even closer to the papacy.

Stein first met Pacelli in the 1920s, when he gave a speech in Speyer, Germany, at St. Magdalen's Convent, where Stein was teaching. She warmly saluted Pacelli in the welcoming speech, and she kept those warm feelings over the years. In her collected letters, there is one dated November 17, 1940, in which Stein wrote: "Next Sunday we will be united with the Holy Father in the prayer campaign."[67] In another letter dated July 10, 1940, she wrote of the tremendous Church struggle and "fight" against Nazism and her prediction of the ultimate "victory" of the Church over Nazism.[68]

On a related note, in an article entitled "The Saint and the Holocaust," in the June 7, 1999 edition of *The New Yorker* magazine, critic and excommunicated former priest James Carroll argued that by declaring Edith Stein a saint, the Catholic Church elevated her death above that of six million Jews and in the process may have "subverted" the value of Edith Stein's life. Carroll argued that Stein was killed because she was Jewish. This is true. Had she not been Jewish, the Nazis would not have deported her at that time. However, if Carroll had quoted the general-commissar's statement mentioned above, he would have had to acknowledge that Stein was deported due to her Catholicism as well.

To make his point, Carroll reported that on her way to Auschwitz, Edith was supposedly offered the opportunity to use her baptism as a shield from deportation. She declined the offer, according to Carroll, saying: "Why should there be an exception made in the case of a particular group? Wasn't it fair that baptism not be allowed to become an advantage?"

This decision to decline an offer of freedom (and, indeed, life itself) seems particularly noble, even saintly. Carroll, however, gives this act of selflessness an unusual interpretation, arguing that in declining this offer, Edith was not being selfless and noble. Rather, Carroll would have us believe that Stein was rejecting her baptism and the Catholicism that she had adopted twenty years earlier and had fully devoted her life to for the previous nine years. This is a very strained interpretation of her reported words.[69] Perhaps more telling is Carroll's willingness to use this statement at all, much less to build a central argument around it.

Carroll acknowledged that the story came forth years after Edith had been deported and killed, and that it came from a Dutch official who claimed to have met Stein in a transit camp on her way to Auschwitz. It is reasonable to be suspect of any unconfirmed, self-serving memory that is asserted years after the fact, but there is an even greater reason to be suspicious in this case.

The focus of Nazi deportation at this time was on Jews who had been baptized into the Catholic Church. Therefore, it is very unlikely that someone would have asked whether one of the numerous Catholic Jews would want to use her *baptism* in order to avoid deportation. Far more likely is the account given by other sources that Stein was offered the opportunity to use her status as a *nun* to avoid the concentration camp. That story, however, would not have fit with Carroll's premise that Stein was rejecting her religion by declining to invoke her baptism.

Relating a story about his study of Edith Stein when he was a young seminarian, Carroll says that "it never occurred to us then that there could be something offensive to Jews in our honoring her as a young woman in search of the truth." He now suggests that there is something wrong with honoring this young woman who went in search of the truth. The only real reason he has given for this position is that she was born Jewish. That seems to be a most inappropriate reason.

––––––––––

In the summer of 1942, the situation in Warsaw was getting worse. In July, the first deportations from the ghetto to concentration camps took place, and the Treblinka camp was opened. The Polish underground, which was strongly influenced by the Catholic Church,[70] was in full swing. Nuns carried secret messages, and priests conducted special Masses behind closed doors.[71] In at least one case, a member of the underground who was about to go on a dangerous mission attended a secret Mass at which the priest, in violation of normal Catholic practices, presented him with a consecrated host. The priest said: "I have been authorized by those in whom the authority of the Church is vested, to present you, soldier of Poland, with Christ's Body to carry you on your journey.... If danger approaches, you will be able to swallow it."[72]

Zofia Kossak-Szcaucka, a well-known writer of historical novels, was also a Catholic and a member of a Catholic organization known as FOP. In the name of that organization, Kossak-Szcaucka wrote an illegal leaflet that was posted around Warsaw. It described the horror of life and death in the ghetto, and called upon those who could not undertake action to at least raise a protest:

> We have no means actively to counteract the German murders; we cannot help, nor can we rescue anybody. But we protest from the bottom of our hearts filled with pity, indignation, and horror. This protest is demanded of us by God, who does not allow us to kill. It is demanded by our Christian conscience. Every being calling itself human has the right to love his fellow man. The blood of the defenseless victims is calling for revenge. Who does not support the protest with us, is not a Catholic.

* * *

> Whoever does not understand this, and whoever dares to connect the future of the proud, free Poland with the vile enjoyment of your fellow man's calamity is, therefore, not a Catholic and not a Pole.[73]

Kossak-Szcaucka followed up this document up with a request to establish an underground organization to save the Jews. By the end of 1942, the Council for Aid to Jews had been established. Later, Kossak-Szczaucka was caught and sent to Auschwitz. She was released after about one year and resumed her underground activity, focusing especially on sheltering Jewish children in convents and other institutions run by the Catholic Church.

----

In September 1942, a report from the Inter-Allied Information Committee claimed that the Nazis had killed 207,373 people in occupied territories, 200,000 of them in Poland.[74] The committee suggested that many more may have been put to death by Hitler, but these numbers could not be officially confirmed.

The word from Germany was also quite bad. In July, Nuncio Orsenigo reported that "the situation of the Jews excludes all charitable interventions" and that he had been warned that "the less he talked about the Jews, the better it would be."[75] Up until this time, the Pope had continued to receive leading members of the National Socialist Party.[76] Now, however, Pius began to follow the lead of Bishop Preysing of Berlin who was a recognized opponent of Nazism. Not only did the Pope send a message congratulating Preysing for his defense of the rights of all people, he also took Preysing's advice when selecting episcopal candidates, avoiding those whom Preysing felt were sympathetic toward the Nazis.[77]

On September 19, an American delegation had an audience with Pius XII. They explained the irrevocable determination of the Allies to "obliterate" Nazism, and to do so in concert with the Soviet Union. The delegation told the Pope that he must drop any idea of a negotiated settlement. The Americans were concerned that the Vatican would support the Axis in an attempt to seek a peace without suffering a defeat. The Americans made it clear that they would accept nothing short of an unconditional surrender.[78]

The Holy See was still concerned about the ultimate aims of Soviet Communism, including the elimination of religion.[79] Pius XII seemed to accept the Allies' position, and he became even more critical and outspoken against the Nazis. On October 26, 1942, a coded telegram to the British War Cabinet from the Madrid Offices reported: "[Serrani] Suñer in his visit to the Pope said that the Germans would win the war and that the Vatican and Spain should adapt their policy accordingly. The Pope replied 'if the Germans win, it will mean the greatest period of persecution that Christians have ever suffered.' "[80]

The Axis leaders recognized Pius XII's bias against their cause. The editor of the Fascist publication *Regime Facista* wrote in October 1942: "The Church's obstruction of the practical solution of the Jewish problem constitutes a crime against the New Europe."[81] According to the *London Tablet* of October 24, out of disgust at the number of Jews that were released from Nazi-occupied areas due to Vatican pressure, the Third Reich circulated ten million copies of a pamphlet saying that Pius XII inspired a lack of confidence in the Catholic world.[82] The pamphlet argued that earlier popes had not been friendly to Jews, but this "pro-Jewish" Pope Pius XII — is the only one who has "found it necessary to make interventions on behalf of Jews."[83] Mussolini, too, vented displeasure over the "anti-dictatorial darts" that appeared in *L'Osservatore Romano*.[84]

---

In September 1942, President Roosevelt sent a message to the Pope detailing reports from the Warsaw ghetto and asking whether the Vatican had any information that would tend to confirm or deny the reports of Nazi crimes.[85] In mid-October, the Holy See replied, stating that it, too, had reports of "severe measures" taken against the Jews, but that it had been impossible to verify the accuracy of the reports. The statement went on, however, to note that "the Holy See is taking advantage of every opportunity offered in order to mitigate the suffering of non-Aryans."[86]

The following month, at their annual meeting in Washington, DC, the U.S. bishops released a statement indicating that the Vatican had come to believe the horrible news coming from Germany and occupied nations:

> Since the murderous assault on Poland, utterly devoid of every semblance of humanity, there has been a premeditated and systematic extermination of the people of this nation. The same satanic technique is being applied to many other peoples. We feel a deep sense of revulsion against the cruel indignities heaped upon Jews in conquered countries and upon defenseless peoples not of our faith.... Deeply moved by the arrest and maltreatment of the Jews, we cannot stifle the cry of conscience. In the name of humanity and Christian principles, our voice is raised.[87]

Critic Daniel Goldhagen attempted to portray this statement as a slap at Pius XII and an "all but explicit rebuke of the Vatican." Actually, the American bishops repeatedly invoked Pius XII's name and teachings with favor ("We recall the words of Pope Pius XII"; "We urge the serious study of peace plans of Pope Pius XII"; "In response to the many appeals of our Holy Father"). Moreover, in a letter written at this very time, Pius expressed thanks for the "constant and understanding *collaboration*" of the American bishops and archbishops.[88]

Parts of the Pope's letter of thanks were published in the very same issue of a Catholic newspaper that contained the bishops' statement.[89] It should be noted that there was a general thanks given to the "hierarchy, clergy, and faithful" for their efforts, but the thanks for "collaboration" was separate and directed to the bishops and archbishops. The bishops replied with a letter pledging "anew to the Holy Father our best efforts in the fulfillment of his mission of apostolic charity to war victims." They also offered a prayer for his collaborators. The very idea that the bishops were trying to insult the Holy Father is *preposterous*. Archbishop (later Cardinal) Francis Spellman of New York said: "Our President and our Holy Father have combined the forces of our country and the forces of religion in a battle for peace."[90]

———

With the Vatican having recognized Nazi atrocities earlier than many other nations and having assisted Western powers during the early hostilities, Allied leaders sought to have the Pope join in a formal declaration concerning the atrocities taking place in Germany and in German-occupied areas. In a message dated September 14, 1942, the Brazilian ambassador, Ildebrando Accioly, wrote: "It is necessary that the authorized and respected voice of the Vicar of Christ be heard against these atrocities."[91] On that same day, British Minister D'Arcy Osborne and American representative Harold H. Tittmann requested a "public and specific denunciation of Nazi treatment of the populations of the countries under German occupation."[92] Interestingly, neither Tittmann nor Accioly mentioned the treatment of Jews by the Nazis. Osborne, who did mention the treatment of Jewish people in his request to the Pope, reported back to London that the coordinated requests to the Pontiff looked like an effort to involve the Pope in political and partisan action.[93]

Pius was noncommittal in response to these requests, and a few weeks later President Roosevelt's representative, Myron Taylor, renewed the request on behalf of the Allies. American representatives ultimately reported back that the Holy See was convinced that an open condemnation would "result in the violent deaths of many more people."[94] A secret British telegram from this same time period reported on an audience with the Pope: "His Holiness undertook to do whatever was possible on behalf of the Jews, but His Majesty's Minister doubted whether there would be any public statement."[95]

Critics have sometimes used this episode to argue that the Allies were upset with Pope Pius XII's stance in the war. Recently, however, the Franklin D. Roosevelt Library posted several wartime documents on the Internet, including an official summary prepared by Myron Taylor of conversations that he had with the Pope on September 19, 22, and 26, 1942. Taylor made it clear that the Holy See and the Allies saw eye-to-eye:

> We have seen how the Vatican and America were not self-seeking, were and are free from materialistic or ambitious motives; how the parallel efforts of His Holiness and President Roosevelt for the maintenance of peace were energized by their very spiritual qualities. We have seen the Encyclical of Pope Pius XI and the allocutions of Pope Pius XII.... All have harmonized in upholding the moral code which aims to protect mankind in freedom and justice under the moral law.[96]

In addressing the Pope, Taylor read from a statement that had been approved by President Roosevelt:

> Before the war became general, President Roosevelt, in parallel effort with the Holy See, explored every possible avenue for the preservation of the peace. The experience of those days of fruitful cooperation, when the high moral prestige of the Holy See was buttressed by the civil power of the United States of America, is a precious memory. Although totalitarian aggression defeated those first efforts to prevent world war, the United States looks forward to further collaboration of this kind when the anti-Christian philosophies which have taken the sword shall have perished by the sword, and it will again be possible to organize world peace.
>
> In the just war which they are now waging, the people of the United States of America derive great spiritual strength and moral encouragement from a review of the utterances of His Holiness Pope Pius XII and of his venerated Predecessor. Americans, Catholic and non-Catholic, have been profoundly impressed by the searing condemnation of Nazi religious persecution pronounced by Pope Pius XI in his "Mit Brennender Sorge;" by the elevated teaching on law and human dignity contained in the "Summi Pontificatus" of Pope Pius XII; by the famous Five Points laid down in 1939 by the same Pope as the essential postulates of a just peace; and by the forthright and heroic expressions of indignation made by Pope Pius XII when Germany invaded the Low Countries. Now that we are fighting against the very things which the Popes condemned, our conviction of complete victory is one with our confidence in the unwavering tenacity with which the Holy See will continue its magnificent moral leading.[97]

Reporting on the Pope's reaction to this statement, Taylor wrote: "The prompt reaction of His Holiness to the positive statements of American attitude was one of surprising satisfaction, of immediate and happy response and the repetition, several times, by His Holiness of words to the effect that America would not compromise but would continue the war until victory was achieved."[98]

Reporting on his second meeting with the Pope (September 22, 1942), Taylor gave more details about Pius XII's attitude:

Despite all propaganda, His Holiness "would never propose or approve of peace by compromise at any cost;" "there can be no compromise of moral principles," and it is gratifying to know that the peace aims of the United States uphold this approach to the ultimate conclusion of the war." He emphatically asserted that "we need have no fear that any pressure from outside the Vatican will ever make it change its course."[99]

The Pope did not join in the 1942 joint Allied statement, perhaps because, as a *New York Times* editorial concluded, it was "an official indictment."[100] Pius did not want to breach the Church's official neutrality by joining in a declaration made by either side, and he was concerned that the Allies' statement would be used as part of the war effort (as happened with some of his earlier radio broadcasts).[101] He did, however, make his position known.

On December 1, 1942, in a front-page article entitled "Appeal to Stay the Butcher's Hand," the *Palestine Post* reported that the Jewish community of Poland had requested that Pius XII intervene on its behalf. Apostolic Delegate Father W. A. Hughes, addressing the extraordinary session of the Elected Assembly of Palestine Jews, assured the assembly that the Pope had received the message and reported that "the Vatican had endeavoured consistently to assist in these matters to the full measure of its possibilities."[102] The Latin patriarch of Jerusalem, Louis Barlassina, associated himself with Pius XII, saying that he was "inspired by his paternal love and sympathy for all suffering and characterized by great charity."[103]

In his 1942 Christmas statement, "The Rights of Man," broadcast over Vatican Radio and reprinted around the globe, Pope Pius XII said that the world was "plunged into the gloom of tragic error," and that "the Church would be untrue to herself, she would have ceased to be a mother, if she were deaf to the cries of suffering children which reach her ears from every class of the human family."[104] He spoke of the need for mankind to make "a solemn vow never to rest until valiant souls of every people and every nation of the earth arise in their legions, resolved to bring society back to its immovable center of gravity in the Divine Law, and to devote themselves to the service of the human person and of a divinely ennobled human society." He said that mankind owed this vow to all victims of the war, including "the hundreds of thousands who, through no fault of their own, and solely because of their nation or race, have been condemned to death or progressive extinction."

Pius condemned totalitarian regimes (Nazi and Communist), which too often replace the ultimate duty owed by individuals to God with another duty owed to the state:

Finally, all those theories are to be shunned which, though in themselves divergent and deriving from opposed ideologies, have this in common that they regard the State, or a group that is representing it, as an absolute or supreme entity exempt from all control and criticism, even when its theoretical and practical postulates result in open and clashing contradiction with essential data of the human and Christian conscience.

The Pope also spoke of human rights that are inherent in God's creation of man in his own image. "By reaffirming these rights, and most importantly their divine source, Pius XII attacked a core Nazi belief: that of superiority of the Aryan race over all others. The arguments that Pius XII set out also served to further condemn genocidal Nazi anti-Semitism."[105] The Pope also condemned totalitarian regimes and acknowledged some culpability on the part of the Church: "A great part of the human race, and not a few — We do not hesitate to say it — not a few even of those who call themselves Christians, bear some share in the collective responsibility for the aberrations, the disasters, and the low moral state of modern society." He urged all Catholics to give shelter wherever they could.[106]

The Polish ambassador to the Holy See thanked the Pontiff, who "in his last Christmas address implicitly condemned all the injustices and cruelties suffered by the Polish people at the hands of the Germans. Poland acclaims this condemnation; it thanks the Holy Father for his words. . . ."[107] British records reflect the opinion that "the Pope's condemnation of the treatment of the Jews & the Poles is quite unmistakable, and the message is perhaps more forceful in tone than any of his recent statements. The Pope informed the United States Minister to the Vatican that he considered his recent broadcast to be clear and comprehensive in its condemnation of the heartrending treatment of Poles, Jews, hostages, etc. And to have satisfied all recent demands that he should speak out."[108]

The Dutch bishops issued a pastoral letter in defense of Jewish people on February 21, 1943, making express reference to the Pope's statement.[109] Moreover, a well-known Christmas Day editorial in the *New York Times* praised Pius XII for his moral leadership in opposing the Nazis:

> No Christmas sermon reaches a larger congregation than the message Pope Pius XII addresses to a war-torn world at this season. This Christmas more than ever he is a lonely voice crying out of the silence of a continent. . . . When a leader bound impartially to nations on both sides condemns as heresy the new form of national state which subordinates everything to itself; when he declares that whoever wants peace must protect against "arbitrary attacks" the "juridical safety of individuals"; when he assails violent occupation of territory, the exile and persecution of human beings for no reason other than race or political opinion; when he says that people must fight for a just and decent peace, a "total peace" — the "impartial judgment" is like a verdict in a high court of justice.[110]

A similar editorial from the *Times of London*, predating the Christmas address and commenting on the Pope's statements in general, said:

> A study of the words which Pope Pius XII has addressed since his accession in encyclicals and allocutions to the Catholics of various nations leaves no room

for doubt. He condemns the worship of force and its concrete manifestation in the suppression of national liberties and in the persecution of the Jewish race.[111]

Obviously, in contrast to what the critics would have us believe, everyone knew to whom the Pope was referring, including the Axis powers.

According to an official Nazi report on the papal Christmas address by Heinrich Himmler's Superior Security Office (the *Reichssicherheitshauptamt* — the main security department of the Nazi government) to Foreign Minister Joachim von Ribbentrop's office:

> In a manner never known before, the Pope has repudiated the National Socialist New European Order.... It is true, the Pope does not refer to the National Socialists in Germany by name, but his speech is one long attack on everything we stand for.... God, he says, regards all people and races as worthy of the same consideration. Here he is clearly speaking on behalf of the Jews.... [H]e is virtually accusing the German people of injustice toward the Jews, and makes himself the mouthpiece of the Jewish war criminals.[112]

An American diplomatic report noted that the Germans were "conspicuous by their absence" at a Midnight Mass conducted by the Pope for diplomats on Christmas Eve following the papal statement.[113] German Ambassador Diego von Bergen, on the instruction of Foreign Minister Joachim von Ribbentrop, warned the Pope that the Nazis would seek retaliation if the Vatican abandoned its neutral position. When he reported back to his superiors, the German ambassador stated: "Pacelli is no more sensible to threats than we are."[114]

————

Critic Susan Zuccotti complained about the translation of the 1942 Christmas statement that appeared in the first edition of this book. At issue is the Italian word *stirpe*, which was used in several official Church pronouncements including the 1942 Christmas statement. Like many authors, I have translated this as "race."[115] On page two of *Under His Very Windows*, however, Zuccotti explains that *stirpe* does not exactly correlate with the English word "race," but should be understood as meaning "descent." Her suggestion is that when the Pope or various Church officials used the word *stirpe*, they were not saying "race" and therefore were not defending Jewish people.

One might question whether in this context the difference between race and descent is significant in any way, but just to be clear: *Cassell's Italian Dictionary* (1979) gives the following as the definition of the Italian *stirpe*: "stock, race, descent, lineage, extraction." ("Race" precedes "descent.") The *Zanichelli New College Italian and English Dictionary* gives: "stock, race, family, lineage, ancestry." ("Descent" is *not* given as an option.)[116] Of greatest importance, the *Nuovo Dizionario della Lingua Italiana*, published in Milan in 1924 (therefore best reflecting Italian usage when Pius XII was a young man) gives *schiatta* ("race") as an *exact synonym* of *stirpe*. It even provides as an illustration of the word's meaning the phrase "*la stirpe semitica*" ("the Semitic race").[117]

The Church did not view people as being racially distinct in the way that the Nazis did. Jewish people were defined by their faith. When it was necessary to refer to them as a group, however, the well-established practice at the Vatican had been to use the word *stirpe*.[118] In fact, *stirpe* had been used throughout Europe for centuries as an explicit reference to Jews.[119] As Desmond Fisher wrote in 1965: "Pope Pius frequently used the word *stirpe* (race) to identify the Jews and no one could be in any doubt about his attitude."[120]

Perhaps more revealing as to the validity of the critic's argument is that Pope Pius XI's anti-Nazi encyclical, *Mit brennender Sorge*, used the German word *Rasse*, which — as Zuccotti concedes — means "race." This time, however, her analysis changes. She argues that since the Church did not actually consider Jews as a distinct race, rather as a religion, "it is unlikely that any reference to observant Jews was intended." Regardless of the word used, she finds a basis for her criticism of the Pope and the Church.[121]

Popes of this era did not speak as directly as a modern American politician might speak. Yet, when Pope Pius XII spoke of "the hundreds of thousands" condemned to death because of their "nation or race" [or descent, or *stirpe*],[122] the press, rescuers, and even the Jewish victims knew what he meant. In making these statements, a pope might use theology or some other background for his message, but all educated Christians (most notably priests and bishops, who would then relate the message to parishioners) understood the papal message. As Pius XII explained after the war: "We know in fact that Our broadcasts... were in spite of every prohibition and obstacle studied by diocesan conferences and expounded to the people."[123]

That people understood the papal messages is reflected in the anger that Pius XII's protests provoked in Nazi ranks. Just twenty days after the broadcast, Ribbentrop said: "If the Vatican should threaten or try out any political or propagandist action against Germany, the Reich would obviously have to retaliate in an appropriate manner.... The Reich would have no lack of effective means...."[124] Radio operator François de Beaulieu (later a Protestant minister) was arrested and imprisoned for carrying a translation of the broadcast and thereby spreading a "subversive and demoralizing document." He was also accused of having a critical view of the war and of being "spiritually attracted to Jewish environments and sympathetic toward Jews." Beaulieu later explained:

> The Pope could not do much more. He would have had to set himself on fire in front of the Vatican to awaken consciences worldwide. Many political leaders knew that there were extermination camps in Hitler's time. Of what use would it have been for the Pope to set himself on fire in front of the Vatican?[125]

Hitler was so angry at Pius that he seriously considered invading the Vatican and seizing the Pope.[126] Karl Otto Wolff, S.S. chief in Italy toward the end of the war, testified to having received the orders to invade the Vatican from Hitler himself.[127] The German ambassador to Italy and an aide to the German ambassador to the Holy See both confirmed that Hitler had such plans.[128] Fortunately, he was dissuaded from them, but the reaction from Hitler and other Nazi leaders is strong evidence about how they viewed the Pope and the Vatican leadership. In fact, in 1944, before the Allies liberated Rome, Wolff approached Pius XII to discuss a possible peace treaty. At that time, Wolff provided Pius with documents regarding Hitler's plans to invade the Vatican.[129]

The Pope felt that his position on the brutal treatment of Jews and others by the Nazis was clear.[130] Others shared his view. The bishops of western Germany and Berlin issued a joint pastoral letter that said:

> The ultimate principles of right are not conditioned by time nor the result of national character so the claim to... such rights cannot be a prerogative of a single people. Whoever bears a human countenance has rights, which no earthly power may take.... All the original rights of man... can and must not be denied to one who is not of our blood or does not speak our language.[131]

That same month, the German bishops, in a joint letter to the government, complained about the treatment of the people of Poland.[132] The *New York Times* reported: "The lesson is by now so clear that in all the occupied countries the most open and defiant opposition to Nazi tyranny comes from the religious leaders. This is strikingly true in Germany itself."[133]

# THIRTEEN

# 1943 and Turning Tides

In January 1943, the Pope met with Nicholas Kallay, the Hungarian premier. According to Kallay, Pius "condemned the system and the methods of the Germans, which independently of the war were inhuman and brutal, especially towards the Jews."[1] Pius further explained that the Church could never cooperate with governments like those in Germany and the Soviet Union. He had long known about the brutality of Russian Bolshevism, but had been painfully surprised to learn that the Germans were capable of similar anti-Semitism and brutality.[2]

This same month, Pius wrote a letter to President Roosevelt in which he expressed his gratitude for the support he had received from the president in his efforts to bring about peace and alleviate suffering. He promised to continue

> to recall to men's minds... those higher principles of justice and Christian morality without which there is no salvation, and to draw men's spirits anew towards those sentiments of charity and brotherhood without which there can be no peace. In the ceaseless furtherance of this, Our program, We feel certain that We may count upon the efficacious comprehension of the noble American people and upon the valid collaboration of Your Excellency.[3]

As the year went on, Pius expressed confidence that a new spirit of collaboration among men and nations would unite men after the war, and despite official neutrality, he conveyed to the American president his desire to continue with parallel endeavors for the alleviation of suffering and for peace.[4]

In terms of the war, the most important development of January 1943 was that President Roosevelt, Prime Minister Churchill, and Charles de Gaulle concluded a ten-day meeting in Casablanca. (Stalin, angry that the Allies had not yet started a second European front, refused to attend.) From this conference, the Allies established a seven-point plan to coordinate their efforts for future military action in the Mediterranean. This included the union of British and American operations in North Africa and an invasion of Sicily. They also agreed that strategic bombing of German industries would be intensified. Perhaps the most controversial decision was the demand for unconditional surrender.

As soon as the policy was announced, critics voiced their objections: unconditional surrender would lengthen the war; it would intensify the German fighting morale; it would also delay the ultimate peace settlement. Some have argued that once Germany was on the run, the main obstacle to peace was this self-imposed barrier. The German ambassador to the Holy See later reported, "I told every official quarter in Rome to which I had access that this formula would cost the lives of many more Allied soldiers."[5] Hitler did not miss the chance to use this demand as propaganda to motivate the German people. In his campaign of "strength through fear," Goebbels focused on unconditional surrender. The German people, he said, had "no choice but to fight or face obliteration."[6]

Pius XII was willing to make certain reasonable compromises in order to achieve a just peace. As such, the unconditional surrender policy was much to his disliking.[7] In fairness to the Allied leaders, however, it should be noted that a conditional surrender had not held up after World War I.[8] In addition, British and American policy makers were concerned that the Soviet Union might seek a separate peace with Germany, and unconditional surrender seemed the best insurance against such an eventuality.[9]

Another decision at Casablanca was perhaps less controversial at the time, but in retrospect may have cost more lives. This was the directive calling for the progressive destruction and dislocation of the German military, industrial, and economic system and the undermining of the morale of the German people. In other words, the directive called for the strategic bombing of civilian targets.

In 1922, three years after World War I had ended, the major powers met at the Washington Arms Limitation Conference. There they adopted rules of warfare that reflected the view that some restraints ought to apply, even in times of war.[10] Article 28 of these rules stated: "The area of bombardment for the purpose of terrorizing the civilian population, destroying or damaging civilian property not of a military character, or injuring non-combatants is prohibited." Both Prime Minister Churchill and British Air Marshal Arthur Harris, however, believed in the effectiveness of bombing civilian targets.[11] The years when the Allies controlled the air (1944-45), were the peak years in terms of the sheer tonnage of bombs dropped. The Allies emphasized aerial bombing in population centers and working-class neighborhoods. This bombing, it was thought, would weaken the German will to fight and reduce German war production. The Americans also applied this tactic in Japan.

Pius, as always, strongly opposed the introduction of warfare into civilian areas.[12] (The Germans asked him to intervene and try to stop the bombing of civilian populations in Germany.)[13] Under Catholic doctrine, war is not in itself unjust.[14] When it meets certain conditions, war can even be virtuous.[15] In order to meet those conditions, however, the nation must have a just reason for entering the war (*jus ad bellum*),[16] and it must fight the war in a just manner (*jus in bello*).[17] The attack on civilian populations typically falls outside of the requirements of a just war.[18]

———

In early 1943, the Vatican received information from the nuncio in Berlin about the deportation and execution of Jewish people.[19] In late April, Pius wrote to Bishop Preysing of Berlin, explaining that he had received news of the atrocities, which had nothing to do with the necessities of war, and it crippled and horri-fied him. He added, "It was for us a great consolation to learn that Catholics, in particular those of your Berlin diocese, have shown such charity towards the suf-ferings of the Jews." He praised the example of Provost Lichtenberg who had been imprisoned for public prayers in support of the Jews. The Pope added:

> In Our Christmas message We have already said something about what is now being done against the non-Aryans in the area of German domination. This was short, but was well understood. We do not now need to give assurances that Our paternal love and paternal care is due in increased measure to the non-Aryan or half-Aryan Catholics who are children of the Church like all the others, now during the collapse of their exterior existence and in their spiritual distress. With the situation such as it is at the moment, We can unfortunately provide them with no effective help except our prayers. We are determined, however, to raise Our voice again on their behalf, according to what the circum-stances demand or permit.[20]

Regarding efforts on behalf of Jewish people, Pius explained: "To the extent it was able, the Holy See has in fact given charitable aid to non-Aryan Catholics and to members of the Jewish religion.... The principal Jewish organizations have expressed to the Holy See their warmest appreciation for its relief efforts." He explained, however, that he left it to local Church officials to decide what could be accomplished in any given area.

Pius sent his nuncio in Berlin, Cesare Orsenigo, to approach Hitler directly and discuss the treatment of Jews in Germany and in occupied areas. Orsenigo reported:

> A few days ago I finally was able to go to Berchtesgaden, where I was received by Hitler; as soon as I touched upon the Jewish question, our discussion lost all sense of serenity. Hitler turned his back on me, went to the window and started to drum on the glass with his fingers... while I continued to spell out our complaints. All of a sudden, Hitler turned around, grabbed a glass off a nearby table and hurled it to the floor with an angry gesture. Faced with this kind of diplomatic behavior, I thought my mission was over.[21]

As others have noted, "the correspondence and documents of the Holy See during the War reveal a growing sense of helplessness and frustration in the face of the persecution of the Jews in Germany and in Poland."[22] The Spanish ambas-sador, Domingo de las Barcenas, reported on a conversation he had with the Pope in the spring of 1943. "His Holiness... said with great emphasis that it must be kept in mind that communism is not the only enemy. I cannot tell you in writ-ing the terms he used in speaking of the *Nazi menace*. He strictly forbade me to do so."[23]

In 1941, before the Final Solution had become official policy, Pius expressed a "special love" for the Germans. He held audiences with German soldiers often,

Protestants as well as Catholics. He said that he had "nothing against" Germany, which he "loved and admired." Regarding Hitler's regime, Pius said it had caused him profound sadness, especially "certain measures" which it had taken, but he still hoped that matters would improve.[24] By 1943, however, he expressed great doubt about any eventual improvement. "Personally," Ambassador Barcenas said, "the Pope, contrary to what is generally believed, in spite of his professed affection for the German people," is angry at the regime.[25] The ambassador reported that the Pope believed the Nazi persecution of religion was "fundamental to the regime; that it is more dangerous than any previous persecution; and that its application to Poland went to inconceivable extremes." Pius also said that "there was no hope for change as long as [Hitler and his top advisers] remain in charge."[26] The Pope warned: "[D]o not underestimate the danger that Rome will be in if the Nazi menace spreads all over Europe."[27]

The Pope's feelings about Nazism were well known inside the German leadership. In the spring of 1943, a group of German officials — including Marschall von Biberstein (an official of the German foreign ministry), Martin Luther (director of the German agency that handled certain domestic affairs), and Walter Schellenberg (a German intelligence officer) — hoped to overthrow Foreign Minister Joachim von Ribbentrop and negotiate a peace treaty with the Allies.[28] They indirectly approached Pius XII, seeking to have him encourage a negotiated peace. The Pope sent an open letter calling for prayers for peace, especially from the children. The anti-Ribbentrop movement stalled, however, when Ribbentrop learned of their plans. He had Luther sent to a concentration camp and other members sent to the front.[29]

That same Easter, the Protestant community in Munich submitted an unsigned petition to their bishop, Hans Meiser. The petitioners denounced anti-Semitism and by implication the Nazi regime, which had approved that policy. "We can as Christians no longer bear it that the church in Germany remains silent regarding the persecutions of the Jews."[30] The duty of the church, according to the petition, was to attest that "the Jewish question is primarily an evangelical and not a political question." The "politically irregular and singular existence and identity of the Jews" existed because God had chosen them as the instrument of his revelation. The church was obliged to bear witness to this by assisting the Jews who "fell among thieves" under the Third Reich. It must also oppose "that 'Christian' anti-Semitism" which speaks of "the 'deserved' curse against Israel." Even more important, the church must denounce the state's attempt "to destroy Judaism" with its "homemade political gospel."[31]

The anonymous petition, like all such statements during the war, had no beneficial impact on the Nazis. The brutality continued.

———

As Germany began to suffer military defeats, it also faced increasing difficulties from underground resistance in occupied nations. At first, resistance was modest, perhaps because many believed the Nazis to be invincible; but after some early Axis setbacks, anti-Nazi activity increased, even in Germany.

One of the best known opposition groups was centered at the University of Munich and went by the name of the White Rose. It was led by philosophy professor Kurt Huber and two students, Hans and Sophie Scholl (who were brother and sister). The group was genuinely high-minded, recklessly daring, and "profoundly Catholic."[32] They often made reference to their faith as they opposed the Nazis.

The White Rose published four pamphlets in quick succession in June and July 1942. The first one, which contained the earliest German account of mass slaughter by the Nazis, told of German troops killing three hundred thousand Polish Jews. It urged readers to: "Offer passive resistance — *resistance*—wherever you may be, forestall the spread of this atheistic war machine before it is too late...."[33] Other pamphlets were even more bold:

> Every word that comes from Hitler's mouth is a lie. When he says peace, he means war, and when he blasphemously uses the name of the Almighty, he means the power of evil, the fallen angel, Satan. He is the foul-smelling maw of Hell, and his might is at bottom accursed.[34]

They promised: "We will not be silent. We are your bad conscience. The White Rose will not leave you in peace!"[35]

The group distributed the leaflets throughout Germany, traveling by train with suitcases full of documents. They would hand them out at night or mail them from addresses that could not be traced. They were so successful that a branch of the White Rose was opened in Hamburg; it ended up surviving the original group.

On February 19, 1943 (the same day that Vatican Radio condemned deportations and forced labor, saying "the curse of God" will fall on those who do these things),[36] the regional Nazi commissar made a presentation at the University of Munich. The students in attendance were primarily women and unfit men. He told the men that they would be put to some "more useful" work; he told the women that they would better serve their country by having babies than by pursuing a higher education. He was shouted down, and the students took their protest out to the street. It was the first openly anti-Nazi protest in wartime Germany.[37]

The White Rose published a new pamphlet following the protests. It said: "For us there is but one slogan: fight against the party.... The name of Germany is dishonored for all time if German youth does not finally rise up, take revenge, and atone, smash its tormentors, and set up a new Europe of the spirit."[38] Hans and Sophie distributed it personally at the university, but they were betrayed by a janitor. The Gestapo reacted immediately.

One hundred fifty people were arrested for membership in the White Rose. The leaders were tortured and interrogated by the Gestapo for three days, tried by the People's Court, and beheaded at the guillotine on the day they were found guilty. All told, eighteen members of the White Rose died at the hands of the Nazis, and dozens were imprisoned until the end of the war. (The Hamburg leaders were executed in 1945.) Today, the main square outside the University of Munich is called *Geschwister-Scholl-Platz* in their honor.[39]

The leaders of the White Rose made a statement for God and for their consciences, but the Nazis were not deterred. The persecution continued unabated.

———

The nation of Slovakia (carved out of the defunct Czechoslovakia) came under Nazi rule on March 16, 1939. Nuremberg race laws were introduced in that country on September 9, 1941. Two days later, Monsignor Burzio, the Vatican's chargé d'affaires in Bratislava (the capital of Slovakia), went to see President Jozef Tiso in order to stress "the injustice of these ordinances which also violate the rights of the Church."[40] Shortly thereafter, Slovakia's representative to the Vatican received a written protest from the Holy See that these laws were "in open contrast to Catholic principles."[41] Several other protests followed.[42]

When Jews were deported from Slovakia in 1942, the Vatican secretary of state immediately filed a protest with the Slovakian government.[43] On March 21, 1942, a pastoral letter was read by episcopal order in all Slovak churches. The letter spoke of the "lamentable fate of thousands of innocent fellow citizens, due to no guilt of their own, as a result of their descent or nationality."[44] Under direct orders from Pius XII, the Slovak minister to the Holy See was summoned and requested to take immediate action with his government.[45] The Vatican also instructed the chargé d'affaires in Bratislava once again to contact Tiso and seek relief.[46] Catholic prelate Paval Machàcek, vice president of the Czechoslovak State Council, said in a broadcast to the Slovak people: "It is impossible to serve simultaneously God and the devil. It is equally impossible to be at the same time a good Christian and an anti-Semite."[47]

Pope Pius XII weighed in on the matter with a letter, dated April 7, 1943, to the Slovak government:

> The Holy See has always entertained the firm hope that the Slovak government... would never proceed with the forcible removal of persons belonging to the Jewish race. It is, therefore, with great pain that the Holy See has learned of the continued transfers of such a nature from the territory of the republic. This pain is aggravated further now that it appears... that the Slovak government intends to proceed with the total removal of the Jewish residents of Slovakia, not even sparing women and children.[48]

The following day, a message went out from the Holy See instructing its representative in Bulgaria to take steps in support of Jewish residents who were facing deportation.[49]

On May 5, 1943, a message went out from the Vatican's secretary of state to the representative in Slovakia condemning "the forcible removal of persons belonging to the Jewish race.... The Holy See would fail in its Divine Mandate if it did not deplore these measures, which gravely damage man in his natural right, merely for the reason that these people belong to a certain race."[50] Shortly thereafter, the secretary of the Jewish Agency for Palestine met with Archbishop Roncalli, "to thank the Holy See for the happy outcome of the steps taken on behalf of the Israelites in Slovakia."[51]

On September 20, 1944, the Vatican again instructed its representative in Bratislava to intervene for the Jews.[52] That same month, the *Jewish Chronicle* (London) editorialized, "The Pope's action is... a striking affirmation of the dictum of one of the Pope's predecessors that no true Christian can be an anti-Semite."[53] Jewish communities around the world soon recognized that the Vatican was an advocate in favor of Jews in Slovakia.[54]

By October 1944, deportations were back underway, and many Jews were in hiding. Tiso reported to the Vatican on October 26: "In spite of all protests the German security forces continue transfer of Jews to Germany."[55] A telegram drafted under the name of the acting secretary of state bears corrections in Pius XII's handwriting. It directed the chargé d'affaires to:

> Go at once to President Tiso and, informing him of His Holiness's deep sorrow on account of sufferings which very large numbers of persons — contrary to principles of humanity and justice — are undergoing in that nation *on account of their nationality or race*, in the name of the August Pontiff bring him back to sentiments and resolutions in conformity with his priestly dignity and conscience.[56]

Between 1941 and 1944, the Vatican sent four official letters and made numerous oral pleas and protests regarding the deportation of Jews from Slovakia.[57]

In November 1944, the Holy See dispatched a note expressing "deep sorrow" and hope that the Slovak government would assure that "Jews who are still in the territory... may not be subjected to even more severe sufferings." The note concluded:

> The Holy See, moved by those sentiments of humanity and Christian charity that always inspire its work in favor of those who are suffering, *without distinction of religion, nationality or race*, will continue also in the future, in spite of the growing difficulties of communications, to follow with particular attention the fate of the Jews of Slovakia, and will do everything in its power to bring them relief.[58]

Tiso ultimately managed to slow down the deportation of Slovakian Jews,[59] but due to his collaboration with the Nazis (albeit under pressure from Hitler), the Slovaks hanged him after the war.

Because he was a priest, some critics have argued that the Vatican supported Tiso, despite his collaboration with the Nazis. Actually, the available evidence demonstrates just the opposite. On the day that Tiso was chosen as the first president of the Slovak Republic (September 26, 1939), the Vatican released a statement expressing its "grave misgivings," and warning that this move would corrupt the relationship between church and state. As reported in the *New York Times*:

> Owing to Slovakia's subservience to Germany it is not doubted that President Tiso will have to visit Berlin and most likely be seen and even photographed with Chancellor Hitler, whom the Vatican regards as a persecutor of Catholics.... It was recalled in this connection that the Vatican, prompted by a similar consideration, refused to sanction the appointment some months ago of a priest as Ambassador to the Holy See from a South American Republic, and the candidate had to be withdrawn.[60]

Despite Pius XII's concern that this move might have a Catholic priest pictured with Hitler, Tiso assumed the office in defiance of the Pope, not with his support.[61] As it was written during the war:

> What followed was strictly according to the Nazi pattern. Persecution of the Jews and imprisonment of every democratic voice; the creation of an Iron Guard to shoot down strikers and saboteurs; the Germanization of the school system; the expropriation of property, the confiscation of grain and foodstuffs; and the dispatch of Slovak youth to the Russian front. From Rome came the thunders of the Holy Father, denouncing these outrages, but Tiso paid no heed to the voice of the Holy Father.[62]

The Secretary of the Congregation of Extraordinary Ecclesiastical Affairs (Monsignor Domenico Tardini) recorded in his notes of October 21 and 23, 1941, that if the pro-Nazi statements attributed to Tiso were actually made by him, the Holy Father wanted his name to be removed from a list of praiseworthy prelates.[63] Later, Tardini wrote: "It is a great misfortune that the President of Slovakia is a priest. Everyone knows that the Holy See cannot bring Hitler to heel. But who will understand that we can't even control a priest?"[64]

———

Hans Frank, the Nazi *gauleiter* (governor) of occupied Poland, declared in 1941, "I asked nothing of the Jews except that they should disappear." His forces then set about trying to accomplish just that: the Nazis refused to allow enough food into the Warsaw ghetto to keep the Jews healthy, forcing most to try to survive for a whole day on a bowl of soup. Soon, several hundred were dying each day from starvation and disease. By July 1942, about 80,000 Jews had perished. That month, the S.S. began a massive "resettlement," taking the Jews out of the ghetto to extermination camps (mainly Treblinka), where they were to be gassed.

In just two months, a total of 310,322 Jews were sent to their deaths. By the end of the year, only 60,000 Jews remained.[65]

On April 19, 1943, Jewish residents of Warsaw staged a desperate uprising in the ghetto. The Nazis countered with a block-to-block search, but they found it difficult to kill or capture the small battle groups of Jews, who would fight, then retreat through cellars, sewers, and other hidden passageways. On the fifth day of the fighting, Himmler ordered the S.S. to comb out the ghetto with the greatest severity and relentless tenacity. S.S. General Juergen Stroop decided to burn down the entire ghetto, block by block. Many victims burned to death or jumped to their death, rather than permit themselves to be caught by the Nazis.

On May 5, 1943, the Vatican secretariat issued a memorandum expressing the reaction of the Roman authorities:

> The Jews. A dreadful situation. There were approximately four and a half million of them in Poland before the war; today the estimate is that not even a hundred thousand remain there, including those who have come from other countries under German occupation. In Warsaw a ghetto had been established which contained six hundred and fifty thousand of them; today there would be twenty to twenty-five thousand. Some, naturally, have avoided being placed on the list of names. But there is no doubt that most have been liquidated. The only possible explanation here is that they have died.... There are special death camps near Lublin (Treblinka) and Brest-Litovsk. It is said that by the hundreds they are shut up in chambers where they [are] gassed to death and then transported in tightly sealed cattle trucks with lime on their floors.[66]

The Jews in Warsaw resisted for a total of twenty-eight days. On May 16, General Stroop reported that "the former Jewish quarter of Warsaw is no longer in existence. The large scale action was terminated at 2015 hours by blowing up the Warsaw synagogue.... Total number of Jews dealt with 56,065, including both Jews caught and Jews whose extermination can be proved."[67] (About 20,000 Jews were killed in the streets of Warsaw and another 36,000 in the gas chambers.) Polish sources estimated that 300 Germans were killed and about 1,000 were wounded.

Not only in Warsaw, but throughout Poland, Jewish people were in hiding. About 200 convents hid more than 1,500 Jewish children, mainly in Warsaw and the surrounding area. This was especially difficult, because Polish nuns in German-occupied areas were often persecuted and forced into hiding themselves.[68] Nuns who lived in Soviet-occupied areas did not have it much better. They were sent to work for the Soviets, in areas as far away as Siberia. As such, the courage of the priests and nuns who provided shelter to Jewish people was truly admirable.

The case of Père Jacques of Jesus (of the Carmelite Order) illustrates the risks that clergy took when they hid Jewish people from the Nazis. Father Jacques was headmaster at a boys' school in Avon, France, when the Nazis invaded. As the deportations began, he agreed to hide Jews, seminarians facing deportation, and fugitive resistance fighters. When he was questioned about taking such chances, he said: "If by chance I were shot, I would be leaving my pupils an example worth more to them than all the instruction I could give." In January 1944, the Gestapo conducted a raid. When Father Jacques and three Jewish boys were being taken away, he called to the remaining children, *"Au revoir, les enfants!"*[69] He died in German custody, having spent his final days comforting other prisoners.[70]

---

The deportation and execution of priests from occupied countries created some very difficult personal dilemmas. For instance, if Nazis were deporting priests, soldiers would be charged with finding them, and the whole community would often help protect them. One technique that the Germans used to uncover those in hiding was to pretend to seek counsel so that the person being sought would come out of hiding.[71] On occasion, however, a Catholic German soldier (or even a Nazi official) would actually seek spiritual counseling from a priest. How would the community decide whether the request to see a priest was real, and how much courage did it take for the priest to come out of hiding to counsel those who might be hunting him? The priests usually did come out to provide counsel,[72] which might help account for the high number of priests who were sent to the concentration camps.

In 1943, the German bishops issued a statement proclaiming: "The extermination of human beings is *per se* wrong, even if it is purportedly done in the interests of society; but it is particularly evil if it is carried out against the innocent and defenseless people of alien races or alien descent."[73] The bishops urged respect for the right to life of all people, including the old and sick, hostages, prisoners of war, and members of a foreign race.[74]

The July 3, 1943 issue of the *Tablet* (London) published part of a transcript of a Vatican Radio broadcast into Germany from the bishops of Slovakia in which they expressly defended the rights of Jews under natural law. Similar broadcasts were made in other nations, but the impact did not always reach into Nazi-controlled areas. For instance, on June 2, 1943 (the feast day of St. Eugenio), in an address to the cardinals that was broadcast on Vatican Radio and clandestinely distributed in printed form within Poland, the Pope expressed in new and clear terms his compassion and affection for the Polish people and predicted the rebirth of Poland:

> No one familiar with the history of Christian Europe can ignore or forget the saints and heroes of Poland... nor how the faithful people of that land have contributed throughout history to the development and conservation of Christian Europe. For this people so harshly tried, and others, who together have been forced to drink the bitter chalice of war today, may a new future dawn worthy of their legitimate aspirations in the depths of their sufferings, in a Europe based anew on Christian foundations.[75]

Pius XII assured his listeners that he regarded all people with equal goodwill. He then, however, provided a bit more insight into his thoughts:

> [D]o not be surprised, Venerable Brothers and beloved sons, if our soul reacts with particular emotion and pressing concern to the prayers of those who turn to us with anxious pleading eyes, in travail *because of their nationality or their race*, before greater catastrophes and ever more acute and serious sorrows, and destined sometimes, even without fault of their own, to exterminating constraints.[76]

The Pope warned the cardinals to be cautious about what they said: "Every word we address to the competent authority on this subject, and all our public utterances, have to be carefully weighed and measured by us in the interests of the victims themselves, lest, contrary to our intentions, we make their situation worse and harder to bear."[77]

Leaders of the Catholic Church in Poland, including some who had asked the Pope to make a statement on behalf of the victims of the Nazis, were very grateful for the address. On June 11, Cardinal Hlond sent his thanks for the "historic words" of the Pope, saying that "the Poles needed this, and they anxiously awaited this statement which put an end to the fables of Hitler's propaganda that the Holy See had simply given up in regard to the situation in Poland."[78] Archbishop Sapieha wrote from Kraków that "the Polish people will never forget these noble and holy words, which will call forth a new and ever more loyal love for the Holy Father... and at the same time provide a most potent antidote to the poisonous influences of enemy propaganda."[79] He also said that he would try to publicize the speech as much as possible by having copies printed, if the authorities would permit it.

––––––––––

The Catholic Pope is also the Bishop of Rome. As such, the safety of Rome was always very close to Pius XII's heart. In May, he sent word to Mussolini that he was prepared to use the authority of his offices to try to extricate Italy from the war.[80] He also had several communications with Roosevelt, seeking assurance that the Allies would not bomb Rome.[81] On May 18, 1943, Pius wrote to Roosevelt:

> The assurance given to Us in 1941 by Your Excellency's esteemed Ambassador Mr. Myron Taylor and spontaneously repeated by him in 1942 that "America has no hatred of the Italian people" gives Us confidence that they will be treated with consideration and understanding; and if they have had to mourn the untimely death of dear ones, they will yet in their present circumstances be spared as far as possible further pain and devastation.[82]

In response, on June 16, Roosevelt wrote:

> Attacks against Italy are limited, to the extent humanly possible, to military objectives.... This may be an opportune time to warn Your Holiness that I

have no reason to feel assured that Axis planes would not make an opportunity to bomb Vatican City with the purpose of charging Allied planes with the outrages they themselves had committed. My country has no choice but to prosecute the war with all force against the enemy until every resistance has been overcome.... Any other course would only delay the fulfillment of that desire in which Your Holiness and the governments and peoples of the United Nations — I believe the people of Italy likewise — are joined — the return of peace on earth.[83]

This was followed within a month by a telegram in which President Roosevelt said: "Churches and religious institutions will, to the extent that it is within our power, be spared the devastations of war during the struggle ahead. Throughout the period of operations the neutral status of the Vatican City as well as of the Papal domains throughout Italy will be respected."[84]

Despite the Pope's pleas, on the morning of July 19, 1943, the Allies bombed Rome. As he did whenever there was an air raid, Pius XII refused to go to a shelter. Instead, he watched the two-and-a-half-hour raid from a window in his study.[85] More than 500 American bombers dropped 1,200 tons of explosives on Rome. The Basilica of St. Laurence Outside-the-Walls, first built in the sixth century by Pope Pelagius, was partially demolished, as was the cemetery of Campo Verano, where the remains of the Pope's parents were blown from their graves. It was estimated that "well over 1,000" people were killed.[86]

As soon as the all-clear was sounded, the Pope withdrew the cash reserves in the Vatican Bank and drove into the city. He said prayers, gave comfort to the injured, and distributed about two million lira.[87] Around dawn, Pope Pius returned to the Vatican and composed a letter to President Roosevelt. It said:

> We call on God, Our sole stay and comfort, to hasten the dawn of that day when His peace will erect the glorious temple built of living stones, the nations of the earth, wherein all members of the vast human family will find tranquillity, security in justice, and freedom and inspiration to worship their Creator and to love their fellow men. It is the day, as Your Excellency says, longed for by all men of good will.... We avail Ourselves of this occasion to renew Our good wishes, while we pray God to protect Your Person and the people of the United States.[88]

He also sent an open letter to the cardinal-vicar of Rome, in which he expressed great disappointment at his failure to persuade Allied leaders not to bomb Rome,[89] and he wrote the Italian government to verify whether they had kept their promise to remove all military targets from the city.[90]

Memories of this day would haunt the Pontiff for years thereafter. In 1948, he recorded his thoughts:

> That day will be known in history as the most sorrowful for the Eternal City during the Second World War. Seldom perhaps have the Shepherd and the

faithful of the Bishopric of Rome been as closely united as in the common mourning of July 19. The air attack had devastated a peaceful section of Rome; the tombs of the cemetery of San Lorenzo were destroyed; the roof of the vestibule, the facade and one of the walls of one of Rome's oldest basilicas had been razed. This day, however, gave us an opportunity to come in close contact with the suffering and frightened population of our beloved native town. Up to the last day of our life we will still remember this sorrowful meeting.[91]

One month after this attack, the district of San Giovanni was bombed, and the Pope was again among the first on the scene.

The Axis leaders expressed great concern over the bombing and offered their condolences to the Holy See. According, however, to a telegram from the American ambassador in Switzerland:

Many Fascists are shedding "crocodile tears." In their hearts they are rejoicing that Papacy has after all proved itself unable [to] protect Rome since loss [of] prestige which they believe Pope will suffer as result will tend to strengthen their own political position with masses. The Germans as well, I understand, have been quick to recognize propaganda possibilities for them.[92]

Axis propaganda agencies characterized the Pope's words as condemning the Allies. In response, Pius "launched a broadcast to Germany denying their propaganda blasts that the Pope had only condemned the Allies. He said that the churches had been destroyed in the whole of Europe. This meant that Nazi Germany had done it."[93] On the night of July 24, Vatican Radio reported (in German) that the Pope did not protest to Roosevelt, did not summon American representatives to his office, and did not question the good faith of the American aviators.[94]

Around this time, Pius was reportedly told that Hitler had ordered his capture and given instructions that the Pope should be shot if he resisted.[95] Pius was urged to move the papacy to a neutral nation, but he resolved to stay in Rome and do what he could to alleviate the suffering. About six months earlier, he had said to the rector at the Gregorian University that the Nazis "want to destroy the Church and crush it like a toad. There will be no place for the Pope in the new Europe. They say that he is going to America. I have no fear and I shall remain here."[96]

In June 1943, Pius released his encyclical *Mystici Corporis Christi* (on the Mystical Body of Christ). At least one of his advisers reportedly urged him to name Hitler as the "barbaric butcher behind the Holocaust,"[97] but the draft as released contained no express references to Hitler or the Nazis. Still, it was an obvious attack on the theoretical basis of National Socialism. As Pinchas E. Lapide, the Israeli consul in Italy, wrote: "Pius chose mystical theology as a cloak for a message which no cleric or educated Christian could possibly misunderstand."[98] "Clerics and educated Christians" would, of course, include priests and bishops who would "translate" messages for other Christians. They recognized that this encyclical was an "unequivocal condemnation of the Nazis 'euthanasia' program."[99]

Historians like to rely upon documentary evidence in original languages. This places a premium on linguistic abilities. Translation issues, however, show that the ability to read a given language is not in and of itself sufficient to come to a full understanding of papal statements.[100] The ability to understand "Vatican-talk" is equally important. Those who look at papal statements without that ability are like someone looking at a language that they do not understand. Unfortunately, critics seem completely lost when it comes to understanding how Vatican leaders have traditionally spoken.

In *Mystici Corporis Christi*, Pius wrote: "The Church of God... is despised and hated maliciously by those who shut their eyes to the light of Christian wisdom and miserably return to the teachings, customs, and practices of ancient paganism." He wrote of the "passing things of earth," and the "massive ruins" of war. He offered prayers that world leaders be granted the love of wisdom and expressed no doubt that "a most severe judgment" would await those leaders who did not follow God's will. Pius appealed to "Catholics the world over" to "look to the Vicar of Jesus Christ as the loving Father of them all, who... takes upon himself with all his strength the defense of truth, justice, and charity." He explained, "Our paternal love embraces all peoples, whatever their nationality or race."

Despite claims by critics that Pius never mentioned Jews in his wartime statements, in this document he made a statement that was quite remarkable for its time: "Christ, by his blood, made the Jews and Gentiles one, 'breaking down the middle wall of partition... in his flesh' by which the two peoples were divided." He noted that Jews were among the first people to adore Jesus. Pius then made an appeal for all to "follow our peaceful King who taught us to love not only those who are of a different nation or race, but even our enemies."[101]

The impact of the encyclical was expanded as it was repeated. In June, Vatican Radio followed up with a broadcast that expressly stated: "He who makes a distinction between Jews and other men is unfaithful to God and in conflict with God's commands."[102] On July 28, 1943, a Vatican Radio broadcast further reported on the Pope's denunciation of totalitarian forms of government and support for democratic ideals. It said:

> The life and activities of all must be protected against arbitrary human action. This means that no man has any right on the life and freedom of other men. Authority... cannot be at the service of any arbitrary power. Herein lies the essential differences between tyranny and true usefulness.... The Pope condemns those who dare to place the fortunes of whole nations in the hands of one man alone, a man who as such, is the prey of passions, error and dreams.[103]

Adolf Hitler's name was not used, but there was no doubt to whom the Pope was referring.

Jewish organizations took note of Pius XII's efforts, and they turned to him in times of need. In July 1943, Grand Rabbi Herzog wrote to Cardinal Maglione on behalf of Egyptian Jews, expressing thanks for the Holy See's charitable work in Europe and asking for assistance for Jews in Poland.[104] On August 2, the World Jewish Congress sent the following message to Pius:

> World Jewish Congress respectfully expresses gratitude to Your Holiness for your gracious concern for innocent peoples afflicted by the calamities of war and appeals to Your Holiness to use your high authority by suggesting Italian authorities may remove as speedily as possible to Southern Italy or other safer areas twenty thousand Jewish refugees and Italian nationals now concentrated in internment camps... and so prevent their deportation and similar tragic fate which has befallen Jews in Eastern Europe. Our terror-stricken brethren look to Your Holiness as the only hope for saving them from persecution and death.[105]

Later that same month, *Time* magazine reported: "... no matter what critics might say, it is scarcely deniable that the Church Apostolic, through the encyclicals and other Papal pronouncements, has been fighting totalitarianism more knowingly, devoutly, and authoritatively, and for a longer time, than any other organized power."[106]

In September, a representative from the World Jewish Congress reported to the Pope that approximately four thousand Jews and Yugoslav nationals who had been in internment camps were removed to an area that was under the control of Yugoslav partisans. As such, they were out of immediate danger. The report went on to say:

> I feel sure that the efforts of your Grace and the Holy See have brought about this fortunate result, and I should like to express to the Holy See and yourself the warmest thanks of the World Jewish Congress. The Jews concerned will probably not yet know by what agency their removal from danger has been secured, but when they do they will be indeed grateful.[107]

In November, Rabbi Herzog again wrote to Pius expressing his "sincere gratitude and deep appreciation for so kind an attitude toward Israel and for such valuable assistance given by the Catholic Church to the endangered Jewish people."[108] Jewish communities in Chile, Uruguay, and Bolivia also sent similar offers of thanks to the Pope.[109]

———

The Allied leaders met in Washington in May 1943, to discuss strategy. Freed from the battles in Africa, Allied troops could look to the north. Churchill wanted to attack Italy "the soft underbelly of the Axis." President Roosevelt agreed. The next month the Allies began their long-awaited invasion of Sicily.

The German forces in Italy put up dogged resistance, and the Italian front soon was marked by the most bitter and bloody fighting of the European war.

Italian cities, which contained some of the most precious memorials of European culture, were ravaged by the prolonged fighting. The Italian people, however, were no longer ready to be led to slaughter by Mussolini. The invasion of Italy was the last straw.

By this time, there were several movements to rid Italy of Mussolini. Pius was anxious to take whatever action he could to help shorten the war, and on May 12 he wrote a note encouraging Mussolini to pursue a separate peace with the Allies.[110] Mussolini thanked the Pope, but replied that "under present condition there is no alternative, and Italy will continue to wage war."[111]

By now the Americans were certain of ultimate victory. Roosevelt had already asked the Vatican to keep him informed of governmental changes within Italy. On May 29, Myron Taylor sent a message to the Vatican in which the Holy See was urged to tell "whoever has the means for acting" that Italy now had to separate itself from Germany and form a new government.[112] The only other alternative was utter devastation.

In early June, Pius agreed to draft a message to the Italian king. Before it was sent, Roosevelt made the information public. He announced in a press conference that the Italian people had to oust the Fascist regime and rid itself of the Nazis. If that were done, Italy could choose its own government and join the family of nations. Otherwise, Italy had to brace for intensive warfare.[113] On June 17, Pius sent his nuncio to see King Victor Emmanuel III and confirm that the United States had sent a substantially similar message to the king through the Vatican's diplomatic offices.[114] The king was not ready to move at that time, but Mussolini did not remain in power much longer.

Following the bombing raid on Rome that took place on July 19, King Victor Emmanuel III scheduled a meeting with Mussolini at the Quirinal Palace. It took place on the night of July 24. When it was over, Mussolini went out to his car, but it was gone. He was directed to a shaded area of the king's villa. Mussolini found himself surrounded by secret police who ordered him into an ambulance. He asked where he was being taken and was told that he would be safe. Without saying anything more, Mussolini got into the vehicle and was driven to a place of imprisonment. He was replaced by Marshal Pietro Badoglio.

Even though the king pledged to continue fighting alongside the Germans, the change in Italian leadership concerned Hitler's high command. They were worried that Badoglio might defect and take sides with the Allies.[115] To prevent this, the Germans seized strategic centers, preparing to occupy an allied nation. Pius, for his part, urged the new Italian government to declare Rome an open city. On July 31, the Badoglio government informed the Vatican that Rome would, in principle, be free and asked the Vatican to forward that message to Washington.[116]

When the news spread that Mussolini had been overthrown, most Italians were delighted.[117] He had led Italy into the war and was blamed for much of the suffering that came with it. On the other hand, as long as Mussolini was in power, Italians did not agree to deportation of Jews from Italy, Italian-occupied

France, or Italian-occupied Croatia.[118] (Some top German leaders blamed the influence of the Catholic Church for the Italian resistance to Jewish deportation.)[119] Now, however, German troops were going to be in charge. "Suddenly the future seemed at risk not only for the forty-three thousand Italian Jews whom Mussolini had protected from deportation, but also for many thousand more Jews who lived, or had found refuge, in [Italian-occupied areas]."[120]

Hitler learned of Mussolini's downfall over the radio. (It was reported that Mussolini had suddenly resigned for health reasons.) He "was furious, especially with the 'Jew-loving' Pope Pius XII, whom he was sure had encouraged the revolt."[121] Napoleon Bonaparte had kidnapped Pope Pius VII in 1809, and Hitler considered doing the same.[122] When someone suggested that this would create a public relations problem,[123] Hitler at first dismissed the concern. Minutes of a meeting that took place that night quote him as saying:

> That doesn't matter, I'll go right into the Vatican. Do you think I worry about the Vatican? We'll take that right off. All the diplomatic corps will be hiding in there. I don't give a damn; if the entire crew's in there, we'll get the whole lot of swine out. Afterward, we can say we're sorry. We can easily do that. We've got a war on.[124]

People living in the Vatican kept their bags packed, fearing that the Germans would enter. They also all used false names, just in case.[125] (Pius told Cardinal Nasalli Rocca, "If the Nazis decide to kidnap me, then they're going to have to drag me away by force. Because I'm staying here.")[126]

(There was even a joke that made the rounds in Vatican City concerning German occupation and Air Marshall Hermann Göring's well-known fondness for uniforms and decorations. According to the story, he had been sent to Rome by Hitler. Shortly thereafter he wired back: "Have placed the Holy See under German protection. All prelates in concentration camp. Pope has fled. Vatican in flames. Cardinal's robe suits me beautifully.")[127]

Fortunately, wiser counsel prevailed.[128] Rome was not stormed by Panzer divisions, and the Vatican was never invaded, but Hitler did send his troops into Rome. They took the city on September 10, 1943, after just two days of fighting.[129]

As soon as it became clear that German troops would occupy Rome, Pius tried to help Jews evacuate the city and made plans for feeding the city's residents. Rome's population was swollen to almost double its size by refugees drawn by what they thought was the protection of an open city. It was, according to one account, "a city of spies, double agents, informers, torturers, escaped war prisoners, hunted Jews, and hungry people."[130] Pius also had the Vatican secretary of state write to the leaders of all religious orders and ask them to help refugees in any way they could.[131]

Upwards of sixty thousand German soldiers entered Rome. A white line on the ground separated occupied Rome from neutral Vatican City. On September

10, at 4:00 p.m., Nazi troopers in full battle dress took up "protective patrol" around the Vatican.[132] On one side of that line, German soldiers carried their machine guns. On the other side, the Vatican's Swiss Guards stood at attention with their largely decorative pikes. (London Radio reported that the Pope was being held hostage.)[133] At first, people could pass freely into Vatican City, but when the Nazis realized that the Pope was offering shelter to Jews and other refugees, they began checking identification. The Church countered by providing fake identification for people wanting to enter the Vatican. Later still, many people made mad dashes to safety after dark.

These Vatican soldiers represented the remnants of an era when the Pope actually commanded a military force. In addition to protecting those in the Vatican, the Holy See's honorary troops, the Swiss Guard and the Palatine Guard, also provided cover for refugees during the war. Membership in the Palatine Guard automatically confered Vatican citizenship.[134] Because of the immunities and privileges that such citizenship implied, the number of Palatine Guards had always been kept low. In early 1942, for instance, there were only about 300 members. By the end of 1943, however, the Palatine Guard had grown to 4,000.[135] The indignation of the German high command "knew no bounds when it was discovered that many hundreds of these papal guards were unbaptised Jews."[136] After receiving the protests and fearing that Vatican citizenship might not be sufficient to protect them, Pius XII ordered that about 250 of them be quartered in the Vatican itself.[137]

————

The Allies bombed Rome on August 19, 1943, and two days later they sent a message to the Holy See. Why, they wondered, had the new Italian government not separated itself from the Germans, and were they being forced to continue the war?[138] There was some concern on the part of the Holy See with regard to the propriety of answering, but the Pope decided to reply. A return cable, sent on August 21, said that Italian cooperation with the Germans was not freely given, but was forced.[139] This information helped the Allies with their next major move in the war.

On September 3, 1943, British and American forces moved across the Strait of Messina to the Italian peninsula. At Algiers, on the same day, the Badoglio regime secretly signed an armistice with the Allies. The Italian capitulation was announced on September 8.[140] The very next day, the newspaper *Il popolo di Roma* reported that the Holy See had an important role in bringing the armistice about, though this was subsequently denied to Nazi authorities.[141] Within a month, southern Italy was under Allied control, and on October 13 the new anti-Fascist government declared war on Germany.

The relief effort undertaken by the Vatican when Hitler moved troops into Italy has been called "probably the greatest Christian program in the history of Catholicism."[142] Pius sent a letter to the bishops, instructing them to open all convents and monasteries throughout Italy so that they could become safe refuges for Jewish people.[143] A nun in Rome recorded in the convent diary: "New demands come in to increase the number of families already welcomed, and there is beginning to be a lack of space, but how can we refuse any of the distressed?"[144] Even more revealing of Pius XII's intent, another wrote in her convent diary: "In these grievous situations the Holy Father wishes to save his sons, also the Jews, and orders that in the convents hospitality be given to those persecuted people, and also the Monasteries of enclosure must adhere to this desire of the Supreme Pontiff."[145]

All available Church buildings — including those in Vatican City — were put to use. One hundred and fifty such sanctuaries were opened in Rome alone. "Shelters were improvised everywhere, in lofts, in storage rooms under stairs, hidden behind blind doors or cupboards, subterranean galleries, ancient Roman doors used as escape routes: all this as soon as the alert sounded — according to agreed signs, such as the convent bells — that a Nazi inspection was approaching."[146] As the Nazis intensified their persecution, the Church also placed Jews in monasteries, parish houses, and private homes.[147] As the *New York Times* reported: "Jews received first priority — Italian Jews and Jews who escaped here from Germany and other countries — but all the hunted found sanctuary in the Vatican and its hundreds of convents and monasteries in the Rome region."[148] Almost five thousand Jews, a third of the Jewish population of Rome, were hidden in buildings that belonged to the Catholic Church.[149] The Vatican provided food and clothes.[150] Catholic hospitals were ordered to admit Jewish patients, even if their ailments were fictitious.[151] Deserting German soldiers were also given sanctuary, as were Allied soldiers who were trapped behind enemy lines.[152] The chief rabbi of Rome reported:

> No hero in history has commanded such an army; an army of priests works in cities and small towns to provide bread for the persecuted and passports for the fugitives. Nuns go into canteens to give hospitality to women refugees. Superiors of convents go out into the night to meet German soldiers who look for victims.... Pius XII is followed by all with the fervor of that charity that fears no death.[153]

Convents were normally closed to outsiders. These rules were very strict and could not have been violated without instructions from high Church authorities. At first, refugees were kept in common areas, out of the cloistered rooms, but as more and more people sought protection from the Germans, all rooms were opened. Still, however, everyone in the convents and monasteries had to abide with strict separation-of-the-sexes rules. As a result, most Jewish families were split up. Priests sometimes had to play "postmen," carrying messages between husband and wife. In rare occasions, Church officials would bend the rules to accommodate married couples.[154] Catholic authorities also made provisions for kosher food and tried to provide decent burials when Jewish people were killed in the war.[155]

Those receiving shelter were required to pledge that they did not have weapons, that they would act in accordance with the Vatican's official neutrality, and that they would follow any rules that were necessary to preserve that neutrality. Jewish religious articles presented particular problems, as they would be sure giveaways if they were discovered by the Germans. There are, however, many accounts of Catholic clergy saving sacred books and copies of the Torah for their Jewish "guests."[156]

Castel Gandolfo, the papal summer home, is worth particular note. This facility was used to shelter hundreds and perhaps thousands of refugees during the war. The papal apartments were used to shelter pregnant women nearing the days of childbirth, and some forty children were born there.[157] The first edition of this book used the (apparently low) number of five hundred Jews sheltered. In fact, photos from Castel Gandolfo show people not only sleeping in the halls, but even up and down the staircases,[158] and some accounts place the number of people sheltered there as high as twelve thousand.[159] A wartime U.S. intelligence document reported that the "bombardment of Castel Gandolfo resulted in the injury of about 1,000 people and the death of about 300 more. The highness of the figures is due to the fact that the area was crammed with refugees."[160] No one but Pope Pius XII had authority to open these buildings to outsiders. As at least one witness testified under oath that the orders came from the Pope.[161]

Susan Zuccotti noted the rescue work at Castle Gondolfo, but she speculated that perhaps none of the people sheltered there were Jewish. Actually, at the liberation of Rome, the *Palestine Post* wrote: "Several thousand refugees, largely Jews, during the week end left the Papal Palace at Castle Gondolfo — the Pope's summer residence near Marino — after enjoying safety there during the recent terror. Besides Jews, persons of all political creeds who had been endangered were given sanctuary in the Palace."[162] Moreover, the director of the papal villa at Castel Gandolfo during the Second World War, Emilio Bonomelli, wrote a book in 1953 in which he discussed caring for Jews and other refugees during the war.[163] According to another account, about three thousand Jews were sheltered there at one time.[164] Today, in Castel Gandolfo, there is on display a beautifully decorated, enormous wooden cross, which was given to Pius XII at the end of the war by the Jews who lived there during those terrifying days.[165]

Blank and forged documents were freely handed out by Church authorities. Many Jews used these to show that they had been baptized into the Catholic faith, and because of the provisions of the 1933 concordat, Germans would usually leave them alone. Pius also assisted Jewish people as they emigrated to safe nations. Many Jewish people with these documents were transported to safety in Spain or Switzerland, but as the border became better secured by the Germans, relocation became more dangerous. Many Jews were dressed in clerical garb and were taught to chant the liturgy.[166] (Some survivors recall switching in mid-prayer from the Hebrew *Shema* to the Latin *Ave Maria* when a stranger approached.)[167] Catholic priests then began personally escorting these "monks and nuns" across the Allied lines.[168] Even later, some were sent in trucks disguised as food-delivery vehicles.

The Catholic Church provided papers indicating Latin American citizenship to many Jews in occupied France. When the papers were discovered to be fraudulent, the Latin American countries withdrew recognition of them. This made the Jews subject to deportation to the concentration camps. Pursuant to a request from the Union of Orthodox Rabbis of the United States and Canada, and working in conjunction with the International Red Cross, the Vatican contacted the countries involved and urged them to recognize the documents, "no matter how illegally obtained."[169]

In a video interview posted on the Internet, Archbishop Giovanni Ferrofino, the former secretary to the apostolic nuncio in Haiti and the Dominican Republic, explained how, at Pius XII's direction, the Church smuggled over eleven thousand Jews out of Europe into the United States through the Dominican Republic. Ferrofino said the Pope "showed a firm determination to save many Jews." He also quoted Pius XII: "'Everything must be done to save such a vibrant community!' *The pope literally said this to me.*"[170]

———

Bruno Ascoli, was born in 1910, and he grew up in the Jewish community in Ancona. He was the son of a mixed marriage and did not practice Judaism. In fact, on October 28, 1938, just after the racial laws went into force, he asked to be baptized. The parish priest tried to help, writing that Ascoli had attended catechism since August of that year, but the response from the government was that whoever had a Jewish parent, and couldn't prove he belonged to another religion at the time when the racial laws went into effect, was considered to be a Jew. Two years later, Bruno was married in the Catholic Church to a Catholic woman, even though the marriage could not have civil effect.[171]

In October 1943, when the Nazis began to round up Roman Jews,[172] Bruno was put on the "wanted" list. He briefly found a place to hide in the repair shop of a tire dealer, but the tire dealer made him leave because it had become too dangerous. That is when he was enlisted into the Palatine Guard and became an auxiliary of the Pope's honor guard. As Bruno's son has written: "[T]here was an organized network of aid and assistance.... I believe that Pope Pacelli chose well: no public denunciations which would have provoked acts of repression — I don't dare imagine what would have happened had the SS entered the Vatican — but rather give concrete help to the persecuted."[173] He added: "I'm not a believer, I don't go to church, but if I found myself before Pius XII I'd get down on my knees, because if my children and I are in existence, we owe it to him."[174]

As the Pope placed himself in danger and sacrificed much to save others, the world Jewish community took note. A note from the Israelite Central Committee of Uruguay to the papal nuncio reported:

> We deem it a high honor to make known to Your Excellency our fondness and support of His Holiness, Pius XII, who already directly suffers the conse-

quences of the actual conflict that strikes the world.... [T]he Community that we represent has always followed the news... of the situation of the Vatican and the August person of His Holiness.... And from the depths of their hearts the Israelites of Uruguay pray [for]... news that assures the cessation of the danger that threatens His Holiness, Pius XII, ardent defender of the cause of those who are unjustly persecuted.[175]

The Germans had a list of priests who had given shelter to Jews, and they tried to capture these priests and send them to concentration camps. As the Nazis moved into Italy, many "listed" priests moved into the Vatican, and they did not re-emerge until the Allies had liberated the city. In northern Italy, where the priests had more difficulty hiding out, the Nazis executed many of them.

———

Ernst von Weizsäcker, German ambassador to the Holy See in the latter part of the war,[176] was not a typical Nazi officer. Outwardly, he conformed to the requirements of a loyal Nazi diplomat, but inwardly, as his confidants testified, he was determined to sabotage and resist:[177]

> Colleagues in the diplomatic corps, such as the British and Italian ambassadors, Sir Nevile Henderson and Bernardo Attolico, and the last [League of Nations] high commissioner to Danzig, Carl Burckhardt, believed he was an honorable and tenacious foe of war, a reasonable, decent German, opposed to Joachim von Ribbentrop and Adolf Hitler on fundamental issues. The vigorous Norwegian primate, Bishop Elvind Berggrav, was convinced that his friend on the Wilhelmstrasse was a noble and sincere Christian, caught in a cruel dilemma by his role as a diplomat in Nazi Germany. Younger foreign office officials — Erich and Theo Kordt, Adam von Trott zu Solz, Albrecht von Kessel — considered the state secretary their mentor in efforts for sane diplomacy. In the resistance, Admiral Wilhelm Franz Canaris and General Hans Oster, both executed after July 20, 1944, included Weizsäcker in their ranks as an opponent of the Nazi regime.[178]

Even before the war, Weizsäcker wanted to oust Hitler.[179] In fact, Hitler had "exiled" Weizsäcker to Rome, where the Nazis thought he could do little harm.[180] Eventually, however, Weizsäcker joined in a military plot to overthrow the *Fuehrer*.[181]

On September 20, a representative from the Fascist government in northern Italy approached Archbishop Schuster of Milan to demand six thousand Jewish "hostages" in exchange for six German soldiers who were killed at a hospital. The Pope's close adviser, Giovanni Battista Montini, the future Pope Paul VI, immediately contacted Weizsäcker. The German ambassador, however, explained to Montini that he did not want to speak of the Vatican when he communicated with Berlin. "At headquarters they are not thinking about the Holy See, and I am afraid that to talk about hostages in the name of the Holy See would provoke grave repercussions against the Holy See," he said.[182] Montini at first rejected this line of argument. Eventually, however, Weizsäcker persuaded Montini to trust him. Montini wrote, "He is a man with a heart, and knows that we must make every effort to dam the flood of hate that threatens to drown the peoples."[183] Eventually, the Germans dropped their demand for Jewish hostages, but Weizsäcker warned that similar cases were likely to follow, and one did within a week.[184]

On September 27, S.S. officials summoned representatives of Rome's Jewish community and demanded fifty kilograms of gold (or the equivalent in dollars or sterling) within thirty-six hours.[185] Otherwise, the Nazis would send two hundred Jews to the concentration camps.[186] In his 1954 memoir, Rabbi Eugenio Zolli gave his account of the Jewish community's approach to the Pope for help:

> The Community had succeeded in gathering together only around thirty-five kilograms of gold. Would I, he asked, go to the Vatican and try to obtain a loan of fifteen kilograms of gold? "Right away," I replied. Dr. [Giorgio] Fiorentino arrived with a car. "I am dressed like a beggar," I remarked. "We shall go in by one of the back doors," he replied. "The Vatican is always guarded by the Gestapo. A friendly person will be waiting for you, and so that you can avoid showing personal documents stamped 'Hebrew Race,' you will be presented as an engineer, called to examine some walls that are being constructed."
>
> ***
>
> The Vatican had already spent millions in aiding fugitive Jews to reach safety. I said, "The New Testament does not abandon the Old. Please help me. As for repayment, I myself shall stand as surety, and since I am poor, the Hebrews of the world will contribute to pay the debt."[187]

The Vatican officials retreated to speak to Pope Pius XII. After just a few minutes, they returned and offered to loan money for the ransom. The time for repayment was left open; there was no interest charge; and everyone knew that it could not be repaid anytime soon.[188]

According to most accounts, sufficient funds were collected from other sources, so the Vatican did not actually make the loan.[189] Nevertheless, the Pope's charitable offer was not forgotten. Rabbi Zolli expressed his thanks to the Pope on behalf of the Jewish community. Following the war, Rabbi Zolli even converted to Catholicism, and he adopted the Christian name Eugenio to honor the man who had done so much to protect others during the war.[190]

The ransom paid to the Germans merely bought a bit of time. The very next day German troops entered the main synagogue in Rome and took a complete list of Roman Jewish families.[191] At about that same time, Herbert Kappler, S.S. commander in Rome, received an order to arrest the eight thousand Jews who were living in the Roman ghetto and send them to northern Italy, where they would face eventual extermination.[192] According to the memoirs of Adolf Eichmann:

> At that time, my office received the copy of a letter that I immediately gave to my direct supervisors, sent by the Catholic Church in Rome, in the person of Bishop Hudal, to the commander of the German forces in Rome, General Stahel. The Church was vigorously protesting the arrest of Jews of Italian citizenship, requesting that such actions be interrupted immediately throughout Rome and its surroundings.[193]

Eichmann explained that "the objections given [by the Church] and the excessive delay... resulted in a great part of Italian Jews being able to hide and escape capture."[194]

Despite the papal protests, on Saturday, October 16, the Gestapo launched an attack on those Jews who had not yet left the city or found safe refuge.[195] Unfortunately, many who might have otherwise left were persuaded to stay because of the earlier ransom payment.[196] Thus, within a short time, 1,259 Jews were captured.[197] The next day, German Ambassador Ernst Von Weizsäcker wired to Berlin that "[t]he Curia is particularly shocked that the action took place, so to speak, under the pope's windows. This reaction would be perhaps softened if the Jews could be used for military work in Italy."[198]

In the 1960s, critic Robert Katz set forth the hypothesis that Pope Pius XII knew of the October 16, 1943, roundup before it took place but did nothing to prevent it.[199] Katz's account has many holes in it.[200] He claimed to have talked to a German diplomat (Eitel Möllhausen) who claimed to have told Ambassador Weizsäcker about the roundup in advance. Katz then suggests that Weizsäcker told Vatican officials and that they *must have* told the Pope. Weizsäcker, however, never mentioned this matter in his memoirs.[201] No wonder that the Congregation for the Causes of Saints' *Positio* ended up quoting the *New York Times* review that called Katz's book "hostile," "uninformed," and "downright offensive."[202]

The only recorded witness to the Pope's reaction upon learning of the roundup was Italian Princess Enza Pignatelli. She went to the Pope to seek help as soon as she learned of the roundup. She reported that Pius was "furious" when he learned of it.[203] "Let's go make a few phone calls," he said.[204]

Pius immediately filed a protest through Cardinal Secretary of State Maglione with German Ambassador Weizsäcker, demanding that the Germans "stop these arrests at once."[205] He also sent his nephew, Carlo Pacelli, to see the rector of the National German Church in Rome, who was known to have close ties to German government officials. Ignoring Weizsäcker's warning, the young Pacelli told the Nazis to suspend all actions against the Jews or risk public condemnation.[206] The rector then forwarded the message on to the military governor of Rome.[207]

The British representative to the Holy See sent a secret telegram to the Foreign Office in which he reported: "As soon as he heard of the arrests of Jews in

Rome Cardinal Secretary of State sent for the German Ambassador and formulated some [sort] of protest."[208] The result, according to the telegram, was that "large numbers" of the Jews were released. "Vatican intervention thus seems to have been effective in saving a number of these unfortunate people."[209]

Cardinal Maglione's demand that Ambassador Weizsäcker intervene on behalf of the Jews for the sake of "humanity and Christian charity" was received with embarrassment. Weizsäcker, who said he knew that the Holy See "has had greater faith in the Allies,"[210] said to Maglione: "I always expect you to ask me, 'So why then are you staying in your position?'" Maglione, who knew of Weizsäcker's efforts to help the Jews, replied:

> No, I simply tell you: Excellency, you have a soft and good heart. Try to save these innocent ones. It is painful to the Holy Father, painful beyond measure, that in Rome itself and under the eyes of the father of us all so many people are made to suffer for the simple reason that they are members of a particular race.[211]

Weizsäcker assured Cardinal Maglione that "a good number" of Jews had been released, but he cautioned that this information was strictly confidential.[212] Any indiscretion would be likely to result in further persecutions. Weizsäcker later explained: "Any protest by the Pope would only result in the deportations being really carried out in the thoroughgoing fashion. I know how our people react in these matters."[213] At the end of the meeting, Weizsäcker asked Maglione for permission not to report this conversation back to his superiors, lest it lead to retaliation. The cardinal replied: "Your Excellency has informed me that he is attempting to do something for the unfortunate Jews. I thank him for this. As to the rest, I leave it to his judgment."[214]

At Adolf Eichmann's 1961 trial, Israeli Attorney General Gideon Hausner said that "the Pope himself intervened personally in support of the Jews of Rome."[215] A Protestant minister, Heinrich Grober, testified at the trial that Pius helped him save Jews.[216] Documents introduced in that trial also show Vatican efforts to put a halt to the arrests of Roman Jews.[217] In upholding Eichmann's conviction, the Israeli Supreme Court noted the Pope's protest regarding the deportation of Hungarian Jews.[218]

In other words, the best evidence suggests that the Pope was *not* warned about this roundup.[219] Nevertheless, Katz's theory has been embraced by critics like Susan Zuccotti, even though she claims to base her analysis on archival evidence.[220] In fact, in her 1986 book, Zuccotti acknowledged that the story about Weizsäcker alerting the Pope might be "untrue."[221] In a footnote, she even noted that Weizsäcker's secretary, Albert von Kessel, did not know whether the Pope had been informed and that Weizsäcker never mentioned the incident in his memoirs.[222] In her 2001 book, however, she dropped all qualifications and cautionary notes and presented Pius XII's foreknowledge as fact.

The raid on Roman Jews ended abruptly at 2 p.m., October 16, after the Nazis had seized about 1,200 of the originally intended 8,000 Jews. Some critics, however, refuse to acknowledge that the Vatican played any part in this decision. Susan Zuccotti, for instance, argues that S.S. chief Himmler could not have learned of the papal protests until the evening of October 16. Therefore, she argues, those protests had nothing to do with the Nazis ending the roundup.[223] According, however, to sworn testimony given by German diplomat Gerhard Gumpert (for the 1948 trial of Baron Ernst von Weizsäcker), Pius XII's personal emissary, Father Pancratius Pfeiffer, delivered a letter of protest to General Rainer Stahel, the German army commander in Rome, "toward noon" on October 16.[224] The general telephoned Himmler shortly after receiving this message.[225] There was therefore plenty of time for Stahel to contact Himmler and for Himmler to order Kappler to end the raids. Indeed, Bishop Hudal reported that on October 17 he received a phone call from General Stahel, who assured him that he had "referred the matter *at once* to the local Gestapo and to Himmler. Himmler ordered that in view of the special character of Rome these arrests were to be halted at once."[226] As the chief rabbi of Rome at the time, Israel Zolli, explained:

> With regard to the probability of persecution in Rome, there was this to be said: the influence of the Vatican was great, and open persecution was certain to produce a great outcry from the Pope. The number of Jews was small, and the Germans had little to gain from their elimination. It was known that the German army was opposed to persecution on political grounds. But reason had little hold on the S.S.[227]

On November 7, 2000, the German Catholic news agency KNA released an interview with Nikolaus Kunkel, a German officer stationed in Rome during the roundup. Kunkel, a lieutenant on the staff of General Rainer Stahel, explained that the Pope forcefully intervened behind the scenes to rescue Rome's Jews and that as a result of the Pope's actions, General Stahel persuaded the Nazi authorities to stop the anti-Jewish raids at once. Kunkel went on to note that if Pius had publicized these efforts, it would have backfired and caused immense harm.[228]

Zuccotti gives Pius no credit for having stopped these raids. She argues that "clearly, there were no plans for continuing the [roundup] action" by the Nazis. That claim, however, is made without any supporting documentation and is flatly contradicted by Jewish historian Michael Tagliacozzo (himself a survivor of the raid). Commenting on Pius XII's actions during the raid, he explained:

> The documents clearly prove that, in the early hours of the morning, Pius XII was informed of what was happening and he immediately had German Ambassador von Weizsäcker called and ordered State Secretary Luigi Maglione to energetically protest the Jews' arrest, asking that similar actions be stopped.... In addition, by his initiative he had a letter of protest sent through Bishop

Alois Hudal [delivered by Father Pfeiffer] to the military commander in Rome, General Rainer Stahel, requesting that the persecution of Jews cease immediately. As a result of these protests, the operation *providing for two days of arrests and deportations* was interrupted at 2 P.M. the same day. Instead of the 8,000 Jews Hitler requested, 1,259 were arrested. After meticulous examination of identity documents and other papers of identification, the following day an additional 259 people were released. Moreover, after the manhunt in Rome on Oct. 16, the Germans did not capture a single Jew. Those who were arrested were handed over by collaborators.[229]

Shortly after the roundup, Pius XII published an article in *L'Osservatore Romano* that made his views clear.[230] The *Jewish Chronicle* of London ran a headline proclaiming: "Jewish Hostages in Rome: Vatican Protests."[231] Commenting on this episode, others have noted: "Those Romans reading between the lines understood that Pius XII wanted Catholics to 'do all they possibly can, to hide and save Jews.'"[232]

––––––––

Papal critics John Cornwell and Robert Katz have argued that the October 16, 1943, deportation did not sufficiently concern Pius XII. Part of the "evidence" they cited was a message sent from U.S. official Harold Tittmann to the State Department regarding a meeting he had with Pius.[233] The message was dated October 19 and reported not the Pope's outrage at the Nazis roundup a few days earlier, but his concern that "Communist bands" might "commit violence in the city." If things were actually as Cornwell and Katz reported them, Pius would indeed have appeared indifferent to this Nazi abuse of Jewish people. Such, however, was not the case.

The Vatican keeps precise records of audiences given by the Pope. The transcribed message to Washington from Harold Tittmann is dated October 19, but this is a mistake. Vatican records show that the meeting between Pius and Tittmann took place on October 14.[234] In fact, *L'Osservatore Romano* of October 15, 1943, reported on page one (top of the first column) that Tittmann was received by the Pope in a private audience on October 14, 1943.[235] Apparently a handwritten "4" was misread as a "9" when the documents were typed. The Pope did not mention the roundup of Jews because it had not yet happened! His concern was that a group of Communists would commit a violent act and this would lead to serious repercussions. Of course, he proved to be exactly correct the following spring.[236]

––––––––

Ambassador Weizsäcker was constantly worried that public statements or open activity by the Church would cause Hitler to order an invasion of the Vatican.[237] "From the time he arrived in Rome, Weizsäcker was determined that his policy would be to avoid any rupture between his government and the Holy

See."[238] As such, he played a "subtle double game,"[239] and sometimes censored messages from the Vatican or sent "tactical lies" to persuade the Nazis that Pius was not a threat.[240] Rather than just forwarding messages to Berlin, he would even occasionally reword them. In fact, Weizsäcker sometimes sent one set of comments to Berlin, while recording a different version in his private notes.[241]

On October 25-26, 1943, the Vatican newspaper printed a major article under the headline "The charitable work of the pope." It said: "The charity of the pope is universal and fatherly. It knows no frontiers of nationality, of religion, of race. The pope's continual activity has been increased in these last days because of the sufferings which have fallen upon so many unfortunates."[242] Concerned that Berlin would be upset by this clear statement of support for the Jews, Weizsäcker sent a notorious telegram to his superiors on October 28. It said:

> Although the Pope is said to be importuned from various quarters, he has not allowed himself to be carried away making any demonstrative statements against deportation of the Jews. Although he must expect our enemies to resent this attitude on his part, he has nevertheless done all he could in this delicate question as other matters, not to prejudice relationships with the German government. Since further action on the Jewish problem is probably not to be expected here in Rome, it may be assumed that this question, so troublesome to German-Vatican relations, has been disposed of. On 25 October *L'Osservatore Romano*, moreover, published a semi-official communique on the Pope's charitable activities in which the statement was made, in the style typical of this Vatican newspaper — that is to say, involved and vague — that the Pope extends his paternal solicitude to all men without distinction of nationality and race. There is no need to raise objections to its publication, since hardly anyone will understand the text as referring specifically to the Jewish question.[243]

Despite what the telegram said, Weizsäcker understood the Pope's message.[244] He knew that thousands of Roman Jews were being sheltered in Church buildings that had been opened at the instruction of Pius XII,[245] and he knew that the Church had provided many Jews with falsified documents showing them to have been baptized as Catholics.[246] His telegram helped dissuade the Nazi leadership from invading the Vatican, and the Nazis did not again attempt a large-scale roundup, but the telegram also misled historians studying this era.[247]

———

In March 2004, St. Bonaventure University awarded a medal to Don Aldo Brunacci, an Italian Catholic priest from Assisi. The award was presented at the Holocaust Memorial Museum in Washington, DC, and was given in recognition of Father Brunacci's having helped save more than two hundred Jews during World War II. On March 31, 2004, National Public Radio broadcast an interview with him. Through a translator, Father Brunacci said: "In September 1943, the bishop of Assisi received a very classified letter from the secretary of state of the Vatican asking the bishop to organize help to take care of all the refugees, especially the Jews." Father Brunacci added that Pope Pius XII "did unbelievable things to save Jews." He also made note of a recently published list of Church organizations and religious communities that helped save Jews during the Nazi occupation.[248]

During the war years, Pope Pius XII frequently confided in the Jesuit Father Giacomo Martegani, director of *La Civilta Cattolica*, who kept a diary of their conversations. The diary shows that the Pope was aware of and approved of the Church's efforts to help Jews threatened with deportation from Rome.[249] In the fall of 1943, when the Nazis were expelling Roman Jews to death camps, Father Martegani recorded that Pius told him that "he has looked into the well-being of the Jews."[250] Some weeks later, after a number of Nazi raids on Church properties that harbored Jews, Father Martegani noted that the Pope "no longer trusted in the safety of the ecclesiastical refugees." The Pope told him that it was important not to push the Nazis to the point where they undertook a generalized shakedown of religious houses in the city.

———

In providing forged documents to victims of the Nazis, the neutral Vatican was actually violating the Geneva Convention. As such, this activity brought occasional complaints from groups such as the International Red Cross, because a compromise of neutrality could jeopardize an organization's ability to carry out its work.[251] Another problem for the Pontiff was that Allied planes routinely machine-gunned trains and cars in German-occupied Italy. Difficulties like this did not prevent the Pope from offering assistance to both sides. A communiqué published by the Vatican in October 1943, explained:

> The August Pontiff… has not desisted for one moment from employing all the means in his power to alleviate the suffering which, whatever form it may take, is the consequence of this cruel conflagration. With the augmentation of so much evil, the universal and paternal charity of the Supreme Pontiff… knows neither boundaries nor nationality, neither religion nor race.[252]

That same month, President Roosevelt announced at a press conference that the Allied campaign in Italy was a crusade to free Rome, the Vatican, and the Pope from Nazi domination. London Radio had already broadcast that the Pope was being held captive,[253] and the Germans were upset by the combination of these stories. Foreign minister Joachim von Ribbentrop sent Weizsäcker to see the Pope, with a statement affirming that the German government had fully respected the sovereignty of Vatican City. The Germans wanted the Pope to issue a similar statement. Eventually, they agreed on a statement that appeared in *L'Osservatore Romano* on October 30. It clarified the information that had been set forth by the Allies and stated that the neutral status of Vatican City had indeed been respected by the Germans.[254]

After the armistice with the Allies, many Italian soldiers were taken as prisoners to Germany. Because of the changing alliances, these soldiers were regarded as "military internees," not prisoners of war. As such, they did not have full rights under the Geneva Convention, and the Allies would not allow the passage of material assistance destined for them. The Pope filled the void by making sure that the soldiers were well cared for by his agents who were already inside Germany.[255]

As the tension in the city grew, Pius became increasingly apprehensive that the Roman citizenry would rebel. Again and again he appealed to the people to refrain from such activity because of the reprisals that would be sure to follow. All the while, he was sending truckload after truckload of food and clothing from Vatican warehouses to the convents and other buildings where Jewish people were being sheltered.[256]

———

Mussolini, under guard since his arrest in the summer, had been moved from place to place by his Italian captors so that the Germans would not discover his whereabouts. Hitler, however, named a special S.S. unit to the task of finding and rescuing him.[257] In early September, just after the occupation of Rome, German commandos located Mussolini in a small mountain hotel at the Gran Sasso. On September 13, 1943, in a carefully scripted rescue, 120 S.S. soldiers flew into the area on gliders. One glider crash-landed; three failed to land in the correct area, but eight succeeded in landing. That was enough to do the job. The Italians guarding Mussolini were surprised and overcome without a single shot being fired. Mussolini was skirted away in a small aircraft that was capable of taking off in a limited area.

On September 23, 1943, Mussolini was put in charge of the new "Italian Social Republic" in the northern part of Italy.[258] From this time until the end of the war, Italy was a divided country. The two governments — one on the side of the Axis, the other on the side of the Allies — each claimed to represent the people. Mussolini was now, however, little more than a Nazi puppet supported with German troops and money. He argued that the Vatican should continue to recognize his Fascist regime due to the Lateran Treaty. The Vatican, however, replied that it made concordats with nations, not with particular governments-in-power.[259] He was no longer recognized by the Vatican.[260]

———

On November 5, 1943, at around eight in the evening, a plane dropped four small bombs on Vatican City. The Germans wanted the Holy See to suspect the Allies (or perhaps be intimidated into embracing the Axis), but the plane is thought to have belonged to an Italian man who was angry at Pius XII for having sided with the Allies.[261] One of the bombs hit the glass roof over the workshop of mosaics. Others smashed holes in the walls of the Vatican railroad station and other nearby buildings. Windows were broken in many buildings.[262]

The German high command offered to enter the Vatican and investigate the whole matter," but Pius turned them down. The Germans next urged Pius to let them escort him to a neutral country in the interest of his "personal safety." He also declined this offer.[263] President Roosevelt labeled Nazi military exploitation of Rome as "an affront to all religions."[264] For the time being, however, the threat of a Nazi invasion of the Vatican had passed.

The Pope's efforts on behalf of Jewish people were beginning to be noticed. On November 5, the *Catholic Review* ran a story on the Pope's efforts to protect Jewish people in Rome, under the title "Holy See Is Eager to Rescue Hebrews."[265] Rabbi Morris S. Lazaron, writing in the *Baltimore Synagogue Bulletin*, affirmed that "[t]he Pope has condemned anti-Semitism and all its works. Bishops of the Church have appeared in the streets... with the Shield of David on their arms.... Indeed, many priests and ministers have been jailed and not a few killed in their effort to protect Jews."[266] As reported on Christmas Day by the *Tablet* (London), Rabbi Lazaron went on

> to quote the Pope's condemnation of anti-Semitism, and the action taken by Bishops and priests throughout occupied Europe to protect Jews "driven like animals" from their homes. "They have shielded and healed them at the risk of their own lives.... But it is more than a mere reciprocal gesture which prompts our prayers for His Holiness. We can place ourselves in the position of our Catholic friends.... We link our prayers with theirs. May God protect and keep His Holiness in strength and all good."[267]

On December 30, the following message was sent to Pius XII:

> With profound gratitude, the Israelite families, fraternally sheltered by the Institute of "Our Lady of Zion," turn their moved thoughts to Your Holiness, who deigned to show them a new proof of benevolence. And while they express their gratitude for the attentive response to the call for help not in vain directed to Your Christian charity, they wish above all to show their confidence and faith for the spiritual comfort received from the Apostolic Blessing paternally imparted to them.[268]

Even more blessings would be needed in the year to come.

FOURTEEN

# 1944 and the Allies Invade

On January 29, 1944, Vatican Radio broadcast a strong condemnation of anti-Semitic legislation.[1] Less than two weeks later, the *New York Times* reported: "Vatican Radio, commenting on the Fascist raid on St. Paul's Basilica last Thursday in which sixty-four Italian officers and Jews who had received sanctuary there were arrested, said tonight that the Church would not yield in offering charity to everyone.... Charity is above human constitutions. On this point, the priest can never yield. It is the demarcation line between good and evil."[2]

Under the terms of the Lateran Treaty, only a limited number of Church buildings were entitled to extraterritorial status. The Italians, however, treated all Church property in Rome as if it were off-limits.[3] When German forces moved into Rome, they initially followed that same approach. Before long, however, they learned that these buildings were being used to shelter Jews and other refugees. (In fact, the Vatican was quite open about its status as a "haven" to *anyone* in need.)[4]

In February 1944, the Fascist police broke into the extraterritorial Basilica of St. Paul Outside-the-Walls. They found that the monastery there was a shelter for Jews, former members of the dissolved *Carabinieri* (military police), and various men avoiding military service with the Fascist army.[5] Somewhere between sixty-four and eighty-two arrests were made.[6] If such raids were to continue, the results would be disastrous. Almost the entire National Committee of Liberation was hidden in the Roman Seminary at St. John Lateran, only "a few paces" from the headquarters of the Gestapo police chief.[7] The Vatican immediately protested to Italian and German authorities, and issued condemnations on Vatican Radio and in *L'Osservatore Romano*.[8] The Pope himself "protested energetically" against the German's interpretation of the Lateran Treaty, which had caused the Nazis to believe that they were authorized to conduct such raids.[9] A *New York Times* headline reported: "Vatican Repeats Pledge of Haven; Church Will Always Provide Sanctuary for All, Radio Comments on Raid."[10] In light of this pressure, the raids came to an end.

Many German officials could now see the writing on the wall. Soon they would be forced out of Rome, and unless things changed, the Allies would be victorious. In an effort to win Vatican support in brokering a separate peace with the Western Allies, the German ambassador to the Holy See, Ernst Von Weizsäcker, met with Cardinal Maglione in January 1944. Weizsäcker cautioned the cardinal that "if Germany, a bulwark against Bolshevism, should fall, all Europe will become Communist." Maglione replied: "What a misfortune that

Germany, with its antireligious policy, has stirred up concerns as serious as these."[11]

As the fighting came closer to Rome, the German high command informed the Pope that if forced to leave the city, the Nazis would practice a "scorched earth" policy, leaving behind only ruins.[12] The Nazis made it clear that the risk to Vatican City was very real, but they offered him safe refuge in Germany. He immediately declined the offer and registered a protest against any violence.[13] Pius then called together all of the cardinals in the Vatican and explained the German threat. Since he had asked bishops in war-torn areas to stay in place as long as possible, he was determined not to leave his post. Others, however, might have felt differently. Reportedly, the Pope released the cardinals from their obligation to stay with him in Rome. Not one accepted the offer.[14]

Pius was also concerned about the impact of war on civilian populations in Rome. The *New York Times* reported in 1944 that Rome's population grew during Nazi occupation because

> in that period under the Pope's direction the Holy See did an exemplary job of sheltering and championing the victims of the Nazi-Fascist regime. I have spoken to dozens of Italians, both Catholics and Jews, who owe their liberty and perhaps their lives to the protection of the church. In some cases anti-Fascists were actually saved from execution through the Pope's intervention.[15]

The article went on to explain that "none doubts that the general feeling of the Roman Curia was anti-Fascist and very strongly anti-Nazi."

On February 10, bombs once again fell on Rome and the Vatican's sacred shrines. They nearly demolished Castel Gandolfo, the Pope's summer residence, where thousands of refugees were being sheltered. More than five hundred people were killed.[16] On February 15, bombs fell on the abbey of Monte Cassino, reducing it to rubble and killing an unknown number of people who had sought refuge there.[17] On March 1, bombs again fell on Vatican City, causing minor damage.[18] Shortly thereafter, Pius XII gave his first public address since the Nazi occupation of Rome. He blasted both the Allies and the Axis for turning Vatican City into a battle zone. His words did little good.

On March 24, the Nazis conducted a massive roundup and execution, which was prompted when the group GAP (*Gruppi di Azione Patriottica*), comprised mainly of Communist students, decided that the time had come for a major gesture.[19] The day before the roundup, GAP had planted a bomb that exploded just as a German unit was marching down Via Rasella in Rome. Thirty-three German soldiers were killed. The high command in Berlin ordered the immediate execution of ten Italians for every soldier who had been killed.[20] According to a direct and personal order from Adolf Hitler, the reprisal was to be completed within twenty-four hours.[21] By noon the next day, a convoy that included Jews, Catholic priests, women, and two fourteen-year-old boys — none of whom had anything to do with the bombing — was directed to some man-made caves on the outskirts of Rome, among the catacombs of the Appian Way. Under the direction of S.S. Lieutenant Colonel Herbert Kappler, these 335 Italians were shot and killed. German engineers then blew up the entrances to the caves, sealing the evidence inside. Months passed before the identities of all the victims were known.

The only record of these executions that has surfaced in the archives of the Vatican Secretariat of State is a memo written by a Vatican secretary reporting a call received at 10:15 a.m. on the day after the explosion (the day of the roundup). The caller described the bombing and reported that "[c]ountermeasures are still not known; it is thought, however, that for every German killed, 10 Italians will be executed."[22]

When Pius first learned of the arrests, he put his head in his hands and moaned: "It is not possible, I cannot believe it." He sent his special liaison officer, Father Pancratius Pfeiffer, S.D.S. superior general, to plead with the German command.[23] He may also have sent his nephew, Prince Carlo Pacelli, to investigate. Unfortunately, the Vatican officials were unable to learn what had happened until it was too late.[24] The German diplomatic corps withdrew into discreet silence, and on March 29 the German ambassador's office said that inquiries about persons taken by the Germans should be addressed to the headquarters of S.S. Lieutenant Colonel Herbert Kappler, the Nazi chief of police in Rome. As Kappler confessed years later, it was a waste of time to come to him; by then the people had all been killed.[25]

―――――

In April 1944, two young men, Rudolf Vrba and Fred Wetzler, escaped from Auschwitz and wrote a very detailed report to warn others of what was going on ("The Auschwitz Protocol"). The report said that 1,750,000 Jews had already been exterminated, and the killings were continuing. In his book, *I Cannot Forgive*, Vrba explained that he gave the report to Jewish officials in Budapest, but that nothing seemed to have come of it. Then one day, several weeks later, he was asked to meet with Monsignor Giuseppe Burzio, chargé d'affaires in Bratislava.[26]

Burzio "cross-examined" Vrba for six hours to confirm what he had written in the protocol. "He went through the report line by line, page by page, returning time after time to various points until he was satisfied that I was neither lying or exaggerating." Finally, the Vatican official found himself weeping. He told Vrba: "I shall carry your report to the International Red Cross in Geneva. They will take action and see that it reaches the proper hands."[27]

Burzio did indeed take the report to the International Red Cross immediately after he had presented it to Pope Pius XII.[28] While informed sources had heard rumors, and many probably had good information about the death camps, this report confirmed the worst to the whole world. Before long, leaders from all the Allied nations were citing the figures set forth in this report. Not only did the Vatican play a significant role in spreading this information to others, Pius also later used this information to put pressure on the regent of Hungary to end the deportation of Jews from that country.[29]

On June 2, 1944 (the feast day of St. Eugenio), the Pope spoke about his war-related efforts: "To one sole goal our thoughts are turned, night and day: how it may be possible to abolish such acute suffering, coming to the relief of all, without distinction of nationality or race."[30] Two days later, the Allies finally made their way to Rome. This was of little strategic value, but it had great psychological benefit. Rome was the capital of one of the original Axis powers and the first European capital to be liberated from the Nazis.

Pius feared that the city would suffer great damage in battle. He said: "Whoever dares to raise his hand against Rome will be guilty of matricide in the eyes of the civilized world and in the eternal judgment of God."[31] He urged the Germans to leave peacefully so as to avoid a terrible battle in the city. Fortunately, despite Hitler's earlier warnings, Mussolini's call for street-fighting, and German General Alfred Jodl's recommendation that the Vatican be destroyed,[32] as the Allies entered on one side of Rome, the Germans left quietly from the other side.[33] In fact, the Germans had moved their military equipment out of Rome in April, and they informed the Allies of this (and the consequent reason to stop bombing Rome) via the Vatican.[34] The German ambassador to the Holy See, Ernst von Weizsäcker, in discussing the peaceful exchange that took place in Rome, gave "chief credit to the ceaseless quiet activity of the Pope."[35]

Both the Italian king and the prime minister had fled to safety in southern Italy when the Germans invaded. Mussolini, having been ousted as dictator, was in northern Italy. As such, during the occupation and at the time of liberation, the Pope was the only authority figure in Rome. Thousands who had been in hiding ran out into St. Peter's Square for the first time in nine months and embraced the soldiers.[36] That evening, families joined other families in a massive, joyous march up to Vatican City, to thank God and Pope Pius for bringing them through the war.[37]

The Romans considered Pius "their bishop." They proclaimed him *Defensor Urbis* and *Defensor Civitatis*.[38] These people had no doubts about where the Pope stood. Books had already been written and speeches had been made documenting the Vatican's support of the Allies and work with the Jews. Crowds streamed into the square and called for *Papa Pacelli*, who appeared on the loggia. He thanked God for saving Rome. "Every phrase of his was punctuated with thunders of applause.... He said that whereas yesterday Rome was still fearful for the fate of her children, today she rejoiced...."[39] He gave a blessing to the crowd and left the balcony. The crowd continued to acclaim him.[40] Mussolini, who had sided with the Nazis, would receive a very different reception the following year.

A few days after the liberation, United States Lieutenant General Mark Clark, commander of the 5th Allied Army, came to pay his respects to the Pope. One of the first things he said was: "I am afraid you have been disturbed by the noise of my tanks. I am sorry." Pope Pius XII's face lit up with a bright smile as he replied: "General, any time you come to liberate Rome, you can make just as much noise as you like."[41]

One of the first things Pius did after the liberation was to pray, alone, in the Jewish cemetery.[42] His standing with Jewish soldiers from the United States is reflected in the bulletin put out by the "Jewish Brigade Group" (U.S. Eighth Army). The June 1944 edition carried a front-page editorial which proclaimed: "To the everlasting glory of the people of Rome and the Roman Catholic Church we can state that the fate of the Jews was alleviated by their truly Christian offers of assistance and shelter."[43] The Committee on Army and Navy Religious Activities of the American Jewish Welfare Board wrote to the Pope:

> Word comes to us from our army chaplains in Italy telling of the aid and protection given to so many Italian Jews by the Vatican and by priests and institutions of the Church during the Nazi occupation of the land. We are deeply moved by these stirring stories of Christian love, the more so as we know full well to what dangers many of those exposed themselves who gave shelter and aid to the Jews hunted by the Gestapo. From the bottom of our heart we send to you, Holy Father of the Church, the assurance of our unforgetting gratitude for this noble expression of religious brotherhood and love.[44]

*Davar*, the Hebrew daily of Israel's Federation of Labor, quoted a Jewish Brigade officer shortly after Rome's liberation: "When we entered Rome, the Jewish survivors told us with a voice filled with deep gratitude and respect: 'If we have been rescued; if Jews are still alive in Rome come with us and thank the pope in the Vatican. For in the Vatican proper, in churches, monasteries and private homes, Jews were kept hidden at his personal orders.'"[45] As a *New York Times* headline proclaimed: "Jews of Rome Thank Pope for Aiding Them."[46]

On July 31, 1944, in front of fifty thousand people at Madison Square Garden, Judge Joseph Proskauer, the president of the American Jewish Committee said: "We have heard... what a great part the Holy Father has played in the salvation of refugees in Italy, and we know... that this great Pope has reached forth his mighty and sheltering hand to help the oppressed of Hungary."[47] Today, in Vatican City, where one enters the porticos of the Sacred Congregation of Bishops just off St. Peter's Square, is a square called "The Square of Pius XII, the Savior of the City."[48] "Savior of the world," is the way some Jewish survivors have preferred to describe him.[49]

In the weeks following Rome's liberation, the Holy Father was to grant daily audiences to large groups of Allied soldiers of every religious persuasion. One of the frequent themes of his presentations was captured in a filmed statement. In English, the Pope said: "You have had experience now of the danger and uncertainty of life in the midst of a war. Make one thing certain — that you keep always close to God."[50] Another film shows him addressing Allied soldiers and saying, "It is a real joy for Us to welcome you all here, within the very old home of the common Father of the Christians...."

At the conclusion of one small audience held for Allied servicemen, an over-joyed American lieutenant called out, "Okay! Let's really hear it for His Holiness," and then led his men in a loud rendition of "For He's a Jolly Good Fellow."[51] Another time, excited Polish soldiers, after presenting the Pope with a beautifully decorated shield, obtained permission to carry him on the *sedia gestatoria*.[52]

In an audience of October 29, former prisoners of an Italian Fascist concentration camp where Jews were treated with relative humanity thanked Pope Pius XII for his "remarkable and generous gifts" twice given through Cardinal Francesco Borgongini Duca, for his open "support [for] our rights to human dignity," and for preventing the prisoners' deportation to Poland in 1942.[53] Later in the year, Pius announced that he would say a Midnight Mass at St. Peter's Basilica on Christmas. The Vatican received terrorist threats that it would be bombed, but Pius would not cancel. Some seventy thousand persons, mostly Allied soldiers, were in attendance, and it came off without incident.[54]

In the months following Rome's liberation, the Germans retreated from one defensive line to another, as Allied troops pushed north through Italy. In fact, the Germans in Italy did not surrender until May 1, 1945. With many Jewish prisoners still in the hands of the Axis powers, the Holy See still had much left to do. Fortunately, due to the Church's efforts and the reluctance of the Italians to enforce racial laws, the Jews in Italy had a far higher survival rate than did those in most other occupied nations.

In June 1944, the chief rabbi of Rome, Israel Zolli, held a service that was broadcast on radio, to publicly express the gratitude of Italian Jews to Pius.[55] The next month, reflecting upon the liberation of Rome from German occupation, Zolli "made a solemn declaration in the Roman synagogue, paying tribute to the Holy See for having condemned the anti-Semitic laws and diminished their effects."[56] The synagogue in Rome was even adorned with a plaque thanking Pius XII for assisting in their defense.[57]

The American Jewish Welfare Board, in July 1944, also expressed its appreciation for the protection that the Pope had given to the Jews during Germany's occupation of Italy.[58] An editorial in the July 27 edition of the *American Israelite*, entitled "True Brotherhood," discussed Vatican efforts in Rome and Pope Pius XII's efforts in Hungary and concluded that "we feel an immeasurable degree of gratitude toward our Catholic brethren." In August, Pulitzer Prize-winning writer Anne O'Hare McCormick issued a dispatch for the *New York Times* from Rome indicating that Pius enjoyed an "enhanced" reputation because, during the occupation, he made "hiding someone 'on the run' the thing to do," and he had given Jewish people "first priority."[59]

---

Cardinal Archbishop Pietro Boetto of Genoa, criticized the British shelling of his city, but he gave his wholehearted support to the Jewish rescue group DELASEM and its clandestine operations on behalf of Jewish people. Boetto asked the Vatican for help, and Pope Pius XII answered by having Monsignor Giovanni Battista Montini send money. In 1945, Boetto urged all Axis forces in the area to surrender rather than endanger the population. It has been estimated that he saved about eight hundred Jewish lives. An article in the Italian paper *Il Nuovo Cittadino*, dated February 3, 1946, called Boetto "the Cardinal of the Jews."[60]

In Rome, Monsignor Hugh O'Flaherty was known for his work on behalf of the Jews and Allied soldiers hiding in Rome. Under Pius XII's direction, he was in charge of a network of hundreds of people who rescued thousands of Jews from the Nazis. Gestapo officer Herbert Kappler was in charge of the German occupation forces. When the Allies liberated Rome, Kappler was captured and sentenced to life imprisonment for war crimes. In the years that followed, he had only one regular visitor, Monsignor O'Flaherty. O'Flaherty and Kappler had been bitter enemies during the occupation, but the priest's compassion following the war impressed the German. In 1959, O'Flaherty baptized Kappler into the Catholic faith.[61]

Papal critic Susan Zuccotti argued that the first edition of this book made "exaggerated claims" because the authors that it cited (Hatch and Walshe) did not say that O'Flaherty sheltered *Jews*. Indeed, Hatch and Walshe did not specifically note that Jews were among O'Flaherty's group, but neither did they deny it. They called him the "Conrad Hilton of the underground" because he had more than sixty apartments (some with as many as twelve rooms) in which he kept *refugees*. In order to find proof that many of the refugees were Jewish, however, one only had to consult any of numerous other sources.

As reported by Jewish author and diplomat Pichas Lapide in 1967, O'Flaherty took care of: "aristocrats, *Jews*, and anti-Fascists who were in danger. He found them clothes and food."[62] Richard Owen reported that O'Flaherty "earned the title 'the Oscar Schindler of Killarney' by hiding 4,000 Jews and escaped Allied prisoners."[63] In fact, O'Flaherty first began smuggling and hiding refugees in the fall of 1942, when the Italians cracked down on prominent Jews and anti-Fascist aristocrats. He later broadened his operation to include escaped British POWs. As the war went on, O'Flaherty did not ask about faith or race. He took care of Jews or anyone else who needed assistance.[64] According to author J. P. Gallagher:

> On the day of the liberation of Rome, the Pimpernel [O'Flaherty] and his associates were looking after about 4,000 people — British, South African, Russian, Greek, American and a score of other nationalities, *quite apart from an uncounted number of Jews whom O'Flaherty personally saved.*[65]

A downed British airman, who was protected by Monsignor O'Flaherty during the war, wrote an account explaining how Allied soldiers, Jewish refugees, and escaped war prisoners were sheltered in the basements and attics of Catholic seminaries and universities throughout Rome. In fact, he quoted O'Flaherty complaining to British soldiers: "Between you fellows and *all my Jews*, I can't get my work done."[66]

Pope Pius recognized Father O'Flaherty's work, on Easter Sunday 1945, by calling together a number of priests who had worked with him during the war. The Pope then offered a deep and sincere tribute to Father O'Flaherty and his assistants for all that they had done to help the Jewish victims who were "particularly dear to my heart." O'Flaherty was also honored by Australia, Canada, and by the United States (as a recipient of the Medal of Freedom).

---

In March 1944, Germany invaded Hungary on the pretext of safeguarding communications, and the last great nightmare of the war began.[67] Hungary had been a haven for refugee Jews, but the Nazis immediately issued anti-Jewish decrees.[68] From almost the first day, Nuncio Angelo Rotta worked to help improve the treatment of the Jews. He was the first foreign envoy to submit a formal diplomatic objection,[69] and he issued baptismal certificates and passports that enabled thousands of Jews and converted Jews to leave Hungary.[70] The Holy See also informed other nations about the conditions in Hungary, and this brought international pressure on the Hungarian government.

Early in the occupation, Rotta received a letter of encouragement from Pius XII in which the Pope termed the treatment of Jews as "unworthy of Hungary, the country of the Holy Virgin and of St. Stephen."[71] From then on, acting always in accordance with instructions from the Holy See and in the name of Pope Pius XII, Rotta regularly intervened against the maltreatment of the Jews and the inhuman character of the anti-Jewish legislation.[72]

The Vatican had direct contact with Jewish organizations, and it agreed to assist the War Refugee Board (a newly created organization linking all Jewish organizations) in its effort to help Jews in Hungary.[73] Not long after the deportations started, the War Refugee Board urged the International Red Cross and six neutral nations (Sweden, Spain, Portugal, Switzerland, Turkey, and the Holy See) to assign additional diplomatic personnel to Hungary. It was thought that foreign observers might act as a restraining influence on the Germans. Sweden and the Vatican complied very quickly. The International Red Cross, fearful that it might antagonize Germany and find itself excluded from its important work for war prisoners, hesitated to intervene, but it eventually complied. Spain, Portugal, Switzerland, and Turkey never did.[74]

In June 1944, at the request of the Vatican, the British News Service representative in Switzerland sent a telegram outlining the brutal treatment of Jews in Hungary and their deportation to Auschwitz. Using abbreviated language to minimize the per-word telegraph charge, it reported a "Dramatic account one darkest chapters modern history revealing how 1,715,000 Jews put death annihilation Camp Auschwitz, Birkenau and Harmansee . . . where also awful destiny HungJews today fulfilling itself."[75] The message ended with the following language: "Absolute exactness above report unquestionable and diplomat Catholic functionaries well-known Vatican desire widest diffusion worldwide."[76]

Sometimes Church officials were embarrassed about how quickly they would convert Jews to Catholicism for the purpose of avoiding persecution. One small church in Budapest averaged about four or five conversions a year before the occupation. In 1944, those numbers shot up dramatically. Six were converted in January, 23 in May, 101 in June, over 700 in September, and over 1,000 in October. Three thousand Jews became Catholics at this one small church in 1944.[77] The Nazi occupying forces soon recognized that these conversions were being done only to avoid deportation, so they started persecuting the "converts."[78] Since it no longer assured protection, the flood of conversions dried up.

By mid-summer, despite the Church's efforts, 437,000 Jews had been deported from Hungary. Then, on June 25, just days after he had seen the Auschwitz Protocol, Pius XII sent an open telegram to the regent of Hungary, Admiral Horthy:

> Supplications have been addressed to Us from different sources that We should exert all Our influence to shorten and mitigate the sufferings that have for so long been peacefully endured on account of their national or racial origin by a great number of unfortunate people belonging to this noble and chivalrous nation. In accordance with our service of love, which embraces every human being, Our fatherly heart could not remain insensible to these urgent demands. For this reason We apply to your Serene Highness appealing to your noble feelings in the full trust that your Serene Highness will do everything in your power to save many unfortunate people from further pain and suffering.[79]

Hungarian authorities also received protests from the nuncio, the King of Sweden, the Swiss press, and the International Red Cross.

In addition to the telegram to Admiral Horthy, Pius sent an open telegram to Hungarian Cardinal Serédi, asking for support from the Hungarian bishops:

> We would forfeit Our moral leadership and fail in Our duty if We did not demand that Our countrymen should not be handled unjustly on account of their origin or religion. We, therefore, beseech the authorities that they, in full knowledge of their responsibility before God and History, will revoke these harmful measures.[80]

The telegram was read publicly in many churches before all copies were confiscated by the government. Nuncio Rotta informed Serédi of Pius XII's desire "that the Hungarian episcopate should publicly take a stand... on behalf of their compatriots who are unjustly hit by racist decrees."[81] Two days after this telegram, Pius requested that Hungarian bishops "intercede publicly on behalf of Christian principles and to protect their fellow citizens, especially Christians, unjustly affected by racial regulations."[82]

On June 28, Archbishop Spellman of New York broadcast a strong appeal to Hungarian Catholics deploring the anti-Jewish measures, which he said, "shocked all men and women who cherish a sense of justice and human sympathy."[83] These measures were, he said, "in direct contradiction of the doctrines of the Catholic Faith professed by the vast majority of the Hungarian people."[84] He called it incredible "that a nation which has been so consistently true to the impulses of human kindness and the teachings of the Catholic Church should now yield to a false, pagan code of tyranny...."[85] *Time* magazine reported: "This week listeners at Europe's 36 million radio sets might have heard New York's Archbishop Francis Joseph Spellman preaching civil disobedience. The Archbishop's... broadcast... eloquently urged Hungary's nine million Catholics to disobey their government's new anti-Semitic decrees."[86] The Allies dropped printed copies of it over Hungary.[87] Spellman later confirmed what most observers had thought: he had made the statement at the express request of Pope Pius XII.[88]

Admiral Horthy complained to the Germans that he was being bombarded with telegrams from the Vatican and others and that the nuncio was calling on him several times each day.[89] In the face of these protests, Horthy withdrew Hungarian support from the deportation process, making it impossible for the Germans to continue. Horthy's reply cable to the Pope said: "It is with comprehension and profound gratitude that I receive your cable and request you to be convinced that I shall do all within my power to make prevail the demands of Christian humanitarian principles."[90] More than 170,000 Hungarian Jews were saved from deportation on the very eve of their intended departure.[91]

Horthy agreed to work against the deportations, and he even signed a peace agreement with the Allies. For once, it appeared that Pius XII's words might actually have had a positive effect. The apostolic delegate in London wrote to the representative of the World Jewish Congress: "At this moment I have a telegram from the Holy See. The Holy Father has appealed personally to the Regent of Hungary... on behalf of your people, and has been assured that the Regent will do all possible to help."[92] The Germans, however, would not be dissuaded by mere pleas.

The Germans arrested Horthy in October, put Hungary under the control of a group of Hungarian Nazis known as the Arrow Cross, and the deportations resumed. The Pope and his representatives then made many more protests to German authorities, issued a report documenting the Vatican's work with the Jews of Hungary, and encouraged Catholics to help the victims.[93] In October, Pius joined in an effort to raise money to support Hungarian refugees, urging all the faithful to redouble their efforts on behalf of all victims of the war, regardless of their race.[94] Almost every Catholic Church in Hungary provided refuge to persecuted Jews during the autumn and winter of 1944.[95]

Nuncio Rotta protested to the German foreign ministry, saying that "from a humanitarian perspective but also to protect Christian morality, the Holy See protests the inhumane attitude adopted toward the Jews."[96] When Nazi officials suggested that Jews were merely being sent to Germany to work, not for any evil purpose, Rotta responded:

When old men of over 70 and even over 80, old women, children and sick persons are taken away, one wonders for what work these human beings can be used?... When we think that Hungarian workers, who go to Germany for reasons of work, are forbidden to take their families, we are really surprised to see that this great favor is granted only to Jews.[97]

Such blunt sarcasm is quite rare in official communications among diplomats.

The nunciature in Budapest had been bombed and half destroyed; communication with the Vatican was extremely difficult, and the lives of those Catholic officials still in the city were in constant danger. Nuncio Rotta sent a message to Rome asking what to do. The reply from Pope Pius was: "If it is still possible to do some charity, remain!"[98] Accordingly, Rotta stayed in Budapest, providing help to the Jewish victims of the Nazis.

The Germans were finally forced out of Budapest two days before Christmas, December 23, 1944. Despite the terrible losses that had taken place during their occupation, most of the Jews in Budapest were saved from the gas chamber, at least in part as a result of the combination of strong protests made by the Pope, the nuncio, and the Hungarian bishops to a government that was willing to listen. To the entire international Jewish community, on December 3, 1944, Romanian Chief Rabbi Safran declared:

My permanent contact with, and spiritual closeness to, His Excellency the Apostolic Nuncio, the Doyen of the Diplomatic Corps of Bucharest, were decisive for the fate of my poor community. In the house of this high prelate, before his good heart, I shed my burning tears as the distressed father of my community, which was hovering feverishly between life and death.[99]

On September 27, 1944, Safran published an article in the newspaper *Mantuirea* under the title: "The apostolic nuncio has seen to it that the deportation of Jews to Transnistrie has been halted. May God reward him for what he has done."[100]

On October 30, Democratic Representative Emanuel Cellers, from New York, wrote a letter to Pius thanking him for his "merciful endeavor" on behalf of Jewish refugees. He wrote: "Your humanitarian and merciful endeavors in behalf of Jewish refugees fleeing death have attracted the deep gratitude and appreciation of the people of America."[101] The following day, President Roosevelt's representative to the Pope, Myron C. Taylor, transmitted a report to the director of the Committee for Refugees in Washington:

I also want to pay tribute to many non-Jewish groups and individuals who have shown a true Christian spirit in their quick and friendly reaction in support of the helpless of Europe.... The record of the Catholic Church in this regard has been inspiring. All over Europe, Catholic priests have furnished hiding places and protection to the persecuted. His Holiness, Pope Pius XII, has interceded on many occasions in behalf of refugees in danger. In this country too, we have received help from many Catholic leaders.[102]

The World Jewish Congress, on December 1, 1944, at its war emergency conference in Atlantic City, sent a telegram of thanks to the Holy See for the protection it gave "under difficult conditions to the persecuted Jews in German-dominated Hungary."[103] Similarly, the American National Jewish Welfare Board sent an expression of deep thanks to Pius:

> From the bottom of our hearts we send to you, Holy Father of the Church, the assurance of our unforgetting gratitude for this noble expression of religious brotherhood and love. We glory in this bloodless victory over the forces of evil that are bent on uprooting religion's eternal teachings of the sacredness of life and the oneness of humanity under God. It is our fervent prayer that your example, your influence and your intervention may yet save some of the remnant of the Jews in other lands who are marked down by the Germans for murder and extinction...."[104]

---

In August 1944, British Prime Minister Winston Churchill traveled to the Vatican to meet with Pope Pius XII. With the war against Germany drawing near an end, both men were very concerned about the danger of Communism. According to the press, the Pope's attitude toward Russia and Communism was one of "benevolent waiting."[105] According to Churchill, "The Pope received me... with the dignity and informality which he can so happily combine."[106] Churchill admired the Pope's "simplicity, sincerity and power."[107] When Churchill informed Pius of Stalin's question: "How many divisions has the Pope?" Pius responded: "When you see Joseph Stalin again, tell him that he will meet our divisions in heaven."[108] After the meeting, Churchill said: "I have spoken today to the greatest man of our time."[109] He would later write, "I have always had the greatest dislike of [Communism]; and should I ever have the honour of another audience with the Supreme Pontiff I should not hesitate to recur to the subject."[110]

The same month that Pius received Churchill, an attempt was made, through the Pope, to save the Jews in German-occupied northern Italy. Sir Clifford Heathcote-Smith (the Intergovernmental Committee's delegate in Italy) and Myron C. Taylor (President Roosevelt's representative to Pius XII) spoke with the Pope. They asked him to urge the German government to stop the deportations from Italy and to release the Jews to the Allied part of the country. The Pope immediately agreed. He told Heathcote-Smith that neither his conscience nor history would forgive him if he did not make the effort. Unfortunately, his approach, made through the nuncio in Berlin, brought only an evasive response from the Germans.[111]

August 1944 was also the month when a group of Roman Jews came to thank Pius for having helped them during the period of Nazi occupation. In response, the Pontiff reaffirmed his position: "For centuries, Jews have been unjustly treated and despised. It is time they were treated with justice and humanity. God wills it and the Church wills it. St. Paul tells us that the Jews are our brothers. They should also be welcomed as friends."[112]

———————

On the eastern front, as the Soviet army followed the retreating Germans, it advanced along an eight-hundred-mile front and did not stop at the national border. By mid-July 1944, the Soviets swept across Ukraine and Poland and up to the gates of Warsaw. With the Soviets approaching, the exiled Polish government called for an insurrection to liberate Warsaw from Germany, similar to the one that led to the liberation of Paris. On August 1, underground units of the Polish Home Army began the insurrection. Almost the entire city fought against the Nazis.

The Germans were ruthless in putting down the rebellion, which could only succeed with support from the Soviets. The British and Americans urged Stalin to help, but he argued that the insurrection had begun without any prior coordination with the Soviet command.[113] As such, the U.S.S.R. would not provide any support.

In August, Pius received a message from a group of women in Poland asking for prayers and moral support. The message went as follows:

> Most Holy Father, we Polish women in Warsaw are inspired with sentiments of profound patriotism and devotion for our country. For three weeks, while defending our fortress, we have lacked food and medicine. Warsaw is in ruins. The Germans are killing the wounded in hospitals. They are making women and children march in front of them in order to protect their tanks. There is no exaggeration in reports of children who are fighting and destroying tanks with bottles of petrol. We mothers see our sons dying for freedom and the Fatherland. Our husbands, our sons, and our brothers are not considered by the enemy to be combatants. Holy Father, no one is helping us. The Russian armies which have been for three weeks at the gates of Warsaw have not advanced a step. The aid coming to us from Great Britain is insufficient. The world is ignorant of our fight. God alone is with us. Holy Father, Vicar of Christ, if you can hear us, bless us Polish women who are fighting for the Church and for freedom.[114]

Pius responded to the president of the Polish Republic, expressing his desire to neglect nothing in his effort to save lives.[115] The message from the Polish women was then forwarded to the American and British representatives, with the request that it be brought to the attention of their governments.[116] It was also published in *L'Osservatore Romano* on September 15.[117] That same week, Pius went on Vatican Radio to send a message to President Wladislaw Raczkiewicz, of the London-based Polish Government in exile, expressing his sorrow over the situation in Poland and praying for Warsaw's liberation.[118]

Unfortunately, the Pope's efforts did not stop the flow of blood. On October 2, the insurgents gave up. Overall, about 216,000 Poles and 2,000 Germans had been killed. Hitler ordered the population removed from the city, the insurgents taken prisoner, and most of Warsaw destroyed.[119]

––––––––––

Nazi persecution of Catholic priests continued, and 1944 was an especially bad year for the Jesuits in Germany. It was said that Jesuits were, first and foremost, enemies and adversaries of the Reich.[120] From the early days of Nazi rule, Jesuits attacked the intellectual basis of Nazism in their publications.[121] This, however, led to severe reprisals, including the Gestapo's publication in 1935 of a document entitled "Safeguarding against the Jesuits" that called the attention of local Nazi leaders to the Jesuit opposition.[122] Nazi pressure eventually led to the closing of the Jesuit presses.[123] The persecution of Catholic priests did not, however, come to an end. In Dachau alone, more than two thousand Catholic priests were murdered or died from the ill-treatment they received.[124]

In October 1944, Mussolini denounced Pius XII as a renegade Italian who had sided with the enemies of his country.[125] The next month, the Vatican sent a letter demanding that the Germans release some Jewish prisoners (sick, elderly, women, and children) and guarantee humane treatment for the rest.[126] Although nothing directly came of it, the people closest to the situation were well aware of the Pontiff's support for Jewish victims.

By February 1943, the Jewish community in Romania had already twice sent its gratitude to the Holy Father for assistance given by the Church during the war.[127] The Holy See once again sent a large donation to Romania "for those civilian internees, excluding the Polish Aryans."[128] About that same time, Dr. Safran, the chief rabbi in Bucharest, sent Pius "the loving respect and the sincere and gracious wishes of the whole community whose members are well aware that the august pontiff regards them with fatherly solicitude."[129] Almost two years later (December 3, 1944), Safran acknowledged that support from the Pope's representative was decisive for the fate of his community.[130] Rabbi Herzog of Palestine also expressed thanks to the Vatican on behalf of the Jewish community for the Church's effort in helping Romanian-Jewish orphans escape to Istanbul. He wrote:

> The people of Israel will never forget what his Holiness and his illustrious delegates inspired by the eternal principles of religion which form the very foundations of true civilization, are doing for us unfortunate brothers and sisters in the most tragic hour of our history, which is living proof of divine Providence in this world.[131]

After the war, Herzog sent "a special blessing" to the Pope for "his lifesaving efforts on behalf of the Jews during the Nazi occupation of Italy."[132] The intermediary, Harry Greenstein, who would later go on to become executive director of the Associated Jewish Charities of Baltimore, reported the Pope's reaction: "I still remember quite vividly the glow in [Pope Pius XII's] eyes. He replied that his only regret was that he was not able to save many more Jews."[133]

―――――

Pius XII's 1944 Christmas address was entitled "Democracy and Peace." In it, he thanked the personal representative of President Roosevelt (Myron C. Taylor) for "the vast work of assistance accomplished, despite extraordinary difficulties."[134] Pius then expressed his confidence in a democratic future:

A healthy democracy, based upon the principles of the natural law and of revealed truth, will resolutely oppose the corrupt notion which attributes to State legislation an authority beyond limit or restraint, and which, despite deceptive appearances to the contrary, will transform even a democratic régime into a system of absolutism pure and simple.[135]

Pius also offered support and suggestions for the democratic ideals of liberty and equality.

As for the leaders of the Axis powers, Pius foresaw what lay in store. In a section entitled "War Criminals," he did not defend them, but said:

As for those who have taken advantage of the war to commit real and proved crimes against the law common to all peoples, crimes for which supposed military necessity may have afforded a pretext but could never offer an excuse — no one, certainly, will wish to disarm justice in their regard.[136]

Pius added that only those individuals who were guilty of these offenses should be punished, not "whole communities." The special European correspondent for the *New York Times*, who was also a member of the paper's editorial board, Anne O'Hare McCormick, wrote: "In the time, circumstances and setting in which it is delivered it stands out as one of the historic utterances of the war."[137]

# FIFTEEN

# 1945 and the End of War

On January 12, 1945, the Soviets initiated a major assault on the German lines in the east. Within five days, they took Warsaw and two days later captured Kraków. On the twenty-seventh, they reached Auschwitz and discovered 220,000 starving prisoners and evidence of the extermination of millions of "undesirable" people. The gas chambers and crematoria had been blown up by the retreating Nazis, but the Germans had kept records, including times and dates of executions, up until the very end.

In all, the Nazis exterminated approximately six million Jews and close to as many non-Jews in their concentration camps.[1] These non-Jewish victims included Poles and Slavs (characterized in Nazi Germany as *Untermenschen*, or sub-humans), Gypsies, mentally-ill people, politicians, intellectuals, ministers, priests, and anyone else who might have been a threat to the occupying Nazi forces. Had the Nazis won the war, all of the concentration camp victims would have eventually faced the gas chambers. As it was, some survived, and Pius was recognized by the Jewish community for his part in helping them.[2]

In February, Roosevelt, Stalin, and Churchill met at the Yalta Conference to consider the fate of postwar Europe. They decided that all territories annexed by the Nazis between 1938 and 1940 would be returned to their former Austrian, Czechoslovakian, or French owners. Germany itself was to be divided into zones that would be administered by the United States, Great Britain, France, and the Soviet Union. The Soviets promised to establish provisional democratic governments and hold free elections in the eastern European areas as soon as possible. In return for their cooperation in Europe, the Soviets were promised an even bigger piece of Poland than Hitler had offered prior to the war.[3] Land from Germany would be used to compensate the Poles. The Soviet Union was also to receive islands in the Pacific.

Pius was not pleased with the results of Yalta. In his wartime correspondence with President Roosevelt, Pius indicated a desire to have the Allies isolate Russia. He also condemned the partition of the world between the great powers and pointed to the failure of settlements in the past based on the distinction between victor and vanquished, rather than true justice. In one filmed statement, he said:

> Do we have peace, true peace? No, merely a postwar period. How many years will it take to overcome the moral suffering? How much effort will it take to heal so many wounds? Today, as the reconstruction begins, mankind is beginning to realize how much care, honesty and charity will be required to rescue

the world from physical and spiritual ruin, and to lead it back to the paths of peace and righteousness.[4]

His objections to the postwar plans of the Allies, however, had little more effect than did his objections to the wartime activities of the Axis powers.

———

As the end of the war drew near, President Roosevelt became the first of the major leaders from the warring nations to pass away, on April 12, though both Mussolini and Hitler would come to their end in that same month. Roosevelt had suffered bad health for a long time; he died from a cerebral hemorrhage while resting up at Warm Springs, Georgia. Pope Pius sent telegrams to Eleanor Roosevelt and Harry Truman:

> The unexpected and sorrowful word of the passing of the President brings to Our heart a profound sense of grief born of the high esteem in which We held this renowned Statesman and of the friendly relations which he fostered and maintained with Us and with the Holy See. To the expression of Our condolences We join the assurance of Our prayers for the entire American people and for their new President to whom We extend Our fervent good wishes that his labors may be efficacious in leading the Nations at war to an early peace that will be just and Christian.[5]

Roosevelt was replaced by Vice President Harry Truman, who had to decide about continued relations between the Holy See and the United States. Myron Taylor, after all, had been the personal representative of the president to the Pope, not an official ambassador. The message came that the new president wanted to continue relations through Taylor. The message was well received in the Vatican.[6]

———

While the Soviets were making their final drive to Berlin, Allied troops liberated numerous concentration camps. In April, they reached Buchenwald and Belsen, where they found forty thousand inmates barely alive and ten thousand unburied corpses. The camp at Dachau revealed even greater horrors. Shock and revulsion ran through the entire world as the reality of Hitler's Final Solution sank in. German civilians, many of whom claimed not to have known what took place in the concentration camps, were escorted through to see the evidence.

As the Axis military power in Europe was collapsing, American, British, and Russian armies were destroying the will of the aggressors and encouraging resistance movements. On April 27, Mussolini and several other Fascists tried to make their escape to Switzerland. Having been once deposed and then made a puppet, Mussolini was only a shadow of his former self. While the Italian people celebrated Pius XII for his brave resistance to Hitler and the Nazis, Mussolini was despised.

The Fascists traveled in a column of vehicles toward the Swiss border, but they were stopped by Italian partisans. Mussolini, disguised in a German coat and helmet, was recognized and taken prisoner. He and his mistress, Claretta Petacci, were shot, and their bodies were taken to Milan, the city where Fascism had first taken root.[7] They were strung up by their heels in the public square and later dragged through the street, with people kicking and spitting on them. One hysterical woman fired five shots into Mussolini's body, screaming, "Five shots for my five murdered sons."

In April 1945, Pius issued the encyclical *Communium Interpretes Dolororum* (an appeal for prayers for peace), in which he encouraged the faithful to pray for peace and to return to Christian morals. As was his style, he appealed to the spiritual side of life, not the secular:

> Change the heart and the world will be changed. Eradicate cupidity and plant charity. Do you want peace? Do justice, and you will have peace. If therefore you desire to come to peace, do justice; avoid evil and do good. This is to love justice; and when you have already avoided evil and done good, seek peace and follow it.[8]

The Holy Father specifically asked his followers to pray for those who had fallen victim to the war:

> We desire moreover that those who heed Our exhortation, also pray for those who are fugitives banished from their homeland and longing to once again see their own homes; also for those in captivity who wait for their liberation after the war; and finally those who lie in numberless hospitals.[9]

Around this time, the Vatican heard rumors that the Germans intended to execute all foreigners under their control (estimated at six hundred thousand Jews). The Pope and other Church officials "worked feverishly" to prevent this massacre.[10]

In fact, Pius XII's efforts in support of Jews drew criticism from some unusual sources. "Catholic" Fascist Roberto Farinacci wrote furious attacks against Pius, culminating with this outburst: "For a few years, Pope Pius XII has fully espoused the Jewish cause.... We never imagined that our Pastor, the Vicar of Christ, the Head of our Church, could one day be regarded as the most influential defender of the interests of the Jewish people."[11]

---

On April 30, just days after Mussolini's execution, Hitler and his longtime mistress, Eva Braun, were married. Early in the war he had lived high in the mountains, in his "Eagle's Nest." Now he lived in a Berlin bunker, emerging only when necessary for meetings or to walk his dog, Blondie. After the wedding, the newlyweds committed suicide rather than face the world in defeat. Their bodies were then taken outside, burned, and buried in a shallow grave. The Nazi propaganda machine announced that he had died fighting with his last breath for Germany and against Bolshevism.[12]

German Admiral Karl Doenitz, Hitler's successor, tried desperately to arrange a surrender to the Western Allies instead of the Soviets, but Eisenhower refused all attempts to put conditions on surrender.[13] Finally, on May 7, representatives of Germany's armed forces capitulated to the Allies at Eisenhower's headquarters in Reims. The formal unconditional surrender came the next day in Berlin, May 8, V-E Day. Hitler's "thousand-year" Third Reich had come to an end. Eisenhower declared: "We come as conquerors but not as oppressors."[14] Stalin had a different view. Three and a half million German soldiers were marched off to the Soviet Union. Half of them were never seen again.[15]

In an allocution to the Sacred College on June 2, 1945, which was also broadcast on Vatican Radio, Pius reviewed the struggle supported by the Holy See, beginning from the time of Pius XI, against Nazism and against the anti-Christian doctrines that it spread. He noted the death of about two thousand Catholic priests at Dachau and described National Socialism as "the arrogant apostasy from Jesus Christ, the denial of His doctrine and of His work of redemption, the cult of violence, the idolatry of race and blood, the overthrow of human liberty and dignity."[16] With "the satanic apparition of National Socialism" out of the way, Pius expressed his confidence that Germany would "rise to a new dignity and a new life."[17] He went on to point out that Nazi persecution of the Catholic Church both in Germany and occupied nations had been continuous and that he had been aware of Nazism's ultimate goal: "[I]ts adherents boasted that once they had gained the military victory, they would put an end to the Church forever. Authorities and incontrovertible witnesses kept Us informed of this intention."[18]

———

The German threat was now over, and by mid-summer 1945 Japan was on the verge of collapse. Since January, Vatican officials had been in contact with Japanese leaders in the hopes of reaching a negotiated settlement.[19] Unfortunately, as the Vatican representatives realized, Japan's demands were beyond anything that the Allies would accept. The war would have to end in some other manner.[20]

Back in August 1939, Leo Szilard wrote President Roosevelt asking him to consider the use of atomic energy in war. Albert Einstein, the most renowned scientist in the world, added his name to the letter, even though he was known as an ardent pacifist. Over the next six years, the American government sponsored a secret two-billion-dollar operation known as the Manhattan Project. On April 25, 1945, Secretary of War Henry Lewis Stimson told President Truman: "Within four months we shall in all probability have completed the most terrible weapon ever known in human history, one bomb of which could destroy a whole city."[21] When Winston Churchill was informed that the Americans had developed the bomb, he said: "This is the Second Coming, in wrath."[22]

On July 26, without mentioning the bomb, Truman, Churchill, and Chinese leader Chiang Kai-shek issued an ultimatum. Surrender had to be complete, include the return of all Japanese conquests since 1895, and provide for Allied occupation of Japan until "a peacefully inclined and responsible government" was established. The alternative was to face "the utter devastation of the Japanese homeland."[23] Surrender, however, was not forthcoming. On July 28, the Japanese prime minister, in a statement designed for domestic consumption, pronounced the Allies' ultimatum "unworthy of public notice."[24]

On August 6, 1945, from an altitude of 31,600 feet, the American B-29 *Enola Gay* dropped a bomb with an explosive force greater than had ever been known. The bomb destroyed five square miles in the center of the Japanese city of Hiroshima. At least seventy-eight thousand people (including the entire Japanese Second Army) were killed outright, ten thousand more were never found, and more than seventy thousand were injured. Almost two-thirds of the city was destroyed. The next day, the Soviets entered into the war against Japan, giving them standing to demand certain postwar concessions.

On August 9, another atomic bomb was dropped on Nagasaki. About forty thousand people were killed, and about the same number were injured. On August 10, Japan sought peace, on the condition that the emperor retain his position as sovereign ruler. The Allies responded that the future status of the emperor would be determined by them. On August 14, Japan accepted the Allies' terms, and a cease-fire was ordered the following day.

———

In terms of loss of life, World War II was the costliest war in history. More than 15 million military personnel were killed in action. Of the Axis powers, Germany lost about 3.5 million soldiers in battle, Japan 1.5 million, and Italy 200,000. Among the Allies, the Soviet Union had the heaviest battle casualties, with about 7.5 million dead; China lost 2.2 million soldiers; the British lost more than 300,000 military personnel; the United States suffered 292,000 losses; and France lost 210,000.[25]

Civilian casualties were even worse, numbering perhaps 20 million. The Soviet Union lost more than 10 million civilians; China lost at least 6 million; France lost 400,000; the United Kingdom 65,000; and the United States 6,000. On the Axis side, Germany lost about 500,000 civilians; Japan lost 600,000; and Italy 145,000. Expenditures for war materials and armaments were enormous. The United States spent about $300 billion on the war effort; Germany spent about $231 billion. Japan, the Soviet Union, Italy, and Britain also each spent billions. Added to these costs was the tremendous material damage done to property of all kinds, including priceless historical sites, art, and buildings.[26]

Most notoriously, an estimated 6,000,000 Jews, mostly from eastern Europe, were killed by the Nazis. Before the Final Solution, there were approximately 9,000,000 Jews north of Spain in continental Europe. By 1945, two-thirds of them had been murdered or died because of the conditions in the German concentration camps. In Germany, Austria, the Baltic countries, and Poland, 90 percent of all Jews were killed.[27] Several million non-Jewish Nazi victims (estimates range as high as 6,000,000) also lost their lives in the death camps.

Many Germans had to face the question of their own role in the course of Nazism, but most of them also suffered from the war. A majority of German families lost members at the front, and most of the rest lost relatives, homes, or possessions in the bombing raids on German cities or on the refugee treks from the east at the end of the war. Many Germans left their country following the war; those who remained suffered from severe hunger.[28] The average caloric intake from 1945 to 1947 was less than 70 percent of that which was deemed adequate.[29] Many took to looting and fighting in the streets. Germany was called "a country where men had lost all hope and women all shame."[30]

---

The Catholic Church was not defeated, but it suffered greatly during the war. Thousands of priests and nuns were killed; millions of Catholics died. In Poland alone, it was estimated that "4 bishops, 1,996 priests, 113 clerics, and 238 female religious were murdered; sent to concentration camps were 3,642 priests, 389 clerics, 341 lay brothers, and 1,117 female religious."[31] According to a report prepared for the prosecution team at Nuremberg, at least 7,000 priests were killed.[32]

This persecution put an enormous strain on Pius. Associates worried about his ability to survive the eighteen-hour days he put in. Although Pius could have lived the style of a king, he put war-time restrictions upon himself and the other citizens of Vatican City. He dispensed with his private secretaries, and he survived on the same rations that were available to everyone in Rome (little food, no coffee, and no heat).[33] By the end of the war, he was emaciated. Although he was more than six feet tall, he weighed only 130 pounds.

Bishop (later Archbishop) Fulton Sheen called Pius a "dry martyr," meaning that he had suffered for the Church in times of persecution, but without having shed blood.[34] He had witnessed terrible suffering up close, and had been unable to stop it:

> Perhaps no Pope in history has seen so many martyred for their faith as has Pius XII. The first 32 Popes, including St. Peter, were martyrs for the faith. They were the wet martyrs. The present Holy Father has seen millions tortured, persecuted, exiled, and martyred under the beatings of the hammer and sickle of communism; he has agonized under the double cross of Nazism and borne in his body the marks of the sticks of fascism.... [A]ll this and other sorrows, he felt as his own.[35]

Additionally, the Pontiff was not pleased about what the future held. He feared that the spread of Communism and Soviet influence would bring the Church and its people throughout the world to their knees.[36] As Sheen said: "To the world, it may seem an honor to be a Pope; but to be a Pope, in these times, is to bear a cross."[37]

Despite the physical strain, Pius stood strong against the Nazis throughout the war. At Christmastime 1941, the *New York Times* wrote: "The voice of Pius XII is a lonely voice in the silence and darkness enveloping Europe this Christmas.... The Pope put himself squarely against Hitlerism."[38] That same paper, one year later wrote: "This Christmas more than ever he is a lonely voice crying out of the silence of a continent...."[39]

In August 1943, *Time* magazine wrote: "... it is scarcely deniable that the Church Apostolic, through the encyclicals and other Papal pronouncements, has been fighting totalitarianism more knowingly, devoutly, and authoritatively, and for a longer time, than any other organized power."[40] Following the liberation of Rome, in October 1944, the *New York Times* wrote: "[U]nder the Pope's direction the Holy See did an exemplary job of sheltering and championing the victims of the Nazi-Fascist regime."[41] This perception of Pope Pius XII as a staunch opponent of the Nazis and a protector of victims, Christian or not, was widely shared from the time of the war until several years after his death. The Nazis despised him, the victims praised him, and the rescuers cited him as their inspiration.

———

The last Allied wartime conference was held at Potsdam, Germany, in July and August 1945. Roosevelt had died in April, so President Truman represented the United States, but Churchill and Stalin were both there for at least part of the conference (Churchill was defeated by Clement Attlee in an election for prime minister that took place during the conference). The Allies agreed at Potsdam that they would prosecute Nazi Party and German military leaders for crimes against humanity and world peace.

Potsdam, like Yalta, called for the Soviet Union to have a very significant role in postwar Europe. This was seen by many (including most people in the Holy See) as a betrayal of the ideals for which the Allies had fought.[42] The Soviet Union emerged from the war with 262,533 more square miles of territory, 22,162,000 more people, and satellite states in Poland, East Germany, Lithuania, Latvia, Estonia, Romania, Bulgaria, Czechoslovakia, and Albania.[43] Ambassador William C. Bullitt said of the Yalta agreement: "No more unnecessary, disgraceful, and potentially disastrous document has ever been signed by a President of the United States."[44] Arthur Bliss Lane, U.S. ambassador to Poland in 1944-47, called the Yalta agreement: "a capitulation on the part of the United States and Great Britain to the views of the Soviet Union on the frontiers of Poland and the composition of the Polish Provisional Government...."[45] Even Winston Churchill ended up calling the results of Yalta "a tragedy on a prodigious scale."[46] The problem with these agreements was not how they were negotiated. Like so much that took place in the war, it had to do with differing ethics and morality.

The Yalta and Potsdam agreements were based on the fallacy that the golden rule would work on the Russian government, which regarded Christian ethics as outmoded."[47]

Pope Pius XII worked with the Nuremberg prosecution. He named Edmund A. Walsh, a Jesuit priest, as expert consultant to the War Crimes Commission and charged him with the responsibility of investigating and tabulating the persecution of religion by the Nazi government. On December 12, 1945, Walsh wrote from Nuremberg:

> The Pope has put at the disposal of the United States an important collection of documents dealing with the persecution of the Church by the Nazi regime. With his permission, and bearing the official authentication of the Papal Secretary of State, they will be offered in evidence before the International Military Tribunal sometime during the first week in January. With charity, but with firmness and justice, the Holy See will then point out the specific measures adopted by the Nazi Government to destroy the Catholic Church in Germany and in the occupied countries. This Vatican evidence will, I am confident, become part of the history of the war.[48]

Despite these efforts, the Pope was concerned about a world that seemed less stable than ever. Uneasy alliances were falling apart, weapons of incalculable power were aimed at key targets around the globe, and governmental power was dangerously centralized. The Soviets, in particular, seemed intent on expanding their influence, by force if necessary. In March 1946, Winston Churchill, speaking at Westminster College in Fulton, Missouri, said: "From Stettin in the Baltic to Trieste in the Adriatic, an Iron Curtain has descended across the Continent."[49]

---

The end of the war saw Pius XII hailed as "the inspired moral prophet of victory,"[50] and he "enjoyed near-universal acclaim for aiding European Jews through diplomatic initiatives, thinly veiled public pronouncements, and, very concretely, an unprecedented continent-wide network of sanctuary."[51] As an author and correspondent who lived in postwar Italy explained:

> Only by the most strenuous means had Pius XII, an extraordinary being, maintained the prestige of the Church. This tall, frail man with piercing black eyes had for twenty-five years conducted an almost incredibly arduous reign. He had literally thrown open the huge bronze doors of the Vatican and invited people to come to him. No longer was the Vicar of Christ unapproachable.... He had seen to it that for the first time since the fourteenth century foreign cardinals outnumbered Italians in the Sacred College and he had severely condemned racialism, anti-Semitism and totalitarian doctrines.[52]

With the end of hostilities, Pius concentrated on trying to help people recover from the ravages of war.[53] In 1947, he was feeding an average of a quarter of a million people a day.[54] Papal money was sent to every war-torn nation and distributed without regard to race, creed, or nationality. With his two personal assistants, Monsignor Giovanni Montini and Domenico Tardini, the Pontiff personally helped to feed and reconstruct western Europe. (Shipments of food, clothing, and medicine continued until June 3, 1966.)

One of Pius XII's biggest postwar projects was helping displaced children and families through the Pope's Children War Relief Program. More than ten thousand children from Austria, Hungary, Germany, Italy, and Switzerland obtained release papers, transatlantic passage, and admission into the United States thanks to this project.[55] Pius also established the International Committee of Catholic Charities. This organization coordinated local and national efforts to assist victims of war and to help return displaced persons to their homes.[56]

Following the war, Pius received numerous guests from the world of entertainment and films, the aristocracy, politics, and religion. Some sought counsel; others merely paid their respects. Among the distinguished groups that were granted audiences shortly after the war were many American officials, including the House of Representatives' Foreign Affairs Committee and more than two hundred senators and congressmen. (Said Indiana Congressman Samuel B. Pettengill: "I am far from being a Roman Catholic, but it sometimes seems to me that the present Pope is the most sane and sagacious leader on the stage of action at this time.")[57]

In 1945, the chief rabbi of Romania, Dr. Alexander Safran, expressed the gratitude of the Jewish community for the Vatican's help and support for prisoners in the concentration camps.[58] Pinchas E. Lapide, the Israeli consul in Italy, wrote:

> The Catholic Church saved more Jewish lives during the war than all other churches, religious institutions and rescue organizations put together. Its record stands in startling contrast to the achievements of the International Red Cross and the Western Democracies.... The Holy See, the nuncios, and the entire Catholic Church saved some 400,000 Jews from certain death.[59]

Lapide later increased his estimate of Jewish lives saved to between 700,000 and 860,000.[60] The World Jewish Congress also expressed thanks and donated two million lira (about $20,000) to Vatican charities.[61] The New York Times reported that the gift was given in recognition of the work of the Holy See in rescuing Jews from Fascist and Nazi persecution. The National Jewish Welfare Board wrote to Pius: "From the bottom of our hearts we send to you, Holy Father of the Church, the assurance of our unforgetting gratitude for your noble expression of religious brotherhood and love."[62] Dr. Joseph Nathen, a representative of the Hebrew Commission, expressing thanks for support during the Holocaust, said: "Above all, we acknowledge the Supreme Pontiff and the religious men and women who, executing the directives of the Holy Father, recognized the persecuted as their brothers and, with great abnegation, hastened to help them, disregarding the terrible dangers to which they were exposed."[63]

On November 29, 1945, Pius received a group of Jews who were serving as delegates to a displaced-persons conference being held in Rome. The Pope laid a foundation for assisting with the establishment of a new Jewish state by reminding the temporal authorities of the need to adhere to moral principles, especially those of solidarity and brotherhood, as they addressed the plight of displaced persons. These principles, the Pope asserted, would provide the framework for resolving the political and territorial issues involved in establishing a homeland.[64] Pius reminded the delegation that the Holy See repudiated the deplorable and dishonorable ideas that had devoured many Jewish victims during the War years. Moshe Sharett, who attended this meeting and was later to become the first foreign minister of Israel, told the Pope that a major reason for the loss of six million Jews was that Jews had no state of their own. He further asserted that there was no real conflict between the interests of the Jews and those of the Church. In return for the moral support of the Church, he indicated that Jews were prepared to honor the holy sites in painstaking fashion. The meeting concluded with an exchange of blessings or best wishes.[65]

In 1947, a delegation of Palestinian Arabs, consisting of Christians and Muslims, traveled to Rome to meet with the Pope. During their audience on August 3, they expressed their views on the difficult situation in Palestine. The contingent asked for papal intervention to help those Palestinian Arabs who might be displaced by Jewish settlers, but Pius would not commit the Holy See to any specifics of the proposal. Instead, he renewed his condemnation of anti-Semitism, which harmed Jew and Arab alike, and he expressed his sincere interest in doing what he could to facilitate a proper and just solution to these difficult problems.[66] He also appealed to both Jews and Arabs to resolve their differences in a peaceful manner.[67]

Some critics say that true feelings of anger were disguised during and after the war to preserve goodwill between the Church and Jews who hoped to form a new state of Israel. That theory, however, is contradicted by a wartime, interoffice memo of the World Jewish Congress, apparently not intended for release to the public. It said:

> The Catholic Church in Europe has been extraordinarily helpful to us in a multitude of ways. From Hinsley in London to Pacelli in Rome, to say nothing of the anonymous priests in Holland, France and elsewhere, they had [sic] done very notable things for us.[68]

William Zukerman, editor of the *Jewish Newsletter* and one of the most distinguished Jewish journalists of the age, called "the rescue of thousands of Jewish Nazi victims by the Vatican... one of the greatest manifestations of humanitarianism in the 20th century as well as a new, effective method of fighting anti-Semitism."[69] On April 5, 1946, the Italian Jewish community sent a message of appreciation to Pope Pius XII:

> The delegates of the Congress of the Italian Jewish Communities, held in Rome for the first time after the Liberation, feel that it is imperative to extend reverent homage to Your Holiness, and to express the most profound gratitude that animates all Jews for your fraternal humanity toward them during the years of persecution when their lives were endangered by Nazi-Fascist barbarism. Many times priests suffered imprisonment and were sent to concentration camps, and offered their lives to assist Jews in every way. This demonstration of goodness and charity that still animates the just, has served to lessen the shame and torture and sadness that afflicted millions of human beings.[70]

Cecil Roth, the leading English authority on the history of Italian Jewry, also paid tribute to the Church's uncompromising stand against racism in his *Encyclopedia Judaica*. The Protestant publication *Christian Century* wrote an editorial on Pius stating that "it is to be regretted that no equally impressive Church statesmanship, no equally commanding message, has as yet come to this postwar world from any other authoritative body or leadership."[71]

Dr. Herman Datyner, a member of the Inter-Allied Conference for Refugees and special representative of Italian Jewish refugee groups and organizations, was granted an audience with Pius XII to thank him for assistance during the war. He memorialized some of the Pontiff's comments. Regarding Jewish suffering, the Pope said:

> Yes, I know, my son, all the sufferings of you Jews. I am sorry, truly sorry, about the loss of your family. I suffered a great deal,... knowing about Jewish sufferings, and I tried to do whatever was in my power in order to make your fate easier.... I will pray to God that happiness will return to you, to your people. Tell them this.[72]

Tributes and kind words, as well as acts of charity, continued for years following the war.[73]

In 1947, King Gustav V of Sweden honored Pius XII with the annual Prince Carl medal, given to the person who has done the most outstanding work in the field of charity. The citation said it was for his "tireless work in relieving the misery of the war victims."[74] The War Refugee Board, representing the united effort of various American Jewish organizations, publicly acknowledged its close relationship with the Holy See and the good work of the Church.[75] Maurice Edelman, president of the Anglo-Jewish Association, visited Pius XII to thank him for his help. According to Edelman, papal intervention "was responsible during the war for saving the lives of tens of thousands of Jews."[76] When the Pope received a large delegation of Roman Jews in the Vatican, he ordered that the "imperial steps" be opened for them to enter. This was an honor usually reserved for crowned heads of state. Noting that his visitors seemed uncomfortable in the

Sistine Chapel, Pius came down from his throne and warmly welcomed them, saying: "I am only the Vicar of Christ but you are His very kith and kin."[77]

In 1955, when Italy celebrated the tenth anniversary of its liberation, Italian Jewry proclaimed April 17 as "The Day of Gratitude." That year, thousands of Jewish people made a pilgrimage to the Vatican to express appreciation for the Pope's wartime solicitudes. The musicians who were to become the Israeli Philharmonic Orchestra even gave a special performance of Beethoven's Ninth Symphony in the Papal Consistory Hall as an expression of gratitude for the Catholic Church's assistance in defying the Nazis.[78] While there, they posed with Pius XII for a photographic portrait.[79]

Before the celebration, a delegation approached Monsignor Montini, the director of Vatican rescue services who later became Pope Paul VI, to determine whether he would accept an award for his work on behalf of Jews during the war. He was extremely gratified and visibly touched by their words, but he declined the honor: "All I did was my duty," he said. "And besides I only acted upon orders from the Holy Father. Nobody deserves a medal for that."[80] Angelo Roncalli (the future Pope John XXIII), wartime apostolic delegate in Istanbul, made a very similar statement concerning his efforts to save Jewish lives: "In all these painful matters I have referred to the Holy See and simply carried out the Pope's orders: first and foremost to save human lives."[81]

By September 1957, the secular *Wisdom* magazine was able to editorialize: "Of all the great figures of our time, none is more universally respected by men of all faiths than Pope Pius XII."[82] When the truth finally came out, it was clear: the driving force behind rescue operations carried out by papal representatives all around the world was Pope Pius XII.[83] The achievement was all the more amazing because it was well understood that Catholics themselves were, as *Reader's Digest* described it: "Nazi Scapegoat Number 2."[84]

Despite the accolades he received, and the high hopes he had for the United Nations,[85] Pius was not pleased with the way the postwar world was shaping up. After the war, more than two million Soviet refugees in western Europe, primarily prisoners of war and slave laborers taken by the Germans, were forcibly repatriated with the assistance of British and American troops.[86] Poles were forced to evacuate from those areas of Poland that had been claimed by the Soviet Union. In return, Poland was given parts of Germany. Seven million Germans disappeared from those regions awarded to Poland; many were killed, many fled, and the rest were driven out. Later, more than three million Germans were expelled from Czechoslovakia.[87] Pius viewed all of this as a continuation of the human rights abuses that had taken place during the war.

All along, Pius had feared that a Soviet victory would mean that eastern Europe would fall to Communism, and much of it did. The Soviets quickly established satellite states — governments that were beholden to (if not dominated by) Moscow — in Poland, East Germany, Lithuania, Latvia, Estonia, Romania, Bulgaria, Czechoslovakia, and Albania. In light of the Church's history with

Communism in Russia, China, and Mexico, Pius was afraid that the spread of Soviet influence would bring the Church to its knees, and in many places that is what happened.[88] He actively worked to limit the Communist influence in western Europe, especially in Italy. Fortunately, the Church emerged from World War II with enhanced strength and prestige within Italy. In fact, the immediate postwar years may have seen the Catholic Church at its most influential since the Reformation.[89] As such, it was able to have a substantial impact on political issues, particularly in postwar elections, when the Pope helped fight off a possible Communist takeover of the Italian government.[90]

————

For Pius, reminders of the war years were particularly disheartening. Not only did the war reveal humans at their most evil, but the suffering was not confined the way it had been in previous wars. Women and children figured very high among the death rolls. Pius was, however, proud of how the Church had maintained its dignity during the war. In his speech at the 1946 consistory, he pointed to the crucial role played by the Church in preserving the civil values that had been so threatened by the war.[91] Speaking to delegates from the Supreme Council of the Arab People of Palestine on August 3, 1946, Pius said: "It is superfluous for me to tell you that we disapprove of all recourse to force and violence, from wheresoever it comes, just as we condemned on various occasions in the past the persecutions that a fanatical anti-Semitism inflicted on the Hebrew people."[92] When it seemed that concerns for humanity were lacking throughout the world, the Church was one entity that continued to exhibit charity and compassion.

Pius served thirteen postwar years, reigning in a style reminiscent of the grand centuries of the papacy. Until failing health forced him to restrict his activities, Pius XII was an extraordinarily accessible pope. He celebrated more public Masses and held more private audiences than any of his recent predecessors had, and each week he held a special audience just for newlyweds.[93] Although he was urged to slow down and take care of his health, he said that it was his duty to fulfill the desires of all those who came to Rome to see the Pope.[94]

During his life, Pius XII was widely regarded as a warm man and a brilliant conversationalist.[95] The Vatican reporter for the *New York Times* described the new Pope in 1939:

> His personality is even more impressive than his precision. No member of the Sacred College so perfectly looks the part of a prince of the church. His tall, slender figure has remarkable dignity. His face is thin and ascetic, with long features and deepset, questioning eyes. He has the manner of a great gentleman, simple, modest and assured. He speaks English clearly and well. His expression is much more lively than the photographs indicate.[96]

Noting that he had a reputation for being austere, she went on to say that she found him to be "smiling, warm, and vivacious." Pius also used television and radio to reach out directly to the people. As the *New York Times* reported, he "exchanged views with more laymen of different creeds and nationalities than any pontiff of modern time."[97] Because of all this, he was known as the "least stuffy" of popes.[98]

After the war, servicemen and celebrities from all around the world came to see the Pope. He tried to talk to everyone. "This was the period of 'open house' at the Vatican when Pius XII met more Americans than any other Pontiff in history or any living ruler."[99] Field Marshal Earl Alexander of Tunis wrote:

> I well remember that, when the Allies were in occupation of Rome, crowds of our soldiers went to the Vatican to see the Pope, who daily gave them his blessing. Thinking that it might be too great a strain on him I said one day: "I hope that all these Allied soldiers are not too great a burden for your Holiness," and added, "although of course, so many of them are Catholics," He replied: "No! No! Let them all come to me — I love them all"[100]

Shortly after Pius XII's death, Field Marshal Montgomery wrote in the October 12 issue of London's *Sunday Times*: "He was a great and good man, and I loved him."[101]

One time a nervous soldier dropped his hat, and the Pope smilingly picked it up for him.[102] Another soldier told the Pope that they shared something in common: "[W]e both used to be Cardinals." Pius asked how that could have been. Joe "Ducky" Medwick of the St. Louis Cardinals baseball team's famed "Gas House Gang" then let the Pope in on his joke. "I guess I really walked into that one," said a smiling Pope.[103]

Many children came to see the Pope. They "pressed close to him and offered him gifts of candy and flowers. His love for these small ones of his flock was very evident in his smiling, affectionate gaze."[104] It was said that he "made himself a child with children."[105] A young mother at a papal audience once asked another woman to hold her crying baby while she approached Pius XII. She returned a moment later, saying: "Let me have him. His Holiness says he doesn't care if the baby *does* cry."[106]

Pius went out of his way to meet with handicapped visitors. A Swiss Guard reported in his memoirs:

> Well I remember a cripple in the audience hall. Unnoticed he squatted behind hundreds at the entrance of the room. He was happy to see the Holy Father from the distance. Pius XII stood up from his throne, approached him with great strides and treated him like a poor brother whom one has not seen for years and who has come back to his home, ill in body and soul.[107]

He also paid special attention to the many widows who brought their children to meet him at an audience.[108] Anne O'Hare McCormick, the *New York Times* correspondent at the Vatican, wrote: "Pius XII is not tired by the innumerable audiences he gives, because he likes people."[109]

"Movie stars, sports heroes, celebrities of every stripe, creed and discipline flocked to [Pius XII's] audiences."[110] "Among prominent Americans he has received are Dwight D. Eisenhower (when he was still in uniform), ex-Presidents Truman... and Hoover and Secretary of State Dulles."[111] When the Harlem Globetrotters visited the Vatican, Pius was filmed tapping his foot to "Sweet Georgia Brown." When Clark Gable came to visit, the Pope discarded his schedule to spend time with his favorite movie star (keeping Angelo Roncalli, the future Pope John XXIII, waiting for two hours).[112] Tyrone Power met the Pope very early in his pontificate. Said the popular movie actor:

> It was the most marvelous experience of my life. There were several hundred of us and it was the surprise of my life to see how we all instinctively reacted. I expected a reverent hush in the presence of a great man. But everyone applauded. He is the most amazing person I have ever seen. I got an impression of tremendous vigor.[113]

U.S. Undersecretary of State Robert Murphy had — along with Pacelli — been a diplomat in Germany during the mid-1920s. When they met after the war, Murphy reminisced about how they both had reported to their governments that Hitler would never amount to anything. In response, the Pope smiled, raised a finger, and joked: "Remember, back then I was not infallible."[114]

One time a group of altar boys visiting the Vatican got lost and ended up in the papal apartment. They were quite surprised to learn that the kindly man they asked for directions was the Pope.[115] Similarly, a lady waiting for an audience did not recognize him. She asked Pius to hold her baby while she primped! He did so with a smile.[116] Pius enjoyed telling these stories on himself. Once, when a non-Catholic wondered aloud whether he should have come to a papal audience, Pius "smilingly asked him to accept the blessing, not of the Pope, but of an old man!"[117] Pius himself even accepted an "honorary membership in the fire department of Newark, New Jersey. Even the good servant must enjoy an occasional smile of wry amusement."[118]

Pius called laughter a gift from God and said that "laughter has no religion.... There should be more of it in the world."[119] In fact, he was remembered by his friend Domenico Cardinal Tardini, as follows:

> Pius XII appeared also to be — and was in reality — happy. He took pleasure in lively conversation, and appreciated fine literary phrases.... As a true Roman, he loved and relished wit, and was quick to see the humorous, so often hidden in the inexhaustible variety of human affairs. When he laughed, with his wide mouth open, his eyes flashing, and his arms raised, he looked — allow me to say so, for I cannot find any other comparison — like a happy child.[120]

Monsignor Hugh Montgomery, an English priest who knew Pope Pius XII well, wrote of him in the *Catholic Herald*: "It must seem absurd to anyone who knew 'Papa Pacelli' at all to hear him described as 'cold.' He had a boyish eagerness of manner which was most attractive and a radiant smile."[121] That personality served him well for the twenty-two years prior to becoming Pope that he spent as an international diplomat in service to the Holy See.[122] (As nuncio in Berlin, he was known as an avid bridge player.)[123]

Pius was able to "introduce an extraordinary intimacy, gentleness, a sense of love into his work and writings.... [He] has been described as a Franciscan with a love for nature and animals."[124] An article in the March 1939 edition of *Reader's Digest* explained:

> Pope Pius XII seems cold and austere, cloaked in an impenetrable dignity, until he comes within five feet of you. Then you see that his blue eyes are wells of understanding, his thin lips turn up slightly at the corners, features that appeared stern become warm and gentle. And when he speaks and uses his hands in gesture he is magnetic and charming. In conversation, his mind and tongue are keenly alive.[125]

In keeping with tradition, Pius XII ate most of his meals alone, but he kept little plates of bird seed on the table for his pet canaries, that would sometimes light on his shoulder.[126] He also spoke "familiarly" with his attendants and had reports read to him.[127] He was the first Pope to use the telephone or an electric razor.[128] He took walks in the garden and used the gymnasium (complete with electric horse, rowing machine, and punching bag) that he had installed in the Vatican Palace when he was secretary of state.[129] He also loved to ride in fast cars; it was suspected that he left late for meetings so that his driver would have to drive fast.[130] It was said that under Pius XII, "the fabric of St. Peter's became as modern as the fabric of New York."[131]

Even in difficult times, Pius XII's personality came through. "To his own friends, the Cardinal was the same warm, sincere, humor-loving person he had always been."[132] In 1933, when Hitler's government forced the Vatican into an agreement that the Nazis never intended to honor, then-Secretary of State Pacelli remarked: "[W]ell, at least they probably can't violate all of the terms at the same time."[133] Later in the 1930s, Pacelli (who is often depicted as being overly devoted to Germans and Germany) was quoted as having said: "I have lived for too long among Germans not to value highly social relations with Frenchmen."[134]

Pius XII was more willing than his predecessors to see positive elements in the ecumenical movement. In December 1949, shortly after the formation of the World Council of Churches, he formally recognized the ecumenical movement and permitted Catholic scholars to dialogue with non-Catholics on matters of faith. That same year the Holy Office issued a decree, with papal approval, stating that actual incorporation into the Catholic Church was not necessary for salvation.[135] He also encouraged Catholic nuns to study theology, Scripture, and psychology,[136] and he shifted the time of certain services, to permit more people to attend Mass.[137]

Pius even considered calling a council, which might have completely changed the face of the Church.[138] He went so far as to set up five preparatory commissions, but he ultimately decided against proceeding in that direction due to the complexities and expense involved.[139] His work, however, encouraged his successor, Pope John XXIII, to convene Vatican II.[140] John's reformation of the Curia followed along the lines set forth by Pius XII over a decade earlier.[141] As others have concluded: "However the pontificate of the Pacelli pope was to be evaluated, it has to be acknowledged that, without him, John's achievement would have been unthinkable."[142]

Vatican II led to the release of the Declaration on the Relation of the Church to Non-Christian Religions. That declaration "commends mutual understanding and esteem" between Christians and Jews, rejects anti-Semitism, and specifically states that God has neither rejected nor cursed the Jews.[143] The *Jewish Post* explained that Pope Pius XII had set the stage for a new understanding between Jews and Christians:

> Organized and institutionalized Christianity realized that the old religious bitterness and hatred between Christians and Jews no longer had meaning or reason and that the failure to remove them in time had almost brought Judeo-Christian civilization to its end. It is to the credit of Pope Pius XII that he, a great leader of Christianity, not only recognized this truth in time, but also that he visualized a positive method of acting upon it in a grand manner: Instead of merely preaching Christianity, he and [other church leaders practice Christian] principles and set an example by their acts and lives, as did the founder of Christianity. This was the uniqueness of the achievement of Pope Pius XII.[144]

Pius was known for making highly informed presentations to representatives from all types of professions.[145] He amazed listeners with his knowledge of various technologies. The Pope worked hard and cared deeply about his research. Illustrating the importance that he attached to accurate citation of authority, he liked to tell the story of one professor who said to another: "I congratulate you. In your latest book — which is really excellent — I found one accurate quotation."[146]

In December 1954, Pius fell seriously ill, and his physicians feared for his life. Cardinals packed their bags, diplomats prepared memos, and journalists speculated about a successor, but he recovered his strength and returned to work.[147] During this illness, Pius reported an apparition of Jesus.[148] While this caused some to question his mental stability, the crowds drawn to him grew even larger.

During his pontificate, Pius expanded and internationalized the Church by creating fifty-seven new bishoprics, forty-five of them in America and Asia.[149] Pius also caused the percentage of Italians in the College of Cardinals to drop to less than half, paving the way for the eventual election of a non-Italian pope. (One of the first new cardinals following the war was German Count von Galen, bishop of Münster and a noted opponent of Hitlerism.)[150]

In 1958, at Castel Gandolfo, Pius XII summoned his last ounce of energy for the necessary paperwork that included nominations for six new auxiliary bishops in Poland. One of the openings was in the Kraków archdiocese. On July 8, Pius XII signed the nomination of Karol Wojtyla to be the titular bishop of Ombia and auxiliary bishop in Kraków. The signing of this nomination fundamentally altered the future of the Church and of Father Wojtyla, who would go on to become Pope John Paul II. It was Pius XII's final great historic act.

––––––––––

On October 3, 1958, the first word of the Pope's illness was released. Six days later, at the age of eighty-two, Pope Pius XII died peacefully in his sleep at Castel Gandolfo. With church bells ringing, a Jesuit priest read the final bulletin: "The Supreme Pontiff is dead. Pope Pius XII, the most esteemed and venerated man in the world, one of the greatest Pontiffs of the century, with sanctity passed away at 3:52 today, October 9, 1958."[151] He had served for nineteen and a half years, the longest pontificate since Pius IX (1846-78). Four days after his death, on Friday, October 13, Pius XII began his final trip to his beloved Rome.

Funeral rites for Pius XII were marked by splendor and reverence that was unusual even for the Vatican. Ceremonies continued for nine days.[152] Hundreds of thousands of tearful people lined the route as the cortege (itself, two miles long) slowly made its way through the Roman countryside and entered the city through the St. John Gate, past the house where Eugenio Pacelli had been born, to the Basilica of St. John Lateran (the cathedral church of Rome) where a contingent of the Swiss Guard led the way to the papal altar. Fifty-three nations sent representatives to the Requiem Mass in his honor.[153]

The fallen Pontiff's last will and testament provided: "I am aware of the failures, of the sins, committed during so long a pontificate and in so grave an epoch. Sufficient it is that my remains should be laid simply in a sacred place — the more obscure the better."[154] He was laid to rest in the Sacred Grotto beneath St. Peter's Basilica, close to the tomb of St. Peter, near most of the 259 popes who had preceded him.[155]

Even at the time of his death, Pius's activity in World War II was the primary focus of attention. Then Israeli representative to the United Nations and future prime minister of Israel, Golda Meir, said: "During the ten years of Nazi terror, when our people went through the horrors of martyrdom, the Pope raised his voice to condemn the persecutors and to commiserate with their victims."[156] Nahum Goldmann, president of the World Jewish Congress, said: "With special gratitude we remember all he has done for the persecuted Jews during one of the darkest periods of their entire history."[157] Rabbi Elio Toaff, who would later become chief rabbi of Rome, said: "More than anyone else, we have had the opportunity to appreciate the great kindness, filled with compassion and magnanimity, that the Pope displayed during the terrible years of persecution and terror, when it seemed that there was no hope left for us."[158] As the *Jewish Post* (Winnipeg) reported in its November 6, 1958 edition:

> It is understandable why the death of Pope Pius XII should have called forth expressions of sincere grief from practically all sections of American Jewry. For

there probably was not a single ruler of our generation who did more to help the Jews in their hour of greatest tragedy, during the Nazi occupation of Europe, than the late Pope.

Similarly, the *Jewish Chronicle* (London), in its October 10, 1958, edition said:

Adherents of all creeds and parties will recall how Pius XII faced the responsibilities of his exalted office with courage and devotion. Before, during, and after the Second World War, he constantly preached the message of peace. Confronted by the monstrous cruelties of Nazism, Fascism, and Communism, he repeatedly proclaimed the virtues of humanity and compassion.

In New York, virtually every major rabbi offered praise for Pius ("an example for all religious leaders" and "man at his highest").[159] Nearly a thousand letters of gratitude from Jewish survivors of the Holocaust poured into the New York archdiocese.[160] President Eisenhower said: "The world is a poorer place with the death of Pius XII."[161] The Anti-Defamation League, the Synagogue Council of America, the Rabbinical Council of America, the American Jewish Congress, the New York Board of Rabbis, the American Jewish Committee, the Central Conference of American Rabbis, the National Conference of Christians and Jews, and the National Council of Jewish Women all expressed sorrow at his passing and gratitude for his good works.[162] Israel sent an official delegation to his funeral, and many people in Israel wrote to newspapers suggesting that a forest in the Judean hills be established in his name.[163]

The cardinals went into conclave sixteen days after Pius XII's death, and Cardinal Angelo Giuseppe Roncalli of Venice (who had been promoted and praised by Pius XII)[164] was elected pope three days later, taking the name of John XXIII. That week, he said he had trouble remembering that when people spoke of "the Pope" they were not talking about "our Holy Father Pope Pius XII, whom I venerated and loved so much."[165] Pope John would soon launch Vatican Council II. From that council would come the Church's teaching that:

All men are endowed with a rational soul and are created in God's image.... [F]orms of social or cultural discrimination in basic personal rights on the grounds of sex, race, color, social conditions, language or religion, must be curbed and eradicated as incompatible with God's design.[166]

---

In 1963, Pope John XXIII passed away and was succeeded by Pope Paul VI (Cardinal Giovanni Battista Montini). In 1965, Pope Paul VI proposed that "his great model," Pius XII, be considered for sainthood.[167] He has been declared "Venerable," and the cause of his beatification is still underway.

# SIXTEEN

# The Play and the KGB Plot

With all of the accolades given to Pope Pius XII during the war, after the war, and even at the time of his death, why do people today question his behavior in World War II? Clearly, the Pope neither sympathized with the Nazis, nor was he indifferent. Just as earlier popes had (and subsequent popes have) avoided designating the aggressor when consoling the victims, Pius did not expressly name Hitler.[1] Nevertheless, his meaning was plain to everyone who read or listened to his words.[2] In Nazi circles throughout the war, it was "axiomatic" that Pius XII "sympathized with the Allies and covertly assisted their cause."[3] In the West, he "enjoyed near-universal acclaim for aiding European Jews through diplomatic initiatives, thinly veiled public pronouncements, and, very concretely, an unprecedented continent-wide network of sanctuary."[4]

While the charge that Pius XII was overly tolerant of the Nazi regime had been leveled earlier, most people trace the issue to a play, *The Deputy* (*Der Stellvertreter*),[5] written by a German playwright named Rolf Hochhuth.[6] Not long after it opened, Pius XII's reputation changed dramatically. This prompted *America* magazine, in 1964, to ask the following questions:

> What has happened since 1958 to erase with one sweep these informed and unsolicited tributes to the memory of Pope Pius XII? Why do they count for nothing when *The Deputy* comes to town? By what dialectic, or through what human fickleness, has a great benefactor of humanity, and of the Jews particularly now become a criminal?[7]

Pope Pius XII's reputation flipped so fully and so fast without *any* new evidence being uncovered — indeed solely on the basis of activity or inactivity that had been fully known for almost two decades.[8] This was not an organic result of honest inquiry. Something else was at play.

*The Deputy* opened in Berlin on February 23, 1963, which coincided closely in time with the Second Vatican Council, the publication of Anne Frank's diary, and the trial and execution of Adolf Eichmann.[9] The play was a scathing indictment of the Pope's alleged indifference to the Holocaust. Although it was fictional, Hochhuth claimed that it was based on "provable facts" and appended a text ("Sidelights on History") in which he argued that his depiction was justified by the historical record.[10] According to one commentator, the German public was "affected by this drama as no trial in Nuremberg or Jerusalem, no study by the Institute for Contemporary History, no matter how extensive, has affected it."[11]

It was long known that *The Deputy* drew upon (or at least parroted) postwar Communist propaganda.[12] Only recently did a former Soviet Bloc official set forth the charge that the KGB sponsored the play in order to discredit Pius XII and through him the Catholic Church.[13] This is a controversial claim, but upon examination the facts fit the charges. Consider:

1. Soviet leaders opposed the Church and took actions against it at other times in history.

    a. The Soviet Union was actively engaged in disinformation campaigns in the late 1950s and early 1960s.
    b. The Soviet Union was also in an active intellectual battle with the West and the Catholic Church at this time, and among its more common weapons were literature and theater.
    c. *The Deputy* certainly draws upon Communist propaganda from the 1940s.

2. The German and American producers of the play, the American publisher, and the French translator were all Communists.

    a. The German producer produced plays under orders from the Communist Party.
    b. The German theater at which *The Deputy* opened was overtly dedicated to pro-Communist propaganda.
    c. The American producer was fined and given a suspended criminal sentence by the House Un-American Activities Committee.
    d. The American publisher considered Communism to be his "religion."
    e. The French translator was a member of the Spanish Communist Party's politburo and had for several years organized clandestine activities for that organization.
    f. The British translator and director both had close professional connections to Communist influences.

3. The play was promoted with Soviet-style propaganda.

    a. Many of the early positive reviewers had Communist ties.
        i. At least one was paid by the KGB.
        ii. Another was a former KGB spy.
        iii. Others were at the time or had previously been members of the Communist Party.
    b. The play would not have opened on Broadway but for support from a "Catholic" magazine that was falling under Communist influence at the time.
        i. The magazine also set forth the Soviet line on the Vietnam War, the Kennedy assassinations, the CIA's funding of student groups, and other issues.

ii. The CIA believed, but could not prove, that Soviet money funded the magazine.

4. Hochhuth seems to have been a likely target for a KGB-style operation.

   a. He was an unknown writer.
   b. His research methods were sloppy at best (resulting in a significant legal verdict against him for his work on a different play).
   c. He has been caught in outright lies.
   d. After *The Deputy* was written, he worked closely with his lifelong friend, a noted Holocaust denier whom Hochhuth has frequently defended.
   e. In 1969, British Intelligence prepared a report noting its suspicion of his efforts to advance ideas designed to undermine the West.

If *The Deputy* was indeed a Soviet plot designed to discredit the Catholic Church, it becomes easier to understand how a play could have helped change Pius XII's reputation so quickly and so thoroughly.

———

*The Deputy* was first staged in Berlin under the direction of Erwin Piscator. Soon translated into many other languages, it received its first English production in London by the Royal Shakespeare Company at the Aldwych Theatre in 1963 under the title *The Representative*.[14] The American version opened on Broadway on February 26, 1964, at the Brooks Atkinson Theater under the English title it is now best known by, *The Deputy*.[15] The play ran for 316 performances. Director Herman Shumlin earned a Tony Award for the production.

The story focuses on two main characters, Kurt Gerstein (based on a real person) and Father Riccardo Fontana. As a prisoner of the Allies after the war, the real Gerstein (a Nazi official) set forth a written statement on which the broad outline of the play was based. It may have been true, but Gerstein was hanged in his cell (perhaps suicide) before his story could be confirmed. As such, he remains an enigmatic figure.[16] Fontana is fictional, though Hochhuth at times said that the character was based upon Father Maximilian Kolbe, Father Bernhard Lichtenberg, and similar self-sacrificing priests.[17]

The basic plot of *The Deputy* involves a good Nazi (Gerstein) who tells a good priest (Fontana) about what the Nazis are doing to the Jews. Fontana, however, is continually thwarted in his efforts to get a message to the Pope. When he finally succeeds, the Pope does not care. Fontana then sacrifices himself by putting on a yellow star and going to a concentration camp, thereby becoming the true deputy of Christ.[18] Recurring themes include the idea that Hitler's war against the Soviet Union was sort of a papal crusade, that Pius and the Jesuits were primarily concerned about their investments in the armaments factories, and papal silence.[19] According to some statements made by the playwright himself, *The Deputy* has no imputation of anti-Semitism, because there was no evidence that Pius was an

HITLER, THE WAR, AND THE POPE

anti-Semite.[20] On the other hand, many viewers have found a clear indication of anti-Semitism in the play.

Obviously, the alleged silence of any character cannot drive a theatrical production, so Pius is not on stage very long. His alleged silence, however, is the subject of much dialogue among the other characters. "Nearly all the other characters discuss among themselves, or at least mention, the Pope's failure to speak out directly and forcefully against Hitler's treatment of the Jews, thus leading up to a direct confrontation consisting of a single pivotal scene, the only one in which the Pope himself appears on stage (Act IV)."[21] In some versions of the production, the Pope's final act is to wash his hands, stained with ink from his editing of a statement that he never makes, in a manner reminiscent of Pontius Pilate.[22]

If it were produced as written, *The Deputy* would take about seven hours to perform.[23] Since that was totally unrealistic, the German producer edited the script into a more manageable length, making very substantial changes along the way.[24] Hochhuth was surprisingly willing to rework his play.[25] When the play was translated into English for the British production, scenes were shuffled and many nuances were lost.[26] When the play came to the United States, a different translation and abridgement were used, and the scenes were shuffled again.[27] (One commentator said it was "like one of those comic-strip versions of a literary classic.")[28] The 2002 motion picture version, *Amen*, provided yet another version.[29]

Although it had some nice runs, *The Deputy* is more noted for its charges against the Pope than for its plot or theatric insight. The play does not develop Pius as a tragic figure, since he is neither tragically indecisive nor torn by his alternatives. Not only does he lack Christian charity, but also simple human decency. *Variety* wrapped it up in its own way: "It's hardly picture material, of course, and doubtful for the road or stock."[30]

———

Immediately after *The Deputy* premiered, Church officials responded, as did Protestant and Jewish leaders. An article by Archbishop Giovanni Battista Montini (who worked closely with Pius XII during the war), written shortly before he became Pope Paul VI and released just after, was published in the London *Tablet* on June 29, 1963. In it, he wrote:

> For my part I conceive it my duty to contribute to the task of clarifying and unifying men's judgment on the historical reality in question — so distorted in the representational pseudo-reality of Hochhuth's play... [which] does not represent the man as he really was: in fact it entirely misrepresents him.

* * *

> Let some men say what they will, Pius XII's reputation as a true Vicar of Christ, as one who tried, so far as he could, fully and courageously to carry out the mission entrusted to him, will not be affected.[31]

Later, the Vatican's weekly publication, *L'Osservatore della Domenica*, devoted a special eighty-page edition to setting the record straight. It began with an introduction that said: "Today a posthumous trial of Pius XII is being conducted. But too many people have forgotten that Pius XII fought with all his might to avoid world conflict... and spare mankind from horrible suffering."[32] The issue contained writings by Pope Paul VI, Pope John XXIII, Cardinal Carlo Confalonieri, Father Robert Leiber, and others. It also included copies of papal protests against Nazi violence and a marked-up draft of the encyclical *Mit brennender Sorge*.

A number of wartime diplomats publicly rejected Hochhuth's characterization of Pope Pius XII, including Wladimir d'Ormesson (a member of the French Academy), Sir Francis D'Arcy Osborne (British minister to the Holy See during the war), Ambassador Grippenberg (from Finland), Ambassador Gunnar Haggelof (from Sweden), and Minister Kanayama (from Japan).[33] In 1963, Albrecht von Kessel, aide to the German ambassador to the Holy See during the war, wrote:

> We were convinced that a fiery protest by Pius XII against the persecution of the Jews would have in all probability put the Pope himself and the Curia into extreme danger, but *would certainly not have saved a single Jew*. Hitler, like a trapped beast, would react to any menace that he felt directed against him, with cruel violence.[34]

Giuseppe Saragat, who was Italian foreign minister at the time, wrote:

> I, myself, am convinced Pius XII was a great Pope and that the campaign against him is orchestrated for partisans. So many years after his death, this is unacceptable not just for Catholics, but for all men of good will.... Innumerable episodes reveal the spirit behind Pius XII's activity, especially here in Rome... where there is living testimony from all citizens on Pius XII's work; moreover, instead of going to a safe place protected by Allied troops... he stayed in his place, in the middle of the storm, giving aid to neighborhoods stricken by the fury of the war, and trying to pry innocent victims away from Nazi barbarism.... In any event, the controversy that has broken out over the memory of Pius XII is not a cultural debate; it is founded on calumnies and lies that have nothing to do with historical and cultural research. In the debates against Pius XII we see the cold, calculating propaganda of those trying to excuse Nazism from horrific crimes by making the Roman Catholic Church co-responsible.[35]

Many writers and commentators have supported this view.[36] "Historically... [*The Deputy*] is open to challenge on many points."[37] "The facts [are] in dispute; the history imperfect; the indictment too severe."[38] Jenö Levai, the leading scholar of the Jewish extermination in Hungary, observed that it was a "particularly regrettable irony that the one person in all of occupied Europe who did more than anyone else to halt the dreadful crime and alleviate its consequences is today made the scapegoat for the failures of others."[39] Other authors, of course, joined in support of Hochhuth.[40]

280 | HITLER, THE WAR, AND THE POPE

In 1964, Pope Paul VI asked a team of three Jesuit historians — Pierre Blet, Burkhart Schneider, and Angelo Martini — to conduct research in closed Vatican archives and publish relevant documents from the war years.[41] A few years later, the three Jesuits were joined by a fourth, Robert A. Graham, S.J. The project was completed in 1981 with the publication of the eleventh and final volume of the *Actes et Documents du Saint Siège relatifs à la seconde guerre mondiale* ("ADSS" or "the Actes").[42]

Publication of these documents seemed to quell the controversy. They clearly showed that the Vatican and the Catholic Church in general were involved in efforts to rescue Jewish and other victims from the Nazis. They also showed that Pope Pius XII was strongly anti-Nazi and that he was concerned about all of the victims. As one early commentator noted, the importance of the ADSS collection

> is fully evident only when one compares it with the facile hypotheses on which some journalist-historians have feverishly constructed certain publications. Fr. Blet and his confreres have allowed the discussion to begin again on sure foundations; they have done their work in such a way that what was only a pastime for journalists may now become the object of serious historical research.[43]

It was called "a model of meticulous editorship."[44] Very little was written about this controversy from 1981 until the release of John Cornwell's book, *Hitler's Pope*, in 1999.

————

In early 2007, Ion Mihai Pacepa, a former Romanian intelligence chief and the highest-ranking official ever to defect from the Soviet Bloc, reported that in 1960 Soviet Premier Nikita Khrushchev approved a plan for destroying the Vatican's moral authority by smearing the reputation of the late Pope Pius XII.[45] Pacepa attributed the idea to KGB chairman Aleksandr Shelepin and Aleksey Kirichenko, the Soviet Politburo member responsible for international policies. "Moscow wanted the Vatican discredited by its own priests, on its home territory, as a bastion of Nazism."[46]

The KGB wanted Vatican documents so that its disinformation experts could work with them and taint the late Pope's reputation. The trick was to get into the Vatican archives. The Soviet Communist Party had been working on churches "from the inside" for several years,[47] and it was "engaged in a systematic program to infiltrate American religious groups."[48] The KGB had been successful in placing spies and disinformation agents in high places in other churches,[49] but Vatican leaders in Rome would be very suspicious of anyone coming from the U.S.S.R. In 1959, however, Soviet intelligence had decided to use the entire Soviet Bloc to further its ends.[50] Accordingly, the Soviet foreign intelligence turned to the Romanian foreign intelligence service (*Departamentul de Informatii Externe*, or "DIE") to help with the plan.

DIE was in a good position to send agents into the Vatican archives due to contacts it had made during earlier projects. This new project was to be code-named "Seat-12," and Pacepa was its "Romanian point man."[51] He was authorized to tell the Vatican that Romania was ready to restore diplomatic relations with the Holy See in exchange for access to its archives and a $1 billion interest-free loan.[52]

In carrying out this mission against Pope Pius XII, Pacepa met with "an 'influential member of the diplomatic corps' who... had begun his career working in the Vatican archives. His name was Agostino Casaroli." Pacepa does not go on to tell us that Pope John Paul II later named Casaroli cardinal secretary of state or that he was indeed known as the Vatican's "secret agent" in Communist Europe. In fact, he was known for dressing in civilian clothes to meet with Communist officials.[53]

Pacepa's foreign intelligence service sent three illegal officers who posed as priests to get access to the Vatican Secret Archives, where they secretly photographed documents and sent the results to the KGB.[54] Nothing they found, however, could be used to fabricate believable evidence that made Pius seem sympathetic to Hitler's regime.[55] The problem was that the Soviets would not control the proceedings as they had been able to do with postwar prosecutions in Hungary, Croatia, and elsewhere. The Vatican's extensive archives would be available to counter and disprove any fabricated evidence. Forged documents would not withstand such scrutiny, and so the original plan could not be successful.[56]

The pilfered documents did, however, give the KGB an idea of what Vatican records looked like.[57] That permitted Soviet experts to use them to develop a reasonable background for a piece of fiction that would charge not bad actions, but failure sufficiently to act and would attribute blame for motivations that would be virtually impossible to disprove.

––––––––––

According to Pacepa, the KGB chief of disinformation took credit for creating an outline for the first draft of *The Deputy*:

> In 1963, General Ivan Agayants, the famous chief of the KGB's disinformation department... told us that "Seat-12" had materialized into a powerful play attacking Pope Pius XII, entitled *The Deputy*.... Agayants took credit for the outline of the play, and he told us that it had voluminous appendices of background documents put together by his experts with help from the documents we had purloined from the Vatican.

Agayants did indeed specialize in writing false histories; he was "Moscow Center's disinformation expert."[58] As Andrew and Gordievsky explain in their book, *KGB: The Inside Story*: "Agaynts owed his appointment as the first head of Department D [the KGB's disinformation department] to his success in sponsoring a series of bogus memoirs and other works."[59]

Hochhuth's papers show that he had the idea for this play in 1958 or 1959, and he had a fairly complete draft by the summer of 1961.[60] Of course, the KGB may have found Hochhuth already working on the play and pushed him in a certain direction.[61] By Hochhuth's own account, Pius XII did not figure into early drafts of the play.[62] His biographer reported: "Hochhuth contributed to the transformation of his play by many directors from a Christian tragedy, as first conceived, into an anti-Catholic polemic."[63]

If the Soviets were capable of doing these things, they were certainly capable of helping write, edit, and stage *The Deputy*. This took place in the time frame when Khrushchev was actively opposing organized churches and using religion to spread Marxism.[64] It was at the height of the Cold War, and the height of Catholic/Communist tensions.[65] Pius had been an avowed opponent of Communism.[66] This type of operation fit well with what the KGB was doing in other nations at that time.[67] In fact, historians at the Vatican have "no doubt" that the KGB helped edit the play and get it produced.[68]

---

A play is just a play, but Hochhuth, or others associated with the play, wanted this to be something more. The printed version of the play contained an appendix entitled "Sidelights on History."[69] It was of enormous importance to the play's historical impact:

> With the postscript, "Sidelights on History," Hochhuth renounced his play's artistic autonomy. He deliberately renounced the enduring alibi Lessing's essays on drama gave to writers of historical plays; his material was not intended to be merely a useful story, exempt from reality and historical truth so as . . . to better serve human potentialities and philosophic truth. On the contrary, his material was explicitly meant to present the historical truth in the artistically useful dramatic form.[70]

According to Hochhuth, the "main thesis" of *The Deputy* was "that Hitler drew back from the extermination program as soon as high German clerics . . . or the Vatican . . . forcibly intervened."[71] Hochhuth defended the historical accuracy of his play, but he also argued that it had a moral truth of its own, separated from historical truth.[72]

"Perhaps never before in history have so many human beings paid with their lives for the passivity of a single statesman,"[73] Hochhuth wrote. *America* magazine responded: "Perhaps never before in history have so many vicious, tendentious and mean imputation of motives been based on such flimsy, distorted and falsified historical arguments."[74] People wondered where he got his information:

> Where did Hochhuth get his facts? He was able to use the evidence presented at the Nuremberg trials and at the Eichmann trial, and to consult U.S. and German historical records and contemporary documents. These provided him

with material for his descriptions of the persecution of the Jews and for his concentration camp scenes. But for his main charges — the contemptible motives he attributes to Pope Pius XII for his silence — he quotes no documentary evidence at all.[75]

Hochhuth said that he spent three months in Rome "studying the atmosphere, talking to Swiss Guards, Romans and Jews who had been hidden in Italian monasteries."[76] He claimed to have posed a series of questions to "an elderly and experienced German-speaking bishop,"[77] but he refused to name the bishop. Instead, he brought suspicion on numerous Vatican officials by purporting to quote "high clerics" and "anonymous eyewitnesses."[78] Hochhuth said that the bishop avoided him for weeks, but ultimately confirmed his suspicions about Pius XII.[79]

The claimed sources of high clerics and an unidentified, elderly bishop are very suspicious. Some people believe that Hochhuth consulted Austrian Bishop Alois Hudal or Monsignor Bruno Wüstenberg (both of whom spoke German),[80] but even this remains uncertain.[81] As one early commentator noted:

Hochhuth went to Rome to collect documentary evidence that the Vatican had betrayed and sold the Jews. Naturally he was not given access to Vatican archives, for, like all state papers, they are not made public until some decades later. Moreover, it takes many years of intensive study for a complete outsider even to fumble his way around in Catholic theology, organization, history, and administration. As Shakespeare said: "Fools rush in where angels fear to tread." How true this is of the Church! Hochhuth was able to dig up some aged informant who could not stand Pius XII. What precisely this old gentleman actually did tell Hochhuth will probably never be known.[82]

A more recent commentator on Vatican policy and intrigue has written:

Many points of view coexist within the Vatican walls, and there are more than a few curialists who like to talk to reporters. Very few if any of these chatty people count, in terms of expressing the settled judgment of the senior leadership of the Catholic Church. That leadership, when it wishes to make a serious point, does so through its major figures, not through the bureaucratic munchkins....[83]

How the Protestant Hochhuth, an unknown aspiring playwright without even a high school diploma, would have managed to get a bishop, even one angry with Pius,[84] to assist with this work is difficult to understand unless Hochhuth had influential assistance.[85] Of course, as will be seen, Hochhuth has a history of citing mysterious sources to support his claims. At least some of those sources seem to have been fabricated, and other charges that he made have been established as fraudulent.

Some of the mistakes that appear in *The Deputy* are not the kind that high clerics or a bishop would have made. Soviet disinformation experts, however, might make such mistakes. Erik von Kuehnelt-Leddihn indentified the following mistakes (and others) in his 1969 book, *The Timeless Christian*:

1. Fr. Fontana is referred to as "Count Riccardo Fontana, a twenty-seven-year-old Jesuit, who works as a young attaché in the Berlin nunciature." First of all, the time needed to prepare for a Jesuit priesthood prevents anyone from becoming a Jesuit at that young age. Additionally, at that time there were no Jesuits in the diplomatic service. Perhaps most obviously, no Jesuit retains his secular titles; they have to give them up.

2. The play mentions a concordat between the Vatican and Japan. No such agreement was ever signed.

3. The play also has Spanish court dress being worn in the Vatican — "the somber beautiful court dress of Henry II." It is simply not true.

4. According to the play, Hitler forbade all measures against the Church. Lots of victims wish those instructions had been obeyed!

5. Pius XII was always alone at the table because he could not abide the sight of a human face. In actuality, Pius followed the custom of taking most meals alone, but he sometimes dined with guests, and he was known as a witty conversationalist.[86]

6. An officer of the Swiss Guard was depicted in full uniform in the center of Rome to summon a cardinal who was visiting Count Fontana. Swiss Guards, however, were not permitted to wear the uniform outside the Vatican.

7. The Society of Jesus is referred to as the "Order of Jesus," and supposedly the "Order of Jesus" supplied the Soviet Union with mercury from Spanish mines.

8. Contrary to the play, there was no papal legate in Washington at that time, only an apostolic delegate.

9. In the scene where Pius tries to forbid Fr. Fontana from pinning the Star of David on his cassock, the Pope says: "We forbid him to do it — forbid it *ex cathedra*!" This is absurd. *Ex cathedra* pronouncements can be made only in respect of dogmatic formulations.[87]

Perhaps the strongest indication of a Soviet hand, however, shows up when the German playwright Hochhuth, for no apparent reason, blames the Katyn Forest Massacre (where thousands of Polish military officers, policemen, intellectuals, and civilian POWs were executed and buried in a mass grave) on the Germans. For a long time, Germany and the Soviet Union blamed each other for this slaughter. Today it is well known that fault lies with the Soviets, but when *The Deputy* was published, this was still an active debate.[88] Disinformation experts would not have missed a chance to score a point for their side.

The "Sidelights on History" has been called the result of "misrepresentation, distortion and prejudice."[89] It has also been described as follows:

Forty-five pages of demonstration and proof! But the quantity is deceptive. The materials are all mixed up higgledy-piggledy; seldom are we told precisely where the arguments and quotations come from. "Solid collections of sources are mentioned only in isolated instances; but evidence and witnesses of dubious value are mentioned frequently.... The work is based on second- and third-hand evidence, on popular books which do not even claim to provide a final clarification...."[90]

If he did write it, as others have said, it reveals "Hochhuth's deep distrust of history."[91]

Even before Pacepa made his claims, people had recognized that Hochhuth's argument was very close to postwar Communist propaganda. Back in 1948, propagandists at the Historical Institute of the Soviet Academy of Sciences in Moscow had hired M. M. Sheinmann to fabricate a report alleging a Vatican-Nazi conspiracy.[92] Sheinmann's report contained details about an alleged "Secret Pact" the Vatican had signed with Hitler.[93] Translated into German as *Der Vatikan im zweiten Weltkrieg* in 1954, this phony report did not attract much attention from a generation that had seen Pius in action.

After *The Deputy* debuted, Monsignor Erich Klausener, Jr., whose father had been the head of Berlin's Catholic Action but was murdered during the Night of the Long Knives, pointed out that Hochhuth's play bore a striking resemblance to Sheinmann's fake report.[94] Similarly, Desmond Fisher, in his book *Pope Pius XII and the Jews: An Answer to Hochhuth's Play "Der Stellvertreter"* wrote: "As has been noted in the London *Tablet* (May 11, 1963), German critics have pointed out how closely Hochhuth follows a Communist publication, *The Vatican and the Second World War*, which appeared in 1955, and which attempted to blacken the Holy See as the instrument of a calculating capitalism."[95] More recently, German scholar Michael Feldkamp noted: "In the summer of 1963 the Vatican pointed out 'numerous similarities' between Hochhuth's play and 'the usual communist propaganda against the Church and the Pope,' among them the charge of a 'common crusade with Hitler against the Soviet Union,' and the claim that the 'enormous economic power' of the Holy See and the Jesuit order explained their abandonment of Christian moral principles."[96] The West German government even expressed its "deepest regret" for such attacks on Pius XII, since he had protested racial persecution by the Third Reich and had "saved as many Jews as possible from the hands of their persecutors."[97]

---

When Pacepa first reported that *The Deputy* was a Soviet-inspired counterintelligence operation, Hochhuth's strongest support came from the British researcher David Irving, who posted the following on his web page:

WHAT an extraordinary story about Hochhuth, and what utter rubbish; he was my best friend in those years and still is a good friend; I have two chapters about him in my memoirs. There was never a hint of Soviet influence — which is not to say he may not have been fed a corrupt dossier in some clever way. He could be very naive.[98]

Similarly, Pacepa charged that "[f]orgeries based on the stolen documents" were part of the play's "historical appendix."[99] Clearly, this is a matter that calls for more investigation. There are, however, some things that we do know.

First of all, we know that Irving is lying. *The Deputy* was written between 1959 and 1961, and it was first produced in 1963. As Irving reports elsewhere on his web page, Hochhuth first approached him after having written *The Deputy*, and they did not meet in person until 1965.[100] Accordingly, they were not "best friends" at the time in question. Irving could not have known about Soviet influence at the time *The Deputy* was being written. Hochhuth and Irving did, however, become great friends. In the mid- to late 1960s, Irving worked as Hochhuth's chief researcher.[101] As Irving went on to become known as the world's foremost Holocaust denier (at least prior to Iranian President Mahmoud Ahmadinejad),[102] his old friend Rolf Hochhuth always stood by him.[103]

We also know that the British government suspected Irving of receiving financial support from the Communists. As he reports on his web page: "The recently relesaed [sic] files in the Public Record office in London show that the Government suspected at that time I too was receiving Soviet financial support, otherwise how could I be living in my fine apartment in Mayfair just on the income of a struggling author."[104] According to a 1992 report prepared by the London Board of Deputies of British Jews (a nongovernmental British agency) and intended for Canadian government files: "Uncorroborated evidence implies that Irving has been the recipient of substantial funding from unknown sources."[105] Irving denies receiving support from the Soviets or from Germans, but his only real accounting for the money is a complaint that the government took it away in 2002.

Irving wrote a controversial biography of Adolf Hitler in 1977, and he famously argued that Hitler knew nothing about the systematic slaughter of six million Jews. In 1992, a judge in Germany fined him the equivalent of $6,000 for publicly insisting the Nazi gas chambers at Auschwitz were a hoax.[106] He has also been quoted as saying there was "not one shred of evidence" that the Nazis carried out their "final solution" on such a scale.[107] "I don't see any reason to be tasteful about Auschwitz," Irving declared in 1991 before a group of neo-Nazis. "It's baloney. It's a legend... more women died on the back seat of Edward Kennedy's car at Chappaquiddick than ever died in a gas chamber in Auschwitz."[108]

Irving raised his profile as a Holocaust denier in 2000, when he sued Deborah Lipstadt of Emory University and Penguin Books over Lipstadt's book *Denying the Holocaust*.[109] Irving charged that the book was part of a "concerted attempt to ruin his reputation as an historian."[110] The defense argued that "it is true that Irving is discredited as an historian by reason of his denial of the Holocaust and by reason of his persistent distortion of the historical record so as to depict Hitler in a favourable light."[111] The British judge sided with Lipstadt and Penguin:

> Having reviewed what appear to me to be the relevant considerations, I return
> to the issue which I defined... above. I find myself unable to accept Irving's

contention that his falsification of the historical record is the product of innocent error or misinterpretation or incompetence on his part. When account is
taken of all the considerations... it appears to me that the correct and inevitable
inference must be that for the most part the falsification of the historical record
was deliberate and that Irving was motivated by a desire to present events in a
manner consistent with his own ideological beliefs even if that involved distortion and manipulation of historical evidence.[112]

The *New York Times* proclaimed: "The verdict puts an end to the pretense that
Mr. Irving is anything but a self-promoting apologist for Hitler."[113]

Irving was again in the news and in court when he was arrested for Holocaust denial in Austria in 2005.[114] Irving eventually plead guilty, saying: "I made
a mistake when I said there were no gas chambers at Auschwitz."[115] The court
sentenced him to three years imprisonment, but he was released after serving
only a short time.[116]

According to the BBC, at the time of his arrest Irving was in Austria to "give
a lecture to a far-right student fraternity."[117] Perhaps more interesting is that he
was also returning from a visit to his longtime friend, Rolf Hochhuth.[118] (In fact,
from prison Irving wrote a note to Hochhuth, suggesting that the arrest and trial
would make a good two-act play.)[119] Hochhuth defended Irving throughout his
Austrian ordeal, calling the allegation that he was a Holocaust denier "simply
idiotic" and calling Irving "a fantastic pioneer of current historiography who has
written terrific books."[120]

When asked about Irving's statement that "more women died on the back
seat of Edward Kennedy's car at Chappaquiddick than ever died in a gas chamber in Auschwitz," Hochhuth said it was just black humor.[121] This caused newspapers in Germany to label Hochhuth an anti-Semite. Paul Spiegel, president
of the Central Jewish Council in Germany, argued that with these statements
Hochhuth himself was denying the Holocaust. The German publishing house
*Deutsche Verlags-Anstalt* canceled publication of Hochhuth's autobiography.[122] Of
course, Hochhuth had defended Irving several times in the past. When Hochhuth praised Irving in his 1996 memoirs, critics asked how anyone could write
words of praise for such a radical. His answer was: "Because I am Hochhuth."[123]
Following the 2005 event, however, Hochhuth eventually issued an apology.[124]

---

When Pacepa's story broke, Hochhuth "denied any KGB influence and
insisted that the play was all his own work."[125] Several people who have studied
the Pius XII controversy (including this author) expressed surprise and some
doubt when the story first appeared.[126] On the other hand, former CIA director
James Woolsey has vouched for Pacepa's personal credibility, and Pacepa's memoir *Red Horizons* formed the basis for the indictment and conviction of Romanian dictator Nicolae Ceausescu, who was executed in 1989.[127] Hochhuth may

not have been a knowing player in any Soviet plot. The facts suggest, however, that he was a good candidate for the Soviets to target as an unknowing dupe.[128]

On the surface, Hochhuth seemed very impressive. The press called him a playwright of conscience ("such a nice young man — and such an idealist!"[129] and "a man of discriminating moral intelligence").[130] At the same time, as his friend David Irving said, he could be "very naive." Irving would know. He worked "hand in hand" as Hochhuth's researcher/historian on his first play after *The Deputy*.[131] That play, entitled *Soldiers*, criticized Great Britain for bombing German cities, and it alleged that British Prime Minister Winston Churchill ordered the assassination of the Polish prime minister-in-exile, General Wladyslaw Sikorski.[132] (Hochhuth would go on to write other plays also critical of actual people for their actions during the war.)[133]

Like *The Deputy*, *Soldiers* was loosely based on an historical event. During World War II, General Sikorski became prime minister of the Polish government-in-exile, commander-in-chief of the Polish armed forces, and a staunch advocate of the Polish cause on the diplomatic scene. He was killed on July 4, 1943, when his plane crashed into the sea immediately on takeoff from Gibraltar. According to Hochhuth, it was murder, and it was perpetrated on the orders of Winston Churchill.

Hochhuth's story is that agents entered the plane in which Sikorski was riding and killed him and others (including Sikorski's daughter, two members of Parliament, and a dozen innocent people) prior to takeoff. The alleged reason for this supposed murder was that Sikorski was creating a problem for the Anglo-American-Soviet alliance.[134] The assassins then abandoned the plane. The pilot intentionally crashed (after taking special precautions for his personal safety), making it look like Sikorski was killed by the impact. Hochhuth's charge was that only the pilot survived the crash, but that he was later killed by British agents to keep him quiet.[135] *Time* magazine called it "a tenuous personal speculation indicative only of a common European fascination with conspiratorial-plot theories of history."[136] A leading Polish literary critic called the allegations "insane."[137]

At a press conference that took place at the Berlin premiere of *Soldiers*, Hochhuth was asked to expand on the "sources of his secret knowledge" about Sikorski's assassination. Hochhuth repeated what he had written for that day's edition of *Der Spiegel*. He claimed that he had "accidentally" received the information.[138] Later investigation, however, would prove that there was *no* substance behind Hochhuth's claims.[139] In fact, according to a profile published in 1970, Irving "spotted a possible clue, checked it at source, found it untrue and discarded it — all the behaviour of a good historian." He went on, however, to give the clue to Hochhuth, who lacked discretion when it came to evidence supporting his conclusions. Thus, the rejected evidence was used to support Hochhuth's fiction.[140]

Hochhuth would shift his premise based upon nothing more than (and often less than) a rumor.[141] He originally claimed that Churchill had General Sikorski killed due to his strong stance against the Soviets. When an article in the Moscow *New Times* (an "undercover magazine of the KGB published in English for Western consumption")[142] made a different argument, he immediately adopted it and suggested that Churchill had Sikorski killed due to his pro-Soviet policies.[143] He did another flip-flop when discussing the British government's desire to implicate or incriminate a certain participant in the plane crash.[144] Hochhuth gave inconsistent answers not only about his theories and the source of his information, but even about why he lived in Switzerland instead of Germany.[145]

Hochhuth was also very quick to rewrite sections of his play and even to eliminate characters.[146] As Lawrence Olivier's wife, Joan Plowright, noted: "There is one thing we all agree on, I'm sure. We have never seen an author so little married to his words."[147] Witnesses complained that "Hochhuth tried to put words in my mouth."[148] He claimed to have a wealth of information (some of which was provided by David Irving, who according to a favorable 1970 profile was open "about his deviousness"),[149] but he was evasive when asked about his sources. Sometimes it was a retired British Intelligence man; other times it was a Polish lady.[150] He claimed to have deposited his proof in a bank vault to be opened fifty years later.[151] Said Hochhuth: *"I know that in fifty years my play will be unassailable."*[152]

Hochhuth's research was sloppy at best, and his analysis was even worse. *Soldiers* was initially banned in England. That generated great debate about the freedom of artists in Britain. It also led actor Carlos Thompson, who was at first interested in helping bring the play to the stage and perhaps film, to write a book exposing the shoddy research and ridiculous theories that Hochhuth set forth.[153] Thompson shows Hochhuth as semi-paranoid[154] and "all-too-eager to believe anything he is told."[155] Thompson, who entitled one chapter "A sad example of Hochhuth's methods," wrote of the "tangled gyrations of Hochhuth's thinking"[156] and said that the playwright's mind worked along "dangerously greased rails."[157]

Julius Firt, one of many witnesses interviewed by Carlos Thompson, said: "I find it difficult to understand what Hochhuth is really after. His play on the Pope was tendentious enough, but this one, marshalling non-existent evidence to prove that Britain killed Sikorski, is one big step further."[158] Polish Prince Lubomirski, another witness, said: "Hochhuth had nothing, and construes everything to his advantage."[159] Yugoslavian dissident Milovan Đilas (whom Hochhuth tried to invoke when questions arose about his research) said: "Hochhuth's quotation of me is a complete distortion."[160] Stanislaw Lesniowski said: "[T]he *Sunday Times* quoted Mr. Hochhuth and through him, quoted me. What I had said to him was totally misrepresented."[161] Lesniowski went on to say that "after reading his play, I find that it is the exact opposite of what he told me."[162]

One witness said: "I have begun to ask myself if Hochhuth does not suffer from delusions. He remembers visiting me in my home, which he never did, and conversations between us that never took place."[163] Thompson wrote: "It was becoming difficult to follow Rolf's gyrations of theory-within-theory."[164] Another time he wrote: "Rolf was beginning to tire. He was forgetting his own invention."[165] When one witness came forth to contradict his theory, Hochhuth attributed it to British disinformation.[166] Another time Hochhuth suggested that witnesses were faking amnesia.[167] Yet another said that Hochhuth simply refused to consider the theory that the Soviets were behind the general's death.[168] Responding to allegations from Sikorski's countrymen that undercut his thesis, Hochhuth said that "all the Poles in London lie."[169]

Hochhuth and Irving claimed that after five years of painstaking research they had "conclusive evidence" of the death of the pilot, Edward Prchal, at the hands of the "Old Firm" in a staged knife fight in Chicago. Their theory was that Prchal was in on the assassination, but that the Old Firm killed him to be certain that he did not reveal the plot.[170] Before long, word surfaced that Prchal was still living in the United States. Hochhuth, however, declined to interview him.[171] Hochhuth claimed that the man in the United States was an imposter, but he and Irving were exposed on British television.

In December 1968, television host David Frost invited Hochhuth as his guest to discuss the play *Soldiers*, which had just opened in London. Hochhuth declined, citing his inability to speak English (despite Frost's offer of a translator).[172] David Irving and theater critic Kenneth Tynan, however, were there as part of what Frost called "the Hochhuth contingent."[173] Central to their case, of course, was that the pilot of the crashed plane, Edward Prchal, had been in on the assassination. When Prchal came on stage, he said: "Mr. Hochhuth is producing a slander of the century."[174] According to Frost, "The credibility of the Hochhuth-Tynan-Irving case went from bad to worse."[175]

After the first show (which was broadcast live), Frost asked the guests to return for the taping of a second show. This gave him and his producers time to investigate some of the Hochhuth contingent's claims and to expose them as lies.[176] When Tynan tried to argue that the play actually enhanced Churchill's reputation, it was noted that he had previously suggested that it was libelous. Asked to explain this contradiction, he said: "It would have libeled him, had he been alive. Since he's dead, it's not a libel."[177]

It went so poorly for the Hochhuth contingent that they tried to stop the second show from being broadcast by demanding unreasonable fees from Frost and his production company. As the TV interviewer later wrote: "It was instructive to see the way in which, when they felt that they had been bested, they moved to suppress the very freedom of expression they proclaimed to be their cause."[178] As one commentator noted: "David Frost, the well-known television interviewer, has stated that possibly his best performance ever was the night he fairly thoroughly dismantled Hochhuth before the cameras, above all for waiting until Churchill's death to make such a foul slander; he also waited until Pius XII was dead...."[179]

Prchal filed suit against Hochhuth for defamation.[180] In fact, according to declassified British files, Prchal's lawyer suggested a criminal prosecution.[181] Prchal won a £50,000 judgment from the playwright.[182] Hochhuth's biographer reported: "Hochhuth's... accusation resulted in a libel action brought by the surviving pilot of the crashed aircraft which involved the author [Hochhuth] and the producers of the play in London in a costly financial settlement."[183] As the relator in Pius XII's sainthood cause has stated: "Hochhuth was publicly disgraced in Britain and elsewhere when, with exactly the same anti-historical methods which he used against Pius XII... he accused Winston Churchill of having ordered the murder of the Polish General Sikorski...."[184]

Of course, there is no apparent reason to suppose that Hochhuth behaved differently when researching and writing *Soldiers* than he had when working on *The Deputy*.[185]

---

When he was working on *The Deputy*, Hochhuth was an unknown publishing house employee. The man who would eventually bring *The Deputy* to the stage, Erwin Piscator, was a very influential producer.[186] He was a founder of the school of drama known as "Political Theatre," whose method was to put living or recently deceased political persons on stage for either pillorying or praising.[187] Piscator was also a devoted Communist who was "heavily influenced by Soviet agitation-propaganda, [and] produced plays which celebrated the imminent demise of capitalist society and of course, capitalism's supposed clerical offshoot, the Catholic Church."[188] It is no surprise that General Ivan Agayants — at that time the head of the PGU (the Soviet foreign intelligence service) *Dezinformatsiya* Department — said that "the producer of *The Deputy* was a KGB influence agent."[189]

In 1925, the German Communist Party (KPD) — which was at that time the largest Communist Party outside of the Soviet Union — asked Piscator to produce a political review.[190] He put together a team including himself, a composer nominated by the party, and a writer/lyricist/producer. They came up with "about a dozen sketches, introduced by a pot-pourri of communist songs" that culminated in a "Victory of the Proletariat" scene.[191] It was enough of a success that the KPD soon demanded that he stage a show for their first party conference. Piscator used the same team and produced a show with an "overwhelmingly documentary approach... virtually every character being historical (and in many cases still alive)."[192]

The KPD was not completely happy with the production. Officials thought it was too factual, which, of course, lessened the propaganda value of the production. "That may be what's wrong, comrade director.... Don't stick so slavishly to 'that's the way it happened,'" an official wrote.[193] Piscator took advice well and learned to fictionalize history. He soon found himself working with the leading Communist playwrights in Germany.[194] He also trained young actors, though it was said that they mainly received "courses by KPD officials; 'one's party card became a certificate of competence.'"[195] In at least one case, Piscator's company declined to produce a play because the author declined membership in the Communist Party.[196] In another case, Piscator invited "representatives of the Soviet embassy and trade delegation and of the KPD and its paper" to one of the final rehearsals of a play, only to be told that he had to rewrite it. He complied, though it meant that opening night had to be delayed by two days.[197]

In the late 1920s, Piscator worked in collaboration with the great German (and Communist) playwright Bertolt Brecht at the Theater am Nollendorfplatz. Together, they created "electrically charged productions of, among others, *Hoppla, Wir Leben* and *Die Abenteuer Des Braven Soldaten Schwejk*."[198] This success, however, raised some questions in high Communist circles about the direction of his work. (His relationship with Nazi Germany's Propaganda Minister Joseph Goebbels, who once submitted a play to Piscator and with whom Piscator considered doing a radio broadcast, may also have puzzled the party hierarchy.)[199] Ultimately, however, his "record as a supporter of the October Revolution and the Soviet Regime was a good one; from the days of the Proletarian Theatre onwards, he had been caught up in the wave of pro-Soviet feeling."[200] His biographer wrote: "The overriding fact remained that he was a communist and subject to party orders."[201]

Piscator defended his ideas in his 1929 book *Das Politische Theater* ("The Political Theatre"). He wrote that "any artistic intention must be subordinated to the revolutionary purpose of the whole: the conscious emphasis and propagation of the concept of the class struggle." Continuing:

> We, as revolutionary Marxists, cannot consider our task complete if we produce an uncritical copy of reality, conceiving the theatre as a mirror of the times.... The business of revolutionary theatre is to take reality as its point of departure and to magnify the social discrepancy, making it an element of our indictment, our revolt, our new order.[202]

Despite the minor difficulties that came up between Piscator and Communist Party officials, he had made a significant mark on the theater. Along with other dramatists, he "stirred up a revolutionary whirlwind in the theater. This stir followed directly in the wake of a successful Communist revolution in Russia."[203]

In 1929, Piscator made his first visit to the Soviet Union, where he worked briefly with the International Association of Workers' Theatres (IATB). As reported in his biography, "Communist artists came increasingly to take their cultural directives from Moscow.... [I]t became natural for German artists not merely to visit Russia but to take jobs there."[204] Accordingly, in 1931, Piscator moved to the U.S.S.R., where his initial desire was to make short propaganda films. Lobbying to get started, he managed to obtain a two-hour meeting with Joseph Stalin's brother-in-law.[205] Piscator was soon elected president of IATB, which then changed its name to the International Association of Revolutionary Theatres.[206]

According to Pacepa, Westerners who were granted political asylum in the Soviet Union "had cooperated, in one way or another, with the KGB, and Piscator sought political asylum in Moscow in the 1930s."[207] In the postscript to a 1934 Soviet edition of one play, Piscator wrote that his theater "was always political, that is to say political in the sense approved by the Communist Party."[208]

In 1936, worried about the Soviet purges, Piscator moved to France, where he married the dancer Maria Ley. In 1939, he came to the United States where he opened the Dramatic Workshop at The New School in New York. This workshop launched the careers of many notable students, including Tennessee Williams,[209] Marlon Brando, Walter Matthau, Rod Steiger, Shelley Winters, Harry Belafonte, Elaine Stritch, Ben Gazzara, and Tony Curtis. Of Piscator, in 1940, *Time* magazine wrote: "He produced great plays frankly as propaganda, stressed all possible class-war angles, emphasized mass effects rather than individual actors. Determined to get his audiences 'into' the plays, he abolished the curtain, had actors play in the aisles, loudspeakers sound from all parts of the house. His theatre became a versatile expressive 'machine,' blending plays, films, radio."[210]

Around 1951 (perhaps due to the Cold War and his Communist ties), Piscator moved to West Germany, where "he was treated as 'The Grand Old Man' who had outlived himself."[211] He spent nine years floating from one theater to another, but around 1960, he got back in touch with Bernhard Reich, a playwright and theater director. Piscator had worked with Reich in the Soviet Union in the 1930s. (In fact, it was Reich who warned Piscator in 1937 not to return to the Soviet Union from France, prompting Piscator's eventual move to the United States.) Reich had been unable to escape from the U.S.S.R. in the 1930s. He was arrested and deported. He returned to Germany in the mid-1950s as a "rehabilitated" Soviet critic."[212] He may have had a role in having Piscator appointed manager and director of the Freie Volksbühne (Free People's Theater) in West Berlin in 1962. The Freie Volksbühne was openly political, along the lines of theaters Piscator had worked with in the 1920s.

---

The idea of a Berlin theater "of the people," which underlies the Freie Volksbühne, can be traced back to an organization of the same name that was founded in 1892. The goal of the organization was to promote the social-realist plays of the day at prices accessible to the common worker. The slogan was *"Die Kunst dem Volke"* ("The Art to the People"). The first theater building was constructed in 1913-14, but World War II reduced it to rubble. It was rebuilt and placed under Piscator's control in the early 1960s. His biographer wrote: "It is striking how far [Piscator] returned to his old interests."[213]

If German theater had been political in the 1920s and 1930s, by the early 1960s it was outright propaganda. Berlin, of course, was divided after World War II. East Berlin was a Communist city, part of East Germany, and affiliated with the Soviet Union. West Berlin was part of West Germany, and it was more closely associated with the United States. The two parts of the city used different currencies, but prior to the construction of a wall separating East and West

Berlin, people passed rather freely from one side to another.[214] At that time, theaters on both sides of the city produced agenda-driven plays, but in East Berlin the agenda was overt: "In setting about to create a socialist society and a socialist theater, the East Germans explicitly rejected... 'bourgeois' assumptions. Their task — to re-educate the East German population to accept this new way of life — was truly overwhelming."[215]

Construction of the Berlin Wall began in August 1961. Once it was completed, people from one side of the city were no longer able to cross over to see productions on the other side. East Berlin theaters would still run productions setting forth the Communist line, but those plays would not be seen by patrons from West Berlin. The Freie Volksbühne was designed to fill that gap. It would present Communist propaganda to viewers in West Berlin. Piscator would run it, and *The Deputy* would be among the first plays produced there.

How an unknown writer like Hochhuth got a famous producer like Piscator even to look at his play is a question in and of itself. According to one of Hochhuth's biographers, in February 1962 (within weeks of Piscator's new appointment), "an unknown thirty-year old author called on Piscator to discuss a play which their common publisher thought might be of interest. This was Rolf Hochhuth and the play *Der Stellvertreter* or *The Representative*."[216] That would be a fairly straightforward story. Piscator, however, gives a more interesting version of how they first met:

A telephone call reached me from Mr. Ledig-Rowohlt: he had received a play from his friend, Karl Ludwig Leonhardt, acting as intermediary, the first work of a young German author, which was really more than "just" a play.... The play was sent to me, not in manuscript as usual, but in galley proofs, set not by Rowohlt publishers [the German publisher of the play] but by a publisher who had to acknowledge, after typesetting, that he lacked the courage for publication."[217]

Hochhuth was "quite convinced that if Piscator had not staged the play at the Freie Volksbühne in Berlin, he would never have had any of his works performed in the German theatre."[218]

Hochhuth said, "*The Deputy* is politics,"[219] and in that play, Piscator found his perfect vehicle for *political theatre*, a school of drama which credits Piscator for its very name. "Thanks to this play," Piscator said of *The Deputy*, "there is some point in working in the theatre."[220] It was the kind of "epic, 'political' theatre such as I have been fighting for for thirty years and more,"[221] Piscator explained, adding: "I don't think I am devaluing those authors who worked with me in the 1920s if I say that the type of play I ideally had in mind at that time is only now being written by people like Hochhuth...."[222]

Of course, if this truly had been an artistic endeavor, and not a political operation, it should have bothered Piscator that — as Hochhuth said — *The Deputy* violated the tenets of the school.[223] The presentation of Pope Pius XII focused on his personality rather than on history. The play tried to make the case that Pius, if not necessarily pro-Nazi during the war, at least feared Communism more than he feared Hitler.[224] There was, of course, no documentary evidence to back up such claims.[225] The play even used an allegorical figure, a nameless doctor (likened by some to the notorious S.S. physician Josef Mengele) who played an important role in the dramatic action.[226] As such, Piscator and Hochhuth were not true to their theatrical format. Instead, they used the play to further a political end.[227]

Before the play could even be staged, Piscator had to significantly rewrite it. At seven to eight hours, the written play simply could not be produced.[228] Piscator ultimately staged the play in a more traditional two- or three-hour format. Although it ran in Berlin for only a few weeks, had mixed reviews at best,[229] and was criticized by virtually every person who had firsthand knowledge of the Pope's wartime activities, the Soviet propaganda machine was able to attract enough attention that the play eventually became an international sensation.[230] Piscator had served his purpose.[231]

———

Despite its short and commercially unsuccessful debut in Berlin, this play by an unknown writer was quickly translated and produced by some of the biggest names in theater.[232] The first French production of *The Deputy* ["*Le Vicaire*"] took place at the Théâtre de L'Athénée in Paris. The translator was Jorge Semprum, an award-winning novelist and playwright. He was also an active Communist Party leader.[233] Semprum had been a Communist militant since his youth, and he joined a Communist resistance group in France during World War II. After the war, while still in France, he joined the exiled Communist Party of Spain (PCE). For nearly a decade in the 1950s and early 1960s, he organized clandestine activities for the PCE.[234] In fact, at the time when he translated Hochhuth's play, he was still an active member of the party's politburo. Only after being expelled from the politburo in 1965 (over strategy differences), did Semprum truly focus on his legitimate writing career.[235]

The French production was co-directed by Francis Darbon and noted British director Peter Brook. Like Piscator, Brook was a theatrical legend. His production of Hochhuth's play ran for about six months in Paris, and it went a long way toward establishing the so-called "Theatre of Fact" in France.[236] Brook, however, did not like the "Theatre of Fact" label. "You can never get to the facts," he said. "I'd rather call it the theatre of myth."[237]

In addition to working in France, Brook was one of the three permanent directors of the new, but highly regarded Royal Shakespeare Company (RSC) at the Aldwych Theatre in London. This company was established by Peter Hall (later, Sir Peter Reginald Franklin Hall), another one of the most influential figures in postwar British theater.[238] He and Brook served as permanent directors along with French director Michel St. Denis.[239] Like many young directors at the time, Hall was deeply influenced by popular theatrical trends, and the

RSC soon came "to be regarded as an avant-garde stronghold."[240] This theater is where Hochhuth's play received its first English production, under the title *The Representative*.

Robert David MacDonald translated the play for the RSC.[241] He had worked as a translator for the United Nations Educational, Scientific and Cultural Organization (UNESCO) in the 1950s. At that time, not only was UNESCO perceived by many as a platform for Communists to attack the West,[242] the KGB used it to place agents around the world.[243] (UNESCO also assisted with the publication of the journal *World Theatre*, which praised Erwin Piscator's courage for bringing *The Deputy* to the stage.)[244] While working at UNESCO, MacDonald met Piscator. Although he had no prior experience, MacDonald "immediately became involved in theatre as a director."[245] He worked with Piscator in Berlin, and the two men formed a close professional relationship. This led to MacDonald translating (and reworking) *The Deputy* into English.[246]

The director who handled *The Deputy* at the Aldwych was Clifford Williams,[247] who added a new scene at the beginning of the play and ended with a film of the Auschwitz victims being buried by bulldozer.[248] Newspaper clippings and other documents were also read over loudspeakers at different points in the play.[249] Of Williams it was written: "Hochhuth's play undoubtedly spurred Williams's interest — at a time of shifting social and theatrical perspectives in theatre that might provoke arguments or disturb complacency."[250] Of course, Williams had come to the RSC from the "left-wing and indeed almost Communist" Theatre Workshop,[251] where he had trained under the noted Communist director Joan Littlewood.[252]

In the United States, *The Deputy* was published in book form by Grove Press in New York. Barney Rosset, a self-proclaimed Communist, purchased the company in 1951, and he turned it into an influential alternative press. Among the radical political thinkers and writings he published in the 1960s were Malcolm X, Che Guevara's diaries (with an introduction by Fidel Castro), and Erwin Piscator's old partner Bertolt Brecht. In 1975, it was revealed that the CIA had been gathering information on Grove Press because the publisher had "intelligence interests" relating to foreign contacts with American dissidents.[253] In a 2006 interview, Rosset was asked about his religion. He replied that he never had a religion: "So I became a Communist. As a religion. And you better believe it."[254]

In addition to Grove Press, Rosset published a literary magazine called *Evergreen Review*, a countercultural journal that pushed the limits of censorship by featuring sex as well as politics. The CIA investigated this magazine, suspicious of its motivation and sponsors. In May 1964, just after *The Deputy* opened on Broadway, *Evergreen Review* help promote the play by publishing an article written by Hochhuth.[255] In addition, not only did the magazine run advertisements for the book version of *The Deputy*, it used cross-marketing and advertised Rudolf Vrba's *I Cannot Forgive*, calling it "an eyewitness report — documenting *The Deputy* — by a man who escaped from Auschwitz."[256]

Herman Shumlin was the American producer who brought *The Deputy* to Broadway. While he was not of the same historic importance as Piscator or Brook, he had a long, successful career in film and on the stage. Among his Broadway productions were *The Last Mile* (1930), *Grand Hotel* (1930), *The Children's Hour* (1934), *The Little Foxes* (1939), *The Male Animal* (1940), *The Corn Is Green* (1940), *Watch on the Rhine* (1941), *The Searching Wind* (1944), *Inherit the Wind* (1955), and *The Deputy* (1964). He was also a Communist.

According to *Time* magazine (February 5, 1940), Shumlin was the only producer who advertised in the Communist *Daily Worker*. The article went on to note that "Mr. Shumlin had almost no friends except Leftist Lillian Hellman." Hellman, with whom Shumlin had a professional and a romantic relationship, was outspoken in her support for Communism.[257] The notes for a play she authored (*The Little Foxes*) report that she was "known both for her mink coats and her outspoken support of the communist party and communist-affiliated organizations."

Shumlin served as chairman of "the leftist Joint Anti-Fascist Refugee Committee" (JAFRC).[258] This organization was "originally formed by Communists to aid Stalinist refugees from Spain."[259] Although JAFRC's charter was to raise money for relief causes, after World War II it sent funds to Yugoslavia, helping the Communists win the first postwar elections. In 1947, JAFRC was investigated for Communist infiltration by the House Un-American Activities Committee. When JAFRC refused to turn records over, a federal judge held Shumlin and fifteen other members of JAFRC guilty of contempt of Congress. Shumlin was given a $500 fine and a suspended three-month jail term.[260]

In 1964, Shumlin received a Tony Award for bringing *The Deputy* to Broadway. This was perhaps due in large part to the perceived bravery it took to stand up against all of those who objected to the characterization of Pope Pius XII. Many critics did not like Shumlin's version of *The Deputy*, but it ran on Broadway for almost a year. That seems not to have been as a result of the theatrical quality of the play. Discussing concern about violence from protestors at the opening, *New York Times* theater critic Frank Rich wrote: "The only bomb was on stage, but the publicity turned the show, now forgotten, into a quasi-hit and earned its producer a Tony for his courage."[261]

*The Deputy* finally made it to film in 2002, in the motion picture *Amen*. The screenwriter for the project was Jorge Semprum, the former member of the Communist Party of Spain's politburo who had translated the play into French.[262] The film's accomplished director was Constantinos Gavras, better known as Costa-Gavras. After World War II, Gavras' Greek father was found to be a Communist and sent to prison. Costa-Gavras was denied a visa to the United States over concern that he was also a Communist. Some of his later politically charged films seemed to confirm that suspicion, but he also made films critical of totalitarian (Soviet) regimes. There is no indication that he was ever a member of the Communist Party.[263]

Like Piscator, Brook, Williams, and Shumlin, Gavras reworked *The Deputy*'s script. Like Shumlin, he cut some of the more violent parts of the play as well as anti-Semitic characterizations of Jews. Explaining Hochhuth's unflattering depiction of Jews, Shumlin said: "He was but a child when these horrible events occurred.... None of these young Germans knew Jews.... There just weren't many left around for them to get to know."[264] In fact, Shumlin expressed surprise at the idea that the youthful Hochhuth could have written *The Deputy*.[265] Of course, he may have had help.

————

The KGB liked to use magazines, newspapers, books, and films to spread its propaganda.[266] On January 10, 1963, Congressman A. S. Herlong, Jr., of Florida introduced into the Congressional Record a list of the Communist Party's goals.[267] Among those goals were:

18. Gain control of all student newspapers.

20. Infiltrate the press. Get control of book-review assignments, editorial writing, policymaking positions.

21. Gain control of key positions in radio, TV, and motion pictures.

Communist agents would find and develop reliable outlets so that they could regularly place the stories that often would be picked up by the mainstream press.[268] Consider this statement regarding KGB operations against the United States during the Vietnam era:

One of its favorite tools was the fabrication of such evidence as photographs and "news reports" about invented American war atrocities. These tales were purveyed in KGB-operated magazines that would then flack them to reputable news organizations. Often enough, they would be picked up. News organizations are notoriously sloppy about verifying their sources. All in all, it was amazingly easy for Soviet-bloc spy organizations to fake many such reports and spread them around the world.[269]

Professor Edward McMillan explained in his 1962 book that "the most readily infiltrated areas of the press are international pages, book and film reviews. The propaganda role of reviewers is important because their opinion encourages many to read the works supporting the Soviet line and ignore unfavorable ones."[270] It certainly seems as if Soviet agents worked to promote Hochhuth's play.[271]

Not only did the Soviets have several reliable magazine outlets for their fabrications, but they also used theatrical productions, movies, and other outlets.[272] One former Soviet spy wrote:

Theaters were immensely useful to the party. For the most part they were motion-picture publicists, advertising men, newspaper writers and editors, and radio executives.... I wrote radio scripts, prepared news releases under party direction.... I organized and staged rallies and fund-raising dinners. So thoroughly respectable was my front that one big Communist-sponsored rally — without the Communist label, of course — I was able to obtain the services of a snappy Catholic Youth Organization band.[273]

Jack Moffitt, a top Hollywood screenwriter, testified before the U.S. House Committee on Un-American Activities and described being told by John Howard Lawson, the founder of the Screen Writers Guild, how he should "try to get five minutes of left-wing doctrine in every script you write."[274]

Former KGB Chief of Counterintelligence Oleg Kalugin advanced through the Soviet system at an early age to become a major general with the KGB.[275] Eventually, he was sent off to be deputy head of the Leningrad KGB.[276] Over his thirty-two-year career, he eventually lost faith in the Soviet Communist system, came to the United States, and wrote the book *The First Directorate: My 32 Years in Intelligence and Espionage Against the West*.[277] Of particular interest in that book is the chapter on the time he spent as a young KGB agent in the United States during the early 1960s.

Kalugin and the other Soviet spies in the United States infiltrated left-leaning magazines and newspapers.[278] They would even, on occasion, finance these journals and then plant stories reflecting the Soviet line, hoping that other news outlets would repeat them. As Kalugin wrote: "I had no qualms about stirring up as much trouble as possible...."[279]

Kalugin developed close ties with M. S. ("Max") Arnoni, a Holocaust survivor, one-time editor of the *Encyclopedia Britannica*, and publisher of the magazine *A Minority of One*. According to Kalugin, "*A Minority of One* was a highbrow magazine for the liberal American elite, and we decided to use Arnoni and his publication to further the Soviet cause in the United States."[280] At first, Kalugin simply relied on his friendship with Arnoni to place KGB-written articles into *A Minority of One*. As Arnoni's financial situation worsened, Kalugin first funded the publication of some letter/ads (often signed by several leftist journalists) in the *New York Times*. Eventually, Kalugin gave Arnoni $10,000 from the KGB. Arnoni hid the source of the funds. "Thus did the KGB infiltrate a small yet influential American publication."[281] Arnoni "unwittingly did the bidding of the KGB."[282]

Arnoni became a strong supporter of *The Deputy*. Not only did he write in support of the play in his own journal, but he also wrote an article for another periodical, *American Dialog*.[283] Beyond discussing Hochhuth's drama, he made inflammatory factual assertions that are demonstrably false, such as: "There are... unassessable numbers of Jewish orphans saved in convents who do not know of their Jewish origin, because the Church keeps obstructing the efforts of Jewish organizations to identify such children."[284] Contrary to the historical record, he even wrote that "the man who was to become Pius XII was deeply involved in the politics of ultra-rightist German parties."[285]

Well-known journalist I. F. Stone published an article/review on *The Deputy* in which he faulted the Catholic Church for its role in the rise of Fascism.[286] (Stone's sister, theater critic Judy Stone, conducted an interview with Hochhuth that was published in *Ramparts* magazine.)[287] There had long been rumors about Stone's association with the KGB.[288] Recently deciphered KGB cables (Venona) show that he was recruited by the KGB and became a Soviet intelligence agent in 1936. He was given the code name "Blin" (Russian for "pancake").[289] He apparently had some fallings-out with the Soviets over the years, but they were still in contact in the 1960s. In the 2009 book *Spies: The Rise and Fall of the KGB in America*, authors John Earl Haynes, Harvey Klehr, and Alexander Vassiliev explain that the Venona cables show that "Stone assisted Soviet intelligence on a number of tasks, ranging from doing some talent spotting, acting as a courier by relaying information to other agents, and providing private journalist tidbits and data the KGB found interesting."[290] Helping promote *The Deputy* was one of those little tasks that served the KGB's interests.

Another of the early articles published in the United States about the play was written by David Horowitz.[291] As he has since explained, he was at that time a practicing Communist.[292] Before eventually becoming a leader of the conservative (or neoconservative) political movement, Horowitz spent time in various leadership positions at leftist *Ramparts* magazine, which played an important role in seeing that *The Deputy* opened on Broadway.[293]

Most of the early reviews, articles, and related works by Arnoni, Horowitz, and others were in magazines or outlets of fairly limited distribution.[294] As the KGB would have hoped, however, the story found its way into major media outlets where authors sympathetic to the Soviet viewpoint continued on with it.[295] For instance, when the *New York Times Book Review* section decided to do a major, front page article on *The Deputy*, it explained that it had turned to a Catholic scholar (George N. Shuster) and a non-Catholic scholar (Robert Gorham Davis).[296] It did not explain that Davis was a former member of the Communist Party who had testified before and "named names" to the U.S. House Committee on Un-American Activities.[297]

---

Max Arnoni shared several interests and had contact with Edward Keating, the founder of *Ramparts* magazine. They both took part in the largest-ever anti-Vietnam "teach-in," which was held on May 21-23, 1965, at the University of California at Berkeley.[298] They both had contributions to the book *Teach-Ins: U.S.A.: Reports, Opinions, Documents*.[299] They also shared an interest in (and wrote about) the Kennedy assassination. Keating wrote articles on *The Deputy* for three publications in 1964: *Ramparts*, *This World* magazine, and the *San Francisco Chronicle*.[300] He also wrote a book, *The Scandal of Silence: A Layman's Powerful Critique of the Catholic Church in America*, which was published in 1965.[301] In early 1964, as the battle over whether *The Deputy* would open on

Broadway was raging, Keating took a leading role in support of the play, discussing the matter on WABC's television program *New York, New York*.[302]

In addition to his contacts with Keating, Arnoni had contacts with Warren Hinckle, the editor of *Ramparts*. Hinckle signed one of Arnoni's protest letters that was funded by the KGB and published in the *New York Times*.[303] It should come as no surprise to find that *Ramparts*, like *A Minority of One*, played a role in helping *The Deputy* have an impact on the American conscience. In fact, *Ramparts'* role was crucial in getting the play staged.

Keating had founded *Ramparts* as a liberal Catholic quarterly.[304] Around 1963, however, Keating became disillusioned with the Church, and he went from a "respectfully orthodox convert to a brazen anti-cleric who would make jokes in public and even in the presence of nuns about 'taking a bite out of the Pope's ass.'" (He reportedly had been offended by some Jesuits and vowed to make the Church pay: "From now on, it's no more Mr. Nice Guy.")[305] The magazine dropped its Catholic identity and began its shift toward a communistic viewpoint. Editor Hinckle explained: "[T]here weren't enough Catholic laymen to write for and to buy the magazine. Besides, we got bored with just the church."[306] In 1967, *Time* magazine would editorialize that "no other left-wing publication in the U.S. pursues shock more recklessly or plays around more with facts."[307] It was particularly hard on the Catholic Church. Editor Hinckle explained that "the ramparts of *Ramparts* were used for attacking the Church, rather than defending it as Keating first intended."[308] Of course, because of its original identity, *Ramparts* had an undeserved credibility when it came to Catholic matters.

By early 1964, when *The Deputy* was about to open on Broadway, so many associates, diplomats, and other informed people had spoken against its thesis that it had caused somewhat of an international scandal. New York's Cardinal Spellman had called *The Deputy* "an outrageous desecration of the honor of a great and good man."[309] The National Council of Catholic Men and the American Jewish Committee were joined by Protestants under name of the National Council of Churches. The three groups all tried to talk the television networks out of promoting the play.[310] Jewish War Veterans even marched on the play's opening to defend the Pope's honor.[311]

With the play's ability to open in serious jeopardy, a little magazine with Catholic roots and a Communist future, *Ramparts*, took the lead in defending it. It may not be too much of a stretch to say that without its support, *The Deputy* would not have played on Broadway. (A few years later, similar concerns about Hochhuth's next play, *Soldiers*, kept it from opening at the National Theatre in London.)[312] Hochhuth later repaid *Ramparts* by granting the magazine one of the very few interviews he gave back then.[313]

It was never really clear why the California-based *Ramparts* decided to promote the New York play or how they could justify the cost. In his memoirs, *Ramparts* editor Warren Hinckle explained that he set out to invent an "ecumenical conspiracy" in support of *The Deputy*. He called Keating and said that the two of them were forming a committee, the Ad Hoc Committee to Defend the Right of The Deputy to be Heard. At first, according to Hinckle, Keating was not sure about the effort. He pointed out that the play was "dramaturgically flawed." Hinckle appealed to Keating's ego, arguing that "he could become famous overnight if he, a Catholic publisher, headed a committee to defend the Pope-baiting play." Keating finally agreed.

Hinckle said that he was able to find "a few prominent Protestants, like John C. Bennett, of the Union Theological Seminary," who would stand with *Ramparts*, but they had trouble finding *any* Catholics who could accept the outrageous assertions set forth in the play.[314] Hinckle spoke to an auxiliary bishop, "highly regarded for his liberalism, who told me he would rather endorse a company that put the picture of Jesus Christ on packages of contraceptives than get involved on the side of the author of *The Deputy*." In desperation, Hinckle signed up some Catholic laymen, sociologist Gordon Zahn and novelist John Howard Griffin.[315] Of course, they did not really participate in the proceedings. Hinckle called them "Catholic window dressing."[316]

Hinckle also drafted two Jews: Rabbi Abraham H. Heschel of the Jewish Theological Seminary and Maxwell Geismar, a critic and literary historian. Of Geismar, Hinckle wrote: "a wonderful man about whom I cannot marshal enough superlatives, who, from our chance meeting during the white-heat controversy over *The Deputy*, was to become almost instantly my closest friend, confidant, foster father, and soul mate, and the most important intellectual influence on the developing *Ramparts*." This "most important intellectual influence" on Hinckle and *Ramparts* was an avowed Marxist who wrote the introduction to Eldridge Cleaver's book *Soul on Ice*, which was a collection of essays written while Cleaver was in prison serving time for drug dealing and rape.[317] Cleaver later became a staff writer for *Ramparts*.

Hinckle, who had never been to New York before, created an event. He threw a catered (Bloody Marys and danish) press conference that was really more of a party. Hinckle explained: "Armed with press release, we marched out to do murder in the Cathedral." He rented space in New York's Waldorf Astoria Hotel. He sent long (and expensive) telegram invitations and then followed up with telegram reminders to "everyone in New York City in possession of a pencil or camera."[318] It took far more money than a small magazine like *Ramparts* normally would be able to devote to such a project to pull this off, but Hinckle attracted a huge crowd. One photographer said it was the biggest press conference he had seen since Adlai Stevenson had conceded in the presidential race. When a reporter questioned why no other members of the "blue ribbon committee" had showed up besides Hinckle and Keating, they said that the "room was too crowded."[319]

*Ramparts'* defense of *The Deputy* overshadowed most of the news critical of the play in the final days and assured that the curtain would go up on opening night. That a "Catholic" magazine would defend the play was big news, but *Ramparts* was already well underway in its rejection of a Catholic identity. More than that, CIA documents released under the Freedom of Information Act confirm that by 1966, *Ramparts* had become a reliable outlet for Soviet Communist propaganda.[320] Eventually, the agency devoted twelve full-time or part-time agents to investigating *Ramparts*. They identified and investigated 127 *Ramparts* writers and researchers, as well as nearly 200 other people with some link to the magazine.[321]

Exactly when the transformation of *Ramparts* from a Catholic magazine to a left-leaning political periodical to a reliable outlet for Soviet propaganda became complete is unclear, but the events surrounding *The Deputy* indicate that a major transformation was well underway by 1964.[322]

———

Some have seen in Hochhuth's work, at least in his first two plays, encouragement for "those who, consciously or not, cannot accept Germany's defeat."[323] Others have concluded that Hochhuth's work was part of a campaign to "absolve Germany from war guilt."[324] British Intelligence, looking at Hochhuth's first two plays and a description of a third that he was working on at the time (with the working title *Anatomy of Revolution or How to Overthrow the US Government from the Inside*), saw both of those motivations and more. A top secret report from Sir Burke Trend to Prime Minister Harold Wilson (with attached Memo by Intelligence Coordinator) said: "There are various grounds for suspecting, but no real proof, that Hochhuth's and Irving's activities are part of a long-term Soviet 'disinformation' operation against the West."[325]

Referencing interviews conducted by Carlos Thompson, another declassified secret report said that "it can also be argued... that Hochhuth is engaged in some 'decomposition' exercise and that he is attempting to destroy the fundamental value of a free society, from its religions to its heroes."[326] The report went on to speculate that Hochhuth "might perhaps be an 'intellectual agent,' writing either on behalf of the East Germans or the Soviets."[327] It concluded: "[W]hether Hochhuth is motivated only by the urge to write historical plays, to rehabilitate the Germans or is up to some more sinister game is difficult to determine at this stage. But the Russians are certainly reaping some of the benefit."[328]

Whatever the motivation, what Anthony Quayle said about Hochhuth's play *Soldiers* applies with equal force to *The Deputy*:

> To write a play, rather than a book, on such a matter, is to me, suspect.... It is an allegation which needs the most careful research and importance — but it needs to be a book, written by a meticulous and scholarly mind. No author could expect to make much money out of such a book, but he'd be making a contribution to history. But a play is a blunt emotional instrument. It is the wrong container for such a grave charge, though it may be more of a money-spinner.[329]

Of course, a play better suited Hochhuth's (or the KGB's) ends.

As one Soviet writer explained: "Convincing, profoundly reasoned propaganda of atheism which does not offend the feelings of believers is the main characteristic of all anti-religious work of the present moment."[330] *The Deputy* plot would have been a quite reasonable anti-religion operation from that era. It brought disrespect on not only Pope Pius XII, but the whole Catholic Church. To a degree, it even shamed Christianity itself. Yet, most viewers of the play could distance themselves from the criticism. From the KGB's perspective, that would have been perfect.

Hochhuth may not have knowingly cooperated with the Soviets, but he was the perfect candidate to be an unknowing dupe. *Time* magazine described him as "one cut above a crank and several cuts below a thinker."[331] His ideology was not far removed from Marxism.[332] He also admitted that he was, at least at times, anti-clerical.[333] He compared Catholicism to Nazism and Bolshevism in its "demand for... unheard-of sacrifices and victims.... They [Church leaders] do not think of the happiness of the living but of generations to come.... [I]t is always terribly inhuman to think in this way"[334] He was particularly opposed to priestly celibacy.[335]

Assuming that his work on *Soldiers* is indicative of his work on *The Deputy*, Hochhuth's sloppy research and willingness to believe whatever story he was told would have made him an excellent target for the Soviets. Moreover, it was the appendix that attracted most of the attention, not the play. That is where he most likely had help. The Soviets had the opportunity to feed bad information to Hochhuth, and they also seem to have had the correct personnel in place. Even Hochhuth's great buddy David Irving said he may have been "fed a corrupt dossier in some clever way. He could be very naive."[336]

The play was certainly supported by Communists and fellow-travelers.[337] The producer who brought *The Deputy* to the stage in Berlin had long carried out orders from the Communist Party. The American producer and publisher were also Communists. Many of the journalists who brought early attention to *The Deputy* had strong ties to leftist (and sometimes Communist) causes. The translator of the play into French was a member of the Communist Party of Spain's politburo, and he had just spent a decade organizing clandestine activities. The magazine that helped assure that the play appeared on Broadway was in the process of becoming a Communist organ.[338] British intelligence, in 1969, concluded: "[N]or can we discount the possibility of long-term efforts by the communists to foster Hochhuth's allegations until they become legend."[339] Certainly, the main point of the play and the hostility to the Church came from the Soviets.

The Italian newspaper *La Repubblica* has reported that archival documents from the former East Germany support Pacepa's eyewitness testimony that the Soviet Union was behind the campaign to calumniate Pius XII. According to Father Peter Gumpel, a historian and the investigating judge in Pope Pius XII's sainthood cause:

These revelations do not add anything to what the Holy See already knows, but it is important for those who have thought and written that Pacelli was "Hitler's Pope." Now there are other documents that show how many false statements have been made about Pius XII. The responsibility of the Soviet Union is also evident in the campaign to calumniate Pius XII.[340]

Gumpel concluded is that there was a "deliberate effort on the part of the Russians to discredit Pope Pius XII."[341] German historian Michael Feldkamp concluded that "Pacepa's report is wholly credible. It fits like a missing piece in the puzzle of communist propaganda and disinformation aimed at discrediting the Catholic Church and its Pontiff."[342] Putting together all of the evidence, it is hard to disagree.[343]

# SEVENTEEN

# The Critics

Since the first edition of this book was published, there have been numerous books and articles critical of Pope Pius XII and the Catholic Church. Authors including Garry Wills,[1] James Carroll,[2] Susan Zuccotti,[3] Michael Phayer,[4] Daniel Goldhagen,[5] David Kertzer,[6] and Robert Wistrich[7] have written highly critical books. John Cornwell, author of the best known anti-Pius book (*Hitler's Pope*), came back with a second book touching on the topic.[8] Robert Katz, author of two books critical of Pius XII back in the 1960s has authored a new book that largely combines his earlier complaints.[9] At least two older books critical of the Pope have reportedly been scheduled for re-release,[10] and Rolf Hochhuth's play *The Deputy* was filmed and released as a motion picture entitled *Amen*.[11] There have also been some more nuanced books[12] and several that applaud Catholic efforts during that era.[13] Numerous articles, of course, have been written on both sides of the debate.

This flurry of attention has resulted in several new allegations, many of which are inconsistent with earlier charges. One book charges that Pius helped Nazis escape to South America. Another book dismisses that, but raises the charge that he was too concerned about centralization of papal power. The next book rejects those charges, but raises new claims. Along the way, Pope Pius XI — traditionally presented by the critics as a strong opponent of the Nazis — has come under heavy (though inconsistent) criticism. The German Catholic hierarchy has also been strongly criticized. The argument eventually reached beyond the Catholic Church and challenged the very foundation of Christianity — the New Testament itself.[14] Of course, as Rabbi David Dalin has noted, many of the critics are not honestly seeking the truth; they are instead distorting the truth in order to influence the future of the Catholic Church.[15]

Too many stories about Pius XII have not been properly traced back to the original source. For instance, in his book *Constantine's Sword*, former priest James Carroll shows an unreasonable eagerness to accept and readily advance a supposed death-bed condemnation of Pius XII by Pope John XXIII.[16] No eyewitness has ever come forward to support that story. "The Postulator of John XXIII's Cause for Canonization, Fr. Luca De Rosa, OFM, states that the story is 'absolutely untrue.' He adds that Pope John was, in fact, 'full of admiration and devotion' for Pius XII."[17] Archbishop Loris Capovilla, formerly private secretary to Pope John, also categorically denies that Pope John ever said any such thing, calling it "a lie."[18]

Throughout his life, John praised Pius. Before he was made pope, John was offered thanks for his wartime efforts to save Jewish refugees. He replied: "In all these painful matters I have referred to the Holy See and simply carried out [Pius XII's] orders: first and foremost to save human lives."[19] When Pius died, the future John XXIII said that he had been like a "public fountain" pouring forth good waters at which all the world, great and lowly, could profitably drink.[20] John's staff had a photograph of Pius published with a prayer on the back asking for his canonization as a saint. The prayer called Pius "a fearless defender of the Faith, a courageous struggler for justice and peace… a shining model of charity and of every virtue."[21] A million of these prayer cards were soon in circulation, and John XXIII (who prayed monthly before the tomb of Pius XII)[22] said in an audience that surely one day Pius would be raised to the Catholic altars.[23]

John even considered taking the name "Pius XIII," and one of the first things that he did upon becoming pope was to have a photo of Pius XII put on his desk.[24] In his first Christmas broadcast to the world after his election, John paid the high honor of saying that Pius XII's doctrinal and pastoral teaching "assure a place in posterity for the name of Pius XII. Even apart from any official declaration, which would be premature, the triple title of 'Most excellent Doctor, Light of Holy Church, Lover of the divine law' evokes the sacred memory of this pontiff in whom our times were blessed indeed."[25] Of course, only a saint can be declared a Doctor of the Church. Yet *Constantine's Sword* is at least the third publication in which Carroll has advanced the fabricated death-bed story, and he did so twice in that book!

Similarly, the claim that Pius was worried about putting Germans into a "conflict of conscience" if he were to condemn Nazism traces back to a highly suspect source.[26] Also, many critics are all too quick to accept Robert Katz's claim that Pius knew of the October 16, 1943, roundup of Rome's Jews before it took place. The "evidence" for this is really nothing more than pure speculation.[27]

After the manuscript of the first edition of this book was substantially completed, Viking Press released *Hitler's Pope: The Secret History of Pius XII*, by British journalist John Cornwell. That book created quite a splash in the popular press, and therefore it had to be addressed. We held up the release of the first edition until I could undertake some additional research in Rome and prepare an epilogue to add on to the end of the first edition.

In his 2004 book, *The Pontiff in Winter*, John Cornwell admitted that *Hitler's Pope* lacked balance. He reported that "in the light of the debates and evidence following *Hitler's Pope*," Pope Pius XII "had so little scope of action" that it is impossible to judge his motives "while Rome was under the heel of Mussolini and later occupied by the Germans."[28] The *Economist* reported that Cornwell was "chastened" by the experience. In an article from the *Catholic Herald* entitled "I've Never Accused Pius of Being a Nazi," Cornwell said: "A lot of people have misunderstood the book, and possibly it's my fault — the title could so easily be misunderstood."[29] He went on to explain: "I've changed my mind about the extent to which one could call in question Pius XII's motives and conscience over his silence." [30] He continued: "I've never accused him of being a wicked man, a Nazi or anything like that." [31] Cornwell remained critical of the centralization of power in the Church, and he said that Pius should have explained himself better after the war, but he essentially recanted his attack on Pius XII's motives.

In 2008, Penguin Press released a new edition of *Hitler's Pope*. The only apparent change was a new preface in which Cornwell admitted that Pius was not a Nazi sympathizer, did not favor Hitler, and was not an anti-Semite. Cornwell also noted that he had qualified his criticism of Pius XII's handling of the roundup of Roman Jews in October 1943, and here he also acknowledged the reality of the threat of an invasion of the Vatican, which he had previously downplayed. [32]

In the new edition, Cornwell still argues that Pacelli was "an ideal church leader" for Hitler to exploit. "I am not inclined to alter this view despite the many citations of Pacelli's alleged deeds of mercy toward Jews and others, or his private criticism of Hitler, or his cautious, even-handed reproaches against both the Axis and the Allied powers." Cornwell now wants to focus on the early 1930s, when Secretary of State Pacelli "entered into a series of negotiations with Hitler, culminating in the Reich Concordat." [33] He also says that Pacelli's postwar claim to have "on various occasions" condemned the "fanatical anti-Semitism inflicted on the Hebrew people" is "a blatant lie." In the end, he reasserts that Pius XII was "a deeply flawed human being from whom Catholics, and our relations with other religions, can best profit by expressing our sincere regret."

---

As the title suggests, *Hitler's Pope* presents a very cynical portrait of Pope Pius XII. [34] The book's thesis is that Eugenio Pacelli was a single-minded Vatican lawyer and diplomat who, from the earliest part of his career, set out to establish the absolute authority of Rome over Europe's Catholic populations. According to this book, Pacelli was vain, beady-eyed, and an overwhelmingly ambitious careerist who dominated Vatican policy long before he was elected pope. Cornwell concludes that Pius XII "was the ideal Pope for Hitler's unspeakable plan. He was Hitler's pawn. He was Hitler's Pope." [35]

To reach his conclusions, Cornwell disregarded much recent scholarship and provided quirky interpretations of well-known facts. [36] As one reviewer (himself a critic of Pius) explained: "Throughout the book Cornwell insists on interpreting every decision and action of Pacelli in a way most inimical to him. The author is so committed to demonstrating or proving everything prejudicial to Pacelli, that he weakens, almost to the point of destruction, his own basic argument." [37] Those who read only *Hitler's Pope* (as did far too many reviewers in the popular press) may think that Cornwell established his case. [38] A fair evaluation of the facts, however, reveals that he failed. [39]

The first cause for suspicion about *Hitler's Pope* is on its cover. The dust jacket of the original British edition shows Nuncio Pacelli leaving a reception given for German President Hindenburg in 1927. The photograph, a favorite of those who seek to portray Pius XII in an unfavorable light,[40] shows the nuncio dressed in formal diplomatic regalia (which could easily be confused with papal garments), as he exits a building. On each side of him stand soldiers of the Weimar Republic. In front of him stands a chauffeur saluting and holding open the square-looking door, typical of automobiles from the 1920s. Those who do not recognize the differences in uniform details could easily confuse the Weimar soldiers with Nazi soldiers because of their distinctive helmets associated with Nazi-era German soldiers.

Use of this photograph, especially when coupled with a provocative title such as *Hitler's Pope*, gives the impression that Pope Pius XII is seen leaving a meeting with Hitler.[41] Making matters even worse is the caption from inside the dust jacket on early British editions of the book, which labels the photograph as having been taken in March 1939.[42] By this time, Hitler was chancellor of Germany, and this was the month Pacelli was made pope. A fair-minded person reading the caption could easily conclude that Cardinal Pacelli paid a visit to Hitler immediately prior to being elected pope.

The American version of *Hitler's Pope* never had the wrong date, but — given that the date might have been an honest error — it is far more revealing about the intentional misinformation that went into the marketing of this book. The U.S. edition uses the same photograph as the British edition, but it is cropped to eliminate two important points of reference: the soldier nearest the camera and the square door of the automobile. Both of those images provide clues to the true date of this photo (1927), and Cornwell apparently did not want that known.[43] The photo also has been significantly darkened, giving it a more sinister feel.[44] Even more telling is the intentional blurring of the background. Looking at this cover, Nuncio Pacelli is in clear focus, but the soldier to his left and the chauffeur are both badly blurred. They are so badly blurred that it is impossible even for a well-trained observer to recognize that the soldier wears a Weimar uniform rather than a Nazi uniform. The chauffeur, due to the blurring and cropping that eliminates the car door, takes on the appearance of a saluting S.S. officer. Even a civilian in the background could seem to be a Nazi official.

Since none of the images on the British edition are blurred, and since Nuncio Pacelli's face is in focus on the U.S. cover but the other images are blurred, the only logical conclusion is that the photo was intentionally altered to support Cornwell's thesis. Unfortunately, this is not the only dishonest aspect of the book.

Inside *Hitler's Pope*, before the text, Cornwell presents a quotation from Thomas Merton, a well-known contemplative monk whose writings have inspired many people. As butchered by Cornwell, the quotation says:

"Pius XII and the Jews.... The whole thing is too sad and too serious for bitterness... a silence which is deeply and completely in complicity with all the forces which carry out oppression, injustice, aggression, war."

This is a fairly shocking condemnation of the Pope from an esteemed Catholic thinker. If Merton had actually written this, it would indeed give one pause. Actually, however, this is not a true quotation. Cornwell manufactured it.

Cornwell gave no citation, so his deception was hard to uncover.[45] The full quotation, which was written by Merton in his personal journal, is a complaint that he had been ordered not to publish his essay on nuclear war. The "silence" about which he complained was the "silence" that had been imposed upon him. It was unrelated to Pius XII. Merton actually wrote:

> A grim insight into the stupor of the Church, in spite of all that has been attempted, all efforts to wake her up! It all falls into place. Pope *Pius XII and the the Jews*, the Church in South America, the treatment of Negroes in the U.S., the Catholics on the French right in the Algerian affair, the German Catholics under Hitler. All this fits into one big picture and our contemplative recollection is not very impressive when it is seen only as another little piece fitted into the puzzle. *The whole thing is too sad and too serious for bitterness.* I have the impression that my education is beginning — only just beginning and that I have a lot more terrible things to learn before I can know the real meaning of hope.
>
> There is no consolation, only futility, in the idea that one is a kind of martyr for a cause. I am not a martyr for anything, I am afraid. I wanted to act like a reasonable, civilized, responsible Christian of my time. I am not allowed to do this, and I am told I have renounced this — fine. In favor of what? In favor of *a silence which is deeply and completely in complicity with all the forces that carry out oppression, injustice, exploitation, war.* In other words silent complicity is presented as a "greater good" than honest, conscientious protest — it is supposed to be part of my vowed life, it is for the "Glory of God." Certainly I refuse complicity. My silence itself is a protest and those who know me are aware of this fact. I have at least been able to write enough to make that clear. Also I cannot leave here in order to protest since the meaning of any protest depends on my staying here."[46]

Cornwell selected the phrases that are italicized above, linked them with ellipses, and committed academic fraud.

Not long after the release of *Hitler's Pope*, the Vatican issued a statement on Cornwell's work in Rome. It denied Cornwell's claim to have been the first person to have access to the archives that he used, denied his claim that he had worked "for months on end" in these archives,[47] denied his claim that a letter he had found had been kept secret prior to his efforts (noting that it had been published in full several years earlier), and stated that these falsehoods had been revealed "to put readers on guard about Cornwell's claims."[48]

When he was asked about these claims in *Brill's Content* magazine, Cornwell replied as follows: "Nowhere in the book do I claim that I spent months on end in the Secretariat of State archive. The quote is taken from a sub-editorial conflation in a newspaper article and was an error of strict fact that actually turns out to be essentially true." This was a brazen effort to obfuscate the issue. Cornwell completely neglected to mention that the newspaper article was one that *he* had written *about his book*! Moreover, he repeated the claim in a piece that *he* wrote *about his book* for *Vanity Fair* magazine![49]

Cornwell's supposed "new information" came not from secret files, but from the open, pre-1922 archives of the Vatican's secretary of state office. This would account for the only "new" pieces of evidence offered in his book, both of which are dated before 1920.[50] He also saw Pius XII's beatification deposition transcripts,[51] but they were also not secret.[52]

Cornwell claimed that these beatification deposition transcripts were "explosively critical matter" and "a priceless biographical resource" that Father Peter Gumpel had made available to him "at great risk." In fact, he said that "in the absence of a devil's advocate [the testimony of Pacelli's younger sister, Elisabetha] should be heeded."[53] One might expect to find controversy in the materials. However, as one plows through the ninety-eight deposition transcripts (not seventy-six, as Cornwell writes), they turn out to be not at all controversial. No witness gave "shocking" testimony. Many spoke of Pius XII's concern for and help given to Jewish people, both before and after he became pope.

The original handwritten transcripts take up just over 1,700 pages which are spread over seven volumes; the printed set that fills two volumes in the *Positio* is just over 900 pages (not a thousand pages, as Cornwell says). Yet, Cornwell has only 30 citations to this material, in which he references only 12 of the 98 witnesses. More telling, however, are the contents of the testimony that he found so devastating.[54]

Cornwell was able to uncover a bit of disharmony between the Pope's housekeeper and his sister (who wanted to be his housekeeper), but other than some petty jealousy — not on the part of Pius — the testimony is not in the slightest negative.[55] Much of it relates to matters such as Pius XII's height, weight, health problems, etc. Cornwell attempts to present these transcripts as controversial by quoting statements favorable to the Pope, then arguing against them. As the Congregation for the Causes of Saints concluded, *Hitler's Pope* is neither scholarly nor honest.[56] Actually, the clear message from each and every witness is that Eugenio Pacelli (Pope Pius XII) was an honest, holy, and charitable man — even saintly.

The following is a chart that covers every citation that Cornwell has to the deposition transcripts. The headings indicate the location of the citation in *Hitler's Pope* (by chapter and page), the page number of the location of the testimony in the printed transcripts, the witness, and a thumbnail sketch of the testimony.

| Hitler's Pope Chapter | Note # in Hitler's Pope | Vatican Transcript Page | Witness | Subject Matter of Testimony |
|---|---|---|---|---|
| Intro | | 229 | Carlo Pacelli (nephew) | Height and weight of Pius. |
| 1 | 7 | 30 | Guglielmo Hentrich (professor) | No heat in Pacelli's child-hood home. |
| 1 | 14 | 109 | Pascalina Lehnert (housekeeper) | Young Pacelli had unusual sense of control over self. |
| 1 | 20 | 3 | Elisabetha Pacelli (sister) | Family brought him food when he was in the seminary. |
| 2 | 4 | 255-56 | Maria Teresa Pacelli (cousin) | Young cousin felt that she could confide in him. |
| 2 | 5 | 256 | Maria Teresa Pacelli | Older, the same cousin found him open, modest, humble, reserved but cheerful, and marked by simplicity. |
| 5 | 26 | 6 | Guglielmo Hentrich | 1920s problem between members of Nuncio Pacelli's domestic staff. |
| 5 | 27 | 6 | Guglielmo Hentrich | Pacelli was pleased when accusations of a romance between him and his house-keeper were disproved. |
| 5 | 28 | 69 | Suora Ignazia Caterina Kayser (member of religious order) | Priest/assistant thought Nuncio Pacelli should fire his housekeeper. |
| 6 | 18 | 54 | Hans Struth (journal-ist) | Pacelli blessed crowds as he left Germany. |
| 7 | 12 | 6 | Elisabetha Pacelli | Domestic quarrel between housekeeper and staff. |
| 11 | 13 | 12 | Guglielmo Hentrich | Pacelli's nephew took a photo of the housekeeper in an embarrassing position with a man. |
| 15 | 3 | 31 | Guglielmo Hentrich | Pius slept no more than four hours a night during the war. |
| 16 | 22 | 85 | Pascalina Lehnert | Pius decides to burn notes of condemnation due to news of the persecution of Jews in Holland. |

| Hitler's Pope Chapter | Note # in Hitler's Pope | Vatican Transcript Page | Witness | Subject Matter of Testimony |
|---|---|---|---|---|
| 17 | 31 | 831 | Gen. Carlo Otto Wolff (S.S. commander) | Wolff talks with Hitler about occupation of the Vatican. |
| 17 | 32 | 832-33 | Gen. Carlo Otto Wolff | Hitler makes "dark threats" against the Vatican. |
| 17 | 33 | 832 | Gen. Carlo Otto Wolff | Hitler orders occupation of Vatican and kidnaping of Pope. |
| 17 | 34 | 834 | Gen. Carlo Otto Wolff | Wolff tries to thwart Hitler's plans. |
| 17 | 35 | 836-37 | Gen. Carlo Otto Wolff | Wolff urges Hitler to drop plans against the Vatican. |
| 18 | 14 | 340 | Quirino Paganuzzi (worked in the Vatican) | Pius got on his knees and apologized to a priest with whom he had been sharp. |
| 20 | 3 | 102 | Pascalina Lehnert | Pius says that a pope must be perfect, but not others. |
| 20 | 4 | 334 | Quirino Paganuzzi | Pius stayed up late to return books and files to their proper places. |
| 20 | 8 | 89 | Pascalina Lehnert | Companion did not share the vision seen by Pius. |
| 20 | 10 | 219 | Carlo Pacelli | There was a rumor that Pius XII's housekeeper interrupted an important meeting. |
| 20 | 13 | 37 | Guglielmo Hentrich | Pius did not think beauty contests were good for women. |
| 20 | 14 | 249 | Virginio Rotondi (journalist) | Pius rejected a candidate for sainthood due to his use of obscene language. |
| 20 | 15 | 210 | Giacomo Martegani (radio and newspaper man) | Pius warned priests to avoid temptation by avoiding trips with young women. |
| 20 | 23 | 229 | Carlo Pacelli | Pius had dental problems. |
| 20 | 26 | 276 | Cesidio Lolli (newspaper writer) | Pius XII's health problems. |
| 20 | 27 | 227 | Carlo Pacelli | Pius changed doctors. |

Not only did each of these witnesses have favorable things to say about Pope Pius XII, but even the portions of testimony cited by Cornwell are not critical of Pius, despite Cornwell's arguments to the contrary. One need not view the deposition transcripts to verify this summary. Just look at Cornwell's citations and compare them with *his* text. The testimonies "are without any exception, positive with regard to the life, activity, and virtue of Pius XII."[57]

In the April 2000 issue of *Brill's Content* magazine, Cornwell addressed the fact that these depositions contain nothing that could possibly put an honest person into a state of moral shock. His only reply was that Pius XII's sister "tells us that he was accused of having had an affair with his housekeeper nun and that the housekeeper in turn had been engaged in a flirtation with the Vatican architect. Is that not explosive?"[58] That testimony (which actually was that Pius immediately ordered an investigation when he heard this rumor and was pleased when it was disproved) has nothing to do with Hitler, the Jews, the Nazis, or the Holocaust. Cornwell's claim of having been left in a "state of moral shock" is preposterous.[59]

Critics claim to have found two pieces of evidence from this era to support the conclusion that Pacelli was an anti-Semite. The first is a letter that the nuncio wrote in 1917. A rabbi had requested Pacelli's assistance in obtaining palm fronds from Italy to be used in a synagogue festival. Pacelli welcomed the rabbi, but — in the middle of a nation torn by world war — it was not easy to comply with his request, especially since the Vatican did not have diplomatic relations with Italy at that time. In his report back to Rome,[60] Pacelli noted the difficulty in offering such help, given that the assistance sought was *not* in a matter pertaining to "civil or natural rights common to all human beings," but rather in a matter pertaining to the ceremony of a "Jewish cult." He indicated that if this matter had pertained to civil or natural rights (e.g., "human rights"), the Church might have been able to do more. Cornwell and the other critics overlook this significant distinction. The rabbi, however, understood the difficulty and thanked Pacelli for his efforts.

Cornwell based much of his argument not on Pacelli's report to Rome, but on the reply sent to him from Cardinal Secretary of State Gasparri.[61] In that reply, Gasparri praised Pacelli's skill ("*destrezza*") in handling a delicate matter. Cornwell, however, mistranslated the word *destrezza* as "shrewdness." Cornwell led his readers to believe that Gasparri was praising Pacelli's shrewdness or praising him for supposedly deceiving the rabbi about the palms and what the Holy See could do. In actuality, Gasparri simply expressed his admiration to Pacelli for his skill in dealing with this complicated, sensitive matter. Thus, Cornwell's reference to Pacelli being "capable of implicating the Holy See in a diplomatic sleight of hand"[62] was pure invention, employed to accentuate his phony translation.

Another linguistic trick that Cornwell tries to use relates to the word *cult*. Given the pejorative meaning that is today associated with that word, Cornwell argues that its use reflects Pacelli's contempt for Judaism. That's a false argument, and Cornwell knew it all along.

The actual Italian word used by Pacelli was "*culto*." The first three meanings for this word in *Webster's 3rd International Dictionary* all deal with religious rites and worship. The *American Heritage Dictionary's* first definition of *cult* is: "A system or community of religious worship or ritual." The word itself is derived from the Latin *cultus*, which means "worship."

The Vatican still uses the word *cult* to refer to the Church's own rites and worship, such as "the cult of the saints" and "the cult of the Virgin Mary." Thus, the word does not carry any derogatory connotation.[63] In fact, Cornwell uses the term in this manner several times in *Hitler's Pope.*[64] To stretch the word to include an anti-Semitic sentiment reveals an ill-disguised motive. In fact, the rabbi's willingness to approach Pacelli for help like this confirms Pacelli's well-deserved reputation for being friendly to Jews.[65]

The other controversial letter was written in 1919. That year, Bolshevik revolutionaries temporarily took power and tried to set up a Soviet republic in Bavaria.[66] Their leaders occupied the royal palace and began operating what might best be described as a rogue government. They created a "Red Army" that killed about 325 people.[67] Of particular concern to all diplomats in Munich was that the Bolsheviks violated the sovereign immunity of foreign missions and representatives. Two legations were invaded, and a car was requisitioned from another. The Austro-Hungarian consul general was arrested without cause and held for several hours.[68]

Many foreign dignitaries left Munich, but Pacelli stayed at his post and became a target of Bolshevik hostility.[69] One time, an angry mob descended on Pacelli's car, screaming insults and threatening to turn the car over.[70] On another occasion, in true gangland style, gunmen in a car sprayed Pacelli's residence with machine-gun fire.[71] When he called in a protest, he was told to leave the city that night or he would die.[72] Not only did Pacelli stay, but he even "mounted the pulpit at the Munich cathedral against the orders of the Red committee."[73]

Concerned for the people under his charge, Nuncio Pacelli sent his assistant, Monsignor Lorenzo Schioppa, to meet with the leaders of the new government. Schioppa, accompanied by a representative from the Prussian legation, met with the head of the Republic of the Councils of Munich, Eugen Levine. Their hope was for Levine (incorrectly identified as "Levien" in the later report) "to declare unequivocally if and how the actual Communist Government intends to recognize and oversee the immunities of the Diplomatic Representatives."[74] Of course, their position demanded that they make a plea, not a demand.[75]

The meeting did not go well. The only "commitment" that the representatives could get from Levine was that the Republic of the Councils would recognize the extraterritoriality of the foreign legations "if, and as long as the representatives of these Powers . . . do nothing against the Republic of the Councils." Schioppa was warned that if the nuncio did anything against the new government, he would be "kicked out."[76] Levine made it clear that "they had no need of the Nunciature."[77]

Pacelli wrote a letter back to Rome, reporting on this meeting. Cornwell translated a few sentences from that letter and set them forth as "proof" that Pacelli was an anti-Semite. Other critics, including Daniel Goldhagen, blindly followed that translation and compounded the error. The key passage, as translated by the critics, described the palace as follows:

> ... a gang of young women, of dubious appearance, Jews like all the rest of them, hanging around in all the offices with lecherous demeanor and suggestive smiles. The boss of this female rabble was Levien's mistress, a young Russian woman, a Jew and a divorcee, who was in charge.... This Levien is a young man, of about thirty or thirty-five, also Russian and a Jew. Pale, dirty, with drugged eyes, hoarse voice, vulgar, repulsive, with a face that is both intelligent and sly.[78]

To the critics, these words (taken from Schioppa's report to his superior, Pacelli) prove that Pacelli was an anti-Semite.[79]

In truth, this translation is grossly distorted. It uses pejorative words, instead of neutral ones that are more faithful to the original Italian. For instance, the most damning phrase in the translation, "Jews like all the rest of them," turns out to be a distorted, inaccurate translation of the Italian phrase "*i primi.*" The literal translation would be "the first ones" or "the ones just mentioned."[80] In context, "also Jewish" would have been appropriate. Similarly, the Italian word "*schiera*" is translated by Cornwell as "gang" instead of "group," the latter of which would be more appropriate. Additionally, the Italian "*gruppo femminile*" should be translated as "female group" or "group of women," not "female rabble" (though in the new edition of *Hitler's Pope*, Cornwell tries to justify this translation as being "true to the overall drift of the letter").[81]

This letter was published in its original Italian in 1992.[82] Church historian John Conway — an Anglican and a distinguished scholar — reviewed the book in which it was included for the *Catholic Historical Review*. Neither he nor anyone else at that time suggested that the letter was anti-Semitic. Considering the centrality of this letter to *Hitler's Pope*, one might have expected (and editors should have demanded) that Cornwell publish it in full.[83] That did not happen, however, perhaps because when the entire letter is read in an accurate translation (see Appendix, p. 390), it is not anti-Semitic. The tone of anti-Semitism is introduced only by a calculated mistranslation.

Any disrespect reflected in the language that was actually used (as opposed to the mistranslation) would not stem from racial or even religious differences, but from the Bolshevik activity in Munich. There was clear animosity between the Church and the revolutionaries, and those revolutionaries are the focus of the comment, not all Jewish people.[84] *In fact, this letter was describing the leaders of a rogue government that presented a threat to the nunciature!* It was written fourteen years before Hitler came to power and the Jewish persecution began. The language used to describe a similar event in 1943 might well have been very different.

Rather than using unfair translations and fabricating an argument, the critics could have looked to direct, relevant evidence from that same period. On May 12, 1917, author, journalist, and board member of the Zionist World Congress Nahum Sokolow wrote a letter to the Executive Committee of the Zionist World Congress regarding meetings he had with Pacelli, Cardinal Secretary of State Gasparri, and Pope Benedict XV regarding the establishment of a Jewish homeland in Palestine. He wrote:

> I was first of all received by Msgr. Eugenio Pacelli, Secretary for Extraordinary Affairs, and had a few days later a long conference with Cardinal Secretary of State Gasparri. Both meetings were extraordinarily friendly and positive.... I don't tend towards credulity or exaggerations and still I can't avoid to stress that this revealed an extraordinary amount of friendship: to grant a Jew and representative of Zionism with such a promptness a private audience which took so long and was of such a warmth and took place with all assurance of sympathy, both for the Jews in general and for Zionism in special, proves that we don't need to expect any obstacles which can't be overcome from the side of the Vatican.... The Pope asked me: Pacelli told me about your mission; do you want to tell me any more details?"[85]

This certainly does not leave the same impression that Cornwell's mistranslation does. Moreover, there is additional evidence from the same time period.

During World War I, the American Jewish Committee of New York petitioned the Vatican for a statement on the "ill-treatment" suffered by Jewish people in Poland. The response came on February 9, 1916, from the office of the secretary of state, where Eugenio Pacelli was working hand-in-hand with Cardinal Secretary of State Gasparri.[86] It said:

> The Supreme Pontiff... as Head of the Catholic Church, which, faithful to its divine doctrine and to its most glorious traditions, considers all men as brothers and teaches them to love one another, he never ceases to inculcate among individuals, as well as among peoples, the observance of the principles of natural law and to condemn everything which violates them. This law must be observed and respected in the case of the children of Israel, as well as of all others, because it would not be conformable to justice or to religion itself to derogate from it solely on account of religious confessions. The Supreme Pontiff at this moment feels in his fatherly heart... the necessity for all men of remembering that they are brothers and that their salvation lies in the return to the law of love which is the law of the gospel.[87]

This pronouncement was published in the *New York Times* on April 17, 1916, under the headline "Papal Bull Urges Equality for Jews." It also appeared in *La Civiltà Cattolica* on April 28 of that year and in the *London Tablet* on April 29. In 1936, when he was visiting the United States as cardinal secretary of state, Pacelli met with two officials of the American Jewish Committee, Lewis Strauss and Joseph Proskauer, and he reaffirmed this teaching, promising to make it better known.[88] The critics fail even to mention it.[89]

In these same years, Cardinal Gasparri sent a telegram to Pacelli in Germany. It was sent at the behest of the "Israelite Community of Switzerland" and related to the deterioration of conditions in Palestine, where Jews were being driven from their homes. Pacelli then sent this request to the responsible German authorities:

> The undersigned Apostolic Nuncio has the honor to inform Your Excellency that the Israelite Congregations of Switzerland asked the Holy Father to appeal for the protection of the sites and the Jewish population of Jerusalem. His Eminence, the Cardinal Secretary of State has ordered the undersigned to act accordingly and with all care, and to draw this subject to the attention of the Imperial [German] Government. The Undersigned requests that Your Excellency enforce the realization of this goal with every resource at your disposal.
>
> Eugenio Pacelli, Archbishop of Sardes, and Apostolic Nuncio[90]

---

While Cornwell has only thirty citations to the deposition transcripts, he has about twice that many citations to Klaus Scholder's two volumes on *The Churches and the Third Reich* (Fortress Press, 1988). In fact, Cornwell says that his "greatest debt, and indeed homage, is to the magisterial scholarship of the late Klaus Scholder." According to Cornwell, Scholder's reputation as a church historian is "unchallenged in German scholarship," but scholars at the Holy See have overlooked him. On both counts, Cornwell is demonstrably wrong.

Scholder has been seriously challenged by many scholars, perhaps most notably by Konrad Repgen. In several works, Repgen has particularly contested Scholder's assertion that there was a connection between the dissolution of the Center Party and the 1933 negotiations that led to a concordat between the Third Reich and the Holy See.[91] Ludwig Volk's work, though published prior to Scholder's, also refutes the latter's contentions, in particular Scholder's claim that the initiative for the concordat came from the Vatican.[92] Much modern scholarship supports Volk over Scholder on this point.[93] In fact, the editors of a collection of Scholder's papers that was published after his death even admitted in the introduction that Scholder's anti-Pacelli thesis could not be supported from the available records.[94]

As for the Vatican's failure to consult Scholder's work, Cornwell reported that in a conversation Gumpel admitted "that not only had he not read Klaus Scholder's extensive and crucial scholarship on the Reich Concordat, but that he was unaware of its existence." Gumpel, of course, has read Scholder's writings.[95] Gumpel attributes Cornwell's error to a misunderstanding that took place when Cornwell visited Rome. "He has a very bad pronunciation of German," Gumpel explained. "He may have asked whether I knew of Scholder's work, but mispronounced the name so badly that I did not recognize it." Gumpel has also explained why Cornwell relies so heavily on Scholder: "Scholder's work relating to the various concordats is 'largely surpassed' by other standard works, but Scholder better supports Cornwell's thesis."[96]

———————

Viking Press marketed *Hitler's Pope* as having been written by a practicing Catholic who started out to defend Pius XII. Most reviewers accepted Cornwell's claim to have been a good, practicing Catholic determined to defend his Church when he began his research. Earlier accounts of Cornwell's background, however, paint a very different picture. More importantly, the time line does not fit. Based on his own account of things, Cornwell could not have been intending to defend the Pope when he started his work.

According to a 1989 report in the *Washington Post*, Cornwell "was once a seminarian at the English College in Rome and knows the Vatican terrain, [but] he has long since left the seminary and the Catholic faith, and thus writes with that astringent, cool, jaundiced view of the Vatican that only ex-Catholics familiar with Rome seem to have mastered."[97] His 2006 memoir *Seminary Boy* is a nice tribute to Cornwell's seminary years. In *The Hiding Places of God* (1993), however, he wrote of his days in the seminary: "I took delight in attempting to undermine the beliefs of my fellow seminarians with what I regarded as clever arguments; I quarreled with the lecturers in class and flagrantly ignored the rules of the house." He declared that human beings are "morally, psychologically and materially better off without a belief in God." He also said that he had lost his "belief in the mystery of the real presence of Christ in the Eucharist." Reviews of that book called Cornwell an agnostic and former Catholic. In fact, in 1989 Cornwell described himself as a "lapsed Catholic for more than 20 years."[98] As late as 1996, Cornwell called himself a "Catholic agnostic," who did not believe in the soul as an immaterial substance.[99]

The importance of this information is that Cornwell claims to have spent six years researching Pius XII.[100] Since his book came out in 1999, that would mean that he started his research by 1993 at the latest. Thus, his claim to have been a practicing Catholic intending to defend the Church when he began his research is at odds with the evidence. The logical conclusion is that he concocted a story to add credibility to his work.

Cornwell claimed that the Vatican assisted him with his research for *Hitler's Pope* both because of his professed desire to defend Pius XII and because of his 1989 book, *A Thief in the Night*, which he says was favorable to the Holy See. David Yallop had written a book entitled *In God's Name*, which alleged that Pope John Paul I had been murdered by Vatican insiders. It is true that Cornwell rejected rumors of a papal-poisoning conspiracy in that book, but it was not friendly to the Vatican. Cornwell blamed the Pope's death on Vatican ineptness and infighting. He argued that no one properly cared for the Pope, and that he died alone in the heart of a cynical, uncaring power structure.[101]

George Weigel, Pope John Paul II's biographer, wrote that *A Thief in the Night* provided a "skewed picture" of the Holy See.[102] Cornwell himself wrote: "The Vatican expected me to prove that John Paul I had not been poisoned by one of their own, but the evidence led me to a conclusion that seems to me more shameful even, and more tragic, than any of the conspiracy theories."[103] In other words, it was not the kind of book that would win friends in high Vatican circles.

Perhaps more revealing about Cornwell's intent as he began this important project was the brief mention of Pope Pius XII in *A Thief in the Night*. On page 50, Cornwell mentioned the "alleged anti-Semitism" of Pius without offering any defensive comment. Then, on page 162, he mocked Pius, saying that he was "totally remote from experience, and yet all-powerful — a Roman emperor." He went on to call Pius an "emaciated, large-eyed demigod."[104] In a 1995 article in London's *Sunday Times*, Cornwell described Pius as a diplomat, a hypochondriac, and a ditherer.[105] The next year — *when by his own account he was supposedly working on his defense of Pius XII* — Cornwell wrote in the *New York Times* of "Pius XII's silence on Nazi atrocities" as an example of a failing by the Catholic Church.[106] In light of this evidence, his claim to have had nothing but the highest regard for Pius XII when he began his research for *Hitler's Pope* is "difficult to accept."[107]

None of this material concerning Cornwell's anti-Catholic background and prior hostility toward Pope Pius XII serves by itself to undermine Cornwell's research. It does, however, raise serious questions about his credibility in relation to the supposed time line. Many, many reviewers took Cornwell at his word about being out to defend the Pope but being left in a state of moral shock. In his next book after *Hitler's Pope*, Cornwell himself explained the importance of that claim: "[T]here is a world of difference between an authentic believing Catholic, writing critically from within, and a 'Catholic bashing' apostate who lies about being a Catholic in order to solicit an unwarranted hearing from the faithful." He claimed to have been in one camp, but the evidence suggests he was in the other.

––––––––

The last chapter of *Hitler's Pope* was entitled "Pius XII Redivivus." In it, Cornwell argued that John Paul II represented a return to a more highly centralized, autocratic papacy, as opposed to a more diversified Church. He wrote that there were early signs of a titanic struggle between the progressives and the traditionalists, with the potential for a cataclysmic schism, especially in North America. Cornwell felt that John Paul II was leading the traditionalists as the Church moved toward this struggle, and he argued that "canonization of Pius XII is a key move in the attempts to restore a reactionary papal absolutism."[108]

The often overlooked truth about *Hitler's Pope* is that it was not ultimately about Pope Pius XII. Cornwell saw the end of John Paul II's papacy coming, and he wrote a book arguing that John Paul had led the Church in a bad direction. Both John Paul and Pius XII were overly-authoritarian, in Cornwell's view, and as Pius XII's leadership led to the Holocaust, John Paul's leadership was leading to catastrophe. The only hope was to elect a very different kind of pope after John Paul.

Any doubt about Cornwell's intent was resolved in March 2000, at the time when Pope John Paul II made an unprecedented and historic trip to the Holy Land. At that time, as Christians and Jews were coming closer together, Cornwell described the Pontiff as "aging, ailing, and desperately frail as he presides over a Vatican that is riven by cliques, engulfed in scandal, and subject to ideological power struggles."[109] To Cornwell, the Vatican was "a nest of nepotism and corruption, sexual depravity, gangsterism, and even murder." Quoting an unidentified "Vatican insider," Cornwell described the Vatican as "a palace of gossipy eunuchs.... The whole place floats on a sea of bitchery."[110]

In his 2001 book, *Breaking Faith*, Cornwell made charges against Pope John Paul II similar to those that he made against Pius XII in *Hitler's Pope*. Cornwell argued that centralization of power under John Paul's authoritarian rule had brought about a fundamental breakdown in communications between hierarchy and laity. "Bullying oppression," Cornwell wrote, was driving people away from the Catholic Church. He blamed virtually all of the Church's modern problems on "the harsh centralized rules of Wojtyla's Church." He called John Paul a "stumbling block" for "a vast, marginalized faithful" and said that the Holy Father had "encouraged an oppressive intellectual culture." Cornwell warned that if a conservative Pope were to succeed John Paul II, the Church would "deteriorate" and push "greater numbers of Catholics toward antagonism, despair and mass apostasy."[111] It is safe to say that he was not at that time hoping for a Ratzinger papacy.

The 2004 book, *The Pontiff in Winter*, was Cornwell's final shot at Pope John Paul II. The full title of the American version of this book is *The Pontiff in Winter: Triumph and Conflict in the Reign of John Paul II*, but the British title is more telling as to Cornwell's intent: *The Pope in Winter: The Dark Face of John Paul II's Papacy*. In this book, Cornwell argued that John Paul had "taken a bit of the Iron Curtain with him" to the Vatican to mold a rigid, authoritarian papacy. Cornwell not only blamed John Paul for the spread of AIDS and global terrorism, but he also said that John Paul had developed a "medieval patriarchalism" toward women and that his "major and abiding legacy... is to be seen and felt in various forms of oppression and exclusion." Cornwell criticized the Pope's positions on the September 11 attacks, the clash between Islam and Christianity, and statements regarding Mel Gibson's motion picture *The Passion*. He charged that the Catholic teachings voiced by the Pontiff have "alienated generations of the faithful" and that "John Paul's successor will inherit a dysfunctional Church fraught with problems."[112]

Cornwell's clear intent was to prevent another orthodox Catholic from becoming pope.[113] His continuing theme was that the Church needed to decentralize its authority. Mainly, however, he advanced the typical laundry list of liberal Catholic demands, including married clergy, women priests, a bigger role for the laity in running the Church, and inclusive language in the Mass.[114] He complained about the Church's teachings on sexuality, particularly Pope Paul VI's encyclical *Humanae Vitae*, which prohibited artificial birth control. Cornwell argued that contraception, homosexuality, divorce, and essentially all extramarital sex are matters to be decided by consenting adults, and that the Church should change its teachings on these matters.[115]

---

At the same time that he lodged criticism from the Left, in *Breaking Faith* Cornwell also raised many of the objections against the Church that one usually hears only from critics on the Right. In fact, one fairly conservative American Catholic magazine, *Crisis*, gave him a friendly profile, noting that many of his objections were in line with complaints regularly made in that periodical.[116] Thus, Cornwell claimed to be concerned about "dumbed-down populism" and wrote negatively of overblown signs of peace, dancing girls at Mass, and a lack of reverence for the Holy Eucharist. He questioned modern music, the architecture of modern church buildings, and he criticized the number of annulments granted to divorced Catholics. Of his return to Catholicism after about twenty years as a lapsed Catholic, he wrote: "Mostly I was appalled at what I encountered. Something was badly wrong with the singing, the translations of the Latin rite, the manner of participation."[117]

When an entity is criticized from two different directions, one might assume that it is somewhere in the middle, probably doing a pretty good job. What, however, is one to make of an individual who criticizes the Catholic Church from both the Left and the Right at the same time? The only constant seems to be that each Pope since Pius XI (with the exception of John Paul I, who did not live long enough to offend Cornwell) is criticized. According to Cornwell, Pius XII — "Hitler's Pope" — was suspicious of democracy,[118] and he suppressed Catholic thinkers. John XXIII was an "archconservative when it came to seminary training." In fact, seminarians, including Cornwell, "could not wait" for the "better days to come" after John's papacy. Paul VI, of course, committed the ultimate sin of authoring *Humanae Vitae* and reasserting traditional Christian teaching against contraception. John Paul II took all types of authoritarian actions that were (according to Cornwell) destroying the Church. According to Cornwell, for Benedict XVI, "'ultra-reactionary' might be too tame an epithet."[119] Cornwell takes every opportunity that he can find to criticize the Catholic Church, regardless of inconsistencies in his argument.

Instead of consistent arguments, Cornwell reviewed opinion surveys suggesting that Catholics have difficulty with Church teachings on contraception, abortion, divorce, and homosexuality. He interpreted this as resistance to papal authority, and the only solution that made sense to him was to weaken the papacy and change the Church's teachings. That, however, is not the Catholic way. As historian Paul Johnson has written:

Catholicism is not a market-research religion. It is not in business to count heads or take votes.... Dogma and morals are not susceptible to guidance by opinion polls. The truth is paramount and it must be the naked truth, presented without cosmetics and exercises in public relations.... The Catholic Church has not survived and flourished over two millennia by being popular. It has survived because what it taught is true. The quest for popularity, as opposed to the quest for truth, is bound to fail.[120]

In contrast to Cornwell's warped approach to Catholicism, consider that of John Henry Newman, who was made a cardinal by Pope Leo XIII in 1879. "Newman would not have condemned any view more strongly than the one holding that opinion polls decide the truth. Nothing would have shocked him more than the thought that the faithful and not the Magisterium decide what is to be believed."[121] As Cardinal Ratzinger (Pope Benedict XVI) famously said: Truth is not determined by a majority vote.

Pope John Paul II, perhaps better than anyone else, recognized the parallels between his efforts and those of Pius XII.[122] John Paul, of course, did not have a horrible world war to contend with, nor was he threatened with the possibility of Vatican City being invaded; but given those differences, the approach each leader took was similar. As John Paul II explained: "Anyone who does not limit himself to cheap polemics knows very well what Pius XII thought of the Nazi regime and how much he did to help countless people persecuted by the regime."[123]

John Cornwell recognized divisions in the Catholic Church today and the similarities between Pius XII and John Paul II, but rather than trying to discuss them honestly, he picked a target that he thought would be easy to attack, created a far-fetched theory, and ignored all evidence to the contrary. Along the way, he revealed a basic misunderstanding of modern history. His books, which purport to be genuine scholarship, are unfortunately much less than that.

———

Saul Friedländer's book *Pius XII and the Third Reich*, published in 1966, was one of the early books critical of Pius XII. As other reviewers noted, Friedländer selectively used documents, eliminating those that were favorable to the Vatican:[124]

In his discussion of German-Vatican relations, Friedländer has omitted the vast majority of these representations [from the Vatican to the Germans] and has referred only to certain unsuccessful gestures by the Nuncio — an omission which conceals the range and extent of the interventions made by the Vatican throughout the years of Nazi persecution. He has also chosen to overlook the most significant of papal protests, which, despite his contention, are to be found in the sources he used. This arbitrariness in selection is matched by a bias in interpretation which extends even to the various editions of his book.[125]

Of Friedländer, Father Robert Graham wrote: "In my reasonably wide reading of professionally written history books, never have I found such massive uncritical use of primary sources, such wholesale arbitrary and ill-informed commentary, such carelessness in checking basic facts on which speculation is based, so many irrelevancies erected into significant events.... This book is not history but a very low level of political mythology."[126]

Despite this apparent unfairness, historians at the Congregation for the Causes of Saints largely forgave Friedländer for his transgressions. One footnote in the *Positio* says: "We should, however, be lenient with respect to the excess and lack of understanding shown by Saul Friedländer, an inexperienced author, using only very unilateral documentation, seeing that he has dedicated his work 'to the memory of my parents, killed at Auschwitz.'"[127]

Over the years, *Pius XII and the Third Reich* has received a good deal of unwarranted attention because it was supposedly endorsed by Cardinal Tisserant. Most readers seemed not to notice that the "endorsement" was nothing but a perfunctory letter of thanks for a copy of the book that Friedlander had sent to the cardinal. In fact, Tisserant's assistant, Monsignor Pedro Lopez-Gallo, recently told an interviewer that Tisserant didn't even read the book or write the letter of thanks. Lopez-Gallo wrote the perfunctory letter. Friedländer and his publishers exploited this "endorsement," reprinting it at the beginning of the book to give the book unwarranted credibility.[128]

---

Critic Susan Zuccotti researched parish archives throughout Italy. Time after time she found that Catholic bishops, priests, nuns, and laypersons fed, sheltered, and clothed Jewish refugees. She claimed, however, to find no evidence of papal help with this rescue work. When overwhelming oral evidence of papal support was pointed out to her, she rejected anything except contemporaneous written evidence. Not finding any, and assuming that the Vatican would have published any such documents if they existed, she assumed that there was no valid evidence of papal involvement in rescue efforts.[129] She was wrong.

Initially, it should be noted that Zuccotti's thesis is illegitimate. She builds her case not on evidence, but on a lack of evidence.[130] In doing this, she violates a Talmudic rule: "[N]ot to have seen is not yet a proof."[131] This has also been called "rule one" of archaeology: "Absence of evidence is not evidence of absence."[132] The same maxim applies to legal analysis.[133] No honest historian should make such an argument.

Holocaust denier (and close friend of Rolf Hochhuth) David Irving once offered a reward to anyone who could find a document linking Hitler to the extermination of Jews. Serious historians rightfully rejected his argument. A lack of existing written evidence is not sufficient to prove that Hitler lacked responsibility for the Holocaust. Everyone who arrested a Jew, informed on those who sheltered refugees, or helped run a concentration camp knew that Hitler approved of this work.[134] By the same token, everyone who helped rescue Jews knew that they were fulfilling the Pope's wishes. He inspired them. He encouraged them.[135]

Zuccotti frequently notes that Pope Pius XII *allowed* his underlings to carry out life-saving work on behalf of the Jews. For instance, on page 214 of *Under His Very Windows*, she reports: "He may not always have known the extent of the rescue work, but… [he] did not prohibit these activities." On page 188, she writes that "he allowed Benedetto's [rescue] activities to continue." On page 236, she informs the reader: "Pius XII did not prohibit [rescue operations in north Italy]." On page 299, one reads: "Pius XII and his advisors undoubtedly knew what Bernardini was doing, and approved." On page 243, she even goes further, saying that rescuers "may have been encouraged" by Pius XII's public statements or by articles about his work that appeared in local parish bulletins. Unfortunately, like Irving, she rejects overwhelming evidence simply because she could not find the written *order*. Zuccotti's theory is bad logic for a Holocaust denier, and it is bad logic for her.

One problem with her argument is that in order for it to be valid, the researcher must have scoured every potential source. Zuccotti assured her readers that she did just that, but subsequent discoveries have established that she did not find all the evidence.

In southern Italy, Giovanni Palatucci was known as "The Policeman Who Saved Thousands of Jews." He was named by Yad Vashem, Israel's Holocaust Martyrs' and Heroes' Remembrance Authority, as a "Righteous Gentile" for helping save five thousand Jewish lives. Palatucci worked in close collaboration with his uncle, Giuseppe Maria Palatucci, bishop of Campagna, a small town where the largest internment camp in southern Italy was located. In 1940, Bishop Palatucci received two letters from the Vatican.

The first letter, sent to the bishop on October 2, 1940, reported that Pope Pius XII had agreed to grant to him the sum of 3,000 lire. The letter, which was signed by Cardinal Maglione, Pius XII's secretary of state, stated: "This sum is preferably to be used to help those who suffer for reason of race" ("*questo denaro è preferibilmente destinato a chi soffre per ragioni di razza*"). The choice of language at this time and place in history was a clear reference to Jews.

In a second letter, the future Pope Paul VI, Giovanni Battista Montini, then an official in the Vatican's Secretariat of State, notified Bishop Palatucci that Pope Pius XII had granted him the sum of 10,000 lire "to distribute in support of the interned Jews" ("*da distribuirsi in sussidi agli ebrei internati*"). These two letters are very clear, and they completely contradict Zuccotti's thesis.[136]

Pacelli wrote a letter complaining about the Nazis as early as 1923. On November 14, 1923, he wrote to Cardinal Pietro Gasparri to report that "followers of Hitler and Ludendorff" were persecuting Catholics.[137] The attacks "were especially focused" on Cardinal Michael von Faulhaber, who was setting a good example because he "denounced the persecutions against the Jews."[138]

Similarly, on April 4, 1933, the Holy See sent a letter, signed by Secretary of State Pacelli, to Cesare Orsenigo, the nuncio in Germany. It said that some requests had come to the Pope asking for his "intervention against the danger of anti-Semitic excesses in Germany." The letter continued: "Given that it is part of the traditions of the Holy See to carry out its mission of universal peace and charity toward all men, regardless of the social or religious condition to which they belong, by offering, if necessary, its charitable offices, the Holy Father asks your Excellency to see if and how it is possible to be involved in the desired way."[139] As others have concluded: "The letter is of decisive value in the debate launched by those who say that Eugenio Pacelli, the future Pius XII, never spoke in favor of the Jews."[140]

In some cases, Zuccotti simply misconstrues the evidence. For instance, in *Under His Very Windows*, she gives considerable attention to a Jewish family's request for permission to stay in an Italian convent.[141] She discusses Montini's note of October 1, 1943, concerning this matter and his efforts on behalf of the Jewish family, but she says nothing of Pius XII's own involvement, which is confirmed by a notation at the bottom of that note (*Ex. Aud. SS.mi.* 1.X.43).[142] The abbreviation stands for "*Ex Audientia Sanctissimi*, 1 Oct. 1943," meaning that it was discussed with the Pope on that date.[143] The term "*Sanctissimi*" stands for His Holiness — in this case Pius XII.

In fact, below this indication that the matter was discussed with the Pope is a further notation: "*Si veda se possible aiutarlo.*" The phrase means roughly "See if he can be helped." Following the notation of the meeting with the Pope, this is an indication of his permission for the convent to admit a male Jew, despite a normal prohibition on men in the convent. Thus, this very document shows direct papal involvement in the sheltering of Jews even prior to the notorious roundup of October 16, 1943.[144] Again, one cannot overlook or fail to understand written exhibits like this and then build a legitimate case arguing that there is a lack of evidence.

––––––––

Several quotations in Zuccotti's book seem to have been truncated so as to eliminate any evidence that might show the Pope's concern for Jewish victims. For instance, pursuant to Pope Pius XII's request, Secretary of State Maglione met to lodge a protest with German Ambassador Weizsäcker after the infamous October 16, 1943, roundup of Jews.[145] Weizsäcker was known to be a friendly voice within the German leadership in Rome, and he was embarrassed about the Nazi treatment of the Jews.[146] Maglione began his memo about the meeting by writing:

> *Having learned that this morning the Germans made a raid on the Jews*, I asked the Ambassador of Germany to come to me and I asked him to try to intervene on behalf of these unfortunates. I talked to him as well as I could in the name of humanity, in Christian charity.
>
> *The Ambassador, who already knew of the arrests, but doubted whether it dealt specifically with the Jews, said to me in a sincere and moved voice: I am always expecting to be asked: Why do you remain in your position?*

Zuccotti deleted the italicized clauses above, thereby eliminating the cardinal's first two express references to the victims being Jewish. She also omitted the entire concluding paragraph, which recounted Maglione's last words to Weizsäcker:

> *In the meantime, I repeat: Your Excellency has told me that you [Weizsäcker] will attempt to do something for the unfortunate Jews. I thank you for that. As for the rest, I leave it to your judgement. If you think it is more opportune not to mention our conversation [to the German high command due to fear of retaliation], so be it.*[147]

So, even though Cardinal Maglione referred explicitly to "Jews" three times, Zuccotti's readers never saw those references; she deleted them.[148]

Similarly, Zuccotti quoted a report written by Nuncio Valerio Valeri to Cardinal Maglione, dated August 7, 1942. This memorandum related to the deportation of Jews from France to unknown areas, probably in Poland. In quoting the report, however, Zuccotti deleted the crucial first line of Valeri's report, where he mentions that he had used his position to *frequently* intervene for Jews in the name of the Pope.[149] This testimony, which would be hard to rebut, is simply omitted.

Zuccotti also quotes Cardinal Tisserant, claiming that in 1939 he questioned whether Eugenio Pacelli was strong enough to be Pope. She does not, however, mention that Tisserant later praised Pius XII's wartime conduct.[150] The full facts are that Cardinal Tisserant sent a private letter to Cardinal Emmanuel Suhard, the archbishop of Paris, in 1940 (two years before the infamous Wannsee conference, at which the Nazi leadership decided upon the "Final Solution" for the Jews), in which he wrote: "I fear that history will reproach the Holy See for having followed a policy of comfort and convenience, and not much else." The letter, never meant for public consumption, was seized by the Gestapo in Paris and later found in their archives. It was made public in 1964 during the debate over *The Deputy*. Tisserant immediately issued a statement unequivocally clarifying his remarks: "The pope's attitude was beyond discussion. My remarks did not involve his person, but *certain members of the Curia*. In the dramatic period of the War, and what a period that was, Pius XII was able to guide the Church with invincible strength."[151] He also told the *New York Times* the following: "It seems evident to me that the principles, reaffirmed by Pope Pacelli in his first encyclical, and repeated forcefully at every circumstance, above all in the Christmas messages of the war years, constitute the most concrete condemnation of the Hitlerian type of absolutism."[152] Robert Graham later interviewed Tisserant about the whole affair, and Tisserant admitted that he had written his 1940 letter in anger ("*ab irato*") and that it was perhaps even unfair to the people in the Curia whom he was criticizing. He underscored that it was written in 1940 when Pius could not "have dealt with the tragedy which was yet to unfold."[153]

Zuccotti tells us that French priest-rescuer Father Pierre-Marie Benoît received virtually no support from Rome, but he is on record as saying just the opposite. "Father Benoît spoke in glowing terms of the Holy Father. In fact on the occasion of the centenary of Eugenio Pacelli's birth, he sent a report which praised the various undertakings of the Pope on behalf of the Jews during the war."[154] Benoît noted that in a face-to-face meeting, Pius listened to his plan to save Jews with great attention and promised to take care of the matter personally. Pius XII's assistant, Robert Leiber, also reported that Pius gave a good deal of assistance to Benoît.[155]

Among the published documents, Zuccotti encountered irrefutable evidence that the Vatican provided money to help Father Benoît.[156] She said this was difficult to interpret and supposed that the amount must have been exceedingly sparse."[157] However, Fernande Leboucher, who worked with Father Benoît as perhaps his closest collaborator, wrote a book about their rescue work. She even called upon him for help in putting the book together.[158] Leboucher estimated that a total of some four million dollars was channeled from the Vatican to Benoît and his operation.[159] The evidence is certainly not as Zuccotti would have us believe.

Actually, the Nazis noted the coordinated efforts of Catholic officials in different areas and speculated that they were acting pursuant to a larger plan. A German Foreign Office agent named Frederic was sent on a tour through various Nazi-occupied and satellite countries during the war. He wrote in his confidential report to the German Foreign Office on September 19, 1943, that Metropolitan Archbishop Andrey Sheptytsky, of the Ukrainian Greek Catholic Church, remained adamant in saying that the killing of Jews was an inadmissible act. Frederic went on to comment that Sheptytsky made the same statements and used the same phrasing as the French, Belgian, and Dutch bishops, as if they were all receiving instructions from the Vatican.[160]

Zuccotti even mischaracterized Pius XII's first encyclical, *Summi Pontificatus*, saying that it "never mentioned Jews. Indeed, despite references to the unity of the human race, it seemed to single out Christians, or perhaps Catholics, for special consideration."[161] In fact, Pius did use the word "Jew" in the context of explaining that there is no room for racial distinctions in the Church.[162]

On April 16, 1943, the *Australian Jewish News* quoted Cardinal Gerlier as saying that he was obeying instructions from Pius XII by opposing France's anti-Semitic measures. Since that claim is not supported by a written order from Pius, however, it does not meet Zuccotti's demand for written documents. It should be noted, however, that she applies that standard quite inconsistently.

Even Zuccotti agrees that Catholic rescuers "invariably believed that they were acting according to the pope's will."[163] He encouraged, inspired, and authorized them to do what they could to help; but in conformity with the Catholic social doctrines of subsidiarity and solidarity,[164] details were usually left to be decided at the local level.[165] That is not to say, however, that Pius was uninvolved in rescue efforts.

Between 1967 and 1974, ninety-eight witnesses who personally knew Pope Pius XII gave sworn testimony, under oath, about his life.[166] This evidence, unlike published Vatican documents, focuses directly on Pope Pius XII's personal efforts on behalf of Jews and others. In other words, these transcripts contain exactly the type of evidence that Zuccotti was seeking, but she did not review them for her book.

No less than forty-two witnesses, including five cardinals, spoke directly of Pius XII's concern for and help given to Jewish people.[167] Some witnesses spoke of papal orders to open buildings. Others testified that Pius knew of and approved of sheltering Jews in Church buildings. The vice director of the Vatican newspaper testified that Pius personally opened Vatican buildings, and he authorized convents and monasteries to welcome outsiders. The clear message from each and every witness was that Pope Pius XII was honest, holy, and charitable.

It may be understandable that a researcher would not consult the deposition transcripts. They have not been translated or widely published. One cannot, however, legitimately overlook this most relevant testimony and then turn around and build a case based upon an alleged lack of evidence.

Pietro Cardinal Palazzini, then assistant vice rector of the Seminario Romano, hid Italian Jews there in 1943 and 1944. In 1985, Yad Vashem honored the cardinal as a Righteous Gentile. In accepting the honor, Palazzini stressed that "the merit is entirely Pius XII's, who ordered us to do whatever we could to save the Jews from persecution."[168] Palazzini also credited Pius for the "great work of charity" of sheltering anyone who needed refuge during the war.[169] In fact, Palazzini wrote: "Amidst the clash of arms, a voice could be heard — the voice of Pius XII. The assistance given to so many people could not have been possible without his moral support, which was much more than quiet consent."[170]

Paolo Cardinal Dezza, head of one of the institutions that sheltered Jews, quoted Pius as saying to him: "Avoid helping the military [who were sheltered at another Vatican institution, the Palazzo Callisto] ... but as for the others, help them willingly, especially help the poor, persecuted Jews."[171] Jewish historian Michael Tagliacozzo, head of the Center on Studies on the Shoah and Resistance in Italy and a survivor of the October 1943 roundup, told about how he was rescued from the Nazis and hidden in the Pope's building in Vatican City. He also said that Pius himself ordered the opening of convents and that Pius was the only person to intervene when the Nazis rounded up Roman Jews on October 16, 1943.[172]

Hungarian rescuer Tibor Baranski was honored by Yad Vashem as a Righteous Gentile for his rescue work in Hungary during World War II. As executive secretary of the Jewish Protection Movement of the Holy See, Baranski officially saved three thousand Jews. He worked closely with Angelo Rotta, papal nuncio in Hungary during the war (who was also recognized by Yad Vashem as a Righteous Gentile). Baranski made clear that these life-saving activities were not the lone actions of himself or Nuncio Rotta. "I was really acting in accordance with the orders of Pope Pius XII." He wrote that charges that Pius was not involved are "simple lies; nothing else," and claims that Pius should have done more for the Jews are "slanderous."

Baranski reported that he personally saw at least two letters from Pius XII instructing Rotta to do his very best to protect Jews but to refrain from making statements that might provoke the Nazis. He added: "These two letters were not written by the authorities at the Vatican, but they were hand-written ones by Pope Pius himself." He went on to note that "all other Nuncios of the Nazi-occupied countries received similar letters." Italian Jews, for instance, were sheltered in monasteries, seminaries, and other Church buildings on the "direct instruction of the Vatican."

Baranski explained that for Pius, the first and foremost concern was saving human lives. "It was precisely because [Pius] wanted to help the Jews" that he refrained from making repeated public condemnations. Pius "intervened in a very balanced way," trying to save lives without provoking retaliation. He did not, however, behave differently depending upon the status of the victims. Baranski noted that these same concerns prevented the Pope from making repeated public appeals when the Nazis killed thousands of Catholic priests.

"The Pontiff did not only encourage the Nuncio to protect Vatican [baptized] Jews," explained Baranski, "but as many persecuted persons as possible, in the ghetto or elsewhere." The nuncio kept Pius well informed of efforts undertaken in collaboration with other embassies, including close work with Swedish diplomat and rescuer Raoul Wallenberg, who also was declared a Righteous Gentile by Yad Vashem.

Baranski, who reported that he was "fantastically near" to Wallenberg, argued that were he alive today, Wallenberg would defend Pope Pius XII and commend the Catholic Church for its work in collaboration with him: "Look, there was no problem or disagreement whatsoever between the Catholic Church and Wallenberg. I personally arranged unofficial, private meetings between Wallenberg and Nuncio Rotta." Baranski reported that Wallenberg "knew Pius was on his side." Rotta, Baranski, Wallenberg, and — yes — Pius XII worked together as a team. Baranski believed that, like the others, Pius XII should be honored at a Righteous Gentile.[173]

Another witness to Pius XII's orders to help Jews was Righteous Gentile Don Aldo Brunacci. Zuccotti spoke to him as part of her research. He told her that the Vatican sent a letter instructing Catholics to assist Jews during the Nazi occupation of Italy, but she discounted his testimony because he did not read the letter of instruction that came from the Vatican; it was read to him by Bishop Giuseppe Nicolini of Assisi. Brunacci, interviewed after Zuccotti's book was published, disputed her analysis:

Q. In her book... Susan Zuccotti, who says that she interviewed you, maintains that you never actually saw the text of the letter from the Vatican to Bishop Nicolini.

BRUNACCI: Ah, Zuccotti! Yes, I did speak with her. What should I say? It is true, I did not make a photocopy of the text.

**Q.** Did you actually see the letter?

**BRUNACCI:** I did not actually see the text of the letter, but look, I was alone with the bishop in the room, he held the letter up and showed it to me. He said he had received the letter from Rome, and he read what it said — that the Holy Father wanted us to see to it in our diocese that something would be done to ensure the safety of the Jews — and the bishop wanted to consult with me on what to do.

**Q.** So you never actually read the letter?

**BRUNACCI:** No, the bishop read the letter to me.

**Q.** Then, as Zuccotti suggests in her book, it might be possible that the letter was not what Bishop Nicolini told you it was, that he was in some way deceiving you?

**BRUNACCI:** (Laughs) Impossible, impossible. (Laughs again) It is not possible that Bishop Nicolini was deceiving me. I am certain of that. Look, we were alone in the room and he read the letter to me. It was clearly from the Vatican, there is no doubt of that. Not from the Pope himself, personally, but from the Secretariat of State.

It was a letter asking the bishop to do all he could to help the Jews, and the bishop wanted me to advise him on the best way to carry out that request. In fact, this same order went out to many other dioceses in Italy....

The work of Pope Pius XII was a majestic work, a work of deeds, not of words. Zuccotti doubts that Pius XII could have issued such an order because she is persuaded by the campaign launched against Pius in 1963. But that campaign has been filled with slanders and calumnies. Still, Signora Zuccotti is persuaded by it, and so cannot accept that this letter was sent out, and she has to invent the story that the bishop deceived me to explain it away. But the letter was sent out. I saw it with my own eyes, in my bishop's hands, as he read it to me. It was a letter from the Vatican asking the bishop to take measures to help protect the Jews. And we took the measures.

Don't take Zuccotti too seriously....[174]

Italian Senator Adriano Ossicini, founder of the Italian "Christian Left,"[175] and Sister Maria Corsetti Ferdininda[176] both told similar stories. In her book *Yours Is a Precious Witness*, Sister Margherita Marchione wrote that in interview after interview she was told that "at the request of Pope Pius XII, doors of convents and monasteries were opened to save the Jews when the Nazis occupied Italy."[177]

It was long known that one thousand German Jews wanted to emigrate to Brazil, and the Pontiff paid out of his own pocket the $800 each needed for the trip. Recently discovered Vatican documents now show that Pacelli, as secretary of state, feverishly tried to arrange for the evacuation of three thousand Jews ("non-Aryans") to Brazil and to get reductions in the price charged to the Jews.[178] In 1939, he organized special operations inside the Vatican Information Office to help Jews persecuted by Nazism.

Author Antonio Gaspari recounted several instances of Pius XII intervening in his personal capacity, through the Vatican state secretariat, to save Jews.[179] Regarding Zuccotti's thesis that Catholic rescue activity took place without papal support, Gaspari expressly said: "This is a thesis that is impossible to defend."[180]

So how does Zuccotti argue that Pope Pius XII had no role in rescue efforts, when so many witnesses testified that he did? The answer is that — time and time again — she discounts or dismisses the testimony of people who were there. In so doing, she denies the legitimacy of the gratitude of the Jewish victims and denies "the credibility of their personal testimony and judgement about the Holocaust itself."[181]

On page 264, she discusses a bishop who claimed to have been holding a letter from Pius in his hands, but she suggests that the bishop falsified this claim because he "may have considered it useful to make his assistants believe that they were doing the Pope's work."

On page 193, Zuccotti suggests that nuns who credited the Pope for having ordered their convents opened to Jewish refugees were "eager that Pius XII receive credit for the work of their order." (She does, however, concede that Pius probably knew these nuns were sheltering Jews.)

On page 143, she discusses a letter from A. L. Eastman, of the World Jewish Congress, thanking the Pope for helping free imprisoned Jews. Zuccotti, however, dismisses this testimony by saying, "Eastman must have known better."

On page 103, she quotes the papal nuncio in Vichy, praising Pope Pius XII for condemning the persecution of Jews and others. Zuccotti accuses him of fabricating the papal responses.

On page 301, she discusses gratitude from Jewish people to the Pope following the war. She attributes their attitude to "benevolent ignorance."[182]

On page 302, in an even more disturbing analysis, she suggests that Jewish chaplains simply lied because they were "anxious to protect and preserve the fragile goodwill between Jews and non-Jews that seems to be emerging from the rubble of the war in Italy."

At other points along the way, she dismisses letters of thanks from Jewish people because "[t]he Holy See had done nothing more for the Jewish Internees than for non-Jews" (p. 85). Favorable accounts of the Pope's efforts to help Jews are dismissed as "less than honest" (p. 272). Testimony from the future Pope Paul VI is dismissed because, according to Zuccotti, he "knew perfectly well" that his statement was wrong (p. 169).[183]

Zuccotti does not show a lack of papal involvement in rescue efforts. All she shows is that she does not believe the limited amount of evidence that she has reviewed.[184] She also engages in unfair and selective analysis of the evidence:

It simply will not do for the beneficiaries of freedom to come after the event and either to disregard the ambiguities and veiled communications or to pick out one of the meanings of a deliberately ambiguous utterance and that *not* the one meant to be conveyed (with as much benefit and immunity as possible in the circumstances) at the time of the transaction, but one that fits a later case. Much of the conflict about the church has been of that kind. People have picked out not only the documents but parts of documents, even parts of meanings of single sentences or of words that suited them.[185]

At the end of the day, we have Zuccotti on one side arguing that there is no evidence of papal involvement. On the other side, we have a mountain of testimony from rescuers, victims, Germans, Jews, priests, nuns, the *New York Times* (and other papers), seven cardinals, and two popes. We also now have the written, archival confirmation of papal involvement in the rescue of Jews that Zuccotti thought did not exist. In other words, the evidence all weighs in favor of Pope Pius XII. To ignore that evidence is to deny history. With this subject, that is a very dangerous thing to do.[186]

––––––––

Some critics have focused on one incident that took place with the liberation of Rome. Just before the liberation, the British minister to the Vatican, Francis D'Arcy Osborne, cabled to England that "the pope hoped that no allied coloured troops would be among the small number that might be garrisoned at Rome after the occupation."[187] Not surprisingly, some have taken this as evidence that the Pope was a racist.[188]

Actually, the Pope's concern was not about "coloured troops," but specific French Moroccan troops who were known to have committed horrible acts of violence in areas where they were stationed.[189] As Bishop of Rome, Pius did not want those soldiers stationed in his city (or anywhere else).[190] Pius expressed his concerns about these specific men (he spoke of "*Marocchini*," not "colored troops") to Osborne, who broadened the statement in his cable back to London, perhaps in order to avoid insulting French allies.

That the Pope was concerned about specific French Moroccan troops is made clear in a now-declassified confidential memorandum from the Office of Stategic Services, Washington, DC,[191] an article that appeared in *L'Osservatore Romano* on October 4, 1944,[192] and a message sent from the Vatican to its representative in France.[193] None of these documents make reference to race, just the Pope's concern over these specific French Moroccan troops. The lack of any other records relating to the request confirm that this was not a racial matter, especially when considered in light of the Pontiff's other statements, actions, and appointments of minority bishops.

The S.S. journal, *Das Schwarze Korps*, published an article arguing that it was a crime against nature to permit black soldiers to fight against white races. It attacked the French for "following the creed of the Vatican, believing that baptism can transform the soul of a man." Vatican Radio replied:

(a) That it is sufficient for a black man to be a human being in order to be able to claim a human soul and human dignity. The black race has proved... that it has been able to fill the gap between the primitive state and civilization. Black men have given proof that they can be a real asset to human culture.

(b) The allegation that it is a crime to allow colored people to fight against the white race reminds us that Germany made Negroes fight during the last war in East Africa.

(c) The movement of the black peoples towards the Catholic Church is becoming very considerable. There are at present over seven million black persons who have embraced the Catholic Faith, and they are among its most valuable members. According to the statement of a well-known missionary... the deep faith and high morals he found in Africa are beyond comparison."[194]

In paragraphs 45-50, of his first encyclical, *Summi Pontificatus* (On the Unity of Human Society), Pius XII dealt with racial matters and expressed his belief that the Church could not discriminate against any given race of people. He expressly stated that all races and nationalities were welcome in the Church and had equal rights as children in the house of the Lord. In paragraph 48, he put meaning to his anti-racist statements by naming new bishops of different races and nationalities. Two weeks later, in *Sertum Laetitiae* (on the 150th anniversary of the establishment of the hierarchy in the United States), Pius wrote of a "special paternal affection" for black Americans.

Shortly after World War II, the pastor of Holy Angels Church in Indianapolis assured his congregation that "no Negro will ever come to Holy Angels." When word of this made its way to Rome, Pope Pius XII immediately had the pastor removed.[195] About this same time (May 27, 1946), Pius addressed the American Negro Publishers Association on the importance of interracial justice and brotherhood.[196]

Against all of this and more, the critics cite only a secondary source that, by all of the best evidence, misreports the Pope's actual request. Once again, a fair analysis of the evidence suggests that the critics are far too willing to accept bad evidence when it meets with their preconceived notions.

———

Guenter Lewy was one of the first authors to write critically about Pope Pius XII. His work has been often cited by modern critics of the Pope. For instance, despite her insistence on original sources, Susan Zuccotti's only source for the old canard holding that Pius XII was unwilling to speak out against the Nazis because this would create a "conflict of conscience" for the German soldiers is Lewy. There is no document to back this story up, and no one who has spent any time trying to know Pope Pius XII can believe that this was a significant influence upon him.[197]

The story according to Lewy is that a correspondent for the *Vatican* newspaper in Berlin, Eduardo Senatra, at a public discussion in Berlin in 1964, said that Pius had told him this.[198] The problem is that Senatra was not from the Vatican newspaper, but from a *Fascist* newspaper. He had no particular relationship with Pope Pius. Senatra, who never made such a claim in his own newspaper, later wrote a letter correcting statements attributed to him at that 1964 occasion. Nevertheless, and despite the lack of *any* supporting documents, this unbelievable story is repeatedly told by those who want to present the worst possible portrait of Pope Pius XII and the Catholic Church.[199]

Lewy, like some critics who followed him, used quotations very selectively. For instance, he quoted the German theologian, historian, and sociologist Ernst Troeltsch (1865-1923) in attempting to explain the Catholic Church's role in society. Lewy wrote: "To use the sociological categories of Ernst Troeltsch, Catholicism is an example of 'that type of organization which is overwhelmingly conservative... it becomes an existing part of the existing order,... [and which knows to attain her end] by a process of adaption and compromise.'"[200] The ellipses and bracket commentary are provided by Lewy. In fact, the second ellipsis covers *eight pages* of Troeltsch's writings![201]

Beate Ruhm von Oppen, writing on this bit of journalistic sleight of hand, explained that if one were to reject the very notion of sacraments (which, of course, would mean rejection of Catholicism), one might go on to make Lewy's argument that the Church has, at times, "retreated behind the cloister walls, and instead of being the salt of the earth has become the force tragically upholding injustice and tyranny."[202] Von Oppen goes on to note, however, that "one cannot use Troelsch for that argument," as Lewy attempted to do with the misleading quotation.[203]

––––––

In the 1960s, Italian writer Carlo Falconi wrote his book *The Silence of Pius XII.*[204] Although the title does not reveal it, Falconi's book is completely centered on Croatia and communications between that nation and the Holy See. In fact, the title of each and every chapter in the book relates to Croatia.[205] In his foreword, Falconi explains that the "central core of the Croatian documents" that had been provided to him "brought to light an entirely new and unsuspected harvest of revelations on the men and the mysterious world" of high Vatican officials. His book was highly critical of Pope Pius XII. Of course, he had no way to know that he was not looking at legitimate documents, but at postwar disinformation.[206]

At the beginning of the Second World War, the area now known as Croatia was part of Yugoslavia. In March 1941, Yugoslavia formally threw in with the Axis side. Two days later, Serbian nationalists seized control of Belgrade and announced that they were siding with the Allies. As a result, Hitler invaded

Yugoslavia and gave his support to Croatian nationalists who declared an independent Croatia.[207] The new Croatian government was led by Ante Pavelić and his Nazi-like party, the Ustashe (also sometimes written as Ustaši or Ustacha).[208] Their brutality shocked even the Nazis.

The leader of the Roman Catholic Church in Croatia at that time was Archbishop (later Cardinal) Aloysius Stepinac. Others have noted that when the brutality began, Stepinac "almost immediately… used his position to speak out against the maltreatment of Jews and Orthodox Christians."[209] He also conducted extensive relief work, including hiding refugees in Church buildings. Stepinac was recognized as a staunch opponent of Fascist leaders, but after the war, he was a threat to the Communist regime that took over. Communist leader Josip Broz Tito put Stepinac on trial, and he was convicted of having supported the Ustashe government's brutality toward Serbs and of having engaged in forcible conversions.[210]

During Stepinac's trial, the prosecution produced a report allegedly sent by the archbishop to the Pope dated May 18, 1943. It bitterly condemned the Serbs and the Orthodox Church. It also showed Stepinac to have been working for the Ustashe and calling on the Pope to arrange for foreign intervention in Yugoslavia.[211] Stepinac denied having written or sent this letter.[212] It was not written on diocesan paper, and it did not have an address or signature. It was in Italian, instead of the formalized Latin style normally used by the archbishop. It referred to Stepinac as "*Metropoleta de Croatiae et Slovoniae*," but Stepinac never referred to himself that way. It contained detailed information about Bosnia and its history, which Stepinac was unlikely to know, especially as Bosnia was not part of his diocese.[213] The Communists claimed that the letter was found in the Croatian Foreign Ministry offices, but Stepinac did not send his reports there. (If he had actually sent such a report there, he would have had the opportunity to remove it before the Communists would have found it.) The prosecutor claimed to have a copy signed by Stepinac, but he never produced it at trial, and it does not appear in the record of court documents.[214]

In December 1941, copies of another letter, this one signed by Dr. Prvislav Grisogono, a well-known Catholic and a respected Croatian politician, came into circulation. It was addressed to Stepinac, and it condemned the Church for permitting priests and monks to kill and torture thousands of Serbs. The writer condemned the sending of nuns, "with a dagger in one hand and a prayer book in the other," to convert the survivors. The letter provided alleged details of priest-led gangs of thugs, of jars of Serbian eyes, strings of tongues, and more. A Serb in the Yugoslav government in London ordered the letter to be broadcast from the Middle East over "Radio Karageorge" to Yugoslavia.[215]

Although this letter was reprinted in many books after the war, it was a forgery. Grisogono, the supposed author, was in the Gestapo prison at Banjica, near Belgrade, at the time that the letter was supposedly written. On his release from prison, Grisogono wrote to Stepinac to disown the letter.[216] After the war, Grisogono's son and daughter also confirmed that the letter was a forgery. The son and daughter of another man, Adam Pribićević, acknowledged that their father had forged the letter. The father's political assistant, Vlastimir Stojanović, confirmed their story.[217]

In 1985, Stepinac's prosecutor, Jakov Blažević, acknowledged that Stepinac had been framed and that he was tried only because he refused to sever ties between Croatians and the Roman Catholic Church.[218] Blažević said that if Stepinac had agreed to head an independent Catholic Church, he would not have been brought to court.[219]

In 1992, Croatia came out from under the thumb of Communism. One of the first acts of Parliament in the newly independent state of Croatia was to issue a declaration condemning "the political trial and sentence passed on Cardinal Aloysius Stepinac in 1946."[220] Stepinac was condemned, declared the Parliament, "because he had acted against the violence and crimes of the communist authorities, just as he had acted during the whirlwind of atrocities committed in World War II, to protect the persecuted, regardless of the national origin or religious denomination."[221]

Nearly forty years after the trial, one of Tito's senior legal officials by the name of Hrnčević, who had put together the original case against Stepinac and arranged the trial, stated: "The indictments were designed rather more for publicity than for legality."[222] Yugoslavian political dissident Milovan Đilas, who had once been close to Tito, said that the problem with "Stepinac was not his policy towards Ustashe, but towards the Communists."[223]

In the 1960s, however, when the Communists were still in control of Croatia, Falconi sought permission from the Yugoslav authorities to conduct research in Croatian archives for a book that he was writing on Pope Pius XII. Many researchers were looking for evidence of what Pius did or did not do, and evidence that had been tested at trial had a certain air of authenticity and importance. It would be most helpful to historical analysis.

Falconi's request to review the court documents left Communist Party officials in a quandary. If they gave Falconi access to the archives, he would be able to see how the evidence had been manufactured and the documents had been altered. On the other hand, refusing to provide any evidence would look suspicious and they would be passing up a chance to spread more disinformation.

The officials eventually decided to give Falconi *some* of the original documents and to provide him with a copy of a book that they had produced for Stepinac's trial containing handpicked and altered documents.[224] The documents, like the book, were forged or "selected and edited in order to do as much damage as possible to the image of the Catholic Church."[225] Falconi was not given access to original materials or archives that could have revealed the truth. Thus, he wrote his book based upon documents "partly forged and all carefully selected to support the government's accusations against Stepinac and the Church."[226]

Falconi's book was extremely successful. It was highly footnoted, and it quoted many documents and shaped much of the early scholarship on Pope

Pius XII. It remains much cited to this day. John Cornwell's *Hitler's Pope* made extensive use of the materials Falconi had used. In fact, Cornwell cited Falconi by name nine times, and he praised Falconi's "painstaking" research.[227] Falconi and the works that built upon his book have tainted the entire investigation into Pope Pius XII. As Croatian scholar Jure Krišto has explained: "The documents which both men [Falconi and Cornwell] used had, of course, been assembled by the Yugoslav secret police, then led by the Serbian Communist Aleksandar Ranković, and fed to Falconi in order to compromise Pope Pius XII as 'Hitler's Pope.'"[228] These documents have confounded scholars of Pope Pius XII for decades.[229]

———

Some critics — including Susan Zuccotti, Michael Phayer, John Cornwell, and Daniel Goldhagen — claim that even after the liberation of Rome, Pius remained "silent" about Jews and anti-Semitism. In making this argument, they ignore or dismiss not only several of Pope Pius XII's later statements, but also earlier Vatican condemnations of anti-Semitism that were issued in 1916,[230] 1928,[231] 1930,[232] 1938,[233] 1942,[234] and 1943.[235] In fact, Pius made several statements in support of the Jews.[236]

One statement was originally reported on April 28, 1944, in the *Palestine Post* (now, the *Jerusalem Post*), the most influential Jewish publication in the world at that time. The article said that the author, an anonymous Jewish man, attended a papal audience in the autumn of 1941. He entered the papal chamber along with numerous other people, including a group of German soldiers. The author was the final individual to approach the Pope that day. He wanted to tell Pius about a group of Jews who were being interned by Italy's Fascist government on an island and were in danger of starvation. Pius listened intently then said: "You have done well to come to me and tell me this. I have heard about it before. Come back tomorrow with a written report and give it to the Secretary of State who is dealing with the question. But now for you, my son, you are a young Jew. I know what that means, and I hope you will always be proud to be a Jew!" Pius then raised his voice so that everyone in the hall could hear it and said: "My son, whether you are worthier than others only the Lord knows, but believe me, you are at least as worthy as every other human being that lives on our earth! And now, my Jewish friend, go with the protection of the Lord, and never forget, you must always be proud to be a Jew!"

As cited earlier, upon the liberation of Rome in 1944, Pius made one of his most fervent pleas for tolerance. "For centuries," he said, referring to the Jews, "they have been most unjustly treated and despised. It is time they were treated with justice and humanity. God wills it and the Church wills it. St. Paul tells us that the Jews are our brothers. Instead of being treated as strangers they should be welcomed as friends."[237] The following year, to an audience in St. Peter's Square, Pius gave a warning to those who had sympathized with Nazi brutality:

To those who allowed themselves to be seduced by apostles of violence, who are now beginning to waken from their illusions, shocked to see where their servility has led them, there remains no way of salvation but to forswear once and for all the idolatry of absolute nationalism, the pride of race and blood, the lust for mastery in the possession of the world's goods, and to turn resolutely to a spirit of sincere brotherhood, founded on the worship of the divine Father of all men.[238]

In a major address to the College of Cardinals on June 2, 1945, Pius XII called National Socialism "a conception of state activity that took no account of the most sacred feelings of humanity and trod underfoot the inviolable principles of the Christian faith."[239] He spoke of the "satanic specter of Nazism" and of the background and impact of the anti-Nazi encyclical, *Mit brennender Sorge*:

In these critical years, joining the alert vigilance of a pastor in the long-suffering patience of a father, our great predecessor, Pius XI, fulfilled his mission as Supreme Pontiff with intrepid courage. But when, after he had tried all means of persuasion in vain... he proclaimed to the world on Passion Sunday, 1937, in his encyclical *Mit brennender Sorge* what National Socialism really was: "the arrogant apostasy from Jesus Christ, the denial of His doctrine and of His work of redemption, the cult of violence, the idolatry of race and blood, the overthrow of human liberty and dignity."[240]

As for his own efforts, the Pope explained:

Continuing the work of Our Predecessor, We never ceased during the war (especially in broadcast messages) to oppose Nazi doctrine and practice the unshakable laws of humanity and Christian faith. This was for Us the most suitable, We may even say the only effective, way of proclaiming in the sight of the world the unchanging principles of the moral law among so much error and violence, to confirm the minds and hearts of German Catholics in the higher ideals of truth and justice. Nor was it without effect. We know in fact that Our broadcasts, especially that of Christmas 1942, were in spite of every prohibition and obstacle studied by diocesan conferences and expounded to the people.[241]

On November 29, 1945, a group of Jewish refugees returning from captivity came to the Vatican as an expression of gratitude for the way the Church's charity had transcended egoism and racial passion. In an audience that he granted to them, Pius spoke of "the brotherhood of man":

Your presence, gentlemen, is an eloquent reflection on the psychological changes, the new directions that the war has brought to maturity. The gulfs of discord and hate, the folly of persecution, which were created among peoples and races by false and intolerant doctrines, opposed to human and Christian spirit, have devoured many innocent victims, including non-combatants. The Apostolic See, faithful to the principles of natural right inscribed by God in every human heart, revealed on Sinai and perfected by the Sermon on the Mount, has never left in doubt at any moment however critical that it repudiated those ideas which history will list among the most deplorable and dishonorable travesties of human thought and feeling.[242]

Pius explained: "[T]he Church, remembering her religious mission, must maintain a wise reserve about particular questions of political and territorial character. But this does not prevent her proclaiming the great principles of humanity and brotherhood which must underlie the solutions of such questions."[243] The Pope went on to note that "In your own persons you have felt the evil and harm of hatred, but in the midst of your trials you have also experienced and benefited from the consolation of love — that love which does not draw its inspiration and nourishment from earthly sources, but from a profound faith in the eternal Father Whose sun shines upon all of every tongue and race. . . ."[244]

Pius named many new cardinals after the war, expanding the College of Cardinals from thirty-eight to seventy, and transforming the College of Cardinals into a "more truly international body."[245] Italian cardinals were outnumbered for the first time in recent history.[246] Many of the nominees were also vigorous opponents of the Nazis. The *New York Times* reported:

> The three new German Cardinals were all outspoken critics of the Nazi regime. The outstanding nominee in France is the venerable Archbishop Saliège of Toulouse, noted for his defiance of the Germans and the collaborationists. Archbishop Sapieha of Cracow is a courageous patriot who shared all the suffering of his people. Archbishop Mindszenty of Hungary was a prisoner of the Nazis.[247]

Pius XII's comment was: "This Church does not belong to one race or to one nation, but to all peoples."[248]

On August 3, 1946, Pius said the following to a delegation of Palestinian Arabs: "There can be no doubt that peace can only come about in truth and justice. This presupposes respect for the rights of others and for certain vested positions and traditions, especially in the religious sphere, as well as the scrupulous fulfillment of the duties and obligations to which all inhabitants are subject." He continued:

> That is why, having received again during these last days numerous appeals and claims, from various parts of the world and from various motives, it is unnecessary to tell you that We condemn all recourse to force and to violence, from wherever it may come, as also We have condemned on several occasions in the past the persecutions which a fanatical anti-Semitism unleashed against the Jewish people.[249]

Pius condemned racism until the end of his life. In June 1957, he received a delegation from the American Jewish Committee. There was a great deal of concern at that time about anti-Semitism and persecution of Jews in Communist nations. A July 2 memo to Chapter and Unit Chairmen of the American Jewish Committee reported on the Pope's words:

> Pope Pius XII, in a private audience granted June 28th to your AJC delegation led by Irving M. Engel, issued a most important statement condemning racial and religious persecution. The Pontiff urged governments to offer asylum to such refugees. The significance of this plea — coming from the supreme spiritual leader of the world's 484,000,000 Catholics — is apparent.[250]

The Committee's representatives described the Pope as a "great friend" in the battle against racism and anti-Semitism in the United States. They later (July 23) drafted a memo suggesting that this statement be used as the basis of a television show. The memo said, in part:

> The Vatican during the reign of Pope Pius XII has on a number of occasions demonstrated concern with discrimination against minorities, and was conspicuous in the efforts to save many Jewish victims from Nazi persecution. Because of this known sympathy on the part of His Holiness, the American Jewish Committee felt that a declaration by the Pope at this time, condemning all forms of bigotry and anti-Semitism and asking for asylum for refugees from persecution, would be both timely and effective.[251]

They concluded by saying that "the historic declaration" was "received with profound gratitude by us. This important step is but another indication of the deep concern of the Vatican for the dispossessed, the afflicted and the persecuted." The Pope, in turn, praised the committee's work.[252]

A decade earlier, on August 26, 1947, Pius wrote a letter to the president of the United States, Harry Truman. The Pope explained:

> Social injustices, racial injustices and religious animosities exist today among men and groups who boast of Christian civilization, and they are a very useful, and often effective weapon in the hands of those who are bent on destroying all the good which that civilization has brought to man. It is for all sincere lovers of the great human family to unite in wresting those weapons from hostile hands. With that union will come hope that the enemies of God and free men will not prevail. Certainly Your Excellency and all defenders of the rights of the human person will find wholehearted co-operation from God's Church.[253]

Shortly after the war, Catholic philosopher Jacques Maritain, who is sometimes presented as a critic of Pius XII's wartime policy, wrote a letter to Monsignor Montini on the need for the Church to address the issue of postwar anti-Semitism. In a key part of the letter, Maritain (whose wife was a Jewish convert to Catholicism) went out of his way to praise "the tireless charity with which the Holy Father has tried with all his might to save and protect the persecuted," and he praised Pius XII's "condemnations against racism that have won for him the gratitude of Jews and all those who care for the human race." Maritain hailed the Pope's wartime diplomacy on behalf of persecuted Jews, recognizing that it was founded upon "very good reasons, and in the interests of a higher good, and in order not to make persecution even worse, and not to create insurmountable obstacles in the way of the rescue that he [Pius XII] was pursuing."[254]

In a related matter, Susan Zuccotti claims that there was a great deal of criticism of Pius XII during and after the war. Almost no one else sees it that way. Historian Peter Novick wrote: "As far as I know, the only comment on Pius's silence during the Holocaust that was made at the time of his death came from a writer for the French Communist newspaper *L'Humanité*"[255] There is simply no legitimate excuse for ignoring the evidence the way that modern papal critics have done.

———

Daniel Goldhagen seems to want nothing less than a renunciation of Christianity. In *A Moral Reckoning*, he accuses Pope Pius XII of collaborating with the Nazis, and like fellow critic James Carroll he treats the cross as a symbol of oppression. He lectures about how portions of the New Testament were fabricated and asserts that the very term "New Testament" is offensive.[256] Echoing the notorious anti-Catholic fundamentalist, Dave Hunt,[257] Goldhagen writes that the Catholic Church's claim to be the people of God is the source of ideological anti-Semitism. His agenda-driven approach, coupled with sloppy fact-checking and poor analysis, results in one of the most unjust broadside attacks launched against Christianity in several generations.[258]

One of Goldhagen's main assertions was that the guilt of *all* Jews for the Crucifixion was a "central Catholic doctrine" — and that during the 1940s, teaching it was "official Catholic Church doctrine." He provided no evidence for this serious charge, nor could he. The *Catechism of the Council of Trent*, published in 1566 and approved by many popes thereafter, was the authoritative statement of Catholic doctrine during the Nazi period. It provided that: "*All sinners* were the authors of Christ's Passion" (emphasis added).

Goldhagen and similar critics focus on those passages of the New Testament that *can* be misunderstood. For instance, they cite the Gospel of John, chapter 8. Here Jesus instructs people to reject Satan and follow him to the Father. "If you continue in my word, you are truly my disciples, and you will know the truth, and the truth will make you free" (Jn 8:31-32). Of those who reject him, however, Christ says:

> You are of your father the devil, and your will is to do your father's desires. He was a murderer from the beginning, and has nothing to do with the truth, because there is no truth in him. When he lies, he speaks according to his own nature, for he is a liar and the father of lies. But, because I tell the truth, you do not believe me. (Jn 8:44-45)

Goldhagen argues that these words are anti-Semitic because Jesus is calling Jews the "children of the devil."[259]

The Gospel says that Jesus was talking to a group of Jews, but that — in context — is like saying he was talking to any group of people who were not his followers.[260] After all, Jesus was born into a Jewish family. His mother was Jewish. His early followers were all Jewish, and the people who first heard him were Jewish. At his triumphal entry into Jerusalem, the crowds thronging around him were made up almost exclusively of Jews.[261] In John, chapter 8, he was trying to convince a group of those people to follow him. *Jesus's words, as recorded in Scripture, were not anti-Semitic!*[262]

Critics are also concerned about Matthew's Gospel, chapter 27, where Jesus is handed over to the Roman authorities, ultimately to face crucifixion. Pontius Pilate offers to free one of the "criminals," and the crowd calls for Barabbas. As Matthew reports:

> So when Pilate saw that he was gaining nothing, but rather that a riot was beginning, he took water and washed his hands before the crowd, saying, "I am innocent of this righteous man's blood; see to it yourselves." And all the people answered, "His blood be on us and on our children!" (Mt 27:24-25)[263]

Goldhagen argues that Matthew here falsely attributes blame for the Crucifixion to all Jews for all times, that this instilled a hatred of Jews into the European psyche, and that Hitler merely had to exploit this pre-existing attitude to his own perverted ends.

The Catholic Church, of course, does not read Matthew or John the way that the critics suggest. A popular Catholic educational book published in 1903 tells the story of Pope Pius IX coming upon an unconscious Jewish man, giving him a ride home, and later sending his personal physician to care for the man. This illustrates the lesson that "It is unworthy of a Christian to refuse aid to any one because he is of a different creed or nationality."[264]

At the Second Vatican Council, the Church reaffirmed its centuries-old teaching by explaining that guilt for Jesus' death is *not* attributable to all the Jews of that time or to *any* Jews of the current times.[265] In fact, at every Mass, whether they recite the Apostles' Creed or the Nicene Creed, Catholics identify *only* the Roman leader Pontius Pilate when it comes to the passion of Christ.[266] As Pope Pius XI said in 1938: "Spiritually, we are all Semites."[267]

Critics who try to force an anti-Semitic interpretation on the Gospels have selected a particularly difficult target in the Catholic Church. Catholics have an authority, a history of scholarship, and a Magisterium. The Holy See's Pontifical Biblical Commission has devoted significant attention to this issue. In a document entitled *The Jewish People and Their Sacred Scriptures in the Christian Bible*,[268] the commission discussed the charges that the New Testament is anti-Semitic. As explained in the introduction:

[T]he reproofs addressed to Jews in the New Testament are neither more frequent nor more virulent than the accusations against Israel in the Law and the Prophets, at the heart of the Old Testament itself. They belong to the prophetic language of the Old Testament and are, therefore, to be interpreted in the same way as the prophetic messages: they warn against contemporary aberrations, but they are essentially of a temporary nature and always open to new possibilities of salvation.

This document, which is 105 pages long, goes on to discuss the historic and generally close relationship between Catholics and Jews. "[T]he main conclusion to be drawn is that the Jewish people and their Sacred Scriptures occupy a very important place in the Christian Bible.... Without the Old Testament, the New Testament would be an incomprehensible book, a plant deprived of its roots and destined to dry up and wither." Quoting Pope John Paul II, the commission explains: "The Jewish religion is not 'extrinsic' to us, but in a certain manner, it is 'intrinsic' to our religion. We have therefore a relationship with it which we do not have with any other religion." All of this, of course, is at odds with what the critics would have their readers believe about the Catholic faith.

It is easy enough to find sloppy interpretations of the Bible or hate-mongers who bend it for their own purposes, but that is not to be found in the official teachings of the Catholic Church.[269] Unfortunately, critics often appear to be unfamiliar with the existing scholarship.[270] Goldhagen, for instance, says that Catholic teaching has always "revised" its essential beliefs. That is certainly *not* true, and it reflects a fundamental ignorance of the topic on which he writes. The documents of Vatican II maintain a clear and unqualified connection with the original Deposit of Faith.[271] The Catholic Church, according to its own teaching, does not have the authority to rewrite Scripture or deny the ultimate divinity of Christ. (*Imagine* the divisions that would take place within Christianity if it tried to do so.)[272]

Certainly no one would suggest that Christians and Jews have gotten along well at all times throughout history.[273] Prior to 1870, when popes had real temporal power, Jews were sometimes treated with religious and political contempt. Many Catholic officials of this period were fearful that Jews would lead Christians away from Christ, or worse.[274] They found reason for their fear in Old Testament passages such as Joshua 6:21 (Jews "utterly destroyed all in the city, both men and women, young and old, oxen, sheep, and asses, with the edge of the sword"), Deuteronomy 20:17 ("... you [Jews] shall utterly destroy them..."), and Deuteronomy 7:1, 2, 5-6:

> "When the LORD your God, brings you [Jews] into the land which you are entering to take possession of... and you defeat them... then you must utterly destroy them; you shall make no covenant with them, and show no mercy to them.... [Y]ou shall break down their altars, and dash in pieces their pillars, and hew down their Asherim, and burn their graven images with fire. For you

are a people holy to the LORD your God; the LORD your God has chosen you to be a people for his own possession...."

Additionally, the "imprecatory" sections of the Scriptures contain prayers or songs for vengeance upon the enemies of the Jewish nation or which end in triumphant praise at their destruction (Ps 5:11; Ps 10:15; Ps 18:38-43; Ps 31:18-19; Jer 15:15; Jer 17:18).[275] In 1564, Pope Pius IV announced that the Talmud could be distributed only on the condition that the portions offensive to Christians were erased.[276] Earlier popes had, at times, banned it altogether.

The incorrect understanding of Scripture did, indeed, breed suspicion and mistrust between Christians and Jews, but even papal critics have acknowledged that throughout the worst periods popes regularly condemned violence directed against Jews and offered protection when they could.[277] A papal bull of Pope Calixtus II (1190) condemned not only violence against the Jews, but also any attempt to forcibly baptize them. This teaching "was confirmed at least *twenty-two times* up to the middle of the eighteenth century."[278] Catholic "anti-Judaism" was a matter of religion, not race. In fact, the more common charges arising out of this history related to efforts directed toward encouraging Jews to convert — *to become Catholics.*

One oft-cited example is that in the past, on Good Friday, Catholics used to pray for the conversion of the "perfidious Jews."[279] This is offensive to the modern ear,[280] but what was it saying? It was a request to God that these people who did not believe in Jesus as Savior be converted so that they could share in eternity. While describing this act of "anti-Semitism," critics never point out that when this prayer was placed into the Good Friday service, "perfidious" did not have the pejorative connotation that it now carries —it simply meant "non-believing."[281]

By contrast, Nazi racial anti-Semitism did not encourage Jews to "join the party." This "scientific" position drew support from biological arguments and *the absence of religion.* Nazis showed films equating Jews, handicapped persons, and other "undesirables" with vermin that needed to be exterminated.[282] This grew out of a Darwinian/scientific ideal and was in direct contradiction to everything that the Catholic Church had always taught about the fundamental dignity of *all* human life.[283] Victor Frankl, who survived the Holocaust, wrote this stinging critique:

> The gas chambers of Auschwitz were the ultimate consequence of the theory that man is nothing but the product of heredity and environment — or, as the Nazis liked to say, "Of Blood and Soil." I'm absolutely convinced that the gas chambers of Auschwitz, Treblinka, and Maidanek were ultimately prepared not in some ministry or other in Berlin, but rather at the desks and in the lecture halls of nihilistic scientists and philosophers.[284]

Does this mean that it was impossible for Hitler to lay claim to Christian teachings as he advanced his evil agenda? Of course not. In *Mein Kampf,* Hitler went to great length about misusing religious imagery to inspire and inflame the masses. Hitler also played to a populist mentality, a racist mentality, a socialist mentality, a chauvinistic mentality, a nurturing/mothering mentality, a scientific mentality, and just about any other mentality that he could think of.[285] Are they all to be condemned because they were capable of being manipulated by Hitler (who also planned to eliminate largely *Catholic* Poland)? The answer is equally clear: Of course not.

———

Goldhagen seems to think the Pope should have set aside all of his foreign intelligence and adopted a confrontational approach to the Nazis — *in each and every location*. That, of course, would have been foolish.[286] The Pope knew of the retaliation following *Mit brennender Sorge*. He had the example of Edith Stein in Holland. He sent an express condemnation into Poland to be read, but the archbishop of Kraków, Adam Sapieha, burned it, saying that it would bring too many reprisals.[287] In fact, the Nuremberg report documents case after case of retaliation against clergy (Catholic and Protestant) following statements or other agitation against the Nazi regime.[288]

Rather than endangering others with grand public gestures, Pius used churches, convents, monasteries, seminaries, and the Vatican itself to run a rescue operation for all victims, without any distinction based on race, religion, or nationality. The last thing a rescue operation wants is attention, particularly when it is likely to bring about reprisals. Goldhagen focuses only on potential reprisals against Jewish people. Such reprisals occurred; but the Pope was also concerned about Catholics. For one thing, Catholic rescue efforts could be harmed, causing further suffering for Jews. More importantly, as Pius said, martyrdom cannot be imposed on someone, but must be voluntarily accepted.[289] Catholic doctrine would not permit the Pope to sacrifice some lives to save others, even if a utilitarian equation might suggest that would be appropriate. The Church did not, however, vary its approach based upon the identity of the victim.

The historical facts show that sometimes a confrontational approach worked with the Nazis, but other times it did not. Robert M. W. Kempner, the deputy chief U.S. prosecutor at the Nuremberg war trials, explained that a public protest against persecution of the Jews could only lead to "partial success when it was made at a politically and militarily opportune moment."[290] He added that Pius made such protests through nuncios when and where possible. Confrontation would not, however, have been advisable with Hitler. "Every propaganda move of the Catholic Church against Hitler's Reich," he wrote, "would have been not only 'provoking suicide'... but would have hastened the execution of still more Jews and priests."[291]

Goldhagen also asserts that Pius did not privately instruct cardinals, bishops, priests, and nuns to save Jews. How could he know that? Catholic rescuers — including people such as Pietro Cardinal Palazzini and Tibor Baranski, who were later recognized by Israel as Righteous Gentiles — testified that they received precisely such orders from the Pope.[292] Several other witnesses also testified that such instructions were sent out in the form of letters.[293] Still others — including Father Benoît, Carroll-Abbing, Pope John XXIII, and Pope Paul VI — all testified that they received such instructions from Pope Pius XII in face-to-face meetings, or through other direct channels.[294]

Goldhagen even tried to link the Vatican and Pacelli with the notorious anti-Semite Julius Streicher. Streicher himself, however, told a different story. He railed against the Pope's support for Jewish people:

> The Jews have now found protection in the Catholic Church, which is trying to convince non-Jewish humanity that distinct races do not exist. The Pope has made his own the false conception of racial equality — and the Jews, with the help of Marxists and Freemasons, are doing their best to promote it. But the Pope's attitude will surprise no one who is familiar with the shrewd schemes of Vatican politics.[295]

Pacelli's opposition to Streicher's worldview was well-known. In *Three Popes and the Jews*, Pinchas Lapide cites a public address by Pacelli in Rome that repeated Pope Pius XI's eloquent statement that "spiritually we are all Semites."[296] Goldhagen's efforts to distort the historical record are simply outrageous.

———

One oft-repeated charge is that the Vatican under Pope Pius XII helped Nazis escape justice in Europe and make their way to South America, via the so-called rat-line. This claim was most fully developed by the self-styled "investigative journalists" Mark Aarons and John Loftus. They first brought it up in their 1991 book, *Unholy Trinity: The Vatican, the Nazis, and the Swiss Banks*. In a later book (*The Secret War Against the Jews*, 1994), Aarons and Loftus expanded their argument and asserted that almost every entity in the world — from the Vatican to the Bush family — is at war with the Jews.[297] Commenting on their argument, Anti-Defamation League director Abraham Foxman called it "so exaggerated, so scantily documented, so overwrought and convoluted in its presentation, that Loftus and Aarons render laughable their claim to offer 'a glimpse of the world as it really is.'"[298]

The Vatican has acknowledged that Bishop Alois Hudal of Austria and a Croatian priest named Krunoslav Draganović helped war criminals escape from Europe.[299] Evidence shows, however, that this was done without approval from Vatican authorities.[300] The Vatican recently permitted Professor Matteo Sanfilippo, a member of the Comision Para el Esclarecimiento de las Actividades Del Nazismo en la Republica Argentina (CEANA), the historical commission that looked into Argentina's role in sheltering war criminals, to examine Hudal's personal papers. Sanfilippo found no evidence that the Pope encouraged Hudal's activities.[301] In fact, Sanfilippo uncovered a letter from Monsignor Montini to

Hudal expressing outrage at his suggestion that the Vatican should help members of the S.S. and the Wehrmacht.[302]

In a letter published in the *New York Times* on March 13, 1984, Nazi hunter Simon Wiesenthal wrote:

> In the 1950's, when I was working on the Eichmann case, I was in Rome and found out how this escape route operated after 1945. I never heard of Dr. Willi Nix, the focus of one of your articles, but I did hear about the German bishop in Rome, Alois Hudal. There is no evidence that Pope Pius XII ordered or knew about this escape route at the time it was run, but Bishop Hudal, in his diary published in 1969, had this to say:
>
> > "... So the Allies' war against Germany had in its last consequence nothing to do with ideals. This was not a Crusade but the rivalry of economic complexes.... Slogans such as democracy, race, religious liberty and Christianity were used as bait for the masses.... (All this) led me after 1945 to devote my charitable efforts mainly to former National Socialists and Fascists, especially to the so-called 'war criminals,' who were being persecuted by Communists and 'Christian Democrats.'"
>
> The bishop recalled that among the Roman Curia he became known as the "Nazi, Fascist Bishop" and that eventually "Vatican politics" regarded him as no longer tolerable....
>
> SIMON WIESENTHAL Jewish Documentation Center Vienna, Feb. 24, 1984

Archival evidence confirms that Wiesenthal was correct: Hudal "acted without Rome's permission or knowledge."[303]

Several writers, including Michael Phayer, have alleged that Hudal enjoyed a close relationship with Pius XII.[304] In his memoirs, however, Hudal frequently complained of the Vatican's "pro-Allied bias" during World War II and how Pius XI, Pius XII, and Monsignor Montini, mistreated him throughout his career.[305] Recently opened archives indicate that Hudal was "kept at arm's length" from positions of responsibility because the Pope and his secretary of state did not trust him.[306] Those same archives, however, show that Pius used Hudal when he could, and Hudal "played a decisive role in the termination of the deportation of the Jews from Rome" in October 1943.[307]

Phayer cited Uki Goni's *The Real Odessa* (2002) for his argument that Pius helped war criminals escape to South America. Goni asserted that Montini asked the government of Argentina to shelter war criminals, and he cited a letter from him to Argentina's embassy at the Vatican as proof.[308] Professor Ignacio Klich, however, the coordinator of CEANA, has denied that Montini's letter requested help for war criminals. Rather, the letter asked Argentina to keep its doors open to all immigrants and refugees. There were hundreds of thousands of refugees made homeless by the war and displaced persons fleeing persecution from Communist countries in Eastern Europe at the time.[309] The Vatican was trying to help these people start new lives in other countries as quickly as possible. There is little doubt that some individuals — including many Soviet spies, whom the Holy See would not have wanted to help — took advantage of the system to avoid justice, but there is no evidence of a widespread Catholic plan to support such efforts.

Like the Vatican, the International Red Cross has been identified as having helped Nazis escape from justice.[310] It is, however, inconceivable that the Nazis revealed their background to the Church or Red Cross officials. It is even less likely that any such information would have reached the upper echelons of these organizations.[311] The logistics of the massive relocation programs simply made it impossible to investigate most individuals who sought help.[312] Besides, "if Pius were actually bent on rolling back the communists rather than containing them, it would have made more sense for him to encourage anti-communists to infiltrate Eastern Europe rather than, as Phayer holds, finance their way from Genoa to Latin America."[313]

Monsignor Karl Bayer, who was liaison chaplain responsible for the 250,000 prisoners of war in the north of Italy, explained:

> "If there really was a screening," he said, "an attempt at detailed research by examining each of the people concerned, it would have required at least a dozen German-speaking priests. I knew them all. There were, of course, quite a few, but they were incredibly busy — too busy, I think, for the kind of supervision of the many people [they dealt with]...."

> "Well, of course we asked questions," he said. "But at the same time, we hadn't an earthly chance of checking on the answers. In Rome, at that time, every kind of paper and information could be bought. If a man wanted to tell us he was born in Viareggio — no matter if he was really born in Berlin and couldn't speak a word of Italian — he only had to go down into the street and he'd find dozens of Italians willing to swear on a stack of Bibles that they knew he was born in Viareggio — for a hundred lire."[314]

In a situation like that, it is hard to fault any relief agency for being deceived.

In 1947, a top secret Department of State memorandum entitled "Illegal Emigration Movements in and Through Italy" identified the Vatican as the largest single organization involved in the illegal movement of emigrants. "Jewish Agencies and individuals" were identified as the second-largest group. The memo, however, made clear that all of the agencies, including the International Red Cross, worked in collaboration with one another and that anyone could take advantage of these programs. In fact, the memo indicated that "no less than 10% of all illegal emigrants passing through Italy are Russian agents," because the Church had no way to identify the politics of the people in the program. Moreover, the memo reported that Vatican and Red Cross passports were easily and commonly falsified by changing the pictures on them.[315]

In his 1944 Christmas message, Pope Pius XII objected to the collective punishment of nations, but he defended the punishment of war criminals. In fact, the Vatican helped prosecute Nazi war criminals. In 1946, the Vatican handed over many of its documents to the International Military Tribunal in Nuremberg, which used them as evidence against the Nazis for persecuting the Catholic Church before and during the war.[316] Although Pius XII asked for clemency for some criminals, including Tojo in Japan, he refused to intervene on behalf of the Nazis who were sentenced to death at Nuremberg. The critics' arguments do not stand up to analysis.

In the end, it must be concluded that the Church, like the Red Cross, was interested in ending suffering. Undoubtedly, some Nazis took advantage of the Vatican's efforts to help dislocated people move about the world.[317] In the chaos of postwar Europe, many war criminals used false names and forged papers to obtain exit visas and travel documents from many civilian relief agencies, including those run by the Church. There is, however, no indication that the Holy See was intentionally involved in trying to help Nazis escape justice following the war.[318] Critics who make this charge have ignored the evidence to advance their case.[319]

---

Several of the papal critics have rejected the findings of Jewish scholars Joseph Lichten and Pinchas Lapide. Lichten was the director of the Intercultural Affairs Department of the Anti-Defamation League of B'nai B'rith. Lapide was a journalist and diplomatic official of the Israeli government. They both wrote blistering responses to the allegations made in *The Deputy*, and they set forth what had been the dominant Jewish view of Pius XII up until that time.[320] Naturally, this work embarrasses modern papal critics.

Critic Susan Zuccotti asserts, without evidence, that Lichten deliberately sacrificed the truth in order to foster good relations between Israel and the Holy See. She argues, for instance, that Lichten "wrote without evidence" that the Vatican offered Jewish scholars teaching posts to protect them from Fascist persecution. In fact, not only did Lichten have supporting evidence, this matter was very well-publicized, and the documentary evidence is included in the Appendix (see p. 396, original French text).[321]

As for Lapide, Zuccotti claims that there is "no evidence offered" for his assertion that Bishop Hudal's letter protesting the roundup of Roman Jews on October 16, 1943, was written at the urging of the Pope.[322] In fact, Hudal's own memoirs reveal that his letter of protest was prompted by Pope Pius XII's personal agent, his nephew Carlo Pacelli.[323] Moreover, the letter was delivered to German General Stahel by Father Pancratius Pfeiffer, Pius XII's personal emissary to the Germans.[324]

The most controversial figure surrounding these Jewish authors is the estimate relating to the number of Jewish lives that were saved by the Holy See under Pope Pius XII. Following months of research at the Yad Vashem archives,

Lapide came up with the estimate that Pius saved 700,000 to 860,000 Jews.[325] While critics have challenged this number, others have come to similar or higher tallies.[326]

Lapide knew both Pope Pius XI and Pope Pius XII. He was the author of at least nine books, and he wrote extensively on religious affairs for journals throughout the world. In World War II, he fought with the British Eighth Army in the North African and Italian campaigns. While serving in southern Italy, he found a group of peasant converts to Judaism, and he spent twenty years serving as their spiritual adviser. His book *The Prophet of San Nicandro*, which tells this story, was translated and published in eight different languages. The Jewish Book Guild of America awarded him a literary prize for it. Lapide also worked for a time with the prime minister's office in Jerusalem. He wrote *A Pilgrim's Guide to Israel* and *An Israeli's Introduction to Christianity*, both of which helped the interfaith movement in Israel. His credentials are (or should be) above question. (Of course, in 2006, Rolf Hochhuth said of him: "He is a liar, he is a Jew, one of the Jesuit overflowed. He is a liar.")[327]

Lapide attributed his estimated number of Jewish lives saved to "[t]he Holy See, the nuncios, and the entire Catholic Church." Seen that way, and recognizing that he was an Israeli diplomat who spent months researching the issue in the Yad Vashem archives, it is not surprising that his figures have become so widely accepted, despite protestations from the critics.[328]

Critics sometimes question why there is not more surviving written evidence of papal involvement and why so many witnesses waited to come forward until the 1960s. Susan Zuccotti, in particular, has even argued that had there been papal involvement in rescue activities, people would have saved written evidence to protect his reputation.

Actually, during the war, almost nothing was committed to paper.[329] Moreover, if written directives existed, anyone who cared for the Pope would have quickly destroyed written evidence of his involvement in rescue activities.[330] It was extremely dangerous to keep papers related to anti-Nazi efforts, and few who worked in the underground did. Italian Senator Adriano Ossicini, founder of the "Christian Left" in Italy, was arrested by Mussolini's Fascists in 1943. Upon his release, he thanked Pius for his intervention with Mussolini and apologized to the Pope because one of the reasons for his arrest was that he was carrying a document that showed how strongly Pius opposed racial laws.[331] Ossicini knew that by carrying the document, he had endangered the Pope and others in the Church.

As discussed earlier, in the spring of 1940, a group of German generals wanted to oust Hitler and make peace with the Allies. Needing a way to communicate with the Allies (mainly the British), they approached Pope Pius XII.[332] Not only did he help with the negotiations,[333] he actually went so far as to inform the Allies about German troop movements.[334] There are, however, no documents on this in the Vatican's published collection. The documents were found only in the British archives.[335]

During Pius XII's pontificate, and particularly during the war, important matters were not kept on paper:

> For every form of communication used within the Roman Curia — memo, letter, phone call, encyclical, Papal bull and smoke signal — the whispered word outranks them all. Millions of words are put to paper or sent over wire. But urgent truths and hot gossip go out by whisper, shot anywhere from two inches to one foot from the ear of the listener.[336]

Any Vatican papers related to the planned coup, like any relating to other anti-Nazi or rescue efforts, were undoubtedly hidden or destroyed. This direct involvement by the Pope in an attempted coup is far more telling than mere words ever could have been.[337]

More importantly, no one at the time thought Pius XII's reputation would need to be protected. As rescuer John Patrick Carroll-Abbing wrote in his 1965 book:

> Never, in those tragic days, could I have foreseen, even in my wildest imaginings, that the man who, more than any other, had tried to alleviate human suffering, had spent himself day by day in his unceasing efforts for peace, would — twenty years later — be made the scapegoat for men trying to free themselves from their own responsibilities and from the collective guilt that obviously weighs so heavily upon them.[338]

In his earlier book, Carroll-Abbing wrote of being inspired by the "luminous sublime example of the Holy Father."[339] He also reported about Catholic assistance to Jews and the Pope's order that "no one was to be refused" shelter.[340] In fact, in an interview given shortly before his death, Carroll-Abbing said: "I can personally testify to you that the Pope gave me direct face-to-face verbal orders to rescue Jews." Asked about the thesis that the rescuers like him acted without papal involvement, he denied it and added:

> But it wasn't just me. It was also the people I worked with: Father Pfeiffer and Father Benoît and my assistant, Monsignor Vitucci and Cardinals Dezza and Pallazzini, and of course Cardinals Maglione and Montini and Tardini. We didn't simply assume things; we acted on the direct orders of the Holy Father.[341]

Although she later changed her argument, in 1987 even Susan Zuccotti acknowledged that "[a]ny direct personal order would have had to be kept very quiet to protect those who were actually sheltered."[342]

The Nazis also understood Pius XII's position during the war. There are numerous instances of Nazi leaders complaining bitterly about the Pope's statements. They even spied on him and many of his assistants.[343] This culminated in an order from Hitler (later retracted at the urging of his staff) to invade the Vatican itself.[344]

Responding to the observation that a more confrontational position might have made things worse for Hitler's victims, Robert Wistrich writes: "I find this argument bizarre as well as speculative." Of course, it is no more speculative than the conclusion that such a position would have made things better.[345] That certainly was a serious concern for Pope Pius XII. American diplomat Harold Tittmann reported back to Washington: "The Holy See is apparently still convinced that an open denunciation by the Pope of the Nazi atrocities, at least as far as Poland is concerned, could have no more result but the violent death of a great many more people."[346] The deputy chief U.S. prosecutor at Nuremberg, Dr. Robert Kempner, agreed: protests did not stop the Nazis, and they often made things worse.[347] As reported by the Congregation for the Causes of Saints following a thirty-nine-year investigation into Pope Pius XII:

> Loud protests achieve nothing and only cause damage.... The only means to save the Jews was, therefore, secret but efficient ways to shelter them, provide them food and clothing, and move them to neutral countries. Pius XII did this in a manner unequaled by any state or organization, as was attested by many Jewish authorities and individuals.[348]

That is the crux of the dispute when it comes to Pope Pius XII. He outlined a course of action in his first encyclical, and he stuck with it. He felt that this was the best way to help save lives, minister to all, and achieve peace. It was also in keeping with papal tradition.

Decisions like this are always subject to after-the-fact speculations, and it is impossible to prove whether a different course of action would have been better or worse. Papal critics, however, too often do more than ask whether the Pope made the correct decision. They suggest that he did not care about the victims, that he was anti-Semitic, or that he was "Hitler's Pope." They attribute evil intentions to him. In doing this, they cease writing history and instead engage in character assassination. That is a terrible disservice to the truth.

---

In a letter to the president of the Pontifical Committee of Historical Sciences, Pope John Paul II wrote:

> Historical research, free of prejudices and linked uniquely to scientific documentation, has an irreplaceable role in breaking down barriers among peoples. Often, great barriers have been built up throughout the centuries due to partiality of historiography and of reciprocal resentment. The consequence has been that even today misunderstandings persist which are an obstacle to peace and fraternity among men and peoples.[349]

Too often, however, critics of the World War II-era Catholic Church are not "free of prejudices," and their works are not based upon valid documentation.

In advancing their arguments, they contribute to the misunderstandings that become obstacles to peace and brotherhood.

The evidence *clearly* shows that Pius was appalled by the Nazis and sympathized with their victims. He intervened where he could, in ways that he thought would be most effective. The Vatican under his rule was certainly more outspoken than it had been under Benedict XV during the First World War.[350] Pius XII's decisions were not based on affection for Hitler, hatred of the Communists, dislike for the Jews, fear for his own safety, or any of the malicious reasons suggested by the critics. Nor were they made without serious reflection. Historical questions about his approach are fair, though his decisions are certainly defensible.[351] When the critics resort to *ad hominem* attacks against Pope Pius the man, however, they simply raise the heat and not the light.

Unfortunately, it may be that some critics are indeed more interested in raising the heat. Critics John Cornwell, James Carroll, Garry Wills, and Daniel Goldhagen have all — in one way or another — called upon the Catholic Church to reform itself.[352] They are critical not only of Pope Pius XII, but also Pope John Paul II, Pope Benedict XVI, traditional Catholic doctrines of papal supremacy, the all-male priesthood, and especially Catholic sexual teachings.[353] In fact, such critics recognize that the Catholic Church stands as perhaps the preeminent voice advancing the very concept of ultimate truth, and that makes it their target. Robert Louis Wilken was writing about James Carroll's *Constantine's Sword* when he penned the following, but it could be applied to many of the modern critics of Pius XII:

> At the end of the day, in spite of the enormous effort to lay bare the sins of the Church over two millennia, *Constantine's Sword* is not really a book about Christian theology of the Jews. Its subject is Christian theology *tout court*, and its polemic springs from the currently fashionable "ideology of religious pluralism" — what might be termed horror at strong opinions. Carroll wants a Christianity that celebrates a "Jesus whose saving act is only one disclosure of the divine love available to all," and calls for a pluralism of "belief and worship, of religion and no religion, that honors God by defining God as beyond every effort to express God." What we have, then, is a rather conventional cultural critique of Christianity. The Jews are the victims *par excellence* of the excesses of revealed religion. But what Carroll forgets is that Jews, too, believe in revelation.... In Carroll's brave new world there will be neither Jews nor Christians.[354]

The critics focused on Pope Pius XII because he seemed to be an easy target for their anger at the Catholic Church and organized religion in general.[355] They were wrong.

Perhaps the most important recent development in understanding Pope Pius XII is the completion of the thirty-nine-year study into his life that was undertaken by historians for the Vatican's Congregation for the Causes of Saints.[356] This report, which fills eight volumes, includes 1,420 pages on his life (*Vita*

*Documentata*); almost 1,000 pages of sworn testimony transcripts given by 98 witnesses (*Summarium*); a 300-page synthetic exposition of his virtues of faith, hope, charity, and prudence (*Informatio*); and a 300-page appendix addressing specific issues in the life of Pius XII, including his work vis-à-vis the Jewish victims of the Holocaust.[357] Cumulatively, these documents are known as the *Positio*.[358]

The particular importance of the *Positio* comes not from the evidence that it reviews, but from the analysis of that evidence. It sets forth a compelling case that Pius XII lived a life of heroic virtue. As for the charges raised by a slew of papal critics, the *Positio* concludes that they are part of a campaign to denigrate his personality and his work.[359]

The evidence that it reviews is essentially the same evidence that has been available to all researchers in this area. The difference is that the Congregation for the Causes of Saints has a history of looking into the lives of important people. It uses reasonable standards of general applicability and tries to apply them fairly. All charges and claims on both sides of the issue are explored, and true scholars take as much time as is necessary to reach the right conclusion. In a forum such as that, the charges against Pope Pius XII fall by the wayside.

# EIGHTEEN

# The Questions and Answers

The first step in assessing the role that Pope Pius XII played in World War II is to consider both his actions and the world situation as it appeared to him in those years. These facts have been explored in the previous chapters of this book. They present a picture of Pius that calls for further analysis to reach an accurate evaluation of his leadership. That analysis can largely be accomplished by addressing ten questions regarding his papacy.

## 1. Was the Pope Anti-Semitic?

The close work of the Vatican, local bishops, and papal nuncios with Jewish groups belies any claim that the Pope discriminated against any race or religion.[1] The Catholic Church saved more Jewish lives than all the other churches, religious institutions, and rescue organizations put together. The 1943-44 *American Jewish Yearbook* reported that Pius XII "took an unequivocal stand against the oppression of Jews throughout Europe." The head of Italian Jewry's wartime Jewish Assistance Committee, Dr. Raffael Cantoni, who subsequently became the president of the union of all Italian Jewish communities, reported: "The Church and the papacy have saved Jews as much and in as far as they could save Christians.... Six millions of my coreligionists have been murdered by the Nazis, but there could have been many more victims, had it not been for the efficacious intervention of Pius XII."[2] Even Pope Pius XII's most severe critics acknowledge that he was personally involved in saving some Jewish victims.[3] In fact, Pius had a lifelong Orthodox Jewish friend, Guido Mendes, with whom, as a boy, he often had Shabbat dinner.[4]

If any restraint on the part of the Vatican were to be attributed to an anti-Semitic attitude on the part of the Pope, then one would expect to see the Church behave in a different manner when a similar situation involving Christians arose. By late in the war, most of the Jews in Poland had been eliminated, and Hitler was concentrating on other victims, the vast majority of whom were Catholic.[5] As early as 1941, the *Palestine Post* reported on the severe treatment of Catholics as well as Jews:

> "Macabre" was how the visitor described the Ghettoes of Poland. In Lodz he saw mobile gallows on wheels. He told how, for lack of fuel, entire families crowded together into one room to sleep, huddling together like animals.... Catholics were served as horribly as the Jews by the Germans. About 60 percent of the Polish Catholic clergy have been murdered by the Nazis, he estimated. One Catholic priest who fell from exhaustion in the snow-covered courtyard of

the prison where he was imprisoned was laughed at by the Nazi guards: "Now, you look like your Christ," they scoffed.[6]

Literally thousands of Catholic priests died in the Nazi camps,[7] but the Pope did not become more vocal or behave differently in these cases than he had when the victims were Jews.[8]

No one who was close to the Pontiff during the war ever imputed any anti-Semitic attitudes to him. Father Leiber, the Pope's private secretary and personal confidant during the war years seems to have put this issue to rest with one brief statement: "The Pope sided very unequivocally with the Jews at the time. He spent his entire private fortune on their behalf.... Pius spent what he inherited himself, as a Pacelli, from his family."[9] Clearly, anti-Semitism did not affect Pius XII's actions during the time of Hitler. Even Rolf Hochhuth and John Cornwell have denied any implication of anti-Semitism on Pius XII's part.

A related issue is the impact of the general anti-Semitic attitude that could be found in much of Christianity prior to the war. After the war, the World Council of Churches issued the following statement: "We have failed to fight with all our strength the age-old disorder which anti-Semitism represents. The churches in the past have helped to foster an image of the Jews as the sole enemies of Christ which has contributed to anti-Semitism in the secular world."[10] In 1998, the Vatican released a fourteen-page document entitled *We Remember: A Reflection on the Shoah*, which acknowledged that centuries of anti-Jewish attitudes in the Church may have contributed to Christians' lack of resistance to Nazi policies. "We deeply regret the errors and failures of those sons and daughters of the Church. This is an act of repentance, since, as members of the Church, we are linked to the sins as well as the merits of all her children."[11] The document was somewhat controversial, however, because in a long footnote, it defended the "wisdom of Pope Pius XII's diplomacy."[12]

Granting that Hitler perverted Christian concepts, is it possible that Christian teaching concerning the "people who rejected Jesus" made it easier for him to develop his extreme racial views or for the German public to accept his ideas? Of course. In a meeting that took place between Hitler and German church officials in 1933, Hitler essentially justified his policies by citing Catholic traditions.[13] Religious differences often create deep divides; however, the evidence for Christianity having shaped Hitler's racial views is very weak.[14]

The Final Solution entailed two elements that were fundamentally new and clearly did not evolve from Christian theology: the view of racial Jewishness, which rendered baptism irrelevant, and the commitment to extermination of the Jewish people.[15] Because of this, Christian leaders who proclaimed the worst anti-Semitic teaching of their faith still were unable to embrace the extreme teachings of the Nazis.[16]

If anti-Jewish teachings from Christian churches were the cause of the persecution of Jews, how does one account for the persecution of Gypsies and Catholic

Poles? Similarly, there was no religious basis for the euthanasia program of the 1930s; Christian Germans were among the first victims. Church teachings also cannot account for persecution of Jehovah's Witnesses or — for that matter — of the bourgeois in Communist nations. These things happened independently of religion, not because of it.

There is no record of Hitler having attended church services at any time after his childhood.[17] Ernst von Weizsäcker, German ambassador to the Holy See during the war, wrote that Hitler "had from his youth been an enemy of the Church."[18] In 1939, Joseph Goebbels wrote:

> The *Führer* is deeply religious, though completely anti-Christian. He views Christianity as a symptom of decay. Rightly so. It is a branch of the Jewish race. This can be seen in the similarity of religious rites. Both (Judaism and Christianity) have no point of contact to the animal element, and they, in the end, will be destroyed.[19]

In 1934, Hitler told a group of Protestant leaders that he was glad to have been brought up Catholic, because it helped him attract votes, but inwardly he felt closest to the Evangelical (Protestant) Church.[20] Privately, he was opposed to any form of Christianity.[21]

Hitler's strong anti-Semitic feelings are thought to have developed in his teens and twenties, after he quit attending Mass. His first known anti-Semitic writing came after the end of World War I, after he had attended the German army's program for veterans, which taught anti-Semitism.

While one can never be certain when re-creating a "what if" scenario, it is completely reasonable to argue that Hitler would never have developed his extreme racist views if only he had continued attending church services into his adulthood.

A distinction should be drawn between antipathy toward the Jewish race (anti-Semitism) and differences with the Jewish faith (sometimes called anti-Judaism). Catholic teaching, like most Christian teaching, says that acceptance of Jesus is the road to salvation. Members of the Jewish faith do not view Jesus as Savior, but people of Jewish heritage are always welcome and encouraged to join the Catholic Church. Thus, Hitler's concept of a lesser race (as opposed to a different faith) is clearly distinct from (and in opposition to) the Catholic Church's teaching.

Many Jews converted to Catholicism during the war as a way to avoid Nazi persecution.[22] The Catholic Church was so open to Jewish converts that some have argued that during the war this was the Church's primary interest. In a Papal Allocution of October 6, 1946, Pope Pius addressed the issue of "forced conversions."[23] He found the best evidence to be a memorandum, dated January 25, 1942, from the Vatican Secretariat of State to the Legation of Yugoslavia to the Holy See. The Pope read from that document:

According to the principles of Catholic doctrine, conversion must be the result, not of external constraint, but of an interior adherence of the soul to the truths taught by the Catholic Church. It is for this reason that the Catholic Church does not admit to her communion adults who request either to be received or to be readmitted, except on condition that they be fully aware of the meaning and consequences of the step that they wish to take.[24]

Canon 750 of the 1917 Code of Canon Law, which was supplemented during World War II by orders from the Holy See, prohibited forced conversions.

A slant on this claim relates to children, particularly those under the age of six. The surest way to protect such young children from the Nazis was by actually baptizing and indoctrinating them, in case they were ever challenged. Both canon law and the Holy See, however, made clear that hidden Jewish children were not to be baptized without parental consent.[25] Even when parents requested the baptism, it was recognized that this was often a matter of duress and was sometimes prohibited.[26] In fact, classes were often established to let the children study their own religion.[27]

[I]t is clear that conversion of Jewish children was undertaken cautiously and often only after special permission was granted by parents or guardians. Moreover, Catholics close to the process explained that, after baptism, Jewish children were more likely to feel Christian and, therefore, had a better chance of avoiding giving themselves and their rescuers away.[28]

In parts of France and Belgium, Church officials forbade the actual baptism of Jewish children. Outward appearances were thought sufficient to deceive the Nazis.[29]

On December 28, 2004, an Italian professor from Bologna named Alberto Melloni published an article in the Italian newspaper *Il Corriere della Sera* entitled *Pius XII to Nuncio Roncalli: Do Not Return the Jewish Children*. The article cited a document that Melloni claimed to have received from an unidentified archive in France. This document, dated October 23, 1946, was said to be "a disposition of the Holy Office" (the Congregation for the Doctrine of the Faith's former name), and it purportedly contained Pope Pius XII's directives to his representative in France — Archbishop Angelo Roncalli, the future Pope John XXIII — on how to handle the Jewish children, especially any who had been baptized by their Catholic rescuers.

According to Melloni, the letter said: "Children who have been baptized must not be entrusted to institutions that cannot ensure their Christian education." Also according to Melloni, the letter said that children whose families survived the Holocaust should be returned, "as long as they had not been baptized." The clear implication was that baptized Jewish children should not be returned to their families. Melloni quoted the letter as saying: "It should be noted that this decision taken by the Holy Congregation of the Holy Office has been approved by the Holy Father."

The *New York Times* reported that the letter was made available to it "on the condition that the source would not be disclosed."[30] This, in and of itself, should have set off alarms. Moreover, the letter was not signed, not on Vatican letterhead, and Vatican officials immediately noted that the words used were not typical for directives from the Vatican. Importantly, the letter was in French, not in Italian as it would have been had this actually been an instruction from the Pope to his nuncio.[31] Moreover, Archbishop Roncalli certainly never acted in a way that this report said he was instructed to act. In fact, he has been repeatedly praised for all he did to assist Jewish refugees, and he gave all credit to Pius XII (whom, according to his private papers, he "venerated and loved").[32] Nevertheless, and despite all of these warning signs, critics like Daniel Goldhagen and Rabbi Shmuley Boteach were quickly in the press explaining how this document proved that Pius was indeed an evil man.[33]

Melloni did not identify the archive from which the French memo came, but Italian journalist Andrea Tornielli and historian Matteo Luigi Napolitano were able to track down the memo in the Centre National des Archives de l'Eglise de France. The French letter that Melloni was promoting as a startling find was not, in fact, a papal directive. It was a summary of an earlier document, a letter from Monsignor Domenico Tardini to the papal nuncio in France, Angelo Roncalli — the future Pope John XXIII.[34]

The instructions from Tardini, approved by Pius XII, said that if institutions (*not families*) wanted to take those children who had been entrusted to the Church, each case had to be examined individually. There was indeed special concern about baptized children. In some cases, their parents (or appointed relatives) had requested baptism, perhaps because they thought that would best protect the children. In those cases, the Church would breach its obligation to the parents if it turned the children over to the wrong institution. Even in those rare cases where Catholic rescuers had baptized Jewish children without consent of the Jewish parents, the Church was still concerned about turning them over to institutions that were not associated with the children's family.

As for the rest of the children, the instructions provided: "... also those children who were not baptized and who no longer have living relatives, having been entrusted to the Church, which has taken them under its care, as long as they are not able to decide for themselves, they cannot be abandoned by the Church or delivered to parties who have no right to them." There were very few facilities fit for children in Palestine or war-torn Europe, and the Pope was concerned for their welfare.

The Tardini document made clear that these instructions related solely to *institutions*, wanting to relocate orphaned children after the war: "*Things would be different if the children were requested by their relatives.*" This qualification of the papal directive changes the entire meaning of the instructions. They did not relate to children being sought by their parents or other relatives. That is completely different from what news reports led people to believe.

Archbishop Loris Capovilla, secretary to Nuncio Roncalli during and after the war, explained the need for close scrutiny of organizations: "It was then natural to screen the situations case by case, paying the highest attention to those who knocked on the door to reclaim the children: What should those [Catholic] families have done? Give the children raised together with their own to those who first presented themselves? The Church did nothing other than to counsel a rule of prudence, and to watch over the protection of the little ones."[35] Archbishop Capovilla said that he was not aware of any case in which a Jewish child was impeded from reentering his or her natural family.

These Vatican instructions regarding the return of Jewish children were prompted by a meeting between the Pope and Chief Rabbi Isaac Herzog of Palestine in March 1946. In a letter sent at that time, the rabbi expressed his profound thanks for the "thousands of children who were hidden in Catholic institutions." Herzog noted that Pius XII "has worked to banish anti-Semitism in many countries" and concluded with an invocation: "God willing, may history remember that when everything was dark for our people, His Holiness lit a light of hope for them."[36]

The *Palestine Post* (March 31, 1946) reported that Rabbi Herzog "told of his audience with the Pope, who had received him on a Sunday early in March. Their conversation... was mainly on the subject of the 8,000 Jewish children in Poland, France, Belgium and Holland who were [being] brought up in monasteries and by Christian families. He had the Vatican's promise of help to bring those children back into the Jewish fold." The Pope must have come through on that promise. As Dr. Leon Kubowitzky, of the World Jewish Congress, said in 1964: "I can state now that I hardly know of a single case where Catholic institutions refused to return Jewish children."[37]

At least one petition from a Catholic parent who did not want to return a Jewish child to her natural parents made its way to the Pope. It was from a Polish Catholic woman named Leokadia Jaromirska, who was later honored as a Righteous Gentile. She sought the Pope's permission to keep the little girl whom she was rearing as a Catholic even though the Jewish father had returned. Pius told Jaromirska to return the girl to her father. The Pope explained that it "was her duty as a Catholic not only to give back the child, but do it with good will and in friendship."[38]

When it comes to Jewish children, critics of the Catholic Church often cite the Finaly affair from France, but they omit many details. That case began on February 14, 1944, when Gestapo agents entered the village of Tronche, France. They arrested two Jewish refugees from Austria, Fritz and Annie Finaly (also sometimes spelled "Finely"). The Finalys were never seen again. Their children (Robert, aged three, and Gerald, aged two) were left behind. A Catholic woman named Antoinette Brun took the two young boys into the Grenoble founding home, which she ran. Eventually, she came to love them, and in 1945 she began the process to formally adopt the boys. In 1948, she had them baptized into the Catholic Church.

The boys' parents were gone, but after the war an aunt from New Zealand wrote a letter asking that they be sent to her. Brun resisted that overture, but in 1949 the Finaly family filed suit to have the boys sent to live with a different aunt in Israel. The lawsuit went on for almost four years, and the evidence was conflicting. The boys' late father had told friends that he wanted to have his sons brought up in France, but there was no clear evidence as to his (or their mother's) religious wishes. For their part, the boys wanted to stay in France with Brun.

The French court ultimately sided with the Finaly relatives, but when the authorities went to pick up the boys, they were missing. Friends and supporters of Ms. Brun, including some Catholic priests and nuns, had spirited the boys off to Spain.

Several arrests were made, and French socialists used this as an opportunity to bash the Catholic Church. Contrary to what critics of the Catholic Church often say, these Catholics were not acting on behalf of the institutional Church. Bishop Alexandre Calliot of Grenoble made a radio broadcast in which he demanded that anyone with information about the boys get in touch with the authorities. One of the first to comply was a priest in Spain who reported on the boys' whereabouts.[39]

Forty-eight hours after the legal appeal was resolved in favor of the Finaly family, a representative of Pierre Cardinal Gerlier, archbishop of Lyon, made the final of several trips into Spain to find the boys. They were waiting in the home of a Spanish provincial governor, and the Church official helped bring them back to France. As *Time* magazine explained, "[T]he Roman Catholic hierarchy had helped in getting the Finely brothers back" to their Jewish relatives.[40]

When critics acknowledge Catholic efforts on behalf of Jews, they often refer to the Holy See's efforts as being directed toward Catholics who converted from Judaism, as opposed to Jews who were not Catholics.[41] In 1963, Joseph Lichten, director of the Intercultural Affairs Department of the Anti-Defamation League of B'nai B'rith, wrote: "There is an element of naïveté" on the part of those who make such allegations, because the Catholic Church issued tens of thousands of blank and forged baptismal certificates during the war.[42] With these documents, any Jewish person could avoid deportation by the Nazis as long as converted Jews were protected.[43]

Vatican officials had legal standing to object to persecution of Catholics. Unfortunately, they did not have similar standing when it came to non-Catholics — be they Protestants, Jews, or others. As it turns out, the Nazis rarely responded positively when protests were made on behalf of Catholics. (German authorities even denied a Vatican request to enter German-occupied areas of Poland to check on Catholic clergy, referring them to the Red Cross.)[44] A regime that would not heed

Church protests on behalf of its own members would certainly never have listened to Vatican protests on behalf of non-Catholics. The best the Church could do was to try to pass off non-Catholic victims as Catholics and try to intervene to save them on that basis.[45]

Documents discovered after the Vatican opened archives in 2003 show that Pope Pius XI and Secretary of State Pacelli were very concerned about Jewish victims, regardless of whether they were baptized. Peter Godman, who reviewed these documents explained: "[B]oth Pius XI and his second-in-command [Pacelli] recognized the Church's duty to intervene in order to alleviate the suffering of German Jews. Not only Jews converted to Catholicism but all people — irrespective of race, rank, or religion — in need of Christian charity."[46] Godman further explained that by 1936 (well before the *Kristallnacht* pogrom) the Vatican understood that Nazi treatment of the Jews violated 'the law of justice toward all races' which the Supreme Tribunal of the Roman Church regarded as a binding principle.[47]

More evidence that Pope Pius XII was concerned about Jewish victims, regardless of whether they were baptized, appeared in the book *The Heresy of National Socialism*. Released in 1941 by the "Publishers to the Holy See" (Burns, Oates, & Washburn), and carrying both an *imprimatur* and a *nihil obstat*, this book laid out a strong condemnation of Nazism, focusing on both Nazi persecution of the Catholic Church and on Hitler's extreme hatred of the Jews.[48] Those who read this book had no doubt about where the Holy See stood.

Perhaps the question of anti-Semitism affecting the Pope's wartime performance can best be answered by Jewish leaders who knew of his efforts during the war. Grand Rabbi Isaac Herzog of Jerusalem wrote:

I well know that His Holiness the Pope is opposed from the depths of his noble soul to all persecution and especially to the persecution... which the Nazis inflict unremittingly on the Jewish people.... I take this opportunity to express... my sincere thanks as well as my deep appreciation... of the invaluable help given by the Catholic Church to the Jewish people in its affliction.[49]

After the war, Rabbi Herzog visited the Vatican to thank Pius and the Holy See for "manifold acts of charity" on behalf of the Jews.[50] Thus, if anti-Semitic prejudice existed within the Catholic Church, it did not affect Pius XII's behavior during the war.

## 2. Was the Pope Blinded by His Hatred of Communism?

In March 1937, Pope Pius XI issued the encyclical *Divini Redemptoris* (of the Divine Redeemer, although it is better known by its subtitle, "On Atheistic Communism"), in which he attacked Communism, which was beginning to spread throughout the world. He wrote that Communism was historically evil, that Communist governments were out to destroy religion, were godless, were violent, denied the individual and the family, and reigned by terror. He concluded that

"Communism is intrinsically wrong, and no one who would save Christian civilization may collaborate with it in any undertaking whatsoever."[51]

The concluding chapter of Michael Phayer's *Pius XII, the Holocaust, and the Cold War* states: "Pius XII's obsession with communism is the key to understanding his papacy." Some have argued that the Church's view of Communism caused Pius XII to turn a blind eye to the Nazis and their Jewish victims. The Vatican certainly had viewed Communism as the Church's greatest threat from the early 1920s until at least the late 1930s.[52] Many British leaders also thought that Communism was a greater threat than Nazism.[53] The Soviet Union not only killed millions of peasants, but made it a policy to persecute the Church and drive religion out of the country.[54] Many Church leaders feared that if Germany were thoroughly de-Nazified, the Communists would take over. The prospect of a communistic Germany was of deep concern to the Catholic hierarchy (as well as to Protestant leaders).[55]

Long before Pacelli became Pope, Hitler and Mussolini were seen by many world leaders (including some Catholics) as the best defense against the spread of Communism.[56] Father Falkan, a Catholic parish priest in Germany, said: "I must admit that I was glad to see the Nazis come to power, because at that time I felt that Hitler as a Catholic was a God-fearing individual who could battle communism for the Church."[57] Of course, this was before the Nazis began their reign of terror and right in the middle of the Soviet terror.[58] Moreover, Church leaders were right to fear Communism. After the Allied victory, the Soviets expanded their sphere of influence (and their persecution of the Church) throughout most of Eastern Europe, including East Germany.[59]

One of the first authors to assert that Pius saw National Socialism as a possible bulwark against Communism was Saul Friedlander. In *Pius XII and the Third Reich: A Documentation*, Friedlander explained:

> It is, perhaps, not altogether outside the realm of possibility that Pius XII believed that a peace between Berlin and London would eventually enable the Reich to turn on the Soviet Union and rid that country of atheistic communism. (It should be made clear that we have no document written in 1940 indicating such an intention, and this is mere hypothesis on my part.)[60]

As his analysis continued, however, Friedlander dropped the cautionary note and presented the Vatican's motivations as a virtual certainty.[61] As Father Robert Graham explained in *America* magazine, Friedlander was "determined to make the facts fit his theory."[62]

Pope Pius XII was not nearly as hostile toward the Communist-Soviet regime as some critics would have their readers believe. On behalf of Pope Pius XI (who was said to possess a "horror of Bolshevism"),[63] Pacelli tried to obtain a concordat with the Soviet Union in the mid-1920s,[64] and he did conclude one with the predominantly Socialist government of Prussia in 1929.[65] In fact, in 1926, Pacelli consecrated a Jesuit bishop in Berlin, Father Michel d'Herbigny, whose task it was to go into the U.S.S.R. to consecrate several bishops secretly and to inform them officially of their appointments as apostolic administrators.[66]

Despite his concern over the spread of Communism, Pius XII also recognized that Nazism presented a similar threat. He still condemned Communism during the war, but as an observer of that time noted, "with it he bracketed Nazism in the same breath, for it strikes, no less ruthlessly, at the individuality of the home, the very heart of religion. Both are tyrannically pagan."[67] In 1942, Pius XII told Father Paolo Dezza, S.J. (made a cardinal in 1991): "The Communist danger does exist, but at this time the Nazi danger is more serious. They want to destroy the Church and crush it like a toad."[68]

When the Allies sought to have Pius speak out against Nazi Germany, he said he was unwilling to do so without also condemning the atheistic government of the Soviet Union, but he also refused Axis requests to bless their "crusade" into the godless Soviet Union.[69] (Father Robert Graham wrote, "As is well known, during the war on Russia the Pope refused by word or gesture to lend any form of moral support to the Nazi or Fascist arms.")[70] In fact, at the request of President Franklin Roosevelt, he stopped all mention of the Communist regime in the Soviet Union.[71] He did, however, provide aid to Soviet prisoners of war.[72] President Roosevelt's representative to the Pope, Myron Taylor, reported back to Washington that Pius XII's concern about the Soviet Union would not present a problem for the American war effort.[73]

In early May 1943, the Spanish ambassador to the Vatican reported that Pius "now regarded Nazism and Fascism, and not Communism, as he used to, as the greatest menace to civilization and the Roman Catholic Church."[74] Minutes from the British high command, dated September 10, 1941, state: "His Holiness is heart and soul with us in the struggle against Nazism, and his attitude as regards the 'anti-Bolshevist Crusade' leaves nothing to be desired."[75] U.S. Representative Harold Tittmann reported to Washington that "the last thing the Vatican would welcome would be a Hitler victory."[76] Tittmann said that "Pius XII himself had joined the President in admitting that Hitlerism was an enemy of the Church more dangerous than Stalinism and that the only way to overcome the former was an Allied victory, even if this meant assistance from Soviet Russia."[77] Others were also aware of the Pope's view. According to a postwar interrogation of Nazi official Joachim von Ribbentrop, Hitler thought that the Catholic Church sometimes worked with the Communists.[78]

In April 1943, Hungarian Prime Minister Nicholas de Kallay met with Pius XII. He recorded:

His Holiness brought up the matter of conditions in Germany. He depicted the conditions prevailing in Germany, which fill him with great sadness, in dramatic words. He finds incomprehensible all that which Germany does with regard to the Church, the Jews, and the people in occupied territories.... He is quite aware of the terrible dangers of Bolshevism, but he feels that, in spite of the

Soviet regime, the soul of the large masses of the Russian people has remained more Christian than the soul of the German people.[79]

In fact, by cooperating with Franklin Roosevelt's request to support extension of the lend-lease program to the U.S.S.R., Pius actually gave economic and military aid to the Soviets, even though this seemed to be in conflict with Pope Pius XI's 1937 encyclical *Divini Redemptoris*, which strictly prohibited Catholics from collaborating with Communists.[80] (Later, Pius XII's appeals on behalf of Ethel and Julius Rosenberg again revealed his ability to look beyond the "Communist" issue.)[81] The failed Catholic-Jewish study group found no evidence to support the conclusion that Pius favored the Germans over the Soviets.[82] As such, the record simply does not support the conclusion that hatred of Communism blinded Pius XII to the evils of Nazism.[83]

## 3. Did the Pope Come Under the Influence of Hitler?

As a former nuncio to Germany for thirteen years, fluent in the German language, and well known to many German leaders, Pius XII certainly had close connections to the Axis powers. He also held the German people in great esteem. Some critics have used his relationship with Germany to charge that the Pope was sympathetic to the German war effort. Even though Pacelli never met Hitler,[84] in the *Sidelights on History*, Hochhuth accused Pius of being influenced by Hitler because as Vatican secretary of state he negotiated the concordat with Germany.[85]

Many people did fall under the influence of Hitler. Some religious leaders at that time thought that the churches were not socialistic enough. They hoped to reform Socialism and retain a political (and national) identity. This was what Hitler offered — National Socialism.[86] Thus, many religious people supported Nazism. Pius, however, understood that Hitler, who wanted to create national "popes" and replace the existing churches with a German Nazi church, was no friend to the Holy See.[87] It is totally at odds with all of the evidence, including the Pope's public pronouncements, all that is known about his wartime activities, and his pre-war attitude, to think that Pius was attracted to Hitlerism. In fact, General Erich Ludendorff, a German national hero and one of Hitler's earliest supporters wrote: "Pacelli was the live spirit which stood behind all the anti-German activities of Rome's policy."[88]

As for the concordat, this was a common diplomatic procedure. Pius XI viewed the concordat process as the best way to safeguard and defend the freedom of worship of the Catholic faithful (especially in countries where they were in a minority) and to defend and safeguard essential elements of Catholic life (such as Catholic schools and Catholic associations). The Holy See had sought such an agreement with Germany for well over ten years. Moreover, although the Nazis immediately began a pattern of ignoring the concordat, on paper it seemed very favorable to the Vatican. Had the Vatican turned it down, the Catholic

Church certainly would have been criticized for having bypassed an opportunity to restrict the Nazis. A few years after the concordat, the Vatican released the encyclical *Mit brennender Sorge*, which was a clear condemnation of the Nazis. It must also be noted that Pacelli was at that time secretary of state for the Vatican. Certainly, he had significant input into the Vatican's international policies, and he probably agreed with the approach, but the ultimate decision to sign and ratify the concordat was not his.[89] As such, the concordat provides no basis to conclude that Pius XII or the Vatican fell under the influence of Hitler.[90]

### 4. Would a Statement by the Pope Have Diminished Jewish Suffering?

This is perhaps the most important question, and yet it is also the one most difficult to answer. Holocaust survivor Elie Wiesel, accepting the Nobel Peace Prize, said: "Take Sides. Neutrality helps the oppressor, never the victim. Silence encourages the tormentor, never the tormented." There are, however, certain assumptions inherent in this observation, and not all of them are applicable to the situation during World War II.

Reading accounts of "rescuers" and resistance fighters in occupied nations, one is struck by how often the people were in their teens or twenties. There might be several explanations for this: older rescuers died long ago, so we do not hear their stories; younger people traditionally are more willing to challenge authority; and younger people are better able to take whatever physical risks that accompany this work. It might also be that as people move into adulthood and assume obligations to others, they are much more reluctant to risk retaliation because of the impact that it might have on others, especially their children.

During the days of the Third Reich, many pastors said that they would be willing to endure imprisonment or death, but they could not do so because of their families. It is one thing for a husband/father to be persecuted; it is quite another to see children suffer a similar fate. Hitler always used a man's family as an inducement for absolute obedience.[91]

Pius was not in the situation of a teenager; he was more like the parent of a very large family.[92] He knew well that any of his acts or comments might bring retaliation — not against him, but against Catholic clergy and laity in Germany and every occupied nation.[93] As one bishop who was imprisoned at Dachau reported:

> The detained priests trembled every time news reached us of some protest by religious authority, but particularly by the Vatican. We all had the impression that our wardens made us atone heavily for the fury these protests evoked… whenever the way we were treated became more brutal, the Protestant pastors among the prisoners used to vent their indignation on the Catholic priests: "Again your big naive Pope and those simpletons, your bishops, are shooting their mouths off… why don't they get the idea once and for all, and shut up. They play the heroes and we have to pay the bill."[94]

With concerns like this, Pope Pius XII had to weigh carefully the force of his words. This threat might not be justification for maintaining neutrality if a different course of action would have saved more lives, but that is far from certain.

Hochhuth suggested that Pius XII could have made 35,000,000 Germans "hostile to the state," perhaps causing the Nazi leaders to rethink their actions.[95] For this to be true, however, the Pope's message would have to reach receptive listeners. That probably would not have happened.

First of all, there is no evidence of any Vatican intervention having any rallying effect on the German people or a moderating effect on the Nazis. *Mit brennender Sorge* certainly did not rally the people, nor did it moderate Nazi behavior.[96] It is interesting to note the comments of Susan Zuccotti on the "Roman Roundup": "[A] specific public Vatican protest... while placing the pope on sounder moral ground, would nevertheless have helped the Jews of Rome very little. The Nazis would never have released the Jews already caught or ceased future arrests."[97]

Clearly, the Vatican held no sway with the Nazis.[98] Pius made several private protests to the German leaders, but they had no lasting impacts.[99] "Hitler showed no respect at all for the intervention of the Pope and the nuncios on behalf of the Jews."[100] Pius knew that a public statement might lead to great damage to the Church, but it would probably not have any impact on the functioning of the Third Reich.[101] In fact, at times German occupation authorities believed that an immediate papal protest might work in their favor.[102] The few times when German authorities were concerned about a public denunciation, such as after the invasion of Rome in 1943, Pius used the threat of a statement to convince the Nazis to reduce persecution of Jews.

At the Nuremberg trials, German Field Marshal Albert Kesselring testified: "If [Pius XII] did not protest, he failed to do so because he told himself, quite rightly: If I protest, Hitler will be driven to madness; not only will that not help the Jews, but we must expect that they will then be killed all the more."[103] The U.S. deputy chief of counsel at the Nuremberg War Crimes Trials,[104] Dr. Robert M. W. Kempner, wrote that "[e]very propaganda move of the Catholic Church against Hitler's Reich would have been not only 'provoking suicide,'... but would have hastened the execution of still more Jews and Priests."[105] Father Robert Leiber, who worked closely with Pope Pius XII for many years, said, "During the war the thought never entered anybody's head that Pope Pius XII could have been able to put a stop to the annihilation of the Jews by means of public protest."[106]

Pius XII's words would have provoked retaliation from the Nazi leaders, but what would the impact have been on the citizenry? Hochhuth argued that the Pope would have been believed by the masses, whereas pronouncements from the Allies were "shrugged off" as propaganda.[107] In all likelihood, however, condemnation would have been kept from the German public by the Nazis. The idea of a free press came to an end in Germany in 1933, and expression was suppressed everywhere else the Nazis went.[108] As others have written: "The very evil to be condemned was sufficiently evil to be able to prevent its condemnation."[109] As even John Cornwell acknowledged: "Pacelli had only limited scope for action. His cables and messages to nuncios around the world could be intercepted. His newspaper could be stopped at the gates of the Vatican. His radio station could be jammed. An encyclical aimed at Germany could be destroyed or altered before publication."[110] Pius himself was aware of these limitations, writing in a letter dated March 1, 1942: "Whereas Our Christmas radio message found a strong echo in the world... We learn with sadness that it was almost completely hidden from the hearing of German Catholics."[111]

In private conversations, too, Pius expressed dismay at the limited impact of his words. Once, to a chaplain who reported to him on the conditions in Poland, the Pontiff remarked:

> Please tell everyone, everyone you can, that the Pope suffers agony on their behalf. Many times I have thought of scorching Nazism with the lightning of excommunication and denouncing to the civilized world the criminality of the extermination of the Jews. We have heard of the very serious threat of retaliation, not on our person but on the poor sons who are under the Nazi domination. We have received through various channels urgent recommendations that the Holy See should not take a drastic stand. After many tears and many prayers, I have judged that a protest of mine not only would fail to help anyone, but would create even more fury against the Jews, multiplying acts of cruelty.[112]

As a British scholar of German history wrote: "Perhaps behind the present criticism of Pius XII lies dread of admitting that he may have been powerless."[113]

According to the U.S. deputy chief of counsel at the Nuremberg War Crimes Trials, the Nazi hierarchy sent their ambassadors a "guideline on silencing the Vatican," which made clear that the Nazi propaganda machine would be put in gear to counter any statements from the Vatican.[114] Such efforts were effective where they were employed. In occupied France, for instance, the media put forth only censored versions of the Pope's proclamations, including his Christmas messages. Thus, when the Allies invaded southern France, General Eisenhower said: "You see this country has suffered an intellectual blackout ever since the fall of France. The people have heard only what the Germans and Vichy wanted them to hear."[115] No outside news reached Poland during the occupation.[116]

Had a statement gotten through, it is very questionable as to whether it would have prompted the citizens of Germany to abandon their allegiance to Hitler. He was wildly popular, and few civilians would have wanted to become martyrs. More likely, German Catholics would have left the Church. After all, the Vatican's efforts to win freedom for its bishops and priests imprisoned in Dachau were all frustrated.[117] That being the case, it is unreasonable to think that the Pope could have been more effective helping Jews. In fact, "in the expert hands of a Goebbels, a pontifical speech could become a choice weapon against Christianity."[118]

Marcus Melchior, the chief rabbi of Denmark during the war, explained that Pius had no chance of influencing Hitler: "I believe it is an error to think that Pius XII could have had any influence whatever on the brain of a madman." He added that if he had been more confrontational, "Hitler would have probably massacred more than six million Jews and perhaps ten times ten million Catholics, if he had the power to do so."[119] Even critic Guenter Lewy concluded that once the inability of the Pope to motivate the faithful into a decisive struggle against the Nazis is accepted as a fact, it may well be that a statement would only have made things worse.[120]

In 1963, Dr. Joseph L. Lichten, director of intercultural affairs for the Anti-Defamation League of B'nai B'rith, wrote an appraisal of the Vatican during the war. He quoted a German Jewish couple whom Pius XII helped escape through Rome to Spain:

> None of us wanted the Pope to take an open stand. We were all fugitives, and fugitives do not wish to be pointed at. The Gestapo would have become more excited and would have intensified its inquisitions. If the Pope had protested, Rome would have become the center of attention. It was better that the Pope said nothing. We all shared this opinion at the time and this is still our conviction today.[121]

Ernst von Weizsäcker, German ambassador to the Vatican during the war, expressed this same sentiment when he informed the Holy See that any protest by the Pope would only make things worse on the Jews:

> A "flaming protest" by the Pope would not only have been unsuccessful in halting the machinery of destruction but might have caused a great deal of additional damage — to the thousands of Jews hidden in the Vatican and the monasteries, to the *Mischlinge*, the Church, the territorial integrity of the Vatican City, and — last but not least—to the Catholics in all of Germany-occupied Europe.[122]

As the official representative of the Nazi government, Weizsäcker's advice would have been very influential. Moreover, this is the same advice that Pius received from his bishops in occupied nations.[123]

A complicating factor in this debate concerns the Vatican's humanitarian work. Chief among its efforts was the so-called Vatican Information Office, established in 1939 for the purpose of ensuring an exchange of news between prisoners and their families.[124] In addition, there were also Vatican efforts to assist in the emigration of Jews. From 1939 on, the Vatican provided financial assistance to organizations that aided in the emigration of Jews.[125] When the Allies invaded Italy, efforts were made to escort victims across Allied lines. As part of the program, the Vatican provided false baptismal certificates and Vatican passports to Jews, which provided them with passage and some legal protection under the terms of the concordat.[126] All of this could have been lost if the Pope provoked Hitler to the point where he would retaliate.

The International Committee of the Red Cross was similarly reluctant in pressing Nazi authorities regarding aid to Jewish prisoners. The official in charge of Jewish matters, Jean-Etienne Schwarzenberg, wrote in 1942 that "there is a great danger that the *good relations the ICRC maintains with… Germany will be compromised, to the detriment of its normal work*, if it insists too much on this delicate question."[127] An International Red Cross statement, released in 1943, addressed its reluctance to issue a protest: "[S]uch protests gain nothing… [and] can greatly harm those whom they intend to aid.… Faced with these numerous difficulties, the International Committee has given up on the question of requests for information.[128] The success of such work depended on the goodwill of the belligerent nations. Any tension in relations could see a disruption in its aid work, particularly if that nation forbade any access to prisoners. Under relatively stable circumstances, the Nazis often refused to grant the Vatican access to prisoners.[129] It was not unreasonable to assume that such difficulties would have been exacerbated if relations worsened. Indeed, as Father Robert Graham noted, "appeals to world opinion, high-sounding though they may appear, would have seemed cheap and trivial gestures to those engaged in rescue work."[130]

It is impossible to reconstruct history and determine what would have happened if only a minor change were made. As such, Pius XII's behavior during the war will always be subject to speculation. We do know that the "survival rates for Jews in Catholic countries were almost invariably higher than for Jews who found themselves under Nazi occupation elsewhere."[131] "Suppose that Pacelli had… made visible and vocal statements condemning Nazism, excommunicated all Catholic Nazis, even died a martyr's death in a concentration camp. What then? Almost certainly, more Jews would have perished than was actually the case."[132] While speculating about what might have been, it is possible to look at the assistance — in terms of information, lines of communication, and influence within Italy — given by the Vatican to the Allies and conclude that if the Pope had spoken, and the German war machine had retaliated, the very outcome of the war would have been adversely affected.

Pius XII's decision to use pastoral action instead of political posturing was neither ill-informed, shaped by prejudice or bias, nor made without serious consideration of the consequences. Perhaps more important, as expressed in his encyclical *Summi Pontificatus*, Pius felt that what he was doing was the appropriate thing for the Church to do. All evidence shows that he believed his approach would best serve the victims of the Nazis. This was what most Jewish leaders advised,[133] as well as Polish Archbishop Adam Sapieha,[134] almost all German religious leaders,[135] the International Red Cross,[136] and several Jewish rescue organizations. A fair evaluation of the evidence suggests that they (and the Pope) were right.

### 5. Was the Pope Afraid of Retaliation Against Himself or the Church?

On one episode of *Investigative Reports*, broadcast on the Arts and Entertainment Television Network, host Bill Kurtis began by posing the question: "Was he a pragmatic hero, or a moral coward?"[137] Some have indeed suggested that the Pope was not more vocal in his Nazi condemnation due to fear of retaliation. Hochhuth condemned Pius XII's moral cowardice.[138] The Vatican, of course, is located within Italy, Germany's first ally and signatory to the "Pact of Steel."[139] Pius was well aware of the Church's vulnerability with regard to the Italian Fascist state, which could violate the Lateran Treaty at any time, treat the Vatican as a subordinate state, and establish national churches apart from the Vatican.[140] He was especially concerned about the ability of the Holy See to provide for the needs of the Church and the people of Rome if the Vatican were under the control of a Fascist government.

A concern like this is reflected in the Pope's letter of April 30, 1943, to Bishop Preysing of Berlin. Pius wrote:

> We are leaving to the pastors, according to each location, the care of evaluating if, and in what measure, the danger of reprisals and pressure, as well as perhaps other circumstances due to the length and psychology of war, warrant restraint — despite the reasons for intervening — so as to avoid greater evils. This is one of the reasons for which We ourselves are imposing limits in Our declarations.[141]

Pius recognized that his words would likely lead to greater persecution of innocent people. Restraint in such a situation certainly cannot be said to reflect moral cowardice.

Critics often dismiss it, but as Dan Kurzman explained in his book *A Special Mission: Hitler's Secret Plot to Seize the Vatican and Kidnap Pope Pius XII*, the possibility of a German invasion of Vatican City was very real. Napoleon had done this in 1809, capturing Pope Pius VII at bayonet point and taking him away.[142] Rolf Hochhuth rejected the notion that Pius XII feared "violence against himself or, say, against St. Peters,"[143] but even he admitted that Hitler considered invading the Vatican. In fact, minutes of a Berlin high-command meeting show that Hitler spoke of wanting to enter the Vatican and "pack up that whole whoring rabble."[144]

Ernst von Weizsäcker, the German ambasador to the Vatican, wrote that he heard of Hitler's plan to kidnap Pius XII.[145] Weizsäcker regularly cautioned Vatican officials not to provoke Berlin.[146] Written statements by the German ambassador to Italy, Rudolf Rahn, also describe the plot and attempts to head it off. "The fact of [the plan's] existence and its target is solidly anchored in my memory," reported Rahn.[147] Albrecht von Kessel, Weizsäcker's closest aide, explained: "All we could do . . . was to warn the Vatican, the church, and the Pope himself against rash utterances and actions."[148]

Karl Otto Wolff, a German general who was the S.S. chief in Italy toward the end of the war reported the following conversation from 1943:

> **HITLER:** Now, Wolff, I have a special mission for you, with significance for the whole world, and it is a personal matter between you and me. You are never

to speak of it with anyone without my permission, with the exception of the Supreme Commandant of the S.S. [Himmler], who is aware of everything. Do you understand?

**WOLFF:** Understood, *Führer*!

**HITLER:** I want you and your troops, while there is still a strong reaction in Germany to the Badoglio treachery, to occupy as soon as possible the Vatican and Vatican City, secure the archives and the art treasures, which have a unique value, and transfer the Pope, together with the Curia, for their protection, so that they cannot fall into the hands of the Allies and exert a political influence. According to military and political developments it will be determined whether to bring him to Germany or place him in neutral Liechtenstein. How quickly could you prepare this operation?[149]

Wolff said that it would take four to six weeks in order to come up with a plan. Hitler replied: "That's far too long. It's crucial that you let me know every two weeks how you are getting on. I should prefer to take the Vatican immediately."[150] Hitler wanted the report back quickly, perhaps so that he could get rid of the Pope as soon as possible.[151]

When someone suggested to Hitler that such an attack would create a public relations problem for the party, he dismissed the concern.[152] When Wolff reported his plan back to Hitler in early December 1943, however, the S.S. general expressed his opinion that an attack would cause the Italian people to defend their Church at all costs and make occupation all the more difficult.[153] Foreign Minister Joachim Von Ribbentrop gave similar advice:

If you send aircraft over to bomb the Vatican, it will be the last move we will make. Our own people can overlook much, even our attacks on priests of other countries; but if we attack the Vatican, we will most assuredly have a civil war in Germany within the hour the first bomb falls.[154]

In light of this advice, Hitler dropped the kidnapping plan.[155] (Wolff, however, felt that it was "essential to persuade the pope to remain silent in public. If he did not... Hitler would carry out the plot.")[156]

On September 26, 1944, Paolo Porta, the Fascist leader in Como, wrote a letter to Vincenzo Costa, the Fascist leader in Milan. In that letter, Porta cited a high S.S. official to the effect that in December 1943, Hitler personally delegated Himmler and Gestapo head Heinrich Mueller to study and execute a plan to eliminate the Pope. (Himmler "was almost as anti-Catholic as he was anti-Semitic.")[157] The plan called for Germans dressed as Italian partisans to attack the Vatican. German troops would then come to the "rescue," with the hope that Pius would be killed in the foray. If he were not killed, he would be sent to Germany for "protection." After the attack, "the persecution of the Catholic Church would begin with mass deportations to Germany of all ecclesiastics in Italy and throughout the world. They are to be considered the cause of ignorance, of domination, of conspiracies. . . ." The reason for the attack was identified as "the papal protest in favor of the Jews."[158]

Hochhuth tried to diminish the threat of an invasion by saying that Hitler made this comment "among his intimates" and suggesting that it was not serious. Hochhuth then went on to discuss "feverish diplomatic activity" on behalf of the Vatican.[159] This would be natural, especially since thousands of Jewish people were being hidden from the Nazis by the Vatican. It would also indicate that the Vatican took the threat very seriously. (President Roosevelt took the threat seriously enough to suggest, in a 1943 White House meeting with Prime Minister Churchill, that the new Allied slogan should be: "Save the Pope.")[160] Pius held a meeting of the cardinals to choose his successor if he were kidnapped.[161]

Sir Francis D'Arcy Osborne, British minister to the Holy See from 1936 to 1947, came to know the Pope quite well during the war years. He denied any cowardice on the part of the Pontiff:

> Pius XII was the most warmly humane, kindly, generous, sympathetic (and, incidentally, saintly) character that it has been my privilege to meet in the course of a long life. I know his sensitive nature was acutely and incessantly alive to the tragic volume of human suffering caused by the War and, without the slightest doubt, he would have been ready and glad to give his life to redeem humanity from its consequences.[162]

Similarly, on June 16, 1944, the chief rabbi in Rome during the German occupation, Israel Zolli, explained that "on many occasions the Pope personally interceded for victims of the Nazis, thus saving their lives or getting mitigation of their penalties."[163] Giovanni Battista Montini (Pope Paul VI) said that "it is utterly false to tax Pius XII with cowardice."[164] John Cornwell even charged Pius with "almost foolhardy valor" due to his involvement with the plan to topple Hitler.[165]

He may not have made repeated public pronouncements, but Pius took affirmative action when there was some chance to make a lasting difference, even though he risked retaliation. He was not afraid of being taken prisoner or of having the Vatican invaded, and he did not hesitate to put himself in jeopardy.[166] It should also be noted that Pius did not change his approach even after the Allies had liberated Rome, Germany was in retreat, and the Vatican was safe. Thus, it cannot be said that cowardice kept Pius from being open about the German abuses.[167]

## 6. Did the Pope Know of the "Final Solution" Before the End of the War?

The general public did not become aware of the extent of Nazi atrocities until after the war. Even today it is hard to comprehend. Recent surveys have indicated that up to 25 percent of the American populace think that the Holocaust might never have happened. Because of the difficulty in understanding the magnitude of this evil, several of Pius XII's defenders have speculated that he did not know of the Holocaust in time to raise a protest. They have even made a pretty good case.

Entities in the West, especially religious institutions, had little information about what was taking place in Germany and the occupied areas.[168] In early 1940, the Vatican began receiving reports of the forced deportation of German Jews, the slaughter of Jews in Slovakia, and the abuse of Jews in Romania. There was not, however, a clear pattern of deadly Nazi violence toward the Jews at this time. The Final Solution was not made official Nazi policy until early 1942. The World Jewish Congress in Geneva first noted an increase in persecutions in March of that year.[169] A Jewish official reported this to the Vatican in August, and about this same time priests also began reporting the massive extermination of Jews by the Nazis.[170] When this was reported to the United States, President Roosevelt sought confirmation from the Vatican, but the Vatican was unable to confirm those reports until late 1942.[171]

As the Allies began to send information about the Nazi abuses to the Vatican, there was reason to question it. The Soviets certainly did not have a good reputation for veracity, and the Vatican would have wanted proof of their allegations. In addition, the Germans tried to disguise the extent of their crimes, and they were fairly successful. Moreover, the Holy See had witnessed Mussolini's activity up close, and Jews in Italy were not subject to the abuses reported from Germany and Poland.[172]

On the other hand, the Vatican had diplomatic representatives in Berlin, Paris, Lisbon, Madrid, and Washington. Priests coming to Rome from various countries brought with them accounts of the events that were taking place everywhere the Nazis went. In addition, the Vatican had innumerable ecclesiastics on both sides of the conflict who reported to Rome via friends or acquaintances and through underground operatives in the various resistance movements.[173] In fact, the Church was widely regarded as one of the best informed sources in the world and had the reputation as the listening post of Europe. German intelligence, which was convinced that the Catholic Church was a worldwide intelligence organization working against the Nazis, had radio operators monitoring Vatican transmissions twenty-four hours a day.[174]

Exactly when the Vatican recognized the pattern of treatment carried out against the Jews is unclear. As early as May 1940, Pius confided in a private conversation to a senior Italian diplomat that "terrible things" were occurring in Poland.[175] There was no set extermination plan at this time, however. In all likelihood, the Vatican learned of the plan shortly after the Nazis themselves decided on it. In February 1942, Archbishop Hlond of Warsaw (who had fled Poland against the Vatican's wishes)[176] informed the Vatican that prisoners in Nazi concentration camps "were deprived of all human rights, handed over to the cruelty of men who have no feeling of humanity. We live in terror, continually in danger of losing everything if we attempt to escape, thrown into camps from which few emerge alive."[177] Certain Poles, exiled in London, called for stronger statements by the Pontiff. Archbishop Adam Sapieha of Kraków, however, was still in Poland. He urged Pius not to speak.[178]

It is, of course, possible — even likely — that not all of the reports were believed when they were first heard.[179] Many Allied agencies doubted the earliest reports. It is virtually certain that most people, hearing the reports for the first time, thought they were exaggerated.[180] It makes no sense, however, to contend that Pius did not receive information about the abuses until after the war. In his 1942 Christmas statement, he spoke of how the Nazis were killing hundreds of thousands of victims.[181] Pius XII did what he thought was most appropriate as the spiritual leader of his people, and he did so with relatively good information.

## 7. Was the Pope Too Willing to Compromise to Achieve Peace?

Prior to the outbreak of the war, many world leaders were willing to compromise with Hitler to avoid further aggression; British Prime Minister Neville Chamberlain was only the most prominent. The League of Nations also followed this course rather than confront Mussolini after his conquest of Ethiopia. The minor sanctions let Hitler know that there was no need to fear retaliation for his early conquests. When Hitler annexed Austria and threatened Czechoslovakia, leaders from France and England agreed to transfer the Sudetenland region of Czechoslovakia to Germany. In return, Hitler assured them that the rest of the country would not be invaded. Hitler was given everything he wanted.

Prior to the war, most Vatican leaders followed the appeasement line. Pius XII was also attached to this policy, at least prior to the outbreak of hostilities.[182] He believed that the continuance of the war was a greater evil than the horrors committed during it.[183] His willingness to negotiate in order to win peace is often portrayed as a willingness to accommodate the aggressive tendencies of Hitler and Mussolini. In a 1942 message to the United States government, however, he expressly stated that

> despite what any propaganda may say to the contrary, We have never thought in terms of a peace by compromise at any cost. On certain principles of right and justice there can be no compromise. In our Christmas allocutions of 1939, 1940, and 1941 the world may read some of these essential principles expressed in unmistakable language, We think they light the path along which We walk and will continue to walk unswervingly.... We shall never approve of, much less further a peace, that gives free rein to those who would undermine the foundations of Christianity and persecute Religion and the Church.[184]

Moreover, while it is certainly true that Pius wanted to bring the war to an end as quickly as possible, that end would also have brought an end to the Holocaust.[185] While appeasement might have been an unwise policy for a warring nation to advance, it was — as modified by Pius XII in the above quoted message — a completely understandable position for a man of God in search of peace.[186]

## 8. Should the Pope Have Made a Statement for the Sake of Appearances?

This question certainly has the look of being a straw man, but Hochhuth suggested that the Pope *should* have considered the impact that a statement would have had on the Church's reputation: "The Pope must surely have realized that a protest against Hitler… would have elevated the Church to a position it has not held since the Middle Ages."[187] Pius XII's dilemma was this:

> Was his own moral reputation more important than the life of a single Jew, or is the life of even one Jew more valuable than justifying his conscience in the eyes of the world? If Pius XII had spoken in this context, no doubt the case against him would have been that, by issuing moral platitudes, he had threatened the lives of others.[188]

Pius understood his situation. He once speculated that a record of his personal actions in helping the Jews might have given him a better place in history. He said, "No doubt a protest would have gained me the praise and respect of the civilized world, but it would have submitted the poor Jews to an even worse fate."[189]

Of course, there could have been no more outrageous sin for the Pope than to sacrifice his ideals and compassion for the persecuted in order to advance the stature of himself or the Church.[190] Such an action would have gone against everything that is known about Pope Pius XII. "Nothing was more opposed to the pope's intentions than to use human suffering as an opportunity to increase his prestige and power."[191] Thus, with full knowledge of the consequences to his reputation, Pius elected to work behind the scenes, instead of making grand pronouncements, though he knowingly risked, and subsequently did incur, much condemnation.[192] He refused "to buy his own good image in the history books at the price of possibly exposing many more human lives to the anger of an egomaniac capable of anything."[193]

In the end, perhaps one must acknowledge the different roles that various agencies play in times of crisis. The Jewish rescue groups did not speak out during the war. Rather, they did their work in relative silence. The same goes for humanitarian groups like the International Red Cross. In order to have any effectiveness in their chosen role, these agencies had to maintain a fairly low profile. The same was true for Pius XII. He chose a role for the Church and carried it out in the best way possible. Condemnations from the pulpit would likely have had no positive effect on the Nazis and would almost certainly have resulted in Hitler putting an end to the Vatican's charitable works and the Holy See's efforts to end the war. As others have written, "If Pope Pius had said anything, the impact would have lasted a day and the Vatican would have lasted 30 minutes."[194]

## 9. Can Responsibility Be Diminished by Pointing to the Failings of Others?

The evil that Hitler symbolizes is so hard to comprehend that there is a desire to find other culprits to share the blame. Thus, there are those who would spread the blame not only to Pius, but also to Roosevelt, the Allies, other churches, and various world organizations and officials.[195] Hochhuth said that Jews could not expect the same help from the Vatican, the Red Cross, or any other nation (with the possible exception of the Danes) that non-Jews would receive.[196] He also blamed the Allies for not acting sooner against the gas chambers in Austria and Poland, asserting that they knew of the atrocities in 1942.[197]

It is not unusual for observers to praise one entity by contrasting it with other institutions. Thus, it has been argued that the Christian churches showed a greater resistance to Hitler and the Nazis than did the judiciary, the universities, or German trade unions.[198] Similarly, a former Israeli consul in Italy stated that "the Catholic Church saved more Jewish lives during the war than all the other churches, religious institutions and rescue organizations put together. Its record stands in startling contrast to the achievements of the International Red Cross and the Western Democracies."[199] Pulitzer Prize-winning author John Toland called the Holy See's silence "deplorable," but he also said that the record of the Allies was far more shameful.[200] Toland argued that the British and Americans, despite lofty pronouncements, not only avoided taking any meaningful action but gave sanctuary to few persecuted Jews.[201]

In 1944, the U.S. secretary of the treasury, Henry Morgenthau, confronted President Roosevelt concerning the government's reluctance to provide aid to European Jews. Ultimately, the president created the War Refugee Board, which helped rescue tens of thousands of Jewish people from Europe.[202] Those who wish to spread Hitler's blame have called it "the great shame" that Roosevelt did not act earlier and rescue America's reputation.[203] Others have condemned the United States Congress for its reluctance to open up immigration limitations or the Allies, particularly Roosevelt, for the unconditional-surrender demand.

In all of these cases, people have tried to shift blame away from Hitler and the Nazis by pointing to others. More often than not, Pius receives the blame when people do this. Some, however, have used this technique in an effort to defend Pius. In other words, they defend him by saying that he is not the only one who treated the Jews improperly.

If Pius XII's actions had been wrong, blaming others would not lessen his sin. It is, however, interesting to note how many individuals and groups have been blamed for the Nazis' actions. The evil is so great that people keep looking for another culprit. Hitler and his top advisers, however, deserve the vast majority — if not all — of the blame. Others who are sometimes named may have in some way contributed to the evil, but action or inaction on their part should not affect the proper allocation of the blame.

## 10. Should the Pope Have Excommunicated Hitler?

As an infant, Hitler was baptized into the Catholic faith, so some have suggested that excommunication would have been an appropriate sanction for him and some other Nazi leaders.[204] Some critics have argued that Hitler might have backed down had Pius XII made the threat. Reportedly, Pius was urged to threaten excommunication in the 1942 Christmas address.[205] In a note from the Pope that was smuggled to Polish priests, Pius said that he had considered excommunication and greater condemnation of the Nazis but had concluded that it would only create more fury against the Jews, multiplying acts of cruelty.[206] As it was, "Pius XI had all but excommunicated Hitler."[207]

It should be noted that excommunication from the Catholic Church is not akin to the process of shunning, where a community turns its back on an individual. Excommunication from the Catholic Church means that the person is prohibited from receiving the sacraments.[208] In cases where this is important to the individual, a mere threat can have a significant impact. Hitler, however, had not been a practicing Catholic since his childhood, and he "hated the Christian religion in which he was reared."[209] Mussolini himself said that appeals to Christianity were meaningless when it came to the Nazis "because they are true pagans."[210]

Hitler did not receive Communion as an adult and had essentially excommunicated himself. The events surrounding Hitler's suicide make clear that the Catholic religion had no influence over him, even at the time of his death. His wedding ceremony was carried out by a justice of the peace, not a priest. In addition, suicide has always been in violation of Catholic doctrine, and would have meant almost certain damnation to a devout Catholic. In 1945, cremation was also in clear violation of the Church's teaching. Moreover, despite his planning and the numerous directions that were left for others to carry out, Hitler made no arrangements for the last rites or any type of Christian burial. If the Catholic faith had meant anything to him, he certainly would have made some type of arrangement along these lines.

The Catholic Church has two forms of excommunication. A *ferendae sententiae* excommunication is imposed by an ecclesiastical judge. The self-executing *latae sententiae* applies without official Church decree, based simply on the acts of the individual. As others have recognized: "Hitler was already excommunicated *ipso facto* for a whole range of crimes and could only have returned to the Catholic faith, even assuming that he would ever have wanted to, by having his excommunication lifted."[211] Thus, it could be argued that the 1917 Code of Canon Law, which the young Eugenio Pacelli helped prepare, set forth the terms of Hitler's excommunication.[212] Of course, this type of excommunication would not necessarily have been drawn to anyone's attention unless Hitler sought to receive one of the sacraments, but there is no record of him having done that.

The Pope, of course, could have announced Hitler's excommunication, even if it were the *latae sententiae* kind.[213] Such an announcement would have amounted to simply making a statement for public consumption, with no positive benefits for Hitler's victims and potentially tragic consequences.[214] As one commentator has written:

To criticize the Pope for failing to excommunicate Hitler is unrealistic since the action would have triggered greater evils. And to criticize Pius XII for his alleged failure to condemn the murderous actions of the Nazis fails to take into account that he had actually done this and that his words had already fallen upon deaf ears.[215]

Pius XII's decision not to announce excommunication of Hitler is not only in keeping with his approach to the war effort, but is also completely understandable.

## The Real Answer

In his first encyclical, *Summi Pontificatus* (On the Unity of Human Society), released in 1939, Pope Pius XII set forth his position on Hitler, the war, and the role that he would play. He made reference to the Nazis as "the ever-increasing host of Christ's enemies" (n. 7), and noted that these enemies of Christ "deny or in practice neglect the vivifying truths and the values inherent in belief in God and in Christ" and want to "break the Tables of God's Commandments to substitute other tables and other standards stripped of the ethical content of [Christianity]." In the next paragraph, Pius charged that Christians who fell in with the enemies of Christ suffered from cowardice, weakness, or uncertainty.

In paragraph 13, Pius wrote of the outbreak of war. "Our paternal heart is torn by anguish as We look ahead to all that will yet come forth from the baneful seed of violence and of hatred for which the sword today ploughs the blood-drenched furrow." In the next paragraph, he wrote of the enemies of Christ (a reference to Hitler's National Socialists) becoming bolder.

Paragraphs 24 through 31 laid out the Pope's belief that prayer (not public condemnation) was the only appropriate response for the Bishop of Rome. Obviously, Pius viewed this as an important act of faith. Moreover, it was the lack of Christianity that he identified as the cause of the "crop of such poignant disasters." Faith and prayer were the things he could contribute to the world at that time, not political or military strength. Pius also expressed his belief in redemption. Thus, even though the enemies of Christ were committing horrible atrocities, it was still possible for even these very evil people to be redeemed. It was fundamental to the Pope's faith that anyone could be forgiven.

Paragraphs 45 to 50 of the encyclical reject the racial policies in both Germany and Italy. Pius expressly stated that all races and nationalities were welcome in the Church and had equal rights as children in the house of the Lord. In paragraph 48, he put meaning to those anti-racist statements by naming new bishops of different races and nationalities. Moreover, he said that the Church must always be open to all:

> The spirit, the teaching and the work of the Church can never be other than that which the Apostle of the Gentiles preached: "putting on the new (man) him who is renewed unto knowledge, according to the image of him that

created him. Where there is neither Gentile nor Jew, circumcision nor uncircumcision, barbarian nor Scythian, bond nor free. But Christ is all and in all" (Col 3:10-11).

The equating of Gentiles and Jews was a clear rejection of Hitler's fundamental ideology.

Paragraphs 51 to 66 set forth Pius XII's view of a just society. Here he asserts that the first reason for the outbreak of war is that people have forgotten the law of universal charity. The second reason is the failure to put God above civil authority. He argues that when civil authority is placed above the Lord, the government fills that void, and problems develop. This is exactly what Hitler had done. (This analysis would also apply to Pius XII's view of the Soviet Union — which at that time had an agreement with Hitler.)

Pius said that nations must have a religious basis. He wrote that the goal of society must be development of the individual, not the power of the state. Again, this was a slap at Hitler's dismantling of religious institutions and development of the state in Germany. In fact, paragraph 60 was a direct answer to Hitler's view of the state as set forth in *Mein Kampf*:

> To consider the State as something ultimate to which everything else should be subordinated and directed, cannot fail to harm the true and lasting prosperity of nations. This can happen either when unrestricted dominion comes to be conferred on the State as having a mandate from the nation, people, or even a social order, or when the State arrogates such dominion to itself as absolute master, despotically, without any mandate whatsoever.

Similarly, Pius presented an answer to Hitler's views of the family and of education in this section of the encyclical.

Pius made note of how "powers of disorder and destruction" stand ready to take advantage of sorrow, bitterness, and suffering in order to make use of them "for their dark designs." This would seem to be a description of how Fascists in Italy and Nazis in Germany took advantage of the chaos following the First World War to rise to power. Pius also responded to the demands of Hitler and Mussolini (and, for that matter, Stalin) for stronger central governments. While acknowledging that there may be difficulties that would justify greater powers being concentrated in the state, the Pope also said that the moral law requires that this need be scrutinized with greatest rigor. The state can demand goods and blood, but not the immortal soul.

Paragraphs 73 to 77 dealt with the Pope's ideas relating to international relations. Here, in paragraph 73, he wrote:

> Absolute autonomy for the State stands in open opposition to this natural way that is inherent in man . . . and therefore leaves the stability of international relations at the mercy of the will of rulers, while it destroys the possibility of true union and fruitful collaboration directed to the general good.

Pius stressed the importance of treaties and wrote of an international natural law that requires that all treaties be honored. With Hitler having recently breached several treaties and the concordat, this must be seen as another swipe at the Nazi leader.

In paragraph 85, Pius accurately described the challenges he would face, and he set forth the code of conduct that he followed throughout the rest of the war:

> And if belonging to [the Kingdom of God], living according to its spirit, laboring for its increase and placing its benefits at the disposition of that portion of mankind also which as yet has no part in them, means in our days having to face obstacles and oppositions as vast and deep and minutely organized as never before, that does not dispense a man from the frank, bold profession of our Faith. Rather, it spurs one to stand fast in the conflict even at the price of the greatest sacrifices. Whoever lives by the spirit of Christ refuses to let himself be beaten down by the difficulties which oppose him, but on the contrary feels himself impelled to work with all his strength and with the fullest confidence in God.

In paragraphs 93 to 95, Pius expressed the importance that he attached to the spirit as opposed to the physical world. Here he made clear that the most important thing would be to open people to Christ. He said that the Church must be protected so that it can fulfill its role as an educator by teaching the truth, by inculcating justice, and by inflaming hearts with the divine love of Christ. Indeed, throughout the war, he would protect the Church so that it could carry out its life and soul-saving functions.

Paragraphs 101 to 106 draw distinctions between the Vatican and other, secular nations and explain the Church's special role in the world. The Church "does not claim to take the place of other legitimate authorities in their proper spheres." Instead, Pius writes, the Church should be a good example and do good works. In paragraph 101, he says that the Church

> spreads its maternal arms towards this world not to dominate but to serve. She does not claim to take the place of other legitimate authorities in their proper spheres, but offers them her help after the example and in the spirit of her Divine Founder Who "went about doing good" (Acts 10: 38).

This same thought is expanded upon when Pius writes "render therefore to Caesar the things that are Caesar's." In other words, the Church plays an important, but limited role in resolving disputes in the secular world. The Pope's obligation is to pray for peace and offer comfort to the afflicted.

Pius expressed his confidence that the Church would always prevail in the long run. Any structure that is not founded on the teaching of Christ, he wrote, is destined to perish. Read in context, this was a promise of the ultimate failure of Nazism. In fact, in paragraph 106, he expressly foresaw that Poland would be resurrected:

This... is in many respects a real "Hour of Darkness,"... in which the spirit of violence and of discord brings indescribable suffering on mankind.... The nations swept into the tragic whirlpool of war are perhaps as yet only at the "beginnings of sorrows,"... but even now there reigns in thousands of families death and desolation, lamentation and misery. The blood of countless human beings, even noncombatants, raises a piteous dirge over a nation such as Our dear Poland, which, for its fidelity to the Church, for its services in the defense of Christian civilization... has a right to the generous and brotherly sympathy of the whole world, while it awaits, relying on the powerful intercession of Mary, Help of Christians, the hour of a resurrection in harmony with the principles of justice and true peace.

This reference to Poland resolved any doubts about to whom the Pontiff was referring.

In paragraphs 107 to 112, Pius wrote that it was his duty to try for peace, and that duty had to be fulfilled even if it meant that the Church was misunderstood in the effort:

While still some hope was left, We left nothing undone in the form suggested to us by Our Apostolic office and by the means at Our disposal, to prevent recourse to arms and to keep open the way to an understanding honorable to both parties. Convinced that the use of force on one side would be answered by recourse to arms on the other, We considered it a duty inseparable from Our Apostolic office and of Christian Charity to try every means to spare mankind and Christianity the horrors of a world conflagration, even at the risk of having Our intentions and Our aims misunderstood. (n. 107)

He encouraged people to keep faith that good will prevail, and he once again expressed his faith in the ultimate triumph of God's will.

———

World leaders well understood Pius XII's message in *Summi Pontificatus*. François Charles-Roux, the French ambassador to the Vatican during the 1930s, lavished praise on the encyclical, because in it Pius XII took a stand "against exacerbated nationalism, the idolatry of the state, totalitarianism, racism, the cult of brutal force, contempt of international agreements, against all the characteristics of Hitler's political system; he laid the responsibility for the scourge of the war on these aberrations."[216]

This encyclical shows that Pius did not waver in his approach to Hitler and the Nazis. In 1939, he laid out his vision, which he followed for the rest of the war.[217] Thus, it was not a matter of fear, nor did Pius change after he learned of the Nazi abuses. All along he thought that the best way to ensure peace was through prayer. Moreover, his primary concern was with the eternal soul, which was always subject to redemption. While it may be hard to call anything associated with Nazi Germany a success, as reported in *Time* magazine, the German Catholic Church "resisted co-operation more successfully than had German Protestantism."[218]

---

In January 2002, documents from the personal archive of General William J. ("Wild Bill") Donovan, who served as special assistant to the U.S. chief of counsel during the International Military Tribunal at Nuremberg, were made public and posted on the Internet by the *Rutgers Journal of Law and Religion*.[219] In a confidential report documenting Nazi persecution of the Church, prepared for the Nuremberg prosecution, the situation surrounding *Summi Pontificatus* was discussed as providing grounds for a separate count against the Nazis. The report noted that priests who read that document were reported to the authorities and that Nazi officials stopped its reproduction and distribution.[220]

Pius followed his first encyclical with a Christmas address that also condemned Nazi aggression. He spoke of "a series of deeds, irreconcilable either with natural law or with the most elementary human feelings.... In this category falls the premeditated aggression against a small, hardworking and peaceful people, under the pretext of a 'threat' nonexistent, not thought of, not even possible."[221] The Pontiff cried out against "atrocities... and the unlawful use of destructive weapons against non-combatants and refugees, against old men and women and children; a disregard for the dignity, liberty, and life of man, showing itself in actions which cry to heaven for vengeance: 'The voice of thy brother's blood crieth to me from the earth'"

By March 1940, *Look* magazine was able to proclaim that "the most important axis of the world is no longer the Rome-Berlin, but the Rome-Washington. This is the peace axis."[222] President Roosevelt praised the Vatican, urging other churches to "synchronize their peace efforts... to the outline of Pope Pius XII of his conception of a just peace"[223] Nazi propagandist Joseph Goebbels, on the other hand, complained in his diary: "The Pope has made a Christmas speech. Full of bitter, covert attacks against us, against the Reich and National Socialism. All the forces of internationalism are against us. We must break them."[224]

---

In 1965, Pope Paul VI proposed that Pius XII be considered for sainthood. In 2007, after forty years of research devoted to every aspect of Pius XII's life and pontificate, the Congregation for the Causes of Saints voted unanimously to recommend that the Church recognize the wartime Pope's "heroic virtues."[225] Father Paul Molinari, the Church-designated advocate for sainthood (the postulator general of the cause), wrote that he has "an excellent case."[226] Father Peter Gumpel, relator for the beatification of Pius XII with the Congregation for the Causes of Saints, has called Pius XII's case one of the strongest he has seen in four decades of working on saints' causes.[227]

In September 2008, at an audience at Castel Gandolfo, at which this author was honored to be present, Pope Benedict XVI said of Pius XII:

> When one draws close to this noble Pope, free from ideological prejudices, in addition to being struck by his lofty spiritual and human character one is also captivated by the example of his life and the extraordinary richness of his teaching. One can also come to appreciate the human wisdom and pastoral intensity which guided him in his long years of ministry, especially in providing organized assistance to the Jewish people.

Referring to a conference on Pius XII that Pave the Way Foundation had just sponsored in Rome,[228] Benedict XVI said: "In the proceedings of your convention, you have also drawn attention to [Pius XII's] many interventions, made secretly and silently, precisely because, given the concrete situation of that difficult historical moment, only in this way was it possible to avoid the worst and save the greatest number of Jews." Benedict expressed his desire for in-depth study of Pius XII's life and his works "in order to come to know the historical truth, overcoming every remaining prejudice."

In December 2009, Benedict signed a decree declaring Pius XII "venerable," affirming the Congregation for the Causes of Saints' finding that Pius led a life of "heroic virtue." The signing also meant that Pius was eligible to be beatified when a miracle was attributed to his intervention. As of this writing, that matter was still being investigated.

It was written during the war that "Pius XII is the Peacemaker who God raised up for this world."[229] The Bible says, "Blessed are the peacemakers, for they shall be called sons of God" (Mt 5:9).

# Appendix

## Contents

1. **English translation of the "palm fronds" correspondence (September 4-28, 1917) between Nuncio Eugenio Pacelli and Cardinal Gasparri.**

*Pacelli wrote the following on September 4, 1917:*

Request for an intervention of the Holy See in favor of the Israelite Community

Your Eminence,

The Israelite community of the German Empire, known as the "Free Interest Community of Orthodox Jewry," based in Frankfurt and represented by Prof. Dr. Werner, the Rabbi of Munich, approached this Nunciature with the following request.

As provided in the Bible, the community celebrates Sukkoth, or the Feast of the Tabernacles (in this year on October 1st), and for this they need palm leaves which they usually get from Italy, but now, unexpectedly and for reasons that I also do not understand, the Italian government has banned the export of the palm leaves even though they are already in Como (at the Swiss border), and they serve no other purpose. Time is short, and the export should take place within days, if the palm leaves are to arrive on time, especially since they must then be distributed throughout Germany.

The Israelite community desires an intervention by His Holiness, with the Italian government, and asked this Nunciature to request such, adding that thousands of members loyal to their religion were praying for a successful result.

It seemed to me that giving aid in this case would not mean helping the Israelite Community in a matter of civil or natural rights common to all men (which would not have been an inconvenience) but would rather mean a cooperative effort, material and remote, providing direct support of the exercise of the Jewish Faith (*culto giudaico*). Therefore, I replied to the Rabbi in all politeness, that, while help might not be possible to send a telegraph (having sent one for a similar affair which, because it is quite extraordinary, would require too much explanation), I would immediately send an urgent report to the Holy See, although I am afraid that because of the duration of communication it might not come in time, and would not know which further action the Holy Father would chose in this matter with the Italian Government.

Therefore I hand over this case to the higher judgment of Your Most Reverend Eminence....

*On September 18, the cardinal secretary of state replied that he "fully agrees with the way in which you acted in this delicate affair, since the Holy See, obviously, cannot follow the request of Prof. Dr. Werner. Please explain this to the gentleman in your reply — the choice of the words is up to you — but stress the fact that the Holy See does not entertain diplomatic relationship with the Italian Government." Pacelli reported on September 28: "Prof. Werner fully understands the reasons which I explained him and thanked me warmly for what we did on his proposal."*

2. **English translation of a letter (dated April 18, 1919) from Nuncio Eugenio Pacelli to Cardinal Gasparri regarding the Bolshevik takeover in Munich.**

Munich, April 18, 1919

Your Eminence,

At the beginning of this week, I had the honor to refer to Your Eminence, with coded letter No. 319, that two Foreign Legations in Munich were invaded by red guards of the Republic of the Councils. Following this event, the Legation of Prussia's automobile was requisitioned, and the Austrian-Hungarian Consul General was arbitrarily arrested and released only after strong protests by the Austrian-Hungarian Chargé d'affaires.

In this regard, because of such deplorable events, it was deemed opportune to call for a reunion of the Diplomatic Corps. After a long discussion it was decided to speak about this directly with Levien, head of the Republic of the Councils of Munich, to force him to declare unequivocally, if and how the actual Communist Government intends to recognize and oversee the immunities of the Diplomatic Representatives. Negotiations were entrusted to the Nunciature and to the Prussian Legation. Since it would have been absolutely undignified for me to present myself to this Gentleman, I sent Monsignor Uditore, who went this morning with the Prussian Chargé d'affaires, Count von Zech (since the Minister, because of the present circumstances, is away from Munich).

Levien installed himself with the State officials, or better stated, with the Council of the Representatives of the people, in the royal palace of the Wittelsbach. The present scenario in the palace is indescribable. The confusion is chaotic, the filth is nauseating, the continual coming and going of soldiers and armed workers, the shouting, the bad words, the cursing, that resounds there, make the building, that was the preferred residence of the King of Bavaria, a truly infernal place. There is an army of clerks, going, coming, transmitting orders, spreading news. Among them, a crowd of young women of doubtful appearance, also Jews, are in all the offices, with provoking attitudes and equivocal smiles. At the head of this group of females, there is Levien's lover: a young Russian Jewess, divorced, who gives the orders. And to this woman the Nunciature, unfortunately, had to bow down to request a permit to enter.

Levien is a young man, also Russian and Jewish, of about 30 or 35 years old. Pallid, dirty, with dull eyes, a voice that is hoarse and coarse: a truly revolting type, yet with an intelligent and clever physionomy. He just about deigned to receive Monsignor in a hallway, surrounded by an armed guard, among whom was an armed hunchback, who is his faithful guard. With a hat on his head and smoking, Levien listened to what Monsignor Schioppa explained to him, while protesting repeatedly and roughly that he was in a hurry and had more urgent business. With a contemptuous tone, he said that the Republic of the Councils recognized the extraterritoriality of the Foreign Legations if, and as long as the representatives of these Powers, friendly or unfriendly (he doesn't care), do nothing against the Republic of the Councils.

When Monsignor asked him to reflect on the position of the Pontifical Representative who merits special consideration because of his Mission, Levien stressed the fact with an ironic tone: "Naturally, it's about protecting the Center!" With that remark, Monsignor Schioppa added energetically that it's about defending the religious interests of Catholics, not only of Bavaria but of all Germany!

The conclusion of the discussion was that he sent Monsignor to Comrade Dietrich, Representative of the people for Foreign Affairs. There he found another crowd of women, of soldiers, and of workers; more screams, more confusion. This improvised Minister of Foreign Affairs was a little less discourteous, but more cutting with his answers. In substance he repeated what Levien said, adding, in a way that would not allow discussion, that, if the Nuncio did anything against the Republic of the Councils or the interests of the proletariat, he would be "kicked out" (weggeworfen), and he repeated Levien's statement that *they had no need of the Nunciature*, since they will adhere to separation of State and Church. Monsignor Schioppa noted that, if the Republic damaged Catholic interests, the Nuncio would betray his Mission by keeping quiet, but that naturally, in other cases, the Papal Representative would not get involved in the politics of the country. Dietrich insisted that extraterritoriality will be respected, as long as the safety of the Republic of the Councils is not endangered. In any event, the Nunciature and the other Legations were granted some sheets, in which extraterritoriality itself is recognized. It is clear that such sheets have but a relative value.

Similar documents had already been given to the Diplomatic and Consular Representatives in Bavaria; however, they did not impede the invasion of the two Legations mentioned above, nor the arrest of the Austrian Consul. Given the complete anarchy that reigns, the interpretation of such documents is made by the military which can present itself wherever it wishes and do whatever it pleases and get away with it. There may be some soldiers who have some intelligence and the capacity to understand the significance of extraterritoriality; but it is clear that most of them do not understand an iota, and are interested solely in capturing and arresting people. Only after this happens, can one invoke the protection of the commissaries of the people.

This is the unprecedented situation of the Apostolic Nuncio, who for future negotiations would have to submit to the undignified humiliation of returning to such authorities in similar circumstances.

It is my duty to fulfill my responsibility and refer this matter to you. With deep veneration, I humbly kiss your ring and have the honor to declare myself

Your humble and devoted servant,

Eugenio, Archbishop of Sardi, Apostolic Nuncio

3. English translation of a letter (dated November 14, 1923) from Nuncio Eugenio Pacelli to Cardinal Gasparri regarding the attempted putsch in Munich.

[*Author's note: This is the English Translation of Pacelli's November 14, 1923 letter denouncing the early version of the Nazis. (Archivio Nunziatura Monaco, protocollo numero #28961.) The translation is by Antonio Gaspari, published by* Inside the Vatican *magazine.*]

Your Eminence:

The facts about the nationalist uprising, which in recent days has disturbed the city of Munich (see dispatches No. 443, 444, and 445) are already known to Your Most Reverend Eminence from the Italian press; I therefore do not need to repeat them in this respectful report. Still, upon one point, which I alluded to already in dispatch No. 444, I believe it opportune to communicate to Your Eminence some further details, that is, regarding the demonstrations of an anti-Catholic character which accompanied the uprising itself, but which have not surprised those who have followed the publications of the papers of the right-wing radicals, like the *Völkischer Beobachter* ("Folkish Observer") and *Heimatland* ("Homeland").

This character was revealed above all in the systematic attacks on the Catholic clergy with which the followers of Hitler and Ludendorff, especially in street speeches, stirred up the population, thus exposing the ecclesiastics to insults and abuse.

The attacks were especially focused on this learned and zealous Cardinal Archbishop, who, in a sermon he gave in the Duomo on the 4th of this month and in a letter of his to the Chancellor of the Reich published by the Wolff Agency on the 7th, had denounced the persecutions against the Jews.

To this was added the unfounded and absurd rumor in the city, probably spread intentionally, that accused the cardinal of having changed von Kahr's mind, who, as is known, while at the beginning in the Bürgerbräukeller (beer hall) had apparently, to avoid violence, adhered to the Hitler-Ludendorff coup d'etat, later came out against it.

Thus it was that, during the confusing events of last Saturday, a numerous group of demonstrators gathered in front of the front door of the bishop's residence, shouting "Down with the Cardinal!" ("*Nieder mit dem Kardinal!*")

His Eminence was by good fortune absent from Munich, having left that day to consecrate a new church in a town near Müldorf; but, when he returned in his car the following evening, he was greeted by a similar hostile demonstration. These anti-Catholic sentiments also manifested themselves in chaotic student gatherings, the day before yesterday, in the university, which were attended by people who did not attend the university (and were not even from Bavaria), obliging the Rector in the end to close the university until further notice. Also in the university, object recently of repeated acts of the charitable solicitude and generosity of the Holy Father on behalf of the students, there were denunciations of the Pope, of the Archbishop, of the Catholic Church, of the clergy, of von Kahr, who, even though he is a Protestant, was characterized by one of the orators as an honorary member of the Society of Jesus (*Ehrenmitglied der Jesuiten*).

4.  **English translation of an instruction (dated April 4, 1933) to intercede on behalf of Jews, sent from the Vatican (Cardinal Secretary of State Pacelli) to Nuncio Cesare Orsenigo in Berlin.**

Your Reverend Excellency:

Important Israeli personalities have appealed to the Holy Father to ask for his intervention against the danger of anti-Semitic excesses in Germany. Given that it is part of the traditions of the Holy See to carry out its mission of universal peace and charity toward all men, regardless of the social or religious condition to which they belong, by offering, if necessary, its charitable offices, the Holy Father asks your Excellency to see if and how it is possible to be involved in the desired way.

I greatly appreciate this encounter and have a sense of distinct and sincere esteem for Your Excellent Rev. Servant. [*Profitto volontieri dell'incontro per rafformarmi con sensi di distinta e sincera stima, di Vostra Eccellenza Rev. ma Servitors.*]

[*Author's note: Pacelli signed the original, and initialed the copy in the left margin, with a "P."*]

5.  **English translations of correspondence (1933) between St. Edith Stein and the Holy See.**

*Letter (undated) of St. Edith Stein to Pope Pius XI*

Holy Father!

As a child of the Jewish people who, by the grace of God, for the past eleven years has also been a child of the Catholic Church, I dare to speak to the Father of Christendom about that which oppresses millions of Germans. For weeks we have seen deeds perpetrated in Germany which mock any sense of justice and humanity, not to mention love of neighbor. For years the leaders of National Socialism have been preaching hatred of the Jews. Now that they have seized the power of government and armed their followers, among them proven criminal elements, this seed of hatred has germinated. The government has only recently admitted that excesses have occurred. To what extent, we cannot tell, because public opinion is being gagged. However, judging by what I have learned from personal relations, it is in no way a matter of singular exceptional cases. Under pressure from reactions abroad, the government has turned to "milder" methods. It has issued the watchword "no Jew shall have even one hair on his head harmed." But through boycott measures — by robbing people of their livelihood, civic honor and fatherland — it drives many to desperation; within the last week, through private reports I was informed of five cases of suicide as a consequence of these hostilities. I am convinced that this is a general condition which will claim many more victims. One may regret that these unhappy people do not have greater inner strength to bear their misfortune. But the responsibility must fall, after all, on those who brought them to this point and it also falls on those who keep silent in the face of such happenings.

Everything that happened and continues to happen on a daily basis originates with a government that calls itself "Christian." For weeks not only Jews but also thousands of faithful Catholics in Germany, and, I believe, all over the world, have been waiting and hoping for the Church of Christ to raise its voice to put a stop to this abuse of Christ's name. Is not this idolization of race and governmental power which is being pounded into the public consciousness by the radio open heresy? Isn't the effort to destroy Jewish blood an abuse of the holiest humanity of our Savior, of the most blessed Virgin and the apostles? Is not all this diametrically opposed to the conduct of our Lord and Savior, who, even on the cross, still prayed for his persecutors? And isn't this a black mark on the record of this Holy Year which was intended to be a year of peace and reconciliation?

We all, who are faithful children of the Church and who see the conditions in Germany with open eyes, fear the worst for the prestige of the Church, if the silence continues any longer. We are convinced that this silence will not be able in the long run to purchase peace with the present German government. For the time being, the fight against Catholicism will be conducted quietly and less brutally than against Jewry, but no less systematically. It won't take long before no Catholic will be able to hold office in Germany unless he dedicates himself unconditionally to the new course of action.

At the feet of Your Holiness, requesting your apostolic blessing,

[*signed*] Dr. Edith Stein,
Instructor at the German Institute for Scientific Pedagogy,
Münster in Westphalia, Collegium Marianum.

### Cover letter (dated April 12, 1933)

*[Author's note: The following was attached to Edith Stein's undated letter, in German, to Pius XI, by Archabbot Raphael Walzer of the Beuron Abbey (Stein's spiritual director at that time), from his original Latin text.]*

The supplicant [Edith Stein] has most urgently asked me that the attached letter which she has given me under seal be transmitted to His Holiness [Pope Pius

XI]. The supplicant is known everywhere in Catholic Germany as a woman of outstanding faith and virtue, and has authored numerous important works, which have gone through several editions. Making use of this good opportunity, I agreed, Your Most Reverend Eminence, in a most humble way, to ask that you should assist us in these most unhappy days.

For, if I am not mistaken, if sober and prudent persons do not intervene, our whole country, and therefore also our Holy Mother Church in Germany, will continue in the greatest danger. The present danger is especially fearful since so many people are being deceived by word and treacherous claims. My only hope here on earth is the Holy Apostolic See. For our part, we will not cease to pray, and to insist and invoke in silence, God's help. I ask in a most humble way for a benediction; and while I kiss the sacred purple, I am your unworthy servant,

Raphael, Archabbot

*Cardinal Pacelli's reply (dated April 20, 1933), from the original German text*

With special thanks I have confirmed to Your Grace the reception of your kind letter of April 12 and the attached document [Edith Stein's letter]. I leave it to you to inform the sender [Edith Stein] in an opportune way that her letter has been dutifully presented to His Holiness [Pope Pius XI]. With you, I pray to God that in these difficult times, He may, in a special way, protect His Holy Church and grant all the children of the Church the grace of fortitude, and generous mentality, which are the presuppositions of our final victory. With the expression of my special estimation, and with my intimate wishes for the entire Archabbey, I am, Your Grace, very devotedly,

Eugenio Pacelli

6. Letter (dated April 13, 1938) from Monsignor Ernesto Ruffini, secretary of the Congregation for Seminaries and Universities, to the rectors and presidents of Catholic universities worldwide (original French text).

S. CONGRÉGATION DES SÉMINAIRES ET UNIVERSITÉS   235

tous dans leur propre pays, dans les nationalités particulières de chacun, dans leur race particulière, les propagateurs de cette idée si grande et si magnifiquement maternelle, humaine, avant même d'être chrétienne. »

### S. CONGREGATION DES SEMINAIRES ET UNIVERSITES

**Lettre de la S. Congrégation, adressée le 13 avril 1938 aux Recteurs des Universités et Facultés catholiques.** — (Reproduite dans *La Croix* du 11 mai 1938, la *Documentation catholique* du 20 mai 1938, col. 579, etc.).

Excellence ([1]),

L'année dernière, à la veille de la nativité de Notre-Seigneur, l'auguste Pontife heureusement régnant, dans son allocution aux éminents cardinaux et aux prélats de la Curie romaine, parla avec tristesse de la grave persécution qui sévit, comme tout le monde le sait, contre l'Eglise catholique en Allemagne.

Mais la principale affliction du Saint-Père vient de ce que, pour excuser une si grande injustice, on fait intervenir des calomnies impudentes et qu'on répand partout les doctrines les plus pernicieuses, faussement colorées du nom de science, dans le but de pervertir les esprits et d'en arracher la vraie religion.

En face de cette situation, la Sacrée Congrégation des études enjoint aux Universités et aux Facultés catholiques d'appliquer tous leurs efforts et leur activité à défendre la vérité contre l'envahissement de l'erreur.

Aussi les maîtres devront-ils s'appliquer, de tous leurs moyens, à emprunter à la biologie, à l'histoire, à la philosophie, à l'apologétique, aux sciences juridiques et morales, des armes pour réfuter avec solidité et compétence les assertions insoutenables qui suivent :

1) Les races humaines, par leurs caractères naturels et immuables, sont tellement différentes que la plus humble d'entre elles est plus loin de la plus élevée que de l'espèce animale la plus haute.

2) Il faut, par tous les moyens, conserver et cultiver la vigueur de la race et la pureté du sang ; tout ce qui conduit à ce résultat est par le fait même, honnête et permis.

3) C'est du sang, siège des caractères de la race, que toutes les qualités intellectuelles et morales de l'homme dérivent comme de leur source principale.

4) Le but essentiel de l'éducation est de développer les caractères de la race et d'enflammer les esprits d'un amour brûlant de leur propre race comme du bien suprême.

5) La religion est soumise à la loi de la race et doit lui être adaptée.

([1]) Le titre varie selon la qualité du destinataire. De même chaque lettre porte une salutation finale (non reproduite ici), différente selon que le destinataire est Cardinal ou évêque ou prélat.

236                    ACTES DU SAINT-SIÈGE

6) La source première et la règle suprême de tout l'ordre juridique est l'instinct racial.

7) Il n'existe que le Kosmos, ou l'Univers, être vivant ; toutes les choses, y compris l'homme, ne sont que des formes diverses s'amplifiant au cours des âges de l'universel vivant.

8) Chaque homme n'existe que par l'Etat et pour l'Etat. Tout ce qu'il possède de droit dérive uniquement d'une concession de l'Etat.

À ces propositions si détestables, on pourra d'ailleurs en ajouter facilement d'autres.

Le Très Saint-Père, préfet de notre Sacrée Congrégation, a l'assurance, Excellence, que vous ne négligerez rien pour amener à leur plein effet les prescriptions contenues dans cette lettre.

                         Ernest RUFFINI, secrétaire.

                         NOTE

Parmi les documents épiscopaux récents, condamnant les hérésies du racisme, signalons particulièrement : Cardinal Van Roey, archevêque de Malines, *Le mystère du sang dans l'économie du salut*, discours adressé aux prêtres du diocèse pendant les retraites ecclésiastiques de 1938, dans *Collectanea Machliniensia*, novembre 1938, p. 573-593 ; reproduit également dans la *Documentation catholique*, 20 décembre 1938, col. 1481 suiv. — Cardinal Verdier, archevêque de Paris, *Lettre au Cardinal Van Roey* du 17 nov. 1938, reproduite dans *La Croix*, des 20-21 novembre 1938 et la *Doc. cath.* 20 déc. 1938, col. 1495 suiv. — Cardinal Schuster, archevêque de Milan, allocution prononcée au Dôme de Milan, le 13 novembre 1938, traduction de la *Doc. cath.*, 20 déc. 1938, col. 1497 suiv. — Cardinal Cerejeira, patriarche de Lisbonne, discours du 18 novembre 1938, traduction de la *Doc. cath.* du 20 déc. 1938, col. 1502 suiv. (1). — Cardinal Faulhaber, archevêque de Munich, discours à la cathédrale de Munich le 6 novembre 1938, traduction de *La Croix* du 15 novembre 1938, reproduction partielle de la *Doc. cath.* du 20 déc. 1938, col. 1510.

---

(1) Ces quatre documents viennent d'être édités en brochure à la *Bonne Presse*, Paris, sous ce titre : *L'Eglise contre le Racisme. Une hérésie anti-romaine*, 64 p., 17 × 9 cm. Prix : 2 frs.

7. **English translation of a memorandum (1938) from Cardinal Pacelli, with a cover letter by American Ambassador Joseph P. Kennedy.**

*Cover letter*

London, April 19, 1938

PERSONAL AND CONFIDENTIAL.

Dear Jimmy:

I enclose a copy of a strictly confidential Memorandum which I have received personally from Cardinal Pacelli. I believe this will be of interest to the President and yourself. Please note particularly the part beginning with the last paragraph on page 3, down to the middle of page 4. That question is one that is bound to come up again and merits very close and serious attention.

With all good wishes,
Yours sincerely,

Joseph P. Kennedy

Enclosure: as stated.
The Honorable James Roosevelt, The White House, Washington, D.C.
HVJ/MW

*Pacelli memorandum*
*[handwritten date: April 1938]*

As to your investigation about some rumors concerning the attitude of the Church towards the new rulers in Austria and the possibility of an agreement in this regard between the Holy See and the Nazi Government, I am happy that you brought up this matter so as to allow me to give you my personal views which of course cannot reflect any positive information from the official circles and are just delivered to your confidential use.

The sudden statement of the Austrian Catholic Hierarchy in reference to the new Government, as it was given to the Press, was evidently the result of some compulsory influences. Their unexpected declaration immediately after the military invasion of the country did not receive any approval neither previously nor afterwards from the Holy See, as the officious [*sic*] Vatican organ, the "Osservatore Romano," stated immediately after the issue of such declaration. One is rather inclined to think that the text of this statement might have been prepared, at least in its main points, by a Governmental Press Bureau, if not by the Government Commissioner Bürckel himself, and that the signing thereof by the Bishops might have been the result of a political pressure rather than of their free initiative and intention. Under this pressure as a matter of fact the Bishops have overlooked to quote in the text of the declaration the fundamental principles of the freedom of the practice of Christian religion, of the respect of the right of the Church and of the abolishment of the anti-Christian propaganda, a clause that in view of the persecution in Germany could have appeared quite natural. Rather on this occasion they should have expressed the hope that the beginning of a Kulturkampf should be avoided in Austria and that the Kulturkampf in Germany should be quieted down, a hope, though, which in consideration of the clear evidence of the facts could not be well founded and which — as it happened at the time of the Saar Plebiscite — would undoubtedly be deluded.

Being confronted with so much confusion and critics among Catholic and non-Catholic circles at such a declaration made by the Austrian Bishops, the Holy See did not delay, through the "Osservatore Romano," to sever itself from the said declaration with great tact and marked firmness.

Upon the Vatican statement immediately followed the call to Rome of Cardinal Innitzer, Archbishop of Vienna, and the same official Vatican paper, the "Osservatore Romano," published his open statement in its original German text (English translation of it follows here below). From the text of this declaration and from the above attitude of the Vatican authorities one can easily understand that the Holy See will never be ready to give its approval to any agreement of any bishop to any Governmental action which might be in contrast with the Divine Law and the freedom and the rights of the Church.

You know that a diplomatic Concordat was concluded and signed between the German Reich and the Holy See a few years ago and that official diplomatic relations do exist as there is an Apostolic Nuncio in Berlin and a German Ambassador to the Holy See. But, no matter what pretexts are set forth by the German Government, the real fact is that since the early time after the Concordat was signed a more or less open attitude against all clauses accepted in the Concordat was adopted by the German Government. The Holy See has used all possible ways to protect the freedom of the Church and of the Catholics, keeping itself ever ready to do the best in order to avoid any more bitter conflict, and being always prompted by the desire of avoiding to make the situation more and more difficult.

Even now, I feel sure that the Holy See would always be willing to agree and to deal fairly with any political authority whatsoever, but before a real understanding is reached there must be at least the beginning of the evidence of good faith on the other side: evidence that so far has been completely lacking in this instance, for which the possibility of an agreement between the two Powers is out of question for the time being.

I think it will be very fine if you will convey to your Friend at home these personal private views of mine. Ever in my personal judgment, no better opportunity than this for trying to carry on the plan that we had thought of while in America and that I know is amongst your aims. It would make the world think over the ever increasing necessity in the present troubles of keeping in touch with the Supreme Moral Powers of the world, which at times feel powerless and isolated in their daily struggle against all sorts of political excesses from the Bolsheviks and the new pagans arising amongst the young "Arian" [sic] generations.

I still think that the planned provision would increase the prestige of the American Government which would appear solely directed to use all means for insuring the peace of all peoples.

You can judge yourself of the inconvenience in this very crucial moment of the European political life that the American Government is without a direct source of information from and a straight and intimate connection with the Vatican circles.

[*Illegible handwritten word or letters; perhaps Pacelli's initials.*]

I am sure that you have seen in the Press the text of the statement issued by His Eminence Cardinal Innitzer, Archbishop of Vienna.

Anyway, the English translation of same is following here below:

[*The word "Quote" is handwritten on the memorandum.*]

> The solemn statement of the Austrian Bishops of the 18th March of this year did not intend evidently to express an approval of what was not and is not reconciliable [*sic*] with the Laws of God, with the freedom and the rights of the Catholic Church. Furthermore that statement cannot be interpreted by the State and the Party as a duty of conscience of the faithful nor must be used for propaganda purposes.

For the future the Austrian Bishops request:

> That in all matters pertaining to the Austrian Concordat no change be made without previous understanding with the Holy See.
>
> That in a particular way all rules in connection with the schools and the educational activities as well as in the training of the youth might be arranged in such a way as to respect the natural rights of the parents and the religious and moral formation of the Catholic youth, according to the doctrine of the Catholic religion.
>
> That the propaganda against religion and the Church be forbidden.
>
> That the rights of Catholics to proclaim, defend and practice Catholic Faith and the Christian Laws in all the fields of human life with all the means allowed by the present progress of our day's science be respected.

Rome, April 6, 1938

Signed: Th. Cardinal Innitzer [*The words "End Quote" are handwritten on the memorandum.*]

[*Author's note: From the Joseph P. Kennedy Collection at the John F. Kennedy Library.*]

8. Confidential memorandum (dated March 3, 1939) from the American Consulate regarding the views of Pope Pius XII.

IN REPLY REFER TO
FILE No. 800 AWK-RM

DEPARTMENT OF STATE

THE FOREIGN SERVICE
OF THE
UNITED STATES OF AMERICA

AMERICAN CONSULATE

Cologne, Germany,
March 3, 1939.

Confidential.

Dear Moffat:

Even at the risk of duplication from other sources, may I transmit to you the following information concerning the new Pope.

I knew Pacelli in Berlin when he was there as Papal Nuncio. Two years ago when I was in Rome on a holiday, I found the Sistine Chapel closed on the only day I was free to see it. I appealed to Pacelli, then Cardinal Secretary of State for special permission to see the Chapel. I got the permission but I did not see the Chapel after all as the Cardinal detained me for three solid hours and we discussed the situation in Germany.

His views, while they are well-known, surprised me by their extremeness. He said that he opposed unalterably every compromise with National Socialism. He regarded Hitler not only as an untrustworthy scoundrel but as a fundamentally wicked person. He did not believe that Hitler was capable of moderation and in spite of appearances would end up in the camp of the left-wing Nazi extremists when he began his career. He told me that he supported the German Catholic bishops in their anti-Nazi stand. The risk of losing a large

part

Jay Pierrepont Moffat, Esquire,
    Chief of the Division of
        European Affairs,
            Department of State,
                Washington, D. C.

- 2 -

part of the Catholic youth in Germany, he said,
was not as great as the consequences to the
Catholic Church in general throughout the world
in surrendering to the Nazis. At that time --
it was two years ago - he did not want the
German Catholics to do more in their opposition
than to practice their religion openly and devoutly but, he added, "if the time comes, and there
is no way out of the dilemma, they (the German
Catholics) will know how to grasp stronger
measures". Pacelli never gave me the impression
of being a "peace at any price advocate"!

He was formerly in favor of the Bavarian
monarchist movement which plans to unite
Bavaria with Austria under the aegis of a
monarch. He always believed that a strong
federal Germany was a real danger to the peace
of Europe, and hence to the Church. He liked
the German people and appreciated their good
qualities but feared them as a strong united
nation regardless of the circumstances.

Pacelli, too, was prominent in the
Vatican's Russian policy. It was in this connection that I first learned to know him. At
that time, I was working on Russian affairs.
He ordained priests and even a bishop in his
private chapel in Berlin, whereupon they left
incognito for Soviet Russia. Their mission
was to train and ordain priests in Soviet
Russia. He was responsible, too, for a private
college in Berlin for the preparation for the
Catholic priesthood of Russians, formerly members
of the Russian orthodox church. The Church plans
to use them in Russia when "Der Tag" comes along.
A good many starved Russian ex-officers and noblemen were enlisted, not only in Germany, but in
other European countries. Among them is a Prince
Obelensky, a distant connection of Mrs. Klieforth.
Pacelli's early anti-Communist slant seemingly trained
him for his later anti-Nazi one.

With my greetings and best wishes, I am,

Very sincerely yours,

A. W. Klieforth
American Consul General

9. **English translation of a letter (dated October 3, 1940) from the Holy See (Cardinal Maglione) regarding money being sent to help imprisoned Jews in southern Italy.**

Secretariat of State of His Holiness

From the Vatican, 3 October 1940

Your Reverend Excellency,

I have submitted to the august attention of the Holy Father the request made in your letter #935 of September 15th on behalf of those who have been interned.

The August Pontiff deigned to consider your request, and has ordered me to see to it that the sum of 3,000 Lire be sent to Your Excellency, which I now do with the attached cheque drawn on the Bank of Rome.

His Holiness, in deference to the intentions of the donors, has also charged me to make you aware that this money should preferably be destined for those who suffer for reasons of race, and to communicate the Apostolic Benediction, which he imparts with his whole heart to Your Excellency and to the flock entrusted to your charge.

I am happy to carry out these august orders. And let me take this opportunity of expressing to you my sincere feelings of esteem.

Your Excellency's servant,

Luigi Cardinal Maglione [*signed by hand*]

10. **English translation of a letter (dated November 29, 1940) from the Holy See (Archbishop Montini) regarding money being sent to help imprisoned Jews in southern Italy.**

From the Vatican, 29th November 1940

With regard to your letter of November 8th, seeking a new sum to be directed for the support of Jews interned in your diocese, I am pleased to tell Your Excellency that the Holy Father has benevolently decided that you should be granted the extra assistance you asked for.

In keeping with this revered instruction, I am sending the enclosed check for 10,000 Lire, asking Your Excellency to be good enough to send to the Secretariat of State, when convenient, an exact, even if brief, report on how this money was used.

I am likewise happy to tell Your Excellency that His Holiness has learned with great pleasure about the energetic charitable activities you have undertaken.

He imparts his Apostolic Benediction to you, your entire diocese and to all those whom you are assisting.

Yours very sincerely,
G. B. Montini [*signed by hand*]

[*Author's note: Montini was then the assistant to the secretary of state, Cardinal Maglione, and later became Pope Paul VI.*]

## 11. Letter (dated April 8, 1942) from Dr. G. Riegner of the World Jewish Congress to Nuncio Philippe Bernadini.

*Original French version*

le 8 avril 1942.

Excellence,

Nous avons reçu votre communication du 2 avril et nous nous empressons de vous remercier très sincèrement d'avoir bien voulu attirer l'attention de la Secrétairerie d'Etat du Saint-Siège sur la situation des Juifs en Europe centrale et notamment en Slovaquie.

Nous avons également pris note avec une vive satisfaction des démarches faites par Son Excellence le Cardinal Maglione auprès des autorités de la Slovaquie en faveur des Juifs de ce pays et nous vous prions de vouloir bien transmettre à la Secrétairerie d'Etat du Saint-Siège l'expression de notre profonde gratitude.

Nous sommes convaincus que cette intervention a produit une forte impression dans les milieux dirigeants de Slovaquie, ce qui semble résulter des nouvelles que nous venons de recevoir de ce pays.

En effet, en date du 27 mars, le Ministre de l'Intérieur et Vice-Président du Conseil, Monsieur Mach, a convoqué la presse locale et étrangère pour lui donner des explications au sujet des mesures prévues contre les Juifs. Nous nous permettons de vous remettre sous ce pli, en double exemplaire, le texte du discours prononcé par M. Mach à cette occasion et dont il ressort que le Ministre a tenté de justifier les mesures cruelles déjà appliquées ou en voie d'être appliquées, en essayant de les présenter comme étant compatibles avec les exigences du droit humain naturel et avec les principes de l'Eglise. Nous croyons que l'étrange interprétation que M. Mach donne des dispositions en question mérite de retenir votre attention et celle de la Secrétairerie d'Etat du Vatican. En effet, dans ce discours, M. Mach insiste sur le plan prévu d'envoyer tous les Juifs dans des camps de travail forcé, tout en passant sous silence les mesures également prévues et déjà en voie de réalisation de confisquer tous leurs biens.

S'il ressort de ce discours que le Gouvernement slovaque a jugé nécessaire tout de même de justifier les mesures en question, on peut en conclure aussi qu'il pourra peut-être amené, dans leur exécution pratique, à se conformer davantage aux voeux exprimés par le Saint-Siège et qui avaient pour but de faire révoquer les récentes dispositions prises contre les Juifs.

En vous renouvelant l'expression de nos sentiments de vive gratitude pour ce que le Saint-Siège, grâce à votre aimable entremise, a bien voulu entreprendre en faveur de nos frères persécutés, nous vous prions, Excellence, d'agréer les assurances de notre très respectueuse considération.

R. Lichtheim
Agence Juive pour la Palestine

Dr. G. Riegner
Congrès Juif Mondial

Son Excellence Mr. Philippe Bernardini,
Nonce Apostolique
Berne

*English translation*

TRANSLATION FROM THE FRENCH

April 8 1942

Excellency:

We have received your communication of April 2nd, and we hasten to thank you very sincerely for so graciously calling the attention of the Secretariat of State of the Holy See to the situation of Jews in Central Europe and specifically in Slovakia.

We also note with great satisfaction the steps undertaken by His Excellenc the Cardinal Maglione, with the authorities of Slovakia on behalf of the Jews of that country, and we ask you kindly to transmit to the Secretariat of State of the Holy See the expression of our profound gratitude.

We are convinced that this intervention greatly impressed the governmental circles of Slovakia, which conviction seems to be confirmed by the inform. tion we have just received from that country.

On the 27th of March, the Minister of Interior and Vice President of the Cabinet, M. Mach, convoked a conference of the local and foreign press for the purpose of clarifying the measures directed against the Jews. We take the liberty of enclosing (in duplicate) the text of M. Mach's speech upon that occasion, from which it is obvious that the Minister attempted to justify the cruel measures, already in effect or about to be applied, and tried to prove their compatibility with the requirements of natural human law and with the principles of the Church. We believe that the strange interpretation applied by M. Mach to the provisions in question, deserves your attention and that of the Secretariat of State of the Vatican. In fact, in his speech, M. Mach stresses the plan to transport all the Jews to forced-labor camps, passing over in silence the measures which have already been drafted and are about to be applied, concerning the confiscation of all Jewish property.

It appears, from this speech, that the Slovak Government finds it necessa. to justify the measures in question. One might therefore conclude that i might be induced – in the application of these measures – to conform more closely to the wishes expressed by the Holy See which desired to revoke t: recent measures against the Jews.

In renewing the expressions of our profound gratitude, for whatever the Holy See, thanks to your gracious intermediation, was good enough to unde. take on behalf of our persecuted brothers, we ask Your Excellency to accept the assurance of our deepest respect.

(Signed) DR. G. RIEGNER
World Jewish Congress

R. LIGHTHEIM
Jewish Agency for Palestine

to: HIS EXCELLENCY M. PHILIPPE BERNADINI
Apostolic Nuncio
Berne, Switzerland

## 12. Message (dated September 10, 1942) from British Minister Francis D'Arcy Osborne to British Foreign Secretary Anthony Eden.

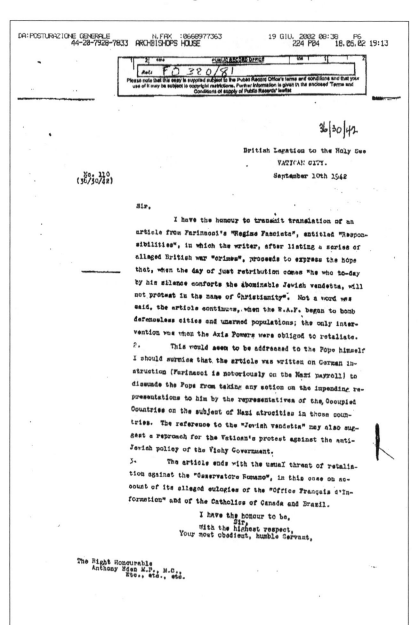

36/30/42

British Legation to the Holy See
VATICAN CITY.
September 10th 1942

No. 110
(36/30/42)

Sir,

I have the honour to transmit translation of an
article from Farinacci's "Regime Fascista", entitled "Responsibilities", in which the writer, after listing a series of
alleged British war "crimes", proceeds to express the hope
that, when the day of just retribution comes "he who to-day
by his silence comforts the abominable Jewish vendetta, will
not protest in the name of Christianity". Not a word was
said, the article continues, when the R.A.F. began to bomb
defenceless cities and unarmed populations; the only intervention was when the Axis Powers were obliged to retaliate.

2.      This would seem to be addressed to the Pope himself
I should surmise that the article was written on German instruction (Farinacci is notoriously on the Nazi payroll) to
dissuade the Pope from taking any action on the impending representations to him by the representatives of the Occupied
Countries on the subject of Nazi atrocities in those countries. The reference to the "Jewish vendetta" may also suggest a reproach for the Vatican's protest against the anti-
Jewish policy of the Vichy Government.

3.      The article ends with the usual threat of retaliation against the "Osservatore Romano", in this case on account of its alleged eulogies of the "Office Français d'Information" and of the Catholics of Canada and Brazil.

I have the honour to be,
Sir,
With the highest respect,
Your most obedient, humble Servant,

The Right Honourable
Anthony Eden M.P., M.C.,
Etc., etc., etc.

13. Telegram (dated September 11, 1942) — and associated documents — to the British War Cabinet from British Minister Francis D'Arcy Osborne confirming that the papal nuncio in France protested against the persecution of the Jews.

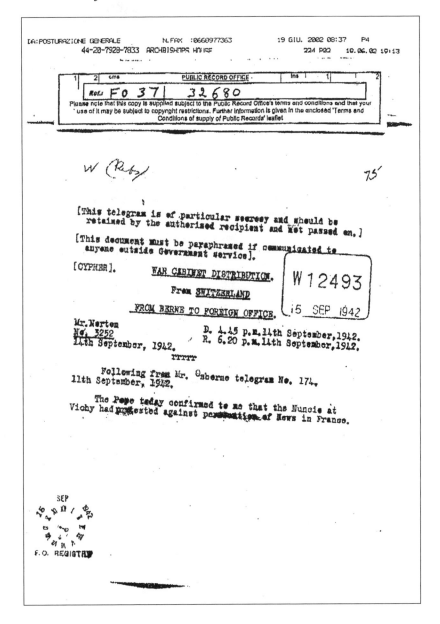

DA: POSTURAZIONE GENERALE          N. FAX : 0660977363          19 GIU. 2002 08:37    P4
44-20-7928-7833  ARCHBISHOPS HOUSE                              224 P02    10.06.02 19:13

PUBLIC RECORD OFFICE
Ref.: FO 37   32680
Please note that this copy is supplied subject to the Public Record Office's terms and conditions and that your use of it may be subject to copyright restrictions. Further information is given in the enclosed 'Terms and Conditions of supply of Public Records' leaflet

W (Ref.)                                                                          75

[This telegram is of particular secrecy and should be retained by the authorised recipient and not passed on.]

[This document must be paraphrased if communicated to anyone outside Government service].

[CYPHER].          WAR CABINET DISTRIBUTION.

From SWITZERLAND                          W 12493

FROM BERNE TO FOREIGN OFFICE.          15 SEP 1942

Mr. Norton
No. 3252                    D. 4.45 p.m. 14th September, 1942.
14th September, 1942.      R. 6.20 p.m. 14th September, 1942.
          rrrr

Following from Mr. Osborne telegram No. 174.
11th September, 1942.

The Pope today confirmed to me that the Nuncio at Vichy had protested against persecution of Jews in France.

SEP
16    1942

F.O. REGISTRY

36/30/42

British Legation to the Holy See
VATICAN CITY.

September 10th 1942

No. 110
(36/30/42)

Sir,

I have the honour to transmit translation of an
article from Farinacci's "Regime Fascista", entitled "Responsibilities", in which the writer, after listing a series of
alleged British war "crimes", proceeds to express the hope
that, when the day of just retribution comes "he who to-day
by his silence comforts the abominable Jewish vendetta, will
not protest in the name of Christianity". Not a word was
said, the article continues, when the R.A.F. began to bomb
defenceless cities and unarmed populations; the only intervention was when the Axis Powers were obliged to retaliate.

2.      This would seem to be addressed to the Pope himself
I should surmise that the article was written on German instruction (Farinacci is notoriously on the Nazi payroll) to
dissuade the Pope from taking any action on the impending representations to him by the representatives of the Occupied
Countries on the subject of Nazi atrocities in those countries. The reference to the "Jewish vendetta" may also suggest a reproach for the Vatican's protest against the anti-
Jewish policy of the Vichy Government.

3.      The article ends with the usual threat of retaliation against the "Osservatore Romano", in this case on account of its alleged eulogies of the "Office Français d'Information" and of the Catholics of Canada and Brazil.

I have the honour to be,
Sir,
with the highest respect,
Your most obedient, humble Servant,

The Right Honourable
Anthony Eden M.P., M.C.,
Etc., etc., etc.

Attached is a copy of the telegram you requested. It is a bit blurred but reads:

"The Pope today confirmed to me that the Nuncio at Vichy had protested against persecution of Jews in France."

Re File number: FO 471 36650, the only reference I could find to this protest was in a note attached to a letter from The Board of Deputies of British Jews, dated 28 December 1942. I have typed out the letter and the relevant section of the note.

There is a further reference to the protest in a letter from Osborne to Anthony Eden, in a letter dated 10 September 1942. I have attached a copy of this. I had to reduce the size to get it through the Fax, and so I hope you can read it all right.

I am continuing to work in the Public Record Office to see what else I can find that may be of use to you and to my thesis.

---

DA:POSTURAZIONE GENERALE     N.FAX :0668977363     19 GIU. 2002 08:38   P5
44-20-7928-7833   ARCHBISHOPS HOUSE        224 P03   19.06.02 19:13

Public Record Office

FO 371 36650

Letter to the British Foreign Secretary, from the Secretary of The Board of Deputies of British Jews, dated 28 December 1942:

> "As you know, a Deputation representing British Jewry was received by Mr Eden last Wednesday. We have sent Mr Eden a note of the points that we raised with him, and we thought it would be useful that you should have a copy, in view of the fact that Professor Brodetsky, Mr Stein and I will have the pleasure of meeting you shortly."

The note accompanying this letter is headed:

"Arising from the Declaration made by His Majesty's Government on 17 December 1942"

Referring, in the note, to the idea of asking the International Red Cross and the Vatican to help in the passing on of information, there is the statement that:

> "The Catholic authorities in France and the Papal Legate intervened when the Laval Government was deporting foreign Jews."

14. Order (dated October 9, 1943) to Herbert Kappler, S.S. commander in Rome, to arrest eight thousand Jews (original German text).

Fernschreiben aus Westfalen Nr.1645 vom
9.10.1943

Gehe... Reichssache

Nur für Ministerbüro.

    Der Herr RAM bittet, Gesandten Rahn und Konsul Moellhausen mitzuteilen, dass auf Grund einer Führerweisung die 8000 in Rom wohnenden Juden nach Mauthausen (Oberdonau) als Geiseln gebracht werden sollen.

    Der Herr RAM bittet, Rahn und Moellhausen anzuweisen, sich auf keinen Fall in diese Angelegenheit einzumischen, sie vielmehr der SS zu überlassen.

                  Sonnleithner.

15. Telegram 2341 (dated March 9, 1944) reporting that Castel Gandolfo was "crammed with refugees" when it was bombed by the Allies.

### Document 3-43

Telegram 2341, March 9, 1944

[This message reports on the Allied bombing of Castel Gandolfo, the location of the summer residence of the Pope.]

According to a trustworthy Vatican source, bombardment of Castel Gandolfo resulted in the injury of about 1,000 people and the death of about 300 more. The highness of the figures is due to the fact that the area was crammed with refugees. Our source says, however, that the village of Castel Gandolfo was packed with Nazi military equipment and soldiers, and the same bombs which caused the college to explode destroyed tanks which were parked before the palace. Again according to our source, the Vatican is looking at the bombing fairly, though it felt forced to protest against this bombardment of its territory.

16. English translation of a letter (dated March 27, 1946) to the Archbishopric Diocese of Münster, from the Jewish Community of the North-Rhine Province, on the death of Cardinal von Galen.

3/27/1946

To the Archbishopric Diocese of
Münster in Westphalia

The undersigned Chairman and representative of the Jewish community of North-Rhine Westphalia permits himself to express his deepest sympathy on the loss of Cardinal von Galen, on behalf of the Jewish community.

The German Jews sympathise with you at the great loss which has befallen you. The deceased was one of the few conscientious men who fought against race hate during most difficult times.

We will keep the deceased in venerable memory.

Yours sincerely [*Hochachtungsvoll*]

The Jewish Community of the North-Rhine Province

[*signed*] Auerbach [*chairman*]

412 | HITLER, THE WAR, AND THE POPE

## 17a. American Jewish Committee memorandum (dated July 2, 1957).

THE AMERICAN JEWISH COMMITTEE

M E M O R A N D U M

TO: Chapter and Unit Chairmen                    July 2, 1957

Copies To {Members of Board of Delegates
{Members of Chapter Executive Committees

FROM: John Slawson

U R G E N T   I N F O R M A T I O N

Pope Pius XII, in a private audience granted June 28th to your AJC delegation led by Irving M. Engel, issued a most important statement condemning racial and religious persecution. The Pontiff urged governments to offer asylum to such refugees. The significance of this plea -- coming from the supreme spiritual leader of the world's 484,000,000 Catholics -- is apparent.

The full text of his statement, printed July 1st in the Vatican paper, L'Osservatore Romano, and carried in today's New York Times, is attached.

May I urge you to help gain for this statement the widest possible attention in your community by:

1) Contacting your local newspaper editor to gain editorial support;

2) Contacting your radio and TV news commentators for similar support;

3) Approaching Catholic clerical and lay leaders for press coverage in diocesan papers and statements from the pulpit and from Catholic rostrums;

4) Contacting leaders of community organizations concerned with: immigration, race relations and community relations.

Your local area office and the national office will be anxious to hear whatever results you may have been able to obtain.

/NOTE: If your Chapter Chairman is away, it would be most helpful if the Vice-Chairman or another officer would take the initiative/.

In the near future, a full report on our mission to Israel, North Africa, Italy and France will be sent to you.

To save time, lists have
not been checked for duplicates,
so you may receive a second copy.

# NEWS

## THE AMERICAN JEWISH COMMITTEE
### 386 FOURTH AVENUE   NEW YORK 16, N. Y.   MURRAY HILL 5-0181

Washington Office: 1625 Eye Street, N.W. • Wash. 5, D.C. • District 7-3204
European Headquarters: 30 Rue La Boetie • Paris 8, France
South American Headquarters: Bulnes 1863 • Buenos Aires, Argentina

HAROLD STEINBERG
*Director of Press Relations*

FOR IMMEDIATE RELEASE

### TEXT OF STATEMENT BY POPE PIUS XII

New York, N.Y. . . . . The following is the full text of a statement by Pope Pius XII, delivered at the Vatican in a private audience to a delegation of American Jewish Committee leaders. The statement was published in the Vatican newspaper L'Osservatore Romano, July 1, 1957.

"The American Jewish Committee, which you honorable gentlemen represent, has just rounded out fifty years of service in behalf of the right and status of those of your race who, with other minority groups, have been subjected to the violation of fundamental rights inherent in the human person.

"Forced to forsake the land of their birth and seek on far-off unfamiliar shores a refuge where they might begin anew a family life, how many have then had to experience the almost desperate situation added to their miseries of not being welcome where they had hoped for hospitality.

"Your desire to visit us this morning is a testimony to your confidence in the interest we have in the sad plight of the peoples just described.

"Again and again, as did our predecessor of happy memory /Pope Pius XI/ before us, we have strongly urged that the fundamental principles of justice and charity and the long-recognized practice of offering asylum to those not guilty of crime be the norm of government conduct today.

"It is a consolation to our paternal heart to know that our appeal has been generously heeded in many countries; and we like to cherish the hope that so long as that evil blight endures, states will not be lacking in their obligation to succor those who have been forced to emigrate.

157-4-57-20M

＊─── MORE ────

- 2 -

"We have been happy to welcome you gentlemen and our heart goes out in a fervent prayer to God that in His bounteous goodness He have pity on those who are suffering injustice and enlighten those who are perpetrating evil."

The Pontiff delivered his plea to resettle refugees in an address to the following American Jewish Committee leaders, Friday, June 28th:

Irving M. Engel, President of the American Jewish Committee, member of Governor Harriman's Committee on Public Employees Security Procedures and former member of the U.S. Committee on Government Contract Compliance;

Herbert B. Ehrmann of Boston, Vice-President of the Committee, member of its Administrative Board, former member of the Massachusetts Judiciary Council and Massachusetts Civil Service Commission;

Martin Gang of Los Angeles, member of the Administrative Board of the American Jewish Committee, former Director of the Jewish Community Council of Los Angeles;

Frederick F. Greenman, Committee Vice-President and member of its Administrative Board, Trustee of the State University of New York and Chairman of its Committees on New Institutions and on the Community Colleges;

James Marshall, Chairman, AJC's Committee on International Organizations, member, Board of Trustees, Institute of International Education, former President New York City Board of Education;

Alan M. Stroock, Committee Vice-President and Chairman of its Foreign Affairs Committee, member of the Board of Legal Examiners;

John Slawson, Executive Vice-President American Jewish Committee and member of the U.S. National Commission for UNESCO.

The fifty-year-old American Jewish Committee is the oldest organization in this country combating bigotry, protecting civil and religious rights of Jews and advancing the cause of human rights everywhere.

# # # # #

No. 63
 A-29
 NP-20
 J-29

# NEWS

**THE AMERICAN JEWISH COMMITTEE**
386 FOURTH AVENUE    NEW YORK 16, N. Y.    MURRAY HILL 5-0181

Washington Office: 1625 Eye Street, N.W. • Wash. 5, D.C. • District 7-3204
European Headquarters: 30 Rue La Boetie • Paris 8, France
South American Headquarters: Bulnes 1863 • Buenos Aires, Argentina

◄ This is the American Jewish Committee:
◄ Founded in 1906.
◄ Pioneer American organization combating bigotry, protecting the civil and religious rights of Jews here and abroad, and advancing the cause of human rights everywhere.
◄ Chapters in 44 principal cities; members in more than 550 American communities.

Officers

IRVING M. ENGEL, President

JACOB BLAUSTEIN
JOSEPH M. PROSKAUER
Honorary Presidents

MURRAY I. GURFEIN
Chairman, Administrative Board

RALPH E. SAMUEL
Chairman, Executive Board

JOHN SLAWSON
Executive Vice-President

HAROLD STEINBERG
*Director of Press Relations*

Background of the Statement by Pope Pius XII

to the

American Jewish Committee Delegation

Anti-Semitism in the Communist orbit and the aggressive anti-Jewish policies of the Nasser regime are responsible for the present plight of tens of thousands of Jewish refugees in Europe and the Middle East. The following are the main areas of oppression and flight:

1. Poland  Die-hard Stalinist forces are provoking and exploiting anti-Semitism as a political weapon. Consequently, the 50,000 Jews remaining in Poland as of October 1956 have been leaving the country at the rate of 2,500 per month.

2. Hungary  The Soviet puppet regime is seeking to solidify its position by ascribing the recent revolution against Communist tyranny and the ensuing Communist massacres to "sinister machinations of the Jews." Of the 140,000 Jews in Hungary in November 1956, 20,000 fled to the free world. The migration is continuing at the rate of 1,000-1,500 per month.

3. Egypt  The Nasser dictatorship has pursued a four-pronged anti-Jewish policy consisting of expulsion, economic strangulation, revocation of citizenship rights, and arrests and imprisonment. More than half of Egypt's 45,000 Jews have been forced out of the country since November 1956. Departures continue at the rate of 1,000 per month.

The delegation of American Jewish Committee leaders was granted a private audience with Pope Pius XII during a 15,000-mile survey and consultative mission to Europe, North Africa and the Middle East.

The American Jewish Committee, which recently marked its fiftieth anniversary, is the oldest organization in this country combating bigotry, protecting the civil and religious rights of Jews, and advancing human rights here and abroad.

157-4-57-20M

17b. Follow-up American Jewish Committee memorandum (dated July 23, 1957), "Suggested Topic With Reference to TV Program on Audience With the Pope."

7/23/57

### SUGGESTED TOPIC WITH REFERENCE TO TV PROGRAM ON
### AUDIENCE WITH THE POPE

The Vatican during the reign of Pope Pius XII has on a number of occasions demonstrated concern with discrimination against minorities, and was conspicuous in the efforts to save many Jewish victims from Nazi persecution. Because of this known sympathy on the part of His Holiness, the American Jewish Committee felt that a declaration by the Pope at this time, condemning all forms of bigotry and anti-Semitism and asking for asylum for refugees from persecution, would be both timely and effective.

We have been distressed at the pernicious use by Communist regimes of anti-Semitism as a political tool employing the age-old tactic of scapegoating. This has occurred in recent years especially in the Eastern European satellite countries, such as Poland and Hungary. We have also been eager to open immigration opportunities to qualified victims of religious, racial and political persecution. Asylum for them becomes an obligation of all freedom-loving people. We hold that the Americas, both North and South, should play a central role in this much needed work of rescue.

Therefore, the historic declaration by His Holiness, made to the delegation of the American Jewish Committee in audience with him on June 28, 1957, was received with profound gratitude by us. This important step is but another indication of the deep concern of the Vatican for the dispossessed, the afflicted and the persecuted.

July 23, 1957

18. Letter with enclosure (dated March 24, 1959) from Monty Jacobs of the World Jewish Congress to Dr. Edgar Alexander.

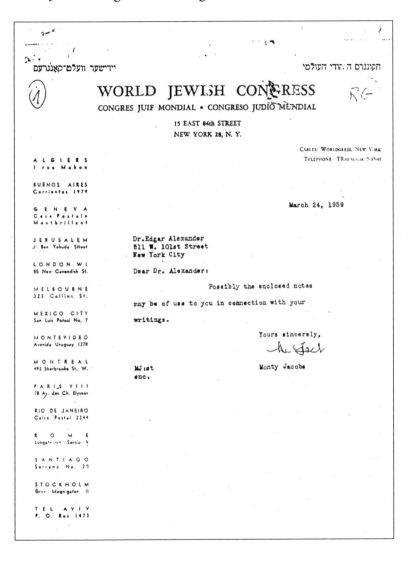

WORLD JEWISH CONGRESS
THE VATICAN AND THE JEWS

March 24, 1959

Throughout the World War II years, and particularly in the period 1943-45, interventions were frequently made with Pope Pius III by the World Jewish Congress in an effort to save, shelter and succor Jews hounded by the Nazis. In all instances, the appeals were graciously and sympathetically received. The responses to these pleas and the subsequent information channeled to the WJC by the Pope's envoys in the USA, Britain and elsewhere, indicated that the action was taken and the machinery of the Vatican put into operation on behalf of Jews.

Constant contact with the Vatican was, for instance, maintained from early 1944 on the question first of Hungarian asylum to Jewish refugees from Poland and Slovakia and, later, on the desperate issue of preventing the mass deportation of Jews from Hungary. As the result of one intervention by Dr. Goldmann early in 1944, the Holy See notified its Nuncios in Budapest and Bratislava to watch the situation and interest themselves, as far as they could in the welfare of Jewish refugees.

About that time, an inter-office memo written by one of the WJC officers closely involved in these matters said:

> "The Catholic Church in Europe has been extraordinarily helpful
> to us in a multitude of ways. From Hinsley in London to Pacelli
> in Rome, to say nothing of the anonymous priests in Holland,
> France and elsewhere, they had done very notable things for us..."

As the situation of the Jews in Hungary deteriorated in 1944, Pope Pius sent the following communication to the WJC:

> "Whenever reports reached the Holy See that the situation of the Jews
> in Hungary was becoming worse, steps were immediately taken to assist
> these people and to alleviate their condition. The Holy See gives assurance that it will continue to act in favor of these Jews. Following instructions from the Holy See, the Apostolic Nunciature in Budapest has repeatedly intervened with the Hungarian authorities so that
> violent and unjust measures would not be taken against the Jews in that
> country. The Bishops of Hungary have engaged in intense activity in
> favor of persecuted Jews. The action on the part of the Nunciature and
> the Bishops will continue as long as necessary. The 29th of October,
> 1944, was designated as a day of prayer for refugees by the Archbishop
> of Strigonia. The Holy Father took this occasion to send a personal
> open telegram to the Cardinal and in this communication His Holiness
> again manifested his heartfelt interest in promoting the welfare of all
> those exposed to violence and persecution because of their race or religion or on account of political motives. The Holy Father gives assurance that he will, in the future, as in the past, do everything in
> favor of these people in Hungary or in any other European country."

In Bratislava, the Papal Nuncio, following up instructions from Pope Pius XII, did at one time succeed in securing a promise from the head of the puppet government

-2-

in Slovakia that Jews would not be deported. A representative of the World Jewish Congress who visited the Apostolic Delegation in Washington to explain the gravity and urgency of the rescue problem, came away with the conviction that the Vatican "will be glad to help whenever possible."

The Pope himself protested the 1943 round-up of Italian Jews. The order for this action was given by the Italian Police but executed by the Germans. The Pope's viewpoint was further expressed in an article in "Observatore Romano," condemning the internment of Jews and the confiscation of their property.

In 1943 and 1944 there were some Jewish refugees in France holding Paraguayan passports. Fearing that Paraguay might withdraw recognition of these passports and thus deprive their holders of Paraguayan protection, the refugees concerned approached the Vatican. As a result, the Apostolic Delegate in Paraguay conveyed these fears to that country's government and was given an assurance that the passports would continue to be recognized.

The Vatican took care of a number of Jewish children in Nazi-occupied Italy whose parents had been killed by the Germans. This action, in which Vatican welfare funds were substantially depleted, brought a WJC expression of "profoundest gratitude for the protecting hand extended by the Pope over the persecuted Jews in this trying period."

There are other instances of Papal help: special documents issued to some Jews in Hungary giving them Vatican protection; intervention once with the Germans so that Jews in Bergen Belsen, holding South American passports, might receive packages of food and clothing.

In recognition of such action, the World Jewish Congress in 1945 made a gift of $20,000 to Vatican charities, in recognition of the work of the Holy See in securing the rescue of Jews from Fascist and Nazi persecution.

## 19. British secret intelligence file on Rolf Hochhuth.

'SOLDIERS' - IRD CONTRIBUTION

### The Author

According to the German Rowohlt edition of October 1967 Rolf Hochhuth was born in Eschwege/Hessen in 1931. (Eschwege, near Erfurt in East Germany, is only just this side of the East/West German border and there are some who say that Hochhuth spent his adolescence in what is now East Germany.) He became at first a bookseller, then a reader for a publisher. His play, "The Representative" was first performed in 1963 by the veteran German producer Erwin Piscator in West Berlin. It has since been translated into sixteen languages and, again according to the publishers note, has been performed in 22 countries. Hochhuth today lives in Basle.

2. According to "Wer ist Wer" of 1967/68, Hochhuth was born on 1 April 1931, is married and has a son. (IRD have seen part of a typescript by Carlos Thompson entitled "Playright Playwrong" which, it is assumed, forms the basis of the book "The Assassination of Winston Churchill" which is shortly to be published in this country. In this version Carlos Thompson says that Hochhuth's wife was a German and was called Marianne He also speaks of Hochhuth's two sons.)

3. Wer ist Wer states that Hochhuth's address is 4125 Riehen b. Basle, Unterer Schellenberg 117.

4. There have been reports in the Swiss press over the last 18 months suggesting that the Swiss authorities were unhappy about Hochhuth's presence in Switzerland but were unable to do much about it because he was still a lecturer at Basle university.

/5.

5.   IRD have no information from secret sources as to
Hochhuth's background.


His Plays.

6.   "The Representative" is a historical drama indthe
tradition of Schiller.   It tells the story of a protestant
SS officer by name of Kurt Gerstein who in the course of
his duties, which included the provison of Prussic acid
for Himmler's extermination camps in Poland, became aware
of the deliberate mass killing of Jews by the Nazis.   As
early as 1942 he approached neutral foreign diplomats in
Berlin (particularly a Swede) and the Papal Nuncio in
Berlin telling them of what he knew and providing proof
with the request to transmit it to their respective
governments of the Vatican reporting with a request for
action.


7.   The Vatican, in the person of Pope Pius XII, however
failed to annul the Concordat with Nazi Germany or to
denounce the German mass murder of the Jews even in the
light of Gerstein's evidence in despite of the fact
that the Vatican had plenty of collateral from their own
sources.   The position of Catholics in Nazi territory was
more important than the lives of Jews.   There is the
clear implication that the Vatican is as guilty of the
crimes committed by the Nazis as the rulers of wartime
Germany themselves.


8.   Gerstein is a historical figure.   A biography by
a German historian has just been published and extracts
appeared in Der Spiegel last December.

/9.

9.  "<u>Soldiers</u>".  This was performed for the first
time at the West Berlin Freie Volksbühne  on 9 October
1967 as Hochhuth's second documentary drama, under the
German title "Soldaten".   The English version now staged
in London does not contain the Prologue which consists
mainly of a plea for a new Geneva Convention to cover
aerial warfare with *and to outlaw* the bombing of
unarmed civilians.

10.  The main play, which falls into three parts -
The Ship, The Bed, the *Garden* - continues this theme
particularly in respect *spent* of the destruction of Hamburg
and Dresden and contains the allegation that Sir Winston
Churchill had at least connived at a plot to do away with *General*
Wladyslav Sikorski, head of the Polish Government-in-exile,
who died in an aircraft crash off Gibraltar on the night
of 4 July 1943, together with his daughter, several members
of his staff, and two British members of Parliament, Colonel
Victor Cazalet, a British liaison officer, and Brigadier
J.P. Whiteley.

11.  The idea for the play, according to Hochhuth came
from a statement by a former member of SIS who told
Hochhuth that "we" (the British) killed Sikorski".
Hochhuth alleges that he has deposited the statement of the
name of his informat in a Swiss bank, to be released in
50 years time, presumably in 2018.   To this day, he has
steadfastly refused to move from this position.   The
British motive for the murder was that Sikorski, because
of his insistence that the International Red Cross
investigate the murder of Polish officers at Katyn, which

which he firmly believed to be a Russian crime, and his
opposition to the seemingly permanent occupation of large
parts of Polish territory by the Soviet Union.

12. It would appear, however, that Hochhuth has also
drawn largely on a book by Jerzy Klimkowski, a former
ADC to General Anders, who returned to Poland from this
country after the war and published in Poland in 1965 under
the title "The Catastrophe at Gibraltar".  Hochhuth
apparently borrowed the book in 1966 when he called on
the General Sikorski Institute in London where he saw
General Kukiel, Chairman of the Institute and at some
time Minister of Defence in the Polish Government-in-exile.

13. In his book Jerzy Klimkowski states that the British
were responsible for the death of General Sikorski
because he had threatened to take his government-in-exile
to Russia and to cooperate with Stalin.

14. The book was given wide publicity in Poland at that
time and is said to have been printed in an edition of
30,000 copies while an edition of 3,000 would be normal.
On 22 October, 1967, the Cracow literary weekly Zycie
Literackie (Literary Life) published an article in which
Olgierd Terlecki, an eminent literary critic, described
Hochhuth's - not Klimkowski's - allegations as "insane".

15. Apart from the alleged "confession" in the Swiss bank
by a former British intelligence officer, and Klimkowski's
book, it is also clear that Mr. David Irving, who has dealt
with the death of Sikorski in a book "Accident" and who
seems to be a close friend of Hochhuth, has done his best
to encourage the latter to proceed with his play.

/16.

✗    16.   While Hochhuth *in his play* /does his best to convince his audience
of the guilt of Sir Winston Churchill, it is the stage
direction and instructions to the actors which are
particularly telling.   In these Sir Winston Churchill
while clearly showing anquish when conniving in the murder
of Sikorski, is depicted as a completely ruthless determined
statesman set on winning the war disregarding the cost to
either his country or its enemies.   The real villain of
the piece and instigator of the plot however, is Lord
Cherwell, the "grey eminence of Downing Street".   Hochhuth
does not say that Lindeman was a Jew.   He does in fact
say that whether he was a Jew or not "no one knows".   He
quotes from Lord Birkenhead who drew a portrait of
Lindemann's father saying that he reminded him of one
of Rembrandt's "wise Jewish heads".   Hochhuth recalls that
Frederick Alexander Lindemann was born of an American
mother in 1886 in Baden-Baden.   With some justification
he could therefore be called a German.   He never forgave
his mother, Hochhuth alleges, for bringing him into the
world there.   Lindemann's wealthy father came from the
✗    Palatinate but was naturalised in Britain as a young man.
Lord Cherwell,who spoke in the precise English of one
who learnt the language at an early age, was the arch
intriguer in Sir Winston Churchill's circle.   He had the
"head of a Cicero, of pronounced evilp male beauty, and
sad brown eyes.   He held his head like a cat carrying a
mouse".   He was an upstart, a snob and an intense hater
of Germany knowing how to manipulate Sir Winston Churchill
with uncanny intuition.   Hochhuth quotes C.P. Snow as
saying about Lindemann: "a man who was no Englishman, who
only became one and who showed the intense patriotism of
a man who had chosen a fatherland which essentially
however was not his".

/EFFORTS

Efforts to Show "Soldiers"in London

17. The play was originally offered to Sir Laurence
Olivier in his capacity as Artistic Director of the
National Threatre and to Mr. Kenneth Tynan, its Literary
Manager, but Sir Laurence Olivier eventually shied off.
Carlos Thompson implies that this is largely due to his
own efforts.   Lord Chandos, Chairman of the Board of
Directors of the National Theatre decided in the end that
the play could not be shown there.   Thereafter Mr. Kenneth
Tynon, according to his own admission, considered
production at the Mermaid Theatre and the Royal Court
on the basis of "club performances".   These efforts failed
until the abolition of censorship when the play was put
on at the New Theatre, St. Martins Lane.

Carlos Thompson's investigations.

18.   From part of a version of a manuscript by Mr. Carlos
Thompson which I.R.D. have seen, it would seem that
Thompson while at first collaborating with Hochhuth in
unearthing facts and material about Sikorski's death,
he soon became suspicious when he found that Hochhuth,
apparently with the authority of Mr. David Irving, told
him that Prchal, the Czechoslovakian pilot of the plane
in which Sikorski crashed in 1943 had been killed by "the
old firm" in Chicago, by which Hochhuth meant by members
of SIS.   ("C's" men incidentally are referred to several
times in "Soldiers" as those who had been in the aircraft
and killed Sikorski.)   Mr. Thompson discovered from a
newspaper cutting that Captain Prchal was alive and lived
in San Francisco.

19.   This set Mr. Thompson on a long trail of enquiries
including checks and counter-checks of Hochhuth's sources
and allegations, most of which proved incorrect.   For
example, Milovan Djilas Was alleged to have said that he
believed Stalin's assertion that the British had killed
Sikorski.   In fact, according to Mr. Thompson, Milovan
(Djilas

Djilas had stated that Hochhuth was "obsessed with destroying the names of greatest man of our time. This meant to destroy Churchill".

20. Prince Eugene Lubomirski, ADC to General Anders during the war, who Mr. Thompson met at the Sikorski Institute in London, said that he never suspected foul play on the part of the British, nor did Mme. Sikorska, or Gen. Kukiel during the same interview. The actor Anthony Quayle denies Mr. Irving's and Hochhuth's story that he had confirmed that the accident was engineered by the British.

21. The controversy meanwhile continues unabated. There was David Frost's programme on 20 December 1968. Extensive extracts from the Daily Telegraph of 21 December 1968, and of the Sunday Telegraph of 22 December 1968 are attached. Libel actions are pending and an exchange of accusations and counter-accusations between Hochhuth and Mr. Thompson continues in the "Welt am Sonntag" in which Hochhuth once again refuses to disclose his sources but insists that Sikorski had to be killed because he endangered the coalition between Britain and Russia. ("Welt am Sonntag" 5 January, 1969). In the same paper of 12 January, Hochhuth challenges Thompson to publish photographs which he was alleged to have obtained from a former British officer, now living in South Africa, showing that the cockpit of the crashed Liberator was intact and had been opened from the inside, thus contradicting the official version that the pilot had been thrown out of the smashed cockpit which caused some of his severe injuries.

/Hochhuth's Themes

Hochhuth's Themes

22.  In "The Representative" he was clearly intending to
put some of the blame for the mass murder of Jews by Nazi-
Germany on to the Vatican, whose inaction was partly
responsible for the continuation of the mass killings.
It is not only the Germans who are guilty.

23.  In "Soldiers" it is the "terror raids", particularly
on Hamburg and Dresden, the total war of our time, which
knows no distinction between front line and hinterland,
soldiers and civilians, which Hochhuth castigates and for
which the British, particularly Lord Cherwell and Churchill,
are responsible.  The men capable of such action would, of
course, also have murdered a troublesome ally such as
Sikorski.  It is doubtful that Hochhuth is in fact
trying to shift the blame away from the Germans, but he
would definitely seem to be attempting to spread the load
of responsibility to all concerned, particularly the British.

24.  The clue to Hochhuth's purposes may well be furnished
by the next play, which according to the "Sunday Times" of
12 January, 1969, he has just completed.  It is called
"Anatomy of Revolution" or "How to Overthrow the US
Government from the Inside".  Hochhuth's thesis, according
to Antony Terry, the paper's Bonn Correspondent, is that
effective revolution by the workers in a big modern
industrialised society is not possible, and that an
"establishment" can only be changed by infiltrating it with,
what Hochhuth calls, "heroic Philbys - men working for their
own people and not selling themselves to another country."
This is exactly what the hero of the play, an American
named Nicholson, through his family contacts, is doing.
The present version according to Terry, however, ends with
the CIA foiling Nicholson's plot, and having him thrown out

of a window of a New York skyscraper. On the other
hand, Hochhuth has also told Terry that the play may
contain a final scene, on which he is now working, and
in which the revolutionaries discuss holding the US
Government to ransom and freeing captured fellow-plotters
with a threat to destroy America's main cities and their
Polaris submarines, whose crews have joined the conspiracy.

25. It can also be argued, as Carlos Thompson has done,
that Hochhuth is engaged in some "decomposition" exercise
and that he is attempting to destroy the fundamental values
of a free society, from its religions to its heroes. In
the version of Mr. Thompson's manuscript, which IRD has
seen, the author asks whether Hochhuth is being used. It
is obvious, he says, that Hochhuth "was after Churchill's
head. By proving him guilty of an unnecessary collective
crime (the bombing of German towns) and of a private one,
he had him on two vital counts". In his talk with Prince
Lubomirski, Thompson confided his thought that Hochhuth
might perhaps be "an intellectual agent, writing either
on behalf of the East Germans, or the Soviets". To these
Prince Lubomirski replies "not impossible". General Kukiel
suspected that it was the Russians who may have been
responsible for the aircrash.

26. Elsewhere in his manuscript Mr. Thompson and some of
his interlocutors regret that the findings of the Courts
of Enquiry following the accident had never been published,
and that it was this fact which particularly helped
Hochhuth.

/27.

27. It can also be argued that the moving spirit in all
this is not perhaps so much Hochhuth but Mr. David Irving.
Carlos Thompson says that originally Hochhuth had alleged
that he learnt of the murder of Sikorski through a member
of SIS.   Later on however, again according to Carlos
Thompson, Hochhuth denied this as "a great error".   He
had hit upon the idea from reading the "letters between
Churchill and Stalin" and other material.   "For three whole
years I have searched with the help - but this only in the
very end - of Irving...".   Touching on the Hochhuth/Irving
relationship.   Thompson claims that at some stage Irving
had denied his collaboration with Hochhuth and the murder
allegation.   Yet, says Thompson, Hochhuth spoke of
having "sent" Irving to Gibraltar.

28. To sum up whether Hochhuth is motivated only by the
urge to write historical plays, to rehabilitate the Germans
or is up to some more sinister game is difficult to
determine at this stage.   But the Russians are certainly
reaping some of the benefit.   The best counter action
would seem the release of the full findings of the courts
of enquiry.

MISS NUNN

## THE SIKORSKI CASE

Mr. Wilson's minute of 13th January raises the question whether the report of the Court of Inquiry was furnished to the Czech pilot.

The answer is that neither the Czech Government in Exile nor the pilot were given a copy of the report. They were only informed that the pilot was exonerated. But, as Mr. Wilson says, the Polish Government was given a copy of the report in 1943.

(D.G. WHITE)

15th January, 1969

MISS NUNN

                    Copy to Sir Dick White ←


        In his minute of 10th January Mr. Gruffyd Jones suggests that the
reply to Captain Roskill should be prepared in the light of the latest
developments on the Hochhuth case; Mr. David Irving is the defendant
in the Roskill matter and was a marginal contact with the Hochhuth case.

        I have already sent a note on the Roskill case, with a draft reply
which should I think be settled by the Treasury Soliciter. In that case
Roskill wishes, before he appears as a witness in the libel action, to
refresh his memory of a Cabinet document on which he based a statement
in his Official History published in 1956; to maintain the reputation
and prestige of the Official histories (apart from Roskill's own
reputation), I think he should be allowed to do so, and if the Court
requires production of the document, privilege might be waived.

        So far as I understand the Hochhuth case, it involves a series of
libel actions by the Czech pilot, with overtones affecting Sir Winston
Churchill. A most relevant document would seem to be the report of the
Court of Inquiry, a copy of which was furnished to the Polish Government
in exile at the time, and to which Mr. Irving appears to have had access
in the writing of 'Accident', and to that extent it is already in the
public domain. I do not recall from the papers (now with Sir Dick White)
whether a copy was supplied to the pilot, but if Oswald Hickson, Collier
& Co. ask for a copy, the question of privilege will arise. If on this
aspect the papers go to the Treasury Solicitor he should be aware that
while Mr. Irving's access to official information in this country has
been tenuous and correct, he has extensive contacts in U.S.A. and in
Germany and appears to have information from those contacts on matters
which are still classified here. (c.f. Virus House and Bombing of Dresden



                              J J Wilson.



13th January 1969

## THE SIKORSKI CASE .

I understand from your Private Office that you are anxious to know what progress is being made on enquiries into the above matter. A search has been made for all relevant papers in the Cabinet Office, Ministry of Defence, Security Service and FCO. I attach a note of the relevant papers so far discovered.

2. Included in the papers retrieved is the record of the official Court of Enquiry into the fatal accident at Gibraltar. Its principal conclusions were as follows:-

    (a) The Court found the accident "to be due to the aircraft becoming uncontrollable for reasons which cannot be established".

    (b) The Court considered that there was "no question of sabotage involved in the crash".

    (c) The Court considered that no blame attached to the Czech pilot.

3. According to Hansard of the 23rd December 1943, Column 458, the Government made an official statement to Parliament on the matter in the following terms:-

### LOST AIR LINER (INQUIRY)

Mr. I. Thomas asked the Secretary of State for Air whether he is now in a position to make a statement on the causes of the crash which resulted in the death of General Sikorski and two hon. Members of this House?

Captain Balfour: The findings of the Court of Inquiry and the observations of the officers whose duty it is to review and comment on them reveal that this most regrettable accident was due to jamming of the elevator controls shortly after take-off, with the result that the aircraft became uncontrollable. After careful examination of all the available evidence, including that of the pilot, it has not been possible to determine how the jamming occurred, but it has been established that there was no sabotage. It is also clear that the captain of the aircraft, who is a pilot of great experience and exceptional ability, was in no way to blame. An officer of the Polish Air Force attended throughout the proceedings.

4. In addition to the fatal accident of 1943 there was a previous incident in 1942 in which it was alleged an attempt was made to sabotage the trans-Atlantic plane in which General Sikorski was flying to Canada. The allegation was made by a Polish official travelling in the same plane who claimed to have discovered a SOE-type incendiary bomb which he managed to prevent igniting. Under interrogation he later confessed that the provision of the bomb and the sabotage story was his own invention. Although both the Canadian (RCMP) and the Americans (FBI) had knowledge

-1-

of this incident at the time, both were subsequently satisfied
that no act of sabotage had been attempted.  The 1942 incident,
therefore, cannot be used to substantiate any charge to the
effect that the British were seeking an opportunity to get rid
of General Sikorski.  In my opinion it can safely be ignored.


5.   I am calling a meeting of those responsible for searching
their own Departmental records on the Sikorski accident on
Thursday afternoon.  It should then be possible to report to
you further on the official documentation and to supply you
with the framework within which you might wish to consider
how best the Government can reply to any possible Parliamentary
questions into Hoocuth's allegations.




                              (D.G. WHITE)


14th January, 1969

## THE SIKORSKI CASE

You asked for a summary of action to date, the papers so far discovered, and the principal facts which can be established from these papers to answer the innuendo that General Sikorski was the victim of assassination not accident.

2. I attach a note of the relevant papers so far discovered as a result of search in the Cabinet Office, Ministry of Defence, Security Service and FCO and the principle useful facts which emerge from the record of the official Court of Inquiry which was convened on 7th July 1943 and reconvened on 3rd August 1943.

3. The Security Service was not directly or officially involved in this enquiry: however, Lord Rothschild, who was engaged on counter-sabotage work for the Security Service at the time, has usefully drawn attention, from memory, to the fact that two Naval divers, Crabbe and Bailey, were concerned in the salvage operation. The Admiralty is now searching for any record of their report and attempting to discover Bailey's whereabouts. The names of the divers were not mentioned in the record of the Court of Enquiry.

4. The overall impression given from all these papers is of an urgent but careful enquiry into the accident which produced the following conclusions:-

(a) The Court found the accident "to be due to the aircraft becoming uncontrollable for reasons which cannot be established". (Page 3, para. 10).

(b) The Court considered that there was "no question of sabotage involved in the crash".

(c) The Court considered that no blame attached to the Czech pilot.

5. Hansard dated 23rd September 1943, Column 458 reads as follows:-

### LOST AIR LINER (INQUIRY)

Mr. I. Thomas asked the Secretary of State for Air whether he is now in a position to make a statement on the causes of the crash which resulted in the death of General Sikorski and two hon. Members of this House?

Captain Balfour: The findings of the Court of Inquiry and the observations of the officers whose duty it is to review and comment on them reveal that this most regrettable accident was due to jamming of the elevator controls shortly after take-off, with the result that the aircraft became uncontrollable. After careful examination of all the available evidence, including that of the pilot, it has not been possible to determine how the jamming occurred, but it has been established that there

was no sabotage.   It is also clear that the captain of the
aircraft, who is a pilot of great experience and exceptional
ability, was in no way to blame.   An officer of the Polish
Air Force attended throughout the proceedings.


(B.T.W. STEWART)


13th January, 1969

MINISTRY OF DEFENCE FILE CS 20396
ACCIDENT AT GIBRALTAR TO LIBERATOR AIRCRAFT IN WHICH
GENERAL SIKORSKI WAS KILLED - COURT OF INQUIRY PROCEEDINGS


Contains minutes, letters and the record of the Air Ministry
Court of Enquiry into the accident. From this file the following
important facts emerge clearly:-

(a) Polish officers, serving in the RAF at the time, were
present throughout the proceedings of the Enquiry.

(b) A copy of the report was passed to the Polish
Government in Exile (Foreign Office 9840/5680/G of
1st September 1943).

(c) The Czech Government in Exile was informed that the
Czech pilot was in no way to blame (Foreign Office
C9840/5680/G of 1st September 1943). They were
not, however, given a copy of the record of the
Court of Enquiry.

(d) The Air Ministry Court of Enquiry convened on the
7th July 1943 found:-

(i) the accident "to be due to the aircraft
becoming uncontrollable for reasons which
cannot be established". (Page 3, para. 10).

(ii) that there was "no question of sabotage
involved in the crash".

(e) The Court was reopened for further technical enquiries
on 3rd August. When after a further series of
questions to the pilot and to variously technically
qualified officers, and practical tests of methods
of jamming Liberator controls the Court confirmed
its opinion that "the elevator controls were jammed
by some means other than the flying controls locking
mechanism, but that there is no further evidence to
show how this jamming occurred", and considered that
Flight Lieutenant Prchal was in no way to blame for
the accident.

(f) That all major wreckage was recovered and examined
both during salvage and ashore in Gibraltar by an
Inspector of the Air Ministry's Inspectorate of
Accidents and aircraft parts were flown back to
the UK for technical examination.

MINISTRY OF DEFENCE FILE ID8/504
ENTITLED CRASHED LIBERATOR AL 523 -
GENERAL SIKORSKI'S PARTY

This reflects the contents of C 20396: and points up
the care with which the investigation was carried out.
It provides much evidence also of the care given to the
question of Czech anxieties over the case.  It is,
however, mainly a record of administrative signals and
correspondence rather than with the circumstances and
cause of the accident.

ANNEX 'C'

PHOTOSTAT COPY OF MINISTRY OF DEFENCE FILE ID8/504
ENTITLED CRASHED LIBERATOR AL 523 - GENERAL SIKORSKI'S PARTY

This is the same as Annex 'B' on the same subject which
overlaps with the other two files and adds nothing of
substance to the picture.

### ALLEGED ATTEMPT TO SABOTAGE GENERAL SIKORSKI'S AEROPLANE ON 21ST MARCH 1942 EN ROUTE FROM PRESTWICK TO CANADA BY WING COMMANDER KLECZYSNKI

Security Service papers on the alleged attempt to sabotage the aeroplane carrying General Sikorski en route from Prestwick to Canada on 21st March 1942.

The papers clearly establish that this was not an attempt to sabotage the General's aircraft.

### WAR CABINET RECORDS

There is nothing in these records about the accident other than references to the death and funeral arrangements. They include a minute of 18th July 1943 from the Prime Minister to CAS asking for an interim report without waiting for the result of the Court of Enquiry.

ANNEX 'Y'

PHOTOSTAT COPY OF WAR CABINET RECORDS

This is a duplicate of Annex 'E' and adds nothing to the picture.

⟨3⟩

*Mr. John Peck*
Sir E. Peck

"Soldiers"

The Intelligence Co-ordinator asked me to call on him
on 8 January. He said that the Prime Minister had told
Sir Burke Trend after the Frost programme on 20 and 21
December that he thought there might be Parliamentary
interest in the matter when Parliament re-assembled. The
Prime Minister had asked for a "précis of the facts", to
which the Co-ordinator thought that he should add inter-
departmentally agreed recommendations about future policy.
2. The Co-ordinator has therefore asked the MOD, the
Security Service and ourselves to attend a meeting on
16 January, bringing background contributions to a paper
which would be completed in the light of discussion at the
meeting and then cleared with the PUS and Sir J. Dunnett
before being put to Sir B. Trend for the Prime Minister. The
Co-ordinator asked me to undertake the drafting of the final
paper.
3. I told the Co-ordinator that this came opportunely for
us, as we had in any case been planning to review policy
ourselves in the immediate future, and that I was sure the
PUS would welcome an agreed paper. I have arranged for the

/preparation

S E C R E T

- 2 -

preparation of brief Foreign Office contributions, and you
have agreed with Mr. John Peck that he and I should be the
FCO representatives at the meeting on 16 January, It
would be useful to consider before the meeting what we think
future policy should be.

4. Sir B. Trend agreed in his letter of 6 December that we
should continue with our previous policy of

- (i) avoiding official comment on "Soldiers" if possible,
  or, if pressed to comment, saying simply that the
  allegations in it are so absurd as not to be worth
  rebutting;

- (ii) providing strictly unattributable help to Mr. Carlos
  Thompson and others, e.g. Mr. Churchill's wartime
  "secret Circle", who have been ready to defend
  Mr. Churchill.

In his minute of 23 December about the Frost programme
Mr. Peck added that he would be strongly opposed to any
governmental intervention, and we may find that this policy
will in any case be forced on us ~~partly by~~ because of the fact
that the pilot of Sikorski's aircraft, Captain Prchal, has
now started legal proceedings in this country over "Soldiers".
For example, Mr. Simpson's initial reaction is that,
depending of course on the exact wording of any PQ, Ministers
might well have to decline to comment on the circumstances
of the accident or on Hochhuth's allegations, because the
matter was now sub judice. On the other hand, I suppose
we cannot exclude the possibility that official witnesses
will be subpoened during the course of any court action and
/that

S E C R E T

S E C R E T

- 3 -

that there may be pressure from one side or the other for
official documents connected with the crash to be disclosed
to the court. This might be difficult to resist and would
probably involve official denial of Hochhuth's allegations
in one form or another. I am discussing with the Co-ordinator
the possible need for legal advice at the meeting on the 16th,
and Mr. Simpson has kindly said he would try to be available
for the meeting if required.

5. For the moment, however, I think it/be easiest to consider
what our policy ought to be if there were no legal complications.
We could then apply any general principles which emerge to
any new situation created by legal developments. I do not
for example think we could in principle recommend the Prime
Minister to rest on the line at (i) above in the event of
Parliamentary Questions. This would hardly be enough for the
House. Indeed the House would probably provide the best and
most sympathetic forum at any time for any official statement
about the affair. There is likely to be widespread support
from both sides of the House for any denial of Hochhuth's
allegations, and this would have an obvious value in terms
of public opinion. There might therefore be something to
be said for inspiring a PQ if we were to favour a more
forward policy (see paragraph 6 below). Meanwhile, in the
event of a spontaneous PQ I think the best line would probably
be a firm denial of the allegations, in as categoric a form as
is possible when trying to prove a negative so long after

/the

S E C R E T

- 4 -

the event. We might also usefully consider publishing the
full proceedings of the Court of Enquiry over the Sikorski
crash if close examination of them suggests that this would
be profitable, and if the Ministry of Defence can be
persuaded to abandon their previous rejection of a similar
proposal in 1958 because the papers were "privileged".

6.   It is also for consideration whether, because of
developments during the past three weeks, the time has not
now come for us to adopt a more forward policy generally,
and to recommend an official denial of the allegations even
if our hand is not forced by a PQ or e.g. the subpoenaing
power of official witnesses in Prchal's libel action.
Hochhuth has already called for a new Government enquiry into
the crash (drawing apparently on an idea originally launched
by Bernard Levin in the Daily Mail for a "court of honour"
to examine the "evidence" which Hochhuth claims to have
lodged in a Swiss bank);  and David Irving has simultaneously
called for the re-opening of the RAF Court of Enquiry. We
must reckon on Hochhuth et al trying to keep the affair alive
as long as possible through stratagems of this kind;  nor
can we discount the possibility of long-term efforts by the
communists to foster Hochhuth's allegations until they become
legend like the story of the Princes in the Tower.  There
is thus a valid argument in favour of trying to pre-empt
any further development of the smear by a strong official
denial as soon as possible.  This could have the additional

/advantage

- 5 -

advantage of providing a definitive statement to which we
could always decline to add in the event of subsequent
attempts by e.g. Hochhuth to get more mileage out of his story.
7.

CLOSED UNDER THE
FREEDOM OF INFORMATION
ACT 2000

(ii) trying to helping to force Hochhuth's "evidence"
into the light of day, provided we were satisfied
that this would not be playing Hochhuth's game for
him by giving the story further publicity or making
it difficult to resist pressure for a new or resumed
Court of Enquiry, which would be quite unacceptable.

S E C  R T
- 6 -

Mr. Winston Churchill has possibly already taken
a further step towards forcing out the evidence
Flag H          with his letter in The Times today.

And it would be useful for us to be
able to deny the evidence, whatever it is, once
and for all.  Against this, there is a danger that
the "evidence" might in some people's minds help
to support Hochhuth's allegations, especially if
it is a good piece of forgery or if by any chance
Hochhuth has got hold of an essentially inoffensive
official document of some kind about Sikorski which
could nevertheless be misinterpreted to suit his
book;

(iii) instituting criminal proceedings against Hochhuth.
Flag I          Mr. Simpson agrees with me that the recent letter
from Prchal's lawyers to The Times could be construed
as an invitation to HMG or other interested parties
to do this.

8.    In considering these possibilities we must, I think,
never lose sight of the fact that any official statement or
intervention is in danger of being labelled by our enemies

/as

S E C R E T

S E C R E T
- 7 -

Flag E

Flag F

as an attempt to whitewash Mr. Churchill.  Hochhuth has already
used this line in relation to the Frost programme, and he
can be expected to develop it if opportunity offers.  Moreover,
my own impression is that Hochhuth's allegations have been
pretty effectively debunked by the many people who have leapt
to Mr. Churchill's defence (cf. the letter from the "secret
circle").  Irving's very poor showing on the Frost programme
has also helped.  Prchal's court actions and Carlos Thompson's
book may further the process.  I feel therefore that there
is a chance that if we continue to say nothing officially
the story will eventually run itself into the ground.
Accordingly my preliminary conclusion is that the policy
we might suggest for consideration at the meeting on 16 January
should be as follows:-

    (i) maintain the policy agreed with Sir B. Trend for
       the time being;

    (ii) nevertheless prepare a strong official statement
       for use if it ever become necessary, e.g. in answer
       to a PQ, and see whether there are any supporting
       documents such as the proceedings of the Court of
       Enquiry which could usefully be published;

  (iii)

CLOSED UNDER THE
FREEDOM OF INFORMATION
ACT 2000

/(iv)

S E C R E T

S E C R E T

- 8 -


(iv) regard sympathetically any private attempts to
     force Hochhuth's evidence into the open, and give
     them unattributable support if this seems desirable;
 (v) investigate the possibility and desirability of
     criminal proceedings against Hochhuth, etc.


(J. E. Jackson)
10 January, 1969


Copied to:
SIR G. PECK.
~~Mr. John Peck~~
Mr. Ewart-Biggs
Mr. John Simpson
Mr. Barker (EESD)


S E C R E T

SIR DICK WHITE

When you invited Lord Rothschild and Mr. Peter Wright to discuss the Sikorski case on 9th January at 3 p.m. the following points arose:-

(a) Mr. Wright produced a photocopy of the RAF Enquiry of 7th July, 1943.

(b) Lord Rothschild reported that although he had no part in the formal enquiry on the accident he remembered discussing the matter with Commander Crabbe who had dived in the area and examined the wreckage. Crabbe was accompanied by Bailey, another diver, at this time. Lord Rothschild was certain that he had formed the impression at the time that the diver had ruled out sabotage as a result of his investigation.

(c) It was agreed that the testimony of the divers, to which no reference was made in the RAF enquiry, should be sought from the Admiralty.

A scrutiny of the RAF document shows that:-

(a) The pilot was "quite satisfied with the disposal of the load".

(b) The pilot had previously experienced the locking of the control column in a Liberator during take off.

(c) Additional security precautions were made for the Liberator in question.

(d) Two RAF officers observing the crash agreed that the plane sank towards the sea with engines under full power. LACs however described the cutting of the engines before the crash.

(e) That there were considerable quantities of mail aboard.

(f) All major wreckage was recovered and taken to the Naval Dockyard (Gibraltar) for examination in detail.

(g) The Court found the accident "to be due to the aircraft becoming uncontrollable for reasons which cannot be established". (Page 3, para. 10).

(h) The Court considered that there was "no question of sabotage involved in the crash".

(j) Unfortunately the Court goes on to note that despite security precautions the 22nd witness was able to remove a mail bag from the Liberator, unobserved by the 23rd witness whose duty it was to guard the plane.

(B.T.W. STEWART)

10th January 1968

SECRET

①

SIR BURKE TREND

"THE SOLDIERS"

With reference to the papers on the above subject sent
to you by Gore-Booth, I find that the Security Service have
a considerable amount of information both about the dramatis
personae and the incident itself.    It is a pity that the
Foreign Office apparently did not consult the Security
Service before compiling the note which has now been
forwarded to you.    I have been briefed by the Security
Service and when you wish to discuss the matter further
I will be in a position to tell you what is known.    The
story is in some respects different from the one given
to you by the Foreign Office and there are some fairly
tricky angles to it.

(D.G. WHITE)

12th December, 1968

# Notes

## Chapter One: The Papacy and the World

1. Once, when asked how many people worked at the Vatican, Pope John XXIII famously replied: "About half of them."

2. Vatican City also has a governor (during World War II this role was filled by Marchese Camillo Serafini). The governor is appointed by the Pontiff and is directly responsible to him. He has day-to-day control over the extensive gardens and technical services of Vatican City.

3. Since the year 2000, this author has had the honor of serving as an adviser to the Holy See's New York mission to the United Nations. There is also a mission and an observer at The Hague.

4. Korn, 125.

5. See Charles Rankin, "Pius the Man and His Efforts for Peace," *The Pope Speaks: The Words of Pius XII*, 14 (Pius XII's father was "dean of the Vatican Bar").

6. This dispute arose when Italian forces ousted the Pope from most of his temporal powers, claiming Church property for Italy. Due to his family's association with the Church, which was in conflict with the Italian government, young Eugenio encountered discrimination in school and elsewhere. Halecki and Murray, 8-11.

7. See p. 23.

8. Hatch and Walshe, 32.

9. Doyle, 4.

10. Barton, 17.

11. The young Pacelli was a handsome man. According to one account, "all the convent girls used to say, 'Who could look at him and not love him!'" Congregation for the Causes of Saints, *Positio*, (Summarium) "Testimony of Maria Teresa Pacelli," before the Tribunal of the Vicariate of Rome, on the beatification of Pius XII (Eugenio Pacelli).

12. See Charles Rankin, "Pius the Man and His Efforts for Peace," *The Pope Speaks: The Words of Pius XII*, 15. ("[I]t was only his father's influence which enabled him to live at home and continue his studies.")

13. Pacelli served as an assistant lecturer in canon law. A young seminarian, Angelo Roncalli — the future Pope John XXIII — was impressed by his "understated brilliance" and felt that Pacelli was marked for a bright future. Elliott, 32.

14. Church law had been built up over a thousand years of edicts, papal encyclicals, instructions, decrees, regulations, and precedents, each of which was applicable to its own era. By the beginning of the twentieth century, Church laws were confused and perhaps even contradictory. This project was designed to reduce the various pronouncements into a single code that could easily be referenced.

15. See Besier, 4-5.

16. See Charles Rankin, "Pius the Man and His Efforts for Peace," *The Pope Speaks: The Words of Pius XII*, 16 (examining prisoner exchanges and other efforts headed by Pacelli).

17. "Technically he was accredited to the Catholic Kingdom of Bavaria, always the most independent State in the German Reich." See Charles Rankin, "Pius the Man and His Efforts for Peace," *The Pope Speaks: The Words of Pius XII*, 17.

18. Besier, 10. The ceremony took place on May 13, 1917, the same day that three young shepherd children in Fátima, Portugal, reported their vision of the Virgin Mary.

19. Deutsch, 109, n. 14 (also noting Howard's distrust of Pope Benedict XV and his evaluation of Cardinal Gasparri as a charming but slippery old man).

20. The plan was controversial in the United States, even among the Catholic hierarchy, because it suggested that the nation was on the wrong path by waging war. One German-Catholic paper in the United States, however, took an editorial position in favor of the plan. This was dangerous in that it arguably violated the "Trading with the Enemy Act" of 1917. See Paul Likoudis, "How Pope's 1917 Peace Proposal Put *Wanderer* Editor at Risk," *Wanderer*, September 20, 2007. That law prohibited, quoting from the *Wanderer*'s October 17, 1917 editorial:

> the printing, publishing, and circulating "in any foreign language of any news item, editorial, or other printed matter respecting the government of the United States, or any nation engaged with the present war, its politics, international relations, the state or conduct of the war, or any matter relating

thereto," unless the printer and publisher either secures a permit issued by the President or has filed before mailing his publication on the form of a proposal unless an English translation of the entire article containing such matter [has been filed] with the local postmaster.

21. Elliott, 73-74. The "Kaiser made it quite clear that he was expecting to win the war and any suggested peace offer was unwelcome." See Charles Rankin, "Pius the Man and His Efforts for Peace," *The Pope Speaks: The Words of Pius XII*, 17. Wilhelm did later, however, express his admiration for Pacelli's "distinguished sympathetic appearance, the high intelligence, and the impeccable manners." The kaiser also called Pacelli "the prototype of a Roman prelate." Halecki and Murray, 37.

22. Hatch and Walshe, 77. The Vatican also proposed the exchange of war prisoners incapable of further military service. When that suggestion was favorably received, the Pope proposed including interned civilians who were unfit to serve in the armed forces. All of these arrangements were negotiated through Pacelli's office. Halecki and Murray, 29.

23. Halecki and Murray, 41-42; Hatch and Walshe, 74.

24. Halecki and Murray, 29; Cornwell (1999), 60 (also noting that Pacelli "declined even a day's vacation" during the first three years of the war).

25. See p. 115.

26. The letter is extensively quoted in chapter 16. See p. 317.

27. Lapide, 84; Hesemann, *The Pope Who Defied Hitler*. Documents related to this section are collected on the web page of Pave the Way Foundation: *http://www.pavethewayfoundation.org/Downloads/Pacelli%20Zionist%201917.pdf*.

28. Hesemann, *The Pope Who Defied Hitler*.

29. Hesemann, "Eugenio Pacelli and the Zionists." ("The decision to delegate this difficult affair to Pacelli was wise indeed. It was more than questionable if an intervention by the Pope himself would have any impact in Constantinople. Only Germany as their most important ally was able to stop the Turks from performing a massacre.")

30. Ibid.; Lapide, 289. A copy of both the draft and the final version is located in the Vatican Secret Archives.

31. Eleven days later, a reply came from Constantinople: "[T]here is no reason to fear that the Turkish authorities in Palestine order measures against the Jewish population. We learned from the Turkish side that the Holy City and all sites which are subject of Christian and Jewish veneration are spared and respected as far as the military necessities by all means allow." Lapide, 289-90.

32. Hesemann, "Eugenio Pacelli and the Zionists." ("Since von Falkenhayn was a man who strictly followed orders, it is reasonable to assume that his 'conduct' was ordered from Berlin.")

33. Lapide, 290-91.

34. Ibid., 291.

35. This translation was provided by Michael Hesemann and is archived on the web page of Pave the Way Foundation: *http://www.pavethewayfoundation.org/Downloads/Pacelli%20Zionist%201917.pdf*. Hesemann also reports that Pacelli intervened in 1917, through the German government, to assure the Jews of Palestine that they would be protected from any harm from the Ottoman Turks.

36. Kurt Blumenfeld, *Living the Jewish Question* (1962); Lapide, 273. In 1926, Pacelli also encouraged Catholics in Germany to join the *Committee Pro Palestina*, which supported Jewish settlements in Palestine.

37. The Italian government, still in conflict with the Vatican, pressured France, Great Britain, and Russia to keep the Holy See out of the postwar proceedings. Halecki and Murray, 27; Hatch and Walshe, 68. See Besier, 8-9.

38. Copeland, 352. The French prime minister, Georges Clemenceau, was not eager to provide Germany with much freedom. Regarding President Wilson's Fourteen Points, he said: "Why, God Almighty only had ten."

39. Ibid.

40. Not counting the territories annexed before and during World War II, Germany was at its largest just prior to the First World War. With the Treaty of Versailles, it lost significant territory to France, Poland, and Czechoslovakia.

41. The Italians also were not pleased with the peace proposal. They had wanted to be given certain lands as spoils of war, but the Allies did not agree. The Italian delegation left Paris in a rage. Though they returned to sign a treaty that did not give them the land they wanted, the incident disrupted the conference. It may also have shaped Italian attitudes about the Allied nations, giving Benito Mussolini a reason to side with Germany in the next war. See generally Arno J. Mayer, *Politics and Diplomacy of Peacemaking: Containment and Counterrevolution at Versailles 1918-1919*, Harcourt (New York, 1967).

42. The Weimar Constitution was widely acclaimed as one of the most democratic in the world. It featured universal adult suffrage; proportional representation; provisions for popular referenda, petition, and recall; and an extensive list of civil liberties. It created a dual executive: a chancellor, as head of government, appointed by the president, and a directly elected president as chief of state. However, it also had a serious flaw: the president had the power to issue decrees in lieu of legislation if there was a state of emergency. This

provision would be used before Hitler came to power, and that use would set the precedent for his later abuses of power.

43. See M. Price, 155 (Hitler exhorts crowd to help Germany by hanging "the criminals of November 1918!"). The majority of Jews in Germany at this time were Social Democrats and were identified with that part of the political spectrum. Friedländer (1997), 75. This linkage of Jews with the group that had agreed to the 1918 surrender and accompanying penalties imposed on Germany was often noted in Nazi propaganda.

## Chapter Two: Hitler and the Postwar World

1. Alois and Klara were second cousins and therefore needed special dispensation from the Church to get married. Kershaw, 10.

2. Lutzer, 64.

3. Later in life, Hitler embraced many aspects of occultism.

4. Vienna of this era spawned "one of the most fertile, original and creative periods in art and architecture, music, literature and psychology, as well as in philosophy." Janik and Toulmin, 9. From this city came Sigmund Freud, Victor Adler, Arnold Schönberg, Adolf Loos, Oskar Kokoschka, Ernst Mach, and Ludwig Wittgenstein.

5. Kershaw, 57.

6. Ibid., 44.

7. According to Hitler, Wagner "had really proclaimed the eternal tragedy of human destiny. He was not merely a musician and a poet; he was the supreme prophetic figure among Germans." Rauschning, 229 (also noting that Hitler attributed his vegetarianism to Wagner's writings on the subject).

8. Hitler would later say: "Whoever wants to understand National Socialist Germany must know Wagner." Shirer (1962), 101.

9. Janik and Toulmin, 54.

10. Kershaw, 58; Lapomarda, 68.

11. Kershaw, 33-34, 58. Hitler came to believe that Schönerer had failed to achieve national prominence by openly opposing the Church and thereby antagonizing the people. Hitler would adopt the attitude, but try not to repeat the mistake.

12. Hannes Stein, "Return of the Gods," *First Things* (November 1999), 34, 37.

13. Ibid.

14. Ibid.; Lutzer, 91.

15. Hannes Stein, "Return of the Gods," *First Things* (November 1999), 34, 37.

16. Payne, 102, 166.

17. Hitler was not really a corporal in American terms. A U.S. Army corporal wears two stripes. Hitler's rank was *Gefreiter*; he had one stripe. Thus, he was the equivalent of a private first class. The British army equivalent, however, is lance corporal, which accounts for the common assertion that he was a corporal.

18. Although he would maintain a largely German staff even after becoming pope, none of them were compromised by German intelligence initiatives during the war. Alvarez and Graham, 175.

19. Fulton J. Sheen, "The Pope as I Saw Him," *Catholic Digest* (October 1955), 62. Pope Leo XIII's 1891 encyclical *Rerum Novarum*, remembered today primarily as the basis of Catholic social justice teaching, said that Marxism was incompatible with Catholicism.

20. Hatch and Walshe, 83.

21. Charles Rankin, "Pius the Man and His Efforts for Peace," in *The Pope Speaks: The Words of Pius XII*, 20 (noting that this once resulted in a threat that the revolutionary leader would come over and shoot him personally).

22. Fulton J. Sheen, "The Pope as I Saw Him," *Catholic Digest* (October 1955), 62.

23. Halecki and Murray, 46 (noting that others were home, but no one was hurt); Cornwell (1999), 78 (noting that more than fifty bullet holes were found in the masonry of the building's facade).

24. Fulton J. Sheen, "The Pope as I Saw Him," *Catholic Digest* (October 1955), 62. See also Hatch and Walshe, 84 (when the intruders demanded his money and food, Pacelli replied: "I have neither money nor food. For, as you know, I have given all I had to the poor of the city"); ibid., 84 (noting that Pacelli later gave the bent cross to Francis Cardinal Spellman of New York); Halecki and Murray, 47 (Pacelli never flinched. He said, "This is a house of peace, not a den of murderers!"); Charles Rankin, "Pius the Man and His Efforts for Peace," in *The Pope Speaks: The Words of Pius XII*, 20 (similar account).

25. Hatch and Walshe, 84-85; Halecki and Murray, 47-48.

26. Korn, 135; Duffy, 263; Stehlin, 41.

27. Hatch and Walshe, 85.

28. As a young man, Luther had been a champion of the Jews. When he failed to win them to the Gospel of Christ, however, he raged at them with violent language. Hitler appropriated these writings for his own purposes, circulating them to counter Christian opposition to his Nazi theories. See p. 96.

29. The difficulty that the Catholic Church was having in the late nineteenth century caused Pope Leo XIII to issue an encyclical entitled *Iampridem* (on Catholicism in Germany, 1886). In it, Leo complained

about how the relationship between Church and state was "thrown into sudden disorder" by certain laws that placed "Catholic citizens in such danger and distress."

30. Rauschning, 236 (Hitler said that anti-Semitism was beyond question the most important weapon in his propagandist arsenal). See also M. Price, 140-41 (discussing the anti-Semitism of emerging nationalist parties in postwar Germany).

31. Rauschning, 234 (among Nazi leaders, Hitler's racial doctrine was called "Adolf's bunkum").

32. Barnett, 15 (quoting Eberhard Bethge).

33. Hatch and Walshe, 81.

34. As a boy, Hitler was proud that his eyes were blue, and his hair was then light brown. Toland (1997), 298.

35. His girlfriend (and later, wife), Eva Braun, has been called the most envied woman in Germany. Nevertheless, she was hidden from the public so well that in 1945, *Newsweek* foreign editor Harry Kern sent a cable asking who she was. Some have speculated that she was hidden in order to keep German women interested in Hitler (he received thousands of love letters), but even some of those close to Hitler were uncertain as to whether he and Eva had a physical relationship. Even when she moved into his Berlin bunker in 1945, Eva had her own small suite next to Hitler's. O'Donnell, 29. There were, however, rumors of love affairs that Hitler had with other women, including filmmaker Leni Riefenstahl.

Several of the women with whom Hitler was romantically involved, including Eva Braun in 1935, attempted suicide; at least one (his niece, Geli Rabble) succeeded. Bullock, 174 (suggesting that this was the true love of his life and that he may have killed her in the course of a jealous argument). Hitler told Eva that he could not marry because he did not have time for a wife and child. "I don't want children. The children of a genius have a hard time in the world. People expect such a child to be a replica of his famous father and don't forgive him for being average. Besides, it's common for them to be mentally deficient." Toland (1997), 314; ibid., 293.

36. The postcard is reproduced in Kershaw (photograph section). Himmler was also an animal lover who opposed hunting. Crankshaw, 18.

37. Toland (1997), 311. Reportedly, he loved all jokes, except political or "dirty" ones.

38. Holmes, 101.

39. Akin, 14; Lapide, 118.

40. Holmes, 101.

41. Halecki and Murray, 59.

42. Holmes, 146-47.

43. Cheetham, 283. It should be noted, however, that Catholic political parties in Germany were subject to sudden shifts in political positions. See M. Price, 106. This is one of the reasons why the Holy See withdrew support from Catholic political parties in the 1920s and 1930s.

44. The Socialists probably would have agreed to an alliance with the Catholics, but the Pope rejected it as a compromise with the powers of evil. Moreover, the Pope made it clear to the priest/leader of the Socialist Popular Party, Father Don Sturzo, that he regarded Sturzo's political activity as incompatible with his priestly duties. Sturzo obediently resigned his leadership of the party.

45. According to a close wartime adviser, Mussolini delighted in calling himself "an unbeliever." *The Ciano Diaries*, 184. "For me," he declared, "Christmas is nothing more than the twenty-fifth of December. I am the man who in all this world feels least these religious anniversaries." Ibid., 424-25.

46. Holmes, 40. Hitler once noted that Fascism came to power despite the opposition of the Church. *Hitler's Secret Conversations*, 422.

47. See Heller and Nekrich.

48. Ibid., 137. In April 1923, Monsignor Konstantin Buchkavich, vicar general of the Roman Catholic Church in Russia, was convicted on the charge of opposing the Soviet government. He was tried along with eighteen other people for engaging in activities "detrimental to the proletarian revolution." Despite foreign protests, the monsignor was shot through the head in the cellar of the Moscow secret police building. *Chronicle*, 301.

49. *Controversial Concordats*, 2.

50. Cheetham, 284-86.

51. Ibid., 286.

52. *Divini Redemptoris*, n. 58.

## Chapter Three: The Spread of Nationalism

1. Halecki and Murray, 56-58.

2. Lutzer, 176.

3. Taylor, 121.

4. Payne, 154.

5. Meltzer, 18.

6. "Adolf Hitler, in an Exclusive Interview, Condemns Berlin Government's 'Liquidation' of Conflict, and Throws Down Gauntlet to Dr. von Kahr," *Christian Science Monitor*, October 3, 1923.

7. Ibid.

8. Ibid.

9. Erich Ludendorff had been a leader of the German army, especially at the end of the First World War. He was a strong supporter of the Nazi Party and agreed to become head of the German army in Hitler's government.

10. This letter is reproduced in the Appendix, p. 392. Its identification in the Vatican archives is: Archivio Nunziatura Monaco, #28961, Busta 396, Fascicolo 7, Foglio 6r-7v. In 1926, Pacelli encouraged German Catholics to join and support the "German Committee Pro Palestine to Support the Jewish Settlement in Palestine," founded in 1926. Among its board members were Albert Einstein and Pacelli's close friend and adviser, the German politician and Catholic prelate Dr. Ludwig Kaas.

11. Archivio Segreto Vaticano, Arch. Nunz. Monaco d.B. 396, Fasc. 7, Pos. XIV, Baviera, p. 75.

12. Archivio Segreto Vaticano, Arch. Nunz. Monaco 365, Fasc. 7, Pos. XIV, Baviera, p. 83.

13. A firsthand account is reprinted in *A History of the Third Reich*, 65.

14. Besier, 32-33.

15. Ibid. (noting Pacelli's disappointment in Catholic associations that failed to defend the Church or the bishop). That same day Albert Einstein fled Berlin to avoid the growing anti-Jewish sentiment. *Chronicle*, 307.

16. Besier, 33.

17. Ibid.

18. *Chronicle* at 314.

19. Besier, 34.

20. Ibid. In a report at that time, Pacelli quoted a newspaper account that said: "We have ceased to be a free people. Non-German powers, the Jew and Rome, shoot their mouths off in our country, and trample our rights under foot." Ibid., 35.

21. Ibid., 34.

22. Ibid., 35.

23. See Kershaw, 262-63; *Chronicle*, 323.

24. Stehlin, 148; Besier, 53. The only problem with this plan, from the German perspective, was that the Danzig government was unprepared to pay the salary of its new Catholic leader, and there was concern that Poland might underwrite the costs and thereby gain influence over Danzig's Catholic administration. Therefore, the German Republic came up with more than fifty thousand marks to help defray O'Rourke's living expenses and maintain the diplomatic advantage that it had gained with appointment of a German-speaking administrator. Later, the Vatican newspaper reported that if Danzig fell to the Nazis, Poland, Romania, and the Balkans would fall shortly thereafter. "Acta Diurna," *L'Osservatore Romano*, May 3, 1934, 1.

25. Hatch and Walshe, 87; Besier, 30.

26. O'Carroll, 31; Halecki and Murray, 63.

27. Besier, 35 (also noting he was the lowest-paid nuncio in the world).

28. Ironically, after working so long to get Pacelli to move to Berlin, German leaders almost sent him away later that year. In November 1925, the nuncios in France and Brazil were recalled to Rome after completing their assignments. As is traditional, they were named cardinals at the next consistory. German leaders, while desiring to retain Pacelli in Berlin, became concerned that he had served longer than either of these other two nuncios, but he was not included on the list for elevation to the Sacred College of Cardinals. This omission was thought to be an indication that the Vatican did not regard the Berlin nunciature of equal stature with those of other nations. These concerns were brought to the Curia's attention, but the Church was able to convince the Germans that this should not be seen as a slight.

29. Hatch and Walshe, 88-89. Foreign correspondent Dorothy Thompson later reported: "In knowledge of German and European affairs and in diplomatic astuteness the Nuncio was without an equal." Halecki and Murray, 63.

30. Conradt, 10.

31. Overy, 284.

32. Hitler, 114. See also Kershaw, 33-34; Janik and Toulmin, 58.

33. The German term *Kulturkampf* is derived from this struggle. This struggle is cited by some as motivation for the Church's 1933 agreement with Nazi Germany. Kevin E. Schmiesing, "Dealing with Dictators," *Crisis*, October 1999, 47 (reviewing *Controversial Concordats: The Vatican's Relations with Napoleon, Mussolini, and Hitler*, Catholic University of America Press [Frank J. Coppa, ed., 1999]).

34. See Kershaw, 33-34, 58.

35. Kershaw, 262. Following Hitler's release from prison, some of his political opponents accused him of having given in to the international power of the Catholic Church. Ibid., 263. In 1928, one rival even accused Hitler of being a tool of the Catholic Church. Ibid., 298.

36. Hitler, 108.

37. Ibid., 108-9.

38. Ibid., 109. "[O]nly an ignoramus could fail to see that an offensive in favor of German interests was something that practically never occurred to the German clergyman." Ibid., 109-10.

39. Ibid., 109.

40. Ibid., 112.

41. Ibid., 113.

42. Ibid., 119.

43. Ibid., 113-14.

44. Ibid., 100.

45. Ibid., 562.

46. Ibid., 561.

47. Taylor, 144.

48. Hitler, 562.

49. Rauschning, 239. Hitler wrote: "Ourselves or the Freemasons or the Church — there is room for one of the three and no more… and we are the strongest of the three and shall get rid of the other two." Ibid., 241.

50. Ibid., 239.

51. Friedländer (1997), 432.

52. Hitler, 459.

53. Ibid., 475.

54. Interestingly, Hitler condemned exactly the same thing that he was proposing: "Worst of all, however, is the devastation wrought by the misuse of religious conviction for political ends. In truth, we cannot sharply enough attack those wretched crooks who would like to make religion an implement to perform political or rather business services for them." Hitler, 268.

55. Rauschning, 239.

56. R. Martin, 183; Matheson, 72; Lapide, 108. Loyola was the founder of the Jesuits.

57. The Nazis, at one point, demanded that *Mein Kampf* replace the Bible in all German churches. See pp. 97, 188-89.

58. Kershaw, 318-22; M. Price, 186.

## Chapter Four: The Lateran Treaty

1. H. Stewart, 108.

2. Cianfarra, 69 (quoting a December 1934 writing by Mussolini).

3. Holmes, 45.

4. Pacelli was largely responsible for negotiating the agreements with Bavaria (1924), Prussia (1929), and Baden (1932). He also started negotiations with the Weimar Republic and attempted to secure an agreement with the Soviet Union. *Controversial Concordats*, 2.

5. See Ronald J. Rychlak, "History Kidnaped?" (reviewing David Kertzer, *The Kidnaping of Edgardo Mortara) Crisis*, May 1997.

6. Pope Pius XI made reference to this in his encyclical *Quinquagesimo Ante* (1929).

7. *Chronicle*, 372.

8. Hatch and Walshe, 94.

9. Ibid., 95-96; Besier, 68-69. Article 34 of the concordat between Italy and the Vatican provided:

> The Italian State, wishing to restore to the institution of marriage — basis of the family — a dignity in conformity with the Catholic tradition of its people, recognizes civil validity to the sacrament of marriage disciplined by canon law.

This provision was to cause controversy later, when Italy adopted racial laws that, inter alia, refused to recognize a marriage between a Jewish person and a non-Jewish Italian.

10. This provision caused some reporters to mistakenly report that the Lateran Treaty gave Mussolini equal say in the appointment of bishops and archbishops in Italy. Actually, bishops had been appointed by the Church subject to the approval of the state before the Lateran Treaty. After the new terms went into effect, the state's role was diminished to having the right to object to an appointee for political reasons only. See Benns, 230.

11. Cianfarra, 298.

12. P. Murphy, 99-100. The Vatican's treasurer, Bernardino Norgara, a layman of Jewish ancestry, invested this money wisely, so that the money from the Lateran Treaty became a vast reserve estimated at hundreds of millions by the mid-1930s.

13. Hatch and Walshe, 96.

14. Holmes, 56.

15. Benns, 231.

16. See Besier, 69. Mussolini's desire to unite all of Italy led him to neutralize the Mafia in Sicily. In fact, Mussolini's war against the Mafia caused many Italian Mafiosi, including a nineteen-year-old future "godfather," Carlo Gambino, to leave Sicily for the United States.

17. Hoar, 149.

18. See Margo Hammond, "Masking the Realities of History," *St. Petersburg* (Florida) *Times*, May 15, 1994, 1D (discussing positive images of Mussolini by Gandhi, the archbishop of Canterbury, and Thomas Edison); Jeffrey M. Landaw, "Gilbert, as in Sullivan: A Victorian Paradox," *Baltimore Sun*, September 29, 1996, 5E (George Bernard Shaw's positive feelings toward Mussolini); Hoar, 237, 240 (Churchill); Yosef Yaakov, "Roots of Fascism," *Jerusalem Post*, February 24, 1995, 23 (Freud). According to some reports, when the Germans invaded Austria in 1938, Mussolini intervened with Hitler and obtained permission for Freud to escape to England. Other reports have it that Freud used his contacts in the United States. Either way, he avoided the concentration camps, where three of his sisters died in the 1940s.

19. Payne, 235. See Jack Epstein, "Digging Up Former Nazis in Argentina: Some say it's finally time to expose war criminals," *San Francisco Chronicle*, July 3, 1994, Sunday Punch, 3 (Hitler's and Perón's respect for Mussolini); Fest, 157 (Hitler's admiration for Mussolini).

20. Holmes, 58-59.

21. Ibid., 58-59; Cheetham, 280.

22. Ray, 28-29.

23. Holmes, 58-59.

24. *Summi Pontificatus*, n. 17.

25. See *The Catholic Church in World Affairs*, W. Gurian and M.A. Fitzsimons, eds. (University of Notre Dame Press: Notre Dame, IN, 1954) (discussing the relationship between the Vatican and Mussolini in light of the Lateran Treaty).

26. Kevin E. Schmiesing, "Dealing with Dictators," *Crisis*, October 1999, 47 (reviewing *Controversial Concordats: The Vatican's Relations with Napoleon, Mussolini, and Hitler*, Frank J. Coppa, ed. [Catholic University of America Press, 1999]).

27. Ibid.

28. Report from Osborne to London, British Public Records Office FO 371/24935 60675 (May 21, 1940).

29. Procacci, 356. The story making the rounds in Rome was that on the day after the agreement was signed, Cardinal Gasparri's car was stopped by a fight in the street. Looking at the two men, the cardinal commented, "I wonder how long ago they signed a concordat." Daniel-Rops, 305.

30. Barzini, 139-40. "It seemed beyond doubt that Mussolini himself had very little faith." Daniel-Rops, 306.

31. Darragh, 4; Daniel-Rops, 310 (Ratti was Pius XI's family name).

32. Daniel-Rops, 310.

33. Charles Rankin, "Pius the Man and His Efforts for Peace," in *The Pope Speaks: The Words of Pius XII*, 12. The risk of Italian censorship of the printed press caused Pacelli to engage in a modernization program that included installation of a radio tower for Vatican Radio broadcasts. Hatch and Walshe, 108.

34. *Non Abbiamo Bisogno*, n. 44.

35. Holmes, 66-67; *Ciano's Diplomatic Papers*, 48 (Mussolini's 1936 statement that "since September 1, 1931, Catholic Action in Italy has practically ceased to exist").

36. Hatch and Walshe, 107.

37. Two months after the encyclical, the Italian leadership reached a compromise agreement with the Holy See. According to one commentator:

> What was at stake was the existence of Catholic Action and its independence of the secular power, and on both these points the Pope obtained satisfaction. The Catholic organizations retained their unique position of freedom from control by the totalitarian machine, as well as the right to recruit members from the rising generation. It was for this principle that Pius XI had fought, and there seems to me no doubt that he saved it.

Darragh, 5 (quoting Daniel A. Binchy, *Church and State in Fascist Italy*, 529). Another commentator said that "the Pope's arrows were barbed, they hurt; and moral victory easily lay with him." Ibid., 4 (quoting Finer, *Mussolini's Italy*, 466). See also Daniel-Rops, 311.

38. In 1926, Pacelli consecrated a Jesuit bishop in Berlin, Father Michel d'Herbigny, "whose task it was to go into the USSR to consecrate several bishops secretly, to inform them officially of their appointments as apostolic administrators." Nichols, 280.

39. It was signed on June 14, 1929. *Controversial Concordats*, 2.

## Chapter Five: Hitler's Rise to Power and the Concordat

1. Payne, 165.

2. Adolf Hitler

> accepted Charles Darwin's theory of "the survival of the fittest" and asserted that man had every right to be "as cruel as nature." Detailed lectures were given in schools and to S.S. troops to prove the inferiority of the Jews. Aryan skulls were compared with those of Jewish ancestry to prove on a scientific basis that the latter were hopelessly inferior. Only the "fittest" had the right to survive.

Lutzer, 80. Leni Riefenstahl, perhaps the most talented female filmmaker of the century, would later turn Nazi propaganda into an art form with films like *Triumph of the Will* and *Olympia*.

3. *Chronicle*, 380.

4. Bullock, 178.

5. Halecki and Murray, 86.

6. Hatch and Walshe, 101. Charles Rankin, "Pius the Man and His Efforts for Peace," in *The Pope Speaks: The Words of Pius XII*, 23 ("Pope Sixtus V wrote: 'He must know everything, understand everything, and say nothing.'")

7. Charles Rankin, "Pius the Man and His Efforts for Peace," in *The Pope Speaks: The Words of Pius XII*, 22.

8. Translated from the original German edition: Sister M. Pascalina Lehnert, *Ich durfte ihm dienen: Erinnerungen an Papst Pius XII*, Würzburg (4th ed., 1983), 42-43.

9. Hatch and Walshe, 90-91; see also Halecki and Murray, 63; Charles Rankin, "Pius the Man and His Efforts for Peace," in *The Pope Speaks: The Words of Pius XII*, 21-22.

10. See Charles Rankin, "Pius the Man and His Efforts for Peace," in *The Pope Speaks: The Words of Pius XII*, 22.

11. Besier, 71.

12. See Charles Rankin, "Pius the Man and His Efforts for Peace," in *The Pope Speaks: The Words of Pius XII*, 27.

13. Stehlin at 318; Ronald J. Rychlak, "Pope Pius XII's Real Personality," 7.5, *Envoy* 28 (2007).

14. Hatch and Walshe, 109; see Halecki and Murray, 65 ("closest possible co-operation").

15. Lutzer, 104. General voting patterns show that Catholics did not support Hitler during his rise to power. See Richard F. Hamilton, *Who Voted for Hitler?* (Princeton University Press: Princeton, 1982); Thomas Childers, *The Nazi Voter* (University of North Carolina Press: Chapel Hill, 1983). Karl Barth, writing about the German Lutheran Church said: "The Church had almost unanimously welcomed the Hitler régime with real confidence, indeed, with the highest hopes." Micklem, 55, quoting Karl Barth in *Cross and Swastika*, 15 (London, Student Christian Movement Press, 1939).

16. Micklem, 55.

17. Stehlin, 353.

18. The original document was obtained by Pave the Way Foundation and at the time of this writing is being prepared to be posted on that organization's web page, *www.ptwf.org*. Later, storm trooper leaders complained that "German mothers have been refused Communion simply because their sons belonged to the Storm Troops." Micklem, 53.

19. "Il partito di Hitler condannato dall'autorità ecclesiastica," *L'Osservatore Romano*, October 11, 1930. (The first line reads: "Belonging to the National Socialist Party of Hitler is irreconcilable with the Catholic conscience, just as belonging to Socialism of any kind is in general irreconcilable with it.")

20. Holmes, 101. Several protests from bishops of this time period are reviewed in Groppe (1983), 24.

21. See Cornwell (1999), 109.

22. Besier, 91.

23. Ibid.

24. Ibid.

25. Stehlin, 353.

26. Holmes, 109-10.

27. Ibid.

28. Ibid. See generally Spicer, *Hitler's Priests*.

29. Kershaw, 418-20.

30. Ibid., 392.

31. After several weeks of negotiations in Switzerland, the European Allies agreed not to punish Germany for this failure to meet its obligations.

32. See Eric Black, "A chilling choice," *Star Tribune* (Minneapolis, MN), February 7, 1993, 23A.

33. *Chronicle*, 411.

34. See Kershaw, 500.

35. Papen's account of these events is reprinted in *A History of the Third Reich*, 57.

36. Palmer, 159; Groppe, 24. Although Papen ultimately played into Hitler's hands and helped his rise to power, he was a devout Catholic and expressed many anti-Hitler sentiments. Hamilton Fish, *The Other Side of the Coin*, 238 (1962).

37. Micklem, 93.

38. Office of United States Chief of Counsel, vol. II, 932.

39. Ibid.

40. On February 12, 1933, the Bavarian bishops' conference, at papal urging, issued pastoral instructions to all their clergy, which said in part: "Leading spokesmen of National Socialism put race before religion, rejecting the Old Testament and even the Mosaic Ten Commandments." All priests were ordered to explain to their congregations that "National Socialism has taken up a position of *Kulturkampf* irreconcilable with

Catholic teaching" and to prohibit the attendance of Nazis in uniform or "with their flags at Divine services, lest people think that the Church has come to terms with National Socialism." Lapide, 98-99.

41. Mr. Kirkpatrick (The Vatican) to Sir R. Vansittart, August 19, 1933, *Documents on British Foreign Policy*, Series II, vol. V, London, 1956, no. 342, p. 524.

42. *Vatican Impressions* (Sweeney, ed.), 260; Lapomarda, 240, n. 36 (Pacelli viewed Hitler's victory as "more fatal than a victory of the socialist left").

43. Rauschning, 49; Groppe, 24.

44. In fact, Hitler's official statements were always conciliatory toward the churches. For instance, in a message that he sent to Cardinal Bertram on April 28, 1933, Hitler wrote that the Reich government "does not desire conflicts with the two churches in Germany, but a sincere cooperation for the good of the state as well also for the good of the churches." *Documents of German Foreign Policy 1919-1945*, Series C (1933-1937), vol. I, no. 196. Nevertheless, Hitler himself explained: "The fact that I remain silent in public over Church affairs is not the least misunderstood by the sly foxes of the Catholic Church, and I am quite sure that a man like Bishop von Galen knows full well that after the war I shall extract retribution to the last farthing." *Hitler's Secret Conversations*, 451. Reichsleiter Bormann suggested to Hitler that Galen be hanged in retaliation for his sermons, but instead thirty-seven members of the clergy were arrested, ten of whom lost their lives. *Three Sermons in Defiance of the Nazis*, 4-5.

45. Micklem, 48.

46. See, e.g., Stehlin, 353.

47. Micklem, 39. ("With church-going and dogmatic theology they were wholly unconcerned; but to destroy atheist Communism, to weld together their broken nation in a fellowship of mutual service, to make the good of the community to prevail over the selfishness of the individual — this was their dream and this, surely, would be Christianity in practice.")

48. Lutzer, 104; Holmes, 102-103.

49. Cornwell (1999), 138.

50. *Office of United States Chief of Counsel*, vol. II, 932-3 (reprinting the full statement by the bishops). There is no evidence of pressure from Rome for this to take place. In fact, Pacelli privately criticized the bishops for lifting the condemnation without first obtaining some sort of assurances from the party. The earlier prohibition is reflected in the minutes of the bishops' conference in Fulda, of August 17, 1932. The relevant passage provides:

> All the gathered bishops have declared that membership in this Party is not allowed because: 1) Portions of its official program, the way they read and as they must be understood without reinterpretation, contain false doctrine; 2) Because the announcements of numerous leading representatives and journalists of the Party contain statements of a character which are opposed to faith, expressing a hostile attitude towards basic teachings and requirements of the Catholic Church, and these statements have not been denied or withdrawn on the part of the highest Party leadership.

At the time of this writing, the original document is being prepared to be posted on Pave the Way Foundation's web page, *www.ptwf.org*. See Groppe, 14.

51. Lapide, 99.

52. The filmed statement can be found in some documentaries on the Nazi era. See Kershaw, 470.

53. "A serious word in serious times," *Berlin Jahrgang*, February 16, 1933.

54. An entry in Goebbels' diary suggests that the burning of the Reichstag surprised Hitler's inner circle. *Time*, September 14, 1987, 44.

55. Micklem, 85. In signing the decree, Hindenburg was acting in accordance with the Weimar Constitution, which stipulated that the president could bypass the Reichstag in the event of an emergency.

56. Ibid., 86.

57. Ibid.

58. *Chronicle*, 416.

59. Lutzer, 33-34.

60. *Chronicle*, 417.

61. Hamerow, 12.

62. The original document was obtained by Pave the Way Foundation and at the time of this writing is being prepared to be posted on that organization's web page, *www.ptwf.org*.

63. Micklem, 88.

64. Peter Hoffman, *Stauffenberg: A Family History, 1905-1944*, Cambridge University Press (Cambridge, 1995), 61. The Enabling Act is largely reprinted in *A History of the Third Reich*, 12.

65. Shortly after the Enabling Act was signed, "the bishops of Cologne, Paderborn, and Osnabrück summoned their dioceses to earnest prayer, not merely for the unity and freedom of the people, but also because, as they said, these were days of severe and bitter suffering for many good and loyal men." Micklem, 89.

66. *Chronicle*, at 418; See Kershaw, 465-67.

67. Micklem, 90-91.

68. Halecki and Murray, 72.

69. *Chronicle*, 417.

70. See "The 1990s; A weekly countdown to the third millennium; 1933," *Fort Worth Star-Telegram*, September 20, 1998 (Life section, 3).

71. *Chronicle*, 419.

72. Ibid.

73. Hamerow, 76.

74. *Chronicle*, 420.

75. Ibid. The genetics movement was very active in Germany, the United States, and elsewhere at the time. See Paul Popenoe and Rosewel H. Johnson, *Applied Eugenics* (The MacMillan Company, 2nd ed., 1935), vii-viii. ("The problem of eugenics is to make such legal, social, and economic adjustments that [1] a larger proportion of superior persons will have children than at present, [2] that the average number of offspring of such superior persons will be greater than at present, [3] that the most inferior persons will have no children, and finally that [4] other inferior persons will have fewer children than now.") Popenoe and Johnson argued that a campaign against abortion would be eugenic, because they assumed that abortions were more common among the upper class, and they suggested that women who underwent abortion might be sterilized, so abortion worked against the "eugenic" benefit to society. Ibid., 279. See also Marie E. Kopp, "Legal and Medical Aspects of Eugenic Sterilization in Germany," *American Sociological Review*, October 1936, 763 (noting that Margaret Sanger, the founder of Planned Parenthood, was deeply involved and held some repugnant views); "Margaret Sanger's Eugenics," *Life Advocate Magazine*, January/February 1998 (discussing how Sanger and other American eugenicists "made their own modest contribution to the plight of the Jews in the Reich"); Robert G. Marshall and Chuck Donovan, *Blessed Are the Barren: The Social Policy of Planned Parenthood* (Ignatius Press, 1991).

76. Doyle, 31. See *Chronicle*, 420.

77. Rauschning, 49.

78. Lutzer, 104.

79. McCabeus, 20; Rauschning, 246.

80. McCabeus, 20; Rauschning, 246.

81. Rauschning, 49; McCabeus, 19.

82. Burleigh, *Sacred Causes*, quoted in Richard John Neuhaus, "As Long As They Spell Our Names Right," *First Things* (November 2007).

83. Rauschning, 53; Barnett, 44.

84. McCabeus, 19.

85. Ibid., 19; Rauschning, 52-53.

86. Bullock, 169; Rauschning, 223.

87. Not long after coming to power, the Nazi authorities conducted a widely publicized campaign for the "purification" of public morals. Bars and cabarets featuring nudity were required to be more modest; commercialized vice became less conspicuous; plays and movies turned from social criticism and bedroom comedy to preaching and moralizing; and gay nightclubs and cafés were closed by order of the police. This history provides the background for the musical play/motion picture *Cabaret*.

88. Hamerow, 54.

89. Ibid.

90. Ibid., 154-55.

91. Ibid., 227.

92. Ibid., 306-307.

93. Ibid.

94. Ibid.

95. Ibid., 364.

96. Ibid., 20-23.

97. Ibid., 73.

98. Ibid., 54.

99. Groppe, 20.

100. It is published in the *Acta Apostolicae Sedis* of September 10, 1933, vol. XXV, no. 14, pp. 389-414. See Rychlak, "The 1933 Concordat." The term "concordat" was important to Pope Pius XI, who preferred it to the word "treaty." Memorandum from Ambassador Bergen to Foreign Minister Neurath, July 3, 1933, in *Documents on German Foreign Policy 1919-1945*, Series C (1933-1937), vol. I, no. 351.

101. Daniel Goldhagen made this charge. He was probably fooled by James Carroll's *Constantine's Sword*. Carroll artfully stated that the concordat was Nazi Germany's first "bilateral" treaty. See Ronald J. Rychlak, "At Cross Purposes" (reviewing James Carroll, *Constantine's Sword: The Church and the Jews*), *Washington Post*, February 12, 2001, C3. Although deceptive, Carroll was technically correct.

102. Two days later, Pius XI made an explicit reference to it in a speech, noting that it was an indication that the international community thought it was necessary to try to negotiate with Germany for the sake of peace. See *Principles for Peace: Selections From Papal Documents, Leo XIII to Pius XII*, 475.

103. John Jay Hughes, "The Pope's 'Pact With Hitler': Betrayal or Self-Defense?" 17 *Journal of Church and State* 63, 69 n. 28 (1975).

104. Gotto, *Die Katholiken und das Dritte Reich.*

105. *Hitler's Rise to Power*, at 26, n.d.; see generally Carr, *A History of Germany.*

106. See Edwin Black, *The Transfer Agreement* (Basic Books, 2001). This agreement was endorsed by the World Zionist Conference in 1935. The immigration of Jews to Palestine was a tolerable solution to the so-called Jewish problem for some in the Nazi leadership, but Hitler did not intend to let Jews survive. In a letter to Haj Amin Al-Husseini, chief mufti of Jerusalem, he wrote:

> Germany stands for an uncompromising struggle against the Jews. It is self-evident that the struggle against the Jewish national homeland in Palestine forms part of this struggle, since such a national homeland would be nothing other than a political base for the destructive influence of Jewish interests. Germany also knows that the claim that Jewry plays the role of an economic pioneer in Palestine is a lie. Only the Arabs work there, not the Jews. Germany is determined to call on the European nations one by one to solve the Jewish problem and, at the proper moment, to address the same appeal to non-European peoples.

Klaus Gensicke, *Der Mufti von Jerusalem und die Nationalsozialisten* (Darmstadt: Wissenschaftliche Buchgesellschaft, 2007), 60-61. According to some accounts, the Nazis would have started the process of eliminating Jews from Palestine but for the defeat of Rommel at the second battle of El Alamein. Ibid.

107. See Besier, 32 (listing nations and dates).

108. *Controversial Concordats*, 2; Besier, 50. See Wright, 1929.

109. The Germans considered Pacelli more "realistic" than Pius XI, who was said to "often create serious obstacles." Confidential Telegram from the Ambassador to the Holy See to the Foreign Ministry, Oct. 16, in *Documents on German Foreign Policy, 1918-1945*, Series C (1933-1937), vol. II, no. 3, at 3.

110. Besier, 62 (emphasis added, internal footnote omitted). See also George O. Kent, *Pope Pius XII and Germany: Some Aspects of German-Vatican Relations, 1933-1943*, 70:1, *The American Historical Review* 59, 60 (October 1964) ("The initiative for the concordat was taken by the German government and particularly by Franz von Papen, who at that time [April 1933] was Vice-Chancellor in the Hitler cabinet"); Micklem, 98 ("Von Papen is the tragic figure of these early days. It was he who was largely responsible for the Concordat.... He believed, or at least he hoped, that the Party would respect the Concordat.")

111. Lutzer, 104. See Morgan, 154.

112. Giorgio Angelozzi Gariboldi, *Pius XII, Hitler e Mussolini: Il Vaticano fra le dittature*, Mursia (Milan, 1995) at 52.

113. Papen explained his thinking in a letter to the German ambassador to the Holy See:

> When it became apparent in January, 1932 [*sic*] that the social collapse of Germany could be prevented only by calling Hitler to power, it was clear for anyone with insight into the situation that assumption of power by the National Socialist movement would necessarily raise a number of fundamental problems. It was clear, above all, that the attitude of the National Socialist movement toward German Catholicism would be one of active opposition. For political Catholicism had fought the movement most bitterly for the preceding 10 years — with the important assistance of the authority of the bishops, at least some of whom had pronounced an anathema against the ideological content of the National Socialist doctrine and had moreover taken action against its followers with the most serious weapons of ecclesiastical disciplinary punishment.
>
>   ... It went therefore without saying that all energies had to be concentrated upon overcoming as far as possible the ideological differences between German Catholicism and the National Socialist movement. This was the basic conviction inspiring my ardent desire to reach as quickly as possible a new arrangement of affairs between the Reich and the Holy See....

Vice Chancellor Papen to Ambassador Bergen, April 7, 1934, in *Documents on German Foreign Policy, 1918-1945*, Series C (1933-1937), vol. II, no. 383.

114. On June 2, 1945, Pope Pius XII [Pacelli] said : "As the offer [to negotiate] came from the Reich Government, the responsibility of a refusal would have devolved upon the Holy See." Lapide, 101. Papen later claimed that the concordat was necessary to protect the Church from Hitler's aggression. *Office of United States Chief of Counsel*, vol. II, 935-36 (indicating that the prosecutors at Nuremberg did not completely believe him).

115. Morgan, 154.

116. R. Stewart, 17.

117. Mr. Kirkpatrick (The Vatican) to Sir R. Vansittart, August 19, 1933, *Documents on British Foreign Policy*, Series II, vol. V, London, 1956, no. 342, p. 524. See also John Jay Hughes, "The Pope's Pact with Hitler," 17 *Journal of Church and State* 63 (1975) (arguing that the Vatican had no real choice but to negotiate).

118. Mr. Kirkpatrick (The Vatican) to Sir R. Vansittart, August 19, 1933, *Documents on British Foreign Policy*, Series II, vol. V, London, 1956, no. 342, p. 524.

119. Telegram from the German Embassy in Italy to the Foreign Ministry, July 4, 1933, in *Documents on German Foreign Policy 1919-1945*, Series C (1933-1937), vol. I, no. 352.

120. Cornwell (1999), 138.

121. Lewy, 77; Secret Memorandum from Vice Chancellor Papen to Chancellor Hitler, July 2, 1933, in *Documents on German Foreign Policy 1919-1945*, Series C (1933-1937), vol. I, no. 347 (reporting on difficulty in negotiations and a promise that violence would end with the signing of the concordat).

122. The charge that Pacelli undermined the party goes back to the memoirs of Germany's last Catholic chancellor, Heinrich Brüning, whose account of the concordat negotiations, written years later, contains numerous factual and chronological errors. In *Hitler's Pope*, John Cornwell presented an interesting twist on this issue. He argued that Secretary of State Pacelli pursued the concordat because he was motivated by the desire to strengthen the papacy. In so doing, Cornwell argued that Pacelli (not Pius XI) eliminated the only power that could have stopped Hitler's rise to total power, the Catholic Center Party. Here, one might note that both the Communists (81) and the Social Democrats (120) had more seats in the Reichstag than did the Center Party (73). The National Socialists held 288 seats. Micklem, 57, 84.

The concordat, according to Cornwell, silenced political priests and bishops who might have held Hitler in check. According to Cornwell, Pacelli wanted to impose papal absolutism on the Church in Germany through the 1917 Code of Canon Law. Cornwell suggests the code was at the heart of this agreement, but the concordat does not even mention the 1917 code.

123. Micklem, 55. See Besier, 77-78 (positive report on the party from Nuncio Orsenigo, written in 1930).

124. "It stands to reason that the members of the Centre Party ... did not suddenly as the result of the turn of the political wheel adopt the principles and admire the practices of their rival, the National Socialist Party." Micklem, 57-58.

125. Burleigh, "The Cardinal Basil Hume Memorial Lectures," 3 *Totalitarian Movements and Political Religions*, 25. See Besier, 66-67. The Catholic Center Party, including former Chancellor Heinrich Brüning, voted in favor of Hitler's Enabling Bill of 1933. This is at least partially due to pressure from the Nazis, who seriously weakened and almost eliminated the Center Party in March 1933.

126. Micklem, 89.

127. On July 5, 1933, two weeks before the concordat was signed, the party voluntarily dissolved in an effort to stop Nazi brutality. Telegraph from Mr. Newton (Berlin) to Sir J. Simon, July 7, 1933, *Documents on British Foreign Policy 1919-1939*, Her Majesty's Stationary Office (E. L. Woodward, ed., London, 1956) (party members believe that dissolution will end arrests, sequestrations, and discrimination against the Catholic press); Congregation for the Causes of Saints, *Positio*, appendix 25, p. 270. Father Robert Leiber, who served as Pacelli's private secretary, believed that the "positive attitude of the Catholic Center party and the Catholic Bavarian People's party toward the so-called enabling laws in 1933 greatly influenced the attitude of the Holy See" regarding the concordat. "This influence was reinforced by the apparent willingness of the German bishops to cooperate with the leaders of the Third Reich, as expressed by them in their meeting of March 28, 1933." George O. Kent, "Pope Pius XII and Germany: Some Aspects of German-Vatican Relations, 1933-1943," 70:1 *The American Historical Review* 59, 60 (October 1964). See Besier, 104. In 1930, the Center Party "increasingly emphasized the impossibility of a politically motivated collaboration with the National Socialists." Besier, 84-85 (quoting a report from Nuncio Orsenigo).

128. See Congregation for the Causes of Saints, *Positio*, appendix 25, p. 270.

129. Ibid. See Dietrich, 105 ("Hitler's original intention had been to use a Concordat to dissolve the Center party, but the clergy themselves deserted the party, which by early July had dissolved itself"); Cheetham, *The Keeper of the Keys*, 283-84; Kershaw, *Hitler: 1889-1936 Hubris*, 478; Robert Leiber, "*Reichskonkordat und Ende der Zentrumspartei*," in *Stimmen der Zeit: Monatschrift für das Geistesleben der Gegenwart*, Verlag Herder-Freiburg im Breisgau, 1960/61, 213; Telegraph from Mr. Newton (Berlin) to Sir J. Simon, July 7, 1933, *Documents on British Foreign Policy 1919-1939*, Her Majesty's Stationary Office (E. L. Woodward, ed., London, 1956) (party members believe that dissolution will end arrests, sequestrations, and discrimination against the Catholic press). The Belgian ambassador in Rome reported that the party had not consulted Rome about its decision to dissolve, and that Pacelli was irritated about how it all took place, believing that the party had disappeared without dignity. Stehlin, 438. The leaders of the Center Party, however, felt that they had to dissolve or they would endanger the Church and risk major clashes with the Nazis, who had already used arrests and intimidation against the party. See Telegraph from Mr. Newton (Berlin) to Sir J. Simon, July 5, 1933, *Documents on British Foreign Policy 1919-1939*, Her Majesty's Stationary Office (E. L. Woodward, ed., 1956). For details on the collapse of the Catholic Center Party, see Robert Leiber, "*Reichskonkordat und Ende der Zentrumspartei*," in *Stimmen der Zeit: Monatschrift für das Geistesleben der Gegenwart*, December 1960, 213.

On July 18, two days before the signing of the concordat, Catholic organizations including the People's Association for Catholic Germany and the Peace-fellowship of German Catholics went into "voluntary liquidation." Micklem, 95.

130. Stehlin, 438. See Giovanni Sale, S.J., "*Roma 1943: occupazione nazista e deportazione degli ebrei*," *La Civiltà Cattolica*," Dec. 6, 2003, 417-429; "Archives Vindicate Vatican on Hitler's Appointment, Says Review" (Zenit News, Dec. 19, 2003). ("[T]he archive sources attest that the Vatican was not informed ahead

of time of negotiations that took place between Hitler and leaders of the Zentrum party on the question of the law of full powers.")

131. Besier, 121. Pacelli went on to complain that the parties dissolved without even informing the Holy See. Ibid.

132. Congregation for the Causes of Saints, *Positio*, appendix 25, p. 270.

133. Stehlin, 46-47 (Pius X "believed the mixture of politics and religion to be the most hybrid and dangerous possible for the Church"). See also Congregation for the Doctrine of the Faith, *Doctrinal Note on Some Questions Regarding the Participation of Catholics in Political Life*, Nov. 21, 2002 (especially section IV), available on the Internet through the Vatican's web page. In 1931, Pius XI wrote an encyclical, *Quadragesimo Anno*, which asserted that the Church has the right and duty "to interpose her authority... in all things that are connected with the moral law." See *The Black Book of Communism*, 29. Regarding political issues unrelated to morality, however, Pius wrote: "[T]he Church holds that it is unlawful for her to mix without cause in these temporal concerns." Modern Church teaching agrees with him. The Second Vatican Council, in its Pastoral Constitution on the Church in the Modern World (*Gaudium et Spes*, n. 76) said: "[At] all times and in all places the Church should have true freedom to... pass moral judgment even in matters relating to politics." The ability of the clergy — of the Church itself — to become involved in politics is limited, however, to situations in which "the fundamental rights of man or the salvation of souls requires it."

134. See generally Rhodes, *The Vatican in the Age of the Dictators: 1922-45*; Besier, 32, 38 (noting Benedict XV's support for concordats). On the other hand, an internal German document indicates that ending the Church's involvement in politics was a very important provision for the Germans. Secret Memorandum from Vice Chancellor Papen to Chancellor Hitler, July 2, 1933, in *Documents on German Foreign Policy 1918-1945*, Series C (1933-1937), vol. I, no. 347. See generally Rhodes.

135. "The Centre Party dissolved itself under pressure in 1933, but the Nazi Party claims that the 'old firm' is still operating under a new name, and that, in particular, Catholic Action is simply the Centre Party in another form, up to a point." Micklem, 55.

136. Report from the British Legation to the Holy See, Feb. 17, 1939, British Public Records Office, FO 371/23789. Documents from recently opened Vatican archives also show that the cardinal-secretary of state followed the orders of Pope Pius XI. Godman, 28-29, 40, 82-84, 164-65. See also Purdy, 20 (Pacelli "was to all appearances a punctilious collaborator of Pius XI, and enjoyed his complete confidence....").

137. George O. Kent, "Pope Pius XII and Germany: Some Aspects of German-Vatican Relations, 1933-1943," 70:1 *The American Historical Review* 59, 60 (October 1964).

138. Purdy, 20. "To Cornwell, Pius XII was too authoritarian, too monarchical, too powerful. It may be argued that the very opposite was true. Pius XII was not sufficiently confident of his power and of his situation." John Lukacs, "In Defense of Pius," *National Review*, Nov. 22, 1999.

139. Hatch and Walshe, 109; see Halecki and Murray, 65 ("closest possible co-operation"); McCormick, 98 ("As the Papal Secretary of State, Eugenio Cardinal Pacelli had admiration amounting to veneration not only for the person but the policy of his chief").

140. See Godman, 28-29, 40, 82-84, 164-65 (reviewing newly opened Vatican archives).

141. Congregation for the Causes of Saints, *Positio*, (Summarium) Testimony of Cardinal Stefano Wyszynski, Oct. 18 and 25, 1968, before the Tribunal of the Vicariate of Rome, on the beatification of Pius XII (Eugenio Pacelli), part II, p. 578; *Controversial Concordats*, 136.

142. Burleigh, "The Cardinal Basil Hume Memorial Lectures," 3 *Totalitarian Movements and Political Religions*, 25 ("the once-mighty Catholic Centre Party was sent to the liquidators after it had voted for the March 1933 Enabling Act").

143. "Justice for Jews," reprinted in *Commonweal Confronts the Century: Liberal Convictions, Catholic Traditions*, 193, 194 (Patrick Jordan and Paul Baumann, eds., 1999).

144. John Cornwell noted that the Vatican could not control the party and that many German Catholics left the Center Party and joined the National Socialists. Cornwell also noted that the Catholic Center Party, including former Chancellor Heinrich Brüning, voted in favor of Hitler's Enabling Bill of 1933. *Hitler's Pope*, 135-36. That was an embarrassment to the Holy See and hardly suggests that the party was willing to battle Hitler to the end. See Ibid., 144, 197.

145. William Rees-Mogg, "The Vatican's holy failure," *Times* (London), Oct. 4, 1999.

146. Besier, 114; see Ibid., 115-16, 152.

147. See Vazsonyi, 58, 148. While all of these points were popular with German people, the term "social justice" had particular meaning to Catholics. This term was regularly used in the United States by both Catholic social activist Dorothy Day and controversial radio personality Father Charles Coughlin, even though they were from different ends of the political spectrum.

148. See Besier, 114-15 (Nuncio Orsegino's report on promises from the new National Socialist regime).

149. Ibid., 116.

150. Ibid., 118-19.

151. Godman, 9, 39. See Official Report by William Donovan, "The Nazi Master Plan; Annex 4: The Persecution of the Christian Churches," July 6, 1945, reprinted in Stein, 272-73. German bishops at one

point considered mediation of the disputes with the Reich, but Secretary of State Pacelli insisted that the concordat was with the Holy See, not German bishops. "Vice Chancellor Papen to Ambassador Bergen," Nov. 11, 1933, in *Documents on German Foreign Policy 1918-1945*, Series C (1933-1937), vol. II, no. 61 (margin note). The likely reason for this insistence is concern that the Nazis would bully local clergy into compliance.

152. Besier, 122.

153. The German bishops spoke out more brazenly than any other group in Germany. Groppe, *The Church's Struggle with the Third Reich*.

154. See Second Vatican Council, Pastoral Constitution on the Church in the Modern World (*Gaudium et Spes*). In 1918, when he was the Holy See's representative in Poland, Cardinal Ambrogio Damiano Achille Ratti (the future Pope Pius XI) argued strenuously against the formation of a single Catholic political party in that nation.

155. Article 16 of the concordat contained a pledge required of new bishops that they "swear and promise to honor the constitutional government and to cause the clergy of my diocese to honor it." Article 32 of the supplementary protocol, however, made clear that German clergy were not prohibited or even limited in preaching about "the dogmatic and moral teachings and principles of the Church." *The Persecution of the Catholic Church in the Third Reich*, 522 (reprinting the supplementary protocol). See *Controversial Concordats*, 209; Groppe, *The Church's Struggle with the Third Reich*.

156. See *The Persecution of the Catholic Church in the Third Reich*, 522 (reprinting the supplementary protocol); Second Vatican Council, Pastoral Constitution on the Church in the Modern World (*Gaudium et Spes*); see also Pius XI, On Reconstruction of the Social Order (*Quadragesimo Anno*) (1931). Hitler verbally attacked the German bishops at a mass rally in the Berlin *Lustgarten*. "The Church and the Jews in the Third Reich," *Fidelity*, November 1983, 21.

157. In 1943, for instance, the German bishops issued a statement saying: "The extermination of human beings is *per se* wrong, even if it is purportedly done in the interests of society; but it is particularly evil if it is carried out against the innocent and defenseless people of alien races or alien descent." Saperstein, 43. Since this type of statement related to morality, it was not restricted by the terms of the concordat.

158. For more on the relatively few Catholic priests who succumbed to Nazism, see Spicer, *Hitler's Priests*; Spicer, *Resisting the Third Reich*.

159. "Ai Margini del Concordato tra la Santa Sede e il Reich Germanico," *L'Osservatore Romano*, July 26, 1933, 1; "Ancora a proposito del Concordato tra la Santa Sede e il Reich Germanico," *L'Osservatore Romano*, July 27, 1933, 2; Congregation for the Causes of Saints, *Positio*, appendix 25, 270.

160. William M. Harrigan, "Pius XII's Efforts to Effect a Détente in German-Vatican Relations," 1939-1940, *The Catholic Historical Review*, July 1963. Even before the concordat was ratified, the Vatican had made many objections to German officials regarding treatment of the Church. "The Papal Secretary of State to the German Ambassador to the Holy See," Oct. 19, 1933, in *Documents on German Foreign Policy 1918-1945*, Series C (1933-1937), vol. II, no. 17, 23 (enclosure); see *Controversial Concordats*, 226.

161. Lapide, 103-4; Holmes, 110. See "Telegram from the Chargé d'Affaires of the Embassy to the Holy See to the Foreign Ministry," dated Sept. 12, 1933, in *Documents on German Foreign Policy 1918-1945*, Series C (1933-1937), vol. I, no. 425 (refusal to accept Catholics of Jewish descent as equal to Catholics of Aryan descent). One of the German officials at the Foreign Office complained that "the Nuncio used to come to me nearly every fortnight with a whole bundle of complaints." Weizsäcker, 282. In December 1933, the German ambassador to the Holy See wrote to German Foreign Minister Neurath that he considered a clash with the Curia quite possible and that the lack of response to the Vatican's charges would look bad to the world. "Ambassador Bergen to Foreign Minister Neurath," Dec. 28, 1933, in *Documents on German Foreign Policy 1918-1945*, Series C (1933-1937), vol. II, no. 152.

162. William M. Harrigan, "Pius XII's Efforts to Effect a Détente in German-Vatican Relations, 1939-1940," *The Catholic Historical Review*, July 1963, 186.

163. "Why 'Hitler and the Vatican' Fails as History: Interview with Father Peter Gumpel, Postulator of Pius XII's Cause," Zenit News Service, March 3, 2004. Gumpel was actually the relator, not the postulator, of Pius XII's cause. The protests were published in the collection: "*Der Notenwechsel Zwischen dem Heiligen Stuhl und der Deutschen Reichsregierung - I. Von der Ratifizierung des Reichskonkordats bis zur Enzyklika 'Mit brennender Sorge,'*" Bearbeitet von Dieter Albrecht. VKZ A 1, Mainz (1965).

164. Stein, 128 (also noting that the concordat was influential in helping the Church oppose other propaganda, including the anti-Semitic book *The Myth of the Twentieth Century*).

165. Graham, *Pope Pius XII and the Jews of Hungary in 1944*, 5-6.

166. Tinnemann, 337, 341. In July 1933, just days after Germany ratified the concordat, the Reich government announced a sterilization law (or the "law to prevent congenitally sick offspring") designed to achieve "perfection of the Aryan race." Besier, 65; *Chronicle*, 422. Germans who were less than perfect were to be sterilized for the glory of Reich. This was in direct conflict with Catholic teaching about the sanctity of human life, including Pius XI's recent encyclical, *Casti Connubii* (on chastity in marriage, 1930). Prominent Church leaders immediately denounced the program. Benns, 266.

167. On March 22, 1937, the *Völkischer Beobachter* said, "Loyalty to a contract cannot be regarded as binding forever and under all circumstances." Micklem, 74. See Ibid., 75-76 (similar articles in the storm trooper publication *Der S.A. Mann*); Godman, *Hitler and the Vatican*, 89 (noting the extensive violations by the Nazis).

168. *Hitler's Secret Conversations 1941-1944*, 449. He also spoke of ending the concordat once the war was over. Ibid., 448. One of his complaints was that "the Catholic Church strives always to seek advantage where we are the weakest by demanding the application to the whole Reich of those of the various Concordats which conform most closely to its aspirations." Ibid., 448.

169. *Das Schwarze Korps* had a circulation of about 200,000. "Those who read this paper will have little doubt that it is as fundamentally anti-Christian as it is openly anti-Church." Micklem, 138.

170. Ibid., 80-82.

171. Ibid., 76.

172. Ibid.

173. Ibid., 77. See "War on Church, German Decrees, Concordat Abrogated, Reich Laws to Govern Relations with Vatican," *The Canberra Times*, Dec. 15, 1938.

174. *Hitler's Secret Conversations*, 449.

175. Shirer, *Berlin Diary*, 296. See also Office of the United States Chief of Counsel, Supp. B, 1238 (Ribbentrop's testimony as to his desire to obtain a new agreement with the Vatican but that "things didn't come off").

176. See Godman, 50; McCormick, 91 (the concordat did not prevent retaliation by the Nazis against Catholic priests). See also "Baptised Jews, Pope's Demand, Germany Agrees," *Courier-Mail* (Brisbane), Sept. 13, 1933 ("before the concordat between Germany and the Vatican was signed Germany pledged herself to accept the terms of the Vatican memorandum demanding full rights for baptized Jews"); "Vatican Concordat: Humane Treatment of Jews," *The Argus* (Melbourne), Sept. 13, 1933 (the memorandum "demanded that Jews be treated with humanity in accordance with the principles of Christian charity").

177. "Pope Signs Pact With Germany: 'Jews Must Be Treated with Christian Charity,'" *Palestine Post*, Sept. 13, 1933.

178. Critic Daniel Goldhagen has asserted that a "secret annex" to the concordat gave the Church's approval to German rearmament. This argument must have been drawn from a misreading of the supplemental protocol. One provision stated that *if* Germany were to revive its army, Catholic soldiers would have access to chaplains. In other words, it was exclusively a matter of protecting the sacraments, not approving German rearmament. See Congregation for the Causes of Saints, *Positio*, appendix 25, 271.

179. Because of this provision, when National Socialists argued that someone baptized into the Catholic faith remained a Jew, it was not just an assault on the Church's authority; it was a breach of the concordat. As such, the Church had a legal basis to protect those who were (or who claimed to be) baptized.

180. *Office of United States Chief of Counsel*, vol. II, 937.

181. Cornwell (1999), 179.

182. Ibid.

183. They are reprinted in *A History of the Third Reich*, 208.

184. Memorandum to General Donovan from Fabian von Schlabrendorff, Oct. 25, 1945. On Innitzer and the Vatican, see pp. 114-15.

185. Memorandum to General Donovan from Fabian von Schlabrendorff, Oct. 25, 1945. See also Schlabrendorff, *The Secret War Against Hitler*.

186. Official Report by William Donovan, *The Nazi Master Plan; Annex 4: The Persecution of the Christian Churches*, July 6, 1945, reprinted in Stein, 272-73.

187. Ibid. Congregation for the Causes of Saints, *Positio*, appendix 25, 271. See pp. 53-55.

188. *Mit brennender Sorge*, n. 3. For a detailed discussion of this encyclical, see Congregation for the Causes of Saints, *Positio (Vita Documentata: L'Enciclica "Mit brennender Sorge")*, pp. 583-621.

189. Lapide, 101; Nichols, 282.

190. See Gallin, *German Resistance to Hitler: Ethical and Religious Factors* (arguing that the concordat helped the Vatican by providing it with a legal basis for its arguments); John Jay Hughes, "The Pope's Pact with Hitler," 17 *Journal of Church and State*, 63 (1975) (without the concordat, Hitler would have been able to persecute the Church without restriction).

191. The concordat "was simply the culmination of efforts Pacelli had begun long before with the Weimar Republic." Purdy, 22, 252.

192. Lewy, 77.

193. Benns, 266.

194. Holmes, 107.

195. "Let's Look at the Record," *Inside the Vatican*, October 1999, X.

196. Fabert, 36; Hamerow, 75-76; Gallin, 210. Moreover, on June 30, 1933, Pacelli's predecessor in office, Cardinal Gasparri, wrote a note urging the Holy See to avoid controversy with the Nazi regime or a struggle with Hitlerism. Besier, 120.

197. Kershaw, 488 ("it was an unqualified triumph for Hitler").

198. "Minutes From the Meeting of the Conference of Ministers," July 14, 1933, in *Documents on German Foreign Policy 1918-1945*, Series C (1933-1937), vol. I, no. 362.

199. Darragh, 15 (quoting Knox, *Nazi and Nazarene*, 9) (emphasis in original); see also Henri Daniel-Rops, *A Fight for God: 1870-1939*, 308 (Dutton: New York, 1965) (similar); Desmond Fisher at 20 (a concordat "is never a friendship pact, as so many non-Catholics believe, but a sign of tension....")

200. Godman, 50.

201. Matheson, 47-48.

202. *Why the Churches Kept Silent*.

203. Original documents, as well as translations and commentary are available on the Internet at: *watch-tower.observer.org/*.

204. Ibid.

205. *Why the Churches Kept Silent*.

206. See Gabriele Yonan, "Spiritual Resistance of Christian Conviction in Nazi Germany: The Case of the Jehovah's Witnesses," 41 *Journal of Church and State*, 307 (March 22, 1999).

207. "Theological principles were adhered to; Witnesses remained 'neutral,' they were honest and completely trustworthy and as such, ironically, often found themselves employed as servants of the S.S." *Watchtower Magazine*, Oct. 1, 1984, 8.

208. *Why the Churches Kept Silent*.

209. Figures from the *Watchtower's* 1974 yearbook.

210. Holmes, 115.

211. This letter is reproduced in the Appendix, p. 393. The Vatican archive reference is: *Sacra Congregazione Degli Affari Ecclesiastici Straordinari, Germania, Anno: 1933-1945, Posizione 643, Fascicolo 158*. As for the translation, most accounts have referred to anti-Semitic "excesses." The actual word used by Pacelli was *"eccessi,"* which can be translated as *"rage"* or *"extremes"* — as in *"andare agli eccessi"* — "to go to extremes;" or *"dare in eccessi"* — "to fly into a rage" — these are the examples given by *Langenscheidt's Standard Italian Dictionary*, 143 (Munich, 1990). Thus Pacelli should not be seen as tolerating a limited amount of anti-Semitic behavior but opposing an excessive amount. Rather, he is condemning the abuse of Jews by the Nazis, which he considers *outrageous*.

212. "New Proofs of Pius XII's Efforts to Assist Jews: 1933 Letter Targets 'Anti-Semitic Excesses' in Germany," Zenit News Service, Feb. 17, 2003. See also Godman, 37-38 ("Orsenigo read the Catholic vice-chancellor, Franz von Papen a lesson on how the legislation represented 'an offense against the divine law.'")

213. Passelecq and Suchecky, 113.

214. Holmes, 109.

215. This filmed statement sometimes appears in documentaries on the Nazi regime.

216. Holmes, 108.

217. Benns, 266-67.

218. See "The German Youth Leader to the Vice Chancellor," Feb. 20, 1934, in *Documents on German Foreign Policy 1918-1945*, Series C (1933-1937), vol. II, no. 272.

219. Holmes, 108.

220. Barnett, 78.

221. "Unsigned Memorandum," reporting on a meeting that took place on Dec. 18, 1933, in *Documents on German Foreign Policy 1918-1945*, Series C (1933-1937), vol. II, no. 133.

222. *Chronicle*, 425.

223. Holmes, 111.

224. Micklem, 101.

225. Ibid., 101.

## Chapter Six: Hitler Battles the Churches

1. Quoted in Matheson, 48-49.

2. Holmes, 108; Oppen, 407. Reverend Martin Niemöller said: "I am convinced that if the Catholic Church had refrained from opposing Hitler it would have been permitted to handle its money affairs in the proper way. And I agree with the Pope that these laws are unethical. They were seized upon as a means of destroying the Catholic Church's prestige." Stein, 130 ("What Pastor Niemöller said of the other charges could be no stronger from the lips of a Catholic priest.")

3. Oppen, 407.

4. According to some reports, Himmler and Göring actually duped Hitler into killing all of their rivals within the party. See Shirer (1962), 305.

5. Speer, 87-89.

6. Fest, 450-51.

7. Kershaw, 348; *The Persecution of the Catholic Church in the Third Reich*, 314 (Hitler claimed to have protected Roehm from violent attacks in the past).

8. The exact figure is unknown. It seems certain that more than 100, and perhaps several hundred people were killed. See Goldston, 80 (suggesting that there might have been more than 1,000 victims).

9. Daniel-Rops, 320. Most priests resisted the Nazis. For instance, in the Archdiocese of Freiburg in southwestern Germany, there were 1,546 ordained priests in 1937. Many had military experience, but only about sixty were considered by the party to be "reliable." Of these sixty, twelve later "ran afoul" of the Gestapo and an additional four were questioned by the Gestapo for reading Pope Pius XI's encyclical *Mit brennender Sorge* to their congregations. In fact, "one can describe only two of the sixty priests as outwardly and ideologically sympathetic to National Socialism." Spicer, *Father Wilhelm Senn*, 295-97.

10. Cornwell (1999), 165.

11. Ibid.

12. Payne, 277-83.

13. *The Persecution of the Catholic Church in the Third Reich*, 336 (reprinting orders to leave the Church).

14. Goldston, 81.

15. The mass starvation that followed was no improvement on the Nazi death camps with their gas chambers disguised as showers. Heller and Nekrich, 233-38.

16. Hollander.

17. Ibid.

18. Ibid.

19. David Remnick, "Gorbachev, Vatican Aide Hold Talks; 'Good Atmosphere' Cited by Casaroli," *Washington Post*, June 14, 1988, A18.

20. Cornwell (1999), 112 ("It became a crime to teach children under sixteen about God").

21. Ibid., 112-13.

22. See Joshua Rothenberg, "The Legal Status of Religion in the Soviet Union," in *Aspects of Religion in the Soviet Union 1917-1967*, Chicago/London (Richard H. Marshall, ed., 1971).

23. James P. Gallagher, "Catholic Church on Rise in Russia: Communism's End Unleashes Repressed Spirit," *Chicago Tribune*, Nov. 26, 1995.

24. Holmes, 94.

25. Hatch and Walshe, 109.

26. Some of the voters viewed Hitler as the best defense against the spread of Bolshevism. Kershaw, 546-47. Others may have been afraid to cast a ballot against a return for fear of what Hitler would do to them if they returned to Germany and he found out.

27. Kershaw, 547.

28. *Chronicle*, 442.

29. Hatch and Walshe, 110-11. This was a very significant international event, and the Argentinian government pulled out all the stops to welcome the Pope's representative. Morgan, 156.

30. O'Carroll, 41. Secretary of State Pacelli took an ocean liner to South America. Relaxing on a deck chair, he laid aside his golden cross and red moire cape. Soon thereafter a young boy grabbed them and began to run up and down the deck with these symbols of majesty. A horrified father witnessed the scene and rushed to grab the items from his young son. "Let him be," said Cardinal Pacelli. "Little children bless all they touch." *The Catholic Treasury of Wit and Humor*, 136 (Hawthorn Books, Inc., New York: 1960, Paul Bussard, ed.)

31. *Controversial Concordats*, 173 (quoting Pacelli to Schulte, Vatican City, March 12, 1935, in Volk, *Akten deutscher Bischöfe*, 2:113-17).

32. Bogle, *Salisbury Review*.

33. Hamerow, 196-97.

34. "'Immorality Trials' Went On For Years," *Wanderer*, Oct. 18, 2007, 5.

35. See Ibid.

36. Ibid.

37. *Persecution of the Catholic Church in the Third Reich*, 275 (reprinting a speech from July 13, 1935). Emphasis in original.

38. "'Immorality Trials' Went On For Years," *Wanderer*, Oct. 18, 2007, 5.

39. *Persecution of the Catholic Church in the Third Reich*, 412.

40. Goldhagen (2002), 118.

41. *Persecution of the Catholic Church in the Third Reich*, 429.

42. Ibid.

43. Ibid., 415.

44. Ibid. The following year, the S.S. newspaper, *Das Schwarze Korps*, published an article entitled: "Dear Vatican, We Beg a Little Greater Indignation!" It said:

> For us Westerners it is difficult to understand the tolerance which Rome shows towards a Bolshevism which disseminates universal destruction from the Kremlin.... They march separately in order to strike down, together, the real enemy of their theories, National Socialism.... *Catholic Action* has never been more closely in line with Bolshevism than today.... It does not matter whether one is

Indian, Hottentot or Anglo-Saxon so long as all acknowledge the Church of Rome; all are equal and equally worthy of Heaven, to which a democratically elected Pope claims the keys....

*The Persecution of the Catholic Church in the Third Reich*, 415 (quoting *Das Schwarze Korps* of April 23, 1936).

45. Ibid.

46. This letter is reproduced in the Appendix, p. 392. See p. 44.

47. Besier, 71.

48. *The Nazi Master Plan: The Persecution of the Christian Churches*, July 6, 1945.

49. Ibid.

50. Ibid.

51. Ibid.

52. Ibid.

53. Ibid.

54. *Summi Pontificatus* is central to Pius XII's approach to the war. See pp. 380-83.

55. *Tablet* (London), April 27, 1940, 398. The *Tablet* reported that "the *Osservatore Romano*, the Vatican's newspaper, published important extracts from Cardinal Faulhaber's recent outspoken pastoral on the Encyclical *Summi Pontificatus*." See "*La figura e l'opera di Pio XII*," *L'Osservatore Romano*, April 14, 1940, 1.

56. Stein, 127.

57. Ibid.

58. Memorandum to General Donovan from Fabian von Schlabrendorff (noting that "quite a number of the lower clerics" who repeated his teachings "ended up in prison or in a concentration camp"). See also Schlabrendorff, *The Secret War Against Hitler*.

59. *Stephen S. Wise, Servant of the People: Selected Letters*. In a wartime editorial, he also spoke well of Pope Pius XII. "Christendom and the Jews," *Jewish Chronicle* (London), Sept. 11, 1942 (praising Pius XI and Pius XII); Wise, *As I See It* (reprinting the 1942 article).

60. Niemöller himself, speaking of a meeting with Hitler [in 1931], said: "I know that from that day on, until our eyes were opened, Hitler had the full support of the Protestant Church in Germany." Stein, 79 (later suggesting that Niemöller's "eyes were opened" in January 1934).

61. *Akten Kardinal Michael von Faulhaber, 1917-1945* (edited by Ludwig Volk, Matthias-Grünewald-Verlag: Mainz, 1975-1978), vol. 1, 705, 726 (these are the official papers of Cardinal Faulhaber). The letter is also cited in Hamerow, 75. Hamerow says of Faulhaber:

> The cardinal's private correspondence during the early months of the Third Reich reveals, moreover, that his sympathies were not confined to the Judaism of antiquity. In a letter to Alois Wurm, editor of a Catholic periodical, he condemned the new government's anti-Semitic campaign. "This action against the Jews is so unchristian that every Christian, not only every priest, would have to stand up against it." Clearly, Faulhaber cannot be accused of being an anti-Semite.

Ibid., 75.

62. Hamerow, 75-76.

63. Ibid. Support from Pacelli has been identified as one of the reasons for Faulhaber's outspokenness. Fabert, 36.

64. *Chronicle*, 446.

65. Taylor, 144.

66. Goldston, 89-90; "Let's Look at the Record," *Inside the Vatican*, October 1999, X.

67. See Goldston, 89-90; Kershaw, 563-65.

68. Micklem, 2.

69. Matthew Berke, "Accomplices to Genocide?" *First Things*, February 1998, 42 (reviewing William D. Rubinstein, *The Myth of Rescue: Why the Democracies Could Not Have Saved More Jews from the Nazis*).

70. Rousmaniere, 116-17.

71. "Polish Bishops, The Victims of Nazi Ideology," January 1995, reprinted in *Secretariat for Ecumenical and Interreligious Affairs*, National Conference of Bishops, *Catholics Remember the Holocaust*, United States Catholic Conference (Washington, 1998).

72. Marchione (1997), 200.

73. *The Persecution of the Catholic Church in the Third Reich*, 19.

74. Ibid., 421 (quoting Julius Streicher's *Stürmer*).

75. Richard J. Neuhaus, "The Public Square," *First Things*, October 1997, 75, 89.

76. Michaelis, 240.

77. Graham (1996), 1.

78. Cianfarra, 112.

79. For a discussion of the economic maneuvers that Hitler was using to keep up appearances within Germany, see Kershaw, 576-78.

80. Goldston, 85.

81. Lutzer, 17.

82. Conradt, 50-51.

83. Lutzer, 17.

84. Conradt, 50-51.

85. This was explained by Sir Neville Chamberlain as an "Anglo-German understanding" for "the two pillars of European peace and buttresses against Communism" (Sept. 13, 1938, in a letter to King George VI).

86. See Payne, 139.

87. See Horst J.P. Bergmeier and E. Lotz Rainer, *Hitler's Airwaves: The Inside Story of Nazi Radio Broadcasting and Propaganda Swing*, Yale University Press (1997).

88. Ibid. These inexpensive radios had great difficulty picking up broadcasts from outside of Germany. Whether by design or luck, this worked in Hitler's favor when he later wanted to suppress information from the Vatican and other nations.

89. *Chronicle*, 429.

90. Ibid., 431.

91. Ibid., 435.

92. Goldston, 98-99.

93. Charles Pichon, *The Vatican and its Role in World Affairs* (E. P. Dutton, New York, 1950), 146.

94. "Uno strano avvenimento a Vienna: Un colpo di sorpresa alla stazione radio fa credere all'avvento dei nazionalsocialisti al potere ed alle dimissioni di Dollfuss," *L'Osservatore Romano*, July 26, 1934; "Il Fallito Colpo di Stato in Austria: Dollfuss corona con la sua morte un'eroica vita consacrata all'indipendenza ed all'elevazione di un popolo," *L'Osservatore Romano*, July 27, 1934; "Dopo la Sanguinosa Giornata Viennese: Il cordoglio e l'indignazione mondiale per l'assassinio del Cancelliere austriaco," *L'Osservatore Romano*, July 28, 1934; "La Riscossa contro il terrorismo Nazionalsocialista: L'Austria riconsacra nella cristiana eredità di Dollfuss," *L'Osservatore Romano*, July 29, 1934. For later commentary on the new Austrian government, see "Il Viaggio del Cancelliere Austriaco," *L'Osservatore Romano*, Feb. 26, 1935; *L'Osservatore Romano*, Feb. 24, 1935; "Austria e Francia," *L'Osservatore Romano*, Feb. 23, 1935; "L'Austria e la cooperazione italo-franco-inglese," *L'Osservatore Romano*, Feb. 22, 1935.

95. *Chronicle*, 453.

96. Kennedy (1961), 93-94. Kennedy suggests that this retooling problem put Britain two years behind Germany.

97. *Chronicle*, 452.

98. German troops received a warm welcome as they entered the Rhineland. Women placed flowers in the road, and priests offered their blessings. Cardinal Schulte offered praise to Hitler for "sending back our army." Kershaw, 588.

99. Hatch and Walshe, 129.

100. Shirer (1962), 402-3.

101. Hitler, 108-9.

102. Speer, 142.

103. Ibid., 142-43.

104. See Geoffrey Reagan, *The Guinness Book of Decisive Battles* (Canopy Books: New York, 1992).

105. Pope Benedict XVI cautioned against this tendency in a speech that created an international incident. See "Papal Address at University of Regensburg: 'Three Stages in the Program of De-Hellenization,'" Zenit News Service, Sept. 12, 2006 (reprinting the text of the speech).

106. Geoffrey Reagan, *The Guinness Book of Decisive Battles* (Canopy Books: New York, 1992). Hitler also said, "If we ever get rid of Christianity, then other nations can have it." Groppe, 13 (quoting the diary of Alfred Rosenberg).

107. Matheson, 43.

108. Shirer (1962), 329; Lutzer, 117. "Hitler spoke of both Protestants and Catholics with contempt, convinced that all Christians would betray their God when they were forced to choose between the swastika and the Cross." Lutzer, 104.

109. Hitler, 213.

110. Saperstein, 38-39 (noting that in 1936 it was published under Nazi auspices and later excerpts from Luther's writings were printed in a pamphlet that was distributed by the Nazis).

111. Quoted in Lutzer, 86. See also Shirer (1962), 326-27. Saperstein makes the point that Luther was calling for the destruction of synagogues, not people, but his choice of language (calling for good Christians to "act like a good physician who, when gangrene has set in, proceeds without mercy to cut, saw, and burn flesh, veins, bone, and marrow") made it easy for the National Socialists to exploit. Saperstein, 39.

112. Saperstein, 39 (quoting Luther, *On the Jews and Their Lies*, 275).

113. Lapide, 96 (noting that such comments appeared until Pope Pius XI put an end to them in 1938).

114. O'Carroll, 73-74.

115. "Nazi laws defining 'Jewishness' were carefully drawn to exclude both Jesus Christ and Adolf Hitler" (who may have feared that one of his grandparents was Jewish). Toland (1997), 288.

116. In 1936, Himmler sent out a memorandum defining new holidays which were based upon paganism and Nazism. They included: Hitler's Birthday (April 20), May Day, Summer Solstice, Harvest Feast, The Beer Hall Putsch Anniversary (Nov. 9), and Winter Solstice. He also devised ceremonies that he hoped would one day replace Christian rituals (Naming Rites, for instance, were to replace Baptism).

> Since Germans had for centuries celebrated Christmas and Easter, Hitler had to reinterpret their meaning. Christmas was turned into a totally pagan festival; in fact, at least for the SS troops, its date was changed to December 21, the date for winter solstice. Carols and Nativity plays were banned from the schools in 1938, and even the name Christmas was changed to "Yuletide." Crucifixes were eliminated from classrooms, and Easter was turned into a holiday that heralded the arrival of spring.

Lutzer, 115.

117. Daniel-Rops, 316.

118. See Alvarez and Graham, 49 ("The Catholic Church, then, joined the Communists, Jews, and Freemasons as one of the 'Transnational Powers' [*Überstaatliche Mächte*) which were the mortal enemies of the National Socialist state."); Kershaw, 560 (citing internal S.A. reports to the effect that Jews, Catholics, and capitalists were their ideological enemies); Daniel-Rops, 319.

119. Lapide, 104.

120. Micklem, 15-16.

121. Besier, 144. This meant that Catholics were forbidden from acquiring, possessing, or reading the book. Ibid. The same day that the book was placed on the index, *L'Osservatore Romano* ran an article calling the book "fanatical," and said it was "anticultural, anti-Christian,... and misanthropic." "Un libro di odiose falsità per la giovent ùtedesca," *L'Osservatore Romano*, Feb. 7, 1934.

122. Micklem, 113. Rosenberg published a response to the Church in June 1935. Ibid., 125 (suggesting that the most important thing this did was offer Hitler the chance to distance the Party from the theories set forth in the book).

123. Speer, 143; Blet, 52 ("official catechism of the new Germanic religion").

124. Shirer (1962), 332-33; Lutzer, 118-19. In 1933, all German newlywed couples were presented with a copy of *Mein Kampf.* Sales were so brisk that Hitler renounced his salary as chancellor and lived on the royalties from the book. Daniel-Rops, 317.

125. Speer, 143; Shirer (1962), 210.

126. Benns, 263.

127. Hitler's radio broadcast explaining this matter is reprinted in *A History of the Third Reich*, 248.

128. Ibid., 264. This accounts for the typical references to "the Protestant Church" in Germany.

129. *A History of the Third Reich*, 106.

130. Benns, 264.

131. Shirer (1962), 326; Rousmaniere, 118.

132. Spicer, *Father Wilhelm Senn*, 298.

133. Poewe, 135.

134. The *Chicago Tribune*, Aug. 6, 1938, published a story entitled "Bible Twisted to Nazi Creed." The article told how Bishop Mueller rewrote the Sermon on the Mount and the Gospel of John. The words *sin* and *grace* were deleted, and the Golden Rule was rewritten to apply only to relationships between Nazi comrades. All references to Old Testament prophets, from Moses to Abraham, were also deleted. See Lutzer, 146.

135. Shirer (1962), 327-28. This synod was held in the Castle Church in Wittenberg, where Matin Luther had nailed his Ninety-Five Theses. Mueller was unanimously elected as Reich bishop right beside the tomb where Luther was buried. Lutzer, 126-27.

136. Lutzer, 113.

137. Shirer (1962), 328.

138. Ibid.; Lutzer, 123 ("One State, One People, One Church").

139. On Sept. 21, 1933, just two weeks after the Brown Synod, Niemöller helped form the Pastors' Emergency League. They pledged to take a stand against the intrusion of Nazism in their churches. They did not take a stand against Nazism as such, only against its invasion of the spiritual sphere. Lutzer, 125.

140. Ibid., 124.

141. Shirer (1962), 325.

142. Lutzer, 124.

143. Shirer (1962), 326.

144. Barnett, 91-92.

145. Ibid.

146. Benns, 265.

147. Barnett, 91-92.

148. The Barmen Confession was drafted by German-Swiss theologian Karl Barth. He had lost his professorship at the University in Bonn because he refused to sign the pledge to put the German state over his religious ideals.

149. Lutzer, 134.

> If the Confessing Church had chosen to break away from the established Lutheran church and become a free church, it would have lost the financial support of the state. That was not a viable option since the Confessing Church declared that it was the true church whose spiritual heritage could be traced back to the Reformation.

Ibid., 135.

150. Rousmaniere, 118-119; Matheson, 45-47.

151. Rousmaniere, 119.

152. Barnett, 84.

153. Hamerow, 207-9; Matheson, 58-62.

154. See Barnett, 84.

155. Matheson, 58-62.

156. Lutzer, 144.

157. As translated in Charles Colson, *Kingdoms in Conflict*, 187 (Zondervan: Grand Rapids, 1987).

158. Saperstein, 42; Hamerow, 228.

159. Saperstein, 42.

160. *Chronicle*, 456.

161. McCormick, 77. See Charles Rankin, "Pius the Man and His Efforts for Peace," in *The Pope Speaks: The Words of Pius XII*, 66 (footnote).

162. Darragh, 6; Hatch and Walshe, 115.

163. McCormick, 67.

164. Henri Daniel-Rops, *A Fight for God: 1870-1939*, 312 (New York: E. P. Dutton and Co., 1965).

165. Darragh, 7-8. See Charles Rankin, "Pius the Man and His Efforts for Peace," in *The Pope Speaks: The Words of Pius XII*, 11-12 (Secretary of State Pacelli adopted a "definite and determined" policy and stood up to Mussolini, who had been used to getting his way).

166. McCormick, 67.

167. Ibid., 77.

168. Ibid., 79.

169. Cardinal Pacelli's speeches as secretary of state (1930-1939) appear in *Discorsi e Panegirici* (*Società Editrice "Vita e Pensiero"*: Milan, 1939). See also F. Murphy, 59; Hatch and Walshe, 116-17 (longer quotation).

170. "Nazis Warned in Lourdes," *New York Times*, April 29, 1935.

171. Besier, 152-53.

172. Marchione, *Pope Pius XII*, 57.

173. Morgan, 158.

174. Lenn and Reardon, 97.

175. Rose Fitzgerald Kennedy, *Times to Remember*, 204-5 (Garden City, NY: Doubleday and Co., 1974).

176. Lenn and Reardon, 98.

177. "Peace & the Papacy," *Time*, Aug. 16, 1943, 55, 56; Hatch and Walshe, 120; *Current Biography, 1941*, Maxine Block, ed., the H. W. Wilson Co., 1971 reissue, 673, 675; Hatch and Walshe, 120; see Morgan, 188-89. See also Letter from President Roosevelt to His Holiness, Dec. 23, 1939, in *Wartime Correspondence*, 4, 19 (letter in which Roosevelt calls Pius "a good friend and an old friend").

178. McCormick, 100.

179. Lenn and Reardon, 61. See Ronald J. Rychlak, "Pope Pius XII's Real Personality," *7.5 Envoy*, 28 (2007) (Belmont Abbey College); Rychlak, *Righteous Gentiles*, 182.

180. Duffy, 256; Gannon, 177.

181. Telegram from the ambassador in France (Bullitt) to the secretary of state, in *United States Department of State, Foreign Relations of the United States, Diplomatic Papers, 1937, vol. I (General)*, United States Government Printing Office (Washington, 1954), 89-91.

182. Shirer (1962), 410.

183. Speer, 172-73; Deighton, 594.

184. Copeland, 513.

185. Ibid., 522.

186. Michaelis, 226.

187. *Divini Redemptoris*, n. 4.

188. Pius XI, *Quadragesimo Anno* (1931).

189. *Divini Redemptoris*, n. 58.

190. Congregation for the Causes of Saints, *Positio*, appendix 25, 273. For the official Latin text of the decree, see the *Acta Apostolicae Sedis*, Volume XX, pp. 103-4.

191. "The Pope's Desire to Help," *Jewish Chronicle of London*, May 12, 1933, 28.

192. "The Pope Denounces Anti-Semitism," *Jewish Chronicle of London*, Sept. 1, 1933.

193. Pope Pius XI recognized the problems, but defended the concordat, saying: "[A]lready when it was concluded on practical grounds we knew what sort of people we had to deal with. But such a measure of disloyalty towards a word pledged we neither believe nor expected. But even under present conditions the concordat is still of value, at least if one takes a stand upon the law." Besier, 165.

194. Ibid., 164.

195. Ibid.

196. Ibid., 165.

197. Lubac, 28, n. 10; Duffy, 260.

198. Besier, 165.

199. "The Pope Yesterday and Today," (Il Papa Ieri e Oggi) *L'Osservatore Della Domenica*, June 26, 1964 (image of marked-up draft); Godman, 144-48 (reviewing different versions of the draft); Besier, 164.

200. "Pius XI's Anti-Nazi Encyclical was Prophetic," *Wanderer* (Zenit), April 19, 2007 (quoting Father Peter Gumpel).

201. *Mit brennender Sorge*, n. 12.

202. Ibid., n. 15.

203. *Mit brennender Sorge*, n. 42. Some critics point out that the complaints focused more on Nazi persecution of Catholics than of Jews, but in 1937, no one "could dream of what would develop" in terms of Nazi persecution of Jews. Sereny, 294.

204. Bogle, *Salisbury Review*; Lapide, 111. "It is enough to read the drafts, not only to confirm that Pacelli was one of the writers but (to see that) the original text has additions in his own handwriting." "World Press Unmasks Fallacies in Book Defaming Pius XII: Exclusive Interview with Reporter of Pacelli's Beatification Cause," Zenit News Service, Oct. 3, 1999 (quoting Father Peter Gumpel).

205. Maccarrone, 163. See Charles Rankin, "Pius the Man and His Efforts for Peace," in *The Pope Speaks: The Words of Pius XII*, 12 (crediting Pacelli for devising this plan to avoid censorship by Mussolini).

206. Some authors have suggested that the encyclical was not actually read in many German churches. A telegram from the German ambassador to the Holy See, dated March 23, 1937, however, reports that "the reading from the pulpits in German churches proceeded without incident." *Documents on German Foreign Policy 1918-1945*, Series D (1937-1945), vol. I, no. 634. Ambassador Bergen went on to write that this encyclical and the way it was distributed "amount to an attempt at intimidation" by the Vatican. Ibid. The Reich and Prussian minister for ecclesiastical affairs wrote to the German bishops complaining that this attack "against the welfare and interests of the German nation" was a violation of the concordat. *Documents on German Foreign Policy 1918-1945*, Series D (1937-1945), vol. I, no. 635.

207. Lubac, 32. According to Dr. Duncan-Jones, the Anglican dean of Chichester, the encyclical was of "shattering force." Darragh, 15 (quoting Duncan-Jones, *The Struggle for Religious Freedom in Germany*, 225).

208. Peter Hoffman, *Stauffenberg: A Family History, 1905-1944*, Cambridge University Press (Cambridge, 1995), 317; Congregation for the Causes of Saints, *Positio (Vita Documentata: L'Enciclica "Mit brennender Sorge")*, 595.

209. *The World's Great Catholic Literature*, 263. The same version was printed in a later edition of the same book. *The World's Great Catholic Literature: A Magnificent Treasury of Catholic Writing*, 289 (George N. Shuster, ed., 1965).

210. *Positio (Vita Documentata: L'Enciclica "Mit brennender Sorge")*, 592-93 (quoting Professor Robert d'Harcourt).

211. "Religion: Nazis: An American Cardinal Champions Pope Pius' Cause," *Newsweek*, May 29, 1937, 18.

212. "Pope Pius' encyclical soon precipitated a fight to the finish. Five weeks later, government-controlled newspapers announced a nationwide campaign to 'clean up' Catholic monasteries, schools, and charity institutions. Screamer headlines proclaimed: THE CLOISTERS HAVE BECOME SINKS OF VICE. Lurid screeds ranted on the immorality of the 'sexual criminals in priestly robes.' One thousand more of Germany's 13,900 Catholic monks and lay brothers were rounded up and charged with sex crimes." ("Religion: Nazis: An American Cardinal Champions Pope Pius' Cause," *Newsweek*, May 29, 1937, 18.) See George O. Kent, "Pope Pius XII and Germany: Some Aspects of German-Vatican Relations, 1933-1943," 70:1 *American Historical Review*, 59, 63 (October 1964) (quoting from German dispatches).

213. "Pius XI's Anti-Nazi Encyclical was Prophetic," *Wanderer* (Zenit), April 19, 2007.

214. *The Nazi Master Plan: The Persecution of the Christian Churches*; Congregation for the Causes of Saints, *Positio (Vita Documentata: L'Enciclica "Mit brennender Sorge")*, 593; Burleigh, "The Cardinal Basil Hume Memorial Lectures," 3 *Totalitarian Movements and Political Religions*, 18 (noting that the encyclical particularly infuriated Hitler because he hated being laughed at, and this document said he was being laughed at in heaven); Eric A. Johnson, *Nazi Terror: The Gestapo, Jews, and Ordinary Germans*, Basic Books (New York, 1999). Payments due to the Church under the terms of the concordat were also reduced. Cianfarra, 100; Holmes, 113; Lothar Groppe, "The Church and the Jews in the Third Reich," *Fidelity*, November 1983, 21. Nazi official Reinhard Heydrich's belief that the Vatican was the archenemy of National Socialism was only strengthened with the release of *Mit brennender Sorge*. Alvarez and Graham, 64.

215. Lapide, 110; Robert Martin, *Spiritual Semites: Catholics and Jews During World War Two*, Catholic League Publications (Milwaukee, 1983).

216. Lapide, 110.

217. *Documents on German Foreign Policy 1918-1945*, Series D (1937-1945), vol. I, no. 633.

218. Lapide, 110.

219. Besier, 167.

220. Ibid., 168.

221. "The Church and the Jews in the Third Reich," *Fidelity*, November 1983, 21. German officials also complained about "the Vatican's harsh policy toward the Third Reich." *Documents on German Foreign Policy 1918-1945*, Series D (1937-1945), vol. I, no. 644.

222. Cornwell (1999), 183.

223. Holmes, 101.

224. Ibid.

225. Bokenkotter, 370-71.

226. Holmes, 113. See Coady, 166 (letter from Jesuit prisoner: "The trial bristled with abusive comments toward the Church and its organizations.... No one believes a Jesuit because he is on principle an enemy of the Reich and above all an enemy of the Nazi Party.") Ibid., 167 (noting an "intense onslaught of hatred against the Church" from the Gestapo).

227. The Pope wanted *Mit brennender Sorge* to be published in Spain, but Franco thought that it was also directed at him. Besier, 167. On March 26, two weeks after the encyclical was issued, Pacelli sent a telegram asking if the document had been published in Spain's daily press. The nuncio in Spain responded that the only public notice of the encyclical was a strong attack on the Vatican's position by German radio. The encyclical was not even published in diocesan bulletins until early the following year. The only periodical in Spain which published the document at the time was the Jesuit monthly, *Razón y Fe*. See Sánchez (2002), 369-70 (also noting that Pacelli, in an interview with the official Spanish agent, the Marqués de Magaz, said that Nazi racism was just as bad as atheistic Communism, and that both systems were lacking spirituality).

228. The third encyclical of March 1937, *Nos es muy conocido* ("It Is Well Known to Us"), dealt with the religious persecution of the Church in Mexico. Pius wrote: "only the teaching and the work of the Church, assisted as it is by its Divine Founder, can furnish a remedy for the very grave ills which burden humanity." One point of instruction is particularly relevant with regard to his successor, Pius XII. Speaking of living conditions for Mexican workers and peasants, Pius XI wrote: "[I]t may be necessary at times to denounce and to blame boldly... at the same time, however, care must be taken to guard against either making violence legitimate... [or] to effects which are more harmful than the evil itself which is intended to be corrected."

229. Kennedy (1961), 80.

230. "Religion: Nazis: An American Cardinal Champions Pope Pius' Cause," *Newsweek*, May 29, 1937, 18.

231. Ibid.

232. "Goebbels Lashes Catholic Church on Morals Issues," *New York Times*, May 29, 1937.

233. William M. Harrigan, "Pius XII's Efforts to Effect a Détente in German-Vatican Relations, 1939-1940," *Catholic Historical Review*, July 1963, 176; Besier, 168.

234. "Religion: Nazis: An American Cardinal Champions Pope Pius' Cause," *Newsweek*, May 29, 1937, 18.

235. Hatch and Walshe, 122.

236. Lapide, 119.

237. Ibid. The article went on to report, "Any other attitude would have made Pius an inconsistent Pope." Other authors noted that Pius XI "needlessly irritated" the German government by praising the zeal of Cardinal Mundelein. William M. Harrigan, "Pius XII's Efforts to Effect a Détente in German-Vatican Relations, 1939-1940," *Catholic Historical Review*, July 1963, 177.

238. "Religion: Nazis: An American Cardinal Champions Pope Pius' Cause," *Newsweek*, May 29, 1937, 18.

239. William M. Harrigan, "Pius XII's Efforts to Effect a Détente in German-Vatican Relations, 1939-1940," *Catholic Historical Review*, July 1963, 176.

240. "Confidential letter to Moffit from A.W. Klieforth," March 3, 1939, File No. 800, AWK-RM (also noting that Pacelli was responsible for a private college in Rome for the preparation for the Catholic priesthood of Russians). See also Charles R. Gallagher, " 'Personal, Private Views:' A newly discovered report from 1938 reveals Cardinal Pacelli's anti-Nazi stance," *America*, Sept. 1, 2003. Klieforth, an American diplomat, went to Rome on the pretext of taking a vacation. He spent a long time with Secretary of State Pacelli and according to Klieforth's son: "[W]hat was divulged was critical, sensitive information because among other things, it proved that the pope-to-be was anti-Nazi and hated Hitler." Ann Aubrey Hanson, "San Diego Diplomat Defends Pope Pius XII," *Southern Cross*, Jan. 15, 2004, 2 (quoting Alexander Klieforth, son of Alfred Klieforth). "Cardinal Pacelli thought the whole Nazi ideology an abomination because it persecuted the Jews and persecuted the Church." Ibid.

241. See Charles Rankin, "Pius the Man and His Efforts for Peace," in *The Pope Speaks: The Words of Pius XII*, 31 (quoting the earlier talk).

242. R. Stewart, 18.

243. F. Murphy, 59-60.

244. *Documents on German Foreign Policy 1918-1945*, Series D (1937-1945), vol. I, no. 672.

245. Ibid., no. 673.

246. F. Murphy, 60.

247. Micklem, 15.

248. Korn, 126.

## Chapter Seven: The Violence Spreads

1. Otto D. Tolischus, "Hitler Says Reich Is Eager for Peace; Conciliatory Greetings Are Exchanged with Diplomatic Corps at Reception," *New York Times*, Jan. 12, 1938.

2. Stephen Schwartz, "Gertrude and the Führer," *San Francisco Chronicle*, June 9, 1996 (noting that Stein also supported Marshal Philippe Pétain, head of the pro-Nazi French occupation regime during World War II); Peter S. Prescott, "The Great Barbarian," *Newsweek*, Sept. 20, 1976, 87.

3. Gilbert (1985), 57.

4. About this time, the Nazis passed a law requiring Jews to wear a yellow Star of David on their clothing. German bishops tried to intervene on behalf of non-Aryan Catholics, i.e., Jews who had been baptized into the Catholic faith. Bishops Heinrich Wienken and Wilhelm Berning both asked that their dioceses be exempt from the Star of David rule, but the Gestapo denied the request. Fogelman, 171.

5. Hatch and Walshe, 126.

6. K. Doyle, 16.

7. On the day following that vote, an editorial in *Der Angriff*, a Nazi newspaper, said: "Radio Moscow and Radio Vatican have conducted full-scale electoral sabotage and vilified the laudable attitude of German Princes of the Church. But all in vain!" Lapide, 112.

8. "Il Cancelliere Schuschnigg indice un plebiscito nazionale per Austria 'libera e tedesca, indipendente e sociale, cristiana e unita,'" *L'Osservatore Romano*, March 11, 1938; "Il fervido consenso della popolazione austriaca al plebisccito nazionale," *L'Osservatore Romano*, March 12, 1938; "Il Cancelliere Schuschnigg dichiara di cedere alla violenza: dopo un 'ultimatum'; e movimenti militari," *L'Osservatore Romano*, March 13, 1938. See also "L' 'Anschluss' dell'Austria, Hitler parlerà stasera al Reichstag," *L'Osservatore Romano*, March 19, 1938; "La Jugoslavia e le minoranze slovene in Austria," *L'Osservatore Romano*, March 22, 1938; "Anschluss e Independenza svizzera," *L'Osservatore Romano*, March 23, 1938; "La situazione religiosa nell' Austria," *L'Osservatore Romano*, March 24, 1938; "La situazione in Austria dopo L' Anschluss," *L'Osservatore Romano*, March 26, 1938.

9. Holmes, 114.

10. Cianfarra, 220. See "The Chargé in Austria (Wiley) to the Secretary of State," March 19, 1938, in *Foreign Relations of the United States, Diplomatic Papers, 1938, vol. I (General)*, United States Government Printing Office (Washington, 1955), 458 (priests arrested).

11. Goldston, 99-100.

12. Besier, 172-73.

13. Ibid., 173.

14. Ibid., 174.

15. According to a report from the American chargé in Austria to the secretary of state:

> Cardinal Innitzer... called in person upon Hitler in the Hotel Imperial and had a fifteen minute interview with him. Subsequently a statement appeared in the press on March 16 which stated that the Cardinal had expressed his joy to Hitler at the "reunion" of German Austria with the Reich.... While Cardinal Innitzer did sign a statement, the text of the one which appeared was not that which he had approved. The Nuncio added that Cardinal Innitzer was a weak man.

"The Chargé in Austria (Wiley) to the Secretary of State," March 19, 1938, in *Foreign Relations of the United States, Diplomatic Papers, 1938, vol. I (General)*, United States Government Printing Office (Washington, 1955), 458.

16. "Memorandum by the Vatican Secretary of State (Cardinal Pacelli) to the American Ambassador in the United Kingdom, April 19, 1938," in *Foreign Relations of the United States, Diplomatic Papers, 1938, vol. I (General)*, United States Government Printing Office (Washington, 1955), 474.

17. Lutzer, 104.

18. Charles Rankin, "Pius the Man and His Efforts for Peace," in *The Pope Speaks: The Words of Pius XII*, 32 (noting that the Vatican distanced Secretary of State Pacelli from this broadcast; it was believed to have come from Pius XI himself).

19. Hatch and Walshe, 126. Internal German records reflect that Nazi leadership wanted to "encourage Cardinal Innitzer and the Austrian bishops in their patriotic attitude." "Message from German Ambassador to the Holy See (Bergen) to the German Foreign Ministry, dated April 2, 1938," *Documents on German Foreign Policy 1918-1945*, Series D (1937-1945), vol. I, no. 699 (also complaining about the Vatican Radio broadcast).

20. Besier, 174.

21. Cornwell (1999), 201.

22. "Confidential Letter to Oliver Harvey from D'Arcy Osborne," Feb. 26, 1947, British Public Records Office, FO 371/67917 60675.

23. "Message from German Ambassador to the Holy See (Bergen) to the German Foreign Ministry, dated April 6, 1938," *Documents on German Foreign Policy 1918-1945*, Series D (1937-1945), vol. I, no. 701.

24. Ibid., no. 702. See Besier, 175 (noting Innitzer's reservations about the new statement).

25. Passelecq and Suchecky, 56.

26. See "Le dichiarazioni dell'Episcopato autriaco lette nelle Chiese," *L'Osservatore Romano*, March 31, 1938.

27. See "Innitzer Guarded, Vatican Aide Says; Cardinal is Declared to be in 'Protective Custody' of Nazis in Vienna; Secret Visit Described; Spokesman For Prelate Denies the Report, but Restriction on Travel is Indicated, Found Rooms in Disorder," *New York Times*, Nov. 10, 1938.

28. Cianfarra, 142-43. The Innitzer matter is examined in the 1963 motion picture *The Cardinal*, which was produced independently and directed by Otto Preminger, who would later challenge playwright Rolf Hochhuth over his depiction of Pius XII. The motion picture presents Innitzer's letter welcoming Hitler, the Holy Father's efforts to have him reverse himself, Hitler's persecution of the Church, Innitzer's changed position, and the crowd storming his residence. The most serious factual flaw in the movie is that it shows Innitzer changing his mind after a meeting with Hitler, rather than after being called to the Vatican.

29. Cianfarra, 143; Holmes, 115.

30. Gallagher, "Personal, Private Views." Kennedy's cover letter and Pacelli's report are included in the Appendix, p. 398.

31. "Pius XI Ordered Catholic Universities to Refute Nazi Racist Theories: 1938 Letter from Sacred Congregation for Seminaries," Zenit News Service, March 4, 2003. The letter was published in *Nouvelle Revue Théologique*, Leuven (Vol. 66), 1939. It is reprinted in the Appendix, p. 396. See also Gallo, 15; "The Inner Forum: Scholars at the Vatican," *Commonweal*, Dec. 4, 1943, 187 ("When he engaged Jewish scholars for the libraries and academies of the Vatican, Pius XII followed in the footsteps of his illustrious predecessor....").

32. Quoted in "The Inner Forum: Scholars at the Vatican," *Commonweal*, Dec. 4, 1943, 188.

33. Ibid. (noting that Pope Pius XII was guided by the same concerns).

34. His successor, Pope Pius XII, let his opposition to the Italian racial laws be known from the very outset of his papacy. "At the beginning of World War II, Pius XII arranged a meeting at the Quirinal Palace with the King of Italy, and specifically excluded Mussolini from the session... the pope's words [were]: 'I don't want anyone present at the meeting who signed the racial laws.'" *L'Avvenire*, June 27, 1996 (as recounted by Adriano Ossicini, a personal friend of Pius XII and an anti-Fascist leader); "More Echoes on Pope Pius XII, Nazi Holocaust," Zenit News Agency, June 27, 1996.

35. Besier, 183.

36. Ibid.

37. Daniel-Rops, 313; Purdy, 22. German officials explained the Pope's slight by saying that he was offended by Hitler's refusal to meet with him, and that is why he left town and closed the museums. "Message from German Ambassador to the Holy See (Bergen) to the German Foreign Ministry, dated May 23, 1938," *Documents on German Foreign Policy 1918-1945*, Series D (1937-1945), vol. I, no. 710.

38. Besier, 182-83.

39. The idea of leaving and closing the museums was apparently Pacelli's. "The present Italian Minister of the Italian Defense... has a note claiming that the Italian government archives show Pacelli as the instigator of the Vatican boycott of Hitler's visit to Rome in May 1938." Purdy, 22. Bishop Alois Hudal of Austria ignored the order to avoid celebrations and took part in one celebration where he was photographed with Hitler at his side. Besier, 183.

40. Besier, 183.

41. Cianfarra, 120-22; Holmes, 73; "Message from German Ambassador to the Holy See (Bergen) to the German Foreign Ministry, dated May 5, 1938," *Documents on German Foreign Policy 1918-1945*, Series D (1937-1945), vol. I, no. 706 (the Vatican press had not reported on Hitler's trip but had reported the Pope's anti-Nazi comments). The idea of closing the museums was Pacelli's. Hatch and Walshe, 128.

42. Holmes, 73; "Message from German Ambassador to the Holy See (Bergen) to the German Foreign Ministry, dated May 5, 1938," *Documents on German Foreign Policy 1918-1945*, Series D (1937-1945), vol. I, no. 706 (relaying the anti-Nazi sentiments of the Pope).

43. Besier, 178.

44. Ibid.

45. Ibid., 179.

46. Letter from Secretary of State Paccelli to Eugenio Cardinal Tisserant, Secretary of the Holy Congregation for the Eastern Church, May 21, 1938, doc. No. 543019.

47. *Principles for Peace*, 540-43. See also Levai, 7-16; ibid., 18 (noting the Pope's early intervention following the occupation of Hungary); Hatch and Walshe, 127. Critic Michael Phayer preposterously tried to turn Pacelli's comments all around. He reported that Pacelli was condemning not the Nazis but the Jews. *Nowhere* in the speech did Pacelli mention "Jews." He spoke of the "*military godless.*" *No one* at the time thought that he was speaking of the Jews. Jenö Levai, the Jewish author of *Hungarian Jewry and the Papacy: Pius XII Was Not Silent* (1968), personally witnessed the speech. As the title of his book implies, he was a great supporter of Pacelli. The anti-Jewish interpretation is pure post-Holocaust reconstruction.

48. See pp. 107-10.

49. Stille, 12; Lamb, 35 (noting that Jewish support for Mussolini survived the imposition of anti-Jewish laws in 1938); Kurzman, 87.

50. Not only Italian writers (many of them Jewish) praised Mussolini, but Ezra Pound (who would broadcast Fascist propaganda during the war and later be indicted for treason), T. S. Eliot, W. B. Yeats, and Wyndham Lewis were all early supporters of Mussolini's brand of Fascism.

51. Holmes, 73. In Turin, a Jewish banker published a Jewish Fascist newspaper, *La Nostra Bandiera*. Lamb, 38.

52. Holmes, 13.

53. Stille, 70; Cianfarra, 126.

54. *L'Osservatore Romano*, July 17, 1938, 1; *New York Times*, July 17, 1938, 1; Daniel-Rops, 313.

55. Groppe, *The Church and the Jews*, 21.

56. The text of the handwritten note is included in the Appendix, p. 398.

57. N.S.W. Board of Jewish Education, "Australian Memories of the Holocaust": *http://www.holocaust.com.au/mm/i_australia.htm.*

58. *Manchester Guardian*, May 23, 1936, cited in A.J. Sherman, *Island Refuge, Britain and the Refugees from the Third Reich, 1933-1939*, 112 (London, Elek Books Ltd, 1973). The only nation to suggest that it would accept more Jewish refugees as permanent residents was the Dominican Republic.

59. *L'Osservatore Romano*, July 23, 1938, 1; *New York Times*, July 22, 1938. See also Cianfarra, 133-34 ("As the enslaved Italian press obeyed Fascist Party instructions to vilify the Jews, Pius XI fought with truly amazing vigor.... The papal appeal contained in the July 21 speech was a signal for a campaign throughout Italy against the racial laws").

60. "La parola del Sommo Pontefice Pio XI agli alunni del Collegio di Propaganda fide," *L'Osservatore Romano*, July 30, 1938, 1.

61. "Arresti e misure antisemite a Danzica," *L'Osservatore Romano*, April 2, 1938, 6.

62. "Parole del Santo Padre in un'udienza a Castelgandolfo," *L'Osservatore Romano*, July 17, 1938, 1 (subheadline: "Errori e pericoli del nazionalismo").

63. "Intorno alla Nazionalità," *L'Osservatore Romano*, July 21, 1938, 2.

64. "Precisazione di Chamberlain sui colloqui di Wiedemann a Londra," *L'Osservatore Romano*, July 23, 1938, 5.

65. "Intorno alla Nazionalità," *L'Osservatore Romano*, August 13, 1938, 2.

66. "Attuali problemi della Piccola Intesa," *L'Osservatore Romano*, Aug. 22-23, 1938, 1 (subheadline: "Questioni minoritarie").

67. "Le controversie slovacco — ungheresi," *L'Osservatore Romano*, Oct. 17-18, 1938, 1.

68. "Colloquio di François Poncet con Hitler," *L'Osservatore Romano*, Oct. 20, 1938, 2.

69. "Mon curé chez les Nazistes," *L'Osservatore Romano*, Oct. 23, 1938, 2.

70. "La situazione religiosa nel Reich," *L'Osservatore Romano*, Oct. 25, 1938, 1.

71. "Attività spirituale e culturale dell'Azione Cattolica Italiana a Città di Castello," *L'Osservatore Romano*, Oct. 26, 1938, 4.

72. "La situazione religiosa nel Reich," *L'Osservatore Romano*, Oct. 27, 1938, 2.

73. "La campagna antisemita nei Sudeti," *L'Osservatore Romano*, Nov. 3, 1938, 2.

74. "Dopo le manifestazioni antisemite in Germania," *L'Osservatore Romano*, Nov. 13, 1938, 6.

75. "La ripercussione delle manifestazioni antisemite in Germania," *L'Osservatore Romano*, Nov. 14-15, 1938, 6.

76. "La sorte degli ebrei in Germania," *L'Osservatore Romano*, Nov, 16, 1938, 6.

77. "Dopo le manifestazioni antisemite tedesche," *L'Osservatore Romano*, Nov. 17, 1938, 1.

78. "Per la soluzione della questione ebracia," *L'Osservatore Romano*, Nov. 19, 1938, 1.

79. "Gli sviluppi della questione ebracia dopo manifestazioni antisemite nel Reich," *L'Osservatore Romano*, Nov. 20, 1938, 6.

80. "La situazione religiosa nel Reich," *L'Osservatore Romano*, Nov. 21-22, 1938, 2.

81. "Gli sviluppi della questione ebraica," *L'Osservatore Romano*, Nov. 23, 1938, 1.

82. "Il Cardinale van Roey e il Cardinale Verdier illustrano la dottrina cattolica di fronte al 'razzismo,'" *L'Osservatore Romano*, Nov. 24, 1938, 2.

83. "Inasprimento della lotta antisemita in Germania," *L'Osservatore Romano*, Nov. 26, 1938,6.

84. "La situazione religiosa nel Reich," *L'Osservatore Romano*, Dec. 25, 1938, 2.

85. "La situazione religiosa nel Reich," *L'Osservatore Romano*, Jan. 19, 1939, 2. See Passelecq and Suchecky, 293-97.

86. Dineen, 201-2.

87. Purdy, 24.

88. A.C. Jemolo, *Chiesa e stato in Italia negli ultimi cento anni*, 680-81 (Einaudi: Torino, 1948).

89. See Krišto, *An American View*, 230 (noting that American Bishop Joseph P. Hurley was instrumental in accomplishing this).

90. A. C. Jemolo, *Chiesa e stato in Italia negli ultimi cento anni*, 703 (Einaudi: Torino, 1948). Papal critic Susan Zuccotti admits: "*L'Osservatore Romano* did object unequivocally and strenuously to the infamous Italian police order number five of December 1, 1943, which declared that all Jews in Italy were to be arrested by Italian police and carabinieri and interned in camps within the country. The objections were commendable." Zuccotti, *Under His Very Windows*, 306.

91. A. C. Jemolo, *Chiesa e stato in Italia negli ultimi cento anni*, 703 (Einaudi: Torino, 1948).

92. *Ciano's Hidden Diary*, 190.

93. Ibid.

94. The Germans were, by now, less concerned about statements from the pulpit, because they knew that they could restrict the spread of information. On Sept. 19, 1938, Rudolf Hess gave a speech in Nuremberg in which he not only called National Socialism "a God-ordained order and institution," but went on to explain:

> Who bothers any longer if, for example, pastoral letters are read from the pulpits of the Catholic churches — however packed they may be with concealed threats, attacks, distortions of the truth, and so on…? Their lordships can read out what they want as long as they have no access to the outside world.

Matheson, 75; see Lapide, 96. At this same time, Alfred Rosenberg said: "I am absolutely clear in my own mind, and I think I can speak for the *Führer* as well, that both the Catholic Church and the Evangelical Confessional Church, as they exist at present, must vanish from the life of our people." *The Persecution of the Catholic Church in the Third Reich*, 277.

95. Stille, 230-31.

96. Ibid., 73-75.

97. Ibid., 75.

98. Ibid., 73. See also "Pope's Attack on Racialism: 'Why Must Italy Copy Germany,'" *Palestine Post*, Aug. 8, 1938.

99. Stille, 134. "The Concordat notwithstanding, unnumbered Church papers have been confiscated or suppressed for printing the pastoral letters of the bishops or the encyclical of the Pope." Micklem, 34-35.

100. Andrea Tornielli, "La lettera inedita: così Pacelli intervenne in favore dei riti ebraici 'La legge che proibisce la macellazione rituale sarebbe una vera persecuzione,'" *Il Giornale*, June 3, 2008.

101. Ibid.

102. Ibid.

103. Dr. Joseph Lichten, himself a Jewish survivor of the Holocaust, who later served as a director for B'nai B'rith, wrote: "When the Nazis forbade ritual slaughter to the Jews, the Pope [Pius XII] sent *shohetim* into Vatican City to perform the ritual slaughter and store food for the Jews sheltered there." *A Question of Judgement: Pius XII and the Jews*, 1963. See also Andrea Tornielli, "La lettera inedita: così Pacelli intervenne in favore dei riti ebraici 'La legge che proibisce la macellazione rituale sarebbe una vera persecuzione,'" *Il Giornale*, June 3, 2008 (papal opposition to Polish legislation that would have made ritual slaughter illegal). Pius also had the papal seal imprinted on the Roman synagogue near the Tiber, in order to protect its inhabitants, as well as its sacred Jewish rituals within. *Davar*, the Hebrew Daily of Israel's Federation of Labour, Oct. 10, 1958. According to the firsthand testimony of Monsignor John Patrick Carroll-Abbing, a close confidante of Pius during the war, the Pope explicitly instructed Carroll-Abbing to rescue and protect persecuted Jews, and to "do whatever is necessary *to permit them to celebrate their sacred Jewish rites.*" *Inside the Vatican*, July-August, 2001.

104. *Chronicle*, 487. S.S. leader Reinhard Heydrich's account of the night is largely reprinted in *A History of the Third Reich*, 185.

105. Matthew Berke, "Accomplices to Genocide?" *First Things*, February 1998, 42 (reviewing William D. Rubinstein, *The Myth of Rescue: Why the Democracies Could Not Have Saved More Jews from the Nazis*) (by 1939, 80 percent of Germany's Jewish population under the age of 40 had fled).

106. Meltzer, 55.

107. At the beatification ceremony, Pope John Paul II read portions of a letter he had written for the event. That letter included the statement: "Anyone who does not limit himself to cheap polemics knows very well what Pius XII thought of the Nazi regime and how much he did to help countless people persecuted by the regime."

108. He was also the first Catholic presidential nominee from any major political party in the United States. He was the Democratic nominee in 1928.

109. Maggie Master, "The Record, the Broadcast and the Nazis: An Archivist's Discovery Rewrites History," *CUA Public Affairs*, Fall 2007.

110. Lapide, 95.

111. "A proposito di un Nuovo Decreto Legge," *L'Osservatore Romano*, Nov. 14-15, 1938.

112. Lapide, 95. Anti-Jewish laws were not officially lifted until Jan. 20, 1944.

113. Some top German leaders blamed the influence of the Catholic Church for the Italian resistance to Jewish deportation. Michaelis, 322-23 (citing a note written by Obersturmführer S.S. Lieutenant Heinz Röthke).

114. Michaelis, 181.

115. "La ripercussione delle manifestazioni antisemite in Germania," *L'Osservatore Romano*, Nov. 14-15, 1938, 6; "La sorte degli ebrei in Germania," *L'Osservatore Romano*, Nov. 16, 1938, 6; "Dopo le manifestazioni antisemite tedesche," *L'Osservatore Romano*, Nov. 17, 1938, 1.

116. "Dopo le manifestazioni antisemite in Germania," *L'Osservatore Romano*, Nov. 13, 1938.

117. "Il Cardinale van Roey e il Cardinale Verdier illustrano la dottrina cattolica di fronte al 'razzismo,'" *L'Osservatore Romano*, Nov. 24, 1938, 2.

118. For the original text as it was delivered in French, see the Belgian publication *La Libre Belgique* (Sept. 14, 1938); the original text also was reproduced in the French documentary news service *La Documentation Catholique*, vol. 39, no. 885 (Dec. 5, 1938, columns 1459-60). Not long thereafter, Secretary of State Pacelli used this same language in a speech in Rome. Lapide, 118; R. Stewart, 21.

119. Critics sometimes complain that various papal statements were not reported in the Catholic press. One must be careful, however, when looking at Catholic publications in Nazi-controlled countries. As one author explained:

> Father Leiber went on to say that... it was impossible to get ideas or articles contrary to the opinion of the Party into even *Catholic* publications. If they included such an item, the Catholic editor was removed and replaced with a National Socialist, but the publication continued to appear as if under Catholic auspices (thereby obviously lulling the reader into a false security).

Sereny, 62. In fact, even in making this statement Pius XI was careful. The story was first reported by Monsignor Picard in *La Libre Belgique*. It was later reprinted in its entirety in *Documentation Catholique* (No. 39, 1938). The pope held a private audience with the monsignor and two other officers of *Radio Catholique Belge*, and it was at that audience the Pope made his statement. Picard wrote:

> At the beginning of the public audience, the Holy Father charged those whom he had just received to tell the others what he had confided to them in private. It is in order to respond to the desire of the Holy Father that we make public the declarations that he made to us in his private office.... Needless to say, we have taken extreme care not to write a single syllable that was not truly pronounced by His Holiness.

120. Lapide, 118; Stewart, 21.

121. *New York Times*, Dec. 12, 1938, 1.

122. Maritain, "The Pagan Empire and the Power of God," *Virginia Quarterly Review*, 161, 167 (1939). Maritain went on to give much analysis of the existing world situation: "Our time offers to homicidal demons unheard-of feasts. Stalin has given them the kulaks; Hitler has given them the Jews. And each of them has given them the Christians." Ibid., 168. He continued: "Never before in the history of the world have the Jews been prosecuted in so universal a fashion; and never before has the persecution fallen, as it does today, upon Jews and Christians alike." Ibid.

123. "Italy: Like Son, Like Father," *National Jewish Monthly*, January 1939, 157, 183.

124. Gallo, 303, n. 1 (citing *New York Times*, Jan. 17, 1939).

125. Arnold Brugmann, "From Ketteler to Catholic Action," *Volk im Werden*, December 1939 (reprinted in "Documentazioni," *L'Osservatore Romano*, Jan. 1, 1939, 2).

126. Ibid.

127. Besier, 186.

## Chapter Eight: The Pre-War Pope

1. Korn, 140. Later, Pacelli, as Pope Pius XII, made similar statements. Hatch and Walshe, 233.

2. Lapide, 115.

3. The Pope, on April 13, 1938, had the Congregation of Seminaries and Universities send a letter to Cardinal Baudrillart, charging Catholic academic institutions to refute the Nazi theories of racism. Copies of this letter were sent to all European cardinals with instructions to act likewise. Lapide, 112. Pope Pius XII renewed this instruction. See "Priest Denounces Race Bias in U.S.," *New York Times*, Nov. 19, 1944 ("Fulfilling the instructions of Pope Pius XII that all Catholic Universities study the race problem, the Alumni Association of the Catholic University of America devoted its third annual forum... to the subject.")

4. Lapide, 115.

5. "Let's Look at the Record," *Inside the Vatican*, October 1999, XI.

6. Ibid.

7. Lapide, 115.

8. This appeared in the *Jerusalem Latin Patriarch* on Feb. 12, 1939.

9. Duffy, 262.

10. Lapide, 118; see Gallo, 27.

11. A 1940 book published with the assistance of Pope Pius XII documented the persecution of the German Catholic Church in the 1930s. It reprinted the following poem, reporting that it had first been published in *Das Schwarze Korps*, the official publication of the S.S., on Jan. 19, 1939.

> Go bury the delusive hope
> About His Holiness the Pope
> For all he knows concerning Race
> Would get a schoolboy in disgrace
>
> ***
>
> Since he regards both Blacks and Whites
> As children all with equal rights,
> As Christians all (whate'er their hues),
> They're "spiritually" nought but Jews.
>
> ***
>
> The banner is at last unfurled
> "Chief Rabbi of the Christian World."

*The Persecution of the Catholic Church in the Third Reich*, 426-27.

12. Otto D. Tolischus, "A 'Political Pope' is Reich Comment," *New York Times*, Feb. 11, 1939. In England, on the other hand, Pius was seen as a "spiritual rather than a 'political' pope." Charles Rankin, "Pius the Man and His Efforts for Peace," in *The Pope Speaks: The Words of Pius XII*, 11.

13. F. Murphy, 57; Duffy, 261 ("stubborn old man"). Count Ciano reported in his diary on Dec. 14, 1938, that Mussolini hoped for the Pope's death in the near future. *The Ciano Diaries*, 204. On Oct. 18, 1938, Mussolini said that all popes named Pius have brought misfortune to the Church and that Pius XI "will leave behind him a larger heap of ruins than any Pope before him." Ibid., 179.

14. *Chronicle*, 490.

15. F. Murphy, 59.

16. Charles Rankin, "Pius the Man and His Efforts for Peace," in *The Pope Speaks: The Words of Pius XII*, 39.

17. See "Report from the British Legation to the Holy See, Feb. 17, 1939," British Public Records Office, F0 371/23789 (reporting on Pacelli's chances); Charles Rankin, "Pius the Man and His Efforts for Peace," in *The Pope Speaks: The Words of Pius XII*, 37-38 (running down all of the likely candidates).

18. Besier, 256, n. 731.

19. Cianfarra, 22-23 (also identifying pressure from the Italian government); see "Report from the British Legation to the Holy See," Feb. 17, 1939, British Public Records Office, F0 371/23789 (reporting that the Nazis were expected to oppose Pacelli). In 1903, the Italian and Austrian governments applied pressure to prevent the election of the Vatican secretary of state, Cardinal Rampolla, who was not elected. Halecki and Murray, 19; Hatch and Walshe, 58.

20. "Enclosure in Mr. Osborne's dispatch No. 37 of February 17, 1939," British Public Records Office, FO 371/23789 57760. The paper of the French Communist Party, *L' Humanité*, happily reported on March 2, 1939: "The insolent veto against him [Cardinal Pacelli] lodged by the Fascist governments of Berlin and Rome has received its proper response." On the next day, *L'Humanité* added:

> Pius XII... is a pope who is an adversary of the racial standpoint and a friend of freedom of conscience and human dignity... for Cardinal Pacelli and the (late) pope could not be separated when it was a matter of condemning the folly of racialism or the persecutions of the Third Reich.... But for the Gestapo Pius XII was already "the pope of Moscow!" The election of Pius XII will undoubtedly be called by them "a Bolshevik machination."

See Lapide, 122. The weekly journal of the Communist International, *La Correspondance Internationale*, wrote, "In calling to succession the one who had demonstrated energetic resistance against the fascists totalitarian ideas that tend to eliminate the Catholic Church, (and) Pius XI's most direct collaborator, the Cardinals made a demonstrative gesture by placing, as head of the Church, a representative of the Catholic resistance movement." See "World Press Unmasks Fallacies in Book Defaming Pius XII: Exclusive Interview with Reporter of Pacelli's Beatification Cause," Zenit News Service, Oct. 3, 1999.

21. See Otto D. Tolischus, "A 'Political Pope' is Reich Comment," *New York Times*, Feb. 11, 1939 (subheadlines: "Hitler Sends Message" and "Reich Holds Successor Should Be Man Who Understands 'Laws of These Times' "). According to at least one account, however, Pacelli was Bergen's personal favorite to become the new Pope (due to his previous ties with Germany). Alvarez and Graham, 65.

22. "Message from the British Legation to the Holy See," Feb. 17, 1939, British Public Records Office FO 371/23789 57760 (also noting that the German ambassador had not appeared at any recent official functions "because of the present deadlock between the Holy See and the Reich government").

23. Alvarez and Graham, 65. "Members of the French and British foreign offices discussed the idea of attempting to influence the conclave in favor of Pacelli." Cornwell (1999), 206. The Spanish ambassador from Franco's regime also indicated that he hoped that the new Pope would not be as obsessed with Nazism as Pius XI had been. Sánchez (2002), 373.

24. "Secret Message from Osborne to Ingram," Feb. 23, 1939, British Public Records Office, FO 371/23789 57760.

25. "Message from the British Legation to the Holy See," Feb. 17, 1939, British Public Records Office, FO 371/23789 57760.

26. Korn, 126. The literal translation is closer to "the Vicar of Christ on the ground." See also Hatch and Walshe, 18; Halecki and Murray, 93; Charles Rankin, "Pius the Man and His Efforts for Peace," in *The Pope Speaks: The Words of Pius XII*, 46 (noting that he had injured his arm in the fall).

27. Holmes, 120.

28. Fabert, 37 ("The only vote cast against him was his own."); Cheetham, 285; see also Hatch and Walshe, 17 (reporting that Pacelli obtained a majority of votes in the second vote, but not the required two-thirds). Angelo Roncalli, the future Pope John XXIII, commented: "I am very pleased with this election, in which we can clearly see the Lord's hand." Elliott, 147.

29. Charles Rankin, "Pius the Man and His Efforts for Peace," in *The Pope Speaks: The Words of Pius XII*, 48.

30. Hebblethwaite, 50. "He was elected, as everyone knew, to be pope in time of total war, a role for which everything about his career — his diplomatic skills, his gift of languages, his sensitivity and his intelligence — equipped him." Duffy, 263.

31. Morgan, 158.

32. Hebblethwaite, 50; Deutsch, 108.

33. Korn, 140; *Vatican Impressions* (Sweeney, ed.), 219; Hatch and Walshe, 20.

34. Cianfarra, 84.

35. Ibid., 85.

36. F. Murphy, 58.

37. Elliott, 270. "Pacelli was everyone's idea of a Catholic saint." Duffy, 263. Mussolini might have preferred a friendlier pope, but on March 3, 1939, he reportedly was "satisfied with Pacelli's election." *The Ciano Diaries*, 36. His "satisfaction," however, should be viewed in light of his statement on March 5: "I don't give a damn about the Pope, the Cardinal Secretary of State, or anybody who occupies such positions." Ibid., 38.

38. See "Report from the British Legation to the Holy See," Feb. 17, 1939, British Public Records Office, F0 371/23789 ("I should myself be very pleased to see Cardinal Pacelli elected Pope"). Osborne went on to report on "the saintliness of character of Cardinal Pacelli, who has been a politician in spite of himself." Ibid.

39. Quoted in *Catholic Mind*, June 1964, 26, 27.

40. "Anti-Nazi Cardinal Elected Pontiff," *Dodge City Daily Globe*, March 2, 1939.

41. "Pius XII," *New York Times*, March 3, 1939. "An important section of American opinion regarded the new Pope as a friend of Democracy, crediting him with being largely responsible for his predecessor's attitude toward the Totalitarian States." Charles Rankin, "Pius the Man and His Efforts for Peace," in *The Pope Speaks: The Words of Pius XII*, 43.

42. "Pius XII," *New York Times*, March 3, 1939.

43. Charles Rankin, "Pius the Man and His Efforts for Peace," in *The Pope Speaks: The Words of Pius XII*, 40 ("As the right-hand man of Pius XI and familiar with his thoughts and intentions, it was clear that Pius XII would continue the policy laid down by his predecessor. That policy was one of courage in the face of international problems confronting the Church.")

44. "Washington Hails Pacelli Election," *New York Times*, March 3, 1939.

45. Besier, 188 (quoting the Polish Catholic Press Agency KAP).

46. "British View the Election as Sign of Continued Resistance to Totalitarianism," *New York Times*, March 3, 1939.

47. "France Applauds Choice of Pontiff," *New York Times*, March 3, 1939.

48. *L'Humanité*, March 4, 1939.

49. "The Election of Pope Pius XII," *Daily Worker*, March 4, 1939.

50. *Palestine Post*, March 2, 1939.

51. *New York Times*, March 3, 1939, p. 5 (quoting Samuel Goldstein).

52. *The Canadian Jewish Chronicle* (Montreal), March 10, 1939 (Pius XII was actually the 260th pope, not the 262nd.)

53. Ibid.

54. *Palestine Post*, March 6, 1939.

55. That same edition of the *Jewish Chronicle* went on to note that "on January 22 [1939], the *Voelkischer Beobachter* published pictures of Cardinal Pacelli and other church dignitaries beneath a collective heading of 'Agitators in the Vatican against Fascism and National Socialism.'"

56. "Jews Express Pleasure at Selection of New Pope," *The Canadian Jewish Chronicle* (Montreal), March 10, 1939, 2.

57. Charles Rankin, "Pius the Man and His Efforts for Peace," in *The Pope Speaks: The Words of Pius XII*, 42.

58. Michaelis, 241.

59. See Lapide, 122.

60. Quoted in Akin, 14. A biography of Pius, published in 1940, began with the words: "It is fortunate, indeed, for the whole world (excepting the dictators of Germany and Russia) that the former Pacelli is now Pope." Charles Rankin, "Pius the Man and His Efforts for Peace," in *The Pope Speaks: The Words of Pius XII*, 3.

61. Cornwell (1999), 218.

62. Ibid.

63. See *Jewish Chronicle* (London), March 10, 1939, 31.

64. *The Goebbels Diaries (1939-1941)*, 10.

65. Lapide, 121.

66. Charles Rankin, "Pius the Man and His Efforts for Peace," in *The Pope Speaks: The Words of Pius XII*, 110-11 (the report went on to say that Hitler thought he might get some high-ranking cardinals to go along with this, and that they could then install the national churches he desired). Italian Fascist leader Roberto Farinacci wrote: "Our enemies are a triumvirate, Stalin, de Gaulle, Pius XII."

67. Congregation for the Causes of Saints, *Positio*, appendix 25, 273.

68. *The Ciano Diaries*, 47 (reporting on March 18, 1939 that Pius XII "was most concerned about Germany and intends to follow a more conciliatory policy than Pius XI"); Deutsch, 110 (citing a German report of March 8, 1939, referring to "very strong hopes" that relations between Germany and the Vatican would improve).

69. Wright, 1930. See "*Le cardinal-archevêque de Munich Faulhaber au pape Pie XII,*" March 31, 1939, *Actes et Documents*, vol. 6, p. 62, no. 8.

70. O'Carroll, 49.

71. Congregation for the Causes of Saints, *Positio*, appendix 25, 273.

72. Smit, 215. In fact, the Vatican leadership seriously discussed breaking off diplomatic relations with Germany. Cornwell (1999), 209, 210.

73. Charles Rankin, "Pius the Man and His Efforts for Peace," in *The Pope Speaks: The Words of Pius XII*, 59.

74. "The New Secretary of State of the Vatican," *Zionist Review* (London), March 16, 1939, 13.

75. Tardini served as the deputy for the Congregation for Extraordinary Ecclesiastical Affairs (foreign relations), and he later became secretary of state to Pope John XXIII.

76. At this time, Montini was the deputy for the Congregation for Ordinary Affairs (domestic matters). Later he became Pope Paul VI.

77. The United States had not maintained a diplomat at the Holy See since 1867.

78. *Documents on German Foreign Policy 1918-1945*, Series D (1937-1945), no. 472 (March 5, 1939) (telegram from the German ambassador to the Holy See to the Foreign Ministry, reporting on a warm meeting with Pius XII). See Besier, 189.

79. *Documents on German Foreign Policy 1918-1945*, Series D (1937-1945), no. 470 (March 2, 1939).

80. *Records and Documents*, 91.

81. Smit, 238-39. Reflecting on this period in a radio broadcast after the war, Pius said:

> The world was then still at peace, but what a peace, and how precarious! With Our heart full of anguish, in perplexity and prayer, We regarded that peace as a person would regard the bed of a dying man, fighting, against all the odds, to save him from the throes of death.

"The Catholic Church and the Third Reich: Pope Pius XII Surveys an Heroic History," *Tablet* (London), June 9, 1945, 268.

82. Korn, 105-6.

83. Ibid.

84. *Chronicle*, 491-92.

85. The "hidden encyclical" was made public in 1972 by the *National Catholic Reporter* and again in 1973 by *L'Osservatore Romano*, not (as Cornwell reported) in 1995. Burkhart Schneider, "Un'enciclica mancata," *L'Osservatore Romano*, April 5, 1973; *National Catholic Reporter*, Dec. 15, 1972. See Vincent A. Lapomarda, *The Jesuit Heritage in New England*, 178 (1977) (citing the *National Catholic Reporter* piece).

86. Sereny, 294.

87. See Gallo, 326-27, n. 56.

88. Besier, 179.

89. Passelecq and Suchecky, 81 ("Gundlach was convinced that the new pope knew nothing about the encyclical project.... Fr. Maher informed LaFarge... that the new pope had not yet become acquainted with [preparatory documents]"); ibid., 82 (Gundlach... once again expressed... his conviction that 'nothing was transmitted' to Pius XII, and, as a result, 'our project has gone the way of all earthly things.'")

90. See pp. 380-83.

91. Cianfarra, 199. LaFarge wrote glowingly about *Summi Pontificatus*. He did, however, call it "dangerous" because it so obviously addressed the racism that was spreading across Europe. Lafarge, "Mankind is called to unity in Christ," *America*, Nov. 11, 1939, 120-121.

## Chapter Nine: 1939 and the Outbreak of War

1. S. K. Padover, "Nazi Scapegoat Number 2," *Reader's Digest*, Feb. 1939, 1 (condensed from *The Forum*). A similar account appears in the religion section of Newsweek, May 29, 1937 (discussing "four years of Church-state strife" in Germany). For an account of an Austrian nun who was beheaded for her opposition to the Nazis, see Hans Knight, "The Nun and the Nazis," *The Catholic Digest*, February 1992, 14.

2. Barnett, 106.

3. A German euthanasia program was first proposed in 1933. "At that time, the German Catholic Church declared uncompromisingly that any kind of legally sanctioned euthanasia was incompatible with Christian morality." Sereny, 60. Cardinals Bertram and Faulhaber both spoke out against euthanasia in 1934 and again in 1940, and Archbishop Gröber did so in 1937. Ibid., 72. Other German Catholic leaders also filed protests:

> Archbishop Gröber and Bishop Bornewasser von Trier, the Bishop of Limburg and of course the infinitely courageous Bishop of Münster, Count Galen — all in 1941; and finally a pastoral letter from all the German bishops, dated September 12, 1943, and certainly remarkable for the period, in which bishops protest not only against euthanasia but against the murder of "innocent hostages, prisoners of war or penal institutions, and human beings of foreign race or extraction."

Ibid., 72 (quoting a circular letter from Bishop Johann Neuhäusler, auxiliary bishop of Munich, "an inveterate opponent of the Nazis who spent most of the war years in Dachau concentration camp, and whose own political integrity is beyond question.")

4. Ibid.

5. Meltzer, 131; McGarry, in *Introduction to Jewish-Christian Relations*, 66. Hitler's ultimate goal was to create a "pure" Volk. See Mary M. Penrose, "Assisted Suicide: A Tough Pill to Swallow," 20 *Pepp. L. Rev.*, 689 (1993).

6. Hoar, 154.

7. See "Assisted Suicide Bill," *Los Angeles Times*, June 4, 1999, part B; page 6 ("In Nazi Germany, the mentally retarded and other sick, who were called 'useless eaters,' were given involuntary euthanasia, as the 'right to die became the duty to die'").

8. Hans Jonas, "The Right to Die," *Hastings Center Report 8*, no. 4 (1978), 31; Marvin Zalman et al., "Michigan's Assisted Suicide Three Ring Circus — An Intersection of Law and Politics," 23 *Ohio N.U.L. Rev.*, 863 (1997); Scott I. Davidson, "But, Why Do We Shoot Horses?: An Analysis of the Right to Die and Euthanasia," 12 *N.Y.L. Sch. J. Hum. Rts.*, 115 (Fall 1994).

9. McGarry, in *Introduction to Jewish-Christian Relations*, 66.

10. Barnett, 106.

11. A total of 70,273 patients appeared on the official lists of those who had been murdered; the actual number is estimated at closer to 105,000. See Rousmaniere, 120.

12. Ibid.

13. *The Nazi Master Plan*, July 6, 1945; *The Persecution of the Catholic Church in the Third Reich*, 421 (quoting Julius Streicher's *Stürmer*).

14. Oudendijk, 179.

15. *Sermon at St. Lambert's Church*, Aug. 3, 1941. The speech is largely reprinted in *A History of the Third Reich*, 179, and in Joanna Bogle, "The Bishop vs. the Nazis," *This Rock*, February 2008, 19. Within a few years, Galen's outspokenness was well-known throughout Germany. When his arrest seemed imminent, peasants came each morning to his residence and called for him to show himself at the window. Arvid Fredborg, *Behind the Steel Wall: Inside Report on Germany 1943*, Viking Press (New York, 1943), portions reprinted in *Reader's Digest*, January 1944, 125, 138-39. According to a wartime book, legends soon spread about his defiance of the Nazis. The best-known legend was that a Nazi official stood up in church one day and shouted that those who did not contribute to Germany's struggle with their own flesh and blood, or that of their children, should remain silent. Galen reportedly scolded the official in a sarcastic manner: "I forbid anyone in this church, whoever it may be, to criticize the *Führer*." Ibid. Galen had previously criticized the Nazis for confiscating Church property and for charging that the Church was anti-science. Bogle, *supra*, 20 ("He referred openly to the Nazis as pagan and urged people not to allow great Catholic traditions to be usurped in the name of progress").

16. Oudendijk, 179; Joanna Bogle, "The Bishop vs. the Nazis," *This Rock*, February 2008 (reprinting one of his sermons).

17. "A l'Evêque de Münster," Feb. 24, 1943, *Actes et Documents*, vol. 2, p. 306, no. 101 (letter from Pius encouraging Galen's "open and courageous pronouncements" and telling him that two letters he had mailed to the Holy See laid the groundwork for the 1942 Christmas message). Even earlier, on Feb. 2, 1942, Pius XII congratulated Cardinal Faulhaber for two bold sermons in the face of Nazism: "Au Cardinal-Archevêque de Munich," Feb. 2, 1942, *Actes et Documents*, vol. 2, p. 235, vol 2, no. 78. In a letter to Bishop Konrad Preysing of Berlin, Pius explained:

> The three sermons of the bishop of Münster and the pastoral letter of the joint episcopacy furnish proof of what can still be achieved within the Reich through public and resolute acts. We stress that because the Church in Germany is all the more dependent on your own public actions because the general political situation in its difficult and often contradictory nature imposes on the head of the entire Church in his public statements a necessary restraint. However, that the bishops who with such courage and at the same time in such irreproachable form stand up for the causes of God and the Holy Church, as did Bishop von Galen, will always find Our support, of that We do not specifically need to assure you and your brothers.

"A l'Evêque de Berlin," Sept. 30, 1941, *Actes et Documents*, vol. 2, p. 229, no. 76. See also "A l'Evêque de Berlin," April 30, 1943, *Actes et Documents*, vol. 2, p. 318, no. 105 (on the difficulty of speaking out without risking reprisals); "A l'Archevêque de Cologne," March 3, 1944, *Actes et Documents*, volume 2, p. 363, no. 1129. In addition to being collected in volume 2 of the *Actes et Documents* collection, Pius XII's wartime letters to the German bishops have been published as *Die Briefe an die Deutschen Bischöfe 1939-1944*, edited by Burkhart Schneider (Grünewald: Mainz, 1966).

18. For Pius XII's Feb. 24, 1943 letter to von Galen, see *Actes et Documents*, vol. 2, p. 306, no. 101.

19. Joanna Bogle, "The Bishop vs. the Nazis," *This Rock*, February 2008, 22. In 2005, Galen was declared "blessed," one step away from canonization as a saint. Ibid.

20. Burleigh, *The Third Reich: A New History*, 400 (regarding the efforts of the Nazi leadership to compel the Church to tolerate euthanasia: "Negotiations collapsed when on 2 December 1940 Pope Pius XII unequivocally condemned the killing of 'life unworthy of life'"). This statement was repeated on Vatican Radio (Dec. 2) and in *L'Osservatore Romano* (Dec. 6). Sereny, 74 (incorrectly reporting that the statement appeared in Latin instead of Italian). See also Gallo, 35 (noting that the Allies were heartened when they learned of this condemnation); Graham, "The 'Right to Kill' in the Third Reich: Prelude to Genocide," LXII *Catholic Historical Review*, 65. Bishop Preysing of Berlin also read it from the pulpit of St. Hedwig's Cathedral on March 9, 1941. Sereny, 74. As early as 1930, in the encyclical *Casti connubii*, Pope Pius XI condemned sterilization and asserted that the right of families to have children overrides the state's desire for eugenically perfect people. See Burleigh, "The Cardinal Basil Hume Memorial Lectures," 3 *Totalitarian Movements and Political Religions*, 30; Meltzer, 131; *Controversial Concordats*, 162 (citing *L'Osservatore Romano* of Dec. 6, 1940).

21. Besier, 74.

22. "A l'Evêque de Berlin," Dec. 15, 1940, *Actes et Documents*, vol. 2, p. 180, no. 58. See Wright, 1930.

23. Graham, *The 'Right to Kill,'* 68. Pius always was close to Preysing, but beginning in 1942, he particularly began following Preysing's lead, even bypassing the papal nuncio to take advice directly from Preysing, a widely recognized opponent of Nazism. See Oppen, 405 ("Preysing received far more correspondence than any of his colleagues; also, the Pope praised his outspoken stand for the rule of law and even-handed justice"). In April 1943, Pius wrote encouraging Preysing to continue his work on behalf of the Jews:

> For the non-Aryan Catholics as well as for Jews, the Holy See has done whatever was in its power, with charitable, financial and moral assistance. Let us not speak of the substantial sums which we spent in American money for the fares of emigrants. We have gladly given these sums, for these people were in distress. Jewish organizations have warmly thanked the Holy See for these rescue operations. As for what is being done against non-Aryans in the German territories, we have said a word in our Christmas radio message.

Quoted in Holmes, 167.

24. Graham, *The 'Right to Kill,'* 68-72; Holmes, 101. Several protests from bishops of this time period are reviewed in Groppe, *The Church's Struggle*, 24. See also Godman, *Hitler and the Vatican* (documenting numerous protests, but arguing that they should have been stronger).

25. Commenting on the mistaken notion that Galen's protests caused the Nazis to halt the "mercy-killing" program, Dr. Robert M.W. Kempner, deputy chief U.S. prosecutor at Nuremberg, wrote:

> "Open protests against the 'Final Solution' would certainly have been effective," so it is now often asserted *après le débâcle*, this is proved by the "success" of the German bishops protests against the so-called "euthanasia" programme. This is not in accord with the facts, for even after the protests this programme of murder was strictly enforced in secret right up to the end of the war. For example,

many thousands of victims were allowed to die of hunger, so that they died a "natural death." … A public protest against the persecution of the Jews could only lead to the partial success of gaining time when it was made at a politically and military opportune moment, like those of the nuncios in Slovakia and Romania.…"

Congregation for the Causes of Saints, *Positio*, appendix 25, 239, 244. Similarly, historian Michael Burleigh comments:

Galen's coruscating verbal assault… had no functional effects.… Although his sermon [condemning euthanasia in the summer of 1941] which enjoyed national and international notoriety, undoubtedly moved some Nazi leaders to contemplate murdering him, its effects on the "euthanasia" programme were minimal. The medical killing of children continued unimpeded; gassing facilities were used to murder concentration-camp inmates; while the "euthanasia" killing of adult psychiatric patients went on by other means down to the final days of the war.

Burleigh, *The Third Reich: A New History*, 723; see also Burleigh, "The Cardinal Basil Hume Memorial Lectures: Political Religion and Social Evil," 3 *Totalitarian Movements and Political Religions*, 32-33.

26. Joanna Bogle, "The Bishop vs. the Nazis," *This Rock*, February 2008, 21.

27. *Three Sermons in Defiance of the Nazis Preached During 1941 by Bishop von Galen of Munster*, 5. Retaliation concerns are justified by statistics from Poland, where, of the 828 priests in the diocese of Posen, 450 were put in camps and 74 were shot. Many of the others fled. Gallo, 34.

28. *Hitler's Secret Conversations*, 520. Hitler also vowed to send Nuncio Orsenigo back to Rome as soon as the war was over. Ibid.

29. Congregation for the Causes of Saints, *Positio*, appendix 25, 245.

30. *The Nazi Master Plan: The Persecution of the Christian Churches*.

31. Ibid. See also Fredborg, "Behind the Steel Wall," 138 (praising Galen's open opposition to Hitler and noting his widespread anti-Nazi reputation).

32. Joanna Bogle, "The Bishop vs. the Nazis," *This Rock*, February 2008, 21-22.

33. Levai, 108 (noting that Galen's comments were not really influential in this decision).

34. Meltzer, 131.

35. Cornwell (1999), 277. One of the primary reasons that the program was driven underground was the impact that it had on morale in the military. Soldiers knew that they might lose a limb in war. If that then meant that they would be put to death, they might be less willing to fight for the Fatherland. When the Nazi hierarchy realized this, they tried to make it look like the program had ended.

36. Barnett, 118.

37. Ibid.

38. "The History Place: World War II in Europe," on the Internet at: *http://www.historyplace.com/world-war2/timeline/threat.htm*.

39. "Anti-Nazi Bishop a Step Closer to Beatification" (Zenit News, Dec. 21, 2003) (von Galen's "heroic virtue" recognized by the Catholic Church, moving him a step closer to beatification).

40. "ADL Applauds Steps to Beatify Anti-Nazi Cardinal," *ADL press release*, Dec. 28, 2004.

41. The Easter homily is reprinted in *The Pope Speaks: The Words of Pius XII*, 126, 131. See also *Records and Documents*, 99; Smit, 205.

42. The letter is reprinted in Charles Rankin, "Pius the Man and His Efforts for Peace," in *The Pope Speaks: The Words of Pius XII*, 106-7.

43. Ibid., 54 ("Presumably the references to the violation of solemnly sanctioned pacts were regarded as unsuitable reading for the German public").

44. *The Ciano Diaries*, 98.

45. Ibid., 111.

46. British authorities suggested that Pius could convince Poland to make certain concessions to Germany. "Great Britain's Minister Osborne to the Secretariat of State," Aug. 26, 1939, *Actes et Documents*, vol. 1, p. 251, no. 134.

47. Cornwell (1999), 230 (quoting Foreign Office Papers, in Public Records Office, Kew 371/23790/283).

48. Address to the Sacred College of Cardinals, reprinted in *The Pope Speaks: The Words of Pius XII*, 137. *Records and Documents*, 151; Smit, 207-8.

49. On Dec. 7, 1939, Pius sent a message to Italy's ambassador to the Vatican, in which he called for peace but also condemned "state doctrines and practices of a disruptive and destructive character that find in the severance of natural law from the divine revelation." "To Italy's Ambassador to the Vatican," Dec. 7, 1939, reprinted in *The Pope Speaks: The Words of Pius XII*, 222.

50. Kennedy (1961), 122, 179, 190-91.

51. Ibid., 122.

52. *The Black Book of Communism*, 367-68.

53. "To Those in Power and Their Peoples," Aug. 24, 1939, in *The Pope Speaks: The Words of Pius XII*, 145. See also Shirer (1962), 746; Hatch and Walshe, 146; Blet, 21; Charles Rankin, "Pius the Man and His Efforts for Peace," in *The Pope Speaks: The Words of Pius XII*, 79-80.

54. Shirer (1984), 434.

55. "Notes de Mgr. Tardini," Aug. 31, 1939, *Actes et Documents*, vol. 1, p. 270, no. 159 (related documents following).

56. Ibid. See Besier, 191 (noting that Pius considered traveling to Warsaw and Berlin).

57. "Telegram from the Ambassador in France (Bullitt) to the Secretary of State, May 9, 1939," in *Foreign Relations of the United States, Diplomatic Papers, 1939, vol. I (General)*, United States Government Printing Office (Washington, 1956), 182-83 (reporting on France's absolute rejection, Poland's reasons for resisting, and Britain's counterproposal); "The Under Secretary of State (Welles) to President Roosevelt, May 16, 1939," in *Foreign Relations of the United States, Diplomatic Papers, 1939, vol. I (General)*, 186-87, United States Government Printing Office (Washington, 1956) (the Pope's report on the negative reaction to his proposal).

58. Mazour and Peoples, 715-17; Morison, 992; Taylor, 162-63.

59. Taylor, 155.

60. "War! Bomb Warsaw!" *Chicago Daily Tribune*, Sept. 1, 1939, 1.

61. Mazour and Peoples, 717; Goldston, 121.

62. Hatch and Walshe, 147.

63. In 1938, Secretary of State Pacelli helped an Italian Jewish family emigrate to Palestine. *Jerusalem Post*, Oct. 10, 1958. By 1940, the Vatican had an organized effort regarding the clandestine immigration of Jews to Palestine. "Notes de Mgr. Tardini, " *Actes et Documents*, vol. 4, p. 422, no. 294. In fact, volume four of the *Actes et Documents* contains numerous messages sent immediately following the outbreak of war about efforts to get Jews out of harm's way, including efforts to obtain travel visas. See, e.g., documents nn. 56, 57, 60, 61, and 96. Most of the other messages during this time concerned protecting refugees, without any indication as to race or religion. Several of them contain the mark "Ex. Aud. SS.mi." This abbreviation stands for "*Ex Audientia Sanctissimi*," meaning that it was discussed directly with the Pope. Michael Berenbaum, president and CEO of the Survivors of the Shoah Visual History Foundation and former Director of Research at the U.S. Holocaust Museum, prepared a memo on the role of Angelo Roncalli (the future Pope John XXIII) during the war. According to that memo:

> Chaim Barlas, the chief delegate from Palestine, wrote that Roncalli cried when told what was happening to the Jews. He said, "I am going to fast and to pray for the people and our people." Teddy Kollek, a delegate from Palestine during the darkest years of the Holocaust who for three years was mayor of Jerusalem, recalled: "he commiserated together with us. He wasn't able to do very much. But what he could, he did."

The memo reports that Roncalli used his authority to pressure Romania to dismantle camps and send some 3,000 children to Palestine. In fact, "working with the Jewish envoys and with Roncalli, by war's end, some 20,000 Jews were transported to Palestine via Turkey."

A biography of Pope John XXIII also confirms that the Church was involved in the process of helping Jews flee to Palestine. Specifically, that book reports, "At the outbreak of hostilities, Pope Pius XII, like Benedict XV twenty-five years before, organized the resources of the Vatican for the relief of Europe's afflicted." Lawrence Elliott, *I Will Be Called John*, 152. That book reports that the German official Papen "had been consistently helpful in *church efforts to spirit doomed Jews away to Palestine*." Ibid., 164. John, of course, always credited Pius for all such efforts. Ibid., 159.

Filippo Cortesi, the nuncio in Warsaw, as well as his assistant Alfredo Pacini, were forced to flee Poland soon after the invasion. They escaped to Romania. There, Cortesi received a letter, dated Sept. 19, from Monsignor Domenico Tardini, of the Vatican Secretariat of State, who communicated to him the Pope's decision that he remain in Romania *to be of assistance to the Poles fleeing there*. (*Actes and Documents*, vol. 6, doc. 69, 147-148). Some of these refugees (most of whom were Jewish) remained, but many left with the Church's help to Palestine, and the *Actes et Documents* collection confirms that the Vatican remained in close contact with this process (see vol. 6, documents 77, 78, 79, 81, 82, and 85).

64. Records indicate that 4,770 Jews were baptized in Budapest during the occupation, but 80,000 baptismal certificates were distributed. O'Carroll, 99, 104; Graham, *Pope Pius XII and the Jews of Hungary in 1944*, 17; Lapide, 159. At the outbreak of war, Roncalli wrote from Istanbul: "Together with Monsignor Testa I have organized several works of social assistance. The Holy Father has sent me half a million lire to begin with." Elliott, 152 (also noting that he was involved in passing clandestine messages to Palestine and elsewhere). By April 1942, the Romanian minister to the Holy See informed the Vatican that the number of Jews being baptized into Catholicism was too great, and it was drawing attention. "Notes du cardinal Maglione," April 18, 1942, *Actes et Documents*, vol. 8, no. 353, 310. The Pope, however, rejected the suggestion that further conversions be suspended until the end of the war. In February 1943, the Jewish community in Romania sent its gratitude to Pius XII for the help of the Vatican and its nunciature.

The memo by Michael Berenbaum (referenced in the previous endnote) reports: "Roncalli worked with Church officials in Hungary who issued papers to individual Jews which said they were under the protection of the Holy See." Yad Vashem is investigating whether Roncalli issued false *baptismal* certificates to Jews, but "it is certain that he passed Certificates to Palestine and quasi-official documents" that helped Jews obtain safe passage. Saul Friedlander, no apologist for Pius XII, writes:

> Monsignor Roncalli spared no effort to succor the Jews of Central Europe and the Balkans.... The Zionist archives contain a large number of documents concerning the incessant activity of Nuncio Roncalli on behalf of the Jews. We should stress, however, that Msgr. Roncalli is reported to have stated that everything he did in this sphere was done at the insistence of the Pope.

*Pius XII and the Third Reich*, 222. In Hungary, Roncalli reportedly referred to this as "Operation Baptism." Ira Hirschmann, a special emissary of the American War Refugee Board, following a visit and interview with Roncalli, reported on the "baptism of thousands of Hungarian Jews in air raid shelters." Elliott, 161 (also noting that Roncalli had "no interest in whether any Jew actually received the sacrament").

It should be noted that the false baptismal certificates were used because Vatican officials had legal standing to object to persecution *of Catholics*. Unfortunately, they did not have similar standing when it came to non-Catholics, be they Protestants, Jews, or unbelievers. As it turns out, the Nazis rarely responded positively when protests were made on behalf of Catholics. A regime that would not heed church protests on behalf of its own members would certainly never have listened to Vatican protests on behalf of non-Catholics. The best the Church could do was to try to pass off non-Catholic victims as Catholics and try to intervene to save them on that basis. Thus when protests or efforts by the Church are directed on behalf of baptized Jews (as is the case in many of the documents sent out from the Vatican following the outbreak of war), it must be remembered that this did not mean only those Jews who actually had been converted.

65. See Keegan (1989), 44-46.
66. Barnett, 176.
67. Polish Bishops, "The Victims of Nazi Ideology," January 1995, reprinted in *Secretariat for Ecumenical and Interreligious Affairs, Catholics Remember the Holocaust.*
68. William J. O'Malley, "Priests of the Holocaust," reprinted in *Pius XII and the Holocaust: A Reader*, 153. Bormann's explanation of the incompatibility of Christianity and National Socialism is reprinted in *A History of the Third Reich*, 229.
69. Morrow, 34; Jim Skowronski, "So Others Will Never Forget," *Columbia*, September 1997, 18; William J. O'Malley, "The Priests of Dachau," in *Pius XII and the Holocaust: A Reader*, 143. "The German opposition counted thousands of priests of every denomination in its ranks; six thousand of them died in the concentration camps or in prison. But Nazism and Christianity were fundamentally at odds, and the Party made little effort to disguise it." Overy, 284.
70. Polish Bishops, "The Victims of Nazi Ideology," January 1995, reprinted in *Secretariat for Ecumenical and Interreligious Affairs, Catholics Remember the Holocaust*. In 1944, Hlond was arrested by the Gestapo. He was liberated by the Allies the following year.
71. Weigel, 73, 74 (noting that Sapieha worked to help Jews escape Nazi persecution). After the war, Pius made Sapieha a cardinal. Ibid., 78.
72. Todd and Curti, 671. So did France and Britain, both of which seriously underestimated Germany's military might. Tenen, 355-56.
73. Hoar, 196-97.
74. Kennedy (1995), 58.
75. Keegan (1989), 47.
76. *Chronicle*, 499.
77. Ibid., 510.
78. Ibid., 500.
79. Blum, 726.
80. Mazour and Peoples, 720.
81. Deighton, 432.
82. Even the German Mennonites, traditionally pacifists, chose not to "exercise the principle of non-defense" at a meeting of elders and ministers on Jan. 10, 1938. See John D. Thiesen, *Mennonite and Nazi? Attitudes Among Mennonite Colonists in Latin America, 1933-1945* (Kitchener, Ontario: Pandora, 1999).
83. Barnett, 163. Pius, through Cardinal Faulhaber, instructed all priests and theology students drafted into the German army to "shun all ideas that are contrary to justice and Christian charity, to profess by action and when necessary also by word their Catholic convictions." Blet, 68.
84. Holmes, 148.
85. Ibid., 149. On Dec. 18, 1939, Count Ciano recorded: "The fight against Catholicism in Germany is being carried on pitilessly and idiotically." *The Ciano Diaries*, 180.
86. *The Ciano Diaries*, 86.
87. Cianfarra, 101-2.

88. Lapomarda, 85, n. 43. Hitler made a speech at the S.S. Ordensburg (youth leader training center) at Sonthofen, where he had screamed that he would crush the Catholic Church under his heel, as he would a toad. Deutsch, 110, n. 1.

89. Holmes, 110.

90. Gallin, 166-67.

91. Holmes, 101; Gallin, 167-68.

92. Gallin, 168 ("At this early date, there was apparently unanimity among the bishops as to the incompatibility of Catholicism and National Socialism, and they were courageous in their denunciation of the errors inherent in the philosophy of which the latter was based."); Lewy, 10-11. Lewy claimed that *after* the Nazis obtained power, the German Catholic bishops abandoned this noble record and began to placate, if not collaborate with, the Nazis. Since Lewy's book originally appeared, however, an abundance of new evidence has become available which has placed the German Catholic bishops' record in proper perspective. Heinz Hürten, *Deutsche Katholiken, 1918-1945* (Ferdinand Schöningh: Paderborn, 1992) contradicts the version supplied by Lewy and his uncritical followers like Daniel Goldhagen. See also, Ludwig Volk, "Zwischen Geschichtsschreibung und Hochhuthprosa: Kritisches und Grundsätzliches zu einer Neuerscheinung über Kirche und Nationalsozialismus," in *Stimmen der Zeit,* vol. 176 (1965), 29-41.

93. Steigmann-Gall, 67.

94. Tinnemann, 334, citing Hans Müller, *Katholische Kirche und Nationalsozialismus, Dokumente 1930-1935,* 13-47 (Munich: *Nymphenburger Verlagshandlung,* 1963).

95. Ibid., 334.

96. Ibid., 339.

97. Ibid.

98. Ibid., 339.

99. Ibid.

100. Oppen, 406. Orsenigo was criticized for being too accommodating to the Nazis. Recently opened archives, however, indicate that he was not as friendly toward the Nazis as had been thought. See Godman, 30-33, 80, 87; Besier, 124 (in 1933, Orsenigo opposed Nazi racial policy); ibid., 128, 131. Though he had been appointed by Pius XI, Pius XII could have removed him. At one point, Pius XII reportedly convened a meeting of the cardinals of the Congregation for Extraordinary Ecclesiastical Affairs, and considered recalling Orsenigo. The Pope, however, determined that the Germans would break off all diplomatic relations if Orsenigo were removed, and they would be unlikely to accept a new nuncio. This would cut off the Vatican's best source of information on Nazi activities in Germany, including the many acts of persecution against the Church. Holmes, 149; Alvarez and Graham, 161; O'Carroll, 138, 150-51; Besier, 75; *The Pius War,* 253 ("Most scholars believe that had Orsenigo been recalled ... the Nazis would have prevented *any* nuncio from remaining in Germany, just as they banned the one in Poland.") Ernst Von Weizsäcker, the German ambassador to the Holy See, later wrote that Orsenigo carried out his duties properly, but that his efforts to avoid angering Hitler caused him to appear more sympathetic to the Nazis than he really was. Weizsäcker, 282-83; see also Rhodes, 343; Besier, 75 ("[T]he Berlin nuncio captured the political moods in Germany excellently, and hence advised caution and reconciliation. Noone [*sic*] in the Curia need follow instructions of this kind.") As evinced by unpublished Nuremberg documents, Osenigo made a constant stream of protests, enquiries, and requests for access, on matters regarding the Germans' treatment of the Church, prisoners, and Jews. See Conway, *The Nazi Persecution of the Churches,* 306. In fact, Orsenigo intervened with leaders in Berlin on behalf of Nazi victims at least 300 times, but it was almost all in vain. Lapomarda, 128. For examples of the nuncio's inquiries over Jewish matters, see *Actes et Documents,* vol. 8, 59-60; ibid., vol. 8, 687. Regarding his request for access to minister to Polish and French Catholic prisoners, Orsenigo's interventions became so frequent that the Foreign Ministry replied that he should confine his complaints only to matters of larger importance. Unpublished Nuremberg Document NG4445. Foreign Minister Ribbentrop was to remark after the war that he had a drawer full of Orsenigo's protests left unanswered. International Military Tribunal, *Trial of the Major War Criminals,* vol. X, Nuremberg, 1947, 140-4.

101. Oppen, 406, quoting *Die Briefe Pius' XII. an die deutschen Bischöfe 1939-1944, Herausgegeben von Burkhart Schneider in Zusammenarbeit mit Pierre Blet und Angelo Martini* (Mainz, 1966), 355-66.

102. When Orsenigo was inclined to make overtures to the Reich government, Pacelli instructed him not to make friendly statements about Hitler and the Nazis. See "Vatican Told Nuncio to Forgo Praise of Hitler: Professor Sees Signs of Opposition to Nazism in 1930s Archives," Zenit News Service, May 1, 2003; Andrea Tornielli, "Interview with Prof. Matteo Luigi Napolitano," *Il Giornale* (Milan, Italy), April 10, 2003.

103. Oppen, 407; see Besier, 111-13 (Orsenigo felt that to support National Socialism would be "naïve and illogical," but he also warned against open confrontation).

104. See Ulrich von Hehl, *Priester unter Hitler's Terror* (Matthias-Grünewald-Verlag: Mainz, 1984) (biographical and statistical survey documenting how up to one-third of the German Catholic clergy were persecuted by the Nazis, experiencing everything from interrogations to imprisonment and execution). Other than Jews and Gypsies, few segments of the German population were persecuted to the same extent as Catholic priests.

105. *The Nazi Master Plan*, July 6, 1945. See also Burleigh, "The Cardinal Basil Hume Memorial Lectures," 3 *Totalitarian Movements and Political Religions*, 29 ("[T]he pastoral letters and sermons of the bishops were punctuated with protests against the myriad incremental measures which added up to systematic religious persecution. The density of complaint can be gauged from a rather impressive book, *The Nazi Persecution of the Catholic Church*, published in London in 1940").

106. *The Nazi Master Plan: The Persecution of the Christian Churches*, July 6, 1945.

107. *Hitler's Secret Conversations*, 83.

108. Ibid., 112.

109. Ibid., 296.

110. Ibid., 583.

111. Ibid., 98-99.

112. "The Church and the Jews in the Third Reich," *Fidelity*, Nov. 1983, 21.

113. *Hitler's Secret Conversations*, 389.

114. Ibid., 48-49.

115. Ibid., 624. Of course, it is impossible to identify a single "Nazi view" of Christianity. See "Ronald J. Rychlak, Book Review: "The Holy Reich: Nazi Conceptions of Christianity, 1919-1945," by Richard Steigmann-Gall, *First Things*, October 2003. Hitler's attitude can be deduced from several semi-private statements that he made: "There is something unhealthy about Christianity." *Hitler's Secret Conversations*, 397. "I shall never come personally to terms with the Christian life.... If my presence on earth is providential, I owe it to a superior will. But I owe nothing to the Church that trafficks [*sic*] in the salvation of souls.... Our epoch will certainly see the end of the disease of Christianity." Ibid., 330. "When one examines the Catholic religion closely, one cannot fail to realise that it is an almost incredibly cunning mixture of hypocrisy and business acumen, which trades with consummate skill on the deeply engrained affection of mankind for the beliefs and superstitions he holds." Ibid., 398. "It is deplorable that the Bible should have been translated into German, and that the whole of the German people should have thus become exposed to the whole of this Jewish mumbo-jumbo." Ibid., 482.

116. Holmes, 149 (quoting Reinhard Heydrich). "Heydrich seems to have had a pathological hatred of the Churches.... He sought to ruin them by discrediting them through a long and sustained campaign of slander, backed up by Gestapo action." Crankshaw, 85.

117. Johann B. Neuhäusler, *Kreuz und Hakenkreuz* (Two Volumes: *Katholische Kirche Bayerns*: Munich, 1946), especially vol. 1, p. 76. An English translation of many of the documents Neuhäusler compiled can be found in *The Persecution of the Catholic Church in the Third Reich; Facts and Documents Translated from the German*. See also George N. Schuster, "Catholic Resistance in Nazi Germany," 22:84 *Thought*, 12 (March, 1947); "The Anti-Christians," *Tablet* (London), Jan. 4, 1941, 12 (reviewing *The Persecution of the Catholic Church in the Third Reich*).

118. Purdy, 254.

119. Ibid. See Lewy, 247, 390; Holmes, 129.

120. Purdy, 254 (noting that the broadcast brought a protest from the German Foreign Office).

121. "First Report of Cardinal Hlond, Primate of Poland, to Pope Pius XII, on the Religious Situation in the Archdioceses of Gniezno and Pozan," reprinted in *The Persecution of the Catholic Church in German-Occupied Poland*, 1-35. Later reports noted the conversion of some Catholic churches into Protestant churches. See Ibid., 40-41.

122. "Second Report of Cardinal Hlond, Primate of Poland, to Pope Pius XII, on the Religious Situation in the Polish Dioceses of Chelmno, Katowice, Lodz, Plock, Wloclawek, and Others Incorporated in the Reich," reprinted in *The Persecution of the Catholic Church in German-Occupied Poland*, 37-65. This report also notes that priests were confined together with Jews in wooden huts, suggesting that Nazis treated priests in the same manner that they treated Jews.

123. Testimony of Cardinal Stefano Wyszynski, Oct. 18 and 25, 1968, before the Tribunal of the Vicariate of Rome, on the beatification of Pius XII (Eugenio Pacelli), part II, p. 578; Halecki and Murray, 142.

124. Graham (1968), 29.

125. "Le primat de Pologne cardinal Hlond au pape Pie XII," Oct. 7, 1939, *Actes et Documents*, vol. 3*, p. 88, no. 21 (including a facsimile of the original handwritten letter).

126. *Tablet*, Sept. 23, 1939, 375. Reprinted in *Principles for Peace*, 587.

127. Reprinted in *Principles for Peace*, 588. He also asked the pilgrims to pray that peace "will again grant the Catholic Church in your beloved fatherland happier days and greater freedom." Ibid.

128. Alvarez and Graham, 142. Hlond's protests from afar brought complaints from Catholics still in Poland. Bishop Karl Maria Splett of Danzig wrote to Pius XII:

> At my inquiry the Gestapo told me that Cardinal Hlond had called for resistance among the Polish population over the Vatican Radio station, and the Gestapo had to prevent him.... They say that Cardinal Hlond called the Polish people to rally round its priests and teachers. Thereupon, numerous priests and teachers were arrested and executed, or were tortured to death in the most terrible manner, or were even shipped to the far east.

Lothar Groppe, "The Church's Struggle with the Third Reich," *Fidelity*, October 1983, 15.

129. *Great Untold Stories of World War II*, 85.

130. Ibid., 82.

131. For accounts of life for priests in a concentration camp, see Lenz, *Christ in Dachau*; Hanley, 37-39 (photos). See generally Bernard, *Priestblock 25487*; Lapomarda, *The Jesuits and the Third Reich* (Lapormarda identifies 152 Jesuits who were killed or who died in Nazi captivity); Coady, *With Bound Hands* (letters written in prison).

132. Polish Bishops, "The Victims of Nazi Ideology," January 1995, reprinted in *Secretariat for Ecumenical and Interreligious Affairs, Catholics Remember the Holocaust*.

133. Certain Poles, exiled in London, directed criticism at the Pope because it was thought that he had clearly spoken on behalf of the Jews, but not on behalf of Catholic Poles. See Gallo, 34.

> The strongest complaint against the Pope came from Karol Radonski, Bishop of Wloclawek, who was in exile in London and in contact with the Polish government in exile. When Maglione [the Cardinal Secretary of State during the War] chastised him for "adding an additional cross" for the Pope to carry, Radonski replied that he had heard that the nuncio in France (Valeri) had told Pétain that the Pope had condemned the persecution of Jews. "Are we less deserving than the Jews?" he asked.

Sánchez, *Pope Pius XII and the Holocaust*, 157. For the original correspondence between Radonski and Maglione, see *Actes et Documents*, vol. 3, 633-636; 713-717; 736-739. For refutations of the charge that Pius XII "turned his back on the Poles" during the war, see *Pope Pius and Poland*, published by the Jesuits at America Press in New York City (1942); Graham, *The Pope and Poland*; John Lafarge, "The Pope is True Holy Father to Poland's stricken people," *America*, Sept. 12, 1943, 622-23.

134. *Vita*, April 15, 1964, as cited and translated by Carlo Falconi in *The Silence of Pius XII*, 149. See "L'archevêque de Cracovie Sapieha au pape Pie XII," Oct. 28, 1942, *Actes et Documents*, volume 3\*\*, 669, no. 437 ("We very much regret that we cannot publicly communicate to our faithful your Holiness' letters, as this would only afford an opportunity for fresh persecutions; and the fact that we have been suspected of being in secret communication with the Holy See has already led to victimization").

135. "A l'Evêque de Berlin," April 30, 1943, *Actes et Documents*, vol. 2, p. 318, no. 105. An English translation of the letter appears in Friedländer, *Pius XII and the Third Reich*, 135-143.

136. "Discours du pape Pie XII en la fête de St. Eugène," May 31, 1943, *Actes et Documents*, vol. 3\*\*, p. 801, no. 510. See also Toland, 864; Holmes, 132. See generally Jakubowski, *Pope Pius and Poland* (documenting Pius XII's actions on behalf of Poland).

137. "L'archevêque de Cracovie Sapieha au cardinal Maglione," June 18, 1943, *Actes et Documents*, vol. 3\*\*, p. 813, no. 523. See also "Le primat de Pologne cardinal Hlond au cardinal Maglione," June 4, 1943, *Actes et Documents*, vol. 3\*\*, p. 803, no. 513. "Le primat de Pologne cardinal Hlond au cardinal Maglione," June 9, 1943, *Actes et Documents*, vol. 3\*\*, p. 807, no. 517.

138. *Summi Pontificatus*, n. 3. The encyclical is reprinted in *The Pope Speaks: The Words of Pius XII*, 148.

139. *Summi Pontificatus*, n. 45. Less than two weeks after publication of *Summi Pontificatus*, in *Sertum Laetitae* (On the Establishment of the Hierarchy in the United States), Pius wrote of a "special paternal affection" for black Americans.

140. *Summi Pontificatus*, n. 7.

141. In addition to being a dictator and a racist, one of Hitler's first actions after assuming power was to denounce and repudiate all treaties he deemed unfavorable to Germany.

142. German Cardinal Michael von Faulhaber used *Summi Pontificatus* to condemn the Nazis, resulting in a headline reading "Cardinal Faulhaber Indicts Hitlerism." "The Church Abroad," *Tablet* (London), April 27, 1940, 398.

143. *Summi Pontificatus*, n. 48.

144. "Pope Condemns Dictators, Treaty Violators, Racism: Urges Restoring of Poland," *New York Times*, Oct. 28, 1939, p. 1, col. 1. The *Times* Vatican correspondent, Camille Cianfarra, similarly remarked:

> Stripped of its religious references, the encyclical was tantamount to a declaration of war on Germany and Russia. By condemning their policies and theories, the Pontiff substantially served notice that he would continue to fight, just as Pius XI had done, those manifestations of the totalitarian regimes that injured religion and the carrying out of the Church's spiritual mission.

Cianfarra, 199.

145. Charles Rankin, "Pius the Man and His Efforts for Peace," in *The Pope Speaks: The Words of Pius XII*, 118.

146. Ibid., 85.

147. Ibid., 85-86 (noting, however, that Vatican Radio broadcast a reading of the complete text).

148. O'Carroll, 53. The German-controlled Polish newspapers took advantage of the lack of communication with the outside world to distort and falsify the attitude of the Holy See. The encyclical was circulated in corrupted versions which seemed to make the Pope blame the Poles for their own predicament. Graham (1968), 34. See Holmes, 124.

149. "SS Group Leader Heydrich to Reich Minister and Chief of the Reich Chancellery Lammers," Federal Archives (Germany), Koblenz, R 43 II/1504 c, typed copy with enclosure (June 22, 1940). Goebbels wrote in his diary on Oct. 28, 1939, that it was "partly very aggressive toward us, though covertly." *The Goebbels Diaries: 1939-1941*, 33.

150. Cornwell (1999), 234.

151. *The Persecution of the Catholic Church in German-Occupied Poland*, 59.

152. Cornwell (1999), 234.

153. "British Legation to the Holy See," Jan. 7, 1941, British Public Records Office, FO 371/3073 56879.

154. "Minutes of November 13, 1939," British Public Records Office, FO 371/23791 56879. Minutes of the following meeting, Nov. 16, 1939, reflect the decision not to thank the Pope, lest Mussolini find out and take offense. Ibid. FO 371/30173 56879 (similar report).

155. O'Carroll, 53.

156. "Le primat de Pologne cardinal Hlond au pape Pie XII," Oct. 7, 1939, *Actes et Documents*, vol. 3*, p. 88, no. 21.

157. Congregation for the Causes of Saints, *Positio*, appendix 25, 273. The Hitler Youth were ordered to collect these copies and destroy them.

158. The *New York Times* even reported on the connection between the two documents when *Summi Pontificatus* was released. Passelecq and Suchecky, 88.

159. Missing also were sections on racism and anti-Semitism from that original paper that would be very offensive by today's standards. The draft paper said that Jews were responsible for their own fate because God chose them to make way for Christ's redemption, but they rejected him and killed Christ. "Blinded by their dream of worldly gain and material success," they deserved the "worldly and spiritual ruin" that came down upon them.

160. LaFarge wrote glowingly about *Summi Pontificatus* in *America* magazine, calling it "dangerous" because it obviously addressed the racism that was spreading across Europe. See Kevin M. Doyle, "The Moral Challenge of the Holocaust in 1998," *New Oxford Review*, July-August 1998, 20, 22. On the "Hidden Encyclical," see pp. 133-34.

161. C. Doyle, 9. For similar reasons, he did not have a single cup of coffee during the war. Gaspari, 26.

162. Smit, 195.

163. "The American Hierarchy" (*Sertum Laetitae*), Nov. 1, 1939, reprinted in *The Pope Speaks: The Words of Pius XII*, 198. See also Charles Rankin, "Pius the Man and His Efforts for Peace," in *The Pope Speaks: The Words of Pius XII*, 87. On Nov. 13, he broadcast a radio message to the Catholic University of America, in which he spoke of the "disconcerting errors of Naturalism and Materialism which, in precipitating the world into an appalling war, give cruel proof of the falsity of a philosophy based on essentially human values." Broadcast to the Catholic University of America, Nov. 13, 1939, reprinted in *The Pope Speaks: The Words of Pius XII*, 216.

164. Holmes, 154.

165. "Cardinal MacRory to Cardinal Maglione," May 19, 1940, *Actes et Documents*, vol. 4, p. 306, no. 201.

166. Holmes, 154. The documents show the emigrants to be Catholic, but testimony and documents make it clear that these were Jews holding false baptismal certificates provided by the Catholic Church. See documents collected on *www.PTWF.org*.

167. Graham, 20.

168. Holmes, 150-51.

169. See "Le cardinal Maglione au ministre de Grande Bretagne Osborne," Oct. 11, 1941, *Actes et Documents*, vol. 8, p. 305, no. 169 (message from Maglione to Osborne regarding distribution of provisions in Greece); "Le nonce à Berlin Orsenigo au cardinal Maglione," Nov. 12, 1941, *Actes et Documents*, vol. 8, p. 347, no. 200 (similar message from Orsenigo to Maglione).

170. Holmes, 150-51. In August 1943, the British government refused the Vatican's request for permission to pass into areas occupied by the Axis powers. The British informed the Vatican that "so long as the Germans have no hope of obtaining supplies through the blockade they are obliged in their own interest to maintain a minimum standard of nourishment from the resources at their disposal in order to prevent the economic collapse of the occupied countries." Ibid., 163-64. The following year, Pius asked for assistance from the Allies in feeding the Roman population, but the Allies took the position that this was the responsibility of the Germans. See "Le délégué apostolique à Washington Cicognani au cardinal Maglione," June 3, 1944, *Actes et Documents*, vol. 10, p. 301, no. 220.

171. Bokenkotter, 373.

172. Smit, 240.

173. Even later in the war, it was clear to many German leaders that peace would only be possible without Hitler. Weizsäcker, 285.

174. "Probably the most feasible plot to depose Hitler during the war." Cornwell (1999), 234.

175. *American Intelligence and the German Resistance to Hitler: A Documentary History* (Jürgen Heideking, ed., Westview Press, 1996), document 65. See Kurzman, 70 ("The military conspirators against Hitler needed the pope to verbally exchange secret information with the British government....")

176. Day, 24. Pius actually preferred the term *impartiality* to *neutrality*. He felt that neutrality implied passive indifference, while impartiality meant judging events according to the truth and justice. "Letter of Pius XII to Cardinal Faulhaber," Jan. 31, 1943, *Actes et Documents*, vol. 2, p. 293, no. 96. See Conway, "The Vatican, Germany and the Holocaust," in *Papal Diplomacy in the Modern Age*, 111-12; Paci, 39.

177. Brown, 181; Alvarez and Graham, 24. The leaders might have been concerned that selection of a Protestant to broker the agreement would be seen as an attempt to advance their religion. Deutsch, 108. He also had a better cover story. Müller had previously carried out various assignments for the Vatican. Ibid., 113. Müller also had met Pius in 1922. Testimony of Dr. Giuseppe Müller, Jan. 24, 1972, 1969, before the Ecclesiastical Tribunal of the Vicariate of Munich, on the beatification of Pius XII (Eugenio Pacelli), Part II, p. 752.

178. Alvarez and Graham, 25; Day, 24. It was reported to Nazi authorities that Müller went to the Vatican to collect information for German intelligence from his sources in the Vatican. Deutsch, 126. In 1941, Müller let Pius know that the Nazis had learned how to decode Vatican messages. Testimony of Dr. Giuseppe Müller, Jan. 24, 1972, 1969, before the Ecclesiastical Tribunal of the Vicariate of Munich, on the beatification of Pius XII (Eugenio Pacelli), Part II, p. 756. Later in the war, another member of German intelligence, Paul Franken, would keep Pius informed on anti-Hitler activity inside of Germany. Alvarez and Graham, 35-36.

179. Leiber was one of Pius XII's closest advisers, and he was known as a strong opponent of the Nazis. Sereny, 61. See also *American Intelligence and the German Resistance to Hitler: A Documentary History* (Westview: Boulder, Colorado, Heideking, Frey, and Mauch, eds., 1996), document 65 (report on the O.S.S. confidential interview with Father Leiber after the liberation of Rome, on Aug. 18, 1944, discussing coordination between the Vatican and the German resistance).

180. Alvarez, 174, 186; Brown, 181-82; Alvarez and Graham, 25; Deutsch, 114. At the Pontiff's request, he did not meet personally with Müller during the war. Deutsch, 122.

181. In 1945, Fabian von Schlabrendorff, a Protestant member of the German resistance, wrote a memorandum to U.S. General William ("Wild Bill") Donovan, in which Schlabrendorff reported that Müller "had orders from the Catholic Church to negotiate with representatives of the Protestant Church in order to harmonize their measures in the struggle against Hitler." Memorandum to General Donovan from Fabian von Schlabrendorff. See also Schlabrendorff, *The Secret War Against Hitler*. As such, Pius became linked to work of noted Protestant resistance leader Dietrich Bonhoeffer, who eventually joined a conspiracy to assassinate Hitler. Bonhoeffer contacted the Allies to seek terms of surrender should the assassination attempt succeed. He also worked on a plan to smuggle Jews out of Germany. Bonhoeffer's close friend and co-resister Eberhard Bethge wrote to him of having had an audience with the Pope. He reported that the Pope looked "older than I expected from the pictures," and added that he (Bethge) "wasn't able to make any more visits." *Dietrich Bonhoeffer: Letters and Papers from Prison*, 214 (Eberhard Bethge, ed., Collier Books, New York, enlarged ed., 1971). In a collection of letters, Bethge explained that this oblique reference related to meetings with Pope Pius XII's close assistants Father Robert Leiber and Monsignor Johannes Schönhöffer "who had been let in on the conspiracy." Ibid., 267, n. 152. This important evidence of contact between Pius XII and the resistance may have been missed by previous researchers because the letter refers only to "the Pope," not to Pope Pius XII, and the index of names misidentifies the Pope in question as Pius XI. Ibid., 428.

182. Alvarez, 175; Brown, 181.

183. Dr. Josef Müller, Affidavit to the Delegate Judge in the Beatification Process of Pope Pius XII, Munich, March 27, 1972, p. 2. See also Michael Hesemann, *High Treason: Pius XII, Stauffenberg and the Conspiracy against Hitler* (Düsseldorf/Germany, 2009).

184. Deutsch, 120; Alvarez and Graham, 27; Thomas J. Craughwell, "Pius Defenders," *Latin Mass*, Winter 1998, 36, 39.

185. Secret memorandum from the British Legation to the Holy See, Jan. 12, 1940, British Foreign Office Document no. FO 371/24405; Secret message from the British Legation to the Holy See, Jan. 12, 1940, British Public Records Office F.O. 800/318; Personal and Confidential Message from the British Legation to the Holy See, Feb. 7, 1940, British Public Records Office, FO 371/24405; Personal and Confidential Message from the British Legation to the Holy See, Feb. 19, 1940, British Public Records Office, FO 371/24405. The first visit took place in September or October 1939. Deutsch, 119.

186. Secret message from the British Legation to the Holy See, Jan. 12, 1940, British Public Records Office, FO 800/318 (reporting on a planned German offensive); Personal and Confidential Message from the British Legation to the Holy See, Feb. 7, 1940, British Public Records Office, FO 371/24405 (reporting on the planned attack on Belgium and future plans for an invasion of France).

187. Lapomarda 240, n. 36 (quoting Owen Chadwick, *Britain and the Vatican During the Second World War*, Cambridge University Press (Cambridge, 1987), 91. Pius begged the British diplomats to keep these

matters "absolutely secret," lest the German generals have their lives put at risk. Secret memorandum from the British Legation to the Holy See, Jan. 12, 1940, British Foreign Office Document no. FO 371/24405.

188. Josef Müller, *Bis zur letzten Konsequenz*, 16 (Munich 1967). Müller was eventually imprisoned by the Nazis, kept in chains, and "forced to eat his food like a dog, from a plate on the stone floor of his prison cell, with his hands tied behind his back." *They Almost Killed Hitler*, 5.

189. Josef Müller, *Bis zur letzten Konsequenz*, 141 (Munich 1967).

190. The declassified Nazi document, the Kaltenbrunner Report to Adolf Hitler of Nov. 29, 1944, on the background of the July 20, 1944, plot, is available at Pave the Way Foundation: *http://www.PTWF.org*.

191. Ibid.

192. Secret memorandum from the British Legation to the Holy See, Jan. 12, 1940, British Foreign Office Document, FO 371/24405.

193. Lapide, 119-20.

194. Secret memorandum from the British Legation to the Holy See, Jan. 12, 1940, British Foreign Office Document, FO 371/24405. See also Personal and Confidential Message from the British Legation to the Holy See, Feb. 7, 1940, British Public Records Office, FO 371/24405.

195. Secret memorandum from the British Legation to the Holy See, Jan. 12, 1940, British Foreign Office Document, FO 371/24405 (Pius did not endorse or recommend the plan, but his conscience "would not be quiet easy" unless he sent it on). See also Personal and Confidential Message from the British Legation to the Holy See, Feb. 7, 1940, British Public Records Office, FO 371/24405.

196. Shirer (1962), 914. Even some of Pope Pius XII's closest advisers thought that "the Pope had gone much too far" and took a foolhardy risk by joining with forces in opposition to the Nazis. Deutsch, 121. Pius was likely encouraged to become involved in this attempt because both Prime Minister Chamberlain and Lord Halifax had assured him that Britain would welcome his cooperation in any peace efforts. Ibid.

197. Secret message from the British Legation to the Holy See, Jan. 12, 1940, British Public Records Office, FO 800/318.

198. Secret Message from Halifax to Osborne, Feb. 17, 1940, British Public Records Office, FO 371/24405. See Woodward, 191. In November 1939, two British intelligence officers were lured to the Dutch frontier by Nazi officers posing as conspirators. They were captured by the S.S. and dragged into Germany. Deutsch, 136. This set negotiations back and caused the British to demand assurances from the Pope. Fortunately, due to the "trust and admiration" that British representatives to the Vatican had for him, Pius was able to reassure British leaders and put the plan back in place. Ibid., 137.

199. Woodward, 189 (citing British Foreign Office documents).

200. Personal and Confidential Message from the British Legation to the Holy See, Feb. 7, 1940, British Public Records Office, FO 371/24405.

201. Ibid.

202. A note from King George reflects that he was approached with this proposal on January 26, 1940. Handwritten note, Feb. 2, 1940, British Public Records Office, FO 371/24405.

203. Deutsch, 103.

204. See Memorandum of February 15, 1940, British Public Records Office FO 371/24405 (discussing a counterproposal).

205. "It was the fear of the generals that immobilized the opposition's revolt." Day, 25.

206. Ibid., 26.

207. Day, 25.

208. Robert McClory, "Tunnel Visions," *In These Times*, Dec. 12, 1999, 40.

209. Kurzman, 6 (arguing that Pius hated Mussolini and the hatred "ran deep").

210. Robert A. Graham, "Foreign Intelligence and the Vatican," *Catholic World Report*, March 1992, 48, 51.

211. Robert McClory, "Tunnel Visions," *In These Times*, Dec. 12, 1999, 40.

212. Robert A. Graham, "Foreign Intelligence and the Vatican," *Catholic World Report*, March 1992, 48, 51.

213. After months of investigation the Gestapo acted. Numerous conspirators were arrested, and most were executed. Müller was one of the few conspirators to avoid execution, even though he was arrested. Brown, 797-98. He endured 200 interrogations in Nazi prisons and concentration camps, but he did not betray the trust of his co-conspirators. This earned him the grudging admiration of his tormentors, who reported that he was "an unusually adroit man of the Jesuit school." Deutsch, 114. Reinhard Heydrich's personal conviction was that Müller was actually a Jesuit priest in disguise. Ibid., 114, n. 32. After the war, Pius held an audience with Müller. The Pontiff gave thanks for Müller's survival, and reminded him: "We have contended with diabolical forces." Thomas J. Craughwell, "Pius Defenders," *Latin Mass*, Winter 1998, 36, 39.

214. This and the official greeting announcing his coronation are the only two messages Pius ever sent to Hitler. Both were sent in 1939.

215. Sigmund von Braun, a postwar German ambassador to the Vatican, also speculated that Pius probably would have liked to see an assassination attempt succeed.

216. Toland, 687.

217. Letter from President Roosevelt to His Holiness, Dec. 23, 1939, in *Wartime Correspondence*, 17, 19 (letter in which Roosevelt calls Pius "a good friend and an old friend").

218. Appointment by President Roosevelt of Myron C. Taylor as the President's Personal Representative to Pope Pius XII, in *Foreign Relations of the United States, Diplomatic Papers, 1939, vol. II* (General, The British Commonwealth and Europe), United States Government Printing Office (Washington, 1956), 869; Letter from President Roosevelt to His Holiness, Dec. 23, 1939, in *Wartime Correspondence*, 17.

219. The designation "personal representative" meant that this was something less than formal diplomatic relations. As such, Taylor's office was established in his apartment in Rome, not inside the Vatican. When, however, Italy declared war on the United States, the office was moved into Vatican City. *Wartime Correspondence*, 6.

220. Morgan, 189-90 (also noting that Taylor had health problems at the time of the appointment).

221. Letter from President Roosevelt to His Holiness, Dec. 23, 1939, in *Wartime Correspondence*, 17, 19. Roosevelt, in internal documents, had also expressed his "personal belief that there will be, in all probability, more Christian refugees than Jewish refugees," and asked whether "the Vatican itself may not desire to take an active interest in helping the Catholic refugees to find homes in wholly new surroundings." Memorandum by President Roosevelt to the Secretary of State, Oct. 2, 1939, in *Foreign Relations of the United States, Diplomatic Papers, 1939*, vol. II (General, The British Commonwealth and Europe), 870, United States Government Printing Office (Washington, 1956).

222. Reply of His Holiness to President Roosevelt, Jan. 7, 1940, in *Wartime Correspondence*, 23.

223. Telegram from the Ambassador in Italy (Phillips) to the Secretary of State, Dec. 24, 1939, in *Foreign Relations of the United States, Diplomatic Papers, 1939, vol. II (General, The British Commonwealth and Europe)*, United States Government Printing Office (Washington, 1956), 874.

224. The Jewish press agreed. Upon Taylor's appointment, the *Jewish Advocate* editorialized:

> The agitation in some Protestant circles to have Myron Taylor recalled from the Vatican is to be deplored.... We can't see any possible infringement on the constitutional guarantees for separation of church and state in this matter; to the contrary we regard it as a personal effort on the part of the President to keep informed on the European situation, to exchange opinions with others who seek peace, and to explore the roads ahead for restoration of a sane world.

Gannon, 168 (quoting the *Jewish Advocate,* April 26, 1940).

225. When Taylor was absent, Harold Tittmann took his place. Morgan, 202. Tittmann was ordered off of Italian territory when the U.S. joined the war. At that time, he and his family moved into the Vatican. Ibid. See generally *Inside the Vatican of Pius XII*.

226. O'Connell, 60; "A Vatican Visit," *London Times*, Oct. 1, 1942 (reporting on a rumor that Taylor was trying to get Pius to serve as a mediator for a possible peace settlement). Count Ciano recorded in his diary on Oct. 26, 1942:

> The Duce was irritated with Myron Taylor and with the Vatican. He attributes to the reports of the American envoy the heavy bombardments of our northern Italian cities. "This buffoon," he said, "went back to America to report that the Italians are on their last legs, and that with one or two hard blows they can easily be beaten." Anyway, "he learned those things from the Holy See, where information comes by way of parish priests. But," says the Duce, "there they don't see that the people who follow the priests are the least courageous, and the worst, always ready to weep and beg." In any case, he wanted me to let the Vatican know that "concordat or no concordat, if Myron Taylor tries to return to Italy he will be put in handcuffs."

*The Ciano Diaries*, 534.

227. *Wartime Correspondence*, xiii.

228. "The Five Point Peace Plan," Christmas Eve, 1939, reprinted in *The Pope Speaks: The Words of Pius XII*, 224. See also *The Goebbels Diaries 1939-1941*, 75. The *Jewish Chronicle* (London) later (March 14, 1940) reported that the Pope's conditions for peace, especially for protection of racial minorities, were a "welcome feature," and it praised him for supporting the "rights of the common man."

229. *The Goebbels Diaries 1939-1941*, 75.

## Chapter Ten: 1940 and the Nazis Press On

1. On the day after his election, Pius XII turned to Vatican Radio to issue his first message to the world. It was a tribute to his predecessor, an expression of compassion for all, and a prayer for peace. "The First Message of Pope Pius XII (*Dum Gravissimum*)," March 3, 1939, in *The Pope Speaks: The Words of Pius XII*, 123.

2. Alvarez and Graham, 142; *Palazzo Pio*, Vatican Radio's production headquarters since 1970, is named after Pope Pius XII; "Catholic Historian's Report Details Perils of 'Martyrs of Vatican Radio,'" *National Catholic Register*, Feb. 1, 1976.

3. Cianfarra, 256.

4. "Notes de Mgr. Montini," Jan. 19, 1940. *Actes et Documents,* vol. 3, p. 24, no. 102 (Montini's notes on Pius XII's directives for Vatican Radio).

5. Quoted in *Great Untold Stories of World War II,* 84. See also Wright, 1930; Charles Rankin, "Pius the Man and His Efforts for Peace," in *The Pope Speaks: The Words of Pius XII,* 93.

6. *New York Times,* Jan. 25, 1940, p. 4.

7. Wright, 1930.

8. Marilyn J. Matelski, *Messages From the Underground,* 6 (Praeger: Westport, 1997). See also Marilyn J. Matelski, *Vatican Radio: Propagation by the Airwaves* (Praeger: Westport, 1995).

9. "Rome and Detroit," *American Israelite,* March 14, 1940.

10. "Notes de Mgr. Tardini," June 13, 1941, *Actes et Documents,* vol. 4, p. 548, no. 401; "Notes de Mgr. Tardini," Nov. 2, 1940, *Actes et Documents,* vol. 4, p. 216, no. 140; "Notes de Mgr. Tardini," May 26, 1941, *Actes et Documents,* vol. 4, p. 514, no. 374. This was in keeping with the Pope's official instruction at the beginning of the war that Vatican Radio would be an independent, autonomous entity and not an organ of the Holy See. "Catholic Historian's Report Details Perils of 'Martyrs of Vatican Radio,'" *National Catholic Register,* Feb. 1, 1976 (citing Robert Graham). This may have contributed to the Gestapo's particular hostility toward the Jesuits. See Coady, 167, 170-71.

11. See Robert Graham, "La Radio Vaticana tra Londra e Berlino: Un dossier della guerra delle onde: 1940-1941," in 1 *La Civiltà Cattolica,* 132 (1976); "Notes de Mgr. Tardini," Jan. 19, 1940, *Actes et Documents,* vol. 3, p. 24, no. 102 (Montini's notes on Pius XII's directives for Vatican Radio). "Catholic Historian's Report Details Perils of 'Martyrs of Vatican Radio,'" *National Catholic Register,* Feb. 1, 1976 (citing a directive dated Jan. 19, 1940, from the Pope ordering German-language broadcasts on the state of the Church in Poland).

12. *La Civiltà Cattolica,* Jan. 17, 1976. "Notes de Mgr. Montini," Jan. 19, 1940, *Actes et Documents,* vol. 3, p. 204, no. 102 (Montini's notes on Pius XII's directives for Vatican Radio). *Pope Pius and Poland,* published by The America Press (New York) in 1942, covers Pius XII's many and explicit condemnations of Nazi atrocities in the first years of the conflict. It provides precise titles and dates of broadcasts and summarizes Vatican Radio's anti-Nazi broadcasts of Jan, 13, 20, 27, April 25, Dec, 20, 1940; and March 28 and April 4, 1941.

13. "Catholic Historian's Report Details Perils of 'Martyrs of Vatican Radio,'" *National Catholic Register,* Feb. 1, 1976.

14. Telegram from the Ambassador in Italy (Phillips) to the Secretary of State, dated Feb. 28, 1940, in *United States Department of State, Foreign Relations of the United States, Diplomatic Papers, 1940, vol. I (General),* United States Government Printing Office (Washington, 1959), 126 (discussing the security of France and England, the mood in Germany and in the German military, Germany's resources in the event of a long war, and Italy's attitude toward war).

15. Alvarez and Graham, 143. See, e.g., "Notes de Mgr. Tardini," Nov. 2, 1940, *Actes et Documents,* vol. 4, p. 216, no. 140.

16. Cornwell (1999), 227.

17. See "Le cardinal Maglione au nonce à Berlin Orsenigo," June 16, 1940, *Actes et Documents,* vol. 3*, p. 255, no. 152 (with enclosure).

18. *Great Untold Stories of World War II,* 85.

19. *Inside the Vatican of Pius XII,* 112.

20. Ibid.

21. "Vatican Radio Denounces Nazi Acts in Poland," *Jewish Advocate* (Boston, Mass.), Jan. 26, 1940.

22. *Jewish Ledger* (Hartford, CT), on Jan. 19, 1940.

23. Daniel Goldhagen, "What Would Jesus Have Done?" *New Republic,* Jan. 21, 2002.

24. "Vatican Radio Denounces Nazi Acts in Poland," *Jewish Advocate* (Boston), Jan. 29, 1940, 1. The entire text of the broadcast of Jan. 21-22, 1940, can be found in *The Persecution of the Catholic Church in German-Occupied Poland,* 115-17. The story was also reported in the Jan. 23 edition of the *New York Times,* under the headline: "Vatican Denounces Atrocities in Poland; Germans Called Even Worse than Russians." A separate story in that same edition of the *Times* reported that a Soviet newspaper had labeled Pius the "tool of Great Britain and France." (At that time, the Soviets were still on better terms with the Germans than with the Allies.)

25. "Vatican Radio Denounces Nazi Acts in Poland," *Jewish Advocate* (Boston), Jan. 29, 1940, 1; Sánchez (2002), 374; Gilbert (1987), 40; Charles Rankin, "Pius the Man and His Efforts for Peace," in *The Pope Speaks: The Words of Pius XII,* 94-95.

26. See Rychlak, *Righteous Gentiles,* 116.

27. Holmes, 129. Similar broadcasts were directed at other nations. Alvarez and Graham, 142 (discussing France).

28. "Vatican Censures Nazis; Broadcast Charges Catholics in Poland Are Oppressed," Nov. 12, 1940.

29. Speaight, 25. The broadcast said that "with violence and with singular ability, this literature has attacked Christianity and the Catholic Church both as a whole and in its personnel and institutions. It has even attacked the most essential dogmas of the Church. This attack has been carried out with the great-

est possible efficiency, while the Church has been hindered from the self-defense it should properly have employed." It continued: "If National Socialism is a Christian movement as *Alcazar* alleges, what is the explanation of the fact that, whereas in 1933 almost the entire Catholic youth was educated in Catholic schools, the whole magnificent school organization is now practically non-existent?" The broadcast concluded with a broad hint to the Spanish Catholics: "There is not in Poland the flourishing religious life the writer of this report would have us believe. Rather the Catholics of Poland have grave need of the Catholics of the whole world to sustain them in their trial." Cianfarra, 256-57.

30. Cianfarra, 256-57.

31. Speaight, 25.

32. *New York Times*, Nov. 20, 1940.

33. See "Notes de Mgr. Tardini," Oct. 20, 1940, *Actes et Documents*, vol. 3\*, p. 315, no. 215; "Le cardinal Maglione au nonce à Berlin Orsenigo," Oct. 23, 1940, *Actes et Documents*, vol. 3\*, p. 316, no. 216; Blet, 98-100 (going into detail regarding the broadcasts and dispute of October 1940).

34. Speaight, 26.

35. "Notes de Mgr. Tardini," Nov. 2, 1940, *Actes et Documents*, vol. 4, p. 216, no. 140.

36. Quoted from a transcript of a Vatican Radio broadcast, in *Tablet* (of London), April 5, 1941, 264.

37. *Great Untold Stories of World War II*, 80. See generally *The Pius War*, 268-270.

38. These pamphlets were published from 1940 until late 1942, with a suspension in publication between May and September 1941. See René Bédarida, "La Voix du Vatican, 1940-1942, Bataille des ondes et résistance spirituelle," in *Revue d'histoire de l'Eglise de France*, vol. 64 (July-December 1978), pp. 215-243. The pamphlets have been hard to find, because only a limited number of each issue was printed (800-900 at first, later about 1,500) and few people kept them due to fear of persecution. It is possible, however, to obtain photocopies of the original publication.

39. Mistiaen had close connections with high members of Pope Pius XII's staff. See Lapomarda, 242. See also Chadwick, *Weizsäcker, the Vatican*, 141-42.

40. See *Actes et Documents*, vol. 4, pp. 18-29 (essay on the radio war).

41. *Ciano's Diplomatic Papers*, 349.

42. "Message to the Cardinal Archbishop of Breslau," March 17, 1940, *Actes et Documents*, vol. 2, p. 131, no. 42.

43. Charles Rankin, "Pius the Man and His Efforts for Peace," in *The Pope Speaks: The Words of Pius XII*, 101.

44. "Message to the Cardinal Archbishop of Breslau," March 17, 1940, *Actes et Documents*, vol. 2, p. 131, no. 42.

> That the two men [Hitler and Mussolini] who had allied themselves with the Bolshevists and had tried all they knew to break the power of the Christian Church in the lands they control, should try to enlist the help of the Pope (whose own followers had so heavily suffered) on a plan which would get the German leaders out of their difficulty, was clearly monstrous.

Charles Rankin, "Pius the Man and His Efforts for Peace," in *The Pope Speaks: The Words of Pius XII*, 102.

45. "Pope Is Emphatic About Just Peace; His Stress on Indispensable Basis for End of Hostilities Held Warning For Reich; Jews' Rights Defended; Pontiff in von Ribbentrop Talk Spoke on Behalf of Persecuted in Germany and Poland," *New York Times*, March 14, 1940. See also Charles Rankin, "Pius the Man and His Efforts for Peace," in *The Pope Speaks: The Words of Pius XII*, 100 (the Pope sought assurances related "not only to the German Catholics, but also to non-Catholics who had been ill-treated in Poland").

46. Charles Rankin, "Pius the Man and His Efforts for Peace," in *The Pope Speaks: The Words of Pius XII*, 100.

47. Following the undersecretary's meeting with Pius, he met with Cardinal Maglione, the cardinal secretary of state. Cardinal Maglione hinted that he was aware of a plan to topple Hitler from within Germany, and he asked Welles whether he knew anything of the plan. Welles essentially declined to answer. Memorandum from Undersecretary of State Sumner Welles, dated March 18, 1940, in *United States Department of State, Foreign Relations of the United States, Diplomatic Papers, 1940, vol. I (General)*, United States Government Printing Office (Washington, 1959), 108 (reporting, contrary to many other accounts, that Ribbentrop "had been exceedingly quiet and moderate in his manner").

48. Lapide, 185; Hatch and Walshe, 150-51; Charles Rankin, "Pius the Man and His Efforts for Peace," in *The Pope Speaks: The Words of Pius XII*, 101 (Ribbentrop reportedly had a nervous breakdown). See also Office of the United States Chief of Counsel, Supp. B, at 1238 (Ribbentrop's testimony as to his desire to obtain a new agreement with the Vatican but that "things didn't come off").

49. *Current Biography, 1941* (Maxine Block, ed., the H.W. Wilson Co., 1971 reissue), 673.

50. See John M. Oesterreicher, "As We Await 'The Deputy,'" *America*, Nov. 9, 1963, 570 (There were "Catholic bishops, priests and students who wore the 'Jewish star' to declare their fellowship with the persecuted.") King Christian may not have ever actually worn the yellow star. Some writers also say that he never even threatened to do so.

All legends to the contrary, King Christian X neither wore nor ever threatened to wear the Jewish star. Nor did he do anything memorable on behalf of the Danish Jews for the simple reason that such a thing was not necessary. No Jew in occupied Denmark was ever obliged to wear the Jewish star. A model satellite, of enormous economic importance to Germany, Denmark was always treated by the Nazis with great consideration.

Istvan Deak, *New York Review of Books*, March 23, 2000. For more information on the treatment of the Danes by the Nazis, see Palle Lauring, *A History of the Kingdom of Denmark*, 241-251 (D. Hohnen, trans., 1960) (explaining that King Christian X's "statement" was continuing the daily rides through town that he had taken prior to the occupation); Hans Kirchhoff's comments in Denmark, *The Holocaust Encyclopedia*, edited by Walter Laqueur (Yale University Press: New Haven, CT, 2000), 145-148.

51. Rousmaniere, 121.

52. Marchione (1997), 178.

53. Istvan Deak, "The Pope, the Nazis and the Jews," *New York Review of Books*, March 23, 2000. Eventually the Germans deported about five hundred Jews from Denmark. Fortunately, many others had escaped by that time. Those who were deported were for the most part sent to a "show" camp at Theresienstadt, where about 90 percent of them survived. Of course, those Jews displaced others who had been living at Theresienstadt. These others were sent on to death camps.

54. "Call to Prayer for the Restoration of Peace Among Nations," April 15, 1940, reprinted in *The Pope Speaks: The Words of Pius XII*, 254.

55. Testimony of Dr. Giuseppe Müller, Jan. 24, 1969, before the Ecclesiastical Tribunal of the Vicariate of Munich, on the beatification of Pius XII (Eugenio Pacelli), Part II, p. 755.

56. Gilbert (1981), 59; Deutsch, 338-39.

57. "Le cardinal Maglione au nonce à Bruxelles Micara et à l'internonce à La Haye Giobbe," May 3, 1940, *Actes et Documents*, vol. 1, p. 436, no. 293.

58. Blet, 94. Similar treatment was given to nuncios in the Balkan States after the Soviet invasion. Ibid.

59. "Le cardinal Maglione au nonce à Bruxelles Micara et à l'internonce à La Haye Giobbe," May 3, 1940, *Actes et Documents*, vol. 1, p. 436, no. 293.

60. See "Notes de Mgr. Tardini," May 9, 1940, *Actes et Documents*, vol. 1, p. 441, no. 298 (with attachment: Télégramme du Governement Français à son Ambassadeur près le Saint Siège); "Notes de la Secrétairerie d'Etat," May 10, 1940, *Actes et Documents*, vol. 1, p. 443 no. 299; "Notes du cardinal Maglione," May 14, 1940, *Actes et Documents*, vol. 1, p. 457 no. 316; "Le nonce à Paris Valeri au cardinal Maglione," May 15, 1940, *Actes et Documents*, vol. 1, p. 457 no. 317.

61. Rumor had it that some paratroopers were disguised as monks and nuns.

62. See Wright, 1930; Charles Rankin, "Pius the Man and His Efforts for Peace," in *The Pope Speaks: The Words of Pius XII*, 113.

63. "Messaggi del Santo Padre, ai Sovrani del Belgio, dell'Olanda e del Lussemburgo," *L'Osservatore Romano*, May 12, 1940.

64. Cianfarra, 226-27; Hatch and Walshe, 152; Charles Rankin, "Pius the Man and His Efforts for Peace," in *The Pope Speaks: The Words of Pius XII*, 114.

65. "Le pape Pie XII au roi des Belges Léopold," May 10, 1940, *Actes et Documents*, vol. 1, p. 444, no. 301.

66. Ibid., no. 302.

67. Charles Rankin, "Pius the Man and His Efforts for Peace," in *The Pope Speaks: The Words of Pius XII*, 113.

68. *The Ciano Diaries*, 248; see Special Distribution from Italy, British Public Records Office, FO 371/24935 60675 (May 30, 1940) (noting strained relations between the Holy See and Italy).

69. Hatch and Walshe, 152; Cornwell (1999), 241 (Mussolini called the Vatican the "chronic appendicitis of Italy.")

70. Holmes, 126. The Belgians needed little incitement beyond that which was provided by Nazi brutality. See Jan-Albert Goris, "Lest We Forget III: We Shall Come Back," *Reader's Digest*, January 1945, 69.

71. Telegram from Mr. Myron C. Taylor, Personal Representative of the President to Pope Pius XII, to President Roosevelt, dated May 17, 1940, in *Foreign Relations of the United States, Diplomatic Papers, 1940*, vol. II (General and Europe), 705, United States Government Printing Office (Washington, 1957).

72. "*Notes de Mgr. Montini*," May 13, 1940, *Actes et Documents*, vol. 1, p. 543, no. 313.

73. Ibid.

74. Ibid.

75. See Paci, 39.

76. "Rome and Detroit," *American Israelite*, March 14, 1940, 4.

77. Cianfarra, 226-27. *The Ciano Diaries*, 248; see Special Distribution from Italy, British Public Records Office, FO 371/24935 60675 (May 30, 1940) (noting strained relations between the Holy See and Italy).

78. Alvarez and Graham, 82.

79. Ibid.

80. Holmes, 126.

81. *The Ciano Diaries*, 248-49.

82. Ibid., 249.

83. Lubac 15, 20.

84. Ibid., 152-53, n. 11.

85. R. Price, 259.

86. Ibid., 255.

87. For an account of one priest who fully embraced Vichy, Monsignor Gabriel Piguet, see Sweets, 56-58.

88. R. Price, 255. Gerlier would later go on to defy the Nazis. See p. 171.

89. "Letter to the Church in France," July 31, 1940, reprinted in *The Pope Speaks: The Words of Pius XII*, 259.

90. Ibid.

91. Lubac, 97.

92. French Catholics may have been particularly willing to oppose the collaborationist aspects of the Vichy government. In the 1790s, between 118,000 and 250,000 Catholics were brutally murdered in Vendée, a region of about 12,000 square kilometers in western France. This was done under the color of state law by the new, post-revolutionary secular government. The stories are horrific — "unparalleled until the advent of Stalin and Hitler." Anne Barbeau Gardiner, "The Heart of Darkness: How Visceral Hatred of Catholicism Turns into Genocide," *New Oxford Review*, May 2004, 39. See Reynald Secher and George Holoch, *A French Genocide* (University of Notre Dame Press, 2003). Because this persecution evolved out of the victims' unwillingness to put the state ahead of their faith, Pope John Paul II beatified many of the victims (Father William Repin and 98 Companions, "the Martyrs of Avrillé") in 1984.

93. *Tablet* (London) Sept. 28, 1940, 252.

94. Michel Riquet, *Chrétiens de France dans l'Europe enchaînée*,98 (SOS: Paris, 1973); Lacouture, 387 (footnote).

95. *La Voix du Vatican* # 23, Vatican Radio broadcast of April 29, 1942. "Cardinal Hits New Order; Van Roey Calls on Belgians to Shun Credos Excluding Christ," *New York Times*, March 11, 1942. Similarly, on Oct. 15, 1942, Father Mistiaen again spoke on behalf of Jewish victims of the Nazis, saying: "All men are the children of the same Father.... They are no longer Jews, Greeks, gentiles, they are only candidates to the universal redemption brought by Jesus Christ." *La Voix du Vatican* # 30, Vatican Radio broadcast of Oct. 15, 1942.

96. See Lubac, 148.

97. Quoted in Leon Poliakov, "Pope Pius XII and the Nazis," *Jewish Frontier*, April 1964, reprinted in *The Storm Over The Deputy*, 222, 230. See also Sweets, 133-34.

98. "Barbarities by Nazis in Poland Denounced by Cardinal Hinsley," *Argus* (Melbourne), July 10, 1942.

99. Lubac, 161-62; Gilbert, *The Holocaust*, 355.

100. Lacouture, 387 (footnote).

101. Lubac, 161-62.

102. Holmes, 164-65. See also George Kent, "Shepherds of the Underground," *Christian Herald*, April 1945. Numerous other courageous statements from French bishops are set forth in Susan Zuccotti, "Pope Pius XII and the Holocaust: The Case in Italy," in *The Italian Refuge*, 257.

103. "Laval Spurns Pope — 25,000 Jews in France Arrested for Deportation," *Canadian Jewish Chronicle*, Sept. 4, 1942.

104. Lubac, 161-62 ("Our bishops were actively supported by the Holy See").

105. *Australian Jewish News*, April 16, 1943.

106. English excerpts as quoted by Lapide, 189-190. For excerpts from the original French text of Saliège's pastoral, see Jaques Duquesne, *Les Catholiques Français sous l'occupation*, 257 (Paris: 1966). For the general background of Saliège's protests, and those of the other French bishops, see Lubac, 157-64.

107. Lubac, 162.

108. *Osservatore della Domenica*, June 28, 1964, p. 28.

109. McCormick, 132 (from a *New York Times* dispatch of Dec. 26, 1945).

110. Holmes, 164.

111. "War News Summarized," *New York Times*, Aug. 6, 1942. This protest has been questioned by some writers, but it is confirmed in a telegram sent from the German ambassador to France. Ambassador Abetz in Paris to the Office of Foreign Affairs, dated Aug. 28, 1942, *Akten Zur Deutschen Auswärtigen Politik, 1918-1945*, Series E, Band III, Vandenhoeck and Ruprecht in Göttingen (1974), no. 242 (discussing a protest from the Nuncio regarding the treatment of the Jews, instructions from the Archbishop of Toulouse telling priests "to protest most vehemently from the pulpit against the deportation of the Jews" and discussing Laval's protest to the Vatican).

112. *New York Times*, Aug. 27, 1942.

113. British Public Records Office, Reference Number 320/81.

114. British Public Records Office, Reference Number 371 32680.

115. Wyman, 34; see "A Spiritual Ally," *California Jewish Voice*, Aug. 28, 1942; "Vichy Seizes Jews; Pope Pius Ignored," *New York Times*, Aug. 27, 1942; and "25,000 Jews Reported Held in South France For Deportation by the Nazis to the East," *New York Times*, August 28, 1942 (noting the Pope's support for appeals made to Vichy leaders by Catholic clergymen).

116. "Laval Spurns Pope — 25,000 Jews in France Arrested for Deportation," *Canadian Jewish Chronicle*, Sept. 4, 1942. See also "Vatican Gives Assurance of Aid to Jews," *California Jewish Voice*, Feb. 12, 1943; "Jewish Hostages in Rome: Vatican Protests," *Jewish Chronicle* (London), Oct. 29, 1943.

117. "Christendom and the Jews," *Jewish Chronicle* (London), Sept. 11, 1942. See Lothar Groppe, "The Church and the Jews in the Third Reich," *Fidelity*, November 1983, 25 (quoting parts of the editorial). See also "Plea for Rights of Mankind: French Archbishops Appeal for Jews," *Palestine Post*, Sept. 16, 1942; Pope Intercedes for French Jews, *The Argus* (Melbourne), Sept. 11, 1942 ("The Pope in a personal message to Pétain has approved of the initiative of French cardinal and bishops in favor of Jews, and has also requested Pétain's personal intervention to prevent continuation of the wave of horror.") "Vatican Condemns Vichy Anti-Jewish Measures: Priests Held for Quoting Warning," *Palestine Post*, Sept. 20, 1942 (quoting Vatican Radio's condemnation of the persecution of Jews in France); "Catholics Join in Protest," *Palestine Post*, Dec. 9, 1942 (Catholic day of prayer in Britain for treatment of Jews in Poland).

118. "*Les persécutions en France contre les Juifs: Une protestation du pape Pio XII*," *Geneva Tribune*, Sept. 8, 1942.

119. McCormick, 107 (dispatch of Sept. 26, 1942).

120. Sweets, 133. Catholic officials also protested governmental efforts to take over youth groups. Ibid., 59-60.

121. *La Voix du Vatican* # 28, Vatican Radio broadcast of Sept. 14, 1942.

122. *La Voix du Vatican* # 26, Vatican Radio broadcast of June 30, 1942.

123. See p. 493, n. 38.

124. Richard F. Crane, "Maritain's True Humanism," *First Things*, Feb. 2005, 17, 19.

125. Quoted in Ibid., 20.

126. Fogelman, 209. See also George Kent, "Shepherds of the Underground," *Christian Herald*, April 1945. For a discussion of how the children were returned to their families, see pp. 359-61.

127. Fogelman, 209.

128. Purdy, 256-57.

129. Lubac, 71-102; Purdy, 257 (suggesting that there may actually have been someone at the Vatican who made such a statement even though it certainly did not reflect the true opinion of the Vatican leadership).

130. Lubac, 71-102.

131. Ibid., 102.

132. A censorship order to the press said, "No mention is to be made of the Vatican protest to Marshal Pétain in favor of the Jews." Groppe, *The Church and the Jews*, 25.

133. "Vatican Scores Nazi Laws: Warned French Bias Against Jews Is Offense Against God," *New York Times*, June 27, 1943; Joseph L. Lichten, "A Question of Judgment: Pius XII and the Jews," in *Pius XII and the Holocaust: A Reader*, 114-15.

134. Stephen S. Wise, "Christendom and the Jews," *Jewish Chronicle* (London), Sept. 11, 1942; Wise, "As I See It" (reprinting the 1942 article).

135. Joseph L. Lichten, "A Question of Judgment: Pius XII and the Jews," in *Pius XII and the Holocaust: A Reader*, 114-15.

136. David S. Wyman, *The Abandonment of the Jews: America and the Holocaust 1941-1945*, Pantheon Books (New York, 1984).

137. Gilbert (1987), 333-50. According to one account, 162 French priests were arrested by the Gestapo, of whom 123 were shot or guillotined. Marchione (2000) (Vatican Documents).

138. Jesuit priests and their publications *Etudes* and *Témoignage Chrétien* were at the center of much of the French underground work. Lapomarda, 275-85.

139. Shirer (author's note).

140. Ibid., 159.

141. Father Christian was later captured by the Nazis and sentenced to death for his work with the underground. He, however, escaped with the help of British intelligence. Ibid., 312, 385. See Ronald J. Rychlak, "Father Christian and the Paris Underground," *Voices (Women for Faith and Family)*, Christmas-Epiphany 2005-2006; *Catholic Response*, January-February 2007, 33 (updated version).

142. The Vatican provided papers indicating Latin American citizenship to many Jews in occupied France. When the papers were discovered to be illegal, the Latin American countries withdrew recognition of them. This made the Jews subject to deportation to the concentration camps. Pursuant to a request from the Union of Orthodox Rabbis of the United States and Canada, and working in conjunction with the International Red Cross, the Vatican contacted the countries involved and urged them to recognize the documents, "no matter how illegally obtained." Graham, 23-24.

143. Blet, 200.

144. Joseph L. Lichten, "A Question of Judgment: Pius XII and the Jews," in *Pius XII and the Holocaust: A Reader*, 116-17.

145. Holmes, 152-53. For further cooperation between DELASEM and the Catholic Church, see Lapomarda, 233-34.

146. *Chronicle*, 576.

147. R. Price, 268. Laval was executed, Pétain was sentenced to death (the sentence was later commuted, and he was exiled), and a handful of other collaborators were imprisoned.

148. "Le général de Gaulle au pape Pie XII," May 29, 1944, *Actes et Documents*, vol. 11, p. 336, document 201.

149. Ibid.

150. Blet, 247-48 (quoting de Gaulle's *War Memories*).

151. "The minister did not want the dean of the diplomatic corps, who once had presented Marshal Pétain with the customary greetings in addresses required by protocol, to offer similar greetings to General de Gaulle." Ibid.

152. Ibid. The Vatican Ministry of State made innumerable requests to foreign governments for exit and entry papers during the occupation of France. Vatican funds were used to help procure transit visas from other nations. The cost for these rescue operations was enormous, totaling in the millions of dollars, and the primary source for this money was the Vatican.

153. Ibid.

154. Lubac, 98.

155. Pope Pius XII reported that "it was with deep satisfaction that We heard of M. De Gaulle's desire not to allow any interruption in the happy relations between France and the Holy See." "The Task of France," *Tablet* (London), May 19, 1945.

156. Fabert, 38-39. See Pope John XXIII (Angelo Giuseppe Roncalli), *Mission to France 1944-1953* (D. White, trans., 1966).

157. "Le pape Pie XII à Mussolini," April 24, 1940, *Actes et Documents*, vol. 1, p. 425, no. 284. See "La Secrétairerie d'Etat à l'ambassadeur Taylor," April 26, 1940, *Actes et Documents*, vol. 6, p. 296, no. 196. See Morgan, 194-96.

158. "Le pape Pie XII à Mussolini," April 24, 1940, *Actes et Documents*, vol. 1, p. 425, document 284.

159. See "Mussolini au pape Pie XII," April 30, 1940, *Actes et Documents*, vol. 1, p. 432, document 290; "Le nonce en Italie Borgongini Duca au cardinal Maglione," May 1, 1940, *Actes et Documents*, vol. 1, p. 433, document 291; "Notes du cardinal Maglione," May 2, 1940, *Actes et Documents*, vol. 1, p. 434, document 292. According to British documents from 1940, Pius reported that the Germans did not reply to him, and he no longer felt that there were favorable prospects for him to help bring about peace talks. Minutes of April 3, 1940, British Public Records Office, FO 371/24407 65042; Personal and Secret Message to the Secretary of State from Osborne, April 3, 1940, British Public Records Office, FO 371/24407 65042.

160. Blum, 719.

161. Hatch and Walshe, 153.

162. Blum, 719.

163. Morgan, 196-97.

164. *Saeculo Exeunte Octavo*, n. 39.

165. Cianfarra, 228, 242.

166. "Letter from His Holiness to President Roosevelt," May 18, 1943, *Wartime Correspondence*, 89-90; ibid., 91-92 (Roosevelt's reply, dated June 16, 1943).

167. "Le délégué apostolique à Londres Godfrey au cardinal Maglione," June 10, 1940, *Actes et Documents*, vol. 1, p. 485, no. 342; Blet, 47 (noting particularly Great Britain's reluctance to give assurances).

168. Graham, 16.

169. Joseph L. Lichten, "A Question of Judgment: Pius XII and the Jews," in *Pius XII and the Holocaust: A Reader*, 123-24.

170. "Reply of President Roosevelt to His Holiness," June 16, 1943, in *Wartime Correspondence*, 91-92.

171. Halecki and Murray, 182-83.

172. This diplomatic practice was done with the cooperation of Allied leaders. See *United States Department of State, Foreign Relations of the United States, Diplomatic Papers, 1944, vol. IV (Europe)*, United States Government Printing Office (Washington, 1966), 1318-1327 (various communications regarding movement of diplomats in and out of the Vatican). Following the war, the Vatican requested that German diplomats be treated with normal diplomatic immunity. Telegram from Mr. Myron C. Taylor, Personal Representative of President Roosevelt to Pope Pius XII, to the Secretary of State, June 8, 1945, in *United States Department of State, Foreign Relations of the United States, Diplomatic Papers, 1945, vol. III (European Advisory Commission; Austria; Germany)*, United States Government Printing Office (Washington, 1968), 787.

173. Cornwell (1999), 241 (noting that the paper's impact was magnified by the practice of priests reading it from the pulpit).

174. Cianfarra, 220, 227-28; Holmes, 127. See General Distribution from Italy, British Public Records Office, FO 371/24935 60675 (May 17, 1940) (vendors and purchasers beaten); Report from Osborne to London, British Public Records Office, FO 371/24935 60675 (May 21, 1940) (report on the ban on the sale of the Vatican newspaper); Special Distribution from Italy, Public Records Office, FO 371/24935 60675 (May 30, 1940) ("agreement has been reached on the circulation within Italy of the present emasculated Osservatore").

175. Cianfarra, 220-21 (quoting Roberto Farinacci, editor of *Regime Fascista*); Charles Rankin, "Pius the Man and His Efforts for Peace," in *The Pope Speaks: The Words of Pius XII*, 100 (the leading Fascist publication accused *L'Osservatore Romano* of "being in the pay of Jews and Freemasons").

176. Report from Osborne to London, British Public Records Office, FO 371/24935 60675 (May 21, 1940).

177. Some dispute does exist over the value of Vatican Radio broadcasts in Soviet-occupied areas. At least some people felt that broadcasts "had no effect other than to rile up the Soviet authorities against the church." Blet, 100.

178. Deutsch, 144. See pp. 153-55.

179. Secret message from the British Legation to the Holy See, Jan. 12, 1940, British Public Records Office, FO 800/318 (reporting on a planned German offensive); Personal and Confidential Message from the British Legation to the Holy See, Feb. 7, 1940, British Public Records Office, FO 371/24405 (reporting on the planned attack on Belgium and future plans for an invasion of France). One of Müller's reports concerned a speech Hitler made at the S.S. Ordensburg (youth leader training center) at Sonthofen, where he had screamed that he would crush the Catholic Church under his heel, as he would a toad. Deutsch, 110, n. 1.

180. See *The Persecution of the Catholic Church in the Third Reich*, 64.

181. Ibid., 62-63.

182. Ibid., 413.

183. Ibid.

184. O'Carroll, 55-56. The material was edited by W. Mariaux and published in 1940 by Burns and Oates under the title *The Persecution of the Catholic Church in the Third Reich*.

185. *The Goebbels Diaries 1942-1943*, 166 (the Pope "thereby gives expression to his enmity for the Axis").

186. Deighton, 256-57.

187. Lapide, 174.

188. Earlier that year, when it had become obvious that Hitler was considering a treaty with the Soviet Union, Mussolini wrote him a letter urging him against it. Payne, 376.

189. Reprinted in *The Persecution of the Catholic Church in German-Occupied Poland*, 121-23.

190. Ibid. See "Il discorso del Cancelliere Hitler," *L'Osservatore Romano*, Dec. 11, 1940; "Il discorso del Cancelliere Hitler," *L'Osservatore Romano*, Dec. 12, 1940; "Ispezione del Cancelliere Hitler sul fronte," *L'Osservatore Romano*, Dec. 28, 1940.

191. This issue also printed Albert Einstein's declaration:

> Only the Church stood squarely across the path of Hitler's campaign for suppressing truth. I had never any special interest in the Church before, but now I feel a great admiration because the Church alone has had the courage and persistence to stand for intellectual truth and moral freedom. I am forced thus to confess, that what I once despised, I now praise unreservedly.

"German Martyrs," *Time*, Dec. 23, 1940, 38.

192. Lubac, 34-35.

193. British diplomats certainly thought so. See Distribution B from Switzerland, Dec. 30, 1940, British Public Records Office, FO 371/30173 56879 (request from Osborne for permission to offer Pius "a personal message of appreciation").

194. "The Pope's Christmas Message," *New York Times*, Dec. 25, 1940, p. 26, col. 2. The editorial added, "If the Pope... had intended to condemn Hitler's system, he could not have done it more effectively than by describing the 'moral order.' "

195. Lubac, 35.

196. Lapide, 186; Robert Martin, "Spiritual Semites: Catholics and Jews During World War Two," *Catholic League Publications* (Milwaukee, 1983) (citing the diary of Emanuel Ringelbaum).

## Chapter Eleven: 1941 and New Enemies

1. "Message to the Bishop of Limburg (Antonius Hilfrich)," Feb. 20, 1941, *Actes et Documents*, vol. 2, p. 198, no. 65.

2. Pope Pius XII also sent President Roosevelt the following Easter greeting by means of telegram:

> We thank Your Excellency for the greetings which you have so kindly sent Us for Easter. In these festive days of joyful commemoration Our heart is particularly saddened by the thought of the massacre and widespread devastation which the present conflict is leaving in its wake. . . . We have found

unbounded sympathy and generous cooperation among Our beloved children of the United States. Not content with this We have felt and We feel it Our duty to raise Our voice, the voice of a Father not moved by any earthly interests but animated only by a desire for the common good of all, in a plea for a peace that will be genuine, just, honorable, and lasting; a peace that will respect individuals, families and nations and safeguard their rights to life, to a reasonable liberty, to a conscientious and fervent practice of religion, to true progress, and to an equitable participation in the riches which providence has distributed with largess over the earth; a peace whose spirit and provisions will tend to revitalize and reinvigorate through new and enlightened organization the true spirit of brotherhood among men today so tragically alienated one from another.

"Message from His Holiness to President Roosevelt," Easter-April 1941, *Wartime Correspondence*, 53.

3. Copeland, 525 (setting forth the entire speech); Smit, 227.

4. Copeland, 525.

5. Ibid.

6. The notes of German Legation Counselor Haidlen, dated Jan. 5, 1942, observed that both Germany and Russia were implied in the message. *Akten Zur Deutschen Auswärtigen Politik, 1919-1945,* Series E, vol. 1, Vandenhoeck and Ruprecht, Göttingen, 1960, no. 95. See also Blet, 119.

7. Vatican Radio explicitly condemned "the wickedness of Hitler" on March 30, 1941, and "the immoral principles of Nazism" on April 5, 1941. Joseph M. McGowan, "'Hitler's Pope' author drew flawed conclusions," *Pantagraph* (Bloomington, IL), Dec. 7, 1999, A10.

8. "Catholic Historian's Report Details Perils of 'Martyrs of Vatican Radio,'" *National Catholic Register*, Feb. 1, 1976 (citing Robert Graham).

9. Owen Chadwick, *Britain and the Vatican During the Second World War*, 147 (Cambridge University Press, Cambridge, 1988).

10. Holmes, 130.

11. Kurzman, 74.

12. Lubac, *Christian Resistance to Anti-Semitism*, 118-22.

13. *Figaro*, Jan. 4, 1964. See also "Letters to the Editor: Pope Pius XII: An Eyewitness," *Inside the Vatican*, January 2000, 10 (a former seminarian in Rome tells of papal orders to shelter Jewish victims and of reports given on Vatican Radio).

14. Lapide, 254.

15. Allied propaganda often contained misleading information about the Church, the Vatican, or the Pope. Alvarez and Graham, 14.

16. Ibid., 17. For a wartime account of British radio propaganda, see William D. Bayles, "England's Radio Blitz," *Saturday Night*, Jan. 29, 1944, reprinted in *Reader's Digest*, April 1944, 61.

17. Alvarez and Graham, 144.

18. Certain Polish bishops, exiled in London, called for stronger statements by the Pontiff. Those who remained in Poland, however, urged him not to speak. Paci, 41; Lamb, 48.

19. "Notes de Mgr. Tardini," Oct. 27, 1940, *Actes et Documents*, vol. 4, p. 205, no. 131.

20. "Mémorandum de la Légation britannique," June 10, 1941, *Actes et Documents*, vol. 4, p. 541, no. 396. See also "La Légation de Grande-Bretagne à la Sécrétairerie d'Etat," Nov. 14, 1940, *Actes et Documents*, vol. 4, p. 243, no. 165; "Notes de Mgr. Tardini," Nov. 16, 1940, *Actes et Documents*, vol. 4, p. 244, no. 166; "Le délégué apostolique à Londres Godfrey au cardinal Maglione," Nov. 16, 1940, *Actes et Documents*, vol. 4, p. 246, no. 167.

21. "Notes de Mgr. Tardini," June 13, 1941, *Actes et Documents*, vol. 4, p. 548, no. 401.

22. "Le cardinal Maglione aux nonces en France, à Berne, à Madrid, à Buenos Aires et à Rio de Janeiro et au délégué apostolique à Washington," Feb. 18, 1941, *Actes et Documents*, vol. 4, p. 389, no. 265.

23. Holmes, 128-29. See p. 192.

24. Hitler's proclamation justifying the action is reprinted in *A History of the Third Reich*, 125. His thoughts on the need for German living space are reprinted in Ibid., 26.

25. William J. O'Malley, "Priests of the Holocaust," reprinted in *Pius XII and the Holocaust: A Reader*, 153.

26. Gilbert (1987), 362.

27. Copeland, 516.

28. "Notes de Mgr. Tardini," Sept. 5, 1941, *Actes et Documents*, vol. 5, p. 182, no. 62. Internal German documents suggest that some German officials felt that Pius XII privately favored their side in the war with the Soviets. According to one 1941 report, Pius was about to condemn Nazi policies in Germany when the war with the Soviet Union broke out. The writer went on to speculate that Pius refrained from condemning Nazi policies so that he would not hurt the German cause in the war. *Documents on German Foreign Policy 1918-1945*, Series D (1937-1945), no. 309 (Secret message from Counsellor of Embassy Menshausen to State Secretary Weizsäcker, Sept. 12, 1941).

29. "Notes de Mgr. Tardini," Sept. 5, 1941, *Actes et Documents*, vol. 5, p. 182, no. 62. Later, Hitler wanted to back off from the "crusade" language, because it might mean that he would have to let churches into occupied areas, and he did not want to do that. Cornwell (1999), 261.

30. "Notes de Mgr. Tardini," Sept. 5, 1941, *Actes et Documents*, vol. 5, p. 182, no. 62.

31. Few priests actually ended up accompanying the German troops. Not only had the Pope opposed their mission, German leadership also opposed them. The Germans feared that the Church might try to use the invasion to gain entry and do missionary work. In July 1941, Reinhard Heydrich circulated a report that the Vatican had a long-term plan to proselytize Russia and encircle the Reich with hostile Catholic states. Hitler ordered that missionary activity was absolutely prohibited, and nonmilitary priests were barred from entering occupied areas to the east of Germany. Alvarez and Graham, 12-13, 124. Most of the priests who did accompany the invasion were shot and killed as deserters or spies. Cornwell (1999), 264.

32. "Notes de Mgr. Tardini," Sept. 27, 1941, *Actes et Documents*, vol. 5, p. 254, no. 105. See Report from Mr. Osborne, Sept. 29, 1941, British Public Records Office, FO 371/30175; see also British Public Records Office, INF 1/893 (pressure being put on the Vatican to declare the German invasion a crusade).

33. Minutes dated September 10, 1941, British Public Records Office, FO 371/30175 57750.

34. Gilbert (1987), 362. A year earlier, Cardinal Maglione, the Vatican secretary of state, was unable to disguise his aversion for the German government as he expressed the opinion that Communism would come to dominate Germany before too long. Memorandum from Undersecretary of State Sumner Welles, dated March 18, 1940, in *United States Department of State, Foreign Relations of the United States, Diplomatic Papers, 1940, vol. I (General)*, United States Government Printing Office (Washington, 1959), 108.

35. Gilbert (1987), 362. British leaders recognized the references to Poland and Germany. Minutes of June 28, 1941, FO 371/30175 57750.

36. Gilbert (1985), 362.

37. O'Carroll, 132.

38. Robert A. Graham, "A Return to Theocracy," *America*, July 18, 1964, 70.

39. "Notes de Mgr. Tardini," Sept. 27, 1941, *Actes et Documents*, vol. 5, p. 254, no. 105. The British leadership used the Vatican's refusal to support the "crusade" for propaganda, even to the extent that they acknowledged "causing the Vatican some embarrassment." Report from Mr. Osborne, Sept. 29, 1941, British Public Records Office, FO 371/30175; see also British Public Records Office, INF 1/893 (secret telegram dated Oct. 26, 1942, to the British War Cabinet reporting on pressure being put on the Vatican to declare the German invasion a crusade).

40. Kurzman, 59.

41. Ibid., 59 (quoting the diary of Alfred Rosenberg).

42. Carol Rittner and John K. Roth, "A Chronology About Pope Pius XII and the Holocaust," in *Pope Pius XII and the Holocaust*, 23.

43. "Le nonce à Berlin Orsenigo au cardinal Maglione," Nov. 12, 1941, *Actes et Documents*, vol. 5, p. 300, no. 139.

44. Carol Rittner and John K. Roth, "A Chronology About Pope Pius XII and the Holocaust," in *Pope Pius XII and the Holocaust*, 23.

45. *Chronicle*, 524. "The first line of Churchill's declaration of support for the Russian people broadcast on the night of 22 June 1941 began with the words: 'The Nazi regime is indistinguishable from the worst features of communism.'" Overy, 285. Likewise, President Roosevelt agreed that on the basic moral issues, Stalin's dictatorship was similar to Hitler's. "The first official statement following the outbreak of the German-Soviet war, approved by Roosevelt and broadcast on 23 June, made no distinction between Nazi Germany and Soviet Russia on the question of 'freedom to worship God.' Both states denied this 'fundamental right.' The atheistic principles of communism were 'as intolerable and alien' as the doctrines of Nazism." Ibid., 283.

46. The roots of the Atlantic Charter have been traced back to a peace proposal that Pius XII presented in an allocution to the cardinals on Christmas Eve 1939. Hatch and Walshe, 150.

47. Germany had several predominantly Catholic regions, and the area under Hitler's control was now overwhelmingly Catholic. Moreover, the German-allied countries of Italy, Slovenia, Slovakia, and Croatia were nearly entirely Catholic, and Hungary was primarily Catholic. This led to several minor disputes between the Reich and the Holy See regarding the application of the concordat (and therefore the rights of the Church) in occupied areas. *Documents on German Foreign Policy 1918-1945*, Series D (1937-1945), no. 241, 260 (memoranda concerning application of the concordat).

48. "If Socialism, like all errors, contains some truth (which, moreover, the Supreme Pontiffs have never denied), it is based nevertheless on a theory of human society peculiar to itself and irreconcilable with true Christianity. Religious socialism, Christian socialism, are contradictory terms; no one can be at the same time a good Catholic and a true Socialist" (Pope Pius XI, *Quadragesimo Anno* [1931]).

In addition, Pope Pius IX, in his 1846 *Syllabus Errorum*, referred to "that infamous doctrine of so-called Communism, which is absolutely contrary to the natural law itself, and if once adopted would utterly destroy the rights, property, and possessions of all men and even society itself." Similarly, Pope Leo XIII defined

Communism as "the fatal plague which insinuates itself into the very marrow of human society only to bring about its ruin." Leo XIII, *Quod apostolici muneris* (1878).

49. Memorandum from the Ambassador in Italy to the Foreign Ministry, Sept. 17, 1941, (Top Secret), enclosing "The Royal Italian Embassy to the Holy See, Subject: Taylor's Conversations at the Vatican, Rome, Sept. 16, 1941 (Secret)," in *Documents on German Foreign Policy 1918-1945*, Series D (1937-1945), no. 330 (Sept. 22, 1934).

50. Ibid.

51. Ibid.

52. Ibid.

53. President Roosevelt "was shocked by a poll of American Catholic clergy which revealed that 90 percent were opposed to US aid to Russia." Lamb, 47.

54. "Letter from President Roosevelt to His Holiness," Sept. 3, 1941, in *Wartime Correspondence*, 61-62. In reply, Pius wrote:

> We are endeavoring, with all the forces at Our disposal, to bring material and spiritual comfort to countless thousands who are numbered amongst the innocent and helpless victims. We should like, on this occasion, to express to Your Excellency Our cordial appreciation of the magnificent assistance which the American people have given, and continue to offer, in this mission of mercy.

Ibid., 63-64 (Reply of His Holiness to President Roosevelt, Sept. 20, 1941). The Holy See at this time was only aware of two Catholic churches that were open in all of the Soviet Union. "Notes du cardinal Maglione," Sept. 11, 1941, *Actes et Documents*, vol. 5, p. 199, no. 72.

55. "Le délégué apostolique à Washington Cicognani au cardinal Maglione," Sept. 4, 1941, *Actes et Documents*, vol. 5, p. 181, no. 60; "L'archevêque de New York Spellman au Pape Pie XII," Sept. 4, 1941, *Actes et Documents*, vol. 5, p. 181, no. 61.

56. "Notes du cardinal Maglione," Sept. 11, 1941, *Actes et Documents*, vol. 5, p. 199, no. 72.

57. Ibid. (noting Archbishop Mooney of Detroit's argument that American Catholics needed direction from Rome).

58. Ibid.

59. Ibid. See "Notes de Mgr. Tardini," Sept. 5, 1941, *Actes et Documents*, vol. 5, p. 185, no. 63 (Tardini's notes: "These Americans — who in reality are already in the war against the Axis… should comprehend that the Holy See is in a very difficult situation…. As for religious liberty in Russia, it is clear that so far it was the most that was trampled upon….").

60. "Mgr. Tardini au délégué apostolique à Washington Cicognani," Sept. 20, 1941, *Actes et Documents*, vol. 5, p. 240, no. 93.

61. Congregation for the Causes of Saints, *Positio*, appendix 25, 270.

62. Langer and Gleason, 796-97.

63. "The Politburo made moderate gestures to the Catholics: it praised the Vatican for condemning Nazi atrocities and freed several Catholic priests who were under arrest, some of whom later functioned as chaplains with Polish troops of the Polish regime in London. The Politburo also stressed freedom of religion in the USSR and did numerous small favors for Father Leopold Braun, a Catholic priest in Moscow, who declared that there was no antireligious persecution in Soviet Russia and urged the Vatican and the Kremlin to combine against the common enemy." Book Review, "The Catholic Church and the Soviet Government 1939-1949," by Dennis J. Dunn, in *Slavic Review*, vol. 38, no. 2. (June 1979), pp. 320-322.

The Allies suppressed information about Stalin's anti-religious actions because it did not fit with the current pro-Soviet propaganda. See Terkel, 113-120. For an example of how the American popular press reported on religion in the Soviet Union, see, "Up from the Russian Catacombs," *Time*, Dec. 27, 1943, reprinted in *Reader's Digest*, March 1944, 94; see also William Philip Simms, "Give Us Your Hand, Russia," *New York World-Telegram*, Nov. 6, 1945 ("Our pulpits and platforms welcome pro-Soviet propagandists."); Terkel, 113-120 (American woman questions pro-Soviet propaganda). See also Blet, 261 ("When *Collier's* magazine printed that about eighteen hundred Catholic churches remained open in Russia, it gave completely false information.") "Letter from President Roosevelt to His Holiness," Sept. 3, 1941, in *Wartime Correspondence*, 61-62.

64. Overy, 283 ("By 1943 the churches of Moscow were so crowded at Eastertime that the congregations spilled out into the surrounding streets… soldiers on leave began to use the churches in large numbers too.")

65. Allocution of Feb. 25, 1946, published in the *Acta Apostolicae Sedis*, vol. 38, p. 154. In his apostolic letter to the Russian people, *Sacro Vergente Anno* (July 7, 1952), Pius was equally explicit:

> Never at that time was heard from our lips a word that could have seemed to any of the belligerents to be unjust or harsh. We certainly reproached, as was our duty, every evil and every violation of rights; but we did this in such a way as to avoid with all care whatever might become, even unjustly, an occasion for greater affliction of the oppressed peoples. Then, when pressure was brought to bear upon us to give our approval in some way, either verbally or in writing, to the war undertaken against Russia in 1941 we never consented to do so.

66. "Bishop Speaks," *Time*, July 14, 1941. Perhaps most interesting was the bishop's view that the president had the sole authority to decide on issues of war and peace.

> It is up to him to safeguard the interests of the nation in times of great emergency.... He must be ready to act fast and decisively should the need arise.... The problem [of entering the war] should be left to the Commander in Chief who alone, in loyal communication with Congress and in consultation with his military and naval advisers, is capable of bringing us safely through....
>
> It is not the business of a churchman to call for war but neither may a churchman do anything other than encourage a government to protect... its sacred national interests.... I believe that our Government in this awful hour may with justice say to certain churchmen: "Render unto Caesar the things that are Caesar's!"

Ibid.

67. Ibid. ("The school may change its curriculum, but the same professors hold the chairs, for they are specialists in the universe of knowledge. Many Catholics are inclined to apologize for them; but I think that is unwise. They are embarrassing but not significant, and quite harmless as long as their tantrums do not lead them to break the furniture. They will disappear in time like those other exhibitionists — the marathon dancers and flagpole sitters — who amused America for a while and vanished.")

68. In 1941, when he was a senator, Truman described the ideal reaction of the still neutral America: "If we see Germany as winning, we ought to help Russia. And if we see Russia is winning, we ought to help Germany. And in that way, let them kill as many as possible." The *Chicago Tribune*, on Sept. 17 of that year, similarly wrote: "The Nazi-Communist War is the only one of the last century that civilized men can regard with complete approval. They hope it will persist until both brutal antagonists have bled to death." Langer and Gleason, 793.

69. Cheetham, 287. Giulio Andreotti, the former prime minister of Italy, said the Pope had to choose "between the Plague and Cholera."

70. Blet, 116.

71. See Winston S. Churclhill, *The Grand Alliance*, 379 (Boston: Houghton Mifflin, 1950).

72. According to the head of the Soviet Parliamentary Commission on Rehabilitation, from 1929 to 1953, 21.5 million people were "repressed." Of these a third were shot, the rest were imprisoned (where many of them died). These figures do not include famine victims and deported ethnic groups. If the victims of politically induced famines and deportations are counted, the total number of Soviet victims is far greater than the Nazi victims. When it comes to the deliberate mass murder of civilians, the Communists are the "blood-stained world champions." Paul Hollander, "Soviet terror, American amnesia: there has been a striking asymmetry between the American responses to the two great mass murders of our century, the Nazi and the Soviet. Why?" *National Review*, May 2, 1994.

73. See *The Foreign Office and the Famine: British Documents on Ukraine and the Great Famine of 1932-1933* (Marco Carynnyk, Lubomyr Luciuk, and Bohdan S. Kordan, eds.; Kingston: Limestone Press, 1988).

74. Holmes, 138.

75. Overy, 285.

76. Gascoigne, 290.

77. Cheetham, 287-88. In December 1941, Hitler disclosed his thoughts on this matter:

> The war will come to an end, and I shall see my last task as clearing up the Church problem. Only then will the German nation be completely safe.... In my youth I had the view: dynamite! Today I see that one cannot break it over one's knee. It has to be cut off like a gangrenous limb.

Cornwell (1999), 261.

78. Toland, 774.

79. Memorandum from the Ambassador in Italy to the Foreign Ministry, Sept. 17, 1941, (Top Secret), enclosing "The Royal Italian Embassy to the Holy See, Subject: Taylor's Conversations at the Vatican, Rome, Sept. 16, 1941 (Secret)," in *Documents on German Foreign Policy 1918-1945*, Series D (1937-1945), no. 330 (Sept. 22, 1934).

80. Deighton, 537.

81. The day that this statement was made, Dec. 8, the first Jews were gassed at Chelmno, Poland. Rousmaniere, 113.

82. Charles J. Gangi, "The Christmas Addresses of Pope Pius XII," *New Oxford Review*, December 2007.

83. Cianfarra, 319-29.

84. Hitler, of course, had pulled Germany out of the League of Nations.

85. "Notes of the Legation Counsellor Haidlen," Jan. 5, 1942, *Akten Zur Deutschen Auswärtigen Politik, 1918-1945*, Series E, Band I, Vandenhoeck and Ruprecht in Göttingen (1960), no. 95.

86. *The Ciano Diaries*, 424. Ciano added, "This is unavoidable, in view of the anti-Catholic policy of the Germans." He also reported that "at the Vatican the Russians are preferred to the Nazis." Ibid.

87. Quoted in Cianfarra, 319-29 (emphasis added).

## Chapter Twelve: 1942 and the Final Solution

1. Office of the United States Chief Counsel, vol. I, 279. Despite the tone of the rejection, the Vatican did express a desire to improve relations between the Holy See and Germany. Ibid., vol. V, 1009.

2. *Hitler's Secret Conversations*, 447.

3. *Chronicle*, 542.

4. "This was where the majority of European Jews lived and, therefore, such a Nazi crime could be better hidden from world public opinion in a country totally occupied and even partially annexed to the Third Reich." Polish Bishops, "The Victims of Nazi Ideology," January 1995, reprinted in Secretariat for Ecumenical and Interreligious Affairs, National Conference of Bishops, *Catholics Remember the Holocaust*, United States Catholic Conference (Washington, 1998).

5. Holmes, 128-29.

6. Minutes, July 21, 1941, British Public Records Office, INF 1/893. See pp. 182-83.

7. Holmes, 129.

8. Groppe, *The Church's Struggle*, 14; see Matheson, 93-94. The Holy See refused to recognize the annexed portion of Poland as part of Germany. Because of this, when it attempted to protest the treatment of people in this area, the Germans refused to recognize the Holy See's standing to voice objections. R. Stewart, 29.

9. Graham (1968), 18.

10. Ibid.

11. R. Stewart, 28.

12. This eventually led to the creation of a dissenting Protestant church. See pp. 99-101.

13. O'Carroll, 132.

14. Graham (1968), 20.

15. Ibid., 20.

16. Robert A. Graham, "Author Questions Pope Pius XII's Vatican Diplomacy," *Pilot* (Boston), Oct. 31, 1970, 1, 16.

17. *Maltreatment and Persecution of the Catholic Clergy in the Western Provinces*, Office of the United States Chief of Counsel, vol. I, 286. See also "A note of His Eminence the Cardinal Secretary of State to the Foreign Minister of the Reich about the religious situation in 'Warthegau' and in the other Polish provinces subject to Germany," March 2, 1943, in Office of the United States Chief of Counsel, vol. V, 1018.

18. Graham (1968), 22.

19. In the un-annexed part of German-occupied Poland (the General Government), the situation was not quite as severe, though religious persecution certainly existed. In Germany itself, where many Polish workers were sent, Poles were refused permission to enter churches that were conducting services intended for Germans, and they were not allowed to use the Polish language in confession. Graham (1968), 20-21.

20. Groppe, *The Church's Struggle*, 14 (citing Walter Adolph, *Im Schatten des Galgens* [Berlin, 1953]).

21. This was necessary because the bishop from Kulm had fled Poland (as had Cardinal Hlond).

22. Groppe, *The Church's Struggle*, 14 (citing Walter Adolph, *Im Schatten des Galgens* [Berlin, 1953]).

23. In protest of the treatment that the Polish Catholic Church suffered at the hands of the Nazis, the Vatican issued a memorandum on Oct. 8, 1942, to the German Embassy:

> For quite a long time the religious situation in the *Warthegau* gives cause for very grave and ever increasing anxiety. There, in fact, the Episcopate has been little by little almost completely eliminated; the secular and regular clergy have been reduced to proportions that are absolutely inadequate, because they have been in large part deported and exiled; the education of clerics has been forbidden; the Catholic education of youth is meeting with the greatest opposition; the nuns have been dispersed; insurmountable obstacles have been put in the way of affording people the help of religion; very many churches have been closed; Catholic intellectual and charitable institutions have been destroyed; ecclesiastical property has been seized.

Office of the United States Chief of Counsel, vol. I, 283; ibid., vol. V, 1017. This and similar protests sent by Catholic officials failed to bring any relief. In fact, they tended to make things worse.

24. See Lukas, *Forgotten Holocaust*, 13-15.

25. William J. O'Malley, "The Priests of Dachau," reprinted in *Pius XII and the Holocaust: A Reader*, 143. See also Lenz, *Christ in Dachau*.

26. Pius mentioned this and other sufferings of priests at Dachau in an allocution to the Sacred College on June 2, 1945. A translation of this whole speech, as it was broadcast on Vatican Radio, can be found in "The Catholic Church and the Third Reich: Pope Pius XII Surveys an Heroic History," *Tablet* (London), June 9, 1945. See Purdy, 45.

27. William J. O'Malley, "The Priests of Dachau," reprinted in *Pius XII and the Holocaust: A Reader*, 143; Holmes, 142, 145. Archbishop Juliusz Nowowiejski of Plock died in a concentration camp in May 1941, followed by his suffragan bishop, Leon Wetmaski. Bishop Kozal of Wloclawek was killed in Dachau. Szulc, 119. See also Lenz, *Christ in Dachau*; Coady, *With Bound Hands* (letters written in prison).

28. O'Malley, "The Priests of Dachau," reprinted in *Pius XII and the Holocaust: A Reader*, 143.

29. Hanley, 15 ("Priests occupied the second lowest rung of the camp ladder. On the lowest were the Jews.")

30. Bernard, 24, 34-35. One message that comes through loud and clear is the absolute joy that the sacraments brought to these men who were in such dire conditions. Although they could be executed if caught, they secretly said Mass and used what little scraps of bread they could find to provide Communion for priests and non-priests alike. Father Bernard wrote: "It is a sea of comfort that pours over the gathering. Comfort and hope and strength for new suffering joyfully accepted." Ibid., 41.

31. Ibid., 28-29.

32. Father Bernard received a highly unusual reprieve when, in February 1942, he was given a nine-day pass. His mother had died, and it seems that the Nazis thought there was an opportunity for some good publicity. It also seems likely that they did not expect Father Bernard to return to Dachau. He, however, recognized their agenda and despite the absolute misery that he knew awaited him, Father Bernard went back to the concentration camp. (This episode, just one chapter in his memoirs, inspired the motion picture *The Ninth Day*.) Later, he declined the Nazis' offer to release him from Dachau if he would only promise to leave the priesthood.

33. Purdy, 45. See also *Maltreatment and Persecution of the Catholic Clergy in the Western Provinces*, Office of the United States Chief of Counsel, vol. I, at 286; "A note of His Eminence the Cardinal Secretary of State to the Foreign Minister of the Reich about the religious situation in 'Warthegau' and in the other Polish provinces subject to Germany," March 2, 1943, in Office of the United States Chief of Counsel, vol. V, 1018; "Recalling the Polish Clergy Imprisoned in Dachau: Interview With Archbishop Emeritus Majdanski of Stettino-Kamien," Zenit News Service, May 2, 2004 ("I was arrested, as were other students and professors of the seminary, for wearing a cassock. The Germans who arrested us did not ask us for our particulars. So it can be said that I was arrested as a Catholic priest.... Our German executioners cursed God, denigrated the Church, and called us the 'dogs of Rome.' They wanted to force us to desecrate the cross and the rosary. To make a long story short, for them we were only numbers to be eliminated.... I saw so many priests die in a heroic way.") See generally Lenz, *Christ in Dachau*.

34. Bernard, 139.

35. Ibid., 144, 146.

36. Ibid., 143.

37. An English translation of this document can be found in *Nazi Conspiracy and Aggression* (Office of United States Chief of Counsel for Prosecution of Axis Criminality, 1946) vol. V, 1018-1029.

38. "The Catholic Church and the Third Reich: Pope Pius XII Surveys an Heroic History," *Tablet* (London), June 9, 1945.

39. This observation alone serves to undercut the argument against Pope Pius XII set forth by Father Martin Rhonheimer, in "The Holocaust: What Was Not Said," *First Things*, November 2003. Rhonheimer's theme (derived in large part from Kertzer, *The Popes Against the Jews*) was that historic anti-Judaism influenced the papal response to the Holocaust and the anti-Semitic activities that preceded it. The Vatican archives that were opened in February 2003, however, clearly show that Pope Pius XI and Secretary of State Pacelli were very concerned about the fate of German Jews. Drafts of statements, not issued on the advice of German clergy because of concern about Nazi retaliation, negate any inference of anti-Semitism or anti-Judaism. Those documents also dispel any notion that the Holy See was concerned only about "baptized Jews." See pp. 358-59. They show that the Pope and the future Pope believed that their statements *were* strong, and the Nazis, the world press, and most importantly the Catholic faithful recognized them as clear condemnations of Hitler's ideology and a call to assist the persecuted victims, including Jews. Rhonheimer himself backed off of the implication of his original article when responding to letters it generated. See "Martin Rhonheimer responds," *First Things*, February 2004, 4-5 ("[M]y article was not about Pius XII and the Holocaust," the Church did far more to help the Jews than any other institution, and "the Church was certainly not responsible for the rise of Nazi anti-Semitism — indeed it did much to counter Nazi ideology.")

40. Telegram from the Chargé in Switzerland (Huddle) to the Secretary of State, Feb. 9, 1942, in *Foreign Relations of the United States, Diplomatic Papers, 1942, vol. III (Europe)*, United States Government Printing Office (Washington, 1961), 778. Japan was widely perceived to be waging a war against Christianity. See Robert Bellaire, "'Christianity Must Go,' Says Japan: The Enemy fights the Christians as viciously as he fights us," Collier's, Nov. 20, 1943 ("Japan is as much at war with Christianity as with the United States.")

41. Holmes, 136. The Japanese were similarly concerned that the Vatican had established relations with China. "Le cardinal Maglione au délégué apostolique à Tokyo Marella," May 11, 1942, *Actes et Documents*, vol. 8, p. 533, no. 373; "La Secrétairerie d'Etat à la Légation de Grand Bretagne," June 6 1942, *Actes et Documents*, vol. 8, p. 553, no. 392.

42. Darragh, 15. See "Le cardinal Maglione au délégué apostolique à Tokyo Marella," May 27, 1942, *Actes et Documents*, vol. 8, p. 546, no. 385 (dealing with the exchange of information regarding POWs).

43. Blet, 130.

44. The Germans may have asked Pope Pius to intervene and try to stop the bombing of civilian populations. *The Ciano Diaries*, 523.

45. Enclosure in Mr. Osborne's Despatch No. 111 of September 11, 1942, British Public Records Office, FO371/334148 56879.

46. Heller and Nekrich, 408.

47. Ibid., 408; Barnett, 166. This is very similar to some of the ideas he had set forth almost 20 years earlier in *Mein Kampf*.

48. Heller and Nekrich, 409.

49. Ibid., 408.

50. García, 19. See generally Scaperlanda, *Edith Stein*; A. G. Harmon, "Authenticating a Miracle: The Case of Edith Stein," in *Things in Heaven and Earth: Exploring the Supernatural* (Harold Fickett, ed., 1997).

51. This caused some difficulty with her mother, who felt that Christians were persecuting the Jews; Edith's sister Rosa was baptized as a Catholic only after their mother had died. García, 19.

52. Freda Mary Oben, "My Journey with St. Edith Stein," *Homiletic and Pastoral Review* (July 2000).

53. Groppe, 23.

54. Fogelman, 172; Holmes, 165.

55. Fogelman, 172; Holmes, 165. A similar letter concerning the situation in the Third Reich was sent by German bishops on July 6, 1941. One of its provisions was: "Never, and under no circumstances, may a man, except in the case of war and legitimate defense, kill an innocent person." O'Carroll, 106.

56. Congregation for the Causes of Saints, *Positio*, appendix 25, 246.

57. Ibid.; *Tablet*, Aug. 29, 1942, 103.

58. Congregation for the Causes of Saints, *Positio*, appendix 25, 246.

59. García, 20.

60. Lapomarda, 261, n. 23.

61. Congregation for the Causes of Saints, *Positio* (Summarium), Testimony of Sr. Pascalina Lehnert, Oct. 29, 1968-Jan. 24, 1969, before the Tribunal of the Vicariate of Rome, on the beatification of Pius XII (Eugenio Pacelli), Part I, pp. 77, 85; Congregation for the Causes of Saints, *Positio* (Summarium), Testimony of Maria Conrada Grabmair, May 9, 1969-May 29, 1969, before the Tribunal of the Vicariate of Rome, on the beatification of Pius XII (Eugenio Pacelli), Part I, pp. 173, 174. In addition to these two sworn testimonies, the relator of Pius XII's sainthood cause, Father Peter Gumpel, told me that a third witness was prepared to testify to this fact, but he passed away before his testimony was taken.

62. Pope Pius XI's 1937 encyclical *Mit brennender Sorge* ("With Burning Anxiety") certainly provided the condemnation of Nazism that Stein wanted. See pp. 107-110. In her July 10, 1940, letter, Stein wrote favorably about a pastoral letter that had been written by Bishop Lemmens (her bishop). Stein mentioned that Lemmens was interrogated by the Nazis, who had just overrun Holland, and she praised him for giving this letter to the Nazis who interrogated him. Stein marveled at his courage and said how right he was to give them the letter which repeatedly invoked and quoted from *Mit brennender Sorge*. *Self-Portrait in Letters 1916-1942*, vol. 5, 327.

63. Heidi Collins and John Allen, "Did Vatican Do Enough to Stop Holocaust?" *CNN Sunday Morning*, Feb. 16, 2003 (comments of John Allen, CNN Vatican analyst).

64. Besier, 126.

65. This letter is reprinted in the Appendix, p. 393.

66. Critics often confuse this point, leading their readers to think that she was a Carmelite nun at the time of the letter. See Godman, 34.

67. *Self-Portrait in Letters 1916-1942*, vol. 5, 327.

68. Ibid.

69. It also completely overlooks her will, in which the saint prays for world peace, the deliverance of Germany, for the Catholic Church and its orders, for the honor of the Immaculate Heart of Mary and the Sacred Heart of Jesus, for the safety of her own family, and that all Jewish people will turn from disbelief to belief. Freda Mary Oben, "Saint Edith Stein and the Meaning of the Cross," *Voices*, Eastertide 2007.

70. Karski, 129-30, 235, 257, 271-72, 387 (firsthand account of the Polish underground); Lapomarda, 132; Mazgaj, 62-63 (priest sent to Auschwitz due to work in the Polish underground).

71. Karski, 167, 180, 352-53.

72. Ibid., 354.

73. Reprinted in Tec, 110-112.

74. F. Murphy, 201-2.

75. "Nuncio in Berlin, Orsenigo, to Cardinal Maglione," July 20, 1942, *Actes et Documents*, vol. 7, p. 604, no. 433.

76. Holmes, 139.

77. Holmes, 149; O'Carroll, 89. See "A l'Evêque de Berlin," March 1, 1942, *Actes et Documents*, vol. 2, p. 251, no. 83.

78. Pius did not favor this approach. He feared that it would cause Axis soldiers to fight to the bitter end, leading to more death. See "Pie XII aux Cardinaux et prélats de la Curie romaine," June 2, 1944, *Actes et Documents*, vol. 11, p. 341, no. 205; "The Pope's Solicitude," *Jewish Chronicle*, July 16, 1943.

79. "Monsignor Tardini to Ambassador Myron Taylor," Sept. 26, 1942, *Actes et Documents*, vol. 5, p. 727-29, no. 492 (discussing suppression of religion in the Soviet Union).

80. British Public Records Office, INF 1/893.

81. Lapide, 137.

82. *Tablet* (London), Oct. 24, 1942, 202 (quoting the *Jewish Chronicle*).

83. Ibid.

84. *The Ciano Diaries*, 537, 538. According to Ciano, Mussolini wanted to "break a few wooden heads," but he had been dissuaded from doing so because "the prestige of the Church is very high." Ibid., 538-39.

85. The President's Personal Representative to Pope Pius XII (Taylor) to the Cardinal Secretary of State (Maglione), Sept. 26, 1942, in *Foreign Relations of the United States, Diplomatic Papers, 1942, vol. III (Europe)*, United States Government Printing Office (Washington, 1961), 775.

86. Telegram from the Minister in Switzerland (Harrison) to the Secretary of State, Oct. 16, 1942, in *Foreign Relations of the United States, Diplomatic Papers, 1942*, vol. III (Europe), United States Government Printing Office (Washington, 1961), 777 (going on to suggest that "there is little hope of checking Nazi barbarities by any method except that of physical force coming from without").

87. *Catholic News*, Nov. 21, 1942, reprinted in Secretariat for Ecumenical and Interreligious Affairs, National Conference of Bishops, *Catholics Remember the Holocaust*, United States Catholic Conference (Washington, 1998), 17.

88. "Holy Father Extends Thanks to American Catholics for Aid," *Catholic News*, Nov. 21, 1942 (emphasis added). See *Catholic News*, Nov. 21, 1942, reprinted in Secretariat for Ecumenical and Interreligious Affairs, National Conference of Bishops, *Catholics Remember the Holocaust*, United States Catholic Conference (Washington, 1998), 17.

89. "Holy Father Extends Thanks to American Catholics for Aid," *Catholic News*, Nov. 21, 1942.

90. Timothy A. Byrnes, *Catholic Bishops in American Politics*, Princeton University Press (Princeton, 1991). In 2002, I was given access to archives containing the papers of Cardinal Spellman at St. Joseph's Seminary in Dunwoodie, New York. They reveal that Spellman played an important role in helping Pius XII coordinate efforts with President Roosevelt. For instance, in the autumn of 1942, Spellman (then archbishop) traveled to Washington, D.C., for a private meeting in the White House with President Roosevelt and Winston Churchill. See Florence D. Cohalan, *A Popular History of the Archdiocese of New York*, 286 (U.S. Catholic Historical Society, 1983). On Oct. 19, Myron Taylor (President Roosevelt's personal representative to Pius) sent a note to Spellman in which he said he would accept Spellman's advice and not take with him to Italy a certain manuscript that Spellman had given to him. Taylor was afraid that it might fall into Fascist hands. The note in question seems to be one contained in the Spellman archives that details Pius XII's close cooperation with Roosevelt.

This was not Spellman's only trip related to the war effort. In 1941 he took a secret trip to Turkey in an effort to negotiate an agreement that might keep the United States out of the war. As reported by an attaché to the German embassy in Ankara, Turkey, who was involved in this failed attempt:

> Shortly before the United States actually entered the shooting war, President Roosevelt had sent Archbishop Spellman, as he then was, on a special mission to the Allied and neutral countries. The Archbishop, of course, was not merely a very high dignitary of the Catholic Church in the United States; he also enjoyed the President's personal confidence, and his mission, evidently blessed by the State Department, was one of the utmost political importance.
>
> At that time a negotiated peace was still not entirely impossible. At least we thought so in Ankara, though von Papen was doubtless well aware that the Allies would never negotiate again with Hitler, and that radical change would have to come about within the Third Reich before anything of the sort could even be started. Indeed, as he realized, this would mean the end of the Third Reich and the beginning of a new Germany, prepared voluntarily to surrender its ill-gotten conquests....

L.C. Moyzisch, *Operation Cicero*, 73-74 (Pyramid Books, 1958). The German ambassador, Franz von Papen, knew Spellman, but it would have looked bad for him to meet with the Archbishop. For that reason, attaché Moyzisch was charged with setting up a meeting between Spellman and an important German described only as "a Catholic, a very eminent lawyer, and a scholar." Unfortunately, the meeting never took place. "Ribbentrop got wind of what was going on and put a stop to it just as ruthlessly as he knew how.... I myself [Moyzisch] was kept on tenderhooks for a considerable time as to whether or not I was to be recalled to Germany to face a treason trial, and probably a firing squad." Ibid., 74. Franz von Papen, in a postscript to this book, verified Moyzisch's account. Ibid., 157. The Nazis knew of Spellman's work for the Pope and against them, so they spied on him. Congregation for the Causes of Saints, *Positio*, appendix 25, 245.

91. "L'ambassadeur du Brésil Accioly au cardinal Maglione," Sept. 14, 1942, *Actes et Documents*, vol. 5, p. 673, no. 466.

92. The British chargé d'Affaires reported back to London that Pius felt that his broadcast of May 13 had already condemned the Nazis, and he had sent messages of consolation to various Polish priests. Pius did not see how he could do more. Enclosure in Mr. Osborne's Dispatch No. 111 of September 11, 1942, British Public Records Office, FO371/334148 56879; Letter from Osborne to Mr. Howard, July 12, 1942, British Public Records Office, FO371/33426 65042 (similar message).

93. See Telegram from the Minister in Switzerland (Harrison) to the Secretary of State, Aug. 3, 1943, in *Foreign Relations of the United States, Diplomatic Papers, 1942, vol. III (Europe)*, United States Government Printing Office (Washington, 1961), 772 (expressing concern over the lack of a statement).

94. Mr. Harold H. Tittmann, Assistant to the President's Personal Representative to Pope Pius, to the Secretary of State, Oct. 6, 1942, in *Foreign Relations of the United States, Diplomatic Papers, 1942*, vol. III (Europe), United States Government Printing Office (Washington, 1961), 776.

95. Outward Telegram, FO 371/34363 59337 (Jan. 10, 1943). See also Political Distribution from Switzerland from Berne to Foreign Office, Jan. 5, 1943, FO 371/34363 59337 (similar).

96. "A Summary of the Conversations between His Holiness Pope Pius XII and Myron Taylor, Personal Representative of the President of the United States to His Holiness Pope Pius XII at Vatican City," Sept. 19, 22, and 26, 1942, 5. Posted on the Internet by the Franklin D. Roosevelt Library: *www.docs.fdrlibrary.marist.edu/psf/box52/a467e01.html.*

97. Ibid., 5-6.

98. Ibid., 11.

99. Ibid., 13.

100. Wyman, 76.

101. Of course, most careful observers saw through the official neutrality. McGurn, 92 ("On World War II and the East-West Cold War Pius was neutral in theory but warmly pro-Western in fact.") He "would not stay neutral in the sense of putting good and evil on the same footing." Ibid., 93. In fact, there was "a virtual wholehearted endorsement of the Allies' World War II Atlantic Charter, Marshall Plan for postwar aid to Europe, the United Nations, the Atlantic Alliance, and the American-advocated drive to unite Western Europe economically and politically." Ibid., 93.

102. "Appeal to Stay the Butcher's Hand," *Palestine Post*, Dec. 1, 1942.

103. Ibid. The Latin Patriarch of Jerusalem is the title possessed by the Latin-rite Catholic Archbishop of Jerusalem. The Archdiocese of Jerusalem has jurisdiction for all Latin-rite Catholics in Israel, Palestine, Jordan, and Cyprus.

104. The original Italian version was published in the official *Acta Apostolicae Sedis* of 1943 (vol. 35, pp. 5-8). For an English version, see *Pius XII: Selected Encyclicals and Addresses*, 275-97 (Catholic Truth Society: London, 1949).

105. Charles J. Gangi, "The Christmas Addresses of Pope Pius XII," *New Oxford Review*, December 2007.

106. A group of 50 Americans of German heritage published an advertisement containing their statement in the last week of December 1942:

> "We Americans of German descent raise our voices in denunciation of the Hitler policy of cold-blooded extermination of the Jews of Europe and against the barbarities committed by the Nazis against all other innocent peoples under their sway," the declaration began. "These horrors... are, in particular, a challenge to those who, like ourselves are descendants of the Germany that once stood in the foremost ranks of civilization." The ad went on to "utterly repudiate every thought and deed of Hitler and his Nazis," and urged the people of Germany "to overthrow a regime which is the infamy of German history."

Rafael Medoff, "Sultan of Swat," *Washington Times*, Dec. 25, 2007. Signatories included Protestant theologian Reinhold Niebuhr, news correspondent and author William Shirer, and baseball legend Babe Ruth.

107. "L'ambassadeur de Pologne Papée au cardinal Maglione," Feb. 20, 1943, *Actes et Documents*, vol. 7, p. 237, no. 123.

108. British Public Records Office, FO 371/34363 59337 (Jan. 5, 1943); Telegram from the Minister in Switzerland (Harrison) to the Secretary of State, Jan. 5, 1943, in *Foreign Relations of the United States, Diplomatic Papers, 1943, vol. II (Europe)*, United States Government Printing Office (Washington, 1964), 91.

109. Lapide, 201. For further details about the anti-Nazi Catholic Resistance in the Netherlands, see L. Bleys, "Resistance in the Netherlands," *Tablet* (London), Oct. 14, 1944, 186 (eyewitness account by a Dutch resistance priest, in which he provides details of how Pius XII communicated his support to Dutch Catholics fighting Nazism). "In no other country, said the Pope, have the Bishops guided the faithful so clearly, so unanimously and so courageously in the battle against the errors of National Socialism." Ibid.

110. *New York Times*, Dec. 25, 1942.

111. "A Vatican Visit," *London Times*, Oct. 11, 1942. See also Gilbert, *The Righteous*, 357-358.

112. Quoted in Rhodes, 272-73 (citing German archives: *A.A. Abteilung Inland*, pak. 17, vol. I, Jan. 22, 1943); see also Holmes, 140. In fact, a Protestant minister who helped circulate this statement was sentenced

to prison for spreading a "subversive and demoralizing document." He was also accused of having a critical view of the war and of being "spiritually attracted to Jewish environments and sympathetic toward Jews." "For Berlin, Pius XII Was a Subversive: Radio Operator's Experience of Spreading Papal Christmas Message," Zenit News Service, May 14, 2002.

113. Telegram from the Minister in Switzerland (Harrison) to the Secretary of State, Jan. 5, 1943, in *Foreign Relations of the United States, Diplomatic Papers, 1943, vol. II (Europe),* United States Government Printing Office (Washington, 1964), 91.

114. Telegram from the German Ambassador (Bergen) to the Reich Minister, dated Jan. 26, 1943, NARA, T-120, Roll 361, 277668-70.

115. See *Under His Very Windows,* 329, n. 3 (noting that this was done by Joseph Lichten, the editors of the *Actes et Documents* collection, and Robert Graham — one of the editors — in a different writing).

116. *Zanichelli's Italian and English Dictionary* has five English translations for the word *stirpe*: stock, birth, family, race, and descent (NTC Publishing Group, Chicago, 1993), 304.

117. See Kenneth D. Whitehead, "The Pope Pius XII Controversy," 31 *Political Science Reviewer,* 374 (2002).

118. Lapide, 251; personal interview with Peter Gumpel, S.J., December 1999, Vatican City.

119. Congregation for the Causes of Saints, *Positio,* appendix 25. 264, 282.

120. Desmond Fisher, 13.

121. Ibid., 282. Zuccotti mischaracterized Pius XII's first encyclical, *Summi Pontificatus,* saying that it "never mentioned Jews. Indeed, despite references to the unity of the human race, it seemed to single out Christians, or perhaps Catholics, for special consideration" (p. 63). In fact, Pius did invoke Scripture to use the word "Jew" in the context of explaining that there is no room for racial distinctions in the Church. *Summi Pontificatus,* n. 84.

122. "The Rights of Man," broadcast of Pope Pius XII, Christmas 1942.

123. The full text of the address appears in Margherita Marchione, *Pope Pius XII: Architect for Peace,* 143-152. See also Office of the United States Chief Counsel, vol. I, 285-86; Shirer, *The Rise and Fall of the Third Reich,* 324-25 (footnote); Purdy, 43.

124. Whitall N. Perry, "Book Review: The Silence of Pius XII, by Carlo Falconi," 5:1 *Studies in Comparative Religion* (Winter 1971).

125. "For Berlin, Pius XII Was a Subversive: Radio Operator 's Experience of Spreading Papal Christmas Message," Zenit New Service, May 14, 2002.

126. See generally Kurzman, *A Special Mission.* Also see pages 372-73.

127. Congregation for the Causes of Saints, *Positio* (Summarium), Testimony of Karl Otto Wolff, March 14, 1972, before the Ecclesiastical Tribunal of Munich, on the beatification of Pius XII (Eugenio Pacelli), 825. Wolff, "against Hitler's will and without his knowledge," played a decisive part in bringing about the surrender of the German armies in Italy. At the time of his first contact with Allied representatives, Wolff had promised to protect the lives of political prisoners in the area under his command. *They Almost Killed Hitler: Based on the Personal Account of Fabian von Schlabrendorff,* 4 (explaining that he did, indeed, protect the prisoners); Simpson, 186 (those in the Vatican knew it was possible that he would invade).

128. Weizsäcker, *Memoirs of Ernst Von Weizsäcker,* 291; Holmes, 155-56; Payne, 485 (quoting Hitler: "Do you think I worry about the Vatican? We can wrap it up at once! The whole diplomatic corps will be there! I don't give a damn!... we'll apologize later. That's all right. There is a war on!") See generally Kurzman, *A Special Mission;* Ronald J. Rychlak, "The Plot to Kidnap Pope Pius XII (Kurzman's 'A Special Mission')," *Crisis* magazine, October 2007.

129. Congregation for the Causes of Saints, *Positio* (Summarium), Testimony of Karl Otto Wolff, March 14, 1972, before the Ecclesiastical Tribunal of Munich, on the beatification of Pius XII (Eugenio Pacelli), 825.

130. Telegram from the Minister in Switzerland (Harrison) to the Secretary of State, Jan. 5, 1943, in *Foreign Relations of the United States, Diplomatic Papers, 1943,* vol. II (Europe), United States Government Printing Office (Washington, 1964), 91; British Public Records Office, FO 371/34363 59337 (January 5, 1943).

131. Telegram from the Minister in Switzerland (Harrison) to the Secretary of State, Jan. 5, 1943, in *Foreign Relations of the United States, Diplomatic Papers, 1943, vol. II (Europe),* United States Government Printing Office (Washington, 1964), 91.

132. Ibid.

133. Quoted in McCormick, 107.

## Chapter Thirteen: 1943 and Turning Tides

1. Kallay, 169.
2. Cianfarra, 301.
3. "Reply of His Holiness to President Roosevelt," Jan. 5, 1943, in *Wartime Correspondence,* 81-82.
4. Explanatory Note by Myron Taylor, in *Wartime Correspondence,* 69-70.
5. Weizsäcker, 297.

6. Toland, 1163; Majdalany, 194-95. In February 1945, General Eisenhower said: "The policy of unconditional surrender faced the German high command with the choice of being hanged or jumping into a cluster of bayonets." Dupuy and Dupuy, 1016.

7. "Pie XII aux Cardinaux et prélats de la Curie romaine," June 2, 1944, *Actes et Documents*, vol. 11, p. 341, no. 205. See "The Pope's Solicitude," *Jewish Chronicle*, July 16, 1943; Hennesey, 282.

8. President Roosevelt explained:

> The trouble is that the reassuring [of conditional surrender] presupposes reconstituting a German state which would give active co-operation apparently at once to peace in Europe. A somewhat long study and personal experience in and out of Germany leads me to believe that the German philosophy cannot be changed by decree, law or military order. The change in German philosophy must be evolutionary and may take two generations. To assume otherwise is to assume, of necessity, a period of quiet followed by a third World War.

Ziemke, 31.

9. Blum, 749. The possibility of a separate peace with the Soviets had been discussed in high Italian circles in January 1943. *The Ciano Diaries*, 565.

10. "Other Soviet Affairs; Japanese claim to islands disputed in Diet," *BBC Summary of World Broadcasts*, March 14, 1979.

11. In 1943, Air Marshal Harris said: "Every ton of bombs dropped on Germany's industries will save the lives of ten United Nations soldiers when the invasion comes." Allan A. Michie, "Germany Was Bombed to Defeat," *Skyways*, August 1945, reprinted in *Reader's Digest*, August 1945, 77.

12. E.g., "The Rights of Man," broadcast of Pope Pius XII, Christmas 1942, reprinted in *Pius XII: Selected Encyclicals and Addresses*, 277.

13. *The Ciano Diaries*, 523.

14. In *Nichomachean Ethics*, Aristotle wrote: "We make war that we may live in peace." War itself can be defined as a state of conflict "between two or more sovereign nations carried on by force of arms." John A. McHugh, O.P., and Charles J. Callan, O.P., 1 *Moral Theology: A Complete Course*, 545 (1929). According to this definition, war involves a *state of conflict*, as opposed to a passing conflict such as a border skirmish or momentary dispute. It also involves sovereign nations, which rules out civil wars, riots, or fights against an individual or group (such an action — or at least one side of such activity — could, of course, be "just"; it would not, however, be just *war*). See George Weigel, "Moral Clarity in a Time of War," *First Things* (January 2003).

15. "As the months went by and Adolph Hitler overwhelmed country after country in Europe, it became clear to me that I was far from being a pacifist and was becoming increasingly convinced that we had a positive moral duty to try to stop Hitler." James O'Gara, "Why I Went to War," *U.S. Catholic* (May 1992).

16. See U.S. Catholic Bishops, "The Harvest of Justice Is Sown in Peace" (1993) (discussing "St. Augustine's classic case: love may require force to protect the innocent.")

17. The *Catechism of the Catholic Church* incorporates these teachings, and under a subsection entitled "Safeguarding Peace (Avoiding War)," it provides:

> **2307** The fifth commandment forbids the intentional destruction of human life. Because of the evils and injustices that accompany all war, the Church insistently urges everyone to prayer and to action so that the divine Goodness may free us from the ancient bondage of war.
>
> **2308** All citizens and all governments are obliged to work for the avoidance of war. However, "as long as the danger of war persists and there is no international authority with the necessary competence and power, governments cannot be denied the right of lawful self-defense, once all peace efforts have failed."
>
> **2309** The strict conditions for *legitimate defense by military force* require rigorous consideration. The gravity of such a decision makes it subject to rigorous conditions of moral legitimacy. At one and the same time:
>
> – the damage inflicted by the aggressor on the nation or community of nations must be lasting, grave, and certain;
> – all other means of putting an end to it must have been shown to be impractical or ineffective;
> – there must be serious prospects of success;
> – the use of arms must not produce evils and disorders graver than the evil to be eliminated. The power of moden means of destruction weighs very heavily in evaluating this condition.
>
> These are the traditional elements enumerated in what is called the "just war" doctrine.
> The evaluation of these conditions for moral legitimacy belongs to the prudential judgment of those who have responsibility for the common good.

**2312** The Church and human reason both assert the permanent validity of the *moral law during armed conflict*. "The mere fact that war has regrettably broken out does not mean that everything becomes licit between the warring parties."

Emphasis in original.

18. See Ronald J. Rychlak, "Just-War Theory, International Law, and the War in Iraq," 2 *Ave Maria L. Rev.*, 1 (2004).

19. Critic Daniel Goldhagen asserted that the Polish ambassador to the Holy See during the War, Casimir Papée, pleaded with Pius in vain for intervention on behalf of the Jews, and that by 1944 Pius XII was so "sick" of hearing about the Jews that he got angry with the ambassador. Goldhagen gave no documentation for this charge. That is hardly surprising, since the charge was untrue. In his book, *Pius XII e Polska* ("Pius XII and Poland"), Papée comprehensively analyzed — and supported — Pius XII's wartime policies. Papée, *Pius XII e Polska*. See also Sereny, 332 (quoting Papée: "He *was* in a very very difficult position. . . . He was — one must appreciate this — surrounded by Fascism: he had very little freedom of movement."); Jakubowski, *Pope Pius and Poland* (documenting Pius XII's actions on behalf of Poland). Moreover, in a postwar interview Papée made clear that his pleas were made on behalf of all Poles, not expressly on behalf of *Jewish* victims, as Goldhagen would have his readers believe. Sereny, 333 (Papée pleaded for a statement on behalf of *Poles*, not *Jews*. He added: "I meant, of course *all* the Poles, including the Jews, most of whom, of course, by this time, were dead.") Pius prepared an express statement on behalf of all the Poles, but he was told by Archbishop Sapieha that it would only lead to bad repercussions. See p. 346.

20. "A l'Evêque de Berlin," April 30, 1943, *Actes et Documents*, vol. 2, p. 318, no. 105.

21. "Book Claims Vatican Official Confronted Hitler on Persecution," *National Catholic Register*, July 5-11, 1998, 6 (quoting Monica Biffi, *Msgr. Cesare Orsenigo: Apostolic Nuncio in Germany [1930-46]*). See also R. Stewart, 11; Rhodes, 343 (relating the same event).

22. Holmes, 166. On Feb. 20, 1941, Pius wrote: "When the pope wanted to cry aloud in a strong voice, waiting and silence were unhappily often imposed. . . ." See "A l'Evêque de Limbourg," Feb. 20, 1941, *Actes et Documents*, vol. 2, p. 198, no. 65. Similarly, on March 3, 1944, he wrote: "frequently it is with pain that a decision is made as to what the situation demands; prudent reserve and silence or, on the contrary, candid speech and vigorous action." "A l'Archevêque de Cologne," March 3, 1944, *Actes et Documents*, vol. 2, p. 363, no. 118.

23. Sánchez (2002), 375 (emphasis in original).

24. Ibid., 374.

25. Ibid.

26. Ibid., 375.

27. Ibid.

28. Apparently several Nazi leaders had problems with Ribbentrop. Weizsäcker, 278, 284 ("[H]is lust for war showed me how dangerous he was, and I honestly hated him.")

29. Alvarez and Graham, 41 (noting that Schellenberg avoided punishment).

30. Hamerow, 310.

31. Ibid.

32. K. Doyle, 16; Keegan (1994).

33. Scholl, 73, 74.

34. Ibid., 85-86.

35. Ibid., 86; Gill, 183-95.

36. "Let's Look at the Record," *Inside the Vatican*, October 1999, XII. See "Vatican Gives Assurance of Aid to Jews," *California Jewish Voice*, Feb. 12, 1943.

37. Moshe Kohn, "Remember the *White Rose*," *Jerusalem Post*, July 9, 1993.

38. Scholl, 91, 92.

39. Gill, 183; Ari L. Goldman, "Anti-Hitler German Students Lauded," *New York Times*, June 30, 1985.

40. Lapide, 138. In the Vatican, the secretary of the Congregation for Extraordinary Ecclesiastical Affairs (Msgr. Domenico Tardini) recorded in his notes of Oct. 21 and 23, 1941, that if the pro-Nazi statements attributed to Tiso were actually made by him, the Holy Father wanted his name to be removed from a list of prelates designated for special praise. "Notes de Mgr. Tardini," Oct. 23, 1941, *Actes et Documents*, vol. 5, p. 273, no. 123.

41. Lapide, 138. See "La Secrétairerie d'Etat à la Légation de Slovaquie," March 14, 1942, *Actes et Documents*, vol. 8, p. 459, no. 305 (Vatican Secretary of State's concern over expulsion of Jews from the Slovak Republic).

42. E.g., The Apostolic Delegate (Cicognani) to the Acting Secretary of State, Feb. 26, 1944, in *Foreign Relations of the United States, Diplomatic Papers, 1944, vol. I (General)*, United States Government Printing Office (Washington, 1966), 995.

43. While Catholics did not face the same fate as Jews, the postwar Czechoslovak *Official Report for the Prosecution and Trial of Major War Criminals* documented Nazi efforts to suppress Catholicism in this area:

At the outbreak of war, 487 Catholic priests were among the thousands of Czech patriots arrested and sent to concentration camps as hostages. Venerable high ecclesiastical dignitaries were dragged to concentration camps as hostages.... Religious orders were dissolved and liquidated, their charitable institutions closed down and their members expelled or else forced to compulsory labor in Germany. All religious instruction in Czech schools was suppressed. Most of the weeklies and monthlies which the Catholics had published in Czechoslovakia had been suppressed from the very beginning of the occupation.... To a great extent Catholic church property was seized for the benefit of the Reich.

Office of United States Chief of Counsel, 283.

44. Lapide, 141.

45. See "Le cardinal Maglione au chargé d'affaires à Presbourg Burzio," March 9, 1943, *Actes et Documents*, vol. 9, p. 179, no. 87 (Vatican direction to impede the deportation of 20,000 Jews from Slovakia).

46. See "Le cardinal Maglione au chargé d'affaires à Presbourg Burzio," March 9, 1943, *Actes et Documents*, vol. 9, no. 87 (Vatican direction to impede the deportation of 20,000 Jews from Slovakia).

47. Jacques Maritain, "Atonement for All," *Commonweal*, Sept. 18, 1942, 509.

48. Holmes, 159-60; See "Notes de Mgr. Tardini," April 7, 1943, *Actes et Documents*, vol. 9, p. 233, no. 136 (regarding the Holy See's concern about the persecution of Jews in Slovakia).

49. "Le cardinal Maglione au délégué apostolique à Sofia Mazzoli," April 8, 1943, *Actes et Documents*, vol. 9, p. 242, no. 141.

50. "La Secrétairere d'Etat à la Légation de Slovaquie," May 5, 1943, *Actes et Documents*, vol. 9, p. 275, no. 176.

51. "Le délégue apostolique à Istanbul Roncalli au cardinal Maglione," May 22, 1943, *Actes et Documents*, vol. 9, p. 306, no. 195. See also Congregation for the Causes of Saints, *Positio*, appendix 25, 246 (protest by the Slovak nuncio, made at the opportune time, led to partial success of delaying deportation). Denis Barton, *Fr. Tiso, Slovakia and Hitler* (Church in History Information Center: Birkenhead, 1990), refutes many accusations about the Catholic hierarchy in wartime Slovakia. Similarly, evidence of the Slovak bishops' appeals for Jews is found in the *Tablet*, June 12, 1943, 283, and July 3, 1943, 8. After the war, the *Tablet* reaffirmed that the Slovak bishops "did in fact, in accordance with the desire of the Holy See, make most emphatic public denunciation of the persecution of the Jews." *Tablet*, Feb. 15, 1947, 108.

52. "La Secrétairerie d'Etat à la Légation de Slovaquie," *Actes et Documents*, Sept. 20, 1944, vol. 10, p. 422, no. 328.

53. *Jewish Chronicle* (London), Sept. 11, 1942.

54. "Le cardinal Maglione au chargé d'affaires à Washington Cicognani," Feb. 16, 1944, *Actes et Documents*, vol. 10, p. 134, no. 60 (directive regarding requests from the World Jewish Congress); "Le cardinal Maglione au chargé d'affaires à Presbourg Burzio," April 22, 1944, *Actes et Documents*, vol. 10, p. 234, no. 159 (similar).

55. Lapide, 147.

56. "Notes de Mgr. Tardini," Oct. 28, 1944, *Actes et Documents*, vol. 10, p. 461-62, no. 378 (Annexe); Robert A. Graham, "Pius XII's Defense of Jews and Others: 1944-45," in *Pius XII and the Holocaust: A Reader*, 65-66 (emphasis added); Lapide, 147.

57. O'Carroll, 106.

58. Robert A. Graham, "Pius XII's Defense of Jews and Others: 1944-45," in *Pius XII and the Holocaust: A Reader*, 66 (emphasis added).

59. Michaelis, 373. The survival of nearly 25 percent of the Slovakian Jews has been attributed to Vatican pressure on Tiso. Lapide, 144.

60. "Tiso Chosen as First President of Slovakia; Vatican Frowns on Priest as Head of State," *New York Times*, Oct. 27, 1939, 1.

61. In attempting to implicate Pius XII in the atrocities carried out in the Nazi satellite states of Slovakia, critic Daniel Goldhagen mentioned the work of Livia Rothkirchen, a respected authority on the annihilation of Slovak Jewry, but he failed to mention that in documenting and appropriately condemning the savageries committed by anti-Semitic Slavs, Rothkirchen emphasized that this was done in spite of, not because of, Pope Pius XII. See Livia Rothkirchen, *The Destruction of Slovak Jewry* (Yad Vashem: Jerusalem, 1961); Livia Rothkirchen, *Vatican Policy and the "Jewish Problem" in "Independent" Slovakia (1939-1945)*, VI Yad Vashem Studies 27-53 (1966); Livia Rothkirchen, "The Churches and the 'Final Solution' in Slovakia," in *Judaism and Christianity under the Impact of National Socialism 1919-1945*, 413-41 (Otto Dov Kulka and Paul R. Mendes-Flohr, eds. 1987) (mentioning several papal interventions for Jews and contrasting them favorably with the behavior of the local populace). To the extent that deportations were minimized in Slovakia, Rothkirchen credited the Pope. Commenting on the decision of the Slovak authorities to suspend deportations in the spring of 1943, Rothkirchen said: "The impact of the Holy See at this phase was undoubtedly a decisive factor. This was known and widely commented upon." Ibid., 419. In fact, she concluded that the several letters of protest delivered by the Vatican during the years 1941-1944 "prove sufficiently that the Vatican objected to the deportation of Jews from Slovakia." Rothkirchen, *The Destruction of Slovak Jewry*, xxxiii; see also Lapide, 148; 358, n. 28 (citing this passage). In volume XV of *Yad Vashem Studies*, John Conway also states that the archival material "confirms the picture already drawn by such Jewish authors as Livia

Rothkirchen and Pinchas Lapide. Where the Nuncios were alert, and the governments susceptible to papal remonstrances, then the interventions succeeded in delaying or reducing the deportations and other acts of persecution towards the Jews." See generally *The Pius War*, 271-73.

62. *War Criminals and Punishment* (Robert M. McBride and Company: New York, 1944), 113.

63. "Notes de Mgr. Tardini," Oct. 23, 1941, *Actes et Documents*, vol. 5, p. 273, no. 123.

64. "Notes de Mgr. Tardini," July 13, 1942, *Actes et Documents*, vol. 8, p. 598, no. 426.

65. See Günther Deschner, *Warsaw Rising*, Ballatine Books (New York, 1972).

66. "Notes de la Secrétairerie d'Etat," May 5, 1943, *Actes et Documents*, vol. 9, p. 274, no. 174. On Aug. 30, the United States secretary of state expressed doubt about the whole matter, sending a message that "there exists no sufficient proof to justify a statement regarding executions in gas chambers." Ibid.

67. See Günther Deschner, *Warsaw Rising*, Ballatine Books (New York, 1972).

68 In a small town near Mir, Poland, the Nazis executed twelve nuns in one day for suspicion of harboring Jews.

69. His story was later made into a motion picture entitled *"Au revoir, les enfants!"*

70. Patricia Treece, "Joyful Martyr," *Crisis*, July/August 1997.

71. See Zolli (1997), 156.

72. Tardini, 165-66. See Francesca Bierens, "Encounter on a Wartime Night," *Catholic Digest*, July 1996, 74.

73. Quoted in Saperstein, 43.

74. Ibid. The letters can be found in *Akten Deutscher Bischöfe über die Lage der Kirche, 1933-1945*, six volumes, edited by Bernhard Stasiewski and Ludwig Volk (Matthias-Grünewald-Verlag: Mainz, 1968-1985). These letters were misrepresented in Guenter Lewy's *The Catholic Church and Nazi Germany*. For English translations of many of the bishops' statements, see Lothar Groppe, *The Church's Struggle with the Third Reich*, 12-15, 23-27; and Groppe, *The Church and the Jews in the Third Reich*, 18-27.

75. "Discours du Pape Pie XII en la fête de St. Eugène," May 31, 1943, *Actes et Documents*, vol. 3**, p. 801, no. 510 (including a facsimile of the original typewritten version with hand corrections by the Pope).

76. This section was suppressed in Italy and Germany. *Tablet* (London), June 12, 1943, 282, n. 1 (reprinting the Pope's words; emphasis added).

77. Toland, 864; Holmes, 132; O'Carroll, 131; Burleigh (2007), 252-53 ("It is easy, with hindsight, to object that matters could not have been much worse, but this is an utterly unhistorical approach to events that for Pius were either in the present or in the future rather than sixty years in the past.")

78. "Le primat de Pologne cardinal Hlond au cardinal Maglione," June 11, 1943, *Actes et Documents*, vol. 3**, p. 809, no. 519; "Le primat de Pologne cardinal Hlond au cardinal Maglione," June 11, 1943, *Actes et Documents*, vol. 3**, p. 810, no. 520.

79. "L'archevêque de Cracovie Sapieha au cardinal Maglione," June 18, 1943, *Actes et Documents*, vol. 3**, p. 813, no. 523.

80. "The Pope Yesterday and Today," *L'Osservatore Della Domenica*, June 26, 1964. See also "Vatican Weekly Defends Pius," *Washington Post*, June 27, 1964.

81. See generally "Appeals of the Vatican to the American and British Governments That They Refrain from Bombing Rome," in *Foreign Relations of the United States, Diplomatic Papers, 1942, vol. III (Europe)*, 791-800, United States Government Printing Office (Washington, 1961); "Appeals of the Vatican to the American and British Governments That They Refrain from Bombing Rome," in *Foreign Relations of the United States, Diplomatic Papers, 1943, vol. II (Europe)*, 910-961, United States Government Printing Office (Washington, 1964).

82. "Letter from His Holiness to President Roosevelt," May 18, 1943, in *Wartime Correspondence*, 89.

83. Ibid., 91 (reply of President Roosevelt).

84. The answer from the British was similar. *The Ciano Diaries*, 552. This prompted Pius to ask Mussolini to remove military commands from Rome. The Italian king favored such a move, but as the demands from the Allies grew, the Italian leaders found it impossible to comply. Ibid., 552, 554, 555, 558-59.

85. Halecki and Murray, 182-83.

86. "Telegram from the Minister in Switzerland (Harrison) to the Secretary of State," July 28, 1943, in *Foreign Relations of the United States, Diplomatic Papers, 1943, vol. II (Europe)*,935-36, United States Government Printing Office (Washington, 1964). Other estimates put the number of dead at 1,500 (Blet, 208) or at 500 (Cornwell, *Hitler's Pope*, 298).

87. Smit, 231.

88 "Reply of His Holiness to President Roosevelt," July 19, 1943, in *Wartime Correspondence*, 95-97.

89. "Pie XII au cardinal Vicaire de Rome Marchetti-Selvaggiani," July 21, 1943, *Actes et Documents*, vol. 7, p. 507, no. 306 (including a facsimile of the typewritten letter with corrections in the Pope's handwriting).

90. "La Secrétairerie d'Etat à l'Ambassade d'Italie," July 23, 1943, *Actes et Documents*, vol. 7, p. 517, no. 311.

91. "Le sollecitudini costanti del 'Defensor Civitatis' nella parola di Sua Santità all'Associazione fra I Romani," *L'Osservatore Romano*, June 21, 1948. The object of the attack was the depot of San Lorenzo, with

its military trains and storehouses. Ibid. The German ambassador to the Holy See wrote: "For us Rome had become a German garrison." Weizsäcker, 290.

92. "Telegram from the Minister in Switzerland (Harrison) to the Secretary of State," July 27, 1943, in *Foreign Relations of the United States, Diplomatic Papers, 1943, vol. II (Europe)*, 934-35, United States Government Printing Office (Washington, 1964). In fact, Italian authorities shortly thereafter announced several steps that they were taking to make Rome a less likely target. "Memorandum from The Apostolic Delegation at Washington to the Department of State," in *Foreign Relations of the United States, Diplomatic Papers, 1943, vol. II (Europe)*, 946-47, United States Government Printing Office (Washington, 1964).

93. Morgan, 201.

94. "Telegram from the Minister in Switzerland (Harrison) to the Secretary of State," July 28, 1943, in *Foreign Relations of the United States, Diplomatic Papers, 1943, vol. II (Europe)*, 935-36, United States Government Printing Office (Washington, 1964); "Vatican Denies Protesting to U.S. or Claiming Basilica Is All Ruins; Protest Is Denied By Vatican Radio," *New York Times*, July 25, 1943, p. 1.

95. See Congregation for the Causes of Saints, *Positio*, (Summarium), Testimony of Karl Otto Wolff, before the Ecclesiastical Tribunal of Munich, on the beatification of Pius XII (Eugenii Pacelli), 827-851. See generally Kurzman, *A Special Mission*. See also pp. 372-74.

96. O'Carroll, 60; Groppe, *The Church's Struggle*, 12 (noting that Pius XII was aware of this statement).

97. P. Murphy, 212.

98. Lapide, 251.

99. Gallo, 48.

100. The numerous translation errors created by papal critics reveal a particular problem with the normal approach to history. Knowledge of a language does not necessarily correlate with an understanding of the nuances of that language. For instance, it seems likely that critic John Cornwell intentionally misrepresented Pacelli's 1919 letter back to Rome. See pp. 315-16. On the other hand, it is unlikely that Susan Zuccotti would have made such a major point over the Pope's use of the word "*stirpe*" (see pp. 207-8) unless she thought that she understood technical differences in the meanings between very similar foreign words.

101. *Mystici Corporis Christi* also strongly condemned the forced conversions to Catholicism that were then occurring in Croatia, which some critics wrongly claim enjoyed Vatican support. See pp. 222-23.

102. *New York Times*, June 27, 1943, 16; *The American Jewish Yearbook, 1943-1944*, 292 (Jewish Publication Society: Philadelphia). When this was reprinted in occupied areas, Axis leaders deleted that section of the allocution. Wistrich, 144-45.

103. Cianfarra, 315-16. Pius also embraced democratic ideals in his 1944 Christmas message. See McCormick, 125-27 (calling the papal message "a deeply pondered pontifical pronouncement in favor of democracy in the interests of the 'individual himself…'").

104. "Le grand rabbin Herzog au cardinal Maglione," July 19, 1943, *Actes et Documents*, vol. 9, p. 403, no. 270 (offering thanks and seeking help for the Jews in Poland).

105. "Mr. Easterman au Pape Pie XII," Aug. 2, 1943, *Actes et Documents*, vol.9, p. 417, no. 282.

106. "Peace & The Papacy," *Time*, Aug. 16, 1943.

107. "Mr. Easterman au délégué apostolique à Londres Godfrey," Sept. 24, 1943, *Actes et Documents*, vol. 9, p. 488, no. 346.

108. "Le grand rabbin Herzog au cardinal Maglione," Nov. 22, 1943, *Actes et Documents*, vol. 9, p. 575, no. 436.

109. See "Le délégué apostolique au Caire Testa au cardinal Maglione," April 6, 1942, *Actes et Documents*, vol. 9, p. 498, no. 340; "Le chargé d'affares à Presbourg Burzio au cardinal Maglione," April 9, 1942, *Actes et Documents*, vol. 9, p. 501, no. 343.

110. "Le Pape Pie XII à Mussolini," May 12, 1943, *Actes et Documents*, vol. 7, p. 331, no. 186. Later, Mussolini did try to negotiate an armistice through Archbishop Schuster of Milan. Barzini, 162.

111. "Notes du cardinal Maglione," May 13, 1943, *Actes et Documents*, vol. 7, p. 334, no. 189; "Notes du cardinal Maglione," May 13, 1943, *Actes et Documents*, vol. 7, p. 335, no. 190.

112. "Le délégue apostolique à Washington Cicognani au cardinal Maglione," May 29, 1943, *Actes et Documents*, vol. 7, p. 377, no. 215.

113. See "Le president Roosevelt au Pape Pie XII," June 16, 1943, *Actes et Documents*, vol. 7, p. 430, no. 251.

114. "Le nonce en Italie Borgongini Duca au cardinal Maglione," June 17, 1943, *Actes et Documents*, vol. 7, p. 431, no. 252.

115. "Notes du cardinal Maglione," July 27, 1943, *Actes et Documents*, vol. 7, p. 524, no. 316; Weizsäcker, 289. According to some accounts, the new Italian leadership did try to reach a settlement with the Allies, but they refused to accept the demanded unconditional surrender.

116. "L'Ambassade d'Italie à la Secrétairerie d'Etat," July 31, 1943, *Actes et Documents*, vol. 7, p. 533, no 322.

117. Procacci, 368.

118. Lamb, 35-39. Goebbels wrote in his diary on Dec. 13, 1942: "The Italians are extremely lax in their treatment of Jews. They protect Italian Jews both in Tunis and in occupied France and won't permit their being drafted for work or compelled to wear the Star of David." *The Goebbels Diaries 1942-1943*, 241; see Crankshaw, 188 ("Many Jews in Italy and the south of France owe their lives to the flat refusal of the Italian Fascist authorities, civil and military, to co-operate with Eichmann, and to their ingenuity in frustrating his plans"); Chadwick (1977), 183 (the Vatican was less pleased with Mussolini's overthrow than was the rest of Rome).

119. Michaelis, 322-23 (citing a note written by Obersturmführer S.S. Lieutenant Heinz Röthke).

120. Gilbert (1981), 152.

121. Kurzman, 5.

122. Lamb , 45.

123. As Joachim von Ribbentrop explained in an interrogation during the Nuremberg war trials, main-taining good relations with the Vatican was an important part of the German foreign policy. Bad relations with the Vatican would negatively impact on Germany's relations with other nations, particularly in South America. Office of the United States Chief of Counsel, Supp. B, 1236. Ribbentrop's concern over relations with the Vatican is reflected in a telegram he sent in January 1943. "Secret Telegram From Ribbentrop to the German Ambassador (Bergen)," dated Jan. 13, 1943, *Akten Zur Deutschen Auswärtigen Politik, 1918-1945*, Series E, Band V, Vandenhoeck and Ruprecht in Göttingen (1978), no. 123.

124. See Congregation for the Causes of Saints, *Positio*, (Summarium), Testimony of Karl Otto Wolff, March 14, 1972, before the Ecclesiastical Tribunal of Munich, on the beatification of Pius XII (Eugenii Pacelli), 837; Toland, 851; Payne, 485.

125. Consider the following statement made by Hitler in mid-July 1941:

> The ideal situation would be to leave the religions to devour themselves.... The heaviest blow that ever struck humanity was the coming of Christianity. Bolshevism is Christianity's illegitimate child. Both are inventions of the Jew. The deliberate lie in the matter of religion was introduced into the world by Christianity....

*Hitler's Secret Conversations*, 6; Cornwell (1999), 261. Similarly, Goebbels wrote in his diary on Nov. 1-2, 1941, "The Catholic Church... has not lost contact with its Jewish origin." *The Goebbels Diaries 1942-1943*, 117.

126. Stefano M. Paci, "Read Father Blet's book on Pius XII," *30 Days*, No. 4, 1998, 40; see Richard Lamb, *War in Italy 1943-1945: A Brutal Story*, 45 (St. Martin's Press, New York, 1993) (similar quote). As early as 1940, however, rumors spread that the Pontiff might leave Rome for a safer location. Charles Rankin, "Pius the Man and His Efforts for Peace," in *The Pope Speaks: The Words of Pius XII*, 108.

127. Cianfarra, 219.

128. "We agreed that carrying out such a plan would have had tremendous consequences and that it had to be blocked at all costs," wrote Ambassador Rahn. As a result, he was instructed to draft a note stating that it was Hitler's wish that "nothing whatever be undertaken against the person of the Pope, the integrity of his entourage and the inviolability of Vatican institutions." Haberman, *New York Times*. See "Kin Says Paul Barred Pius Kidnapping," *Washington Post*, Feb. 11, 1964 (Pope Paul VI persuaded the German envoy not to carry out the plot).

129. The German ambassador to the Holy See seems to have taken pride in his efforts to preserve Rome, noting that the German occupying forces were reduced to a "ridiculously small minimum." Weizsäcker, 289, 291-93.

130. Katz (1973), 6.

131. Graham, 14.

132. "Capital Is Shelled; 'Protection' of Vatican Assumed by Germans as Badoglio Flees[.] Cabinet With Allies[;] Threatens War on Reich — Landing by Invaders at Ostia Reported[.] Rome Is Shelled, Occupied by Nazis," *New York Times*, Sept. 11, 1943.

133. Blet, 213.

134. Leboucher, 138. See also Andrea Tornielli, "E Pio XII arruolò l'ebreo per salvarlo dai nazisti," *Il Giornale*, Nov. 15, 2007 (Father John Zuhlsdorf, trans.).

135. Between 1942 and December 1943, the Pope's Palatine Guard increased in number from 300 to over 4,000, "not due to any militarist expansion, but [as] a means of distributing Vatican passports to refu-gees." Gerald Warner, "Twisted Interpretation of History Blames Pius XII for the Plight of the Jews," *Scot-land on Sunday*, Sept. 26, 1999.

136. Leboucher, 138.

137. Ibid.

138. "Le délégué apostolique à Washington Cicognani au cardinal Maglione," Aug. 19, 1943, *Actes et Documents*, vol. 7, p. 567, no. 355.

139. "Le cardinal Maglione au délégué apostolique à Washington Cicognani," Aug. 21, 1943, *Actes et Documents*, vol. 7, p. 569, no. 357.

140. "L'Ambassade d'Italie à la Secrétairerie d'Etat," Sept. 8, 1943, *Actes et Documents*, vol. 7, p. 609, no. 385.

141. Chadwick (1977), 185 (noting that the denial appeared in *L'Osservatore Romano* on Sept. 10).

142. P. Murphy, 203.

143. Zolli, 141; Holmes, 152. Citing "Vatican records," the *Sunday Times* (London) reported: "During the second world war, on hearing that the Germans were exterminating Jews, Pope Pius XII secretly ordered the religious houses of Rome to shelter them from persecution." Simon Caldwell, "Sainthood bid for British nun Mother Ricarda who saved Jews," *Sunday Times* (London), Feb. 8, 2009. See Leon Poliakov, *Harvest of Hate* (Philadelphia, 1954), 293 ("We do not know what were the exact instructions sent by the Holy See to the churches in the different countries, but the coincidence of effort at the time of the deportations is proof that such steps were taken.") Years later, when the Israeli press asked why Christian rescuers had risked their lives for others, they frequently referred to Vatican orders "to save lives by all possible means." Lapide, 134-35. See "When Rome's Religious Houses Saved Jews," Zenit News Service, Jan. 21, 2005. Pius was in charge of the overall relief effort. Zolli, 141; Holmes, 152. He could have obtained credit for opening the buildings if he had made an announcement, but the likely reaction of Hitler's Nazis would have been to invade the buildings and seize those being protected.

144. Gallo, 143. Mother Ricarda Beauchamp Hambrough played an important role in saving the lives of more than 60 Jews by smuggling them into her convent. Her order, the Brigittines, has sought permission from the Vatican to examine her life and writings for evidence of "heroic virtue," the first step toward beatification. Simon Caldwell, "Sainthood bid for British nun Mother Ricarda who saved Jews," *Sunday Times* (London), Feb. 8, 2009.

145. *Memoriale delle Religiose Agostiniane Ven. Moastero dei SS Quattro Coronati* (Rome, 1943), http://www.ptwf.org/Downloads/Nun%27sDiary.pdf.

146. "Glimpse at How Religious Houses Helped the Jews: Research Presented on Wartime Efforts in Rome," Zenit News Service, Sept. 18, 2006 ("Documented historical research revealing this reality was carried out by Sister Grazia Lopaco of the pontifical Faculty Auxilium of Rome, and presented Friday in the context of the congress of the Italian Association of Church History Professors entitled 'Women in the Church in Italy.'")

147. Holmes, 152; Fogelman, 172.

148. McCormick, 118 (from a *New York Times* dispatch of Aug. 24, 1944). Having received assurances that its properties in Rome would be regarded as extraterritorial, not part of German-occupied Italy, the Holy See posted signs on the buildings to warn German soldiers that they should not search them. Papal critic Susan Zuccotti complained that the Vatican put protection notices on *all* of its buildings, instead of just the 160 or so where refugees are known to have been hiding. From this she concluded that the Church was protecting its property, not the refugees. She suggested that the warnings should have been put on *only* those churches, monasteries, and schools that contained Jews or other refugees. That, however, would have been nothing but a clear indication to the Nazis that refugees were hidden therein. If the Nazis had been provided with such information and they had used it to deport more Jews, the Vatican would indeed have been responsible. Besides, by putting signs on every building, Jews and other refugees were informed that these buildings were safe, and they could be entered on a moment's notice.

149. See Lapomarda, 234-35, n. 17 (referring to a list of 4,447 Jews who had been sheltered by religious groups). See generally Marchione (1997); Cardinal Pietro Palazzini, *Il clero e l'occupazione tedesca di Roma* (Editrice Apes: Rome, 1955); Antonio Gaspari, *Nascosti in convento. Incredibili storie di ebrei salvati dalla deportazione, Italia* 1943-1945, (Editrice Áncora: Milan, 1999). Monsignor Giovanni Ferrofino, secretary of the nuncio in Haiti during the war, said that more than 11,000 Jews were saved by Pius XII's continual requests for visas from General Trujillo, president of the Dominican Republic. He also said that the numbers showing up in documents were often in code and therefore drastically understated the number of people actually assisted. A video interview is archived at http://ptwf.org/Projects/Education/Pope%20Pius%20XII%20Videos.htm.

150. Gallo, 144. The Vatican also helped Jews escape to unoccupied areas. Ibid.

151. This rarely noted act was reported by Senator Adriano Ossicini, founder of the "Christian Left" in Italy, who was arrested in 1943 due to his opposition to the Fascist regime. "More Echoes on Pope Pius XII, Nazi Holocaust," *Catholic World News*, June 27, 1996 ("On the eve of one massive police sweep... the hospital received direct orders from Pope Pius XII to admit as many Jews as possible immediately.")

152. The Pontiff also granted audiences to German soldiers, many of whom suffered from guilty consciences, until an order from the German High Command prohibited them from entering the Vatican. In his diary, on April 5, 1942, Joseph Goebbels wrote that he urged the *Führer* to forbid German soldiers from visiting the Pope because Pius was using these opportunities for propaganda that was in conflict with Nazi aims. *The Goebbels Diaries 1942-1943*, 161. "The SS was certain that the Vatican was the center of anti-German espionage." Gallo, 146.

153. Zolli, 187; Lapide,132-33.

154. Stille, 270.

155. Ibid., 270-71. Stille tells the story of a woman who had not revealed that she was Jewish to the nuns sheltering her. The mother superior severely reprimanded her when she discovered this fact. The woman offered to leave, but the mother superior said: "No, it's not that, we just need to know so that if they come for you, we can take you down a secret passageway." Ibid., 216 ("[T]he nuns were incredibly good and courteous to us.") See also Editorial, *Congress Weekly, The Official Journal of the American Jewish Congress,* July 14, 1944 (the Vatican had provided kosher food).

156. Marchione (1997), 73. See also *Examining the Papacy,* 100-102 (newspaper clippings reporting on efforts to shelter Jews).

157. "Castel Gandalfo Celebrates 400 Years as Papal Residence," *Catholic World News,* Dec. 31, 1996 ("During the pontificate of Pius XII in World War II, for example, 12,000 people took refuge in Castel Gandolfo, and the papal apartments were opened up to shelter pregnant women nearing the days of childbirth; some 40 infants were born there."); Jason Berry, "Papal Lives: Biographies of Pius XII and John Paul II examine 2 of the century's most controversial men of the cloth," *Chicago Tribune,* Oct. 24, 1999, section 14, p. 1.

158. See Marchione, *Yours Is a Precious Witness* (photo section); *Examining the Papacy of Pope Pius XII,* 100 (photos of Jews being sheltered).

159. "Castel Gandalfo Celebrates 400 Years as Papal Residence," *Catholic World News,* Dec. 31, 1996. See *From Hitler's Doorstep: The Wartime Intelligence Reports of Allen Dulles, 1942-1945,* 237 (Pennsylvania State University Press, Neal H. Peterson, ed., 1996) (Document 3-43, Telegram 2341, March 9, 1944) ("crammed with refugees").

160. *From Hitler's Doorstep: The Wartime Intelligence Reports of Allen Dulles, 1942-1945,* 237 (Pennsylvania State University Press, Neal H. Peterson, ed., 1996) (document 3-43, Telegram 2341, March 9, 1944). This document is reprinted in the Appendix, p. 411.

161. Congregation for the Causes of Saints, *Positio,* (Summarium), Testimony of P. Guglielmo Hentrich, before the Ecclesiastical Tribunal of Rome, on the beatification of Pius XII (Eugenio Pacelli).

162. "Sanctuary in the Vatican," *Palestine Post,* June 22, 1944.

163. Emilio Bonomelli, *I Papi in Campagna,* 439 (Gherardo Casini Editore, Rome, 1953). When American soldiers (Special Forces) were housed in Castel Gandolfo, they "liberated" some of the Pope's furniture and other property. When the officers found out, they made sure that all of the property was returned. Robert H. Adleman and Col. George Walton, *The Devil's Brigade,* 205-6 (1966).

164. Leboucher, 137.

165. Timothy O'Donnell, president of Christendom College, reported: "I myself, during a private tour of the gardens of Castel Gandolfo . . . visited a number of areas which are not open to the public. Under the papal residence are the ruins of the palace of the Emperor Tiberius. Here in these hidden chambers Pius XII hid thousands of Jews during the Second World War who were to be deported to German concentration camps. On the walls one can still see the darkened ash where these fugitives from the Nazi fury lit fires to cook food and keep warm. In the dark stillness of this subterranean vault stands an enormous wooden cross, beautifully decorated. This Christian symbol of suffering love was given to Pius XII at the end of the war by the Jews who lived there during the those terrifying days. It was their way of expressing their deep gratitude and veneration for this Pope who had heroically defied the Gestapo and had saved their lives." Marchione, *Pope Pius XII: Architect for Peace,* 134 (citing John S. Rader and Kateryna Fedoryka, *The Pope and the Holocaust*).

166. Holmes, 153.

167. Mary DeTurris, "The Vatican and the Holocaust," *Our Sunday Visitor,* May 18, 1997.

168. Father Peter Gumpel, the relator of Pope Pius XII's sainthood cause took part in this activity, escorting Jews from Holland to Belgium.

169. Graham, 23-24; Blet, 238.

170. See *PTWF Press Release,* "Newly Discovered Documents proves Pope Pius XII was the best friend of the Jewish People before, during and after WWII," Feb. 18, 2009 (emphasis in original). A transcript and a video of the interview are posted on the Internet: *http://www.barhama.com/PAVETHEWAY/ferrofino.html.* See also Zenit News, "Group Gives New Proof of Pius XII's Help for Jews; Says Pope Worked to Save Lives Before, During, After War," Feb. 20, 2009.

171. Andrea Tornielli, *"E Pio XII arruolò l'ebreo per salvarlo dai nazisti," Il Giornale,* Nov. 15, 2007.

172. See "Jewish Hostages in Rome: Vatican Protests," *Jewish Chronicle* (London), Oct. 29, 1943.

173. Andrea Tornielli, *"E Pio XII arruolò l'ebreo per salvarlo dai nazisti," Il Giornale,* Nov. 15, 2007.

174. Ibid.

175. "Le nonce à Montevideo Levarne au cardinal Maglione," Oct. 14, 1943, *Actes et Documents,* vol. 9, pp. 501-502, no. 364.

176. Weizsäcker replaced von Bergen, the German ambassador, in July 1943. "L'ambassadeur d'Allemagne Weizsäcker au pape Pie XII," July 5, 1943, *Actes et Documents,* vol. 7, p. 465, no. 277.

177. See "Notes du cardinal Maglione," Sept. 20, 1943, *Actes et Documents,* vol. 9, p. 505, no. 368; Chadwick (1977), 190-91; Robert Graham, "La strana condotta di E.von Weizsäcker ambasciatore del Reich in Vaticano," *La Civiltà Cattolica,* vol. II, del 1970; see also Weizsäcker, 277-78. When he learned that German troops would take over Rome, Weizsäcker expressed depression at the thought of it. Chadwick (1977),

183-84. One priest reported that when others tried to report the names and places were Jews were being sheltered, Weizsäcker turned them away. Chadwick (1977), 199. When several conspirators were arrested in a failed coup attempt, they were questioned by Nazi officials as to whether Weizsäcker was involved in the plot. Weizsäcker, 295-96. Weizsäcker, though he was a Protestant, asked for the Vatican post because he thought that would give him the best opportunity to work for peace. Weizsäcker, 286. He would have liked to have followed custom and have a priest attached to his embassy, but German authorities offered him only a priest who had left the Church. "I had no difficulty in deciding between this plan and not having an ecclesiastical advisor at all." Weizsäcker, 294; see Hatch and Walshe, 166; Katz, 12 ("Weizsäcker… was considered by the Vatican and others, including himself, to be secretly anti-Nazi"). He was convicted at the postwar Nuremberg trials, but was released from prison after only 18 months. Chadwick (1977), 181.

178. Leonidas E. Hill III, "The Vatican Embassy of Ernst von Weizsäcker, 1943-1945," 39:2 *Journal of Modern History*,138 (June 1967).

179. Kurzman, 69.

180. Ibid., 73.

181. Ibid., 69.

182. "Notes du cardinal Maglione," Sept. 20, 1943, *Actes et Documents*, vol. 7, p. 631, no. 410; Chadwick (1977), 187.

183. Chadwick (1977), 187.

184. "Notes du cardinal Maglione," Sept. 20, 1943, *Actes et Documents*, vol. 7, p. 631, no. 410 (appendix, "Notes du Mgr. Montini").

185. This demand was the brainchild of Herbert Kappler, who was in charge of the S.S. and Gestapo in Rome. According to at least one hypothesis, he was afraid that deportation of Jews would make occupation harder, so he invented this ransom idea to convince his Nazi superiors in Berlin not to order deportation. Lamb, 40-41. He refused payment in lira, saying: "I could print as many of them as I like." Chadwick (1977), 187-88.

186. Michaelis, 355. Apparently, such a demand was not unprecedented. See Mazgaj, 71 (similar demand in Polish town of Klimontow in 1942).

187. Zolli, 160-61.

188. Ibid., 161, 206; Holmes, 155; Michaelis, 355; "Israelis Defend Name of Pope Pius XII," *Jewish Chronicle*, Oct. 11, 1963 (citing "a report by Dr. Ugo Foa, president of Rome's Jewish community, describing how Pope Pius offered the congregation gold to help pay the ransom demanded by the Germans in 1943 and how he subsequently instructed Catholic institutions in Italy to give refuge to Jews threatened with deportation").

189. O'Carroll, 95; Chadwick (1977), 188.

190. Zolli always explained that his conversion was a matter of faith, not just an effort to thank the Pope or the Catholic Church. Zolli, 185. The choice of his Christian name, however, was to pay tribute to Pius XII.

191. Lamb, 41.

192. The order is reprinted in the Appendix, p. 410. The facts are also confirmed in Adolf Eichmann's memoirs, which were made public in March 2000, after being guarded by the Israeli government for almost 40 years. See "Dragnet: The Last Acceptable Bigotry," *This Rock*, April 2000, 7, 9 (quoting Eichmann's memoirs); Elli, Wohlgelernter, "Memory — and the Nazi master plan," *The Jerusalem Post*, March 3, 2000, 5B; "Eichmann's Diary Reveals Church's Assistance to Jews," Zenit News, March 2, 2000. The memoirs were released in order to help defend a lawsuit brought by David Irving. "Historian's Holocaust Libel Suit Dismissed by Judge in London," *New York Times*, April 11, 2000; Leonidas E. Hill III, "The Vatican Embassy of Ernst von Weizsäcker, 1939-1945," 39 *Journal of Modern History*, 138, 148 (1967). See p. 234.

193. See "Dragnet: The Last Acceptable Bigotry," *This Rock*, April 2000, 7, 9 (quoting Eichmann's memoirs); Elli, Wohlgelernter, "Memory — and the Nazi master plan," *The Jerusalem Post*, March 3, 2000, 5B; "Eichmann's Diary Reveals Church's Assistance to Jews," Zenit News, March 2, 2000.

194. See "Dragnet: The Last Acceptable Bigotry," *This Rock*, April 2000, 7, 9 (quoting Eichmann's memoirs).

195. Scrivener, 38 (diary account of what took place).

196. Chadwick (1977), 188.

197. Susan Zuccotti, "Pope Pius XII and the Holocaust: The Case in Italy," in *The Italian Refuge*, at 254.

198. This message is the source of the title of one of Zuccotti's books. The memo was actually an attempt by Weizsäcker to convince Berlin not to launch an attack on the Vatican. He downplayed the papal reaction for that purpose. Congregation for the Causes of Saints, *Positio*, appendix 25, 273; Ivo Herzer, *The Italian Refuge*, 121 (Catholic University Press of America, 1989); Gallo, 136; Leonidas E. Hill III, "The Vatican Embassy of Ernst von Weizsäcker, 1939-1945," 39 *Journal of Modern History*, 138, 150 (1967).

199. Katz (1969), 134-39. The Pacelli family successfully sued Katz for defamation. See p. 233.

200. See Congregation for the Causes of Saints, *Positio*, appendix 25, 264.

201. Ernst Von Weizsäcker, *Memoirs of Ernst Von Weizsäcker* (H. Regnery Co., Chicago, J. Andrews, trans., 1951).

202. Congregation for the Causes of Saints, *Positio*, appendix 25, 264 (quoting a *New York Times* book review on Aug. 31, 1969). For the Vatican's record during the roundup, see Giovanni Sale, "Roma 1943: occupazione nazista e deportazione degli ebrei romani," *La Civiltà Cattolica*, 2003, vol. 4, 417-29.

203. See Chadwick, *A History of Christianity*, 190; Owen Chadwick, "Weizsäcker, the Vatican, and the Jews of Rome," 28 *Journal of Ecclesiastical History*, 179 (April 1977) ("The pope was obviously surprised. He said that the Germans promised that they would not hurt the Jews, and knew of the 50 kilograms of gold."); Robert Graham, "La Strana Condotta di E. Von Weizsäcker ambasciatore del Reich in Vaticana," *La Civiltà Cattolica*, June 6, 1970, 455-471; Gallo, 134; Congregation for the Causes of Saints, *Positio*, appendix 25, 260.

204. Princess Enza Pignatelli Aragona Cortés, taped interview for the documentary "History Undercover: Pope Pius XII and the Holocaust" (1997, A&E Home Video); Dan Kurzman, *The Race for Rome*, XXXI (Doubleday: Garden City, 1975). See also "La carità del Santo Padre," *L'Osservatore Romano*, Oct. 25-26, 1943 ("With the augmentation of so much evil, the universal and paternal charity of the Supreme Pontiff has become, it might be said, ever more active; it knows neither boundaries nor nationality, neither religion nor race."); Zuccotti, "Pope Pius XII and the Holocaust: The Case in Italy," in *The Italian Refuge*, 255.

205. Congregation for the Causes of Saints, *Positio*, appendix 25, 261; "Notes du cardinal Maglione," Oct. 16, 1943, *Actes et Documents*, vol. 9, p. 505, no. 368 (including a facsimile of the handwritten version). An editorial in the *Jewish Chronicle* (London), Oct. 29, 1943, entitled "Jewish Hostages in Rome: Vatican Protests," said: "The Vatican has made strong representations to the German Government and the German High Command in Italy against the persecution of the Jews in Nazi-occupied Italy."

206. Blet, 216.

207. Ibid.

208. Diplomatic (Secret) Telegram from Osborne to Foreign Office, Oct. 31, 1943, British Public Records Office, FO 371/37255 56879.

209. Ibid.

210. "Notes du cardinal Maglione," Oct. 16, 1943, *Actes et Documents*, vol. 9, p. 505, no. 368 (including a facsimile of the handwritten version).

211. Ibid.

212. Ibid.; Blet, 215-16 (also noting that the Vatican undertook efforts to help the Jews who were not released); Lamb, 42.

213. Weizsäcker felt that "if it were possible to do anything at all for peace, it could be done at or through the Vatican." Weizsäcker, 277.

214. "Notes du cardinal Maglione," Oct. 16, 1943, *Actes et Documents*, vol. 9, p. 505, no. 368 (including a facsimile of the handwritten version); Chadwick (1977), 191; "Notes de la Secrétairerie d'Etat," Oct. 23, 1943, *Actes et Documents*, vol. 9, p. 519, no. 383. See "La Secrétairerie d'Etat à l'Ambassade d'Allemagne," Oct. 23, 1943, *Actes et Documents*, vol. 9, p. 521, no. 385; "Le nonce à Berlin Orsenigo au cardinal Maglione," Oct. 23, 1943, *Actes et Documents*, vol. 9, p. 522, no. 386.

215. State of Israel Ministry of Justice, *The Trial of Adolf Eichmann: Record of Proceedings in the District Court of Jerusalem (Vol. I)*, 83 (Jerusalem, 1992). A report from Rome to Berlin, dated Oct. 26, 1943, confirmed that the "Vatican has apparently for a long time been assisting many Jews escape. The fear is growing that further actions to transport factory hands and workers are planned." *National Archives and Records Administration, CIA Selected Documents, 1941-1947*, Box 4, Group XIII/52, Rome to Berlin, RSS 210.26.19/43.

216. Gaspari, *Gli ebrei salvati da Pio XII*; "New Revelations on Jews Saved by Pius XII," Zenit News Service, Feb. 16, 2001.

217. State of Israel Ministry of Justice, *The Trial of Adolf Eichmann: Record of Proceedings in the District Court of Jerusalem (Vol. IV)*, 1504-5 (Jerusalem, 1992).

218. Antonio Gaspari, *The Jews Saved by Pius XII (Gli ebrei salvati da Pio XII)* (2001); "New Revelations on Jews Saved by Pius XII," Zenit News Service, Feb. 16, 2001.

219. According to the Jesuit magazine *La Civiltà Cattolica*, the Pope was informed of the roundup only after it had been completed. The Pope immediately sent his nephew to intercede with influential German Church officials in Rome, to attempt to help the detained Jews and to prevent another such operation in the city. Whatever the reasons, the magazine reported that the roundup ended immediately and about 8,000 Roman Jews "miraculously had their lives saved." John Thavis, "Jesuit journal cites new evidence that Pius XII helped save Jews," *Catholic News Service*, Dec. 4, 2003; Giovanni Sale, *La Civiltà Cattolica*, Dec. 5, 2003.

220. Professor Owen Chadwick of Cambridge dismissed Zuccotti's arguments as "not history but guesswork." "Pius XII's Terrifying Dilemma: Put Yourself in His Shoes," *Tablet* (London), June 30, 2001, 950-951.

221. Zuccotti, *The Italians and the Holocaust*, 127.

222. Ibid., 303, n. 69.

223. Thus, she argues, "clearly there were no plans for continuing the action" by the Nazis. Zuccotti, *Under His Very Windows*, 169.

224. Congregation for the Causes of Saints, *Positio*, appendix 25, 261; Andrea Tornielli, *Pio XII. Papa degli ebrei* (Piemme, 2001); see also Leonidas E. Hill III, "The Vatican Embassy of Ernst von Weizsäcker, 1939-1945," 39 *Journal of Modern History*, 138, 148 (1967) ("Gumpert remained in General Stahel's service and thus was one of the first German diplomats to learn that the roundup of the Jews had commenced on October 16. Gumpert telephoned Kessel… and arranged with him that a trusted Vatican dignitary would present a letter of protest to Stahel that morning. The letter would reflect the Vatican's disgust at the measures against the Jews.")

225. Congregation for the Causes of Saints, *Positio*, appendix 25, 237 (noting that this was confirmed by one of Stahel's assistants in an interview with the German news agency KNA). See also *L'Osservatore Romano*, Dec. 8, 2000, 4.

226. "Mgr. Hudal au général Stahel," Oct. 16, 1943, *Actes et Documents*, vol. 9, p. 509, no. 373, n. 4 (emphasis added). General Stahel had signs posted forbidding German troops from entering the Holy See's property. Images of the sign are posted on the web page of Pave the Way Foundation, *www.ptwf.org*.

227. Zolli, 140.

228. See "Most of Rome's Jews Were Saved from Hitler's Final Solution," *L'Osservatore Romano*, weekly edition in English, Jan. 24, 2001, 11 (translation of Kunkel's interview with KNA).

229. Interview, Zenit News, Oct. 26, 2000 (emphasis added). See Congregation for the Causes of Saints, *Positio*, appendix 25, p. 291; Besier, 146-47 (Hudal "played a decisive role in the termination of the deportation of the Jews from Rome.")

230. "La carità del Santo Padre," *L'Osservatore Romano*, Oct. 25-26, 1943.

231. "Jewish Hostages in Rome: Vatican Protests," *Jewish Chronicle* (London), Oct. 29, 1943.

232. Gallo, 135 (citing *L'Osservatore Romano* of Oct. 25, 1943). "La carità del Santo Padre," *L'Osservatore Romano*, Oct. 25-26, 1943. This issue of *L'Osservatore Romano* is listed in the index to the CD-ROM set of *L'Osservatore Romano* under Oct. 26.

233. Cornwell, *Hitler's Pope*, 309 (citing Robert Katz, *Black Sabbath*, 259). In an example of circular scholarship, Cornwell and Zuccotti relied on Katz's work, which predated the release of most relevant documents. In his newest book, Katz relied on Cornwell and Zuccotti.

234. This is made clear in the diary of the *Maestro di Camera* (master of the chamber). The *Maestro di Camera* arranges audiences and pontifical ceremonies, and he keeps very detailed records of these matters. See also "Note de Mgr. Tardini," Oct. 21, 1943, *Actes et Documents*, vol. 7, p. 678, no. 442 (footnote 1, noting Tittmann's mistake); "Le délégué apostolique à Washington Cicognani au cardinal Maglione," Sept. 25, 1943, *Actes et Documents*, vol. 9, p. 489, no. 347 (footnote 2, noting the meeting on Oct. 14).

235. "Nostre Informazioni," *L'Osservatore Romano*, Oct. 15, 1943, 1. Tittmann's memoirs confirm that the resistance from within Germany encouraged Pope Pius XII *not* to make more express condemnations regarding Nazi brutality. Writing of German lawyer Joseph Mueller, who was very active in the resistance, Tittmann reported:

> Dr. Mueller said that during the war his anti-Nazi organization in Germany had always been very insistent that the Pope should refrain from making any public statements singling out the Nazis and specifically condemning them and had recommended that the Pope's remarks should be confined to generalities only. Dr. Mueller said that he was obliged to give this advice, since, if the Pope had been specific, Germans would have accused him of yielding to the promptings of foreign powers and this would have made the German Catholics even more suspected than they were and would have greatly restricted their freedom of action in their work of resistance to the Nazis.

Tittmann's ultimate conclusion was: "I cannot help but feel that the Holy Father chose the better path and thereby saved many lives." Tittmann, *Inside the Vatican of Pius XII*.

236. Perhaps even worse than Cornwell's development of this argument is that critic Robert Katz repeated it several years after it had been exposed. Katz, *The Battle for Rome*, 113-14.

237. Robert A. Graham, "A Return to Theocracy," *America*, July 18, 1964, 72; Chadwick (1977), 195. When the Nazis first occupied Rome, Weizsäcker sent his second-in-command, Albrecht von Kessel, into the Vatican so that he would be able to calm things down if German troops should invade. Ibid., 185.

238. Blet, 212.

239. Cornwell (1999), 312.

240. Holmes, 156; Blet, 213.

241. Holmes, 156.

242. "La carità del Santo Padre," *L'Osservatore Romano*, Oct. 25-26, 1943, 1.

243. Holmes, 157-58.

244. Weizsäcker had long served in Germany's diplomatic service, and probably knew Pius XII's attitudes toward Nazism better than anyone else in the German government. He had no doubt about where Pius stood. He said to Hitler on the day he left for Rome as German ambassador to the Vatican: "I am actually leaving for enemy country." Lapide, 123. On Jan. 25, 1940, while he was the German secretary of state in the foreign

office, Weizsäcker wrote to the ambassador from the Holy See, "To be sure the Vatican does express itself in general terms, but it is totally clear who is meant." Groppe, *The Church and the Jews*, 25.

245. In 2009, a note was discovered in a cloistered monastery near the Coliseum in Rome, and it lists the names of 24 people who were taken in by the nuns "in accordance with Pius' desire." "Vatican Radio: document shows Pius XII helped Jews" (AP), March 4, 2009; "Vatican document shows Pius XII saved Jews" (JTA), March 5, 2009. Found in the historical journal of the Augustinian Community of Santi Quattro Coronati, the note said: "The Holy Father wants to save his children, including the Jews, and orders that hospitality be shown to these persecuted people in the convents." John Thavis, "Document confirms Pope Pius XII's efforts to save Jews, expert says," *Catholic News Service*, March 5, 2009. Relevant portions of the document include the following:

> Having arrived at this month of November we must be ready to render services of charity in a com-pletely unexpected way. The Holy Father Pius XII, of paternal heart, feels in himself all the sufferings of the moment. Unfortunately with the Germans entry into Rome, which happened in the month of September, a ruthless war against the Jews has begun, whom they wish to exterminate by means of atrocities prompted by the blackest barbarities. They round up young Italians, political figures, in order to torture them and finish them off in the most tremendous torments. In this painful situa-tion the Holy Father wants to save his children, also the Jews, and orders that hospitality be given in the convents to these persecuted, and that the cloisters must also adhere to the wish of the Supreme Pontiff....
>
> * * *
>
> At the end of the war, the goodness of the Holy Father was spoken about, who had helped and caused many to be saved, both Jews and young people and entire families. The press filled its columns and in a Catholic paper, *L'Osservatore Romano*, we read an article by Professor Tescari who knew well how much had been done in the cloistered convents for the salvation of so many persecuted.
>
> * * *
>
> Those who write the history of the most recent German Fascist oppression in Rome will have to devote a special chapter to the generous, vast, multiform work, deployed in favor of the persecuted by the religious. Parochial offices transformed into true and proper placement-refuge offices (I was in one where, in the few minutes I was there, I saw a multitude of men and women of every class, of every age, converge, and the parish priest listen, take notes, direct, promise, give generously), priests' homes become hotels for fugitives (I still hear the housekeeper of one of them grumbling that there wasn't anything in the house anymore, etc.); complaints unusually peopled by faces shaped by new and strange confusion, but in this field of charity those who showed themselves real heroines, were the nuns who dressed up Jewish women (guilty of nothing else except being blood of Jesus and Mary) as fellow sisters, who violated the sacred cloister to shelter men persecuted for reason of politics or race, who took in children of fugitives, who gave themselves to the forging of personal documents getting them themselves or facilitating their acquisition....

246. Holmes, 158. After the war, Father Pierre-Marie Benoît of Marseilles was given an award by the Ital-ian Jewish Union for his work in protecting about 1,000 Jews in Rome. Upon receiving his gold medal from the Italian Jewish Union, Father Benoît paid tribute to Ambassador Weizsäcker, "who undoubtedly knew that the institutions of Rome were packed with Jews," but did not reveal this to his superiors. Ibid., 152-53.

247. As others have noted, "[I]t is ironical that Pius XII became the unintended victim... of this maneu-ver that saved the lives of thousands of Roman Jews." Robert A. Graham, "A Return to Theocracy," *America*, July 18, 1964, 72. Chadwick calls this "the very nub of the problem." Was Weizsäcker telling the truth or try-ing to dissuade the Nazi leadership in Berlin from invading the Vatican? Graham ultimately concludes that it was the latter. See also Chadwick (1977), 194 ("This telegram did as much as any other single document to lower the postwar reputation of Pius XII. Looked at in terms of the reign of terror, and of Weizsäcker trying to do what he could for the Jews, it was beautifully drafted.") That is one of the great difficulties in trying to uncover the truth. In postwar Europe, scholars know of at least one particularly notorious manufacturer of false information, but they don't know how many others there might have been. See Winks, 386.

248. National Public Radio, *Morning Edition*, Father Don Aldo Brunacci discusses his efforts to save 200 Jews during World War II, March 31, 2004. See also Mae Briskin, "Rescue Italian Style," *Jewish Monthly*, May 1986, 22 (similar quote from Brunacci). Father Brunacci was arrested by the Nazis, but they moved him to Rome shortly before its liberation, and he spent less than three weeks in captivity. Ibid. See also Congrega-tion for the Causes of Saints, *Positio*, appendix 25, 280.

249. John Thavis, "Jesuit journal cites new evidence that Pius XII helped save Jews," *Catholic News Ser-vice*, Dec. 4, 2003; Giovanni Sale, *La Civilta Cattolica*, Dec. 5, 2003.

250. Ibid.

251. Holmes, 163-64.

252. "La carità del Santo Padre," *L'Osservatore Romano*, Oct. 25-26, 1943.

253. Blet, 213.

254. "Nostre Informazioni," *L'Osservatore Romano*, Oct. 30, 1943. See also "Border Not Crossed, Vatican Says," *New York Times*, Sept. 22, 1943, 4.

255. Graham, 10-11.

256. The Vatican was supplying up to 100,000 meals per day to the people hardest hit by food shortages.

257. Gilbert (1987), 447.

258. *The Italian Refuge*, 6.

259. Holmes, 134.

260. Pius had encouraged Mussolini and King Victor Emmanuel III to abandon Germany and seek a separate peace agreement with the Allies. Blet, 17. Later, Mussolini tried to negotiate an armistice through Archbishop Schuster of Milan. Barzini, 162. The weakness of Mussolini vis-à-vis Hitler was reflected in January 1944, when Hitler forced Mussolini to execute his son-in-law, Count Ciano, former Italian ambassador to the Vatican. Hitler believed Ciano to be guilty of betraying the Axis cause by seeking a separate peace through the mediation of Pope Pius XII.

261. "Rome Radio Reports Vatican City Bombed; Confirmation Lacking — Germans Blame Allies — 1941 Ruse Cited," *New York Times*, Nov. 6, 1943, 5. On Nov. 9, 1943, Joseph Goebbels wrote in his diary:

> The dropping of some enemy bombs on Vatican City still creates a world sensation. Under the pressure of commentary in the neutral press the English have been compelled to deny any guilt and to attempt to blame us. They are doing that, however, in such a clumsy and transparent manner that nobody will believe them. Their lies are too transparently foolish....

> Unfortunately the *Osservatore Romano* assumes only a very moderate attitude concerning this event. Obviously the Pope does not want to forego the possibility of acting as mediator between the Reich and the western enemy powers, at least not for the present, although there isn't the slightest occasion for such mediation at the moment.

*The Goebbels Diaries 1942-1943*, 503. A few days later, Goebbels expressed resentment about the Germans' inability to use the Vatican's complaint to their political advantage. Ibid., 514.

262. See "Bombing of Vatican 'Planned,' Pope Says; He Indicates Knowledge of the Identity of Nov. 5 Attacker," *New York Times*, Dec. 28, 1943.

263. Korn, 145. See "Germany Pledges Pontiff's Safety; Ambassador Says Nazis Will Respect Rights of the Pope and His Official Family," *New York Times*, Oct. 30, 1943. When the Germans again urged Pius to leave Rome in 1944, he said, "If Rome really is an open city, why don't you leave?" Hatch and Walshe, 176.

264. Korn, 146.

265. *Catholic Mind*, June 1964, 26.

266. Ibid.; *Tablet* (London), Dec. 25, 1943, 306 ("[W]e can well imagine the anxiety in the hearts of our Catholic fellow-citizens in these days when the head of their Church again becomes prisoner in the Vatican.")

267. *Tablet* (London), Dec. 25, 1943, 306.

268. "Des familles juives au pape Pie XII," Dec. 30, 1943, *Actes et Documents*, vol. 9, p. 636, no. 490 (Jewish families thank Pope Pius XII).

## Chapter Fourteen: 1944 and the Allies Invade

1. *Is the Catholic Church Anti-Social? A Debate Between G.G. Coulton and Arnold Lunn*, 193 (The Catholic Book Club: London, 1947).

2. "Vatican Repeats Pledge of Haven," *New York Times*, Feb. 9, 1944.

3. Roberto Ronca served as rector of the Roman Seminary during the war. In February 1944, during the German occupation, he met with Pope Pius XII, who offered support and encouragement for these efforts. Marco Tosatti, "PIO XII: ospitava ebrei in Laterano," *La Stampa*, May 22, 2009 (report from Monsignor Giuseppe Simonazzi, who was present at the meeting). This testimony contradicts Zuccotti's claim (*Under His Very Windows*, 206-210) that Pius XII gave no support to Ronca's lifesaving efforts and may have been hostile to them. In 1948, Pius appointed Ronca as a bishop.

4. See "Vatican Repeats Pledge of Haven," *New York Times*, Feb. 9, 1944.

5. Scrivener, 106 (quoting a dispatch from *Popolo di Roma*).

6. "Vatican Repeats Pledge of Haven," *New York Times*, Feb. 9, 1944 (64 arrests); "Fascists Slay Six Seized in Church," *New York Times*, Feb. 11, 1944 (82 arrests).

7. Graham (1987), 12.

8. Scrivener, 106. See "Extraterritorialità e mimmunità diplomatica nei riguardi della Basilica di San Paolo e degli edifici annessi," *L'Osservatore Romano*, Feb. 10, 1944.

9. "Vatican Repeats Pledge of Haven," *New York Times*, Feb. 9, 1944. "Fascists Slay Six Seized in Church," *New York Times*, Feb. 11, 1944 (82 arrests) ("strong and immediate protest by Pope Pius XII").

10. *New York Times*, Feb. 9, 1944 ("The Vatican radio, commenting on the Fascist raid on St. Paul's Basilica last Thursday in which sixty-four Italian officers and Jews who had received sanctuary there were arrested, said tonight that the church would never yield in offering charity to everyone.")

11. Scrivener, 106.

12. In October 1943, the Department of State urged President Roosevelt to try to avoid destroying Rome when liberating it from the Germans. Memorandum by the Under Secretary of State (Stettinius) to President Roosevelt, Oct. 7, 1943, in *Foreign Relations of the United States, Diplomatic Papers, 1943, vol. II (Europe)*, United States Government Printing Office (Washington, 1964), 948.

13. Smit, 234.

14. Ibid., 234-35; O'Carroll, 70; Hatch and Walshe, 173-74. But see Robert A. Graham, "Author Questions Pope Pius XII's Vatican Diplomacy," *Pilot* (Boston), Oct. 31, 1970, 1, 16 (suggesting that this is an apocryphal story).

15. Herbert L. Mathews, "Happier Days for Pope Pius: Shadows of war are lifting for a Pontiff whose greatest interest is world peace," *New York Times*, Oct. 15, 1944, 8.

16. The Vatican had received word that the Allies might bomb in and around Castel Gandolfo, so in mid-February 1944, the apostolic delegate in Washington contacted the United States secretary of state to assure the American government that "no German soldier was ever admitted within the precincts of the Pontifical Villa and that no German military whatsoever are now within the villa." The Apostolic Delegate in Washington (Cicognani) to the Secretary of State, Feb. 16, 1944, *United States Department of State, Foreign Relations of the United States, Diplomatic Papers, 1944, vol. IV (Europe)*, United States Government Printing Office (Washington, 1966), 1277; see Ibid., 1279. See also p. 338.

17. General Mark W. Clark later wrote:

> I say that the bombing of the Abbey... was a mistake — and I say it with full knowledge of the controversy that has raged around this episode. The official position was best summed up, I suppose, in a State Department communication to the Vatican's undersecretary of State on October 13, 1945, saying that "there was unquestionable evidence in the possession of the Allied commanders in the field that the Abbey of Monte Cassino formed part of the German defensive system."

> I was one of the Allied commanders in the field and the one in command at Cassino, and I said then that there is irrefutable evidence that no German soldier, except emissaries, was ever inside the Monastery for purposes other than to take care of the sick or to sightsee.

Gannon, 228-29.

18. "Vatican Bombed by Single Plane; Craft Unidentified," *New York Times*, March 3, 1944.

19. The abbreviation is sometimes shortened to GAPO.

20. According to Father Peter Gumpel, relator of Pope Pius XII's sainthood cause, Hitler originally ordered a 100-to-1 reprisal, but he was talked into the more traditional 10-to-1. Some of those executed were people who had already been condemned to death for other offenses.

21. See O'Carroll, 242.

22. "Notes de la Secrétairerie d'Etat," March 24, 1944, *Actes et Documents*, vol. 10, p. 189, no. 115.

23. Carroll, 242.

24. This event was later depicted in an Italian motion picture entitled *La Rappresaglia* (1973), which was highly critical of Pope Pius XII. In 1974, a niece of Pius XII sued the writer, producer, and director of the film alleging calumny. Testimony established that the killings were carried out within 24 hours of the bombing and were done in complete secrecy. There was no opportunity for intervention by the Pontiff. The court held in favor of the plaintiff, requiring the defendants to pay fines and handing out one (suspended) prison sentence. See p. 233.

25. Graham (1987), 12. This explanation has not satisfied some critics, who argue that the Pope intentionally avoided making a protest. See Katz (1973), 218 (citing Rolf Hochhuth's play *The Deputy*). Following the war, the German generals who ordered the executions were tried for war crimes, found guilty, and sentenced to death. Ibid., xii.

26. Graham (undated), 9-12.

27. Ibid.

28. Burzio had protested against Nazi treatment of the Jews as early as Sept. 11, 1941. Lapomarda, 104, n. 34.

29. Graham (undated), 9-12; see pp. 248-51.

30. "Pie XII aux Cardinaux et prélats de la Curie romaine," June 2, 1944, *Actes et Documents*, vol. 11, p. 341, no. 205. See "The Pope's Solicitude," *Jewish Chronicle*, July 16, 1943. Pius also took this opportunity to caution against the problems associated with unconditional surrender, which displeased President Roosevelt.

31. "Pie XII aux Cardinaux et prélats de la Curie romaine," June 2, 1944, *Actes et Documents*, vol. 11, p. 341, no. 205. See "The Pope's Solicitude," *Jewish Chronicle*, July 16, 1943. See also "Perspectives on History: Pope Pius XII," a 1963 made-for-television biography, hosted by Mike Wallace.

32. Kurzman, 56.

33. The German ambassador to the Holy See tried to approach the Allies through the Vatican to coordinate the transfer. He presented his proposal to the Vatican the night before the Allies moved into Rome. Weizsäcker, 292. See Smit, 237; Blet, 234.

34. "L'Ambassade d'Allemagne à la Secrétairerie d'Etat," April 13, *Actes et Documents*, vol. 11, p. 276, no. 156.

35. Weizsäcker, 293. "Although he failed to obtain any formal bilateral agreement, he did inspire both sides, as Weizsäcker wrote, with a type of reverential respect for Rome." Blet, 234.

36. Scrivener, 201.

37. Ibid., 202 (placards all around town read: "Come to St. Peter's at six o'clock to thank the Pope.") German ambassador Weizsäcker noted how no one thought of the King of Italy. Chadwick, "Weizsäcker, the Vatican, and the Jews of Rome," 183.

38. See "Le sollecitudini costanti del 'Defensor Civitatis' nella parola di Sua Santità all'Associazione fra i Romani," *L'Osservatore Romano*, June 21, 1948.

39. Scrivener, 203.

40. Ibid.

41. Hatch and Walshe, 179.

42. Cornwell (1999), 316.

43. Lapide, 131; see Weizsäcker, 297.

44. "Le National Jewish Welfare Board au pape Pie XII," July 21, 1944, *Actes et Documents*, vol. 10, p. 358, no. 272.

45. Lapide, 131. The *Jewish News* (Detroit) reported on July 7, "It is gradually being revealed that Jews have been sheltered within the walls of the Vatican during the German occupation of Rome." An editorial in the July 14 edition of the *Congress Weekly*, the official journal of the American Jewish Congress, noted that the Vatican had provided kosher food.

46. "Jews of Rome Thank Pope for Aiding Them," *New York Times*, June 17, 1944.

47. Dimitri Cavalli, "How Pope Pius XII was made a villain," *Riverdale Press* (Bronx, NY), July 16, 1998, A11. See also "Le délégué apostolique à Washington Cicognani au cardinal Maglione," Aug. 9, 1944, *Actes et Documents*, vol. 10, p. 378, no. 295 (expressing thanks from the American Jewish Committee and the Committee to Save Jews in Europe to "the Holy Father and Your most Reverend Eminence for the decided improvement obtained in Hungary.... The aforementioned committees recognize that everything is owed to the Holy Father").

48. In addition, as one enters St. Peter's Basilica, to the right, just beyond Michelangelo's *Pietá*, stands a large statute of Pius XII.

49. Korn, 151. On Oct. 29, 1944, elder survivors from a concentration camp in Ferramonti, Italy, presented Pius a letter which said, in part:

> Now that the victorious Allied troops have broken our chains and liberated us from captivity and danger, may we, the Jewish internees of Ferramonti, be permitted to express our deepest and devoted thanks for the comfort and help which Your Holiness deigned to grant us with fatherly concern and infinite kindness throughout our years of internment and persecution.
>
> Your Holiness has as the first and highest authority upon earth *fearlessly raised his universally respected voice*, in the face of our powerful enemies, in order to defend openly our rights to the dignity of man.... When we were threatened with deportation to Poland, in 1942, Your Holiness extended his fatherly hand to protect us, and stopped the transfer of the Jews interned in Italy, thereby saving us from almost certain death. With deep confidence and hope that the work of Your Holiness may be crowned with further success, we beg to express our heartfelt thanks while we pray to the Almighty: May Your Holiness reign for many years on this Holy See and exert your beneficent influence over the destiny of the nations.

> [signed] The President and community of Jewish internees of the former camp at Ferramonti-Tarsia.

Lapide, 129-30. In March 1945, the Italian Jewish community honored Pope Pius XII with a plaque that was displayed at the Museum of Liberation. A photo and full translation of the plaque can be found in *Examining the Papacy of Pope Pius XII*, 115. See also "Le nonce en Italie Borgongini Duca au cardinal Maglione," March 4, 1942, *Actes et Documents*, vol. 8, p. 449, no. 294 (Vatican efforts on behalf of the internees at Ferramonti); "Le cardinal Maglione au nonce en Italie Borgongini Duca," Feb. 17, 1943, *Actes et Documents*, vol. 9, p. 131, no. 55 (Vatican concern over internees at Ferramonti); "Le cardinal Maglione au nonce en Italie Borgongini Duca," June 13, 1943, *Actes et Documents*, vol. 9, p. 338, no. 228 (Vatican concern over Yugoslavian Jews interned in Italy).

50. "Perspectives on History: Pope Pius XII," a 1963 made-for-television biography, hosted by Mike Wallace.

51. Korn, 151. See also Charles Rankin, "Pius the Man and His Efforts for Peace," in *The Pope Speaks: The Words of Pius XII*, 8-9, 10 (discussing Pius XII's interaction with crowds).

52. O'Carroll, 140. The *sedia gestatoria* is the portable papal throne used in certain pontifical ceremonies. It consists of a richly adorned armchair, fastened on a platform, which twelve footmen (*palafrenieri*) typically carry on their shoulders. While Pius sometimes rode in it, "he was embarrassed by the manifestations of filial devotion showered on him.... He was humiliated and mortified when he had to appear with great solemnity and pomp." Marchione, *Pope Pius XII*, 44.

53. *L'Osservatore Romano*, June 4, 2009 (reviewing *Ferramonti di Tarsia*, by Mario Rende).

54. Doyle, 34.

55. Later Zolli (who had approached the Pope to obtain gold to pay the Nazi's ransom demand in 1943) converted to Catholicism (along with his wife), asked Pope Pius to be his godfather, and took Eugenio as his Christian name in honor of the Pontiff. *Popes of the Twentieth Century*, 53; see generally Zolli, *Why I Became a Catholic*. Zolli's daughter, Myriam Zolli, said that "the world's Jewish community owes [Pius XII] a great debt." EWTN Vatican Update, March 31, 1998.

56. Nazareno Padellaro and Robert L Reynolds, "His Reign," *Wisdom*, September 1957, 26.

57. Interview: "The Jews, Pius XII and the Black Legend — A Book Tells the Story of Jews Saved From the Holocaust" Zenit News Service, Dec. 8, 1998. For a similar plaque, see *Examining the Papacy of Pope Pius XII*, 115.

58. Holmes, 158.

59. Anne O'Hare McCormick, "Position of Pope in Italy has been Enhanced by War," *New York Times*, Aug. 21, 1944. Some critics have tried to argue that Pius was more concerned about buildings and artifacts in Rome than with the people. This absurd argument is rebutted by any of the number of appeals made to spare Rome because "house to house combat in the city would entail tremendous losses to both the attacking and the defending forces, and of course principally to the innocent civilian residents." Letter to President Roosevelt from Apostolic Delegate, Archbishop Cicognani, March 13, 1944 (original document posted on the Internet by the FDR Library).

60. See Lapide, 134. See also "Churchmen & The War," *Time*, Feb. 24, 1941; "Milestones," *Time*, Feb. 11, 1946.

61. This story is told in the Gregory Peck motion picture *The Scarlet and the Black* (1992, LIVE Home Video), and in the book *The Scarlet Pimpernel of the Vatican*, by J. P. Gallagher. See also Hatch and Walshe, 170-72.

62. Lapide, 134 (emphasis added).

63. Richard Owen, "Vatican war hero may have been Nazi 'mole,'" *Times* (Europe), July 3, 2000 (noting that German files show that O'Flaherty may have provided inaccurate information to the Germans during the war).

64. "During Rome's occupation by the Nazis, the number of people Monsignor O'Flaherty helped ran well into the thousands. He never asked a person to name his religion. That would not have been like him. Besides, under the Nazi regime if a Jew told the truth about his religion, he would automatically be calling himself a criminal, for to the Nazis, to be a Jew was the biggest crime of all!" Madden, 104-5. See also J. P. Gallagher, *Scarlet Pimpernel of the Vatican* (Souvenir Press, 1967); Brian Fleming, *The Vatican Pimpernel. The wartime exploits of Monsignor Hugh O'Flaherty* (Cork: The Collins Press, 2008).

65. Gallagher, *Scarlet Pimpernel of the Vatican* (emphasis added). Gallagher notes that those Vatican officials who had been inclined to prudence were radicalized by the Gestapo. "Even the most conservative men in the Vatican were prepared now to give the trouble-shooting Monsignor quite a bit more rope." Pope Pius XII knew about O'Flaherty's lifesaving activities, and it was a clear breach of neutrality that could endanger the Vatican. Nevertheless, he "continued to turn a Nelsonian blind eye to the figure on St. Peter's steps, a figure he could see from his own study window as well as anyone else." Ibid., 63. Pius and Cardinal Ottaviani, "the stern disciplinarian of the Holy Office and O'Flaherty's direct superior," kept their eyes "tightly closed" in order to let the "obstreperous Irish Monsignor" carry out his lifesaving operations. Ibid., 174.

66. Simpson, 78 (emphasis added). Simpson was a Presbyterian from Scotland.

67. "The extermination of more than 400,000 Hungarian Jews was the last act of the historical tragedy...." Congregation for the Causes of Saints, *Positio*, appendix 25, 248. See generally *The Pius War*, 260-61.

68. Anti-Semitic laws had been proposed in Hungary prior to the occupation. Jusztinián Cardinal Serédi, the primate, openly protested on the Senate floor:

> Should your hearts, seized by race-hatred, drive you to vote for this law, hear my words — words which the Lord Himself suggests to me at this fateful moment. In truth I say to you: all the tears, all the victims, all the massacred martyrs will accuse you when your time comes to give an account before the Lord of your infamous act of this day. Remember the warning of Bernard of Clairvaux: "Do not touch the Jews for they are the apple of God's eye." In the name of Almighty God I shall vote against this infamous law.

Purdy, 263-64.

69. Lapide, 151; Graham (undated), 14 (footnote). See "Le cardinal Maglione au nonce à Budapest Rotta," April 5, 1944, *Actes et Documents*, vol. 10, p. 206, no. 133 (instruction to intervene on behalf of the

Jews); "Mgr. Tardini au nonce à Budapest Rotta," Dec. 4, 1944, *Actes et Documents*, vol. 10, p. 506, no. 412 (letter expressing the Holy Father's "deep pain" and enclosing money to support Rotta's work on behalf of the persecuted).

70. Lapide, 159; O'Carroll, 99. The official records indicate that 4,770 Jews were baptized in Budapest during this time, but that 80,000 baptismal certificates were distributed. Graham (undated), 17; O'Carroll, 104.

71. Lapide, 151. "Le cardinal Maglione au nonce à Budpest Rotta," April 5, 1944, *Actes et Documents*, vol. 10, p. 206, no. 133.

72. Graham (1987), 5 (quoting Jenö Levai). See "Le cardinal Maglione au nonce à Budpest Rotta," April 5, 1944, *Actes et Documents*, vol. 10, p. 206, no. 133 (delegating "intervention by the Holy See" to Rotta and instructing him to "judge which further steps are possible and opportune to achieve at the moment"); "Mgr. Tardini au nonce à Budapest Rotta," Oct. 21, 1944, *Actes et Documents*, vol. 10, p. 452, no. 365 (asking Rotta to inform the Vatican concerning the threat to the Jews); Gerhard M. Riegner, "The Holocaust and Vatican Diplomacy," *Reform Judaism*, Fall 1984, 42, 44 (noting that "the Pope personally intervened" in Hungary and the Vatican "contributed to saving many Jewish lives").

73. Almost as soon as the Nazis moved into Hungary, organizations began asking the Vatican for help. See, e.g., "Le World Jewish Congress au Cardinal Maglione," July 21, 1944, *Actes et Documents*, vol. 10, p. 359, no. 273 (thanking the Pope for help in other areas, and asking for more assistance in Hungary); "La Légation de Grande Bretagne à la Secrétairerie d'Etat," April 1, 1944, *Actes et Documents*, vol. 10, p. 205, no. 132, footnote 1; "L'archevêque de Westminster Griffin au cardinal Maglione," July 3, 1944, *Actes et Documents*, vol. 10, p. 341, no. 253.

74. Wyman, 237; Graham, 25. The Board also appealed to the five neutral nations to grant protective citizenship documents to Hungarian Jews who had family or business ties to their countries. Turkey did not participate, but the cooperation of the other four countries helped save thousands of Jews. Wyman, 237. The War Refugee Board sent a message to the Vatican in June 1944, in which it acknowledged that Pius "has labored unceasingly to reinculcate a decent regard for the dignity of man," and the "tireless efforts of His Holiness to alleviate the lot of the persecuted, the hunted and the outcasts." Telegram from the Secretary of State to the Consul General at Naples (Brandt), June 13, 1944, in *Foreign Relations of the United States, Diplomatic Papers, 1944, vol. I (General)*, United States Government Printing Office (Washington, 1966), 1068-69.

75. Gilbert (1981), 248-49 (quoting Jenö Levai, *Zsidosors Europaban*, Budapest 1948, pp. 68-72).

76. Ibid.; Harmansee is a village in Poland that served as a farm labor-camp annex for the Auschwitz Camp. Ibid., 248, n. 4.

77. *Investigative Reports* (Bill Kurtis, A&E Network).

78. This was a direct affront to the Church. On May 15, the papal nuncio wrote to the Hungarian prime minister and the Foreign Ministry, arguing:

> The very fact of persecuting men merely on account of their racial origin is a violation of the natural law. If God has given them life, no one in the World has the right to take it from them or refuse them the means of preserving it, unless they have committed crimes. But to take anti-Semite measures, not taking into account at all the fact that many Jews have become Christians through reception of baptism, is a serious offense against the church and in contradiction with the character of the Christian state, such as Hungary is proud to profess itself, even today.

"Le nonce à Budapest Rotta au Cardinal Maglione," May 23, 1944, *Actes et Documents*, vol. 10, p. 283, no. 207 (enclosures 1 and 2).

79. "Le pape Pie XII au regent de Hongrie Horthy," June 25, 1944, *Actes et Documents*, vol. 10, p. 328, no. 243.

80. Holmes, 163; "Le nonce à Budapest Rotta au Cardinal Maglione," June 24, 1944, *Actes et Documents*, vol. 10, p. 327, no. 242.

81. Lapide, 153-54; "Le nonce à Budapest Rotta au Cardinal Maglione," June 24, 1944, *Actes et Documents*, vol. 10, p. 327, no. 242. See "Le nonce à Budapest Rotta au Cardinal Maglione," June 24, 1944, *Actes et Documents*, vol. 10, p. 351, no. 265.

82. Levai, 68.

83. "Memo by Monsignor Tardini," Oct. 18, 1944, *Actes et Documents*, vol. 10, p. 446, no. 357 (footnote 4); Graham (undated), 5-6 and footnote.

84. Graham (undated), 5-6 and footnote.

85. Ibid.

86. *Time*, July 3, 1944.

87. "Memo by Monsignor Tardini," dated Oct. 18, 1944, *Actes et Documents*, vol. 10, p. 446, no. 357 (footnote 4).

88. Graham (undated), 5-6 and footnote. See also Roger Butterfield, "Cardinal Spellman," *Life*, Jan. 21, 28, 1946 (Spellman "became the Pope's radio expert"). According to the Italian periodical *Regime fascista*, Spellman was an "agent of American Jews, someone who sends any amount of dollars to the Vatican in

exchange for an anti-Fascist policy approved by the Holy See." Blet, 105. Anne O'Hare McCormick complained about "moral surrender" to the Nazis. "The worst thing the Germans could do," she wrote, "is to dehumanize other people and silence the voices that protest against cruelty and injustice." She was concerned that if the Nazis were to "stifle moral indignation," they would "win their war against the spirit of man." She encouraged others to remain strong by noting that "the Pope does not think it is hopeless." Anne O'Hare McCormick, *New York Times*, July 15, 1944.

89. Gilbert (1981), 266 (citing Report of Veesenmayer to Ribbentrop, July 6, 1944, Nuremberg Trial Documents, NG 6584).

90. Lapide, 153.

91. Gilbert (1987), 50; see Blet, 189-99.

92. Lapide, 156. Rabbi Maurice Perlzweig, also of the World Jewish Congress, wrote to the apostolic delegate in Washington, Amleto Cicognani, on Feb. 18, 1944, as follows:

> It is scarcely necessary for me to assure Your Excellency that the repeated interventions of the Holy Father on behalf of Jewish communities in Europe has evoked the profoundest statements of appreciation and gratitude from Jews throughout the world. These acts of courage and consecrated statesmanship on the part of His Holiness will always remain a precious memory in the life of the Jewish people.

"M. Perlzweig, au délégué é Washington Cicognani," Feb. 18, 1944, *Actes et Documents*, vol. 10, p. 140, no. 67.

93. See "Le nonce à Bucarest Cassulo au minister des Affaires étrangères M. Antonescu," Feb. 18, 1944, *Actes et Documents*, vol. 10, p. 140, no. 68; "Le cardinal Maglione au nonce à Bucarest Cassulo," March 2, 1944, *Actes et Documents*, vol. 10, p. 167, no. 89; "Le nonce à Bucarest Cassulo au ministre des Affaires étrangères M. Antonescu," March 11, 1944, *Actes et Documents*, vol. 10, p. 176, no. 100; "Le nonce à Bucarest Cassulo au cardinal Maglione," March 16, 1944, *Actes et Documents*, vol. 10, p. 179, no. 104.

94. "Le nonce à Bucarest Cassulo à Mgr. Tardini," Oct. 2, 1944, *Actes et Documents*, vol. 10, p. 428, no. 68.

95. Lapide, 161.

96. "Notes de la Secrétairerie d'Etat," June 7, 1944, *Actes et Documents*, vol. 10, p. 304, no. 223 ; Blet, 197.

97. "Le nonce à Budapest Rotta au cardinal Maglione," June 10, 1944, *Actes et Documents*, vol. 10, p. 308, no. 227 (appendix); "Le nonce à Budapest Rotta au cardinal Maglione," May 23, 1944, *Actes et Documents*, vol. 10, p. 283, no. 207 (with appendices); "Mgr. Tardini au nonce à Budapest Rotta," May 29, 1944, *Actes et Documents*, vol. 10, p. 297, no. 216. See Lapide, 152.

98. "Mgr. Tardini au nonce à Budapest Rotta," May 29, 1944, *Actes et Documents*, vol. 10, p. 297, no. 216. See "Mgr. Tardini au nonce à Budapest Rotta," Dec. 4, 1944, *Actes et Documents*, vol. 10, p. 506, no. 412; "Le nonce à Budapest Rotta à la Secrétairerie d'Etat," Dec. 11, 1944, *Actes et Documents*, vol. 10, p. 509, no. 415; "Le nonce à Budapest Rotta et les représentants des puissances neutres au Ministère hongrois des Affaires étrangères," Dec. 23, 1944, *Actes et Documents*, vol. 10, p. 519, no. 424.

99. Graham, 20. Earlier, Rabbi Safran paid tribute to the Catholic Church's activities on behalf of Romanian Jews in a letter to the papal nuncio, in which he wrote:

> In these harsh times our thoughts turn more than ever with respectful gratitude to what has been accomplished by the Sovereign Pontiff on behalf of Jews in general and by Your Excellency on behalf of the Jews of Romania and Transnistria.
>
> In the most difficult hours which we Jews of Romania have passed through, the generous assistance of the Holy See, carried out by the intermediary of your high person, was decisive and salutary. It is not easy for us to find the right words to express the warmth and consolation we experienced because of the concern of the supreme Pontiff, who offered a large sum to relieve the sufferings of deported Jews, sufferings which had been pointed out to him by you after your visit to Transnistria. The Jews of Romania will never forget these facts of historic importance.

Joseph L. Lichten, "A Question of Judgment: Pius XII and the Jews" in *Pius XII and the Holocaust: A Reader*, 130. See also "Le grand rabbin Herzog au délégué apostolique à Istanbul Roncalli," Feb. 28, 1944, *Actes et Documents*, vol. 10, p. 161, no. 83 (thanks from the Grand Rabbi of Jerusalem); "Le grand rabbin Herzog au visiteur apostolique à Zagreb Marcone," Feb. 28, 1944, *Actes et Documents*, vol. 10, p. 161, no. 84 (similar); "Le nonce à Bucarest Cassulo au cardinal Maglione," May 25, 1944, *Actes et Documents*, vol. 10, p. 291, no. 211 (appendix II, thanks and request from the Grand Rabbi of Jerusalem regarding the fate of Jews concentrated in Transnistria).

100. Blet, 200.

101. "Lauds Pope's Help to Jews: Representative Celler Sends Letter of Appreciation to Vatican," *New York Times*, Oct. 31, 1944.

102. "Memo by Monsignor Tardini," Oct. 18, 1944, *Actes et Documents*, vol. 10, p. 446, no. 357 (footnote 4).

103. "Le National Jewish Welfare Board au pape Pie XII," July 21, 1944, *Actes et Documents*, vol. 10, p. 358, no. 272.

104. "Le World Jewish Congress au cardinal Maglione," July 21, 1944, *Actes et Documents*, vol. 10, p. 359, no. 273. Unfortunately, the Soviets followed the Nazis, and they persecuted the Church and its leaders in Hungary, particularly Cardinal Mindszenty. See generally József Cardinal Mindszenty, *Memoirs* (New York: Macmillan & Co., 1974).

105. "Churchill Talks with Pope on Peace: Vatican Quarters Gratified at Outcome Said to Promise a Profound Effort on Terms," *New York Times*, Aug. 28, 1944.

106. Churchill (1953), 115-16.

107. McCormick, 123 (from a *New York Times* dispatch of Sept. 6, 1944). For his part, Pius described Churchill as "very able and large-minded." Ibid.

108. Hatch and Walshe, 184.

109. Anton J. Gahlinger, *I Served the Pope*, 6 (The Mission Press, Techny, IL, 1952). See "Churchill Talks With Pope on Peace; Vatican Quarters Gratified at Outcome Said to Promise a Profound Effect on Terms," *New York Times*, Aug. 26, 1944.

110. Churchill (1953), 115-16.

111. See Telegram from the Ambassador in the United Kingdom (Winant) to the Secretary of State, Aug. 14, 1944, in *Foreign Relations of the United States, Diplomatic Papers, 1944, vol. I (General)*, United States Government Printing Office (Washington, 1966), 1123; ibid., 1140.

112. Joseph L. Lichten, "A Question of Judgment: Pius XII and the Jews," in *Pius XII and the Holocaust: A Reader*, 127; R. Stewart, 60.

113. Heller and Nekrich, 415-16.

114. Churchill (1953), 143.

115. "Le pape Pie XII au président de Pologne Raczkiewicz," Aug. 31, 1944, *Actes et Documents*, vol. 10, p. 398, no. 311.

116. "La Secrétairerie d'Etat à l'ambassadeur Taylor," Sept. 1, 1944, *Actes et Documents*, vol. 10, p. 401, no. 313*.

117. "Notiziario Internazionale," *L'Osservatore Romano*, Sept. 15, 1944.

118. "Pope Is Sorrowful Over Poles' Plight; Vatican Message Prays for the Deliverance of Warsaw," *New York Times*, Sept. 12, 1944.

119. The Soviets had installed their own Polish government as they had pushed into Poland, but the Polish government-in-exile planned to take control after the war. The uprising, however, greatly weakened the exiled government and made it easier for the Soviets to claim Poland after the war.

120. Holmes, 146; Coady, 170-71 ("The actual reason for my condemnation was that I happened to be, and chose to remain, a Jesuit.") See Lapomarda, 38, n. 5 ("One can note that no Jesuit was ever a member of the Nazi party.") Lapomarda also lists the names of 152 Jesuit priests who were killed by, or died as result of, the Nazis. Ibid., 313-18. Himmler, who admired certain aspects of the Jesuit order, also considered them to be one of the Nazis' most formidable enemies. Matheson, 72. He told the wife of Germany's ambassador to the Holy See that the National Socialists "would not rest until we have rooted out Christianity." Weizsäcker, 281. Late in the war, German Jesuits had the following stamp on their identification papers: "Jesuit: not fit for military service." Similar imprints were put on the identification cards of Jews and others deemed undesirable by the Nazis. C. Ryan, 25. The Gestapo reportedly had plans to round up all German Jesuits and send them to concentration camps. Alvarez and Graham, 51.

121. Lapomarda, 11-12.

122. Ibid., 12.

123. Ibid., 11-12.

124. William J. O'Malley, "The Priests of Dachau," reprinted in *Pius XII and the Holocaust: A Reader*, 143; Holmes, 142, 145. See p. 259.

125. Michaelis, 425.

126. Graham (1987),11.

127. Blet, 184. See also "Le cardinal Maglione au nonce à Bucarest Cassulo," Jan. 14, 1943, *Actes et Documents*, vol. 9, p. 81, no. 15 (noting efforts made on behalf of Romanian Jews).

128. "Le cardinal Maglione au nonce à Bucarest Cassulo," Feb. 15, 1943, *Actes et Documents*, vol. 9, p. 129, no. 53.

129. "Le nonce à Bucarest Cassulo au cardinal Maglione," March 2, 1943, *Actes et Documents*, vol. 9, p. 162, no. 72 (conveying the rabbi's message).

130. Graham (1987), 20.

131. "Le grand rabbin Herzog au cardinal Maglione," July 13, 1943, *Actes et Documents*, vol. 9, p. 403, no. 270; Graham (1987). 20. In April 1942, the Romanian minister to the Holy See informed the Vatican that the number of Jews being baptized into Catholicism was too great, and it was drawing attention. Ibid. The Pope, however, rejected the suggestion that further conversions be suspended until the end of the war. Ibid. In February 1943, the Jewish community in Romania asked Archbishop Cassulo to send their gratitude to Pius XII for the help of the Vatican and its nunciature. Joseph L. Lichten, "A Question of Judgment: Pius XII and the Jews," in *Pius XII and the Holocaust: A Reader*, 112.

132. Joseph L. Lichten, "A Question of Judgment: Pius XII and the Jews," in *Pius XII and the Holocaust: A Reader*, 128.

133. Ibid.

134. Pius XII, *Selected Encyclicals and Addresses*, 317.

135. Ibid., 310. "Intellectual developments found expression in 20th-century papal thought, which gradually embraced the idea of the 'juridical' (or constitutional) state, a state whose principal function is 'to safeguard the inviolable rights of the human person, and to facilitate the performance of his duties.'" Kenneth L. Grasso and Robert P. Hunt, "Dignitatis Humanae and The Catholic Human Rights Revolution," 3 *Faith and International Affairs*, 3, 7 (2005-2006) (quoting Pius XII's radio message of June 1, 1941, in *Acta Apostolicae Sedis*, 33 (1941): 200). In his 1944 Christmas message, Pius XII set forth the formulation that man "is the origin and end of human society." "The democratic form of government," he noted, "appears to many a postulate of nature imposed by reason itself." Ibid.

136. Reprinted in Pius XII, *Selected Encyclicals and Addresses*, 315.

137. Quoted in Charles J. Gangi, "The Christmas Addresses of Pope Pius XII," *New Oxford Review*, December 2007.

## Chapter Fifteen: 1945 and the End of War

1. Barnett, 176.

2. In 1942, Hertz, the Grand Rabbi of the British Empire, wrote to Cardinal Maglione asking for assistance in protecting the Jews of Slovakia. "Le grand rabbin Hertz au cardinal Maglione," June 2, 1942, *Actes et Documents*, vol. 8, p. 551, no. 389. On Jan. 1, 1945, Hertz wrote a letter of thanks to Msgr. William Godfrey, apostolic delegate in the United Kingdom, as follows:

> All the deeper is our appreciation of the sympathy that His Holiness the Pope, and all those associated in the leadership of the Vatican, have shown in the fate of our doomed brethren. The whole House of Israel will be ever mindful of the many and persistent efforts that have been made by Roman Catholic authorities to rescue Jews threatened with barbarous murder.

"Le nonce à Bucarest Cassulo à Mgr. Tardini," Dec. 14, 1944, *Actes et Documents*, vol. 10, p. 513, no. 419 (in footnote 6); "L'ambassadeur des Etats Unis Taylor à la Secrétairerie d'Etat," Nov. 15, 1944, *Actes et Documents*, vol. 10, p. 484, no. 396 (referencing this message).

3. Hoar, 206-7. Roosevelt was not as cooperative as Stalin had hoped. Stalin came to believe that this was due to Cardinal Spellman's influence. Andrew and Gordievsky, 339-40 (also noting that Stalin thought Spellman was at Yalta in disguise).

4. This filmed statement is included in some documentaries relating to the Church and the war.

5. "Message from His Holiness to President Harry S. Truman," April 13, 1945, in *Wartime Correspondence*, 125.

6. Ibid. In fact, Taylor was better received at the Vatican than were ambassadors from some nations. Ibid. (conclusion). Truman ended up using Taylor to communicate with various religious leaders. See Letter of Oct. 2, 1947 from President Truman to Bess Truman, in *Dear Bess: The Letters from Harry to Bess Truman, 1910-1959* (Robert H. Ferrell, ed., 1983), 551. Taylor later wrote:

> My work involved not only frequent Papal audiences but also conferences with Vatican officials, and consultations with envoys of other governments to the Holy See and with many other persons, both in Rome and en route. Two immediate matters were uppermost in the minds of the President and of His Holiness at the outset of my mission. One was an effort to prevent the spread of war to southern Europe. The other was to help alleviate suffering caused by the war…. The parallel endeavors of President Roosevelt and of His Holiness were directed toward theses ends.

*Correspondence Between President Truman and Pope Pius XII* (Myron C. Talyor, ed., Kessinger Publishing, 2005).

7. Mussolini's widow lived quietly in Italy until her death in October 1979.

8. *Communium Interpretes Dolororum*, nn. 2 and 3.

9. Ibid., n. 7.

10. Graham (1987), 32-33; Blet, 263-67.

11. *Regime Fascista*, Jan. 17, 1945.

12. Hitler's propaganda minister from 1933 on, Joseph Goebbels, also committed suicide. He remained hidden in Hitler's bunker until May 1, 1945, when he poisoned his six children before he and his wife took their own dose of cyanide. Soviet forces later found all the bodies.

13. Morison, 1041. One of the last messages between the warring parties to pass through the Vatican was a memorandum from the German ambassador to the Holy See to President Roosevelt recommending a new democratic and federal constitution and suggesting that only American and British troops occupy Berlin. "That Allied armies should all advance to meet in Berlin was, I said, politically undesirable." Weizsäcker, 298.

14. Proclamation to the German People, Sept. 28, 1944, reprinted in Snyder, 389.

15. See Keegan, 533.

16. Office of the United States Chief Counsel, vol. I, 285-86; Shirer (1962), 324-25 (footnote). A translation of this whole speech, as it was broadcast on Vatican Radio, can be found in "The Catholic Church and the Third Reich: Pope Pius XII Surveys an Heroic History," *Tablet* (London), June 9, 1945.

17. Lukacs, 265, criticizes Pius for attributing National Socialism to an "apparition," thereby diminishing human (and Catholic) responsibility. Had Lukacs quoted the whole statement, however, his criticism would have been harder to support.

18. Paci, 43.

19. Memorandum by the Director of the Office of Far Eastern Affairs (Ballantine) to the Under Secretary of State (Grew), Jan. 30, 1945, in *United States Department of State, Foreign Relations of the United States, Diplomatic Papers, 1945, vol. VI (The British Commonwealth; The Far East),* United States Government Printing Office (Washington, 1969), 475.

20. Japan demanded retention of Hong Kong and Hainan, an independent Phillipines, and more.

21. Henry Stimson's Memorandum to President Truman, April 25, 1945. See "Barton J. Bernstein, Roosevelt, Truman, and the Atomic Bomb, 1941-1945: A Reinterpretation," 90 *Political Science Quarterly,* 23 (Spring 1975).

22. Morison, 1044.

23. Ibid., 1043. The American position was that war was not being waged on civilians, but that this was the only way to destroy Japan's ability to build planes and make war. Frederick C. Patton, "Why We Must Bomb Japanese Cities," *Reader's Digest,* May 1945, 82; Thomas M. Johnson, "Doom Over Japan," *American Mercury,* August 1945, reprinted in *Reader's Digest,* August 1945, 89.

24. Blum, 756; Mazour and Peoples, 740.

25. A comprehensive accounting of the damage, costs, and deaths caused by World War II can be found in "World War II," *Encyclopedia Americana/CBS News Audio Library* (print material, 169-71) (1974).

26. See Lewis F. Gittler, "Life in a German City," *American Mercury,* October 1945, reprinted in *Reader's Digest,* October 1945, 25 (describing the devastation of most German cities).

27. Rousmaniere, 113.

28. Jürgen Moltmann, "Wrestling with God: A Personal Meditation," *Christian Century,* Aug. 13-20, 1997, 726.

29. Conradt, 16. The caloric intake of almost everyone in postwar Europe, including Allied soldiers, was limited. Vida, 57. See "Europe: From Freedom to Want," *Fortune,* May 1945 ("liberated Europe is fed, clothed and sheltered worse even than under German occupation").

30. Prittie, 54.

31. Blet, 70-71.

32. "Maltreatment and Persecution of the Catholic Clergy in the Western Provinces," Office of the United States Chief of Counsel, vol. I, 286. See also "A note of His Eminence the Cardinal Secretary of State to the Foreign Minister of the Reich about the religious situation in 'Warthegau' and in the other Polish provinces subject to Germany," March 2, 1943, in Office of the United States Chief of Counsel, vol. V, 1018.

33. See "Vatican City Heating Cut Off," *New York Times,* Jan. 13, 1944; Charles Rankin, "Pius the Man and His Efforts for Peace," in *The Pope Speaks: The Words of Pius XII,* 104.

34. Fulton J. Sheen, "The Pope as I Saw Him," *Catholic Digest,* October 1955, 62.

35. Ibid.

36. Other officials had similar concerns. The chargé in the Soviet Union (Kennan) to the Secretary of State, Feb. 8, 1945, in *United States Department of State, Foreign Relations of the United States, Diplomatic Papers, 1945, vol. V (Europe),* United States Government Printing Office (Washington, 1967), 1119-21 ("How this anti-Catholic tendency will affect Soviet policy in Poland, Hungary and Croatia is however still not apparent."); "Le délégué apostolique à Washington Cicognani à Mgr. Tardini," March 9, 1945, *Actes et Documents,* vol. 10, p. 557, no. 466 (enclosing Archbishop Sapieha's appeal concerning Soviet occupation).

37. Fulton J. Sheen, "The Pope as I Saw Him," *Catholic Digest,* October 1955, 62.

38. *New York Times,* Dec. 25, 1941. See Cianfarra, 319-29.

39. *New York Times,* Dec. 25, 1942.

40. "Peace & the Papacy," *Time,* Aug. 16, 1943.

41. Herbert L. Mathews, "Happier Days for Pope Pius: Shadows of war are lifting for a Pontiff whose greatest interest is world peace," *New York Times,* Oct. 15, 1944, 8.

42. Protestant religious leaders in the United States opposed Vatican involvement in the postwar peace process. Gannon, 169.

43. Hoar, 203. See Demaree Bess, "Will Europe Go Communist After the War?" *Saturday Evening Post,* Jan. 22, 1944 (American concern over Soviet expansion).

44. Hoar, 208.

45. Ibid. The word "Yalta" became a pejorative term, resulting in boos and hisses when mentioned at certain events. Morison, 1049. See Frederic Sondern, Jr., "We Are Bungling the Job in Germany," *Reader's Digest,* February 1946, 87, 89 (criticizing the Potsdam Protocol).

46. Hoar, 208.

47. Morison, 1049.

48. Louis J. Gallagher, *Edmund A. Walsh, S.J., Founder of the Foreign Service School, Georgetown University*, Benziger Brothers (New York, 1959). See also O'Carroll, 138 (suggesting that a memorandum authorized by Pius XII influenced the terms of one charge).

49. *Chronicle*, 609.

50. F. Murphy, 64.

51. K. Doyle, 16.

52. M. Davis, 101.

53. He supported the Marshall Plan to rebuild Europe by sanctioning a positive article that appeared in *L'Osservatore Romano*. Cornwell (1999), 330.

54. Hatch and Walshe, 182.

55. Benzinger (preface). See generally "Inter Arma Caritas: L'Ufficio Informazione Vaticano per i Prigionieri di Guerra Istituito da Pio XII (1939-1947)" (vol. I and II), *Archivio Segreto Vaticano: Città del Vaticano*, 2004.

56. Holmes, 150. One of the particular difficulties related to the many victims who had been exposed to tuberculosis and were therefore not welcome in most countries. Vida, 112.

57. C. Doyle, 48, 62. The Pope also shared words of concern about world peace with Connecticut Congresswoman Clare Boothe Luce. Hatch and Walshe, 184.

58. Graham (1968), 20.

59. Holmes, 158.

60. Lapide, 269.

61. Lapide, 226. In a letter dated Oct. 27, 1945, Msgr. Montini (the future Pope Paul VI) gave a detailed account of a private audience between Pius XII and Leo Kubowitzky, then-secretary general of the World Jewish Congress. Kubowitzky expressed gratitude to the Pontiff for his work in support of persecuted Jews. *Corriere della Sera*, August 1999. See also "M. Perlzweig au délégué apostolique à Washington Cicognani," Feb. 18, 1944, *Actes et Documents*, vol. 10, p. 140, no. 67 (World Jewish Congress representative expresses gratitude for "the repeated interventions of the Holy Father on behalf of Jewish communities throughout the world. These acts of courage and consecrated statesmanship on the part of His Holiness will always remain a precious memory in the life of the Jewish people.")

62. "Le National Jewish Welfare Board au pape Pie XII," July 21, 1944, *Actes et Documents*, vol. 10, p. 358, no. 272.

63. Margherita Marchione, "Pope Pius XII and the Jews," *Crisis*, January 1997, 20, 23; John Thavis, "Many Jews Once Defended Pius and Documentary Evidence Supports Him," *Inside the Vatican*, April 1998, 30.

64. *New York Times*, Nov. 30, 1945, p. 10.

65. Lapide, 277.

66. *L'Osservatore Romano*, Aug. 15, 1946, p. 1.

67. *New York Times*, Aug. 4, 1946, p. 22. As the tensions built up within the Middle East over Palestine and armed conflict erupted, Pius XII issued three encyclical letters on Palestine in one year — *Auspicia Quaedam* (May 1, 1948); *In Multiplicibus Curis* (Oct. 24, 1948); and, *Redemptoris Nostri Cruciatus* (April 15, 1949). In the first encyclical, the Pope stated that Palestine should be dear to every cultured person, a place where from antiquity wisdom shone forth to men and where Christ lived and died so that peace could be enjoyed by all nations who would know how to live in harmony.

68. Quoted in a World Jewish Congress memorandum dated March 24, 1959, and enclosed in a letter from Monty Jacobs of the World Jewish Congress to Dr. Edgar Alexander, also dated March 24, 1959.

69. *Jewish Post*, Nov. 6, 1958.

70. "Un messaggio delle Comunità Israelitiche Italiane a Sua Santità Pio XII," *L'Osservatore Romano*, April 5, 1946. Reuben R. Resnick, director of the Joint Distribution Committee, said: "Thousands of Jews in Italy owe their lives to Italian citizens and the Catholic Church." *Jerusalem Post*, Jan. 22, 1946.

71. C. Doyle, 62.

72. Joseph L. Lichten, "A Question of Judgment: Pius XII and the Jews," in *Pius XII and the Holocaust: A Reader*, 100.

73. At a conference in St. Louis, on March 16, 1946, William Rosenwald, chair of the United Jewish Appeal for Refugees, Overseas and Palestine, said: "I wish to take this opportunity to pay tribute to Pope Pius for his appeal in behalf of the victims of war and oppression. He provided aid for Jews in Italy and intervened in behalf of refugees to lighten their burden."

74. "Significativo omaggio del Re di Svezia al Sommo Pontefice," *L'Osservatore Romano*, March 1, 1947, 1; "Il ringraziamento del Santo Padre al Re Gustavo di Svezia," *L'Osservatore Romano*, March 2, 1947. Even today, one of the highest awards that a Catholic Boy Scout can receive is the Pope Pius XII medal. Among the things that this award is intended to stimulate is an examination of how being a Christian affects daily life in the real world.

75. Telegram from the Secretary of State to the Consul General at Naples (Brandt), June 13, 1944, in *Foreign Relations of the United States, Diplomatic Papers, 1944, vol. I (General)*, United States Government Printing Office (Washington, 1966), 1068-69.

76. P. Murphy, 208.

77. Bogle, *Salisbury Review*.

78. "Israelis Defend Name of Pope Pius XII," *Jewish Chronicle*, Oct. 11, 1963. "Conductor Paul Klecki had requested that the Orchestra on its first visit to Italy play for the Pope as a gesture of gratitude for the help his church had given to all those persecuted by Nazi Fascism." *Jerusalem Post*, May 29, 1955.

79. *Examining the Papacy of Pope Pius XII*, 116 (reprinting the photo).

80. Lapide, 137.

81. O'Carroll, 20; Lapide, 316.

82. "Acknowledging the Men and Women of Wisdom," *Wisdom*, September 1957, 2.

83. O'Carroll, 104.

84. S. K. Padover, "Nazi Scapegoat Number 2," *Reader's Digest*, February 1939, 1 (condensed from *The Forum*). A similar account appears in the religion section of *Newsweek*, May 29, 1937 (discussing "four years of Church-state strife" in Germany). See also *The Persecution of the Catholic Church in German-Occupied Poland; The Persecution of the Catholic Church in the Third Reich*.

85. As early as 1944, Pope Pius XII expressed interest in joining the "International Organization." Telegram from Mr. Myron C. Taylor, Personal Representative of President Roosevelt to Pope Pius XII, to the Secretary of State, Oct. 6, 1944, in *Foreign Relations of the United States, Diplomatic Papers, 1944, vol. I (General)* United States Government Printing Office (Washington, 1966), 963.

86. The Holy See tried to intervene and prevent repatriation of citizens who did not want to come under Soviet domination. Confidential Note from the Assistant to the President's Personal Representative at Vatican City (Tittmann) to the Secretary of State, July 5, 1945, in *United States Department of State, Foreign Relations of the United States, Diplomatic Papers, 1945, vol. I (The Conference of Berlin)*, United States Government Printing Office (Washington, 1960, 797, discussing the Vatican's efforts on behalf of Ukrainians who were in Germany); Telegram from the Acting Secretary of State to the United States Political Adviser for Germany, July 13, 1945, in *United States Department of State, Foreign Relations of the United States, Diplomatic Papers, 1945, vol. II (General: Political and Economic Matters)*, United States Government Printing Office (Washington, 1967), 1176. Pius also issued an appeal in favor of a group of German internees who were being sent back to Germany (from the United States) rather than to Costa Rica, where their families were. The Apostolic Delegate (Cicognani) to the Secretary of State, in *United States Department of State, Foreign Relations of the United States, Diplomatic Papers, 1945, vol. IX (The American Republics)*, United States Government Printing Office (Washington, 1966), 281.

87. Taylor, 192.

88. "All over Soviet-dominated Europe, Christian people suffered for their allegiance to Rome. Church schools were closed, all Christian teaching outside church services forbidden, seminaries starved of funds or students, or closed altogether, key clergy targeted as anti-social or treacherous. There was a series of spectacular show-trials." Duffy, 266.

89. Conradt, 32; Douglas Woodruff, "Mediterranean Enquiry: The Church in Italy," *Tablet* (London), June 9, 1945. See F. Murphy, 14, 64; M. Davis, 93 ("Through the years of dismay and despair, the Church had acted as a spiritual beacon. Now it was menaced in its spiritual mission by the Communists, more numerous in Italy than anywhere west of the Iron Curtain."); ibid., 94-95 (on the prestige of the postwar Church).

90. See J. Hughes (1994), 255 ("Faced... with the most powerful communist party in the Western world, the Pope in 1949 approved a decree of the Holy Office which excommunicated those who voted for communist candidates in Italian elections"); F. Murphy, 14, 64; M. Davis, 93 (the Church was the only organized group strong enough to combat the "new strength of the Left"); ibid., 94, 97 (noting that despite the excommunication decree, about one-third of the Italian Catholics voted for Communist candidates). See also Dunn, 142-43.

> The persecution in Hungary was a factor in the Vatican's decree of condemnation of Communism in 1949, which many of the East European Church leaders did not like because the Vatican decree did nothing to assuage Communist persecution. In fact, it gave the Communists a reason to intensify pressure against the Churches. The Polish Catholic leaders, in particular, thought the condemnation was counterproductive.... Nonetheless, the decree allowed the Vatican to vent its anger over the situation in Eastern Europe and it aroused world public opinion, particularly in the West, to the struggle that confronted civilization and helped crystallize Catholic voting blocks into bastions of anti-Communism and solidify Catholic support for the United States in the Cold War and to its effort to contain Communism. It also put Italians on notice that the Communist Party in Italy, which was a potent political force, was unacceptable as a governing agent.

Ibid.

91. F. Murphy, 64-65.
92. Cornwell (1999), 297.
93. Cheetham, 291; Pepper, 178; C. Doyle, 29; Hatch and Walshe, 210-11 (calling him the "least stuffy" of Popes). See also Ronald J. Rychlak, "Pope Pius XII's Real Personality," *Envoy*, vol. 7.5 (2007).
94. Constantine, 28.
95. "Cardinal Pacelli belongs among the most impressive personalities that I have ever met in my life as man, as intellect, as priest, in short as the prototype of a timeless but at the same time very modern prince of the Church." Kurt von Schuschnigg, *Austrian Requiem*, 107 (1946) (as identified on the title page, Schuschnigg was "Chancellor of Austria and Prisoner of Hitler").
96. McCormick, 99.
97. Ibid., 130 (from a *New York Times* dispatch of Dec. 26, 1945).
98. Hatch and Walshe, 210-11. John Cornwell criticized Pius for appearing in film and suggested that this indicated an egocentric side to his personality. Actually, this was just a matter of technology catching up with the papacy. See James W. Demers, *The Last Roman Catholic?* 20 (1991) ("[W]e saw more of [Pope John XXIII] in a short year than we ever saw of Pius XII in the whole of the '50s.")
99. McCormick, 150.
100. Earl Alexander, *The Alexander Memoirs: 1940-1945*, 122 (New York: McGraw-Hill, 1962).
101. Montgomery kept two photographs in his bedroom: one of his father and one of Pius XII. Peter Gumpel, "Cornwell's Pope: A Nasty Caricature of a Noble and Saintly Man," Zenit News Service, Sept. 16, 1999.
102. Burton, 141.
103. John M. McGuire, "Play on Words: Paul Dickson's Books Are a Feast of Slang, Lingo and Great Quotations," *Everyday Magazine, St. Louis Post-Dispatch*, July 18, 1991, 1E; Marchione, *Pope Pius XII*, 63.
104. Burton, 142.
105. Jean Guitton, *The Pope Speaks: Dialogues of Paul VI with Jean Guitton*, 83 (1968).
106. Ibid.
107. Anton J. Gahlinger, *I Served the Pope*, 45 (The Mission Press: Techny, IL, 1952).
108. Ibid.
109. McCormick, 144.
110. James W. Demers, *The Last Roman Catholic?* 26 (1991) ("He raised the papacy to a level of popular recognition never before reached.")
111. *The Story of the Pope*, 35.
112. In contrast, when the Nazis had attempted to score a diplomatic coup by having former World Heavyweight Champion boxer Max Schmeling meet with the Pope, Pius refused to grant him a private audience. Simpson, 146-47.
113. Charles Rankin, "Pius the Man and His Efforts for Peace," in *The Pope Speaks: The Words of Pius XII*, 76.
114. Marchione, *Pope Pius XII*, 64.
115. Ibid., 67.
116. Ibid., 62.
117. Lenn and Reardon, 122.
118. Emmet John Hughes, "The Papacy's Awesome Task," *Life*, Oct. 20, 1958, reprinted in *Great Reading from LIFE: A Treasury of the Best Stories and Articles Chosen by the Editors* (Bonanza Books: New York, 1960), 590, 593.
119. Marchione, *Shepherd of Souls*, 64.
120. Tardini, 34; see also Lenn and Reardon, 130 ("he often smiles").
121. *Catholic Herald*, May 24, 1963.
122. Kaiser Wilhelm, who met Pacelli in 1917, gave the following description of him: "Pacelli is an attractive and distinguished man, of high intelligence with very fine manners: he is the perfect model of an eminent prelate of the Catholic Church." Quoted in Purdy, 12. Pius was also a strong advocate for his causes. The cover story in a wartime issue of *Time* magazine identified him as "one of the world's most hardheaded statesmen." "Peace & the Papacy," *Time*, Aug. 16, 1943, 55.
123. Ann Aubrey Hanson, "San Diego Diplomat Defends Pope Pius XII," *The Southern Cross*, Jan. 15, 2004, 2. When he was in Berlin he was one day asked why Italians did not follow the same strict discipline that was common in German churches. Specifically he was asked why Romans behaved in church as if they were in the theater. He replied: "For the same reason that Germans behave in the theater as if they were in church." Kurt Klinger, *A Pope Laughs*, 74 (1964).
124. Marchione, *Pope Pius XII*, 83.
125. Joseph F. Dinneen, "Pope of Peace," *Reader's Digest*, June 1939, 83.
126. Burton, 143. See John Tagliabue, "Obituary: Paul Hofmann, Author and Foe of Nazis, Dies at 96," *New York Times*, Dec. 31, 2008 ("One of them… was a goldfinch named Gretel that the pope had found as a fledgling in the papal gardens and had affectionately tamed.")

127. Doyle, 101.

128. Priests, who were accustomed to kneeling when addressing a Pope, did not know how to act when speaking to Pius on the phone. Some knelt, which led to the ridiculous charge leveled by John Cornwell that the Holy Father demanded this of all to whom he spoke on the phone.

129. Lenn and Reardon, 130; *Current Biography, 1941* (Maxine Block, ed., the H. W. Wilson Co., 1971 reissue), 673, 675.

130. *Current Biography, 1941* (Maxine Block, ed., the H. W. Wilson Co., 1971 reissue), 673, 675. He replaced the Vatican automotive fleet with new cars that were gifts of manufacturers. "Peace & the Papacy," *Time*, Aug. 16, 1943, 55, 56.

131. "Peace & the Papacy," *Time*, Aug. 16, 1943, 55, 56 (quoting "a Catholic commentator").

132. Lenn and Reardon, 59.

133. Mr. Kirkpatrick (The Vatican) to Sir R. Vansittart, Aug. 19, 1933, *Documents on British Foreign Policy*, Series II, vol. V, London, 1956, no. 342, p. 524; Congregation for the Causes of Saints, *Positio*, appendix 25, 270.

134. Lapide, 120, quoting Erich Ludendorff, *General and Cardinal — On the Policy of the New Pope Pius XII 1917-1937*, 64. About this same time, Pacelli complained that Germany made more work for him than the rest of the world combined. William M. Harrigan, "Pius XII's Efforts to Effect a Détente in German-Vatican Relations, 1939-1940," *Catholic Historical Review*, July 1963, 175. As Pope, he caused the German ambassador to complain following an audience: "Why does he insist on talking French [the official diplomatic language] when he speaks German as well as I do?" Purdy, 12.

135. Fogarty, in *The Papacy and the Church in the United States*, 126.

136. With this encouragement, more and more religious women earned advanced degrees. In many cases, this led to a broadened sense of service, causing many nuns to become active in the civil rights struggle in the United States and similar struggles elsewhere. Briggs, 26, 78.

137. *The Story of the Pope*, 33.

138. His statement, "The laity are the Church," emerged as a major theme of Vatican II. See Weigel, 553-54.

139. J. Hughes (1994), 267.

140. F. Murphy, 67, 79.

> Pius XII was the real architect and promoter of Vatican Council II. He was the one who created the Commission that was to prepare the sessions, but the situation had not matured and Pacelli was already ill. In any event, suffice it to read the Council's minutes to discover that, after Sacred Scripture, Pius XII is the most quoted author. In his encyclicals and addresses he focused on all the problems that would later be addressed by Vatican Council II.

"World Press Unmasks Fallacies in Book Defaming Pius XII: Exclusive Interview with Reporter of Pacelli's Beatification Cause," Zenit News Service, Oct. 3, 1999 (quoting Father Peter Gumpel). Regarding the importance of Pope Pius XII's writings during Vatican II, see R. P. Paolo Molinari, "La Présence de Pie XII, au Concile Vatican II," in *Pie XII et la Cité: La Pensée et l'action politiques de Pie XII*, Presses Universitaires d'Aix-Marseille (Jean Chélini and Joël-Benoît d'Onorio, eds., 1988).

141. F. Murphy, 106. The annotations to the documents of Vatican II contain over 200 references to Pius XII's works, more than for any source other than the Bible. O'Carroll, 182, n. 8 (also noting that there are many other quotations from Pius XII's writing that were not attributed to him); ibid., 226, n. 20; see generally *Pie XII et la Cité: Actes du Colloque de la Faculté de Droit d'Aix-en-Provence*, Presses Universitaires d'Aix-Marseille (Jean Chélini and Joël-Benoît d'Onorio, eds., 1988).

142. F. Murphy, 71; see also O'Carroll, 174 (similar quotation from Cardinal Bea, former head of the Rome Biblical Institute).

> "Without the Christmas messages of Pius XII during the war years, and particularly those of 1941 and 1942 and that of 1944 on democracy, without the same pope's profound reflections on the state, economic and social affairs, the encyclical *Pacem in Terris* would be scarcely thinkable. There is a clear line of continuity between Pius XII and John XXIII."

François Refoule, *The Church and the Rights of Man*, The Seabury Press (New York, 1979), 78-79.

143. See generally Committee for Religious Relations with the Jews, *Guidelines on Religious Relations with the Jews* (n. 4), Dec. 1, 1974.

144. *Jewish Post* (Winnipeg), Nov. 6, 1958.

145. He was both brilliant and able to relate to children:

> Pius XII's intelligence entered into details: That was his charm; he refined and cultivated it. He really learned new languages. He spoke of agriculture with agriculturists, of atomic science with atomic scientists, of obstetrics with midwives, of the law with solicitors. He made himself a child with children. And, inversely, as if to compensate for this incarnation in a technique, a profession, a circumstance, a case, he rose up to Tabor. He gazed at heaven. He *saw*.

Jean Guitton, *The Pope Speaks: Dialogues of Paul VI with Jean Guitton*, 83 (1968). Emphasis in original.

146. Tardini, 64.

147. Hebblethwaite, 51. It has been reported that he was never the same man after this illness. Elliot, 221.

148. For details of the vision and the Pontiff's amazing recovery from illness, see Hatch and Walshe, 235, 238-39.

149. Congregation for the Causes of Saints, *Positio*, (Summarium), Testimony of Cardinal Stefano Wyszynski, Oct. 18 and 25, 1968, before the Tribunal of the Vicariate of Rome, on the beatification of Pius XII (Eugenio Pacelli), Part II, p. 580. See Anne O'Hare McCormick, "Abroad; Influence of Vatican Policy Shows in Italy," *New York Times*, Dec. 26, 1945 (discussing "the revolutionary transformation announced on Christmas Eve in the character and composition of the College of Cardinals").

150. See "A l'Evêque de Münster," Feb. 24, 1943, *Actes et Documents*, vol. 2, p. 306, no. 101 (letter from Pius encouraging Galen: "It is always a comfort to Us when We learn of an open and courageous pronouncement on the part of a single German bishop or all of the German bishops together.") See pp. 136-38.

151. Elliott, 1.

152. Cornwell reports that Pacelli's body began to decompose prematurely. Cornwell (1999), 358. A firsthand account, which includes a photograph of the body lying in state, mentions no similar problem. Dora Jane Hamblin, *That Was the Life*, George J. McLeod Ltd. (Toronto, 1977), 38-39.

153. Elliott, 2; Korn, 154.

154. Marchione (2000) (*Death of Pius XII*).

155. Elliott, 2. In St. Peter's Basilica, about halfway down to the left, is an ornate grillwork above his crypt which pays homage to the former Pontiff. His crypt is immediately to the left as one files down the stairs from within the basilica.

156. Joseph L. Lichten, "A Question of Judgment: Pius XII and the Jews," in *Pius XII and the Holocaust: A Reader*, 129. See also Emmet John Hughes, "The Papacy's Awesome Task," *Life*, Oct. 20, 1958, reprinted in *Great Reading from LIFE: A Treasury of the Best Stories and Articles Chosen by the Editors* (Bonanza Books: New York, 1960), 590, 593.

157. Akin, 17; Lapide, 118.

158. Joseph L. Lichten, "A Question of Judgment: Pius XII and the Jews," in *Pius XII and the Holocaust: A Reader*, 129; Gallo, 293; Lapide, 228. Roman Jews also hung a plaque in their synagogue in honor of Pius XII's efforts to save them. "Interview: 'The Jews, Pius XII and the Black Legend' — A Book Tells the Story of Jews Saved from the Holocaust," *Zenit News*, Dec. 8, 1998.

159. K. Doyle, 16.

160. George Sim Johnston, "The 'Hitler's Pope' Canard," *New York Post*, Sept. 21, 1999.

161. Cardinal Thomas Winning, "Pius XII — Friend of the Jews and Hitler's Foe," *The Daily Telegraph* (London) Oct. 5, 1999. Former President Harry Truman said: "I'm sorry to hear of the passing of Pope Pius XII, whom I consider the greatest statesman in the Vatican in 200 years." William Doino, Jr., "John Paul II: 'Read Father Blet,'" *Inside the Vatican*, October 1999. Former President Herbert Hoover said: "The world has lost a great man. I have reason to know the breadth of his spiritual leadership. This world has been better for his having lived in it." Ibid. Secretary of State John Foster Dulles said: "The passing of this great spiritual leader, who has ever been in the forefront of the defense of Christian civilization, is a profound loss for all peoples of the world." Ibid. Adlai Stevenson said: "All of mankind feels, with the oneness he helped give it, an overpowering loss at this saintly man's being gone." Ibid.

162. Rabbi Theodore L. Adams, president of the Synagogue Council of America, said: "The late pontiff, throughout his long career, ceaselessly fought the forces of racism and bigotry." William Doino, Jr., "John Paul II: 'Read Father Blet,'" *Inside the Vatican*, October 1999. Rabbi Jacob P. Rudin, president of the Central Conference of American Rabbis, said: "His broad sympathy for all people, his wise social vision and his compassionate understanding made his a prophetic voice for righteousness everywhere." Ibid. Dr. Israel Goldstein, chairman of the Western Hemisphere Executive of World Jewish Congress wrote: "In Rome last year, the Jewish community told me of their deep appreciation of the policy which had been set by the Pontiff for the Vatican during the period of the Nazi-Fascist regime, to give shelter and protection to Jews wherever possible." Ibid. Rabbi Joachim Prinz, national president of the American Jewish Congress, said: "The Pontiff will be remembered wherever men of good will gather for his profound devotion to the cause of peace and for his earnest efforts in the rescue of thousands of victims of Nazi persecution, including many Jewish men, women and children." Ibid.

163. Memorial forests were planted for Winston Churchill, King Peter of Yugoslavia, and Count Bernadotte of Sweden. The proposal was that Pius XII's forest would have 800,000 trees one for each Jewish life he was credited with having saved. Graham (1987), 34. This number was based upon the testimony of the postwar government of the State of Israel, and it is a larger total than all other European Jewish relief organizations combined. Akin, 17. "The Catholic Church, under the pontificate of Pius XII, was instrumental in saving at least 700,000, but probably as many as 860,000 Jews." Lapide, 269.

164. Bernstein and Politi, 111; Roncalli had likewise been very pleased when Pacelli became Pope Pius XII. Elliott, 147.

165. J. Hughes (1994), 265.

166. Vatican II, *Gaudium et Spes* (Pastoral Constitution on the Church in the Modern World), n. 29.

167. During the war, Pius XII and Montini were "intimate friends" in daily contact with one another. Fabert, 13, 87. In fact, they had a father-son relationship, and it was thought by many that Pius was grooming Montini to one day become pope. Ibid., 37, 45, 48. The two had somewhat of a falling out over political matters in 1954, however, and Pius appointed Montini archbishop of Milan without naming him a cardinal. See Ibid., 46-52. Nevertheless, upon his election, it was said that Paul VI was closer to Pius XII, intellectually and emotionally, than he was to Pope John XXIII, his immediate predecessor. Ibid., 66.

## Chapter Sixteen: The Play and the KGB Plot

1. In fact, the Vatican had a "long-standing papal practice in wartime of not condemning wartime atrocities by name and only in general terms. The reasons for this practice are... based on experience." Robert A. Graham, reviewing *Vatican Diplomacy and the Jews During the Holocaust: 1934-1943* (by John F. Morley), in *America*, Aug. 9, 1980, 56, 57. Myron Taylor, President Roosevelt's representative to Pope Pius XII early in the war apparently understood this. He denied having asked Pius to identify Hitler by name. Blet, 134 ("I never asked for that, I never asked that Hitler be named.")

2. Many anti-Hitler intellectuals in Germany chose the same indirect technique for criticizing Hitler. Knowing that a direct attack would only result in further oppression, they would write about Cromwell, Robespierre, Philip of Macedon, or Napoleon and still "hit the target." *The United States at War: The Audio Classics Series.* See also *The Ciano Diaries*, 493 (an article in *L'Osservatore Romano* was expressly written about Greek philosophy, but "the real purpose was evident" to Mussolini, who became "very hostile to the Vatican"); ibid., 497-98 (Mussolini considered arresting the director of *L'Osservatore Romano* due to articles which contained "a subtle vein of poison against the regime.")

3. Alvarez and Graham, xi. "The Nazis considered the Catholic Church in general and the Vatican in particular to be their archenemies beyond any hope of accommodation, let alone collaboration." Ibid., xii.

4. K. Doyle, 16.

5. See Congregation for the Causes of Saints, *Positio*, appendix 25, 236.

6. Mr. Hochhuth declined to be interviewed for this project, even though the author offered to conduct it in person, by phone, by e-mail, or by traditional mail. Hochhuth did, however, agree to permit an American scholar, Mark Ruff from St. Louis University, to review his papers.

7. "Editorial: Character Assassination," *America*, March 7, 1964, reprinted in *The Storm Over The Deputy*, 39.

8. "Most amusing are anti-Catholic authors Avro Manhattan and Paul Blanshard. They both published books in 1949 accusing the pope of pro-Nazi sympathies. But neither author mentioned his 'silence' during the Holocaust. Of course, after 'The Deputy' came out, both of them suddenly remembered that he was silent as well." E-mail note to the author from Dimitri Cavalli, June 2, 2009.

9. See Giovanni Sale, "The birth of the 'black legend' of Pius XII," *La Civiltà Cattolica*, March 21, 2009 (noting the importance of the Eichmann trial to the changed perception of Pius XII).

10. Wright, 1929.

11. Golo Mann, "The Real Accomplishment," *Basler Nachrichten*, Sept. 17, 1963, reprinted in *The Storm Over The Deputy*, 217, 219 (Golo Mann is the son of German writer and Nobel Prize recipient Thomas Mann, one of Hochhuth's heroes.) See also Gad Kaynar, "The Liturgical Theatre of the Holocaust on the Israeli Stage – Holy Scripture, Myth, Ritual," in *Theatre and Holy Script* (Sussex Academic Press, Shimon Levy, ed., 1999) (giving insight to the power of theater in matters like this).

12. See Lapomarda, 172, 195, n. 8; Giovanni Sale, "The birth of the 'black legend' of Pius XII," *La Civiltà Cattolica*, March 21, 2009.

13. For some people, at least, the play did indeed discredit not only the Catholic Church, but Christianity itself. Consider the following passage:

> I began attending the Unitarian Church, where I felt at home in the liberal intellectual ambience. In those days of desegregation and social change, it was good to feel a part of throwing off the old order. One of the sermons I recall most vividly cited Rolf Hochhuth's play, *The Deputy*, which I now know is the fictional source for much of the disinformation about Pope Pius XII's role in World War II. The sermon fed my sense of outrage and probably contributed to my mistrust of institutional Christianity. I still considered myself a Christian, but not in the sense taught in churches; I felt I would have to invent my own religion to feel completely satisfied, and I even made some notes as to its projected beliefs and practices.

Terrye Newkirk, "The Long and Winding Road," *This Rock*, September 1996, *http://www.catholic.com/thisrock/1996/9609conv.asp*.

14. In England, the title is usually translated as *The Representative*, but sometimes as *The Vicar*. The program from the original London production says: "It is not, as has been widely construed and rumoured, a gratuitous and vicious attack on the Catholic Church — almost every page proves this accusation to be

absurd." Director Clifford Williams included an essay in which he wrote: "I have examined all the facts which the play contains and I have found no instance of Hochhuth deliberately distorting verifiable information." Pope Paul VI's defense of Pius XII is also reprinted. See p. 278.

15. Later that year, *The Comforter* was performed at Blackfriars' Theatre in New York (on Oct. 13, 1964). Written by Redemptorist priest Edward A. Molloy, it presented Pius XII as a humane man, depicting how much he did in defense of the Jews during the Holocaust.

16. See Pierre Joffroy, *A Spy for God: The Ordeal of Kurt Gerstein* (New York: Harcourt Brace, 1969, N. Denny, trans.).

> Gerstein's "eye-witness" accounts, and further argumentation based thereon, appear very untrustworthy indeed. One does not have to be a fanatical supporter of Nazism or Fascism (your reviewer, when a student in Italy in the 1930's, was strongly anti-Fascist, and still is) to recognize the extent to which, all unsuspecting, we have been tricked into believing Gerstein's assertions, especially through the deceit practised on us by Rolf Hochhuth in *Der Stellvertreter*.

Robert A. Hall. Jr., "Book Review: *Il Rapporto Gerstein: Anatomia Di Un Falso* (The Gerstein Report: The Anatomy of a Fraud), Carlo Mattogno." Sentinella d'Italia (Via Buonarroti, 4, Monfalcone, Italy, 1985), *Journal of Historical Review* (2002).

17. Hochhuth dedicated the play to the memory of Kolbe and Lichtenberg, two priests who were killed for standing up against the Nazis. While this can be seen as a sign of respect for the Catholic Church, it is more clearly a statement of contrast, designed to advance Hochhuth's criticism of Pius XII.

18. Discussing a similar, overly dramatic scene in a different play, Justus George Lawler wrote: "This was a dramatic *inventio* worthy of Rolf Hochhuth." Manuscript, working title: *Were the Popes Against the Jews?*

19. D. Fisher, 9, 29.

20. Hochhuth, 331. Patricia Marx, Interview with Rolf Hochhuth, WNYC Radio (February 1964), reprinted in *The Storm Over The Deputy*, 52, 59-60.

21. Ward, 29.

22. See ibid., 34.

23. Ibid., 27. Hochhuth called for individual actors to play different parts in different scenes.

24. "Piscator's production... reduced the fifth act to a short epilogue, making Riccardo's development into a tragic hero unclear.... It shifted the emphasis back to the confrontation with the Pope in Act IV and away from the question posed at the beginning of the final act: 'Where Are You, God?'" Ward, 29 (noting that many other productions deleted the fifth act entirely). It also eliminated one of Hochhuth's most offensive passages, when Pius first appears and says: "With burning sorrow for Our factories." See D. Fisher, 7.

25. Thompson, 15 ("We have never seen an author so little married to his words.") According to Hochhuth's papers, he and Piscator differed over the editing. In 1963, he "submitted to the criticism that Auschwitz could not be produced on the stage by writing an alternative conclusion" in which Fontana was not a tragic hero but a mere victim. Ward, 29 (this version was prepared for a production in Basle).

26. John Simon, "The Deputy and Its Metamorphoses," *Nation*, March 16, 1964, reprinted in *The Storm Over The Deputy*, 109, 114.

27. Ibid., in *The Storm Over The Deputy*, 109, 115 (highly critical of the American version). Robert Brustein, writing in the *New Republic* explained: "The New York production of his play... preserves no integrity at all, and I have confined my discussion to the printed text because the Broadway performance is beneath discussion." Robert Brustein, "History as Drama," *New Republic*, March 14, 1964, reprinted in *The Storm Over The Deputy*, 23.

28. John Simon, "The Deputy and Its Metamorphoses," *Nation*, March 16, 1964, reprinted in *The Storm Over The Deputy*, 109, 116.

29. See Ronald J. Rychlak, "The Church and the Holocaust," *Wall Street Journal* (Europe), March 28, 2002.

30. Quoted in Hinckle, 67. See Jerry Glenn, "Faith, Love, and the Tragic Conflict in Hochhuth's 'Der Stellvertreter,'" 7:3 *German Studies Review*, 481 (October 1984).

31. See Congregation for the Causes of Saints, *Positio*, appendix 25, 237 (discussing Paul's defense of Pius that appeared in the *Tablet* and in *L'Osservatore Romano* on June 29, 1963). Montini's letter was received in London an hour after he became pope. Rhodes, 352, n. 28. It is reprinted in *The Storm Over The Deputy*, 66. Montini was an off-screen character in the play. Ibid., 9 (editor's foreword).

32. "Il Papa Ieri e Oggi," *L'Osservatore della Domenica*, June 26, 1964. See also "Vatican Weekly Defends Pius," *Washington Post*, June 27, 1964.

33. During Paul VI's visit to Israel in 1964, he declared:

> Everybody knows what Pius XII did for the defense of all those who were caught in [World War II's] tribulations, without distinction. And yet you know suspicions and even accusations have been leveled against this great Pontiff. We are happy to have the opportunity to state on this day and in this place that there is nothing more unjust than this slight against such a venerated memory. Those who intimately knew this admirable man know how far could go his sensibility, his compassion for

human suffering, his courage, his delicacy of heart. Those who after the war came with tears in their eyes to thank him for saving their lives also knew it.

2 *Insegnamenti di Paolo VI*, 53-54 (Libreria Editrice Vaticana: Città del Vaticano). See also *New York Times*, Jan. 6, 1964, 1 ("The pope's defense of Pope Pius XII's efforts to save Jews during World War II were widely and favorably commented on both privately and publicly [throughout Israel].")

34. *Die Welt*, April 6, 1963 (emphasis added). Reprinted in "The Pope Yesterday and Today," *L'Osservatore della Domenica*, June 26, 1964. See O'Carroll, 21, 81.

35. "Additional Evidence of Pius XII's Help to Jews: Church Saved One Million Jews from Certain Death," Zenit News, March 15, 1999.

36. "I would like to say quite plainly that I regard *The Deputy* as a shameless and inexcusable attack upon a defenseless dead man who, in view of the laws operative in most 'civilized states,' cannot be given protection against the calumny of this theatrical web of lies." Kuehnelt-Leddihn, 184-85. "This portrait of a callous, money-minded, cynical and selfish man is contradicted by everything in the German and British Foreign Office documents." Rhodes, 351.

37. "Echoes of The Deputy," *New York Post*, editorial, March 6, 1964. "Throughout Hochhuth's career, prominent drama critics, scholars, and teachers of literature have dismissed his works as artistically flawed and morally simplistic." Book Review: Margaret Ward's *Rolf Hochhuth*, 52 *German Quarterly*, 293.

38. "Silence," *New York Times*, editorial, Jan. 28, 1964.

39. Harold Burke-Sivers, "Has the Church Sinned?: The Holy Catholic Church and the Issue of the Jewish Holocaust," *Aurem Cordis*, Oct. 30, 2005; Gerald Warner, "Twisted Interpretation of History Blames Pius XII for the Plight of the Jews," *Scotland on Sunday*, Sept. 26, 1999.

40. See Friedländer, *Pius XII and the Third Reich*; Katz, *Black Sabbath*; Katz, *Massacre in Rome*; Lewy, *The Catholic Church and Nazi Germany*; Falconi, *The Silence of Pius XII*. Of course, Katz was eventually criminally convicted for having unfairly slandered Pius XII, see p. 306, and much of Falconi's work was later shown to have come from doctored documents provided to him by Tito's Communist government in Yugoslavia, see pp. 335-38.

41. Congregation for the Causes of Saints, *Positio*, statement of the relator, p. 9. Like most world governments, the Holy See keeps records confidential for an extended period of time to make certain that secret governmental information will not be revealed and that living people will not be embarrassed by disclosure of private information. Only recently were most (not all) of the American OSS World War II files made public, and similar French and British files also remain secret.

42. Volume three is split into two books, which accounts for occasional references to 12 volumes.

43. Quoted in *Positio*, appendix 25, 251, note 3.

44. Oppen, 400. Eugene Fisher, the Catholic coordinator of the International Catholic-Jewish Historical Group that analyzed the 11 volumes from 1999 to 2001, said that the documents were "objectively and well selected." E-mail to author from Eugene Fisher, March 13, 2009.

45. Pacepa, *Moscow's Assault on the Vatican*. Pacepa was one of Romanian President Nicolai Ceaucescu's most trusted lieutenants. As head of the foreign intelligence service ("DIE"), Pacepa was well-versed in much of what the KGB was involved in, met regularly with representatives from the other European Communist security services, and had a very good idea of what went on inside the Soviet Bloc. In the months following his defection, a third of the Romanian ruling Council of Ministers was demoted, 22 ambassadors were replaced, more than a dozen high-ranking security officers were arrested, and several dozen more simply vanished from sight. Much of the Warsaw Pact's spy service in the West was decimated. Ceaucescu subsequently ordered Pacepa killed. Pacepa is still in the CIA's witness protection program. His book *Red Horizons* caused Ceaucescu to impose a second death sentence on him. The dictator also made it clear that anyone in the country found with a copy of the book would be shot. The principal message of the book was that Ceaucescu had devised a system, "Red Horizons," to dupe the West into believing that he was a different sort of Communist, and that Romania was a different sort of country than the rest of the Soviet Bloc. In theory, Romania was independent of Moscow, more interested in trade with the West, and less repressive than other Warsaw Pact countries. Pacepa exposed this myth, and Radio Free Europe broadcast *Red Horizons* into Romania in the fall of 1989, just as the first anti-government demonstrations were beginning. Within weeks, a revolution spread across the country, and on Christmas Day 1989, Ceaucescu and his wife were executed by a firing squad. The next day, the principal Romanian newspaper began serializing *Red Horizons* on the front page. The paper explained that the broadcast by Radio Free Europe had inspired the rebels. It concluded: "The publication of this book played an uncontested role in revealing in all its hideousness the true face of a dictatorship, which with diabolical cunningness had managed to outfox a part of the world." See Alfred S. Regnery, "Book Inspired Counter-Revolution: How *Red Horizons* Helped Bring Freedom to Romania," *Human Events*, Oct. 22, 2001.

46. Pacepa, *Moscow's Assault on the Vatican*. Khrushchev had also initiated a campaign against the Russian Orthodox Church, forcing the closure of about 12,000 churches.

47. "All important Soviet religious organizations were... subordinated to the KGB, and all important religious servants working for them were... on the KGB's payroll." Pacepa, *The KGB use of Religion for Dez-*

538 | Hitler, the War, and the Pope

*informatsiya* (copy on file with author). Pacepa reported that "the Department of Cults, which coordinated the entire religious activity in the country, became my DIE's front. In a couple of years, every priest holding an official job, starting with Romania's patriarch and the country's metropolitans, became either DIE undercover officers or paid collaborators. Every Romanian representative in international religious organizations was also on my payroll." Ibid.

48. See Hoover, 324-25 ("Members [of the Communist Party] are being told: 'Join churches and become involved in church work.'")

49. Golitsyn, 292.

50. Ibid., 91, 295 (establishment of coordinating machinery for the bloc in 1959).

51. Pacepa, *Moscow's Assault on the Vatican*. While the Soviets and the Romanians were supposedly at odds with one another at this time, former Soviet intelligence officer Anatoliy Golitsyn reports that this was just another piece of disinformation. Golitsyn, 186.

52. There is no evidence that such a loan was ever made. The Vatican archives that could confirm or disprove the Romanian request are sealed. The Vatican Secretariat of State reports:

> It would seem extremely unlikely that Romania would have asked for a loan from the Vatican. No relations existed between the Government and the Vatican after the expulsion of the apostolic nuncio in 1946 and the closure of the nunciature in 1950. Furthermore such a petition would be inconsistent especially when one considers the severe persecution that the Catholic Church, especially the Greek Catholic Church, endured during the Communist regime.

Letter to the author from Monsignor Gabriele Caccia, Assessor, Vatican Secretariat of State, Feb. 2, 2008. Pacepa's case, however, seems to anticipate this concern: "Romania's relations with the Vatican had been severed in 1951, when Moscow accused the Vatican's *nunciatura* in Romania of being an undercover CIA front and closed its offices. The *nunciatura* buildings in Bucharest had been turned over to the DIE, and now housed a foreign language school." Pacepa, *Moscow's Assault on the Vatican*. A loan would provide cover and explain why Romania was changing its position vis-à-vis the Holy See. Ibid. In private correspondence with this author, Pacepa wanted to make clear that his statement to the Vatican representative that "Romania was ready to restore diplomatic relations with the Holy See in exchange for access to its archives" was an "invented reason." Pacepa explained: "Ceausescu did not intend to restore diplomatic relations with the Vatican. To enforce that lie, I was also instructed to tell the Vatican that Romania needed access to these archives to find historical roots that would help the Romanian government publicly justify its change of heart toward the Holy See." Correspondence from Ion Pacepa to Ronald J. Rychlak, May 18, 2009.

53. During his life, it was thought that Casaroli was pro-Communist. His posthumously published memoirs show that he permitted this perception to exist because it helped him with international relations. In reality, he was strongly anti-Communist.

54. Father Peter Gumpel, relator of Pius XII's sainthood cause, remembered a young German priest who was in Rome at the appropriate time. He drove a sports car that seemed incongruous with his status, and few people seemed to know his background. Father Gumpel also said, however, that there is no evidence that anyone managed to get into the archives and steal or manipulate any documents.

55. Father Sergio Pagano, prefect of the Vatican Secret Archives, has explained that during the years Pacepa describes, "the letters of Pius XII were no longer in the Vatican Secret Archives. The documents they were interested in were to be found in the archive of the Secretary of State." Zenit News Service, "Relator of Pius XII's Case Is Wary of Report: Father Gumpel Urges Prudence Over Defector's Tale," Feb. 18, 2007. Father Gumpel, relator of Pope Pius XII's sainthood cause, speculated that Soviet spies, unfamiliar with how things work in the Vatican, might have confused "the Vatican Secret Archives with the Archive of the Secretary of State." Ibid.

56. After Mikhail Gorbachev's departure in August 1991, there was a brief period of time during which the KGB archives were opened. Among the documents that were uncovered was a report apparently written by Bishop Alexis of Tallin, Estonia, concerning information he had gathered in Rome for the KGB in the 1960s. Among his most important findings was the library at the Jesuit-run Oriental Institute. "Alexis was awed by their library: bound copies of *Pravda* and *Izvestia* from 1917 on; all the decrees promulgated since the Russian Revolution; all the reviews; volumes and documents that would be rarities at home." The importance of this information was that this would make it impossible for the KGB to rewrite history to suit political convenience. For example, the Jesuits knew exactly what happened at the pseudo-synod of the Ukrainian Catholic Church in 1946. Peter Hebblethwaite, "The Russian Orthodox, KGB, and Vatican: Patriarch Alexis report reveals old dilemmas," *National Catholic Reporter*, May 27, 1994 (noting that in 1990 Alexis was named patriarch of Moscow and of all Russia and that the Ukrainian Catholic Church has denied that Alexis was a KGB agent). Andrew and Mitrokhin, however, report that Alexis was formally recruited by the KGB in February 1958 "on the basis of patriotic feelings," and was given the code name "Drozdov." According to a document found in the Estonian KGB archives, "Drozdov" was a highly successful agent who "pacified" rebellious monks. He was also granted an Honorary Citation by the KGB chairman in 1988. Andrew and

Mitrokhin, 498-99. Regardless of who wrote this report from Rome, the important point is that it would have been hard for the KGB to fabricate history in light of the Vatican's well-known archives and records.

57. Correspondence from Ion Pacepa to Ronald J. Rychlak, June 10, 2009.

58. Andrew and Gordievsky, 503 (he was involved in the creation of many fake documents).

59. Ibid., 463. On Department D, see Golitsyn, 50-51.

60. In an interview, Hochhuth said that his work on the play had begun by 1956 or earlier. Patricia Marx, Interview with Rolf Hochhuth, WNYC Radio (February 1964), reprinted in *The Storm Over The Deputy*, 52. According to Hochhuth's papers, however, there is no evidence of work on it prior to the second half of 1958. Daily work on it began in 1959. Ward, 25. A biographer reports that he wrote it between 1959 and 1961. Taëni, 54; Victor Gaetan, "Historians, diplomats cast doubts on KGB plot against Pope Pius XII," *Catholic News Service*, Feb. 28, 2007.

61. General Agayants was sometimes accused of claiming credit for documents that were actually prepared by others. Andrew and Gordievsky, 463.

62. Ward, 25 ("In the early stages of its conception... the Pope did not figure in the play.")

63. Ibid., 41-42 ("This was particularly true of the sensationalized adaptation of Jerome Rothenberg used in the New York production by Herman Shumlin.").

64. Khrushchev wanted to export the Communist revolution to many areas, including South America. "The majority of South Americans were unsophisticated religious peasants, and Khrushchev intended to infiltrate Marxism into their continent with the help of a new religious movement [called Liberation Theology]." Pacepa, *The KGB Use of Religion for Dezinformatsiya* (copy on file with author). The KGB also sent "a few trusted priests working for the DIE to South America to see how 'we' should tune" the theology "to make it palatable to the local priests." Ibid. Pope John Paul II denounced liberation theology at the January 1979 meeting of the Latin American bishops' council (CELAM), held in Pueblo, Mexico: "This conception of Christ as a political figure, a revolutionary, as the subversive of Nazareth, does not tally with the Church's catechism."

65. See Patrick N. Allitt, "Catholic Anti-Communism," *Crisis Magazine Online*, http://insidecatholic.com/Joomla/ (April 4, 2009) ("[I]t was in the twenty years of the 'high' Cold War era, 1945-1965, that Catholic anti-Communism reached its climax.")

66. Hennesey, 289 (quoting Pius XII's 1956 Christmas message, in which he suggested that it was pointless to talk to the Communists). Khrushchev said, "We remain the Atheists we have always been; we are doing as much as we can to liberate those people who are still under the spell of this religious opiate." Hoover, 321.

67. Here are a few excerpts from KGB documents released by Father Gleb Yakumin, vice chairman of a Russian parliamentary commission that investigated the KGB's manipulation of the church, primarily by influencing the World Council of Churches (WCC) toward liberation theology:

> **August 1969:** Agents "Svyatoslav," "Adamant," "Altar," "Magister," Roschin," and "Zemnogorskiy" were sent by the KGB to England for participation in the work of the Central Committee of the World Council of Churches. The agency [KGB] managed to thwart hostile activity [against the Liberation Theology], and agent "Kuznetsov" managed to penetrate the WCC directorate.

> **February 1972:** Agents "Svyatoslav" and "Mikhailov" went to New Zeeland and Australia for sessions of the Central Committee of the WCC.

> **July 1983:** 47 agents of the KGB organs among religious authorities, clergy, and technical personnel from the USSR delegation were sent to Vancouver (Canada) for the 6th WCC General Assembly.

> **July 1989:** In accordance with a plan authorized by the leadership of the KGB of the USSR, agency-operatives and organizational measures were undertaken for ensuring state security in the period of preparation for and conduct of measures during a meeting of the World Council of Churches in Moscow.... Eight declarations and 3 messages corresponding to the political line of the socialist countries were adopted as a result of measures rendered by the executive committee of the WCC.

> **August 1989:** The Central Committee of the WCC organized a special session on perestroika.... Now the agenda of the WCC is also our agenda.

Pacepa, *The KGB Use of Religion for Dezinformatsiya* (copy on file with author), citing *New Times*, July 25-31, 1989. See also *Religion and the Cold War: Cold War History Series* (Dianne Kirby, ed., New York: Palgrave Macmillan, 2003).

68. Telephone conversation between the author and Father Peter Gumpel, relator of Pius XII's sainthood cause.

69. Many reviewers found it more interesting than the drama. See Carl Amery, "The Harassed Pope," *Süddeutsche Zeitung*, March 2-3, 1963, reprinted in *The Storm Over The Deputy*, 149, 151; Ward, 29.

70. Rolf C. Zimmermann, "Drama or Pamphlet: Hochhuth's *The Deputy* and the Tradition of Polemical Literature," *Der Streit um Hochhuth's "Stellvertreter"* (1963), reprinted in *The Storm Over The Deputy*, 123, 124. This is the same basic technique Dan Brown used with his books *The DaVinci Code* and *Angels*

*and Demons.* They were both fictional, but they made enough truth claims that many readers believed the outlandish claims.

71. Hochhuth, 328. Quite inconsistently, Hochhuth suggests that the Vatican never did forcefully intervene. For instance, while recounting the events of the fall and winter of 1942, including the Allies' Dec. 17 announcement, Hochhuth trivialized the Pope's 1942 Christmas message. Regarding the Pope's statements in general, Hochhuth described them as: "carefully insipid, flowery, vaguely moralizing and generalizing speeches, or rather assemblages of clichés about the events of the war. In none of them did he ever specifically name a statesman, a country — aside from Poland — or even the fact of the deportations which had been going on for years." Ibid., 349. Hochhuth criticized Pius for everything from having makeup applied to his face when he appeared in a film (Ibid., 351), to being sympathetic to Hitler as evidenced by the concordat (Ibid., 296), to not being seriously disturbed when Hitler persecuted priests who spoke out against Nazism. Ibid., 305. He also faulted the Church for profiting from both sides by continuing to trade with them during the war. Ibid., 350. Ignoring Nazi persecution of Catholic clergy, Hochhuth argued that Himmler concentrated his policy of extermination on Jews, Slavs, Gypsies, Jehovah's Witnesses, and Communists because this would not damage relations with the Holy See. Ibid., 306.

72. Ward, 47; ibid., 142 ("he has continually stressed that his plays are works of art — not reportage"). In 1967, Jenö Levai, who testified as an expert witness in the Adolf Eichmann trial, released his book *Hungarian Jewry and the Papacy: Pope Pius XII Did Not Remain Silent.* Levai was outraged that Hochhuth had cited him as a source and criticized what he thought was a dishonest use of historical sources. See Dimitri Cavalli, "How Pope Pius XII Was Made a Villain," *Riverdale Press* (Bronx, NY), July 16, 1998, A11.

73. Hochhuth, 304.

74. "Editorial: Character Assassination," *America*, March 7, 1964, reprinted in *The Storm Over The Deputy*, 39.

75. D. Fisher, 11.

76. Interview with Rolf Hochhuth, *Ramparts*, Spring 1964, reprinted in *The Storm Over The Deputy*, 42. His book on Busch sold well, and while he did not receive royalties, his publisher sent Hochhuth and his wife to Rome as a reward for the book. Taëni, 14.

77. Friedrich Heer, "The Need for Confession," *Commonweal*, Feb. 20, 1964, reprinted in *The Storm Over The Deputy*, 166.

78. "Even Pius XII's longtime secretary, Father Robert Leiber SJ, was charged with betrayal." Michael Feldkamp, "Hochhuth Exposed," *Association of Contemporary Church Historians*, July/August 2007 (John Jay Hughes trans.).

79. Interview with Rolf Hochhuth, *Ramparts*, Spring 1964, reprinted in *The Storm Over The Deputy*, 42.

80. Hudal and Wüstenberg were both "on the outs" with the Vatican leadership. Hudal was angry with the way Pius XII kept him away from positions of power (see pp. 347-48), and some people suspected that Wüstenberg, "a German priest in the papal Secretariat of State whom Pius XII had refused to promote" because he disapproved of his lifestyle, "had sought revenge." Michael Feldkamp, "Hochhuth Exposed," *Association of Contemporary Church Historians*, July/August 2007 (John Jay Hughes trans.). Pius later sent Wüstenberg to Japan. Father Peter Gumpel, the relator of Pius XII's sainthood cause, reports that Pius always kept Wüstenberg "at a great distance on account of his reputation." Private correspondence to author, Jan. 8, 2008.

81. "For more than forty years the Pope's 'silence' has supplied headlines for the media. The same media however have never questioned Hochhuth's silence, even though he still refuses to identify his Vatican contacts. While Hochhuth is clearly concerned for his own good name, and that of his Roman informants, he has never hesitated to defame others. But his readers should know that his readiness to tamper with historical veracity is by now well established. They can't claim that they haven't been warned against such a long-term manipulator of the facts." Michael Feldkamp, "Hochhuth Exposed," *Association of Contemporary Church Historians*, July/August 2007 (John Jay Hughes trans.).

82. Erik von Kuehnelt-Leddihn, *The Timeless Christian* (Franciscan Herald Press, 1969). "Hochuth's affirmation that he posed 'a series of questions' to an undisclosed bishop resulting in 80 pages of secret documents attached to his play is at least as ridiculous as the KGB's insinuation that the CIA killed President Kennedy." Correspondence from Ion Pacepa to Ronald J. Rychlak, May 18, 2009.

83. George Weigel, "Parsing the Vatican Newspaper," *National Review Online*, May 21, 2009.

84. See p. 283.

85. Pacepa reports: "At about that same time I used to visit the Vatican fairly regularly as an accredited messenger from a head of state, and I was never able to get any talkative bishop off into a corner with me — and it was not for lack of trying." David Irving, who later worked with Hochhuth and who was suspected by British Intelligence of working with the Soviets, was also known for his ability to locate documents that others could not find (and of interpreting them in controversial, anti-British ways). Susan Barnes, "David Irving: Portrait of a Gentleman," *Sunday Times Supplement*, London, Sept. 6, 1970 (It is "freely admitted by historians of excellent reputation, that Irving is a remarkable researcher who has discovered documents of great importance. But some of them think he unduly emphasizes some words to distort their meaning and

denigrate Britain.") See also David Irving Deportation from Canada file, 1992 (documents released under the Access to Information Act by the Canadian Department of Citizenship and Immigration in 1994), available on the Internet: *http://www.fpp.co.uk/Canada/FDCIfile/BoDSmear1990a.html* (suggesting that he "received funding, material assistance, and access to private archives" in writing his first three books"). In fact, "His correspondence... points at the fact he received assistance from at least 1961." Ibid.

86. Rychlak, *Righteous Gentiles*, 188.

87. Kuehnelt-Leddihn, 191-93.

88. In 1943, Nazi Germany announced the discovery of mass graves in the Katyn Forest in Russia. The victims had been executed. Many of them were Polish officers; others included Polish landowners, factory owners, lawyers, priests, and government officials. The Nazis blamed the Soviets, and this led to the end of diplomatic relations between Moscow and the London-based Polish government-in-exile. The Soviet Union denied the massacres until 1990, when it finally acknowledged the perpetration by the NKVD and the subsequent cover-up. The total number of victims is estimated at about 22,000. See Allen Paul, *Katyń: Stalin's Massacre and the Seeds of Polish Resurrection* (Annapolis, Md.: Naval Institute Press, 1996).

89. D. Fisher, 47. "Hochhuth has been able to produce no support for his subjective speculations and these, in fact, seem to be based on bias and a deliberate attempt to seek a scapegoat for the guilt of others." Ibid.

90. Levai, 5-6 (quoting Albert Wucher, "Der Stellvertreter und die historische Wirklichkeit," in the *Süddeutsche Zeitung*, Munich, April 19, 1963).

91. Rolf C. Zimmermann, "Drama or Pamphlet: Hochhuth's The Deputy and the Tradition of Polemical Literature," *Der Streit um Hochhuth's "Stellvertreter"* (1963), reprinted in *The Storm Over The Deputy*, 123, 124.

92. *Tablet* (London), March 16, 1963. See also Graham (1996).

93. See, e.g., Mikhail Markovich Sheinmann, *Der Vatikan im Zweiten Weltkrieg* (Dietz: Berlin, 1954; first published in Russian in 1948). For an analysis of Soviet propaganda, see Graham, *The Vatican and Communism During World War II*.

94. *Petrusblatt* (March 3, 1963). *Petrusblatt* was a weekly publication in Berlin.

95. D. Fisher, 29.

96. Michael Feldkamp, "Hochhuth Exposed," *Association of Contemporary Church Historians*, July/August 2007 (John Jay Hughes, trans.).

97. Ibid.

98. AR Action Report Online: *http://www.fpp.co.uk/docs/Irving/Hochhuth/Times_200207.html*.

99. Pacepa, *Kerry's Soviet Rhetoric*.

100. Irving's web page also contains the following content on his relationship with the German playwright:

> Mr Hochhuth had first approached Mr Irving after reading his 1963 best-seller *The Destruction of Dresden*; soon after, the German had written his sensational play *The Representative* (*Der Stellvertreter*), critical of Pope Pious' [*sic*] WW II tolerance of Nazi persecution of the Jews. The two writers' friendship began when they met in the Hamburg offices of *Der Stern* magazine in January 1965; Rolf Hochhuth stayed with the Irvings in their London flat (then in Paddington), and Mr Irving often stayed with the Hochhuths — Rolf, his first wife Marianne and second, Dana, in Switzerland. They remained the closest of friends until circumstances drove them geographically apart — Hochhuth no longer able to travel to Britain, and Mr Irving banned from Germany in 1993.

*http://fpp.co.uk/online/98/09/Hochhuth010498.html*. Actually, Irving did travel to see Hochhuth in 2005, and he was arrested. See p. 287.

101. Irving is often presented as a man of the right, and Hochhuth as a man of the left. Their politics are not really that easy to describe. One of Hochhuth's biographers explained him as "a pessimistic leftist with conservative tendencies." Taëni, 36. See Ibid., 38. His "self-assumed title" is "material idealist." Ibid., 41. Ultimately, however, his "stance is not far removed from that of Marxist ideologies, and Hochhuth would probably not deny this himself." Taëni, 42.

102. Perhaps a third "denier" has joined their ranks. Bishop Richard Williamson, one of the four bishops from the Society of St. Pius X who had been excommunicated, made international news when, just after Pope Benedict XVI lifted the excommunication, it was revealed that he had given an interview in which he denied the gas chambers and suggested that the number of Jews killed in the Holocaust had been greatly exaggerated. Interestingly, when trying to figure out how to explain his views, Williamson contacted Irving for advice. See "Holocaust row bishop Richard Williamson contacts David Irving," *U.K. Telegraph*, Feb. 27, 2009 ("Bishop Richard Williamson contacted Mr Irving by email, asking how to present his views without causing an angry backlash.") Said Irving: "He is obviously a very intelligent man who did not realise the danger of talking to the press.... He is not a Holocaust denier. Like me, he does not buy the whole package." Ibid.

103. British intelligence took note of their friendship. See Declassified Secret Memorandum: Soldiers, to Mr. John Peck & Sir E. Peck from J.E. Jackson, Jan. 10, 1969 ('Soldiers' — IRD Contribution) (Irving "seems to be a close personal friend of Hochhuth.")

104. AR Action Report Online *http://www.fpp.co.uk/docs/Irving/Hochhuth/Times_200207.html*. A 1970 profile said: "Irving is ruefully aware of rumours about the source of his income." Susan Barnes, "David Irving: Portrait of a Gentleman," *Sunday Times Supplement*, London, Sept. 6, 1970.

105. This is part of the *David Irving Deportation from Canada* file, 1992 (documents released under the Access to Information Act by the Canadian Department of Citizenship and Immigration in 1994), available on the Internet: *http://www.fpp.co.uk/Canada/FDCIfile/BoDSmear1990a.html*. ("Irving enjoys an opulent lifestyle, and has done for many years. It does not seem that he could maintain such a standard of living without source of income other than his books. [This is particularly true for his apparent wealth during the 1970s.]")

106. William J. Kole, "Historian Charged With Denying Holocaust," *Washington Post*, Nov. 17, 2005.

107. Oliver King and agencies, "David Irving Arrested in Austria," *Guardian Unlimited*, Nov. 17, 2005.

108. Ibid.

109. *Irving v. Penguin Books and Lipstadt*, In the High Court of Justice, Queen's Bench Division, April 11, 2000.

110. Ibid.

111. Ibid.

112. Ibid.

113. Quoted in Deborah Lipstadt, *History on Trial: My Day in Court with David Irving*, 283 (2005).

114. This is the term used in the popular press. Irving was charged under Austria's 1945 "*Verbotsgesetz*" (Banning Law). The technical charge was minimizing the Holocaust. See "David Irving Arrested in Austria," *Guardian*, Nov. 17, 2005; William J. Kole, "Historian Charged With Denying Holocaust," *Washington Post*, Nov. 17, 2005.

115. "Holocaust denier Irving is jailed," BBC News, Feb. 20, 2006: *http://news.bbc.co.uk/2/hi/europe/4733820.stm*. After being sentenced, Irving said that he had been a Holocaust denier but that he changed his views after seeing Adolf Eichmann's files. In a talk at Colorado University, however, his former litigation adversary, Deborah Lipstadt, still referred to him as a "hardcore denier." Gary Black, "Lipstadt gives pointed speech for Holocaust Awareness Week," *TheCampusPress.com*, March 7, 2007.

116. "Holocaust denier Irving is jailed," BBC News, Feb. 20, 2006: *http://news.bbc.co.uk/2/hi/europe/4733820.stm*. Karen Pollock, chief executive of the UK's Holocaust Educational Trust, said: "Holocaust denial is anti-Semitism dressed up as intellectual debate. It should be regarded as such and treated as such." Ibid. However repugnant Holocaust denial may be, the punishment of speech runs counter to the American system. See *The United States Mission to the European Union*, "Hateful Ideas Can Spread, But Also Be Refuted, on Internet," June 16, 2004: *http://useu.usmission.gov/Article.asp?ID'CA693D5C-2CCD-45D4-897A-A64C43296C49* (also containing the text of this author's statement at the OSCE Meeting on the Relationship Between Racist, Xenophobic and Anti-Semitic Propaganda on the Internet and Hate Crimes, Paris, France, June 16, 2004).

117. "Holocaust denier Irving is jailed," BBC News, Feb. 20, 2006: *http://news.bbc.co.uk/2/hi/europe/4733820.stm*.

118. Oliver King and agencies, "David Irving Arrested in Austria," *Guardian Unlimited*, Nov. 17, 2005.

119. David Irving, "Banged Up, What I Went Through and Thought as a Political Prisoner in Austria," online publication, 2008: *http://www.fpp.co.uk/books/Banged/index.html*.

120. "Die Würde des Ortes respektieren," *Junge Freiheit*, Feb. 18, 2005; Justus George Lawler, "Terror Bombing: Historians Take another Look," *America*, Aug. 28, 2006.

121. Karl Pfeifer, "Rolf Hochhuth: Lob für einen notorischen Holocaustleugner," *Hagalil*, Feb. 21, 2005. The speech was screened in a video during Irving's libel trial.

122. "Rolf Hochhuth's autobiography will not be published," *NZ Web Newspaper GmbH*, March 23, 2005.

123. Von Florian Felix Weyh, *Literature in German Radio, Reviewing Wellin by Rolf Hochhuth* (radio broadcast of April 1, 1998). The German transcript is available at: *http://fpp.co.uk/online/98/09/Hochhuth010498.html*.

124. *Wie ein Blinder von der Farbe — Hochhuth hatte keine Ahnung*, N-TV, Feb. 25, 2005.

125. *Sunday Times* (London), Feb. 18, 2007, reprinted on AR Action Report Online: *http://www.fpp.co.uk/docs/Irving/Hochhuth/Times_200207.html*.

126. Victor Gaetan, "Historians, diplomats cast doubts on KGB plot against Pope Pius XII," *Catholic News Service*, Feb. 28, 2007. An unnamed former intelligence officer also raised some serious questions about Pacepa's account: "Between 1960 and 1962, when he pretends he ran Vatican spies, he was in Bucharest, assigned as a deputy in the techno-scientific section of Securitate (the Romanian secret police), where he stayed until he defected in 1978." Ibid. The officer continued: "In 1959, Pacepa was in Germany under diplomatic cover. He was a captain in Cologne with a degree in chemistry and belonged to the techno-scientific section. Again, the KGB generals wouldn't have taken him into consideration," said the source, who believes

Pacepa is trying to build a "mysterious aura" for himself in his later years. Ibid. See also "Relator of Pius XII's Case is Wary of Report," *Zenit News*, Feb. 18, 2007 ("[O]ne needs to be extremely prudent and try to verify the facts.")

127. Rabbi Michael Samuel, "Was Pope Pius XII's reputation smeared by the KGB?" May 27, 2009: *http://rabbimichaelsamuel.com/*.

128. Hochhuth has shown himself to be willing to use government-supplied information when it serves his purpose. In 1978 he claimed to have "toppled" the minister-president of Baden-Württemberg, Hans Filbinger. After the fall of the Berlin Wall, "we learned that at least in the case of Hans Filbinger, Hochhuth had used reports from the secret police of the German Democratic Republic." Michael Feldkamp, "Hochhuth Exposed," *Association of Contemporary Church Historians*, July/August 2007 (John Jay Hughes, trans.).

129. *The Storm Over The Deputy*, 8 (editor's foreword).

130. Ibid., 24 (quoting Robert Brustein from the *New Republic*).

131. See Thompson, 5 (Irving conducted "countless interviews" on Hochhuth's behalf); ibid., 12 (Irving helped gather the evidence); Rolf Hochhuth, *Soldiers* (Robert D. MacDonald, trans., 1968). For the "hand in hand" quote, see Thompson, 143, 155. In addition to Hochhuth and Irving, British theater critic Kenneth Tynan and Sir Laurence Olivier got involved in promoting the play. They were, respectively, the first artistic director and the full-time literary manager of the British National Theatre. They saw their effort to have the play produced as a battle against censorship.

132. Rolf Hochhuth, *Soldiers* (Robert D. MacDonald, trans., 1968).

133. Hochhuth's play *Jurists* dealt with the resignation of Hans Filbinger as minister-president of the southern West German state of Baden-Württemberg. As a judge under the Nazi regime, Filbinger had pronounced death sentences against Wehrmacht soldiers even after the German capitulation. Shortly thereafter, Hochhuth wrote *Physicians*, which denounced the pharmaceutical industry for sacrificing human lives for the sake of profit. In 2004, Hochhuth's play *McKinsey Is Coming* raised the questions of unemployment, social justice and the "right to work." One scene that put the chairman of the Deutsche Bank in a line with leading businessmen who had been murdered by left-wing terrorists and also with Gessler, the villainous bailiff killed by William Tell, was seen by many as excusing, if not advocating, violence against economic figures. See Ulrich Rippert, " 'McKinsey Is Coming': A feeble warning to the German business and political establishment by playwright Rolf Hochhuth," *World Socialist Web Site*, March 9, 2004 ("The most striking feature of this play is the stark contrast between the author's self-confident claim to stand in the tradition of the Enlightenment and his inability to come anywhere near these standards") *http://www.wsws.org/articles/2004/mar2004/hoch-m09.shtml*.

134. According to Hochhuth, the recent discovery of the mass graves containing dead Polish soldiers caused the London-based Polish government to mistrust the Russians. Sikorski pointed out that Britain entered the war to defend Poland; Churchill, on the other hand, argued that the Soviet commitment to the defeat of the Axis had changed things.

135. Hochhuth argued that the pilot "habitually never wore" his Mae West life preserver, but he had uncharacteristically put it on that day. A witness who was familiar with the pilot's practices, however, said: "Wherever I flew with Eddy, he always had his Mae West on." Thompson, 209.

136. "Soldiers," *Time*, May 10, 1968.

137. Declassified Secret Memorandum: Soldiers, to Mr. John Peck & Sir E. Peck from J.E. Jackson, Jan. 10, 1969 ('Soldiers' — IRD Contribution) (citing the Oct. 22, 1967, edition of *Zycie Literackie* (Literary Life) and an article by Olgierd Terlrcki).

138. Thompson, 185.

139. In the Nov. 20, 1967, issue of *Der Spiegel*, Irving reported on an interview he conducted with Douglas Martin, the radio operator who was on duty the night of the plane crash. According to Irving, Martin said that the plane landed in a perfectly horizontal position. In other words, it was an emergency landing (which would have let the pilot survive — Sikorsi having been killed with an axe prior to the crash). *Der Spiegel* also reported that Martin had seen the silhouette of a figure wearing a "Mae West" life preserver crawl out of the wreckage a few seconds after impact and walk along one of the wings. Irving wrote: "I have spoken to Martin personally and I am convinced of his absolute reliability as a witness." Thompson, 272. When Irving's account was relayed to Martin, he acknowledged that Irving had called him and asked a few questions, and also acknowledged having written a letter to Irving, but he denied the story of the horizontal landing, saying "those are not my words." Ibid., 271. Martin acknowledged that he witnessed the crash and that it was not a nose-dive, but he rejected any suggestion that there had been evasive action or an emergency landing. Ibid. As for the silhouette, he said "I didn't say that at all." Ibid., 272. Martin later sent a letter to Thompson in which he stated: "The filling in — or the colouring of my words has in fact been done by Mr. Irving; although I did state that the plane ended up on the water on its 'tummy', *I did not refer to an 'emergency landing'* and at no time did I mention a person *wearing a Mae-West life-jacket*." Ibid., 279 (emphasis by Thompson).

In his book *Accident*, Irving left the impression that he had interviewed the pilot, Edward Prchal, face-to-face. In reality they had only spoken twice on the phone. Thompson, 309. According to Prchal, Irving had claimed to have "seventeen pounds of evidence on my desk." When Prchal asked to see it, however, Irving said that he did not have any. Frost, 412. Similarly, General Sikorski's widow was reportedly "very upset" with Irving because he wrote in *Accident* that she thought the Russians had killed her husband. In reality, "she has never said that they or the British did it, or anybody else in particular — for the simple reason that *she does not know.*" Thompson, 285 (statement of Mrs. Lisiewicz, the wife of Colonel Lisiewicz and a friend of the widow). Thompson concluded that he needed to "have patience" with researchers like Hochhuth and Irving "who work on the two-plus-two makes five basis." Ibid., 337.

140. Susan Barnes, "David Irving: Portrait of a Gentleman," *Sunday Times Supplement*, London, Sept. 6, 1970. According to Irving, "he and Hochhuth exchanged information as their investigations progressed. On each occasion when a trail pursued by Irving subsequently came to an end, he warned Hochhuth in good time. If Hochhuth did not accept the advice, 'that's his responsibility, not mine.'" Ibid.

141. As his biographer wrote, he "is not slow to come to conclusions, which he does without fear or favour." Taëni, 19.

142. Pacepa, *The KGB Use of Religion for Dezinformatsiya* (copy on file with author).

143. Thompson, 131-32.

144. Ibid., 149.

145. Ibid., 78 (Hochhuth told Thompson that he wanted to live in Germany, but his wife preferred Switzerland. He told another witness that he chose to live in Switzerland because the Church was too powerful in Germany, and they would make life too unpleasant due to *The Deputy*.) According to a declassified British secret dossier on Hochhuth, in 1968-69 there were reports in the Swiss press "suggesting that the Swiss authorities were unhappy about Hochhuth's presence in Switzerland...." Declassified Secret Memorandum: *Soldiers*, to Mr. John Peck & Sir E. Peck from J. E. Jackson, Jan. 10, 1969 ('Soldiers' — IRD Contribution).

146. Thompson, 14-15. Hochhuth acknowledged: "In the early stages of its conception... the Pope did not figure in the play." Ward, 25.

147. Thompson, 15. In this context, it is interesting to note the major rewriting that went into the various productions of *The Deputy*. See Sidney F. Parham, "Editing Hochhuth for the Stage: A Look at the Major Productions of *The Deputy*," 28 *Educational Theatre Journal*, 347.

148. Thompson, 82.

149. Susan Barnes, "David Irving: Portrait of a Gentleman," *Sunday Times Supplement*, London, Sept. 6, 1970.

150. Thompson, 6. Thompson wondered: "When had Rolf Hochhuth thrown out his 'Polish Lady', in exchange for his "Intelligence man'? And... why had he never told [Laurence] Olivier that there were two interchangeable 'original sources'?") Ibid., 65-66.

151. Taëni, 75. Hochhuth claimed to have given his "most sacred word of honour" not to reveal the man's name. "Were his name to be revealed, he would be killed within forty-eight hours." Ibid., 6. See Frost, 410 (the Churchill family was "particularly unimpressed by Hochhuth's claim that he kept in a Swiss bank vault a document containing the name of the person who had allegedly given him first-hand proof"). At least once, Hochhuth was caught secretly tape-recording witnesses. Ibid., 63. He admitted to doing it another time. Ibid., 86. Responding to this claim, Winston Churchill's son, Randolph Churchill, said: "Of course, the only thing about these lies is that once they get started it is very difficult indeed to nail them down.... You cannot kill a lie completely. I'm afraid that my father, careful though he was with his papers, did not leave a long, carefully typed-out list of all the Generals whom he did not assassinate. I could, of course, say that I have such a document in a strong vault in Switzerland *à la* Herr Hochmut [*sic*], but I haven't anything like that." Frost, 410 (explaining that Churchill referred to Hochhuth as Hochmut as a play on the word *Hochmut*, which means cheek).

152. Thompson, 106 (emphasis in original). It is unclear when the 50-year time period began to run. At least one author of a letter to the editor thought that it began in 1943, meaning that the vault should have been opened in 1993. Ibid., 171 (reprinting a letter published in the *Daily Telegraph* [London], May 10, 1967). On the other hand, British intelligence seems to have considered the time to have started running in 1968. Declassified Secret Memorandum: *Soldiers*, to Mr. John Peck & Sir E. Peck from J.E. Jackson, Jan. 10, 1969 ('Soldiers' — IRD Contribution) ("Hochhuth alleges that he had deposited the statement of the name of his informant in a Swiss bank, to be released in 50 years time, presumably 2018.")

153. Carlos Thompson, an Argentine-born German writer and actor, made his first film at age 16. In the 1950s, he was the epitome of the Latin lover. Among his movies were: *Valley of the Kings*, starring Yvonne de Carlo, and *The Flame and the Flesh*, in which he played opposite Lana Turner. He also starred in *El Tunel*, based on the novel by the noted Argentine writer Ernesto Sabato. In 1957, he married writer Lilli Palmer, the former wife of actor Rex Harrison. Thompson said that the book "imposed itself" upon him and that Hochhuth "has only himself to blame for it." Ibid., 48.

154. Thompson, 6, 9-10, 21, 87-88 (describing his fear of assassination); ibid., 81 ("[H]e lived with the notion that the British world was a vortex of dark secrets.")

155. See Ibid., 82 (discussing Hochhuth's "keenness on *any* anecdote which he thought indicted the morality of the West during the last war").

156. Ibid., 308.

157. Ibid., 122.

158. Ibid., 266. Whether it is truly "one big step further" is a matter of debate.

159. Ibid., 134 (statement of Prince Lubomirski).

160. Ibid., 149. See Harry de Quetteville, "Did British double agent Kim Philby murder Polish war hero General Sikorski?" *London Telegraph*, July 1, 2008.

161. Thompson, 192.

162. Ibid., 193.

163. Ibid., 133 (statement of General Marian Kukiel). Thompson reported that one of Hochhuth's main shortcomings was that "he was so busy 'knowing,' that he did not have the time or the energy to travel a bit and find out what was really what." Ibid., 125. Thompson continues: "All humour aside, this symptom promised anything but laughs." Colonel John Codrington of British Intelligence said:

> Hochhuth says that Intelligence killed Sikorski. Well if that is the case, then you are talking to the man who would have done the job. I was Assistant Chief of Staff to Governor Mason Macfarlane. I was in charge of Military Intelligence. I repeat, if we had arranged to kill Sikorski, I would have been the one to do it.

Ibid., 287. Codrington said: "Hochhuth simply doesn't know what he is talking about." Ibid., 278.

164. Ibid., 95.

165. Ibid., 100.

166. Ibid., 101.

167. Ibid., 130. When asked about Hochhuth's claims that witnesses were faking amnesia, Kukiel called it a "silly invention." He added: "I am sorry that such a good writer as David Irving should allow himself to be dragged into Hochhuth's theory.")

168. Ibid., 213.

169. Ibid., 214.

170. Ibid., 14, 18. Irving once disassociated himself from the "birth" of the murder theory, but he ultimately did embrace it. Ibid., 115.

171. Instead, Irving "reacted by working to discredit Prchal, claiming to have a wealth of evidence against him." Frost, 411.

> So far this whole affair is outlandish. Hochhuth goes around informing us that Prchal was killed by a knife in a bar-brawl in Chicago; then, a few months ago, when the scandal of his play breaks out in England, the *Sunday Express* publishes an interview given by Prchal denying the charges. Irving must know of the interview as well as I do... I have a feeling that by seeing Prchal I will also learn things about Irving. Do remember, Hochhuth maintains that it is he who provides him with the proofs that it was murder.

Thompson, 71.

172. Frost, 410-11.

173. Ibid., 415.

174. Ibid., 412.

175. Ibid., 412. Kenneth Tynan was a supporter of the play in Great Britain.

176. Ibid., 413. Consider this exchange between Prchal and Irving:

> **Prchal:** There is another thing, Mr. Irving, may I interrupt?... You say in your book that [according to the Court of Inquiry] my injuries were very light.
>
> **Irving:** I quoted the Court of Inquiry.
>
> **Prchal:** According to the Court of Inquiry? Read [handing Irving the report].
>
> **Irving:** I also traced the doctor that examined you.
>
> **Prchal:** Read the first page.
>
> **Irving:** The first page of the Court of Inquiry which I have here says: "The first pilot, extent injured: seriously."
>
> **Prchal:** Thank you.

Ibid., 414.

177. Ibid., 415.

178. Ibid., 415.

179. O'Carroll, 151; Michael O'Carroll, "Saviour of the Jews," *Irish Family*, Feb. 3, 1995 ("[H]e was demolished in a BBC programme by David Frost.") See Declassified Secret Memorandum: *Soldiers*, to Mr. John Peck & Sir E. Peck from J.E. Jackson, Jan. 10, 1969 ('Soldiers' — IRD Contribution) (noting the television program and other events that were keeping the controversy active).

180. Frost, 415-16. Those who knew Prchal knew that he could never have taken part in such a plot:

Prchal would never have gone into a thing like that (to try to kill Sikorski) knowing perfectly well that he only had a one to a million chance of surviving it — he simply was not that type of man. He was brave and extremely efficient as a pilot, but he was not an adventurer, he was not foolhardy. He was the opposite of the man needed for such a thing. Hochhuth is just talking nonsense.

Thompson, 324 (statement of General Janoušek).

181. Declassified Secret Memorandum: *Soldiers*, to Mr. John Peck & Sir E. Peck from J.E. Jackson, Jan. 10, 1969 (copy on file with author) ("[T]he recent letter from Prchal's lawyers to the Times could be construed as an invitation to [institute criminal proceedings against Hochhuth].")

182. Taëni, 140, 149. Prchal "was vindicated in court and damages were awarded." Frost, 416. For details on the verdict against Hochhuth, see "Pilot of General Sikorski's Aircraft Claims Libel Damages from German Playwright," *Times of London*, May 3, 1972, 3; "£50,000 Award to General Sikorski's Pilot," *Times of London*, May 4, 1972, 1; "$130,000 Awarded to Pilot for Libel in Hochhuth Play," *New York Times*, May 4, 1972, 48. Thompson, 17-18.

183. Martin Esslin, "Rolf Hochhuth," in *Makers of Modern Culture*, 233 (1981).

184. Peter Gumpel, "Pius XII as He Really Was," *Tablet*, Feb. 13, 1999.

185. In a television interview, David Irving suggested that Hochhuth should provide more information about the statement that was provided by his secret source. Hochhuth declined, responding: "My play is not at all based on this statement. After I heard it, quite accidentally, I went after the thing and found such an amount of circumstantial evidence." Reacting to this statement, Carlos Thompson wrote: "To say that this play is not based on his informant's statement is the complete reversal of the guarantee he offered to Olivier to convince him that he should present his play." Thompson, 186-87.

186. "Second only to Hochhuth — he provided the occasion for all subsequent statements about *The Deputy*." *The Storm Over The Deputy*, 10 (editor's foreword).

187. Robert A. Graham, lecture delivered to the Theological College, Catholic University of America, Oct. 10, 1989, reprinted in the *Catholic League Newsletter* 11, vol. 16, no. 12, December 1989. See Willett, 45 ("Piscator came to be the great advocate of politics in the theatre.") Defining the school in his book, *Strategies of Political Theatre*, author Michael Patterson explains:

> In the twentieth century, theatre with an intention to convert to a new way of thinking, or at least challenge the old modes of thought, became more overtly political, questioning not so much social morality as the fundamental organization of society, with the emphasis on economics rather than ethics. Usually informed by Marx's analysis of capitalism, a number of directors and playwrights, most notably Erwin Piscator and Bertolt Brecht, sought to use the state to promote socialist alternatives to the injustices of the world about them. In so doing they helped to define what we have now come to term "political theatre," the actual title of Piscator's 1929 book on his work in the theatre.

Patterson, 1. See also La Vern J. Rippley, "Brecht the Communist and America's Drift from Capitalism," 14:3 *Twentieth Century Literature* 143 (October 1968).

188. Karol Jozef Gajewski, "Winning the War over Pius XII," *Inside the Vatican*: *http://www.insidethevatican.com/articles/review-pius-xii.htm#G1267821342821*.

189. Correspondence from Ion Pacepa to Ronald J. Rychlak, May 18, 2009.

190. Terence Smith, Performance, Space and Technology, Stanford University Drama Department, November 1998: *http://homepages.tesco.net/~theatre/tezzaland/webstuff/piscator.html*.

191. Willett, 50-51. See also Smith, 6.

192. Willett, 53.

193. Ibid., 55.

194. Ibid., 104.

195. Ibid., 121 (quoting Franz Jung).

196. Ibid., 75.

197. Ibid., 96.

198. Leo Kerz, "Brecht and Piscator," 20:3 *Educational Theatre Journal*, 363 (October 1968).

199. Ibid., 123. The German Communist Party was not all that opposed to Hitler as he and the National Socialists rose to power. Andrew and Gordievsky, 177, 193.

200. Willett, 124.

201. Ibid., 126.

202. Quoted in Smith, p. 9.

203. La Vern J. Rippley, "Brecht the Communist and America's Drift from Capitalism," 14:3 *Twentieth Century Literature* 143 (October 1968).

204. Willett, 41.

205. Ibid., 131.

206. Ibid., 132.

207. Correspondence from Ion Pacepa to Ronald J. Rychlak, May 18, 2009 ("The first chief of the *Securitate* [Communist Romania's political police], NKVD General Panteleymon Bondarenko... told me

repeatedly that Stalin did not give a *kopek* for any foreign Communist granted asylum in Moscow who was not worthy of being co-opted by the NKVD.")

208. Willett, 122, quoting the postscript to the Soviet edition of Piscator's play *Das p. T.* (Moscow, 1934).

209. Ibid., 165 (noting that the use of a narrator and projections in *The Glass Menagerie* "clearly reflects Piscator's methods").

210. "Revival in Manhattan," *Time*, Dec. 23, 1940.

211. Leo Kerz, "Brecht and Piscator," 20:3 *Educational Theatre Journal*, 363, 368 (October 1968).

212. Willett, 180.

213. Ibid., 181.

214. See Carl Weber, "Crossing the Footbridge Again or: A Semi-Sentimental Journey," 45 *Theatre Journal* 75 (March 1993).

215. Merritt, 206.

216. Willett, 177.

217. *The Storm Over The Deputy*, 13. See also Taëni, 14 (more in accord with Piscator's account).

218. Taëni, 14. See Ibid., 20 ("it really is doubtful whether *The Representative* would ever have seen the light of day if it had not come into the hands of such a famous producer as Erwin Piscator"); ibid., 135 (similar).

219. Ward, 17 ("I have learned that the poet always must be active in politics. That he is always responsible. *The Deputy* is politics.")

220. Willett, 180.

221. Ibid.

222. Ibid., 182.

223. In the play's afterword, Hochhuth admitted that "the action does not follow the historical course of events" and "I allowed my imagination free play." Hochhuth, "Sidelights on History," pp. 287, 348.

224. Robert P. Lockwood, "Deconstructing *The Deputy*," *Catalyst*, June 2000. Lockwood explains:

> For the most part, this was based on the pope's opposition to the Allied demand for unconditional German surrender. He believed such a demand would only continue the horror of the war and increase the killing. That stand was later interpreted as a desire on the pontiff's part to maintain a strong Germany as a bulwark against communism. Hochhuth's charge of papal "silence" fit that revisionist theory.

225. "The characterization of Pacelli as a money-grubbing hypocrite is so wide of the mark as to be ludicrous. Importantly, however, Hochhuth's play offends the most basic criteria of documentary: that such stories and portrayals are valid only if they are demonstrably true." Cornwell (1999), 375.

226. Ward, 38 (calling this "the most striking example" of Hochhuth's "departure from 'Realism'" and noting that Hochhuth rejected the Mengele comparison).

227. "Hochhuth does what no man can do; he inserts himself into the mind of Pius and draws only the worst conclusions. He is guilty of the worst kind of McCarthyism, and only the staggering immensity of his charge has kept people from seeing this fact." James O'Gara, "The Real Issue," *Commonweal*, Feb. 28, 1964, reprinted in *The Storm Over The Deputy*, 219, 221. Twenty-five years after Piscator's production, German director Claus Peymann (known for "a radical style which had its roots in the political dreams of the late sixties") produced *The Deputy* in Austria to coincide with a visit by Pope John Paul II. Peymann said that he did not like the play, but he produced it as a political challenge. Gitta Honegger, "Tales from the Imperial City," 11:2 *Performing Arts Journal*, 45, 50 (1988).

228. See Sidney F. Parham, "Editing Hochhuth for the Stage: A Look at the Major Productions of *The Deputy*," 28 *Educational Theatre Journal*, 347.

229. See "Reviews," XII:2 *World Theatre*, 140 (Summer 1963) ("somewhere between a spoken report with scenes of great realism... and a fast-paced discussion"); Sidney F. Parham, "Editing Hochhuth for the Stage: A Look at the Major Productions of 'The Deputy'," 28:3 *Educational Theatre Journal*, 347, 353 (October 1976) ("How then should we judge Hochhuth as a playwright? The formal shape of his script suggests that he wishes to be judged by traditional dramatic standards, and by these standards one cannot speak well of him.")

230. Piscator was working again with Hochhuth and planning to stage the play *Soldiers* at his theater in Berlin when he died in 1966. See the dust jacket of Rolf Hochhuth, *Soldiers* (Robert D. MacDonald, trans., 1968). West Berlin gave him a state funeral at which Heinar Kipphardt, author of the play *In the Matter of J. Robert Oppenheimer*, spoke on behalf of many assembled authors: "We all come from your theatre," he said, raising his hand a bit, "So long, Erwin." Leo Kerz, "Brecht and Piscator," 20:3 *Educational Theatre Journal*, 363 (October 1968).

231. Pacepa said: "I have little if any doubt that Piscator was maneuvered by Moscow." Correspondence from Ion Pacepa to Ronald J. Rychlak, May 18, 2009. Lest this discussion be taken as trying to diminish Piscator's unquestioned talent as a director, this passage from the set designer for the Berlin production of *The Deputy* is worthy of consideration:

Piscator's production of *The Deputy*, apart from becoming the biggest post-war theatre event and because of it, started a debate which affected and revised the views of philosophers, clergy, politicians, and historians in every corner of the world. It touched upon the conscience of the Catholic Church and, without a doubt, influenced what happened at the last Ecumenical Council. Piscator had caught up with Brecht and proved that the theatre can contribute to the shaping of history as well as being shaped by history.

Leo Kerz, "Brecht and Piscator," 20:3 *Educational Theatre Journal*, 363 (October 1968).

232. Justus George Lawler's recently completed manuscript (Working title: *Were the Popes Against the Jews?*) refers to the "*hallucination publicitaire* spawned by *The Deputy*."

233. Kustow, 136 (noting that *Le Monde* magazine thought that Semprum's edit of the story was superior to Piscator's).

234. Gary Prevost, "Review: The Autobiography of Federico Sanchez and the Communist Underground in Spain by Jorge Semprun," 75:3 *American Political Science Review* 819 (September 1981).

235. See Kathleen A. Johnson, "The Framing of History: Jorge Semprun's La Deuxième Mort de Ramon Mercader," 20 *French Forum*, 90 (January 1995).

236. See Dan Isaac, "Theatre of Fact," 15:3 *Drama Review: TDR* 109 (Summer 1971). Brook essentially used symbolic designs for his production. "The stage was kept bare, no backdrops were used. Each of the actors had an identical blue suit over which he put some distinguishing costume piece, such as a Nazi armband or a priest's cassock. This design stressed the interchangeability of oppressor and oppressed in the modern age." Sidney F. Parham, "Editing Hochhuth for the Stage: A Look at the Major Productions of 'The Deputy'," 28:3 *Educational Theatre Journal* 347, 352 (October 1976).

237. Kustow, 87.

238. See Simon Trussler, "Shakespeare: The Greatest Whore of Them All: Peter Hall at Stratford 1960-1968," 13:2 *Drama Review* 169 (Winter 1968). See also La Vern J. Rippley, "Brecht the Communist and America's Drift from Capitalism," 14:3 *Twentieth Century Literature*, 143 (October 1968).

239. St. Denis was no stranger to the use of media for political purposes. In World War II, he directed the BBC's *Radio Diffusion Française* (established by de Gaulle's government in exile) under the pseudonym of Jacques Duchesne.

240. Irving Wardle, "London's Subsidized Companies," 11:2 *Tulane Drama Review*, 105, 111 (Winter 1966).

241. Michael Coveney, "Obituary: Robert David MacDonald," *Guardian*, May 24, 2004. MacDonald adapted at least three of Hochhuth's plays: *The Representative* (or *The Deputy*), *Soldiers*, and *Judith*. David Irving's web page shows a photo of Irving, Hochhuth, and Macdonald together: *http://www.fpp.co.uk/Irving/photos/Hochhuth/image3.html*.

242. See Thomas G. Gulick, "UNESCO, Where Culture Becomes Propaganda," *Heritage Foundation Backgrounder #233*, Dec. 13, 1982. In the 1950s, two former UNESCO officials identified UNESCO's ancestor as "The Soviet All Union Society for Cultural Relations with Foreign Countries," whose goals included "the world union of intellectual forces for the triumph of genuine world culture," so as to inspire intellectuals to "fight the war danger [and] agitate for peace." Walter H.C. Laves and Charles A. Thompson, *UNESCO: Purpose, Progress, Prospects* (Indiana University Press, 1957). As early as 1952, the Knights of Columbus urged that their fellow Americans give a "close and careful scrutiny" to the operations of UNESCO. "Knights of the Church," *Time*, Sept. 1, 1952; see William R. Kintner and Joseph Z. Kornfeder, *The New Frontier of War: Political Warfare Present and Future* (Chicago: Henry Regnery Company, 1962). Years after MacDonald worked there, the KGB reportedly still had several agents on UNESCO's payroll, at least one of whom was working as a translator. Steve Farrell, "Coalition or Bust! Virtue or Vice?" *Meridian Magazine* (2002). The United States eventually withdrew from UNESCO over its perceived anti-Western bias.

243. Andrew and Mitrokhin, 466; Oleg Kalugin, *Spymaster: My Thirty-Two Years in Intelligence and Espionage Against the West*, 123, 192-93 (Da Capo Press, 2009); Milton Rosenberg, *An American Trapped In A Communist Paradise: An Historical Autobiography*, 45 (Moose Hide Books, 2003); *KGB: Russia's Old Boychiks*, Feb. 6, 1978.

244. "Piscator had the courage to tackle this difficult subject from a text which if performed in total would have lasted six or seven hours." *XII World Theatre*, 140 (Summer 1963).

245. Michael Coveney, "Obituary: Robert David MacDonald," *Guardian*, May 24, 2004.

246. In 1971, MacDonald became a co-director of the Citizen's Theatre in Glasgow, Scotland. He ran this theater in much the same way Piscator operated his *Freie Volksbühne*. Plays were often political, and tickets were priced so that the workers could attend. "For years, a sign declaring 'All seats 50p' blazed over what was then a slum area," "Obituary: Robert David MacDonald," *Daily Telegraph*, May 21, 2004. See Interview: The Citizens Company in Glasgow: "Four Hundred Miles from Civilization", 5:1 *Performing Arts Journal*, 50 (1980) ("Our theatre is actually socialist theatre in the sense that it's the only theatre in Britain which has a seat price that enables absolutely anybody to come in. And I think that's a kind of practical socialism.") While some critics considered the Citizen's Theatre exciting and influential, "others disapproved of what

they saw as high camp, mannered performances and a preference for Left-wing European dramatists." *Daily Telegraph*, May 21, 2004.

247. See Chambers, 233, n. 17.

248. Like Piscator, he also had a program supplement discussing the charges against Pius XII.

249. Sidney F. Parham, "Editing Hochhuth for the Stage: A Look at the Major Productions of 'The Deputy'," 28:3 *Educational Theatre Journal*, 347, 351-52 (October 1976) ("Reviewers generally thought that this concentration on the documents worked against the text.")

250. "Obituary: Clifford Williams, Theatre director with comedic talent and an awesome staging flair," *Independent*, Aug. 23, 2005.

251. Phyllis Hartnoll and Peter Found, "Theatre Workshop," in *The Concise Oxford Companion to the Theatre* (1996). It had grown out of a group known as "The Red Megaphone," which had an overtly political manifesto. Dominic Shellard, *British Theatre Since the War*, 60-61 (Yale University Press, 1999). The Theatre Workshop was an "acknowledged influence" on Peter Hall (and thus the Royal Shakespeare Company). Chambers, 12. Hall even invited Littlewood to direct for the company. Ibid. At about this same time, he did hire John Bury away from the Theatre Workshop to be the Royal Shakespeare Company's main designer. Ibid., 34-35; Martin Esslin, "Brecht and the English Theatre," 11:2 *Tulane Drama Review*, 63, 65 (Winter 1966).

252. Along with Peter Brook, Littlewood was among the most important theatrical personalities in the UK at this time. Shortly before her death in 2002, she said: "I've always been a communist." "Obituary: Joan Littlewood," *Daily Telegraph*, Sept. 26, 2002.

253. S. E. Gontarski, *The Grove Press Reader, 1951-2001*, xxxi (Grove Press, 2001).

254. Jerry Tallmer, "You Can't Print That! (but he did, he does)," *Thrive*, vol. 1: 9, January 1-31, 2006.

255. Rolf Hochhuth, "The Berlin Antigone," *Evergreen Review*, May 1964, 70.

256. *Evergreen Review*, August-September 1964, 97. According to the book, in June 1942, 17-year-old Rudolf Vrba was shipped to Auschwitz. Fighting against starvation, typhus, and almost unbelievable brutality, he kept a complete record of Nazi horrors. Finally he managed to escape and bring his message to the outside world. See Rudolf Vrba and Alan Bestic, *I Cannot Forgive : The Amazing True Story of a 17-Year-Old Jewish Boy Who Defied the Germans at Auschwitz and Escaped to Alert the World to the Nazi Horror Camps!* (New York, Bantam Books, 1964). Apparently Vrba performed poorly under cross-examination at a Canadian trial over Holocaust denial, and he admitted that he had taken "artistic license." *Queen v. Zündel*, 2 S.C.R. 731 (1992). He is now often cited by Holocaust deniers as an example of how people make things up about the Holocaust.

257. She wrote several plays he produced, including *The Children's Hour* (1934), *The Little Foxes* (1939), and *Watch on the Rhine* (1941).

258. *Time*, July 7, 1947.

259. *Time*, Sept. 16, 1946.

260. *Time*, July 7, 1947.

261. *New York Times*, Oct. 17, 1998, p. A-15. Regarding outbursts during productions, see Kustow, 136.

262. See Daniel Robert Epstein, Costa-Garvis Interview, UGO Online: *http://www.ugo.com/channels/filmTv/features/costagavras/* ("I saw the play back in 1964 in Paris. My scriptwriter, Jorge Semprún, wrote an adaptation back then. It was the play to see back then, and it was a huge controversy. I wanted to make the film in the 1970s, but the rights were taken.") See Ronald J. Rychlak, "The Church and the Holocaust," *Wall Street Journal* (Europe), March 28, 2002 (reviewing *Amen*).

263. "Gavras doesn't march behind the banner of political cinema. All cinema is political, he says, even action movies showing 'heroes saving the Earth only with a gun.'" Maya Jaggi, "French resistance: Costa Gavras," *Guardian*, April 4, 2009. "My mother used to say stay away from politics, because my father went to prison. But we can't not be involved. By not taking a position, you take a position." Ibid.

264. Hinckle, 58.

265. Ibid.

266. See, e.g., Andrew and Gordievsky, 463; Andrew and Mitrokhin, 540 (bogus documentary to discredit Pope John Paul II). See generally *The Strategy of Deception: A Study in World-Wide Communist Tactics*.

267. The list was derived from W. Cleon Skousen, *The Naked Communist* (1958), reprint ed., Buccaneer Books (1994).

268. See Yuri B. Shvets, *Washington Station: My Life as a KGB Spy in America*, 13, 39 (Simon and Schuster, 1994) (being a journalist is a "convenient cover" and notation about writing articles); Kalugin, 53 (KGB measures in New York "included the infiltration of left-wing and black nationalist movements. Several colleagues and I had good contacts in some black organizations, and even financed one Afro-American journal, *The Liberator*. We planted stories....") See also Christopher Lehmann-Haupt, "Books of The Times; Prying the K.G.B.'s Secrets Loose," *New York Times*, Oct. 22, 1990 (reviewing Christopher Andrew and Oleg Gordievsky, *K.G.B.: The Inside Story* (1990) and discussing various Soviet disinformation projects).

269. Pacepa, *Kerry's Soviet Rhetoric*. See also "Solzhenitsyn v. the KGB," *Time*, May 27, 1974 (similar tactics used against Soviet writer). Journalists were very important to this effort:

The KGB recruited journalists in part for their access to inside information and sources on politics and policy, insights into personalities, and confidential and non-public information that never made it into published stories. Certain journalistic working habits also lent themselves to intelligence tasks. By profession, journalists ask questions and probe; what might seem intrusive or suspect if done by anyone else is their normal *modus operandi*. Consequently, the KGB often used journalists as talent spotters for persons who *did* have access to sensitive information, and made use of them to gather background information that would help in evaluating candidates for recruitment.... There was also much less risk that a journalist having contact with a government official or engineer would attract the attention of security officials than would a KGB officer under Soviet diplomatic cover. And even if security officials did notice such a meeting, it would be much easier to provide a benign explanation for contact with a pesky American journalist than with a Soviet diplomat.

Klehr, Harvey; Earl, John; Vassiliev, Alexander, "I. F. Stone, Soviet Agent — Case Closed," *Commentary* magazine (May 2009). Perhaps most importantly, "the KGB could use journalists for 'active measures' — the planting of a story in the press or giving a slant to a story that served KGB goals."

270. Edward McMillan, *Communist versus Americanism (Democracy): Questions and Answers*, 20 (Alexandria, LA, 1962) (also noting the tactic of using letters to the editor to generate interest).

271. According to Pacepa: "I did not do any research to see if Moscow had a hand in promoting *The Deputy*, but it is more than likely that the KGB and the Soviet disinformation machinery promoted it with articles and reviews." Correspondence from Ion Pacepa to Ronald J. Rychlak, May 18, 2009.

272. See Moshe Deeter, *The Profile of Communism: A Fact-by-Fact Primer* (Collier Books: New York, 1966); Miller, 157-66 (reporting on how the party used a writer in the United States); ibid., 173 ("The Communists, you will have read before, would clearly like to get a foot into the communications area, followed if possible by every other inch of the anatomy.")

273. Herbert A. Philbrick, *I Led 3 Lives: Citizen "Communist" Counterspy*, 90-91 (McGraw-Hill, 1952).

274. David Usborne, "Revealed: how Hollywood stars queued to expose 'pinkos,'" *Independent*, Aug. 26, 2001.

275. Andrew and Gordievsky, 483 ("dynamic"); ibid., 535 (one of the two "most brilliant and level-headed analysts of British and American policy"); ibid., 542 ("young and dynamic"); Kalugin, 121 (promotion).

276. Kalugin, 287; Andrew and Gordievsky, 543.

277. In a letter to this author, Kalugin explained his move to the United States as follows:

I am not a defector. I came forward publicly against the Soviet system and the KGB when I worked within that system. I was charged with treason in 1990 but was never convicted because the people of Russia elected me a member of the Supreme Soviet and I obtained immunity from prosecution.

In the post Soviet years I enjoyed excellent reputation with the Eltsin's regime and played significant role in reforming the KGB.

I came to the USA in 1995 as vice-president of a major Russian telecommunication company on 3 years contract to run a Russian-American joint venture. In 1998 I had airline ticket to fly back to Moscow, but Mr. Putin, the FSB chief and my former subordinate, called me publicly "traitor." I responded by publicly, calling him "war criminal." From that moment on I had no choice but to ask for political asylum in the USA.

In 2002 I was convicted by the Russian court to 15 years of jail. Two years later I was granted U.S. citizenship. That's my story in brief.

Letter to the author from Oleg D. Kalugin, dated March 20, 2008.

278. Kalugin, 53.

279. Ibid. (discussing racial "trouble" in the United States). This is very close to what *Ramparts* editor Warren Hinckle did when he invited numerous publications to a press conference/party in support of *The Deputy*. See pp. 301-2.

280. Kalugin, 53.

281. Ibid., 54.

282. Ibid., 53. When Soviet handlers controlled American Communists, the Americans were at the beck and call of their handlers. See Miller, 16.

283. "Not Only the Deputy," *Minority of One*, April 1964; M.S. Arnoni, *American Dialog*, July-August 1964.

284. Ibid. See pp. 359-61.

285. "Not Only the Deputy," *Minority of One*, April 1964.

286. I. F. Stone, "What Some People Have Forgotten About God's 'Deputy,'" *I. F. Stone's Weekly*, March 9, 1964, reprinted in *The Storm Over The Deputy*, 234.

287. Interview with Rolf Hochhuth, *Ramparts*, Spring 1964, reprinted in *The Storm Over The Deputy*, 42.

288. See "The Attack on I. F. Stone: An Exchange," *New York Review of Books*, Dec. 3, 1992; Miriam Schneir, "Stone Miscast," *Nation*, Nov. 11, 1996; Cassandra Tate, "Who's out to lunch here? I. F. Stone and

the KGB," *Columbia Journalism Review*, November/December 1992; D.D. Guttenplan, "Izzy an Agent?" *Nation*, Aug. 3/10, 1992.

289. Herbert Romerstein and Eric Breindel, *The Venona Secrets: Exposing Soviet Espionage and America's Traitors*, 432-35; 435-36; 437-39 (Regnery Publishing, 2000).

290. John Earl Haynes, Harvey Klehr, and Alexander Vassiliev, *Spies: The Rise and Fall of the KGB in America*, 159 (New Haven: Yale University Press, 2009), translations by Philip Redko and Steven Shabad (concluding that "from 1936 to 1939 I.F. Stone was a Soviet spy," and that an "effort was made by Soviet intelligence to reestablish that relationship in 1944-45; we do not know whether that effort succeeded"). See also Klehr, Harvey; Earl, John; Vassiliev, Alexander, I. F. Stone, "Soviet Agent — Case Closed," *Commentary* magazine (May 2009) ("One might ask why the KGB would recruit a journalist like Stone, then an editorial writer for the *New York Post*, with no access to government or industrial secrets. In fact, the KGB recruited a great many journalists.") In the 1960s, KGB agent Oleg Kalugin still had dealings with Stone.

291. David Horowitz, *Ohio Jewish Chronicle*, March 20, 1964 (cited in *The Storm Over the Deputy*, 249).

292. David Horowitz, who grew up in New York City as the son of two lifelong Communists, was a founding member of the New Left. During the 1960s, he was a prominent editor of *Ramparts*, but not until after the controversy surrounding *The Deputy*. See David Horowitz, *Radical Son* (The Free Press, 1997). Lionel Abel, who wrote about the play in *Dissent* magazine (Spring 1964), is usually considered a Trotskyite. Alan Wald, "Farrell and Trotskyism," 22:1 *Twentieth Century Literature*, 90, 93 (Feb. 1976); John F. Diggins, "Four Theories in Search of a Reality: James Burnham, Soviet Communism, and the Cold War," 70:2 *American Political Science Review*, 492 (June 1976). See Lionel Abel, "Stalin's Advocate," 2 *Politics* 146 (May 1945).

293. See pp. 301-3.

294. Nathan Cohen, Canada's premier theater critic in the 1960s, wrote a review in the *Toronto Daily Star* (March 11, 1964). His Communist ties from the 1940s frequently kept him from reviewing shows in the United States. While some have expressed uncertainty over whether Cohen was ever a "card-carrying member," Joe Gershman, editor of the *Wochenblatt*, later stated: "[D]uring the years he was a member [of the Communist Party — in the 1940s], he was a rebel against certain postulates held by the party.... He felt a writer should be given a chance to explore and write freely what he thinks and sees, rather than follow the party line. Nathan was, in nature, a rebel, even when he was in the Communist Party." *http://www.allan-gould.com/magazines/profiles/nathancohen/magazines_profiles_nathancohen.html*.

295. In June 1964, George L. Mosse wrote a piece on *The Deputy* for the *Progressive*, an influential left-wing magazine. That periodical opposed the growth of the U.S. military, opposed the United Nations police action to prevent a Communist takeover of Korea, and opposed U.S. intervention to prevent a Communist takeover in South Vietnam. In 1954, it published a huge exposé of McCarthyism, and it was sympathetic to the revolutionary dictatorship of Marxist Fidel Castro, who seized power in Cuba in 1959. All of these are defensible positions, but they also indicate that this was the type of magazine that Soviet influence-makers would have tried to influence.

296. Robert Gorham Davis and George N. Shuster, "Of Gross Ends and a Man's Choice," *New York Times Book Review*, March 1, 1964.

297. "Obituary: Robert Gorham Davis," *New York Times*, July 17, 1998. See also "Obituary: Hope Hale Davis, 100; Author, Writing Teacher, Feminist and Communist," *Los Angeles Times*, Oct. 7, 2004 (obituary of Davis' widow).

298. The event was organized by the Vietnam Day Committee (VDC). In addition to Keating and Arnoni, participants included: Dr. Benjamin Spock; Norman Mailer; Dick Gregory; Hal Draper (Marxist writer and a socialist activist); Levi Laud (Progressive Labor Movement); Jack Barnes (National Chair of the Young Socialist Alliance), and others. See Norman Mailer et al., *We Accuse: A Powerful Statement of the New Political Anger in America* (Berkeley and San Francisco: Diablo Press, 1965).

299. *Teach-Ins: U.S.A.: Reports, Opinions, Documents* (edited by Louis Menashe and Ronald Radosh); Edward M. Keating, Book Review, *San Francisco Chronicle*, March 1, 1964 (Praeger, 1967).

300. Edward M. Keating, "The Voice of Pius Was Silent," *This World*, March 1, 1964; Edward M. Keating, Book Review, *Ramparts*, Summer 1964; Edward M. Keating, Book Review, *San Francisco Chronicle*, March 1, 1964.

301. Edward M. Keating, *The Scandal of Silence: A Layman's Powerful Critique of the Catholic Church in America* (Random House 1965).

302. Tom Prideaux, "Homage and Hate for The Deputy," *Life*, March 13, 1964, reprinted in *The Deputy Reader*, 208.

303. "Protest," *New York Review of Books*, March 14, 1968.

304. Hinckle, 47.

305. Ibid., 50-51.

306. "A Bomb in Every Issue," *Time*, Jan. 6, 1967.

307. Ibid.

308. Hinckle, 50-51.

309. Cooney, 282. He said that the play had been written to "drive a wedge between Christians and Jews." Ibid.

310. Hinckle, 58.

311. Ibid., 58. See "Israelis Defend Name of Pope Pius XII," *Jewish Chronicle*, Oct. 11, 1963 (discussing the Jewish reaction to the play's opening in London). See Trude Weiss-Rosmarin, "Second Thoughts on 'The Deputy,'" *Ramparts*, Summer 1964, 95 (emphasis in original) (detailing how the play insulted Jews). As one of the play's most important early supporters explained: "The serious rejoinders to Hochhuth's charges against the Pope were handled by the Jews, which was the reason for the surprising defense of Pius XII by B'nai B'rith." Hinckle, 58. See also Alfred Kazin, "The Vicar of Christ," *New York Review of Books*, March 19, 1964, reprinted in *The Storm Over The Deputy*, 102, 105.

312. Declassified Secret Memorandum: *Soldiers*, to Mr. John Peck & Sir E. Peck from J.E. Jackson, Jan. 10, 1969 (see Appendix, p. 439) ("Lord Chandos, Chairman of the Board of Directors of the National Theatre, decided in the end that the play could not be shown there.")

313. "Interview with Rolf Hochhuth," *Ramparts*, Spring 1964, reprinted in *The Storm Over The Deputy*, 42.

314. Bennett's most important publication at that time was the book *Christianity and Communism Today* (1948, rev. 1960). He was known for supporting civil rights, protesting the Vietnam War, opposing nuclear weapons, and (later) advocating for gay and lesbian rights. In 1961, *Time* magazine wrote: "Dr. Bennett has long warned Christians against thinking that God is automatically on the side of the West." "Whose Side Is God On?" *Time*, Nov. 10, 1961. The article went on to quote him:

> The very atheism of Communism is a judgment upon the churches, which for so long were unconcerned about the victims of the Industrial Revolution and early capitalism and which have usually been ornaments of the status quo, no matter how unjust it has been. The temptation to turn the cold war into a holy crusade is ever with us. . . .

Ibid.

315. Zahn was a conscientious objector to World War II and co-founder of Pax Christi USA. His most famous work at the time was *German Catholics and Hitler's War* (1962). It led to some serious clashes with Catholic leaders and his departure from the Jesuit Loyola University. Griffin, a convert to Catholicism, was best known for his work on racial strife in the United States and his book *Black Like Me* (concerning his trip through Southern states disguised as an African-American).

316. Hinckle, 64.

317. Upon release from prison, Cleaver joined the Black Panthers and was appointed their minister of information. Despite the great success of *Soul on Ice* and the acclaim Cleaver garnered, he was arrested in 1968 in a shootout with police. One Panther was killed, and Cleaver and a police officer were wounded. Rather than face charges, Cleaver fled the country and began a seven-year tour of Communist and Muslim countries, including Cuba, Algeria, North Vietnam, and the Soviet Union, where he was welcomed as a celebrity political prisoner. In 1975, disenchanted with the workings of Communism, he returned to the United States to face charges. The most serious of the charges were dropped, and he was sentenced to serve 1,200 hours of community service. Cleaver ultimately became a Christian and started giving lectures about his conversion.

318. Hinckle reported that "in length [the telegram invitation was] somewhere between the Gettysburg Address and the Declaration of Independence, and kept the Western Union lady on the telephone for nearly three hours, as I dictated to her the names and addresses of an eclectic group of invitees drawn at whim and whimsy from the Yellow Pages." Among the recipients of the telegrams were not only the major publications, but also *The American Organist, Bedside Nurse, Casket and Sunnyside, Detergent Age, Elementary Electronics, Floor Covering Weekly, Foreign Affairs, Greeting Card Magazine, Hebrew Weekly, Hardware Age, Hospital Management, Hot Rod Magazine, Irish Echo, Intimate Story, Iron Age, Jack and Jill, Jewish Braille Review, Kosher Food Guide, Journal of Nuclear Medicine, Little Flower Magazine, Metal Finishing, Mobile Homes Magazine, Model Airplane News, Modern Concrete, New York Daily Fruit and Vegetable Reporter, Oriental Rug Magazine, Paris Match,* The Polish Press Agency, *Personal Romances, Plastic Laminating, Professional Barber, Progressive Grocer, Refuse Removal Journal, Rubber Age, Saucer News, Scholastic Coach, Sexology, Solid Wastes Management,* and other similar publications. This was a typical approach of the KGB, which would place stories in small papers and journals, hoping that other outlets would pick them up. See Yuri B. Shvets, *Washington Station: My Life as a KGB Spy in America*, 13, 39 (Simon & Schuster, 1994); Kalugin, 53.

319. In his memoirs, Hinckle admitted that the "Ad Hoc Committee to Defend the Right of *The Deputy* to be Heard" was "in the finest tradition of Potemkin villages." It "barely had as many members as words in its cumbersome title."

320. (Subject Deleted) Memo to the White House re Ramparts, case no. EO-1996-00609, pub. Date 5/19/1966; release date 11/4/1997 (noting dramatic expansion and Communist ties of key personnel). Memorandum to Bill Moyers, White House from Richard Helms, DD/CIA (Subject Del), case no. EO-2004-00392, pub. date 5/19/1966; release date 5/17/2004 (same document).

321. Ibid.

322. In his memoirs, Hinckle acknowledged suspicion about the source of some of the information received at the magazine, suggesting that it was either the KGB or a rogue operation from inside of the CIA. Hinckle, 255. Hinckle eventually took to setting up secret meetings and using code language. Finally, *Ramparts* collapsed in part because it could not sustain itself while operating in the Communist model.

> Without a formal hierarchy at *Ramparts*, every issue that came up had to be debated. The need to justify decisions was not only time-consuming for us, but at times cruel to others, as I discovered when we attempted to reduce the mailroom budget at *Ramparts* and were met with a political revolt. The mailroom was staffed by members of Newsreel, a "collective" of radicals who had made promotional films for the Black Panthers and the Vietcong. They had no respect for our publication. The revolution's pecking order had again shifted to the left, and we could not overcome the view that *Ramparts* was part of the power structure that needed to be overthrown.

David Horowitz, "Spy Stories: The Wen Ho Lee Cover-Up," *FrontPageMagazine.com*, Oct. 3, 2000. When it collapsed, Hinckle was editor of the *City of San Francisco*, a radical weekly newspaper owned by Francis Ford Coppola.

323. Thompson, 275 (statement of Zdenek Fierlinger, former president of Czechoslovakia).

324. Ibid., 171 (reprinting a letter published in the *Daily Telegraph* [London], May 10, 1967).

325. Quoted in David Irving, *Churchill's War* (rev. ed. 2007), appendix III, p. 851, note 55.

326. Declassified Secret Memorandum: *Soldiers*, to Mr. John Peck & Sir E. Peck from J.E. Jackson, Jan. 10, 1969. (See Appendix, p. 439).

327. Ibid.

328. Ibid. (concluding that the "best counter action [to the charges implicating Churchill] would seem the release of the full range of the courts of enquiry").

329. Thompson, 36.

330. Hoover, 330 (quoting a "Soviet writer").

331. "Soldiers," *Time*, May 10, 1968.

332. Taëni, 42. He was deeply committed to social change, and he explained: "I am convinced that reform — or even revolutionary change — can only be realized in a modern industrial society on the basis of infiltration." Taëni, 34-35.

333. "In certain historical periods, one must be anti-clerical." Judy Stone, Interview with Rolf Hochhuth, in *The Storm Over The Deputy*, 42. Other times, he denied being anti-clerical. See Friedrich Heer, "The Need for Confession," *Commonweal*, Feb. 20, 1964, reprinted in *The Storm Over The Deputy*, 166, 167.

334. Patricia Marx, Interview with Rolf Hochhuth, *Partisan Review*, Vol. XXXI, No. 3, Summer 1964. He claimed, however, that his "best school friend" was a strict Catholic. "In fact, so strict a Catholic that his parents were very much afraid that he would enter the priesthood." Friedrich Heer, "The Need for Confession," *Commonweal*, Feb. 20, 1964, reprinted in *The Storm Over The Deputy*, 166, 1667.

335. In a 1964 interview, Hochhuth revealed a sense of drama in his personal life, when he described "the most terrifying experience I had since the publication of my play." He reported that a "very intelligent, older, and quite well-known Jesuit priest" came to visit him. Hochhuth never gave the name of the priest, but reported that the Jesuit tried to make a point (rather convoluted as reported by Hochhuth) that human life is not all that important when it is contrasted to eternity. Hochhuth took an interesting lesson from that encounter:

> And on this Sunday I became cognizant for the first time of what bottomless cunning lurks in the Church's insistence on celibacy. That these priests are obliged to live alone, that they do not have a single human being to whom they can get thoroughly attached. They have no child, no wife, and this gives them that unbelievable hardness, which enables them to reckon years not in the terms of a human life, but incommensurably under the aspect of eternity. They are not permitted to live. They are not permitted to have a life of their own, and therefore life itself, the life of other people, is not the same consequence to them as life is for those to whom that is all there is.

Patricia Marx, Interview with Rolf Hochhuth, WNYC Radio (February 1964), reprinted in *The Storm Over The Deputy*, 52, 60-61. Clearly he did not understand or appreciate Catholicism. "This is a Protestant play. Who but a Protestant would have made the Pope the chief target of a work dealing with the extermination of the Jews by mainly Protestant Germans?" Lionel Abel, "Rolf Hochhuth's The Deputy," *Dissent*, Spring 1964, reprinted in *The Storm Over The Deputy*, 81, 84.

336. *AR Action Report Online*: *http://www.fpp.co.uk/docs/Irving/Hochhuth/Times_200207.html*.

337. "The term 'fellow traveller' needs some explanation. It originated in revolutionary Russia, where it was used first in a non-pejorative way for intellectuals who did not oppose the Bolshevik Revolution, although not able to propagandise for it actively. By the end of the 1920s, however, such demonstrations of individualism had become equated with counter-revolution. In the West, the term came into common usage in the early Cold War to denote communist sympathisers. If not exactly Soviet spies or card-carrying party members, they were thought to have contact with menacing forces inside the Soviet Union while maintaining the innocence of their aims: they were the enemy within." Larraine Nicholas, "Fellow Travellers: Dance

and British Cold War Politics in the Early 1950s," 19:2 *Dance Research: The Journal of the Society for Dance Research*, 83, 85 (Winter 2001).

Communists considered any liberal to be a potential party member, and they often were able to use such people for their political advantage even though the people may not have been aware of it. See Miller, 146, 170. Even at American Communist Party meetings, members were reluctant to admit being a Communist. Ibid., 73. As such, it is hard to prove whether some individuals were party members or just fellow travelers.

338. One agent who worked undercover in the American Communist Party at this time wrote:

> We speak of "fellow travelers" *much* too carelessly. It is a term with a wide range, and fellow travelers under the Communists' brave new world serve the cause as Communists never could and hard-core Americans never will. It is they who smudge the link so it becomes undecipherable, so that origins never can be traced back. They serve a cause most of them do not comprehend because they are fatheads, brilliant fatheads, influential fatheads, beguiling fatheads. Naturally a few know perfectly well what they're serving and may be said not to be fatheads but evil, twisted men. But most are infatuated fatheads, adolescents in love with a scheming dazzler who is not for them.

Miller, 175 (emphasis in original).

339. Declassified Secret Memorandum: *Soldiers*, to Mr. John Peck & Sir E. Peck from J.E. Jackson, Jan. 10, 1969 (see Appendix, p. 439). British intelligence was more directly concerned with the allegations in *Soldiers*, but it also noted that *Soldiers* and *The Deputy* seemed to be part of a larger, unified plan. Ibid.

340. "Pius XI's Anti-Nazi Encyclical Was Prophetic," *Wanderer* (Zenit), April 19, 2007.

341. Zenit News Service, "Relator of Pius XII's Case Is Wary of Report: Father Gumpel Urges Prudence Over Defector's Tale," Feb. 18, 2007.

342. Michael Feldkamp, "Hochhuth Exposed," *Association of Contemporary Church Historians*, July/August 2007 (John Jay Hughes, trans.) ("That Pacepa is unable, after forty years, to remember just which Vatican archive was the source for the falsified documents does nothing to destroy his credibility.")

343. As this chapter is going to print, this author is working with Pacepa on another book project which will permit greater exploration of these issues.

## Chapter Seventeen: The Critics

1. Wills, *Papal Sin: Structures of Deceit* (2000).

2. Carroll, *Constantine's Sword: The Church and the Jews: A History* (2001).

3. Zuccotti, *Under His Very Windows: The Vatican and the Holocaust in Italy* (2001).

4. Phayer, *The Catholic Church and the Holocaust, 1930-1965* (2001).

5. Goldhagen, *A Moral Reckoning* (2002).

6. Kertzer, *The Popes Against the Jews* (2001), is overly dependent on the work of Italian scholar Giovanni Miccoli. Justus George Lawler recently completed a manuscript (Working title: *Were the Popes Against the Jews?*) that dissects this book and Kertzer's arguments, both in terms of logic and evidentiary proof. When Lawler first approached me to look over the manuscript, I wondered whether Kertzer's book was worthy of a book-length treatment. After reading both books, it is clear that Lawler's book is much more important than its principal subject.

7. Wistrich, *Hitler and the Holocaust* (2002).

8. Cornwell, *Breaking Faith* (2001). In *The Pontiff in Winter* (2004), Cornwell did not focus on Pope Pius XII, but he retracted the central thrust of *Hitler's Pope*. See pp. 307-8. In 2008, he came out with a second edition of *Hitler's Pope*, the only apparent change being in the preface.

9. Katz, *The Battle for Rome*. See also Katz, *Black Sabbath*; Katz, *Massacre in Rome*.

10. Lewy, *The Catholic Church and Nazi Germany* (1964); Morley, *Vatican Diplomacy and the Jews during the Holocaust 1939-1943* (1980).

11. See Ronald J. Rychlak, "The Church and the Holocaust," *Wall Street Journal* (Europe), March 28, 2002 (reviewing *Amen*).

12. Sánchez, *Pius XII and the Holocaust: Understanding the Controversy* (2002); Steigmann-Gall, *The Holy Reich: Nazi Conceptions of Christianity, 1919-1945* (2003); Godman, *Hitler and the Vatican: The Secret Archives That Reveal the Complete Story of the Nazis and the Vatican* (2004); *Pope Pius XII and the Holocaust* (Rittner and Roth, 2002).

13. Rychlak, *Righteous Gentiles* (2005); McInerny, *The Defamation of Pius XII* (2001); Burleigh, *The Third Reich: A New History* (2001); Stephen M. DiGiovanni, *Pius XII and the Jews: the War Years* (monograph, 2000); Gaspari, *Gli ebrei salvati da Pio XII* (2001); Lawler, *Popes and Politics: Reform, Resentment, and the Holocaust* (2002); Löw, *Die Schuld: Christen und Juden im Urteil der Nationalsozialisten und der Gegenwart* (2003); Marchione, *Man of Peace: Pope Pius XII* (2003); Marchione (2003); Marchione, *Shepherd of Souls: A Pictorial Life of Pope Pius XII* (2002). Andrea Tornielli, *Pio XII. Papa degli ebrei* (2001); *Pius XII, The Holocaust and the Revisionists*, (P. Gallo, ed. McFarland & Co., 2005); *The Pius War* (Lexington Press: Lanham, MD, Dalin and Bottum, eds., 2004); David Dalin, *The Myth of Hitler's Pope* (2005).

14. See, e.g., Daniel J. Goldhagen, "What Would Jesus Have Done?" *New Republic*, Jan. 21, 2002.

15. David Dalin, "Pius XII and the Jews," *Weekly Standard*, Feb. 26, 2001, 31-39. See also Ronald J. Rychlak, "Misusing History to Influence the Future," *Forum Focus*, Summer 2002.

16. The origin of this story seems to be in the following statement: "There is finally the report that in the months preceding his death he was given Hochhuth's play *The Deputy* to read and then was asked what one could do against it. Whereupon he allegedly replied: 'Do against it? What can you do against the truth?'" Hannah Arendt, *Men in Dark Times*, 63 (Harcourt Brace: New York, 1968).

17. Felicity O'Brien, Letter to the Editor, *Catholic Times* (Manchester, England), July 20, 1997.

18. Private correspondence from Loris Francesco Capovilla to the relator of Pius XII's sainthood cause, dated May 18, 2002.

> With regard to the actions in favor of the Jews, affected particularly in Istanbul in the years 1935-1944, which was recognized and praised by Hebrew communities in Jerusalem, Istanbul, and the United States, it is obligatory to recognize that Roncalli was and declared himself the executor of the thought and the directives of Pius XII. He repeated, in fact: "The papal representative is the eye, the ear, the mouth, the heart and the effective hand of the Pope."

Ibid. Capovilla also said that Roncalli's rescue efforts on behalf of Jews make sense "only if they are referred above everything else to Pius XII, of whom Roncalli was the careful and most faithful interpreter. Any strictly personal action, even though it be heroic, of Roncalli himself, would otherwise be inconceivable." Ibid.

19. In the first edition of this book, I reported that the Pope's order was "first and foremost to save *Jewish* lives." I gave the quote the way it was reported in O'Carroll, 20, and I cited O'Carroll. O'Carroll cited Pinchas Lapide for his authority, but Lapide says "*human* lives." After this was brought to my attention, I contacted O'Carroll through a friend. He stands by the accuracy of his quote, saying that in context there is no difference in the two terms. He also says that his information came not only from Lapide, but also from Chief Rabbi Isaac Herzog of Israel. O'Carroll reports that Herzog was close to Pius XII and heard him give orders to save *Jewish* lives.

O'Carroll has a point about the context of the quote, but it is more appropriate for the Pope to have said "human lives" without distinction. A Pope should not give priority to a particular group of people in need. Certainly an order "first and foremost" to save "human lives" encompasses saving Jews. So, the "human lives" quote actually speaks better for Pope Pius XII than does the quotation that I originally used.

20. McGurn, 88. "In the autumn of 1958 the world showed little doubt that one of its great ones had departed, and none showed less doubt than Angelo Roncalli [the future John XXIII]." Purdy, 7.

21. McGurn, 99.

22. Pius died on Oct. 9, 1958. Pope John XXIII knelt in prayer before Pius XII's tomb on the ninth of each month. *The New Catholic Treasury of Wit and Humor*, 193-94 (Meredith Press, New York: 1968, Paul Bussard, ed.).

23. *Discorsi* I, p. 101.

24. McGurn, 36, 39.

25. *Discorsi* I, p. 101; *Days of Devotion*, 12 ("Pope John's programme and its concern for the modern world naturally enough found much of its inspiration in Pope John's predecessor under whom he served for 19 years, and from whom came much of the intellectual foundation on which the Council is built. No one was more generous in acknowledging this debt than Pope John himself.")

26. Lewy, 303-4. See pp. 334-35.

27. See p. 233.

28. See "Exonerated," *National Catholic Register*, Jan. 23-29, 2005, p. 1 ("[T]he author most responsible for spreading the 'Hitler's Pope' myth admits he was wrong."); John Conway, "Book Review: Gerard Noel, Pius XII: The Hound of Hitler," XV *Association of Contemporary Church Historians Newsletter*, March 2003 ("*Hitler's Pope*... has by now been largely discredited, as Cornwell himself has acknowledged.") Cornwell still faults Pius for not being more outspoken following the end of the war. For more discussion of that charge, see pp. 338-39.

29. "I've never accused Pius of being a Nazi," *Catholic Herald*, July 27, 2007.

30. Ibid.

31. Ibid.

32. He also admits that he may have misdated the October meeting between Hitler and Tittmann. See p. 236.

33. Aside from noting that concordats are properly attributed to the reigning Pope, not the secretary of state, and pointing out the many positive things that came from the concordat (see pp. 70-80), it is important to say that Pacelli never met Hitler. See Charles Rankin, "Pius the Man and His Efforts for Peace," in *The Pope Speaks*, 21. They certainly did not negotiate face-to-face. Cornwell ignores that the concordat approach was the long-standing policy of Pope Pius XI, and that it was employed with other nations. He also wrongly attributes the collapse of the Center Party to pressure from Pacelli. See pp. 72-74. Cornwell builds his case almost exclusively on an account provided by Heinrich Brüning, the German chancellor from 1930

to 1932 and leader of the German Catholic Center Party. As others have noted, however, "Brüning's account has little foundation in reality." Heinz Hürten, *Stimmen der Zeit*, March 2000, pp. 205-208. Brüning's own biographer agrees that Brüning "was misguided... to insinuate that the Vatican bore responsibility for his fall as chancellor or the dissolution of the Center Party in 1933.... There is no evidence that the Vatican undermined Brüning's position." William Patch, *Heinrich Brüning and the Dissolution of the Weimar Republic*, 327 (Cambridge University Press, 1998). As reported by the head of the Commission for Contemporary History in Bonn, Germany, the newly released archives of Pius XI's pontificate, which encompass the Concordat/Catholic Center Party demise period, vindicate Pacelli and destroy Cornwell's speculative claims. Karl-Joseph Hummel, *"Der Historischen Wahrheit Auf Der Spur: Vor fünfzig Jahren starb Pius XII. – Zum Stand der Debatte nach der Öffnung der vatikanischen Archive,"* *Die Tagespost*, Sept. 10, 2008.

34. One can take issue with many of Cornwell's assertions. Cornwell, for instance, reports that Pope Pius XI and Secretary of State Pacelli were determined that "no accommodation could be made with Communism, anywhere in the world." Cornwell (1999), 114. The Vatican tried, however, (through Pacelli) to obtain a concordat with the Soviet Union in the mid-1920s, and it did conclude one with the predominantly Socialist government of Prussia in 1929. Pius also cooperated with President Roosevelt's request that he try to change the American-Catholic attitude toward extension of the lend-lease law to the Soviet Union, and he did what he could to help Soviet prisoners of war. Pacelli "ordained priests and even a bishop in his private chapel in Berlin, whereupon they left incognito for Soviet Russia. Their mission was to train and ordain priests in Soviet Russia." Confidential letter to Moffit from A. W. Klieforth, March 3, 1939. File No. 800, AWK-RM (noting that Pacelli was responsible for a private college in Berlin that prepared men to be Catholic priests in Russia).

On pages 259, 281, and 376-77, Cornwell refers to a memorandum from Gerhard Riegner for transmission to the Holy See, dated March 18, 1942. It described Nazi persecution of Jewish people, and Cornwell points out that this memorandum was not published by the Vatican in its collection of wartime documents (*Actes et Documents*). By the same token, the letter of thanks that Riegner sent to Nuncio M. Philippe Bernadinion April 8, 1942, was also not published. In that letter, Riegner stated:

> We also note with great satisfaction the steps undertaken by His Excellence the Cardinal Maglione, with authorities of Slovakia on behalf of the Jews of that country, and we ask you kindly to transmit to the Secretariat of State of the Holy See the expression of our profound gratitude.
>
> We are convinced that this intervention greatly impressed the governmental circles of Slovakia, which conviction seems to be confirmed by the information we have just received from that country....
>
> It appears... that the Slovak Government finds it necessary to justify the measures in question. One might therefore conclude that it might be induced — in the application of these measures — to conform more closely to the wishes expressed by the Holy See which desired to revoke the recent measures against the Jews.
>
> In renewing the expressions of our profound gratitude, for whatever the Holy See, thanks to your gracious intermediation, was good enough to undertake on behalf of our persecuted brothers, we ask Your Excellency to accept the assurance of our deepest respect.

The reason that neither the memo nor the letter of thanks were printed in the *Actes et Documents* collection is that they were classified as "unofficial." Moreover, the memo was rather long and did not report a definite source of information, but reported on persecutions that were "more or less known to the public at large." "Judging Pius XII," *Inside the Vatican*, February 2000, 61, 66 (quoting Father Blet, who noted that the memorandum had been published in a well-known book prior to the Vatican's collection being published). Riegner's memo is, however, mentioned in the *Actes et Documents* collection. "Le nonce à Berne Bernardini au Cardinal Maglione," March 19, 1942, *Actes et Documents*, vol. 8, p. 466, no. 314. In fact, a footnote was added just to draw attention to receipt of the memo. It was certainly never hidden, concealed, or missing.

Many of Cornwell's other errors are minor to the point of being trivial, or they are discussed in earlier chapters of this book. For a few examples: The title of the encyclical *Mit brennender Sorge* is properly translated as "With Burning Anxiety," not "With Deep Anxiety"; Cornwell completely misrepresents Pacelli's visit to Budapest to speak at the International Eucharistic Congress in 1938; Pius was not silent during September 1939; he intervened early — not late — in France, Hungary and every occupied nation; during the war foreign diplomats used the same doctor as did the Pope; the German ambassador to the Vatican did not plead for a public condemnation, precisely the opposite; Nicholas Horthy was not president but regent of Hungary, and he was a Calvinist not a Catholic, and Pacelli did appeal to him to stop the deportations; the motion picture filmed in 1942 (*Pastor Angelicus*) was completed at the request of Catholics around the world (particularly the United States) who had never seen the Pontiff, not in order to satisfy his ego; no one with whom this author spoke in Rome took calls from Pius on his or her knees (certainly there was no instruction to do so and it was not a widespread practice); and Pius XII's 1942 Christmas address was demonstrably more than "a paltry statement." For an answer to the allegation of racism by Pius XII following the liberation of Rome, see pp. 333-34.

35. Cornwell (1999), 297.

36. "Most of his sources are secondary and written by Pacelli's harshest critics. Errors of fact and ignorance of context appear on almost every page. Cornwell questions Pacelli's every motive, but never doubts those who tell a different story." Kenneth L. Woodward, "The Case Against Pius XII: A new biography is scalding—and deeply flawed," *Newsweek International*, Sept. 27, 1999.

> It is difficult to know where to begin to criticize this work because it is replete with innuendo, guilt by the most tenuous association, cleverly phrased non sequiturs and blatant use of any work critical of Pius. He used those works that make Pius look bad, or silly, or imperious, or whatever suits his argument at the moment, even to the extent of repeating the hoary canard that "Vatican officials took phone calls from [Pius] upon their knees" presumably because Pius ordered them to do so.

José M. Sánchez and Kelly Cherry, "Pacelli's Legacy," *America*, Oct. 23, 1999, 25. See Cornwell (1999), 324 ("Vatican officials took telephone calls from Pacelli upon their knees").

37. John F. Morley, "Pacelli's Prosecutor," *Commonweal*, Nov. 5, 1999, 27, 28. Another reviewer wrote: "*Hitler's Pope* is a malign exercise in defamation and character assassination. The author has, in my view, consistently misread and misunderstood both Pacelli's actions and the context in which they occurred." William D. Rubinstein, "Books in Review: The Devil's Advocate," *First Things*, January 2000, 39.

38. "Cornwell, a serious Catholic author who has written many books sympathetic to the Vatican and who once studied for the priesthood, set out to disprove the accusation that Pius XII was soft on Nazism." *Sunday Herald* (London), Sept. 19, 1999.

> Cornwell's great achievement is to make it impossible any longer for Pacelli's defenders to say that it is only Jewish historians with axes to grind who have put their hero in the dock. Cornwell is himself a Catholic, but he has gone where the documentary evidence has taken him, having originally thought that Pacelli was unfairly criticized.

Frank Mclynn, "A Far from Pious World View: A Biography Which Reveals the Shameful History of the Wartime Pope," *Herald* (Glasgow), Sept. 23, 1999.

39. One reviewer concluded that, his charges "should be laughed out of the court of public opinion." "Cornwell's Popes," *Commonweal*, Nov. 5, 1999, 5, 6 (lead editorial).

40. It was also used to illustrate James Carroll, "The Silence," *New Yorker*, April 7, 1997; James Carroll, "The Holocaust and the Catholic Church," *Atlantic Monthly*, October 1999, 107; the German version of Peter Godman's book *Der Vatikan und Hitler: Die geheimen Archive* (Droemer, 2004); and Matteo L. Napolitano and Andrea Tornielli, *Il Papa Che Salvò Gli Ebrei* (Piemme, 2004) (an Italian book favorable to Pius XII that uses this photo as a response to *Hitler's Pope*).

41. Some reviewers of *Hitler's Pope* did assert that Pius met with Hitler. See Linda Massarella, "Book Paints WWII Pope as Hitler Ally — Author: Vatican Files Show Pius Hated Jews," *New York Post*, Sept. 7, 1999, 12.

42. Congregation for the Causes of Saints, *Positio*, appendix 25, 268. The error was corrected in later versions of the dust jacket. "It was only after repeated protests that the publisher provided a new dust jacket for the books not yet sold." Peter Gumpel, "A Journalist Purporting to Be a Scholar," *Die Furche*, January 6, 2000, 1.

43. Cornwell approved the photograph. "Vatican Chronicles: A Different Read," *Brill's Content*, April 2000, 60, 120.

44. *Time* magazine received some criticism when it did the same thing to O. J. Simpson during his trial for the murder of Ron Goldman and Nicole Brown Simpson. Les Payne, "An O. J. Portrait Gets Media Sneer," *Newsday*, July 31, 1994, 42.

45. The dishonesty was uncovered by Prof. Robert Gorman, who presented a paper on this topic at the October 2001 meeting of the Society of Catholic Social Scientists at Ave Maria Law School in Ann Arbor, Michigan.

46. Merton, *Dancing in the Water of Life*, 84 (emphasis added). This passage was written in anger. The following day, Merton tempered his comments about having been ordered not to publish his essay.

47. The Secretariat of State authorized Cornwell to consult the archive of the section on Relations with States, which he did for some three weeks. The topic of his research was relations with Bavaria (1918-1921); Austria, Serbia, and Belgrade (1913-1915). Cornwell was neither the first nor the only one to consult the archives of those years. He had no access to the "closed period," beginning in 1922. Congregation for the Causes of Saints, *Positio*, appendix 25, 265.

48. "Una doverosa precisazione in merito ad un libro recente," *L'Osservatore Romano*, Oct. 13, 1999 (reprinted in Congregation for the Causes of Saints, *Positio*, appendix 25, 267). It was also reported on Vatican Radio.

49. The "sub-editorial conflation" language was edited out of the *Brill's Content* piece when it was published. The only other time I saw this term used, despite numerous searches on Lexis-Nexis, was in an early negative review of the first edition of this book posted on *Amazon.com* by an "anonymous reader from London" who complained that the book was simply an attack on John Cornwell.

50. See Congregation for the Causes of Saints, *Positio*, appendix 25, 266.

51. This refers to the transcript of testimony given by 98 witnesses between the years 1967 and 1974. There are two "original" handwritten files containing these documents, but edited versions have been typed, indexed, and printed. They now form the *Positio*'s Summarium.

52. Congregation for the Causes of Saints, *Positio*, appendix 25, 274 ("The Acts of the Cause of Beatification and Canonization of Pope Pius XII are not at all secret. Cornwell is not telling the truth....") See Kenneth Woodward, "The Case Against Pius XII," *Newsweek* (International), Sept. 27, 1999, 66 ("I have seen [the files] myself."); Felicity O'Brien, "Looking Back on Pius XII," *Newsweek*, Oct. 25, 1999, 18 ("In the late 1980's I studied the sworn testimonies gathered for the Canonization Cause of Pius XII in Rome.") Deposition transcripts are kept secret while testimony is actively being taken, so that later witnesses are not "tainted" by hearing the testimony of witnesses who came earlier. Once depositions are ended, the files are no longer officially secret.

53. John Cornwell, "Look at the Facts: John Cornwell Replies," *Tablet* (London), Sept. 25, 1999.

54. Appendix 25 of the *Positio* reports:

> We have to in every manner make clear that Prof. Ronald J. Rychlak, in his excellent book *Hitler, the War, and the Pope* (2000), added an epilogue addressing the book *Hitler's Pope*, including 197 endnotes. This epilogue is a detailed and well-documented refutation of the falsehoods in Cornwell's book; it is a final and definitive demolition of that work.

55. At least one author has argued that Pius XII's housekeeper, Sister Pascalina Lehnert, dominated the Vatican under Pope Pius XII. See Paul Murphy, *La Popessa*; Gerald Noel, *Pius XII: The Hound of Hitler* (2008) (relying on Murphy). Cornwell largely accepted this depiction, even though it was inconsistent with the picture of Pius that Cornwell presented throughout *Hitler's Pope*. Certainly Sister Pascalina did not present a similar depiction in her testimony. Congregation for the Causes of Saints, *Positio* (Summarium). Nor did she suggest anything like that in her memoirs. See Sister Pascalina Lehnert, *Ich durfte ihm dienen: Erinnerungen an Papst Pius XII* (Würzburg, 1982); Sister Pascalina Lehnert, *Pio XII* (Rusconi Libri: Milan, 1984) (Italian translation). As one author noted: *La Popessa* is a world apart from the genuine memoirs of the nun; it is a world of arbitrary invention, carried at times to the wildest extremes." O'Carroll, 244. Those who knew Pius XII's Vatican well did not think that Sister Pascalina dominated the Pope. See Sereny, 310, quoting Monsignor Karl Bayer. See also Robert A. Graham, "Will the Real Sister Pascalina Please Step Forward," *Columbia Magazine*, November 1983, 9.

56. Congregation for the Causes of Saints, *Positio*, appendix 25, 265.

57. Ibid., 274.

58. "Vatican Chronicles: A Different Read," *Brill's Content*, April 2000.

59. As for Cornwell's publicity campaign, see Ibid., 265.

60. The text of the letter (Sept. 4, 1917) is in the Appendix, p. 389.

61. Vatican Secretariat of State Archive, Fasc. 852, et al., folios 2-5.

62. Cornwell (1999), 71.

63. The derogatory meaning of *cult* is reflected in the *American Heritage Dictionary*'s secondary definition: "Obsessive devotion to a person or ideal; a group of persons sharing such devotion." As used by Pacelli, however, the word "was not a pejorative term." Marilyn Henry, "How Pious was Pius XII?" *Jerusalem Post*, Oct. 1, 1999, 7B (quoting Eugene Fisher). "It has nothing to do with personal animosity toward Jews." Ibid.

64. *Hitler's Pope*, 174 (cult of St. Thérèse); ibid., 344 (cult of the Assumption and cult of the Virgin Mary); ibid., 345 (the Fátima cult); ibid., 382 (noting that beatification "indicates that the Pope has sanctioned a local cult of the individual's sainthood").

65. See Bruno Walter, *Theme and Variations: An Autobiography*, 221 (Knopf: New York, 1966) (Nuncio Pacelli helped a wrongly imprisoned Jewish musician during World War I); "Relief Man," *Time*, March 13, 1939 ("Bruno Walter... told reporters a story: ... Walter's friend, Russian Pianist Ossip Gabrilowitsch, was imprisoned on charges of espionage. Gabrilowitsch got a message to Walter, who spoke to Pacelli, who whispered in someone's ear. In not much more time than it takes to play a Bruckner symphony, Gabrilowitsch was free.")

66. Besier, 18-23.

67. Fulton J. Sheen, "The Pope as I Saw Him," *Catholic Digest*, October 1955, 62.

68. Nuncio Pacelli's letter of April 18, 1919, sent to Cardinal Secretary of State Gasparri (reprinted in the Appendix, p. 390). See Besier, 19-23.

69. See p. 33.

70. Hatch and Walshe, 84; Halecki and Murray, 47-48.

71. Fulton J. Sheen, "The Pope as I Saw Him," *Catholic Digest*, October 1955, 62; Halecki and Murray, 46 (noting that no one was hurt). For a description of the havoc the Communist revolutionaries were causing in Germany at the time, see Kershaw, 109-16.

72. M. Martin, *The Decline and Fall of the Roman Church*, 219 (noting that several people had been killed, so the threat could not be taken lightly).

73. Fulton J. Sheen, "The Pope as I Saw Him," *Catholic Digest*, October 1955, 62.

74. Nuncio Pacelli's letter of April 18, 1919, sent to Cardinal Secretary of State Gasparri (reprinted in the Appendix, p. 390).

75. See Besier, 23

76. Nuncio Pacelli's letter of April 18, 1919, sent to Cardinal Secretary of State Gasparri (reprinted in the Appendix, p. 390).

77. Ibid.

78. Cornwell, *Hitler's Pope*, 74-75. Even worse were press reports that Pacelli described "Jews" (not a specific group of revolutionaries) as "physically and morally repulsive, worthy of suspicion and contempt." Cathy Lynn Grossman, "Catholic scholar casts Pius XII as 'Hitler's Pope,'" *USA Today*, Sept. 7, 1999. Pacelli certainly did not do that. See Ronald J. Rychlak, "Cornwell's Errors: Reviewing Hitler's Pope," *Catalyst*, December 1999, 8.

79. In the second edition of *Hitler's Pope*, Cornwell tries to explain that the fact the report was not directly made by Pacelli, but by his assistant Schioppa, does not diminish the reflection on Pacelli's "stereotypical anti-Semitic contempt" or his "antipathy" toward the Jews. Cornwell bolsters his conclusion by citing the 1917 letter regarding a rabbi's request for palm fronds. *Hitler's Pope* (2nd ed.), xxiii. See p. 314.

80. Ibid. Daniel Goldhagen's statement that "the Communist revolutionaries, Pacelli averred, were 'all' Jews" is wrong. The word "all" appears only in Cornwell's mistranslation.

81. The German edition of *Hitler's Pope* has an even worse translation. "Group" is translated as "scum," so the passage at issue reads: "The boss of this female scum was Levien's mistress...." See Rainer Decker, book review: John Cornwell. "*Pius XII. Der Papst, der geschwiegen hat*," *H-Soz-u-Kult* (February, 2000).

82. Cornwell claims that the letter was first brought to attention in his 1999 book, but the original letter appears in Emma Fattorini, *Germania e Santa Sede. Le nunziature di Pacelli fra la Grande guerra e la Repubblica di Weimar*, 322-25 (Società editrice il Mulino: Bologna, 1992). See Congregation for the Causes of Saints, *Positio*, appendix 25, 266.

83. The same holds true for Daniel Goldhagen and his publisher. The translated letter is reprinted in the Appendix, p. 390.

84. In an interview with a French newspaper, Pacelli described the situation in Munich in 1919:

> I am one of the few non-German eye-witnesses of the Bolshevik régime that ruled Munich in April 1919. At the head of this "Soviet" government were native Russians; every idea of justice, freedom and democracy was suppressed; only the Soviet press was available. Even the nuncio's official residence was part of the republican government; armed bandits forced their way in here and when I protested energetically against this violation of international law, one of them threatened me with his pistol. I am well aware of the objectionable circumstances under which the hostages were massacred....

Sereny, 305, citing an interview with the French newspaper *Le Matin*.

85. File A 18/25 in the Main Archive of Yad Vashem.

86. Cornwell continually argues that Pacelli was responsible for matters done in the name of Gasparri. See *Hitler's Pope*, 31 (they worked "in tandem"); ibid., 38 (Gasparri was Pacelli's "boss and close confidant"); ibid., 41 (Gasparri and Pacelli were "principal architects" of the Code of Canon Law); ibid., 44 (an idea "became clear to Gasparri and Pacelli"); ibid., 46 (Gasparri referring to Pacelli: "one of my trusty staff in the Secretariat of State, in whom I had particular confidence"); ibid., 55 ("Gasparri, Pacelli's guide and mentor"); ibid., 56 (Pacelli as Gasparri's "protégé"); ibid., 61 ("Gasparri would not hear of Pacelli's leaving Rome until the new code had been published.")

87. Cardinal Gasparri, Secretary of State, Replies to the Petition of the American Jewish Committee of New York, Feb. 9, 1916, in *Principles for Peace: Selections from Papal Documents, Leo XIII to Pius XII*, 198-99; *La Civiltà Cattolica*, April 28, 1916.

88. Cohen, 180, 214-15, 578. Cohen's sources are the archives of the American Jewish Committee and statements by AJC members who were directly involved in Catholic-Jewish relations at the time. See Marchione, *Man of Peace*, 73, n. 3. See also "The Anti-Semitic Movement Denounced by the Pope," *Argus* (Melbourne), March 11, 1895 (anti-Semitism condemned by Pope Leo XIII); "Blood Ritual: The Holy See's Attitude," *Mercury* (Hobart), Oct. 29, 1913 (the Vatican reconfirms Pope Innocent IV's condemnation of the alleged Jewish "blood ritual" as "an invention"); "The Pope and the Jews," *Adviser* (Adelaide), Sept. 27, 1915 (Pope Benedict XV promises that the Holy See, as in the past, will always act "according to the dictates of justice in favor of the Jews.")

89. Likewise, the critics ignore Pacelli's friendship with and assistance provided to Zionist leader Nahum Sokolow in 1917 and later. See p. 317.

90. This document can be accessed at the web page of the Pave the Way Foundation: *www.ptwf.org*.

91. A brief summary of Repgen's work can be found in *Controversial Concordats: The Vatican's Relations with Napoleon, Mussolini, and Hitler*, 236-38 (The Catholic University of America Press, Frank J. Coppa, ed., 1999). His works include: Konrad Repgen, *Das Ende der Zentrumspartei und Entstehung des Reichskonkordats, Militärseelsorge*, 2 (1970), and later reissued in *Historische Klopfsignale für die Gegenwart*, Münster:

Verlag Aschendorff, (1974) (concluding that the Center Party was not traded for the concordat); Konrad Repgen, *Dokumentation. Zur Vatikanischen Strategie beim Reichskonkordat, Vierteljahrshefte für Zeitgeschichte*, 31 (1983) (the prohibition of clergy from party politics took place after the dissolution of the party); Konrad Repgen, *"Hitlers Machtergreifung und der deutsche Katholizismus. Versuch einer Bilanz,"* in *Katholische Kirche im Dritten Reich*, edited by Dieter Albrecht, Mainz: Matthias-Grünewald-Verlag (1976) (absolving Ludwig Kaas and the Vatican of initiating concordat negotiations and of making a deal to vote for the Enabling Act); Konrad Repgen, *Über Umlaut! die Entstehung der Reichskonkordats-Offerte im Frühjahr 1933 und die Bedeutung des Reichskonkordats, Vierteljahrshefte für Zeitgeschichte* 25 (1978), 499-534 (providing a detailed critique and refutation of Scholder's thesis that concordat negotiations influenced the Center Party's vote for the Enabling Act). See also Konrad Repgen, *"Reichskonkordats-Kontroversen und historische Logik,"* in *Demokratie und Diktatur. Geist und Gestalt politischer Herrschaft in Deutschland und Europa. Festschrift für Karl Dietrich Bracher* (Düsseldorf, 1987), ed., Manfred Funke, et al., pp. 158-77.

92. Congregation for the Causes of Saints, *Positio*, appendix 25 at 269. See Ludwig Volk, *Das Reichskonkordat vom 20. Juli 1933*, Mainz: Matthias-Grünewald-Verlag (1972); *Controversial Concordats*, 241-42 (calling *Das Reichskonkordat* "the most scholarly study of the subject" and briefly summarizing Volk's other work).

93. Alfons Kupper, *Staatliche Akten über die Reichskonkordatsverhandlungen* (Mainz, 1969) (collection of documents showing that the initiative for the concordat came from the Reich government); John Jay Hughes, "The Pope's Pact with Hitler," 17 *Journal of Church and State*, 63 (1975). See *Controversial Concordats*, 233-34 (synopsis of Kupper). See also p. 72-74.

94. *A Requiem for Hitler*, xii-xiii (Trinity: Philadelphia, Gerhard Besier, ed., 1989).

95. I have seen well marked-up copies of Scholder's work in Gumpel's office.

96. Peter Gumpel, "Cornwell's Pope: A Nasty Caricature of a Noble and Saintly Man," Zenit News Service, Sept. 16, 1999 (also discussing Cornwell's "blind faith" in the suspect memoirs of Heinrich Brüning).

97. Michael Novak, "Death Comes for the Pontiff," *Washington Post*, Dec. 24, 1989 (Final Edition). Cornwell's writing has not changed much. As one generally positive review of *Hitler's Pope* noted:

> So unsympathetic is the portrait of Pius XII — among other things, Cornwell portrays him as a spiritual egotist — that it's hard to believe the author was ever much of an admirer of the man. *Hitler's Pope* is informed by a view of the Church that shows every sign of being long held, and the book uses the case of Pius XII, who reigned from 1939 to 1958, primarily to bolster that view.

Philip Marchand, "Hitler's Pope unsympathetic portrait of Pius XII," *Toronto Star*, Oct. 8, 1999.

98. Michael Novak, "Death Comes for the Pontiff," *Washington Post*, Dec. 24, 1989 (Final Edition).

99. Christian Tyler, "A Philosopher's Tale: Science critic finds U.S. trial raises deeper moral questions," *Financial Post* (Toronto), Sept. 28, 1996. See also Ian Thomson, "Possession: nine-tenths of the lore; The mysterious visions and spooks which led John Cornwell to travel the world in search of supernatural," *Independent* (London), Nov. 16, 1991 (Cornwell proclaims himself an "agnostic investigator"). The term "Catholic agnostic," was used by the British writer Graham Greene to describe himself in an interview that he gave to John Cornwell in 1989. William Tuohy, "Reflections; The author's view of Graham Greene; A 1989 discussion revealed much about how the leading British writer, who died last week, felt about religion, sex and death," *Los Angeles Times*, April 9, 1991. Greene, while typically described as a "Catholic writer" was rebuked by the Vatican for some of his work, and much of his later work seems to have taken on a "liberation theology" slant, which left him at odds with the Catholic Church. Robert Royal, "The (Mis)Guided Dream of Graham Greene," *First Things*, November 1999, 16.

100. Victoria Combe, *Daily Telegraph* (London), Sept. 17, 1999.

101. One reader of *A Thief in the Night*, wrote:

> Cornwell lets his private journalistic ambition sully his integrity as a writer of supposed "history." This man has a clear agenda: vilify the Vatican in every possible way, cast aspersions on those who cannot defend themselves, and where possible make the Catholic Church generally and the Vatican "establishment" in particular look like a bunch of powerhungry egomaniacs and a den of thieves.

This review was available on the *Amazon.com* website in late 1999.

102. George Weigel, "Not by the hand of conspirators," *Washington Times*, Nov. 23, 1989.

103. "Nonfiction in Brief," *Los Angeles Times*, Dec. 10, 1989.

104. Cornwell's other books have also been unfriendly to the Church. His 1993 novel, *Strange Gods*, is about Father Nicholas Mullen, a Jesuit priest in his late forties who keeps a mistress on whom he lavishes caviar and champagne, goes on golfing holidays in Barbados, and takes lithium for manic-depressive swings. He supports his lifestyle by absolving a wealthy Catholic benefactor from his own sins of the flesh. Although unhappy with his emotional, sexual, and spiritual lot, Father Mullen lacks the courage and imagination to do anything about it. The *Independent* (London) called the priest "a cut-out model of a sexually tortured Catholic." Mary Loudon, "Book Review / The missionary's position; 'Strange Gods,'" *Independent*, Aug. 29, 1993. Driven by fear and desperation, he deserts his pregnant mistress in favor of a dangerous, immoral venture in an obscure part of Latin America. There, he encounters Father Christian O'Rourke, an Irish Jesuit whose fanatical attempts to indoctrinate natives into the One True Faith are by turns comical and sinister. Ultimately,

Mullen returns to England, his faith transformed into what one reviewer called "a soggy Christian humanism." Piers Paul Read, "To Hell and back through the faith jungle," *Mail on Sunday* (London), July 18, 1993, 45.

105. See Felicity O'Brien, "Looking Back on Pius XII," *Newsweek* (International), Oct. 25, 1999, 18.

106. Cornwell, "Outfacing his critics," *Sunday Times* (London), Oct. 6, 1996.

107. Kenneth Woodward, "The Case Against Pius XII," *Newsweek* (International), Sept. 27, 1999, 66. "The spin Cornwell puts on all this tends to contradict his claim to evenhanded, objective scholarship. Virtually everything Pius XII did, said or thought about is skewed to portray him as a Machiavellian schemer, a moral coward and a pompous hypocrite. Even the most neutral reader would be hard pressed to stifle the suspicion that Cornwell doth protest too much." Robert McClory, "Tunnel Visions," *In These Times*, Dec. 12, 1999, 40.

108. Cornwell, "Hitler's Pope: The Fight to reveal the secrets that threaten the Vatican," *Sunday Times* (London), Sept. 12, 1999, l.

109. *Jerusalem Post*, March 23, 2000 (online edition).

110. Ibid. In *The Pontiff in Winter*, Cornwell refers to his own inside-the-Vatican, deep throat: Monsignor *Sotto Voce*. Taking Cornwell at his word, and accepting his description of Monsignor *Sotto Voce*, *The Pontiff in Winter* is based upon an "inside account" from a disgruntled and burned-out Vatican official who trades secrets for a good meal and a couple of bottles of wine. The great advantage for Cornwell, of course, is that this lets him write almost anything, and unlike *Hitler's Pope*, no one can prove it is false.

111. See Ronald J. Rychlak, "Guess Who's Back?" *Catalyst* (January-February 2002) (reviewing *Breaking Faith*); Ronald J. Rychlak, "*A Broken Faith:* John Cornwell's New Book," *St. Austin Review*, July/August 2002.

112. Cornwell presented the excommunication of Sri Lankan theologian Father Tissa Balasuriya as an example of the harshness of John Paul's "authoritarian rule." Balasuriya was excommunicated for theological aberrations, barely mentioned by Cornwell, that included the assertion that Christianity is on the same level as other religions, the denial of the virgin birth of Christ, and the rejection of the Holy Trinity. See Ronald J. Rychlak and Father Kevin Slattery, "A Clear-Cut Case for Excommunication," *New Oxford Review*, April 1997. Cornwell used the excommunication to argue that John Paul was insensitive and out-of-touch with the modern world. He did not, however, even mention the extended negotiations between Balasuriya and the Vatican that preceded the excommunication. More incredibly, he failed to mention that one year after the excommunication was imposed, it was lifted. At that time, Balasuriya signed a statement expressing regret for perceptions of error in his work and agreed to submit future writings to bishops for approval prior to publication. This resolution to the matter, unknown to most readers of *Breaking Faith*, severely undercuts Cornwell's thesis *and* his credibility.

113. He has not hidden his disappointment with Pope Benedict XVI: "The Pope is emerging as an ultra-reactionary." Cornwell, "Profile: Pope Benedict XVI," *New Statesman*, Feb. 12, 2009. The most shocking part of this article is that Cornwell presents himself as a great fan of Pope John Paul II, contrasting the late Pope with the current one.

114. Similarly, James Carroll's resolution to this history, as set forth in *Constantine's Sword* (p. 555-58), involves the convening of Vatican III, at which (in addition to rejection of papal infallibility, ordination of women, election of bishops, and relaxation of sexual rules) the Church would acknowledge errors in the Gospels, learn to preach against those errors, and reject the belief that Jesus is the only way to salvation. Similar themes were also advanced by critic Daniel Goldhagen. In his memoir *An American Requiem*, Carroll wrote with scorn about his father's distress over his [Carroll's] excommunication from the Catholic Church. Apparently, however, Carroll has reconciled with the Church. In a contribution to Kerry Kennedy's *Being Catholic Now* (2008), Carroll wrote: "I worship in the Catholic tradition and honor the Catholic institution, even while much of what I believe would disqualify me from a more rigid notion of what it is to be a Catholic. I don't believe in the infallibility of the pope, for example." He also wrote: "My beloved Roman Catholic tradition is full of things I reject."

115. On a television appearance he claimed to be completely in agreement with the Church's teaching on abortion, but at one point in *Breaking Faith* he refers to it as "a painful choice to be made by individual women."

116. Deal Hudson, Crisis Interview with John Cornwell, *Crisis*, March 2002.

117. Cornwell also took the opportunity to argue that the first edition of this book was about *him*. That led to this letter, published in the April 2002 issue of *Crisis*:

If John Cornwell thinks that my book (*Hitler, the War, and the Pope*) is primarily or even significantly about him, he didn't read it.

I would much rather debate the substance of Cornwell's arguments than the stories he has told about himself. He, however, interjected an *ad hominem* aspect to this debate by testifying about his personal emotions and being left in a state of moral shock. I responded fairly. He now uses this as a reason to dodge the issues and avoid the debate.

For the record: My book was completed and at the publisher when I first saw *Hitler's Pope*. We held up production so that I could go to Rome and inspect the documents that he said left him in a state of "moral shock." Upon reviewing those documents, it was clear that nothing he saw would have had such an impact on an unbiased researcher. I wrote a 44-page epilogue (including endnotes) explaining what I found. About two of these pages deal with the 20-plus years Cornwell spent as a self-described "lapsed Catholic." It is a rather trivial part of my book, but it is a legitimate matter to discuss.

During this time, much of Cornwell's writing was openly hostile toward the Church. Some of it was expressly critical of Pius XII. This was in direct contradiction to the claims made in conjunction with the marketing of *Hitler's Pope*. In fact, until my book came out, Cornwell gave no indication in conjunction with the marketing of his book that he had ever been anything other than a devout, practicing Catholic.

Cornwell has now admitted that his claim to have spent "months on end" in the Vatican archives was false. He has also conceded that, contrary to earlier claims, the archives he saw were not secret. The 1919 letter on which he built so much of his case, and which he said had previously been unknown, actually had been published in full several years before the badly translated excerpt that Cornwell included in his book. He also admits to having written in 1993 that people are "morally, psychologically and materially better off without a belief in God." Couple this information with the doctored cover photo (reprinted in *Crisis*), the butchered quotation from Thomas Merton in the opening pages of *Hitler's Pope*, the blatant misrepresentations about the beatification transcripts, and one must question the reliability of anything Cornwell says.

As I clearly stated in my book: "None of this material concerning Cornwell's anti-Catholic background and prior hostility towards Pope Pius XII serves by itself to undermine Cornwell's research. It does however raise serious questions about his credibility."

I stick by that assessment.

Ronald J. Rychlak
Professor of Law
Associate Dean for Academic Affairs
University of Mississippi

118. In actuality, Pius embraced democratic ideals, particularly in his 1944 Christmas message. See McCormick, 125.

119. Cornwell, "Profile: Pope Benedict XVI," *New Statesman*, Feb. 12, 2009 (in which Cornwell purports to have been a fan of Pope John Paul II). In fact, when Cardinal Ratzinger, the future Benedict XVI, spoke at John Paul II's funeral, expressing a traditionalist view of Christianity, Cornwell said that Ratzinger had given up hope of being made pope.

120. Quoted in *New Oxford Review* (2002).

121. Stanley L. Jaki, "Newman: Myths & Facts," *New Oxford Review*, November 2001, 19.

122. Regarding the similar tactics employed by Pius XII and John Paul II, see "Bill O'Reilly Gets in Over His Head," *Catalyst*, April 2003 (quoting a press release from the Catholic League for Religious and Civil Rights):

Just last Saturday Fidel Castro presided over the inauguration of a new convent of nuns in Cuba. He did so as a fitting tribute to the fifth anniversary of Pope John Paul II's visit to Cuba.... The pope was able to accomplish this without ever having a position on Fidel Castro. Come to think of it, the pope never had a position on any of the Soviet Union's officials, yet even Gorbachev credited the Holy Father with bringing about the implosion of the U.S.S.R.

123. Alan Cowell, "Demonstrators and Devout Greet the Pope In Germany," *New York Times*, June 24, 1996, section A, p. 3.

124. Oppen, 399 (citing Conway's *The Nazi Persecution of the Churches 1933-45*). Oppen further discusses sloppy or intentional mistranslations that magnified Friedländer's argument, to the detriment of the truth. Oppen, 400-402.

125. Conway, *The Nazi Persecution of the Churches 1933-45*, 449-50.

126. Father Robert A. Graham, "The Latest Charges Against Pius XII," *America*, May 21, 1966. See also Pierre Blet, S.J., *Civiltà Cattolica*, May 1, 1965 (reviewing Friedländer's book).

127. Congregation for the Causes of Saints, *Positio*, appendix 25, p. 250, note 3. One wonders whether they feel the same following Friedländer's most recent work. See William Doino, "The Silence of Saul Friedländer," *First Things Online*, July 24, 2007.

128. This interview was conducted by William Doino, Jr. It has not been published as of the time of this writing.

129. See Congregation for the Causes of Saints, *Positio*, appendix 25, 279. An interesting letter, which confounds Zuccotti's thesis, can be found in *Dietrich Bonhoeffer: Letters and Papers from Prison* (Eberhard Bethge, ed., Collier Books, New York, enlarged ed., 1971). The letter, to Bonhoeffer from a co-conspirator in the resistance, was worded so vaguely that the true message — about meeting with papal assistants who

had been "let in on the conspiracy" — is decipherable only because the author of the letter also edited the collection of letters and was able to explain it in a footnote. Ibid., 214.

130. In addition to the archives, Zuccotti reviewed the Vatican's published documents on the Holy See and the Second World War (*Actes et Documents*). In her introduction, she explained her belief that all of the good evidence about Pope Pius XII appears in these published documents. She wrote that if there were a papal order to help Jews, it "would almost certainly have been preserved by someone clever enough to understand that it might someday help the Pope's reputation." Failing to find a written order from Pius among those documents, she assumed that he did not participate in rescue efforts. She thus rested her case on the absence of documents, not the existence of evidence. *Nowhere* in the book did she cite a single Italian priest, nun, or bishop who criticized Pope Pius XII by name for an alleged failure to assist Jews.

131. Eugenio Zolli, *The Nazarene: Studies in New Testament Exegesis*, 9 (Cyril Vollert, trans., 1999).

132. Kenneth C. Davis, *Don't Know Much About the Bible: Everything You Need to Know About the Good Book but Never Learned* (2001).

133. See Alana M. Fuierer, "The Anti-Chlorine Campaign in the Great Lakes: Should Chlorinated Compounds Be Guilty Until Proven Innocent?" 43 *Buffalo L. Rev.*, 181 (1995) (citing the rule); Ronald Bayer, Lawrence O. Gostin, and Deven C. Mcgraw, "Trades, AIDS, and the Public's Health: The Limits of Economic Analysis," 83 *Geo. L.J.*, 79 (1994) (same).

134. See Ian Buruma, "Depravity Was Contagious," *New York Times* (Books), Dec. 10, 2000 (reviewing Ian Kershaw, *Hitler 1936-45: Nemesis*).

135. See *Dietrich Bonhoeffer: Letters and Papers from Prison*, 214 (Eberhard Bethge, ed., Collier Books, New York, enlarged ed., 1971). Bethge, active in the German resistance and a collaborator of Bonhoeffer, noted in a wartime letter that Catholic leaders could express their opposition to the Nazis without words: "How easy it is for Catholics now, as they can largely dispense with words and preach with their dress and gestures." Ibid. See also McCormick, 118 (from a *New York Times* dispatch of Aug. 24, 1944) ("What the Pope did was to create an attitude in favor of the persecuted and hunted that the city was quick to adapt, so that hiding someone 'on the run' became the thing to do.")

136. The letters are reproduced in the Appendix, p. 403.

137. Erich Ludendorff had been a leader of the German Army, especially at the end of World War I. He was an early supporter of the Nazi Party.

138. This letter is reproduced in the Appendix, p. 392.

139. This letter is reproduced in the Appendix, p. 393.

140. "New Proofs of Pius XII's Efforts to Assist Jews: 1933 Letter Targets 'Anti-Semitic Excesses' in Germany," Zenit News Service, Feb. 17, 2003. "It is significant that the first initiative of the Holy See toward the government in Berlin concerned the Jews. As early as April 4, 1933, 10 days after the Enabling Act, the Apostolic Nuncio in Berlin [Orsenigo] was ordered to intervene with the government of the Reich on behalf of the Jews and point out all the dangers involved in an anti-Semitic policy." Robert Leiber, *"Mit brennender Sorge: März 1937-März 1962,"* in the March 1962 issue of *Stimmen der Zeit*, (vol. 169), 420. See Godman, 37-38 ("Orsenigo read the Catholic vice-chancellor, Franz von Papen, a lesson on how the legislation represented 'an offense against the divine law.' ") Similarly, famed Italian bicyclist Gino Bartali helped rescue 800 Jews at the direction of Pope Pius XII, according to other newly discovered documents. "Pius XII's Directive Helped Save 800 Jews in 3 Cities, Papers Reveal," Zenit News Service, April 8, 2003. For other new evidence that undercuts Zuccotti's thesis, see the discussion of Adolf Eichmann's memoirs and the events of Oct. 16, 1933, pp. 232-33.

141. Zuccotti, *Under His Very Windows*, 180.

142. "Notes de Mgr. Montini," Oct. 1, 1943, *Actes et Documents*, vol. 9, p. 496, no. 356.

143. Congregation for the Causes of Saints, *Positio*, appendix 25, 281.

144. In a later article, Zuccotti acknowledged this meaning of these indications. Susan Zuccotti, "Pope Pius XII and the Rescue of the Jews in Italy: Evidence of a Papal Directive?" 18 *Holocaust and Genocide Studies*, 255 n. 9 (Fall 2004).

145. Zuccotti somehow tries to diminish this intervention by reporting that it "should be described not as an official diplomatic protest of the roundup but as a desperate plea for Weizsäcker's intervention to save the victims." *Under His Very Windows*, 160.

146. See Day, 22 (listing him among the anti-Nazi German leaders who were willing to risk their lives to topple the regime).

147. Italics added for consistency.

148. Zuccotti, *Under His Very Windows*, 159; see "Notes du cardinal Maglione," Oct. 16, 1943, *Actes et Documents*, vol. 9, p. 505, no. 368. Even critic James Carroll gave Maglione's entire text in his book *Constantine's Sword*, 525-526.

149. Zuccotti, *Under His Very Windows*, 103. Zuccotti accused Valeri of manufacturing papal interventions on behalf of the Jews. See also Blet, 234-35.

150. See "Talk on Racial Stand by Pius XII Is Published," *New York Times*, April 4, 1964 ("Excerpts from a wartime address by Eugène Cardinal Tisserant show that the late Pope Pius XII often underlined the

doctrine that 'men have the same rights, whatever their origin might be' and that 'many times he helped those who were being persecuted because of their birth.'")

151. Tisserant, Interview, *Informations Catholiques*, April 15, 1964. See also O'Carroll, 14, 69.

152. "French Cardinal Condemned Nazis," *New York Times*, Feb. 26, 1964, p. 41.

153. Tisserant, Interview, *Informations Catholiques*, April 15, 1964; O'Carroll, 14, 69.

154. See Stewart, 74.

155. Robert Leiber, "Pio XII e Gli Ebrei di Roma, 1943-1944," *Civiltà Cattolica*, Feb. 1961, vol. 1, 449.

156. "Le père Marie-Benoît à Mgr. Montini," Nov. 5, 1943, *Actes et Documents*, vol. 9, p. 344, no. 412.

157. Both Waagenaar and Zuccotti cite an obscure article, attributed to Father Benoît, suggesting that he received no real assistance from the Vatican. "*Alcune precisazioni di Padre Benedetto,*" *Israel XLVI*, 36, July 6, 1961, 5. The article does not, however, appear to be credible. Not only does it contradict Benoît's other statements and those of his closest collaborator, Fernande Leboucher, it also is contradicted by Vatican archival records. See "Note of the Secretariat of State," Jan. 9, 1944, *Actes et Documents*, vol. 9, p. 544-45 (attached to document 412). Perhaps most importantly, it refers to Monsignor Antonio Riberi as the apostolic nuncio to Italy — a post he never held. All rescuers in wartime Italy — and certainly Benoît — would have known that this post was held by Francesco Borgongini-Duca.

158. Congregation for the Causes of Saints, *Positio*, appendix 25, 282; Leboucher (introduction).

159. Ibid., 141, 167-68. See also James Rorty, "Father Benoît: Ambassador of the Jews," *Commentary*, December 1946, 507, 513 ("The Nazis were never sure how much support Benoît was getting, or would get, from the Vatican. The record shows that he got a good deal.")

160. Lapide, 187-88, citing Document No. CXLV a-60 in the Archives of the Centre de Documentation Juive in Paris. See also Catholic Information Network, "In the Spirit of Christianity: Exhibition Online (History)," *The Holocaust World Resource Center*, copyright 1999-2000: *http://www.hwrc.org/inthespirit/vatican.html* .

161. Zuccotti, *Under His Very Windows*, 63.

162. *Summi Pontificatus*, n. 48. See pp. 380-93.

163. Zuccotti, *Under His Very Windows*, 308.

164. The doctrine of subsidiarity teaches that "it is an injustice, a grave evil and a disturbance of right order for a larger and higher organization to arrogate to itself functions which can be performed efficiently by smaller and lower bodies." Pope Pius XI, *Quadragesimo Anno* (1931).

165. Pius wrote specifically about this issue in a letter to Bishop Preysing on April 30, 1943. *Letters de Pie XII aux Evêques Allemands, 1939-1944, Actes et Documents*, vol. 2, p. 318. See Sereny, 297 (noting that Pius also thanked Preysing for a bold sermon on the rights of all men, regardless of race or nationality). See *Actes et Documents*, vol. 2, p. 322. See also Congregation for the Causes of Saints, *Positio*, appendix 25, 246 (reprinting the prologue to Levai, *Hungarian Jewry and the Papacy: Pope Pius Did Not Remain Silent*) ("A public protest against the persecution of the Jews could only lead to the partial success of gaining time when it was made at a politically and militarily opportune time....")

166. Congregation for the Causes of Saints, *Positio* (Summarium). See p. 558, note 51.

167. Among the witnesses quoted by the Congregation for the Causes of Saints in appendix 25 to the *Positio* (which deals with the kind of charges Zuccotti leveled) are: Pascalina Lehnert, Giovanni Stefanori, Maria Conrada Grabmair, Riccardo Lombardi, Giacomo Martegani, Carlo Pacelli, Cesidio Lolli, Enrico Galeazzi, Igino Giordani, Quirino Paganuzzi, Angelo Martini, P. Paolo Dezza, Cardinale Pietro Palazzini, and P. Giacomo Martegani. Congregation for the Causes of Saints, *Positio*, appendix 25, 285-90. There are also discussions of statements made by John Patrick Carroll-Abbing, Michael Tagliacozzo, and Adolf Eichmann. Ibid., 290-93 (quoting Ronald J. Rychlak, "Comments on Zuccotti's *Under His Very Windows*," 7 J. *Modern Italian Studies*, 218 (2002).

168. *Inside the Vatican*, June 1997, 25 (quoting Father Peter Gumpel).

169. Pietro Palazzini, *Il clero e l'occupazione tedesca di Roma: Il ruolo del Seminario Romano Maggiore*, 19, 29 (Apes: Rome, 1995).

170. Ibid., 16-17; see Ibid., 35.

171. *Osservatore della Domenica*, June 28, 1964, 68-69.

172. Paolo Dezza, *Osservatore della Domenica*, June 28, 1964, 68-69. See also Carol Glatz Pius (CNS), "Pius XII feared outcry against atrocities would worsen situation," Feb. 2, 2010 (reprinting portions and quoting from the 1964 article written by Paolo Cardinal Dezza) ("When the Germans occupied Rome in 1943, the late Italian cardinal said Pope Pius encouraged him to use the pontifical university as a refuge for 'civilians, Jews and the persecuted.'")

173. Personal correspondence with the author. See Ronald J. Rychlak, "A 'Righteous Gentile' Defends Pius XII," *Zenit News*, Oct. 5, 2002; Religious News Service, "Holocaust Hero Defends Papacy," *Wanderer*, Sept. 30, 1983. See also Harvey Rosenfeld, *Raul Wallenberg: Angel of Rescue*, 72-81 (Prometheus: Buffalo, 1982); Kay Lyons, "Hungarian Catholic Given Highest Honors in Israel," *Western New York Catholic Visitor*, March 4, 1979, 6A-7A.

174. Interview with Don Aldo Brunacci: "The Secret Letter," *Inside the Vatican*, January 2004, 74. Quite similarly, Prof. Michael Tagliacozzo a Jewish historian who survived the infamous roundup of Oct. 16, 1943, said: "Susan Zuccotti is a very clever writer but ambiguous and tendentious. She widely writes of documentations regarding events and circumstances near what she thought herself, while she only allows a limited space for her opponent's documentations. In fact, she is prejudiced towards Pope Pius XII's work." Alberto De Marco, Interview of Prof. Michael Tagliacozzo: *www.PTWF.org* (Emilia Palmieri Collins, trans.).

175. *Avvenire*, June 27, 1996 (direct order from Pius to admit Jews to hospital prior to police sweep); *CWN*, "More Echoes on Pope Pius XII, Nazi Holocaust," June 27, 1996.

176. Antonio Gaspari, *The Jews Saved by Pius XII (Gli ebrei salvati da Pio XII)* (2001); "New Revelations on Jews Saved by Pius XII," Zenit News Service, Feb. 16, 2001.

177. Marchione, *Yours Is a Precious Witness*, 6.

178. The new documents are archived on the web page of Pave the Way Foundation: *www.PTWF.org*.

179. Gaspari, *Gli ebrei salvati da Pio XII*.

180. "New Revelations on Jews Saved by Pius XII," Zenit News Service, Feb. 16, 2001. See also *Encyclopedia of the Holocaust* (Macmillan, New York, 1990) ("In many monasteries, churches, and ecclesiastical buildings in Italy, Jews were saved during the Nazi occupation, and the simultaneous opening of so many Catholic institutions could have taken place only under clear instructions of Pius XII.") This entry was written by Professor Israel Gutman, the chief historian at Yad Vashem.

181. Rabbi David Dalin, "Pius XII and the Jews," *Weekly Standard*, Feb. 26, 2001, 39.

182. See the inter-office memo written by a World Jewish Congress officer "closely involved in these matters" that is reprinted in the Appendix, p. 418. See also p. 265.

183. On Feb. 26, 2001, Zuccotti and I debated at Trinity College in Hartford, Connecticut. It was recorded and later broadcast on C-SPAN2's Book TV. In that debate, she also dismissed the testimony of Rabbi Zolli simply because he later became a Catholic. See p. 232.

184. "Zuccotti and [Michael] Phayer have ignored (not the "big picture" — but that too) clear evidence which refutes their basic contentions." Justus George Lawler, "Review Symposium: Proleptic Response," 20 *U.S. Catholic Historian*, 89, 93 (2002).

185. Oppen, 409.

186. See Rychlak, "A Dangerous Thing to Do," Chapter 3 in *The Pius War*. Justus George Lawler, author of *Popes and Politics: Reform, Resentment, and the Holocaust*, noted an injustice in Zuccotti's analysis:

It is noteworthy that when *L'Osservatore Romano* publishes an antisemitic sermon, it speaks not just for its editors but for "Vatican officials," "if not for the pope himself," — the very mention of the pope, of course, unsubtly suggests, "but yes possibly also for him." (And the homily is that of [in Zuccotti's words] "a *mere* bishop in the *prestigious* Osservatore Romano.") When, however, that journal publishes — to take an example from current critics of Pius — two attacks on the antisemitism of Kristallnacht, it is dismissed as "an unofficial voice," that does not represent "the views of the Vatican," *much less* of the pope.

Justus George Lawler, "Review Symposium: Postscriptum Response," 20 *U.S. Catholic Historian*, 96, 113 (2002). Lawler goes on to explain that against this background, Zuccotti's statements "are at best disingenuous." Ibid. He notes her "cagey gambit of heavily footnoting her flying headers into the conjectural ether" — particularly her derogatory conclusions from *ex silentio* arguments which lead to "reliance on unverifiable" assumptions such as, "but he [Maglione] never denied the report." He elaborates: that is, "escalation by insinuation. And when it is a tactic that runs through an entire book, it is called bias. Whether it is virulent depends on whether and how effectively one has been inoculated against falsehood." Ibid., 117. Lawler provides this example:

Whereas the entire world of Vatican officialdom is depicted as knowledgeable in 1941 of the Nazi concentration camps and, less than a year later, of the beginning of the extermination process, in *The Holocaust, the French, and the Jews* virtually no one seemed to know of the camps. The French are exonerated by succumbing to "a failure of imagination." In the summer of 1943, according to Zuccotti, the head of the largest Jewish organization in France when informed of the mass execution of Jews, "still found it unimaginable." Whereas in Italy in that same summer, she tells us, "Vatican officials *were perfectly aware* of the fact [that] *millions* of European Jews had been murdered in the Soviet Union and in Poland."

Ibid., 115. Lawler explains that in Zuccotti's earlier book:

[S]he cites the opinion of Leon Poliakov and others, that the Vichy government knew of the exterminations by mid-1943. She then adds: "These statements, however, all address the question of factual knowledge rather than emotional belief. To his own statement, Poliakov adds tellingly, 'I did not believe it myself until April 1945.' "

Ibid., 116. In *Under His Very Windows*, as Lawler notes, neither Pius nor anyone else at the Vatican is allowed this distinction between factual knowledge and emotional belief. Lawler openly implies that Zuccotti has a virulent bias against the Vatican or the Pope and that she is incapable of objectivity when writing about them. The disconnect between her two books is given as "only one example of such bias." Lawler, 20 *U.S. Catholic Historian*, 116.

187. Cornwell, *Hitler's Pope*, 95.

188. See Robert G. Weisbord and Michael W. Honhart, "A Question of Race: Pope Pius XII and the 'Coloured Troops' in Italy," *Historian*, December 2002, 403-17.

189. "Monsignor Tardini to the Nuncio in France, Roncalli," Feb. 26, 1945, *Actes et Documents*, vol. 10, p. 547, no. 455 ("It is known here that the French government has planned to occupy... northern regions of Italy with Moroccan troops. The Holy See has been sincerely asked to intervene... on account of the acts of violence already done by the above-mentioned troops in various parts of southern and central Italy.") See also "Eccessi delittuosi," *L'Osservatore Romano*, July 28, 1944 (report of brutality by Moroccan troops against women).

190. "Monsignor Tardini to the Nuncio in France, Roncalli," Feb. 26, 1945, *Actes et Documents*, vol. 10, p. 547, no. 455. In fact, Pius did not want any troops to engage in unlawful activities. He was similarly critical of atrocities committed by white troops on both sides of the war. E.g., O'Carroll, 18-19, 134-36. On the other hand, he complimented the conduct of Allied troops who were in Italy. "Pope Compliments Army: Pope Praises Fine Example and Conduct of Allied Troops," *New York Times*, Aug. 20, 1944.

191. Memo dated Nov. 4, 1944 (stamp number 101307).

192. "Notizie Italiane," *L'Osservatore Romano*, Oct. 4, 1944, 1.

193. "Monsignor Tardini to the Nuncio in France, Roncalli," Feb. 26, 1945, *Actes et Documents*, vol. 10, p. 547, no. 455.

194. *Tablet* (London), Oct. 5, 1940, 269; Speaight, 27.

195. Dan McFeely, *Indianapolis Star*, June 2, 2003, 1B.

196. This was reprinted in *L'Osservatore Romano* on May 28, 1946, 1. See also "Pope Pius XII and the Negro," *Interracial Review*, Dec. 1939, 179.

197. Zuccotti treats her readers to an extended discussion of an order that went out to expel refugees from Church properties. Only after a long, speculative discussion about pressures put on refugees to leave Vatican properties does she explain that the order was not enforced within the Vatican and had virtually no impact anywhere (those affected by it were referred to other Church properties). It is obvious to anyone giving it a fair reading that the unenforced order was nothing more than a means of appearing to comply with Nazi orders while still protecting the Jews. Congregation for the Causes of Saints, *Positio*, appendix 25, 283. Such deception was necessary at that time. Considering her focus on original documents, it is worth noting that Zuccotti was unable to find any document linking Pius to the expulsion order. See Ronald J. Rychlak, "Comments on Zuccotti's *Under His Very Windows*," 7 *J. Modern Italian Studies*, 218 (2002), cited as the definitive response to Zuccotti in Congregation for the Causes of Saints, *Positio*, appendix 25, 279.

198. Lewy, 303-4, 400 n. 147.

199. See Sánchez, *Pius XII and the Holocaust: Understanding the Controversy*, 98-99.

200. Lewy, 336.

201. Compare Ernst Troeltsch, *The Social Teachings of the Christian Churches*, trans. by Olive Wyon (New York, 1960).

202. Lewy, 336.

203. Oppen, *Nazis and Christians*, 394-95 (1969).

204. Falconi probably was confused by the contradictory evidence that he found. Consider this observation from an early review critical of the book: "[T]here are excellent citations in the book, especially by Pius XII, giving all the defense needed. But these are patronizingly explained away on psychological grounds." Whitall N. Perry, "Book Review: The Silence Of Pius XII, by Carlo Falconi," 5:1 *Studies in Comparative Religion* (Winter 1971).

205. Consider, **Chapter 1**: The Collapse of Yugoslavia in 1941; **Chapter 2**: Croatia in the Twenty Years of Yugoslav Rule; **Chapter 3**: How the NDH was Received by the Catholics; **Chapter 4**: The Persecution of the Orthodox Serbs; **Chapter 5**: The Croatian Catholic Episcopate Between Intransigence of Principle and Adaptation to Reality; **Chapter 6**: The Vatican Was Aware of Ustaše Crimes; **Chapter 7**: The Contradictory Attitude of the Vatican Towards Forced "Re-Baptism" and the Persecution of the Orthodox Serbs.

206. "Some of the heaviest-handed documentation comes in the 134 pages on the Croatian episode." Whitall N. Perry, "Book Review: The Silence of Pius XII, by Carlo Falconi," 5:1 *Studies in Comparative Religion* (Winter 1971).

207. Prior to the German invasion of Yugoslavia (April 6, 1941), the Diocese of Maribor consisted of 654,000 members, 254 parishes, 474 members of the secular clergy, and 109 members of the religious clergy. Within three months of the German invasion, the Gestapo arrested, killed, or expelled 85 percent of the clergy. Of the original 254 parishes, only 91 remained, each headed by a single priest. The others were closed or taken over by German authorities. The district of Ptuj originally had 30 parishes and 57 priests. It was left with just one active and two retired priests to minister to 80,000 Catholics. Similarly, in the Diocese of Ljubljana, the area occupied by the Germans had 128 parishes. By the end of June 1941, 137 priests had been

killed, 74 were expelled and 37 others had fled. That left only 9 priests to minister to 215,000 Catholics. Cianfarra, 266.

208. The full original name of the organization was *Ustaša — Hrvatska revolucionarna organizacija* or UHRO (Ustaša — Croatian revolutionary organization). In 1933, it was renamed as *Ustaša — Hrvatski revolucionarni pokret* (Ustaša — Croatian revolutionary movement). The name comes from the word *ustati* which means "to rise" or "to stand up." Accordingly, *ustaša* meant an insurgent or a rebel. It did not have Fascist connotations during the party's early years. On the formation of Croatia, see Krišto, *The Catholic Church in Croatia and Bosnia-Herzegovina*, vol. 1, 39, 51-53.

209. Heffron, *Croatia's Fearless Defender*. See generally Ronald J. Rychlak, "Cardinal Stepinac and the Roman Catholic Church in Croatia During the Second World War," in *Stepinac: A Witness to the Truth*, 53 (English) and 213 (Croatian).

210. Some critics also charge that the Croatian Catholic Church hid war criminals after the war and helped Nazi gold make its way from Croatia to the Vatican. As for the allegations regarding gold and money taken abroad from the independent Croatian state during 1944-45, author Jere Jareb examined all the relevant documents. He found no evidence that Pavelić or the Ustashe deposited stolen gold at the Vatican, much less that Pius XII approved of such acts. Jere Jareb, *Zlato i novac Nezavisne Države Hrvatske izneseni u inozemstvo 1944 i 1945* (Hrvatski institut za povijest Dom i svijet: Zagreb, 1997); see "Croatian Catholics and Jewish Gold," *Inside the Vatican*, August-September 1998, 11. A lawsuit based on this claim (*Emil Alperin, et al., Plaintiffs, v. Vatican Bank, et al., Defendants*) was dismissed by the U.S. District Court for the Northern District of California on Dec. 27, 2007. On forced conversions, see pp. 358-59.

211. Pattee, 211.

212. Ibid., 211-12.

213. Alexander, *The Triple Myth*, 113.

214. Barton.

215. Ibid.; see "Prvislav Grisogono and an Apocryphal Letter to Archbishop Stepinac": *http://www.churchinhistory.org/pages/leftpane/documentation/grisogono.htm*.

216. Barton; Lackovic, 19.

217. Barton; Krišto, "The Catholic Church in Croatia," 88, n. 185 ("When today some authors sensationally announce that they have discovered new proofs about the harbouring of war criminals by the Vatican … they do not reveal that their sources are often those very accusations of the Communists from Yugoslavia and other countries under Communist dictatorship.")

218. Savor; Barton; Hinshaw, 26. Stepinac's innocence is now recognized by virtually all scholars. See generally *Stepinac: A Witness to the Truth*. For a collection of documents vindicating Stepinac, see *Proces Alojziju Stepiincu* (Marina Štambuk-Skalić, et al., eds.) Kršćanska sadašnjost: Zagreb, 1997. For Stepinac's anti-Nazi wartime sermons, see *Propovijedi, govori, poruke* (J. Batelja and C. Tomić, eds), AGM: Zagreb, 1996; and *Three Sermons Against Racism by Archbishop Stepinac* (Church in History Information center: Birkenhead, 1998). See also Aleksa Benigar, *Alojzije Stepinac, hrvatski kardinal* (Ziral, Zagreb, 2nd ed. 1993); Ivan Mužić, *Pavelić i Stepinac* (Logos: Split, 1991) (the archbishop's struggle against Pavelić); "Vatican Book Justifies Cardinal Stepinac: Example of Opposition to Fascism, Nazism and Communism," Zenit News, March 10, 1999; Alain Finkielkraut, "*Msgr. Stepinac et les deux douleurs de L'Europe*," *Le Monde*, Oct. 7, 1998 (rebuking critics of Stepinac).

219. Alexander, *The Triple Myth*, 147; Barton. "He was a man who was disliked by the Nazis as well as the Communists for refusing to compromise the interests of the Catholic Church to the regimes of the moment. Stepinac was aware of the fact that both the Nazis and the Communists were plotting to kill him." Gitman, 70.

220. "Assembly Condemns Communist Treatment of Cardinal Stepinac and Andrija Hebrang," *BBC Summary of World Broadcasts*, Feb. 17, 1992.

> The newly elected Croatian parliament rehabilitated Cardinal Stepinac by annulling the results of all Bolshevik-style trials under the former Yugoslav Communist regime. The parliament specifically stated that the only reason for the cardinal's conviction was Stepinac's refusal to lead a schism.

Stilinovic.

221. "Assembly Condemns Communist Treatment of Cardinal Stepinac and Andrija Hebrang," *BBC Summary of World Broadcasts*, Feb. 17, 1992; Peter Hebblethwaite, "John Paul's uphill pilgrimage to Zagreb," *National Catholic Reporter*, Sept. 23, 1994, 7.

222. Alexander, *The Triple Myth*, 138; Barton.

223. Sabrina P. Ramet, *Balkanski Babilon* 113 (Zagreb: Alinea, 2005). See also Tanner at 180; Barton.

224. Krišto, "The Catholic Church and the Jews," 44.

225. Ibid.

226. Ibid.

227. Cornwell, *Hitler's Pope*, 47, 169, 173, 251, 254, 259, 262, 321, 352.

228. Krišto went on to explain: "Ronald J. Rychlak responded at length to Cornwell in *Hitler, the War, and the Pope*.... For understandable reasons, not even Rychlak knew that both Falconi and Cornwell based their judgments on the Catholic Church in Croatia and on Pope Pius XII on falsified documents from the Yugoslav secret police." Krišto, *The Catholic Church and the Jews*, 44, note 150. Former KGB counterintelligence agent Anatoliy Golitsyn was speaking in general terms, but he could have been talking about the Stepinac evidence when he explained: "While observers in the noncommunist world sometimes showed some awareness that information was reaching them through channels under communist control, there was virtually no recognition of the fact that the information had been specially prepared behind the Iron Curtain for their benefit." Golitsyn, 310.

229. Historians rely on documents to understand what happened at a given time. Great credibility is attributed to contemporaneous written evidence. In most cases, that makes perfect sense. As this episode reveals, however, when governmental agencies engage in intentional disinformation campaigns, contemporaneous written evidence may be very misleading. Noncontemporaneous fictionalized plays, like *The Deputy*, are even more misleading.

230. "The Catholic Church... considers all men as brothers and teaches them to love one another.... This law must be observed and respected in the case of the children of Israel, as well as of all others...." Cardinal Gasparri, Secretary of State, Replies to the Petition of the American Jewish Committee of New York, Feb. 9, 1916, in *Principles for Peace*, 198-99.

231. On March 25, 1928, an official decree of the Holy Office condemned anti-Semitism: "Moved by the spirit of charity, the Apostolic See has protected the people [of Israel] against unjust persecutions, and since it condemns all jealousy and strife among peoples, it accordingly condemns with all its might the hatred directed against a people which was chosen by God; that particular hatred, in fact, which today commonly goes by the name anti-Semitism." For the official Latin text of the decree, see the *Acta Apostolicae Sedis*, Volume XX, pp. 103-104.

232. On Oct. 11, 1930, the Vatican's newspaper, *L'Osservatore Romano*, decreed in an editorial: "The Party of Hitler Stands Condemned by the Ecclesiastical Authorities.... Belonging to the National Socialist Party of Hitler is irreconcilable with the Catholic conscience."

233. Both Pius XI and Secretary of State Pacelli argued that "spiritually we are all Semites." See pp. 123-24.

234. See pp. 205-7, 215. Out of disgust at the number of Jews that were released from Nazi-occupied areas due to Vatican pressure, the Third Reich circulated 10 million copies of a pamphlet saying that Pius XII inspired a lack of confidence in the Catholic world. *Tablet* (London), Oct. 24, 1942, 202 (quoting the *Jewish Chronicle*).

235. As reported by the *Tablet* (London), Rabbi Lazaron

> goes on to quote the Pope's condemnation of anti-Semitism, and the action taken by Bishops and priests throughout occupied Europe to protect Jews "driven like animals" from their homes. "They have shielded and healed them at the risk of their own lives, and indeed many priests have been killed and not a few killed in their effort." But it is more than a mere reciprocal gesture which prompts our prayers for His Holiness. We can place ourselves in the position of our Catholic friends.... We link our prayers with theirs. May God protect and keep His Holiness in strength and all good.

Quoted in the *Tablet* (London), Dec. 25, 1943, 306. Rabbi Morris S. Lazaron, writing in the *Baltimore Synagogue Bulletin*, affirmed that "the Pope has condemned anti-Semitism and all its works. Bishops of the Church have appeared in the streets... with the Shield of David on their arms.... Indeed, many priests and ministers have been jailed and not a few killed in their effort to protect Jews." *Catholic Mind*, June 1964, 26.

236. Such statements were consistent with the Vatican's official and well-publicized condemnations of anti-Semitism, including Vatican Radio's explicit defense of Jews (January 1940); Pius XII's defense of Jews during his confrontational meeting with Ribbentrop (March, 1940); Pius XII's order that the pro-Jewish pastorals of the French bishops be read over Vatican Radio; and many other statements in *L'Osservatore Romano* and in papal Christmas messages. See Besier, 79 (Pacelli's personal interest in *L'Osservatore Romano*).

237. Halecki, 340; Joseph L. Lichten, "A Question of Judgment: Pius XII and the Jews," in *Pius XII and the Holocaust: A Reader*, 127; Stewart, 60. Pius had a lifelong Jewish friend, Dr. Guido Mendes. In 1939, Pius helped the Mendes family escape to Palestine. *Jewish Chronicle*, Oct. 11, 1963.

238. Quoted in Purdy, 42.

239. Ibid. The strength of this anti-Nazi statement was noted by U.S. Representative Harold Tittmann. *Inside the Vatican of Pius XII*, 213 (memo dated June 4, 1945, and referring to the Pope "attacking the Nazis in public").

240. Office of the United States Chief Counsel, vol. I, at 285-86; Shirer, *The Rise and Fall of the Third Reich*, 324-25 (footnote).

241. The full text of the address appears in Margherita Marchione, *Pope Pius XII: Architect for Peace*, 143-152. See also Office of the United States Chief Counsel, vol. I, at 285-86; Shirer, *The Rise and Fall of*

*the Third Reich*, 324-25 (footnote); Purdy, 43. Cornwell criticized Pius for diminishing the number in his 1942 Christmas statement. Pius referred to hundreds of thousands of victims, instead of millions. Surely no responsible party in the free world knew that the victims numbered in the millions by 1942. In September 1942, a report from the Inter-Allied Information Committee claimed that the Nazis had killed 207,373 people in occupied territories. F. Murphy, 201-2. In fact, the Allied statement that Pius declined to join in also referred to "hundreds of thousands," not millions.

242. *La vostra presenza*, Nov. 29, 1945. Extracts were published in the *Tablet*, Dec. 8, 1945. Quoted in Purdy, 262; *Acta Apostolicae Sedis*, 37 (Dec. 23, 1945), 317-18; *L'Osservatore Romano*, Nov. 30, 1945, 1; *Tablet*, Dec. 8, 1945, 277. See also Pius XII's address to representatives of the United Jewish Appeal, on relief work in Europe and Palestine, Feb. 9, 1948, *L'Osservatore Romano*, Feb. 9-10, 1948; *Tablet*, Feb. 14, 1948, 105; *New York Times*, Feb. 10, 1948, 13. See "Jewish Leaders Have Papal Audience," *Catholic World*, January 1946, 370.

243. "Jewish Leaders Have Papal Audience," *Catholic World*, January 1946, 370.

244. Ibid.

245. McCormick, 134 (from a *New York Times* dispatch of Feb. 20, 1946). McCormick reports that Pius told her that he planned to accomplish this internationalization project well before the nominations were announced. Ibid.

246. The largest group of nominees came from the United States, and there were several from other North American countries, causing some Europeans to complain about the "Americanization" of the Church. McCormick, 131.

247. McCormick, 132 (from a *New York Times* dispatch of Dec. 26, 1945).

248. James W. Demers, *The Last Roman Catholic?* 24 (1991), citing Francis X. Murphy, *The Papacy Today*, 15 (1981); McCormick, 134 (similar quote).

249. *Tablet* (of London), Aug. 24, 1946, at 97 (excerpts). The full text of the allocution, entitled, *Nous sommes heureux*, appears (in its original French) in the Vatican's official *Acta Apostolicae Sedis*, vol. 38, 1946, pp. 322-323; also published, in Italian, in *L'Osservatore Romano*, Aug. 15, 1946, and English excerpts in the *New York Times*, Aug. 15, 1946, p. C-3.

250. The memorandum is included in the Appendix, p. 412.

251. The memorandum is included in the Appendix, p. 416.

252. "Pontiff Deplores Racial Injustices; He Tells U.S. Jewish Group That He Supports Its Fight for the Rights of Man," *New York Times*, June 29, 1957; Dimitri Cavalli, "The Good Samaritan: Jewish Praise for Pope Pius XII," *Inside the Vatican*, October 2000, 76. See "Pope Asks World to Aid Refugees: Tells American Jewish Unit He Opposes "Evil Blight" of Racial Persecution," *New York Times*, July 29, 1957.

253. Letter from His Holiness to President Truman, August 26, 1947, reprinted in *Correspondence Between Presisdent Truman and Pope Pius XII* (Myron C. Talyor, ed., Kessinger Publishing, 2005).

254. Letter of July 12, 1946, to Montini, quoted in the *Ecumenist*, 39 (Spring 2002), 1-3. Maritain went on to request a new Papal statement against anti-Semitism, and within weeks Pius XII issued his aforementioned Aug. 3, 1946 condemnation.

255. Peter Novick, *The Holocaust in American Life*, 316, n. 77 (Houghton Mifflin, 1999); "Dulles to Attend Rites for Pontiff," *New York Times*, Oct. 11, 1958, 2 (same).

256. The claims of Catholic anti-Semitism that surrounded the release of Mel Gibson's movie *The Passion of the Christ* merely brought to public attention a charge that had already been made repeatedly in the Pius XII debate. Why is it that the Catholic Church and its leaders have been singled our for this charge? Because the Catholic Church is responsible for the New Testament as we know it today. These critics argue that the Gospels are not historically accurate and that the story of Christ was revised to include anti-Semitic messages in order to advance certain political agendas long after the Crucifixion. These critics, including Goldhagen and Carroll, want the Catholic Church (and, presumably, other Christians) either to modify the Gospels or to acknowledge that they contain error and to preach against those portions of Scripture. They seem to be urging an ancient heresy called Marcionism, which eliminated politically unwelcome passages from the Bible. See Donald Attwater, *A Catholic Dictionary*, 305 (1958).

257. See W. Robert Aufill, "A Look at Dave Hunt, Leading Anti-Catholic Fundamentalist," *New Oxford Review* (January 1999), 30.

258. Illustrative of his biased analysis, Goldhagen twists Pacelli's 1933 promise not to interfere "in Germany's internal political affairs" into "the Church's intention to let the Germans have a free hand with the Jews." See Ronald J. Rychlak, "Daniel Goldhagen's Assault on Christianity," 4 *Totalitarian Movements & Political Religions*, 184 (2003); Ronald J. Rychlak, "Goldhagen v. Pius XII," *First Things*, June/July 2002, 37-54.; Ronald J. Rychlak, "Book Review: A Moral Reckoning: The Role of the Catholic Church in the Holocaust and Its Unfulfilled Duty of Repair, by Daniel Goldhagen," *Catholic Historical Review*, April 2003; Ronald J. Rychlak, "Another Reckoning: A Response to Daniel Goldhagen's *A Moral Reckoning*," *Crisis*, January 2003.

259. Joseph Cardinal Bernardin delivered a notable lecture at the Hebrew University in Jerusalem on March 23, 1995. It was entitled "Antisemitism: The Historical Legacy and the Continuing Challenge for

Christians," and in it the cardinal acknowledged that portions of the Gospels, particularly the Gospel of John "remain open to anti-Judaic interpretation." Bernardin, however, drew on historical research, modern Catholic teaching, and current biblical interpretation to show how anti-Semitic arguments come from a misunderstanding of the original contexts of the texts, not from the Gospels themselves. In the end, Bernardin sided with those scholars "who have insisted that 'the Holocaust was the work of a thoroughly modern, neopagan state,' not merely a 'transformed' medieval antisemitism rooted in Christian teachings." Ibid.

260. "Even in John's Gospel, where he refers to these people on occasion simply as 'the Jews,' he makes clear that he is referring to the elite leadership of the second-Temple." David B. Currie, "Are the Gospels Anti-Semitic?" *This Rock*, March 2004, 6, 7 (citing John 7:25-32, 48; 8:13, 22; 11:45; 12:42; 18:3, 14).

261. Luke 19:41-44; 22:2.

262. "Jesus never lost his obvious compassion for and identification with the crowds of Jewish people. In fact, that is what drove his anger with the leaders: They were leading their flock away." David B. Currie, "Are the Gospels Anti-Semitic?" *This Rock*, March 2004, 6, 8.

263. Because of the controversy over this line, it was eliminated from Mel Gibson's movie *The Passion of the Christ*.

264. Francis Spirago, *Anecdotes and Examples for the Catechism* (Roman Catholic Books: Fort Collins, CO., 1903). The wording once again makes clear that Catholics saw Jewishness as an issue of faith, not race.

265. See *Catechism of the Catholic Church* (no. 597).

266. "Pilate holds a preeminent place of moral culpability in this tragic affair. We are reminded of his failure each time we recite the Apostles' Creed." David B. Currie, "Are the Gospels Anti-Semitic?" *This Rock*, March 2004, 6, 8.

267. See pp. 123-24.

268. This is available on the Internet through the Vatican's web page. See also Rosalind Moss, "It Was Sin That Killed Our Savior: Reflections on Mel Gibson's *The Passion of the Christ*," *This Rock*, April 2004, 8.

269. "The long and short of it is that modern anti-Semitism does not find fertile soil in those with a full understanding of the New Testament and its teaching.... According to the New Testament, twenty-first-century Jews are no more nor less responsible for Christ's death than the Catholic sinner writing this article." David B. Currie, "Are the Gospels Anti-Semitic?" *This Rock*, March 2004, 6, 9.

270. This was not true of Jewish leadership during the Nazi era. Jewish leaders recognized a serious difference between Christian and Nazi beliefs. A book published by the Jewish Publication Society of America, Marvin Lowenthal, *The Jews of Germany: A Story of 16 Centuries*, 416 (1939), explained why a Jew could never accept the Nazi idea of God: "The new gods of the racial cult are not, like the Christian Deity, his own under another rubric."

271. After Holy Scripture, the writings of Pope Pius XII are the most cited source in the documents of Vatican II. See Congregation for the Causes of Saints, *Positio*, appendix 18: *Documenti del Concilio Vaticano II Nei Quali si fa Riferimento a Testi di Pio XII*, p. 147-72 (reprinted from *Pie XII et la Cité: La pensée et l'action politiques de Pie XII*).

272. Those who are interested in learning more about Catholic teaching regarding relations with Jews (which should include *every* reader who treated Goldhagen's book with any degree of respect) are advised to read *Nostra Aetate*, the Second Vatican Council's renewal of the Church's condemnation of anti-Semitism. This author has taken part in interfaith dialogue and was a signatory to the *Nashville Declaration on the Church and the Holocaust* (honored at the U.S. Holocaust Museum, Feb. 6, 2007).

273. See Joseph R. Estes, "Jewish-Christian Dialogue as Mission," *LXVIII Review and Expositor: Religious Dialogue in the Modern World*, 5 (Winter 1971) ("The history of Jewish-Christian relations is one of almost unbroken conflict from the apostolic era to modern times.")

274. St. John Chrysostom wrote a number of sermons that preached against "the Jews," but patristics scholars have shown that he (like St. Paul in Galatians) was speaking to Christians who clung to Jewish observances as an expression of a false doctrine of grace and salvation. St. John Chrysostom and St. Paul both used sarcasm in their sermons, but "they were not 'anti-Semetic' in the modern sense of the term." Hugh Barbour, "Has the Church Ever Taught That the Jews Should Be Persecuted and Segregated?" *Ad Veritatem*, March 2004.

> In the early centuries it was the Jews who persecuted the Christians. The Talmud composed back in those days contains slanders against the Christians that easily rival those directed by modern anti-Semites against the Jews. Early Christian writers were well acquainted with such slanders when penning replies to them in kind for which they are today reproached as anti-Semitic.

Kenneth D. Whitehead, "Prominent Conservatives Join the Chorus Against 'The Passion,'" *Catalyst*, April 2004, 8, 9.

275. For a recent expression of different perceptions of Christians and Jews, see Meir Y. Soloveichik, "The Virtue of Hate," *First Things*, January 2003 (Rabbi Soloveichik is shocked by Christ's last words from the Cross, asking forgiveness for those who crucified him, and suggests an alternative prayer: "Father, forgive

them not; they know full well what they are doing.") Compare Alice von Hildebrand, "The Wounded Heart Forgives: A Catholic Response to the Claim That Hate Is a Virtue," *This Rock*, May/June 2003.

276. An Internet search will reveal many alleged quotations from the Talmud that seem very hostile to Christianity. With further effort, one can find more appropriate translations and interpretations of the Talmud. The Talmud certainly contains many references to righteous gentiles whose behavior is held up as a model for all people (e.g., Dama ben Netina). Nevertheless, there has long been concern over some passages in the Talmud. See Steinsaltz, 82-85.

277. "[I]t was the Church, particularly the popes, that were often the protectors of the Jews from popular outbreaks against them. Pope St. Gregory the Great (590-604) strongly condemned violence against them, called for respect for their worship and liberty of conscience, and counseled equity and kindness towards them. Quite a while before Vatican II, the Second Council of Nicaea (787) decreed that the Jews should be allowed to 'be Hebrews openly, according to their own religion.'" Kenneth D. Whitehead, "Prominent Conservatives Join the Chorus Against 'The Passion,'" *Catalyst*, April 2004, 8, 9.

278. Ibid.

279. A version of the full prayer went like this:

Let us pray also for heretics and schismatics: that our Lord and God would be pleased to rescue them from their errors; and recall them to our holy mother, the Catholic and Apostolic Church. Let us pray. Let us kneel. (Arise.) Almighty and eternal God, Who savest all, and wouldest that no one should perish: look on the souls that are led astray by the deceit of the devil: that having set aside all heretical evil, the hearts of those that err may repent and return to the unity of Thy truth. Through our Lord Jesus Christ, Who livest and reignest with God the Father in the unity of the Holy Ghost, through all endless ages. Amen.

Let us pray also for the perfidious Jews: that our God and Lord may remove the veil from their hearts; that they also may acknowledge Our Lord Jesus Christ. Let us pray. Let us kneel. (Arise.) Almighty and Eternal God, Who dost not exclude from Thy mercy even the perfidious Jews: hear our prayers, which we offer for the blindness of that people; that acknowledging the light of Thy Truth, which is Christ, they may be delivered from their darkness. Through the same Lord Jesus Christ, Who livest and reignest with God the Father in the unity of the Holy Ghost, through all endless ages. Amen.

Let us pray also for the pagans: that Almighty God take away iniquity from their hearts: that leaving aside their idols they may be converted to the true and living God, and His only Son, Jesus Christ our God and Lord. Let us pray. Let us kneel. (Arise.) Almighty and Eternal God, Who seekest always, not the death, but the life of sinners: mercifully hear our prayer, and deliver them from the worship of idols: and admit them into Thy holy Church for the praise and glory of Thy Name. Through our Lord Jesus Christ, Who livest and reignest with God the Father in the unity of the Holy Ghost, through all endless ages. Amen.

280. A modern version of the prayer is as follows:

Let us pray for God's ancient people, the Jews, the first to hear his word: for greater understanding between Christian and Jew; for the removal of our blindness and bitterness of heart; that God will grant us grace to be faithful to his covenant and to grow in the love of his name. (Silent prayer.) Lord, hear us. Lord, graciously hear us. Lord God of Abraham, bless the children of your covenant, both Jew and Christian; take from us all blindness and bitterness of heart, and hasten the coming of your kingdom, when Israel shall be saved, the Gentiles gathered in, and we shall dwell together in mutual love and peace under the one God and Father of our Lord Jesus Christ. Amen.

281. Jacques Maritain, "A Letter on Anti-Semitism," *Commonweal*, Feb. 27, 1948 (referring to "translations of the phrase *perfidia Judaica*... which are no more than vulgar misreadings, for in the language of the Church this word signifies 'unbelief' and not 'perfidiousness.'"); Alexis Bugnolo, "A Note on the Latin Phrase *perfidus Iudaeus*," *Seattle Catholic*, June 27, 2003 ("[T]o transfer this proper meaning to racial categories would be both heretical and diabolic.... If some Catholics have altered this term to racial categories... they have justly merited to be condemned by all the faithful and especially by the Pope.")

282. "Hitler... accepted Charles Darwin's theory of 'the survival of the fittest' and asserted that man had every right to be 'as cruel as nature.' Detailed lectures were given in schools and to SS troops to prove the inferiority of the Jews. Aryan skulls were compared with those of Jewish ancestry to prove on a scientific basis that the latter were hopelessly inferior. Only the 'fittest' had the right to survive." Lutzer, 80.

283. This was the ultimate conclusion of Cardinal Joseph Bernardin when he delivered his lecture, "Anti-semitism: The Historical Legacy and the Continuing Challenge for Christians," at the Hebrew University in Jerusalem on March 23, 1995. See supra note 259, p. 569. Similarly, *Dabru Emet: A Jewish Statement on Christians and Christianity*," a document signed by nearly 170 Jewish scholars, was published in the *New York Times*, Sept. 10, 2000, 23, reprinted in *First Things*, November 2000, 39-44. The document repudiated the effort to blame the Holocaust on Christianity and explicitly declared: "Nazism was Not a Christian

Phenomenon." See also Laurie Goodstein, "Leading Jewish Scholars Extend a Hand to Christians," *New York Times*, Sept. 8, 2000.

284. Victor Frankl, *The Doctor and the Soul: Introduction to Logotherapy* (New York: Knopf, 1982), quoted in Ravi Zacharias, *Can Man Live Without God?* 25 (Dallas: Word, 1994).

285. Hitler also used Hindu doctrines to justify the "Final Solution." Lutzer, 96 ("The cruel doctrine of the caste system, based on mythical ideas about blood, became even more cruel under Hitler's leadership.")

286. Pacelli's view that difficult decisions that could involve the risk of life had to be left to the individuals involved is reflected in an account provided by Dietrich Von Hildebrand, widely regarded as one of the great Catholic philosophers of the 20th century and a noted opponent of Nazism. He visited Cardinal Pacelli during the Nazi era. Pacelli "said that there could be no possible reconciliation between Christianity and racism; they were like 'fire and water.' The interview gave von Hildebrand great satisfaction. He was confident that Cardinal Pacelli was fully aware of the gravity of the situation in Germany." Hildebrand, 285-86.

287. See p. 148.

288. *The Nazi Master Plan: The Persecution of the Christian Churches*.

289. Hildebrand, 285-86.

290. Congregation for the Causes of Saints, *Positio*, appendix 25, 246 (quoting the prologue to Levai, *Hungarian Jewry and the Papacy: Pope Pius Did Not Remain Silent*).

291. Ibid.

292. Religious News Service, "Holocaust Hero Defends Papacy," *Wanderer*, Sept. 30, 1983; Antonio Gaspari, *The Jews Saved by Pius XII (Gli ebrei salvati da Pio XII)* (2001); "New Revelations on Jews Saved by Pius XII," Zenit News Service, Feb. 16, 2001. See also p. 333.

293. Several sources argue that Pius XII wrote an extraordinary secret letter to the Catholic bishops of Europe entitled *Opere et caritate* ("By Work and by Charity"). Author/rescuer Fernande Leboucher wrote of Pius XII's 1942 "command addressed to all Christians, and particularly to the clergy, to the effect that every means available must be employed to save as many lives as possible." Leboucher, 141. Rabbi Zolli wrote: "The Holy Father sent by hand a letter to the bishops instructing them to lift the enclosure from convents and monasteries, so they could become refuges for the Jews." Zolli, *Why I Became a Catholic*, 186. Cardinal Elia Dalla Costa, the archbishop of Florence, reported:

> I've been in Rome long enough to understand the Pope's position. Instead of making meaningless declarations that would only antagonize the Germans, perhaps even make them occupy the Vatican itself, he issued orders — to save Jewish lives. We received his message loud and clear. How would Pietro Boetto in Genoa, Nicolini in Assisi, I here [in Florence] and so many other archbishops and bishops all over Italy, provide a sanctuary of Jews, if we did not feel that that is what His Holiness would wish us to do?... In his own diocese — don't forget that the Pope is also Bishop of Rome — over a hundred convents and over fifty churches and theological seminaries are hiding four thousand Jews, half of the Jews of Rome....

Alexander Ramati, *The Assisi Underground*, 50 (Stein and Day: New York, 1978). Recently, researchers discovered the handwritten archives detailing the 1943 order received directly from Pope Pius XII to help hide the Jews in Rome. It also lists the names of the Jews who were sheltered. The original document can be seen on the web page of Pave the Way Foundation: *www.PTWF.org*. Similarly, when Monsignor Giuseppe Maria Palatucci, the bishop of Campagna, and R. P. Alfonso Palatucci, the provincial of the Franciscan Order in Puglie, were asked what had made them risk their lives for others, both referred to Vatican orders issued in 1942 "to save lives by all possible means." Lapide, 134-35.

294. See Congregation for the Causes of Saints, *Positio*, appendix 25, 290. See also p. 333.

295. This quotation was translated from a Nazi journal and printed in the *Tablet* (of London), vol. 172, 301 (1938).

296. Lapide, 118. This has been called one of the Pope's "most fervent pleas for tolerance." Halecki, 340.

297. According to the authors: "The major powers of the world have repeatedly planned covert operations to bring about the destruction of Israel." During the Six Day War, "[t]he U.S. and British governments, while pretending to be on Israel's side, were giving all of Israel's secrets to the Arabs." Particularly appalling is their discussion of the attack on the *USS Liberty* during the Six Day War. See James M. Ennes, Jr., *Book Review: The Secret War Against the Jews by John Loftus and Mark Aarons*, St. Martin's Press, 1994 ("In the end, the only thing Loftus and Aarons seem to have gotten right is the fact that the attack was no accident.")

298. Byron York, "Liberal Radio and Its Dark Angel: Meet the Amazing Sheldon Drobny," *National Review*, Oct 27, 2003.

299. As revealed in newly unsealed archives, Hudal, who helped Nazi war criminals escape justice at the end of the war, was not a supporter of the Nazis early in the war. Later, he was "kept at arm's length" from positions of responsibility because the Pope and his secretary of state did not trust him. Godman, 169.

300. Robert A. Graham, "Another Phony Chapter on 'Pius and the Nazis,' " *Columbia Magazine*, May 1984, 4; Sereny, 302 (the Vatican had no money to support such an initiative). In fact, Bishop Hudal had connections with the Red Cross and may have used their assets. See Sereny, 306. The moral issue of aiding

Nazis who might be persecuted by Allied forces following the war is raised in the Gregory Peck movie *The Scarlet and the Black* (Avid Home Entertainment, 1983). In this account, based on the true story of the Nazis' occupation of Rome, Gestapo officer Herbert Kappler, in charge of the Roman occupation asks Monsignor Hugh O'Flaherty, a leader of Vatican resistance, to help relocate his family as the Allies are entering Rome. When the priest balks, the German accuses him of being a hypocrite because he had promised to help anyone in need. For a discussion of O'Flaherty's rescue efforts, see pp. 247-48.

301. It might also be noted that — at least according to one witness who was involved in the relocation project — Hudal "helped Jews before he ever helped SS men; he helped more Jews than SS men." Sereny, 314 (quoting Monsignor Karl Bayer). See Lapomarda, 234, n. 16 (dismissing allegations that the Vatican was involved in the moving of Nazis).

302. Sanfilippo's article and others on similar issues can be accessed on CEANA's website, at *www.ceana. org.ar.*

303. Godman, 169; Besier, 144 (Pacelli published an article to distance the Curia from Hudal).

304. See Michael Phayer, "The Silent Pope?" *Moment*, April 2004, 48.

305. In his memoirs, Hudal admitted that he helped war criminals, but he made it clear that this was done without the encouragement or knowledge of the Pope. Alois Hudal, *Römische Tagebücher: Lebensbeichte eines alten Bischofs* (Leopold Stocker Verlag: Stuttgart, 1976).

306. Godman, 169. See also Vincent Lapomarda, *Catholic Historical Review* (October 1992); Sereny, 303.

307. Besier, 146-47. Hudal seems to have wanted the Church to work with Hitler and have a moderating influence on the philosophic side of National Socialism, of which Hudal "never disguised his rejection." Ibid., 146-49.

308. For a strong rebuttal of Goni, see Heinz Schneppen, *Odessa and the Fourth Reich: Myths of contemporary history* (Metropolitan-Verlag, Berlin 2007).

309. Klich's article and others on similar issues can be accessed on CEANA's website, at *www.ceana. org.ar.*

310. Dr. Josef Mengele, notorious for his genetic experiments at Auschwitz, is thought to have escaped from Germany with papers from the International Red Cross. Like Eichmann, he moved to Argentina where he found employment for a period of time working as an abortionist. Mengele died under an assumed name without ever being brought to justice.

311. See BBC News, "Nazis 'swindled' Red Cross," Feb. 18, 1999. Discussing the Vatican and the International Red Cross, German ambassador Weizsäcker said: "It is a matter of course and everybody knows it, that these two agencies of world significance and reputation and worldwide influence would have undertaken any possible step that they considered feasible and useful to save the Jews." O'Connell, 80.

312. One might legitimately wonder why the Vatican or the Red Cross would be involved after the war in moving great numbers of people to nations that clearly were not their homelands. Monsignor Karl Bayer explained that there were four "waves" of help provided to dislocated persons:

> The fourth wave — no doubt the largest by far — came after April-May 1945. This one included nationals of many countries who were in Italy, in POW camps and elsewhere, at that time, and didn't want to return to their communist-controlled homelands; German POWs, some of whom would eventually go home, but many of whom didn't wish to at the time; the Polish Army; the Russian Vlasov army (including 15,000 Ukrainians); large numbers of people fleeing from Yugoslavia, Rumania, Hungary, Austria; and then, of course, the comparatively small group of SS personnel who are the people you are particularly referring to.

Sereny, 308 (footnotes omitted); ibid., 303 (The number of Nazis escaping justice "were very few compared with the huge number of other refugees helped by Catholic institutions, and helped with every justification. No one could question in any way the Vatican's motives in giving money towards helping refugees in general — on the contrary.") For a detailed discussion of an earlier wave, see generally Simpson, *A Vatican Lifeline*.

313. Vincent A. Lapomarda, "Pius XII as 'Phayer's Pope,'" *New Oxford Review*, April 2009. Cornwell's claim that if Pius is given credit for Jews surviving in Rome, he must be implicated in the ratline is a total *non sequitur*. There is hard evidence that Pius gave direct instructions to rescue Jews; but there is no evidence that Pius consciously assisted Nazi war criminals.

314. Sereny, 308 (quoting Monsignor Karl Bayer).

315. Department of State, "Illegal Emigration Movements in and Through Italy," Office of American Republic Affairs, July 14, 1947 (Top Secret, declassified in 1988; USNA:RG59; FW 800-0128/5-1547).

316. Pius put at the disposal of the prosecution an important collection of documents dealing with the persecution of the Church by the Nazi regime. Louis J. Gallagher, *Edmund A. Walsh, S.J., Founder of the Foreign Service School, Georgetown University*, Benziger Brothers (New York, 1959). See also O'Carroll, 138 (suggesting that a memorandum authorized by Pius XII influenced the terms of one charge).

317. Adolf Eichmann is one of the former National Socialist leaders who allegedly escaped Europe with a forged Vatican passport that identified him as one "Ricardo Klement." He also took advantage of monasteries, "where, for centuries, travelers have been given food and shelter by monks." Lyttle, 22. As head of

the Gestapo's Jewish section from 1939 until 1945, Eichmann was responsible for the murder of millions of Jews during the war. After the war, he fled to Argentina, where President/Dictator Juan Perón (perhaps best known today in the United States as the husband of "Evita") welcomed Nazis. Eichmann was captured by the Israeli Secret Service in 1960, deported to Israel, tried, convicted, and executed. Documents from his trial reveal the Vatican's efforts to oppose the Nazis. See p. 34.

318. John Cornwell, who presumably looked very hard for such evidence, found nothing to indicate that the Vatican was intentionally involved in helping Nazis escape justice. Cornwell, 267. See "Declaration on Nazi Refugees After World War II," *Vatican Information Service*, Feb. 14, 1992 (denying any intent to assist war criminals).

319. The Vatican issued a formal denial that it had helped Nazis escape Europe during the war. According to a 1984 news report:

> This response is partly to reports about former SS Colonel Walter Rauff, now in Chile. Rauff reportedly told Chilean authorities his escape after the war included 18 months sheltered in Vatican-run convents in Italy. Father Antonio Weber, who directed the Vatican-run refugee protection project during and after the war, told us today some 20,000 Jews and others fleeing from Hitler were housed in Vatican-owned property off-limits to German troops, like this building which housed 400 people and in many others scattered throughout Rome and Italy. Absolute identification of refugees, he said, was rarely possible in those times, but he insisted no Nazi war criminals were ever knowingly helped by his operation. And in Vienna this morning, Nazi hunter Simon Wiesenthal told ABC News that contrary to *London Sunday Times* reports last week, he has no evidence that Vatican sister Pasqualina, nor the Pope she served, Pius XII, were ever involved in helping Nazis escape.

Peter Jennings, *World News Tonight*, Jan. 30, 1984 (Bill Blakemore reporting).

320. Pinchas E. Lapide, *Three Popes and the Jews* (Hawthorn Books: New York, 1967; Sands and Co.: London, 1968); "The Pope Yesterday and Today," *L'Osservatore Della Domenica*, June 26, 1964 (Lapide article); Joseph L. Lichten, "A Question of Judgment: Pius XII and the Jews," in *Pius XII and the Holocaust: A Reader* (Catholic League Publications: Milwaukee, 1988 reprint).

321. See *New York Times*, Jan. 10, 1940 (the Vatican appointed two Jewish scholars to the Vatican Academy of Science). In March, the Vatican appointed another Jewish professor to the Vatican Library to restore ancient maps, twelve hours before the new Italian laws went into effect prohibiting Jews from all professional life. *New York Times*, March 2, 1940. The letter instructing Catholic academic institutions to accept Jewish scholars is included in the Appendix, p. 396.

322. Lapide documents the intervention by citing an article on Father Pfeiffer's lifesaving efforts (accomplished under the direction of Pius XII) published in the June 28, 1964, *L'Osservatore della Domenica*.

323. Alois Hudal, *Römische Tagebücher: Lebensbeichte eines alten Bischofs* (Leopold Stocker Verlag: Stuttgart, 1976). The Pope, who typically kept Hudal at a distance because of his political views, exploited Hudal's talents here, knowing that the Germans would listen to him.

324. "Notes du cardinal Maglione," Oct. 16, 1943, *Actes et Documents*, vol. 9, pp. 505-6, no. 368 (footnote 3) ("As soon as he heard of the arrests of Jews in Rome Cardinal Secretary of State sent for the German ambassador and formulated some [sort?] of protest. The Ambassador took immediate action with the result that large numbers were released...."); "Mgr. Hudal au général Stahel," Oct. 16, 1943, *Actes et Documents*, vol. 9, p. 510, no. 373 (footnote 4). See O'Carroll, 96-97 (1980).

325. Lapide, 269. At a 1975 Holocaust conference in Hamburg, Germany, Lapide said that his estimate "was based on six months of research in the Yad Vashem, the Holocaust archive in Jerusalem." *Catholic Historical Review*, April 1999, 269-270.

326. See Malachi Martin, *The Keys of This Blood: The Struggle for World Domination Between Pope John Paul II, Mikhail Gorbachev & The Capitalist West*, 637 (1990) (Pius XII "personally saved over 1.5 million Jews"); Michael Burleigh, "The Cardinal Basil Hume Memorial Lectures: Political Religion and Social Evil," 3 *Totalitarian Movements and Political Religions*, 38 ("hundreds of thousands"); John S. Conway, *Yad Vashem Studies* XV (1983), 327-345 (primary archival material "confirms the picture already drawn by such Jewish authors as Livia Rothkirchen and Pinchas Lapide"). Sir Martin Gilbert would place the number of Jews saved at about 500,000. "Historian Sir Martin Gilbert Defends Pius XII; Goebbels Saw in Him an Enemy of Nazism," Zenit News Service, Feb. 20, 2003 ("the test for Pacelli was when the Gestapo came to Rome to round up Jews. And the Catholic Church, on his direct authority, immediately dispersed as many Jews as they could"); "The Untold Story: Catholic Rescuers of Jews," *Inside the Vatican*, August 2003, 31 (interview with Gilbert, conducted by William Doino). In its 1998 document on the Holocaust, "We Remember: A Reflection on the Shoah," the Holy See spoke of "what Pope Pius XII did personally or through his representatives to save hundreds of thousands of Jewish lives." Ibid., section IV; n. 16.

327. Interview with Rolf Hochhuth, BR-alpha forum (translated version).

328. Vincent Lapomarda comments:

> Susan Zuccotti, in her work *Under His Very Windows* (2000), sought to disprove Lapide but failed to do so. Unwittingly, she lent at least partial support to his view when she showed how helpful were

the nuns, monks, priests, bishops and archbishops in saving the Jews in Italy's major cities, especially since these rescuers were, according to her, convinced that they were really doing what the pope wanted.

*America*, Feb. 25, 2002, 38.

329. Alvarez, 177.

330. See Ibid., 187.

331. *Avvenire*, June 27, 1996; *CWN*, "More Echoes on Pope Pius XII, Nazi Holocaust," June 27, 1996.

332. "Customarily the most deliberate of men, Pius XII on this occasion made up his mind with little if any hesitation." Deutsch, 120.

333. Congregation for the Causes of Saints, *Positio*, appendix 25, 271. See also Jacques Nobécourt, *Le Vicaire et L'Histoire*, 194 (Paris, 1964).

334. A very good account of this whole matter can be found in Conway, "The Vatican, Germany and the Holocaust" in *Papal Diplomacy in the Modern Age*, 105-120. Also see pp. 163-64.

335. See Gallo, 30-32.

336. Pepper, 77. See also Tittmann, 95 ("[I]t was only rarely that records were kept by the Vatican officials of conversations the Pope had....")

337. In 1945, Fabian von Schlabrendorff, a Protestant member of the German resistance, wrote a memorandum to U.S. General William ("Wild Bill") Donovan, in which Schlabrendorff reported that: "Joseph Müller had orders from the Catholic Church to negotiate with representatives of the Protestant Church in order to harmonize their measures in the struggle against Hitler." Memorandum to General Donovan from Fabian von Schlabrendorff, Oct. 25, 1945 (Subject: Relationship of the German Churches to Hitler). See also Schlabrendorff, *The Secret War Against Hitler*.

338. Carroll-Abbing, *But for the Grace of God*, 48.

339. Carroll-Abbing, *A Chance to Live*, 77.

340. Ibid., 141, 82. See Congregation for the Causes of Saints, *Positio*, appendix 25, p. 290.

341. William Doino, "The Witness of the Late Monsignor John Carroll-Abbing," *Inside the Vatican*, July 12, 2001. Doino played portions of his tape recording of this interview for me.

342. Zuccotti, *The Italians and the Holocaust*, 304.

343. Congregation for the Causes of Saints, *Positio*, appendix 25, 245-46.

344. See pp. 372-73.

345. William M. Harrigan, "Pius XII's Efforts to Effect a Détente in German-Vatican Relations, 1939-1940," *Catholic Historical Review*, July 1963, 191 (Pius XII's "prudence helped to avert an immediate extension of the war"); Gallo, 150 (a protest would not have made things better); Sereny, 283 (By the time the extermination camps were ready for the mass murder of Polish Jews, a protest from the Pope "could have had no practical effect.")

346. Quoted in Purdy, 258 (noting that the time could come when this conviction could change). The background for the Holy See's concern was the message sent to Poland by Pius that was rejected by Archbishop Sapieha out of fear that it would lead to more persecutions. Ibid. See p. 220.

347. Congregation for the Causes of Saints, *Positio*, appendix 25, 245.

348. Ibid., 274. See "Most of Rome's Jews Were Saved from Hitler's Final Solution," *L'Osservatore Romano*, weekly edition in English, January 24, 2001, 11 (German officer reports that a higher profile protest would have backfired).

349. Letter to Msgr. Walter Brandmueller, president of the Pontifical Committee of Historical Sciences, April 2004, quoted in "Pope Says Ignorance of History Leads to Crisis" (Vatican Information Service), *Wanderer*, April 29, 2004.

350. McGurn, 64.

351. After-the-fact analysis is, of course, of limited value. See Henry Kissinger, *Diplomacy*, 27 (1994) ("[T]here is a vast difference between the perspective of an analyst and that of a statesman.... The analyst runs no risk.... The statesman is permitted only one guess.... The statesman must act on assessments that cannot be proved at the time that he is making them....")

352. Interestingly, Wills and Cornwell are former seminarians, and Carroll was a priest prior to being excommunicated.

353. Ralph McInerny (*The Defamation of Pius XII*) argues that the root of the attack on Pius is hatred for the Catholic Church — in particular, hatred for Catholic teachings against the "culture of death" as represented, above all, by abortion-on-demand. He argues that the critics are being morally inconsistent by attacking Pius for allegedly not doing enough to oppose the "Final Solution" while they simultaneously support what many consider the "Final Solution" for today's unwanted pregnancies. It is, of course, very difficult to assess the motivation of authors, except in cases where they make it evident. Critics Carroll, Wills, and Cornwell all made their motivations evident, and McInerny seems to have analyzed their motivations correctly.

354. *The Pius War*, 31.

355. Doris L. Bergen, "An Easy Target? The Controversy About Pius XII and the Holocaust," in *Pope Pius XII and the Holocaust*, 195. Bergen notes the important fact often overlooked by critics: Pius XII was no

more vocal when the victims were Catholic priests than he was when they were Jewish paupers. While she faults Pius for his approach, she does understand that this seriously undercuts any charge of anti-Semitism. See also Dunn, 103 (Pius did not "publicly condemn the Nazi attack upon the Catholic Church in Poland, even though the Nazis were murdering priests and believers.")

356. Such a study is undertaken on every candidate for sainthood, though due to the length of his papacy and the complexity of the issues involved, this study took somewhat longer than most.

357. *La campagna denigratoria nei riguardi della persona e dell'opera di Pio XII*, Congregation for the Causes of Saints, *Positio*, appendix 25, 236-93; see Ibid., Statement of the Relator, 1-2, 13-14.

358. Congregation for the Causes of Saints, *Beatificationis et Canonizationis Servi Dei Pii XII (Eugenii Pacelli) Summi Pontificis (1876-1958): Positio Super Vita, Virtutibus et Fama Sanctitatis* (Rome, 2004). The volumes that make up the *Positio* were prepared by the postulator, Father Paul Molinari, with the help of various collaborators. The work was carried out under the supervision of the relator, Father Peter Gumpel. The *Positio* was assembled with a view to the discussions to be carried out by theologians, ordinaries, and bishops as to the heroic virtue of Pope Pius XII's life. It will one day be made public, but for now it remains confidential. I was given extraordinary access and permission to quote from the document due to my previous work on the subject.

359. *La campagna denigratoria nei riguardi della persona e dell'opera di Pio XII*, Congregation for the Causes of Saints, *Positio*, appendix 25, 236-93; see Ibid., Statement of the Relator, 1-2, 13-14. This should not, I think, be taken as an orchestrated campaign of critics working in conjunction. Rather, many of the critics share a view of the world that runs counter to the Catholic Church, and they have tried to advance their view and discredit the Church by denigrating Pope Pius XII. These critics are not really trying to find the truth; they are advancing a political agenda. See F. David Dalin, "Pius XII and the Jews," *Weekly Standard*, Feb. 26, 2001, 31-39; Justus George Lawler, "Review Symposium: Proleptic Response," 20 *U.S. Catholic Historian*, 89; Ronald J. Rychlak, "Misusing History to Influence the Future," *Forum Focus*, Summer 2002. Other critics seem to have acted in good faith but were either deceived by ill-motivated authors, wrote before all of the evidence was available, or misunderstood the evidence that they saw. See p. 326. On March 8, 1999, Cardinal Secretary of State Angelo Sodano spoke against "the calumnies launched after the war against the Servant of God Pius XII of venerable memory.... This is a deceitful, treacherous persecution." *Positio*, appendix 25, 272. The papal critics specifically identified as being involved in this campaign include: Rolf Hochhuth, Günter Lewy, Saul Friedländer, Robert Katz, John Cornwell, and Susan Zuccotti. Ibid., Statement of the Relator, 14. See Ibid., appendix 25, 276 (noting that the list could be longer).

## Chapter Eighteen: The Questions and Answers

1. "In the final analysis, what the nuncios and bishops as well as the priests, nuns and other religious did for the Jews had the approval and support of the Pope himself as the acts and documents of the Holy See... testify." Lapomarda, 306. "It would have been impossible for the hundreds of priests and nuns to carry forward their work of mercy and rescue if their Pope had forbidden it." Ibid., 310, n. 6 (quoting Abram L. Sachar, *The Redemption of the Unwanted*, St. Martin's Press [New York, 1983], 97). The Nazis were at least suspicious that Pius was behind the various activities of the bishops. One report to Hitler, giving the details of an interview with Cardinal Szeptyckyj, the Ukrainian archbishop, said: "[H]is ideas are the same as the French Bishops, the Belgian Bishops and the Dutch Bishops, just as if they all received identical instructions from the Vatican." R. Stewart, 12.

2. Lapide, 133.

3. For instance, in *Hitler's Pope*, Cornwell criticized Pius for failing to help enough Jews, not for failing to help any Jews.

4. "A Jewish Boyhood Friend," *Inside the Vatican*, October 1999, XXIV. Additional documentation can be found on the web page of Pave the Way Foundation: *www.PTWF.org*.

5. Nearly as many Catholic Poles died at the hand of the Nazis as did Jewish Poles. In fact, it seems clear that Poles were marked by the Nazis for eventual extermination. Lapomarda, 151, n. 84 (noting that 400 nuns, mostly Polish, died in concentration camps). For an interesting account, see Richard C. Lukas, *The Forgotten Holocaust: Poles Under German Occupation, 1939-1944* (rev. ed., 2001). Lukas argues that Hitler's hatred of Poles was quite similar to his feeling toward the Jews, and that, until 1942, Christian Poles in German-occupied Poland were treated worse than Jewish Poles. From the very beginning, Polish bishops, priests, and nuns were arrested and tortured. Ibid. See also "The Victims of Nazi Ideology," January 1995, reprinted in Secretariat for Ecumenical and Interreligious Affairs, National Conference of Bishops, *Catholics Remember the Holocaust*, United States Catholic Conference (Washington, 1998); Bohdan Wytwycky, *The Other Holocaust: Many Circles of Hell* (1980); *Forgotten Survivors: Polish Christians Remember the Nazi Occupation* (Richard C. Lukas, ed. 2004); Andrew Hempel, *Poland in World War II: An Illustrated Military History* (Hippocrene Books, 2000); Haskell Nordon, *The Education of a Polish Jew: A Physician's War Memoirs* (D. Grossman Press, 1982).

6. "United Poland Waits for Victory: Jews and Catholics Singled Out by Nazis," *Palestine Post*, Dec. 17, 1941.

7. It is estimated that in Poland, by the end of the war, more than 10,000 clergy members had been murdered by the Nazis. Kathryn Oates, "What did the pope do about the Holocaust?" *Catholic Digest*, April 2009, 70, 72. About 2,500 priests died at Dachau alone. Patrick O'Hannigan, "Why the Shoah Still Matters," *American Spectator*, Sept. 13, 2007.

8. See Dunn, 103 (Pius did not "publicly condemn the Nazi attack upon the Catholic Church in Poland, even though the Nazis were murdering priests and believers.")

9. Lapide, 168. This was apparently not an insubstantial amount. According to one account, the future Pope inherited $100,000 in the mid-1930s. Cornwell (1999), 178.

10. Rousmaniere, 123.

11. This is reprinted in Secretariat for Ecumenical and Interreligious Affairs, National Conference of Bishops, *Catholics Remember the Holocaust*, United States Catholic Conference (Washington, 1998).

12. Ibid., footnote 16. Releasing the document, Cardinal Edward Idris Cassidy explained: "As for Pope Pius XII, it is our conviction that in recent years his memory has been unjustly denigrated." "Reflections Regarding the Vatican's Statement on the Shoah," reprinted in Ibid., 61, 72. Archbishop Oscar Lipscomb, chair of the U.S. Bishops' Committee on Ecumenical and Interreligious Affairs, wrote: "Pope Pius XII maintained this teaching of his predecessor [as reflected in *Mit brennender Sorge*] throughout his pontificate.... The American, French, and other bishops of the world who joined the condemnations of Nazi genocide believed themselves to be following the lead of the Holy Father." "Commemorating the Liberation of Auschwitz," January 1995, reprinted in Secretariat for Ecumenical and Interreligious Affairs, National Conference of Bishops, *Catholics Remember the Holocaust*, United States Catholic Conference (Washington, 1998).

13. *Documents on German Foreign Policy 1918-1945*, Series C (1933-1937), vol. I, no. 188.

14. "The intellectual origins of Nazi antisemitism are to be found in pseudo-scientific racist and mystical-romantic-traditionalist ideologies of the nineteenth century, not in the teachings of Augustine, Innocent III or even Martin Luther." Saperstein, 40-41.

15. Ibid., 41.

16. Ibid. In fact, a 1940 book commissioned by Pope Pius XII and designed to analyze the treatment of the German Catholic Church by the National Socialists concluded that religious persecution "is determined and actuated by the *very nature and essence of the National Socialist totalitarian system*." *The Persecution of the Catholic Church in the Third Reich*, 515 (emphasis in original).

17. Hitler is only known to have attended one church service in his adulthood — a funeral for Polish Marshal Pilsudski at the Berlin Cathedral, but he ostentatiously avoided kneeling and did not attempt to receive Communion.

18. Weizsäcker, 281. Lenin, Hitler, and Mussolini were noted for their similar intense dislike of religion. H. Stewart, 108. A number of Hitler's closest accomplices shared his hatred toward the Church and his desire to destroy it. The best known among them were Bormann, Himmler, Heydrich, Rosenberg, and Goebbels. In fact, "Himmler's profession became destroying Jews, liberals and priests." Groppe, 29, quoting Gerhard Reitlinger, *Die SS-Tragödie einer deutschen Epoche* (Munich, 1977), 29.

19. *The Goebbels Diaries 1939-1941*, 77. See also Sigrid Schultz, "Germany's Part-Time Brides," *McCall's*, April 1946 (quoting a German woman: "Nazism freed me of the fetters of Christian inhibitions. I'm through with that Christian stuff; I'm going to bring up my children according to my own ideas.") Goebbels was "equally anti-Christian." Kurzman, 55.

20. Matheson, 43. "He said it was downright horrifying that a religion could ever have been possible which literally gobbled up its God in communion." Groppe, 12, 13 (quoting the diary of Alfred Rosenberg).

21. *Hitler's Secret Conversations*, 49 ("I didn't know that Julian the Apostate had passed judgement with such clear-sightedness on Christianity. You should read what he says on the subject."); ibid., 52 (similar); ibid., 274 (Feb. 8, 1942: "The evil that's gnawing our vitals is our priests, of both creeds.")

22. There is also evidence of the effectiveness of this approach. According to statistics put forth by a Catholic charity organization shortly after the war, 7,200 of 8,000 "Catholic" Jews in Vienna survived the war. Only 4,000 of the 152,000 other Jews survived. Vida, 73. See generally Marchione (2000) (Overview) (the Church was often oppressive in its effort to convert Jews, but it always taught that it was wrong to harm or kill Jewish people).

23. See pp. 358-59.

24. *Allocution to the Rota*, Oct. 6, 1946 (AAS 38, 1946) 391-397; *Papal Allocutions to the Roman Rota 1939-1994* (St. Paul University: Ottowa, W.H. Woestman, ed., 1994).

25. As a young priest, the future Pope John Paul II refused to baptize a Jewish child who had been sheltered by a Catholic family for this very reason. "When Karol Wojtyla Refused to Baptize an Orphan," Zenit News Service, Jan. 18, 2005.

26. Lapide, 210.

27. Tec, 187 (also noting that most Jewish survivors who had been sheltered by the Catholic Church "derived much comfort from the Catholic religion"); Stille, 262.

28. Tec, 187. 2007 Nobel Peace Prize nominee Irena Sendler, a Polish Catholic woman, smuggled 2,500 Jewish children out of the Warsaw ghetto between 1942 and 1943 and set them up with Polish families.

She buried lists of the children's names so they could be reunited with their families when the war was over. Badly beaten by the Gestapo, she escaped and survived the war in hiding. The Holocaust Project: *http://www. auschwitz.dk/rescuers/id17.htm*.

29. Lapide, 210. Even when parents requested the baptism, it was recognized that this was simply a matter of duress. Ibid.

30. Elaine Sciolino and Jason Horowitz, "Saving Jewish Children, but at What Cost?" *New York Times*, Jan. 9, 2005.

31. See Ronald J. Rychlak, "Postwar Catholics, Jewish Children, and a Rush to Judgment," *beliefnet.com* (posted Jan. 18, 2005) and reprinted in *Inside the Vatican*, March 2005; Mary Jo Anderson, "Pius XII: Saintly Defender of European Jews," *WorldNetDaily*, Jan. 17, 2005.

32. See 306-7.

33. Daniel Jonah Goldhagen, "If This Is a Saint…," *Forward*, January 2005. In this article and in the Italian newspaper *Il Corriere della Sera*, Goldhagen called for the establishment of an international commission to investigate the Catholic Church's handling of Jewish children. He used the new memo to call Pius XII an "antiSemitic pope" who was "one of the most rampant would-be kidnappers of modern times." Goldhagen argued that the memo "reveals that the pope's and the church's policy was, in effect, to kidnap Jewish children, perhaps by the thousands…. Its plain purpose was to implement a plan that would cruelly victimize the Jews a second time by depriving these bodily and spiritually wounded survivors of the Nazi hell of their own children." He concluded by telling the Church of today that it "should cease efforts to canonize Pius XII." Rabbi Boteach wrote that "Pius ordered the mass kidnapping of hundreds of thousands of Jewish children…." Shmuley Boteach, "Pius XII: Collaborator and Kidnapper," *WorldNetDaily*, Jan. 13, 2005. He repeated similar charges on a radio program he hosted, insisting that this author, who was his guest, was damaging his own credibility by questioning the legitimacy of the documents (which were later proved to be fraudulent).

34. See Edward Pentin, "Pius XII Postulator Dismisses Jewish Baptism Document as 'Hoax,'" *National Catholic Register*, Jan. 23-29, 2005, 4.

35. "Experts React to a Row Over Jewish Children Rescued by Church Doubts Raised About Alleged Vatican Document," Zenit News Service, Jan. 11, 2005.

36. "1946 Document on Jewish Children Tells a Different Story: Undercuts Tale That Vatican Tried to Keep Them From Their Families," Zenit News Service, Jan. 12, 2005.

37. Lapide, 209-10.

38. Hellman, 69.

39. *Time*, March 16, 1953.

40. *Time*, Nov. 7, 1955. See Ronald J. Rychlak, "Jewish Children after World War II: A Case Study," *beliefnet.com*, Jan. 18, 2004.

41. As this wording implies, to the Catholic Church, and in contrast with Nazi philosophy, Jewishness is a matter of religion, not race.

42. Joseph L. Lichten, "A Question of Judgement: Pope Pius and the Jews," originally released in pamphlet form by the National Catholic Welfare Conference. It was reprinted in *Pius XII and the Holocaust: A Reader*, Catholic League Publications (Milwaukee, 1988). See also Meir Michaelis, *Mussolini and the Jews: German-Italian Relations and the Jewish Question in Italy 1922-25*, 1978 (some 5,000 Italian Jews sought baptismal papers in hopes of surviving the Holocaust).

43. In a cable sent on April 15, 1939, by Cardinal Maglione, Pius XII's secretary of state, to the nuncio in Warsaw, Mgsr. Cortesi, Maglione spoke about four petitions by Polish Jews seeking to emigrate from Poland. Maglione said that many Jewish organizations were operating in London and in New York City, and that Catholics in England, America, and the Netherlands had formed committees that assisted primarily converted Jews. He added, however, that "if Your Excellency, after having taken appropriate steps, believes that some of these cases [involving Jews who had not converted] deserve the Holy See's attention, the Secretariat of State would be well ready to consider it benevolently." No distinction was made by Pius XII's Vatican between converted and non-converted Jews, and this was well before the war began. Matteo Luigi Napolitano, *The Vatican Files* (*www.vaticanfiles.splinder.com*).

44. Charles Rankin, "Pius the Man and His Efforts for Peace," in *The Pope Speaks*, 88.

45. E.g., Lapide, 159; O'Carroll, 99. The official records indicate that 4,770 Jews were baptized in Budapest during this time, but that 80,000 baptismal certificates were distributed. Graham, *Pope Pius XII and the Jews of Hungary in 1944*, 17; O'Carroll, 104. Obviously, false certificates were unnecessary for actual Jewish converts to Catholicism who possessed authentic ones.

46. Godman, 33.

47. Ibid. See also Ronald J. Rychlak, "Hitler and the Vatican," *First Things*, May 2004; Ronald J. Rychlak, "Hitler and the Vatican – Reopening the Case," *Crisis*, April 2004, reprinted in *Newsmax* magazine, May 2004.

48. Irene Marinoff, *The Heresy of National Socialism* (Burns, Oates, and Washburn, "Publishers to the Holy See," 1941) (with a foreword by Archbishop Richard Downey of Liverpool).

49. "Le grand rabbin Herzog au délégué apostilique à Istanbul Roncalli," Nov. 22, 1943, *Actes et Documents*, vol. 9, p. 575, no. 436.

50. "Le grand rabin Herzog au cardinal MacRory," May 19, 1940, *Actes et Documents*, vol. 6, p. 306, no. 204.

51. *Divini Redemptoris*, n. 58.

52. During the war, *Time* magazine reported that "if Catholic-Fascist relations have been warm in the case of Spain, tolerable in the case of Italy, bearable in the case of Germany, relations with the democracies have been downright friendly." "Peace & the Papacy," *Time*, Aug. 16, 1943, 55, 59-60.

53. Kennedy (1961), 62-63. According to some accounts, however, Pius XII was convinced that Nazism was a graver threat to Catholicism than Communism, by British Prime Minister Neville Chamberlain and his foreign affairs secretary, Viscount Halifax, in 1939. Krišto, "An American View," 230 (citing Gallagher, *Vatican Secret Diplomacy*).

54. The Soviets even made plans to execute Catholic activists after the war. Andrew and Gordievsky, 297.

55. Barnett, 221.

56. Cianfarra, 99.

57. Lutzer, 106.

58. In 1932-33, Stalin's Soviet Union orchestrated a famine (the *Holodomor*) that killed at least 7.5 million Ukrainians, and perhaps as many as 14 million. *Holodomor: Reflections on the Great Famine of 1932-1933 in Soviet Ukraine* (Lubomyr Y. Luciuk and Lisa Grekul, eds., Kashtan Press, 2008). See Marta Baczynsky, "Holodomor exhibit at the United Nations," *Ukrainian Weekly*, Nov. 30, 2003.

59. The treatment of Polish citizens by the Soviets after Poland (a predominantly Catholic country) was "liberated" also seems to justify any hesitation the Vatican may have felt about siding with the Soviet Union. See Deschner, 7.

60. Friedlander (1966), 61.

61. See Ibid., 176.

62. Father Robert A. Graham, "The Latest Charges Against Pius XII," *America*, May 21, 1966.

63. Micklem, 79.

64. *Controversial Concordats*, 2; Cheetham, 284-86.

65. Pope Pius XI had not given up on the hope of establishing better relations with the Soviet Union. In 1929, he sent a letter to all seminarians, "especially our Jesuit sons," asking for men to enter a new Russian center being started in Rome to prepare young clerics for work in the U.S.S.R. Walter J. Ciszek, *He Leadeth Me: An Extraordinary Testament of Faith*, 13 (Doubleday, 1973). Ciszek entered the seminary and was later arrested in the Soviet Union, charged with being a spy for the Vatican.

66. "The Generals of the Society of Jesus," available on the Internet at *http://www.sogang.ac.kr/~gesukr/sj/sjgen15.html*.

67. Van Hoek, 90.

68. Paolo Dezza, "Pius XII's Alleged Silence," *L'Osservatore della Domenica*, June 28, 1964, 68-69. See also Carol Glatz Pius (CNS), "Pius XII feared outcry against atrocities would worsen situation," Feb. 2, 2010 (reprinting portions and quoting from the 1964 article written by Paolo Cardinal Dezza).

> During a lengthy audience with Pope Pius in December 1942, the cardinal [Dezza] said the pontiff was pained by the Nazi atrocities unfolding in Germany and was distressed by criticisms that he was not speaking out publicly against them. The pope had recently sent letters to three bishops in Poland in which he deplored the Nazi's criminal acts, but the bishops had written back, first thanking the pope for his concern, but adding that they would not make the letters public "because it would worsen the situation," according to the late cardinal. "If I speak out, I will do them harm," the pope said, according to Cardinal Dezza.
>
> The cardinal said the pope told him: "People lament that the pope doesn't speak out. But the pope can't speak out. If he did it would be worse."
>
> When the Germans occupied Rome in 1943, the late Italian cardinal said Pope Pius encouraged him to use the pontifical university as a refuge for "civilians, Jews and the persecuted."

Ibid.

69. *Inside the Vatican of Pius XII*, 63; *Current Biography, 1941*, Maxine Block, ed., the H.W. Wilson Co., 1971 reissue, 673; Overy, 284 (noting that some American Catholics had expected him to bless such a "crusade").

70. Father Robert A. Graham, "The Latest Charges Against Pius XII," *America*, May 21, 1966.

71. Gallo, 326, n. 54.

72. German authorities were almost completely uncooperative with Vatican efforts on behalf of prisoners of war — "even their own." Purdy, 33.

73. Gallo, 35, 40. When German troops invaded the Soviet Union, Pius even instructed the American bishops to make a statement making clear that the Vatican's opposition to the Soviet government did not reflect opposition to the Soviet people. Ibid., 37. "By 1943, the Churches of Moscow were so crowded at

Eastertime that the congregations spilled out into the surrounding streets. Though Stalin did not go so far as to allow chaplains to accompany the troops, it was noticed that soldiers on leave began to use the churches in large numbers too." Overy, 283.

74. Message from the British Embassy in Madrid, May 10, 1943, British Public Records Office, FO 3711 37538.

75. Minutes dated September 10, 1941, British Public Records Office, FO 371/30175 57750.

76. *Inside the Vatican of Pius XII*, 42. Nicolas Cheetham, in *The Keeper of the Keys*, said that Pius blessed the German "crusade" into the U.S.S.R., but there is no citation, and there is no evidence of this. Cheetham is wrong.

77. *Inside the Vatican of Pius XII*, 64-65.

78. Office of the United States Chief of Counsel, Supp. B, 1233.

79. Graham (1996), 156-57 (citing the archives of the Hungarian Foreign Ministry). See also Pius XII to Kallay, April 3, 1943, in the National Archives, Washington, Hungarian Selection/T973/1/1-201/1153ff; Nicholas de Kallay, *Hungarian Premier: A Personal Account of the Second World War*, 169 (1954).

80. Congregation for the Causes of Saints, *Positio*, appendix 25, 271-72. See p. 187.

81. At the time of Pius XII's death, the Communist *Daily Worker* commented: "Progressives throughout the world will remember Pius XII with gratitude for his reiterated appeals on behalf of Ethel and Julius Rosenberg, an intervention unprecedented in Vatican history." See the *Tablet* (London), Oct. 25, 1958. See also McGurn, 16 (noting that a significant Communist population was tolerated in Castle Gandolfo); ibid., 70 (Pius regularly read the Italian Communist newspaper).

82. See the International Catholic-Jewish Historical Commission, "The Vatican and the Holocaust: A Preliminary Report Submitted," question 42 ("The case has repeatedly been made that the Vatican's fear of communism prompted it to mute and limit its criticism of Nazi atrocities and occupation policies. We are struck by the paucity of evidence to this effect...."). See also Rychlak, *A Response to: "The Vatican and the Holocaust."*

83. Some critics have made the charge that Pope Pius XII opposed the Nazis late in the war (once he realized that they would lose), but did not strongly stand against them early in the war. If that were true — which it is not — it would suggest that he moved *with* the Soviets, as they switched from being unofficial allies with the Germans to joining with the Western powers. This is but another inconsistency in the arguments put forth by papal critics.

84. Lapide, 118.

85. Hochhuth, 296.

86. On Oct. 11, 1930, *L'Osservatore Romano* editorialized that membership in the National Socialist Party was "incompatible with the Catholic conscience, just as it is completely incompatible with membership in socialist parties of all shades."

87. According to the *London Tablet*, Nov. 29, 1941, the head of the Gestapo in Yugoslavia told a priest: "Don't you know that our *Führer* wishes to stamp out all Jews and priests? I suppose you know how priests are treated at [the camp at Begunje], like dogs." See Lapomarda, 209, n. 6.

88. Lapide, 120, quoting Erich Ludendorff, *General and Cardinal — On the Policy of the New Pope Pius XII 1917-1937*, 64. See also Duffy, 265.

89. Ratification was the most important event. See Micklem, 96.

90. See p. 80.

91. Lutzer, 182.

92. "A person may take martyrdom and death upon himself — often a man is obliged to do so — and this is a personal act; but no man may decree that another bear testimony in blood, especially if he himself is exempt. Only a tyrant would do that, but never a *Papa*, a true father." Kuehnelt-Leddihn, 190.

93. "Pius XII could easily have made this gesture, *at no risk at all to himself.* The Nazis had learned... not to lay hands on the bishops and archbishops. It was the little people — simple priests, monks, nuns, laymen — who had to pay the price of "freedom" enjoyed by the hierarchy under the swastika. Hitler, whose hatred of Christianity and especially of the Catholic Church knew no bounds, knew exactly how to attack: *he did not want heads to roll, but to cut away the roots.*" (Kuehnelt-Leddihn, 189).

Bishop Clemens August, Count von Galen was well known for three outspoken sermons he gave against National Socialism. He was, however, "deeply dejected" when the result was that 37 members of the clergy were arrested in retaliation, and ten of them lost their lives. "Three Sermons in Defiance of the Nazis," *Church in History Information Centre* (Birkenhead, U.K.), 4-5.

94. O'Carroll, 127. See also Bernard, 24, 34-35 (Protestant minister in camp complaining about brutal treatment following the papal statement).

95. Hochhuth, 298.

96. Wright, 1930.

97. Susan Zuccotti, "Pope Pius XII and the Holocaust: The Case in Italy," in Ivo Herzer, Klaus Voight, and James Burgwyn (eds.), *The Italian Refuge: Rescue of Jews During the Holocaust*, Catholic University of America Press, Washington, 1989, p. 258.

98. "Everyone knows that the Holy See cannot bring Hitler to heel." "*Notes de Mgr. Tardini*," July 13, 1942, *Actes et Documents*, vol. 8, p. 597, no. 426. In a public letter addressed to Cardinal Maglione on Aug. 5, 1943, Pius wrote: "[S]ince no heed is paid to the words which We have with trepidation uttered, We raise Our heart and Our eye to the Father of Mercy." "The Church and the Italian Crisis," *Tablet* (London), Aug. 14, 1943, 76. Rabbi Steven S. Wise, who has been called the foremost Jewish leader in America during the war years, agreed that Pius could not wield any real authority when it came to the Nazis. Wyman, 47, 69.

99. G. M. Gilbert, 39 (Ribbentrop, during a recess from the Nuremberg Trials, admitted that there were several protests from the Vatican, but Hitler ignored them. Göring confirmed Ribbentrop, saying: "But that was our right! We were a sovereign State and that was strictly our business.") See "Notes de la Secrétairerie d'Etat," Sept. 6, 1943, *Actes et Documents*, vol. 9, p. 470, no. 325 (notes reflecting German opposition to the Holy See's right to protest on behalf of Jews).

100. Levai, 30. Those times when protests had some success were situations where the German S.S. had not yet fully taken over. Ibid., 111-12.

101. Robert M. W. Kempner, the Deputy Chief U.S. Prosecutor at the Nuremberg war trials, explained that a public protest against prosecution of the Jews could only lead to partial success when "it was made at a politically and military opportune moment." He further explained that Pius made such protests through the nuncios in Slovakia and Romania when the time was opportune. Similar protests would not have been effective with Hitler. Levai, xi (Kempner's prologue). Congregation for the Causes of Saints, *Positio* (Summarium), Testimony of Cardinal Stefano Wyszynski, Oct. 18 and 25, 1968, before the Tribunal of the Vicariate of Rome, on the beatification of Pius XII (Eugenio Pacelli), Part II, 574, 578 (no international authority would have been able to deter the Nazis).

102. Cornwell (1999), 316.

103. Hochhuth, 326 (suggesting that this testimony was false). "When Clemens August von Galen, bishop of Münster, wanted to speak against the persecution of the Jews in Germany, the Jewish elders of his diocese begged him not to because it would only damage them." Congregation for the Causes of Saints, *Positio*, appendix 25, 271-72.

104. One of the counts charged against the defendants at the Nuremberg trials reflected the Allies' view of the relations between the Vatican and the Nazis.

> The Nazi conspirators, by promoting beliefs and practices incompatible with Christian teaching, sought to subvert the influence of the Churches over the people and in particular over the youth of Germany.... They avowed their aim to eliminate the Christian churches in Germany and sought to substitute therefor Nazi institutions and Nazi beliefs and pursued a programme of *persecution of priests, clergy, and members of monastic orders* which they deemed opposed to their purposes, and *confiscated church property.*

O'Carroll, 138 (suggesting that a memorandum authorized by Pius XII influenced the terms of this charge).

105. Graham (1996), 36 (quoting Dr. Robert M. W. Kempner).

106. "History on the Stage: Could Pius XII Have Stopped Hitler Killing the Jews?" *London Tablet*, March 16, 1963.

107. Even during the war, many people in the Nazi-dominated areas knew that the civilized world would never believe their horror stories. Karski, 322-23. This included many American soldiers. See Richard Joseph with Waverly Root, "Why So Many GIs Like the Germans Best," *Reader's Digest*, March 1946, 5, 6 9 ("[M]any an American soldier carried his defense of the Germans to the point of accusing the American authorities of having invented the atrocity stories.")

108. Morgan, 155 (noting Secretary of State Pacelli's opposition to Hitler's press censorship); Micklem, 84-85 (Shortly after coming to power, Hitler "promulgated a decree for the Protection of the German People in which the rights of public meeting and of the Press... were radically curtailed.") Under the Decree for the Protection of the German People, newspapers were suppressed for treason, civil disobedience, insulting governmental leaders, or insulting legally recognized religious leaders. Ibid.

109. Holmes, 168.

110. Cornwell (1999), 244.

111. "A l'Evêque de Berlin," March 1. 1942, *Actes et Documents*, vol. 2, p. 251, no. 83.

112. Robert Martin, "Spiritual Semites: Catholics and Jews During World War Two," Catholic League Publications (Milwaukee, 1983), quoting Father Scavizzi, in *La Parrochia*, June 15, 1964; Whitall N. Perry, "Book Review: *The Silence of Pius XII*, by Carlo Falconi," 5:1 *Studies in Comparative Religion* (Winter 1971).

113. Wright, 1932.

114. Graham (1996), 35 (quoting a letter to *Commentary*, June 1964, from Dr. Robert M. W. Kempner).

115. See Lubac, 24 (and footnote).

116. Congregation for the Causes of Saints, *Positio* (Summarium), Testimony of Cardinal Stefano Wyszynski, Oct. 18 and 25, 1968, before the Tribunal of the Vicariate of Rome, on the beatification of Pius XII (Eugenio Pacelli), part II, 577.

117. Lapomarda, 97 (making this same argument).

118. Blet, 285.

119. Reproduced by the Danish press and cited by *L'Osservatore della Domenica*, June 28, 1964, 49; see also Lapide, 266, 366, n. 221; Marilyn Henry, "How Pious Was Pius XII?" *Jerusalem Post*, Oct. 15, 1999; Kenneth D. Whitehead, "The Pope Pius XII Controversy," 31 *Political Science Reviewer*, 310 (2002).

120. Lewy, 304-5. See also Day, 21 (the Poles feared papal statements because they provoked Gestapo reprisals).

121. Joseph L. Lichten, "A Question of Judgment: Pius XII and the Jews," *in Pius XII and the Holocaust: A Reader*, 99.

122. Michaelis, 372 (footnote omitted). Another time, discussing the Vatican and the International Red Cross, Weizsäcker said: "It is a matter of course and everybody knows it, that these two agencies of world significance and reputation and world-wide influence would have undertaken any possible step that they considered feasible and useful to save the Jews." O'Connell, 80.

123. O'Carroll, 129.

124. See *Wartime Correspondence*, 78.

125. See p. 80.

126. See William Rubinstein, *The Myth of Rescue*, Routledge, New York, 1997, p. 194.

127. Jean-Claude Favez, *The Red Cross and the Holocaust*, John Fletcher and Beryl Fletcher (eds.), Cambridge University Press, Cambridge, 1999, p. 59-60 (emphasis added).

128. Blet, 161-2.

129. Blet, 140. See also Falconi, 134.

130. Sánchez (2002), 120 (quoting Father Graham).

131. William D. Rubinstein, "Books in Review: The Devil's Advocate," *First Things*, January 2000, 39, 40.

132. Ibid. Unfortunately, this did not stop one author from writing a novel based upon the premise that a more outspoken Pope was able to reduce the suffering of the Holocaust. José Sánchez, *Pope Gabriel* (2007).

133. F. Murphy, 70; "How to Manufacture a Legend: The Controversy over the Alleged 'Silence' of Pope Pius XII in World War II," in *Pius XII and the Holocaust: A Reader*, 18-19.

134. Early in the war, Sapieha had asked the Pope for a forceful statement, but he later changed his mind and recalled his letter. See Paci, 41; D. Fisher, 18. See pp. 148-49.

135. Lutheran pastor Dietrich Bonhoeffer was executed for his part in trying to eliminate Hitler. He is often used to contrast Pacelli's "silence." However, during the war, "Bonhoeffer never gave public condemnations of the Nazis. On the contrary he feigned public approval. The reason — not to draw attention to illegal activities — is the same reason given by Pacelli." Charles Ford, "Invidious Comparisons," *First Things*, January 2000, 67.

136. The Geneva Red Cross decided that a public protest would have no beneficial effect and would compromise what good the Committee was already doing for the internees. Robert A. Graham, "How to Manufacture a Legend: The Controversy over the Alleged 'Silence' of Pope Pius XII in World War II," in *Pius XII and the Holocaust: A Reader*, 20.

137. The Pope and the Nazis, *Investigative Reports*, broadcast on the Arts and Entertainment Television Network, Aug. 11, 1995. One of the points noted in the program was that when the Allies bombed Rome and the Pope went to inspect the damage, it was a very rare opportunity for the people of Rome to see the Pope since "he spent almost the entire war inside the Vatican." The implication seemed to be that he was hiding. In truth, Pius spent most of his time in the Vatican, even during times of peace. He normally traveled away from the Vatican during the summer, but during the war he decided to stay in the Vatican year-round, even though he knew Rome was subject to attack. The saying in Rome was: "The Pope is our best anti-aircraft." Hatch and Walshe, 176. When bombs did fall on Vatican City, Pius refused to enter the air-raid shelter. Thus he placed himself at greater risk. In fact, there were many who had urged him to relocate and get out of harm's way, but Pius refused.

138. In 1978, in a Norwegian newspaper, Hochhuth dismissed Pius as "a common coward." Groppe, 18.

139. It was reported early in the war that Pius approved and blessed a day of national prayer for an Italian victory. In actuality, he called for a day of prayer for the protection of Italian soldiers, and there was no mention of a papal blessing. Outward Telegram Distribution B to Switzerland, Feb. 3, 1941, British Public Records Office FO 371/30173 56879. See p. 489, note 181.

140. Paci, 40. During the war, 27 of the Holy See's 46 cardinals were Italian. Rhodes, 355.

141. *Actes et Documents*, vol. 2, 324, no. 105. See Lubac, 121-22, n. 12; O'Carroll, 89. Pius frequently encouraged Preysing in his resistance work. See "A l'Evêque de Berlin," Dec. 15, 1940, *Actes et Documents*, vol. 2, p. 180, no. 58; "A l'Evêque de Berlin," April 30, 1943, *Actes et Documents*, vol. 2, p. 318, no. 105; "A l'Evêque de Berlin," Sept. 5, 1943, *Actes et Documents*, vol. 2, p. 342, no. 112. See also Lubac, 145; O'Carroll, 89. In fact, Pius was the only world leader who took the resistance seriously. Charles Ford, "Invidious Comparisons," *First Things*, January 2000, 67.

142. Alan Schom, *Napoleon Bonaparte*, 458 (Harper Perennial, New York, 1997).

143. Hochhuth, 351; Rolf Hochhuth, "The Playwright Answers," *Die Welt*, April 6, 1963, reprinted in *The Storm Over The Deputy*, 76, 77 ("It is impossible to assume – and no one in the Vatican did, either in 1943 or 1959 – that Hitler would have made a 'martyr' of the Pope.") He also, however, said that the possibility of retaliation should not have been considered by the Pope. Patricia Marx, Interview with Rolf Hochhuth, WNYC Radio (February 1964), reprinted in *The Storm Over The Deputy*, 52, 59. American documents from 1943 suggest that most people in the Vatican at that time felt that Germany would not invade the Vatican unless Hitler had "a sudden outburst of anger against the church" and he overruled wiser counsel. The same report also noted that a minority was completely convinced that Hitler would invade the Vatican. Telegram from the Minister in Switzerland (Harrison) to the Secretary of State, Oct. 29, 1943, in *Foreign Relations of the United States, Diplomatic Papers, 1943, vol. II (Europe)*, United States Government Printing Office (Washington, 1964), 951-52.

144. Clyde Haberman, "Magazine Says Hitler Planned to Abduct Pope," *New York Times*, July 21, 1991, sec. 1, p. 7. At other times, Hitler made similar threats about the Catholic Church in Germany. See p. 514, note 125.

145. Weizsäcker, 291; "Notes de la Secrétairerie d'Etat," Oct. 1, 1943, *Actes et Documents*, vol. 9, p. 493, no. 355; "Notes de la Secrétairerie d'Etat," Dec. 20, 1943, *Actes et Documents*, vol. 9, p. 611, no. 474. See also Dan Kurzman, "Hitler's Plan to Kidnap the Pope," *Catalyst*, June 2007; "The Pope Yesterday and Today," *L'Osservatore Della Domenica*, June 26, 1964 (Kessel discussing the plan).

146. See Chadwick, *Weizsäcker, the Vatican, and the Jews of Rome*, 187-88, 195.

147. Clyde Haberman, "Magazine Says Hitler Planned to Abduct Pope," *New York Times*, July 21, 1991, sec. 1, p. 7; Holmes, 155-56.

148. Michaelis, 377.

149. Congregation for the Causes of Saints, *Positio* (Summarium), Testimony of Karl Otto Wolff, March 14, 1972, before the Ecclesiastical Tribunal of Munich, on the beatification of Pius XII (Eugenio Pacelli) at 832. See also Kurzman, 12. In 1944, when the Allies liberated Rome, Wolff approached Pius XII to discuss a possible peace treaty. At that time Wolff provided Pius with documents regarding Hitler's plans to invade the Vatican. Ibid. The documents are reprinted along with Wolff's testimony in the *Positio*, 831. Peter Gumpel, S.J., the relator of the cause for Pope Pius XII's sainthood, told me that General Wolff was instrumental in freeing Gumpel's mother in 1938 when she was arrested by the Nazis.

150. Congregation for the Causes of Saints, *Positio* (Summarium), Testimony of Karl Otto Wolff, March 14, 1972, before the Ecclesiastical Tribunal of Munich, on the beatification of Pius XII (Eugenio Pacelli), 832. See Ronald J. Rychlak, "The Plot to Kidnap Pope Pius XII," *Crisis*, October 2007.

151. Kurzman, 15.

152. See Congregation for the Causes of Saints, *Positio* (Summarium), Testimony of Karl Otto Wolff, March 14, 1972, before the Ecclesiastical Tribunal of Munich, on the beatification of Pius XII (Eugenio Pacelli), 837; Toland, 851; Payne, 485.

153. Haberman, *New York Times*. Goebbels recorded in his diary on July 27, 1943, that Hitler at first intended to seize the Vatican, but decided against it when Ribbentrop and Goebbels pointed out the impact that such actions would have on world opinion. *The Goebbels Diaries 1942-1943*, 409.

154. *Great Untold Stories of World War II*, 95. As Ribbentrop explained in an interrogation during the Nuremberg war trials, maintaining good relations with the Vatican was an important part of the German foreign policy. Bad relations with the Vatican would negatively impact on Germany's relations with other nations, particularly in South America. Office of the United States Chief of Counsel, Supp. B, 1236. Ribbentrop's concern over relations with the Vatican is reflected in a telegram he sent in January 1943. Secret Telegram from Ribbentrop to the German Ambassador (Bergen), dated Jan. 13, 1943, *Akten Zur Deutschen Auswärtigen Politik, 1918-1945*, Series E, Band V, Vandenhoeck and Ruprecht in Göttingen (1978), no. 123.

155. Congregation for the Causes of Saints, *Positio*, (Summarium) Testimony of Karl Otto Wolff, March 14, 1972, before the Ecclesiastical Tribunal of Munich, on the beatification of Pius XII (Eugenio Pacelli), 836-37. Wolff said that he intentionally avoided any sentimental argument and focused on practicality, because he knew that is what would persuade Hitler. Kurzman, 52.

156. Kurzman, 53.

157. Ibid., 40, 44-45.

158. Ibid. See also Marchione, *Pope Pius XII: Architect for Peace* (Hitler's Plan).

159. Hochhuth, 324.

160. Kurzman, 64.

161. Kurzman, 75 (also noting that the cardinals were instructed to keep a bag packed in case they were deported). See "Vatican planned to move to Portugal if Nazis captured wartime Pope," *Telegraph*, April 21, 2009 ("Pope Pius XII told senior bishops that should he be arrested by the Nazis, his resignation would become effective immediately, paving the way for a successor, according to documents in the Vatican's Secret Archives. The bishops would then be expected to flee to a safe country — probably neutral Portugal — where they would re-establish the leadership of the Roman Catholic Church and appoint a new Pontiff.")

584 | Hitler, the War, and the Pope

162. *Times* (London), May 20, 1963; see Confidential Letter to Oliver Harvey from D'Arcy Osborne, Feb. 26, 1947, British Public Records Office, FO 371/67917 60675. See also Tardini, 83 ("Pius was strong. He did not fear criticism, opposition, complaints, or accusations. We saw him go along the road that God and his conscience pointed out for him.")

163. "Jews of Rome Thank Pope for Aiding Them," *New York Times*, June 17, 1944.

164. O'Carroll, 69. See Telegram from the German Ambassador (Bergen) to the Reich Minister, dated Jan. 26, 1943, NARA, T-120, Roll 361, 277668-70 ("Pius XII is as little susceptible to threats as we ourselves."); Lapomarda at 232, n. 9 ("Pius XII was fearless in the face of hostile threats from both the Fascists and the Nazis.")

165. Cornwell (1999), 380. See also Day, 24 ("hazardous to the point of being almost foolhardy").

166. F. Murphy, 70-71; Paci, 39; Day, 22.

167. See Day, 24 ("the Roman pontiff had no lack of moral courage").

168. See Bishop Arthur J. Moore, *Christ After Chaos: The post-war policy of The Methodist Church in foreign lands* (Bureau of Missions and Church Extension, The Methodist Church, 1944).

169. Gerhard M. Riegner, "The Holocaust and Vatican Diplomacy," *Reform Judaism*, Fall 1984, 42.

170. Ibid.

171. See Ibid. ("The Vatican understood only very late the full extent of the catastrophe.")

172. Ibid., 80 (noting the difficulty the author had in 1945 convincing Vatican officials of the extent of Nazi abuse).

173. F. Murphy, 61-2.

174. Kahn, 192, 473; Alvarez and Graham, 142-43. Axis intelligence suspected that Vatican Radio was transmitting intelligence information to the Allies, and apparently it was. Alvarez and Graham, 136, n. 1. Some members of the German intelligence believed that Pius XII was personally involved in intelligence work. Ibid., 61.

175. Szulc, 104.

176. Besier, 192.

177. Szulc, 104.

178. Paci, 41. See also Day, 21 (The Poles "feared papal outcries against the Nazis because of Gestapo reprisals.")

179. It is probable that no one in the Vatican knew about the "slaughter on an industrial scale" that the Holocaust actually turned out to be. Paci, 42. Congregation for the Causes of Saints, *Positio* (Summarium), Testimony of Cardinal Stefano Wyszynski, Oct. 18 and 25, 1968, before the Tribunal of the Vicariate of Rome, on the beatification of Pius XII (Eugenio Pacelli), Part II, p. 578 (arguing that no one knew Hitler's intent at first).

180. Rhodes, 346. This is made clear in Jan Karski's *Story of a Secret State* (1944).

181. See pp. 205-6.

182. See Besier, 191.

183. Some writers have suggested that if the Allies had been willing to go along with the peace plans supported by the Pope, there would have been a favorable end to the war in 1943. John Dombrowski, "The Greatest War Crime," *Culture Wars*, December 1997.

184. "Le pape Pie XII à l'ambassadeur Myron Taylor," Sept. 22, 1942, *Actes et Documents*, vol. 5, p. 692-94, no. 476 (footnote 6).

185. O'Carroll, 74 (discussing how Hitler's theory required war to justify the killing of Jews and noting that without the war fewer Jews would have come under his control).

186. As this issue is considered, one must also remember that Pius supported postwar punishment of the perpetrators, and he cooperated with the prosecution at Nuremberg. See p. 263.

187. Hochhuth, 351. See also Patricia Marx, Interview with Rolf Hochhuth, WNYC Radio (February 1964), reprinted in *The Storm Over The Deputy*, 52, 59 (he should have made a statement regardless of retaliation); D. Fisher, 32 (responding to Hochhuth on this point).

188. Holmes, 168.

189. Graham, 2-3 (quoting Pius XII).

190. "Would history have judged Pius differently if he had hurled anathemas at Hitler's regime, and wallowed martyr-like in the blood of his own people and the Jewish people?

"Would it truly have been a sign of goodness to put his own reputation before the lives of men, women and children? There can be only one answer to these questions — questions which commentators and best-selling authors, in recent years have, alas, chosen not to ask themselves" (Cardinal Thomas Winning, "Pius XII — Friend of the Jews and Hitler's Foe," *Daily Telegraph* [London], Oct. 5, 1999).

191. Blet, 288.

192. Guenter Lewy wrote:

Finally one is inclined to conclude that the Pope and his advisors... did not view the plight of the Jews with a real sense of urgency and moral outrage. For this assertion no documentation is possible, but it is a conclusion difficult to avoid.... All things told, did not the murder of several million Jews demand a "candid word"?

Lewy, 305.

193. Day, 26.

194. Peter T. Farrelly, Jr., "The Vatican and the Allies," *Our Sunday Visitor*, May 18, 1997 (quoting William Simpson, author of *A Vatican Lifeline* [1997]).

195. "For too many historians, the Nazis appear in accounts of the Holocaust as some inexplicable force of nature whose destructive powers it is pointless to question, while criticism focuses on the alleged inadequacies of those who could not prevent the slaughter. That this is utterly unfair should be evident, yet library shelves are filled with works on the 'failures' of the Allies, as they are with works critical of Pacelli. At the very best such books deflect attention from the real criminals; at worst they imply a moral equivalency between mass murderers and those who tried, whether effectively or not, to stop them." William D. Rubinstein, "Books in Review: The Devil's Advocate," *First Things*, January 2000, 39.

196. Hochhuth, 317.

197. Ibid., 315, 316.

198. Holmes, 141.

199. Ibid., 158.

200. Toland (1976), 687, 689, 865.

201. Ibid., 865.

202. The War Refugee Board sent a message to the Vatican in 1944, in which it acknowledged that Pius "has labored unceasingly to reinculcate a decent regard for the dignity of man," and the "tireless efforts of His Holiness to alleviate the lot of the persecuted, the hunted and the outcasts." Telegram from the Secretary of State to the Consul General at Naples (Brandt), June 13, 1944, in *Foreign Relations of the United States, Diplomatic Papers, 1944, vol. I (General)*, United States Government Printing Office (Washington, 1966), 1068-69.

203. Wyman, 5.

204. Mussolini suggested this to Vatican officials as late as 1938. Besier, 184.

205. See "Nazi Reprisal Against Jews Held: Fear of Pope Pius XII," *Religious News Service*, May 20, 1963 (report of comments by Pius to a chaplain who had been stationed with the Italian troops along the Russian front).

206. Robert Martin, "Spiritual Semites: Catholics and Jews During World War Two," *Catholic League Publications* (Milwaukee, 1983), quoting Father Scavizzi, in *La Parrochia*, June 15, 1964.

207. Morgan, 159.

208. "If a competent ecclesiastical authority imposes or declares the excommunication, then the offender is removed from all liturgical functions; invalidly exercises any governing authority he previously possessed within the church; forfeits his ecclesiastical office, position, and pension; and cannot assume any other position or function within the Church" (Pete Vere, "Strong Medicine: Canon Law and Excommunication," *This Rock*, November 2007, 22, 23).

209. Morison, 988. Hitler "never allowed a member of the clergy to a Party meeting or to the burial of a member of the Party.... He said it was downright horrifying that a religion could ever have been possible which literally gobbled up its God in communion." Groppe, 12, 13 (quoting the diary of Alfred Rosenberg).

210. *"Le nonce en Italie Borgongni Duca au cardinal Maglione,"* Oct. 25, 1942, *Actes et Documents*, vol. 5, p. 284, no. 130.

211. Bogle, *Salisbury Review*; Michael Schwartz, "Are Christians Responsible?" *National Review*, Aug. 8, 1980, 956 (noting that Hitler incurred this type of excommunication under the canon law then in force when he served as best man in Goebbels' wedding, which took place in a Protestant church). Had the occasion arisen, Hitler almost certainly would have been denied a Christian burial. Michael Schwartz, "Are Christians Responsible?" *National Review*, Aug. 8, 1980, 956, 957.

212. See Marchione (2000) (Overview) (citing Canons 2332 and 2342 of the Code of Canon Law that was then in effect).

213. See Pete Vere, "Strong Medicine: Canon Law and Excommunication," *This Rock*, November 2007, 22, 23.

214. The 1949 excommunication of Communist supporters in Italy seems not to have accomplished its intended objective, and it led to some negative consequences. Moreover, "as in the case with the Nazi persecution of the Church, Pope Pius XII did not publicly denounce the Communist persecution. He continued to believe the public censure would enflame the attacks." Dunn, 103.

215. Lapomarda, 47, n. 28. "People are deluding themselves if they think that the halberds of the Swiss Guard or a threat of excommunication would have stopped the *Wehrmacht* in its tracks." Cardinal Thomas Winning, "Pius XII — Friend of the Jews and Hitler's Foe," *Daily Telegraph* (London) Oct. 5, 1999 (quoting Pierre Blet). Excommunication can backfire. See Rhodes, 342-43.

216. François Charles-Roux, *Huit Ans au Vatican, 1932-1940*, 351-52 (Flammarion: Paris, 1947).

217. Pius "never altered his view throughout the war, returning again and again to this explanation in his various addresses throughout the war and adding a plea to the world's powers to build a postwar order based on the principles of natural law and divine revelation." Dunn, 105.

218. David van Biema, "The Turning Point," *Time*, April 24, 2005 (also noting that Pope Benedict XVI reached this conclusion).

219. See Claire Hulme and Michael Salter, "The Nazis' Persecution of Religion as a War Crime: The OSS's Response Within the Nuremberg Trial's Process," 3 *Rutgers Journal of Law and Religion*, 4 (2001/2002).

220. *The Nazi Master Plan: The Persecution of the Christian Churches.* See also Harrigan, 185 (It was read in the Catholic churches but the Gestapo prevented further distribution.)

221. Address to the Sacred College of Cardinals on December 24, 1939, *Acta Apostolicae Sedis*, vol. 32, 5-13; *L'Osservatore Romano*, Dec. 26-27, 1939, 1-2.

222. Drew Pearson and Robert S. Allen, "Peace by Spring... The Goal of the Pope and Roosevelt," *Look*, March 26, 1940, 33.

223. "Roosevelt Aims at Sound Peace," *Christian Science Monitor*, Dec. 27, 1939.

224. *The Goebbels Diaries 1939-1941*, 75 (entry for Dec. 27, 1939).

225. On December 19, 2009, the Vatican issued a decree, approved by Pope Benedict XVI, proclaiming the heroic virtue of Pius XII and bestowing upon him the title of "Venerable." The only remaining steps in the sainthood cause relate to miracles. If one miracle attributable to his intercession is recognized by the Holy See, Pius will become "Blessed"; and if a second is so approved, he will be canonized as a saint.

226. Lewy, 305.

227. "Judging Pope Pius XII," *Inside the Vatican*, June 1997, 12. Father Gumpel said, "After reading 100,000 pages of the documents for the process of beatification, I am more and more convinced that Pius XII was a saint." "Cardinal Cassidy: 'We Cannot Be Chained to the Past,'" *EWTN News*, March 25, 1999.

228. A record of that conference and numerous supporting documents are available on the web page of the Pave the Way Foundation: *www.PTWF.org*.

229. Van Hoek, 5.

# Bibliography

*Actes et Documents du Saint Siège Relatifs à la Seconde Guerre Mondiale*, Volumes I-XI (Libreria Editrice Vaticana: Città del Vaticano, 1965-81); English edition (Volume I only; Gerard Noel, ed.; Corpus Books: Washington, DC, 1967-77). Volume III is split into two books, thus some authors refer to twelve volumes instead of eleven.

Akin, Jimmy, "How Pius XII Protected Jews," *This Rock*, February 1997.

Akmadža, Miroslav, "The Position of the Catholic Church in Croatia 1945-1970," *Review of Croatian History* 2/2006, no. 1, 89.

*Akten Deutscher Bischöfe über die Lage der Kirche, 1933-1945* (Bernhard Stasiewski and Ludwig Volk, eds.; Matthias-Grünewald-Verlag; six volumes dated 1968-1985).

Alexander, Stella, "Croatia: The Catholic Church and Clergy, 1919-1945," in *Catholics, the State, and the European Radical Right, 1919-1945* (Columbia University Press: New York, 1987).

————, *The Triple Myth: A Life of Alojzije Stepinac* (East European Monographs, 1987).

Alvarez, David, *Spies in the Vatican: Espionage & Intrigue from Napoleon to the Holocaust* (University Press of Kansas, 2002).

————, and Robert A. Graham, *Nothing Sacred: Nazi Espionage Against the Vatican 1939-1945* (Frank Cass: London, 1997).

Ambrosini, Maria Luisa, *The Secret Archives of the Vatican* (Barnes & Noble Books: New York, 1996).

*American Intelligence and the German Resistance to Hitler* (Heideking and Mauch, eds.; Westview: Boulder, CO, 1996).

*The American Jewish Yearbook, 1943-1944* (Jewish Publication Society: Philadelphia, 1944).

Andrew, Christopher, and Oleg Gordievsky, *KGB: The Inside Story* (Harper Collins: New York, 1990).

————, and Vasili Mitrokhin, *The Sword and the Shield: The Mitrokhin Archive and the Secret History of the KGB* (Basic Books: New York, 1999).

Barnett, Victoria, *For the Soul of the People: Protestant Protest Against Hitler* (Oxford University Press: Oxford, 1992).

Barton, Dennis, *Croatia 1941-1946* (The Church in History Information Centre 2006).

Barzini, Luigi, *From Caesar to the Mafia: Sketches of Italian Life* (The Library Press: New York, 1994).

Beales, A. C. F., *The Pope and the Jews: The Struggle of the Catholic Church Against Anti-Semitism During the War* (Sword of the Spirit: London, 1945).

Bemporad, Jack, and Michael Shevack, *Our Age: The Historic New Era of Christian-Jewish Understanding* (New City Press: Hyde Park, NY, 1996).

Benns, F. Lee, *Europe Since 1914 in Its World Setting* (Appleton, Century, Crofts: New York, 1949).

Benzinger, Marieli G., *Echoes Across the Alps* (Benzinger Sisters: Altadena, CA, 1978).

Bernard, Jean, *Priestblock 25487: A Memoir of Dachau* (Deborah Lucas Schneider, trans.; Zaccheus Press, 2007).

Bernstein, Carl, and Marco Politi, *His Holiness: John Paul II and the Hidden History of Our Time* (Doubleday: New York, 1996).

Besier, Gerhard, and Francesca Piombo, *The Holy See and Hitler's Germany* (Palgrave Macmillan: New York, 2007).

*The Black Book of Communism: Crimes, Terror, Repression* (Jonathan Murphy and Mark Kramer, trans.; Harvard University Press: Cambridge, MA, 1999).

Blet, Pierre, *Pius XII and the Second World War* (Lawrence J. Johnson, trans.; Paulist Press: New York, 1999).

Blum, John M., et al., *The National Experience: A History of the United States* (Harcourt, Brace, & World: New York, second edition 1968).

Boatner III, Mark M., *The Biographical Dictionary of World War II* (Presidio Press: Novato, CA, 1996).

Bogle, James, "The Real Story of Pius XII and the Jews," *Salisbury Review*, Spring 1996.

Bonomelli, Emilio, *I Papi in Campagna* (Gherardo Casini Editore: Rome, 1953).

Bozanić, Cardinal Josip, *The Most Illustrious Figure of the Church in Croatia: Pastoral letter on the occasion of the centenary of the birth of the Servant of God Cardinal Alojzije Stepinac*, March 1, 1998 (reprinted in Cardinal Josip Bozanić, *Blaženi Alojzije Stepinac, Baština koja obvezuje* [Glas Koncila, 2008]).

Brent, Jonathan, *Inside the Stalin Archives* (Atlas & Co.: New York, 2008).

Briggs, Kenneth A., *Holy Siege: The Year that Shook Catholic America* (Harper: San Francisco, 1992).

Brown, Anthony Cave, *Bodyguard of Lies* (Harper & Row: New York, 1975).

Brüning, Heinrich, *Memoiren, 1918-1934* (Deutsche Verlags-Anstalt: Stuttgart, 1970).

Bulajic, M., *The Role of the Vatican in the Break-up of Yugoslavia* (Belgrade, 1994).

Bullock, Alan, *Hitler: A Study in Tyranny* (Bantam: Chicago, 1962).

Burleigh, Michael, "The Cardinal Basil Hume Memorial Lectures: Political Religion and Social Evil," 3 *Totalitarian Movements and Political Religions* 1 (Autumn 2002).

———, *Death and Deliverance: Euthanasia in Nazi Germany, 1900-1945* (Cambridge University Press: New York, 1994).

———, *Earthly Powers: The Clash of Religion and Politics in Europe From the French Revolution to the Great War* (Harper Collins: New York, 2006).

———, *Sacred Causes: The Clash of Religion and Politics, From the Great War to the War on Terror* (Harper Collins: New York, 2007).

———, *The Third Reich: A New History* (Hill & Wang: New York, 2001).

Burton, Katherine, *Witness of the Light: The Life of Pope Pius XII* (Longmans, Green: New York, 1958).

Byrnes, Timothy A., *Catholic Bishops in American Politics* (Princeton University Press: Princeton, 1991).

Carlen, Claudia C., *The Papal Encyclicals* (Pierian Press: Ann Arbor, MI, 1990).

Carr, William, *A History of Germany* (Edward Arnold: London, 1979).

Carroll, James, *Constantine's Sword: The Church and the Jews: A History* (Houghton Mifflin Co.: Boston, 2001).

———, "The Silence," *New Yorker*, April 7, 1997.

Carroll-Abbing, John Patrick, *But for the Grace of God — The Houses Are Blind* (Delacorte Press: New York, 1965).

———, *A Chance to Live: The Story of the Lost Children of the War* (Longman, Green & Co.: London, 1952).

*Catholics Remember the Holocaust* (United States Catholic Conference: Washington, DC, 1988).

Chadwick, Owen, *A History of Christianity* (St. Martin's Press: New York, 1995).

———, *Britain and the Vatican During the Second World War* (Cambridge University Press: Cambridge, 1986).

———, "Weizsäcker, the Vatican, and the Jews of Rome," 28 *Journal of Ecclesiastical History* 179 (April 1977).

Chambers, Colin, *Inside the Royal Shakespeare Company: Creativity and Institution* (Routledge: London and New York, 2004).

Cheetham, Nicolas, *The Keeper of the Keys: A History of the Popes from St. Peter to John Paul II* (Macdonald: London, 1982).

*Chronicle of the 20th Century* (C. Daniel, ed.; Chronicle Publications: Mount Kisco, NY, 1986).

Cianfarra, Camille, *The Vatican and the War* (Literary Classics, Inc., distributed by E. P. Dutton & Company: New York, 1944).

*The Ciano Diaries* (Hugh Gibson, ed.; Doubleday & Company, Inc.: New York, 1946).

Clonmore, Lord, *Pope Pius XI and World Peace* (Dutton: New York, 1938).

Coady, Mary Frances, *With Bound Hands, A Jesuit in Nazi Germany: The Life and Selected Prison Letters of Alfred Delp* (Loyola Press: Chicago, 2003).

Cohalan, Florence D., *A Popular History of the Archdiocese of New York* (U.S. Catholic Historical Society: New York, 1983).

Cohen, Naomi W., *Not Free to Desist: A History of the American Jewish Committee, 1906-1966* (The Jewish Publication Society of America: Philadelphia, 1972).

*Commonweal Confronts the Century: Liberal Convictions, Catholic Traditions* (Patrick Jordan and Paul Baumann, eds.; Touchstone Books: New York, 1999).

Congregation for the Causes of Saints, *Beatificationis et Canonizationis Servi Dei Pii XII (Eugenii Pacelli) Summi Pontificis (1876-1958): Positio Super Vita, Virtutibus et Fama Sanctitatis* (Rome, 2004) [the *Positio*].

Conradt, David P., *The German Polity* (Longman: New York, 1978).

Constantine, Prince of Bavaria, *The Pope: A Portrait from Life* (D. Pyke, trans.; Allan Wingate: London, 1954).

*Controversial Concordats: The Vatican's Relations with Napoleon, Mussolini, and Hitler* (Frank J. Coppa, ed.; The Catholic University of America Press: Washington, DC, 1999).

Conway, John S., *The Nazi Persecution of the Churches 1933-45* (London: Weidenfeld and Nicolson, 1960; and New York: Basic Books, 1969).

———, "The Silence of Pope Pius XII," in *The Papacy and Totalitarianism Between the Two World Wars* (Charles F. Delzell, ed.; Wileys: New York, 1974).

———, "The Vatican, Germany and the Holocaust," in *Papal Diplomacy in the Modern Age* (Peter C. Kent and John F. Pollard, eds.; Praeger: Westport, 1994).

———, "The Vatican, Great Britain, and Relations with Germany, 1938-1940," XVI *Historical Journal*, 147 (1973).

Cooney, John, *The American Pope: The Life and Times of Francis Cardinal Spellman* (Times Books: New York, 1984).

Copeland, Lewis, *The World's Great Speeches* (Garden City Publishing Co.: New York, 1942).

Cornwell, John, *Breaking Faith: The Pope, the People, and the Fate of Catholicism* (Viking Press: New York, 2001).

———, *Hitler's Pope: The Secret History of Pius XII* (New York: Viking Press, 1999).

———, *The Pontiff in Winter* (New York: Doubleday, 2004).

Crankshaw, Edward, *Gestapo* (Pyramid Books: New York, 1957).

Dalin, David G., *The Myth of Hitler's Pope: How Pope Pius XII Rescued Jews from the Nazis* (Regnery: Washington, DC, 2005).

———, "Pius XII and the Jews: A Defense," *Weekly Standard*, February 26, 2001.

Daniel-Rops, Henri, *A Fight for God: 1870-1939* (E. P. Dutton and Co.: New York, 1965).

Darragh, James A., *The Pope and Fascism* (John S. Burns & Sons: Glasgow, 1944).

Davis, Kenneth C., *Don't Know Much About the Bible: Everything You Need to Know About the Good Book but Never Learned* (Harper Trade: New York, 2001).

Davis, Melton S., *All Rome Trembled* (G. P. Putnam's Sons: New York, 1957).

Day, Edward, "Pius XII and the Hitler Plot," *Liguorian*, October 1968.

*Days of Devotion: Daily Meditations From the Good Shepherd Pope John XXIII* (John P. Donnelly, ed.; Penguin reprint: New York, 1998).

Deighton, Len, *Blood, Tears and Folly: An Objective Look at World War II* (Harper Collins: New York, 1993).

*Der Streit um Hochhuth's "Stellvertreter"* (Basilius Presse: Basel/Stuttgart, 1963).

Deschner, Günther, *Warsaw Rising* (Ballantine Books: New York, 1972).

Deutsch, Harold C., *The Conspiracy Against Hitler in the Twilight War* (University of Minnesota Press: Minneapolis, 1968).

*Die Briefe. an die Deutschen Bischöfe 1939-1944* (Burkhart Schneider, ed.; Grünewald: Mainz, 1966).

*Die Katholiken und das Dritte Reich* (Klaus Gotto and Hans Günter Hockerts, eds.; Matthias-Grünewald-Verlag, Mainz, 1990).

Dietrich, Donald J., *Catholic Citizens in the Third Reich: Psycho-Social Principles and Moral Reasoning* (Transaction: New Brunswick, NJ, 1988).

DiGiovanni, Stephen M., *Pius XII and the Jews: The War Years* (monograph) also published in: 6 *Catholic Social Science Review* 341 (2000).

Dinneen, Joseph F., *Pius XII: Pope of Peace* (Robert M. McBride and Company: London, 1939).

Doyle, Charles Hugo, *A Day with the Pope* (Doubleday: Garden City, 1950).

Doyle, Kevin M., "Robert Graham, S.J.," *First Things*, June/July 1997, 16.

Duffy, Eamon, *Saints & Sinners: A History of the Popes* (Yale University Press: New Haven, 1997).

Dunn, Dennis J., *The Catholic Church and Russia: Popes, Patriarchs, Tsars and Commissars* (Ashgate: Burlington, VT, 2004).

Dupuy, Trevor N., and R. Ernest Dupuy, *The Encyclopedia of Military History* (Harper & Row: New York, 1970).

Duquesne, Jacques, *Les Catholiques Français sous l'occupation* (Grasset: Paris: 1966).

Elliott, Lawrence, *I Will Be Called John: A Biography of Pope John XXIII* (Berkley Publishing Corp.: New York, 1973).

*Encyclopedia of Catholic Social Thought, Social Science, and Social Policy* (Michael L. Coulter et al., eds.; The Scarecrow Press, Inc.: Lanham, MD, 2007).

*Encyclopedia of the Holocaust* (Macmillan: New York, 1990).

Esterovich, Francis H., "Spiritual Portrait of Cardinal Stepinac," *Crown and Cross* (September 1962).

*Examining the Papacy of Pope Pius XII* (Pave the Way Foundation: Rome, 2008).

Fabert, Andre, *Pope Paul VI* (Monarch Books: Derby, CT, 1963).

Falconi, Carlo, *The Silence of Pius XII* (B. Wall trans., Little Brown: Boston, 1970).

Fattorini, Emma, *Germania e Santa Sede: Le nunziature di Pacelli tra la Grande Guerra e la Repubblica di Weimar* (Il Mulino: Bologna, 1992).

Feldkamp, Michael F., *Der Teufelspakt des Anti-semiten* in *Frankfurter Allgemeine Zeitung*, January 10, 2000, 7.

Fest, Joachim C., "Hitler's German Enemies," *Sunday Telegraph*, July 10, 1994.

Fisher, Desmond, *Pope Pius XII and the Jews: An Answer to Hochhuth's Play* Der Stellvretter *(The Deputy)* (Paulist Press: Glen Rock, NJ, 1965).

Fisher, Eugene J., *Faith Without Prejudice: Rebuilding Christian Attitudes Toward Judaism* (The American Interfaith Institute: New York, 1993).

Fogelman, Eva, *Conscience & Courage: Rescuers of Jews During the Holocaust* (Anchor/Doubleday: New York, 1994).

Fontenelle, René, *His Holiness, Pope Pius XI* (Burns, Oates and Washbourne: London, 1923).

*Forgotten Survivors: Polish Christians Remember the Nazi Occupation* (Richard C. Lukas, ed.; University of Kansas Press: Lawrence, KS, 2004).

Fredborg, Arvid, "Behind the Steel Wall," *Reader's Digest*, January 1944, 125.

Friedländer, Saul, *Nazi Germany and the Jews, Volume I: The Years of Persecution, 1933-1939* (Harper Collins: New York, 1997).

———, *Pius XII and the Third Reich: A Documentation* (C. Fullman, trans.; Knopf: New York, 1966).

*From Hitler's Doorstep: The Wartime Intelligence Reports of Allen Dulles, 1942-1945* (Neal H. Peterson, ed.; Pennsylvania State University Press: University Park, PA, 1996).

Frost, David, *An Autobiography* (Harper Collins: New York, 1993).

Gallagher, Charles R., "'Personal, Private Views': A newly discovered report from 1938 reveals Cardinal Pacelli's anti-Nazi stance," *America*, September 1, 2003.

———, *Vatican Secret Diplomacy: Joseph P. Hurley and Pope Pius XII* (Yale University Press: New Haven, CT, 2008).

Gallin, Mary Alice, *German Resistance to Hitler: Ethical and Religious Factors* (The Catholic University of America: Washington, DC, 1961).

Gallo, Patrick, *For Love and Country: The Italian Resistance* (University Press of America: New York, 2003).

Gannon, Robert I., *The Cardinal Spellman Story* (Doubleday & Company: Garden City, NY, 1962).

García, Laura, "Edith Stein — Convert, Nun, Martyr," *Crisis*, June 1977, 18.

Gaspari, Antonio, *Gli ebrei salvati da Pio XII* (Edizioni Logos: Rome, 2001).

Gilbert, Martin, *Auschwitz and the Allies* (Holt, Rinehart, & Winston: New York, 1981).

———, *The Holocaust: A History of the Jews of Europe During the Second World War* (Holt, Rinehart, & Winston: New York, 1985).

———, *The Righteous: The Unsung Heroes of the Holocaust* (Henry Holt & Company, Inc.: New York, 2003).

———, *The Second World War: A Complete History* (Henry Holt & Company: New York, 1987).

Gill, Anton, *An Honourable Defeat* (Henry Holt & Co.: New York, 1994).

Gitman, Esther, "A Question of Judgment: Dr. Alojzije Stepinac and the Jews," *Review of Croatian History* 2/2006, no. 1, 47.

Godman, Peter, *Hitler and the Vatican: The Secret Archives That Reveal the New Story of the Nazis and the Vatican* (Free Press: New York, 2004).

*The Goebbels Diaries: 1939-1941* (Fred Taylor, trans.; G. P. Putnam's Sons: New York, 1983).

*The Goebbels Diaries: 1942-1943* (Louis P. Lochner, trans.; Doubleday & Co.: New York, 1948).

Goldhagen, Daniel J., *Hitler's Willing Executioners: Ordinary Germans and the Holocaust* (Alfred A. Knopf: New York, 1996).

———, *A Moral Reckoning: The Role of the Catholic Church in the Holocaust and Its Unfulfilled Duty of Repair* (Alfred A. Knopf: New York, 2002).

Goldston, Robert, *The Life and Death of Nazi Germany* (Fawcett Publications: Greenwich, CT, 1967)

Golitsyn, Anatoliy, *New Lies for Old: The Communist Strategy of Deception and Disinformation* (Dodd, Mead & Co.: New York, 1984).

Gonella, Guido, *The Papacy and World Peace: A Study of the Christmas Messages of Pope Pius XII* (Hollis and Carter, Ltd.: London, 1945).

Graham, Robert A., *Pius XII's Defense of Jews and Others: 1944-45* (Catholic League Publications: Milwaukee, 1987). This is also reprinted in *Pius XII and the Holocaust: A Reader* (Catholic League Publications: Milwaukee, 1988).

———, *The Pope and Poland in World War Two* (Veritas: London, 1968).

———, *Pope Pius XII and the Jews of Hungary in 1944* (United States Catholic Historical Society, undated).

———, "The 'Right to Kill' in the Third Reich: Prelude to Genocide," LXII *Catholic Historical Review* 56, 65 (January 1976).

———, *The Vatican and Communism During World War II: What Really Happened?* (Ignatius Press: San Francisco, 1996).

———, "Vatican Radio Between London and Berlin, 1940-41," *Journal of English Jesuits*, April 1976.

*Great Untold Stories of World War II* (Phil Hirsch, ed.; Pyramid: New York, 1963).

Griech-Polelle, Beth A., *Bishop von Galen: German Catholicism and National Socialism* (Yale University Press: New Haven, CT, 2002).

Groppe, Lothar, "The Church's Struggle with the Third Reich" (IBW Journal, Alan F. Lacy trans.), *Fidelity*, October 1983.

———, "The Church and the Jews in the Third Reich," *Fidelity*, November 1983.

Gwynn, Dennis, *Pius XI* (Holmes: London, 1932).

Halecki, Oscar, *Eugenio Pacelli: Pope of Peace* (Creative Age: New York, 1951; revised edition 1954).

———, and James F. Murray, Jr., *Pius XII: Eugenio Pacelli, Pope of Peace* (Farrar, Straus and Young, Inc.: New York, 1954).

Hamerow, Theodore S., *On the Road to the Wolf's Lair: German Resistance to Hitler* (Harvard University Press: Cambridge, MA, 1997).

Hanley, Boniface, *Maximilian Kolbe: No Greater Love* (Ave Maria Press: South Bend, IN, 1982).

Harrigan, William M., "Pius XII's Efforts to Effect a Détente in German-Vatican Relations, 1939-1940," *Catholic Historical Review*, July 1963.

Hassell, Ulrich von, *The von Hassell Diaries: The Story of the Forces Against Hitler Inside Germany, 1938-1944* (Doubleday: New York, 1947).

Hatch, Alden, and Seamus Walshe, *Crown of Glory: The Life of Pope Pius XII* (Hawthorn Books: New York, 1957).

Hebblethwaite, Peter, *The Next Pope* (Harper San Francisco: San Francisco, 1995).

Heffron, Christopher, "Croatia's Fearless Defender of Life," *St. Anthony Messenger*, February 2007.

Heller, Mikhail, and Aleksandr M. Nekrich, *Utopia in Power: The History of the Soviet Union from 1917 to the Present* (Summit Books: New York, 1986).

Hellman, Peter, *When Courage Was Stronger Than Fear: Remarkable Stories of Christians and Muslims Who Saved Jews from the Holocaust* (Marlowe & Co.: New York, 2004).

Hennesey, James, *American Catholics: A History of the Roman Catholic Community in the United States* (Oxford University Press, 1981).

Hesemann, Michael, "Eugenio Pacelli and the Zionists: New discoveries in the Vatican Secret Archives confirm that the man who became Pope Pius XII intervened in favour of the Jewish settlers in Palestine," Pave the Way Foundation (2009): *http://www.pavethewayfoundation.org/Downloads/Eugenio%20Pacelli%20an%20the%20 Zionists.pdf*.

———, *The Pope Who Defied Hitler. The Truth About Pius XII* (St. Ulrich: Augsburg, 2008).

Hildebrand, Alice von, *The Soul of a Lion: The Life of Dietrich von Hildebrand* (Ignatius Press: San Francisco, 2000).

Hinckle, Warren, *If You Have a Lemon, Make Lemonade: An Essential Memoir of a Lunatic Decade* (G. P. Putnam's Sons: New York, 1974).

Hinshaw, Rick, "Cardinal's Past," *Chicago Tribune*, October 17, 1998, 26.

*A History of the Third Reich, Vol. 4, Primary Sources* (Jeff T. Hays, ed.; Greenhaven Press: San Diego, CA, 2003).

Hitler, Adolf, *Mein Kampf* (Ralph Manheim, trans.; Houghton Mifflin: Boston, 1971).

*Hitler's Rise to Power* (Church in History Information Center, undated).

*Hitler's Secret Conversations 1941-1944* (Octagon Books: New York, 1972; Signet edition, 1961).

Hoar, William P., *Architects of Conspiracy: An Intriguing History* (Western Island Publishers: Boston and Los Angeles, 1984).

Hochhuth, Rolf, *The Deputy* (Richard and Clara Winston, trans.; Grove Press: New York, 1964).

———, *Soldiers* (Robert David MacDonald, trans.; Grove Press: New York, 1968).

Hoek, Kees van, *Pope Pius XII: Priest and Statesman* (Philosophical Library: New York, 1944).

Hoffmann, Peter, *German Resistance to Hitler* (Harvard University Press: Cambridge, MA, 1988).

———, *Stauffenberg: A Family History, 1905-1944* (Cambridge University Press: Cambridge, MA, 1995).

Hollander, Paul, "Soviet Terror, American Amnesia," *National Review*, May 2, 1994.

Holmes, J. Derek, *The Papacy in the Modern World 1914-1978* (Crossroad: New York, 1981).

*The Holocaust Encyclopedia* (Walter Laqueur, ed.; Yale University Press: New Haven, CT, 2000).

Hoover, J. Edgar, *Masters of Deceit* (Pocket Books: New York, 1961).

Horowitz, David, *Radical Son: A Generational Odyssey* (Free Press: New York, 1997).

Hughes, John Jay, *Pontiffs: Popes Who Shaped History* (Our Sunday Visitor: Huntington, IN, 1994).

Hughes, Phillip, *Pope Pius the Eleventh* (Sheed and Ward: New York, 1937).

Hürten, Heinz, *Deutsche Katholiken, 1918-1945* (Ferdinand Schöningh: Paderborn, 1992).

*Inside the Vatican of Pius XII: The Memoir of an American Diplomat During World War II* (Harold H. Tittmann III, ed.; New York: Doubleday, 2004).

The International Catholic-Jewish Historical Commission, *The Vatican and the Holocaust: A Preliminary Report Submitted to the Holy See's Commission for Religious Relations with the Jews and the International Jewish Committee for Interreligious Consultations* (October 2000), posted on the Internet at *http://www.ccjr.us/dialogika-resources/themes-in-todays-dialogue/p12/599-the-vatican-and-the-holocaust-a-preliminary-report.*

*Introduction to Jewish-Christian Relations* (Michael Shermis and Arthur Zannoni, eds.; Paulist Press: New York, 1991).

*The Italian Refuge: Rescue of Jews During the Holocaust* (Ivo Herzer, ed.; The Catholic University of America Press: Washington, DC, 1989).

Jakubowski, Zygmunt, *Pope Pius and Poland* (America Press: New York, 1942).

Janik, Allen, and Stephen Toulmin, *Wittgenstein's Vienna* (Touchstone Books: New York, 1973).

Jansen, H., *Pius XII: chronologie van een onophoudelijk protest* (Kampen: Uitgeverij kok, 2003).

Jareb, Jere, *Zlato i novac Nezavisne Države Hrvatske izneseni u inozemstvo 1944 i 1945* (Hrvatski institut za povijest Dom i svijet: Zagreb, 1997).

Jenkins, Philip, *The New Anti-Catholicism: The Last Acceptable Prejudice* (Oxford University Press: New York, 2003).

*The Jewish People and Their Sacred Scriptures in the Christian Bible*, by the Holy See's Pontifical Biblical Commission (available through the Vatican's website, *www.vatican.va*).

John Paul II, *Crossing the Threshold of Hope* (Alfred A. Knopf: New York, 1994).

Kahn, David, *Hitler's Spies: German Military Intelligence in World War II* (Macmillan: New York, 1978).

Kallay, Nicholas, *Hungarian Premier: A Personal Account of a Nation's Struggle in the Second World War* (Greenwood Press: Westport, CT, 1970).

Kalugin, Oleg, *The First Directorate: My 32 Years in Intelligence and Espionage against the West* (St. Martin's Press: New York, 1994).

Karski, Jan, *Story of a Secret State* (Houghton Mifflin: Boston, 1944).

Katz, Robert, *The Battle for Rome: The Germans, the Allies, the Partisans, and the Pope* (Simon and Schuster: New York, 2003).

———, *Black Sabbath: A Journey Through a Crime Against Humanity* (Macmillan: New York, 1969).

———, *Massacre in Rome* (Ballantine: New York, 1973) (originally released as *Death in Rome*).

Keegan, John, *The Second World War* (Penguin Books: New York, 1989).

Kennedy, John F., *Why England Slept* (Dolphin Books: Garden City, NY, 1961).

Kent, Peter C., "A Tale of Two Popes: Pius XI, Pius XII and the Rome-Berlin Axis," 23 *Journal of Contemporary History* 589 (1988).

Kershaw, Ian, *Hitler: 1889-1936 Hubris* (W. W. Norton & Company: New York, 1998).

Kertzer, David I., *The Kidnapping of Edgardo Mortara* (Knopf: New York, 1997).

———, *The Popes Against the Jews: The Vatican's Role in the Rise of Modern Anti-Semitism* (Knopf: New York, 2001).

Konopatzki, Ilse-Lore, *Eugenio Pacelli: Pius XII, Kindheit und Jugend in Dokumenten*, (Universitätsverlag Anton Pustet, Salzburg und München: Salzburg, 1974).

Korn, Frank, *From Peter to John Paul II: An Informal Study of the Papacy* (Alba House: New York, 1980).

Krišto, Jure, "An American View of the Belgrade Episode of Archbishop Joseph P. Hurley," *Review of Croatian History* (Hrvatski institut za povijest, Zagreb, Republic of Croatia, 2008), 218.

———, "The Catholic Church and the Jews in the Independent State of Croatia," *Review of Croatian History*, 3/2007, no. 1, 13, 16.

————, "The Catholic Church in Croatia and Bosnia-Herzegovina in the Face of Totalitarian Ideologies and Regimes," in *Religion Under Siege: The Roman Catholic Church in Occupied Europe (1939-1950)* (L. Gevers and J. Bank, eds.; Peeters Publishers: Wilsele, Belgium, 2007).

Kuehnelt-Leddihn, Erik von, *The Timeless Christian* (Franciscan Herald Press: Chicago, 1969).

Kupper, Alfons, *Staatliche Akten über die Reichskonkordatsverhandlungen* (Matthias-Grünewald-Verlag: Mainz, 1969).

Kurzman, Dan, *A Special Mission: Hitler's Secret Plot to Seize the Vatican and Kidnap Pope Pius XII* (Perseus Books Group, 2007).

Kustow, Michael, *Peter Brook: A Biography* (St. Martin's Press: New York, 2005).

*La Conciliazione Ufficiosa: Diario del barone Carlo Monti "incaricato d'affari" del governo italiano presso la Santa Sede (1914-1922)* (Antonio Scotta, ed.; Vatican Press: Vatican City, 1997).

Lackovic, Stephen, *The Case Against Tito* (memorandum, 1947).

Lacouture, Jean, *The Jesuits: A Multibiography* (Jeremy Leggatt, trans.; Counterpoint: Washington, 1995).

Lamb, Richard, *War in Italy 1943-1945: A Brutal Story* (St. Martin's Press: New York, 1993).

*Langenscheidt's Standard Italian Dictionary* (Langenscheidt Publishing Group: New York, 1990).

Langer, William L., and S. Everett Gleason, *The World Crisis and American Foreign Policy: The Undeclared War 1940-1941* (Harper Torchbooks: New York, 1953).

Lapide, Pinchas E., *Three Popes and the Jews* (Hawthorn Books: New York, 1967; Sands and Co.: London, 1968).

Lapomarda, Vincent A., *The Jesuits and the Third Reich* (Edwin Mellen Press: Lewiston, NY, 1989).

Lawler, Justus George, *Popes and Politics: Reform, Resentment, and the Holocaust* (Continuum Pub. Group: New York, 2002).

————, "Review Symposium: Proleptic Response," 20 *U.S. Catholic Historian* 89 (2002).

Leboucher, Fernande, *The Incredible Mission of Father Benoît* (J. F. Bernard trans.; William Kimber: London, 1970).

Lemkin, Raphael, *Axis Rule in Occupied Europe: Laws of Occupation, Analysis of Government, Proposals for Redress* (Carnegie Endowment for International Peace: Washington, DC, 1944).

Lenn, Lottie H., and Mary A. Reardon, *Pope Pius XII: Rock of Peace* (E. P. Dutton & Co.: New York, 1950).

Lenz, John M., *Christ in Dachau or Christ Victorious: Experiences in a Concentration Camp* (Vienna, 1960).

Levai, Jenö, *Hungarian Jewry and the Papacy: Pius XII Did Not Remain Silent* (Sands and Co.: London, 1968).

Lewy, Guenter, *The Catholic Church and Nazi Germany* (McGraw-Hill: New York, 1964).

Ley-Piscator, Maria, *The Piscator Experiment: The Political Theatre* (James H. Heineman, Inc.: New York, 1967).

Lichten, Joseph L., "A Question of Judgment: Pius XII and the Jews," in *Pius XII and the Holocaust: A Reader* (Catholic League Publications: Milwaukee, 1988).

Löw, Konrad, *Die Schuld: Christen und Juden im Urteil der Nationalsozialisten und der Gegenwart* (Gräfelfing: Resch, 2003).

Lowenthal, Marvin, *The Jews of Germany: A Story of 16 Centuries* (Jewish Publication Society of America: Philadelphia, 1939).

Lubac, Henri de, *Christian Resistance to Anti-Semitism: Memories from 1940-1944* (Ignatius: San Francisco, 1990).

Lukacs, John, *The Hitler of History* (Knopf: New York, 1997).

Lukas, Richard C., *Forgotten Holocaust: The Poles under German Occupation 1939-1944* (Hippocrene Books: New York, 2001).

Lutzer, Erwin W., *Hitler's Cross* (Moody Press: Chicago, 1995).

Lyttle, Richard B., *Nazi Hunting* (Franklin Watts: New York, London, Toronto and Sydney, 1982).

Maccarrone, Michele, *Il nazionalsocialismo e la Santa Sede* (Studium: Rome, 1947).

Madden, Daniel M., *Operation Escape: The Adventure of Father O'Flaherty* (Hawthorn Books: New York, 1962).

Majdalany, Fred, *The Fall of Fortress Europe* (Curtis Books: New York, 1968).

Malcolm, Noel, *Bosnia — A Short History* (Macmillan London Limited, 1994).

Manhattan, Avro, *The Vatican in World Politics* (Gaer Associates: New York, 1949).

Marchione, Margherita, *Crusade of Charity: Pius XII and POWs 1939-1945* (Paulist Press: New York, 2006).

———, *Man of Peace: Pope Pius XII* (Paulist Press: New York, 2003).

———, *Pope Pius XII: Architect for Peace* (Paulist Press: New York, 2000).

———, *Shepherd of Souls: A Pictorial Life of Pope Pius XII* (Paulist Press: New York, 2002).

———, *Yours Is a Precious Witness: Memoirs of Jews and Catholics in Wartime Italy* (Paulist Press: New York, 1997).

Maritain, Jacques, "The Pagan Empire and the Power of God," 15 *Virginia Quarterly Review* 161, Spring 1939.

Martin, Malachi, *The Decline and Fall of the Roman Church* (Bantam: New York, 1983).

———, *The Keys of This Blood: The Struggle for World Dominion Between Pope John Paul II, Mikhail Gorbachev and the Capitalist West* (Simon & Schuster: New York, 1990).

Martin, Robert, *Spiritual Semites: Catholics and Jews During World War Two* (Catholic League Publications: Milwaukee, 1983).

Matheson, Peter, *The Third Reich and the Christian Churches* (T & T Clark: Edinburgh, 1994).

Matijevic, Margareta, "Religious communities in Croatia from 1945 to 1991: Social causality of the dissent between Communist authorities and religious communities' leadership," *Review of Croatian History* 2/2006, no. 1, 117.

Mazgaj, Marian S., *Visiting Home in Poland After 33 Years and World War II True Stories* (McClain Printing Company: Parsons, WV, 1996).

Mazour, Anatole G., and John M. Peoples, *A World History* (Harcourt, Brace, Jovanovich: New York, second edition 1971).

McCabeus, Jude, "Hitler: A Pioneer for the Politically Correct," *New Oxford Review*, October 1997.

McCormick, Anne O'Hare, *Vatican Journal 1921-1954* (Farrar, Straus & Cudahy: New York, 1957).

McGurn, Barrett, *A Reporter Looks at the Vatican* (Coward-McCann: New York, 1962).

McInerny, Ralph, *The Defamation of Pius XII* (St. Augustine's Press: South Bend, IN, 2001).

Meltzer, Milton, *Never to Forget: The Jews of the Holocaust* (Harper & Row: New York, 1976).

Memorandum to General Donovan from Fabian von Schlabrendorff, dated October 25, 1945 (Subject: Relationship of the German Churches to Hitler), posted on the Internet by Rutgers Law School and Cornell University at *http://library2.lawschool.cornell. edu/Donovan/show.asp?id=426&query=*. This memorandum is also printed in Leo Stein, *Hitler Came for Niemoeller [Niemöller]: The Nazi War Against Religion*, 253-57 (Penguin Publishing Co.: New York, 2003 reprinted).

Merritt, Richard L., "Politics, Theater, and the East-West Struggle: The Theater as a Cultural Bridge in West Berlin, 1948-61," 80 *Political Science Quarterly*, 186 (June 1965).

Merton, Thomas, *Dancing in the Water of Life* (Harper: San Francisco, 1998).

Michaelis, Meir, *Mussolini and the Jews: German-Italian Relations and the Jewish Question in Italy 1922-25* (Clarendon: Oxford, 1978).

Micklem, Anthaniel, *National Socialism and the Roman Catholic Church: Being an Account of the Conflict between the National Socialist Government of Germany and the Roman Catholic Church 1933-1938* (Oxford University Press: Oxford, 1939).

Miller, Marion, *I Was a Spy* (Boss-Merrill: Indianapolis and New York, 1960).

Mindszenty, József Cardinal, *Memoirs* (Macmillan & Co.: New York, 1974).

Morgan, Thomas B., *The Listening Post: Eighteen Years on Vatican Hill* (G. P. Putnam's Sons: New York, 1944).

Morison, Samuel E., *The Oxford History of the American People* (Oxford University Press: New York, 1965).

Morley, John F., *Vatican Diplomacy and the Jews during the Holocaust 1939-1943* (Ktav Pub. House: New York, 1980).

Morrow, Carol Ann, "Franciscan Maximilian Kolbe: Auschwitz Prisoner #16670," St. Anthony Messenger, August 1996.

Müller, Joseph, *Bis zur letzten Konsequenz* (Süddeutscher Verlag: Munich, 1975).

Murphy, Francis X., *The Papacy Today* (Macmillan: New York, 1981).

Murphy, Paul I., *La Popessa* (Warner Books: New York, 1983).

Napolitano, Matteo L., and Andrea Tornielli, *Il Papa Che Salvò Gli Ebrei* (Piemme, 2004).

*The Nazi Master Plan: The Persecution of the Christian Churches*, documents prepared for the postwar Nuremberg trials, prepared by the Office of Strategic Services (OSS) Research and Analysis Branch, posted on the Internet by the *Rutgers Journal of Law & Religion*: *http://camlaw.rutgers.edu*.

Neuhäusler, Johann B., *Kreuz und Hakenkreuz* (Katholische Kirche Bayerns: Munich, 1946).

Nevins, Albert J., *The Story of Pope John XXIII* (Grosset & Dunlap: New York, 1966).

Nichols, Peter, *The Pope's Divisions: The Roman Catholic Church Today* (Faber & Faber: New York, 1981).

Noble, Thomas F. X., *Popes and the Papacy: A History, Volumes one and two* (The Teaching Company audiotape, 2006).

Novick, Peter, *The Holocaust in American Life* (Houghton Mifflin: Boston, 1999).

O'Brien, Count Anthony Henry, *Archbishop Stepinac: The Man and His Case* (The Newman Bookshop: Westminster, MD, 1947).

O'Carroll, Michael, *Pius XII: Greatness Dishonored* (Laetare Press: Dublin, 1980).

O'Connell, Hugh J., *Putting Vatican II into Practice* (Liguorian Pamphlets: Liguori, MO, 1966).

O'Donnell, James P., *The Bunker: The History of the Reich Chancellery Group* (Houghton Mifflin: Boston, 1978).

O'Reilly, Charles T., *The Jews of Italy: 1938-1945* (McFarland & Co.: Jefferson, NC; and London, 2006).

Oppen, Beate Ruhm von, "Nazis and Christians," 21 *World Politics* 392 (1969).

Oudendijk, Piet, *Pope Pius XII and the Nazi War Against the Catholic Church* (Martin W. Kennedy: Brisbane, 1944).

Overy, Richard, *Why the Allies Won* (W. W. Norton & Co.: New York and London, 1995).

Pacepa, Ion Mihai, "Moscow's Assault on the Vatican: The KGB made corrupting the Church a Priority," National Review Online, January 25, 2007.

Paci, Stefano M., "Read Father Blet's book on Pius XII," *30 Days*, 1998:4, 38.

Padellaro, Nazareno, *Pio XII* (Editrice S.A.I.E.: Torino, 1956).

———, *Portrait of Pius XII* (J. M. Dent & Sons: London, 1956).

Palazzini, Pietro, *Il clero e l'occupazione tedesca di Roma: Il ruolo del Seminario Romano Maggiore* (Apes: Rome, 1995).

Palmer, Alan, *Who's Who in Modern History 1860-1980* (Holt, Rinehart, and Winston: New York, 1980).

Papée, Casimir, *Pius XII e Polska* (Editrice Studium: Rome, 1954).

Paris, Edmond, *Convert or Die* (Chick Publications: revised edition, 1990).

Passelecq, Georges, and Bernard Suchecky, *The Hidden Encyclical of Pius XI* (Harcourt Brace & Co.: Boston, 1997).

Patch, William L., Jr., *Heinrich Brüning and the Dissolution of the Weimar Republic* (Cambridge University Press: Cambridge, MA, 1998).

Pattee, Richard, *The Case of Cardinal Aloysius Stepinac* (The Bruce Publishing Co.: Milwaukee 1953).

Patterson, Michael, *Strategies of Political Theatre: Post-War British Playwrights* (Cambridge University Press: Cambridge, MA, 2003).

Payne, Robert, *The Life and Death of Adolf Hitler* (Popular Library: New York, 1995).

Pepper, Curtis, *An Artist and the Pope* (Giniger Books: New York, 1968).

*The Persecution of the Catholic Church in German-Occupied Poland: Reports by H.E. Cardinal Hlond, Primate of Poland, to Pope Pius XII, Vatican Broadcasts and Other Reliable Evidence* (Longmans Green & Co.: New York, 1941).

*The Persecution of the Catholic Church in the Third Reich: Facts and Documents Translated from the German* (Burns and Oates: London, 1940; reprinted by Roger A McCaffrey Publishing: Fort Collins, CO, 2002).

Pfister, Pierre, *Pius XII: The Life and Work of a Great Pope* (Studio Publications, in association with Thomas Y. Crowell Co., 1955).

Phayer, Michael, *The Catholic Church and the Holocaust, 1930-1965* (Indiana University Press: Bloomington, IN, 2001).

Piscator, Erwin, *The Political Theater* (H. Rorrison, trans.; Eyre Methuen: London, 1963).

Pius XI, *Divini Redemptoris* (of the Divine Redeemer) (1937).

———, *Mit brennender Sorge* ("With Burning Anxiety") (1937).

*Pius XI und der Nationalsozialismus. Die Enzyklika 'Mit brennender Sorge' vom 14 März 1937* (Heinz-Albert Raem, ed.; Ferdinand Schöningh: Paderborn, 1979).

Pius XII, *Mystici Corporis Christi* (on the Mystical Body of Christ) (1943).

———, *Summi Pontificatus* (On the Unity of Human Society) (1939).

*Pius XII, the Holocaust and the Revisionists* (P. Gallo, ed.; McFarland & Co.: Jefferson, NC, 2005).

*Pius XII and the Holocaust: A Reader* (Catholic League Publications: Milwaukee, 1988).

*Pius XII: Selected Encyclicals and Addresses* (Roman Catholic Books: Harrison, NY, undated).

*The Pius War: Responses to the Critics of Pius XII* (Joseph Bottum and David G. Dalin, eds.: Lexington Press: Lanham, MD, 2004).

Poewe, Karla, *New Religions and the Nazis* (Routledge: New York and London, 2006).

*Pope Pius and Poland: A Documentary Outline of Papal Pronouncements and Relief Efforts in Behalf of Poland, Since March, 1939* (The America Press: New York, 1942).

*Pope Pius XII and the Holocaust* (Carol Rittner and John K. Roth, eds.; Continuum: New York, 2002).

*The Pope Speaks: The Words of Pius XII* (Harcourt, Brace and Company: New York, 1940).

*Popes of the Twentieth Century* (St. Paul Editions: Boston, 1983).

Portmann, Heinrich, *Cardinal von Galen* (Jarrolds: London, 1957).

Powers, Thomas, *Intelligence Wars: American Secret History from Hitler to al-Qaeda* (Review Books: New York, 2002).

Prcela, John, *Archbishop Stepinac in His Country's Church-State Relations* (Associate Book Publishers: Scottsdale, AZ, 1990).

Price, Morgan Philips, *Dispatches from the Weimar Republic: Versailles and German Fascism* (Pluto Press: London, 1999).

Price, Roger, *A Concise History of France* (Cambridge University Press: New York, 1993).

*Principles for Peace: Selections from Papal Documents, Leo XIII to Pius XII* (Harry C. Koenig, ed.; National Catholic Welfare Conference: Washington, DC, 1943).

Prittie, Terence, *Germany* (New York: Life World Library, 1962).

Procacci, Giuliano, *History of the Italian People* (A. Paul, trans.; Weidenfeld & Nicolson: London, 1970).

Purdy, W. A., *The Church on the Move: The Characters and Policies of Pius XII and John XXIII* (Hollis & Carter: London, 1966).

Radosh, Ronald, and Allis Radosh, *Red Star Over Hollywood: The Film Colony's Long Romance with the Left* (Encounter Books: San Francisco, 2005).

Rauschning, Hermann, *Hitler Speaks* (Putnam: New York, 1940).

Ray, John, *Men Who Made History: Hitler and Mussolini* (Heinemann Educational Books: London, 1974).

Raymond, Rev. M., *The Man for This Moment: The Life and Death of Aloysius Stepinac* (Alba House: Staten Island, NY, 1971).

*Records and Documents of the Holy See Relating to the Second World War: The Holy See and the War in Europe, March 1939-August 1940* (Pierre Blet, Angelo Martini, and Burkhart Schneider, eds.; Corpus Books: Washington, DC, 1965).

Repgen, Konrad, "Das Ende der Zentrumspartei und Entstehung des Reichskonkordats" (*Militärselsorge*, 1970).

———, "Dokumentation. Zur Vatikanischen Strategie beim Reichskonkordat" (*Vierteljahrshefte für Zeitgeschichte*, 1983).

———, "Über Umlaut! die Entstehung der Reichskonkordats-Offerte im Frühjahr 1933 und die Bedeutung des Reichskonkordats" (*Vierteljahrshefte für Zeitgeschichte*, 1978).

Rhodes, Anthony, *The Vatican in the Age of the Dictators: 1922-45* (Hodden and Stoughton: London, Sydney, Auckland, and Toronto, 1973).

Rhonheimer, Father Martin, "The Holocaust: What Was Not Said," *First Things*, November 2003.

Riebling, Mark, Was the Pope a Nazi? (*http://www.catholicfidelity.com/apologetics-topics/pope-pius-xii/was-the-pope-a-nazi-by-mark-riebling/*).

Rothkirchen, Livia, "The Churches and the 'Final Solution' in Slovakia," in *Judaism and Christianity under the Impact of National Socialism 1919-1945* (Otto Dov Kulka and Paul R. Mendes-Flohr, eds.: The Historical Society of Israel and Zalman Zhazar Center for Jewish History: Jerusalem, 1987).

———, *The Destruction of Slovak Jewry* (Yad Vashem: Jerusalem, 1961).

———, "Vatican Policy and the 'Jewish Problem' in 'Independent' Slovakia (1939-1945)," VI *Yad Vashem Studies* 27 (1966).

Rousmaniere, John, *A Bridge to Dialogue: The Story of Jewish-Christian Relations* (Paulist Press: New York, 1991).

Rychlak, Ronald J., Book Review: *The Defamation of Pius XII*, by Ralph McInerny, *Catholic Historical Review*, January 2003.

———, Book Review: *Pius XII und Deutschland*, by Michael F. Feldkamp, *English Historical Review*, June 2003, 840.

———, Comments on Zuccotti's *Under His Very Windows*, 7 *Journal of Modern Italian Studies* 218 (2002).

———, "Daniel Goldhagen's Assault on Christianity," 4 *Totalitarian Movements & Political Religions* 184 (2003).

———, "The 1933 Concordat Between Germany and the Holy See: A Reflection of Tense Relations," 2001 *The Digest* 23 (Syracuse University).

———, "Postwar Catholics, Jewish Children, and a Rush to Judgment," Beliefnet.com, posted Jan. 18, 2005 (including sidebar: "Jewish Children After World War II: A Case Study"), also reprinted in *Inside the Vatican*, January-February 2005.

———, *A Response to: "The Vatican and the Holocaust: A Preliminary Report by the International Catholic-Jewish Historical Commission,"* The Catholic League for Religious and Civil Rights web page, posted Nov. 2000.

———, *Righteous Gentiles: How Pope Pius XII Saved Half a Million Jews from the Nazis* (Spence Publishing: Dallas, 2005).

Sale, Giovanni, *Hitler, La Santa Sede e Gli Ebrei* (Jaca Book: Rome, 2004).

Sánchez, José M., *Pius XII and the Holocaust: Understanding the Controversy* (Catholic University of American Press: Washington, DC, 2002).

———, "The Popes and Nazi Germany: The View from Madrid," 39 *Journal of Church and State* 365 (1996).

Saperstein, Marc, *Moments of Crisis in Jewish-Christian Relations* (SCM Press/Trinity Press International: London/Philadelphia, 1989).

Savor, Michael, *Cardinal Aloysius Stepinac, "A Servant of God and the Croatian People"* (revised edition 2001) (*http://www.croatianhistory.net/etf/stepinac.html*).

Scaperlanda, María Ruiz, *Edith Stein: St. Teresa Benedicta of the Cross* (Our Sunday Visitor: Huntington, IN, 2000).

Schlabrendorff, Fabian von, *The Secret War Against Hitler* (Hilda Simon, trans.; Pitman Publishing: New York, 1965).

Scholder, Klaus, *The Churches and the Third Reich* (Fortress Press: Philadelphia, 1988).

———, *A Requiem for Hitler and Other New Perspectives on the German Church Struggle* (Trinity Press International: Philadelphia, 1989).

Scholl, Inge, *The White Rose: Munich 1942-1943* (A. Schultz, trans.; Wesleyan University Press: Hanover, NH, 1983).

Scrivener, Jane, *Inside Rome with the Germans* (The Macmillan Company: New York, 1945).

Secretariat for Ecumenical and Interreligious Affairs, National Conference of Bishops, *Catholics Remember the Holocaust* (United States Catholic Conference: Washington, DC, 1998).

*Self-Portrait in Letters 1916-1942 (The Collected Works of Edith Stein, Sister Teresa Benedicta of the Cross, Discalced Carmelite, 1891-1942)* (J. Koeppel trans.; ICS Publications: Washington, DC, 1994).

Sereny, Gitta, *Into That Darkness: An Examination of Conscience* (Vintage Books: New York, 1983).

Shevchenko, Arkady N., *Breaking with Moscow* (Alfred A. Knopf: New York, 1985).

Shirer, William L., *Berlin Diary: The Journal of a Foreign Correspondent 1934-1941* (Alfred A. Knopf: New York, 1941).

——, *The Rise and Fall of the Third Reich: A History of Nazi Germany* (Fawcett Publications: Greenwich, CT, 1962).

——, *20th Century Journey, A Memoir of a Life and the Times, Vol. II: The Nightmare Years, 1930-1940* (Little, Brown & Co.: Boston, 1984).

Simpson, William C., *A Vatican Lifeline* (Sarpedon: New York, 1995).

Smit, Jan Olav, *Angelic Shepherd: The Life of Pope Pius XII* (James H. Vanderveldt, trans.; Dodd & Mead: New York, 1950).

Snyder, Louis L., *The War: A Concise History 1939-1945* (J. Messner: New York, 1960).

Speaight, Robert, *Voice of the Vatican: The Vatican Radio in Wartime* (Sands and Co.: London, 1942).

Speer, Albert, *Inside the Third Reich* (R. Winston and C. Winston, trans.; Avon: New York, 1970)

Spicer, Kevin, "Father Wilhelm Senn and the Legacy of Brown Priests," 22 *Holocaust and Genocide Studies* 293 (Fall 2008).

——, *Hitler's Priests: Catholic Clergy and National Socialism* (Northern Illinois University Press: DeKalb, IL, 2008).

——, *Resisting the Third Reich: The Catholic Clergy in Hitler's Berlin* (Northern Illinois University Press: DeKalb, IL, 2004).

——, "Selective Resistance: The German Catholic Church's Response to National Socialism," in *Confronting the Holocaust: A Mandate for the 21st Century* (Stephen Feinstein, Karen Schierman, Marcia S. Little, eds.; University Press of America: Lanham, MD, 1998).

Stehlin, Stewart A., *Weimar and the Vatican 1919-1933: German-Vatican Diplomatic Relations in the Interwar Years* (Princeton University Press: Princeton, NJ, 1983).

Steigmann-Gall, Richard, *The Holy Reich: Nazi Conceptions of Christianity, 1919-1945* (Cambridge University Press: Cambridge, MA, 2003).

Stein, Leo, *Hitler Came for Niemoeller [Niemöller]: The Nazi War Against Religion* (Penguin Publishing Co.: New York, 2003 reprint edition).

Steinsaltz, Adin, *The Essential Talmud* (Bantam: New York, 1976).

*Stephen S. Wise, Servant of the People: Selected Letters* (Carl H. Voss, ed.; Jewish Publication Society of America: Philadelphia, 1969).

*Stepinac: A Witness to the Truth* (Željko Tanjić, ed.; Zagreb: Glas Koncila, 2009).

Stewart, Herbert L., "The Great Secularist Experiment," *The Hibbert Journal*, January 1944.

Stewart, Ralph, *Pope Pius XII and the Jews* (St. Martin de Porres Dominican Community and St. Joseph Canonical Foundation: New Hope, KY, 1990).

Stilinovic, Josip, "Cardinal Alojzije Stepinac — A True Catholic Nationalist!" *Catholic World Report* (1998).

Stille, Alexander, *Benevolence and Betrayal: Five Italian Jewish Families Under Fascism* (Picador: New York, 1991).

*The Storm Over The Deputy* (Eric Bently, ed.; Grove Press: New York, 1964).

*The Story of the Pope* (Peter Alan Meyerson, ed.; New York: Dell Publishing, 1957).

*The Strategy of Deception: A Study in World-Wide Communist Tactics* (Jeane J. Kirkpatrick, ed.; Farrar, Straus and Company: New York, 1963).

Sweets, John F., *Choices in Vichy France: The French Under Nazi Occupation* (Oxford University Press: New York, 1994).

Szulc, Tad, *Pope John Paul II: The Biography* (Simon & Schuster: New York, 1995).

Taëni, Rainer, *Rolf Hochhuth* (Modern German Authors Series) (Oswald Wolff: London, 1977).

Tanner, Marcus, *Croatia: A Nation Forged in War* (Yale University Press: New Haven, CT, 2001).

Tardini, Domenico, *Memories of Pius XII* (The Newman Press: Westminster, MD, 1961).

Taylor, A. J. P., *From Sarajevo to Potsdam* (Thames & Hudson: London, 1966).

Tec, Nechama, *When Light Pierced the Darkness: Christian Rescuers of Jews in Nazi-Occupied Poland* (Oxford University Press: Oxford, 1986).

Tenen, I., *This England: Part III, Hanoverian and Modern Periods (1714-1940)* (Macmillan & Co.: London, 1952).

Terkel, Studs, *The Good War* (Ballantine Books: New York, 1984).

*Theologians Under Hitler*, DVD (Vital Visions, 2006).

*They Almost Killed Hitler: Based on the Personal Account of Fabian von Schlabrendorff* (Gero v. S. Gaevernitz, ed.; Macmillan Co.: New York, 1947).

Thompson, Carlos, *The Assassination of Winston Churchill* (Colin Smythe Ltd., 1969).

*Three Sermons in Defiance of the Nazis Preached During 1941 by Bishop von Galen of Munster* (The Church in History Information Center: Birkenhead, United Kingdom, undated).

Tinnemann, Ethel Mary, "Attitudes of the German Catholic Hierarchy Toward the Nazi Regime: A Study in German Psycho-Political Culture," 22 *The Western Political Quarterly* 333 (1969).

Todd, Lewis P., and Merle Curti, *Rise of the American Nation* (Harcourt Brace Jovanovich: New York, 1982).

Toland, John, *Hitler* (Ballantine Books: New York, 1984).

Tornielli, Andrea, *Pio XII. Papa degli ebrei* (Piemme: Casale Monferrato, 2001).

*Vatican Council II: The Conciliar and Post Conciliar Documents*, new revised edition, edited by Austin Flannery, O.P. (Costello Publishing: Northport, NY, 1992).

*Vatican Impressions* (Francis Sweeney, ed.; Sheed & Ward: New York, 1962).

Vazsonyi, Balint, *America's Thirty Years War: Who Is Winning?* (Regnery: Washington, DC, 2000).

Vida, George, *From Doom to Dawn: A Jewish Chaplain's Story of Displaced Persons* (Jonathan David: New York, 1967).

*Voix du Vatican* (Vatican Radio broadcasts into France during World War II). The documents that I have are photocopies of what appear to be original pamphlets.

Volk, Ludwig, *Das Reichskonkordat vom 20. Juli 1933* (Matthias-Grünewald-Verlag: Mainz: 1972).

————, "Zwischen Geschichtsschreibung und Hochhuthprosa: Kritisches und Grundsätzliches zu einer Neuerscheinung über Kirche und Nationalsozialismus," in *Stimmen der Zeit,* vol. 176 (1965).

Waagenaar, Sam, *The Pope's Jews* (Open Court: LaSalle, 1974).

Walsh, Michael, *An Illustrated History of the Popes: Saint Peter to John Paul II* (St. Martin's Press: New York, 1980).

*War Criminals and Punishment* (Robert M. McBride and Company: New York, 1944).

Ward, Margaret E., *Rolf Hochhuth* (Twayne Publishers: Boston, 1977).

*Wartime Correspondence Between President Roosevelt and Pope Pius XII* (Myron C. Taylor, ed.; Macmillan: New York, 1947. Reprint edition from Da Capo Press: New York, 1975).

Weigel, George, *Witness to Hope: The Biography of Pope John Paul II* (Cliff Street Books: New York, 1999).

Weizsäcker, Ernst von, *Memoirs of Ernst von Weizsäcker* (J. Andrews, trans.; H. Regnery Co.: Chicago, 1951).

Whitehead, Kenneth D., "The Pope Pius XII Controversy," 31 *Political Science Reviewer* 283 (2002).

"Why the Churches Kept Silent," *Awake* (Watchtower Bible and Tract Society), August 22, 1995.

Willett, John, *The Theatre of Erwin Piscator: Half a Century of Politics in the Theatre* (Eyre Methuen: London, 1978).

Wills, Garry, *Papal Sin: Structures of Deceit* (Doubleday: New York, 2000).

Winks, Robin W., *Cloak & Gown: Scholars in the Secret War, 1939-1961* (William Morrow & Co.: New York, 1987).

Wise, David, and Thomas B. Ross, *The Espionage Establishment* (Random House: New York, 1987).

Wise, Stephen S., *As I See It* (Marstin Press: New York, 1944).

Wistrich, Robert, *Hitler and the Holocaust* (Modern Library: New York, 2002).

Wolff, R. J., *Catholics, the State and the European Right* (Columbia University Press: New York, 1986).

*World Fascism: A Historical Encyclopedia* (Cyprian P. Blamires, ed.; ABC-CLIO: Santa Barbara, CA, 2006).

*The World's Great Catholic Literature* (George N. Shuster, ed.; Roman Catholic Books: Harrison, NY, 1942).

Wright, J. R. C., *Pius XII and the Nazi Challenge* (History of the 20th Century Series) (BPC Publishing, Ltd., 1969).

Wyman, David S., *The Abandonment of the Jews: America and the Holocaust 1941-1945* (Pantheon Books: New York, 1984).

Zahn, Gordon C., *German Catholics and Hitler's Wars* (University of Notre Dame Press: Notre Dame, IN, 1962).

Ziemke, Earl F., *The Battle for Berlin: End of the Third Reich* (Ballantine's Illustrated History of World War II; battle book no. 6, 1968).

Zolli, Eugenio, *The Nazarene: Studies in New Testament Exegesis* (Cyril Vollert trans.; Urbi et Orbi/Remnant of Israel: New Hope, KY, 1999).

———, *Why I Became a Catholic* (Urbi et Orbi/Remnant of Israel: New Hope, KY, 1997), previously released as *Before the Dawn* (Sheed and Ward: New York, 1954).

Zubrinic, Darko, *Cardinal Alojzije Stepinac and saving the Jews in Croatia during the WW2* (Zagreb, 1997) (*http://www.croatianhistory.net/etf/jews.html*).

Zuccotti, Susan, *The Holocaust, the French, and the Jews* (Basic Books: New York, 1993).

———, *The Italians and the Holocaust* (University of Nebraska Press: Lincoln, NE, 1987).

———, "Pope Pius XII and the Holocaust: The Case in Italy," in *The Italian Refuge* (Catholic University of America Press: Washington, DC, 1990).

———, *Under His Very Windows: The Vatican and the Holocaust in Italy* (Yale University Press: New Haven, 2001).

# Index

# About the Author

RONALD J. RYCHLAK is Mississippi Defense Lawyers Association Professor of Law and Associate Dean for Academic Affairs at the University of Mississippi, School of Law, where he has been on the faculty since 1987. He is a graduate of Wabash College (B.A., 1980, *cum laude*) and Vanderbilt University (J.D., 1983, Order of the Coif). Prior to joining the faculty, Ron practiced law with Jenner & Block in Chicago, and he served as a clerk to the Hon. Harry W. Wellford of the U.S. Sixth Circuit Court of Appeals.

Ron is an adviser to the Holy See's delegation to the United Nations, is a member of the committee appointed by the Mississippi Supreme Court to revise that state's criminal code, and serves on the editorial boards of *Engage*, of the *Journal of the Federalist Society Practice Groups*, and of the *Gaming Law Review*. Ron is also a member of the Mississippi Advisory Committee to the U.S. Civil Rights Commission, and he serves as the chair of the University of Mississippi Athletics Committee and as the university's Faculty Athletic Representative. He is on advisory boards for the Catholic League for Religious and Civil Rights, the Society of Catholic Social Scientists, the International Solidarity and Human Rights Institute, and the Catholic University of Zagreb.

In 2004, the U.S. State Department sent Ron to Paris to address the Organization for Security and Cooperation in Europe regarding the importance of free speech on the Internet. In 2005, he was named as an Academic Fellow by the Foundation for the Defense of the Democracies, and he attended an associated program on counterterrorism in Israel. In 2005 and 2006, he was involved in international diplomatic talks regarding peace in the Middle East. In 2008, he spoke at the cathedral in Zagreb, where he received a Blessed Cardinal Stepinac medal.

Ron is the author or co-author of seven books, including *Righteous Gentiles: How Pius XII and the Catholic Church Saved Half a Million Jews from the Nazis*. He is a columnist for *Crisis* magazine online (hosted on *InsideCatholic.com*), and he has been published in *Notre Dame Law Review*, *UCLA Law Review*, *Boston College Law Review*, *Environmental Law* (Lewis & Clark Law School), the *Stanford Environmental Law Journal*, *First Things*, the *Washington Post*, the *Wall Street Journal*, and several other periodicals and journals. He lives in Oxford, Mississippi, with his wife, Claire, and their six children.